The Business of Sports

Second Edition

Edited by

Scott R. Rosner

Practice Assistant Professor, Legal Studies and Business Ethics Department
Associate Director, Wharton Sports Business Initiative
University of Pennsylvania

Kenneth L. Shropshire

David W. Hauck Professor at the Wharton School
Director, Wharton Sports Business Initiative
University of Pennsylvania

JONES & BARTLETT
L E A R N I N G

FR. LEONARD ALVEY LIBRARY
BRESCIA UNIVERSITY

No Longer Property of
Fr. Leonard Alvey Library
Brescia University

World Headquarters
Jones & Bartlett Learning
40 Tall Pine Drive
Sudbury, MA 01776
978-443-5000
info@jblearning.com
www.jblearning.com

Jones & Bartlett Learning Canada
6339 Ormindale Way
Mississauga, Ontario L5V 1J2
Canada

Jones & Bartlett Learning International
Barb House, Barb Mews
London W6 7PA
United Kingdom

Jones & Bartlett Learning books and products are available through most bookstores and online booksellers. To contact Jones & Bartlett Learning directly, call 800-832-0034, fax 978-443-8000, or visit our website, www.jblearning.com.

Substantial discounts on bulk quantities of Jones & Bartlett Learning publications are available to corporations, professional associations, and other qualified organizations. For details and specific discount information, contact the special sales department at Jones & Bartlett Learning via the above contact information or send an email to specialsales@jblearning.com.

796.0691
B979

Copyright © 2011 by Jones & Bartlett Learning, LLC

All rights reserved. No part of the material protected by this copyright may be reproduced or utilized in any form, electronic or mechanical, including photocopying, recording, or by any information storage and retrieval system, without written permission from the copyright owner.

Production Credits
Publisher, Higher Education: Cathleen Sether
Senior Acquisitions Editor: Shoshanna Goldberg
Senior Associate Editor: Amy L. Bloom
Editorial Assistant: Prima Bartlett
Production Manager: Julie Champagne Bolduc
Production Editor: Jessica Steele Newfell
Associate Marketing Manager: Jody Sullivan
V.P., Manufacturing and Inventory Control: Therese Connell
Project Management: Thistle Hill Publishing Services, LLC
Composition: Dedicated Business Solutions, Inc.
Cover Design: Kristin E. Parker
Photo and Permissions Associate: Emily O'Neill
Cover Images: (top) © Monkey Business Images/Dreamstime.com; (bottom) © Mike Flippo/ShutterStock, Inc.
Printing and Binding: Courier Kendallville
Cover Printing: Courier Kendallville

Library of Congress Cataloging-in-Publication Data
The business of sports / editors, Scott R. Rosner, Kenneth L. Shropshire. — 2nd ed.
   p. cm.
  Includes bibliographical references and index.
  ISBN-13: 978-0-7637-8078-4 (pbk.)
  ISBN-10: 0-7637-8078-2 (pbk.)
  1. Sports administration—United States. 2. Professional sports—United
States—Management. I. Rosner, Scott. II. Shropshire, Kenneth L. III. Business of sports.
  GV713.B87 2010
  796.06′91—dc22
          2010024220

6048

Printed in the United States of America
14 13 12 11   10 9 8 7 6 5 4 3 2

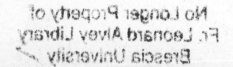
No Longer Property of
Fr. Leonard Alvey Library
Brescia University

Contents

Preface

"Within the framework of what you've been taught, this business makes no sense."

—Wendy Lewis, Vice President, Strategic Planning, Recruitment and Diversity, Major League Baseball, at MBA Media and Entertainment Conference, Stern School of Business, New York University, February 21, 2003

THE BUSINESS OF SPORTS: THE FOUNDATIONS OF A UNIQUE INDUSTRY

Honda and Toyota operate under a general business model of selling as many vehicles as possible with the greatest profit margin possible. In the end, Honda and Toyota are competitors that want to sell product. There is no interest, and it is in fact illegal, to cooperate in a manner that allows both companies to be more profitable. Any traditional business could be used to illustrate the contrast that is important here. Yet, as the epigraph notes, the sports business has been different from the beginning.

In almost every sports venture, the competitors must cooperate for the venture to be profitable. In the nascent stages of team sports, the hat was passed among the spectators at local playing fields. A percentage of the take was distributed among the still sweat-drenched and muddy players from the two squads, and the man (it was almost always a man) who organized the outing took a higher percentage. It was in everyone's interest to have a bigger pie to split, but, even if they cooperated to make attendance as high as possible, they still competed vigorously to be the sole winner on the field. Following the competition, all went back to their jobs during the week. This competitive–cooperative model is now the standard in the National Football League (NFL), Major League Baseball (MLB), the National Basketball Association (NBA), the National Hockey League (NHL), and other sports leagues and professional sports ventures around the world.

Other visionaries saw ways to exploit athletes labeled amateurs by putting together athletic spectacles and reaping the profits. The cash was kept away from those amateurs. The value and need for amateurism was embellished by Greek mythology and class-centered Victorian logic. These amateurism concepts would eventually evolve into the National Collegiate Athletic Association (NCAA) and the Olympic Games. The modern Olympiad was founded by Baron Pierre de Coubertin in 1896, and almost a decade later the NCAA was founded by a group of college presidents convened by then-U.S. President Theodore Roosevelt. The application of the amateur ideal took hold, and student-run sports were taken over by universities, and so, too, were the revenues. From the labor standpoint, a large segment of the sports industry has found a way, unlike the automobile and other industries, to avoid paying for labor.

But winning at any cost is not allowed at any level, at least when the cost is something other than money. Every modern sports business has a set of defined rules and regulations that may even, in many instances, be grounded in law. For example, even if it could be argued that steroids and dietary supplements can make athletes better players, most sports business enterprises have banned their use.

Profit at any cost is similarly problematic. At various times studies have shown that, at the margin, an additional white player on a squad will bring in more fans than an additional black player. Most sports businesses will go for the win rather than the racial slight.

As these ventures grew, new players became part of the industry: radio, television, commercial endorsers, licensees, and sponsors. Lawyers and agents came into the picture to pull these deals together. The business went beyond just what happened during the competition. The business model was expanding. The primary revenue source was no longer limited to just the fans who could put money in the hat or, later, the fans who bought tickets.

By the time sport began to be referred to as a business, it was also clearly entertainment; as such, different rules of business and law applied. Not all parties were able to move away from the concept of these businesses being little more than glorified games. The conflict about whether the business of sports should be treated differently continues today.

The stadiums and arenas where teams played or wanted to play became big parts of the business, too. Interestingly, public money has been used to build many of these facilities. Most companies can only dream of the type of aid that sports franchises receive from the public coffers.

Athletes, too, have realized that it is more than a game, and they have unionized in the team sports, like much of the rest of working class America. That became an ironic position as average salaries surpassed $1 million per year in all of the major North American professional leagues (and much more in some). Without a doubt, the highest paid unions in the world are those involved in professional sports leagues. Unlike most other industries, where employers endeavor to prevent their employees from unionizing, employers in professional sports leagues can derive significant financial and legal benefits from unionization of their workforces. Namely, they can blatantly include anticompetitive measures that help ensure the financial success of the business, such as salary caps and entry drafts, into their collective bargaining agreements. These measures hold up to legal scrutiny, despite the fact that the leagues can all be described as having a monopolistic hold over their respective sports. This is due to the existence of a judicially created exception to the United States antitrust laws known as the nonstatutory labor exemption.

A variety of social issues are unique to the sports industry as well. These see the light of day in sports more than elsewhere, because the business is subject to constant scrutiny. Beat writers and bloggers cover every aspect of the game, looking for unique stories, and those stories go far beyond whatever is happening on the field, court, or ice.

As in other industries, women are still not treated with parity in sports. Initially, it was not "appropriate" for women to participate in sports. Apart from their absence in any highly visible professional sport, the disparity was especially visible in the Olympics. It was not until 1984 at the Olympics in Los Angeles that women competed in a marathon event. Health, decorum, and the need for women to be at home with their families were cited as reasons for this. The passage of Title IX in 1972 helped create new business opportunities in women's professional sports by allowing women to participate in sports in a meaningful way. Many women's leagues have started and failed. A long dominant men's league, the National Basketball Association, started and financed the Women's National Basketball Association (WNBA). The reasons for doing so were all based on business. Beyond professional sports, Title IX has also had a dramatic effect on the business of collegiate sports. It is now an ingrained part of the sports culture, with a full generation of women who have benefited from it and now expect their daughters to be able to do the same.

Many argue that sports led the way for American business on diversity with the racial integration of Major League Baseball (MLB) in 1947 and that sports are still leading the way today. In 2008, 27% of the players in the big leagues were Latino, 10% were African American, and 2% were Asian. However, diversity is still lacking in the upper levels of management. Although there was an all-time high of 2 Latino and 3 African American general managers and 10 field managers of color on opening day in 2009, there were no African Americans or Latinos and only 2 women (one of whom was the owner's wife) serving as a team president or CEO of an MLB team.

Professional sport has become a global business in a manner similar to, yet different from, other businesses. Sports leagues have definitely benefited from larger markets and cheaper labor. In the NBA, NHL and MLB, the expanded talent pool is a genuine reality as well.

Issues that make headlines in this industry include the sharing of revenues, salary caps, luxury taxes, luxury boxes, and the search for the next corporate sponsor. The business model for the automobile may have evolved since the Model T, but not with the same level of public scrutiny and angst as has occurred in sports. Unique to this business is the extraordinary level of dependence on the selling of a product to broadcasters, as opposed to getting customers to "purchase" the product by walking in the gate.

With that said, many of the rules are the same. The bottom line of the enterprise is ultimately important. As applied to team sports, there is just a different way of getting there. This is the case even though some individual owners (whether people or entities) can afford to lose seemingly endless amounts of money, citing reasons ranging from marketing the larger enterprise, to controlling content for the enterprise, to fattening up the enterprise for sale.

The Business of Sports, Second Edition, is designed for current and future sports business leaders as well as those interested in the inner workings of the industry. Through original introductions, carefully selected readings with the editors' notes updating relevant text, and incisive questions, this book gives the reader insight into this unique business. The business of sports is interdisciplinary in nature. As such, the major business disciplines of management, marketing, finance, information technology, accounting, ethics, and law are all encompassed in the materials that follow. The readings provide this insight from the perspective of a variety of stakeholders in the industry. We have attempted to edit the selections in the book in a manner such that the reader will not be overburdened with the jargon of any specific discipline. Where possible, cumbersome citations have been deleted to provide for a smoother read. Where we deemed it necessary for reference purposes, the citations were retained. The original note numbering is retained in the selections, though the numbering of tables, charts, and figures has been changed from the originals in the name of organization and uniformity.

This book is not meant to cover all aspects of every topic involved in the sports industry. Nonetheless, it does provide the reader with a fairly comprehensive overview of many of the major sports business issues. In order to do so most effectively, the book has been divided into three broad sections: professional, Olympic, and intercollegiate sports. The major issues that impact each of these broad categories of sports are subsequently addressed within each section. In addition, there are separate chapters on gender equity, race, and ethics. These three sections include all three of the aforementioned categories of the sports business—professional, Olympic, and intercollegiate sports. Though all sports are not discussed in each section, the message that is gleaned from a selected reading is typically instructive for understanding the issues as they impact other sports.

As the *Second Edition* of the first comprehensive collection of readings to focus on the business of sports, it is our hope that this book will continue to provide a framework for understanding the business of sports and the dilemmas faced by today's sports business leaders. Although this is a *Second Edition*, in many ways it is an entirely new work. Approximately three-quarters of the articles excerpted are new, most of which were published since the *First Edition* was released in 2004. The articles that remain from the *First Edition* are more seminal in nature; they generally remain as timely in 2010 as they were when first published—and any relevant facts have been updated to reflect the current situation. New chapters on global sports leagues and teams have been added to this edition, while the chapters on accounting and taxation, licensed products, and the future that appeared in the *First Edition* have been removed. Those latter topics have been addressed in the context of other chapters. In addition, the chapter on individual sports has been removed from the hard copy of the book and can now be found exclusively in the online materials found at www.jblearning.com. We have also slightly tweaked the order of the chapters to present the information in a more logical manner, a lesson learned from using the *First Edition* of the book in numerous courses at the Wharton School and elsewhere.

However, we recognize that no work is perfect. This book is no different. The information found in this book is current as of January 2010, and, in some cases, was updated to reflect changes that occurred as the book was moving through production. Doubtless some of the information will have changed by the time the book is printed. In researching this *Second Edition* of the book, we continued to find a dearth of existing works on the business aspects of the Olympic Games and intercollegiate athletics, even though much attention has been given to the sociological aspects of both of these topics. Similarly, a glaring lack of attention has been given to the ethical aspects of the business of sports, as well as the involvement of Latinos, women, and people with disabilities. These shortcomings are likely a product of the fact that the serious study of sports as a business is relatively new, with the first academic articles appearing in the 1950s and the advent of college sports management programs occurring little more than a generation ago. Nonetheless, these neglected subjects warrant further study.

Our hope is that both current and future business leaders will take both the facts and viewpoints expressed here and apply their own creativity to take their particular focus in sports to an even higher level.

Acknowledgments

This book is the culmination of thousands of hours of thinking, researching, talking, and writing about the business of sports. We have attempted to provide a comprehensive overview of this industry in a novel manner. In interspersing our own narrative with significant existing works, we seek to "tell the story" of the business of sports so that it is accessible to a wide audience. It is our hope that sports industry practitioners, academics, students, business people, and sports fans alike will find this to be a useful resource and learning tool.

This project could not have been completed without the help of many others. Tamara English and Cherly Vaughn-Curry provided outstanding administrative and editorial assistance on this edition of the book. Lowell Lysinger provided valuable technological assistance. It is difficult to imagine a more talented, dedicated, or nicer group of support staff anywhere. Wharton Sports Business Initiative research fellows Glenn Valli, Alex Wong, and Matt Obernauer as well as research assistants Jeremy Fink, Benjamin Freeman, Ryan Brush, and Will Conroy all spent a significant amount of time researching, editing, and providing important feedback on the drafts of the book as well as the ideas and model answers for many of the discussion questions. Matt provided model answers to the discussion questions found in the Instructor's Manual. All of their work was universally exceptional. The members of the Wharton School's spring 2008 MBA sports business management class conducted research on the early draft of this edition.

We would like to thank the reviewers of the *First Edition*, who provided valuable feedback to make that edition a success: Warren K. Zola, JD, MBA, Boston College; Jeffrey R. Meyer, Wayne State College; John Wolohan, JD, Ithaca College; Aaron W. Clopton, PhD, Louisiana State University; and James Riordan, PhD, Florida Atlantic University.

We also have a list of individuals that we'd like to thank on a personal basis.

For Ken:

This book—more than any other work I am involved in—reminds me of how massive the sports business field has become. As always, thanks to my family for their support, time, and otherwise in allowing me to complete this project. As I wrote in the *First Edition*, this is probably the best place to acknowledge that the lion's share of the effort in this book is Scott's. I certainly hauled a great deal of the water, but Scott's name goes first on this for more than alphabetical reasons. Even with that, I'll share the blame for any perceived shortcomings.

For Scott:

Upon the completion of the *First Edition* of the book, I channeled my inner Apollo Creed and remarked to Ken, "Ain't gonna be no rematch," to which he found his inner Rocky Balboa and responded, "Don't want one." However, here we are again 6 years later with a *Second Edition*. This would not have occurred had the students enrolled in the undergraduate and MBA sports business courses and a number of people working in the sports industry not responded so enthusiastically to the book over the years. In many ways, we were left with no choice but to do it again! For this, I thank my students and those in the industry profusely, as I have certainly learned more from them than I have taught them.

Of course, this book also would not have happened without the authors whose works we have included. We are grateful for their diligence and contributions to the "business of sports."

Working with Ken Shropshire on this as well as on a number of other projects both over the prior 14 years and presently continues to be a highlight of my career, and it remains an honor for me to do so.

I have dedicated this edition of the book to my family. My parents, Sandy and Jay Rosner, and my other parents, Phyllis and Ken Konner, have offered unending encouragement, support, and world class grandparenting. My wife and best friend, Kim Rosner, is an amazing woman whose remarkable ability to successfully balance career and family while (usually) maintaining her sense of humor is inspiring. She would make any man's life complete. I am lucky that I get to be the one. (And I'm not just writing that because I have to . . .)

My family has doubled in size and exponentially more so in happiness since the *First Edition* was published with the arrival of my two children. Logan and Harrison are truly wonderful kids who make their dad very proud on a daily basis. Their willingness to periodically sacrifice their father to *The Business of Sports* is greatly appreciated. And yes, Logan, daddy is done writing and doesn't have to go to the coffee shop, so I can play now.

Reading Credits

CHAPTER 1

Page 8: James P. Quirk and Rodney D. Fort. *Hard Ball: The Abuse of Power in Pro Team Sports*, pp. 96–116. Copyright © 1999 by Princeton University Press. Reprinted by permission of Princeton University Press.

Page 12: Andrew Zimbalist. Sport as Business. *Oxford Review of Economic Policy.* Vol. 19, Issue 4, pp. 503–511, 2003. Reprinted by permission of Oxford University Press.

Page 18: Rodney Fort. The Value of Major League Baseball Ownership. *International Journal of Sport Finance.* Vol. 1, Issue 1, pp. 9–20. Used with permission from Fitness Information Technology.

Page 26: Genevieve F.E. Birren. NFL vs. Sherman Act: How the NFL's Ban on Public Ownership Violates Federal Antitrust Laws. *Sports Lawyers Journal.* Vol. 11, Issue 1, p. 121. Used with permission.

Page 31: Ryan Schaffer. A Piece of the Rock (or the Rockets): The Viability of Widespread Public Offerings of Professional Sports Franchises. *Virginia Sports and Entertainment Law Journal.* Vol. 5, 2006, p. 201. Used with permission.

Page 42: Edward N. Coulson and Rodney Fort. Tax Revisions of 2004 and Pro Sports Team Ownership. *Contemporary Economic Policy.* Published online January 21, 2010 by John Wiley & Sons, Inc. Used with permission.

CHAPTER 2

Page 51: Kenneth Shropshire and Scott Rosner. On the Global Economic Downturn and Sports. *Entertainment and Sports Lawyer.* Vol. 27, Issue 2, pp. 2–3. Copyright © 2009 American Bar Association. Used with permission.

Page 53: Michael N. Danielson. *Home Team: Professional Sports and the American Metropolis*, pp. 83–96. Copyright © 1997 by Princeton University Press. Reprinted by permission of Princeton University Press.

Page 55: Roger G. Noll. The Economics of Promotion and Relegation in Sports Leagues: The Case of English Football. *Journal of Sports Economics.* Vol. 3, Issue 2, pp. 169–203, copyright © 2002 by SAGE Publications. Reprinted by Permission of SAGE Publications.

CHAPTER 3

Page 66: The Economist. Local Heroes. © The Economist Newspaper Limited, London (July 31, 2008).

Page 69: India Knowledge@Wharton. Cricket in India: Moving Into a League of Its Own. Wharton School of the University of Pennsylvania. March 20, 2008. Used with permission.

Page 71: Christopher Hyde and Adrian Pritchard. Twenty20 Cricket: An Examination of the Critical Success Factors in the Development of Competition. *International Journal of Sports Marketing and Sponsorship.* Vol. 10, Issue 2, pp. 132–142. Used with permission.

Page 76: Arsenal Football Club. Arsenal Holdings Plc Statement of Accounts and Annual Report 2007/2008. Used with permission.

Page 84: Scott R. Rosner and William T. Conroy. The Impact of the Flat World on Player Transfers in Major League Baseball. *University of Pennsylvania Journal of Business Law.* Vol. 12, Issue 1, p. 79. Used with permission.

CHAPTER 4

Page 104: Tim Bezbatchenko. Bend it for Beckham: A Look at Major League Soccer and its Single Entity Defense to Antitrust Liability after the Designated Player Rule. *University of Cincinnati Law Review.* Vol. 76, Winter 2008, pp. 611–644. Used with permission.

Page 114: Marc Edelman and Elizabeth Masterson. Could the New Women's Professional Soccer League Survive in America? How Adopting a Traditional Legal Structure May Save More Than Just a Game. 19 *Seton Hall Journal of Sports and Entertainment Law,* 283 (2009). Copyright © 2009 by Marc Edelman. Used with the authorization of Marc Edelman. All rights reserved.

Page 123: Marc Edelman and C. Keith Harrison. Analyzing the WNBA's Mandatory Age/Education Policy from a Legal, Cultural, and Ethical Perspective: Women, Men, and the Professional Sports Landscape. *Northwestern Journal of Law and Social Policy.* Vol. 3, Issue 1, pp. 1–28. Copyright © 2008 by Marc Edelman and C. Keith Harrison. Used with the authorization of Marc Edelman and C. Keith Harrison. All rights reserved.

Page 128: Keith Willoughby and Chad Mancini. The Inaugural (and Only) Season of the Xtreme Football League: A Case Study in Sports Entertainment. *International Journal of Sports Marketing and Sponsorship.* Vol. 5, Issue 3, pp. 227–235. Used with permission.

Page 132: Michael C. Davis. Called up to the Big Leagues: An Examination of the Factors Affecting the Location of Minor League Baseball Teams. *International Journal of Sport Finance.* Vol. 1, Issue 4, pp. 253–264. Used with permission from Fitness Information Technology.

CHAPTER 5

Page 147: Richard G. Sheehan. *Keeping Score: The Economics of Big-Time Sports*, pp. 155–179. Copyright 1996 by Diamond Communications, an imprint of Taylor Trade Publishing. Used with permission. All rights reserved.

Page 151: Allen R. Sanderson and John J. Siegfried. Thinking about Competitive Balance. *Journal of Sports Economics*. Vol. 4, Issue 4, pp. 316–348. Copyright © 2003 by SAGE Publications. Reprinted by permission of SAGE Publications.

Page 159: Clay Moorhead. Revenue Sharing and the Salary Cap in the NFL: Perfecting the Balance Between NFL Socialism and Unrestrained Free-Trade. *Vanderbilt Journal of Entertainment and Technology Law*. Vol. 3, Issue 3, pp. 641–686. Used with permission.

Page 172: Adapted, with permission, from S. Kesenne, 2006, "Competitive balance in team sports and the impact of revenue sharing," *Journal of Sport Management* 20(6): 39–51.

CHAPTER 6

Page 186: Jack Williams. The Coming Revenue Revolution in Sports. *Willamette Law Review*. Vol. 42, Issue 4, pp. 669–708. Used with permission.

Page 193: David J. Berri, Martin B. Schmidt and Stacey L. Brook. Stars at the Gate: The Impact of Star Power on NBA Gate Revenues. *Journal of Sports Economics*. Vol. 5, Issue 1, pp. 33–50. Copyright © 2004 by SAGE Publications. Reprinted by permission of SAGE Publications.

Page 199: Robert Lawson, Kathleen Sheehan, and E. Frank Stephenson. Vend It Like Beckham: David Beckham's Effect on MLS Ticket Sales. *International Journal of Sport Finance*. Vol. 3, Issue 4, pp. 189–195. Used with permission from Fitness Information Technology.

Page 202: Dennis Coates and Brad R. Humphreys. Ticket Prices, Concessions and Attendance at Professional Sporting Events. *International Journal of Sport Finance*. Vol. 2, Issue 3, pp. 161–170. Used with permission from Fitness Information Technology.

Page 205: Adapted, with permission, from D.A. Rascher, C.D. McEvoy, M.S. Nagel, and M.T. Brown, 2007, "Variable ticket pricing in major league baseball," *Journal of Sport Management* 21(3): 407–437.

Page 211: John S. Hill and John Vincent. Globalisation and Sports Branding: The Case of Manchester United. *International Journal of Sports Marketing and Sponsorship*. Vol. 7, Issue 3, pp. 213–230. Used with permission.

Page 220: Forest City Enterprises, Inc., Nets Sports and Entertainment, LLC and Subsidiaries. Consolidated Balance Sheets at June 30, 2009 and 2008, and Consolidated Statements of Operations, Consolidated Statements of Members' Equity (Deficit), and Consolidated Statements of Cash Flows for the fiscal years ended June 30, 2009, 2008 and 2007, including the Notes thereto. Courtesy of EDGAR and the U.S. Securities and Exchange Commission.

Page 223: Nets Sports and Entertainment, LLC and Subsidiaries. Notes to Consolidated Financial Statements, June 30, 2009, 2008 and 2007. Courtesy of EDGAR and the U.S. Securities and Exchange Commission.

CHAPTER 7

Page 230: Martin J. Greenberg. *The Stadium Game*, ScheerGame. ScheerGame Sports Development, LLC. Copyright 2000 by ScheerGame Sports Development, LLC. Used with permission. All rights reserved.

Page 238: Marc Edelman. Sports and the City: How to Curb Professional Sports Teams' Demands For Free Public Stadiums. *Rutgers Journal of Law and Public Policy*. Vol. 6, Issue 1, pp. 35–77. Copyright © 2008 by Marc Edelman. Used with the authorization of Marc Edelman. All rights reserved. Excerpts from this article have previously appeared in the author's Spring 2003 *Virginia Sports & Entertainment Law Review* article, How to Curb Professional Sports' Bargaining Power Vis-à-Vis the American City, 2 *Va. Sports & Ent. L.J.* 280 (2003).

Page 243: Martin J. Greenberg and April R. Anderson. The Name is the Game in Facility Naming Rights. *The Sports Lawyer*. 2000. Used with permission.

Page 247: Brad R. Humphreys. Public Financing for Construction and Operation of Sports Stadiums and Economic Revitalization and Development in Urban America. Testimony for the Domestic Policy Subcommittee Hearing on Taxpayer Financed Stadiums, Convention Centers, and Hotels. March 29, 2007. Courtesy of the U.S. Committee on Oversight and Government Reform.

Page 251: Neil Demause. Testimony for the Domestic Policy Subcommittee Hearing on Taxpayer Financed Stadiums, Convention Centers, and Hotels. March 29, 2007. Courtesy of the U.S. Committee on Oversight and Government Reform.

CHAPTER 8

Page 264: Ronald A. Cass, Mark Abbott, Irwin Kishner, Brad Ruskin, and Alan Vickery. Symposium: The Seventh Annual Symposium on Legal Issues in Professional Sports, Panel I: The Future of Sports Television. *Fordham Intellectual Property, Media and Entertainment Law Journal*. Vol. 14, Issue 3, pp. 645–693. Copyright 2004 *Fordham Intellectual Property, Media & Entertainment Law Journal* and Ronald A. Cass, Mark Abbott, Irwin Kirshner, Brad Ruskin, and Alan Vickery. Used with permission.

Page 273: "NFL Agenda-Setting, the NFL Programming Schedule: A Study of Agenda-Setting" by John A. Fortunato, is reproduced from *Journal of Sports Media* with permission from the University of Nebraska Press. Copyright 2008. Vol. 3, Issue 1, pp. 27–49.

Page 280: Norm O'Reilly and Ryan Rahinel. Forecasting the Importance of Media Technology in Sport: The Case of the Televised Ice Hockey Product in Canada. *International Journal of Sports Marketing and Sponsorship*. Vol. 8, Issue 1, pp. 82–97. Used with permission.

Page 287: Diana Moss. Regional Sports Networks, Competition, and the Consumer. *Loyola Consumer Law Review*. Vol. 21, 2008, p. 56. Used with permission.

Page 295: Irving Rein, Philip Kotler, and Ben Shields. The Future of Sports Media. *THE FUTURIST*. Vol. 41, Issue 1, pp. 40–43. Originally published in *THE FUTURIST*. Used with permission from the World Future Society, 7910 Woodmont Avenue, Suite 450, Bethesda, Maryland 20814 USA. Telephone: 301-656-8274; www.wfs.org.

CHAPTER 9

Page 301: Andrew P. Hanson. The Trend Toward Principled Negotiation in Major League Baseball Collective Bargaining. *Sports Lawyers Journal*. Vol. 15, Spring 2008, p. 221. Used with permission.

Page 310: Andrew Zimbalist. Labor Relations in Major League Baseball. *Journal of Sports Economics*. Vol. 4, Issue 4, pp. 332–355. Copyright © 2003 by SAGE Publications. Reprinted by permission of SAGE Publications.

Page 314: Ryan T. Dryer. Beyond The Box Score: A Look at Collective Bargaining Agreements in Professional Sports and Their Effect on Competition. *Journal of Dispute Resolution*. Vol. 2008, Issue 1, pp. 267–292. Used with permission.

Page 328: Paul D. Staudohar. The Hockey Lockout of 2004-05. 128 *Monthly Labor Review*. 12 (2005). Courtesy of the Bureau of Labor Statistics.

CHAPTER 10

Page 338: James Quirk and Rodney D. Fort. *Pay Dirt: The Business of Professional Team Sports*, pp. 213–225, 238–239. Copyright © 1992 by Princeton University Press. Reprinted by permission of Princeton University Press.

Page 342: Lawrence M. Kahn. The Sports Business as a Labor Market Laboratory. *Journal of Economic Perspectives*, 14 (3) pp. 75–94, Summer 2000. Copyright by American Economic Association. Used with permission. All rights reserved.

Page 349: David J. Berri, Stacey L. Brook, Martin B. Schmidt. Does One Simply Need to Score to Score? *International Journal of Sport Finance*. Vol. 2, Issue 4, pp. 190–205. Used with permission from Fitness Information Technology.

Page 356: Jahn K. Hakes and Raymond D. Sauer. An Economic Evaluation of the *Moneyball* Hypothesis. *Journal of Economic Perspectives*. Vol. 20, Issue 3, pp. 173–185. Used with permission.

Page 361: Bill Gerrard. Is the *Moneyball* Approach Transferable to Complex Invasion Team Sports? *International Journal of Sport Finance*. Vol. 2, Issue 4, pp. 214–230. Used with permission from Fitness Information Technology.

Page 369: Andrew Healy. Do Firms Have Short Memories?: Evidence From Major League Baseball. *Journal of Sports Economics*. Vol. 9, Issue 4, pp. 407–424. Copyright © 2008 by SAGE Publications. Reprinted by permission of SAGE Publications.

Page 374: Stephen M. Yoost. The National Hockey League and Salary Arbitration: Time for a Line Change. *Ohio State Journal on Dispute Resolution*. Vol. 21, p. 485. Used with permission.

Page 390: Richard A. Kaplan. The NBA Luxury Tax Model: A Misguided Regulatory Regime. *Columbia Law Review*. Vol. 104, pp. 1615–1624. Copyright 2004 by Columbia Law Review Association, Inc. Reproduced with permission of Columbia Law Review Association, Inc. in the formats Textbook and Other book via Copyright Clearance Center.

Page 400: William Duffy. Football May Be Ill, but Don't Blame Bosman. *Sports Lawyers Journal*. Vol. 10, 2003, p. 295. Used with permission.

CHAPTER 11

Page 414: Mitchell Ziets and David Haber. The Financial Valuation of Sports Franchises, from *The Business of Sports: Perspectives on the Sports Industry*, Brad R. Humphreys and Dennis R. Howard, eds. Copyright © 2008 by Brad R. Humphreys and Dennis R. Howard. Reproduced with permission of ABC-CLIO, LLC.

Page 423: Chad Lewis, Jessica Soltz Rudd, Laurence Monnier, and Cherian George. Fitch Criteria Report, Criteria Report Global Sports Rating Guidelines, May 9, 2007, pp. 1–18. Reprinted by permission of Fitch, Inc.

Page 436: Brad R. Humphreys and Michael Mondello. Determinants of Franchise Values in North American Professional Sports Leagues: Evidence from a Hedonic Price Model. *International Journal of Sport Finance*. Vol. 3, Issue 2, pp. 98–105. Used with permission from Fitness Information Technology.

Page 440: Donald L. Alexander and William Kern. The Economic Determinants of Professional Sports Franchise Values. *Journal of Sports Economics*. Vol. 5, Issue 1, pp. 51–66. Copyright © 2004 by SAGE Publications. Reprinted by permission of SAGE Publications.

Page 446: Jeffrey S. Phillips and Jeremy L. Krasner, CFA. Professional Sports: The Next Evolution in Value Creation. *The SRR Journal*. Fall 2008, pp. 16–19. Copyright © 2008 by Stout Risius Ross, Inc. (www.srr.com). Used with permission.

CHAPTER 12

Page 457: Jean-Loup Chappelet. Management of the Olympic Games: The Lessons of Sydney. *Olympic Review*, 2000. October–November, Vol. XXVII, No. 35, pp. 43–47. Used with permission.

Page 460: Brad Humphreys and Andrew Zimbalist. The Financing and Economic Impact of the Olympic Games, from *The Business of Sports: Perspectives on the Sports Industry*, Brad R. Humphreys and Dennis R. Howard, eds. Copyright © 2008 by Brad R. Humphreys and Dennis R. Howard. Reproduced with permission of ABC-CLIO, LLC.

Page 470: Chrysostomos Giannoulakis and David Stotlar. Evolution of Olympic Sponsorship and Its Impact on the Olympic Movement. *Eighth International Symposium for Olympic Research*. 2006, pp. 180–190. Used with permission.

CHAPTER 13

Page 480: Rodney K. Smith. A Brief History of the NCAA's Role in Regulating Intercollegiate Athletics. *Marquette Sports Law Review*. Vol. 11, Fall 2000, pp. 9–22. © Marquette University, reprinted with permission.

Page 485: Lisa Pike Masteralexis, Carol A, Barr, and Mary A. Hums. *Principles and Practice of Sport Management*, pp. 145–169. Copyright © 2009, Jones & Bartlett Learning, Sudbury, MA, www.jblearning.com. Used with permission.

Page 494: Ray Yasser, James R. McCurdy, C. Peter Goplerud and Maureen A. Weston. *Sports Law: Cases and Materials*, 4th ed., pp. 92–99. Reprinted with permission. Copyright 2002 Matthew Bender & Company, Inc., a member of the LexisNexis Group. All rights reserved.

CHAPTER 14

Page 507: Roger C. Noll. The Business of College Sports and the High Cost of Winning. *Milken Institute Review*, pp. 24–37, Third Quarter, 1999. Copyright by The Milken Institute Review. Used with permission. All rights reserved.

Page 516: Jack Copeland. Unbound: How a Supreme Court Decision Tore Apart Football Television and Rippled Through 25 Years of College Sports. *Champion Magazine*. Summer 2009, pp. 38–45. © National Collegiate Athletic Association. 2008-2010. All rights reserved.

Page 520: Myles Brand. The 2009 NCAA State of the Association Speech, as Delivered by Wallace I. Renfro, NCAA Vice President and Senior Advisor to President Myles Brand, January 15, 2009. © National Collegiate Athletic Association. 2008–2010. All rights reserved.

Page 526: National Collegiate Athletic Association. NCAA 2008–2009 Revenue Distribution Plan. © National Collegiate Athletic Association. 2008–2010. All rights reserved.

Page 530: National Collegiate Athletic Association. NCAA Financial Report, August 31, 2008. © National Collegiate Athletic Association. 2008–2010. All rights reserved.

CHAPTER 15

Page 544: James J. Duderstadt. *Intercollegiate Athletics and the American University: A University President's Perspective*, pp. 126–145. Copyright © by the University of Michigan 2000, 2003. Used with permission. All rights reserved.

Page 551: University of Michigan Athletic Department. University of Michigan Department of Athletics Operating Budgets, 2009–2010. Used with permission.

Page 555: Knight Commission on Intercollegiate Athletics. Faculty Perceptions of Intercollegiate Athletics Survey, Executive Summary, Knight Commission's Faculty Summit on Intercollegiate Athletics. Used with permission.

Page 559: Jonathan M. Orszag and Peter R. Orszag. The Physical Capital Stock Used In Collegiate Athletics. Commissioned by the National Collegiate Athletic Association, April 2005, funded in part by the Mellon Foundation. Reprinted with permission of the authors.

Page 564: Jonathan M. Orszag and Peter R. Orszag. The Empirical Effects of Collegiate Athletics: An Update. Commissioned by the National Collegiate Athletic Association, April 2005. Reprinted with permission of the authors.

Page 567: Robert H. Frank. Challenging the Myth: A Review of the Links Among College Athletic Success, Student Quality, and Donations. Prepared for the Knight Foundation Commission on Intercollegiate Athletics, May 2004. Used with permission.

Page 577: Devin G. Pope and Jaren C. Pope. The Impact of College Sports Success on the Quantity and Quality of Student Applications. *Southern Economic Journal*. Vol. 75, Issue 3, pp. 750–780. Used with permission.

Page 584: Jeffrey L. Stinson and Dennis R. Howard. Scoreboards vs. Mortarboards: Major Donor Behavior and Intercollegiate Athletics. *Sport Marketing Quarterly*. Vol. 13, 2004, pp. 129–140. Used with permission from Fitness Information Technology.

Page 591: National Collegiate Athletic Association. The Impact of Reclassification from Division II to I-AA and from Division I-AA to I-A on NCAA Member Institutions from 1993 to 2003. © National Collegiate Athletic Association. 2008-2010. All rights reserved.

Page 599: Willie J. Burden and Ming Li. Circumstantial Factors and Institutions' Outsourcing Decisions on Marketing Operations. *Sport Marketing Quarterly*. Vol. 14, 2005, pp. 125–131. Used with permission from Fitness Information Technology.

Page 603: Kristy Piccinini and Dennis Zimmerman. A CBO Paper: Tax Preferences for Collegiate Sports. May 2009. Courtesy of the Congressional Budget Office.

CHAPTER 16

Page 616: Scott R. Rosner. The Growth of NCAA Women's Rowing: A Financial, Ethical and Legal Analysis. 11 *Seton Hall Journal of Sports Law*, 297 (2001). Copyright by Seton Hall University School of Law. Used with permission.

Page 622: Office for Civil Rights. Clarification of Intercollegiate Athletics Policy Guidance: The Three-Part Test. January 16, 1996. Courtesy of the U.S. Department of Education.

Page 627: Mary Frances O'Shea. Letter Clarifying Apportionment of Financial Aid in Intercollegiate Athletics. July 23, 1998. Courtesy of the U.S. Department of Education.

Page 630: Gerald Reynolds. Further Clarification of Intercollegiate Athletics Policy Guidance Regarding Title IX Compliance. July 11, 2003. Courtesy of the U.S. Department of Education.

Page 631: Deborah L. Rhode and Christopher J. Walker. Gender Equity in College Athletics: Women Coaches as a Case Study. *Stanford Journal of Civil Rights and Civil Liberties*. Vol. 4, April 2008, pp. 1–50. Copyright 2008 by *Stanford Journal of Civil Rights and Civil Liberties*. Reproduced with permission of *Stanford Journal of Civil Rights and Civil Liberties* in the format Textbook via Copyright Clearance Center.

CHAPTER 17

Page 648: Kenneth L. Shropshire. Legislation for the Glory of Sport: Amateurism and Compensation. 1 *Seton Hall Journal of Sport Law* 7 (1991). Copyright by Seton Hall University School of Law. Used with permission.

Page 652: Peter Goplerud III. Symposium: Sports Law as a Reflection of Society's Laws and Values: Pay for Play College Athletes: Now More Than Ever. 38 *S. Texas Law Review* 1081 (1997). Used with permission.

Page 658: Christopher A. Callanan. Advice for the Next Jeremy Bloom: An Elite Athlete's Guide to NCAA Amateurism Regulations. *Case Western Reserve Law Review*. Vol. 56, Issue 3, pp. 687–694. Used with permission.

Page 661: James L. Shulman and William G. Bowen. *The Game of Life: College Sports and Educational Values*, pp. 258–267. Copyright © 2001 by Princeton University Press, 2002 paperback edition. Reprinted by permission of Princeton University Press.

Page 666: Knight Commission on Intercollegiate Athletics. A Call to Action: Reconnecting College Sports and Higher Education, 2001 Report. Used with permission.

Page 677: Knight Commission on Intercollegiate Athletics. Quantitative and Qualitative Research with Football Bowl Subdivision University Presidents on the Costs and Financing of Intercollegiate Athletics: Report of Findings and Implications, October 2009. Used with permission.

CHAPTER 18

Page 689: Edward Rimer. Discrimination in Major League Baseball: Hiring Standards for Major League Managers, 1975–1994. *Journal of Sport and Social Issues*. Vol. 20, Issue 2, pp. 118–133. Copyright © 1996 by SAGE Publications. Reprinted by permission of SAGE Publications.

Page 694: N. Jeremi Duru. The Fritz Pollard Alliance, the Rooney Rule, and the Quest to "Level the Playing Field" in the National Football League. *Virginia Sports and Entertainment Law Journal*. Vol. 7, 2008, p. 179. Used with permission.

Page 700: Kenneth L. Shropshire. Diversity, Racism and Professional Sports Franchise Ownership: Change Must Come from Within, 67 *University of Colorado Law Review* 47 (1995). Reprinted with permission of the author and the University of Colorado Law Review.

Page 702: Lawrence M. Kahn. The Sports Business as a Labor Market Laboratory. *Journal of Economic Perspectives*, 14 (3) pp. 75–94, Summer 2000. Copyright by American Economic Association. Used with permission. All rights reserved.

Page 704: Michael Ryan, *The European Union and Fan Racism in European Soccer Stadiums: The Time has Come for Action*, 20 Fla. J. Int'l L. 245–78 (2008). Used with permission.

CHAPTER 19

Page 720: Mary A. Hums, Carol A. Barr and Laurie Gullion. The Ethical Issues Confronting Managers in the Sport Industry. *Journal of Business Ethics*. Vol. 20, 1999, pp. 51–66. © 1999 Kluwer Academic Publishers. With kind permission from the authors and Springer Science+Business Media.

Page 723: John Milton-Smith. Ethics, the Olympics and the Search for Global Values. *Journal of Business Ethics*. Vol. 35, 2002, pp. 131–142. © 2002 Kluwer Academic Publishers. With kind permission from Springer Science+Business Media.

Page 725: Richard H. McLaren. Corruption: Its Impact on Fair Play. From the Symposium "Doping in Sports: Legal and Ethical Issues." *Marquette Sports Law Review*. Vol. 19, Fall 2008, pp. 15–38. © Marquette University, reprinted with permission.

Part I

Professional Sports

Ownership

INTRODUCTION

In the United States and in professional sports around the globe, the individuals or entities that own various sports enterprises have been instrumental in setting the direction of the sports business. As long as there have been professional sports, there have been investors motivated by profits, public attention, winning, and community impact. As described in Don Kowet's 1970s classic *The Rich Who Own Sports*,[1] chariot races in ancient Rome were structured as a league, with corporations owning each of the four teams that competed at Circus Maximus—the Whites, Blues, Reds, and Greens—whose drivers dressed in the appropriately colored tunics. As the Roman Republic became the Roman Empire, the popularity of the races led to an expanded schedule—more races—and the gradual addition of 12 teams, with expansion fees in the millions of *sesterces* (the currency of the day). Owners of the chariot teams ran a profitable business.

The United States has seen several generations of professional team owners. The "original" generation of owners was largely composed of men (and it was all men) who had playing and/or coaching backgrounds. They typically wore multiple hats—owner, general manager, and coach, for example. The National Football League (NFL) had George Halas of the Chicago Bears and Curly Lambeau of the Green Bay Packers; Major League Baseball (MLB) had Connie Mack of the Philadelphia A's, Charles Comiskey of the Chicago White Sox, Clark Griffith of the Washington Senators, and John McGraw of the New York Giants.[2] Other owners bought teams with the goal of making their team the focus of their entrepreneurship. The team was their business. Though not inconsequential, their monetary investments in their teams was paltry by today's standards, and their ownership occurred during the start-up days of their leagues—an era marked by franchise and league instability. Without the

determination and foresight of these owners, the leagues would not have survived.

The second generation of league owners was comprised largely of men who had made money in other industries and whose interest in sports led them to purchase a franchise. Multimillionaires such as Ray Kroc, Ewing Kauffman, Charlie Finley, and Gene Autry invested part of their fortunes in MLB teams. The second generation of owners blazed a trail for the current, third generation. This third generation is marked by individuals who have accumulated vast fortunes through outside business interests and who have purchased sports organizations for any number of different reasons—from business to pleasure. Corporations are also an important part of this third generation, with entities such as Red Bull, Comcast, and Cablevision joining the ownership ranks (**Table 1**). These corporations look to use their sports holdings to improve their core businesses.

The individual equity ownership model of sports organizations can take one of two forms. The first form involves a single, independently wealthy owner, such as "new school" owners Dan Snyder, Mark Cuban, Paul Allen, and Jeffrey Lurie, who can take either a passive or active role in the club's decision making. The owner's role may change over time as he or she becomes less or more interested in team operations. The second form involves a group of individuals who pool their resources to acquire ownership of the team. League rules usually require that one individual be deemed the majority owner and/or specify that one individual be labeled as the final decision maker. For example, in the NFL the majority owner's family must have a 30% stake in the team; in the NBA the requirement is 15%. An investment syndicate document typically outlines the rights and responsibilities of each investor. Although this model can be quite successful—witness the Boston Celtics "Banner 17 LLC" group of Wyc and Irving Grousbeck, Stephen

Table 1   List of High-Profile and Publicly Traded Corporations that Own Sports Franchises

Company	Symbol	Teams
Cablevision Systems	CVC	NY Knicks, NY Rangers
Comcast Corporation	CMCSK	Philadelphia 76ers, Philadelphia Flyers
Liberty Media Corporation	LCAPA, LCAPB	Atlanta Braves
Nintendo Company	NTDOY	Seattle Mariners
Rogers Communications	RCI	Toronto Blue Jays

Source: Based on records of the *Sports Business Resource Guide and Fact Book* (2009).

Pagliuca, and Robert Epstein—it can be fraught with danger if the members of the syndicate develop philosophical or personal differences. The demise of the Atlanta Spirit LLC group and the antagonistic relationship between the Liverpool Football Club's owners Tom Hicks and George Gillett are instructive.

League operators have long preferred to work with individuals who they can look directly in the eye at a meeting and with whom they can make decisions on the spot. League commissioners and owners prefer to deal with individuals rather than corporations and their often unwieldy boards of directors. Leagues want to make decisions now, not when the schedules of two dozen corporate boards allow or, worse yet, those of thousands of shareholders. However, with the exception of the NFL, all leagues now allow teams to be owned by both individuals and corporations, despite the fact that the latter is operationally less desirable. Allowing corporate ownership provides the leagues with greater access to capital markets (i.e., the pool of potential buyers). This helps keep franchise sale prices high.

Although it is debatable whether the evolution from individual to corporate ownership is good or bad for the sports industry, there can be no doubt what is motivating this change: money. Although owners have always been wealthy, escalating franchise prices and operating costs have made ownership by the individual "moms and pops" that embodied the first and second generation of owners more difficult. The game has become too risky and expensive for many of them to play. In the United States, estate planning has also led to the divestiture of sports franchises by individual owners. Even when individual owners have remained, the rationale for their involvement may have changed. Although some venerable first- and second-generation owners remain, such as the descendants of the Mara and Halas families of the NFL's New York Giants and Chicago Bears, respectively, the new breed of individual owners such as Paul Allen, Phil Anschutz, Bob McNair, Jerry Jones, Ted Leonsis, and Jeff Vanderbeek has infused professional sports. Having

representatives from all three generations of ownership creates an interesting dynamic within the ownership ranks of each league.

A number of taxation issues are particular to the sports industry. These issues arise primarily upon the transfer of a sports franchise and involve the accounting concepts of amortization and depreciation. A significant part of the acquisition of a professional sports franchise involves intangible assets, such as the league membership agreement, the facility lease, contracts with season ticketholders, media contracts, and player contracts. The preferential treatment that professional sports franchises receive under the federal tax code—especially with respect to player contracts—is controversial, because it provides their already wealthy owners with a lucrative tax shelter for a period of years after the purchase transaction. The resulting tax benefits associated with ownership of a professional sports franchise help to keep the marketplace robust. Along with the consumption value of team ownership and the opportunity for operating profits and overall capital appreciation, the generous tax treatment of professional sports franchises encourages investment in this industry. Thus, it is important for prospective and current owners to understand the applicable taxation principles. In this chapter's final excerpt, Coulson and Fort provide an excellent overview of these tax issues.

In addition to the financial benefits that can result from the ownership of professional sports franchises in terms of the possible generation of operating profits, tax benefits, and asset appreciation, a very high consumption value is involved as well. Individual owners have long received significant psychological benefits from ownership, such as boosted egos, publicity, access to athletes and other powerful individuals, the chance to be a "winner" on the field, retaining or enhancing a community asset, membership in an exclusive fraternity or club, and the fun of being a real-life "fantasy team" owner. The motivations of some individual owners have changed in recent years, as there is an ongoing shift in focus to the synergies that ownership can provide. Some individuals, such as former owners Bruce Ratner of the NBA's New Jersey Nets and Victor McFarland of Major League Soccer's D.C. United, are motivated by the real estate opportunities surrounding the playing facility. The team serves as a means to accomplish the end goal of maximizing the returns on the larger real estate play. For others, team ownership provides valuable networking opportunities. Bob Johnson, the former owner of the NBA's Charlotte Bobcats, explained it this way:

It's not the sports side of me that drives ownership, it's the business side. Owning an asset like this creates the potential for opportunities beyond the business itself. There are opportunities to develop relationships with other team owners. These are entrepreneurs who like to do things outside of the box. There may be other things I can do with [Dallas Mavericks owner] Mark

Cuban or [Denver Nuggets owner] Stan Kroenke. It's just a good club to belong to.[3]

Other, lower-profile owners use the team to increase their visibility in the local marketplace. Robert Nucci, the owner of the now defunct Arena Football League's Tampa Bay Storm, said, "The investment is in the community and in the value of the franchise. By owning this franchise, you're very involved in the community. Your business becomes more well-known, your overall connections increase. You meet people you haven't met before. I think it's a very good investment."[4]

Some owners are motivated by a desire to win on the field. Owners are usually very competitive individuals, and this competitive nature has helped them to accumulate the vast amount of wealth that it now takes to acquire a professional sports franchise. The ability to compete for a championship provides them with a high-profile outlet for their competitive streak. Roman Abramovich, the Russian billionaire oligarch and owner of the Chelsea Football Club, said, "The goal is to win. It's not about making money. I have many much less risky ways of making money. I don't want to throw my money away, but it's really about having fun and that means success and trophies."[5]

Despite having the business acumen that it takes to accumulate enough wealth to afford a professional sports franchise, a number of owners have struggled to be successful in sports. Donald Trump, the owner of the New Jersey Generals of the long-defunct United States Football League (USFL), once said, "I watch the owners suffer. They have businesses and they're very successful, but when it comes to sports, it's like they lose a lot of business judgment."[6]

It is important to understand why this is the case. The sports industry is an industry of nuance. First, entrepreneurs in other industries are motivated by one thing—making money. However, entrepreneurs in the sports industry are pursuing victories in addition to profits. Craig Leopold, the owner of the NHL's Minnesota Wild, has stated:

Owning a sports franchise, I would say, is a departure from conventional wisdom. It's a different business, a different business model, although you use the same principles of management. That is, you get the best people that you possibly can and you let them do their jobs. But ultimately the end game is different: You're trying to win something, and the value of the asset is getting larger and larger even though your losses may continue. That's not a normal business model.[7]

Robert Kraft, owner of the NFL's New England Patriots concurs:

I learned early on that you come in as a fan, but there's no on-the-job training for owning an NFL franchise. You have to get in it and get roughed up by it. You go through a learning curve, understanding the nuances of the business that are different. At the same time, I

think it's important that when you run and manage a franchise, that you use the same core values that you use in your other businesses. You always have to decide what is right for you and your system, develop a strategic plan and follow it even when things don't go your way. It's pretty cruel in the short term when you lose and things don't go right, but as long as you believe you have a good plan, you have to stick with it and back the key people in your system.[8]

Second, most owners are not used to losing in their entrepreneurial ventures, and like most other entrepreneurs, they do not like to do so. Owners do not buy sports franchises envisioning that they will lose a lot of games. However, the binary nature of sports means that every game has a winner and a loser. There is a lot of emotion associated with the games, and it can be very difficult to separate this emotion from logic, especially when the team is losing a lot. Mark Richardson, the former president of the NFL's Carolina Panthers, explains it this way, "Until you get into it, I don't think you truly understand it. You don't realize the impact (an NFL team) has on your community. You don't understand the depth of emotion that goes with the fans and the team. You don't realize how hard it is to win."[9] Perhaps the best way for the owners to keep from making emotional decisions is to let others handle the daily operations of the franchise. In many cases, this is contrary to how many owners run their nonsports businesses, and for some it takes the fun out of owning a team. But the NHL's Chicago Blackhawks chairman Rocky Wirtz agrees: "You realize tomorrow is a new day, so you can't let your emotions control your better judgment. The owner needs to not get in the way. Too many times the owners in sports tend to let their egos get ahead of them and that is not good. You have to run this as a business."[10]

Third, being an owner of a professional sports franchise is a high-profile position that is dissimilar to what most owners have experienced in their other endeavors. Mickey Arison, owner of the NBA's Miami Heat, explains:

Before you get into it, you don't realize how high-profile it is and how much focus there is on you personally. I'm better known in the community for the team than [for] Carnival [the cruise line that he owns], and that doesn't make a whole lot of sense when you think about it. But the reality is that before I owned the team, I could go out to a restaurant and walk around town and people didn't know who I was. That changed dramatically, and even more so more recently.[11]

Although some owners enjoy the publicity and thrive on it, others are far more reluctant to spend time in the spotlight. When John Moores owned the San Diego Padres, he once said:

The worst part of owning the club is the public part of it. It's just tacky. It's a little bit of a freak show.

But being held up to public scrutiny just comes with the territory of owning any baseball team or public enterprise. It means people care. What would disturb me would be the opposite. If you're not criticized, it means people don't care. Then I would really worry. But people do care. They care a lot. People in this town care a lot about the Padres, and I'm glad they do.[12]

In recent years, the ownership entity has evolved from the gritty, individual model embodied by Art Rooney and George Halas to the presence of both individuals and corporations—particularly media, entertainment, and communications companies—looking for synergies to exploit. It seems that the trend towards corporate ownership is waning, with many of the media, entertainment, and communications companies selling their sports holdings in recent years. Indeed, 10% of all teams in the NBA, MLB, NFL, and NHL are owned in the majority by corporations. Corporations own a minority share of 16% of the teams in the NBA, MLB, NFL, and NHL. A recent count shows that 12 MLB, NBA, and NHL teams are owned by corporations. Rogers Communications, Liberty Media, Comcast, and Cablevision are among the media companies that are involved in the ownership of sports franchises. Traditionally, ownership of professional sports franchises is attractive to corporations with interests in the media, communications, and entertainment business, because sports team programming has significant content value due to the franchise's strong audience loyalty and brand visibility.

Viewing sports franchises as entertainment assets, corporations have attempted to use them to garner additional revenues through the team's playing facility and media rights. In theory, the ownership of the team and its playing facility and programming rights enable the corporate owner to enhance the team's value through the exploitation of a wide range of synergies, including cross-promotional opportunities, the creation of additional distribution outlets, and higher visibility in the marketplace, as well as risk reduction and cost savings through economies of scale. For this reason, as revenues and costs grow larger and values keep increasing, theoretically the number of corporate owners should increase. However, this strategy has not been successful for every corporation that has attempted it, and nationally focused media companies have trended away from sports ownership as a result. It is likely that corporate owners with a local or regional focus will be more successful than those with a national or global focus. Politician Tip O'Neill's statement that "all politics is local" seems to apply to corporate ownership of professional sports franchises as well.

Some notable flameouts have occurred among nationally focused corporate owners. Former team owners Disney, News Corporation, Tribune Company, and Time Warner abandoned their "sports strategies," at least partially because they were unable to capitalize on their ownership of professional sports franchises. Disney's failure is likely attributable to its inability to effectively capture the media-related revenues available through its sports franchises, which resulted in the company incurring a $100 million loss during its ownership tenure of the Anaheim Angels MLB team and Anaheim Mighty Ducks NHL team. To Time Warner, the value of owning professional sports franchises was in its ability to charge national advertising rates for the broad cable distribution of local team broadcasts via its TBS Superstation. When this value diminished as the company grew from a local broadcasting interest to a global venture through a series of mergers and acquisitions, and investor pressure grew for the company to reduce its debt load in a difficult economy, Time Warner withdrew from ownership of its sports franchise holdings. Ironically, the Atlanta Braves were sold to another media company, Liberty Media, as part of a larger stock swap transaction between the companies. Liberty Media is widely expected to sell the team after the tax requirements associated with its acquisition of the team are satisfied. News Corp. acquired the Dodgers from its longtime owners, the O'Malley family, in 1997 for a then-record price of $311 million. In doing so, the company was able to secure the team's broadcasting rights far into the future. Beyond that, however, the Dodgers were never a great fit for the Fox Entertainment Group, the News Corp. subsidiary that operated the team. The team was never part of its parent company's core business, and the managerial skill of the parent company's executives was misplaced when focused on the team side. The Dodgers became lost within the larger entity, and as the team struggled to make the playoffs and began to incur substantial operating losses, News Corp. soon tired of owning the team. When the parent company made the additional acquisition of satellite operator DirecTV for over $6 billion, the Dodgers and its related properties were sold to real estate mogul Frank McCourt, in part to help finance the purchase.

A final hurdle facing large corporate entities that own sports teams is investor and analyst pressure. When the parent company is facing financial difficulties, investors and analysts often place pressure on the company to return to its core businesses. The team is rarely part of that core. In addition, the revenues that are generated by sports franchises do not create regular quarterly earnings before interest, taxes, depreciation, and amortization (EBITDA, a measure of cash flow); instead, revenues are highly seasonal in nature and vary significantly from quarter to quarter. However, public companies are under quarterly pressure to report EBITDA growth; thus, sports teams are not necessarily a good fit for publicly traded corporations.

With the exception of a handful of teams, local sports franchises do not have much impact on a national or international level, where audience loyalty is unlikely to be strong and cross-promotional opportunities limited. Locally focused corporations avoid these problems and can retain the additional revenues that are available through the ownership of professional sports franchises. This is especially true if the corporation is the dominant cable provider in the local marketplace. Companies such as Comcast (owner of the Philadelphia Flyers and 76ers) and Cablevision (owner of the New York Rangers and Knicks) can realize the benefits of vertical integration. By owning the team, its playing facility, and its local media distribution channel, the company captures the lion's share of revenue generated by the team. It is able to dominate the local marketplace, where fans are most passionate about the local teams and can be most effectively monetized.

In addition to this mix of old-school and corporate owners are anomalies such as the Green Bay Packers, a franchise long held in a public ownership form and a grandfathered exception to the NFL's rules against corporate ownership. In the 1980s and 1990s, a smattering of other public offerings cropped up as well. The public-offering structure has provided a cash infusion to existing sports enterprises, including several North American franchises and numerous European soccer clubs. The investment merit of these offerings is somewhat dubious; they turned out to be outlets for fan affinity rather than opportunities for real financial returns.

Some private equity (PE) investment has occurred in professional sports. Although there seems to be some trending away from PE investment in sports, such investment has been significant in value when it has occurred. PE investments in major professional sports leagues have presented a number of problems. Operating within a sports league environment is not a great fit for the traditional PE model of purchasing a distressed property, slashing costs, increasing short-term revenue, and exiting for large profit, typically after a 5-year period. The challenges for PE returns are daunting. Growth areas are limited by league rules covering everything from the team's exclusive and limited geographical territory to marketing prohibitions. Existing long-term local media and sponsorship deals also limit growth opportunities. Cost reduction is difficult because of the presence of collective bargaining agreements negotiated on a leaguewide basis with the players' unions that establish team and individual player salary floors. An additional concern is whether PE firms are too focused on the short term to be effective team owners. Finally, the exit strategy can prove difficult. Given the aforementioned restrictions, the appreciation of the sports asset may not increase substantially in the window preferred by the PE firm. Thus, it may be that ancillary sports deals are somewhat better suited to PE investment. Indeed, firms such as IMG, Route 2 Digital, Falconhead Capital, and Spire Capital have invested in entities such as rodeo, beach volleyball, cricket, and a number of sports media companies. Minor league baseball and hockey, indoor football and soccer, and lacrosse may offer additional investment possibilities.

Several American sports leagues have recently adopted the single-entity structure. MLS was the first entity to use this model, in which an entire league is controlled by a single operating company. Investments are made in the company, rather than in a particular franchise. This format was developed to avoid the self-destructive behavior displayed by owners in other nascent sports leagues whose desire to win has led them to pay more than they could afford for athlete services. This behavior contributed to the demise of these leagues, because so many teams went out of business that the leagues could no longer survive. By adopting a single-entity structure, competitive bidding among owners for players is eliminated, and a major cause of league failure is sidestepped. In addition, this structure allows sports leagues to evade the application of antitrust laws in management–labor disputes.

Following the lead of MLS, most new leagues have since adopted this operating structure. Despite its strengths, the model may not prove to be an effective method of running a mature league. The single-entity structure places a disincentive on individual investors to engage in entrepreneurial behaviors, because the benefits of such tactics are likely outweighed by their costs. The whole may be weaker than the sum of its individual parts. More on the single-entity model can be found in Chapter 2.

As the sports world has become "flatter," there has been an influx of foreign ownership in sports leagues throughout the world. While the NBA's New Jersey Nets were purchased by Russian oligarch Mikhail Prokhorov in 2010, this has been especially prevalent in the English Premier League (EPL), widely regarded as the top soccer league in the world. English clubs Manchester United, Aston Villa, Liverpool, Arsenal, and Derby County are controlled by Americans; Manchester City and Portsmouth (at the time of this writing) are owned by investors from Abu Dhabi and Saudi Arabia, respectively; Fulham is owned by an Egyptian; Chelsea is owned by a Russian; Birmingham City is owned by someone from Hong Kong; and Sunderland is owned by an Irish consortium. The global popularity of the EPL and the more relaxed league rules concerning revenue opportunities and growth make it appealing to foreign investors. Similarly, an entire league, the Indian Premier League (IPL), played its second season in 2009 in South Africa rather than India. The season was moved largely for security reasons, but the action is illustrative of the shrinking sports globe.

The readings that follow examine these various ownership models and the business issues impacting individuals involved in each. There is an emphasis on the functionality of each model. Beyond impact and functionality, the valuable lessons come from understanding who the successful owners have been and who the most successful owners of the future might be.

The chapter opens with an excerpt from Quirk and Fort's classic, *Hard Ball: The Abuse of Power in Pro Team*

Sports, which touches on ownership history and also provides an overview of modern-day owners. The excerpt also focuses on how these owners fit into the modern-day sports league. This is a discussion that will be carried out in more depth in Chapter 11, "Sports Franchise Valuation." Note that the excerpt discusses the "why" of ownership, both in monetary and nonmonetary terms. Noted sports economist Andrew Zimbalist is excerpted from next, providing an excellent overview of the reasons that investors seek out professional sports. Rod Fort examines the value of owning an MLB team in the third selection. The fourth and fifth excerpts focus on initial public offerings (IPOs). This format, which has received a good deal of attention, seems to be more of a novelty than an important long-term business model. These are faceless owners, but similar to the broader corporate model used for raising funds for business success. After a brief flurry, it seems that the use of this novel approach to ownership has fizzled in North America, although the model endures in Europe.

Among the related readings in other sections of the book, three might be of particular interest. In Chapter 8, "Media," there is a discussion of vertical integration. In Chapter 4, "Emerging and Niche Leagues," a selection focuses on the single-entity model of league operation. In Chapter 18, "Race," the excerpt from the article "Diversity, Racism, and Professional Sports Franchise Ownership: Change Must Come from Within" focuses on the diversity issue as it relates to ownership.

Notes

1. Random House, 1977, pp. 3–8.

2. Quirk and Fort, *Hard Ball.*

3. Phil Taylor (quoting Bob Johnson), "Franchise Player," *Sports Illustrated,* May 5, 2003, 36.

4. Bruce Goldberg (quoting Robert Nucci), "So, You Want to Buy into the AFL? Here's How," *Sports Business Journal,* February 25, 2008, 18.

5. Alexander Wolff (quoting Roman Abramovich), "To Russia with Love," *Sports Illustrated,* December 15, 2008.

6. Peter Fitzsimons (quoting Donald Trump), "Select Policy Pays off for Swans," *The Sydney Morning Herald,* October 1, 2005.

7. (Quoting Craig Leipold), "The Daily Goes One-on-One with Wild Owner Craig Leipold," *Sports Business Daily,* November 25, 2008.

8. Jim Chairusmi (quoting Robert Kraft), "Top of His Game," *The Wall Street Journal,* December 2004.

9. (quoting Mark Richardson), "Panthers Celebrate 15th Anniversary in NFL Amid Ups, Downs," *Sports Business Daily,* October 28, 2008.

10. (quoting Rocky Wirtz), "Chicago Sports Leaders Gather to Discuss Local Market," *Sports Business Daily,* September 18, 2008.

11. John Lombardo (quoting Mickey Arison), "The Man Behind the Scenes," *The Sports Business Journal,* April 30, 2007, 1.

12. Barry M. Bloom (quoting John Moores), "Moores Reclaims Active Role with Padres," mlb.com, September 18, 2008.

PERSONALITIES AND MOTIVATIONS

HARD BALL: THE ABUSE OF POWER IN PRO TEAM SPORTS

James P. Quirk and Rodney D. Fort

The payoffs to a rich owner from owning a sports team might come mainly from the fun of being involved with the sport itself and with the players and the coaches, rather than from the profits the team generates. There is also the publicity spotlight that shines on the owner of any team—Carl Pohlad [late owner of the Minnesota Twins] is much better known in the Twin Cities for the Twins than for his Marquette National Bank. . . . And all of the fun and publicity is that much more intense when the team you own is a winner.

This view of owners as "sportsmen" ignoring bottom-line considerations has its attractions, and there have been owners who really seem to have fit this image—Tom Yawkey of the Boston Red Sox of the 1930s and 1940s is one who comes immediately to mind. Still, it pays to be a little skeptical. Billionaires don't get there by throwing their money around recklessly—they tend to be the people who let someone else pick up the tab for lunch. As important

as winning is to them, it might well be a matter of ego and personal pride that they manage to do this while pocketing a good profit at the same time.

A competing view of the owners is that, their loud protestations to the contrary, they actually are minting money from their teams' TV contracts and high-priced luxury boxes and preferred seating licenses. According to this view, owners would very much like to field winning teams if there's any money in it, but otherwise, they're quite content to load up the roster with low-priced talent and have no qualms about moving the team if fans don't flock to watch a second-division turkey.

Whatever view you have of the matter, there is no doubt that almost all of the huge amount of money that pro team sports generates, through gate receipts, TV income, stadium revenues, and sales of memorabilia, passes first through the hands of the owners. But how much stays there, and how much gets passed on in the form of player and coaching salaries, traveling expenses, administrative costs, stadium rentals, and the like? To answer this question authoritatively would require access to the books of sports teams and their owners. Unfortunately, we do not have that access. There are a few—the Boston Celtics, Cleveland Indians, and Florida Panthers—that are publicly traded businesses, so their revenues, costs, and profits are public information. [*Ed. Note: All three teams have since been purchased by private individuals and taken off the public market.*] But most sports teams are closely held businesses, organized as limited partnerships or subchapter S corporations, with no legal requirement to open their books to the rest of us. What we have instead is a set of estimates of income of the various sports teams, prepared on an annual basis since 1990 by *Financial World* [and now *Forbes*] magazine.

. . . .

The first thing that is abundantly clear . . . is that, with just a handful of exceptions, pro team sports does not appear to be a terribly profitable business.

. . . .

The figures seem to make mockery of the notion that owners are making out like bandits. At most only a few teams in each league are showing impressive book profits, and they are generally the ones that all of us would have predicted . . .

Another aspect of the financial picture of sports leagues . . . is the division between the haves and the have-nots. . . .

The large numbers of have-nots in baseball and hockey reflect the fact that winning is more important to the bottom line in these sports than in basketball or football. NFL and NBA teams derive most of their gate revenue from season ticket sales, whereas in baseball, walk-in ticket sales are an important share of the team's gate revenues and are much more sensitive to the team's won–lost record. In the NHL, there are the regular season and the "second season," the play-offs. Playoff ticket sales are a critical part of any NHL team's finances, so missing the playoffs almost certainly means financial problems for the team.

Add to this the fact that the value of local TV rights is sensitive to the playing success of a team and that local TV plays a larger role in baseball and hockey than in the other two sports. Thus, a larger share of revenue is sensitive to the won–lost record of baseball and hockey teams, which tends to increase the value of star players to teams, so that salary costs are adversely affected as well.

The large number of have-not teams also provides a clue as to why it was Major League Baseball and the NHL that experienced long debilitating work stoppages in 1994 and early 1995 [*Ed. Note: and again in 2004–2005*], with the have-not owners holding out for radical changes in the rules governing their leagues' player markets. . . .

What does this suggest about the profit orientation of team owners? We would argue that the pressures that free agency has imposed on the bottom line in sports, as indicated by operating income figures, have made it all the more important for teams to act like profit maximizers, ferreting out every possible source of revenue and exploiting it to the hilt, while paring away at costs with a vengeance. It is much more expensive to be a sportsman-owner today than it was in Tom Yawkey's days, and this lesson is well known to everyone who owns a sports team. The drive for stadium subsidies and tax rebates and the hard-line stands in labor negotiations are just a few of the obvious consequences of the tightening of profit margins in sports.

Does this mean that we should be passing the hat again for Paul Allen . . . , or that we should erect statues to owners for their profitless task of bringing quality athletic entertainment to the masses? Well, maybe not. Let's try to count some of the ways in which an owner can still break even or do better than that, even with an operating income that is negative or barely on the plus side.

First, it is commonplace for an owner to take on a salaried job with his team, as president or chairman of the board. It's the owner's team so he can pay himself whatever salary he wishes. . . .

In the years when Calvin Griffith owned and operated the Minnesota Twins, it was widely reported that there were Griffith relations galore on the payroll of the team. There is nothing illegal or immoral about this, of course; in fact, to the contrary, it makes Griffith seem like what he in fact was, a very family-oriented person. However, it does mean that book figures on team revenues, costs, and profits for the Twins understated the income that the owner and his family derived from the team.

Second, more and more often, team owners today have complex financial interrelationships with their teams. . . .

In the case of the Florida Marlins, when Wayne Huizenga owned the team, he also owned the stadium in which the team played as well as the Miami TV station that aired Marlin game telecasts. Into which of Huizenga's several pockets did the stadium rental or the local TV revenue go? Questions like this have become much more than merely academic matters for the players in the NFL and NBA operating under salary cap rules, because those rules guarantee players a stated minimum percent of league revenues. League revenues will vary depending on whether the team gets the full market value of its TV revenues, or instead a part is transferred to the station, network, or superstation owned by the team owner. (See **Table 2** for a list of the wealthy individuals that are involved in the sports industry.)

. . . .

Third, ownership of a sports team provides tax sheltering opportunities that are not available to most other businesses, so that what appears to be a before-tax loss by the team can, in certain circumstances, be converted into an after-tax profit for the owner. The idea behind the tax shelter was one more contribution to the sports industry by the fertile and conniving mind of Bill Veeck, baseball's greatest hustler and team owner. Back in 1950, Veeck was

Table 2   Sports Interests Among Forbes' Top 200 Billionaires in the World

Rank	Name	Country	Net Worth (in Billions)	Sports Interests
3	Warren Buffett	United States	$47.0	Triple-A PCL Omaha Royals Principal Owner
4	Mukesh Ambani	India	$29.0	Indian Premier League (IPL) Mumbai Indians Owner
5	Lakshmi Mittal	India	$28.7	English soccer club Queens Park Rangers Co-Owner
6	Larry Ellison	United States	$28.0	ATP/WTA BNP Paribas Open, Indian Wells Tennis Garden Owner; BMW Oracle Racing Owner (America's Cup)
37	Paul Allen	United States	$13.5	Trail Blazers, Seahawks Owner
39	Mikhail Prohorov	Russia	$13.4	New Jersey Nets Owner
50	Roman Abramovich	Russia	$11.2	EPL Club Chelsea Owner
52	Phil Knight	United States	$10.2	Nike Chair
64	Ernesto Bertarelli	Switzerland	$10.0	Team Alinghi Owner (America's Cup)
74	Silvio Berlusconi	Italy	$9.0	Serie A Club AC Milan Owner
100	Lee Kun-Hee	South Korea	$7.2	IOC Exec BOD Member
100	Alisher Usmanov	Russia	$7.2	EPL Club Arsenal Investor
117	Rupert Murdoch	United States	$6.3	News Corp. Chair & CEO
123	Phil Anschutz	United States	$6.0	AEG Chair
127	Masayoshi Son	Japan	$5.9	Japanese Baseball Club Fukuoka Hawks Owner
136	Leonid Fedun	Russia	$5.5	Russian Soccer Club FC Spartak Moscow Owner
148t	Charles Ergen	United States	$5.2	EchoStar Chair
148t	Rinat Akmetov	Ukraine	$5.2	Ukrainian Soccer Club FC Shakhtar Donetsk Owner
154	Jim Kennedy	United States	$5.0	Cox Enterprises Chair
167	Hiroshi Mikitani	Japan	$4.8	Japanese Baseball Club Rakuten Eagles Owner
176	Rich DeVos	United States	$4.5	Magic Owner
189	Mickey Arison	United States	$4.4	Heat Owner

Sources: "Forbes' Sports Interests Among Forbes' Top 200 Billionaires in the World," *SportsBusiness Daily,* March 23, 2010. Billionaire rankings reprinted by permission of Forbes Media LLC © 2010. Sports information has not been validated by Forbes.

in the process of selling his Cleveland Indians team to a syndicate headed by his friend Hank Greenberg, the great Tiger outfielder. Veeck convinced the IRS that the purchaser of a team should be allowed to assign a portion of the purchase price of the team to the player contracts that the team owned, and then to treat this as a wasting asset, depreciating the contracts over a period of five years or less. That was an important bit of convincing, because the IRS already had in place rules allowing teams to write off as current costs signing bonuses, scouting costs, losses of minor league affiliates, and all the other costs incurred by a team in replacing its current roster of players with young players coming into the sport.

. . . .

Owners typically plead poverty by quoting net operating losses as the value of the team. And, for people in their wealth class, even 7 percent does not seem like an extraordinary return. Harold Seymour, the eminent baseball historian, quotes Charles Ebbets on baseball operations: "The question is purely one of business; I am not in baseball for my health." But before we agree that sports are not a high-return investment for rich people, let's remember the other values of owning a team. Profit-taking can occur under the "other salaries" heading. Most of the rest of the costs may actually be

revenues, or generate even larger revenues, in other nonsports business operations of the owners. Business and government associations made during ownership tenure are valuable. And there is, after all, the fun of owning a team. Given all of these benefits, a 7 percent rate of return generating $5 million annually after taxes looks pretty good to us. Now, if only we could come up with that initial $75 million. . . .

A team can show a book loss, yet pay owner-management quite well while they run the team, generate many other values not captured in the team's income statement, and end up as a very valuable commodity at sale time.

. . . .

Finally, offsetting the bad news about operating income is the good news about the continuing increases in the prices of sports teams themselves. The capital gains that an owner gets from selling his team can more than offset the losses, if any, that the team has shown from its ongoing operations. In fact, this has been true in practically all cases involving recent sales of sports teams.

. . . .

The fact that the market prices of teams keep going up, even while operating income figures remain at very low levels, raises the question as to whether what we are observing is a "bubble," much like the bubble in California real estate in the 1980s. In a bubble, the current price of an asset is determined not by what the asset is expected to earn in the future, but by what people today think buyers in the future will be willing to pay for the asset. A bubble is fueled by the "greater fool" argument: "Sure, I know this house isn't worth $300,000, but a year from now, I'll be able to sell it to some other real estate speculator for $500,000 because he'll be expecting the price the year after he buys it to be $600,000." The price is what it is today because everyone expects a "greater fool" to come around tomorrow to take the item off your hands at an even higher price.

All that economists know for sure about bubbles is that, eventually, they burst, and it's like the old game of musical chairs—whoever gets stuck with the overvalued asset at the time the bubble bursts has nowhere to get rid of it. There is a classic story about the stock market that goes something like this:

A broker touted a small company's stock to a client and convinced him to buy 1,000 shares at $10 per share. A week later, the broker reported that the price was up to $12, and the client opted for another 1,000 shares. The price kept going up and the client kept buying for several more weeks. When the broker reported the price at $25 per share, the client said, "I'm not greedy. I'll just take my profits now. So sell my shares." There was a pause and then the broker asked, "To whom?"

If it really is a bubble that we are observing in the market for sports teams, the problem is that there isn't any way to know beforehand just when the bubble will burst. Those unlucky people who happen to be holding title to the overvalued team franchises will simply have to eat their losses and live with them. But if it is a bubble, it's been going on for quite a long time. Historical records of franchise sales in sports indicate that over the past thirty years or so [Ed. Note: from approximately 1970–2000], on average, NBA teams have been increasing in price at a rate of around 26 percent per year, MLB teams at around 14 percent per year, and NFL teams at around 22 percent per year.

The fact that the rates of increase in franchise prices in the 1990s, while in the double-digit range, still are lower than those in earlier years indicates that if there is a bubble in these markets, at least it is tapering off. Actually, over the period of the mid-1990s, investors were making a better rate of return simply "buying the market" with an indexed stock fund than were sports entrepreneurs with their high-visibility team investments.

Rather than being simply a bubble phenomenon, the continuing increase in team prices in sports and the capital gains being captured by owners no doubt reflect a range of factors at work in the sports industry. There are the "fun and games" and publicity aspects of ownership of a sports team. These have been increasing over time along with the media exposure that sports receives. The "spill-over" benefits of owning a sports team, those after-tax returns identified earlier that don't show up as operating income for a team, have been increasing over time as well, and get reflected in higher team prices. And there is undoubtedly something of a speculative bubble present as well, a common belief among present and prospective owners that because almost no one in the past has sold a team for less than its purchase price, future capital gains are more or less assured.

In summary . . . the current owners of sports teams are, by and large, very wealthy individuals. But, with teams being as expensive as they are, ownership of a team is a significant investment, even for a wealthy owner. The returns to ownership, as measured by operating income, are below market rates of return from investments of comparable risk in all sports with the possible exception of the NBA. A prime reason for the weak operating income performance of teams is free agency and the continuing escalation of player salaries. This suggests that bottom-line considerations play a critical role in team decision making, perhaps looming larger for today's owners than for owners of the past. On the one hand, this provides incentives for owners to act as aggressively as possible in attempting to exploit whatever local monopoly power the team possesses—if we don't squeeze out every cent of money from local fans and taxpayers, how can we afford to compete with the teams that do? On the other hand, the concentration on the bottom line makes it more difficult for teams to act cooperatively as members of a sports league in addressing problems of mutual interest to all teams in the league. What team can afford to sacrifice some of its income for the "common good" in a world in which lots of red ink is waiting just around the bend for any team that loses a star player to injury or ticket sales to bad weather?

There have been exceptional owners such as Phil Wrigley, who refused to schedule night games at Wrigley Field when he owned the Cubs, to keep nighttime noise, traffic, and confusion out of the north side neighborhood of the park; and Ewing Kauffman, who heavily subsidized his Kansas City Royals when he was alive and then set up a committee of leading local citizens to operate and then sell the team after his death, to ensure that the team stayed in town. But everything about the current and historical record of pro sports suggests that if you are trying to understand what is going on in sports, your best bet is to assume that owners will be motivated by bottom-line considerations, however wealthy they are. Wayne Huizenga's decision to sell off his Florida Marlins, one by one, and then the team franchise itself after the team won the 1997 World Series but reportedly lost $30 million at the gate, fits the mold nicely.

The contribution of owners to the problems of pro team sports does not arise, however, because they operate their teams to make money. After all, one of the fundamental reasons why we in America enjoy the living standards we do is that all those businessmen out there are free to operate to make as much money as they can. The argument in favor of a free enterprise, profit-oriented economy is that the way a businessman makes money is by producing the goods that consumers want, in the style and quantity that they want, at the lowest possible price. And if a businessman doesn't do this, he should be prepared to be steamrollered by other businessmen who do a better and cheaper job of producing that product.

Once again, the problem with the sports industry is the fact that leagues operate as monopolies, so that team owners in sports are not subject to the same intense market pressures to perform well as if they had to face competition from rivals. The local monopoly power of teams is limited, of course, by the availability of substitutes. NFL football has to compete with the college game, with other pro sports such as the NBA and the NHL, and with alternative forms of entertainment. But, when combined with the monopoly power of the league it belongs to, the local monopoly power of a team is certainly significant, as evidenced, for example, by the success of teams in their campaigns for new, highly subsidized stadiums financed by cities and states. . . .

SPORT AS BUSINESS

Andrew Zimbalist

I.   INTRODUCTION

Unlike businesses in other industries, professional sports teams in a given league both compete against and cooperate with each other. The success of a league is, to some extent, affected by the degree of uncertainty of outcome of its contests and its seasonal competitions, or, stated differently, by the degree of balance among its teams.

Professional sports leagues also differ from other industries in the degree of public exposure they garner. The daily game results are reported upon extensively in the local print, audio, and video media, and discussed widely and passionately by millions of fans.

Do these unique features of sporting leagues lead team owners to behave differently from owners of other businesses? Preeminent sportswriter Leonard Koppett (1973, p. 11), writing in the *New York Times Magazine* 30 years ago, suggested that they do:

> *Club owners are not ordinary businessmen. To begin with, profit in itself is not the owner's primary motive. Any man with the resources to acquire a major league team can find ways to make better dollar-for-dollar investments. His payoff is in terms of social prestige. . . . A man who runs a $100m-a-year business is usually anonymous to the general public; a man who owns even a piece of a ball club that grosses $5m a year is a celebrity. His picture and comments are repeatedly published in newspapers known in every corner of his community. . . . This does not mean, of course, that ball clubs don't seek profits . . . but the driving force is to be identified with a popular and successful team . . . and that motivation leads to important variations from 'normal' business behavior.*

To be sure, many economists agree with this perspective. Peter Sloane, in his well-known piece on English football (soccer), writes:

> *It is quite apparent that directors and shareholders invest money in football clubs not because of expectations of pecuniary income but for psychological reasons as the urge for power, the desire for prestige, the propensity to group identification and the related feeling of group loyalty. (Sloane, 1971, p. 134)*

He then goes on to quote a 1966 report on the English Football Association (FA) that found the objective of a club owner was 'to provide entertainment in the form of a football match. The objective is not to maximize profits, but to achieve playing success whilst remaining solvent.' Sloane suggests an owner-objective function with playing success, average attendance, health of the league, and minimum profits as its arguments.

At the time Sloane was writing, a large share of FA clubs carried payrolls that were above 80 per cent of team revenues and FA rules stipulated maximum dividend pay-outs to shareholders for the minority of teams that were publicly held.[2] Indeed, it became commonplace among economists to associate FA club ownership with utility—rather than profit maximization. In a 1999 article, for instance, Stefan Kesenne and Claude Jeanrenaud state matter-of-factly: "The most important difference between the USA and Europe is that American clubs are business-type companies seeking to make profits, whereas the only aim of most European clubs so far is to be successful on the field." Kesenne and Jeanrenaud are joined in this view by a sizeable list of others. . . .

Of course, the presumption that club owners do not profit maximize is also found in the literature on US sporting leagues. For their book on the baseball business, Jesse Markham and Paul Teplitz (1981, p. 26) interviewed ten owners as well as various other club executives and concluded that owners "were motivated to enter the baseball industry more out of reason of personal gratification, love of the game, devotion to professional sports generally, or out of civic pride than by the prospects of profits." Markham and Teplitz claim that owners "satisfice," that is, they seek "good enough" performance—analogous to utility maximization subject to a minimum profit constraint or, as the English football report put it, "playing success whilst remaining solvent."[3]

There is no dearth of newspaper articles or television shows where one can find pious ownership claims about their motives. Joe Maloof, owner of the National Basketball Association (NBA)'s Sacramento Kings, for instance, on 13 May 2003, appeared on Jim Rome's ESPN show and stated: "We have one goal in mind and that's to win a title. We're not going to rest until we have that for the city of Sacramento and for our franchise. We've never had a title and that's what we need to get."[4]

Another line of economic analysis of sports leagues holds either that team owners fundamentally maximize profit or that analyzing leagues under the profit-maximization assumption provides a useful efficiency standard against which to assess actual performance.

. . . .

Most economists do not accept at face value assertions from ownership to the effect that they are motivated strictly or mostly by civic pride or eleemosynary goals. Interviews and survey data that produce self-proclaimed, non-selfish motives can be found among executives in many industries.

Because of this distrust of the survey interview methodology, some economists have attempted to seek empirical confirmation of ownership motivation. Noll (1974) finds that ticket prices are set where the price elasticity of demand is sufficiently close to unity, so that the hypothesis of profit maximization cannot be rejected. . . . Of course, it is possible that teams follow profit-maximizing behaviour with regard to ticket pricing, and utility-maximizing behavior with regard to player salaries (by offering above competitive salaries). Furthermore, as Kesenne and Pauwels (2002) point out, profit and win maximizers are likely to follow identical pricing rules.[7]

Hunt and Lewis (1976) study the level of individual team dominance in MLB with respect to what level of dominance produces profit maximization and what level produces revenue maximization. They find that the actual level of attained dominance is consistent with profit maximization but below the level that would yield revenue maximization.

Scully's findings (1974, 1989) that baseball teams pay players below their marginal revenue products are consistent with profit-maximizing behaviour, as is Zimbalist's (1992a) estimate—using a modified Scully methodology—that on balance players are roughly paid their marginal revenue products.

Szymanski and Hall (2003) analyse the performance of 16 FA clubs that went public since 1995 to see if their behaviour changed along with ownership. The hypothesis is that if clubs were utility maximizers when privately held, then when they went public there would be increased pressure for them to perform on the bottom line. They, however, found no significant evidence of modified performance. This finding is consistent either with the argument that FA clubs are still utility maximizers after going public or the argument that clubs were always profit maximizers.[8]

While some of the empirical results in the literature have been consistent with the hypothesis of profit maximization, the results have not been conclusive. Indeed, Fort and Quirk (2002) find that without holding revenue and labour demand functions constant, it is not possible to find a definitive test to discern whether owners in a league are profit or win maximizing. Still another hypothesis was suggested by author James Michener in his book *Sports in America* (1976, p. 441):

> *In the early years of every professional sport, the owners were men of great dedication and expertise. . . .Their type was soon superseded, however, by the business tycoon who made his fortune in trade, then dabbled in sports ownership both as a means of advertising his product and finding community approval. The beer barons—Jacob Ruppert with his New York Yankees and Augie Busch with his St Louis Cardinals—were prototypes; they became famous across America and the sales of their beer did not suffer in the process. It is interesting that when William Wrigley, the Chicago tycoon, wanted to buy into the National League, he was strongly opposed by Colonel Ruppert, who feared such ownership might be used to commercialize chewing gum.*
>
> *Then came a third echelon of ownership, the corporate manager who bought a club not only to publicize his business enterprises but also to take advantage of a curious development in federal tax laws.*

One could easily quibble with aspects of Michener's taxonomy. What are particularly interesting for our purposes, however, are the notions that: (a) ownership motives might change over time, particularly as franchise values skyrocket—it being one thing to treat a sports club as a plaything when it is purchased for $1m, yet quite another when it is purchased for $800m, and (b) within a given league, ownership motives may vary.

II. WHY DO OWNER OBJECTIVES MATTER?

The behaviour of clubs and the performance of sporting leagues may be affected by objectives of owners. If club owners are profit maximizers, then they would invest in team success up to the point where the expected marginal revenue from an additional win is equal to the marginal cost. In contrast, if owners are utility or win maximizers, then they may invest beyond this point.[9] Thus, if some clubs in a league are utility maximizers and others are profit maximizers, it may provide an additional source of competitive imbalance.[10] Of course, if it is the owners of small market teams that utility maximize (while the owners of large market teams profit maximize), then playing balance may be enhanced.

Rottenberg (1956) argued that a league with profit maximizing owners will be more mindful of the need to maintain a certain level of balance and, hence, will be more restrained in labour-market spending.[11] In contrast, a league of individual utility maximizers will prioritize winning over league success and spend more aggressively on the players' market, even if it renders certain teams perennially dominant.

While this logic suggests that profit-maximizing behaviour will lead to greater competitive balance, El Hodiri and Quirk (1971) show that this generally will not be the case as long as market size and revenue potential remain disparate across the teams. Underscoring this point, a recent article by Burger and Walters (2003), using data from MLB during 1995–9 and respecifying the traditional revenue equation, find that profit-maximizing teams in the largest markets will value a player six times more than teams in the smallest markets, and that, within a given market, when a team is in contention, it can raise a player's value sixfold.

In theory, whether owners in a league are profit or utility maximizers may also affect the success of policies to promote competitive balance. If we assume that owners maximize winning and, therefore, they spend any available revenue on improving their team, then the collective selling of television or Internet rights or other revenue-sharing schemes will improve league balance (Cairns et al., 1986; Kesenne, 1996).[12] This is so because collective selling will result in less money for rich teams and more money for poor teams, and, by assumption, this will yield greater equality in payroll spending across teams. Conversely, if we assume that owners maximize profits and that fan attendance depends only on the relative quality of the home team, proportional revenue sharing will not alter the relative marginal revenues from winning and, thus, will not alter the relative payrolls or talent distribution (although all salaries would be reduced under most revenue sharing schemes) (Fort and Quirk, 1995; Vrooman, 1995; Marburger, 1997).[13]

There is one potentially significant caveat to the last assertion. When teams sign a free agent, they do not know how the player will perform and what impact his performance will have on revenues. They can only estimate a player's marginal revenue product. Hiring players, then, comes along with risk. Teams with higher revenues may be less risk averse and more willing to be aggressive in the free-agent market. Revenue sharing, although it may not alter the expected relative marginal revenue product of a player, may change owner behaviour by providing poorer teams with a larger financial cushion and making them less risk averse. It may also increase the risk aversion among owners of high-revenue teams. Insofar as revenue sharing promotes either of these results, it may promote competitive balance.[14]

Although owners' objectives will affect behavior and league success, existing literature does little more than suggest possible tendencies. Most observed behaviour is consistent with a variety of objective functions. In his 1971 piece on English football, Sloane observes that an owner's objective could be "rationalised so that it is consistent with almost any type of behaviour and therefore tends to lack operational significance." And Cairns et al. (1986, p. 10) conclude that "there are great difficulties involved in distinguishing between the competing hypotheses."[15]

To be sure, owners themselves seem to have difficulty distinguishing between different objectives. Listen, for instance, to Robert Kraft, owner of the National Football League (NFL)'s New England Patriots: "And if you're passionate about winning and you help put an organization in place that can win, the business part will follow." And listen to Robert Johnson, founder of the BET network and [then] owner of the expansion NBA Charlotte Bobcats: "I'm first and foremost a business guy and I don't see a distinction between a winning team and a profitable team." Or to Mark Cuban, owner of the NBA's Dallas Mavericks, expressing a somewhat more enlightened view:

> There's a misconception that people look at sports and say the real people who focus on the business side are just the ones that reduce costs, that the only way to really reflect running it as a business is to keep your player costs low when the reality is if I increase my sales enough it doesn't matter what my costs are.[16]

The likelihood is that owner-objective functions are both more nuanced and more varied than is allowed in the literature attempting to model sports leagues. In the next section, I suggest a more complex view of what today's club owners seek to maximize.

III.   WHAT DO OWNERS REALLY SEEK?

Owners, in fact, take their returns on sports franchises in a number of ways. As indicated above, one obvious aspect of their return is the fun, perquisites, power, and ego gratification they receive. Ownership, in part, is a consumption good. Thus, it would make sense to think of owners as maximizing their total (consumption and investment) return, not just their financial profit.

A significant part of the investment return is indirect. For instance, team ownership provides opportunities to develop new business relationships and to leverage political influence—potentially benefiting the owner's other investments as well as the sports team. . . .

With few exceptions, franchise ownership also produces substantial capital gains. According to Fort's estimates (2002, p. 389), during the 1990s the average annual rates of franchise appreciation were 11.3 per cent in MLB, 17.7 per cent in the NBA, 10.7 per cent in the National Hockey League (NHL), and 12.7 per cent in the NFL. Moag (2002, p. 2), using a different methodology and updating through mid-2002, estimated the annual rate of return to owning a baseball franchise to be 12.44 per cent from 1960 to 2002, which would put it well above the return to common stock ownership for the same period (6.91 per cent for the S&P 500 through 30 June 2002).[18] According to Szymanski and Kuypers (1999, p. 19), an investor who paid 385 pence for a share of Manchester United stock in 1991 and sold the share in mid-1998 would have experienced a capital gain of £24.40 on the single share for an annual rate of return of above 30 per cent.

In each of these instances—consumption value, business connections, political ties, tax benefits, and capital gains—the investment return will not show up on the income statement and is long term in nature. Other than the tax shelter, each of these returns is enriched by having a winning team. This suggests that owners' objective functions may contain both wins and profits. It may also include accumulation of star players.

There is also a great many ways for an owner to take short-run and pecuniary returns.[19] First, an owner can boost other companies in his or her portfolio through favoured contracting with the team. Many team owners today own entities (such as TV, cable, or radio stations, and facility management, concessions, or chartering companies) that do business with the team. When the owner does business with himself he can charge whatever prices he likes—it is money in one pocket or the other. This practice, known as a related-party transaction or transfer pricing, can reduce reported franchise revenues substantially. Consider the example of MLB's Chicago Cubs.

According to 2001 figures that MLB Commissioner Bud Selig delivered to the U.S. Congress, the Chicago White Sox's income from local TV, radio, and cable was $30.1m, and that of the Chicago Cubs was $23.6m. Yet, everyone knows that the Cubs are by far the more popular team in the Windy City, and TV ratings bear this out: in 2001 the Cubs' average ratings were 6.8 on over-the-air broadcasting and 3.8 on cable; the White Sox's were 3.6 and 1.9, respectively. And this does not take account of the fact that the Cubs games are shown on super-station WGN which reaches 55m-plus homes nationally.

So, how can we understand Selig's figures? The Cubs are owned by the Tribune Corporation, which also owns WGN. [*Ed. Note: The team and its related properties were sold to Tom Ricketts in 2009 for $845 million.*] The Tribune Corporation, in effect, is transferring revenue away from the Cubs and lowering the costs of WGN. It does this by using related party transactions, which are entirely lawful and widely used in the sports industry and across business generally. According to *Broadcasting & Cable,* the industry's authoritative source, the estimated value of the Cubs' local media earnings in 2001 was $59m. If the Cubs reported this figure instead of $23.6m, then their reported $1.8m loss would become a $33.6m profit in 2001![20]

Why would the Cubs (and all other baseball teams) want to reduce their reported revenues? There are several possible reasons. First, since 1996, MLB has had a revenue-sharing system that levies a tax on a team's net local revenues. In 2001 this tax was at 20 per cent (in 2003 the effective marginal tax rate is close to 40 per cent) (Zimbalist, 2003, ch. 5). Thus, for every dollar in local revenue not reported in 2001, the team saved just under 20 cents.[21] Since WGN pays no such tax to the broadcasting industry, it is preferable for the parent corporation, Tribune, to have the profits appear on WGN's books.

Second, baseball teams (and even the Cubs, who were seeking public permission to erect higher leftfield stands in 2002) seek various kinds of public support for their facilities. They may believe that the more impecunious they appear, the more likely it is that such support will be forthcoming.

Third, every few years the owners negotiate with the players over a new collective-bargaining contract. The owners always seek new restrictions in the labour market to lower salaries. One of the justifications for these restrictions commonly is that the teams are losing money. Whether or not the Players Association is persuaded by such arguments, it appears to be permanently fixed as part of the owners' opening gambit.

Fourth, MLB is the only professional sport in the United States that has a presumed antitrust exemption. Periodically, MLB is called before Congress to justify this special treatment. One of the arguments that MLB has repeatedly trotted out—most recently by Selig before the U.S. Congress in December 2001—is that the industry cannot possibly be abusing its market power because it is not profitable.

Fifth, ownership may believe that claims of poverty may help to justify higher ticket or concessions prices to the fans.

As in the example of the Chicago Cubs, many MLB teams and teams in other sports make extensive use of related party transactions. In each case, the team's true financial return is unlikely to be found on the bottom line. Hence, a cursory glance at a team's income statement is unlikely to reveal ownership motives.

More generally, it is common for owners to treat sports teams as part of their entire investment portfolio. Often, the team itself is not managed as a profit centre, but rather as a vehicle for promoting the owner's other investments. Owners can take their investment returns in a number of ways. For instance, George Steinbrenner used his New York Yankees to create the YES regional sports network in the nation's largest media market. In 2001, YES had a market value upward of $850m. Rupert Murdoch admitted that his purchase of the Dodgers paid off because it enabled him to prevent Disney from creating a regional sports network in southern California. In 1998, Disney had signed up its MLB Angels and NHL Mighty Ducks to a 10-year cable contract with Fox Sports Net West II for a seemingly well-under-market $12m a year. It is not unlikely that Disney received other benefits from the News Corp. (such as carriage at an attractive price for Disney's many cable channels on the News Corp.'s worldwide satellite distribution systems).

Tom Hicks hopes to use his ownership of the Texas Rangers to develop some 270 acres of commercial and residential real estate around the ballpark in Arlington and to grow his Southwest Sports Group, among other things. [*Ed. Note: These efforts proved unsuccessful, and Hicks sold the Rangers in 2010.*] Dick Jacobs exploited his ownership of the Indians to promote the value of his downtown real estate. And so on. Once again, the team's income statement will not tell the whole story.

One important implication of the preceding discussion is that competitive balance may be more elusive to sporting leagues. Not only may different owner objective functions and team-specific revenue potentials engender imbalance, but team synergies with related business interests may exacerbate inequalities. For instance, when Tom Hicks signed Alex Rodriguez to a 10-year deal for $25.2m annually, he was thinking about the return A-Rod would bring to all of his businesses, not just to the Rangers. Thus, what might appear as utility-maximizing behavior by an owner is really global (portfolio-wide) profit-maximizing behavior. Put differently, owners may find that the best way to profit maximize globally is to win maximize at the team level.[24]

When owner investment in players yields returns to both the ball club and to other businesses of the owner, this may be a significant additional source of league imbalance. Under such circumstances, leagues may be justified in imposing constraints on the legal form of ownership, such as proscribing corporate ownership.

In the United States, however, other than the general and welfare-diminishing prohibition on municipal ownership in all leagues, the NFL is the only league to limit systematically the ownership form. It does so by outlawing corporate ownership. There is an irony here, because the NFL, with its relatively hard salary cap and extensive revenue sharing, is probably the only U.S. league that does not have to worry about competitive balance.

. . . .

In sum, one obvious conclusion to draw from the foregoing discussion is that owners maximize global, long-term returns and that these are very different from a team's reported annual operating profits. While, at today's stratospheric franchise prices, it is problematic for most owners to be pure sportsmen—maximizing utility without a financial constraint—it is almost a certainty that different owners give different weights to the variety of arguments in their objective functions. The next task for modelling the behaviour and performance of sports leagues is to take fuller account of this probable diversity of ownership objectives within a given league.

References

Brower, J. (1977), 'Professional Sports Team ownership: Fun, Profit and Ideology of the Power Elite', *Journal of Sport and Social Issues,* 1(1), 16–51.

Burger, J., and Walters, S. (2003), 'Market Size, Pay, and Performance: A General Model and Application to Major League Baseball', *Journal of Sports Economics,* 4(2), 108–25.

Cairns, J., Jennett, N., and Sloane, P. J. (1986), 'The Economics of Professional Team Sport: A Survey of Theory and Evidence', *Journal of Economic Studies,* 13, 3–80.

Dabscheck, B. (1975a), 'Sporting Equality: Labour Market versus Product Market Control', *Journal of Industrial Relations,* 17(2), 174–90.

—— (1975b), 'The Wage Determination Process for Sportsmen', *Economic Record,* 51(133), 52–65.

Daly, G., and Moore, W. (1981), 'Externalities, Property Rights and the Allocation of Resources in Major League Baseball', *Economic Inquiry,* 19(1), 77–95.

Davenport, D. S. (1969), 'Collusive Competition in Major League Baseball: Its Theory and Institutional Development', *American Economist,* 13, 630.

Demmert, H. G. (1973), *The Economics of Professional Team Sports,* Lexington, MA, D. C. Heath.

El Hodiri, M., and Quirk, J. (1971), 'An Economic Model of a Professional Sports League', *Journal of Political Economy,* 79(6), 1302–19.

Ferguson, D. G., Stewart, K., Jones, J. C. H., and LeDressay, A. (1991), 'The Pricing of Sports Events: Do Teams Maximize Profit?', *The Journal of Industrial Economics,* 34(3), 297–310.

Fort, R. (2002), *Sports Economics,* Upper Saddle River, NJ, Prentice Hall.

—— and Quirk, J. (1995), 'Cross Subsidization, Incentives and Outcomes in Professional Team Sports Leagues', *Journal of Economic Literature,* 33(3), 1265–99.

—— (2002), 'Owner Objectives and Competitive Balance', Washington State University, unpublished manuscript.

Hunt, J. W., and Lewis, K. A. (1976), 'Dominance, Recontracting and the Reserve Clause: Major League Baseball', *American Economic Review,* 66(5), 936–43.

Jones, J. C. H. (1969), 'The Economics of the National Hockey League', *Canadian Journal of Economics,* 2(1), 1–20.

Kesenne, S. (1996), 'League Management in Professional Team Sports with Win Maximizing Clubs', *European Journal for Sports Management,* 2, 14–22.

—— (2000), 'Revenue Sharing and Competitive Balance in Professional Team Sports', *Journal of Sports Economics,* 1(1), 56–65.

—— and Jeanrenaud, C. (1999), 'Introduction', in S. Kesenne and C. Jeanrenaud (eds), *Competition Policy in Professional Sports,* Antwerp, Standard Editions.

—— and Pauwels, W. (2002), 'Club Objectives and Ticket Pricing in Professional Team Sports', Department of Economics, University of Antwerp, unpublished manuscript.

Koppett, L. (1973), 'A Strange Business, Baseball', *The New York Times Magazine,* 2 September.

Lewis, M. (2003), *Moneyball: The Art of Winning an Unfair Game,* New York, Norton.

Marburger, D. (1997), 'Gate Revenue Sharing and Luxury Taxes in Professional Sports', *Contemporary Economic Policy,* 15, 114–23.

Markham, J., and Teplitz, P. (1981), *Baseball Economics and Public Policy,* Lexington, MA, D. C. Heath.

Michener, J. (1976), *Sports in America,* New York, Random House.

Moag, J. (2002), *Moag & Company Industry Analysis,* Spring.

Neale, W. (1964), 'The Peculiar Economics of Professional Sports', *Quarterly Journal of Economics,* 78, 1–14.

Noll, R. G. (1974), 'Attendance and Price Setting', in R. G. Noll (ed.), *Government and the Sport Business,* Washington, DC, Brookings.

Rascher, D. (1997), 'A Model of a Professional Sports League', in W. Hendricks (ed.), *Advances in the Economics of Sport,* Vol. 2, Greenwich, CT, JAI Press, 27–76.

Rottenberg, S. (1956), 'The Baseball Players' Market', *Journal of Political Economy,* 64, 242–58.

Schofield, J. A. (1982), 'The Development of First-class Cricket in England: An Economic Analysis', *Journal of Industrial Economics,* 30(4), 337–60.

Scully, G. (1974), 'Pay and Performance in Major League Baseball', *American Economic Review,* 64(6), 915–30.

——— (1989), *The Business of Professional Baseball,* Chicago, IL, University of Chicago Press.

——— (1995), *The Market Structure of Sports,* Chicago, IL, University of Chicago Press.

Sloane, P. J. (1971), 'The Economics of Professional Football: The Football Club as a Utility Maximiser', *Scottish Journal of Political Economy,* 17(2), 121–46.

Szymanski, S., and Hall, S. (2003), 'Making Money Out of Football', The Business School, Imperial College, London, unpublished manuscript.

——— and Kuypers, T. (1999), *Winners and Losers: The Business Strategy of Football,* London, Viking Books.

Vrooman, J. (1995), 'A General Theory of Professional Sports Leagues', *Southern Economic Journal,* 61, 971–90.

Zimbalist, A. (1992a), 'Pay and Performance in Major League Baseball: Beyond the Scully Model', in P. Sommers (ed.), *Diamonds Are Forever,* Washington, DC, Brookings Institution Press.

——— (1992b), *Baseball and Billions,* New York, Basic Books.

——— (2003), *May the Best Team Win: Baseball Economics and Public Policy,* Washington, DC, Brookings Institution Press.

Notes

. . . .

2. In their excellent overview of English soccer, Stefan Szymanski and Tim Kuypers (1999, p. 16) write that the FA first imposed dividend limitations in 1896. The first limit was 5 per cent of paid-in capital. It was raised to 7.5 per cent in 1920 and to 15 per cent in 1983, but most teams had ceased to pay dividends in the 1950s.

3. The most common formalization of this approach is to assume win maximization subject to a break-even constraint.

4. Quoted in the *Sports Business Daily,* 14 May 2003, p. 20.

. . . .

7. This result may be altered if home-field advantage is partially based on attendance.

8. Szymanski and Kuypers (1999, p. 19) point out that when Manchester United went public in 1991, it organized a holding company that received most of the team's revenue. Among other things, the holding company was a way to avoid FA regulations over the appointment of directors and limitations on dividend pay-outs.

9. This point is nicely exposited by Szymanski and Hall (2003). Depending on one's assumptions, if clubs are constrained win maximizers, they may evince the same labour-market behaviour as profit maximizers. If owners were unconstrained win maximizers, they presumably would invest in increments to player talent until the last player had zero productivity.

10. Fort and Quirk (2002), however, point out that, assuming concavity in teams' revenue functions, the level of competitive imbalance in a profit-maximizing or constrained win-maximizing league is indeterminate.

11. Rottenberg (1956) also argued that diminishing returns to additional star players would support the appropriate level of competitive balance.

12. Kesenne (1996) finds this to hold if the owner maximizes wins subject to a break-even financial constraint. Kesenne (2000) finds it to hold even without a break-even constraint. Still another possibility not considered in the literature is that owners will spend revenues from sources other than their sports franchises to improve team quality.

13. In contrast, if we assume profit maximization and that attendance is a function of the quality of both the home and visiting teams, then increased revenue sharing will equalize the distribution of talent (Marburger, 1997). Rascher (1997) posits an objective function with both profits and wins as arguments and shows that if clubs assign different weights to winning, revenue sharing will promote league balance.

14. To the extent that risk aversion differs between profit- and utility-maximizing owners, the relationship between payroll size and ownership objectives becomes still more complicated.

15. This conclusion is also reached by Fort and Quirk (2002) and by Kesenne and Pauwels (2002).

16. Quoted in the *Sports Business Daily,* 16 May 2003.

. . . .

18. Using data through the early 1990s, Scully (1995, ch. 6, pp. 118–25) finds even higher annual rates of return on sports franchise ownership.

19. What follows in the text is not intended as an exhaustive list of the ways ownership can manipulate the results on an income statement. Another common practice is for an owner to lend money to a partnership and then have the partnership buy the team. The owner in this case receives his return via interest payments on his loan and these interest payments enter the income statement as costs, lowering team book profits. It is also common for the owner to receive financial returns by benefiting from salary, consulting fees, or perquisites, and by hiring family members.

20. It is possible that this figure should be adjusted for the super-station payments that the Cubs make to MLB, which are probably in the order of $15m annually. It is also possible, however, that the Broadcasting & Cable figure is conservative.

21. The reason the net tax was just under 20 cents was that the team gets back roughly one-thirtieth of every dollar it contributed.

. . . .

24. To the extent that this is true, of course, the win-maximization assumption would be appropriate for modelling ownership behaviour in a sports league.

. . . .

**FR. LEONARD ALVEY LIBRARY
BRESCIA UNIVERSITY**

THE VALUE OF MAJOR LEAGUE BASEBALL OWNERSHIP

Rodney Fort

Major League Baseball (MLB) owners have always made the same claims. There's never enough left-handed pitching. And nobody ever makes any money with a baseball team. According to Scully (1989, p. 126), "Whining about lack of profit from owning a baseball club has been a sacred tradition among owners from time immemorial." He cites a case back to 1880 and other famous quotes abound (these were gleaned from USAToday.com's "Antitrust Quotes"):

> *Unless something happens, we're all going to be out of business. When you have as many teams as there are losing money, something has got to give.* —*Cleveland Indians chairman Patrick J. O'Neill, February 27, 1985.*
>
> *We have a remarkable number of teams losing a lot of money.*—*Milwaukee Brewers owner Bud Selig in testimony to a House subcommittee, September 22, 1994.*
>
> *Professional baseball is on the wane. Salaries must come down or the interest of the public baseball must be increased in some way. If one or the other does not happen, bankruptcy stares every team in the face.* —*Chicago White Stockings owner Albert Spalding, 1881.*

More recently, Commissioner Selig's report on finances for 2001 (*Street & Smith's Sports Business Journal*, December 10, 2001, p. 44) showed 19 MLB teams in the red to the tune of $362.3 million (prior to revenue sharing). Since there were 11 teams $130.1 million to the good, consolidated losses were reported at $232.2 million for that season.

The findings in this paper shed light on these claims based on basic finance principles. . . . Data limitations prohibit a direct assessment of the value of professional team sports ownership. But, given that competition over the purchase of MLB teams appears to be brisk, team sale prices should approximate the expected discounted future value of ownership. Further, the observed growth rate in team prices should also be at least as large as the next best alternative growth that owners could enjoy.

An alternative view is that owners don't care about cash flow, or pursue other goals. This view suggests that they are sports consumers with budgets so large that they simply buy the objects of their consumption affection. While some owners no doubt derive consumption value, the vast majority of owner behavior reveals them to be thoroughly professional business people with a keen eye toward the bottom line (Fort, 2003, Chapter 1). Further, as is quite well known, there are other monetary values to owning a team that are not captured on their income–expense reports.

These principles lead to two main findings on actual MLB team sale prices. First, the mean and median growth in team sale prices over the modern history of MLB easily exceed a standard comparison, namely, 3% real growth in the economy at large. Second, the expected growth rate from time of purchase to time of sale has fluctuated over time. The average real growth rate in team sale prices exceeded the 3% typical growth rate in the economy at large from the 1900s through the 1940s. Indeed, prior to the 1930s, growth rates were over three times this comparison value. The 1950s through the 1970s were, indeed, a down period below the 3% comparison. But a strong rebound occurred in the 1980s. Recently, in the 1990s, the growth rate was essentially zero. This roller-coaster ride reveals that owner claims are partly consistent with the data, but not always.

There are other interesting findings as well. First, as with other financial assets, there is a strong relationship between risk, measured by the variance in team sale prices, and expected return, measured by average sale prices. Second, owners appear to have learned over time how to price expansion franchises closer to a reasonable estimate of the expected discounted value of future profits. Third, omitting the tumultuous decade surrounding World War II, the period of ownership fell dramatically in the 1960s and again in the 1990s. Finally, the portion of the value of ownership that is not associated with annual operations appears to be significant, possibly in the tens of millions of dollars.

The paper proceeds as follows. In Section II, the approach to analyzing the value of team ownership is presented and some insights are offered on the popular *Financial World/Forbes* annual team valuations. Section III presents the historical growth of team sale prices and expansion fees. The analysis also yields some estimates of the values of ownership beyond team annual operating profits. Conclusions round out the paper in Section IV. Formal modeling of the determination of team prices would improve our understanding greatly, but the length of such an analysis precludes its inclusion here.

THE VALUE OF TEAM OWNERSHIP

Those seeking to analyze the value of team ownership should keep this warning from Scully (1989, p. 129) well in mind:

> *To the researcher, the analysis of profit in baseball is a particularly difficult undertaking, because uniform audited financial data from the clubs generally is not available, because expended items frequently cover some portion of profits, and because the financial return to ownership is multifaceted.*

The value of owning a pro sports team clearly exceeds annual operating profits. The following is a more complete categorization of ownership values:

1. Annual operating profits.
2. Shelters from federal income taxes.

FR. LEONARD ALVEY LIBRARY
BRESCIA UNIVERSITY

3. Spillovers to other wealth generating elements of the owner's portfolio.

4. Profit taking from the expense side.

5. League revenue sharing, including future expansion fees.

Throughout this section, EBITDA refers to earnings before interest, taxes, depreciation, and amortization and ITDA will be used as shorthand for those deductions from earnings.

Item 1 should be clear enough. After all is said and done, even after ITDA, there may be annual operating profits. But these can be difficult to discern and, to see why, let's turn immediately to Items 2 and 3. The sports accounting practices that come into play have been allowed by the IRS since 1959 (Scully, 1989, p. 130). Okner (1974) was the first to treat these practices academically more than 30 years ago. And despite the fact that they were treated academically again by Scully (1989) and Quirk and Fort (1992), and are now the stuff of sports economics textbooks (Fort, 2003), these accounting practices are completely neglected in the popular analysis of sports team profits.

While there are other nuances concerning tax restructuring and capital gains (covered in detail in the works just cited), the easiest tax shelter to see is produced by the so-called "roster depreciation allowance" (henceforth, RDA). In 1959, Bill Veeck bought the Chicago White Sox for the first time. He argued that players "waste away" like livestock and, since livestock could be depreciated, why not players? The IRS agreed and the RDA was born.

After a few investigations of subsequent use of the RDA by other owners, the IRS finally settled in the late 1970s on the following. An owner could allocate 50% of the purchase price of a team to a five-year depreciation schedule without challenge. Any deviation had to be justified by the taxpayer. That ruling held until just recently and federal tax law amendments now allow 100% of the team sale price to be depreciated for 15 years.

While the merits of Veeck's argument are debatable (again, see the works just cited), and why it is that players can be both depreciated and expensed has not been addressed, the results for sports team owners have been valuable to say the least. The RDA, coupled with structuring the team as a pass-through for tax purposes, generates a tax shelter as follows. I buy a team for about the average price through the current decade, $255 million. I can depreciate the entire $255 million over 15 years. For easy presentation, suppose a flat schedule at $17 million per year. This $17 million annually is my RDA. Suppose my EBITDA in year one is $25 million and interest, actual physical depreciation, and amortization equal $20 million. Annual operating profits subject to taxation would be $5 million. But now my RDA comes into play—subtracting the $17 million RDA generates a $12 million loss for the year. My tax liability from the team is erased.

But what really happened? The $5 million subject to taxation is never really lost; it's a paper reduction according to allowable IRS rules. So I enjoy that $5 million tax-free. But it gets better still. If the team is originally structured as a pass-through (e.g., a Subchapter S Corporation), then the $12 million paper loss goes through to my 1040 Form and shelters other income according to my marginal tax rate. Owners surely pay the top 35% marginal tax rate so about $4.2 million in other earnings is sheltered. From the owner's perspective, this is the best kind of $12 million "loss" possible. In *The Hustler's Handbook,* Bill Veeck jokes, "We play the Star-Spangled Banner before every game. You want us to pay taxes, too?"

Let's move on to Items 3 through 5. Spillovers to other wealth generating items in the owner's portfolio occur along a spectrum of complexity. The more pedestrian include the value of entertaining that might lead to future business dealings; nothing like a night in the owner's box for lively business interaction. More complex is access to information concerning future government decisions that can affect the current and future business dealings of an owner. And then we get to the deeply complex, as in the following example offered by Zimbalist (1998).

The Florida Marlins won the 1997 World Series. Then owner Wayne Huizenga claimed losses of $30 million for that year. But Huizenga also owned the stadium where the Marlins played and the regional media carrier of the team's locally broadcast games. Zimbalist (1998) presents an argument that shifting reported revenues between the team, stadium, and media unit could reduce the amount of revenue shared with other MLB owners as well as produce a tax savings. By Zimbalist's account, the $30 million loss could easily be a $13.8 million gain.

The last two values of ownership are much more straightforward. Profit taking on the expense side is common in all business structures; health care benefits, transportation, and entertainment expenses commonly displace similar expenditures that owners would otherwise have to take on themselves. And low-rate loans from "the team" to "the owner" are common. Finally, membership in a pro sports league entitles team owners to net revenue sharing amounts dictated by league sharing rules (of course, this might be negative if the team is in a relatively larger-revenue market) as well as an equal share of future expansion fees.

The foregoing provides the basic model for an approach to analyze team sale prices and expansion fees. The most anyone should pay for a team (or expansion franchise) should be the real discounted net present value (DNPV) of the stream of returns: . . . . what can reasonably be referred to as the stand-alone asset value of ownership and should be equal to the discounted stream of real annual operating profits alone. While it is only one of the ownership values, it is the object of attention in much of the discussion of MLB owner profits . . . [and] was clearly the object of analysis in

Commissioner Selig's presentations during the last labor–management negotiations in 2001. And independent assessments also focus on this amount. For example, in personal correspondence with Michael Ozanian, one of the authors of the *Financial World–Forbes* (henceforth, FW-F) team valuation reports, it was revealed that those reports are a "multiple of revenues" estimate, adjusted for specific stadium/arena lease factors estimated by those authors.

The usefulness . . . is that both actual team sale values. . . and reports on team valuations . . . are available. And that means we can approximate values of ownership other than annual operating profits, namely, by simple subtraction. This approach helps us sidestep one of Scully's warnings that ownership is multifaceted and still get an estimate of that value.

But we should proceed with caution in this type of comparison. Under the "multiple of revenues" approach, a benchmark is set at some multiple of a team's revenues over time. Lately, reputable finance houses have raised this multiple from around 3.0 to 5.5 (Kaplan, 2004). But revenues can be shifted for some teams, as in the preceding Marlins example, so that reported revenues used in the "multiple of earnings" approach are understated. This means that teams with higher spillover values and understated reported revenues will have artificially understated estimates. . . .

As an aside, the "discounted cash flow" approach to team valuation estimates team sale prices as the amount someone is willing to pay today in order to receive the anticipated cash flow in future years. . . . But, with the RDA and other tax complications, then Blue Jays President and COO Paul Beeston instructs us as follows (found at the same USAToday.com location cited earlier in the section):

> *Anyone who quotes profits of a baseball club is missing the point. Under generally accepted accounting principles, I can turn a $4 million profit into a $2 million loss, and I can get every national accounting firm to agree with me.*

It is straightforward sports accounting to show negative cash flows, rendering the "discounted cash flow" method without its required data.

THE GROWTH IN MLB FRANCHISE PRICES

The aims of this section are to 1) assess the growth of team sale prices and expansion franchise fees, and 2) calculate ownership value other than annual operating profits as in expression (2). The data used to analyze team sale prices and expansion team prices are from popular sources and are listed at the author's webpage, http://www.rodneyfort.com (click on the "Sports Business Data Area" link). Expansion episodes are reserved for separate treatment since that price isn't really the price of a team.

The transaction data were constructed as follows. If a team sells at time t for P_t and then sells again at time $t+$

for P_{t+}, then the buy and sell pair for this transaction at $t+$ is (P_t, P_{t+}). Throughout the data, the actual owner at time t is not necessarily the owner that sells at time $t+$. In many cases, there were intervening transactions for which there are no data. Purchases of less than 100% were adjusted to full-purchase price. No transactions that included other inseparable purchases (real estate, broadcasting ventures, teams in other leagues, and stadiums) were included.

The unit of analysis is the franchise, not the location. For example, the history of the value of the MLB Braves includes their travels from Boston (1901–1952) to Milwaukee (1953–1965) and on to Atlanta (1966–present). This follows since a foresighted owner knows full well that moving a team to a new location is within the realm of possibility and certainly can affect the growth in value of the franchise. In addition, transactions that occurred in steps are treated as a single transaction, including the CBS purchase of the New York Yankees that occurred from 1964–1967.

Only one subjective judgment was made on a transaction—the buyout of the final Marge Schott estate holding of 1/15 of the Cincinnati Reds produced a team value that simply was unbelievably too low. The result is 95 separate transactions for 28 different teams over the period 1902–2004. All values are adjusted to 2004 U.S. dollars (some deflators for the earliest sales were extrapolated).

In the literature, Scully (1989, 1995) examines profitability and return for MLB teams, but only for a few years each time. Quirk and Fort (1992) compare nominal rates of return to the rate of return on industrial common stocks for the same data used here, through 1990, and then extend that calculation in nominal terms to sales episodes during the 1990s (Quirk & Fort, 1995). Zimbalist (1992) produces an overall nominal and real growth rate, for the entire period of the 1910s through the 1980s. But all of these works included sales with inseparable purchases other than the team. Here, those episodes are omitted and real growth rates are compared to the typical real growth rate in the economy of 3%.

Table 3 shows all of the transactions organized by franchise. The clear observation is that there was astronomical growth for some transactions. The truly fabulous all involve the earliest purchases of the older teams, although there have also been handsome growth rates in more recent times, with a few just breaking into double digits relative to the comparison 3%. This observation is consistent with imputation of monopoly power into the purchase price; subsequent returns may still be large relative to 3%, but there's nothing like being the earliest owners to capture monopoly profits (the Cardinals price grew at a 124.6% rate from 1920–1925; the Boston Braves price increased 62.5% in one year, 1910–1911). There also were some large declines in some of the transactions (the 1965 sale of the Senators2 and the 1973 sale of the Indians, and the White Sox decline of 11.1% in 1975 and then, subsequently, another 13.6% in 1981). But on balance the mean and median are well in excess of the 3% comparison.

Table 3 MLB Team Sale Prices and Growth Rates (2004) (in Millions)

Team	t	$t+$	Length	P_t	P_{t+}	Growth
Angels	2000	2003	3	$207.2	$191.4	−2.6%
Astros	1979	1992	13	$50.0	$140.1	8.3%
Athletics	1954	1960	6	$47.6	$24.3	−10.6%
	1960	1980	20	$24.3	$29.5	1.0%
	1980	1995	15	$29.5	$106.3	8.9%
	1995	2005	10	$106.3	$172.8	5.0%
Blue Jays	1991	2000	9	$187.6	$194.3	0.4%
Braves	1906	1910	4	$1.5	$2.3	10.0%
	1910	1911	1	$2.3	$3.7	62.5%
	1911	1919	8	$3.7	$4.4	2.3%
	1919	1923	4	$4.4	$5.6	6.0%
	1923	1925	2	$5.6	$4.2	−12.8%
	1925	1941	16	$4.2	$15.0	8.2%
	1941	1962	21	$15.0	$39.2	4.7%
	1962	1976	14	$39.2	$40.3	0.2%
Brewers2 (Pilots)						
	1970	1981	11	$54.1	$27.3	−6.0%
	1981	2005	24	$27.3	$211.2	8.9%
Cardinals	1920	1925	5	$0.2	$13.6	124.6%
	1925	1949	24	$13.6	$26.7	2.8%
	1949	1953	4	$26.7	$26.8	0.1%
Cubs	1905	1915	10	$2.2	$9.5	15.8%
Dodgers	1912	1944	32	$3.9	$15.1	4.3%
	1944	1945	1	$15.1	$15.9	5.7%
	1945	1950	5	$15.9	$32.5	15.3%
	1950	1998	48	$32.5	$363.9	5.2%
	1998	2004	6	$363.9	$371.0	0.3%
Expos	1990	1999	9	$125.6	$164.3	3.0%
	1999	2002	3	$164.3	$127.2	-8.2%
Giants	1903	1919	16	$2.6	$19.4	13.3%
	1919	1976	57	$19.4	$28.6	0.7%
	1976	1977	1	$28.6	$32.1	12.5%
	1977	1992	15	$32.1	$136.0	10.1%
Indians	1916	1927	11	$8.8	$11.0	2.1%
	1927	1932	5	$11.0	$7.0	−8.7%
	1932	1946	14	$7.0	$15.7	6.0%
	1946	1949	3	$15.7	$20.1	8.6%
	1949	1956	7	$20.1	$27.8	4.8%
	1956	1966	10	$27.8	$47.1	5.4%
	1966	1972	6	$47.1	$49.4	0.8%
	1972	1973	1	$49.4	$30.7	−37.8%
	1973	1986	13	$30.7	$60.9	5.4%
	1986	2000	14	$60.9	$358.5	13.5%
Mariners	1981	1989	8	$27.3	$123.2	20.7%
	1989	1992	3	$123.2	$170.0	11.3%
Marlins	1999	2002	3	$182.3	$167.5	−2.8%
Mets	1980	1986	6	$48.7	$140.4	19.3%
	1986	2002	16	$140.4	$318.0	5.2%
Orioles2 (Brewers1-Browns)						
	1902	1915	13	$1.1	$9.9	18.7%
	1915	1936	21	$9.9	$4.5	−3.7%
	1936	1945	9	$4.5	$15.3	14.7%
	1945	1951	6	$15.3	$16.2	0.9%
	1951	1979	28	$16.2	$34.5	2.7%
Orioles2 (Brewers1-Browns) cont.						
	1979	1988	9	$34.5	$140.9	16.9%
	1988	1993	5	$140.9	$228.4	10.1%
Padres	1974	1990	16	$46.4	$109.5	5.5%
	1990	1995	5	$109.5	$105.0	−0.8%
Phillies	1903	1909	6	$4.2	$7.0	8.8%
	1909	1943	34	$7.0	$3.9	−1.7%
	1943	1981	38	$3.9	$63.0	7.6%
Pirates	1946	1950	4	$24.5	$12.8	−15.0%
	1950	1985	35	$12.8	$39.3	3.3%
	1985	1996	11	$39.3	$112.2	10.0%
Rangers (Senators2)						
	1963	1965	2	$52.0	$30.3	−23.7%
	1965	1969	4	$30.3	$54.3	15.7%
	1969	1971	2	$54.3	$52.3	−1.8%
	1971	1989	18	$52.3	$122.1	4.8%
	1989	1998	9	$122.1	$292.5	10.2%
Red Sox	1912	1913	1	$5.8	$7.7	32.0%
	1913	1923	10	$7.7	$12.8	5.2%
	1923	1933	10	$12.8	$5.1	−8.7%
	1933	1978	45	$5.1	$93.5	6.7%
Reds	1902	1929	27	$3.1	$13.5	5.6%
	1929	1962	33	$13.5	$29.8	2.4%
	1962	1984	22	$29.8	$44.2	1.8%
	1984	1999	15	$44.2	$210.5	11.0%
Rockies	2001	2004	3	$159.5	$142.9	−3.6%
Royals	1983	2000	17	$43.1	$106.6	5.5%
Tigers	1903	1920	17	$1.2	$4.8	8.4%
	1920	1935	15	$4.8	$27.9	12.5%
	1935	1956	21	$27.9	$38.6	1.6%
	1956	1983	27	$38.6	$101.8	3.7%
	1983	1992	9	$101.8	$111.5	1.0%
Twins (Senators1)						
	1912	1919	7	$5.3	$10.0	9.6%
	1919	1964	45	$10.0	$64.3	4.2%
	1964	1984	20	$64.3	$81.0	1.2%
White Sox	1959	1961	2	$32.8	$34.7	2.9%
	1961	1967	6	$34.7	$97.0	18.7%
	1967	1975	8	$97.0	$37.9	−11.1%
	1975	1981	6	$37.9	$15.8	−13.6%
Yankees (Orioles1)						
	1903	1915	12	$0.4	$8.7	29.8%
	1915	1922	7	$8.7	$34.1	21.5%
	1922	1948	26	$34.1	$52.8	1.7%
	1948	1967	19	$52.8	$86.2	2.6%
	1967	1973	6	$80.1	$43.0	−9.8%
	1973	1999	26	$43.0	$690.0	11.3%
Minimum			1.0	$0.2	$2.3	−37.8%
Maximum			57.0	$363.9	$690.0	124.6%
Average			13.4	$44.6	$82.1	6.2%
Median			10.0	$27.9	$38.6	5.0%
Standard Deviation			11.5	$57.4	$106.3	16.9%

Sources: Author's webpage, http://www.rodneyfort.com (click on "Sports Business Data Area" link). Previously published in *International Journal of Sport Finance*. Used with permission from Fitness Information Technology.

Notes: The transaction time endpoints are (t, $t+$); buy and sell prices for each transaction are (P_t and P_{t+}); growth is calculated over the length of time between t and $t+$. The formula simply solves the standard discounted present value formula for the rate that would change prices from P_t to P_{t+} over the period t to $t+$.

The aggregation in **Table 4** covers beginning and end results for each franchise as opposed to separate transactions for insights into longer-term ownership. The Cardinals, Cubs, and Mariners top the list, each over five times the 3% comparison. As with the individual transactions, the team-level aggregates have both average and median growth rates well in excess of the 3% comparison. And, of course, there have been clubs, decline in price. There are seven losers relative to the 3% comparison (Angels, White Sox, Rockies, Marlins, Athletics, Expos, and Blue Jays). But an actual decline in the purchase price only happens for four of these franchises (Angels, White Sox, Rockies, and Marlins). And of these four, only one is over any reasonable amount of time to judge (the White Sox at 22 years, while the period for the rest is only three years). So, we can be pretty sure that 21 franchises did as well or better than the comparison 3% (and some very well, indeed) and that four franchises did not: the White Sox, Athletics, Expos, and Blue Jays. The following conclusion is a fair one: Owning a MLB franchise almost always generates growth in the sale price that exceeds the 3% comparison, and typically (at the median) by about 50%.

One item of interest, relevant to whether or not a market is producing results in line with standard finance notions, is whether or not there is a relationship between risk and return. At the team level, one can calculate the mean growth for teams with more than one transaction and the variance. The correlation between the means of sale prices (MEAN P_{t+}) and their variance (VAR P_{t+}) is 0.516. And a simple regression across teams yields the following:

$$\text{MEAN } P_{t+} = 39.2 + 0.003 \quad \text{VAR } P_{t+}, R^2 = 0.152$$
$$(7.85) \qquad\qquad (0.001)$$

Standard errors are in parentheses and the F-value of the regression is significant at the 95% level. While clearly much of the variation in mean sale prices remains to be explained, there is some support that higher variance leads to higher mean prices consistent with the risk-return explanation.

Formal time series modeling of the behavior of team sale prices is beyond the aims of this particular paper, so we end with the preceding conclusions. But there is one more observation that can be made by aggregating across teams over time. While no market participant can buy a portfolio of baseball teams (the few sales of shares have been mostly gimmick short-term fund-raisers and almost immediately bought back), or speculate on some "index value" of baseball teams, they can use the aggregated information to guide their assessment of the value of purchasing any particular team. And this is especially true for the purchase of an expansion franchise.

But let's be clear. I might ask myself what the expected net discounted present value of ownership might be. This would be associated with similarly situated teams; in the comparison for expansion teams that follows, the average should be an over-statement since expansion teams in MLB typically look more like smaller-revenue market teams.

The behavior of prices, from this perspective, is shown in **Table 5**. If an owner bought in a given decade, what rate of growth did they enjoy to eventual sale (sort Table 3 by P_t and take averages by decade)? Again, the highest growth rates were captured by the earliest owners. Coupled with the observations around Table 4, baseball was simply a booming business through its first 40 modern years. Growth over time moderated considerably for those buying teams in the 1950s through 1970s. And then there's a fascinating episode for the 1980s. The average for those buying in the 1990s is essentially zero. The verdict is still out on those buying in the 2000s; only two of them sold their teams and they didn't hold them for very long.

A standard approach in evaluating owner choices is to compare to a buy-and-hold strategy. For example, suppose a team purchased in a given decade was held the average period that owners actually held their teams purchased in that decade. This strategy beats the decade average growth actually observed in the 1970s and 1990s (two low periods for buyers). But following this strategy would have been the height of foolishness through the first five decades of MLB and in the 1990s. While owners are typically on the ball relative to this objective buy-and-hold strategy, learning why growth is relatively so low in the 1970s and 1990s remains for future work. An obvious explanation is that if all owners sold according to this strategy, franchise prices may not be the actually observed average P_{t+} used in the buy-and-hold calculation.

It is worth noting two other observations generated by this look at decade aggregates. First, the average period of ownership drops off sharply during the War years, as might be expected in a time of high uncertainty. But it also drops off dramatically in the 1960s and again in the 1990s.

Second, this look at aggregates by decade also shows that taking on higher risk purchases yields a greater mean return. The correlation between the mean and variance of decade-average sell prices is 0.823. Running a regression similar to the earlier one for team observations, one finds the following:

$$\text{MEAN } P_{t+} = -2825 + 1.464 \quad \text{YEAR} + 0.0051 \quad \text{VAR } P_{t+}, R^2 = 0.861$$
$$(939.3) \qquad (0.4805) \qquad\qquad (0.0018)$$

The variables are as before with YEAR the last year in the decade where there was a sale. Standard errors are in parentheses and the F-value of the regression is significant at the 99% level. Even accounting for the significant trend over time, there is a significant positive relationship between risk and return and very little of the variation in mean return remains to be explained. Let's see how the information in Table 5 can inform us about expansion franchise fees.

Table 6, Panel A, shows the fees and averages for the five MLB expansion episodes, along with growth rates from episode to episode and over the entire period where any expansion is observed. While not really a team sale

Table 4   MLB Summary (2004) (in Millions)

Team	t	t+	T	P$_t$	P$_T$	Growth
*Angels**	2000	2003	3	$207.20	$191.40	−2.6%
*Astros**	1979	1992	13	$50.00	$140.10	8.3%
Athletics	1954	2005	51	$47.60	$172.80	2.6%
*Blue Jays**	1991	2000	9	$187.60	$194.30	0.4%
Braves	1906	1976	70	$1.50	$40.30	4.8%
Brewers2 (Pilots)	1970	2005	35	$54.10	$211.20	4.0%
Cardinals	1920	1953	33	$0.20	$26.80	15.4%
Cubs	1905	1915	10	$2.20	$9.50	15.8%
Dodgers	1912	2004	92	$3.90	$371.00	5.1%
*Expos**	1990	2002	12	$125.60	$127.20	0.1%
Giants	1903	1992	89	$2.60	$136.00	4.5%
Indians	1916	2000	84	$8.80	$358.50	4.5%
*Mariners**	1981	1992	11	$27.30	$170.00	18.1%
*Marlins**	1999	2002	3	$182.30	$167.50	−2.8%
*Mets**	1980	2002	22	$48.70	$318.00	8.9%
Orioles2 (Brewers1-Browns)	1902	1993	91	$1.10	$228.40	6.1%
*Padres**	1974	1995	21	$46.40	$105.00	4.0%
Phillies	1903	1981	78	$4.20	$63.00	3.5%
Pirates	1946	1996	50	$24.50	$112.20	3.1%
Rangers (Senators2)*	1963	1998	35	$52.00	$292.5	5.1%
Red Sox	1912	1978	66	$5.80	$93.50	4.3%
Reds	1902	1999	97	$3.10	$210.50	4.4%
*Rockies**	2001	2004	3	$159.50	$142.90	−3.6%
Royals	1983	2000	17	$43.10	$106.60	5.5%
Tigers	1903	1992	89	$1.20	$111.5	5.2%
Twins (Senators1)	1912	1984	72	$5.30	$81.00	3.9%
White Sox	1959	1981	22	$32.80	$15.80	−3.3%
Yankees (Orioles1)	1903	1999	96	$0.40	$690.00	8.1%
Minimum			3.0	$0.2	$9.5	−3.6%
Maximum			97.0	$207.2	$690.0	18.1%
Average			45.5	$47.5	$174.6	4.8%
Median			35.0	$25.9	$141.5	4.5%
Standard Deviation			34.3	$63.5	$139.1	5.3%

Source: Author's webpage, http://www.rodneyfort.com (click on "Sports Business Data Area" link). Previously published in *International Journal of Sport Finance.* Used with permission from Fitness Information Technology.
Notes: See Table 3. In addition, T is the length of time between the first buy and last sell for each franchise. *Denotes expansion teams used for calculations in the text (Senators2 to 1971).

Table 5   Growth in P$_t$ by Decade Average Period of Ownership and Buy-And-Hold to 1999 (2004) (in Millions)

Decade (#Obs)	Growth Min	Growth Ave.	Growth Max	Ave. P$_t$	Ave. P$_{t+}$	Ave. Period	Growth Ave. Period
1900s (9)	−1.7%	12.1%	29.8%	$2.6	$8.3	15.4	10.7%
1910s (12)	−3.7%	12.2%	62.5%	$7.5	$8.3	17.0	2.3%
1920s (9)	−12.8%	13.6%	124.6%	$11.1	$12.4	15.1	4.0%
1930s (4)	1.6%	7.2%	14.7%	$11.1	$11.1	22.3	3.9%
1940s (10)	−15.0%	3.5%	15.3%	$20.5	$20.0	10.8	2.1%
1950s (7)	−10.6%	1.8%	5.4%	$29.7	$25.8	22.3	1.8%
1960s (11)	−23.7%	−0.7%	18.7%	$50.3	$50.7	10.0	−1.3%
1970s (11)	−37.8%	1.6%	16.9%	$41.7	$44.2	11.7	5.3%
1980s (13)	1.0%	10.4%	20.7%	$73.0	$76.1	11.7	9.5%
1990s (7)	−8.2%	−0.4%	5.0%	$177.0	$210.0	6.4	3.0%
2000s (2)	−3.6%	−3.1%	−2.6%	$183.3	$214.7	3.0	

Source: Author's webpage, http://www.rodneyfort.com (click on "Sports Business Data Area" link). Previously published in *International Journal of Sport Finance.* Used with permission from Fitness Information Technology.

Table 6   MLB Expansion Fees (2004) (in Millions)

Year	Team	Panel A Fee	Ave. Fee	Growth Over Last Expansion
1960	Astros	$11.6		
	Angels	$13.5		
	Mets	$11.6		
	Senators2	$13.5	$12.6	
1968	Royals	$28.9		
	Expos	$65.0		
	Padres	$65.0		
	Pilots	$27.6	$46.6	17.8%
1976	Mariners	$21.0		
	Blue Jays	$23.5	$22.3	−8.8%
1991	Marlins	$133.0		
	Rockies	$133.0	$133.0	12.7%
1997	Diamondbacks	$154.7		
	Devil Rays	$154.7	$154.7	2.6%
			Growth 1960–1997	7.0%

Expansion	Estimated Present Value	Panel B Franchise Fee	Difference	Ratio Fee: Estimate
1960	$47.2	$12.6	$34.6	0.3
1968	$47.2	$46.6	$0.6	1.0
1976	$63.3	$22.3	$41.1	0.4
1991	$216.0	$133.0	$83.0	0.6
1997	$220.8	$154.7	$66.1	0.7

Source: Author's webpage, http://www.rodneyfort.com (click on "Sports Business Data Area" link). Previously published in *International Journal of Sport Finance.* Used with permission from Fitness Information Technology.

price, expansion fees are reflective of a prospective owner's anticipation of collecting the type of values listed in Section II, and detailed in Table 5. And let's remember that expansion fees are low-end estimates of ownership value since expansion should occur into economically marginal territories; otherwise, existing owners would want to move there.

Over the full sample period, real expansion fees rose from a 1960 average of $12.6 million to $154.7 million in 1997. That's a real annual growth rate of 7.0% over 37 years but includes a significant decline in the 1976 expansion. This overall high rate of growth relative to the growth rate in the general economy might be explained by recognition on the part of prospective owners that the returns to expansion franchises are more risky. And there is some evidence to support this view.

All expansion franchises except the Pilots and the most recent Diamondbacks and Devil Rays appear in Table 4. Seven of the 11 are below average and all of the observations with negative growth rates (except the White Sox) were expansion franchises. And the overall average for the 11 expansion teams (including the Senators2 to 1971 with a growth rate essentially equal to zero) with observations in Table 4 is 3.4%.

But the evidence isn't complete on the idea that expansion franchises are quite risky prospects. For example, the Astros (8.3%), Mets (8.9%), and Royals (5.5%) are all strong performers and the Mariners (18.1%), thanks to the dot.com boom in the Seattle area, show the highest rate of real growth of all teams in Table 4. In addition, the Pilots, arguably the worst experiment in modern MLB history, sold for $54.1 million in 1970 when the average sell price was $44.2 million (Table 5). So, while risky on average, there were some true gems in the expansion mix. This begs an alternative explanation and one does present itself.

Table 6, Panel B, compares an estimated present value of profits to franchise fees. The estimated present value is found as follows. Suppose an existing team were purchased at the same time as the 1960 expansion. Given that the average period of ownership for those buying in the 1960s was 10.0 years (Table 5), and the rate of growth for buyers in the 1960s was −0.7%, and the sale price in the 1970s averaged $44.2 million, then what original buy price in 1960 solves $P_{1960}{}^{*}[44.2/(1 - 0.7)^{10.0}]$? This estimated buy price should be the discounted present value of profits for such a team. These values are shown in Panel B, column 2. Of course, when one buys an expansion franchise, there is still the player roster, stadium arrangement, and other operating expenses to incur. Especially for marginal territories, the franchise fee should be less than the estimated present value of the eventual team that takes the field. But it is the pattern of the fees that proves interesting, not their absolute level.

As an alternative to the idea that expansion teams are riskier than others, Panel B suggests that the overall 7% growth rate is overblown because the franchise fee in the 1960 expansion is only 30% of the estimate of net present value of profits! An explanation for this "mistake" by the league owners in 1960 could simply be "learning by doing." After all, this was their first experiment with expansion in the modern period. The 1960s expansion involved only one city of unknown potential (Houston) but the price was only 30% of the reasonable estimate. Subsequently, for the 1968 expansion, the price jumps to equal the reasonable estimate, but this price is too high for an expansion franchise for the reasons just noted—the owner still needs to buy players, a stadium arrangement, and the rest of their operations. And after the 1968 over-charging, the expansion franchise cautiously rises from 40% to 70% of the estimated present value of profits. This is consistent with learning over time.

Panel B also suggests the following for expansion team owners. Since the expansion of 1976, it appears that owners have been zeroing in on the estimated present value of profits for potential expansion owners. And this really doesn't bode well for potential owners of expansion teams since they must then earn back a discounted present value of profits to cover the expansion fee and their net rate of return. Perhaps the below-average growth rates for the seven of 11 expansion teams in Table 4 is due to this added burden in territories that already were marginal in terms of expected profitability.

Think about this: It appears that the most reasonable conclusion is that owning MLB teams is, with a few notable exceptions, quite profitable and nearly always beats the growth rate in the economy at large. These results, along with the ability of owners to use the RDA or revenue transfers to mask actual operating profits, cast serious doubts on claims of poverty voiced by MLB owners. And expansion franchises appear to be less and less valuable on net, over time, once the original purchase price is imputed into the result.

Finally, what can we learn about ownership values other than operating profits by employing expression? The FW-F valuations are $DNPV_1$, the other values of ownership are $\sum_{i=2}^{5} DNPV_i$, and actual sale prices should be DNPV. So we should be able to find the other values of ownership as:

$$\sum_{i=2}^{5} DNPV_i = P_{t+} - DNPV_1$$

There are 27 transactions from Table 3 that occurred over the period of the FW-F data. Actual sale prices (P_{t+}), FW-F valuations (DNPV1), and differences are shown. . . . The difference between average actual sale prices and average FW-F valuations is only $1.3 million, or about 0.63%. If we toss out the three largest FW-F misses (Seattle, Montreal, and Colorado) the average difference is less than $1 million.

But, the variation is broad in the FW-F estimates; the average percentage difference across all of the observations is about –8.5% (–3.9% without the three biggest misses). So the FW-F estimates are less than actual sale prices as hypothesized in Section II with the conclusion that other ownership values average about 8.5% of actual sale prices. At the average of all actual sale prices, the other values of ownership would be 8.5% of $208.4 million, or about $17.7 million.

But by the discussion in Section II and [the equation], the differences should all be negative. . . . Perhaps heroically, let's focus only on the 15 transactions where the difference is negative and assume that the estimates in those cases are somehow more accurate than the rest. For those 15 transactions, the average difference is $42.1 million. Since the average actual sale price for these transactions is $218.9 million, then other ownership values would be about 19.2% of the actual average sale value.

CONCLUSIONS

Since believable profit data are not provided by MLB owners, one way to track the value of ownership is through actual team sale prices. If owners maximize economic return and competition is brisk, sale prices should approximate the discounted net present value of ownership. Further, observed growth rates in these prices should indicate the next best alternative growth that team owners can obtain.

Examining these growth rates for MLB franchises, it appears that MLB team ownership, once all values to ownership are included in the analysis, is profitable in the aggregate. At the level of individual transactions, the average rate of growth in sale prices is twice the 3% typical growth rate in the economy at large and the median is 1.6 times larger. The average real growth rate in sale prices aggregated at the franchise level is 4.8% and 4.5% at the median. Again, both values are well in excess of the 3% real growth rate in the economy at large. Further, there is a strong risk and return relationship in these prices suggesting that the market for franchises reward those buying higher risk teams.

Without any formal time series analysis, all that can be said is that the behavior of growth rates aggregated at the decade level has been a roller-coaster ride, dramatically high in MLB's earliest decades, falling below the 3% comparison rate from the 1950s through 1970s, bouncing back handsomely in the 1980s, and falling off again in the 1990s to essentially zero. While some of these periods are consistent with owner laments of losses, not all periods back up these claims. And there is an even tighter risk-return relationship at the decade averages (statistically speaking, based on the significance of the regression and coefficient estimates).

In addition, owners appear to have learned over time how to price expansion franchises closer to a reasonable estimate of the expected discounted value of future profits. This may help explain why the growth rates in sale prices for the vast majority of expansion teams are so weak. And, omitting the tumultuous decade surrounding World War II, the period of ownership fell dramatically in the 1960s and again in the 1990s. Finally, the portion of the value of ownership that is not associated with annual operations appears to be significant, possibly in the tens of millions of dollars. Even at its generous length, the paper fails to address some obvious and important issues. The results in Tables 3 and 4 cry out for formal modeling and estimation of the price determination process, perhaps along the lines begun by Alexander and Kern (2004). And surely solid time series techniques can inform us about the interesting roller-coaster ride for sale price growth rates in Table 3. The explosion in the 1980s is consistent with the dramatic expansion of cable TV. But why are growth rates so phenomenal early on only to fall into the doldrums from the 1950s through the 1970s? And why did the fall off to essentially zero growth rates in the 1990s occur? Finally, there is the puzzle of the two fairly distinct points in time where the average period of ownership drops substantially. Related to time series issues, perhaps regime changes based on structural alternations occurred; changes in the tax value of owning teams is one possibility worth exploring.

The analysis suffers from the absence of actual profit data. In the absence of those data, we are left with our suspicions and the results that can be determined from available data. And the results here suggest that few owners actually do experience negative cash flows in the first place since 1) team sale prices increase at rates in excess of the growth rate in the economy at large, and 2) riskier prospects do, indeed, receive higher mean returns. Outside of a few very remote theoretical oddities (Quirk & Fort, 1992, pp. 72–77), claims of negative cash flow appear to be an artifact of acceptable accounting practices. The roster depletion allowance and the ability to shift revenues between multiple operations generate paper losses only. And that is what owners report.

My favorite quote about MLB is attributed variously to Hall of Fame Manager Leo Durocher, "Baseball is like church. Many attend. Few understand." And on the business side of the game, it is no wonder. It is relatively straightforward to list the elements of ownership value. But our ability to untangle values other than operating profit depends on data we rarely get to see. And to date the popular media reports of team sale prices and *Financial World/Forbes* team valuations are what we have to work with. The analysis should be extended as just suggested and revisited as it is here if additional data ever become available.

References

Alexander, D. L., & Kern, W. (2004). The economic determinants of professional sports franchise values. *Journal of Sports Economics, 5*, 51–66.

Fort, R. (2003). *Sports economics.* Upper Saddle River, NJ: Prentice Hall.

Kaplan, D. (2004) Franchise value a multiple-choice question: In analysis of valuation methods, Lehman Bros. finds nearly $1B gap between extremes for Bengals. *Street & Smith's Sports Business Journal,* May 17, 2004, p. 3.

Okner, B. A. (1974). Taxation and sports enterprises. In R. G. Noll (ed.), *Government and the sports business.* Washington, D.C.: The Brookings Institution.

Quirk, J., & Fort, R. D. (1992). *Pay dirt: The business of professional team sports.* Princeton, NJ: Princeton University Press.

Quirk, J., & Fort, R. D. (1999). *Hard ball: The abuse of power in pro team sports.* Princeton, NJ: Princeton University Press.

Scully, G. W. (1989). *The business of Major League Baseball.* Chicago, IL: University of Chicago Press.

Scully, G. W. (1995). *The market structure of sports.* Chicago, IL: University of Chicago Press.

Zimbalist, A. (1992). *Baseball and billions: A probing look inside the big business of our national pastime.* New York, NY: Basic Books.

Zimbalist, A. (1998). Just another fish story. *New York Times,* October 18.

ALTERNATIVE MODELS

NFL VS. SHERMAN ACT: HOW THE NFL'S BAN ON PUBLIC OWNERSHIP VIOLATES FEDERAL ANTITRUST LAWS

Genevieve F. E. Birren

I. INTRODUCTION

In 1991 William H. Sullivan sued the National Football League (NFL), accusing the NFL of violating federal antitrust laws.[1] Sullivan, the owner of the New England Patriots, wanted to sell forty-nine percent of his team to the public in the form of stock.[2] The stock sale never happened and Sullivan sold his team.[3] Sullivan claimed that the NFL rule against public ownership was an antitrust violation.[4]

In the NFL Constitution, there are several rules that result in the ban on public ownership of teams. Rule 3.2(a) prohibits nonprofit corporations from owning a team.[5] This rule includes a "grandfather clause," which allows the Green Bay Packers to operate as a public corporation and still be a member of the NFL. At the time the old NFL and the American Football League (AFL) merged, the Patriots, a member of the AFL, were also publicly owned.[6] The Patriots were also grandfathered into the newly merged NFL.[7] However, in 1976 Sullivan bought all the public shares and became the sole owner of the Patriots.[8] This acquisition of all public stock apparently eliminated the Patriots' right to public ownership under the grandfather clause, at least in Sullivan's mind. In 1987, when the Patriots were in financial trouble and Sullivan wanted to sell public ownership interests again, he sought NFL approval for the sale.[9] The Green Bay Packers, on the other hand, neither needed, nor sought, league approval for any of their four stock sales.[10] If Sullivan believed that he had the right to sell public interests without NFL approval, he would have done so without seeking league approval first.

A combination of other rules makes team ownership by a for-profit public entity a "practical impossibility."[11] Rule 3.3(A)(1) requires "the names and addresses of all persons who do or shall own any interest or stock" in an NFL team.[12] Rule 3.3(A)(2) requires written financial statements from all persons who will have ownership interests, including stockholders.[13] Rule 3.3(C) states that "each proposed owner or holder of any interest in a membership, including stockholders . . . must be individually approved by the . . . members of League."[14] Finally, rule 3.5[15] prohibits certain types of transfers of ownership interests, "effectively precluding any kind of public ownership."[16]

. . . .

[*Ed. Note: Author's discussions of the applicability of the antitrust laws, standards of antitrust analysis and relevant markets are omitted.*]

V.   RULE OF REASON ANALYSIS

A.   Economic Aspects of Public Ownership

There is an agreement among most NFL owners that the sale of stock will substantially increase revenue for the teams that do so.[105] But this does not mean that the owners are correct.

In Sullivan, various NFL owners testified that publicly owned teams would have access to more money than privately owned teams and that privately owned teams would be unable to compete.[106] Theoretically, the publicly owned teams would gain such an economic advantage from their stock sales that private owners would have to sell their ownership interests to the public in order to compete.[107]

This theory does not appear to be accurate. A 2002 news article reported the Green Bay Packers' 2001–2002 net annual income at just $3.75 million, placing the Packers 20th in the league.[108] The Packers' net income increased dramatically during the 2002–2003 football season, totaling a franchise record $18.8 million, making the team 10th in the NFL for the 2002–2003 season.[109] This increase is largely attributed to the renovations that were made to the Packers' stadium, Lambeau Field.[110] Even with increased stadium revenues, the Packers' economic viability depends on the NFL's revenue sharing.[111]

The Packers would have a potentially continuous, inexhaustible source of revenue if they sold stock all the time. However, this continuous revenue is unlikely. Although the 1997–1998 stock sale sold 120,010 shares, 400,000 were available for sale to the public.[112] If there were not sufficient buyers for 400,000 shares, then an unlimited supply of shares would not likely result in unlimited revenue. Although the 1997–1998 stock sale was only for a limited period of time and more time could have resulted in all 400,000 shares being sold, it is unlikely that sales of undefined amounts of stock could continue indefinitely.

Another potential argument against public ownership is that even if all the teams sold public interests, some teams would be at an economic advantage because of the team's location. Although some teams may be located in larger economic markets at the local level, those teams usually share the market with other professional sports teams, including other NFL teams (i.e., New York City and the San Francisco area). Some individual teams may bring in more money from the cities in which they are located but other teams will generate more national income.

To prevent this type of potential inequity, the NFL has adopted rules against public ownership. The First Circuit concluded that were public ownership available, there would be pressure on the teams to compete for public income and this competition is prevented only by the NFL's rules.[113]

Dividends could create another potential economic imbalance. The NFL rules imply a distinction between stocks that pay dividends and ones that do not.[114] The outright ban on nonprofit organizations owning teams is essentially an outright ban on dividend-free stock.[115] There is no such outright ban on stock that pays dividends, but as discussed in the introduction, other rules make it virtually impossible to set up a for-profit public ownership scheme.

It makes sense that the league's primary concerns would be about dividend-free stock. This type of stock allows the team to retain all the revenues from stock sales, whereas stock that pays dividends lowers the income value of the stock to the team. A team that pays dividends on public stock will need to take that into account when looking at the price of the stock and overall team revenue. The NFL has never had a publicly owned team that paid dividends, so there is no example to examine.

The Green Bay Packers do not pay dividends to the shareholders of team stock.[116] This has not resulted in significantly more revenue for the Packers, and to do so could severely hurt the team financially since the total net income is only a few million a year.[117]

B.   Efficiency of Team Management

In a publicly owned corporation, the ownership and the management are different parties. This can make decision-making difficult if there are a large number of owners that need to agree on a specific course of action.[118] Conversely, a privately owned corporation has ownership and management consolidated into one party, expediting decision-making.[119]

However, the above description of a public corporation's management is misleading. Publicly owned corporations generally vest their power in a Chief Executive Officer (CEO) or president, a single person who makes the daily business decisions.[120] The president carries out the directions of a governing board.[121] This is what the Packers have done. The Packers have a board of directors and an executive committee.[122] Although the shareholders have voting rights, they do not make decisions regarding the everyday affairs of the team. There is an annual meeting where the stockholders elect the board of directors, and the board of directors elects the executive committee, which includes the president.[123] Stockholders also vote on whether to increase stock shares and conduct a sale.[124]

This arrangement, which is fairly similar to many other publicly owned corporations, is functional and efficient. There is no indication that this form of ownership has inhibited the Green Bay Packers management efficiency; if it had, then it would not have been reasonable for the shareholders to approve the sale of up to one million shares in 1997.[125] A business, even a professional football team, would not choose to expand a certain form of management if that form had been inefficient at a smaller size.[126]

Furthermore, the NFL exercises a great deal of control over the individual teams, preventing the owners from unilaterally making any decisions they want. The league limits what the owners can do with their ownership interest and requires league approval for any ownership sale or transfer.[127] Private owners cannot act as though they were autonomous corporations. All of this said, there is no evidence that a publicly held team is any less efficient then a privately owned team.

C.   The Role of Relocation

It is in the interest of NFL teams to be able to relocate. If teams can relocate, then cities have an incentive to build new football stadiums and give teams gratuitous leases on publicly owned facilities. If teams cannot relocate, then the teams, and thus the league, lose an important bargaining advantage over cities.

The NFL regulates franchise relocation with rule 4.3.[128] Rule 4.3 requires a three-fourths vote of approval by the other teams before any team can relocate.[129] The NFL admits that the purpose of the rule is to restrain competition between the teams for franchise location.[130] In *Raiders*, the NFL argued that the rule was necessary for league and franchise stability.[131] This rule gives the impression that the NFL does not want teams to be able to relocate. But history indicates that the NFL has not made strong efforts to prevent its franchises from moving.[132]

There have been twenty-three relocations of NFL teams since 1921.[133] Seven of these relocations are merely the team moving to a nearby town or suburb, not changing the city with which the team is associated.[134] For example, both the New York Giants and New York Jets have moved to Rutherford, New Jersey,[135] but they are still considered to be teams located in New York City. The team changed its name to the new city for the other seventeen relocations but only seven of those have occurred since the NFL/AFL merger in 1966,[136] an average of one relocation every five years and three months.[137] Even if the NFL tries to maintain the stability of franchise locations, a team's ability to relocate is also important to the league.

Los Angeles, the second largest city in the country, currently has no NFL franchise. Los Angeles is considered to be the most appealing market for an NFL franchise.[138] There is a great deal of speculation that many teams are interested in relocating to Los Angeles . . . .[139]

Due to the intricacies of public ownerships, it is unlikely that the Green Bay Packers will ever be able to relocate. A majority vote of stockholders is necessary to relocate the team.[143] Since ninety percent of the Packers shareholders live in Wisconsin, it is highly unlikely that the needed majority could ever be achieved.[144] If all of the teams in the NFL could be prevented from relocating, the teams and the NFL could be bound to less lucrative cities than if they could relocate.

Teams that have the potential to move are in a position of power relative to their current city. Teams have tried the threat of relocation to get the team's current city to agree to build a new stadium.[145] New stadiums and tax breaks offered by cities trying to keep their teams increases the individual team's revenue, and due to revenue-sharing, the league's revenue.[146]

While the SBA gave the NFL the right to merge and become a monopoly, it does not grant the NFL complete antitrust exemption.[147] If the revenue increases for NFL teams through NFL rules because prices for tickets, concessions, parking, and merchandise all go up, the league may have abused its position as the only major professional football league in the country and abused the leniency it received under the rule of reason because collusion is necessary for the league to function.

D.   Majority vs. Minority Ownership by the Public

The Green Bay Packers are the only NFL team whose majority interest is owned via stock.[148] In the Packers case, the entire team is owned by the public in the form of stock.[149] This is the type of ownership to which the NFL seems to refer when it cites the difficulty of getting many owners to agree and the potential problems this creates in making management and relocation decisions. As previously discussed, these concerns are invalid.

The NFL's other main concern with public ownership is the potential financial windfall for a team with public stock.[150] A team that is entirely owned in stock could split its shares ad infinitum, if the stock holders approved, as the Packers did in 1997, splitting stock shares 1,000 to 1 and selling 400,000 of the resulting million to the public.[151] The Packers shareholders could vote to split the current 4,748,910 shares[152] again and again. This has the potential to be an inexhaustible resource, but, as discussed earlier, the demand must exist for the quantity of stock that would become available. Without buyers, the available stock is of no economic value to the team.

Even if the NFL's concerns about majority public ownership were valid and the courts assumed them to be true, those concerns do not explain the ban against minority public ownership.[153] When only a minority public ownership in a team exists, the problem of getting enough owners to agree and make decisions is moot. One person still has control over the team. Even if the public owns 49% of a team, the one individual who owns 51% makes all the decisions. If that one owner wants to hire a certain coach or general manager or relocate the team, even if every stockholder votes no, there is still 51% voting yes. The majority owner still runs the team as though he were the sole owner.

There are teams in the NFL other then the Green Bay Packers that have divided ownership. Two have minority owners that own fairly large interests. Al Davis owns 28% of the Oakland Raiders, with several other parties owning the remaining 72%.[154] However, there is no question that Al Davis runs the Raiders. . . .

The percentage division in the Ravens ownership is identical to the division Sullivan wanted to make by selling the Patriots. Sullivan wanted to sell 49% of the team to the public.[156] There appears to be no significant difference between having the minority ownership, if 49% is held by one person . . . or many, potentially thousands of people, as it could have been with the Patriots. In either situation, the team is still run as though it is individually owned.

The fine line drawn between minority ownership by individuals or a small group and minority ownership by the public is too fine. There is no practical business justification for allowing one and not the other. The NFL's concerns with multiple minority owners should be the same regardless of who those owners are. The dissimilar treatment of private and public holding indicates the NFL's true goal: restraining a product, NFL team ownership, from a willing market, the public.

VI. CONCLUSION

The NFL policy banning public ownership interests in NFL teams is intended to restrain competition by excluding a particular type of owner: the public owner. The ban, although proclaimed to have pro-competitive effects that justify the policy, does not correct any competitive advantage either method of team management may have had over the other.

Relocation is substantially affected by the ban because it preserves teams' ability to relocate; an ability that might be lost with publicly owned teams. The economic windfalls presumed to accompany public ownership are nonexistent. The fine line drawn between allowing minority ownership by an individual or group of people and allowing minority ownership by a large group of the public has no justification. The NFL was created by a group of individual owners who shared control over a large financial enterprise the public wants: football. To allow the public to become owners potentially takes away from the economic benefits and the prestige of team ownership individual owners currently enjoy. The only purpose the NFL ban on public ownership seems to serve is the preservation of the NFL as a private group, composed of private owners.

Notes

1. See *Sullivan v. NFL, 34 F.3d 1091, 1096 (1st Cir. 1994)*.

2. See id. at 1095.

3. See id. at 1096.

4. See id.

5. See NFL Constitution and Bylaws art. 3.2(a) (2003). This rule also includes a "grandfather clause" for teams already in the league when the rule was created. See id. This exception is how the Green Bay Packers are able to continue to operate as a nonprofit corporation against league rules.

6. See *Sullivan, 34 F.3d at 1095*.

7. See id.

8. See id.

9. See id. *at 1095–96*.

10. See Packers Stock and Financial History, available at http://www.packers.com/history/stock_history/. The Green Bay Packers stock sales have been held in 1923, 1935, 1950, and 1997–1998.

11. Lynn Reynolds Hartel, Comment, Community-Based Ownership of a National Football League Franchise: The Answer to Relocation and Taxpayer Financing of NFL Teams, *18 Loy. L.A. Ent. L.J. 589, 604 (1998)*.

12. NFL Const. art. 3.3(A)(1).

13. See id. art. 3.3(A)(2).

14. Id. art. 3.3(C).

15. See id. art. 3.5.

16. Hartel, supra note 11, at 605. n104.

105. See *Sullivan, 34 F.3d at 1099-1103*; see also John E. Lopatka & Jill Boylston Herndon, Antitrust and Sports Franchise Ownership Restraints: A Sad Tale of Two Cases, *42 Antitrust Bull. 749, 780–82 (1997)*.

106. See *Sullivan, 34 F.3d at 1100*.

107. See Lopatka & Herndon, supra note 105, at 782.

108. Richard Ryman, Packers' Net Income $3.75 Million, at http://www.packersnews.com/archives/news/pack_4527676.shtml (last visited Sept. 27, 2003).

109. Daniel Kaplan, Pack Earnings Hit a Record $18.8 Million, *Street & Smith's Sports Bus. J.,* June 16–22, 2003, at 1.

110. See id. at 37.

111. See id.; see also Ryman, supra note 108; Hartel, supra note 11, at 595.

112. See Packers Stock and Financial History, supra note 10.

113. See *Sullivan v. NFL, 34 F.3d 1091, 1100 (1st Cir. 1994)*.

114. See generally NFL Const. art. 3.

115. See id. art. 3.2(a).

116. See Green Bay Packers Stockholders Information, available at http//www.packers.com/stockholders/ (last visited Sept. 27, 2003).

117. See Ryman, supra note 108.

118. See Lopatka & Herndon, supra note 105, at 778–79.

119. See id.

120. See Robert W. Hamilton, *The Law of Corporations* 323 (5th ed. 2000).

121. See id. at 330–31.

122. See Packers Stock and Financial History, supra note 10; see also Green Bay Packers Stockholder Information, supra note 116.

123. See Packers Stock and Financial History, supra note 10.

124. See id.

125. See id.

126. There is a difference between having efficient management and having a good on-field team. Just like an individual owner and their general manager, a corporate president and general manager can make bad decisions in coaching staff, draft picks, salaries, and trades. These decisions probably account more for the Packers lack of success throughout the 1970s, 1980s and early 1990s than a failure of the actual type of management structure the team used.

127. See NFL Const. art. 3.5.

128. See id. art. 4.3.

129. See id.

130. See *L.A. Mem'l Coliseum Comm'n v. NFL, 726 F.2d 1381, 1395 (9th Cir. 1984)*.

131. See id.

132. See John Wunderli, Squeeze Play: The Game of Owners, Cities, Leagues and Congress, *5 Marq. Sports L.J.. 83, 90,* (1994).

133. See Cozzillio & Levinstein, supra note 20, at 557–58.

134. See id.

135. See id.

136. See id.

137. The current NFL has existed for thirty-seven years. There have been nine franchise relocations with name changes in that time, averaging a relocation every 5.28 years.

138. See G. Scott Thomas, The 10 Most Appealing Markets in America for New Sports Teams, *Sports Bus. J.,* Jan. 6–12, 2003, at 26.

139. See Sam Farmer, Group Extends Hand to Chargers; Pro Football: Posturing Begins as Anschutz Representatives Query Team About Relocation to L.A., *L.A. Times,* May 30, 2002, at Sports, part 4, page 9. The San Diego Chargers, Minnesota Vikings, Buffalo Bills, New Orleans Saints, and Indianapolis Colts are all teams that have been mentioned to have an interest in relocating to Los Angeles, and the Oakland Raiders are involved in lawsuits to allow the team to return to Los Angeles. See id.

140. See Jay Weiner, Easier Said Than Done: Relocating an NFL Franchise Takes Some Shifty Maneuvering, *Star Trib.* (Minneapolis), Sept. 1, 1999, at C1; Jeff Duncan, Saints Seek Stadium Solution, *Times-Picayune* (New Orleans), Nov. 17, 2000, at National, page 1.

141. See Weiner, supra note 140.

142. See Duncan, supra note 140.

143. See Hartel, supra note 11, at 594.

144. See id.

145. See Vikings and Gophers Continue Work on Stadium, at http://www.Vikings.com/News/StadiumUpdate723.htm (last visited July 22, 2002); Weiner, supra note 140.

146. See Kevin M. Bahr, The Business of Sports and Small Market Viability: The Green Bay Packers and the Milwaukee Brewers, at http://www.uwsp.edu/business/CWERB/1stQtr01/SpecialReportQtrl_01.htm (last visited Sept. 27, 2003).

147. See *15 U.S.C. 1291,* 1294 (2000).

148. See Packers Stock and Financial History, supra note 10.

149. See id.

150. See *Sullivan v. NFL, 34 F.3d 1091, 1100 (1st Cir. 1994)*.

151. Packers Stock and Financial History, supra note 10.

152. Id.

153. See *Sullivan, 34 F.3d at 1091*. The whole premise of this case is that Sullivan wanted to sell a minority interest in the Patriots to the public and the NFL indicated that it would prevent such a sale.

154. NFL Franchise Directory, at http://www.sportsfansofamerica.com/Directory/Football/NFL1.htm (last visited Sept. 27, 2003).

155. Id.

156. See *Sullivan, 34 F.3d at 1094*.

A PIECE OF THE ROCK (OR THE ROCKETS): THE VIABILITY OF WIDESPREAD PUBLIC OFFERINGS OF PROFESSIONAL SPORTS FRANCHISES

Ryan Schaffer

INTRODUCTION

In each professional sport, the gap between the "haves" and the "have-nots" has increased exponentially over the past fifteen years. . . . The increasing gap has led to a competitive imbalance in professional sports in which only a handful of teams have a true opportunity to win a championship at the outset of a season.

Some of the difference in payroll can be attributed to the varying degree of deep pockets and willingness to dig into those deep pockets among the owners. However, the single greatest factor accounting for the differing ability of teams to spend money remains locally generated revenues. In baseball, 80 percent of a team's revenue is generated locally from ticket sales and local broadcast fees, with the remaining 20 percent coming from national television contracts and licensing fees.[7] The reason that the New York Yankees can spend $208 million on player salaries is because they sell out every game and the money generated from local television broadcast fees is much greater than that of other teams.[8]

With such a disparity, professional team owners should first explore every avenue in attempting to max out their locally generated revenues in order to compete effectively. However, the Milwaukee television market is not likely to grow anytime soon, and the Kansas City Royals are not going to sell more tickets until they get a better team on the field. Owners must be creative then in their search for other sources of capital to make up for the disparity in locally generated revenue. One strategy to be explored is the widespread public ownership of professional sports franchises. By conducting an initial public offering (IPO) of some percentage of a franchise, a professional team owner could tap into an important source of capital without ceding any control of the organization, thereby shrinking the competitive gap.

In this Note, I explore the possibility of conducting an IPO of a professional sports franchise. Part I examines the various types of public ownership possibilities and distinguishes a true "stock market team" from other forms of ownership involving either indirect public ownership or complete community ownership. Part II addresses the question of whether a widespread public offering is a viable option under the current rules of each of the major professional leagues. Part III then considers the idea from the point of view of the team owner and the fan-investor in order to understand whether this would be an attractive option for either or both of these groups. Finally, Part IV examines the unique motives that drive a professional sports franchise in the context of considering what fiduciary duties would be owed to shareholders after a sale of stock.

I.   STRUCTURING PUBLIC OWNERSHIP

Various types of public ownership structures have been utilized by professional sports franchises in the past. In order to differentiate the type of widespread public ownership contemplated by this Note from other forms of public ownership, an examination of the various forms is in order.

A.   Stock Market Teams

A stock market team constitutes the primary source of revenue and profits for the corporation that owns it.[9] Marketable securities are sold to the public and then traded on an exchange. Professional teams in the United States that have embraced this form of ownership include the Boston Celtics (NBA), Cleveland Indians (MLB), and Florida Panthers (NHL).

In 1998, the Cleveland Indians became the first professional baseball team to go public, when the Cleveland Indians Baseball Company raised $60 million by selling four million shares of stock at an initial offering price of fifteen dollars per share.[10] The shares were listed for trading on NASDAQ, and consequently fell under the rules and regulations of the National Association of Securities Dealers. The Indians were sold to a private investor in 2000 for $320 million.[11] The transaction was structured as a cash-out merger, which meant that all of the shareholders were required to tender their shares back to the company for cash consideration of $22.61 per share.[12]

Florida Panthers Holdings Inc., the parent holding company of the NHL's Florida Panthers, carried out an initial public offering on the NASDAQ exchange in November of 1996 at $10 a share under the ticker symbol "PUCK."[13] The IPO netted approximately $66 million, which was primarily used to pay down debt or retained for working capital. Arguably, the Panthers fell outside the definition of a "stock market team" soon after their IPO. Before long, Panthers Holdings began buying hotels and resorts and the company's name was changed to Boca Resorts, Inc. to better reflect its focus on hotels, as opposed to hockey.[14] The sale of the Panthers became official in 2001, and put the team back in private hands.[15]

The Boston Celtics were the last major independently-owned public sports franchise.[16] Between 1986 and 2002, the Celtics were owned by a limited partnership, Boston Celtics LP, which was traded on the New York Stock Exchange (NYSE). In 2002, the Celtics were sold to a group of private investors, leaving the current United States land-scape void of any true stock market teams.

B.   General Corporate Ownership

A number of professional sports franchises are or have been owned by large publicly-traded corporations. The difference between these teams and pure "stock market teams" lies in the fact that for the "general corporate ownership" teams, the sports franchise makes only a minor contribution to the parent company's financial performance.[17]

Public corporations (often from the media, entertainment and communications industries) purchased sports franchises throughout the late twentieth century.[18] The Tribune Company bought MLB's Chicago Cubs in 1981 [*Ed. Note: and sold the team in 2009*] and Rupert Murdoch's News Corp purchased the Los Angeles Dodgers in 1998 [*Ed. Note: and sold the team in 2004*].[19] Some media companies engaged in cross-ownership, seeking to leverage their production capability to the fullest extent. Comcast Corporation currently owns the NBA's Philadelphia 76ers and the NHL's Philadelphia Flyers, while Cablevision Systems owns the NBA's New York Knicks and the NHL's New York Rangers. AOL Time Warner bought [*Ed. Note: and then sold*] the NHL's Atlanta Thrashers, the NBA's Atlanta Hawks, and MLB's Atlanta Braves, while Walt Disney owned MLB's Anaheim Angels and the NHL's Anaheim Mighty Ducks. In Canada, publicly traded Rogers Communications purchased 80% of the Toronto Blue Jays from Labatt Brewing Company, Ltd in 2000.[20]

Though they are publicly traded, these organizations differ tremendously from stock market teams. Because stock market teams are the primary source of revenue and profits for the corporation that owns them, the team's financial results will largely determine how the company's stock performs.[21] Investor interest in a pure stock market team will be dictated solely by the interest in investing in the team itself. Sports franchises owned by large media companies consti-tute an entirely different proposition for investors. While the decision to buy a share of Cleveland Indians Baseball Com-pany stock may come from your love of the team, "buying Disney when one is thinking about the [Anaheim] Angels is a bit of a stretch."[22] For professional sports franchises with general corporate ownership, both financial performance and performance on the field will barely register when it comes to the financial results of the parent company.

C.   Community Based Ownership

A third form of public ownership exists in community ownership, where non-marketable securities are sold and the public owns a majority of the stock. In the case of com-munity ownership, the team is set up as a publicly-owned non-profit corporation.[23]

The Green Bay Packers initiated the phenomenon of stock sales by a professional sports franchise in 1923. Four additional sales of stock (in 1935, 1950, and twice in 1997) have left the Packers with almost 112,000 shareholders, hold-ing a total of 4.75 million shares of stock.[24] As a means of running the corporation, a board of directors is elected by the stockholders. The board of directors in turn elects a seven-member executive committee of the corporation, consisting of a president, vice president, treasurer, secretary and three mem-bers-at-large. The president is the only officer who receives compensation. The balance of the committee is sitting gratis.[25]

Purchasers of the Packers' stock received a stock certifi-cate and were drawn in by the team's promise that "purchas-ers of Common Stock will. . . become a part of the Packers' tradition and legacy."[26] However, shares of ownership in the Packers include significant limitations. Shareholders receive no dividends and no season ticket privileges of any kind attach to ownership of the stock.[27] The shares are not mar-ketable, as they may only be transferred to members of the stockholders' immediate family by gift or following death.[28] Further, the articles of incorporation prohibit any individual from owning more than 200,000 shares of stock, in order to prevent someone from taking control of the team.[29]

While the Packers are currently the only major-league team in the United States to utilize the community owner-ship structure, a number of other organizations have shown interest in using this structure to protect against the prob-lems of contraction and franchise relocation.[30] One of the most significant features of the Packers' bylaws is that a majority vote of the shareholders is necessary to relocate the franchise.[31] With over 90% of the shareholders residing in Wisconsin, all of whom are probably avid Packers fans, it is extremely unlikely that any shareholder would ever vote to relocate the team.[32] Within the past decade there have been several attempts on both the state and federal level to introduce legislation promoting the expansion and growth of community ownership in professional sports.[33] . . . a bill was introduced in the Minnesota House of Representatives proposing a process by which MLB's Minnesota Twins would become a community owned organization.[34] The bill provides in part that at least 50% of the common stock must be sold to the general public in a general solicitation, with no individual owning more than 1% of the outstanding common stock.[35] Further, the bill states that "the governing documents must provide that the franchise may not move outside of the state or agree to voluntary contraction without approval of 75% of the shares of common stock, and sev-enty-five percent of the shares of preferred stock. The 75% requirements may not be amended by shareholders or by other means."[36] Community ownership represents not only an opportunity for fans to feel more connected to their lo-cal team, but also an opportunity to protect that community from having its team whisked away on the whim of a greedy owner in search of a new and better stadium deal.

II.   COULD THEY?

Before examining whether owners of professional sports franchises should consider conducting an initial public of-fering of some portion of their franchise, it is important to determine whether this is even a viable option given the current state of rules and regulations in each of the major professional sports leagues.

Each of the professional sports leagues has policies regarding the transfer of ownership of teams. Owners have typically been discouraged from selling a stake in their team to the public.[37] While some of these policies are codified in league by-laws and constitutions, others come from "unwritten rules" which the league expects owners to follow.[38] Despite this seemingly high hurdle, selling shares to the public may be a viable option as a number of leagues have shown a willingness to endorse limited public ownership, while the league with the strongest policy against public ownership [the NFL] may stand on tenuous legal ground.[39]

Major League Baseball owners voted in 1997 to change an existing guideline discouraging public ownership and to authorize teams to register with the U.S. Securities and Exchange Commission to sell equity.[40] However, the new guideline states that no more than 49% of a team can be distributed by way of a public offering, and voting rights of publicly-held shares must be restricted.[41] The intended effect of the guideline is to allow some percentage of ownership to be sold to the general public, while guaranteeing that a controlling voting bloc of shares remains in private hands. The Cleveland Indians became the first (and to this point, only) team to take advantage of this new guideline with their public offering in 1998.[42]

Similarly, while the NHL must review owners' proposals to offer shares to the public, the league has generally proved willing to endorse such plans if the proposal complies with a by-law requiring that one shareholder have ultimate voting control.[43] In the case of both the NHL and the MLB guidelines, the owners appear concerned only that there is a singular voice able to speak for the organization and vote on matters of league importance. While the owners are concerned with voting rights, they appear less concerned that all the economic rights of ownership should inure to one (or only a few) parties.[44]

The NFL is the professional league with the strongest anti-public ownership stance. The NFL Constitution prohibits corporate ownership of franchises, and 75% of NFL owners must approve all transfers of ownership interests in NFL clubs.[45] Furthermore, there is an uncodified league policy that prohibits public offerings of shares in NFL clubs.[46] NFL owners have not shown the same willingness to bend this guideline as their fellow owners in the other major professional sports leagues.

Despite this seemingly insurmountable hurdle, there is some question as to whether the NFL policies concerning public ownership would withstand a challenge under the Sherman Anti-Trust Act. In the late 1980's, the owner of the New England Patriots, William Sullivan, sought approval by NFL owners for a sale of 49% of the team in a public offering. After Sullivan saw the Boston Celtics complete a public offering in December 1986, he sought to use the same instrument to raise capital in order to alleviate some of his financial problems, while still retaining control of the Patriots.[47]

Sullivan asked his fellow owners for a modification or waiver of Article 3.5 of the NFL Constitution,[48] but was told by the Commissioner that league approval was "very dubious."[49] After being rebuffed, Sullivan was forced to sell the team in 1988.[50] Subsequently, Sullivan sued the NFL, claiming among other things that the NFL had violated the Sherman Act by preventing him from selling 49% of the Patriots to the public in an equity offering.[51] Sullivan alleged that this policy constituted an illegal restraint on trade in the market for ownership of a National Football League franchise in general, and in the New England Patriots, in particular.[52] The jury agreed, and rendered a verdict for Sullivan in the amount of $38 million.[53]

On appeal, the verdict was eventually reversed and remanded due to procedural errors that occurred during the trial. However, in addressing the antitrust argument that the NFL's prohibition on public ownership constitutes an illegal restraint on trade, the circuit court left the door open to further challenges. "We accept the NFL's claim that its public ownership policy contributes to the ability of the NFL to function as an effective sports league. . . .We disagree, however, that these factors are sufficient to establish as a matter of law that the NFL's ownership policy does not unreasonably restrain trade in violation of Section 1 of the Sherman Act."[54] From this opinion, it seems at least plausible that a team owner could conduct a successful challenge to the NFL's public ownership policy in an attempt to conduct an equity offering.

The relaxations of ownership rules in Major League Baseball and the National Hockey League may illustrate a trend towards a greater embrace of public ownership. Furthermore, despite its steadfast policy against public ownership, the NFL's policy may be open to legal challenge. Though an owner contemplating such a move would undoubtedly receive some resistance from other owners in his league, it appears that a motivated owner would not be legally prohibited from completing a public offering of a limited share of his organization.

III. SHOULD THEY?

In this Part, I consider first whether the widespread public offering of shares is a good idea for owners of professional sports franchises, addressing the pros and cons of such a strategy. I proceed to conduct the same analysis from the point of view of the fans, who will play a vital role in such an offering as the purchasers of the stock. Should a widespread public offering of an ownership interest in their favorite sports franchise be something that the fans want and are willing to pay for? The question of "should they" is taken entirely apart from the question of "could they," which was addressed above in Part II.

A. Advantages for Current Owners

Often, a corporation will arrange to sell stock to the public in order to fund business activities that cannot be readily financed through other means (e.g., from profits generated by the corporation, from the pockets of the owner of the corporation, or from borrowed funds).[55] As with any other corporation, professional franchise owners may consider selling stock for the very same reasons.

i.   Construction Activity

Over the past twenty years, professional sports stadiums have become palaces of overindulgence. Rather than serving the utilitarian purpose of providing a venue for the playing and viewing of a professional sports match, these stadiums have become full service family entertainment facilities, providing greater amenities and aesthetically pleasing architecture to fans and players alike. Not surprisingly, the cost of building these facilities has skyrocketed. U.S. Cellular Field, home of MLB's Chicago White Sox, was built in 1991 for an estimated cost of $167 million.[56] Less than thirteen years later, Citizens Bank Ballpark was built in Philadelphia for more than double that price.[57] The explosion in cost has not been limited to baseball, as the cost of constructing stadiums for the other major professional sports has increased exponentially during the same time frame.[58]

Whatever the sport, the cost of upgrading a current facility or building a new one has become prohibitive. A number of British soccer teams have carried out IPOs with the express purpose of generating funds required to improve their existing stadiums or to build new facilities.[59] Might owners of a professional sports franchise in the U.S. consider navigating a similar path, conducting an IPO with the explicit purpose of using the funds on construction or maintenance of their facility?

At first glance, it seems as if team owners in the United States are not faced with the same capital needs as the owners of British soccer clubs. Most British soccer teams own their own stadiums and correspondingly pay for construction as well as any upgrades to the facilities.[60] By contrast, the majority of professional teams in the United States do not own their own stadiums. Instead, they typically play in venues that have been partially or completely funded by the public. During the twentieth century, approximately $20 billion was spent on such facilities and nearly $15 billion of this came directly from local government subsidies.[61] Owners are able to coax these stadiums out of cities through threats of relocation. Owners are generally willing (and able) to pick up and move their franchises to a city that will offer them the most advantageous financial and stadium package, regardless of the degree of local support and fan loyalty they leave behind.[62] If owners are generally able to get their stadiums publicly financed with minimal commitment of their own funds, then an IPO in order to raise such funds would be unnecessary.

However, there is some evidence that this gravy train may be slowing down. The prospect of local governments subsidizing the commercial pursuits of wealthy team owners is fostering resistance.[63] There is widespread voter antipathy to new taxes implemented to raise money for the building of sports facilities, and in the recent past, voters have defeated such funding initiatives in a number of American cities.[64] Perhaps the best evidence that there is some movement away from public financing: Gillette Stadium, home of the NFL's New England Patriots, was completed in 2002 for an estimated cost of $325 million.[65] One hundred percent of the cost of the facility was financed with private funds.[66]

The lone example of the Patriots does not prove that public funding of stadiums is coming to an end. Indeed, public funding constituted 86% of the financing of the recently constructed Great American Ballpark in Cincinnati.[67] However, the Patriots and a few other recent examples do perhaps signal a shifting of the tide.[68] Team owners need to seriously consider the possibility that they will have to build their own facilities, or at least pay some of the cost as part of a public/private partnership agreement.[69] Raising capital through the sale of equity in a portion of the team may be one strategy an owner faced with this new reality might choose.

ii.   Financing Other Team Activities

In addition to financing stadium construction and maintenance, funds from the sale of stock in a professional sports franchise can be used for other team purposes in order to increase the competitive advantage of some teams and keep others from falling behind.

British soccer teams utilize the stock market to raise funds for reasons other than stadium construction, such as financing the purchase of players in order to "buy success" and strengthen their teams.[70] The explicit buying of players does not typically occur in the United States because of tight restrictions enacted by the leagues on the sale of players for cash.[71] However, the need for cash on hand to pay players still exists for professional teams in the U.S. Teams typically stock their rosters through the draft, trades, and increasingly, through free agency. In the NFL, contracts are typically structured so that a substantial signing bonus is paid up front to players in order to entice them to sign a contract.[72]

The amount of cash available to pay to a free agent in the form of a signing bonus may be the difference between landing a free agent and watching him sign a contract with another team. Though the NFL has a "salary cap," the cap is really for accounting purposes only.[73] The amount of money spent on payroll (the amount of cash actually paid out in a year from a team to its players) can vary dramatically. During the 2004 season, the Washington Redskins had a total payroll of almost $118 million, while the San Francisco 49ers registered a total payroll of $63 million.[74] The reason that the Redskins are able to spend more money on payroll than the 49ers is a direct result of disparity in revenue.[75] Simply put, the Redskins have more cash on hand to pay players than the 49ers do. This disparity may come from a number of sources (owner wealth and willingness to spend, team marketing revenue, stadium deals, etc.) but the result may be a long term decrease in competitive balance throughout the league.

A sale of stock to the public may be one strategy through which owners of teams falling behind in revenue have the opportunity to stay competitive in the market for free agents. The Green Bay Packers, though not a stock market team per se, have conducted four stock offerings to the public, with the most recent one taking place in 1997.[76] During the 1997 offering, the Packers sold roughly 120,000 shares of stock and took in over $24 million.[77] The $24 million influx doubled the team's financial reserves and virtually assured that the team would remain afloat for the next twenty-five years.[78] A similar influx of cash could help lower-revenue teams like the 49ers level the playing field by allowing them to go after free agents more aggressively, thus maintaining the competitive balance that the NFL itself has deemed crucial to the league's success.[79]

iii. Making Investment Liquid

Shareholders of any privately-held corporation usually cannot sell their equity readily because of the high transaction costs often involved with finding a suitable purchaser and negotiating satisfactory terms without a market price for shares.[80] By going public owners can more easily liquidate at least part of their investment.[81]

In professional team sports, the same idea would hold true. For owners of professional sports franchises, much of the worth of their investment lies in the overall franchise value, as franchises in most professional sports do not generate significant earnings from operations each year. MLB commissioner Bud Selig testified to Congress that the league's thirty teams suffered cumulative operating losses of more than $1.4 billion from 1995 through 2001, with only the New York Yankees and the Cleveland Indians making money over that time.[82] It is true that wealthy individuals are often motivated to own a professional sports franchise for reasons other than pure investment, such as ego, sense of civic duty, or love of the game.[83] Nevertheless, owners may soon be unwilling to blindly subsidize these losses from their own pocket. As the then-head of the sports finance group at Lehman Brothers explained:

> A lot of the owners are not as wealthy, not as liquid as they were five years ago. In the past, a lot of owners have been willing to subsidize their teams, but as annual losses rise to $10 million, $20 million, or more, some owners are being stretched to the breaking point.[84]

Going public may provide owners with additional capital to offset these losses from operations, and give the owners the opportunity to liquidate part of their investment without giving up control of the franchise. The prospect of creating an exit option has helped to foster the public ownership trend in British soccer.[85] Owners of British soccer clubs have on numerous occasions relied on the liquidity provided by a move to the stock market in order to cash in a portion of their investment.[86]

Structured appropriately, franchise owners could receive the influx of capital from a public offering without giving up anything in the way of control over the operations of the team or facing the risk of a hostile takeover. In a sense, a widespread public offering of some portion of a professional sports franchise contains the prospect of "free money" or "early money" for the owner. The public offering of the Cleveland Indians in 1998 provides a constructive example.

In 1998, the Cleveland Indians Baseball Co raised $60 million by selling four million shares at an initial public offering price of $15 per share.[87] The company's shares were then listed for trading on NASDAQ, the "over the counter" stock market operated under the supervision of the National Association of Securities Dealers.[88]

Each of the four million Class A Common Shares offered for sale to the public were entitled to a single vote concerning company operations.[89] Following the offering, Dick Jacobs, the owner of the team, retained beneficial ownership of 2,281,667 Class B Common Shares, each share being entitled to 10,000 votes.[90] Consequently, Mr. Jacobs retained 99.88% of the Company's total voting control. Because he suffered minimal dilution in voting rights over the company, Mr. Jacobs did not expose himself to the risk of a hostile takeover present in most public offerings. Major League Baseball ownership guidelines require that an individual or group of no more than twenty individuals maintain at least a 10% economic interest in the company and a ninety percent voting interest in the company at all times.[91] By structuring the offering in this way, Mr. Jacobs complied with MLB guidelines, retained almost complete voting control over the organization, and was able to raise $60 million without the promise of anything in return.[92] In this way, Mr. Jacobs was able to realize a portion of the value of his investment without selling his franchise.[93]

Because Mr. Jacobs sold his ownership of the Indians within a few years of the public offering, the capital he received was better characterized as "early money" rather than "free money." Without the public offering, the $60 million that Mr. Jacobs received would have been realized by him upon the sale of the team two years later. But with this strategy, Mr. Jacobs was able to get access to the money earlier while giving up no control over his organization. Other owners may view this strategy as a unique source of capital having little downside risk, and attempt to follow suit. For those looking to sell in the short term, the public offering process can offer a chance at "early money," but for those with no plans to sell (but rather to keep ownership in their family) the public offering process truly represents the prospect of "free money."

iv. Capturing Market Ownership

Offering a portion of the local professional sports franchise for sale to the members of the community may give rise to an ancillary benefit of increasing the number of loyal fans. Admittedly, there is a bit of chicken-and-egg argument here, as it is arguably only the very committed fans who would buy stock in the team in the first place.[94] However, these committed fans may also purchase and give stock as a gift, or pass the stock on to their children, which would allow the network of committed fans to grow.

Despite the fact that little economic value is derived from such acts, owners of stock in all kinds of companies often purchase products from that company as a matter of habit. The owner of fifty shares of Procter & Gamble stock may make sure that Tide (a P&G product) is his detergent of choice. The owners of fifty shares of Home Depot may drive an extra few miles to get to a Home Depot store rather than "supporting" Lowe's, Home Depot's strategic competitor. Similarly, ownership of stock in a professional sports franchise may serve to create or deepen the same kind of brand loyalty to the franchise among the fan-investors. This brand loyalty may manifest itself through increased purchase of team merchandise, increased visits to the team website, or a higher season ticket base, all of which serve to increase team revenue.

Admittedly, these effects are uncertain and likely small. Any deepening of brand loyalty would not, by itself, constitute enough of a reason for an owner to conduct a public offering. However, taken on top of the other benefits associated with a public offering, increased brand loyalty may become part of a compelling case for an owner to seriously consider such a strategy.

B. Disadvantages for Current Owners

Despite the many advantages and opportunities offered by a sale of stock to the public, current owners of professional sports franchises would face a number of risks and obligations that may prompt them to seek alternatives to a public offering as a source of additional capital.

i. League Opposition

As noted in Part II, owners seeking to "go public" may face significant objections and hurdles from their leagues and other owners. Some leagues have more stringent policies against public ownership than others. While the NHL reviews the proposals of owners to offer shares to the public, the league has generally proved willing to endorse such plans if the proposal complies with a by-law requiring that one shareholder have ultimate voting control.[95] Major League Baseball owners, as discussed in Part II, voted in 1997 to change an existing guideline discouraging public ownership. Under the new regime, up to 49% of a team can be distributed by way of a public offering though voting rights of publicly held shares must be restricted.[96] This rule change paved the way for the 1998 public offering of the Cleveland Indians.

The NFL, with its uncodified policy against public share offerings, stands out as being more firmly opposed to public ownership of teams than other leagues.[97] As discussed in Part II, there is considerable doubt about the legality of this rule. An owner who wishes to contest this rule on antitrust grounds may very well bring a successful challenge. However, there are costs associated with bringing such a challenge. An owner would certainly have to figure such costs into his calculus of whether he wanted to proceed down this path.

Aside from the legal costs of the challenge, an owner would have to decide whether he wanted to sue the league of which he is part and the other NFL owners who are his colleagues. A sitting owner taking the NFL to court is not unprecedented. Jerry Jones, the owner of the Dallas Cowboys, sued the NFL in 1995 over the signing of separate sponsorship deals for the Cowboys, and Al Davis has sued the NFL on a number of occasions. In 1980, Davis sued the NFL after the league attempted to block the move of his Raiders from Oakland to Los Angeles.[98] In each of those instances, the owners decided that the risk of suing the league and alienating both the commissioner and the other team owners was worth the potential reward and proceeded forward. An owner considering a challenge to the NFL's ban on public ownership would have to make a similar decision, taking into account the strong stance that the league has taken against such a move.

ii. Costs

Despite the possibility that conducting a public offering nets "free money" to the principal owner selling off a share of his equity, there are costs in both time and money associated with conducting a public offering that can significantly cut into the profits generated.

Generally, the expenses of an IPO will amount to 15% or more of the proceeds.[99] For the IPO of the Cleveland Indians, though not quite that high, the expenses amounted to $6 million, out of $60 million raised.[100] Most of those expenses go to investment bankers who agree to serve as underwriters for the transaction. The underwriters are responsible for the pricing, marketing and selling of the company's shares and generate a sizable fee for their work.[101] Attorneys also play a pivotal role during the process of going public, drafting filings made to the Securities and Exchange Commission and answering the inquiries of the regulators in order to move the process along. Accountants will also be needed to prepare and certify the financial documents that will become part of the company's filing and prospectus. Legal and accounting fees will contribute significantly to the cost of the IPO.

Apart from the monetary cost of conducting a public offering, there will be a significant cost in terms of the time commitment required of key personnel. During the process of going public, senior executives will need to discuss relevant issues with lawyers, accountants and financial advisers at length. Additionally, the management team usually takes part in meetings, known as "road shows" which are designed to sell the investment community on the company.[102] Dealing with these issues takes key personnel away from the day-to-day operations of running the franchise, which may cause them a short-term competitive disadvantage. Typically, the process of going public is not a short one. Before a corporation can carry out a public offering, it must prepare and file the necessary documentation and then wait for approval from the SEC. This delay is rarely less than three months and can exceed six months or more.[103] The time cost for management personnel can be just as significant as the monetary cost during the public offering process.

The costs of being a public company do not end once the IPO is complete. The Securities Exchange Act of 1934 governs the regulation of secondary markets. Section 13 of the Exchange Act imposes periodic reporting requirements on publicly traded companies.[104] These reporting requirements are normally satisfied in the form of 10-K (annual) and 10-Q (quarterly) reports. The services of lawyers and accountants will again be needed for each of these reports, and they will charge accordingly. Further costs will be borne in setting up annual shareholder meetings, distributing materials to shareholders, soliciting shareholder proxies for voting, and maintaining a registry of shareholders. Management will need an investor relations department in order to deal with shareholders and financial analysts who cover the company's stock. The costs and headaches of keeping up with SEC disclosure requirements can be significant if management is not prepared. For example, when the Boston Celtics went public, the result was "an expensive administrative nightmare" due to the fact that 90% of shareholders owned ten shares or less, greatly increasing the paperwork involved.[105]

Franchises considering a public offering may be deterred by the high administrative cost and hassle experienced by the Celtics, or they may learn from the Celtics' mistakes. In 1997, the Sacramento Kings of the NBA admitted that the team had given serious consideration to a public share offering, but that the idea had been shelved because of the high administrative cost it would have entailed.[106] The Kings' president specifically cited the problem of dealing with so many small stockholders. "The problem is you have 40,000 people each owning one share as souvenirs. The cost associated with that would be incredible."[107] The Florida Panthers, undeterred by the Celtics' experience, pressed on with a public offering but sought to reduce administrative costs through such measures as a minimum purchase requirement.[108]

The costs of conducting an IPO and remaining a public franchise may be significant and could be the strongest argument against conducting such an offering in the minds of professional sports team owners. At the end of the day, owners must determine if the capital and other benefits gained outweigh the costs in dollars and human capital that they will incur as part of the process.

iii. Disclosure

The disclosure requirements discussed above may deter an owner of a professional sports team from going public for reasons wholly apart from the costs associated with such disclosure. The prospect of disclosing a wide range of previously confidential information can deter business owners of all kinds from selling shares on the market.[109] Public corporations must provide detailed information on numerous components of their business, including their sales and profits, the compensation of top executives, and the activities of certain key shareholders.[110]

It is understandable that in an age of sports talk radio, internet chat rooms and 24/7 coverage of local sports teams, some franchise owners may be hesitant about making any more information than is necessary available to the public. Making this information publicly available may also harm the franchise at the negotiating table. Disclosure would allow the inspection of team finances by the media, government officials, or players seeking background information for contract negotiations. Owners are generally reluctant to issue stock because they do not want to share financial information about their clubs.[111] It would be more difficult for a team owner to cry poverty as a negotiating ploy with a player if the player's agent could easily find team revenue and operating income information simply by logging on to the SEC website and downloading the company's latest 10-K. Negotiations with a city on sweetheart stadium deals, a key component in the current sports landscape, would likewise be more contentious if the public was able to see exactly where the team stood financially.

The costs in privacy of conducting an IPO are not to be overlooked. The external scrutiny faced by the franchise would likely increase, as critics would simply have more information with which to work. Some privately-held British soccer teams chose to forgo the stock market and not go public due to their disinterest in dealing with such heavy scrutiny.[112] For instance, in 1995 the chairman of the Glasgow Rangers, a very successful Scottish soccer club, refuted speculation that a stock market flotation was imminent by saying "I want to own and run Rangers."[113] The same may hold true for owners of sports franchises in the United States. These privacy costs may be just as significant a deterrent to owners considering an IPO as the actual monetary costs associated with such an offering.

C. The Fans

When a public share offering is likely to fail because of lack of investor interest, any organization in any industry will typically abandon its plans before shares are actually offered to the public. Thus, though the owner is the one ultimately making the decision on whether to offer shares in his franchise to the public, it is important to note the advantages and disadvantages of such a move for fans, in order to accurately gauge whether there would be a market for the shares. Can sports stocks inspire investor confidence?

Some of the most important benefits for a fan-investor are psychic rather than tangible. It is the feeling of ownership of a treasured civic asset, of being part of the history and tradition of the team that they love. As one Boston Celtics fan and stockholder put it, "the stock is about being part of the rock and owning part of your team."[114] Often, there is additional psychic pleasure in being able to pass on that membership to family members and friends. The same fan passed up the t-shirt and game ball when buying his fifteen-year-old son a birthday gift, instead buying him fifteen shares of the Boston Celtics, stating: "I hope he'll never sell it because it's sentimental."[115]

The right to attend annual meetings is an important tangible benefit to shareholders. At the first annual meeting of shareholders for the Cleveland Indians, around one thousand shareholders showed up at Jacobs Field, the team's home stadium.[116] Not only was each shareholder provided with a proxy statement and an annual report, but they were given a ticket with an actual assigned seat at the ballpark which they needed to gain entry to the shareholder meeting. The Green Bay Packers 2005 annual meeting attracted a crowd of 9,700 and a special, shareholders-only practice held the day before attracted over 14,000 people.[117]

The argument most commonly invoked against conducting a public offering of shares of a professional sports franchise is that the shares constitute a bad investment.[118] Purchasers of these shares are likely to receive little in the way of financial return from their investments. During their initial offering, both the Cleveland Indians and the Florida Panthers made it very clear to potential investors that they did not intend to pay any dividends at all for the foreseeable future.[119] Although the Boston Celtics did start out paying dividends to their investors, they offered no dividends after 1998 before they were acquired by private investors in 2002.[120] Purchasers of these stocks are also likely to face restrictive voting rights. Though they are owners of the team, they have little or no voice as to how the team and the company are run.

Some have commented that the only real opportunity for a professional sports stock to become more valuable is during the consideration and completion of a sale of the organization.[121] This has in fact been the case for some of the previously publicly traded franchises. The Cleveland Indians stock was languishing for a year after its public offering, losing over 60% of its value,[122] but the stock rallied on the announcement by team owner Dick Jacobs that he was seeking a buyer. In a single day, the stock price rose 64%, trading ninety times average daily volume.[123] After the sale was completed, investors in the Indians ended up making a return on their original $15 per share investment. Based on the evidence, however, the sale of the team was the one and only cause of this return. Generally, the sale of a team is an uncommon occurrence. . . . Investors purchasing sports stocks with a view towards the sale of the team may have to wait for a long time to realize any investment gains.[125]

Conventional investors in search of undervalued companies with growth potential or companies with the ability to expand their operations are unlikely to be satisfied with an investment in a professional sports franchise.[126] Though the capital influx may result in the production of some competitive advantage, the onus of the transaction is raising capital to make up for a shortfall in revenue, a situation that traditional investors avoid. As the critics note, under all of the traditional tests of what makes a good investment, sports stocks are likely to fail.

What these critics fail to recognize, however, is that most purchasers of stock in a professional sports franchise are not likely interested in the stock as a pure investment, but rather as a memento. These offerings are more or less marketed exclusively to the fan-as-investor rather than to the conventional investor or to the investment community as a whole.[127] Sports stocks are better understood as being analogous to the purchase of a team t-shirt or hat rather than an investment on Wall Street.[128] Persons willing to invest in sports stocks enter these situations with their eyes wide open. Disclosure rules found in the Securities Act of 1933 and the Exchange Act of 1934 and enforced by the SEC assure that investors have the opportunity to be well informed about the risks inherent in any stock purchase. As financial analyst Jeff Phillips commented, "You can always come up with a better pure (financial) investment. The bigger issue is what are people's expectations? It's a memento. If you're looking at it to put a stock certificate on the wall, then you're doing it for the right reason."[129]

[*Ed. Note: Author's discussion of the structuring of a public offering for a sports franchise is omitted.*]

CONCLUSION

Conducting a public offering of stock is only one among a number of alternatives for professional sports team owners with capital needs. The National Basketball Association runs a . . . credit facility, which makes low interest rate loans available to teams.[155] . . . The facility uses the collective collateral of the league and its teams to negotiate for lower rates than most clubs could secure on their own.[156] Similar programs exist in Major League Baseball and the National Football League.[157] Alternatively, an owner in need of capital or looking to liquidate part of his investment may have little problem locating a single private investor or small group of private investors to meet such needs.

A public offering of stock, however, offers some clear advantages to owners over these and other alternatives. By financing through equity rather than debt, the owner is not forced to repay with interest the capital he raises. Following the lead of other teams that have gone public in the past, the owner can make it clear to investors that there are no plans to pay dividends at any time in the foreseeable future. Thus, the owner gives up none of the economic rights associated with ownership. As for taking on another private investor, it is unlikely that a single, sophisticated investor or small group of investors would be willing to invest a large chunk of capital under lopsided terms that grant no voting or economic rights, season ticket privileges, or other perks. Thus, despite some obstacles and drawbacks, conducting an IPO of some portion of a franchise may allow an owner to receive an influx of capital without giving up any of the economic control or voting rights associated with ownership. Dick Jacobs did exactly this, pocketing $60 million in 1998 while giving up nothing in terms of control over the Cleveland Indians, and owners may take heed of his example in the future.

From the fan's perspective, the purchase of stock should be looked at not as a financial investment, but as another way to show support for the team. Disclosure requirements enacted in the Securities Act of 1933 and the Securities Exchange Act of 1934 would force disclosure to fans about the nature of the investment they are making, though there is little evidence that fans would be deterred by the prospect of a poor financial investment. Sports fans are a rabid bunch, willing to shell out money for anything with the team logo on it. The more unique the item, the more they are willing to pay. One Red Sox fan demonstrated the kind of attitude a team contemplating a stock sale would seek in investors:

> *If somebody wants a census of RSN (Red Sox Nation) Citizens nationwide or measure interest in the Red Sox, just have the Sox offer stock and see how fast it would sell out. . . . Each season, we RSN Citizens see the Yankees buy more high priced free agents and their payroll climb over $200 million. Theo [Epstein, the team General Manager] wouldn't have to burn up his calculator wrestling with new contracts versus a budget limitation . . . or . . .use the money for a New Fenway? . . . . Most every Sox fan would really enjoy owning a little piece of their team—even if it's only 50 or 100 shares, even if there's never a financial dividend, just as long as the franchise is strong with more latitude to make deals and operate.*[158]

It is this kind of loyalty among the fan population that may make widespread public offerings of professional sports franchises a viable option now and in the future.

Notes

. . . .

7. Martin Wolk, Is Baseball a Bad Business?, http://www.msnbc.msn .com/id/3073502/ (August 11, 2005).

8. Andrew Zimbalist, Baseball and Billions: A Probing Look Inside the Big Business of Our National Pastime, 49 (1992). The Yankees have by far the highest average attendance of any MLB team since 2003. ESPN MLB Attendance Report: 2006, at http://sports.espn.go.com/ mlb/attendance (last visited May 15, 2006).

9. Brian R. Cheffins, Playing the Stock Market: "Going Public" and Professional Team Sports, 24 J. Corp. L. 641, 648 (1999).

10. Daniel Kadlec, An Unhittable Pitch, Time, June 15, 1998, at 50.

11. Bill Lubinger, Jacobs & Dolan: How they Haggled on Tribe, Plain Dealer (Cleveland), Jan 7, 2000, at 1A.

12. Cleveland Indians Baseball Co., Proxy Statement 8 (Proxy), at 20 (Jan 5, 2000).

13. Scott Lascari, The Latest Revenue Generator: Stock Sales By Professional Sports Franchises, 9 Marq Sports L.J 445, 454 (1999).

14. Sarah Talalay, Public Ownership Doesn't Rake in Dough, S. Fla. Sun-Sentinel, July 29, 2001, at 7C.

15. Id.

16. Daniel Kaplan, Public Firms Retreat from Owners Box, Street & Smith's Sports Bus J., Oct 7–13, 2002, at 1.

17. Cheffins, supra note 9, at 647–48.

18. Paul J. Much, Inside the Ownership of Professional Sports Teams 27–28 (Team Marketing Report, Inc., Chicago 1997).

19. Tribune Company continues to own and operate the Cubs. News Corp sold a controlling interest in the Dodgers to Boston businessman Frank McCourt in January 2004. See Dodgers Team History, http://losangeles.dodgers.mlb.com/NASApp /mlb/la/history/ timeline12.jsp (last visited May 15, 2006); Cubs team history, http://chicago.cubs.mlb.com/NASApp/mlb/chc/history/timeline12 .jsp (last visited May 15, 2006).

20. Toronto Blue Jays Franchise History, http://en.wikipedia.org/wiki/ Toronto_Blue_Jays (last visited May 15, 2006).

21. Cheffins, supra note 9, at 648.

22. Id. In 2003, Disney sold the Anaheim Angels to Arte Moreno, taking ownership out of public hands. Disney completely exited the ownership of pro sports franchises with the 2005 sale of the Anaheim Mighty Ducks. See Mark Whicker, Disney Departs Pro Sports Ownership, Orange County Register, Feb 26, 2005.

23. Green Bay Packers Shareholders, http://www.packers.com/ stockholders/ (last visited May 15, 2006).

24. Green Bay Packers Stock & Financial History, http://www.packers .com/history/fast_facts/stock_history/ (last visited May 15, 2006).

25. Id.

26. See Green Bay Packers, Inc. 1997 Common Stock Offering Document (Nov 14, 1997) [hereinafter Packers' Offering Document].

27. Green Bay Packers Stock & Financial History, supra note 24.

28. See Packers' Offering Document, supra note 26, at 5. Immediate family refers to the spouse, child, mother, father, brother(s), sister(s), or any lineal descendant of the stockholder. See id.

29. Green Bay Packers Shareholders, supra note 23.

30. Additionally, a number of minor-league teams currently use community based ownership: Toledo Mud Hens, Appleton Timber Rattlers, Harrisburg Senators, Memphis Redbirds, Rochester Red Barons, Syracuse Sky Chiefs. See New Rules Project, http://www.newrules .org/sports/ (last visited May 15, 2006).

31. Lynn Reynolds Hartel, Community-Based Ownership of a National Football League Franchise: The Answer to Relocation and Taxpayer Financing of NFL Teams, 18 Loy. L.A. Ent. L. J. 589, 594 (1998).

32. See id.

33. Brad Smith, How Different Types of Ownership Structures Could Save Major League Baseball Teams from Contraction, J. Int'l Bus. & L. 86, 104 (2003).

34. See Community Ownership of Minnesota Twins, H.F. 1368 (April 6, 2005), available at http://www.house.leg.state.mn.us/hrd/bs/84/ hf1368.html (last visited May 15, 2006).

35. H.F. 1368 Bill Summary, available at http://www.house.leg.state
.mn.us/hrd/bs/84/hf1368.html (last visited May 15, 2006).

36. Id.

37. Brian R. Cheffins, UK Football Clubs and the Stock Market: Past
Developments and Future Prospects: Part I, 18 Comp. Law. 66, 70,
n. 3 (1997).

38. See Brian R. Cheffins, Sports Teams and the Stock Market: A
Winning Match?, 3 U.B.C. L. Rev. 271, 279 (1998) (citing the
NFL's uncodified policy prohibiting public offerings of shares
in NFL clubs).

39. See Sullivan v Nat'l Football League, 34 F.3d 1091, 1095 (1st Cir.
1994).

40. Baseball Owners OK Sale of Stock to Public, The Fort Worth Star
Telegram, Sept. 19, 1997 at S5.

41. See Tom Nawrocki, Investing in Diamonds, Sports Illustrated, Sept.
29, 1997 at 18.

42. Kadlec, supra note 9.

43. See Jac MacDonald, Peter Puck is Selling Part of His Empire—Will
There Be Any Takers?, Edmonton J. (February 6, 1997); Cheffins,
supra note 38, at 279.

44. Cheffins, supra note 38, at 282.

45. Id. at 279.

46. Id.

47. Sullivan v Nat'l Football League, 34 F.3d 1091, 1095 (1st Cir.
1994).

48. Id. (noting that Article 3.5 of the NFL Constitution codifies the
policy against public ownership).

49. Id at 1096.

50. Id.

51. Id.

52. See id.

53. Id. (The judge in the trial reduced the verdict through remittur to
$17 million. Pursuant to 15 U.S.C. 15, which provides for treble
damages for antitrust violations, the court entered a final judgment
for Sullivan of $51 million.)

54. Id at 1102.

55. Brian Cheffins, supra note 9, at 649.

56. Ballparks by Munsey & Suppes, http://www.ballparks.com/baseball/
index.htm (last visited May 15, 2006).

57. Ballparks by Munsey & Suppes, Citizens Bank Park, http://www
.ballparks.com/baseball/national/phibpk.htm (last visited May 15,
2006). Citizens Bank Ballpark is the current home of baseball's
Philadelphia Phillies. The estimated cost to build was $346 million.

58. In the NFL, Invesco Field at Mile High (home of the Denver Broncos) was completed in 2001 at an estimated cost of $364 million.
Ballparks by Munsey & Suppes, Invesco Field at Mile High, http://
football.ballparks.com/NFL/DenverBroncos/newindex.htm (last
visited May 15, 2006). In the NBA, the FedEx Forum (home of the
Memphis Grizzlies) was completed in 2004 at an estimated cost of
$250 million. Ballparks by Munsey & Suppes, Fed Ex Forum, http://
basketball.ballparks.com/NBA/MemphisGrizzlies/index.htm, (last
visited May 15, 2006).

59. See Jane Fuller, A Fixture that Sets Even Tougher Goals, Fin. Times
(London), April 22, 1991, at 26; Matthew Rowan, Down in the
Valley They Keep Their Eye on the Ball, Indep. (London), May 3,
1998, Bus., at 5; Peter Sloane, The Economics of Sport: An Over-

view, Econ. Affairs, Sept. 1997, at 2, 3; Patrick Tooher, Sunderland
Scores on Trading Debut, Indep., Dec. 26, 1996, at 19.

60. Paul Dempsey & Kevan Reilly, Big Money, Beautiful Game 40–43
(1998).

61. Raymond J. Keating, Sports Pork: The Costly Relationship between
Major League Sports and Government, Pol'y Analysis, April 5,
1999, at 1, 11–15, available at http://www.cato.org/pubs/pas/
pa-339es.html (last visited May 15, 2006).

62. Katherine C. Leone, No Team, No Peace: Franchise Free Agency
in the National Football League, 97 Colum. L. Rev. 473, 476–77
(1997); see Adam Teicher, NFL Teams Walk When Money Talks:
Cleveland Browns' Plan to Move Makes Fans Worry About Own
Teams, Kan. City Star, Nov. 12, 1995 at A1. When the Cleveland
Browns moved to Baltimore, they left behind a legion of loyal and
heartbroken fans (including the Author).

63. Cheffins, supra note 9, at 650.

64. Meredith J. Kane, Stadium Financing Increasingly Using Private
Fund Sources, N.Y.L.J., Jan. 19, 1999, at S4; Jonathan Rand, Voters
Tell Owners to Pay for Stadiums, Kan. City Star, Mar. 29, 1998, at
C8; see also Don Bauder, Liberals, Conservatives Gang Up on Team
Owners, Copley News Serv., Dec. 8, 1997; Jim Murray, Such Glut-
tony is Hard to Digest, L.A. Times, Nov. 6, 1997, at C1.

65. Ballparks by Munsey and Suppes, http://football.ballparks.com/
NFL/NewEnglandPatriots/newindex.htm (last visited May 15, 2006).

66. Id.

67. Ballparks by Munsey and Suppes, http://www.ballparks.com/
baseball/national/cinbpk.htm (last visited May 15, 2006).

68. For example, nearly one-third of the financing for Petco Park in San
Diego (opened in 2004) came from private funds while roughly half
of the financing for Citizens Bank Ballpark in Philadelphia (opened
in 2004) came from private funds. See Ballparks by Munsey and
Suppes, http://www.ballparks.com/baseball/national/sdobpk.htm
(last visited May 15, 2006); see also Ballparks by Munsey and
Suppes, http://www.ballparks.com/baseball/national/phibpk.htm (last
visited May 15, 2006).

69. Cheffins, supra note 9, at 651.

70. Brad Smith, How Different Types of Ownership Structures Could
Save Major League Baseball Teams from Contraction, J. Int'l Bus.
& L. 86, 92–93 (2003).

71. Cheffins, supra note 38, at 276.

72. For instance, the first overall pick in the 2005 NFL Draft, Alex
Smith of the University of Utah, signed a contract with the San
Francisco 49ers which included over $20m in the form of a signing
bonus.

73. The amount of a player's signing bonus, though paid immediately
to the player upon the signing of the contract, is prorated across the
length of the contract for salary cap purposes. For example, assume
Player A signs a 5 year contract with a $20 million signing bonus
and salaries of $1 million for each of the five years. The amount
paid to Player A in year 1 is actually $21 million. However, because
of the signing bonus proration, the amount that Player A counts
against the salary cap is $5 million in year 1.

74. See USA Today Salaries Databases, supra note 1.

75. The Washington Redskins took in $245 million in revenue in 2004,
while the San Francisco 49ers took in $151 million. See The Busi-
ness of Football, Forbes Magazine, January 27, 2005, available at
http://www.forbes.com/2004/09/01/04nfland.html (last visited May
15, 2006).

76. Scott C. Lascari, The Latest Revenue Generators: Stock Sales by Professional Sports Franchises, 9 Marq. Sports L.J. 445, 447–8 (1999). Rather than being a stock market team, the Packers are a community-owned non-profit entity. The differences are explored in Part I, supra.

77. Tom Silverstein, Packers Happy with Stock Sale, but 120,000 Shares Sold Falls Short of Goal, Milwaukee J. Sentinel, Mar. 18, 1998, at C1.

78. See id. at C7.

79. See Mackey v Nat'l Football League, 543 F.2d 606, 621 (8th Cir. 1976) ("The destruction of competitive balance would ultimately lead to diminished spectator interest, franchise failures, and perhaps the demise of the NFL, at least as it operates today").

80. Frank H. Easterbrook & Daniel R. Fischel, The Economic Structure of Corporate Law 230 (1991).

81. Cheffins, supra note 9, at 653.

82. Wolk, supra note 7, http://www.msnbc.msn.com/id/3073502/ (last visited May 15, 2006).

83. Cheffins, supra note 9, at 655.

84. See id.

85. Jimmy Burns, The Transfer Market, Fin. Times (London), Apr. 29, 1997, at 2; Roger Cowe, Float Values Club at More than £150m, Guardian (London), Jan. 17, 1997, at 22.

86. See Cheffins, supra note 37, at 68–69.

87. Kadlec, supra note 10, at 50.

88. Mark Veverka, IPO by Cleveland Indians Not Exactly a Hit With Investors, San. Fran. Chron., June 5, 1998, at B1.

89. Cleveland Indians Baseball Co., Inc., 1998 Prospectus 1, 8 (1998), available at http://www.sec.gov/Archives/edgar/data/1059019/0000950152-98-005093.txt (last visited May 15, 2006) [hereinafter 1998 Prospectus].

90. Lascari, supra note 76, at 460.

91. Id.

92. The Company noted in the 1998 Prospectus that the Company did not intend to pay dividends to holders of either Class A or Class B Common Stock for the foreseeable future, and that all future earnings would be retained for reinvestment into the business. See 1998 Prospectus, supra note 89, at 15.

93. Mr. Jacobs ultimately agreed to sell the Indians in 1999 to Larry Dolan for $320 million. This transaction was structured as a cash-out merger, which meant that all shareholders were required to tender their shares back to the Company for cash consideration of $22.61 per share. When the merger closed in February 2000, the Cleveland Indians ceased to be a publicly traded organization. See Eugene Stroz, Public Ownership of Sports Franchises: Investment, Novelty, or Fraud?, 53 Rutgers L. Rev. 517, 528–29 (2001).

94. Due to, among other things, the fact that compared to other investments, sports franchise stock ownership is likely to yield a much lower return. See Part IIIC, infra.

95. Cheffins, supra note 9, at 657.

96. See Part II, supra.

97. Cheffins, supra note 9, at 657.

98. Davis was successful in his case, and moved the team. The team has since moved back to Oakland.

99. Gregory M. Kratofil, Jr., Direct Public Offerings Can Fill Business' Capital Needs, Kansas City Bus. J., June 25, 1999, at D1 (reporting costs of traditional intermediated offering as 15% while costs of a direct disintermediated offering are only 6%); More Companies Than Ever Do Their Own IPOs, Bus. Wire, Apr. 2, 1999 (reporting that the cost of a traditional IPO is usually about 15% of the total amount raised, compared to 3% on a typical $1 million direct public offering).

100. See 1998 Prospectus, supra note 89, at 20.

101. Carl Schneider, Joseph Manko & Robert Kant, Going Public: Practice, Procedure, and Consequences, 27 Vill. L. Rev. 1, 8–9 (1981).

102. Cheffins, supra note 9, at 661.

103. C. Steven Bradford, Transaction Exemptions in the Securities Act of 1933: An Economic Analysis, 45 Emory L.J. 591, 605 (1996).

104. 15 U.S.C.A. 78(m) (2006).

105. Larry Lebowitz, Panthers Stock: $1,000 Minimum, Sun-Sentinel (Fort Lauderdale, Fla.), Sept. 26, 1996, at D1.

106. Cheffins, supra note 9, at 662.

107. Id. (citing Gary Delsohn, Questions and Answers Surrounding the Kings' Existence in Sacramento, Sacramento Bee, Jan. 23, 1997, at C1).

108. See Lebowitz, supra note 105, at D1.

109. Cheffins, surpa note 38, at 279.

110. Id. at 280.

111. Professional Sports Team Stocks Suddenly Seem to be on a Roll, The Tampa Trib., Feb. 18, 1997, at B7.

112. Cheffins, supra note 38, at 282.

113. Id. (citing John Ivison, Murray Rules Out Suggestions of Share Flotation for Rangers, The Scotsman, Oct. 27, 1995, at 21).

114. Allison Romano, For Fans, Value of Owning Stock Comes in Sentiment, Not Dollars, Chicago Daily Herald, June 9, 1999, at 5.

115. Id.

116. See Leigh Allan, Meeting Passes Mustard for Cleveland Indians' Stockholders, Dayton Daily News, June 5, 1999, at 1B. A spokesman from a New York Stock Exchange Company interviewed for the same story stated that perhaps 200 of the company's more than 400,000 investors actually showed up to its annual meeting. Id.

117. Jeff Fedotin, Packers Showcase Practice Skills for Shareholders, July 27, 2005, http://www.packers.com/news/stories/2005/07/27/2/ (last visited May 15, 2006); see also Jeff Fedotin, Packers Deliver Team Report at Annual Shareholders' Meeting, July 27, 2005 http://www.packers.com/news/stories/2005/07/27/1 (last visited May 15, 2006).

118. See generally Eugene Stroz, Public Ownership of Sports Franchises: Investment, Novelty, or Fraud?, 53 Rutgers L. Rev. .517 (2001).

119. Lascari, supra note 76, at 458.

120. Daniel Kaplan, Public Firms Retreat from the Owners Box, Street & Smith's Sports Bus. J., Oct. 7–13, 2002, at 1.

121. See Stefan Fatsis, Cleveland Indians Are Put on the Block by Jacobs, and Stock Price Soars 64%, Wall St. J., May 14, 1999, at B (citing comments by Paul Much, consultant with Chicago investment firm Houlihan Lokey Howard & Zukin).

122. See id.

123. Id.

124. Chris Isidore, Firing Team Owners?, CNN Money, December 20, 2004, http://money.cnn.com/2004/12/16/commentary/column_sportsbiz/sportsbiz/ (last visited May 15, 2006). Al Lerner, the

owner of the Cleveland Browns, died in 2003 but left the team to his son Randy who has assumed ownership rather than selling the team. Wikipedia, http://en.wikipedia.org/wiki/Cleveland_Browns (last visited May 15, 2006).

125. The example of the Boston Celtics is illustrative of this fact. The Celtics went public in 1986 at a unit price of $18.50. The club was finally sold in 2002, at which time, owners of shares in Boston Celtics LP received $27.00 per share. This represents an annual average return of 2.39% during a time of unprecedented growth in the stock market. See Peter May, New Team Officially in Place, Boston Globe, Jan. 1, 2003, at F3.

126. See Stroz, supra note 118, at 540.

127. Id. at 539.

128. Id. at 54 (quoting Dean Bonham, a noted sports marketing consultant).

129. Sarah Talalay, Public Ownership Doesn't Rake in the Dough, South Florida Sun-Sentinel (Ft Lauderdale, Fla.), July 29, 2001, at 7C (quoting Jeff Phillips, senior vice president of an investment banking firm which advises sports teams).

155. Daniel Kaplan, Cool with Pool: NBA to Renew Credit Facility, Street & Smith's Sports Bus. J., May 2, 2005, at 4.

156. Id.

157. Daniel Kaplan, Vikes Get $125m from NFL Pool, Street & Smith's Sports Bus. J., July 21, 2003, at 5.

158. Quote on Red Sox message board http://bostondirtdogs.boston.com/Headline_Archives/2005/01/barks_bites_1.html (last visited May 15, 2006).

TAX CONSIDERATIONS

TAX REVISIONS OF 2004 AND PRO SPORTS TEAM OWNERSHIP

Edward N. Coulson and Rodney Fort

I. INTRODUCTION

Major League Baseball (MLB) entrepreneur Bill Veeck claims that he convinced the IRS that the roster of players was a depreciable asset following his purchase of the Cleveland Indians in 1946 (Veeck, 1962). Okner's (1974) assessment of this "roster depreciation allowance" (RDA) first appeared nearly 20 years later. The point of Okner's work, and subsequent work after nearly another 20 years by Quirk and Fort (1992), was to demonstrate the RDA by example, illuminating its illogical foundations, and highlight its ongoing consequences. Despite these flaws, the RDA has endured. The effects of the most recent change in tax policy governing the RDA under the tax revisions of 2004, effective 2005, is the point of this paper.

Under previous 1976 tax laws, from 1977 to 2004, sports team owners were allowed to treat 50 percent of the team purchase price as an asset depreciable over no more than 5 years, what we refer to as the "50/5 Rule." The 2004 revision set the RDA at 100 percent of the purchase price depreciable over no more than 15 years, what we will refer to as the "100/15 Rule." All interested parties agreed that administrative enforcement costs would be driven to zero since, under the lavish percentage and depreciation period of the 100/15 Rule, no real legal challenges would be raised. Controversy over this revision did arise over the impacts on both team owner tax payments and team values.

Congressional supporters argued that owners would pay more taxes. A report by the Congressional Joint Committee on Taxation said the revisions would increase owner tax bills $381 million over 10 years. Industry experts disagreed, stating flatly that the revisions would generally lower tax payments by owners (Wilson, 2004, p. 2). To round out the controversy completely, a lobbyist-spokesman for MLB stated that tax payments would remain unchanged (Wilson, 2004, p. 3).

Turning to franchise values, members of Congress were silent but the same industry experts claimed the RDA revisions would raise the capital values of sports franchises. Lehman Brothers publicly stated that the revisions would add about 5 percent to sports team values across all leagues. Raymond James & Associates more vaguely agreed that team values would "increase" (Wilson, 2004, p. 3).

League officials, their lobbyists, and team owners were much less committal. They agreed there would be some advantages but chose instead to downplay the tax advantages and focus on the issue of owners suffering true net operating losses (Rovell, 2004, p. 1). Both Jeff Smulyan, previous owner of MLB's Seattle Mariners, and David Samson, President of MLB's Florida Marlins, voiced that the benefits of depreciation are small consolation for owners facing true operating losses. Ted Leonsis, owner of the NHL's Washington Capitals, said, "I look forward to the day where (write-offs are) an issue for me."

While its public statements downplayed the value of the RDA, MLB actively lobbied for the revisions and the National Football League (NFL) also publicly supported them. The National Basketball Association (NBA) and National Hockey League (NHL) remained neutral. Ostensibly, the reason for this lobbying was more about saving on legal fees than on raising franchise values. William H. Schweitzer, a managing partner of the Washington law firm that promoted the revisions for MLB, said they would have a slightly positive impact, varying from club to club. The revisions would eliminate IRS disputes without significantly changing taxes. Indeed, he offered that MLB had not specifically evaluated how the revisions would affect franchise values (Wilson, 2004, p. 3).

We present a model of tax policy and the RDA whose implications allow us to sort through these conflicting opinions, empirically. The model shows the impact of the RDA on team value and the impact of *changes in the RDA* on team values and taxes paid by owners. We hold all other values of team ownership constant and allow owners to either hold the team or sell it after the expiration of the RDA. Thus, we are able to 1) show the value of the RDA in terms of team operating profits, 2) provide comparative static results for parameters of the RDA, 3) explore the role of the "other values" held constant, and 4) apply our findings to the controversy just detailed.

Our findings suggest that supporters in Congress were qualitatively correct (though we cannot comment quantitatively on their $381 million over 10 years); taxes paid by owners should have increased. In addition, while MLB team values should have increased, outside analysts appear to have under-estimated franchise values by half. Since our model shows that the value of the RDA increased under the 2004 revisions *even though taxes increased*, it is small wonder that MLB and the NFL lobbied in favour of the 2004 revision.

. . . .

The paper proceeds as follows. In Section II we describe the RDA in more detail. Section III contains our model of the impact of the RDA on team value, including sensitivity of team values to tax policy changes that affect the RDA and other parameters determining team values. Section IV employs actual data on the parameters in our model to show relative team values and tax payments, under each of the ownership approaches, for the case at hand. Assessment of the actual impacts of tax policy governing the RDA is in Section V. Conclusions round out the paper.

II. THE ROSTER DEPRECIATION ALLOWANCE

The purchase of a professional sports franchise consists mainly of the rights to intangible assets. Some derive from league membership (territorial rights, revenue shares from attendance and television, and shares of future expansion fees). Others derive from their relationship with state and local hosts (revenues from tickets, parking, and concessions). Finally, there are "other values" like related business opportunities, accounting costs that are actually profit-taking, revenue-shifting tax advantages from joint ownership, and, the point of this paper, tax advantages through the RDA. Fort (2006) discusses all of these other ownership values in detail, including those from the RDA, and esti-

mates that they might be upwards of 18 percent of actual recent sale values.

Historically, the assignment of value to particular assets evolved arbitrarily. Bill Veeck describes how he wrested the RDA from the IRS after he bought the Cleveland Indians in 1946 (Veeck, 1962; Quirk and Fort, 1992). Essentially, Veeck assigned the bulk of the firm's value (90 percent) to the intangible player roster asset and devised a depreciation schedule (5 years) to reduce his taxable obligation on the team. A possible parallel is the depreciation of livestock purchased for work, breeding, or dairy purposes but not kept in an inventory account. Apparently, these types of livestock "wear out" in their relative productive roles and the IRS allows them to be treated as depreciable assets for tax purposes.

Okner (1974) and Quirk and Fort (1992) criticize this RDA for three reasons. First, while some players may be in the declining end of their careers, still other players are appreciating in value; it is not at all clear that "the roster" itself depreciates. Second, it is relatively easy to conceive a value in *player contracts*, but team owners *do not own players* as breeders own livestock. Third, the depreciation allowance surely involves double counting since the salaries and player development costs that create the asset are already treated as expenses at market determined values. But far from recognizing these inconsistencies, the IRS even changed its treatment of contracts to allow depreciation of individual player contracts, subject to capital gains if held long enough (Ambrose, 1985, p. 173).

There were IRS challenges of subsequent large RDA claims by other owners. One of the more famous involved the current MLB Commissioner, Bud Selig. A group led by Selig bought the bankrupt Seattle Pilots in April of 1970 for $10.8 million and moved them to Milwaukee. The IRS challenged Selig's claim that 94 percent of the purchase price could be attributed to the player roster and demanded a large tax adjustment. Selig sued and won the case (*Selig v. U.S.*, 565 F. Supp. 524). Eventually, tax reform legislation in 1976 set the 50/5 Rule and revisions in 2004 set the 100/15 Rule. The point of what follows is to assess changes in team values and owner tax bills following the tax policy that implemented the 100/15 Rule.

III. THE MODEL

We assume the team is structured as a pass through (e.g., subchapter S corporation; limited partnership) so that all tax savings occur at the individual income tax rate. In most cases, the size of the depreciation is easily enough to eliminate any taxes that would have been paid on the team's net operating revenues, and actually to shelter income from other endeavors besides team ownership. We choose to focus on this tax shelter value of the pass-through to the individual tax forms of team owners.

Table 7   Comparative Statics Summary

		Parameters					
	Value	**Y**	**i**	**T**	**a**	**b**	**c**
(1)	z_2	0	−	+	−	+	0
(2)	R_2	+	−	+	−	+	0
(3)	z_3	0	(*)	+	(*)	(**)	−
(4)	R_3	+	(*)	+	(*)	(**)	−

Source: Contemporary Economic Policy. Used with permission.
Notes: Only outcomes for $z3 > 0$ are calculated. *Negative for sufficiently small values of c. **Positive for sufficiently small values of c.

While the tax-saving value of the RDA is one of the "other values" of ownership mentioned in the last section, there is no reason that changes in the RDA would have any cross-effect on any of the rest of the other values. . . .

Since all other values are held constant, the model is based on the tried-and-true assumption that the fundamental value of the firm is equal to the discounted flow of operating profits and, in the case of the RDA, tax savings on team operations and pass-through shelter of taxable income from other endeavors besides team ownership. In this setting, we further assume net operating revenue, nonroster depreciation, amortization and remaining parameters of the model remain constant over time. We will also assume that net revenue after subtracting nonroster depreciation and amortization is positive, but less than the value of roster depreciation. This assures that the pass-through value of the RDA is positive. Finally, we'll use simple straight-line depreciation.

Our approach is to define the model first for the case of no RDA and then introduce the RDA to the model under two alternative ownership strategies. We do not model the choice (although we examine it empirically, later), but owners can hold the team into perpetuity after the RDA expires (henceforth, the "hold strategy") or sell the team after the RDA expires (henceforth, the "sell strategy").

. . . .

A summary of our model findings is as follows. First, team value increases unambiguously with the RDA under the hold strategy (relative to no RDA), even though taxes paid also will increase. Second, our theory alone cannot dictate if team values or owner tax bills are higher under the sell strategy or not. Data on the parameters of our model are required to settle the issue. Third, all else constant, an increase in the personal income tax rate *raises* the relative value of the hold strategy and owner tax bills, but increases in the parameters of the RDA, itself, have conflicting effects on both of these. Finally, team value and owner tax bills for the sell strategy with respect to the length of the RDA period and the percentage of purchase price attributed under the RDA are the same as for the hold strategy *only for sufficiently small values of the capital gains rate.* Settling this last issue also requires attention to the data on the parameters of interest (see **Table 7**).

IV.   THE RELATIVE VALUES OF THE HOLD AND SELL STRATEGIES

To settle the ambiguities detailed in the last section and gain insight into the controversy outlined in the introduction, we turn to data on the interest rate, personal income tax rate, and capital gains tax rate. Given the income levels of owners, we focus only on the rates paid by top income earners. The capital gains rate has been less than the income tax rate except for a brief period when they were equal, 1988–1990. The data (and sources) are shown for representative years in **Table 8**—the effective date of the 50/5 (1977), halfway between the 50/5 Rule imposition and the 100/15 Rule imposition (1990, also representative of that short period when personal income and capital gains tax rates were equal), the year just prior to the creation of the100/15 Rule (2003), and the effective date of the 100/15 Rule (2005). Lacking verifiable cash flow data, we must examine relative values of the hold and sell strategies. We examine each strategy separately and then compare the two in order to facilitate the policy assessment in the next section. The results are in **Table 9** for each of the years in Table 8.

The Hold Strategy

Compared to the codification of the 50/5 Rule effective in 1977, the relative value of the hold strategy was 20.4 percent

Table 8   Model Parameters for Various RDA Episodes

	50/5 Rule			100/15 Rule
Parameter	**(1977)**	**1990**	**2003**	**(2005)**
i	6.13%	6.44%	0.91%	3.98%
T	70%	28%	35%	35%
a	5 years	5 years	5 years	15 years
b	50%	50%	50%	100%
c	39.9%	28%	15%	15%

Sources: i = 13-week T-Bill yield index from the Global Financial Data (2008); a and b are known from Quirk and Fort (1992), Rovell (2004), and Wilson (2004); c and T are from the Citizens for Tax Justice (2008); and K is from the text, expression (3). Reproduced from *Contemporary Economic Policy.* Used with permission.
Notes: All values are actual values except that i and c are averaged over the 1971–76 period (the income tax rate was constant during the period).

Table 9   Team Values Relative to V_1, Various RDA Episodes

		50/5 Rule			100/15 Rule
	Approach	**(1977)**	**1990**	**2003**	**(2005)**
(1)	"Hold"	1.42	1.13	1.21	1.35
(2)	"Sell"	2.30	1.06	−0.81	1.66
(3)	Sell Advantage	62.0%	−6.2%	∞	23.0%

Source: Contemporary Economic Policy. Used with permission.
Notes: Calculated from Expressions (1) through (4) in the text using the parameters in Table 7.

lower in 1990, 14.8 percent lower in 2003, and returned to within 95 percent of its 1977 value for the codification of the 100/15 Rule effective in 2005.

. . . .

For 2003, both the continued decline in the interest rate and the increase in the personal income tax rate raised the relative value of the hold strategy.

Second, the impact of the RDA parameter changes under the 100/15 Rule are in opposite directions (raising the percentage of the purchase price should raise the relative value of the hold strategy but increasing the length of the depreciation period should have an offsetting effect). Further, an increase in the interest rate should decrease the relative value of the hold strategy. For the imposition of the 100/15 Rule, the increase in the percentage of the purchase price must have dominated since the relative value of the hold strategy increased.

The Sell Strategy

Given the data in Table 8 on the relationship between the capital gains tax rate and the personal income tax rate (required since our theoretical implications depend on it), our comparative static results again paint a compelling picture. First, the relative value of the sell strategy should *increase* with the percentage of the purchase price applied under the RDA. Second, the relative value of the sell strategy should *decrease* in the interest rate, *except for* 2003 where it *increases* in the interest rate. Finally, the relative value of the sell strategy should *decrease* in the length of the depreciation period under the RDA.

For 1990, the effects of the increased interest rate and decline in the personal income tax rate offset the effects of the decline in the capital gains tax rate since the relative value of the sell strategy declined. To return to a negative value in 2003, the effect of the interest rate had to overcome the effects of an increase in the personal income tax rate and a decline in the capital gains tax rate. Finally, the last decline in the relative value of the sell strategy with the imposition of the 100/15 Rule cannot be attributed solely to the imposition of that rule. One element of the newest rule, increasing the length of the depreciation period under the RDA, should reduce the relative value of the sell strategy, but the other element, increasing the percentage of the purchase price applied under the RDA, should increase the value. Further, increased interest rates would also act to lower the relative value of the sell strategy.

Comparing Hold and Sell

The only exception is 1990, but the results of our model in the last section help explain this outcome. While the increasing interest rate may well have been an important kicker and the relative values of both the hold and sell strategies fell, it is also true that the personal income tax rate and the

capital gains tax rate both fell and became equal to each other (Table 8). . . .

V. POLICY ASSESSMENT

Since we do not model the hold or sell decision, and the impact on team value and owner tax payments depends on it, we cannot address the controversy in the introduction until we examine whether owners actually hold or sell their teams at the expiration of whatever RDA. In **Table 10**, we compare a variety of statistics on holding periods and the like for all MLB owners purchasing teams during the reign of the 50/5 Rule, 1977–2004, and their predecessor owners. There are insufficient observations for any statements about actual owner choice after the 100/15 Rule. In addition, it is useful to separate expansion team transactions from others since the number of expansion teams is different in each period. Finally, teams that were purchased during the 50/5 Rule period but not sold again to date require special attention (see the notes to Table 10).

Two things are interesting to note in Table 10. First, compared to the preceding 30 years when the RDA was evolving, excluding expansion team transactions, the number of sales increased 7 percent, the holding period declined 39.9 percent, and the vast majority of teams (65.2 percent) were held for a shorter number of years under the 50/5 Rule. Second, the vast majority of teams also were held longer than the duration of the RDA; 22 out of 26 longer than five years (84.6 percent). Other than selling like hotcakes relative to the preceding period (by a factor of 2.75), the story is the same for expansion teams as it is for the rest under the 50/5 Rule. Thus, it is safe to say that owners during this period clearly were not choosing the sell strategy. Indeed only four owners (including 3 expansion team owners) during this period actually did so. If all remaining purchases yet to be resold did so within 5 years of purchase, there would be 8 more but even 15 would be well below a majority of the 49 total sales.

But if teams really were as we have modeled them, owners clearly should be adopting the sell strategy. Our explanation for this behavior is to return to our assumption that all "other values" of ownership were constant. Fort (2006) makes it clear that other values loom large and the results in Table 10 suggest that owners overwhelmingly reject the sell strategy in order to hold on to these other values. This is reasonable since it is highly likely that other values rose during the reign of the 50/5 Rule.

First, there has been a dramatic change in the type of ownership from single individuals to corporations after 1977 and other values should be both larger and easier for corporations to capture. Second, Fort (2006) shows that other values (for our purposes, unfortunately, including the value of the RDA) can represent upwards of 18 percent of recent sale prices. He also documents 5.3 percent and 9.5 percent real rates of growth in team sale prices for average

Table 10   Team Holding Statistics, MLB, 1977–2004

	Last Owner	New Owner
New Expansion Teams		4
Without Expansion Team Transations		
Total Purchases		26
Omitted	0	3
Held ≤ 5 Years	3	1
Held 6–10 Years	8	11
Held > 10 Years	15	11
Average Years Held	20.5	12.3
Sales w/Decreased Hold		15
% Increase in Sales		7.0%
% Decline in Average Hold		−39.9%
% w/Decline in Hold		65.2%
Expansion Team Transactions		
Total Purchases		15
Omitted	0	5
Held ≤ 5 Years	3	3
Held 6–10 Years	4	3
Held > 10 Years	8	4
Average Years Held	11.9	9.1
Sales w/Decreased Hold		6
% Increase in Sales		275.0%
% Decline in Average Hold		−23.5%
% w/Decline in Hold		60.0%

Sources: Compiled from data in appendices of Quirk and Fort (1992), data at Fort (2008), and the most recent MLB team valuations in Ozanian and Badenhausen (2008). Reproduced from *Contemporary Economic Policy.* Used with permission.

Notes: There were 27 purchases excluding expansion franchises for 1946–1976, 10 new expansion teams, and 4 expansion team purchases (after the original entry franchise price). Percentage increase in the number of sales is on a per year basis since the earlier period is three years longer. 23 teams had not been resold as of 2004 so that hold durations for new owners were not evident (2 for 1946–1976 and 21 for 1977–2004). If the team had been held longer than 5 years as of 2004, their hold is stated as of 2004 and they are included in subsequent calculations. If the team had been held 5 years or less as of 2004, they are in the "Omitted" category in the table and omitted from subsequent calculations where relevant.

holding periods over the 1970s and 1980s, respectively (relative to 2.5 percent to 3 percent for the economy at large). Finally, Humphreys and Mondello (2008) show that a quality-adjusted index of major league sport franchise prices practically exploded beginning in the late 1970s. But an examination of "typical revenues in MLB" (Fort, 2008) over this period shows an annual real rate of growth around 4.3 percent for 1974–1980. The upshot of all of this is that rest of the explosion in team prices seems reasonably to have been fueled by increases in "other values" held constant in our analysis.

And that brings us finally to our chance to inform the controversy detailed in the introduction. Supposing that the hold strategy continues to dominate during the reign of the new 100/15 Rule, team values and owner tax payments

should rise about 11.6 percent (1.21 to 1.35 in Table 9, row 1). So, supporters in Congress were precisely correct; taxes would increase under the 100/15 Rule. Our model does not allow us to cast judgment on the $381 million *increase* over 10 years since we do not know of any starting values for tax payments. However, even though they were right qualitatively, outside observers were decidedly low in their quantitative estimate of impacts on franchise values; our 11.6 percent calculation is fully 2.3 times their 5 percent claim.

It is small wonder that major leagues were at worst neutral (NBA and NHL) and at best highly supportive (MLB and NFL) of the 2004 revisions. Their costs and benefits are easily isolated looking at what happened immediately to the first crop of team sales in 2005. The 2005 team sales were $600 million for the NFL's Minnesota Vikings, $375 million for the NBA's Cleveland Cavaliers, $220 million and $180 million for MLB's Oakland Athletics and Milwaukee Brewers (respectively), and $75 million for the NHL's Anaheim Mighty Ducks.

On the cost side, we know of no other data on tax payments than those offered by the Congressional Joint Committee on Taxation cited in the introduction. Their estimate of an *additional* $381 million in tax revenues over ten years yields 381/10 = $38.1 million per year ignoring discounting. That would be an additional $10.0 million for the 32-team NFL, or about $312,500 per owner annually. For the three remaining 30-team leagues, including MLB, each league total is $9.5 million, or about $316,700 per owner annually. These additional average taxes are at least indicative of the cost to the first crop of owners that sold their teams in 2005.

On the benefit side, the predicted 11.6 percent increase would be immediately capitalized into observed sale prices. The 11.6 percent increases are thus $69.6 million for the Vikings owner, $43.5 million for the Cavaliers owner, $25.5 million for the Athletics owner, $20.9 million for the Brewers owner, and $8.7 million for the Mighty Ducks owner. Across all four pro leagues, benefits clearly swamp costs. Indeed, we are left wondering why either the NBA or the NHL remained neutral.

It is tempting to label the downplayed claims by owners and their lobbyist in the introduction as disingenuous. For example, Mr. Leonsis dismisses write-offs like those under the RDA as insignificant to him. He purchased his NHL Washington Capitals in 1999 for a reported $85 million (Ozanian, Badenhausen, and Settimi, 2007), or $99.5 million 2005 dollars. Even if there were no other increase in the team price except an inflation adjustment to 2005, our calculation says that the increase would represent 0.116 × 99.4 = $11.5 million. This increase would have been large enough to recoup 11.5 percent of the $100 million in losses attributed to Leonsis' ownership to 2004 (Rovell, 2004, p. 1).

Put another way, by the Joint Committee report of *additional* taxes, the average tax payment for each NHL owner, as stated above, would have increased about $316,700 from 2004 to 2005. If this is the 11.6 percent increase suggested by our results, the average tax bill for NHL operations in 2004 would have been 316,700/.116 = $2.7 million. Using 33 percent for the top tax bracket puts average taxable net revenues on operations of 2.7/0.33 = $8.2 million in 2004. Since Mr. Leonsis apparently is far below the average, his *worst-case* franchise value gain of $11.5 million is 40% greater than the average taxable NHL net revenue.

But rather than label them disingenuous, it is perhaps fairer to try to determine what else pro team owners and their advocates might have had in mind. For example, the value of our model parameters beyond the outset of the 100/15 Rule is subject to uncertainty. Expectations about interest rates and personal income tax rates (but probably not capital gains tax rates since the hold strategy seems to be the order of the day) may have been behind their downplayed claims. But even this argument is slightly diversionary. Statements based on expectations about these other parameters are beside the point from the perspective of the RDA! Those other parameters have nothing to do with a statement about changes in either the percentage of purchase price attributed under the RDA or the length of its depreciation period.

As a last general observation in this day and age where preferential economic treatment of wealthy owners is highly criticized, we note the following. Suppose government policies toward the other values enjoyed by owners were so tight that owners viewed their teams as stand-alone assets. In this case, "other values" would be minimal and the value of team ownership would be as we have it modeled. In such a world, it seems safe to say that the sell strategy would dominate. But if so, the imposition of the 100/15 Rule would have had dramatically different impacts!

From Table 9, row 2, the value of the sell strategy would have fallen under the 100/15 Rule (from the anomalous case in 2003 to a smaller value in 2005). But even so, the value of the sell strategy would still be 23 percent higher than the hold strategy (1.66 > 1.35), a fact that generates the following final insight. If "other values" are obtained politically by investment in the welfare of politicians that keep these other values flowing, then these other values must be at least as much as the 23 percent potential gain in Table 10. The opportunity cost to owners of their enjoyed "other values" is the 23 percent increase they could have employing the sell strategy for teams that are more like stand-alone assets. Investment in all types of policy toward sports leagues, not just tax policy, clearly has a payoff.

VI. CONCLUSIONS

The "roster depreciation allowance" (RDA) allows pro sports team owners to count a percentage of their team purchase price as a depreciable asset over a specific number of years. The RDA impacts the value of sports team ownership by reducing team tax obligations and providing pass-through tax shelter of an owner's income from other endeavors besides team ownership. Tax law revisions of 2004 increased the amount of team purchase price attributed to the RDA from 50 percent to 100 percent and the allowed depreciation period from 5 to 15 years. Supporters claimed this would practically eliminate costly legal oversight by the IRS and increase owner tax bills. Government officials remained silent on team value impacts but outside analysts argued they would rise and both MLB and the NFL lobbied in favour of the revisions.

Modeling the RDA impact on the value of team operations, we investigate this policy change. Holding all "other values" of ownership constant, we formalize the value of operating a sports team and enjoying the financial benefits of the RDA for both a strategy where the team is held after the RDA runs out and a strategy where the team is sold after the RDA runs out. Applying actual data on the parameters of our model suggests that supporters in Congress were absolutely correct. Tax payments by owners should have increased. Those arguing that tax payments would decrease may have expectations about future cash flow, personal income tax rates, and/or interest rates that are different than the levels at the time of the revision in 2004. But none of those pertain to the revisions of the RDA, itself, under the 2004 revisions. Further, outside analysts missed the mark substantially. Increases in team values attributable to the RDA were likely to be just over twice their claims. Even though MLB remained silent on the impact on team values, our findings help explain support for the revisions by MLB and the NFL.

On a closing note, many of the "other values" of team ownership could be reduced by other types of policy intervention. If these interventions rendered teams more as stand-alone assets that do not generate substantial "other values," owners would be more likely to follow the strategy of selling their team at the expiration of the RDA depreciation period. Interestingly, if such were the case, the value of teams would reasonably have been predicted to fall, instead, under the 2004 revisions. But since returns under the sell policy are 23 percent higher, and owners could reasonably bargain their "other values" politically for this higher return *on operations*, then "other values" must be worth more than the gain under the sell strategy. Policy toward sports team owners is a remarkably many-splendored thing.

References

Ambrose, J.F. 1985. "The Impact of Tax Policy on Sports." In A. Johnson and J. Frey (eds.), *Government and Sport*. Totowa, NJ: Rowman and Allenheld, pp. 171–186.

Citizens for Tax Justice. 2008. "Top Federal Income Tax Rates on Regular Income and Capital Gains since 1916." Web Page URL (last accessed July 7, 2008): http://www.ctj.org/pdf/regcg.pdf.

Fort, R. 2006. "The Value of Major League Baseball Ownership." *International Journal of Sport Finance* 1:9–20.

Fort, R. 2008. Rodney Fort's Sports Business Data Pages. Web Page URL (last accessed July 7, 2008): www.rodneyfort.com/SportsData/BizFrame.htm.

Global Financial Data. 2008. "CBOE 13-Week U.S. Treasury Bill Yield Index." Web Page URL (last accessed July 7, 2008): http://www.globalfinancialdata.com/index.php3?action=Search&seriestype=Treasury_Bill_Yields&country=USA&starttime=1000&endtime=3000.

Humphreys, B.R., and Mondello, M. 2008. "Determinants of Franchise Values in North American Professional Sports Leagues: Evidence from a Hedonic Price Model." *International Journal of Sport Finance* 3:98–105.

Okner, B.A. 1974. "Taxation and Sports Enterprises." In R.G. Noll (ed.), *Government and the Sports Business*. Washington, D.C.: Brookings Institution, pp. 159–184.

Ozanian, M.K., Badenhausen, K., and Settimi, C. 2007. "The Business of Hockey." *Forbes* Web Page URL (last accessed July 7, 2008): http://www.forbes.com/2007/11/08/nhl-teamvalues-biz-07nhl_cx_mo_kb_1108nhl_land.html.

Ozanian, M.K., and Badenhausen, K. 2008. "The Business of Baseball." *Forbes* Web Page URL (last accessed July 7, 2008): http://www.forbes.com/2008/04/16/baseball-teamvalues-biz-sports-baseball08-cx_mo_kb_0416baseballintro.html.

Quirk, J., and Fort, R.D. 1992. *Pay Dirt: The Business of Professional Team Sports*. Princeton, NJ: Princeton University Press.

Rovell, D. 2004. "New Owners' Tax Break Losing Value." ESPN.com, April 15, 2004. Web Page URL (last accessed July 7, 2008): http://sports.espn.go.com/espn/sportsbusiness/news/story?id=1782953.

Veeck, B. (with E. Linn). 1962. *The Hustler's Handbook*. New York, NY: G.P. Putnam's Sons.

Wilson, D. 2004. "Bill would Raise Franchise Value of Sports Teams." *New York Times*, August 2, 2004. Web Page URL (last accessed July 7, 2008): http://www.nytimes.com/2004/08/02/sports/02tax.final.html.

Discussion Questions

1. What is the likely view of public ownership by league commissioners? By existing owners?
2. Why do small investors buy shares of sports franchise stocks?
3. What are the unique characteristics of the Green Bay Packers public ownership structure?
4. Do you think public ownership of sports franchises will continue to increase?
5. How does sports franchise ownership differ from corporate ownership?
6. Is sports franchise ownership profitable?
7. Are sports franchise owners still "sportsmen"?
8. Which sports are the most profitable? Why?
9. What single factor has proven to be the most important in the "boom" of professional sports?
10. Discuss the difference in importance in winning hockey and baseball games versus football and basketball games. What are the major reasons for this difference?
11. Is the bottom-line motivation of most owners bad for sports?
12. Bill Veeck asserted that a club's players were depreciable assets. What would be a viable counterargument to his claim?
13. What are the potential advantages/disadvantages to owners of selling minority interests in a public offering?
14. If you were running a sports league, would you allow for public ownership of franchises (either majority or minority interest)?
15. Irrespective of whether it is good public policy, is it good for sports leagues to have myriad tax shelters available to owners? Does it free up money for owners to invest in their teams, or does it draw ownership groups that are interested in the ancillary tax benefits rather than the good of the club?
16. Is there a speculative bubble for sports franchises? What are the arguments for or against?
17. How can you determine whether an owner is a profit-maximizer or a win-maximizer, or some combination of both?
18. How do we reconcile the prolonged, substantial increase in franchise values across sports with the slim, or sometimes negative, profit margins reported by many clubs?
19. If such figures were publicly available, could you get a true picture of a franchise's value from the club's profit/loss statement?
20. Do you agree with the contention that selling off 49% to the public while retaining controlling interest is a (relatively) cost-free way of injecting liquidity into a club/franchise?
21. What are the potential advantages/disadvantages of selling minority interests in a public offering?

Leagues: Structure and Background

INTRODUCTION

Professional sports leagues are unique business structures in a free market economy. As was mentioned in the introduction to this book, leagues combine elements of cooperation and competition and allow independent team owners to seek monetary gains that might otherwise be unavailable if pursued unilaterally through the playing of disparate contests. Indeed, it is doubtful whether professional team sports could survive in the absence of leagues. Leagues offer an enticing, profit-maximizing structure to teams both on and off the playing field. Though professional sports teams are clearly competitors on the field, leagues benefit owners by providing organized regular and championship seasons of play and offering a unitary set of playing rules, both of which are designed to maximize fan interest and, consequently, team profits. Off the field, competition among teams is generally limited to the pursuit of scarce playing and managerial talent. Professional sports leagues are cooperative endeavors away from the playing field, with teams jointly engaging in numerous practices that maximize the profits of the collective entity. Sports leagues, like other forms of entertainment, also deliver a unique product. In essence, the competition that is delivered to the consumer serves as a diversion from everyday life. In that sense, and because of the historic accessibility—whether at the gate or via broadcast—the business has been argued to be "recession proof."

Each of the major professional sports in the United States has one league. This has important public policy implications. The closed league structure typical of U.S.–based sports leagues allows teams to establish constitutions that govern the locations of their franchises, conditions of entry into the league and relocation within the league, the labor market for players, and rules of the game, as well as permitting teams to pool their broadcast rights for negotiation and sale. This cartel behavior has been widely criticized.

However, it is possible that this off-the-field cooperation among teams allows the on-field competition between teams to endure. It is also important to note that, in a free market economy, professional sports leagues have adopted many characteristics of an alternative economic system—socialism—particularly with respect to planning and the redistribution of income. Indeed, it seems that the higher the degree of socialism, the stronger the league. The collective strength of the league is more important than that of the individual teams within the league. Revenue sharing in leagues is discussed in Chapter 5.

American sports leagues have also adopted the single-entity structure. Major League Soccer (MLS) was the first entity to use this model, in which an entire league is controlled by a single operating company. Investments are made in this company, rather than in a particular franchise. This format was developed for several reasons. First, it helps to avoid the self-destructive behavior displayed by owners in other nascent sports leagues whose desire to win led them to pay more than they could afford for athlete services. This ultimately contributed to the demise of these leagues, because so many teams went out of business that the league could no longer survive. By adopting a single-entity structure, competitive bidding among owners for players is eliminated, sidestepping a major cause of league failure. It also can help a league to avoid many of the problems that can arise from having discrepancies in managerial expertise across teams, particularly in areas such as talent evaluation and marketing acumen. In addition, this structure allows sports leagues to evade the application of antitrust laws in management–labor disputes. The single-entity seems to be quite helpful in allowing a league to survive its startup phase.

Following the lead of MLS, most new leagues have since adopted this operating structure. Despite its strengths, the model may not prove to be an effective method of running a mature league. It places a disincentive on individual investors to engage in entrepreneurial behaviors, because the benefits of such tactics are likely outweighed by their costs. The whole may be weaker than the sum of its individual parts. The WNBA and the NBA D-League, two leagues that began as single entities, altered their structure to a traditional league model as they matured. Even MLS has morphed a bit towards the more traditional model as it has evolved, allowing teams an increased amount of autonomy in recent seasons. MLS teams can sell sponsorships in an increased number of categories (including jersey sponsorships), because league-sponsor categories are no longer exclusive with each team. In addition, teams can retain the transfer fees of players that they develop and sell. The league also adopted a designated-player rule (aka the "Beckham rule") that currently allows teams to be assigned up to three star players with only a minimal amount ($335,000) paid for by the league counting against its team salary cap; the rest of the player's salary above the $335,000 level is the team's responsibility.

Globally, two additional league structures warrant discussion. The model most typical of sports leagues outside of North America is that of promotion and relegation. This open model of competition provides for teams to enter and depart the lower leagues within a domestic league's hierarchy depending on their competitive success or failure. Rather than the league making periodic strategic decisions to expand to new markets, as occurs in North America, the number of teams at each level of the hierarchy remains constant in the open league structure, but the membership of each league changes every year as teams migrate between levels of competition based on their previous season's performance. Although the benefits of an open model of competition are numerous and include increased competition, a reduction of the league's monopoly power, and, arguably, a better economic model, it is highly unlikely that any of the established closed leagues will ever migrate to such a model. The reason? Money. Although teams that are promoted to a higher level of competition may realize a financial windfall, the opposite is also true. Given the risk-averse nature of the owners, it is difficult to imagine them adopting the open league structure that is prevalent throughout the world.

The final league structure addressed here is the "super-league." In one version of this model, the top teams from each country's top domestic league in a particular geographic region compete against each other for regional sporting supremacy. The highest profile league of this type is the Union of European Football Associations (UEFA) Champions League. This extremely lucrative annual tournament of the top European clubs has been held in various formats since 1955–1956 and has morphed into the most prestigious club event in soccer. Teams qualify for the event based on their previous season's performance in their respective leagues and the strength of their domestic league, with the highest ranked European leagues receiving up to four places and the lowest ranked only receiving one. Up to 77 European teams compete in the league, which is a combination of qualification play, a round-robin group stage, a home-and-away knockout tournament phase, and a final game. The UEFA Champions League generates a significant amount of revenue through the sale of television rights, sponsorships, and new media deals. In 2008–2009, these revenues totaled EUR 825–850 million. Note that this sum does not include gate receipts or other locally generated revenues, which are kept entirely by the home club.

The league has a revenue sharing system in place through which the majority of the central revenues are shared among the participating clubs based on their performance in the Champions League, the strength of each team's domestic league, and the performance of the team in that league. The revenue sharing system rewards the strongest teams from the strongest leagues an excess share of the rewards. The remainder of the UEFA Champions League revenues is shared among the national associations, leagues, and clubs that comprise UEFA through a "solidarity" fund and covers UEFA's organizational and administrative costs. The effect of this aspect of the revenue sharing plan is to give more money to the lesser national associations. Overall, it is fair to conclude that the super-league model is highly capitalistic in nature and monetizes the stronger European clubs that participate in it. This can lead to the participating teams furthering their competitive advantage over the non-participants from their domestic league—in other words, the rich are getting richer. Other examples of this structure in global *futbol* are the Copa Libertadores (South America and Mexico), the CONCACAF Champions League (North and Central America and the Caribbean), the CAF Champions League (Africa), and the AFC Champions League (Asia). Some additional global league issues will be examined in Chapter 3.

No matter the structure, all professional sports leagues are concerned with the same two issues: competitive balance and revenue sharing. Although both topics are addressed at length in Chapter 5, it is appropriate to address competitive balance briefly here. Perhaps the best way to think about competitive balance is in its alternative—competitive imbalance. Competitive imbalance can take several different forms, all of which are arguably bad for the league as a collective.[1] The first is if one team dominates the top position in a league over an extended period of time (i.e., dynasties). This is bad for the league, because although casual fans may be drawn to the league because of the excellence of the one team, this interest will almost certainly wane over time because there is little uncertainty of outcome. In addition, fans of the other teams in the league may unite for a period of time to rally against the dynasty, but their interest will wane if their team does not have a realistic chance of winning a championship over a prolonged period of time. A predictable league ultimately becomes of little interest to its followers. Closely related to this is the second form of competitive imbalance: domination of the top of a league by the same teams over an extended period. For example, Celtic or Rangers have won the Scottish Premier League title every year since 1986. Again, there is little uncertainty of outcome, and fans of other teams will ultimately lose interest. A final form of competitive imbalance is the domination of the bottom of a league by the same teams over an extended period. This is bad for a league, because fans of those teams will lose interest in the team and sport, and bringing them back into the fold will require a substantial on-field improvement—contending for a championship. Habitually losing teams also impose costs on the rest of the teams in the league in that their contests against the weaker teams are less attractive and thus typically prevent them from maximizing their revenues in these games.

Leagues use a number of mechanisms to promote competitive balance, including a reverse-order draft in which the worst teams are given an increased opportunity to select the best incoming talent in the league's entry draft; salary caps and floors, which are designed to compress the range of team spending on playing talent such that all teams are spending relatively close to one another on their athletes; luxury taxes, which penalize teams that spend beyond a proscribed threshold on player salaries and are thus meant to rein in teams inclined to spend excessively; relegation and promotion, which incentivize teams to win championships so that they may be promoted to a higher level of competition and reap the financial rewards and disincentivize losing contests to prevent the financial harms associated with demotion to a lower level of competition; and revenue sharing, which theoretically provides teams with an increased ability to spend more on player salaries and thus remain more competitive than they would be in the absence of the receipt of these revenues.

In the first reading, Shropshire and Rosner look at how sports survived the economic downturn that began in late 2008. In "On the Global Economic Downturn and

League revenues
- NFL—(2009) $8.0 billion
- MLB—(2009) $6.5 billion
- NBA—(2008–2009) $3.7 billion
- EPL—(2008–2009) $3.4 billion
- NHL—(2008–2009) $2.65 billion
- Serie A—(2008–2009) $2.0 billion
- Bundesliga—(2008–2009) $2.0 billion
- La Liga—(2008–2009) $2.0 billion
- Ligue 1—(2008–2009) $1.4 million

Sports," Shropshire and Rosner maintain that even the sports industry is vulnerable to a long-term recession. In the second reading, Michael Danielson provides a comprehensive analysis of the role of leagues in the business of professional sports. After giving an overview of league structures, the author then discusses the importance of both on-field competition and territorial exclusivity for the individual teams within the league. Danielson subsequently addresses the issue of geographic exclusivity in professional sports leagues in great detail. In the concluding excerpt, Roger Noll elaborates upon one specific alternative to the closed league structure embraced by North American professional sports that is embraced by much of the rest of the world, the open league model of promotion and relegation. He reviews this model through the lens of the English Premier League, widely considered the top soccer league in the world.

Notes

1. George Foster, Stephen Greyser, and Bill Walsh, "The Business of Sports."

POSITIONING OF SPORTS IN THE U.S. ECONOMY

ON THE GLOBAL ECONOMIC DOWNTURN AND SPORTS

Kenneth Shropshire and Scott Rosner

This has been an unprecedented time. Bear Stearns, Lehman Brothers and Washington Mutual failed, the U.S. automotive market is in disarray, Merrill Lynch was forced to marry Bank of America, AIG, Fannie Mae and Freddie Mac were bailed out and a federal rescue package was implemented that delivered nearly one trillion dollars to the distressed global economy.

On a visit to the Wharton School in 2009, Sam Zell was asked about how the economic downturn will impact the sports industry. He responded, "I don't know. I think we're going to find out. [On the] corporate side of sports [there are] usually less suites than demand. We'll see [if that continues]. We'll also see in about a month with the sale of the Cubs." This hesitation and uncertainty is unusual in the sports industry. Broadly, the old logic seemed to be that sports, movies and other low cost forms of entertainment would always serve as a form of diversion, particularly during hard times. However, as tickets have become increasingly expensive and significant sports sponsors and advertisers have withered, the more problematic that premise has become. Historically, sports properties, teams, successful leagues and the like have been an asset that appreciates in value, provided an owner is able to hold on long enough and have deep enough pockets to withstand the somewhat inevitable operating losses. But the ongoing financial crisis is having a real impact on merger and acquisition activity and an operational impact on ownership. The longer these economic hard times go on, the harder it will become for some owners to maintain their grip given their reduced liquidity. Expect owners to be on the hunt for capital. But who to borrow from? With the elimination of investment banks and constipated credit markets, borrowing is harder than ever. If you are in need of operational cash for your business, most likely the prudent move is to take a reasonable deal from a lender if it is available today, as the offer may not be available tomorrow. And if these deals are unavailable, who to sell to? Deal flow may slow to a trickle, as there is likely to be a decrease in the supply of interested buyers. Thus, it is fair to conclude that with regard to stock and credit markets, the sports industry is no different than any other industry. Both are long term propositions on which the short to medium term financial crisis is having a real impact.

Most sports franchises should expect an operating downturn, with decreased spending by both individual and corporate customers and sponsors likely to be the norm as a result of the financial crisis. However, these operational impacts will not be felt equally across all teams (even within the same league). It should be mentioned that all teams are different, because all markets are different—some markets are going to get hit worse than others. The automotive woes hit Detroit, the financial sector struggles hit New York City, and other cities where the housing glut is unlikely to abate any time soon like Miami, Phoenix and San Diego are feeling the pinch even more. To the extent that all teams in a league rely heavily on local revenues (less in NFL, more in NHL, NBA, MLB), this could be bad news for teams in the impacted cities. Decreased corporate spending means fewer luxury box rentals (for the ones not rented for upcoming season(s) via long-term deals) and fewer, less lucrative team sponsorship sales (again, only for those categories that the team is selling now, not the ones locked in to long term deals). With the opening of two new ballparks in New York City and one in Dallas it is clear that sales of seats and suites are not as vigorous as they were in better economic times. There is a point at which the 'sports as diversion' theory becomes problematic. Consumers have to make tough decisions and between tickets to the game or food on the table, we all know what wins. Discretionary income is labeled as such for a reason. Declines in individuals' discretionary income means decreased ticket sales (especially day of game sales in MLB) and decreased concessions sales (fans that do go may spend less on food, drink, etc.). There even exists the possibility that local media rights fees could decrease (but again only if these rights are on the market). Oh, and that

new facility that provides a transformational moment in the economics of the franchise, funded in part (or increasingly rarely, entirely) by public money? Highly unlikely. Politics, budget shortfalls and higher order governmental priorities will stand in the way.

On the larger level, the impact of the financial crisis on league operations will again vary, as it affects all leagues somewhat differently. The longer market unrest goes on, the greater the chance of impact. It's cyclical too, with the amount of pain endured depending on when your bigger sponsorship or television deals are up for renewal. Now would not be a good time, for example, to seek to renew your AIG deal.

Looking at a sampling of sports enterprises, NASCAR seems to be getting hurt the most in the short-term because of volatile gas prices and the depressed auto industry, with the LPGA and PGA Tours' medium term prospects a bit more uncertain because of the nature of its sponsorships relating to the financial services industry. In the short-term, NBA and NHL season ticket sales were not terribly hurt in 2008–09 because their selling season came before the downturn occurred, but they too will get hurt in 2009–10 if the recession endures through their next selling season. Both leagues' day-of-game sales should take a hit in 2009–10. The NFL may have less immediate concern for the 2009 season because it requires less dollar commitment for tickets but sponsorship sales in their open categories should become more and more difficult should the economy not make a positive turn. The issues are similar for MLB, except that their business has a greater dependence on revenues from ticket sales, and 2009 leaguewide attendance was down 7%. All of the major North American leagues have their national television deals locked in for the next several seasons (and the NFL even managed to extend its deals with Fox, CBS and DirecTV for additional seasons). The networks are clearly banking on the advertising market rebounding in the distant future.

At the collegiate level, the economic downturn is impacting not only endowments, but the level of giving during this current period. The largest impact is on construction of new facilities, with the constipation in the credit markets taking a toll on facility financing. Long term broadcast and sponsorship deals, again, are less problematic. The BCS television negotiations led to a lucrative long-term deal with ESPN, with the latter putting enough faith into the future of its monthly subscriber fees and advertising marketplace for the demographically attractive college sports product so as to allow the annualized rights fee payments to increase well into the double digits.

Unfortunately at the lowest levels of the sports pyramid, the impact is likely to be the most severe. From parents having to make the decision not to pay that Little League fee, to school districts having to decide between books or the gymnastics program, to cash-strapped local municipalities dramatically scaling back and in some cases even shuttering recreational facilities and programs, sports is likely to be the loser. In all circumstances too, the sports world is flat. Sponsors locked in for both the 2012 Olympics in London and 2010 World Cup in South Africa, bear close watching. If problems hit them, replacements could be hard to come by.

So the answer to the question of whether the sports industry is recession-proof is 'No.' If it ever was appropriate to refer to sports as recession (or even depression) proof, those days are clearly gone. There is perhaps a level of resistance due to the emotional involvement of sports fans with their teams, but the business does not have endless elasticity. That is particularly the case if you need to sell an asset now, have ticket inventory to move, or have new broadcast or sponsor deals to renegotiate. This is clearly not the ideal moment. However, all is not lost. Like the stock market, in the long run, the basic long term philosophy about the strength of the sports industry seems true. Wharton professor Jeremy Siegel provides the following guidance on the broader economy. "It is foolish to pick the bottom of either the stock or other financial markets in today's environment. In the short term, anything can happen, since emotion dominates economics. Yet at these levels it is virtually certain that stocks will be a rewarding investment for long term investors."

The power of sport is in its enduring emotional value to the consumer. The simplicity, enjoyment and the diversionary power are enjoyed by all. That is harder to pull away from and is different from the decision to pull away from the gas guzzler SUV and move to the hybrid. For the best qualities in sport, there is no substitute and the financial foundation of the game—the fan—is grounded in the fanaticism that is the basis of that label. While it is doubtless affected by current macroeconomic conditions, the sports industry will remain vibrant in the long-term.

OVERVIEW OF THE PROFESSIONAL MODEL

HOME TEAM

Michael Danielson

The business of professional team sports requires organization of teams into leagues. Leagues bring together a set of places that provide the primary market for the collective product; they provide the framework in which teams meet to produce games; they structure games into seasons, play-offs, and championships. Customers prefer organized games among teams competing for pennants, division titles, or a place in postseason play. As Commissioner Pete Rozelle constantly reminded NFL owners, "if you didn't belong to a league, and just had teams arranging scrimmages against one another, you couldn't expect many people to watch."[1]

The necessity for teams to be organized as leagues structures relations between professional sports and places. Leagues exercise controls over the location and relocation of teams, territorial rights, suitability of places for teams, the number of places that can have franchises, and who can own teams. They determine how revenues will be shared among members, negotiate national broadcasting arrangements, and bargain collectively with players. These league activities raise complicated issues of public policy, whose outcomes shape the way places connect with teams and leagues.

STRUCTURING THE GAME

In performing their functions, leagues have developed a common organizational structure, composed of individual teams operating collectively under direction of a commissioner. . . .

Leagues are associations of teams rather than independent entities; they exist to promote the common interests of their member teams, which are separately owned and operated firms. League rules are determined by member teams, and are only effective as long as individual teams abide by them. Teams collectively make league decisions on relocation, expansion, revenue sharing, and network broadcasting contracts. Extraordinary majorities usually are required on important questions like moving or adding teams. These special voting requirements increase the power of individual owners or small groups of teams with common interests, such as large-market teams desirous of protecting their territories from competition and their revenues from sharing arrangements.

Team interests often conflict with the collective welfare of a league. Revenue sharing reduces income for some clubs in the interest of lessening economic differences among all teams in a league. Few teams can resist the attractions of unshared revenues from luxury boxes, better stadium and concessions deals, and broadcasting income outside league control, even though these revenues tend to increase disparities within a league. Conflict has been intensified by the rapidly increasing economic stakes of professional team sports. Newer owners who pay hefty prices for their teams and carry substantial debts are particularly interested in maximizing team revenues, which intensifies conflicts within leagues over revenue sharing, broadcasting deals, labor contracts, and expansion fees.

Differences among league members are amplified by the people who own major league franchises. Most are rich and powerful individuals who have been successful in other businesses and are used to having their way. Strong egos and personal animosities among owners exacerbate conflicts within leagues over relocation, expansion, and sharing revenues. Baseball owners, in the words of one, "never learned how" to be "both competitors and partners off the field."[2] Owners in the NFL have been more willing to subordinate individual for collective interests; they were the first to adopt an amateur playing draft, and developed the most extensive revenue-sharing arrangements in professional team sports. Still, sustaining collective concerns has been a constant struggle within the NFL . . . .

Leadership has been an important factor in the interplay of league and team interests. Formidable political and public relations skills enabled Pete Rozelle to expand league authority despite an increasingly diverse and contentious set of NFL owners. Another strong leader, David Stern, revitalized the NBA, turning a league plagued by drugs, weak franchises, and declining television appeal into a vibrant organization that pioneered the development of salary caps and league marketing, while expanding successfully and securing lucrative network television contracts. Under Stern, the NBA has emphasized league interests and league services to teams in marketing, promotions, and local broadcasting. National broadcasting revenues also have boosted the power of league officials. The dependence of NFL owners on the commissioner's ability to make good television deals greatly enhanced Rozelle's authority over all aspects of the game.

. . . . League officials are concerned about a set of places; they worry about market coverage and being in major markets. Increasingly, the focus of leagues is national and international, while teams are preoccupied with their metropolitan and regional market. David Stern promotes the NBA as an entity rather than a set of teams. . . . In Stern's approach, individual teams become units of the business like Disneyland or Disney World, and places where they play are the sites of particular business units in the same sense that Anaheim and Orlando are for the Disney empire. Of course, there are critical differences between the NBA and Disney; each of the NBA's . . . teams is individually owned and operated, most play in public arenas, and the owners collectively hire and fire the league commissioner as well as pass judgment on league decisions affecting ownership of teams, relocation of franchises, expansion of leagues, suitability of arenas, national broadcasting deals, and sharing of revenues.

COMPETITIVE LEAGUES

Professional teams have a collective interest in producing games that involve enough uncertainty to sustain the interest of their customers. Competitive leagues are good business; close pennant races and more teams in contention for postseason play increase attendance and broadcast audiences. A league's ability to produce competitive games, teams, and seasons determines how many places will have successful teams at least some of the time. . . .

A league's collective interest in competitiveness coexists uneasily with the desire of individual teams to be successful. Team success means doing better than other clubs by winning more games and championships. Winning teams attract more customers, command more local broadcast revenues, earn additional revenues from postseason play, and make more money for their owners. Both winning teams and competitive leagues are good for business, but teams that win most of the time reduce league competitiveness. This situation leads to arguments that teams have a rational interest in winning, but not so often as to dominate a league and undermine the viability of weaker teams. . . . Winning, however, can be a profitable business strategy even if a team dominates its league. Great teams and dynasties usually are good business for the triumphant team, if not the league. . . .

For most teams, the incentives to win also are more powerful than the rewards of increased competitiveness. Although closely contested games, pennant races, and championships are collectively desirable, individual teams understandably are wary of the risks inherent in highly competitive enterprises. . . . Noneconomic considerations reinforce the attractions of winning teams over competitive leagues. Most people who own teams are highly competitive; they are used to success, and success in professional sports is measured by won–lost records and championships rather than profits and losses. . . . Fans reinforce the drive for victory; fans care more about rooting for winners than whether the home team plays in a competitive league. And winning itself increases pressures to win again, heightening expectations of players for bigger contracts, of fans for another victorious season, and of owners for the thrill of another championship.

Among the four sports, the NFL has been most committed to increasing competitiveness. League control of television and sharing of most revenues were acceptable to NFL owners because these policies promised a more attractive product by increasing the ability of teams to compete regardless of market size. The NFL also uses scheduling to increase competitiveness, matching teams for games outside their division with opponents with similar records during the previous season. . . . However . . . only one team can win the World Series, Super Bowl, Stanley Cup, or NBA championship. Leagues, however, can create more winners by increasing opportunities to participate in postseason play. Leagues can be subdivided into conferences and divisions whose winners make the playoffs, and "wild card" teams can be added to increase the number that advance to postseason play.

. . . .

[Ed. Note: The author's discussion of owners is omitted. See Chapter 1 for a discussion of this topic.]

TERRITORIAL RIGHTS

Teams in a league have substantial shared interests in the location of franchises. As a result, league control of franchise locations has been a cardinal feature of professional team sports from the start. The National League limited franchises to cities with populations of 75,000, with each team granted exclusive territorial rights in its market area. The National League and American Association agreed in 1883 to preserve exclusive territories for teams in each league. Contemporary territorial rights generally include the city where a team plays and the surrounding area within fifty or seventy-five miles of the team's home turf. Each NFL team has "the exclusive right within its home territory to exhibit professional football games played by teams of the League," with two teams in the same territory, as in the New York area, having equal rights.[20] Territorial rights include broadcasts within a team's area, except for games covered by league contracts with national networks.

Territorial exclusivity enables teams to avoid competition for local fans, viewers, media, and broadcasting and advertising dollars. Exclusive territories focus fan loyalty and support for the home team. . . . Territorial controls are the basic instruments by which teams and leagues regulate their relations with places. Exclusive franchises are based on the notion that places belong to a league and its teams; territories are staked out and controlled by private league rules. Territorial controls are vigorously defended as indispensable to professional team sports. . . . Without these protections, professional sports are seen as facing economic ruin and places could lose their teams. . . .

Territorial rights have been relatively static during the rapid expansion of metropolitan areas and urban regions. Fifty or seventy-five miles, which once extended the control of most teams well beyond the urbanized portion of their home territory, now encompass a diminishing portion of the far-flung regions that supply teams with customers and viewers. . . .

Territorial rights have the most substantial impact on the location of professional teams in large metropolitan areas; with or without exclusive territories, smaller areas can sustain only one team in a sport.

. . . .

Because territorial exclusivity primarily protects franchises in the largest markets from competition, these rights reinforce the advantages of teams in the major urban centers. Limiting the number of teams in large metropolitan areas exacerbates market differences by forcing most owners to operate in smaller areas with less revenue potential. League controls also severely constrain the ability of small-market teams to move to larger markets that could sustain another franchise or support a more successful team. . . . The other side of this coin, of course, is that more places have teams because the number of franchises in the largest metropolitan areas is limited by leagues.

Territorial restrictions also reduce competition among teams to be in a particular place, thus increasing the leverage of teams on places. Most places have to deal with a single team in each sport. In the absence of competition from other teams for stadiums and arenas, holders of exclusive franchises are able to drive harder bargains with public agencies for leases, tax concessions, and other subsidies. Franchise controls, however, do not guarantee that a team will be able to capitalize on its market monopoly.

References

1. Ross Atkins, "With Super Bowl Settled, Comes Another Showdown," *Christian Science Monitor,* Jan. 26, 1981.

2. John Fetzer of the Detroit Tigers, quoted in Thomas Boswell, "Baseball: Riches or Ruin?" *Washington Post,* Dec. 21, 1980.

. . . .

20. National Football League, Constitution & Bylaws, Sec. 4.2 (1970).

. . . .

AN ALTERNATIVE MODEL

THE ECONOMICS OF PROMOTION AND RELEGATION IN SPORTS LEAGUES: THE CASE OF ENGLISH FOOTBALL

Roger G. Noll

Unlike in the United States, most of the world's major professional sports leagues are not composed of a permanent roster of teams. Instead, major leagues promote and demote teams at the end of the season. The primary criterion for promotion and relegation is on-field success: The best teams in the highest ranking minor league are promoted to the major league, and the worst teams in the latter are reassigned to the former.[1] In larger countries, several lower leagues are organized hierarchically and the same promotion and relegation system applies down the line. In English football (soccer), for example, the hierarchy involves seven levels of leagues, and the bottom two levels are further divided into hierarchical divisions.

The primary difference between a system of leagues with fixed membership and a promotion/relegation system is that the latter permits a form of entry that is not feasible under the former. In leagues of fixed membership, entry occurs through expansion of a league or the formation of a new, competitive league. In the United States, expansion has been the primary means of entry into major leagues, although at some time during the 20th century the four most popular team sports experienced successful entry in that at least some of teams in a new league merged into the established league.[2] Entry and exit of leagues are substantially more common for minor league sports.

To prospective entrants, expansion and league entry have disadvantages. Expansion requires super-majority approval from established teams and entails paying a substantial entrance fee. Entry by an entire league requires that the incumbent league has left several viable franchise locations unexploited and that several entrants—not just one—are willing to suffer significant financial losses in the early years while the new league becomes established.

Promotion and relegation do not rule out these forms of entry, but this system makes other forms of entry feasible. First, an entrepreneur can buy a minor league team, hire high-quality players and coaches, and earn promotion to a higher league. Second, an entrepreneur can form a new team, enter into the bottom league, and then gain promotion to higher levels. In both cases, after a few years of successful play a team can be promoted all the way to the major league, although in the case of de novo entry in England this strategy requires at least eight promotions and therefore takes at least a decade.

These forms of entry require no approval by, and no payment of expansion franchises to, existing major league teams.[3] The main disadvantages of this form of entry are that teams must start at the bottom rather than immediately enter at the league level that they seek and then must dominate lower leagues to gain promotion, which implies that they may have to field teams that are too good (and too expensive) for the leagues in which they play.

The purpose of this article is to explore how promotion and relegation affect the economics of a sports team and league. Two questions are theoretical: Under what conditions will leagues with promotion and relegation experience more entry? and How does promotion and relegation alter the business strategy of established teams and leagues? The other questions are empirical: Does promotion and relegation produce measurable effects on entry and operations? To answer the second set of questions, this article examines the history of English football.

. . . .

THEORETICAL ISSUES

Entry in team sports has two distinct components. One is entry of a team into a specific location, and the other is a net increase in the number of teams that play in a league. Although the second type of entry requires the first, the first does not require the second. That is, a team can enter a particular location by changing the place it plays its home matches (relocation), or a new team can enter one location while an old team in another location exits the industry. . . . Note that both relocation and promotion/relegation require entry and exit in different local markets. Alternatively, entry can cause a net increase in the number of teams (expansion, new leagues).

Promotion and relegation are a substitute for either relocation or expansion. In the first case, a higher league enters a new city (the home of the promoted team) while simultaneously exiting the home of the demoted team, whereas the lower league does the opposite. In the second case, a higher league promotes more teams than it demotes. If every league in the hierarchy follows this practice, the effect is net entry for the sport through the creation of new teams at the bottom of the hierarchy of leagues. Likewise, leagues can demote more teams than they promote as a means of contraction.

Team Strategies

The strategic decisions of a team are first whether to enter or exit the industry and then, conditional on entering (or not exiting), the level in the hierarchy of leagues to seek. The tactical decisions include picking the optimal team quality—that is, acquiring players and coaches of appropriate skill—to achieve the target league. Although the sequence of decisions is first to make the entry/exit decision, then the decision about league level, and finally a sequence of annual team quality decisions, logically each earlier decision is based on expectations about the financial consequences of later decisions, so it makes sense to discuss decisions about league attainment and team quality before examining the entry decision.

Team Quality

The effects of promotion and relegation on team quality depend on how movement between leagues affects team profits. In principle, promotion and relegation can affect profits in two ways: A team's revenues and costs may differ in different leagues, and the presence of relegation and promotion may affect the interest of fans (and hence revenues).

Conceivably, good and bad teams could benefit from the promotion and relegation system. For the best teams, the reason is clear: Promotion is an additional reward for winning, and so conceivably can increase fan interest in games, assuming that fans prefer that their home team compete at a higher level. For the worst teams, the prospect of relegation also conceivably could increase interest because more is at stake in late-season games and because fans expect that in the next season the average quality of opponents may be lower. Whether these effects are present, of course, is an empirical matter, but if they are then sports that make use of promotion and relegation will earn higher revenues.

The other effect of promotion and relegation on team profits has to do with whether a team actually is better or worse off financially by being promoted to a higher league. To understand why promotion may not be profitable requires delving into the standard economic theory of a sports league. A sports team operates in two types of markets: a local market for selling tickets and concessions and a national or even international market for selling broadcast and licensing rights. In both cases, the demand for a team's products depends on its absolute quality, the quality of its opponents, and the team's tradition (or playing history). In addition, especially for local products, demand depends on exogenous demographic attributes of the city in which the team plays home games. In general, teams in more populous, wealthier markets will generate more revenue, holding constant the quality of the team and its opponents and the number and quality of its local competitors. All else being equal, a team in a better market will have a higher marginal revenue product of increments to team quality, so that teams that play in the best locations generally have a higher optimal quality than teams in worse locations.

Ignoring the possibility that the existence of the promotion and relegation system increases demand and taking as exogenous the number of teams in each league, the optimal distribution of teams among a hierarchy of leagues is for the best league to contain the teams that face the most intensive demand for the sport and for each league in the hierarchy to contain the teams with the best markets among those remaining after higher leagues have been filled. A promotion and relegation system forces a departure from the optimal allocation of teams at least half the time (and most likely virtually all of the time), given the unavoidable uncertainty associated with won–lost records during a league season as well as the requirement to relegate some teams even if the composition of the league is optimal. Thus, promotion/relegation inevitably has costs in terms of sportwide profitability.

Promotion and relegation reduce total revenues in a sport in the following way. When a team in a better market is demoted while a team in a worse market is promoted, all teams except the promoted team are likely to suffer financially. The demoted team will have an optimal relative quality in the lower league that is stronger than the team that was promoted, and so its demotion will reduce the expected won–loss record and hence the revenues of every team in the lower league. Likewise, the promoted team will have a lower optimal relative quality in the higher league than the team that was demoted. Hence, every other team in the higher league must play one home game with a team that has lower average quality than the team it replaced, causing each to have lower revenues. In both leagues, therefore, promotion/relegation reduces outcome uncertainty (competitive balance) and thereby reduces the demand for the other teams.

Although promotion/relegation inevitably creates a cost, this cost could be small. That is, if the differences in local market demand are small among a large number of teams, the revenue loss from distributing teams

suboptimally is likely to be small and may be offset by the demand-enhancing effects of promotion and relegation as described above. Indeed, the most plausible explanation for the widespread adoption of promotion/relegation systems, given that they are certain to cause a suboptimal distribution of teams among leagues, is that the demand enhancing effect is present and that differences in market conditions are small among lower echelon teams in a stronger league and higher echelon teams in a weaker league.

Although theory does not yield a robust qualitative prediction about the effect of promotion on a team's profits, a team in a lower league may have an incentive to seek promotion to a higher league than the one to which it would be assigned if the sport maximized joint profits. Whether such an incentive exists depends on two factors. One factor is the possibility that a promotion and relegation system causes an increase in the demand for games involving teams that are candidates to change leagues, as discussed above. The other factor is the effect of promotion on team specific revenues and costs.

In general, promotion into a league that is too strong for the market in which the team is located will have two economic effects. On the plus side, because the team's opponents are better and the higher league receives more attention from the press (basically, free advertising), the demand for the team's products should increase. On the negative side, the optimal quality of the team will be higher in absolute terms but lower in relation to other teams in its league. Promotion increases the marginal revenue product of quality and so causes the team to spend more on players if it joins a higher league. But a team from a market that, under an optimal assignment of teams to leagues, would be assigned to the lower league will have a higher optimal relative quality in the lower league than its optimal relative quality in the better league. Thus, a team that should be in a lower league from the perspective of sportwide profit maximization expects to finish higher in the standings in the lower league but spend more money for players in the better league.

Whether promotion is profitable to a team, then, depends on the net effect of all of these factors. Specifically, are the benefits of promotion (more revenues from playing better opponents, more exposure, and the possible demand-enhancing effects of the prospect of promotion in the year in which promotion is earned and of demotion later when the team returns to its optimal league) greater or less than the costs (higher salaries and a lower finish in the better league)? As a practical matter, this question is empirical, not theoretical, but the answer almost certainly is in the affirmative, for teams never refuse to be promoted.

. . . .

[T]he equilibrium spread in team quality in the top league is lower than it would be in a league of the same teams with fixed membership. In other words, the effect of promotion and relegation is to increase competitive balance in the top league among the teams that are members; however, because the teams in the top league may not be the optimal allocation of teams to that league, this effect could be offset by the presence of teams in weak markets that have low optimal relative quality in the top league.

The extent to which promotion/relegation improves the overall quality of play depends on the supply of inputs for all teams in the market. The assumption that the supply of inputs is not perfectly inelastic is unexceptional for all inputs except players. For players, supply elasticity has two elements. One component is related to whether children decide to devote themselves to developing their athletic skills and then, as teens, to launch a career in sports. Presumably this elasticity is tiny, especially in the short run. The other element is the nationwide supply of existing players to professional teams. Because soccer is the primary sport in much of the world (most of Europe, Latin America, and Africa), even for a soccer power like England the supply of professional soccer talent is likely to be reasonably elastic, although not perfectly so if players prefer to play in their home country. Hence, the preceding simple model yields two important conclusions:

1. Holding the demand for soccer constant across countries and team locations within those countries, a nation with promotion/relegation will have stronger teams than a nation with leagues of fixed size. For example, the primary soccer league in the United States, Major League Soccer (MLS), always will be weaker than the top European leagues even if soccer becomes as popular in the United States as it is in Europe because MLS does not practice promotion and relegation.

2. The adoption of a promotion/relegation system will increase the wages of players as long as the world supply of professional soccer players is not perfectly elastic. This effect is not due solely to the possibility that promotion/relegation may increase demand but is a consequence of the fact that expenditures on players today are an investment in that they are a cost of gaining entry into a better league (or of avoiding demotion to a lower league), which causes this year's players to have greater value than they would without promotion and relegation.

Entry and Exit

The preceding model has implications with respect to the simultaneous entry of one city and exit of another in a league. Recall that promotion/relegation generates more of this form of entry and exit than does voluntary relocation in a league of fixed size. A team moves from one location to another while staying in the same league because it believes that the new location is sufficiently more profitable that it will offset the costs of relocating. Because the cost of quality is the same in all locations, the source of profit differentials is

differences in the intensity of demand. Hence, team relocation in closed leagues tends to be from weaker to stronger markets. By contrast, in a promotion/relegation system, a new city is added to a higher league because the team in that city does well on the field and perceives its profits to be enhanced by joining a better league, whereas the new city in the lower league is added coercively—the entrant has been forced to exit a more profitable league because of its poor on-field performance. In at least some cases, the demoted team would not want to relocate to the city of the team that replaced it through promotion/relegation.

Another form of entry into a league, whether from de novo creation of a new team or a permanent change in the league assignment of an existing team, arises when the entering team operates in a more lucrative local market than the worst existing team. Exogenous changes in the geographic distribution of people and wealth affect team revenue functions and so alter the set of optimal locations for teams in a league. In a world of perfect information, incumbent teams in a league would be able to identify these locations, and teams could relocate as soon as demographic shifts changed the list of optimal team locations. But if local market responsiveness in areas without a team is uncertain, local entrepreneurs plausibly can detect a favorable shift in local demand before teams that are located elsewhere. Under these conditions, an old team is likely to start to improve or a new team is likely to be formed in a growing local market before another existing team detects that the area is more profitable than its current location.

The preceding argument provides an unobvious economic explanation for a phenomenon that, among sports aficionados, is regarded as a cultural difference between North America and the rest of the world: In other nations, major league teams virtually never relocate. The absence of team movements is attributed to the deep roots that a team has in its local community and, as a result, the unacceptability of relocation to its fans—even in the United States, fans have deeply resented some relocations (e.g., the Brooklyn Dodgers and Cleveland Browns). In any case, this observation, if true, can be interpreted as an assertion that in most of the world relocation costs are higher relative to the costs of forming a new team than they are in the United States. De novo entry can be cheaper under promotion/relegation for two reasons: Expansion fees are avoided and information costs associated with assessing new markets may be lower for residents of an emerging market. Hence, the absence of team relocation is a plausible consequence of a system of promotion and relegation.

League Strategies

The principal strategic decision of a league is to determine its size. The decision to expand is a response to growing demand, which makes an increasing number of locations viable franchise sites. But expansion is not usually in the interests of the most successful teams. Expansion entails increasing the number of teams in smaller markets that have no serious chance of winning a championship. Hence, on average, expansion reduces the average revenue of teams because it reduces the average market potential of teams and hence the average quality and consequentiality of matches. Moreover, expansion requires adding competitors in national markets like broadcasting and licensing or, if national rights are pooled by the league, sharing the revenues from these rights among more partners. Thus, if expansion teams have, on average, weaker demand than incumbents, expansion reduces the national revenue of incumbents.

For the most part, leagues expand not because doing so is in the best interests of incumbents but because they are forced to do so. One purpose of expansion is to inhibit entry by competitive leagues. Another purpose is to satisfy demands from political officials in return for their support for favorable policies regarding sports, such as favorable tax treatments, antitrust exemptions, and stadium subsidies.[8]

New leagues are formed to take advantage of two sources of excess demand for professional sports. First, monopoly leagues usually do not place multiple teams in areas in which demand is sufficient to support more than one or two teams and, by setting monopoly prices, undersupply demand for products in national markets, such as television broadcasts. Second, monopoly leagues typically do not place teams in all financially viable franchise locations.

In leagues of fixed size, both types of excess demand arise for three reasons. First, teams either have exclusive territorial rights or, collectively, teams in areas that could support entrants can veto territory-invading expansion or relocation if either requires a supermajority vote of incumbent teams. Second, incumbent leagues set a monopoly price for an expansion team that exceeds that which is justified by the revenue potential of some otherwise viable locations. Third, relocation costs and imperfect information prevent efficient team relocation and league identification of all financially attractive expansion sites. In deciding on expansion, then, leagues seek to balance the benefits to incumbents of expansion and a lower probability of successful entry by competitive leagues against the cost of adding to the number of teams in weak markets or increasing competition in strong markets. Inevitably, this calculation leads a monopoly league to be smaller than the number of teams that would exist under competition or the absence of league-created entry barriers.

The promotion/relegation system reduces pressures to expand by providing a mechanism whereby teams in markets that have become stronger due to demographic shifts can enter an established league. Promotion/relegation has two benefits to incumbents: The system creates a barrier to entry by new leagues into unoccupied attractive markets (a team in a lower league is already there and likely to seek promotion itself if the market warrants it) and it provides a mechanism for limiting the total number of teams in the league that play in weak markets. Whereas this system denies incumbents the opportunity to charge expansion fees, it

compensates them by not forcing them to play more games against weak teams and to share national markets with more teams. But regardless of whether promotion/relegation is more or less profitable for the best teams than expansion, the one unambiguous prediction is that leagues using this system ought to be less inclined to expand.

The last effect of a decision to adopt promotion/relegation pertains to its effects on player costs. Abstracting from the demand-enhancing effects of the system, leagues have a good reason to adopt fixed membership—doing so reduces equilibrium quality and, if player supply is not perfectly elastic, player wages. Yet all major European soccer powers use promotion/relegation, which seems to be at odds with the assumption that leagues maximize profits.

Two explanations for this phenomenon are consistent with the standard economic model of a for-profit sports league.

First, until very recently, the world market for soccer players was monopsonized. Players were signed to their first contracts while still in their midteens, sometimes by an amateur or semiprofessional team that was owned and operated by the professional team in their home neighborhood. Subsequently, if a player switched teams after a contract expired, the new team was forced to pay compensation— a transfer fee—to the old team. For strong professional players, transfer fees typically ran in the millions of dollars, which was an order of magnitude more than the players' salaries. These fees applied to international transfers as well as movements within the same country and were enforced by the international governing body of soccer, the Federation Internationale de Football Associations (FIFA). Thus, secure monopsonization of the player market ensured that at least some of the demand-enhancing effect of promotion/relegation would be passed on to teams.

This explanation for promotion/relegation may have disappeared. In December 1995, the European Court held that the transfer fee system violated the single-market principle by inhibiting free movement of labor (see Jeanrenaud & Késenne, 1999). As a result, European players can move freely within Europe after their contracts expire. . . .

A second explanation for the dominance of promotion/relegation arises from the fact that an extremely lucrative part of professional soccer is international matches, especially between the best teams in the top leagues. In Europe, the top teams in national Division 1 leagues qualify for the Champions League in the following season, which involves playing several very lucrative matches. Leagues want their best teams to be competitive in the Champions League to make participation in these matches more profitable. Hence, it makes sense to adopt a system that, all else equal, produces stronger teams. Thus, adoption of promotion/relegation is much like an arms race: Conceivably, all teams and top leagues would be better off without it, but once one nation adopts the system, the others have a financial incentive to follow.

THE ENGLISH NATIONWIDE FOOTBALL LEAGUE

England is widely regarded as having one of the most successful sports leagues in the world—the English Premier League. . . .[T]he English Premier League is roughly comparable to Major League Baseball (MLB), the National Basketball Association (NBA), and probably behind only the National Football League (NFL) in profits per team and average franchise value, while its best teams are comparable to the best in any league, including the NFL.

The basic institutional structure of English football has been stable for several decades. As in all countries, the overall governing body for English soccer is FIFA, located in Switzerland. FIFA determines the eligibility of teams and players for international competitions, such as the World Cup, and insists that internationally sanctioned teams must play only other sanctioned teams or else they and their players lose eligibility for international competition. Because international competition is very important to players and teams, this sanctioning power enables FIFA to regulate the business activities of soccer.

Below FIFA is the Union of European Football Associations (UEFA), which sets rules for European Football that are not dictated by FIFA, organizes international competitions within Europe, and supervises national football organizations. The Football Association (FA) represents all of the British Isles in UEFA, including Ireland as well as England, Northern Ireland, Scotland, and Wales. Each of these political jurisdictions has its own top (Division 1) league, its own hierarchy of minor leagues, and its own national team for competing in the World Cup, the Olympics, and other international championships. The FA sanctions and governs all professional and amateur football leagues and teams in the British Isles.

The Premier League stands at the top of the hierarchy of English leagues. Below it three other leagues collectively are called the Nationwide Football League and individually were called Divisions 2, 3, and 4 until 1992 but since have been called Divisions 1, 2, and 3. Historically, all four leagues collectively were called the Nationwide Football League until 1983, when the leagues began to sell their names to corporate sponsors. The leagues were known as the Canon League Divisions 1 through 4 from 1983–1986, the Today League in 1986–1987, and the Barclays League from 1987–1992, when the Premier League decided to withdraw from the Nationwide Football League. In the 1992–1993 season, the lower leagues became Divisions 1, 2, and 3 and retained the name Barclays League, whereas the top league became the English Football Association Premier League.

. . . .

Entry

The purpose of this section is to examine entry and exit in the top four English leagues to see if this history supports the theoretical arguments about the effect of promotion and relegation on entry into a major league and to determine the extent to which promotion and relegation cause instability in league membership through entry and exit. To summarize, the core predictions of the theory of a sports league are that the system of promotion and relegation reduces the rate of expansion and the entry of new major leagues but provides opportunities for new teams to enter or for teams in more rapidly growing markets to improve their quality and earn promotion while teams in declining markets gradually descend the hierarchy of leagues.

Unfortunately, the effect of promotion and relegation on the entry of new leagues is not observable because of the institutional rules of football. In England, as elsewhere, entry of top-ranking leagues is essentially impossible in the present environment. One of FIFA's rules is that if a national team or any professional and amateur team wants to compete internationally, whether in major championships or just friendly (exhibition) matches, it must have a national governing body that enforces FIFA rules, grants franchises to leagues and teams, and certifies the eligibility of players. Another FIFA policy is that each country should have only one major league, usually called Division 1, although in England it has been called the Premier League since 1992. In the United States, MLS is the designated Division 1 league. Thus, entry of competing major leagues is precluded because FIFA and the English soccer authority are unlikely to sanction one. Nevertheless, FIFA and its subsidiary bodies (including the FA and the U.S. Soccer Federation) do allow entry of competing minor leagues. In England, monopoly leagues occupy the first five levels of the hierarchy, but the lower levels have competitive leagues.

An important aspect of the history of English football is that neither leagues nor the FA recognizes territorial rights. Teams can form anywhere, can move their home venues, and can be promoted into a league with a nearby local competitor. The only limitations are league rules regarding the suitability of a playing site in terms of the size and quality of the field and stadium. Because territorial rights are not enforced, large cities have many teams. . . . The absence of territorial rights reduces the "big market, small market" demand disparity; however, this check is limited because the most successful teams enjoy some immunity to competition due to the fan attachments that they have accumulated during their histories.

. . . .

In essence, the size of top professional football in England has remained roughly the same for more than three fourths of a century. . . . no net entry has occurred, either from new leagues at this level of quality or expansion of existing leagues. The economic growth of the past 50 years, the arrival of television with its new major source of revenues, the creation of lucrative international competitions for professional teams, and the boom in sports since the mid-1970s have substantially increased the demand for English football and the revenues of the teams. But this growth in demand has not led to growth in the number of teams in the top four professional leagues. By contrast, the number of teams in the four major professional sports in the United States has more than doubled in this period. Nine new leagues have entered, six of which have survived by being merged into the established league, and all four leagues have added expansion teams every few years since the 1960s. Thus, for more than half a century, the behavior of the top four leagues in England and the four American major leagues is consistent with the theoretical prediction that a system of promotion and relegation reduces the propensity of new leagues to enter and old leagues to expand.

. . . .

The main benefit of promotion and relegation is that it enables entry of teams into high-quality leagues; however, extensive entry is not guaranteed. Instead, the same small core group of teams could simply rotate membership in the leagues, with neither entry nor exit among this group.

. . . .

[Ed. Note: Author's review of the history of promotion and relegation practices in England is omitted.]

The history of the Premier League reveals two core facts. First, a few teams have rarely spent any significant time out of the Premier League and account for most of its championships. Second, there is considerable turnover in Premier League membership among teams that are not frequent challengers for the Premier League championship. Premier League championships have been relatively concentrated.

. . . .

[T]he teams that played in the Premier League fall into three basic categories: a core of more or less permanent members, a group that is referred to as yo-yo teams because they move up and down with regularity, and a group of teams that only occasionally make the Premier League (and then for only 1 or 2 years).

. . . .

[T]urnover within the three divisions is extensive. Except for Premier League members, teams cannot conveniently be divided into a large majority that have a stable league assignment and a minority that are on the margins between two leagues and so alternate back and forth. The dramatic rise and fall of about one fourth of the teams in a decade, and the slower but real turnover that takes place among the teams that do not stay in the Premier League for long runs, show that during the course of a decade the promotion and relegation system has a substantial effect on the composition of all of the leagues. A surprisingly large fraction of teams in the lower leagues occasionally have runs

that last several years in which they ascend to Division 1, and maybe even the Premier League for a few years, before falling back to Divisions 2 and 3. The next section examines recent history to determine the financial consequences of these runs.

. . . .

Recall that the economic theory of a sports league points to an inefficiency of turnover: An assignment of teams among the leagues may not be a good match with relative local market demands. . . many of the teams that were promoted in these years were not among their league's leaders in revenues. Had promotion been based on revenues rather than on-field performance, fewer than half of these teams would have been promoted.

. . . [E]ach league shows very large revenue disparities among teams in the league. In the Premier League, Manchester United has far more revenues than any other team. . . . In all leagues, revenue disparities are larger than for major leagues in the United States. . . .

The substantial overlap in team revenues among the leagues reflects two factors. First, in every year a fairly large number of teams play in lower leagues than their market demand justifies. Second, the revenue data are consistent with the hypothesis that the promotion/relegation system has a positive benefit for at least some teams in that revenues are enhanced by the prospect of promotion. A more formal econometric model is necessary to disentangle these effects completely but quite a bit can be discerned from the raw data.

The financial data provide clear evidence that league assignment affects revenues and so creates a powerful incentive to seek promotion. . . . In every case both revenues and attendance increase when a team is promoted, with the average increase nearly £5 million. Attendance at home league matches is probably a better indicator of the revenue effect of league status than is revenues, for the latter reflects many other revenue sources, such as participation in tournaments and international matches and the "parachute" policy of giving some of the television revenues of the Premier League to teams that have been demoted in the previous 2 seasons. Hence, revenues can vary from year to year for extraneous reasons. On average, a promotion to the Premier League was accompanied by an increase in home attendance of about 6,000 per game. Of course, revenues and attendance in both leagues were growing during this period but not by nearly this amount.

Interestingly, demotion is not always accompanied by a drop in revenues and attendance. . . . In all cases but one, demotion was accompanied by a drop in attendance, typically by a few thousand per game. Thus, demotion usually causes teams to be worse off financially; however, the drop in revenues and attendance is less than the gains from promotion, so that teams end up better off in the demotion year than they would have been had they not played in the Premier

League in the previous season. These facts confirm that promotion has a hysteresis effect: The benefits of promotion persist after a team is demoted and average more than £4 million in the first year after relegation.

The meaning of the data on transfer fees and wages is not as clear as it is for revenues and attendance. Wages include all employees, not just players, and in particular the salaries of management. Hence, movements in wage data do not necessarily reveal the trend in total player salaries. Transfer fees reveal the attempt of teams to . . . improve their team (a positive number) or to sell quality players (a negative number); however, these numbers also are affected by extraneous events, such as injuries, retirements, and unevenness through the years in the number of players who seek employment with another team after their contracts expire. In some cases, teams seriously seek to improve themselves to stay in or return to the Premier League, as reflected in large expenditures on player transfers and higher wage bills.

Notwithstanding the caveats, the data indicate that teams do not all pursue the same strategies in response to promotion and relegation. In some cases, teams take advantage of their promotion to sell the players that made promotion possible and consequently stay briefly in the Premier League. In other cases, teams on the cusp between Division 1 and the Premier League put forth great effort to gain and keep promotion. . . .

. . . .

The propensity of some teams to weaken themselves after promotion is to be expected from the fact that some promoted teams are not among the revenue leaders of the league from which they were promoted. The yo-yo teams plausibly operate in markets that cannot sustain competitive teams in the Premier League, so when they are promoted they do not make a serious attempt to stay. In this case, the motivation for promotion is not to obtain a permanent place in the higher league but to take advantage of the hysteresis effect in attendance. For teams in lower leagues that have higher revenues than some teams in higher leagues, the incentives are likely to be different. Their best assignment is likely to be in the higher league, and so they are more likely to make the expenditures that are necessary to increase their chance of staying in the higher league. . . .

IMPLICATIONS

The financial and playing field experiences of the four leading British football leagues are generally consistent with the predictions of the theoretical model that can be tested using the financial data that are available. Promotion/relegation clearly has led to turnover in league membership among the four leading leagues; however, promotion and relegation between Division 3 and the National Conference has led to very little successful entry into the top echelon of teams. Apparently the combined size of the four leading leagues is sufficiently large that almost all viable franchise locations—especially for the top two leagues—were occupied early in the 20th century. Nevertheless, turnover between the Premier League and lower leagues is substantial in the time frame of a decade. Teams that play in rapidly growing markets or that switch from poor to strong management can rapidly ascend from Division 3 to the top leagues.

The financial information indicates that promotion is financially attractive as well as desired by fans. Both revenues and attendance at league matches tend to increase substantially when teams are promoted. Moreover, the reward from promotion seems to endure for a while after a team is demoted, giving teams that are marginal for a higher league a financial incentive to field teams that bounce back and forth between a higher and lower league.

Of course, this article is only a beginning. The next step is to estimate econometric models of team performance, revenues, attendance, wages, transfer fees, and other financial variables to provide more precise estimates of the effects described above and to determine whether the noisy indicators of player costs can sustain tests of the effects of promotion and relegation on team strategies regarding players.

Applications to North America

Drawing conclusions about United States and Canadian sports from the experience of English football is hazardous and, as a practical matter, probably irrelevant because North American leagues are not likely to experiment with so dramatic a change in format as the introduction of promotion and relegation. Nevertheless, the English football system seems to be a very attractive solution to the perpetual problem of leagues with substantial disparities in on-field success and revenue among their teams.

Promotion and relegation have three significant advantages and one significant disadvantage. On the plus side, this system allows the top league to be smaller, have higher average revenues, and be more balanced competitively, although the latter effect is muted by the yo-yo teams that seek only occasional, brief promotion to profit from the hysteresis effect on revenues. On the negative side, teams that are relegated do worse financially than they would if they finished in the bottom group of teams in the higher league. This disadvantage may be offset by the advantages but the issue cannot be resolved without running an experiment.

A promotion/relegation system can be implemented in two ways: by constructing a lower league from the existing minor league system or by dividing the existing major league. Sports with independent minor league teams are the most likely candidates for the first method.

Changing relations with minor leagues is not likely to be viewed favorably in baseball. The vast majority of minor league baseball teams, and all in the top two classifications, operate as farm teams for major league franchises. This structure enables major league teams to monopsonize the market for players who have any serious chance of becoming major leaguers through the amateur draft. Farm teams are expensive . . . but this cost is more than offset by the salary suppression that arises from the fact that players must have 3 years of major league experience before they qualify for salary arbitration and 6 years before they become unrestricted free agents. In addition, baseball has some attractive open markets that are valuable as potential expansion sites . . . which would be lost if minor league teams in those areas could qualify for promotion to the majors. Thus, baseball does not appear to be a good candidate for rearranging its minor league structure to accommodate promotion and relegation.

. . . .

The second approach to implementing a promotion/relegation system is to divide the existing major leagues to create a significantly smaller top league. The basic idea would be to shrink the top "major-major" league to something between 16 and 20 teams. Perhaps in tandem with expansion or promotion of some minor league teams, the remaining major league teams would be placed in a "minor-major" league with a comparable number of teams. All teams in both leagues would be treated as a "major league" in that all would participate in league governance, would have the same relationship with minor leagues, and would participate in the market for major league players. As the Premier League did when it shrunk to 20 teams and Division 2 did when it reorganized from two coequal leagues to the present Divisions 2 and 3, leagues would implement this system by demoting the major league teams with the weakest records in the season before the plan was implemented. To make the system more palatable to owners, players, and fans of demoted teams, the system could promote the 4 best teams in the lower league at the end of each season.

. . . .

Notes

1. Secondary criteria are a team's stadium quality, revenue potential, and adherence to league rules. In some cases relegated teams are not those with the worst records, and teams are denied promotion because of operational shortcomings.

2. New U.S. leagues that managed to have at least one team enter an established major league were the American League and the Federal League in baseball, the Basketball Association of America, the first American Basketball League (1947–1949) and the American Basketball Association in basketball, the All-American Football Conference and the American Football League in football, and the World Hockey Association in hockey. Only one entrant, the Basketball Association of America (BAA), has managed to supplant the incumbent as the dominant league. In the late 1940s, the BAA merged with the incumbent National Basketball League and the first American Basketball League to form the National Basketball Association. Most of the teams in the merged entity were from the BAA. See Noll (1991) for a history of this era.

3. Entry into the lowest league requires approval, but low leagues do not charge high entry fees.

. . . .

8. For example, to obtain an antitrust exemption for their merger, the National Football League and American Football League granted an expansion franchise to New Orleans, the home of Senator Russell Long, who sponsored the legislation.

. . . .

References

Jeanrenaud, C., & Késanne, S. (Eds.). (1999). *Competition policy in professional sports: Europe after the Bosman case*. Brussells, Germany: Standard Editions.

Noll, R. G. (1991). Professional basketball: Economic and business perspectives. In P. D. Staudohar & J. A. Mangan (Eds.), *The business of professional sports* (pp. 18–47). Urbana: University of Illinois Press.

Ross, S. A., & Szymanski, S. (2000). *Open competition in sports leagues*. Retrieved from http:// papers.ssrn.com/paper.taf?abstract_id=243756.

Discussion Questions

1. Advise a potential team owner of both the benefits and concerns of league membership that he or she will face as an owner of a professional sports team.

2. If you were the commissioner of a new professional sports league, what considerations would you have to keep in mind to ensure both a competitive and a profitable league?

3. In which sport is there the greatest likelihood that a rival league will emerge to challenge the established league? Explain.

4. How is the sports industry affected by negative changes in the macroeconomic climate?

5. How can a team owner respond effectively to an economic downturn?

6. What are some examples of how leagues use their monopolistic power?

7. Why do leagues expand into new territories?

8. Explain how consumers are both benefited and harmed by restrictions on the number of sports leagues and league teams.

9. Does the open league structure (with promotion and relegation) improve or harm competitive balance between teams? Does it create a different kind of balance altogether?

10. What incentives exist for individual franchises to win?

11. Why aren't there more barnstorming teams like the Harlem Globetrotters?

12. How does a team operating within a league structure resemble that of another entertainment company, such as Disney? What are the advantages of a team operating within a league structure resembling another

entertainment company, such as Disney? What are the disadvantages?

13. Are dynasties good or bad for sports leagues?

14. Explain the dichotomy that exists between winning and not completely dominating a league.

15. What are the effects of winning versus not dominating a league on franchises? On owners? Players? Leagues?

16. What are the advantages and disadvantages of the system of promotion and relegation?

17. Is a transition to a system of promotion and relegation feasible in the established North American leagues? Is it feasible in a newly created league? Why or why not?

18. How would the adoption of the system of promotion and relegation in Major League Baseball affect the existing minor leagues? How would it affect NCAA Division I basketball and football?

19. What are the advantages and disadvantages of the single-entity league structure? At what point (if any) should a league consider moving away from this structure? What might be some guideposts that would signal doing so?

20. What would be your preferred league structure for a startup league? What is your preferred structure for a mature league? Explain.

21. What remedies can you offer to protect the competitive balance of leagues amid the rise of "superleagues," such as the UEFA Champions League?

22. Of all the ways the sports industry will be affected by the economic downturn, as described by Rosner and Shropshire, which do you think will have the greatest impact? Why?

23. Many of the authors in this chapter described leagues as cartels that employ monopolistic behavior we would never condone in other kinds of businesses. Do you believe that monopolies are necessary for sports industries to survive/thrive, or is this an example of a segment of society that has carved for itself the ultimate sweetheart deal?

24. Should sports leagues be run as a business coordinating competition between, but existing independently of, the clubs within the league (i.e., the NASCAR model)?

Global Leagues

INTRODUCTION

This chapter takes a brief look at sports leagues based outside of the United States as well as further introducing the reader to concepts of interaction related to leagues based in different countries. Many of the issues related to ownership and leagues discussed in Chapters 1, 2 and 5 are relevant here. In fact, apart from variations in scale, the broad concepts relating to the importance of issues such as centralized governance, revenue sharing, integrity, and agents are very similar. It is the unique product and delivery distinctions that must be examined in order to understand the best business practices for leagues around the globe.

The first article, "Local Heroes," provides an overview of sports labor markets around the globe. It takes an introductory look at how the various sports leagues are becoming more assertive in finding labor for their teams, no matter the country of origin of the athlete. In the United States, this is seen most clearly with the increased number of foreign-born players playing in MLB, the NHL and the NBA. There is certainly an increasing number, although still quite modest, in the NFL as well. Globally, in soccer the use of foreign players has long been present, with South American powerhouses Brazil and Argentina being a major provider for European-based clubs. Over the past decade or so, the African continent has been a provider of global soccer talent as well.

The next two articles look at the sport of cricket. "Cricket in India: Moving into a League of Its Own," examines the origins of the Indian Premier League and the commercialization of the game in that country, which in some ways has mimicked the commercialization of sports taking place around the globe. The inaugural season was played in India to largely positive reviews as an entertaining version of the sport. The article examines the thinking and buildup behind that first season. A business decision was made to play the 2009 season in

South Africa due to security concerns after the terrorist attack in Mumbai. That season, too, received positive reviews, and the entity has returned to India. This is an interesting example of a sports enterprise seeking success on multiple continents, albeit not necessarily by choice.

That second article on cricket, "Twenty20 Cricket: An Examination of the Critical Success Factors in the Development of Competition," examines an even more dramatic development related to this classic sport. Twenty20 cricket is essentially a shorter, faster, and potentially more commercially viable version of the game. The article provides valuable insights in contemplating revisions to sports to seek a broader audience. It takes a close look at various marketing studies on the changes made to cricket and the success achieved.

The next excerpt is from Arsenal Football Club's 2008 Annual Report. It provides a "micro" look at the global side of sports by looking at the finances of one of the top clubs in what is widely recognized as the best soccer league in the world, the English Premier League (EPL). According to Deloitte's "Annual Review of Football Finance," covering the 2007–2008 season, the EPL's 20 clubs generated revenues of EUR 2.4 billion in 2007–2008, while its closest European competitors—Spain's La Liga and the Germany's Bundesliga—generated EUR 1.4 billion each, followed by Italy's Serie A, with just under EUR 1.4 billion, and France's Ligue 1, with EUR 1.1 billion. EPL revenues can be segregated into three categories: broadcasting of EPL and Champions League matches (accounting for 48% of the total revenues); match-day revenues, such as gate receipts and concessions (29%); and commercial revenues, including advertising and sponsorships (23%). Like their U.S. counterparts, the European leagues' biggest expense is player salaries, accounting for 62% of EPL revenues in 2007–2008. The highlights of Arsenal's Annual Report presented here provide the reader with a good overview of the finances of most of the leading global soccer clubs and delivers a good introduction to, and comparison of, a European team's revenues with North American–based franchises. The 2009 Annual Report was published too late to be included in this book, but it does provide additional insight into the impact of the global recession on a high profile club. For a broader "macro" picture of soccer finances, the reader might examine additional highlights from Deloitte's "Annual Review of Football Finance," which is available at http://www.deloitte.com/assets/Dcom-UnitedKingdom/Local%20Assets/Documents/Industries/UK_SBG_ARFF2009_Highlights.pdf.

The final article in this chapter, "The Impact of the Flat World on Player Transfers in Major League Baseball," looks more deeply at the global labor market, with a focus on the interactions of the player markets in the United States and Japan. It also looks at player transfer rules in other sports, as well as how the rules used in baseball might be improved. In reading this article, it is important to reflect on the rules of interaction that leagues around the globe must develop as the labor market flattens out for the players and they more readily view globally competing leagues as options.

OVERVIEW

LOCAL HEROES

Sporting Labour Markets Are Becoming Global. But What About Sports Themselves?

The Economist

The weather is perfect, with just enough breeze to freshen a warm June [2008] evening. Shea Stadium is bubbling this Friday night, with fans and food vendors, music and pre-game presentations. On the big screen the New York Mets introduce themselves: Jose Reyes, shortstop, from the Dominican Republic. . . Carlos Beltran, centre fielder, Puerto Rico. . . Endy Chavez, right fielder, Venezuela. . . Oliver Perez, pitcher, Mexico. Mets fans have had a frustrating season, with rather fewer wins than losses. By Tuesday, the team's manager will have been fired. But tonight they leave Shea unusually content. The Mets beat the Texas Rangers 7-1. Mr. Perez pitches solidly and bats in two runs. Mr. Beltran and Mr. Chavez both score one and bat one in. The speedy Mr. Reyes scores two and steals his 24th base of the year.

What is not unusual is the Mets' cosmopolitan make-up: six of the nine starters were born outside the United States. The Mets are a prime example of the globalisation that has swept through sport's labour markets in recent years. Now many sports are trying to pull off a more difficult trick: globalising their product markets too.

Start, though, with labour—and with baseball. In recent seasons, the proportion of players in the major leagues who were born outside America has been nearly 30%, up from 20% ten years ago. Dominicans are the biggest group, followed by Venezuelans. There are several Japanese players, and New York's other team, the Yankees, has a star Tai-wanese pitcher.

In the minor leagues the proportion is even higher: close to half. Among the legionnaires is Loek van Mil, a

Dutch pitcher who stands 2.16 metres (7′ 1″) tall. If he fails on the mound, he might want to join Mr. Yao playing basket-ball: in recent years foreigners have accounted for around 80 of the 430-odd players on the NBA's rosters. In ice hockey, North Americans no longer think Europeans too weak, with sticks or fists, for the NHL. Over 30% of NHL players come from outside America and Canada. This year's [2008] Stanley Cup winners, the Detroit Red Wings, were captained by Nicklas Lidstrom, a Swede and one of 13 Europeans in a 28-man roster.

In other sports a global labour market may seem less of a novelty. English cricket has long relied on the old empire. In football, the Italian and Spanish leagues were graced by several fine foreign players in the 1950s and early 1960s. Both countries then banned foreigners in the hope of helping their national teams. Spain's ban was lifted in 1974 and Italy's in 1980.

Thirty years ago, when Tottenham Hotspur, a London football club, signed two members of Argentina's World-Cup-winning squad, English fans marvelled at such boldness. Now imports are so common that FIFA and UEFA, the governing body in Europe, would like to cap them, but under European Union labour law players must be able to move freely between member states. The transformation in England, with the richest television contracts in the sport, has been remarkable. More than half the players in the Premier League are from outside Britain, up from one-quarter ten years ago. English clubs employed almost one-eighth of the players in the Euro 2008 tournament this June, even though the national team failed to qualify. Only German clubs were better represented.

The supply side of football's labour market has shifted too. Brazil has long been a big exporter. Most of the clubs in this year's Asian Champions League, for instance, have at least one Brazilian. Over the past decade or so there has been a scramble for Africans. French and Belgian clubs had been using Africa as a cheap source of talent for years, but lately the English have been keen buyers, often via Belgium or France, of such talents as Ghana's Michael Essien and Togo's Emmanuel Adebayor.

Ten years ago just under half the players at the African national championships played in their own leagues and two-fifths were with clubs in Europe. Of the 146 men involved, 41 worked in France and only three in England. At this January's [2008] tournament, less than one-third were with domestic teams, mainly in North Africa. Well over half were working in Europe: 202 in all, 57 of them in France and 41 in England.

Virtuous Circle

It is not surprising that sport's labour markets are globalising. The most talented people are gravitating towards the richest employers, whose ability to pay has been enhanced further by juicy television contracts. In turn, the best players make the sport more enjoyable to watch, bringing in more fans and more revenue.

The television money and fan base attract capital too. The globalisation of sport's capital markets may not have gone as far as that of its labour markets, but it is under way. Several English football clubs are owned by foreigners, among them owners of American baseball and football franchises. In cricket, one franchise in the Indian Premier League has owners based in Australia and Britain.

Now several sports—and sports leagues in particular—are trying to expand their product markets beyond their borders as well, by staging games abroad. This is easier said than done. Sport, says Andrew Zimbalist, an economist at Smith College in Massachusetts, is different from other industries: "You can't produce your product in one country and sell it in another. You can do it with laptop computers, but you can't do it with a game."

It is possible to export sport indirectly, by selling media rights. Most globalising leagues hope to make their money from fans in front of television sets rather than inside stadiums, and games abroad are one way of building a brand. But it may not work, because local loyalties matter. "It's hard to get people interested in a baseball team on the other side of the world," Mr Zimbalist says. "It's an emotional thing."

There are other potential obstacles. American football, for example, is not played much outside America and requires a lot of explaining. Soccer needs no introduction, but any league wanting to expand abroad faces another problem. Under FIFA rules it needs the permission of the national association of its host country. That association may well want to protect its own league from imports.

None of this is putting off prospective exporters. "US sports are rushing to get first into globalisation," says David Stern, commissioner of the NBA. All of them, he explains, try to make money in roughly the same ways: by staging events, including games; by building television audiences; through digital media; through marketing partnerships; and

by selling merchandise. European football and its top clubs are doing much the same thing, with the English to the fore.

Would-be globalisers have a success story to ponder: F1 motor racing, which has been stretching from its old haunts in western Europe, the Americas and Japan towards the fast-growing economies of the Middle East and Asia. This year the United States Grand Prix (GP) was dropped from the calendar. One race is scarcely enough to compete with NASCAR, and other countries have been eager to get their own GPs.

A Malaysian GP was added in 1999; races have been held in Bahrain and China since 2004 and in Turkey since 2005. In September the first Singapore GP—and the first F1 race at night—is due to take place. India, which already has an F1 team, is due to stage its first GP in 2010. According to Bernie Ecclestone, F1's boss, races in Russia and South Korea may follow.

"We go where the markets for the manufacturers are," Mr. Ecclestone noted last year, "where they are going to sell their cars in the future." The sponsors whose logos festoon the cars and drivers' firesuits are doubtless pleased to see the sport spreading around the world. And there are no protective local federations to worry about. On the contrary, more countries seem to want the glamour of their own GPs than can be fitted into the calendar.

On the face of it, American football has much in common with F1. It already has dedicated fans in its main target market (Europe, and chiefly Britain). It is seen as an upmarket sport. The NFL faces no protected competitors abroad, and its product is scarce. The NFL's 32 teams play only 16 regular-season games each; those that reach the Super Bowl play a further three or four. Almost all games sell out. Ten teams have a 25-year waiting list for season tickets.

HOW TO GO GLOBAL

One big difference, though, is that F1 is already a global sport, whereas American football is not, and past efforts at exporting it have stuttered. Lots of exhibition matches have been played. In the 1990s the NFL set up a European league, which is now defunct. It has decided that there is no point in offering second-rate fare. "It's got to be the NFL," says Mark Waller, the Briton who oversees the NFL's international operations. "It can't be the European league."

So last October [2007] the NFL went to Wembley Stadium in London, where the New York Giants (eventual winners of the Super Bowl) beat the Miami Dolphins 13-10. This year [2008] it will bring the New Orleans Saints and the San Diego Chargers to Wembley. Last year's game was a sell-out. When tickets went on sale this May, 40,000 were snapped up within 90 minutes.

Though a great treat for Londoners, the NFL's jaunts abroad are less fun for fans of the "home" team (the Dolphins last year, the Saints this time). Unless they can afford a foreign trip, they must forgo one of only eight regular-season home games. Mr. Waller admits this is a problem. "We've got to find a way to get more games," he says. His preference would be to add an extra game for everyone, to be played on neutral ground. That would be fair on all the teams, and there would be 16 games to be spread around: perhaps in Toronto (where the Buffalo Bills are already due to play once a season), Mexico City (where a game was staged in 2005) or American cities without an NFL team, as well as London. New venues might see four games a year.

Meeting pent-up demand in America may prove easier than generating new interest abroad. Still, the test for the NFL is whether live games bring in more British enthusiasts who will stay with the sport. To fans, the game's technicalities are part of the attraction. The problem is to get newcomers hooked. The NFL has always used television inventively, and Mr Waller thinks that high-definition television, in combination with its website, can help to explain the game to newcomers by getting them close to the stratagems and the sweat. "The only way you could do that before was to get on a field. You can do that all digitally," he says.

MLB and the NHL may be luckier, in that they have more games to spare and are preaching to the converted. The NHL plans four regular-season games in Prague and Stockholm at the start of next season. MLB first went abroad in 1999, to Mexico. This season began with a series between the Boston Red Sox and the Oakland Athletics in Tokyo. Next year [2009] will see the second World Baseball Classic, a sort of baseball world cup, in which many MLB players take part.

Mr. Stern's NBA played regular-season games in Japan 18 years ago. Now, all its foreign games are friendlies. Yet it may be best placed of all the ball-playing organisations to build a business abroad—notably in China. Basketball is already popular, roughly on a par with football, according to CSM Media Research in Beijing. It is also simple to play, and the Chinese government has a five-year plan to put a basketball court (and a table-tennis set) in every village. The Olympic baseball stadiums in Beijing are only temporary structures. The nearby basketball arena is anything but.

HOME-GROWN ATTRACTIONS

Better still, in Mr. Yao the NBA has a local hero who draws in viewers by the million. It also has another Chinese star in Yi Jianlian, now of the New Jersey Nets. Its games are shown on CCTV's main free sports channel and it has another 50 television deals in the country. Not everything is predictable: during the three-day mourning period for the Sichuan earthquake, CCTV took the NBA playoffs, along with other forms of entertainment, off the air and resumed coverage only slowly afterwards—albeit in time for the finals. Earlier this year the NBA sold 11% of its Chinese subsidiary to a group of five investors, including ESPN, for $253m. Eventually, thinks Mr. Stern, there may be potential

for the NBA to form a partnership with a Chinese enterprise to launch an NBA-affiliated league. Expansion to Europe is also on the horizon.

Of all the leagues with grand globalisation plans, the Premier League has probably caused the most fuss. Its Asia Trophy has been staged every other year since 2003. Now it is wondering how to expand its activities abroad. Earlier this year Richard Scudamore, the league's chief executive, floated the idea of an "international round", to be played in the middle of the season, in which all 20 teams would play an extra league match abroad with points at stake. This caused uproar.

One reason was that English fans cherish the symmetry of their football leagues: every team plays every other one twice, once at home and once away. The international round would upset that symmetry. (American sports leagues, by contrast, typically have unbalanced schedules.) Secondly, the Premier League has to deal with foreign football associations. Perhaps taking umbrage at the lack of warning, the Asian Football Confederation (AFC)—a potential host—said it did not like the idea of the English inviting themselves over. However, it has since softened its tone, saying that the Premier League would be welcome after all.

Mr. Scudamore explains that things are still up in the air. "All the clubs agreed to take a look at this over a long period," he says. "The clubs are still keen to see us developing some kind of international strategic play. I sit here not knowing in what variant it will come back, but it will come back." One selling point for some of them may be that foreign games will help financially to even up a lopsided league in which the top four are entrenched. Unlike domestic television revenues, foreign fees are shared evenly among the clubs.

In China, potentially the biggest market, the Premier League lacks the draw of a local star. Zheng Zhi, captain of the Chinese national team, does play in England—but his club, Charlton Athletic, was relegated from the league in 2007. The only Chinese player in the Premier League last season, Sun Jihai of Manchester City, started a mere seven games. He has just moved to Sheffield United, one level below.

Some have also questioned the wisdom of selling television rights for the three seasons to 2009–10 to WinTV, a pay-television company. Mr. Scudamore says that WinTV won a tender fair and square, and that it is "doing well from a low base". WinTV says that since it started to show English football its subscriber base has increased "significantly", to nearly 2.5m (some buying its channels singly, others as part of a package). It expects the number to double in 2008–09. People also mocked the sale of domestic rights to BSkyB when the league started, Mr. Scudamore says—and look how that turned out.

"If they are going to be interested in sport," Mr. Scudamore says of potential fans in emerging economies, "we hope they'll be interested in our sport. If they're going to be interested in our sport, we hope they'll be interested in us." Most would-be exporters of sporting spectacles would no doubt say the same. They offer sport of the highest quality, whereas the standard of play in local leagues is often pretty ropy. But quite possibly, those fans, just like those in America and Europe, will eventually prefer to see their own local teams—the more so as standards improve.

Already, notes Seamus O'Brien, chief executive of World Sport Group, a sports-marketing firm based in Singapore, games involving national football teams draw far bigger audiences in Asia than do matches beamed from Europe "in the middle of the night". Mr. O'Brien, who counts the AFC among his clients, thinks Asian football associations should treat the game at club level as an infant industry. They should shell out cash on bringing in foreign players— as Western sports have been doing for years, and as Major League Soccer did to bring Mr. Beckham to America. He proposes that South-East Asian countries pool resources to form their own regional super-league, which would be stronger than national competitions. There is money to pay for this: the second-placed bids for Premier League football rights in Asia, he says, amounted to $600m.

Eventually, believes Mr. O'Brien, "Chinese football will be bigger in England than English football is in China," because the number of Chinese expatriates wanting to watch games from back home will outnumber their English counterparts. That may be some time off. But in the sports business developed countries no longer call all the shots. The strongest evidence for that comes not from baseball, basketball or football, but from another of the world's great games: cricket.

CRICKET

CRICKET IN INDIA: MOVING INTO A LEAGUE OF ITS OWN

India Knowledge@Wharton

Corporate cricket in India has never been of a particularly high standard. At the bottom end of the leagues, companies form makeshift teams from their own ranks. Anyone who has ever wielded a bat is enlisted to play. You bat a bit, bowl a bit and then disband for beer. (The demon bowler who could mess up the proceedings by being too "professional" is given beer before the match, not after.) "Save for Mumbai teams . . . inter-corporate matches in India have never been very serious," says Sandeep Bamzai, the author of *Guts and Glory: The Bombay Cricket Story.*

Come April 18 [2008], it will be a different ballgame. Eight companies are vying for top honors in the Indian Premier League (IPL). They include Mukesh Ambani's Reliance Industries, Vijay Mallya's UB Group, India Cements, GMR Holdings, filmstar Shah Rukh Khan's Red Chillies Entertainment, and some makeshift alliances such as actor Preity Zinta and Ness Wadia, joint managing director of Bombay Dyeing, a leading textile manufacturer. These companies and combines have bid for and won franchises for eight major Indian cities. The tournament, to be played over 44 days in a 20-overs-a-side (Twenty20) format, will pit these eight teams against one another.

The marketers have already swung into action. The Bangalore team—owned by Mallya—has been named Royal Challengers, after one of the liquor baron's popular whisky brands. Khan has called his Kolkata (formerly Calcutta) team the Knight Riders, "inspired by the phrase knight in shining armor." The Chennai team, owned by India Cements, will be known as the Super Kings. (India Cements has brands such as Coromandel King.) Others, too, are rolling out elaborate plans.

They need to do that. By Indian standards, they have already paid large sums for these teams. The franchises for the eight cities were auctioned by the Board of Control for Cricket in India (BCCI). The auction took place in an extravaganza worthy of a Twenty20 match. Against a floor price of $50 million, Ambani won Mumbai with a bid of $111.9 million. Other winners included Mallya (Bangalore; $111.6 million), Hyderabad (Deccan Chronicle; $107.01 million), Chennai (India Cements; $91 million), Delhi (GMR; $84 million), Mohali (Preity Zinta and Ness Wadia; $76 million), Kolkata (Shah Rukh Khan; $75.09 million), and Jaipur (Emerging Media; $67 million). Incidentally, one of the losing bidders has offered to pay $130 million for a team if any of the franchisees is willing to sell. [The IPL added two teams in 2010, with expansion fees of $370 million for a team based in the city of Pune and $333 million for a team based in Kochi.]

GOING, GOING. . .

The payment for the teams was just the beginning. That auction was followed by bidding for the players. The best cricket players from all over the world were up for grabs. The top bid was for India's Twenty20 and one-day cricket captain, Mahendra Singh Dhoni, who went to Chennai for $1.5 million. Andrew Symonds of Australia was bagged by Hyderabad for $1.35 million. Other rounds of bidding are still on.

With each team needing 16 men (11 players, a 12th man and four reserves), the price tag will keep climbing. Team Hyderabad, for instance, has already paid some $6 million for 11 players and will need to fork over more for the rest. The bids would have been higher, but for the fact that some iconic players—former India captains Sachin Tendulkar, Sourav Ganguly and Rahul Dravid—weren't available. They are captains of the cities they are associated with (Mumbai, Kolkata and Bangalore, respectively) and will be paid 15% more than the highest-paid player in their teams.

These fees for players are hardly unusual by international standards. For example, *Forbes* magazine estimates golfer Tiger Woods' annual income at $100 million. But for cricket—and not just in India—this is big money. Australian Ricky Ponting, the highest-paid cricketer in the highest-rated country team, takes home only $800,000 a year. Sponsorships bring this up to $4 million.

These large deals are already attracting criticism. Left-wing political parties have demanded an investigation into the "sources of hundreds of crores of black money spent on the auction" and why the government has condoned such "outrageous gambling." Not to be outdone, the right-wing Shiv Sena party has described the auction as the "gambling of industrialists."

The auctions, though, are a small part of the money machine. The BCCI had earlier sold the 10-year television rights to Sony Entertainment, the Indian subsidiary of Japan's Sony, and World Sports Group (WSG), an Asia-focused sports marketing and management agency, for more than $1 billion. Together with the other takings, IPL is already a $2 billion business. As Lalit Modi, BCCI vice-president and chairman and match commissioner of the IPL, says: "IPL is the best thing that has happened to cricket. Corporate India is convinced about the product and the revenue model and has shown the appetite and passion for cricket."

MONETIZING THE GAME

Modi, scion of a business family that owns tobacco-maker Godfrey Phillips, is the new face of the Indian cricket establishment. He studied marketing at Duke University in North Carolina, where he learned about the major U.S. sports leagues. "We have succeeded in monetizing the game," he says.

"Yes, priorities have changed for a segment of the population," says Sridhar Samu, professor of marketing at the Indian School of Business (ISB), Hyderabad. Adds Bamzai: "Cricket today is a metaphor for change." According to Ashish Kaul, executive vice-president of the Indian Cricket League (ICL), a rival to IPL: "We as a country have reached a stage where entertainment is a basic necessity and not a leisure activity. Cricket is the lowest common denominator of this country and perhaps the largest entertainer."

Corporate India—in the form of the new cricket leagues—will give the fans all the change they want. The game in its

Twenty20 format has metamorphosed a great deal from its traditional five-day test match version. The first innovation—the 50-over-a-side, one-day variety—offended the purist; Twenty20, for them, is sheer slam-bam. But so what? "People anyway watch only the last 20 overs of a one-day match," says Modi. "We are giving them concentrated cricket, concentrated entertainment."

The franchisees are working overtime to ensure that the new format works. In Hyderabad, Deccan Chronicle is talking about hiring special trains to bring in fans from the hinterland. The train ride will be an experience in itself, with marketing men salivating at the thought of such a focused and captive audience, which also has time on its hands during the journey. In Kolkata, Shah Rukh Khan is planning a special women's stand, while he makes the occasional guest appearance. Meanwhile, the Delhi team has hired an Indian Institute of Management (Ahmedabad) alumnus, a 45-year-old former colonel in the Indian Army, as assistant vice-president (operations). Corporatization and professionalization are clearly the watchwords of the day.

The key question is: Will the IPL benefit all stakeholders? The cricketers certainly stand to gain; they are seeing the sort of money they could only dream about earlier. This is particularly true of countries outside the Indian subcontinent where cricket has not been such a passion. Elsewhere, cricketers have to compete with stars in football, rugby and so on. In India, for all practical purposes, there is money only in cricket.

There could also be casualties, such as English county cricket. Which players would want to spend a season there when there is so much more money in the IPL? "County cricket is a page in the history books," says Bamzai. And, though the BCCI says it will fix IPL schedules in consultation with the International Cricket Council (ICC), there have already been fears that money may have changed power equations. Indian cricket today earns as much as the rest of the cricketing world put together.

. . . .

WHY EYEBALLS MATTER

BCCI's Modi is confident that people are bored with soaps and that IPL will be a huge draw. Not everybody is so sure. "This will only work if you get the eyeballs," says Bamzai. "I am not too sure if IPL will."

Kaul of ICL is another skeptic. (ICL was started by the Zee Group, a television major, and IPL is actually the official response from BCCI.) "Perhaps BCCI and IPL may not lose anything as they are just selling a commodity," he says. "But will the market be able to afford the rates? IPL is just an inter-corporate tournament—in a way, Mukesh Ambani vs. Vijay Mallya with 1,500 seconds (of advertising time) to be sold." By his calculations, Sony and WSG could lose almost $10 million in the first year.

The bigger question around getting the necessary eyeballs—and thus being able to charge high ad rates—is whether Indian audiences will develop loyalty towards city-based teams. State-level cricket matches in India draw no audiences and are largely ignored by television. Will audiences be passionate in their support for Mumbai, except while local hero Tendulkar is batting? Or is the whole IPL extravaganza a marketing exercise that will fizzle out after a few matches?

Modi argues that city-level cricket can succeed in India for several reasons. "The league has been designed to provide opportunities to upcoming cricket stars to showcase their talents while sharing a platform with some of the world's best cricketers," he says. "It will be the first time we have a Twenty20 format for our fans and the first time the game will pit a city against another city. It also marks the first time international players of the stature of Shane Warne, Sanath Jayasuriya and Ricky Ponting will participate in a domestic Indian league. Indian corporations and Bollywood actors will be involved. The cricket matches will be covered globally."

"Marketing muscle and money will play a role," agrees Krishnamachar of WSG. "But eventually, the real maturity will come from the television viewers who turn around and say that they want to watch the best cricket and that it doesn't matter if it is India vs. Australia or something else."

"It is not just marketing hype," says Samu of ISB. "There is significant substance with top players in the teams.

It is a good product which is now getting marketing support. Indian cricket is certainly headed in the same direction as football in the UK and baseball in the U.S." He agrees, however, that it will be a challenge to get audiences to watch city teams, since they have ignored state-level cricket.

Samu disagrees with the politicians who have been complaining about the large sums being spent on cricket. "One should not think in terms of too much money going to cricket being detrimental for other sports," he says. "In fact, it may work to the advantage of other sports. Cricket is now moving to a different league and the other sports could learn from it and follow in its footsteps. They could look at adapting the same formats."

Former test cricketer Syed Kirmani has a suggestion. "Other sports should be taken care of," he says. "If one sport is overflowing with money, it should distribute some to other sports." BCCI is, in fact, doing just that. It has just announced that it will set aside $25 million for the development of other sports.

As D-day approaches, the excitement is building up. It is not just among fans. "There are already enquiries from private equity players to team-owners asking them if they would be willing to sell a share of the pie," says Krishnamachar of WSG. Srinivasan of India Cements is talking about an initial public offer (IPO) and listing his team. "It's going to be a great carnival," says Kirmani.

TWENTY20 CRICKET: AN EXAMINATION OF THE CRITICAL SUCCESS FACTORS IN THE DEVELOPMENT OF COMPETITION

Christopher Hyde and Adrian Pritchard

EXECUTIVE SUMMARY

The Twenty20 cricket competition is a shortened, faster version of traditional four-day and one-day cricket. It was launched in England and Wales in 2003 in an attempt to reverse dwindling interest in the sport. Games were to be completed in three hours and were augmented with off-field entertainment.

The study reviews literature concerning the launch of new sporting products and services, and investigates the critical success factors behind successful launches and also factors that led to failures. Most of the research conducted has been in American and Australian sport, with academic models developed in these countries, particularly America. The authors believe the models to be useful, but felt there

were likely to be differences in England and Wales because of the sporting culture and calendar.

Attendance figures were gathered from a number of sources to quantify the success of the competition in terms of spectator numbers. These clearly show that crowds are a lot higher for this form of cricket. A short open-ended questionnaire was developed from the literature review in order to investigate the likely critical success factors. This was then sent to the marketing departments of the 18 counties who participate in the competition.

The secondary research and the comments received from respondents identify a number of factors that were attributed to being critical to the success of the competition. These include the use of market research and the application of marketing techniques, media coverage, a reputation for being fast and entertaining, and the length of the game. These factors lie within the three strategic factors affecting the diffusion rate model.

However, the model excludes two important factors that are contextual to cricket: competition timing and the weather. There are two elements that respondents felt were important in the competition's timing: that the games are at a convenient time for spectators to attend, and that they avoid competition from other sports, particularly football. The implementation of this timing strategy might have helped gain increased audience interest. Other contextual factors that were identified as impacting on diffusion and requiring further investigation are saturation, in terms of length of the competition, and crowd involvement.

. . . .

The research was qualitative, and only industry experts from counties' marketing departments were interviewed. The primary research did not take account of spectators' opinions, and further research is recommended to obtain their views on the competition and the factors that motivate them to attend matches.

INTRODUCTION

The authors investigated the issues involved in making a new sport successful. What factors determine whether people are likely to attend a new sporting event and become interested in it? Compared to other forms of cricket, the competition appears to have been successful at bringing in spectators, but what have been the critical factors in this success?

BACKGROUND TO TWENTY20

Cricket in England and Wales is governed by the England and Wales Cricket Board (ECB). The 18 domestic counties receive income from the ECB, which generates its revenue from international cricket via the sale of tickets, merchandise and television rights. ECB turnover in 2004 was £75.12 million, up from £73.5 million in 2003. Cricket is highly dependent on broadcasting revenue, which represents 80% of ECB income. The counties are subsidised by the ECB, with some earning up to 75% of their income from the source. The size of the cricket market is considerably smaller than football, where in 2005/6 six English football teams alone had a turnover greater than £85 million, Manchester United being the biggest at £167.8 million.

The English county cricket season begins in mid-April and concludes in September. Before 2003 it consisted of one-day championship games (lasting up to eight hours per day) and one-day games (lasting between six and eight hours) depending on the competition played. . . .

A proposal to improve interest in the game through the new Twenty20 competition format was put to the first-class counties forum in 1998. The idea of a reduced version of the game was snubbed, but in 2001 problems in the domestic game were still apparent (*The Economist* 2003) and attendances were falling (English 2003). A £200,000 survey was undertaken by the ECB in 2001 in an attempt to collate information as to how to satisfy customers, gain interest from a younger market and help the game as a whole. This was undertaken in three key phases. First, there was a complete examination of statistics throughout cricket, which were analysed to identify trends and patterns. This was followed by interviews with a wide cross-section of demographic groups. A mixture of current and potential spectators was involved in the process to gain a greater depth and knowledge of the target audience. The final part of the strategy involved a large random quantitative survey. A programme of 4,000 15-minute face-to-face interviews revealed that about two-thirds of the population either disliked or had no interest in cricket. Prominent among the rejectors were children, young people aged 16–34, women, ethnic minorities and members of the lower social strata.

The first-class counties agreed to a shorter form of the game, with the aim of attracting these rejectors. ECB marketing manager Stuart Robertson was responsible for the creation of the competition and the research programme. He believed it should be launched with the primary aim being that the competition is market-driven. It was therefore necessary to apply basic marketing techniques to cricket. The rules were not intended to be radically different, because it was hoped that it would be a stepping stone for people to watch the longer versions of cricket (Twenty20 official site).

Twenty20 was launched on 13 June 2003, and played by the 18 first-class counties in England and Wales. The counties were split into regional groups, with the winners of each group progressing to a finals day in July. In 2004, an additional quarter-final stage was added to increase the number of games.

The games were designed to last for approximately 2 hours 45 minutes, thus creating a shortened, fast paced version of the traditional one-day game. It was deliberately staged in the middle of June, the hottest month of the year and also the period with the longest daylight hours. Most games started at 5.30pm, the aim being to become a major summer social attraction targeting a younger post-work crowd and offering a great family evening out. Additional entertainment was featured in the form of music and interactive crowd events; £250,000 was spent on marketing but no sponsor was found. However, pay-TV operator Sky screened the competition on satellite television, and terrestrial broadcaster Channel 4 covered cricket in general with a half-hour Saturday morning programme throughout June and a live game on 14 June.

LITERATURE REVIEW

New product development is generally agreed to be risky for a variety of different reasons, and the majority of new products/services fail. Also, the degree of novelty in new products and services tends to vary. Booz et al (1982) classify new developments into four categories: product replacements, additions to existing lines, new product lines, and products that are new to the world. Twenty20 would probably be classified by the model as an 'addition to the existing lines' of four-day and one-day cricket. Others might classify it as a 'new to the world product' if it is viewed as a new sports activity (Harness & Harness 2007).

Rogers (1983) examined the speed of adoption of products and services citing the five characteristics: differential advantage, compatibility with customer values, complexity in terms of ease of understanding, divisibility in terms of ease of trying the product/service and communicability of the benefits. Though the model is a generic one, it can, to some extent, be applied to Twenty20 cricket. Differential advantage is in the form of the speed of the game, with the shorter duration being compatible with consumer values and easier to trial. The limited changes to the rules means that it is not complex (Twenty20 official site 2003). Bridgewater (2007) claims that the complex rules of cricket make it difficult to expand its appeal, and one-day cricket is not suited to trial because of the length of the game. Higgins and Martin (1996) considered diffusion in a sports context and formulated a model to assess the diffusion rates of sporting innovations. They claim that there are three components that affect the rate of acceptance:

- The characteristic of the innovation as discussed above (Rogers, 1983)

- The perceived newness of the innovation, be it a change in rules, location of the event or a combination of both

- Sources of influence used to communicate the idea (Mahajan et al, 1990a; Mahajan et al, 1990b). The authors did not comment on the extent to which changes in rules or location impact on likely success. However, Papadimitriou et al (2004) evaluated perceived fit in sports brand extensions in Greece. Their research provided support for the hypothesis that perceived fit is higher for sports-related extensions and results in a more positive evaluation and higher intention to purchase.

Twenty20 has been televised live by Sky on a subscription channel. The second day of the competition was also covered live on Channel 4 on free-to-air terrestrial television. The importance of television coverage in terms of finance, commercial rationale and organisational skills is generally accepted within the literature.

Garland et al (1999) investigated the marketing of cricket in New Zealand in the 1990s and the adoption of marketing techniques to meet customer requirements. New Zealand Cricket Inc conducted telephone interview research in 1991 to discuss the barriers to cricket. These were identified as 'a boring game that takes too long to finish, with rules that are difficult to understand and in which New Zealand did not perform well'. Further problems identified were poor facilities, unruly behaviour at grounds, and a preference for television coverage. The research also made it clear that the barriers could be 'circumvented' by marketing strategies that made use of:

- The atmosphere of one-day internationals

- The more serene atmosphere of test matches

- The success of New Zealand teams

- The excitement of watching live sport

- National pride

- The quality of teams and individual performances.

After three years, the New Zealand Cricket Council was able to see increases in attendance, television ratings, media coverage and revenue. The authors claim that research shows there is a clear distinction in the customer profile in New Zealand between test match and one-day international supporters, though they offered no empirical evidence.

The authors went on to look at the launch of Cricket Max, a version of the traditional game—mainly intended for pay-TV audiences—that was launched by Martin Crowe, a former New Zealand captain, in 1996. Crowe's rationale (Cricinfo, 1996) was to provide a game that was short, very colourful, kept some old traditions and highlighted the best skills in the game in three hours of cricket. It was launched with live satellite coverage and sponsorship from Pepsi Max and BNZ [Bank of New Zealand]. McConnell (2004) noted that it did not compete against the country's number one sport, Rugby Union. In comparing factors in different hemispheres, he stated that the longer twilight conditions in England offered advantages that could only be matched in the South Island of New Zealand.

Cricket Max has not been played since 2001, although there has never been an official announcement as to why not. Some of the ideas of Cricket Max were borrowed by Twenty20, the three-hour time slot being probably the most significant.

Haigh (2007) argues that the most successful variations of the traditional game have been those that looked more traditional and kept rule changes to a minimum. Cricket Max made changes in numbers of players and scoring; Twenty20 has not. He argues that the promotion of Twenty20 as 'being for those who do not like cricket' is for this reason misleading.

Paton and Cooke (2005) used attendance figures to investigate spectator numbers at domestic one-day and four-day games in England and Wales. The findings demonstrate that attendances were higher for games that didn't clash with internationals, when games were played in the evening under floodlights, and when the games were played at festival grounds (those that are not the county headquarters, where most fixtures were played).

Funk et al (2001) devised the Sport Interest Inventory (SII) to measure the motivation for spectators to attend sporting events. It was originally applied to women's professional soccer in the US (Funk et al, 2002). The model has also been applied in the context of Japanese and Australian sport (Neale, 2006). However, the authors have pointed out the need to survey consumers in a specific situation before using motives to develop marketing strategy.

The models of Higgins and Martin (2006) and Funk et al (2001) were both developed in the context of American sport. The SII was not used by the authors, as the research is of an exploratory nature and is not a quantitative study. An amended version could, however, be applied in the next stage of research when spectators are interviewed.

English sports have a different calendar, culture and spectator tastes from American sports, and the authors believe that the factors of timing and weather might impact upon a decision to attend an event. Further research was needed to find out if they are vital factors in the success of Twenty20. The aim of the research was to investigate these factors. The authors felt that timing was a factor in the success of the launch, as there were no other major sporting events in the summer of 2003, such as an Olympics or World Cup. A comparison can be drawn here with Rugby League. In 1996 the sport introduced an innovation with the creation of the Super League. The changed timing of the event, from a winter to a summer calendar, proved successful, as evidenced by a 19% rise in attendances when launched (Mintel, 2003).

The model for the research was developed by adapting the Higgins and Martin (1996) 'three strategic factors affecting the diffusion rate' model. The perceived newness component is re-titled 'perceived newness of sport' for reasons of clarification. A fourth component is added to include contextual factors. In the case of cricket it was thought that weather and timing would be important in determining the likely success of the innovation, though there may be additional factors that emerge from respondents' comments. An example of the impact of contextual factors, and the benefits to marketers of exploiting them, can be seen in the positive impact of the World Cup in 2002 on attendances in the Japanese football J League (Funk et al, 2006).

Objectives

- To measure the success of the competition in terms of attendances
- To identify the critical success factors of the competition
- To examine how the critical success factors identified in Twenty20 sit alongside the three strategic factors affecting the diffusion rate model of Higgins and Martin (1996)

Methodology

A two-stage approach was adopted. Details of attendances were gathered from secondary information sources to compare attendances across competitions (Mintel, 2006; Wisden, 2004, 2005, 2006, 2007).

The authors also approached industry experts for their views on the competition. Because the research was of an introductory nature, an open-ended questionnaire was mailed to the marketing departments of the 18 first-class county cricket clubs in March 2005. Six questions were asked, the first two covering the areas of competition timing and the influence of weather, as discussed above. Respondents were also asked a further four questions regarding critical success factors to date, future critical success factors, the competition's impact on finances, and whether the format had attracted a new audience. A final question allowed respondents to make further comments. Responses were received from seven of the counties. The respondent counties were all located in the middle and south of England. There was a noticeable absence from the northern counties.

. . . .

QUESTIONNAIRE RESPONSES

Timing

All the respondents believed that the timing of the event was critical to the competition's current success. Indeed timing was identified as crucial in different ways. The date range was selected because it would theoretically coincide with optimal weather conditions. The time of day was also a factor. A key objective was to make the event accessible to target markets, and the 5.30pm start enabled school children and the majority of workers to attend without encroaching on work time. Two respondents pointed out that the combination of these factors allowed families to attend. It was also felt that without other major sporting events occurring simultaneously, Twenty20 received more media coverage.

Weather

Respondents believed that the weather had an impact on initial success, although one pointed out that weather is crucial to all cricket competitions. However, the weather had not been as good in 2004 as in 2003. One respondent claimed that despite this, attendances increased in 2004 mainly through excitement. Another felt that good weather attracted a new audience in addition to established cricket fans.

Critical Success Factors

Respondents listed a number of factors here. Five mentioned the good entertainment provided by the competition. One respondent described the competition as having a reputation for fast and lively cricket. Satellite television and media coverage were mentioned four times, and the length of the game three times. Also mentioned were:

- The use of extensive market research
- Family orientation
- No other competition at the same time
- Early evening timing
- A result is gained
- Word-of-mouth advertising

- Attraction to women and children
- Extra activities leading to crowd involvement.

Future Critical Success Factors

Media interest was mentioned by five respondents in terms of maintaining satellite coverage and keeping the media interested. Five respondents also pointed out the problem of over-exposure of the format and the need to avoid saturation by having too many games. Two respondents mentioned the need to maintain the current format and keep it to a sensible calendar window slot.

Other factors highlighted were the competition from international Twenty20 cricket, which started in 2005 (Coward, 2007), weather, the need for counties to invest in marketing activities to sustain success, and the moving of games away from headquarters to other areas of the county.

Finances

All seven respondents agreed that the Twenty20 competition has made all the counties' finances healthier, and some have come to rely on it to boost their income. For some counties, Twenty20 fixtures are the only games to sell out, and they bring in a big percentage of revenue. One respondent also pointed out that revenue was boosted not only by ticket sales and satellite coverage, but by secondary spending in catering outlets, beer sales, soft drinks etc. Another mentioned corporate hospitality as a good source of revenue.

New Audience

All respondents felt the competition has attracted a new audience: women and children (cited twice) families, non-county members, corporates, young people, people turned off by one-day cricket, 18-35 year olds, and sports fans in general.

Further Comments

One respondent attributed some of the success to crowd interaction, stating that it added to the atmosphere and general overall enjoyment. Another pointed out that Twenty20 led to more people attending other formats of the game, particularly floodlit matches.

CONCLUSIONS

The competition has proved to be a success in its first four years. The reasons for this can be seen in aspects of the three strategic factors affecting the diffusion rate model. In particular the characteristics of a shortened, three-hour version of the game were compatible with consumer needs, and sources of influence were gained through the media.

The timing and weather are not included as factors in the model. However, the findings from the primary and secondary data suggest strongly that these contextual issues need to be added to the model. There appear to be two aspects of timing that contributed to the success of the competition. First, that the competition is played at a time that is convenient for people to attend, and second, that it avoids competition with other sports, particularly football.

Further issues were mentioned and require more research, most notably the level of interaction of the sport. Some of the interaction is caused by events that are part of the match entertainment but not directly part of the game (*Economist*, 2003; Pryor 2004), but do these events contribute to the motive for attending?

FURTHER RESEARCH AND LIMITATIONS

The survey included only the county marketing teams. Research needs to be conducted among those who have attended games to investigate the issues discussed in the models, and in particular their motivation for going to matches. The SII model could be applied, but it needs to be adapted to take account of the contextual issues of timing in terms of convenience of attending, competing sports and the weather. The issue of crowd involvement in entertainment activities that are not part of the main game also requires investigation.

Further research is also needed to monitor the success of the competition following the introduction of international games in 2005. A World Cup was held in South Africa in 2007, but this did not coincide with English and Welsh domestic competition. Research is also required into the area of saturation. At what point is the game likely to reach saturation level, and what is the optimum number of games per season?

References

Booz, Allen & Hamilton (1982) *New Product Management for the 1980s*, New York: Booz, Allen and Hamilton, Inc.

Bridgewater, S. (2007) 'International Marketing Mix' in Beech, J. & Chadwick, S. (eds), *The Marketing of Sport*, FT-Prentice Hall.

Coward, M. (2007) 'Traditionalists man the barricades', *The Australian*, 7 November.

Cricinfo (1996) Cricket Max—The Game Invented By Martin Crowe, available from: http://content-eap.cricinfo.com/ci/content/story/67577.html [20 November 2007]

England and Wales Cricket Board (2005). About ECB and Twenty20, available from: http://www.ecb.co.uk/ecb/about/about-ecb.html [10 November 2004]

English, P. (2003) 'Attention all non-cricket lovers' *Wisden Cricket Monthly*, 17 June.

Funk, D.C., Mahony, D.F., Nakazawa, M. & Hirakawa, S. (2001) Development of the Sport Interest Inventory (SII): implications for measuring unique consumer motives at sporting events, *International Journal of Sports Marketing and Sponsorship* 3(3), 291–316.

Funk, D.C., Mahony, D.F. & Ridinger, L.L. (2002). 'Characterizing consumer motivation as individual difference factors: augmenting the Sport Interest Inventory (SII) to explain specific sport interest', *Sport Marketing Quarterly* 11, 1, 33–43.

Funk, D.C., Nakazawa, M., Mahony, D.F. & Thrasher, R. (2006) The impact of the national sports lottery and the FIFA World Cup on attendance, spectator motives and J. League marketing strategies, *International Journal of Sports Marketing and Sponsorship* 7(3) 267–285.

Garland, R., Inkson, K. & McDermott, P. (1999) 'Sports Marketing' in *Sport Business Management in New Zealand* in Trenberth, L. & Collins, C. Palmerson North: The Dunmore Press.

Haigh, G. (2007) 'Shorter, simpler, sillier'. Available from: http://content-eap.cricinfo.com/ci/content/story/ 309625.html?wrappertype=print [22 December 2007].

Harness, D. & Harness, T. (2007) 'Managing sports products and services' in Beech, J. & Chadwick, S. (eds) *The Marketing of Sport*. FT-Prentice Hall.

Higgins, S.H. & Martin, J.H. (1996) 'Managing sport innovations: A diffusion theory perspective, *Sport Marketing Quarterly* 5(1), 43–48.

Mahajan, V., Muller, E. & Bass, F.M. (1990) New product diffusion models in marketing: a review and directions for research, *Journal of Marketing* 54, 1–26.

Mahajan, V., Muller, E. & Srivastava, R.K.(1990) Determination of adopter categories by using innovation diffusion models, *Journal of Marketing Research* 27, 37–50.

McConnell, L. (2004) 'Twenty20 in the land of Super Max'. Available from: http://content-eap.cricinfo.com/ci/content/story/135060html?wrapper type=print [22 December 2007].

Mintel (2003) UK Spectator Sport—April, available from http://academic.mintel.com, Mintel International Group Ltd, London.

Mintel (2006) Cricket and Rugby-UK—February. Available from: http:// academic.mintel.com, Mintel International Group Ltd, London.

Neale, L. (2006) Investigating motivation, attitudinal loyalty and attendance behaviour with fans of Australian football, *International Journal of Sports Marketing & Sponsorship* 7(4), 307–17.

Papadimitriou, D., Apostolopoulou, A. & Loukas, I. (2004) The role of perceived fit in fans' evaluation of sports brand extension, *International Journal of Sports Marketing & Sponsorship* 6(1), 31–48.

Paton, D. & Cooke, A. (2005) Attendance at county cricket: an economic analysis, *Journal of Sports Economics,* 6(1), 24–45.

Pryor, M. (2004) 'Swift love affair that knows no boundaries', *The Times,* 2 July, p.87.

Rogers, E.M. (1983) *Diffusion of Innovations* (3rd Edn). New York: Free Press.

The Economist (2003) 'Adapt or die', 21 June, p.33.

Twenty20 Cup Official Site, (2003) 'Robertson wary of Twenty20 buzz'. Available from: http://www.thetwenty20cup.co.uk/news/newsitem .asp?NewsID=172 [2 April 2005].

Wisden Cricketers' Almanack, (2004) 141st Edn, Edited by Engel, M. John Wisden, 833–42.

Wisden Cricketers' Almanack, (2005) 142nd Edn, Edited by Engel, M. John Wisden, 887–98.

Wisden Cricketers' Almanack, (2006) 143rd Edn, Edited by Engel, M. John Wisden, 890–96.

Wisden Cricketers' Almanack, (2007) 144th Edn, Edited by Engel, M. John Wisden, 922–44.

Wisden Cricketer Monthly, (2003) July (71). Wisden Cricket Magazines.

SOCCER

ARSENAL FC ANNUAL REPORT, 2008

Chairman's Report

P. D. Hill-Wood, Chairman, 18 September 2008

I am pleased to report another year of satisfactory progress against our key objectives of delivering long-term stability and success through the operation of the Club as a business which is self-sustaining. The annual accounts, which show a pre-tax profit of £36.7 million (2007—£5.6 million), clearly confirm the strength of the Group's financial position following the move to Emirates Stadium. Your Board strongly believes this financial strength establishes the best possible foundation from which the Club can achieve footballing success long into the future.

During the 2007/08 season, the team played some highly entertaining and stylish football. The Club made a strong challenge for the Barclays Premier League title but eventually finished the season, just four points behind the winners, in a respectable third place. In addition, the Club reached the quarter-final stage of the UEFA Champions League and the semi-final stage of the Carling Cup.

. . . Our successful leverage of Emirates Stadium's facilities is providing opportunities for the Group over and above those derived from the core business of staging the Club's competitive fixtures. There is no doubt that Emirates Stadium has become a serious contender for the staging of major nonfootball events. . . . The stadium's standing as a first class venue was further enhanced in March when it played host to a summit between Gordon Brown and French President Nicolas Sarkozy; the two political leaders held a joint press conference with the world's media in attendance.

At the end of May music legend Bruce Springsteen played to two nights of sell-out audiences immediately establishing a reputation for Emirates Stadium as a nonfootball entertainment venue. Although the window between the end of the playing season and the start of work on renovating the pitch for the new season is relatively short, the staging of music events is certainly something we will consider again for the future. We have now successfully staged two Emirates Cups, in pre-season 2007 and 2008, and in March 2008 we played host to a third international friendly—Brazil v Sweden. We hope to continue with both the Emirates Cup and high quality non-Arsenal fixtures as regular features in the Emirates Stadium calendar.

We recognise that the Club's operations have an impact on the local, national and global environment and during the year we have introduced a number of initiatives in order to try and operate as a more environmentally friendly organisation. We now have a dedicated recycling area in the stadium's underground car park and on average we are recycling 10 tonnes per month of glass, cardboard and plastic which would previously have been sent to landfill.

Other new initiatives in the year included progression of our supporter Contact Centre project. This brings together box office, home shopping, tours, travel and Junior Gunners operations for both telephone and e-mail handling and is designed to ensure an enhanced level of service is available to all of our supporters. The initial responses to the roll-out of this project have been encouraging.

. . . .

I am delighted to confirm that E. Stanley Kroenke has accepted the Board's invitation to become a non-executive director of Arsenal. Mr. Kroenke fully supports the approach the Board has taken in setting the direction of the Club and we believe his experience in sports team commercial management, sports marketing, media and new media rights as well as real estate development will be of great value. Mr. Kroenke is not a party to the "lock-down" arrangement entered into by the other members of the Board.

Mr. Kroenke is the shareholder in Kroenke Sports Enterprises (KSE), the leading live sports and entertainment group based in Denver, Colorado. In April this year KSE acquired from ITV plc a 50% share in Arsenal Broadband Limited and at the same time entered into a strategic partnership with the Club through Colorado Rapids, the KSE franchise.

. . . .

ON THE FIELD

A look back at the first team's 2007/08 season elicits mixed emotions. There is no doubt that the football played by Arsène Wenger's side was often at a truly exceptional level, however, despite winning many plaudits, trophies were again to prove elusive.

The Premier League campaign yielded 83 points, some 15 points more than the previous season, and only three defeats yet only a third-placed finish. A fine 'double' over Tottenham Hotspur and an emphatic away win against Everton were particular highlights.

International call-ups and injuries—not least that which was suffered by our Croatian forward Eduardo at, perhaps, a pivotal point of his debut season—depleted the squad in the new year and this proved telling in the months of February and March when four consecutive draws considerably hampered the title challenge. Despite taking the lead in both games, the team then slipped to narrow defeats at Stamford Bridge and Old Trafford, which confirmed that the championship would not be heading to Emirates Stadium.

In the UEFA Champions League, a relatively straightforward Group Stage was followed by the glamour of a tie with reigning holders AC Milan. The excitement and pride felt by everybody connected with the Club following a famous 2-0 win at the San Siro, which secured progress to the quarter-finals, was considerable. However, domestic rivals Liverpool put an end to the European campaign on a dramatic night at Anfield in which a late Emmanuel Adebayor goal seemed to have earned us a place in the last four, only for two further strikes by the hosts to decide otherwise.

There were mixed fortunes in the domestic cups. Another fine Carling Cup run emphasized again the quality and depth of young talent which the Club is developing. The semi-finals were reached in some style although Tottenham Hotspur then prevailed through to the final. Early FA Cup successes against Burnley and Newcastle United were offset when a weakened side was beaten at Old Trafford in the fifth round of the competition.

Despite the disappointment felt at a season without winning a trophy, there can be no denying that progress was made in 2007/08. It is notable that Emirates Stadium is proving to be a significant factor in the team's success—we remained unbeaten in all the 28 home matches played last season and, in fact, only one competitive game has been lost of the 58 played at our new home.

. . . .

COMMERCIAL PARTNERS

Arsenal has continued to develop its commercial partner programme over the 2007/08 season. From a sponsorship perspective we are fortunate to be in a position where we are working closely with many high profile brands. During the year, Ebel joined our partner programme as official timing partner and we are also delighted to welcome Citroën, as the Club's official car partner, for the start of the 2008/09 season.

We delivered our most successful merchandise figures ever during the 2007/08 season on the back of new second and third choice Nike kits and continuing excellence in own brand apparel, gifts and souvenirs delivered by S'porter, our retail partner. These results were assisted by a temporary store established in Enfield for the period ahead of Christmas 2007. A major overhaul of our Finsbury Park shop has been undertaken and a new store has recently been opened in St Albans. Further off-site stores are planned for the future.

Internationally, our merchandise business is also growing. Our Thai partner BEC Tero now has fourteen retail outlets for Arsenal merchandise, including a new flagship store in Phuket, Thailand. More distribution partnerships will be established for official club merchandise in other territories in the coming financial year.

Arsenal has been involved in other international activity which both improves the profile of the Club and drives revenues. Tiger Beer will continue to be Arsenal's Official Beer in South East Asia for another three years. In Vietnam, the Club has secured sponsorship with Vinamilk, Gree Electrics and ICP, which will positively impact on the Club's local profile. Financial service partnerships have been secured in Indonesia and Nigeria with Bank Danamon and UBA respectively. Local language official Arsenal websites in

China, Korea, and Thailand continue to be used by over 300,000 local fans each month.

The international Arsenal Soccer Schools programme continues to advance. High quality facilities have opened in Bangkok, Thailand and Ho Chi Minh City, Vietnam and represent further grassroots investment. Arsenal now has sixteen affiliated Soccer Schools abroad. The Club has made its first major entry into India with a high profile Arsenal football roadshow supported by Tata Tea.

Closer to home, Emirates Stadium has hosted a wide range of organisations for a variety of conference, banqueting and meeting events. The stadium provides a flexible and unique venue and along with our catering partner Delaware North we have become expert in hosting high quality functions. In addition, Emirates Stadium welcomed over 80,000 visitors on a variety of stadium tours during the 2007/08 season.

Emirates Stadium also hosts the production facility and studio used to broadcast Arsenal TV, which was successfully launched in January. The channel is part of the Setanta Sports package of channels and is also available through Virgin Media reaching approximately 5 million homes in the UK and Eire. We are extremely pleased with the quality of the programming and presentation, with much credit going to our production partner Input Media. Feedback from fans has been positive and consequently broadcasting hours have been increased for the 2008/09 season.

Our joint venture partner in the Arsenal.com website business changed, following ITV's sale of their 50% shareholding to KSE, and we now look forward to further developing this already successful website operation alongside KSE.

During the year we also ended our own commercial relationship with ITV. All commercial development, including the Arsenal licensing programme, is now undertaken in house. We would like to thank ITV for all the hard work expended on the Club's commercial programme and their contribution to our commercial success over the last few years.

CHARITY OF THE SEASON

Treehouse, the national charity for autism education, became Arsenal's nominated charity for season 2007/08 taking over from The Willow Foundation. Treehouse was established in 1997 by a group of parents of autistic children and it aims to transform the lives of all children with autism and the lives of their families, by increasing the quantity and quality of autism education. The Club's partnership with Treehouse . . . was a great success raising a record breaking £519,000 for the charity.

PROSPECTS

The property side of the business will inevitably be of considerable significance to the Group over the next year, with a large number of apartment sales scheduled to complete at Highbury Square and progression of the redevelopment plans for Queensland Road. We will be closely monitoring all stages of the sales completion process. Over 2008/09 the proceeds of Highbury Square sales will largely be used for the repayment of the related bank loans, consequently reducing the Group's net debt from its current peak level. The two sides of the Group's business are financed independently of each other and both the property and football business segments start the year from very sound financial bases.

On the field the new season has got off to a promising start. We have successfully negotiated the qualification round of the 2008/09 UEFA Champions League to ensure participation in the Group Stage and this is important to the Club both in competitive and financial terms.

This Club is ambitious for success and as always, at the start of the season, our expectations are high. We look forward to supporting the team, as it challenges for trophies, throughout the course of the season.

In closing, I would like to pay tribute to my fellow directors, our management team and our entire staff for all of their hard work and dedication over the last year. I would also like to thank our Highbury Square project team and all of our other professional advisers for the support they have provided.

Finally thank you for the fantastic support given to the Club by all of our shareholders, supporters, sponsors and commercial partners. I look forward to welcoming you all again to Emirates Stadium over the course of the new season.

FINANCIAL REVIEW

K. J. Friar, Managing Director, 18 September 2008

The results for the year show a very satisfactory outcome and provide a further confirmation of the strong financial position which the Group occupies following its move to Emirates Stadium.

Overall the Group increased its turnover from £200.8 million to £223.0 million and recorded a profit before taxation for the year of £36.7 million compared with £5.6 million (stated after exceptional charges of £21.4 million) in the previous year (see **Tables 1** and **4**).

Continued growth in revenue and profit in our core football business, including the benefit of the new Premier League TV contracts for season 2007/08, was balanced by a year of lower sales activity and a break-even operating return in the Group's property development business. The results of the football and property development segments will be considered in more detail later in this review.

In terms of the Group's balance sheet, the most significant change reflects the progress made toward completion of the Highbury Square residential development and the investment in this project was the main reason that the carrying value of development property stocks increased during the year to £188.0 million (2007 – £100.1 million).

Table 1   Financial Overview

	2008 £m	2007 £m
Group turnover	223.0	200.8
Operating profit before depreciation and player trading	59.6	51.2
Player trading	5.2	0.2
Depreciation	(11.6)	(9.6)
Joint venture	0.5	0.4
Ordinary finance charges	(17.0)	(15.3)
Profit before tax and exceptional items	36.7	26.9
Profit before tax after exceptional items	36.7	5.6

Source: Arsenal Football Club. Used with permission.

The Group's overall net debt position rose to £318.1 million (2007 – £268.2 million). This increase in debt, which was anticipated both in last year's annual report and this year's interim statement, reflects the loans drawn down in funding the Highbury Square construction works. This level of net debt is expected to represent a peak for the Group with the level diminishing throughout 2008/09 as sale completions occur at Highbury Square.

The Highbury Square bank loan is included, on the basis of its projected repayment profile from receipts of sale completions, as part of creditors falling due within one year although the actual term date for the repayment of this loan facility extends to April 2010 (see **Table 2**).

Football Segment

The football business increased its turnover to £207.7 million (2007 – £177.0 million). This increase was mainly driven by the new Premier League domestic and overseas TV deals. The uplift in the value of these contracts, together with the levels of live coverage associated with our prominent challenge for the title and favourable exchange rates on £:_conversion of UEFA Champions League distributions to the quarter final stage, meant that total broadcasting revenues rose by some £24 million to in excess of £68 million. The main component of our turnover continues to be gate and match day revenue which at £94.6 million (2007 – £90.6 million) represents some 45% of total football revenues and 42% of the Group's total revenues. There were 28 first team home fixtures in season 2007/08 which is one more than in the previous year and the average attendance was 59,720 (2007 – 59,850). We have been very successful in generating event income from our new home outside of the competitive first team fixture list; during the year Emirates Stadium hosted the inaugural Emirates Cup pre-season tournament which generated more than £4 million of ticket sales over two days, an international friendly fixture between Brazil and Sweden and two Bruce Springsteen concerts.

The continued growth in our retail turnover to £13.1 million (2007 – £12.1 million) and commercial revenues to £31.3 million (2007 – £29.5 million) has been referred to in the Commercial Partners section of the Chairman's Report.

We remain firmly committed to sustained investment in the development of the playing squad in a market-place where the income from the new Premier League TV contracts has inevitably created a significant upward pressure on both transfer prices and players' wage expectations. During the year we have improved and extended the contract terms of a large number of first team players and, of course, of Arsène Wenger himself. As a result, for the first time, the Group's wage bill has exceeded nine figures at £101.3 million (2007 – £89.7 million). The wage/turnover

Table 2   Segmental Operating Results

	2008 (£m)	2007 (£m)
Football		
Turnover	207.7	177.0
Operating profit*	59.6	42.2
Profit before tax and exceptional items	39.7	20.8
Property development		
Turnover	15.3	23.8
Operating profit*	—	9.0
(Loss)/profit before tax and exceptional items	(3.0)	6.1
Group		
Turnover	223.0	200.8
Operating profit*	59.6	51.2
Profit before tax and exceptional items	36.7	26.9

*Operating profit before depreciation and player trading costs.
Source: Arsenal Football Club. Used with permission.

ratio for the year, on a football segment basis, remained broadly stable at 48.8% (2007 – 50.6%) and continues to fall within our target range.

Taking into account these changes in revenues and operating costs, the operating profit (before depreciation and player trading) from football increased to £59.6 million (2007 – £42.2 million).

Property Segment

Revenue in the property segment fell to £15.3 million (2007 – £23.8 million) as sales activity was limited to the granting of certain leasehold interests and contracting work within the social housing element of the Highbury Square development. The previous year contained the sale of a major development site at Drayton Park.

Profit from this Highbury Square sales activity was balanced by the carrying costs of our development site at Queensland Road such that the overall operating result from property was break-even (2007 – profit of £9.0 million).

We have now secured all of the land interests in the Queensland Road site, which lies to the south of Emirates Stadium, and we continue to progress the design of an appropriate redevelopment scheme and detailed permission for the site. This is proving to be a complex process—blending a mix of residential, commercial and regenerative elements—and we will not be able to finalise an on-sale of the site until it is complete.

Construction work at the Group's main development site, Highbury Square, has continued at an intensive level throughout the year and remains very much on a schedule which will see the completion of the majority of the residential units over the next year. We are, of course, mindful and vigilant of the difficult conditions, which currently exist in the property and mortgage markets in general. That said, we remain confident that Highbury Square represents a genuinely unique residential scheme in an excellent location. This view is supported by the sales position to date, which continues to be positive. We have so far marketed 655 of the development's 680 private residential apartments and 598 of these are the subject of exchanged sale contracts. The first wave of 65 finished apartments in the South Stand was released at the end of July and sales have so far completed on apartments having a revenue value of £18.7 million. Sales as achieved will be included in the Group's 2008/09 financial results.

Player Trading

A profit of £26.5 million (2007 – £18.5 million) from the sale of player registrations means that overall player trading produced a surplus of £5.2 million for the year (2007 – £0.2 million).

The main contributions to the disposal profit came from the sales of Thierry Henry, Freddie Ljungberg, Jose Antonio Reyes, Jeremie Aliadiere and Lassana Diarra which I believe highlights the fact that selling players at a profit

is a by-product of Arsène Wenger's astute management of the long-term development of the playing squad rather than an objective in itself. The terms of certain past sales mean that we continue to gain additional fees as a number of former players, such as Fabrice Muamba and David Bentley, achieve success in their post-Arsenal careers.

The Board's policy continues to be that the proceeds of any player sales are always made available for re-investment back into the development of the team.

Finance Charges

The net interest charge for the year was £17.0 million (2007 – £15.3 million of ordinary charges and £21.4 million of exceptional charges). The increase reflects a full year's charge on the stadium financing bonds, whereas in the previous year interest costs on this debt were capitalised up to the date of Emirates Stadium's opening.

Finance costs of £5.0 million attributable to bank loans drawn specifically to fund property development expenditure during the year were capitalised within property development stocks.

Profit After Tax

The tax charge for the period was £10.9 million (2007 – £2.8 million). The effective rate of tax at 29.8% is impacted by the change in the rate of corporation tax from 30% to 28% for the last two months of the financial year and the conversion of the Group's deferred tax provisions to this new rate of tax.

The retained profit for the year of £25.7 million (2007 – £2.8 million) was the Group's second best ever financial result, bettered only by 2000/01 which was the year in which the Group reported exceptional profits from the part sale of Arsenal.com.

Cash Flow and Treasury

In order to properly review the Group's cash flow for the year it is necessary to separate out the investment in property development and the related bank funding (see **Table 3**).

The positive cash flow for the year means that the Group had total cash balances of £93.3 million at 31 May 2008 (2007 – £73.9 million). Whilst this is clearly a very healthy position it should be remembered that there is a strong element of seasonality to the Group's operational cash flow with season ticket renewals during May having a positive impact. In addition, balances of £31.5 million (2007 – £32.9 million) within the total cash position are debt service bank deposits which form part of the security for the Group's listed bonds and the use of these deposits is restricted.

As mentioned above the Group's overall net debt position rose to an overall £318.1 million (2007 – £268.2 million) and this was an expected increase given the use of bank debt to fund the construction works at Highbury Square. . . .

Table 3   Cash Flow

	£m
Cash from operations before property stock	61.9
Investment in property stock	(82.9)
Bank loan funding of property stock	74.9
	(8.0)
Net receipt from sale of players	4.0
Payment of taxation	(4.2)
Investment in fixed assets	(6.9)
Net interest payments	(19.7)
Repayment of debt	(7.7)
	(27.4)
Increase in year-end cash	**19.4**

Source: Arsenal Football Club. Used with permission.

The largest part of the Group's debt is £250.2 million of long-term bonds with fixed rates of interest which have been in place since the refinancing exercise completed in the summer of 2006. A repayment of £5.0 million was made during the year in accordance with the terms of the bonds. The annual debt service costs for these bonds, including repayment of capital, is approximately £20 million and this figure must always be considered in the context of the significantly increased levels of football operating profit which the Group is achieving following the move to Emirates Stadium.

The main element of property development financing is the Highbury Square loan balance which was £133.5 million at the balance sheet date (2007 – £62.9 million). This loan, which is repayable from the sale proceeds of the development, is ring-fenced from the Group's football activities and the related financing arrangements. Some 73% of this loan balance is at fixed rate by virtue of interest rate swaps in place for that purpose.

The Group's debt facilities are expected to be sufficient to fund the completion of its property development projects for the foreseeable future and its operations generally for the long-term. These facilities were put in place before the start of the 2007/08 financial year and, accordingly, the Group has not, to date, experienced any significant direct adverse impact on its financing arrangements as a result of the "credit crunch" and the related turbulence in the financial markets.

Risks and Uncertainties

There are a number of potential risks and uncertainties which could have a material impact on the Group's long term performance. These risks and uncertainties are monitored by the Board on a regular basis.

Football

The Group's income is affected by the performance and popularity of the first team. Significant sources of revenue are derived from strong performances in the Premier League, FA Cup and UEFA Champions League (or UEFA Cup) and the level of income will vary dependent upon the team's participation and performance in these competitions. A significant amount of the Group's income is derived from ticket sales to individual and corporate supporters who attend matches involving the first team at Emirates Stadium and elsewhere. The level of attendance may be influenced by a number of factors including the level of success of the team, admission prices, broadcasting coverage and general economic conditions. Demand for tickets is currently very high and all season tickets, including approximately 7,000 premium Club Level seats and 150 executive boxes have been sold out for the 2008/09 season. The Club currently has in excess of 47,000 supporters on its waiting list for season tickets.

The first team's success is significantly influenced by the performance of members of the playing staff and the performance of the football management team and, accordingly, the ability to attract and retain the highest quality coaching and playing staff is important to the Group's business prospects. The Group insures the members of its first team squad but such insurances may not be sufficient to mitigate all financial loss, such as fees from a potential transfer, in the event of a serious injury. The Group enters into employment contracts with each of its key personnel with a view to securing their services for the term of the contract. However, the Group operates in a highly competitive market in both domestic and European competition and retention of personnel cannot be guaranteed. In addition, the activities of the Group's main competitors can determine trends for market rates for transfers and wages that the Group may be required to follow in order to maintain the strength of its first team squad.

The Club is regulated by the rules of the FA, Premier League, UEFA and FIFA. Any change to FA, Premier League, UEFA and FIFA regulations in future could have an impact on the Group as the regulations cover areas such as: the format of competitions, the division of broadcasting income, the eligibility of players and the operation of the transfer market. The Group monitors its compliance with all applicable rules and regulations on a continuous basis and also monitors and considers the impact of any potential changes.

Commercial Relationship

The Group derives a significant amount of revenue from sponsorship and other commercial relationships. The Group aims to enter into long term arrangements with its key commercial partners thus securing certainty over the main components of its commercial income in the medium term. The Group's most important commercial contracts are: naming rights and shirt sponsorship contracts with Emirates Airline which expire in 2021 and 2014 respectively, a kit sponsorship contract with Nike which expires in 2011 and a catering contract with Delaware North which expires in 2026.

Table 4   Five-Year Summary

	2004	2005	2006	2007	2008
Profit and Loss Account	£000's	£000's	£000's	£000's	£000's
Group Turnover	156,887	138,395	137,237	200,843	222,970
Operating profit before player trading and exceptional costs	36,162	32,631	11,323	41,614	48,018
Operating expenses—player registrations	(19,637)	(14,993)	(15,262)	(18,238)	(21,285)
Operating expenses—exceptional	(6,269)	—	—	—	—
Operating profit/(loss)	10,256	17,638	(3,939)	23,376	26,733
Share of results of joint venture	(67)	204	499	435	469
Profit on disposal of player registrations	2,282	2,894	19,150	18,467	26,458
Net interest—ordinary	(1,894)	(1,471)	175	(15,304)	(16,992)
Net interest—exceptional	—	—	—	(21,401)	—
Profit before tax	10,577	19,265	15,885	5,573	36,668
Profit after tax	8,152	8,293	7,902	2,816	25,726
Earnings per share	£138.29	£138.91	£127.01	£45.26	£413.49
Earnings per share (excluding exceptional items)	£138.29	£138.91	£127.01	£286.05	£413.49
Balance Sheet					
Tangible fixed assets	209,615	314.822	451,501	455,376	449,923
Intangible fixed assets	34,989	28,983	66,555	64,671	55,665
Net current assets/(liabilities)	(7,479)	28,149	(38,166)	61,231	(5,527)
Long term creditors and provisions	(152,762)	(249,298)	(349,332)	(447,904)	(340,961)
Net assets	84,363	122,656	130,558	133,374	159,100
Share capital	59	62	62	62	62
Share premium	—	29,997	29,997	29,997	29,997
Reserves	84,304	92,597	100,499	103,315	129,041
Shareholders' funds	84,363	122,656	130,558	133,374	159,100
Net assets per share	£1,431.17	£1,971.45	£2,098.46	£2,143.69	£2,557.18
Playing record					
FA Premier League	Champions	2nd	4th	4th	3rd
FA Challenge Cup	Semi-finalists	Winners	4th round	5th round	5th round
Europe	Quarter finals Champions League	1st K/O round Champions League	Finalist Champions League	1st K/O round Champions League	Quarter finals Champions League

Source: Arsenal Football Club. Used with permission.

Broadcasting and certain other revenues are derived from contracts which are currently centrally negotiated by the Premier League and, in respect of European competition, by UEFA; the Group does not have any direct influence, alone, on the outcome of the relevant contract negotiations. The Premier League currently sells its TV rights on a 3 year contract basis and 2007/08 was the first year of a new contract.

Foreign Exchange and Treasury

The Group enters into a number of transactions, relating mainly to its participation in European competition and player transfers, which create exposure to movements in foreign exchange. The Group monitors this foreign exchange exposure on a continuous basis and has facilities in place to hedge any significant exposure in its currency receivables and payables.

The Group's policy is to eliminate, as far as possible, all of the interest rate risk which attaches to its outstanding debt finance balances. Where debt balances are subject to floating rates of interest the Group enters into interest rate swaps which serve to fix the rate of interest.

The financing arrangements for the Group's football and property business segments operate independently of each other. As a consequence, the transfer of cash between the two business segments can, in general, only occur in circumstances governed by the terms of the applicable bank/debt finance arrangements. In addition, certain minimum bank deposits are required to be maintained as part of the security for the Group's bank/debt finance balances. The Group monitors its compliance with the applicable terms of its bank/debt finance arrangements on a continuous basis and regularly reviews its forecast cash flow to ensure that both its business segments hold an appropriate level of bank funds at all times.

Where income from commercial contracts or other material transactions, such as player transfers, is receivable on an installment basis then the Group will usually seek to obtain an appropriate bank or similar guarantee.

Property

The Group expects to derive income from the sale of certain property development sites over the next two years—the main element of this being the sale of some 680 private residential apartments at Highbury Square. The achievement of these sales may be affected by the current downturn in the UK property market and the difficult conditions in the mortgage lending sector. The Group is monitoring the position closely.

The bank facilities which the Group has used to fund the Highbury Square development are ring-fenced from the financing of the football segment of the business. The final profits and cash to be released to the Club on completion of these property developments has not been budgeted by the Club and will be treated as a "bonus" when received—accordingly, there is no commitment to use any such profits and cash at any specific time for any specific purpose.

Outlook

The Group has made a sound start to the new financial year. We have made a modest ticket price increase for season 2008/09 (2.8% on a weighted average basis) following which general admission and Club Tier season ticket renewals have once again been at the maximum level.

The second staging of the Emirates Cup has again proved to be a great commercial success with near capacity attendances to both days of the competition.

The sales of Alexander Hleb, Justin Hoyte and a sell-on share receivable on David Bentley's transfer from Blackburn will make a significant contribution to the profits to be reported on the sale of player registrations.

The most significant aspect of the 2008/09 results will be the sale completions to be reported on Highbury Square. Legal completions from the first phase of 65 apartments, released at the end of July, have so far generated sales proceeds of £18.7 million. We will continue to monitor sales closely over the coming months as the construction of more units is completed ready for release. The sales proceeds will be used to fund construction costs to complete and to repay the Highbury Square loan facility and this will result in a reduction in the Group's overall net debt.

In conclusion, both the property and football business segments start the 2008/09 year in a strong financial position, providing the sound financial platform which underpins our long-term strategy for the Club.

THE IMPACT OF THE FLAT WORLD ON PLAYER TRANSFERS IN MAJOR LEAGUE BASEBALL

Scott R. Rosner and William T. Conroy

I. INTRODUCTION

Globalization has indeed made the world "flat," and the sports industry is no exception. In particular, the exporting of the business of United States-based professional sports leagues is both desirable and irreversible. Throughout the last two decades, the leagues have attempted with varying degrees of success to create global product markets. The impact of this internationalization can be seen everywhere—from the success of the World Baseball Classic in 2006 and 2009 to the exploding popularity that has led the National Basketball Association ("NBA") to announce the creation of NBA China, a Chinese subsidiary league in partnership with Disney and other local partners. Perhaps the most significant of these effects, however, is that the current player pool for most of the top professional sports leagues is no longer domestic in nature. This sea change is well underway, with international players comprising significant portions of current professional sports rosters across the sporting spectrum. There can be no doubt that the labor markets in professional sports are now global in nature. Partly as a result of domestic market saturation, and partly as a result of the sports leagues attempting to become export products, individual clubs are forced to look—and think—globally when seeking top-notch talent. The importation of playing talent into the United States-based professional sports leagues facilitates the exportation of these leagues, as fan affinity in a foreign market is likely to be greater when there is a player from that market in the league. The hope is that the establishment of global labor markets will help the leagues create global product markets.

Major League Baseball ("MLB") has a unique approach to this global labor scene. This approach is evidenced by the system that was created to transfer players' rights from Japanese professional baseball (known as Nippon Professional Baseball ["NPB"]) to MLB teams following the departures of several high profile players in the mid-1990's. Over the last 13 years, a system has evolved whereby the transfer of players from the NPB to MLB is governed by a jointly developed process that allows owners of NPB teams to receive compensation for their less experienced players who are still under contract but desire to leave for MLB before they are eligible for free agency in NPB. When a player in the Japanese professional baseball leagues is under contract with a team in NPB and wishes to sign a contract with an MLB team, he must go through the "posting process."

PLAYER MARKETS

High-profile players such as Ichiro Suzuki and Daisuke Matsuzaka have joined MLB through this system; as such, there has been an understandable amount of public attention directed towards the posting process. While significant media attention was focused on the staggering amount the Boston Red Sox paid for the right to negotiate with Matsuzaka—$51,111,111.11—there has been scant attention paid to the suboptimal nature of the posting process for at least two of the three stakeholders. The issue of player transfers is pressing in the National Hockey League ("NHL") as well, which means that two of the three North American-based professional sports leagues that draw from a global player pool are having issues regarding their player transfer system; the National Football League has struggled to establish an international pipeline for player talent. Furthermore, there are several alternatives to the posting process that can address the suboptimality of the status quo. A more efficient posting process is important for historical reasons as well, with the Negro Leagues serving as an example of how an inadequate player transfer system can help lead to the demise of a league.

II. THE POSTING PROCESS

A. History

A brief examination of the history of the posting process, and the events that led to its development, is essential for understanding why the process exists in its current form. The movement of three players—Hideo Nomo, Hideki Irabu, and Alfonso Soriano—from NPB to MLB spurred the two leagues to complete a formal arrangement for the transfer of players. In short, the posting system was devised to try to keep Japanese players from leaving NPB in the first place and to provide compensation to the NPB teams in the event that they did.

The first Japanese player to appear in MLB was Masanori Murakami. His debut was the product of an exchange program between the Nankai Hawks and the San Francisco Giants, whereby Nankai sent three players to play in the Giants' minor league system in 1964. Murakami performed so well in the minor leagues that the Giants promoted him to the major leagues later that season, where his continued strong performance led the Giants to seek his return for the 1965 season. While Nankai originally balked at the prospect of doing so, they ultimately capitulated on the condition that Murakami be permanently returned after the season. Despite a successful 1965 season, he was returned to the Japanese team. This led to a "Gentlemen's Agreement" between MLB and NPB in 1967, whereby MLB teams agreed that they would not sign NPB players unless they were free agents. Though a number of American players pursued careers in NPB (typically after their MLB careers were over), no

Japanese players moved to MLB until Hideo Nomo left the Kintetsu Buffaloes for the Los Angeles Dodgers in 1995.

Nomo was the first bona fide star to move to MLB from the Japanese professional leagues. In 1995, he used a legal technicality in his NPB contract in order to "retire" from his NPB team at the age of 26 so that he could avoid the free agency restrictions of his native baseball league. Nomo's retirement allowed him to sign a three-year, $4.3 million contract with the Los Angeles Dodgers, a lucrative move that understandably had a profound impact on both the MLB and NPB franchise owners.

More significant than the Nomo retirement, at least in terms of providing the impetus for an agreement for the transfer of players from NPB to MLB, was the movement of star pitcher Hideki Irabu from the Chiba Lotte Marines to the New York Yankees. Prior to the existence of the formal posting process, the relationship between NPB teams and MLB teams was done on an ad hoc basis, with the parties sometimes developing "working agreements" between individual clubs. At the time, Irabu's Japanese team, the Marines, had developed a working agreement with the San Diego Padres of MLB; the working agreement gave the Padres the right to buy the exclusive right to negotiate a contract with Irabu—which the Padres did. However, Irabu was unaware of his sale until it was completed without his permission; he then declared his intention to only play for the New York Yankees, ultimately maintaining this stance until a trade was worked out between the Padres and Yankees before the 1997 season. Again, the transfer of the Japanese player, and the way in which the process transpired, raised sufficient concern on both sides of the Pacific to move the two leagues closer to a formal arrangement.

Alfonso Soriano was the protagonist in the final player transfer to occur prior to the adoption of the posting system. In 1998, following the inability of Soriano to reach agreement on a contract with his NPB club, Hiroshima Toyo Carp, he attempted to retire, much in the same way Nomo had done three years earlier. But NPB had closed the loophole that Nomo had exploited previously, and the Japanese league believed that it had exclusive rights to Soriano. Over the protests, threats and objections of the NPB, Soriano signed a contract with the New York Yankees after a declaration by the MLB Commissioner's Office that Soriano was, in fact, a free agent capable of signing with any team he desired. For the NPB, this was a clear-cut sign that a formal agreement between NPB and MLB was the only way to stem the tide of wholesale player defections to MLB.

B. Description of the Posting System

There are three primary actors in the posting process who have a direct stake in the resulting outcome—the NPB team that "transfers" the player, the MLB team to whom the player is transferred, and the player himself. (There is potentially a fourth actor, the player's agent, but because the agent's interests are aligned with the player's in the posting scenario, we consider just the player here.) Japanese players do not become international free agents until after they have played nine years in NPB; after their ninth year, they are free to sign a contract with any club, including those in MLB, without any transfer fee paid to the former NPB club. Conversely, any Japanese player who has not yet attained nine years of experience in NPB may not sign with an MLB team, because that player has not yet attained international free agent status under NPB rules. However, a player with less than nine years of experience who wishes to sign with a MLB team may ask his Japanese team to "post" him. If the NPB team agrees to post the player, it notifies the office of the NPB Commissioner, who then notifies the MLB Commissioner, at which point all 30 MLB teams are notified that the player is available.

Once individual MLB teams have been notified that the player has been posted, a four-day period begins during which MLB teams compete in a sealed-bid auction for the exclusive right to negotiate a contract with the posted player. After the expiration of the four-day period, all bids are collected by the MLB Commissioner's office and opened. The NPB team is then notified of the amount of the highest bid (but not the identity of the MLB team) and has a four-day period to decide whether or not the winning bid will be accepted, though in each situation where a bid has been submitted by a MLB team, the highest bid has always been accepted by the NPB team. The amount of the bid is considered the "transfer fee" associated with the movement of the player. Following the acceptance of the highest bid by the NPB club, the MLB team that won the auction then has 30 days to negotiate a contract with the player. Should the contract negotiation yield a signed deal, the amount of the transfer fee is then paid to the NPB team by the MLB team, and the player becomes a member of the MLB team. If the player and the MLB team do not come to an agreement, however, the NPB team does not receive the transfer fee and the player returns to the NPB under the terms of his original contract with the club. It should be noted that the posting system is unilateral in nature, as it does not apply to MLB players seeking employment in Japan.

Table 5 is a complete representation of each player that has been successfully posted, along with the MLB team that "won" the auction and the price that team paid for the player.

An example of the posting process is illustrative. Matsuzaka, a star pitcher for the Seibu Lions, had established himself as the premier Japanese professional baseball pitcher. The Boston Red Sox outbid both the New York Mets (who bid a reported $39 million) and the New York Yankees (who bid $33 million) by determining that the right to negotiate with Matsuzaka was worth an unprecedented $51.1 million. Following the announcement of the Red Sox' winning bid, the team then had 30 days during which it could negotiate a player contract with Matsuzaka, with the Seibu Lions receiving the $51.1M upon the signing of the contract between the pitcher and the Red Sox. Ultimately, the Red

Table 5   Posting Fees Paid by MLB

Date	Player	MLB Team	Transfer Fee ($US)
2/1999	Alejandro Quezada	Cincinnati Reds	$400,001
11/2000	Ichiro Suzuki	Seattle Mariners	$13,125,000
1/2003	Kazuhisa Ishii	Los Angeles Dodgers	$11,260,000
2/2003	Ramon Ramirez	San Diego Padres	$300,050
11/2003	Akinori Otsuka	San Diego Padres	$300,000
1/2005	Norihiro Nakamura	Los Angeles Dodgers	Unknown
12/2005	Shinji Mori	Tampa Bay Devil Rays	$1,000,000
11/2006	Daisuke Matsuzaka	Boston Red Sox	$51,111,111.11
11/2006	Akinori Iwamura	Tampa Bay Devil Rays	$4,500,000
11/2006	Kei Igawa	New York Yankees	$26,000,194

Source: Modified from Baseball-Reference.com, Posting System, http://www.baseball-reference.com/bpv/index.php?title=Posting_system. Previously published in *University of Pennsylvania Journal of Business Law.* Used with permission.

Sox and Matsuzaka agreed upon a 6-year, $52M contract, putting the total expenditures by the Red Sox to $103.1M for <u>one</u> player.

III.   THE SUBOPTIMALITIES OF THE POSTING PROCESS

There are several reasons why the posting process is suboptimal, including: 1) it creates windfall profits for the NPB transfer team; 2) the first-price-sealed-bid auction inflates winning bids by MLB teams; 3) individual players are unable to realize their full market value in contract negotiations; 4) individual players have no ability to choose the MLB teams for which they play; 5) the system could adversely affect the competitive balance of MLB teams; and 6) the loss of marquee players negatively impacts NPB as a league. This section is divided into five sub-sections that each address the posting process and its impact on the actors involved. These sections also explore whether recent developments will alter the relationship between MLB and NPB.

[*Ed. Note: Authors' discussion of the windfall for NPB clubs and lost player value and freedom of choice are omitted.*]

. . . .

C.   The Impact on MLB Competitive Balance

If large-revenue MLB teams are the only teams with the financial means to successfully bid on Japanese players,

especially when the posting fees for certain players reach into the $50 million territory, only certain teams will have access to this market for players. Of the 10 players who have been successfully posted and transferred to MLB teams, only five have been transferred to large-revenue teams. However, larger revenue clubs have paid the four largest fees, suggesting that they have increased access to the most desirable talent. While the empirical evidence seems to suggest that this issue has not yet reached the level of being a problem requiring immediate attention, the manner in which the Matsuzaka auction was won raises concern for some. If only the largest revenue teams have access to NPB stars in the posting process, then there is at least the possibility that an unbalanced distribution of talent in MLB could result. This is particularly concerning because the posting fee paid by the MLB team does not count against the team's luxury tax number, and thus, is not subject to a luxury tax penalty. Had the Red Sox signed a free agent pitcher from another team within MLB for the $103.1 million they paid for Matsuzaka, all $103.1 million of that contract would have been subject to the 40% luxury tax aimed at leveling the playing field in MLB. However, because $51.1 million of the money paid for Matsuzaka was allocated as a transfer fee (and not subject to the luxury tax), the Red Sox luxury tax figure for the Matsuzaka signing was only $52 million. This legal loophole circumvents precisely the problem that the luxury tax was aimed at fixing, and furthers the problem of competitive balance in MLB. Given that signing a player from NPB has less of a luxury tax impact than signing a similar MLB free agent, there is credible risk that only large-market MLB teams will have access to the posting process.

D.   The Impact on Japanese Baseball

While the NPB team that successfully posts a player receives short-term windfall profits by doing so, the additive loss of marquee players has a deleterious effect on the overall NPB league product and on the medium and long-term business of the posting team itself. The migration of Nomo to the Los Angeles Dodgers had a strong influence on both Japanese baseball and MLB. Though Nomo was initially treated as a pariah when he left NPB for America, fans grew to accept his departure and tuned in en masse as the NHK public television network broadcast his games live throughout Japan. His success with the Dodgers increased Japanese interest in MLB and created opportunities for future Japanese players to play in the United States. Since Nomo's 1995 debut, 36 Japanese players have played in MLB regular season games, including 16 who were on MLB Opening Day rosters in 2008.

Legendary Japanese baseball player Sadaharu Oh stated, "It's been a great plus for baseball in Japan. Thanks to Nomo, kids in high school and junior high now have dreams of playing in M.L.B. Going to America and directly competing over there is a much better way to improve the level of play here than the good-will-type all-star exhibition series they used to hold when I was a player. Japan's still inferior to America in baseball, but as more players aim to play over there, the gap will continue to close." With respect to how Nomo created opportunities for Japanese players in the United States, Oh stated, "He showed that the level of Japanese baseball was not that different from the major leagues."

Though Nomo's successful MLB career positively impacted baseball in both Japan and the United States, Japanese baseball has suffered from the cumulative effect of the loss of a number of popular star players to MLB through both free agency and posting. Despite three NPB teams generating a combined $81.6 million by posting Matsuzaka, Igawa and Iwamura prior to the 2007 season, there was despair at the NPB offices over losing such popular players. There seems to be some recognition that the pursuit of the short-term revenues generated by posting could lead to a long-term decrease in revenues. . . .

With NPB players leaving for the challenge of playing in MLB, as well as its increased salaries and better living and working conditions, NPB is likely to lose even more of its players to MLB in the future. The high fee paid for Matsuzaka and his potential for long-term MLB success is a portent for Japanese baseball, as the fact that the MVP of the Japanese national team left with great fanfare for a successful MLB team that paid him nearly what the top MLB free agent pitchers in the market secured is likely to lead to more NPB players pursuing careers in MLB, which will only further the uncertainty surrounding the future of NPB. This is heightened by the fact that there is no longer a stigma attached to players leaving NPB and fans are okay with it, as they can still watch their favorite Japanese players play on television or online rather than in person. In fact, most Japanese fans are proud of these transfers' accomplishments and identify with them, rather than feeling resentment. It is simply not practical to expect that MLB teams will cease their pursuit of Japanese players, just as it was impractical to think that Japanese automakers would not pursue the U.S. market. To that end, MLB scouts have descended upon Japan's high schools, colleges and leagues in search of talent. Japanese baseball officials are hopeful that a role model effect might be possible, with more of the best young Japanese athletes choosing to play baseball because of the success of the Japanese players in MLB.

The NPB team receives a windfall profit when it successfully posts one of its players. However, this short-term cash infusion may be offset by the subsequent impact of the loss of the player on the team's on-field performance, attendance, public relations and television ratings—all of which could have a deleterious effect on the team's revenues in the medium to long-term. It is reasonable to expect that an NPB team would be negatively impacted in both winning percentage and attendance when a player is lost through the posting system, as the team is losing what is typically a high-caliber player who helped the team win games and served as a gate attraction for the fan base. The economic benefits that NPB clubs receive from the transfer fees are not necessarily conducive to helping their future on-field success. Japanese teams tend to be more focused on the short-term than on the long-term because of their corporate ownership. As a result, the posting fees received by the teams are either filtered back to the parent corporation or are intended to provide the team with a needed infusion of capital to reduce what is usually a significant cash shortfall; typically, the posting fee is not intended to be used to sign another player in the hope of replacing the lost production of the defected player. Unlike in MLB, where a team may seek to replace a star lost through free agency with another high caliber player, the limited movement of impact free agents seen in NPB makes it very difficult to replace a lost player even if the team and its parent corporation were so inclined.

A closer look at the impact of losing a posted player on the on-field performance of their former NPB team yields mixed results. It is difficult to estimate the impact of the loss of these players on the teams' win-loss record, as there are clearly a number of other factors that affected their performance. Nonetheless, of the 10 players who have been successfully posted, the former team had a worse record in the season immediately after the posting on six occasions and a better record on four occasions. The impact of losing players through the posting system on the attendance of their former NPB teams is also difficult to judge with accuracy because of the lack of reporting standards prior to the 2005 season. Before 2005, NPB teams simply estimated attendance, and these estimates were typically much higher than the actual number of fans who appeared to be in the stadium. It is also reasonable to expect that the team would suffer in its public relations as a result of transferring a star performer. Much as American sports fans protest the loss of a favorite player to another team via free agency by voicing their anger at the team, a Japanese team that posts a player risks incurring the wrath of its fan base. If this manifests itself in fans staying away from the ballpark and not tuning into television broadcasts, then the team's revenues will suffer. While fans tend to be forgiving over the occasional loss of a player, a team that regularly posts players will not be as fortunate.

Finally, the television ratings for NPB games have fallen significantly as an increasing number of its better players have moved to Major League Baseball. Meanwhile, MLB games are broadcast daily in Japan and MLB games receive detailed coverage in Japanese newspapers, with many Japanese fans following MLB closely. More people in Japan watched Matsuzaka pitch his Red Sox games in 2007—all of which were broadcast on NHK-BS satellite that is available in 13 million Japanese homes—than watched his televised Seibu Lions games in 2006 (which was estimated to be 100,000 fans). MLB has successfully monetized this increased interest, resulting in nearly 70 percent of MLB's international revenue coming from Japan. MLB currently receives close to $100 million annually from the Japanese marketplace—slightly less than $50 million from Dentsu (a Japanese advertising agency) and NHK in television rights fees, and approximately $50 million additionally from licensing, sponsorships and advertising.

There is an element of belief that a continual draining of the talent pool in NPB will ultimately lead to the demise of NPB. It is far more likely, however, that with the appropriate reforms to its currently flawed operating structure, NPB will endure; there remains a strong fan interest in and passion for the league, it has a long history, it still produces numerous high quality players, and it may be the only country in the world where baseball is still the national sport. To retain their viability, however, the NPB and its teams need to alter their priorities and organization, as currently their structures are suboptimal for both business and player development.

NPB teams are operated in a manner that is quite different than their MLB counterparts. Rather than being stand alone companies, as are the vast majority of professional sports teams in MLB, Japanese baseball teams are part of larger corporations that use the team to market and sell their products. For example, the Hokkaido Nippon Ham Fighters are owned by the Nippon Ham meat processing company and exist primarily for the purpose of selling its products. The underlying rationale for using the baseball teams in this fashion is that Japanese companies believe it is cheaper to purchase and run the team and get in the media every day through the coverage of the games than it is to advertise on Japanese prime-time television. This is reflected in the selection and deployment of their managerial talent. Unlike their American counterparts, Japanese baseball club executives typically are not baseball experts; instead, they rotate through the team from the parent company's headquarters. The league's fragmented structure is reflected in its flat growth over the past two decades, with attendance hovering around 20 million per year and total league revenues at approximately $1 billion. Historically, two NPB teams have done well on and off the field; the Yomiuri Giants and Hanshin Tigers both draw 3 million fans annually and are estimated to generate ¥20 billion annually, primarily through gate receipts and television rights fees. The teams hand their profits over to their parent companies. Most other teams suffer operating losses even when successful on the field. For example, the Nippon Ham Fighters won the title in 2006, drew 1,635,410 fans and still needed a multimillion dollar bailout from its parent corporation. The Chiba Lotte Marines were estimated to have lost over ¥2 billion in 2005 when it won the title and the Chunichi Dragons won the Central League pennant in both 2005 and 2006, but were estimated to have lost more than ¥10 billion during that period. The decentralized league structure—where there is little cooperation between the teams, no league-wide media, marketing or licensing contracts, and no revenue sharing—results in stark contrasts between revenues generated by individual teams. The revenue disparity is evidenced by television rights deals: Yomiuri sold its 2006 television rights fees for ¥100 million per game and Hanshin for ¥50 million,

but Chunichi did the same for only ¥10 million, Nippon Ham for ¥3.8 million, Seibu Lions for ¥700,000 and Chiba Lotte a mere ¥150,000. Critics place the blame for this anachronistic league business model on the Yomiuri Corporation's unwillingness to cede control as the most powerful team in NPB.

Another area in which there is a significant difference between MLB and NPB is in its playing facilities. Whereas most MLB teams either own their own playing facilities or have very favorable lease agreements that allow them to control most of the revenue generated by the facility, NPB teams generally do not own their stadiums (though Seibu does and it still loses money) or control ancillary revenue streams such as concessions and sponsorships and must pay hefty rents for their facilities. NPB teams are slowly beginning to become more focused on the business-side of the game. For example, following the lead of the Softbank Hawks, all of the NPB's Pacific League teams are now streaming its home games live over the internet for free, the Chiba Lotte Marines are running pre- and post-game promotions and the league adopted interleague play in 2005 and postseason playoffs leading up to the Japan Series in 2007. In addition, mimicking the longstanding practice of the North American sports leagues that has allowed their media rights fees to grow exponentially over time, all of the Pacific League teams sold their broadcasting rights to a subsidiary of Softbank which in turn, negotiated with broadcasting stations to give licenses. Though the prices agreed in these deals are not made public, the Pacific League should see a long-term increase in its rights fees if the North American leagues are any indication. These efforts are all an attempt to generate more revenues from the on-field product.

There are also significant differences in player development between the Japanese and American professional leagues. Most MLB teams have six American minor league teams with a total of 125–150 players in the farm system at any one time, an arrangement that costs the average MLB team $20 million annually. American minor leaguers spend more time playing games than they do practicing. In contrast, there is comparatively little investment by the NPB teams' parent companies in the minor league system, with each team having only 70 players in minor league system and just one farm team that plays close to 100 games each season. Japanese minor leaguers spend most of their time practicing rather than playing games. While it could be a reflection of different philosophies of player development, it is likely that the NPB parent companies do not want to spend the money on their minor league systems that their American counterparts do. This has a huge impact on player development in Japan and is manifested in a dearth of young stars available to replace players who leave Japan for MLB.

Overall, it appears that NPB is in need of a revamped structure where the clubs are treated as profit-oriented businesses in and of themselves and the league operations are more centralized. In addition, although it is highly likely that the top Japanese players will continue to leave for MLB, if Japan can improve its player development system and NPB its minor leagues so as to develop more highly skilled players, and perhaps complementing them with high quality players from other Asian countries like Taiwan and South Korea, then Japanese culture should maintain its passion for baseball and NPB will be well-positioned to monetize its fan base and remain a viable business. This is reminiscent of the many successful domestic soccer leagues globally; while they cannot compete with the top European leagues in England, Spain, Italy, Germany and France, they remain financially viable nonetheless.

[Ed. Note: Authors' discussion of the possible Tazawa effect omitted.]

. . . .

IV. ALTERNATIVE METHODS OF INTERNATIONAL PLAYER TRANSFER

Various player transfer systems exist to facilitate the global movement of athletes across professional sports leagues. The following describes the various systems for the transfer of professional athletes in basketball, soccer and hockey, all of which are possible alternatives to the current MLB-NPB transfer system.

A. Basketball

The ability for professional basketball players across the world to move to a team in another country is governed by the regulations set out by the world basketball governing body, the International Basketball Federation ("FIBA"). These standards are permissive and focus on facilitation of player transfer. In addition, international players may be drafted to American leagues through an acquisition of rights system.

The governing regulations state that "any basketball player shall have the right to play basketball in any country in the world, within the limits established by [FIBA]. . . ."[1] The process by which this occurs is fairly straightforward. A player seeking transfer to a team in a foreign country must receive a "letter of clearance" from the basketball national governing body in his home country. This letter of clearance details the player's playing history, but also includes an attestation by the player that he has fulfilled "all contractual obligations stipulated in any and all contracts between myself and any team. . . ."[2] Once a player receives the letter of clearance, the only way that the letter can be rejected by the national governing body is if that individual player has not fulfilled his contractual obligations to his transferee team. In essence, the letter of clearance is the final step towards a successful transfer of the player to a team in another country.

As it pertains to the National Basketball Association ("NBA"), the rights to international players may be acquired through the annual NBA Draft, an option not available to MLB teams wishing to acquire players from NPB or much of the rest of the world. This draft is a global one, where individual NBA teams are free to draft any player who meets the requirements of Article X of the NBA Collective Bargaining Agreement. Once the NBA team has drafted the rights to the player, that team has exclusive negotiation rights with that player for a period of one year.

In both of the acquisition situations—where a player requests a letter of clearance to join a foreign team, or where that player is drafted by an NBA team (*after* acquiring the letter of clearance)—the individual player is the party negotiating with his own team for his release from the contract. Perhaps the highest profile international transfer to date is that of Yao Ming. The Chinese star was drafted with the No. 1 pick in 2002 by the Houston Rockets, at which time the Rockets began discussions with Yao's Chinese team for his contractual release (discussions also included the Chinese government, because of Yao's required playing service for the Chinese national team). Ultimately the Rockets paid Yao's former team a $350,000 transfer fee for the ability to sign Yao to a NBA playing contract. Unlike the MLB–NPB transfer agreement, where the acquiring team is bidding for the rights to negotiate with the player (which operates as the buy-out provision of the player's contract), the FIBA system allows for the two teams to directly negotiate with one another, a more efficient process than the first-price bidding. The player transferred to the NBA is then free to negotiate a playing contract within the confines of the NBA's collective bargaining agreement with the team possessing his rights.

B. Hockey
1. Background
The National Hockey League ("NHL") workforce was almost exclusively Canadian until the 1972–73 season when a group of Swedish players broke through and became regular contributors to their teams. The initial influx of European players was limited to Swedes and Finns for approximately 15 years until the fall of the Iron Curtain, when Russian, Czech and Slovakian players began to migrate to the NHL. In the 2007–2008 season, over 33% of the players who appeared on an NHL roster hailed from outside of North America. For international hockey, then, the global labor market makes it critical that a transfer agreement be in place to regulate and control the flow of players across international leagues. The NHL, NHLPA, International Ice Hockey Federation ("IIHF"), and the national hockey federations of Sweden, Finland, Russia, Slovakia, Switzerland, Germany, and the Czech Republic reached their first Player Transfer Agreement in 2001. Covering the 2001–2004 playing seasons, this system regulated the transfer of players from one national league to another, although this transfer happened primarily when players moved from non-North American teams to teams within the NHL. The agreement provided that an NHL team would compensate its European

counterpart whenever a European player was signed. This agreement led to NHL teams paying European teams $28.8 million for the right to sign 185 players during its term. This deal was followed by a two-year agreement that began after the conclusion of the 2004–05 NHL lockout. Notably, however, the Russian Ice Hockey Federation opted not to participate in the agreement due to its dissatisfaction with the amount of financial compensation owed by the NHL team upon signing the player, as well as the limitations on the number of players that could be signed and the deadline for signing such players. This two year deal was followed by an agreement that again excluded the Russian Federation and was scheduled to be in effect from 2007–11. However, the European nations exercised a contractual right to opt out of the deal after the 2007–08 season. As of this writing, no new agreement has been reached and, while there have been no negotiations of late with the Russian Federation, the other European nations are still in talks with the NHL.

2. Problems with the Previous Transfer Agreement

The IIHF Player Transfer Agreement (along with the NHL Collective Bargaining Agreement) governed the global movement of players, with the specific intention of compensating non-NHL teams when their star players left for the riches of the NHL. Players who were not currently under contract to an IIHF team were free to sign with any NHL team that they wished (or any other team for that matter). If, however, an NHL team drafted a player while that player was under contract to an IIHF team (or while an IIHF team held the player's rights) from a federation that had signed the Player Transfer Agreement and the NHL team ultimately signed that player, the NHL paid that country's governing body a flat fee of $200,000 in exchange for that player being free to leave his contract and come to the NHL. This was in addition to the value of the playing contract that the player ultimately signed with the NHL club.

For many European nations and for the Russian Federation in particular, the problem with the previous system was the perceived inadequacy of the payment for players. The flat fee of $200,000 was perceived as insufficient to compensate the former club for the loss of particularly talented star players like Evgeni Malkin and Alexander Ovechkin. Russian Ice Hockey Federation president Vladislav Tretiak stated, "Russian teams would rather lose players to the NHL for nothing than sign a contract that pays them what they consider a disrespectful amount of money." Russia did not sign either the 2005–07 or 2007–11 IIHF–NHL Player Transfer Agreements; as a result, neither the NHL, nor the Russian Federation, nor the players, were bound by the terms of the Transfer Agreement when a Russian player was drafted by an NHL team. Neither Malkin's (2nd overall pick in 2004 NHL Draft) nor Ovechkin's (1st overall pick in 2004 NHL Draft) former teams received any compensation when their star players left for the NHL; instead, the players abruptly left their former employers and the NHL did not

have to compensate their former teams for this loss because no agreement existed. The lack of Russian participation in the Player Transfer Agreement signaled a problem that is the complete opposite of that faced by the NPB and MLB: in hockey, the transferee team receives too little compensation.

Though the controversy centers primarily around compensation, the European federations have other issues surrounding the Player Transfer Agreement. First, the fact that many players signed away from the European leagues languish in the minors without ever making it to the NHL indicates that NHL clubs have been stockpiling young European players in the minor leagues (most European players signed by NHL teams do not ever play in the NHL). In 2007–08, there were 59 European players who signed with NHL teams; six played in the NHL that season, seven were returned to their European teams, and 46 played in North American minor leagues. The underlying reason for this stockpiling is likely a clause in the 2005 NHL–NHLPA collective bargaining agreement that requires European players to be signed within two years of being drafted lest the NHL team lose its rights. The European federations believe that this has a deleterious effect on player development, with young players leaving their home environments prematurely and never reaching their potential. In addition, the European teams lose the services of young talented players who could become attractions in their home countries instead of playing in North American minor leagues for a few seasons. While a player under the age of 20 who was under contract to an IIHF team had to be offered back to his European team under the 2007–11 agreement, the European federations would like to increase this age requirement to 22. The second issue for the European federations involves the transfer deadline for players to sign with NHL teams. The June 15 deadline that existed under the previous agreement made it somewhat difficult for European teams that lost players to NHL clubs to replace those players for the upcoming season; thus, they would like to see an earlier deadline that allows them ample time to find a replacement. The third issue for the European federations is related to compensation. Transfer fees under the previous agreements were paid in American dollars, but the decline of the dollar against the Euro and other European currencies means that the $200,000 fees that were being paid were worth substantially less in 2007 than they were in 2005. Given these concerns, the European federations are in search of corrective measures.

3. Implications of the Absence of a Player Transfer Agreement

Fifty-one Russians played in the NHL in 2005–06 while the rights to 41 Russian players were transferred to NHL teams under the 2001–04 Player Transfer Agreement. In addition, 13 Russian players signed contracts with NHL teams during the 2005–07 agreement; however, the exclusion of the Russian federation from this agreement made these transfers 'free'—that is, NHL teams paid no compensation to their Russian counterparts for signing their players instead of paying them a combined $2.6 million. The expiration of the most recent Player Transfer Agreement means all European hockey teams now face the potential loss of their players to NHL teams without compensation. If there was a duplication of the 59 players signed by NHL teams in 2007–08, this would save NHL teams $11.8 million (59 players at $200,000 per player). There also exists the very real possibility of the unregulated landscape leading to a lack of mutual respect of contracts—that is, teams signing (or "stealing") players who have valid and binding contracts with other teams. This has already occurred with a handful of players signed by Russian teams despite the existence of valid contracts with NHL teams. Most notably, Alexander Radulov of the NHL's Nashville Predators signed a deal with Salavat Yulyev Ufa of the Russian Kontinental Hockey League (KHL) in 2008 despite the fact that his contract with Nashville did not expire until 2009. An IIHF investigation found the existence of a valid contract with Nashville but also determined that the IIHF was powerless under its by-laws and in the absence of a valid player transfer agreement between the NHL and the Russian Federation to sanction the player from playing hockey in a domestic league. While the Russian Federation would prefer a FIFA-styled system requiring the NHL teams to negotiate directly with Russian teams over the terms of player transfers, the NHL has understandably balked at such a request. NHL teams are prevented from negotiating directly with European clubs by the terms of its Collective Bargaining Agreement, which prevents circumvention of the deal under threat of severe penalties, including significant fines and loss of draft picks. Any prolonged period without a player transfer agreement could impact the number of European players selected in the NHL entry draft, with NHL teams reluctant to waste valuable draft picks on players who they may be unable to sign. This scenario has already manifested itself with Russian players: only 15 were selected in the 2006 NHL entry draft and nine in both the 2007 and 2008 versions, compared with 44 in 2000.

The long-term impact of the absence of a player transfer agreement will be felt by the NHL and its teams, the KHL and other European leagues, the various European federations and the players themselves. Though NHL teams are realizing the savings of a free transfer system in the near term, the long-term costs could be troublesome. If the migration of talented European players to the NHL slows dramatically—as has already happened with Russians—the drop-off in talent may be reflected in lower quality of play. This in turn could have a negative impact on league revenues, as fans might find NHL hockey less entertaining. Nonetheless, if the most talented Europeans continue to pursue their dreams of playing in the top hockey league in the world and earning the larger contracts that come with it, then this is unlikely to occur. Conversely, while the KHL and other European leagues would certainly lose out on the compensation received when their top players are lost, they could see an increase in their overall quality of play as more players stay at home. The increased quality of play would make the sport more attractive to consumers and revenues could be expected to increase. This is likely to be of some benefit to the KHL as it attempts to grow. Ultimately, if it is successful in the long term in developing young Russian players, can keep them at home, and can attract talented European players, the KHL could compete with the NHL to be the top hockey league in the world. Not surprisingly, the dispute between the NHL, KHL and the Russian Federation over the Player Transfer Agreement is really most likely about each league's desire to create an increasingly global product market and realize the attendant revenue increase.

. . . Though the NHL has long attempted to tap the European market, it has increased these efforts substantially in recent years. In addition to playing regular season games in select cities, the NHL has established the Victoria Cup preseason competition and participates in a marketing partnership with the European Champions Hockey League. These efforts could be a prelude to the NHL investing in the Champions Hockey League and eventually placing franchises in Europe. Though still in its infancy, the KHL is similarly eyeing a future European expansion. Despite all of this activity, the players themselves could be the biggest losers in the long-term if a player transfer agreement does not come to fruition. Though salaries could increase due to the presence of multiple bidders for their services, players may suffer in that it could be far more difficult for them to be able to play for the team and in the league that they desire in the absence of a player transfer agreement that establishes a smooth process for doing so. In addition, there is currently no agreement for the NHL to allow its players to participate in the 2014 Olympics in Sochi, Russia as they have done since the Nagano Games in 1998. The Russian Federation would obviously greatly prefer that the best players be available to participate in what will be one of the showcase events of the Games. However, given the tenuous relationship between the NHL, KHL and the Russian Federation, NHL player participation in the 2014 Olympic tournament is anything but certain. It is clear that a 'Cold War' in international hockey leads to multilateral losses in the long-term and must be remedied.

C. Union of European Football Associations (UEFA)

There are few similarities and numerous differences between the European soccer transfer system and the baseball posting system. The transfer of European soccer players from one team to another closely resembles a free market system and is more efficient than any of the aforementioned systems. In the Union of European Football Associations ("UEFA") the transferor team is permitted to negotiate directly with the transferee team, a direct business-to-business negotiation. Although there are restrictions governing which players may be transferred, the fact that more than one transferor team can solicit the services of the individual player allows for the possibility of an ascending price auction.

In similar fashion to the MLB–NPB posting process, following the conclusion of the playing season, individual teams produce a list of players who are available for transfer to other clubs. These players are currently under contract to the listing club and without being transferred would be forced to play out the duration of their contracts with their current club. Once the player is eligible to be transferred (i.e. his name has been listed by his current club), and there is another team interested in acquiring the player, then the two teams can begin negotiating the transfer price of the player. The transfer fee associated with the movement of a player is preliminarily set by the listing team, with the final transfer value the product of direct negotiation.

An interesting component of the UEFA system also addresses the apprehension felt by the Europeans under the former NHL-IIHF agreement: compensation for the training of younger players. A specific formula is in place to determine extra compensation paid to a transferee team when a player under the age of 23 is being transferred. This formulaic compensation only applies to the transfer of players under this age threshold, but this system is in place in order to compensate the typically lower revenue clubs for the development, and subsequent loss via transfer, of star players to typically higher revenue teams. The loss of promising young players who tend to be less expensive than older players of comparable skill, especially if they have not yet attained free agency, can promote competitive imbalance where the transferee teams are typically smaller, lower revenue clubs. Thus, the extra payment for players under 23 seeks to remedy the perceived imbalance that could result from these transfers of players.

In the absence of the additional payment for younger players, teams are free to negotiate whatever transfer fee they can for their players. There are currently two windows during the year that teams can transfer players—one during the summer and another during the middle of the playing season. Traditionally, teams attached a transfer value to each of the players who had been listed for transfer, and this transfer value was the baseline for negotiations. Unlike the baseball transfer system, where the bidding teams must bid in secrecy in a sealed bid auction, UEFA's system allows for more full market participation, because each of the interested teams will know the transfer price attached to the player by the listing team. Football teams can negotiate with an unlimited number of other teams over the transfer fee and the result is typically a winning bid that is minimally above the next highest bid. The inefficiencies of the MLB system, where the Red Sox bid almost $12 million more than the next highest bidder for Matsuzaka, would never occur in the UEFA system because the winner would theoretically bid just $1 more than the next highest bidder.

Much like the NBA system, the transferee team and the individual player are the beneficiaries of this type of transfer system. Though the transferee team loses the services of a player who has marketable skills, it nonetheless receives financial compensation for this loss. Given the alternative—that the player leaves via free agency after the expiration of his contract without any compensation being paid to his former team—receipt of payment for the transfer of the player is a positive outcome, even if it is not optimal. For the individual player, the transfer system is an excellent lever to increase financial outcomes. In the absence of the transfer mechanism (and free agency), a player whose rights were initially acquired by a small market team would be subject to the budgetary restraints of that team his whole career. The transfer system almost surely guarantees that a player will be moving to the team that most highly values his services; often this will be a larger, more highly monetized team with deeper pockets with which to pay its players.

There is also an argument to be made that the transfer system is better for the transferor team (the team paying the transfer fee) as well. If the transferor team is a large revenue club that is not particularly adept at developing its talent from within, and instead focuses its efforts on placing the highest quality team on the field at any given moment, then the transferor team may view the payment of the transfer fee as simply a cost of acquiring talent. Although signing a player as a 12-year old with potential is less expensive than signing a 23-year old superstar, for a large revenue team without the skill to develop that 12-year old, payment of the transfer fee may be the best option for fielding the best team.

V.   ALTERNATIVES TO THE CURRENT POSTING PROCESS

A.   Worldwide Draft

One alternative to the current posting process between NPB and MLB is to have a worldwide draft, an option that MLB is likely to pursue in the next collective bargaining negotiations with the MLBPA as the 2011 expiration of the current agreement approaches. In both the NBA and NHL, an individual team is allowed to draft players from any country in the world, so long as those players meet the criteria of that league's collective bargaining agreement (i.e. minimum age requirements in both leagues). For MLB teams, however, the pool of players from which the teams can draft is confined to those players who are American citizens (or from American territories), Canadian citizens, or anyone who has attended either high school or college in the United States. Because the MLB teams are not allowed to draft foreign players, the resulting framework is a collection of individual agreements with foreign federations regarding the way in which foreign players are transferred to MLB teams. In most instances, MLB teams are free to sign players from foreign countries in a way that very closely approximates a free transfer system. These transfers, though, are subject to the agreements that MLB has in place with the governing federations, as is the case with both Japan and Korea.

Because of the suboptimality of the current posting process for the transfer of players from NPB to MLB, there is room for improvement in this system. A worldwide draft would change the economics of global talent acquisition, though it is unclear as to exactly how this would occur. Proponents of a worldwide draft believe that it would decrease prices paid for high quality international players and reduce signing bonuses by providing MLB teams with leverage over them, since the clubs would have exclusive negotiating rights with the player rather than allowing the player to engage the clubs in a competitive bidding situation. Those opposed to a worldwide draft believe that it would increase player development costs by eliminating the possibility of signing a large number of players to low cost contracts and would disincentivize teams from scouting internationally, since the players they develop would be subject to selection by another team. The reality is that both parties are correct to some degree. Prices for high-end talent would likely fall due to the exclusive nature of the drafting rights, but the finite (and likely decreased) number of draft rounds would still allow teams to mine baseball rich countries for undrafted talent at a reasonable price. A worldwide draft would also eliminate a great deal of the malfeasance surrounding the signing bonuses paid to high-end international players. The FBI has been investigating whether scouts and team executives have skimmed money off the top of the bonuses paid to Latin American prospects.

A worldwide draft, or at least a United States and Japan draft, would partially alleviate the suboptimality issues of the current system by allowing MLB teams to assign a quasi-market value to Japanese players whose services were desired by MLB teams. By drafting the rights to NPB players in a draft that includes American players as well, MLB teams would be able to assign a value to the NPB players that approximated the player's market value by drafting more valuable players in earlier rounds and less desirable players in later rounds.

The movement of players between NPB and MLB would increase as a result of a worldwide draft because more players would move to MLB, or the MLB minor leagues, than under the current system. By allowing more players to move from one league to another, the artificial premium currently paid for Japanese players under the posting process would be reduced as more and more NPB players move across the Pacific. MLB teams, instead of having to pay upwards of $50 million just for the chance to negotiate with a NPB player, would instead be able to draft that player, a much more efficient and lower cost method of acquiring the rights. A draft where all 30 MLB teams are participating against one another to acquire the rights to the best talent allows clubs to understand the markets for individual players more fully, because the system of drafting players is public and each team knows the relative values placed on players by the drafting teams.

There are, however, several significant hurdles to overcome before such a system could be implemented, as both the MLBPA and the NPB owners would have concerns that would need to be addressed. In exchange for subjecting a larger number of future union members to a draft system (where an MLB team acquires the rights to that player for at least six years), the MLBPA would likely want the number of rounds of the draft shortened from its current maximum length of 50 rounds to something significantly shorter. This would allow the MLBPA to get more prospective players inked to contracts with teams that had demonstrated needs for that player, instead of the player being forced to sign with the team who drafted his rights; or, in the alternative, not sign with the drafting team and be eligible for the draft in the following year.

Even more significant are the concerns of the NPB team owners. Under the current posting process system, they are the constituency for whom the posting fee pays the greatest dividend; thus, the NPB owners are the group least likely to desire change from the status quo. While the short-term interests of the NPB are arguably maximized when MLB teams pay posting fees for the rights to NPB players, an argument can be made that having NPB players eligible for the MLB Draft is in the long-term best interests of the NPB. That is, subjecting NPB players to a worldwide draft in which MLB teams could draft the rights to Japanese players would almost surely guarantee long-term survival for the NPB—even if only as an unofficial minor league for MLB. The focus of the NPB, and many other professional leagues whose players were subject to the MLB Draft, could become more focused upon player development as a pseudo-minor league system. While the NPB owners may be reluctant to move to this type of model, it could be their best long-term option.

Undoubtedly, the long-term dilemma facing the NPB is a difficult one: try to forestall the internationalization of the game and risk losing even more star players to MLB, or accept the globalization of the game as reality and preserve a meaningful role. Though unlikely to occur, the greatest risk for the NPB is the possibility that it could lose its relevance following the continued loss of major talent to MLB. Unlike the Negro Leagues (which folded soon after integration led to most of the best black players moving to MLB), extinction is not as grave a risk for the NPB because of the geographic boundaries separating the two leagues. After integration of American baseball, many times the Negro League and MLB teams were competing in the same cities for the same fans, at a moment when the talent of the MLB teams was far superior. In the hypothetical situation of the best Japanese players moving en masse to MLB, the NPB is protected by the Pacific Ocean. Although technological advancements allow Japanese fans to watch Japanese players who are playing in MLB, this does not mean that those same Japanese fans can see their favorite players in person. If for no other reason than ensuring the continuation of the culturally important performance of live professional baseball in Japan, the NPB will still have a niche.

B.   Flat Fee Paid by MLB to NPB

The presence of a strong Japanese professional baseball league is of great benefit to MLB. Beyond serving as a pool of playing talent for MLB clubs, the league keeps the sport of baseball culturally relevant and popular in Japan. That which is good for baseball is good for MLB, especially in the ever-flattening global sports marketplace. The fact that the sport is ingrained into Japanese culture clearly makes the selling of American baseball in Japan a much easier task than it is in countries where the game does not have a fervent fan base. Just as the minor leagues serve a grassroots function for MLB within the United States, NPB allows fans to develop a passion for the sport and experience it in a way that is otherwise unavailable through the mere watching of televised games. It is easier to sell MLB—the top professional baseball league in the world—to a country that already has a strong interest in the sport. An NPB that is so weakened by player defections to America that fan interest in NPB dissipates is self-defeating for MLB, and the league must remain sensitive to this issue. To this end, it would make sense for MLB to pay NPB an annual fee to allow its players to be selected in the MLB Rule 4 draft. NPB could allocate this money amongst its teams however it wanted, with the desired result being that the teams reinvest the money back into player development budgets so as to maintain a high quality of play in the league. The annual fee paid by MLB could take several forms. It could be a fixed amount, or based on the number and placement of the players selected in the MLB draft, or a combination of both. It is worth noting that it may be difficult to convince the Japanese teams of the merits of this system because the corporate operating structure makes the owners less likely to reinvest these funds into the teams themselves and much more likely to extract the proceeds from the teams.

C.   Per-Player Transfer Fee to be Negotiated by Individual Stakeholders

A third way to address the suboptimality of the NPB–MLB posting process is to have the transferor and transferee teams negotiate directly with one another for the appropriate transfer fee, in a similar fashion to the current system in place in the NBA and UEFA. This system would ideally be layered upon a worldwide draft, such that the transferor team in MLB would have already drafted the rights to the individual player (giving the MLB team exclusive negotiating rights vis-à-vis other MLB teams) and would then engage in a direct, face-to-face negotiation with the player's former team.

Unlike the posting process, where there is no direct negotiation between the NPB and MLB teams involved in the player transfer, this system would allow the two teams to bargain over terms of the transfer fee. In strict financial terms, the benefactors of this proposed system would be the MLB teams, because rather than overbidding for players as a result of the first-price-sealed-bid auction, the MLB team would only have to spend the precise value that the NPB team attached to the individual player in order to acquire the player's rights. In the example of Matsuzaka and the Red Sox, instead of offering a transfer fee that was $12M more than the next highest bidder, the Red Sox would only have had to spend $1 more than the value which the Seibu Lions had attached to Matsuzaka. There is no definitive evidence to prove that $51.1 million, the price paid by the Red Sox to negotiate with Matsuzaka, was the precise value assigned by Seibu to Matsuzaka. In fact, many commentators, prior to the revelation that the Red Sox had bid $51.1 million to win the rights, had said the transfer fee would probably be between $20–30 million. There was little to no indication by any of the same commentators that a bid in the $20–30 million range would have been unacceptable to the Seibu Lions; in fact, because Matsuzaka would have become a free agent after the 2008 season, the Lions wanted to ensure that they received some compensation for Matsuzaka and probably would have accepted a bid substantially lower than $51.1 million. Had the Red Sox been able to directly negotiate with the Lions, after having drafted Matsuzaka's rights, the dollar value of the transfer fee would have more accurately represented what the two sides felt Matsuzaka's value really was. Instead of the Lions capturing the entire inefficiency of the posting process, the Red Sox could have reduced the inefficiencies within the transfer fee by bargaining directly with Seibu.

A potential concern regarding the implementation of the individually negotiated transfer fees is that the NPB team could dictate to which team the player is transferred by refusing to negotiate with certain MLB teams or declaring his price prospectively. For example, a NPB team seeking to prevent its star pitcher from going anywhere but the Red Sox or Mets could effectively put information into the marketplace that teams other than the Red Sox or Mets should abstain from drafting the rights to the pitcher, because the only two teams with which the NPB team would negotiate are the Red Sox or Mets. From an economic standpoint, it is in the best interest of individual NPB teams, and the Japanese leagues as a whole, to have the NPB players drafted exclusively by MLB teams with high payrolls because on the whole, the transfer fees paid by large revenue teams like the Red Sox, Mets and Yankees can be higher than those paid by smaller revenue clubs like the Tampa Bay Rays, Florida Marlins, Pittsburgh Pirates or Kansas City Royals. This unilateral power of NPB teams to dictate the teams to which their players are transferred could seriously undermine the efficacy of the draft and individually negotiated transfer fees to promote an efficient marketplace for the exchange of player services.

Should the individual NPB team be able to effectively control to which teams the Japanese player can be transferred, problems arise not only with the NPB team being unnecessarily powerful, but also with the implication this has for competitive balance in the MLB. Smaller revenue MLB clubs, like the aforementioned Rays, Marlins, Pirates or Royals will not benefit from the talents of NPB players in the same way that the larger revenue clubs could. The existence of the worldwide draft would be far more equitable in the distribution of talent across MLB teams, but this equity could be eviscerated if NPB teams (who have a direct financial incentive) strong arm negotiations so that only the large revenue teams have a realistic chance to sign NPB players.

D.   Per Player Transfer Fee; Uniform

A fourth alternative to the current posting system is to have a transfer agreement that mandates a fixed per-player transfer fee that is paid each time a player under contract with the NPB team is signed by a MLB club. A variation of this model was used by the NHL in its most recent Player Transfer Agreement with the European hockey federations (minus Russia)—for each player under contract that was signed by an NHL club, the transferee team received $200,000.

Whether or not this system contributed to the prevalence of international players in the NHL is uncertain, but one thing the uniform transfer fee certainly did was reduce the transaction costs of player movement to the NHL. Because all three parties knew that $200,000 was the amount the transferee team would receive each time one of their players under contract signed a deal with an NHL club, there was no negotiating that needed to take place. This uniform transfer fee was not the most desirable option for the transferee team; however, it was preferable to the current system where there is the possibility of the transferee team receiving no compensation for the loss of its star players.

The NHL team and transferred player both directly benefitted in instances where the $200,000 fee represented less than market value for the transfer of the player. This was typically in instances where the player being transferred was an international star, or where the player demonstrated the potential to be an NHL star. It was also these instances where the transfer is suboptimal for the transferee team. The NHL team, however, captured the inefficiencies of this transaction because it did not have to pay the "true" transfer value of the player and could instead acquire the rights to the player for less than what they would have had to pay in an open marketplace. If this system were applied to the NPB–MLB relationship, MLB teams would prefer the uniform transfer fee arrangement to both the current posting process and the individually negotiated transfer fee systems, because the uniform transfer fee system, like that used in the NHL, best allows the transferor team to protect its financial interests.

The individual players being transferred also prefer the uniform transfer fee to both the posting process and the individually negotiated transfer fee because it allows the player to capture more of his market value once the player and the transferor team begin contract negotiations. The value a team places on a player will be measured by the total amount of money that the team is willing to spend on the acquisition of the player (both transfer fee and eventual player contract), and if a team spends less than market value on the transfer fee, it follows that the team then has more money to spend on the eventual player contract. Matsuzaka was valued by the Red Sox at $103.1 million, and if the Red Sox paid less than $51.1 million on the transfer fee, there would have been more than $52 million left to negotiate an actual contract with the player. While Matsuzaka probably would not have captured his full $103.1 million value under the uniform player transfer fee, it is reasonable to surmise that the contract the pitcher ultimately received would have represented more than the 50% of the pitcher's overall value that he received under the existing system.

The clear loser under this framework is the transferee team. Teams will not sign players whose value is less than the uniform transfer fee, and will instead focus on players whose value is significantly greater than the predetermined transfer fee amount. While there would undoubtedly be an increase in the overall number of transfers from NPB teams to MLB teams, the overall value of the transfer fees would not approximate the value under the current system. Assuming that the NHL transfer fee of $200,000 per player is adopted, it would take 250 player transfers for the Seibu Lions to get the same amount as they did under the Matsuzaka transfer!

In order for a uniform player transfer fee to be effective, the system must be implemented by all of the countries from which the foreign players are drawn. This has been a major issue faced by the IIHF and the implementation of the International Player Transfer Agreement. Because the Russian Federation was not party to the Agreement, the signing of players under contract with a Russian club by a NHL team did not require the payment of a transfer fee. The major stumbling block preventing the signing of the agreement by the Russians was that the compensation for their star players like Alex Ovechkin and Evgeni Malkin fell woefully short of the players' actual value.

E.   Per Player Transfer Fee; Uniform with Classes of Players

A fifth alternative to the posting process is to utilize the uniform per player transfer fee, but have several different levels of transfer fees based upon the varying degrees of a player's performance and skill set. Teams transferring star players would receive significantly more in transfer fees than would the team losing an older marginal player. Likewise, the transferor team would have to pay a premium for star players, which is precisely what would happen in the open marketplace. Although this system is not optimal for the player being transferred, it does represent a middle point on the continuum between strictly uniform transfer fees and the current posting process.

Formation of this system would require input from both the NPB and MLB on the classification of a player, particularly if the amount of the transfer fee is dependent upon a classification of the individual player's skill level. First, a classification scheme would have to be created, with varying compensation figures attaching to the different types of players. For example, a star right handed pitcher like Matsuzaka would have a higher transfer fee than an older utility infielder. Placement of a player amongst the various levels, however, is where the creation of this system becomes most difficult. Therefore, it will be necessary to have an independent third-party, selected using criteria agreed upon by both the NPB and MLB, as the final decision maker on disagreements of player classification. Particularly with regards to determining the differences between star and superstar players, these classifications could have significant financial impacts.

This proposed system addresses the concerns a NPB team would have regarding the uniform player transfer fee; namely, that the team is not being compensated fairly for loss of its best players. With regards to the IIHF–NHL Transfer Agreement, lack of fair compensation for star players was the precise reason given by the Russian Federation for not being party to the agreement. While these levels of player transfer fees will be both over-inclusive and under-inclusive, this system would yield a more efficient transfer fee than would a uniform transfer fee. At the same time, the individual player's ability to capture his true market value would again suffer as a result of the transferor team being forced to pay a sizeable portion of the player's value to someone other than the player himself.

F.   Percentage System

Another proposal for reform of the current NPB–MLB transfer system is to have the transfer fee amount determined as a percentage of the ultimate contract signed by the player with the MLB team. Under this system, the NPB team would again only receive compensation if the player signed a contract with the MLB team, and that compensation would be subject to the market forces of direct contract negotiation. Unlike the current system, where only one team may negotiate with the NPB player, this system would allow for direct solicitation of the player's services by any and all teams that desired the player's services. The percentage payment to the NPB team would be in addition to, and not subtracted from, the final contract amount received by the player. The cost of signing the player, then, is the value of the contract plus the percentage-based transfer fee.

This proposed system is the most optimal for the player, and represents a far superior outcome than is achieved in the current posting process. Rather than have situations where MLB teams are calculating player values using dollar amounts paid to the NPB team and not the player (Matsuzaka received a contract for far less than his market value because the Red Sox incorporated the $51.1 million posting fee into his value), the player in this system would receive very near his market value. This is especially true if more than one team is permitted to negotiate with the player. But there is still the possibility that the ultimate contract received does not represent the player's true market value, if teams incorporate the percentage fee into the amount it is willing to pay the player. Despite this possibility, this system does not impact the total amount of the compensation received by the player nearly as much as the current posting system, especially if the new system is implemented with multiple suitors permitted for each player.

NPB owners may not prefer this proposed system to the one currently in place, but there are structural factors built into the proposal that ensure the NPB teams are fairly compensated for the caliber of player lost. Because the payment to the NPB team is a function of the total value of the contract given to the player by the MLB team, it follows that the NPB team will receive more money when it loses a star player compared with when it loses a role player. While a percentage-based payment would almost surely not yield the same possibilities of payments as does the current system, from the NPB's perspective, the percentage system ensures that the loss of the best players yields the highest transfer payments.

Whether or not the MLB teams prefer a percentage-based payment model depends entirely on the percentage payment required of the MLB team. Should the percentage rise above 25%, it is conceivable that the MLB teams would prefer, or at least be impartial to, the current system. The preferred aspect of this proposed system, from the perspective of MLB teams, is that individual teams can negotiate with the player directly, without the sealed bidding of the current auction. This transparency will prevent the type of overbidding evidenced by the Red Sox $12 million overpayment for Matsuzaka's services. This system, however, still has limitations. NPB teams could hijack the transfer of players, and skew the MLB competitive balance, by only negotiating with deep-pocketed teams. This system may lead to competitive balance issues if small market teams are entirely excluded from this labor pool.

VI.   Historical Precedent

This is not the first instance of a player transfer system being critical to determining the relationship between MLB and another league. As noted earlier, after Jackie Robinson integrated MLB in 1947, the relationship between MLB and the Negro Leagues was forever changed by the influx of African-American players into MLB. Had a more comprehensive and effective transfer system been in place, it is possible that the Negro Leagues would not have vanished as a viable economic entity. There is undoubtedly an irreversible trend of NPB players coming across the Pacific to the riches of MLB, and if the trend continues, the Japanese league risks becoming a league bereft of its star players.

A formal relationship never existed, pre-integration, between MLB and the Negro Leagues, and this lack of protocol was one of the main reasons the Negro Leagues diminished in popularity and ultimately folded in 1957, ten years after Jackie Robinson's historic feat. There was no posting process and no system of payment for the transfer of players. Negotiations were typically between the Negro League player and the MLB team, and in many cases the Negro League club with whom the player was under contract was omitted from the conversation entirely. This was particularly true during the earliest player signings. As was typically the case in the Negro Leagues at the time, Jackie Robinson was reportedly operating under an oral agreement with his Negro League club, the Kansas City Monarchs. The contract that he signed to play for the Brooklyn Dodgers' top minor league affiliate in Montreal in 1946 provided him with a salary of $600 per month and a $3,500 signing bonus, but more importantly it contained a clause stating that he was free of any obligation to any other club with no compensation owed from the Dodgers. While the white owners of the Kansas City Monarchs alleged that the club had a written contract with Robinson and threatened both to protest to MLB Commissioner Albert 'Happy' Chandler and to file a lawsuit against the Dodgers, they backed down from these threats amidst public pressure from the African-American community and media desiring integration and agreed to allow Robinson to play for the organization; nonetheless, they did publicly state that they felt the Dodgers owed them compensation.

Though no litigation was ever commenced, these complaints were subsequently echoed by other Negro League owners, who ultimately argued to Commissioner Chandler that MLB teams should negotiate with Negro League clubs directly rather than with the player, explaining "that while they were 'glad to see our players get the opportunity to play in white baseball, [we] are simply protesting the way it was done.'"[3] The Negro Leagues' commissioners requested the leagues be formally recognized by MLB as either minor or major leagues, which would have allowed them to participate in the compensation scheme that had been established between MLB and its affiliated minor leagues. These complaints were met with derision by MLB Commissioner Chandler. Though no formal player transfer agreement or protocol was ever reached between the leagues, subsequent signings of Negro League players by other MLB teams began to be negotiated between the respective clubs rather than between the player and the MLB team. Negro League owners hoped to realize significant revenues by selling players to MLB, but this never came to fruition because the Negro Leagues were unable to respond adequately to the MLB teams raiding its rosters by doing so in kind, and they had no other outlet with which to

align themselves. Thus, MLB teams rarely paid a fair market transfer fee, in large part because the Negro League clubs felt that they lacked the leverage to negotiate. After the owner of his Negro League team was rebuffed in an attempt to sell his rights to the New York Yankees for $100,000, Larry Doby became the first African-American to play in the American League in 1947 after MLB's Cleveland Indians purchased his rights from his Negro League team for $10,000 plus an additional $5,000 bonus, payable if he was able to complete thirty days on Cleveland's roster. The rights to Satchel Paige were sold by the Kansas City Monarchs to the Cleveland Indians in 1948 for a mere $5,000. Nonetheless, these laughably small transfer fees became a needed source of revenue for the Negro League clubs, and the exodus of players to MLB clubs accelerated in 1948. This caused the quality of play in the Negro Leagues to decrease and fans stopped coming to the ballparks and supporting their favorite Negro League teams as a result. Negro Leagues attendance dropped precipitously from 1946 (the last season pre-integration) to 1948; for example, the Newark Eagles' home attendance declined 71 percent. By 1949, there were 36 former Negro Leaguers in MLB and their former league was well into its demise. When taken in combination with the desire of African-American baseball fans to support an interracial business that more closely reflected their goal of an integrated society, the poor organizational structure of the Negro Leagues and the typically bad team management, the Negro Leagues finally had too many obstacles to overcome. The Negro National League folded after the 1948 season, with two of its clubs disbanding and a third focusing on barnstorming. While the Negro American League reconstituted itself and continued to plod along, a lack of interest combined with the other obstacles to undermine the viability of the league as a whole and it struggled until the last Negro League game was played in 1957. Ultimately, while there is no doubt that society as a whole benefited from the integration of the major leagues, integration was not without its costs to the Negro League fans, owners and former players who did not make it to MLB.

The current MLB–NPB system presents many of the same issues, especially with regards to player movement and the impact that movement has on the health of the individual leagues. There is a compelling argument that it is in the best interests of MLB to preserve the long-term health of NPB, unlike what happened with the Negro Leagues, because NPB (and not MLB) is the best cultivator of Japanese talent. The owners of NPB teams have an interest in preserving the health of their league, while MLB owners have a similar interest in their own league. Any player transfer agreement would seemingly have to address both of these competing desires, although the place on the spectrum between where the self-preservation ends and the actual agreement falls will be the product of negotiation.

As previously noted, one critical difference between the circumstances surrounding the disappearance of the Negro Leagues and the current state of the NPB is the geographic proximity of the competitor league. During the late 1940s, after MLB had been integrated, many Negro League teams competed in the same cities as their MLB counterparts. In an era when gate receipts were the primary source of team revenue, the fact that many fans went to the higher quality MLB games had a direct effect on the lack of monetization for the Negro Leagues. In the current situation, however, it cannot be said that fans are choosing to attend MLB games instead of NPB games. A more accurate characterization may be that NPB fans are now following former NPB players who have signed with MLB teams (at the expense of following an NPB team) through digital media. But to what extent the following of MLB via digital media will destroy a revenue base (gate receipts) for NPB is uncertain. Another difference in the current situation is cultural. Baseball has long been a very important part of the fabric of Japanese culture and it remains the national pastime. There is simply too much pride in Japanese baseball to allow the long-standing, deep-pocketed professional league to fail. Despite the conceptual similarities, there are substantial differences between the Negro Leagues and Nippon Professional Baseball that are likely to lead to a different end result and allow NPB to survive notwithstanding the suboptimality of the player transfer agreement.

VII.   CONCLUSION

In the ever-flattening world, the challenge for MLB and NPB is to create a transfer system that is more efficient than the current model, while at the same time preserving NPB's status as a viable economic entity. It is imperative for the sport of baseball that NPB remain intact; the demise of the second-strongest professional baseball league in the world would have a deleterious effect on the global growth of the sport and, ultimately, on MLB. The triumvirate of key stakeholders must all agree to effectuate any of the proposed alternatives, and there is an implicit tension between the desires of NPB, MLB and the MLBPA. Notwithstanding their input, there seem to be two alternatives that stand out from the others. The first is a global draft layered upon a NBA/UEFA-esque system of team-to-team negotiation. The second is a percentage based system, where the transfer fee amount paid to the NPB team is determined as a percentage of the ultimate contract signed by the player with the MLB team. It is left to the stakeholders to determine the system that best fits their needs.

Notes

1. *Regulation H—Rules Governing Players, Coaches, Support Officials, and Players' Agents*, Federation Internationale de Basketball, 6.

2. USA Basketball Application for Letter of Clearance, http://www.hunbasket.hu/docs/USA_loc-application.pdf (last visited Dec. 30, 2007).

3. Mark Ribowsky, A Complete History of the Negro Leagues, 1884 to 1955, 285 (1995).

Discussion Questions

1. How is the global market for athletic talent different/the same as traditional business?
2. What elements do most global sports leagues have in common with North American–based sports leagues?
3. What factors motivated the creation of the Indian Premier League?
4. What distinguishes Twenty20 cricket from the traditional version? Why was the revised version of the sport developed?
5. What is the role of non-football revenues for Arsenal? How do you think this compares with U.S.–based NFL teams?
6. Describe the current baseball posting rules.
7. If a viable American–style football league began to flourish in Brazil, what player transfer rules would you suggest the National Football League and the Brazilian Football League agree to? Explain.

Emerging and Niche Leagues

INTRODUCTION

In the United States, beyond the four major professional team sports leagues and individual sports, such as NASCAR, golf, and tennis, a number of start-up leagues and niche sports are competing for space on the professional sports landscape. An early 2010 count of such entities found 272 baseball teams competing in 24 affiliated and independent minor leagues, 75 basketball teams playing in 4 basketball leagues, 4 football leagues featuring 74 teams, 7 hockey leagues with 122 teams, 7 soccer leagues housing 166 teams, 2 lacrosse leagues, and various softball and team tennis leagues. In addition to those disparate leagues are athletes competing in individual sports such as horseracing, rodeo, beach volleyball, various motor sports, fishing, billiards, bowling, mixed martial arts, and action sports, embodied largely in festival-type atmospheres such as the X Games and Dew Tour.

The varying sports discussed in this chapter can best be described as belonging to at least one of four nonexclusive categories, with some accurately described by multiple categories. The first of these categories is *minor leagues*, in which the league does not represent the top level of competition in its sport. Minor leagues may serve three functions: player development, entertainment, and grassroots marketing. With regards to the player development function, athletes are trained for a potential future career at the sport's top level of competition. Examples of leagues serving in this capacity are the affiliated minor leagues in baseball, with Major League Baseball (MLB) teams involved in a relationship with teams at the AAA, AA, A, and Rookie levels. These teams act as the MLB's player development system.

A minor league may also serve an entertainment function, with a focus on providing fans with low-cost, family entertainment at the stadium. Although affiliated minor league baseball serves in this capacity as well, independently owned and operated minor league baseball, hockey, basketball, and football leagues focus on this function, rather than serving as a vertically integrated player development system. The proliferation of unaffiliated independent minor leagues over the past decade indicates that entrepreneurs believe that the demand for low-cost, family entertainment outstrips the available supply of these entertainment options.

Minor leagues may also serve a grassroots marketing function. Primarily located in smaller markets, affiliated minor leagues have historically provided large segments of the population located in secondary and tertiary markets with access to professional sports that would otherwise be unavailable. Thus, along with television, they help allow interest in a sport to continue in these markets. Recently, independent minor league franchises have been established in close proximity to major media markets, providing a lower-cost alternative to the major leagues and allowing segments of the population to have increased access to sports that may be available geographically but not economically. MLB teams have responded to this strategy by placing some of their affiliated minor league teams on the outskirts of their home territories. This allows the MLB teams to capitalize on cross-promotional opportunities, promotes brand domination by the MLB teams throughout their home markets, and makes it easier to closely monitor the progress of their prospects. Fans have the opportunity to follow players closely as they progress to the big leagues.

Leagues in the remaining categories of emerging and niche sports often aspire to become the next major professional sports league in the United States. The second category that these leagues fall into is those emerging and niche sports that represent the *top level of competition in their respective sport*. These sports often have large numbers of recreational participants. This combination of high-level competition and recreational participation would seem to bode quite well for the future of professional competition in these sports. However, this has yet to translate into financial success in anything but action sports. Examples of leagues fitting into this category are Major League Soccer (MLS); Women's Professional Soccer (WPS) and its predecessor, the now defunct Women's United Soccer Association (WUSA); Major League Lacrosse; World Team Tennis; the Women's National Basketball Association (WNBA); and National Pro Fastpitch, a professional women's softball league. The challenge for sports industry leaders is to convert the large number of participants in these sports into commercial users. It remains to be seen whether this can be accomplished, or whether the popularity of these sports is limited to participation rather than as a spectator.

A third category of emerging and niche sports involves leagues that are *indoor variations* of traditionally outdoor sports. Seeking to capitalize on the popularity of established outdoor leagues, entrepreneurs have created separate indoor leagues that utilize a different (and usually less-talented) pool of athletes than the outdoor leagues and that adopt modified playing rules to tailor the sport to a smaller playing field. Typically played in hockey and basketball arenas, these leagues allow the operators of these facilities to host events when the facility otherwise would have been unused, thereby generating additional revenues in the forms of rental payments and ancillary activities. Examples of these leagues include the Arena Football League (AFL), the National Indoor Soccer League (NISL), and the National Lacrosse League. Although it is possible for these leagues to achieve financial success, it is unlikely that they will ever eclipse their outdoor counterparts in either revenues or popularity. The demise of the AFL and several indoor soccer leagues are instructive.

The fourth category of emerging sports is the *gender-specific leagues* that offer women the opportunity to participate in their own league in a sport in which there is a separate men's league. These leagues are attempting to take advantage of an opportunity created by the increased buying power of women resulting from societal changes and the increased female participation rate and interest in sports resulting from Title IX. None of the women's leagues that have been established—including the WNBA, WPS, World Team Tennis, NPF and various women's football leagues—have been profitable thus far, and most have mounted substantial losses. The future viability of these sports on the professional level is dependent on a change in the financial status of the leagues, which must translate women's increased buying power, participation, and interest in sports into involvement in their products as paying spectators, television viewers, and consumers of league sponsors.

In general, emerging sports are monetized from four different sources: gate receipts, parking and concessions, broadcast-related revenues, and sponsorships. The importance of these revenue sources varies according to the sport. For example, minor league baseball teams rely very heavily on gate receipts, parking fees, and concessions sales, whereas many action sports, such as the X Games, do not rely on admission fees. Correspondingly, broadcast-related revenues are important to action sports and are insignificant to most minor league baseball teams; sponsorships are important to both.

Sponsorships may impact an emerging sport in several ways. At both the national and local levels, sponsorships can serve multiple roles: not only do they provide the property with revenues, but a sponsorship that provides products-in-kind that are necessary to support team and league operations allows teams and leagues to conserve their scarce resources. In addition, sponsorships can provide emerging and niche leagues with invaluable exposure when activation of the sponsorships occurs, allowing the sport to receive broad distribution at little cost. For sponsors, relationships with emerging and niche sports allow them to attempt to reach a particular demographic in a cost-effective manner. The appeal of these sports is their lower cost and the quality of the individuals reached rather than the quantity reached, because the overall audience is generally small compared to established sports. Emerging sports can thus prove to be a good value for sponsors.

Similar to other businesses, start-up costs for emerging sports leagues can be substantial, with expenditures reaching well into the millions of dollars. Once initiated, the primary operating costs for emerging sports are the playing facility, administration, and athletic talent. In recent years, many start-up leagues have adopted a unique, single-entity structure in order to help them control costs. Although the single-entity structure has been somewhat effective in controlling costs (particularly with respect to expenditures on athletic talent), thereby allowing a league to survive the start-up phase, it is sufficiently flawed such that it may be an ineffective long-term structure. See Chapter 2 for further discussion of the single-entity structure.

For an emerging sport to achieve long-term financial success, it must possess several characteristics. First, the sport must be appealing to an audience. Although it may seem obvious that a sport lacking in audience appeal will likely fail, what makes a sport attractive to an audience is unclear. The presence of a transcendent athlete aids greatly in this process. An athlete whose singular excellence in the sport and compelling storyline outside of the sport can singlehandedly lift the entire sport and bring it into the mainstream, allowing revenue growth. Although athletes such as Lance Armstrong, Tiger Woods, Tony Hawk, Michael Phelps, Mia Hamm, and the Williams sisters are few and far between, their transcendence brought their respective sports historically unmatched levels of attention. At a minimum, it must be interesting to watch highly skilled participants compete in the sport, and the general population must have a significant participation rate in the sport. In other words, the sport must be fun to watch and people must be interested in playing it to allow for a large enough following. Although the presence of both of these elements does not guarantee success, the absence of either one will ensure long-term failure.

The second important factor is a television presence. Television is very important to emerging sports, because it provides the sport with the exposure needed to grow interest. This exposure drives attendance figures upward. The increased attendance, in turn, can lead to increases in both local and national sponsorship revenues and ancillary, facility-driven revenues such as concessions and parking. Sponsorship revenues can be increased, because a larger audience is reached, making an affiliation with the sport more valuable. Facility-driven revenues can be increased because a larger audience will lead to increased consumption of concessions and parking spaces.

Continuous improvements in technology have led to a dramatic increase in the number of cable television networks. The increased size of the cable universe has created broadcasting opportunities for sports that were previously unavailable, because these networks need programming content. Sports are attractive to cable television networks because of the potentially strong demographics, even if the overall audience size is small. Thus, the opportunity for emerging sports leagues to receive broad television exposure is greater than ever. Even if a television presence is not possible, at a minimum a sport can stream its events over the Internet at a fairly low cost. The audience size will be considerably smaller, but it provides a platform from which it can begin to reach consumers.

The third important factor for emerging sports to possess is deep-pocketed ownership. Not unlike other entrepreneurs, owners in emerging sports must be both willing and able to withstand substantial start-up costs and significant operating losses in at least the first several years. Unwilling or undercapitalized ownership leads to franchise instability or suboptimal management practices, either of which can lead to the ultimate failure of the entire league enterprise. It is important that the league consider this issue when selecting ownership. It is perhaps better for the league to begin play with a smaller number of well-financed franchises than with a larger number of thinly capitalized ones. In addition, the sport must consider the amount of the entrance fee that it will charge to prospective owners. The franchise fee must be sufficient to support league operations yet not lead to owners becoming overleveraged.

The fourth factor is that the sport must access appropriate markets. This is dictated by the desire to be located in major markets, the regional popularity of the sport, and ownership preferences. These determinants of franchise location often conflict. Location in major markets historically has been the primary determinant of franchises in emerging sports leagues. The impetus behind this idea is the notion that media outlets are only interested in broadcasting sports with broad audience appeal that can generate meaningful ratings, which is more likely in large population centers. Having placed itself in these centers, the league would thus be able to sign a lucrative national television contract. In addition, attendance is likely to be higher in larger markets. Location in major markets also allows for increased attention from both the national media and potential advertisers, because it lends a sense of cultural relevance to the sport that makes it worthier. More *potential* fans and more *potential* sponsorship dollars are available. However, there is a hubris associated with locating an emerging sport in major markets. Operational costs are likely to be significantly higher in major markets, and there is increased competition for fan and media attention in the form of other sports franchises. This may render the emerging sport irrelevant on the landscape of the large markets, making it a "small fish in a big pond."

Location that is driven by the regional popularity of an emerging sport may allow the sport to have large attendance revenues and local sponsorship revenues. Operational costs are likely to be lower in smaller markets, and the existing interest will allow the sport to avoid many of the costs associated with developing a fan base. This is the equivalent of "fishing where the fish are." In addition, there is likely to be less competition for fan and media attention in the local marketplace. Yet location that is based on a sport's regional popularity will likely place it in smaller markets where it will be unable to generate a meaningful national television rating, which will make it unattractive to national broadcasters. This could relegate the sport to fringe status, with revenue growth limited because of the regional nature of the sport. This could also make the sport less appealing to investors, because it may lack the glamour of a "big league" sport.

A final determinant of franchise location in emerging sports leagues is investor preference. An owner may choose to eschew major markets or regions where a sport is popular in favor of another location. Sports ownership has a high consumption value, and factors such as an individual's ego, desire to foster civic pride in the city of residence, or an opportunity to exploit the potential synergies available through the existing ownership of other investments may dictate location in a particular market. However, an owner's preferences may conflict with the best interests of the sport. An emerging sport requires investors, but it must consider the long-term impact of its decisions. The short-term investment in the league by a willing and able individual may have negative repercussions in the long term if the sport is located in inappropriate markets.

The fifth factor is that an emerging sport must have strong leadership. Although it is desirable to have an independent leader free from any involvement with any individual team or athlete that could create a conflict of interest, it is just as important that the leadership possess other characteristics. The leadership must have the vision to guide the long-term direction of the league. The leadership must also be able to build consensus among the entity's ownership interests while addressing their conflicting agendas; coordinate and negotiate league-wide broadcasting, marketing, and sponsorships; and generate enthusiasm for the sport.

While the aforementioned elements are necessary for an emerging sport to be successful, the athletes participating in these sports remain an essential component. Unlike many of the athletes competing in established sports, the athletes competing in emerging sports typically earn low salaries as a group, although the top athletes may earn substantial incomes. There are several reasons for this disparity. First, emerging sports do not generate sufficient revenues to justify significant expenditures by ownership on athlete compensation. Second, athletes competing in emerging sports typically do not unionize. There are some exceptions to this rule; athletes competing in the WNBA, MLS, AFL, and minor league hockey and baseball have unionized. These efforts to seek increased bargaining power through a collective voice may be shortsighted, however. Although unionization may result in increased compensation for athletes, it may lead owners to incur increased operating losses. Ultimately, those increased operating losses may lead to the market failure of the emerging sport, which would render the union members unemployed. Third, the organization of many emerging sports leagues into single-entity structures decreases athlete compensation. Because athletes are signed by the league itself and then allocated to a particular franchise in this model, this precludes competition for athlete services among league teams. Thus, single-entity leagues act as a monopsony, with only one purchaser of athletic talent. This prevents athlete compensation from reaching competitive levels in leagues structured in this manner.

The original version of the Arena Football League (AFL) is a defunct sports league that was founded in 1987. Its two decade lifespan ended when the league cancelled its 2009 season and filed for Chapter 11 bankruptcy protection. A different league playing under the same name launched in 2010. Most AFL clubs struggled financially from the league's inception, with numerous teams sold after suffering staggering losses, including the Orlando Predators, a franchise that lost nearly $6 million in 2002 before its sale in 2003. Other teams that were poorly managed or undercapitalized either folded or relocated, with a migration to larger markets from second-tier cities. The AFL's financial situation began to improve in 1999, when the National Football League (NFL) purchased a 3-year option to buy a 49% stake in the AFL. Although the option to buy was not exercised, three individual NFL owners purchased AFL expansion teams at a 50% discount, and others held options to buy AFL expansion teams in the future. This lent the AFL a sense of credibility that proved somewhat valuable.

The revenue sources for AFL teams were similar to other emerging sports. Beginning in 2003, the AFL entered into a 3-year television deal with NBC that was the first of its kind in professional sports and offered hope that it could bring the AFL the exposure that it needed to become the fifth major league. The agreement required NBC to broadcast 70 regular-season AFL games and 5 playoff games. The financial aspect of the deal was unique. NBC did not pay the AFL a rights fee in the initial 3-year contract, which it had the right to renew in perpetuity. The parties agreed to a revenue-sharing partnership in which NBC received the first $8 to $10 million in revenues to offset its production costs. After NBC's production costs were covered, the AFL received the next $3 million in revenues, after which the parties shared all advertising revenues equally. In its first year, the advertising revenue stream was sufficient to allow the parties to reach this final level of revenue sharing. The contract offered little risk to NBC and allowed it to avoid the potentially untoward situation of developing the AFL into a valuable property and then having to pay an inflated rights fee in the future as a result of the league's increased value. The AFL deal also provided NBC with a near-guarantee that it would not lose money on the deal and potentially high returns if the league became popular with viewers. Although this did not occur and average ratings never reached a significant number, the potential upside could not be ignored. Despite this, NBC dropped its coverage of the AFL after the 2006 season, when ESPN/ABC agreed to purchase a stake in the league and reached a 5-year deal in 2007—even playing AFL games on Monday nights. The ratings story there was much of the same. For the AFL, the NBC and ABC/ESPN exposure helped lead to an increase in attendance, which increased the value of local sponsorships. Combined with the additional revenues yielded by the television contract, franchise values increased, with average valuations reaching approximately $20 million in 2007 from $500,000 in 1998. The AFL conceded its long-term television revenues for short-to-medium term growth and exposure. This benefitted both franchise owners and NBC, as the network reaped 5% of the sale price for any franchise that sold for more than $12 million. Although, as noted, television ratings for AFL games on NBC and ABC/ESPN were quite low, AFL per game attendance increased from 9,155 in 2001 to 12,957 in 2008. Finally, AFL sponsorships also increased, with league-wide sponsors reportedly paying fees in the mid-to-high six-figure range. Notwithstanding its growth, AFL teams lost a reported $24 million in both 2007 and 2008, and the league cancelled its 2009 season due to a combination of the recession and the failure of the team owners to come to a consensus on reorganizing from a traditional league structure to a single-entity structure. The league subsequently filed for bankruptcy. Despite the recent struggles of the AFL and failures of a number of football leagues in prior decades (the XFL, USFL, WFL and NFL Europe, to name a few), entrepreneurs continue to believe that there is sufficient pent up demand to support a new professional football league. Four leagues were in various stages of development in late 2009: another iteration of the AFL, the All American Football League, the United National Gridiron League, and the United Football League. Although the business models vary, all four face an uphill battle for survival.

In the aftermath of the 1999 Women's World Cup, WUSA initiated play in 2001 with an initial $40 million commitment to the venture. WUSA's investors were seeking to exploit the opportunity created by the combination of this highly successful event, the high participation in the sport for girls, the increased interest in sports by women, and the substantial buying power of women. Similar to other start-up leagues, WUSA was organized as a single-entity structure with teams located in eight cities. With revenues derived from attendance, sponsorships, and television, WUSA struggled financially, and lost an estimated $100 million during its existence. Spurred by a 30% decrease in costs, the league's losses decreased 45% from 2001 to 2002, yet WUSA remained far from profitability. In 2003, the players agreed to cooperate with WUSA's cost-saving measures. The league's financial situation was considered dire enough that WUSA's top players accepted a 25% pay cut from $80,000 to $85,000 to $60,000. They were not alone in their sacrifice, as the league's average salary decreased approximately 20% to $37,000 and roster sizes were decreased by two. Including complimentary tickets, league attendance decreased from 8,103 in 2001 to 6,957 in 2002, a 14% decrease. Although these figures exceeded league expectations, attendance needed to improve for WUSA to survive. League-wide sponsorship revenues were between $5.5 million and $12 million, with two charter sponsors paying between $1 million and $2.5 million each, and seven league sponsors paying between $500,000 and $1 million each, depending on the sponsorship category and details. The league's television revenues and ratings were below expectations. After the 2001 season, in which games broadcast on the highly visible cable networks TNT and CNN/SI resulted in 0.3 Nielsen ratings, WUSA's shift to the better time slots offered by the relatively obscure PAX network yielded a 0.1 rating in 2002, as it competed head-to-head with MLS broadcasts on ESPN on a weekly basis. Although it is debatable whether WUSA partnered with the appropriate channels, these moribund ratings had to improve if WUSA games were to continue to be broadcast on broadly distributed cable networks. Several league games were broadcast on ESPN2 in 2003. Perhaps an even greater challenge for WUSA was to differentiate itself from two other competitors—MLS and the WNBA. Although WUSA and MLS competed in the same sport during the same calendar months and their games were often broadcast at the same time, they targeted largely different audiences. MLS consumers are primarily young men of various ethnicities; WUSA targeted families and younger females. In this sense, the WNBA seemed to be the most significant competition for WUSA. With both leagues competing for the same consumers during the same time of year, the marketplace could not support both the deeper-pocketed WNBA and the WUSA. WUSA folded after completing its third season in 2003. The void in women's professional soccer in the United States was filled when Women's Professional Soccer

(WPS) launched in seven cities in 2009, with each team losing approximately $1.5 million, and had 8 teams in 2010. The league operates with a traditional league structure, as opposed to the single-entity structure used by WUSA.

Action sports have emerged as the most significant of all of the sports described in this chapter. These sports, which include snowboarding, skateboarding, BMX biking, in-line skating and aerial skiing, as well as their various sub-disciplines, have entered the sporting mainstream but have been the subject of little academic research. Exciting, fast-paced, and dangerous, action sports are particularly appealing to 12- to 34-year-old males, a target market that is highly desirable to advertisers. Skateboarding and snowboarding are the fastest-growing sports among 7- to 17-year-olds.

Youth participation and interest in most team sports is slowly declining. Although the overall audience for action sports is still much smaller than that for the more traditional sports, its desirable demographics and increasing participation rates and interest levels should concern the leaders of the traditional "stick-and-ball" sports. Faced with a potential long-term erosion of their fan bases as these youths mature into adults, the traditional sports cannot merely hope that there will be a migration back to them when they become adults or that action sports will fade away. Recognizing this, each of the "big four" sports leagues has responded to the threat posed by action sports by adopting grassroots marketing programs aimed at youths.

Long participated in on an informal basis and considered to be part of the counterculture, action sports began to enter the mainstream in 1995 with the creation of the Extreme Games by ESPN. An amalgamation of competition in nine different sports, the 8-day, Olympic-style event provided ESPN with its own low-cost programming during a lull in professional sports, when only regular season baseball is available. Simultaneously, the Extreme Games introduced an organized platform for action sports. Largely ignored and mocked by both broadcasters and leaders of mainstream sports, ratings were surprisingly strong, resulting in a 1.0 Nielsen rating on ESPN and 0.5 on ESPN2. In 1996, ESPN changed the name to "X Games" in order to gain greater audience appeal and allow for easier international marketing. As the popularity of the summer event increased, the Winter X Games were added in 1997 to fill a similar void in ESPN's programming and to further exploit the increasing demand in the marketplace. The X Games are monetized through television advertising and sponsorships. ESPN's ownership of its programming inventory allows it to reap directly the revenues generated from the sales of advertising and sponsorships. Top-level sponsors of the Summer X Games pay in the low-to-mid seven figures, and second-tier sponsors pay in the low seven figures; sponsors of the Winter X Games paid $2 million in 2009, with second-tier sponsors paying $1 million. ESPN regularly sells out most of its sponsorship packages and generated $30 million in sponsorship revenues in recent years, along with an additional $10 million in advertising revenues. Despite total event attendance that regularly exceeds 200,000 in the summer and approximately 80,000 in the winter, the X Games charges admission fees ranging from $10 to $100 based on the event, the time of day, and the age of the fan. The X Games have generated annual profits of approximately $12 million over the past several years. ESPN has expanded the X Games brand globally by adding competitions in Latin America, the Middle East, Asia, and Europe. It has also added global team competitions, as well as qualifying events for all X Games competitions, Junior X Games, and touring skate park events.

Given its extraordinary success, it should not be surprising that competitors to ESPN's X Games have emerged. Other entities have focused on presenting action sports tours, with live music acts joining in with the athletic demonstrations in festival-like events. NBC and MTV Networks own Alli, the Alliance of Action Sports. Alli owns a number of action sports properties, including the multi-stop Dew Tour and Winter Dew Tour and the lower-level Free Flow and Winter Free Flow tours, the King of Wake tour, the AMA Pro Motorcross tour, and single events such as the China Invitational. Despite these efforts, the X Games remain the dominant brand in action sports.

Athletes competing in action sports receive compensation primarily in the form of endorsements, with top athletes earning well over $1 million a year and very good athletes earning between $250,000 and $500,000. Athletes also receive income in the form of prize money earned in competitions, with the X Games offering over $1.5 million in prize money in 2008. However, this pales in comparison to the profits generated by the owners of these events.

Action sports now appear to be a permanent part of the sports landscape, but the genre has not yet achieved first-tier status. Action sports have strong demographics that attract top-tier sponsors, an increasing participation rate, a year-round presence, and strong product extensions, such as video games, music, and toys. Its lifestyle appeal is undeniable. However, the lifestyle that action sports embraces has strong anticorporate roots. Its notoriously fickle fans and athletes have traditionally shunned the mainstream and could abandon the mass presentation and media coverage of action sports as the genre becomes further embraced by the corporate world. In addition, action sports are unlikely to generate revenues comparable to established sports properties until this occurs. The irony is that the same corporate embrace that could send revenues skyrocketing could also lead to the demise of action sports. Thus, leaders of the action sports properties face an interesting dilemma: how is big business made out of a sport whose fan base, participants, and athletes have traditionally avoided big businesses?

This chapter looks at various emerging leagues and niche sports in detail. In the first selection, Tim Bezbatchenko reviews MLS and its single-entity structure in depth. The second article, by Marc Edelman and Elizabeth Masterson, examines Women's Professional Soccer. An article by Marc Edelman and Keith Harrison then details the business of the WNBA. Keith Willoughby and Chad Mancini provide an obituary for the dearly departed Xtreme Football League. The final excerpt is Michael Davis' examination of the determinants of location for minor league baseball teams.

MLS

BEND IT FOR BECKHAM: A LOOK AT MAJOR LEAGUE SOCCER AND ITS SINGLE ENTITY DEFENSE TO ANTITRUST LIABILITY AFTER THE DESIGNATED PLAYER RULE

Tim Bezbatchenko

I. INTRODUCTION

[*Ed. Note: As this book was going to publication in early 2010, MLS and its players union reached a new 5-year collective bargaining agreement that extends the Designated Player Rule to 3 players per team, whose first $335,000 in annual salary is paid for by the league and counts against the team salary cap. The remainder is paid for by the player's team. MLS has announced that it will add teams in Portland and Vancouver in 2011 and Montreal in 2012, bringing the league to 19 teams.*]

Major League Soccer (MLS or the league) has undergone many changes since 2002 when, in *Fraser v. Major League Soccer, L.L.C.,* a federal appeals court rejected the players' claim that the league's organizational structure violated antitrust law and granted MLS single entity status.[1] No longer a young league with an uncertain future, MLS has established an identity in the United States with its proven ability to maintain a consistent fan base and expand into new geographic markets.[2] Recent developments in league policy, one of which permitted David Beckham's new contract,[3] highlight the league's maturity and growth potential in its adolescent years. Yet these developments likely affect the league's existing defense to antitrust liability under section 1 of the Sherman Antitrust Act.[4] Specifically, by changing league rules, MLS's single entity distinction hangs in the balance.

Most notable among the recent league's developments is the implementation of the Designated Player Rule (the

Rule).[5] Created in November 2006, the Rule allows MLS teams to sign players whose salaries extend beyond otherwise restricted team salary budgets.[6] Unlike non-designated players, the cost of designated players above $400,000 is the financial responsibility of the club rather than the league itself.[7] As soon as the Rule was announced, clubs' player recruitment personnel began scouring the globe in search of designated players.[8] Predictably, news of the Rule drove speculation that many world soccer stars would sign with MLS.[9] Indeed, within two months, MLS experienced a watershed moment when, in January 2007, David Beckham signed with the league. Beckham inked a $250 million deal to play for Major League Soccer's Los Angeles Galaxy.[10] The media quickly hailed it the "Beckham Rule," believing the ability to attract David Beckham to MLS provided the catalyst for the rule change.[11]

Also predictable, but much less discussed, was the effect the Designated Player Rule had on MLS's vulnerability to antitrust liability. In 2002, MLS declared victory against its players[12] in *Fraser v. Major League Soccer, L.L.C.,* a lawsuit that began in 1997 when the players claimed that the league's centralized structure violated federal antitrust law.[13] In its defense, MLS used the "single entity" enterprise rationale to garner antitrust protection. The league successfully convinced the district court to hold that MLS was a single entity. Therefore, its teams could not illegally conspire under section 1 of the Sherman Antitrust Act.[14] Immunity from section 1 as a single entity does not preclude section 2 liability for unlawful monopolization. However, a jury determined that a lack of market definition by the plaintiffs precluded a finding that the league attempted to monopolize under section 2.[15] On appeal, the U.S. Circuit Court of Appeals for the First Circuit affirmed the district court's market definition holding and ruled in favor of MLS. Nevertheless, the First Circuit was ambiguous in its holding regarding the status of MLS as a single entity for section 1 purposes.[16] Instead of plainly affirming the district court's single entity holding, the First Circuit side-stepped the issue by ruling that the players' claim failed because of the lack of a defined market, a prerequisite for antitrust liability.[17]

Vulnerability to antitrust lawsuits would pose problems for a league that has yet to make profits during its twelve years.[18] Antitrust litigation resulting in a forced restructuring of the league and player salaries would impact the future of professional soccer in this country and have ramifications on other professional sports leagues. All professional sports leagues are subject to scrutiny under antitrust law (the one exception being Major League Baseball). So MLS will be closely watched should the players decide to re-challenge the league's single entity status. A player victory in court would sound the warning bells to all professional sports leagues considering changing league policies and to any person or entity contemplating a new professional sports league.

This Comment discusses the ramifications of the Designated Player Rule and other recent developments on Major League Soccer's single entity defense. . . . Part III provides background information on MLS, describing the formation of the league and the details of its organizational structure. Part III also discusses the *Fraser* decisions from the district court and the First Circuit. In light of recent developments in Major League Soccer, Part IV of this Comment analyzes the impact of the recent developments and changes to the league as they relate to antitrust liability, paying particular attention to the Designated Player Rule. Part IV discusses whether the Designated Player Rule creates enough divergent interests among the league's teams to extinguish MLS's claim that it operates as a single entity enterprise. Next, this Comment discusses the ramifications of MLS losing its single entity status as well as the future of Major League Soccer following the Designated Player Rule. Part V concludes by examining the broader legal implications imposed by a single entity structure and its continued use by future professional sports leagues.

[*Ed. Note: Author's discussion of antitrust principles under the Sherman Act and the single entity defense is omitted.*]

. . . .

III. MAJOR LEAGUE SOCCER BACKGROUND AND LEGAL HISTORY

This Part provides background information on MLS, including the formation of the league and the details of its organizational structure. . . .

A. Organizational Structure

In exchange for permission to host the 1994 World Cup soccer tournament from the Federation Internationale de Football (FIFA), the United States Soccer Federation (USSF) promised to establish a viable Division I professional soccer league in the U.S.[97] The USSF took advantage of the success of the 1994 World Cup and created Major League Soccer the following year.[98] The North American Soccer League (NASL), the country's former pro soccer league, failed in the 1980s due to financial difficulties and a lack of centralized management.[99] In an attempt to avoid the past failures caused by excessive spending and decentralized management, a key feature of the newly created MLS was its unique organizational structure.[100] Alan Rothenberg, the President of USSF, consulted with antitrust counsel to create a league with a highly concentrated management structure—one that could avoid the antitrust issues the National Football League encountered and the financial costs that the NASL experienced.[101] Eventually, Rothenberg and other founders organized the league as a limited liability company owned by a number of independent investors and managed by a committee known as the board of governors.[102] Instead of a league composed of independently owned franchises like most other professional sports leagues, MLS established itself as a "single entity," where the league retained control over all individual teams and players.[103]

MLS's structure and operation is governed by its Limited Liability Company Agreement (LLC Agreement).[104] Rather than teams owned by individuals, the league's investors hold the rights to all thirteen [*now sixteen*] teams.[105] MLS's ownership umbrella covers all intellectual property rights that relate to the league, its teams, tickets, and broadcasting rights.[106] Moreover, the league supplies equipment, sets team schedules, negotiates stadium leases and liabilities, and pays the salaries of referees and other league personnel.[107]

The league itself is owned by independent investors ranging from corporations or partnerships to individuals.[108] Some of the investors are passive investors, while others are active investors who help operate the league.[109] Under MLS's LLC Agreement, the active investors form what is known as the Management Committee.[110] Of the active investors, some are called "investor-operators" since they play a key role in the management and operation of specific teams.[111]

Investor-operators enter into an "Operating Agreement" with MLS in which investor-operators own a financial stake in the league, not just in their individual team.[112] For example, the Kraft Sports Group, as the investor-operator of the MLS's New England Revolution, holds an ownership stake in MLS itself and a considerable interest in the Revolution as the "operator" of the team.[113] As part of the Operating Agreement, these investors have the "exclusive right and obligation to provide Management Services for [the] Team within its Home Territory."[114] Thus, the league surrenders some control to these investor-operators to allow them to run the teams and personally benefit financially from them.[115] The investor-operators:

> *hire, at their own expense and discretion, local staff (including the general managers and coaches of their respective teams), and are responsible for local office expenses, local promotional costs for home games, and one-half the stadium rent . . . . In addition, they license local broadcast rights, sell home tickets, and conduct all local marketing on behalf of MLS.*[116]

The agreements concerning these issues are independent from the league and do not require prior league approval.[117] In exchange for the investor-operators' investment and services, MLS pays each of them a "management fee."[118] In 2002. . . the management fee included 50% of local ticket sales and concessions, the first $1,125,000 of local broadcast revenues, 100% of revenues from overseas tours, 50% of net revenues from the MLS Championship Game, and a share of exhibition game revenues.[119] Thus, an investor-operator's profits and losses will differ depending, at least in part, on the team's performance.[120]

Under strict rules established by the league, investor-operators play a limited role in choosing players for their teams.[121] For example, while they cannot independently bid for players against MLS, investor-operators may trade players with other MLS teams upon league approval.[122] In choosing its players, no single team can exceed the team salary budget that the board of governors establishes, which is currently around $2 million.[123] The league's residual revenues are split equally among all investors, both passive and active.[124]

[*Ed. Note: Author's discussion of the district court's opinion in* Fraser v. MLS *is omitted.*]

. . . .

2. The First Circuit: Avoiding the Issue

On appeal, the First Circuit affirmed the district court jury decision that the plaintiff's claims failed because they were unable to define a distinct, relevant market.[152] . . .

Even though the court left the single entity issue unanswered, the court's detailed discussion . . . went a long way towards rejecting MLS's single entity status.[157] . . . . First, investor-operators have a "diversity of entrepreneurial interests that goes well beyond the ordinary company" . . . . For example, the investor-operators independently hire and fire management, preserve a large part of the teams' revenues, and hold the sale rights for their team that relate to "specific assets and not just shares in the common enterprise."[160] Second, the court noted that the structure more closely resembled a joint venture than a single entity because the investor-operators effectively controlled MLS since they had a majority of the board's votes and were not just "mere servants."[161] Nonetheless, the court stopped short of denying MLS single entity status.[162] Instead, it ruled that MLS's organizational structure was a "hybrid arrangement, somewhere between a single company . . . and a cooperative arrangement between existing competitors."[163] . . .

IV. EROSION OF THE LEAGUE'S SINGLE ENTITY STATUS

MLS is on the move. Barely a week goes by without new headlines concerning developments in MLS. For the first time in league history, MLS managed to sign a lucrative television package for the 2007 season.[166] Additionally, a number of new investors, both domestic and foreign, have made long-term commitments to the league.[167] These investors include well-known organizations such as Red Bull Inc. and the English soccer club Chelsea FC. The rise of soccer-specific stadiums has increased the viability for teams to make profits as well as improve the entertainment level of the game.[168] Soccer-specific stadiums provide each team a place to call "home" and allow the fans to enjoy the game in an intimate setting. Additionally, the league publicized that it expects to earn a profit in the year 2010.[169] And the January 2007 signing of David Beckham to the Los Angeles Galaxy sent shock waves through the entire sporting community.[170] But what do these developments have to do with MLS's single entity status?

As mentioned above . . . the crucial factors that courts use to determine if a single entity exists: (1) the degree to which a subsidiary has interests separate and apart from the whole and beyond an ordinary company, also called "entrepreneurial interests"; (2) market development and the degree of competition that exists for players, coaches, fan support, ticket sales, etc.; (3) investor autonomy and the degree to which a league pays player salaries; (4) the competitive balance among teams in the league; and (5) the disparity of profits and losses among teams.[173]

A series of changes in the league have eradicated the league's unified interests, which are necessary to justify its single entity defense to section 1 liability. . . . Although other factors may affect MLS's single entity status, the Designated Player Rule is most likely to erode the league's single entity nature.[174] This Part concludes by examining the consequences of MLS losing its single entity status on the MLS as well as other professional sports leagues.

A. The Designated Player Rule and Legal Ramifications

According to the Designated Player Rule, each MLS team may sign one "designated" player without regard to each team's budget cap, currently around $2 million per team.[175] The cost of a designated player's salary above $400,000, which is the amount the league is willing to pay for each player, is the financial responsibility of the club's investor-operator.[176] In other words, the league covers the first $400,000, but the investor-operator pays the remaining amount.[177] Therefore, a designated player's salary should reflect the market and, specifically, how much an investor-operators values a designated player.[178] Although clubs receive only one designated player slot, these slots may be traded to gain additional slots.[179] However, no team may hold more than two designated players.[180]

The David Beckham transaction provides a helpful example for understanding the Designated Player Rule.[181] The investor-operator of the Los Angeles Galaxy, Anschutz Entertainment Group (AEG), signed Beckham to a deal allegedly worth $250 million.[182] Initially, this scared soccer pundits who believed that MLS would be footing the bill for the entire amount, which would threaten to bankrupt the league.[183] However, under the Designated Player Rule, MLS only pays the first $400,000, and the rest of the money is the responsibility of AEG as the team's investor-operator.[184] Therefore, most of the risk was assumed by AEG, not the MLS.

1. "Entrepreneurial Interests" Apart from the Whole

To start off, the Designated Player Rule predominantly serves the entrepreneurial interests of the wealthier, riskier investor-operators of MLS that operate in larger markets. By allowing investor-operators the ability to use unlimited resources to sign players, the Designated Player Rule cuts directly against the theory of the single entity enterprise, that is, that unified subsidiaries act under a common conscience. Small market teams, such as Kansas City and Columbus, may lack the wealth or the appeal to draw star-studded

names to their markets. The large market teams, Los Angeles and New York, were the first teams to sign designated players. First, David Beckham signed with the Los Angeles Galaxy for a whopping $250 million. A few weeks later, Claudio Reyna, the most decorated soccer player in United States' history, signed with the New York Red Bulls.[185] Two months passed before another team signed a designated player to a contract.[186] This time it was the Chicago Fire that signed Mexican soccer icon Cuauhtemoc Blanco.[187] The New York Red Bulls later signed a second designated player, Juan Pablo Angel.[188] Small market teams whose investor-operators lack the deep pockets of companies such as Red Bull Inc. and AEG act with less of an entrepreneurial interest in the Designated Player Rule simply because they are unable to pay exorbitant prices for players in the competitive global market. The league's ability to control costly salaries through its centralized structure was paramount in the district court's single entity analysis.[189] However, the freedom to contract openly with "designated" players directly erodes this foundation.

On the other hand, the Designated Player Rule protects the interests of the league and other investor-operators in addition to protecting the interests of deep-pocketed investor-operators. Therefore, this factor alone does not sufficiently crack the league's unity of interest and disqualify its single entity status. The entire league, including the small market teams, benefit from increases in the level of talent, media exposure, and revenue that result from signing designated players. Moreover, by bringing global stars to the United States, the league's overall credibility increases.[190] Signing players such as David Beckham and Cuauhtemoc Blanco is a tremendous stride in the areas of talent and media exposure. For example, a week after Beckham's signing, news reports all over the globe covered the story.[191] This exposure can only help the league's overall image, which is crucial as MLS competes with the NFL, NBA, MLB, and NHL in today's saturated sports market. Even though the exposure benefits the entire league to a degree, little doubt remains that the Designated Player Rule benefits the wealthier teams more than others.

2. Market Competition for Players, Coaches, Fan Support, and Ticket Sales

The competition for players can be separated into two different forums: the general marketplace for professional soccer players in the U.S. and the competition for players among teams. In terms of the professional soccer market itself, MLS essentially created an entirely new market for players.[192] Alluding to the failed NASL, the First Circuit in *Fraser* noted that MLS was an "arrangement formed as a risky venture against a background of prior failure."[193] The court ruled that the forming of the league and its structure actually created a market for the competition for players since no Division I soccer league existed.[194] Past attempts at a professional soccer league in the U.S. had failed from financial shortcomings.[195] The court seemed willing to grant MLS single entity status in part because of the security investors received through the centralized structure and the benefits conveyed to professional soccer players through the formation of the league.

It is not difficult to see why the court ruled this way. After all, MLS created opportunities for players in a Division I environment, and the resulting economic effect was to raise salaries for soccer players above existing levels.[196] However, twelve years have passed and MLS has changed dramatically, particularly with the implementation of the Designated Player Rule. MLS is no longer a new league struggling for survival. The Designated Player Rule is evidence that the league is willing to expose itself to market forces and the higher costs associated with a freer market. Thus, with the passage of time and the implementation of the Designated Player Rule, the arguments that MLS created a new market and that the league needs to tightly control its economics through a single entity structure are less convincing.

Additionally, the second factor also measures the level of actual competition for players within the labor market between investor-operators. By permitting investor-operators to compete freely for "designated" players, the Designated Player Rule exposes the weakness in the league's unity of interest claim. Scholars suggest that professional sports leagues do not operate as single entities in the labor market because individual owners compete for players and therefore have divergent interests.[197] This theory can now be applied to MLS. Under the Designated Player Rule, individual investor-operators in MLS may now compete and bid up player salaries to obtain the most desirable designated player. When investor-operators begin competing for players like they are now, the structure resembles conventional professional sports leagues, which consist of individual owners competing for players in a joint venture. In other words, the more teams compete for players, the less their interests align. As interests diverge, it becomes increasingly difficult for MLS to argue that it operates as a single enterprise with a common conscience. Moreover, competition among teams for coaches, ticket sales, media revenues, and team apparel sales further separates the interests among teams and makes a single entity claim more difficult to defend.

3. Investor Autonomy and the Degree to which the League Pays Player Salaries

Naturally, the single entity structure frees investor-operators from the burden of paying player salaries. The organizational structure of the league is set up in such a way that the league carries this burden. The league's responsibility for player salaries was a pivotal reason for the *Fraser* court's decision that MLS operated as a single entity enterprise.[198] The district court opinion underscored how the "surrender of autonomy, together with the attendant benefit of lower and more controlled player payrolls . . . will help MLS to succeed where others, notably NASL, failed."[199] The court opined how this feature served the interests of the whole league rather than the ulterior interests of individual investor-operators.[200] Conversely, the Designated Player Rule directly opposes this feature and encourages autonomous action by investor-operators. The Rule loosens the league's control over player payrolls and effectively serves the ulterior interests of individual investor-operators. The Rule allows investor-operators to autonomously scour the global market for designated players and offer expensive contracts to selected players. By approving the Rule, the league encourages competition among investor-operators for players like David Beckham. In an open, laissez-faire soccer market, competition for players is the driving force for market equilibrium as supply and demand naturally converge to establish the fair market value for players. However, a large degree of competition among teams within a single entity enterprise contradicts the essence of the single entity theory. The league no longer acts with a "single conscience" as investor-operators actively compete for players.[201] Prior to the Rule, the court classified the structure as a "hybrid arrangement, somewhere between a single company . . . and a cooperative arrangement between existing competitors."[202] After the Rule, the league looks more like the latter, a cooperative arrangement.

4. The Competitive Balance Among Teams

On its face, the Designated Player Rule is non-discriminatory. Every team holds an equal opportunity to sign players. The Rule allows market forces to dictate where players end up. The competition for designated players is substantially less regulated or laissez-faire. However, assuming that larger market teams will be able to afford the most desirable players, the competitive balance that helps characterize MLS's single entity nature will decline. As it stands, the L.A. Galaxy, New York Red Bulls, and the Chicago Fire have acquired arguably four of the world's finest soccer players. These acquisitions effectively disturb the parity among the league's teams, particularly for teams that are unable to sign such star players.[203] So, although it may be non-discriminatory on its face, beneath the surface, the Designated Player Rule fosters discrimination by alienating teams that cannot financially support this caliber of player. As a result, the Rule hinders small market teams' ability to compete on the field. Therefore, the fourth factor flies in the face of a single entity's prize attribute: competitive balance among teams.

For example, Hugo Sanchez, Mexico's national soccer team coach and former MLS player, believes the Designated Player Rule will improve the league's talent and widen the existing gap between the United States and Mexico.[204] He stated that Major League Soccer is "getting better day by day and year by year. Now, with the new policy of bringing big stars, it's going to get better much quicker."[205] Yet, Sanchez's expectations apply only to teams that can afford to buy expensive international stars. The remaining clubs must settle with their current rosters or sign less expensive players into their designated player slots. The wealthier clubs will improve at a faster rate, leaving other clubs behind. For instance, after signing its two designated players in 2007, the New York Red Bulls became the first team to start a season with four consecutive shutouts.[206]

An increase in the level of talent in any professional sports league is positive for the fans, the players, and the league. MLS has been criticized for delivering a dull product, a reflection of the level of talent on the field.[207] These critics applaud the Designated Player Rule for the positive effects it will have on MLS's pool of talent from which it selects players. Nonetheless, the structural changes caused by the Designated Player Rule may create an environment where the larger MLS clubs reap the benefits to the detriment of smaller MLS clubs. If this happens, the league may become plagued with the same problems as the North American Soccer League. In the NASL, the success of the wealthiest club, the New York Cosmos, came at the cost of the other clubs and ultimately led to the league's demise.[208]

5.   The Disparity of Profits and Losses Among Teams

The disparity in profits and losses among teams was one argument stated for denying the NFL single entity status in Los Angeles Memorial Coliseum Commission v. National Football League.[209] Applying this rationale to MLS, David Beckham's Designated Player contract with the Los Angeles Galaxy will create a disparity of profits and losses among the teams in MLS because the Galaxy will benefit the most from the popularity of David Beckham. For example, Galaxy clothing apparel alone will be worth millions of dollars.[210] Local television revenues also will bring in millions of dollars for Galaxy's investor-operators. Although MLS policy mandates that some revenues be shared with the league, a significant percentage remains with AEG.[211] Teams without household names such as David Beckham will lag behind the Los Angeles, New York, and Chicago teams in terms of revenue. The profit disparity further fuels the claim that the Designated Player Rule creates divergent interests among teams and undermines the league's single entity status.

B.   Designated Player Rule Limitations

As noted earlier, the Designated Player Rule addresses MLS's need to increase the standard of talent that currently exists. The Rule challenges the league's conventional behavior regarding player salaries by giving up some of the league's control to the investor-operators. However, the league implemented specific stopgaps and limitations that mitigate the Rule's impact.[212] The league shrewdly recognized the dangers potentially caused by the Rule, such as competitive inequality and exorbitant spending. To help thwart these dangers, the league placed a temporal limitation on the Designated Player Rule so that it automatically expires after three years.[213] The three-year experimental period allows MLS to step back and reflect on the changes the Rule causes, and if needed, it allows MLS to tweak the Rule. Next, the Rule only permits two [now three] designated players per team.[214] This limitation assuages the fears of the "New York Cosmo effect"[215] that the wealthiest team has the best players on its roster. These two limitations lessen the overall impact of the Designated Player Rule. As such, the limitations are a step back in the single entity direction because they reduce the divergent interests generated by the Rule.

C.   Legal Consequences of Losing Single Entity Status: MLS as a Joint Venture

The implementation of the Designated Player Rule is a significant development for Major League Soccer. The Rule reveals the league's commitment to improve talent on the field and its willingness to take risks in order to increase the league's popularity. The Rule also is an important development from a legal perspective. . . . [t]he Designated Player Rule exposes flaws in MLS's single entity claim by generating divergent interests among the league's investor-operators. By encouraging teams to compete for designated players, a court will have a difficult time deciding that the investor-operators operate with similar goals and under a common conscience. Consequently, a court likely will determine that MLS and its investor-operators form a joint venture. As a joint venture, the cooperation between MLS and the investor-operators would meet the agreement requirement, and MLS would become vulnerable to antitrust liability under section 1.

. . . .

As a single entity, MLS currently receives immunity from section 1 antitrust liability. However, liability aside, there are additional benefits from MLS's single entity status that may be in jeopardy if it were to lose this distinction. The principal benefit the league receives from this classification is the ability to keep costs down by suppressing salaries to affordable levels for investor-operators. This salary suppression is accomplished through the centralized structure by which players sign contracts with the league rather than with each independent team. Over the past twelve years, the cost savings associated with this structure has helped the league survive and prevented the problems that plagued the financially troubled NASL. For that reason, MLS has an incentive to keep its single entity status beyond merely preserving its section 1 immunity.

Yet, changes in the league, such as the Designated Player Rule, suggest MLS is heading in a new direction, one that closely resembles a joint venture. If MLS continues to encourage autonomous behavior from the investor-operators, it must also accept the downside risk of section 1 liability. Nevertheless, the exposure to section 1 liability would be alleviated by the benefits provided by a joint venture. Specifically, teams in a joint venture would be permitted to employ the best players money can buy. The most frequent criticism of MLS is that the quality of soccer on field is second-tier in comparison to its European counterparts.[217] The Designated Player Rule is a direct attempt to bridge the gap in talent by enticing the world's best players to come to the United States. Moreover, recent developments such as the MLS's television contract, shirt sponsorships, soccer stadiums, and new investor-operators provide new sources of revenue that would help alleviate the cost burdens associated with joint ventures.

Emerging professional sports leagues attempting to organize as a single entity enterprise will surely scrutinize MLS and its ability to maintain its single entity status. Given that MLS has taken advantage of the benefits provided by its single entity status for twelve years, other entrepreneurs looking to launch professional sports leagues will likely follow MLS's lead: start as a single entity in order to keep costs down, then slowly move to a decentralized structure as the quantity of investors increase and the league solidifies its foundation. The single entity model could be utilized as a temporary structure for developing a professional sports league but is unlikely to continue as the league grows and moves beyond the "hybrid" spectrum.

Likewise, current professional sports leagues will examine how a court classifies MLS in future antitrust litigation. When the players decide to challenge the league's single entity distinction and, as argued above, likely win their claim, it may have a chilling effect on other leagues' ability to change league rules. In particular, leagues will be less likely to modify existing rules in fear of suffering the consequences imposed by antitrust litigation. . . .

V. CONCLUSION

As new leagues and businesses follow the MLS's single entity framework, it will become increasingly necessary for a court to set the parameters for single entity status. It is imperative that a court directly and unambiguously decide the legality of the hybrid arrangement. . . .

The survival and growth of Major League Soccer is crucial for the continued growth of soccer in this country. To ensure its survival, the league has taken calculated risks that aid in the creation of new soccer fans and help attract existing soccer fans to MLS games. The Designated Player Rule may be the type of risk that is essential to elevate the talent in the league. Amid this change, MLS should be conscious of the legal ramifications. . . . [T]hese changes strongly suggest MLS is less of a single entity and more of a joint venture. MLS must bear in mind how the First Circuit's *Fraser* opinion strongly hints at a future reevaluation and that MLS is walking on thin ice with its hybrid arrangement. Further, the league cannot forget that historically few courts have awarded single entity status to professional sports leagues. In addition to the Designated Player Rule, the creation of soccer-specific stadiums and the new television package

are indications that the league is drifting away from the characteristics associated with single entities. As such, the league should be conscious of each new decision or rule modification because it may compromise MLS's protection from antitrust immunity under section 1.

Notes

1. *Fraser v. Major League Soccer,* L.L.C., 284 F.3d 47, 54 (1st Cir. 2002). Single entity status is a term describing entities that cannot illegally conspire in violation of antitrust laws because parties are deemed one entity rather than multiple entities acting together. Joseph P. Bauer & William H. Page, *Kintner Federal Antitrust Law* 92 (2d ed. 2002).

2. Jon Weinbach, U.S. Soccer League Finally Hopes to Score, *Wall St. J.,* Mar. 23, 2007, at B1.

3. "We can hit these numbers" will be remembered as the words that revolutionized professional soccer in the United States. Grant Wahl, Anatomy of a Blockbuster: The Story Behind the Beckham Deal and the Economics, *Sports Illustrated,* Jan. 17, 2007, http://sportsillustrated.cnn.com/2007/writers/grant_wahl/01/17/beckham.qa/index.html. These words, spoken by Tim Leiweke of Anschutz Entertainment Group (AEG), symbolize the impact the AEG executives believed David Beckham would have on MLS development. Press Release, Major League Soccer, Global Icon David Beckham Signs with the Los Angeles Galaxy in Landmark Deal: World's No. 1 Soccer Star to Make Galaxy Debut in Summer 2007 (Jan. 11, 2007), available at http://www.mlsnet.com/news/mls_news.jsp?ymd=20070111&content=81619&vkey=pr_ mls&fext=.jsp. These "numbers" referred to the $250 million spent to lure David Beckham to Major League Soccer's L.A. Galaxy from world renowned soccer club Real Madrid. *Id.* With the deal completed, David Beckham, the most recognized athlete on the planet, was coming to America. *Id.* The English professional soccer player's name was searched on Google more than any other sporting personality in 2003 and 2004. See Google, 2003 Year-End Google Zeitgeist (2003), available at http://www.google.com/press/zeitgeist2003.html; Google, 2004 Year-End Google Zeitgeist (2004), available at http://www.google.com/press/zeitgeist2004.html. Also in 2004, *TIME Magazine* listed David Beckham in its 100 most influential global icons. Press Release, *TIME Magazine, TIME* Names the World's Most Influential People (Apr. 18, 2004), available at http://www.timewarner.com/corp/newsroom/pr/0,20812,670354,00.html. Thus, the news that he had signed with MLS came down like thunder in the media and throughout the global community. Within two days of the announcement, Major League Soccer's L.A. Galaxy had sold 5,000 additional season tickets. Wahl, *supra.* The Beckham announcement "has generated more interest in Major League Soccer than any other event in league history," said MLS commissioner Don Garber. Associated Press, Promise of Beckham Helps MLS Ticket Sales Skyrocket, ESPNsoccernet, Jan. 16, 2007, http://soccernet.espn.go.com/news/story? id=400229&cc=5901.

4. See Hoover's Profile, Major League Soccer, L.L.C., http://www.answers.com/major%20league%20soccer (last visited Dec. 4, 2007) (highlighting the league's history).

5. Press Release, Major League Soccer, MLS Implements Designated Player Rule and Other Competition Initiatives (Nov. 11, 2006), available at http://web.mlsnet.com/news/mls_events_news.jsp?ymd=20061111&content_id=78396&vkey=mlscup2006&fext=.jsp.

6. The salary budget, also known as a salary cap, is "the maximum amount of money that can be spent on salaries for a sports team or other group." *Webster's New Millennium Dictionary of English* (pre-

view ed., vol. 0.9.7, 2006), available at http://dictionary .reference.com/browse/salary%20cap.

7. Press Release, Major League Soccer, *supra* note 5.

8. Associated Press, MLS OKs 'Beckham Rule' to Attract Superstar Players, ESPNsoccernet, Nov. 11, 2006, http://soccernet.espn .go.com/news/story?id=391320&cc=5901.

9. *Id.*

10. Press Release, Major League Soccer, Global Icon David Beckham Signs with the Los Angeles Galaxy in Landmark Deal: World's No. 1 Soccer Star to Make Galaxy Debut in Summer 2007 (Jan. 11, 2007), available at http://www.mlsnet.com/news/mls_news .jsp?ymd=20070111&content_id=81619&vkey=pr_ mls&fext=.jsp.

11. Steve Davis, Ownership Diversity Drove the Beckham Rule, ESPNsoccernet, Nov. 14, 2006, http://soccer.espn.go.com/ columns/story? id=391763&root=mls&&cc=5901.

12. More specifically, MLS declared victory against Ian Fraser, Steve Trittschuh, Sean Bowers, Mark Semioli, Rhett Harty, David Scott Vaudreuil, Mark Dodd, and Mark Dougherty. See *Fraser v. Major League Soccer, L.L.C.,* 97 F. Supp. 2d 130 (D. Mass. 2000), aff'd, 284 F.3d 47 (1st Cir. 2002).

13. *Fraser v. Major League Soccer, L.L.C.,* 284 F.3d 47 (1st Cir. 2002).

14. *Id.* at 54–55.

15. *Id.* at 55.

16. *Id.* at 60–61.

17. *Id.*

18. Tim Lemke, MLS: Franchises to Profit by 2010, *Wash. Times,* May 11, 2006.

. . . .

97. *Fraser v. Major League Soccer, L.L.C.,* 284 F.3d 47, 54 (1st Cir. 2002).

98. *Id.*

99. *Id.* at 52.

100. *Fraser v. Major League Soccer, L.L.C.,* 97 F. Supp. 2d 130, 132 (D. Mass. 2000), aff'd, 284 F.3d 47 (1st Cir. 2002).

101. *Id.*

102. *Fraser,* 284 F.3d at 53, 70.

103. *Id.* at 70.

104. *Fraser,* 97 F. Supp. at 132.

105. *Fraser,* 284 F.3d at 53.

106. *Id.*

107. *Id.*

108. *Id.*

109. *Id.*

110. *Id.* at 53–54.

111. *Id.*

112. Major League Soccer, General Overview, http://www.mlsnet.com/ about (last visited Jan. 5, 2008).

113. *Id.*

114. *Fraser,* 284 F.3d at 53.

115. *Id.* at 54.

116. *Id.*

117. *Id.*

118. *Id.*

119. *Id.*

120. *Id.* Currently, there are nine investor-operators, two of which hold operating rights for multiple teams. Major League Soccer, General Overview, *supra* note 112. The principal investor-operator is Phil Anschutz & the Anschutz Entertainment Group (AEG) which operates the Chicago Fire, Houston Dynamo, D.C. United, and the Los Angeles Galaxy. *Id.* [*Ed. Note: AEG now operates the L.A. Galaxy and half of the Houston Dynamo. There are 14 investor-operators.*]

121. *Fraser,* 284 F.3d 47 at 54.

122. *Id.*

123. *Id.*

124. *Id.*

. . . .

152. *Fraser v. Major League Soccer, L.L.C.,* 284 F.3d 47, 60-61 (1st Cir. 2002). Along these lines, the circuit court described how an amendment on the appeal by the players to allege a broader market than just United States Division I would likely have been futile given the insufficient time period remaining after summary judgment was entered. *Id.* The court opined how allowing the plaintiffs to allege a new market theory would require new discovery and expert analysis and would substantially "[alter] the contours of the case." *Id.* at 60.

153. *Id.* at 59.

. . . .

157. *Id.* at 57.

158. *Id.*

159. *Id.*

160. *Id.*

161. *Id.* This factor was particularly important to the court because the operator-investors are potential competitors with MLS and each other. *Id.* MLS serves a dual purpose: to control its own assets and revenues and to "arguably" create horizontal coordination by limiting competition among investor-operators. *Id.*

162. *Id.* at 59.

163. *Id.* at 58.

. . . .

166. Mike Reynolds, MLS Sets TV Deals, Multichannel News, Aug. 7, 2006, http://www.multichannel.com/article/CA6360146.html.

167. On March 9, 2006 Red Bulls Inc. acquired the New York Metrostars. See New York Red Bulls, Timeline, http:// redbull.newyork.mlsnet .com/t107/about/timeline.jsp (last visited Jan. 5, 2008). The club's name was changed to the New York Red Bulls. *Id.* Also, Adidas made a nine-figure investment in MLS. Wahl, *supra* note 3.

168. Lemke, *supra* note 18.

169. *Id.*

170. Press Release, Major League Soccer, *supra* note 3.

. . . .

173. Factors (1) and (2) are from the *Fraser, Sullivan,* and *Los Angeles Memorial Coliseum* opinions. Factors (3) and (4) are also from the *Fraser* decisions. Factor (5) is from *Los Angeles Memorial Coliseum.* See *supra* Parts II, III.

174. As MLS moves forward, it is worth mentioning that there are other changes the MLS must consider beyond the Designated Player Rule that concern its single entity status. Much like the Designated Player Rule, these changes may not be in the interest of all the investor-operators.

    First, MLS's new soccer stadium initiative of constructing stadiums with a capacity between 20,000 and 30,000 fans conflicts with investor-operators who prefer larger stadiums that can be shared with other sports teams. Major League Soccer, General Overview, *supra* note 112 ("These facilities usually hold between 20,000 and 30,000 people and share design concepts with some of the finest soccer venues in Europe. In 2007, seven of the [l]eague's 13 teams will compete in stadiums built specifically for professional soccer. In addition, Red Bull Park will debut in 2008."). See also Thomas D. Stuck, Comment, Facility Issues in Major League Soccer: What Do Soccer Stadiums Have To Do with Antitrust Liability?, 14 *Marq. Sports L. Rev.* 551 (2004). For instance, the Kraft Sports Group prefers its 68,000 seat stadium that can be shared by both the New England Patriots and the Revolution. See New England Patriots, Stadium Fact Chart, http://www.patriots.com/stadium/index.cfm?ac=factchart (last visited Jan. 5, 2008).

    Second, MLS's new long-term television contract with ESPN and other networks, estimated to be worth $15 million annually, may benefit larger markets more than the smaller market teams. See Ben Grossman, Major League Soccer on ABC/ESPN, *Broadcasting & Cable,* Aug. 4, 2006, http://www.broadcastingcable.com/article/CA6359744.html. See also Jason Halpin, TV Deal Highlights State of the League Address, MLSnet.com, Aug. 4, 2006, http://web.mlsnet.com/news/mls_news.jsp?ymd=20060804&content_id=68212&vkey=news_ mls&fext=.jsp (noting that the ABC/ESPN deal is worth around $7–8 million per year, the Fox Soccer Channel deal is worth $5 million per year, and the HDNet deal is worth $2–3 million per year).

    Third, an increase in the number of investor-operators from three to twelve [now fourteen] and the diversification among investor-operators challenges MLS's claim that it acts with a common conscience. See Wahl, *supra* note 3. After all, it is much easier for three investor-operators than twelve to maintain unified interests. In addition to the numeric increase, the investor-operators have also diversified in composition as a number of them are international investors or corporations.

175. Jason Halpin, New MLS Competition Initiatives Unveiled, MLSnet.com, Nov. 11, 2006, http://web.mlsnet.com/news/mls_news.jsp?ymd=20061111&content_id=78445&vkey=news_mls&fext=.jsp.

176. Press Release, Major League Soccer, *supra* note 5.

177. *Id.*

178. *Id.*

179. *Id.*

180. *Id.* ("The salaries of players above the maximum salary budget have been the financial responsibility of the collective group of MLS investors. Players such as Landon Donovan (Los Angeles), Carlos Ruiz (FC Dallas) and Eddie Johnson (Kansas City) will be 'grandfathered' for one year after which they, too, will assume Designated Player status. . . . The Designated Player Rule is a three-year initiative that will conclude after the 2009 MLS season when its future will be reviewed.").

181. Tim Leiweke, the president of AEG, began courting David Beckham to MLS back in 2005 when he met with Beckham to discuss the opening of a soccer academy in Los Angeles to be called David Beckham's Soccer Academy. Wahl, *supra* note 3. At the time, David Beckham was under contract with Real Madrid. *Id.* Beckham's contract continued for two additional years at which point, during the fall of 2006, Beckham began negotiating a contract extension with Real Madrid. *Id.* After contract negotiations between Beckham and Real Madrid failed in January 2007, Tim Leiweke and AEG seized the opportunity to sign Beckham to an MLS contract. *Id.*

182. Recent publications suggest that the base salary is more in the $5 to $10 million range with the remaining money coming from endorsements and other performance and advertising contingencies. See *id.*

183. *Id.*

184. *Id.*

185. Jonathan Nierman, Reyna Coming Home to Join Bulls, MLSnet.com, Jan. 24, 2007, http://www.mlsnet.com/news/mls_news.jsp?ymd=20070124&content_id=82387&vkey=news_mls&fext=.jsp.

186. David Brown, Fire Excited by Blanco Arrival, MLSnet.com, Apr. 3, 2007, http://chicago.fire.mlsnet.com/news/team_news.jsp?ymd= 20070403&content_id=87240&vkey=news_chf&fext=.jsp&team=t100.

187. *Id.*

188. Jonathan Nierman, Red Bulls Call on Striker Angel, MLSnet.com, Apr. 17, 2007, http://web.mlsnet.com/news/mls_news.jsp?ymd=20070417&content_id=89240&vkey=news_mls&fext=.jsp.

189. *Fraser v. Major League Soccer, L.L.C.,* 97 F. Supp. 2d 130, 137 (D. Mass. 2000), aff'd, 284 F.3d 47 (1st Cir. 2002).

190. See Wahl, *supra* note 3 ("Leiweke showed Anschutz the offer he wanted to make to Beckham. According to Leiweke, Anschutz initially hadn't liked the idea for the designated-player rule. 'Phil doesn't believe at the end of the day that you build great long-term championship franchises around buying the biggest superstar,' Leiweke says. 'But when we finally got it passed in November, he turned to me and said, 'You're right, this is a good idea. We need to do this for the league, because if we're ever going to expand our rating and our audience and get credibility in our country we're going to need a star to break through.'").

191. See, e.g., Richard Bright, MLS Rule Fuels More Beckham Rumours, *Daily Telegraph* (London), Nov. 13, 2006, at Sport 4; Stephen Ellis, US Soccer's Big Bet on Beckham Follows Own Goals, *Weekend Australian,* Jan. 20, 2007; Jack Bell, Takeoff for MLS, With Beckham in the Wings, *N.Y. Times,* Apr. 4, 2007; Morgan Campbell, Vend It Like Beckham, Soccer Superstar's Arrival in MLS Already Selling the Game and Season Tickets in North America, *Toronto Star,* Jan. 12, 2007.

192. *Fraser v. Major League Soccer, L.L.C.,* 284 F.3d 47, 59 (1st Cir. 2002).

193. *Id.*

194. *Id.*

195. *Id.*

196. Before MLS, the only option for soccer players was in the United Soccer League, formerly called the A-League.

197. Nathaniel Grow, Note, There's No "I" in "League": Professional Sports Leagues and the Single Entity Defense, 105 *Mich. L. Rev.* 183, 187 (2006). Grow argues that the circuit courts have failed to distinguish between lawsuits involving non-labor disputes and those involving labor disputes between players and team owners. According to Grow, there is a unity of interest that exists among teams in the league when it comes to non-labor disputes. *Id.* at 188. By separating the non-labor from the labor disputes, Grow astutely recognizes the economic interdependence of teams that exists in a non-labor context. *Id.* Specifically, he asserts the traditional argument that professional sports teams combine to produce a single product,

the league. *Id.* at 191. He emphasizes the only true competition between teams is on the field, whereas, for the most part teams do not compete for media attention, fans, and tickets sales. *Id.* at 192. In contrast to non-labor disputes, Grow asserts that professional sports leagues are not single entities for purposes of labor disputes between players and team owners. *Id.* at 206. At its core, sports leagues do not have a unity of interest among teams because all teams have an interest in obtaining the best players. *Id.* Having the best players on the team, Grow continues, leads to winning which in turn leads to increased ticket sales and greater profits overall. *Id.* Therefore, the interests of teams diverge in the labor context, effectively blocking a single entity exception. *Id.* Additionally, the article states how single entity status for leagues in labor disputes potentially injures the players because of the possibility of collusion amongst owners and the resulting artificially suppressed player salaries. *Id.* at 207.

198. *Fraser v. Major League Soccer, L.L.C.,* 97 F. Supp. 2d 130, 137 (D. Mass. 2000), aff'd, 284 F.3d 47 (1st Cir. 2002).

199. *Id.*; Lisa Dillman, MLS Says Signing Is Strategic; Owners and Experts See Beckham's $250-Million Deal as a Controlled Cost, Different From a Former League's Failed Spending, *L.A. Times,* Jan. 13, 2007 ("'In the NASL days, because there were no control mechanisms, the spending was not rational,' MLS deputy commissioner Ivan Gazidis said . . . . 'It was not strategic. It was not well-considered. That's not the case now.'").

200. *Fraser,* 97 F. Supp. 2d at 137.

201. Interestingly, the increased competition in this case leads to increased antitrust vulnerability. The Designated Player Rule's effect is to increase competition. However, the increased competition may cause MLS to lose its single entity status and become subject to section 1 liability.

202. *Fraser v. Major League Soccer, L.L.C.,* 284 F.3d 47, 58 (1st Cir. 2002).

203. Reyna was selected as a top sixteen player in the 2002 World Cup. Associated Press, Reyna Earns All-Star Selection, Soccernet.com, June 28, 2002, http://soccernet.espn.go.com/wc/story?id=219492&lang=us. David Beckham has made 99 appearances for the England National Team. Wenger: Becks Still Had It in Training, Soccernet.com, Feb. 1, 2008, http://soccernet.espn.go.com/news/story?id=504131&cc=5901. Beckham captained the England National Team at the 2006 World Cup in Germany. Beckham Quits As Captain after England's World Cup Exit, USAToday.com, July 2, 2006, http://www.usatoday.com/sports/soccer/worldcup/2006-07-02-beckham-quits-captain_x.htm.

204. Grahame L. Jones, Leap of Faith: Hugo Sanchez, Who Was an Acrobatic, Scoring Star for Real Madrid, Sees Quality on Mexico's Team, *L.A. Times,* Mar. 28, 2007, at D8.

205. *Id.* As Mexico's national team coach and the United States nemesis in the CONCACAF soccer region, Sanchez is worried about the improvement to MLS that will result from the Designated Player Rule. *Id.* The United States has dominated Mexico as of late. See U.S.

Men Continue Unbeaten Run at Home Against Mexico with Exciting 2-2 Draw in Houston, USSOCCER.com, Feb. 6, 2008, http://www.ussoccer.com/articles/viewArticle.jsp_5308416.html. Historically, Mexico has dominated the CONCACAF region. Only in the past eight years has the United States caught and eclipsed Mexico as the region's dominant soccer country. *Id.* As such, Sanchez's comments exemplify the anxiety and frustration with the United States' continued improvement. According to Sanchez, the Designated Player Rule will widen the gap between the countries. See Jones, *supra* note 204, at D8.

206. Steve Hunt, Run Continues as Red Bulls Top FCD, MLSnet.com, Apr. 26, 2007, http://redbull.newyork.mlsnet.com/news/team_news.jsp?ymd=20070426&content_id=90714&vkey=news_rbn&fext=.jsp&team=t107.

207. Ian Plenderleith, The Road to Positive Soccer, USSoccerPlayers, Mar. 27, 2007, http://www.ussoccerplayers.com/exclusives/mls/index.html? article_id=212.

208. *Fraser v. Major League Soccer, L.L.C.,* 284 F.3d 47, 52 (1st Cir. 2002); Dillman, *supra* note 199 ("If the NASL is viewed as a cautionary tale, the Cosmos was the poster child of the league's rise and fall, a dream team assemblage of Pele, Franz Beckenbauer and Giorgio Chinaglia. In fact, a documentary about the Cosmos' fast times and hard fall, 'Once in a Lifetime,' was released last year and appeared in movie theaters.").

209. 726 F.2d 1381, 1389-90 (9th Cir. 1984).

210. Jen Chang, Debunking the Myths Behind Beckham's Contract, ESPNsoccernet, Jan. 12, 2007, http://soccernet.espn.go.com/columns/story? id=399597&root=mls&cc=5901 ("It's rumored that Adidas will be paying an additional $5 million to $6 million a year just to sponsor the Galaxy's jersey, ironic since they already manufacture them. If that doesn't tell the story of Beckham's endorsement appeal, nothing else will—and presumably Beckham will get a cut of that fee.").

211. *Fraser,* 284 F.3d at 52.

212. Press Release, Major League Soccer, *supra* note 5; Dillman, *supra* note 199 ("The playing side of his contract is extremely rational and makes business sense. This was a smart, strategic, well-thought-through move. It's not wild, out-of-control spending. Or owners trying to be the big man on the block.").

213. *Id.*

214. *Id.*

215. See *supra* note 208 and accompanying text (explaining the "Cosmos Effect").

. . . .

217. Plenderleith, *supra* note 207.

218. *Fraser v. Major League Soccer, L.L.C.,* 284 F.3d 47, 58 (1st Cir. 2002).

COULD THE NEW WOMEN'S PROFESSIONAL SOCCER LEAGUE SURVIVE IN AMERICA? HOW ADOPTING A TRADITIONAL LEGAL STRUCTURE MAY SAVE MORE THAN JUST A GAME

Marc Edelman and Elizabeth Masterson

INTRODUCTION

On July 10, 1999, over ninety thousand screaming fans watched from the Rose Bowl stands as Brandi Chastain hammered a left-footed penalty kick past the reach of China's goaltender Gao Hong to win the World Cup for the U.S. Women's Soccer Team.[1] A euphoric Chastain then celebrated by falling to her knees, stripping down to her sports bra, and clenching her fists into the air.[2] The image was featured on the covers of *Time*, *Newsweek* and *Sports Illustrated* magazines.[3] It was a symbol of "girl power," achievement, and the synergy of feminism with athleticism.[4] Immediately, women's soccer had captivated the hearts of many Americans.[5]

On the heels of Team USA's Women's World Cup victory, Discovery Communications CEO John Hendricks announced plans to launch the Women's United Soccer Association ("WUSA")—the first American women's soccer league of its kind.[6] Much like the Women's National Basketball Association ("WNBA"), the WUSA originally adopted a centrally planned legal structure, featuring shareholder ownership in the league overall, rather than ownership in individual clubs.[7]

However, despite strong initial fan interest, the WUSA soon began to struggle.[8] Fan attendance declined significantly during the 2002 and 2003 seasons.[9] Then, on September 16, 2003, the league unceremoniously suspended operations.[10]

The WUSA's demise signaled a loss of athletic opportunities for women[11]—a troubling outcome for a society that has for so long discriminated against women's athletics.[12] With the late integration of women into professional sports, the recent role of the professional female athlete has proven especially important in terms of providing young women with positive role models.[13] Indeed, studies show that female student-athletes graduate from college at a higher rate than any other student group in American higher education.[14]

In 2007, a subgroup of WUSA investors, known as the Women's Soccer Initiative, Inc. ("WSII"),[15] announced plans to launch a new women's professional league.[16] [*Ed.*

Note: The league is now known as Women's Professional Soccer, or WPS.] WSII investors believe that a women's professional soccer league could succeed if investors implement a more traditional team-based legal structure.[17] Many others remain skeptical.[18]

This article analyzes whether a new women's professional soccer league, operating under a more traditional legal structure, is more likely to succeed than its centrally planned predecessor. Part I of this article explores the history of women's soccer, including the game's transition from a recreational activity into a professional sport. Part II explains the different legal structures that are available to American sports leagues. Part III explains why implementing a traditional legal structure maximizes the new women's professional soccer league's likelihood of success.

. . . .

C.   Launch of a Women's Professional Soccer League

The exciting 1999 Women's World Cup finals set the stage for investors to launch America's first women's professional soccer league. Using momentum from the 1999 U.S. World Cup victory, an investor group led by Discovery Communications CEO John Hendricks officially launched the WUSA in February 2000.[52] Initially, Hendricks's investor group placed teams in eight cities: Atlanta, Boston, New York, Philadelphia, Orlando-Tampa, San Diego, San Francisco, and Washington, D.C.[53] If the league succeeded, Hendricks planned to add more teams.[54]

Although the WUSA placed all of its teams in the United States, the league hired players from around the world.[55] The New York Power, for example, signed two players from Norway.[56] The Atlanta Beat, meanwhile, used its first overall draft pick to select Chinese superstar Sun Wen.[57]

During the league's first season, the WUSA averaged 8,547 fans per game[58]—far above the league's originally projected attendance.[59] Among the WUSA teams, the Washington Freedom performed especially well, averaging an astounding 18,242 fans per game during its first four home games.[60]

By 2003, however, both WUSA attendance and television ratings had declined.[61] For the 2003 season, the WUSA's average game attendance had fallen to below 6,700 fans per game.[62] This drop was most dramatic in two of the league's largest markets, Boston and New York.[63] In New York, the 2003 average game attendance fell below 4,300.[64]

The WUSA's financial struggles hit investors' pockets hard. During the league's first three seasons, WUSA investors lost close to $90 million: $46 million in year one, $24 million in year two, and $19 million in year three.[65] Before the 2003 season began, WUSA investors decreased players' annual pay from an average of $46,000 to a $37,000 average.[66] Even after this pay cut, the league still was unable to balance its budget.[67]

In a final effort to save the WUSA, investors after the 2003 season announced plans to restructure the league into a more traditional legal structure that would include individual club ownership rather than centrally planned ownership.[68] League President Lynn Morgan believed this proposed restructuring would help to lure new investors.[69] However, just one month later, before the WUSA could implement any changes, the WUSA entirely suspended operations.[70]

D. Women's Soccer Initiative, Inc.

After the WUSA suspended operations, the over 150 women's professional soccer players waited, hoping that a new league would soon form.[71] The following year, players on the highly popular Washington Freedom formed a team in the amateur W-League.[72] Other former WUSA players joined existing teams in the W-League, the Women's Premier Soccer League ("WPSL"), and various overseas leagues.[73]

In November 2004, some of the original WUSA investors launched WSII.[74] Led by Yahoo, Inc. executive and former Stanford University women's soccer player Tonya Antonucci, WSII began to explore opportunities to revive women's professional soccer.[75] In September 2007, WSII announced plans to launch a new women's professional league that would begin play in the spring of 2009.[76] Antonucci, who had chaired the reorganization committee, was named as the league's first commissioner.[77]

The new professional women's soccer league intends to replace the WUSA's centrally-held league structure with a more traditional club ownership structure.[78] According to Antonucci, "franchise ownership would encourage entrepreneurial investment and do away with an overly large, overly controlling league office that would inhibit teams' ability to move quickly and set the strategies necessary for their markets."[79]

II. THE FOUR DIFFERENT LEGAL STRUCTURES OF AMERICAN PROFESSIONAL SPORTS LEAGUES

Although it is unknown whether the WUSA would have succeeded if it implemented a different legal structure, there are powerful arguments suggesting that the WUSA's original structural choice was a mistake.[80]

In America, a new professional sports league can choose between four different legal structures: (a) the club-based private property structure (as appeared in very early professional baseball); (b) the single-entity centrally planned structure (as envisioned but never implemented by the founders of the American men's professional soccer league, Major League Soccer ("MLS")); (c) the mixed-mode centrally planned structure (as actually implemented by MLS); and (d) the mixed-mode private property structure (as implemented by each of the four premier men's sports leagues—Major League Baseball ("MLB"), the National Basketball Association ("NBA"), the National Football League ("NFL"), and the National Hockey League ("NHL")).[81]

A. Club-Based Private Property Structure

The earliest-known property rights structure in American professional sports is the club-based private property structure.[82] Under this structure, sports clubs are privately owned, privately operated, and minimally cooperative with one another.[83] In other words, each club is wholly autonomous.[84]

Today, the club-based private property structure is almost obsolete.[85] Although American professional baseball began under this structure, most baseball clubs eventually shifted toward a more cooperative business model.[86] A major blow to the club-based private property structure came in 1876 when Chicago baseball promoter William Hulbert launched what most regard as a superior system: National League Baseball.[87] Although the National League did not initially reallocate many property rights to the league level, its creation marked the beginning of a gradual shift away from the entirely autonomous sports club.[88]

B. Single-Entity Centrally Planned Structure

On the opposite end of the spectrum, other sports leagues have implemented a single-entity centrally planned structure, in which league investors share all property rights in common.[89] The single-entity structure consists of a limited liability company that houses all of the league's teams.[90] Investors own an undivided interest in this company.[91] Investors thus are responsible for financing and operating the entire league.[92] They also act as the league's board of directors.[93]

First envisioned by MLS founder Alan Rothenberg, the single-entity structure was intended to create a "single-entity league" for purposes of avoiding antitrust liability under Section 1 of the Sherman Act.[94] To avoid liability under this section for what would otherwise be anticompetitive conduct, the league's structure needed to establish a "unity of interest" among all investors.[95] In attempting to obtain "unity of interest," the league structure included important economic differences from more traditional sports structures.[96]

Beyond antitrust considerations, one of the most important features of the single-entity structure is that all property rights reside at the league level.[97] As a result, investors "avoid the pitfalls that can be associated with a maverick owner doing what he sees fit for his particular club."[98] These pitfalls may include filing a lawsuit which attempts to block league-wide pooling or reallocation of sponsorship rights,[99] television rights,[100] or even Internet rights.[101]

C. Mixed-Mode Centrally Planned Structure

A third potential legal structure is the mixed-mode centrally planned structure.[102] In form, the mixed-mode centrally planned league looks much like the single-entity league, with investors conducting all functions at the league level.[103] However, in substance, each investor in a mixed-mode centrally planned league also operates the business functions of a single team.[104]

Under the mixed-mode centrally planned structure, each investor-operator owns a share of the league overall. However, investors do not share all league revenues equally.[105] For example, MLS, which operates as a mixed-mode centrally planned league,[106] redistributes league revenues with each team's investor-operator receiving a management fee consisting of a percentage of the local revenues of the franchise which that investor operates.[107]

According to the First Circuit Court of Appeals, even though the mixed-mode centrally planned league, in form, looks like the single-entity centrally planned league, it does not qualify for the single-entity defense to Section 1 of the Sherman Act because, in substance, investors lack "unity of interest."[108] As a result, while the mixed-mode centrally planned league enjoys some of the economic benefits of the single-entity league, it does not enjoy any of the legal advantages.

D. Mixed-Mode Private Property Structure (the Traditional Model)

The fourth legal structure that appears in American professional sports is the mixed-mode private-property structure.[109] The mixed-mode private property structure is the most common league structure, and it is the structure implemented by each of America's four premier professional sports leagues: MLB, the NBA, the NFL, and the NHL.[110] Because this structure appears most commonly, some academics simply call it the "traditional model."[111]

The mixed-mode private property structure consists of individual club owners who each possess independent property rights, but who agree contractually to share some of these rights with each other.[112] For example, in a mixed-mode private property league, club owners may vote to share licensing rights, national television broadcast rights, and Internet intellectual property rights.[113]

Indeed, the interests of individual club owners under the mixed-mode private property structure are never perfectly aligned.[114] Club owners in larger markets typically want to keep more property rights, while owners in the smaller markets typically want to collectivize these rights.[115] As a result, the mixed-mode private property structure may lead to lawsuits between individual club owners and the league overall, such as the one recently filed over the ownership of Internet IP rights between the New York Rangers and the

NHL.[116] Nevertheless, despite these occasional asymmetric incentives, the mixed-mode private property structure provides an opportunity for club owners to enjoy a balance between business cooperation and business competition.[117]

III. WHY THE NEW WOMEN'S PROFESSIONAL SOCCER LEAGUE SHOULD ADOPT A MIXED-MODE PRIVATE PROPERTY STRUCTURE

Although during the past decade most sports executives favored adopting centrally planned structures, the new women's professional soccer league actually has the greatest likelihood for success if it adopts a traditional, mixed-mode private property structure.[118] As explained by Jeffrey Kessler, Co-Chairman of the Sports Litigation Department at Dewey & LeBoeuf, "the [centrally planned league structure] is a wonderful example of how the legal system and lawyers can mess up a business structure in this country."[119] Indeed, when balancing the benefits of a traditional league structure with those of a single-entity structure, the traditional model, in most instances, seems to work better.

A. Benefits of the Traditional League Structure

The mixed-mode private property structure enjoys four important benefits over centrally planned league structures: (1) better ability to attract investors; (2) greater success at promoting innovation; (3) improved ability to "think globally but act locally;" and (4) greater success at convincing fans that game results are natural.

1. Attracting Investors

First, deep-pocketed investors are more likely to invest in traditional sports leagues than in centrally planned leagues. This is because investors, under the traditional structure, are fully able to control individual club operations and compete for league championships.[120] By contrast, under centrally planned league structures, investors do not have the ability to fully control any team, nor the opportunity to compete to the same extent for championship glory.[121] According to Wharton School of Business Legal Studies Professor Kenneth Shropshire, "[m]ost problematic for the [centrally planned] structure is figuring out how to tell the large-ego set of owners that this league is going to be a little bit different, and that as a [centrally planned league], one of the owners . . . will not have the opportunity to be out front [raising a championship trophy]."[122]

Because the centrally planned league lacks certain elements of both control and rewards, it is at a substantial disadvantage when attempting to raise funds.[123] In addition, the lack of these two features helps to explain why investors in centrally planned leagues are generally more willing to abandon their investment than owners in traditionally structured leagues.[124]

2. Promoting Innovation

The traditionally structured league is also better positioned to promote innovation.[125] Innovation is typically superior in traditionally structured leagues because independent club owners are able to implement their own diverse business plans, rather than implementing a single plan approved by the league.[126] This greater flexibility often improves business performance by allowing individual club owners to try different business tactics.[127]

Although not every individualized business plan succeeds, most club owners eventually adopt other clubs' best practices.[128] For example, after a few MLB clubs experimented successfully with variable priced ticketing, many other clubs that would not have initially favored this strategy adopted it.[129] According to Milwaukee Brewers owner Mark Attanasio, whose club was one of the laggards to adopt variable ticket pricing, "[w]e don't need to reinvent the wheel. If somebody else is doing something, the fans seem to like it and we can make some money, we'll do it."[130] This is the beauty of individual club decision-making.

3. Thinking Globally, Acting Locally

The traditionally structured league also encourages club owners to "think globally, but act locally."[131] Under the traditional league structure, each club owner controls his own local sponsorship market and hires employees to address needs within the local community.[132] This, in turn, promotes friendlier business relations.[133] By comparison, the centrally planned league is less adept at meeting local community needs because business planning occurs exclusively at the national, league-wide level.[134] At that level, targeted marketing is simply infeasible.

4. Producing Natural Results

Finally, some experts even believe that fans prefer to watch games played in traditionally structured leagues.[135] This is because some fans perceive these games as having more natural results.[136] According to Jeffrey Kessler, "[t]he absence of control over players and rosters is something that is a detriment, not a positive, because you create an image that there is one giant fantasy [sports] game that someone plays in the league office in which players get ripped from their fans by a central authority and reallocated around the country."[137] Although this argument may be somewhat overstated, Kessler fairly points to the collapse of the Continental Basketball Association almost immediately upon adopting a centrally planned structure as evidence of fans' distrust of this type of league.[138]

B. Purported Benefits of the Centrally Planned Structure

Indeed, the centrally planned structure may have certain legal and economic benefits over the traditional model; however, these benefits are almost always overstated.

1. Purported Legal Benefits of the Centrally Planned League

From a legal perspective, the centrally planned league's most frequently claimed benefit is a total exemption from liability under Section 1 of the Sherman Act.[139] This exemption, if obtained, would allow owners to unilaterally set ticket prices, pool broadcasting and licensing rights, and allocate player contracts among teams.[140]

Recent case law, however, calls into question this purported legal benefit for three reasons: (1) not all centrally planned leagues actually are single-entities for purposes of antitrust laws; (2) according to one court, even certain traditionally structured leagues may qualify within IP markets as single entities; and (3) even if a startup sports league does not qualify for the single-entity defense, it still might qualify for other defenses against antitrust liability.[141]

a. Not All Centrally Planned Leagues Qualify as Single Entities

Although early founders of centrally planned leagues had assumed the single-entity defense insulated all centrally planned structures from liability under Section 1 of the Sherman Act, recent case law indicates that the single-entity defense only applies to true single-entity leagues, and not to mixed-mode centrally planned leagues.[142] This is because clubs in mixed-mode centrally planned leagues lack "unity of interest."[143]

Importantly, in *Fraser v. Major League Soccer*, the First Circuit Court of Appeals explained that even though a single-entity league can never be found to conspire with itself, owners in a mixed-mode centrally planned league such as MLS are still capable of illegally conspiring with one another.[144] This is because, even though a mixed-mode centrally planned league does not seem to have separate ownership in form, the league's investor-operators act in the "role as team managers, [and] not as ordinary stockholders."[145] Further, investor-operators "retain a large portion of the revenues from the activities of their teams; and each has limited sale rights in its own team that relate to specific assets and not just shares in the common enterprise."[146]

. . . .

[*Ed. Note: Authors' discussion of how traditionally structured leagues may qualify within IP markets as single entities and how a start-up sports league might qualify for other defenses against antitrust liability is omitted.*]

2. Purported Economic Benefits of the Centrally Planned League

The economic advantages of adopting a centrally planned structure are similarly overstated. Although advocates of adopting a single-entity structure are quick to point out the structure's ability to reduce shareholder risk and lower operating expenses,[157] these advantages are unlikely to outweigh the structure's disadvantages, as evidenced by the number of sports leagues that in recent years have abandoned the centrally planned structure.[158]

The most well-documented sports league to abandon a centrally planned structure is the WNBA, which made its transition away from the centrally planned structure based on both labor unrest and the difficulty obtaining local sponsorships.[159] According to the Chief Operating Officer of one WNBA team, the traditional structure is one in which "teams should have a better chance to survive."[160] In addition, according to one WNBA owner, the traditional structure is preferable because "teams will be accountable where they weren't totally in the past and that accountability will result in better decisions and better results."[161]

Another more recent example of a sports league that has transitioned away from the centrally planned structure is the Major Indoor Soccer League ("MISL"), which, until recently, was cited as a major success story of central league planning.[162] On May 31, 2008, MISL investors decided to suspend all operations, citing the need to move to a different legal structure that would better allow investors to contain costs.[163] According to attorney Jeff Rotwitt, who was one of the MISL's investors, the MISL decision to cease operations was triggered by investors' preferences to move away from a "foolhardy option."[164]

CONCLUSION

The ultimate fate of the new women's professional soccer league is contingent upon more than just the sport's on-the-field product. The league's fate also depends upon the founders' choice of legal structure. Although the WUSA originally launched as a centrally planned league, that legal structure has failed to attract sufficient investors, sponsors, and fans. Therefore, the new women's professional soccer league should seek an alternative structure. From a societal perspective, reviving professional women's soccer is an important goal because it increases athletic opportunities for women and creates a renewed supply of role models for American girls. A professional women's soccer league also demonstrates the physical strength and ability of women throughout society. The role of the female athlete has evolved mightily since eighteenth century Scotland when women competed in soccer only as a way to meet potential husbands. Today, when strong and qualified women excel on the soccer field, females of all ages seek to emulate their work ethic, passion, and healthy lifestyle. Men also begin to perceive women as being strong, capable, and qualified.

With American society benefiting from having a vibrant women's professional soccer league, it would be a shame if the proposed league fails because "lawyers . . . mess up [the] business structure."[165] Although some believe that there is simply no market in America for women's professional sports,[166] the success of the Women's World Cup and Women's Tennis Association events indicate that women's professional sports can succeed under proper

legal structures.[167] Given the continued success of men's professional sports leagues that apply the mixed-mode private property structure, it makes sense for founders of the new women's professional soccer league to adopt a similar approach. By choosing a more traditional legal structure, league founders give the new women's professional soccer league a bona fide chance to survive.

Notes

1. *See* Shira Springer, *Shot of Brandi Provides Boost: Winning Penalty Kick Completes Journey for Veteran Chastain*, BOSTON GLOBE, July 11, 1999, at E12; George Kimball, *Soccer World Cup; Inspirational Akers Leads Way for Thankful Teammates*, BOSTON HERALD, July 11, 1999, at B03; Philip Hersh, *World Cup Final Quite an Inspired Feat*, CHI. TRIB., July 11, 1999, at 1; Barry Wilner, *A Shot of Brandi: Chastain's Penalty Kick Wins It*, CHI. TRIB., July 11, 1999, at 1.

2. *See* Kimball, *supra* note 1, at B03; Tim Dahlberg, *She Scores! U.S. Wins Cup in Storybook Finish*, LEXINGTON HERALD-LEADER, July 11, 1999, at A-1.

3. *See* Brandi Chastain, WIKIPEDIA, *available at* http://en.wikipedia .org/wiki/Brandi_Chastain. (last visited Apr. 9, 2009).

4. *See* Donna Leinward, *Heroin's Resurgence Closes Drug's Traditional Gender Gap*, USA TODAY, May 9, 2000, at 1A (girl power); *Celebrating Female Athletes*, HARTFORD COURANT, Sept. 21, 2001, at A14 (achievement); Rick Reilly, *Bare in Mind*, SPORTS ILLUSTRATED, Sept. 4, 2000, at 112 (synergy of feminism and athleticism).

5. *See, e.g.*, Wilner, *supra* note 1, at 1.

6. *See, e.g.*, George Vescey, *Sports of the Times; A Kickoff Brings Joy and Thanks and Roars*, N.Y. TIMES, Apr. 15, 2001, at 8-1; Editorial, *A League of Their Own*, N.Y. TIMES, May 1, 2001, at A22; *WUSA's Brief History (10th Anniversary Special)*, SPORTS BUS. J., Apr. 28, 2003, at 30; Bill King, *What's Up with Women's Sports?* SPORTS BUS. J., Apr. 25, 2005, at 18 ("The WUSA launched on the strength of circumstances so perfect, it had to be kismet. It had Mia Hamm, a transcendent star who only wanted to create more stars. It had the grandest of stages, a 1999 World Cup that drew 90,125 fans—including the sitting U.S. president, Bill Clinton—and captured a television audience of more than 40 million. Then it had a reprise, a silver medal in the 2000 Olympics, just to remind everyone of 1999.").

7. *See* Lacie Kaiser, *The Flight from Single-Entity Sports Leagues*, 2 DEPAUL J. SPORTS L. & CONTEMP. PROBS. 1, 1 (2004) ("Sports leagues such as the Women's National Basketball Association (WNBA), Women's United Soccer League (WUSA) and Major League Soccer (MLS) organized themselves as single entities when they first came into existence."); Marc Edelman, *Why the "Single Entity" Defense Can Never Apply to NFL Clubs: A Primer on Property-Rights Theory in Professional Sports*, 18 FORDHAM INTELL. PROP. MEDIA & ENT. L.J. 891, 900-903 (2008) [*Ed Note: hereinafter "Edelman, Single Entity"*] (describing the centrally owned league model or "common property system"); John Lombardo, *A New Play for the AFL?*, SPORTS BUS. J., Feb. 25, 2008, at 1.

8. Jere Longman, *Women's Soccer League Folds on World Cup's Eve*, N.Y. TIMES, Sept. 16, 2003, at A1.

9. *See id.*

10. *Id.*

11. *See generally* Traci A. Guiliano et. al., *Gender and the Selection of Public Athletic Role Models*, 30 J. SPORT BEHAV. 161 (June 1,

2007), *available at* 2007 WLNR 10339494 (discussing the importance of women's athletics on society overall in terms of producing positive role models).

12. Marc Edelman & C. Keith Harrison, *Analyzing the WNBA's Mandatory Age/Education Policy from a Legal, Cultural and Ethical Perspective: Women, Men, and the Professional Sports Landscape*, 3 NW. J.L. & SOC. POLICY 1, 2 (2008); *see also* Mary Crawford & Rhonda Unger, *Women & Gender: A Feminist Psychology* 44-46 (3d ed. 2000).

13. *See* Edelman & Harrison, *supra* note 12, at 2-3; *see also* Editorial, *A League of Their Own*, N.Y. TIMES, May 1, 2001, at A22 ("If successful, the league could join the WNBA as a much-needed source of inspiration for millions of girls across the country. Female professional athletes as role models, particularly in team sports, have been in short supply over the years.").

14. Edelman & Harrison, *supra* note 12, at 3.

15. *See* Jack Bell, *Another Go at a Women's League, But not Going at It Alone*, N.Y. TIMES, Apr. 25, 2007, at D2 (describing Women's Soccer Initiative, Inc.); Lombardo, *supra* note 7, at 1.

16. *See* Terry Lefton, *New Women's Soccer League will Look to MLS*, SPORTS BUS. J., Mar. 5, 2007, at 5; Lombardo, *supra* note 7, at 1.

17. *See id.* ("[T]he WUSA folded in 2003 after losing nearly $100 million as a single-entity league. The newly launched Women's Professional Soccer League will return in 2009 with a traditional league structure with local owners.").

18. *See, e.g.*, Evan Weiner, *Women's Soccer League Faces Tough Obstacles*, THE NEW YORK SUN, Sept. 12, 2007, *available at* http://www.nysun.com/sports/womens-soccer-league-faces-tough-obstacles/62455 (last visited Apr. 9, 2009).

. . . .

52. *See* Lena Williams, *A Plan Is Unveiled for a Women's League*, N.Y. TIMES, Feb. 16, 2000, at D5. [hereinafter *Plan Unveiled*] ("The other investors are Amos B. Hostettler Jr., former chairman of Continental Cablevision, Brian L. Roberts, president of Comcast Corporation, James Kennedy, chairman of Cox Enterprises, Joseph J. Collins, chairman of Time Warner Cable, Amy Banse, vice president of programming investments for Comcast and Fred M. Dressler, senior vice president of programming for Time Warner Cable.").

53. *Plus: Soccer–Women's United Soccer Association; DiCicco Is Named As Commissioner*, N.Y. TIMES, Apr. 27, 2000, at D7.

54. *See* Jayda Evans, *Cup Quest: Chastain, Team Make Qualifying Stop in Seattle*, SEATTLE TIMES, Oct. 27, 2002, at D7 ("Seattle, Portland and Los Angeles are being looked at as possible WUSA expansion cities. Currently, the eight-team professional soccer league has only two teams on the West Coast: the San Diego Spirit and Chastain's San Jose CyberRays."); Williams, *supra* note 52, at D5 ("The new league will have a minimum of 8 teams and may expand to as many as 12.").

55. *See* Evans, *supra* note 54, at D7 (all teams located in the United States); *Norwegians Taken in WUSA Foreign Draft*, TULSA WORLD (Tulsa, Oklahoma), Oct. 31, 2000, at B6 (discussing worldwide talent); *see generally* Amy Shipley, *U.S. Women Want Soccer to Go Pro; Others Question a League's Viability*, WASH. POST, July 8, 1999, at D1 ("Certainly, a women's pro soccer league in the United States would attract talented players from around the world. Perhaps largely because of their experiences during this tournament, many international stars view the United States as women's soccer nirvana.").

56. *See Norwegians Taken in WUSA Foreign Draft*, TULSA WORLD (Tulsa, Oklahoma), Oct. 31, 2000, at B6.

57. Wendy Parker, *Soccer: Beat Picks Sun, China's Top Player*, ATLANTA JOURNAL & CONSTITUTION, Dec. 11, 2000, at E11.

58. *See* John Haydon, *WUSA Pleased with Early Progress*, THE WASH. TIMES, June 23, 2001, at C6 [hereinafter *WUSA Pleased*] (denoting actual year one attendance average of 8,547 fans per game).

59. Williams, *Plan Unveiled*, *supra* note 52, at D5 (denoting expected year one attendance average of 6,500 fans per game).

60. *WUSA Pleased*, *supra* note 58, at C6.

61. *See* Jennifer Lee, *WUSA's Third Season Posts Mixed Results*, SPORTS BUS. J., Aug. 18, 2003, at 9.

62. *See* Longman, *supra* note 8, at A-1; Jennifer Lee, *Coming Months Crucial for WUSA Rebirth*, SPORTS BUS. J., Apr. 19, 2004, at 19.

63. Lee, *supra* note 62, at 9.

64. *Id.*

65. Longman, *supra* note 8, at D-5.

66. Christopher Lawlor, *Teams Losing Money, But WUSA Wants to Expand*, USA TODAY, August 12, 2003, at 3-C.

67. Longman, *supra* note 8, at A-1.

68. Lawlor, *supra* note 66, at 3-C.

69. *Id.*

70. *See Women's Soccer League Collapses*, CHI. TRIB., Sept. 16, 2003, at 20; Jim Barrero & David Wharton, *The Nation: Women's Soccer League Folds After 3 Seasons*, L.A. TIMES, Sept. 16, 2003, at 1.

71. *See* Michelle Kaufman, *U.S. Team Has Multiple Goals*, MIAMI HERALD, Sept. 21, 2003, at D-4 ("Players are hoping the Cup will spark interest among deep-pocketed corporations. I hope the World Cup perhaps can bring more sponsors so they can restart the league," Sweden coach Marika Domanski-Lyfors said of the league's closing. "Girls need opportunities to be pro players, and this is a country that can provide that.").

72. The W-League is a highly competitive amateur soccer league that consists of forty-one teams in four conferences both in the United States and Canada. *See About USL and Franchise Information*, OFFICIAL USL WEBSITE, http://www.uslsoccer.com/aboutusl/franchise/index_E.html; *see also The League: About Us*, OFFICIAL WPSL WEBSITE, http:// www.wpsl.info/about. Currently, international and former professional stars compete in the league, as well as elite college players. *See id.*

73. *See* Soccerway Women Soccer, http:// www.women.soccerway.com; *see also* Women's World Football Rankings, http:// www .womensworldfootball.com.

74. An Introduction to Women's Soccer Initiative Inc., http://wsii .typepad.com/wsii/about.html.

75. *Id.*

76. *Women's Professional Soccer to Launch in 2009*, PR NEWSWIRE, Sept. 4, 2007, http://www.active.com/soccer/Articles/Women_s_ Professional_Soccer_League_to_Launch_in_2009.htm.

77. *Id.*

78. *See* John Lombardo, *A New Play for the AFL?*, SPORTS BUS. J., Feb. 25, 2008, at 1.

79. *See* Tripp Mickle & Terry Lefton, *Several Leagues Later, Debate on Single-Entity Model Still Lively*, SPORTS BUS. J., Aug. 4, 2008, at 8.

80. *See supra* notes 70-72 and accompanying text; *see also* Kaiser, *supra* note 7, at 12 ("In 2001, the [WUSA] structured under the sin-

gle-entity model, played its first season. However, the league was receiving insufficient revenue from core areas of the business and failed to attract the sponsorship support needed to achieve its goal to break even by its fifth season.") (internal quotations and citations omitted); *see generally* Michael J. Cozzillio et. al, SPORTS LAW: CASES AND MATERIALS 26 (1997) [hereinafter SPORTS LAW: CASES AND MATERIALS] (discussing how most of the centrally planned sports leagues launched over the past 15-20 years have been a mistake).

81. *See* Edelman, *Single Entity, supra* note 7, at 897-904 (combining the two centrally planned models as the "common property system"). Indeed, in Europe a fifth and highly popular league structure involves an "open league" with promotion and relegation. *See* Cain & Haddock, *supra* note 35, at 1119. However, it is highly unlikely that an American investment group would ever choose the promotion/relegation model given the greater economic power, and less competition, that teams in a closed league maintain. *See* Marc Edelman, *How to Curb Professional Sports' Bargaining Power vis-à-vis the American City*, 2 VA. SPORTS & ENT. L.J. 280, 303-05 (2003) (explaining how an open professional sports league would be one way to reduce the bargaining power of professional sports in America); Marc Edelman, *Sports and the City: How to Curb Professional Sports Teams' Demands for Free Public Stadiums*, 6 RUTGERS J. OF L. & PUB. POLY. 35, 62-63 (2008); Cain & Haddock, *supra* note 35, at 1119 ("When teams agree to form a league, it would seem advantageous for them to opt for the closed cartel now common in North America."). Therefore, "open league" structures are not considered further in this paper.

82. Edelman, *Single Entity, supra* note 7, at 897.

83. *See* Edelman, *Single Entity, supra* note 7, at 897; *see also Panel III: Restructuring Professional Sports Leagues*, 12 FORDHAM INTELL. PROP., MEDIA & ENT. L.J. 413, 419 (2002) [hereinafter *Panel III*] (quoting Kenneth Shropshire).

84. *See Panel III, supra* note 83, at 419 (quoting Kenneth Shropshire) ("Many of you know that originally sports in America, especially the team sports, started off as individual clubs. You have stories of George Halas sitting around with the rest of the football team, passing the hat around after games to collect funds to divide amongst the team.").

85. This is because, as explained by the U.S. Supreme Court, the marketing of sporting events would be "completely ineffective if there were no rules on which the competitors agreed to create and define the competition to be marketed." NCAA v. Board of Regents, 468 U.S. 85, 101 (1984).

86. Edelman, *Single Entity, supra* note 7, at 898; *see generally* Cain & Haddock, *supra* note 34, at 1121 (noting that the club-based private property model "failed miserably to develop an orderly process for teams to contest a championship and balance their books, so the *Chicago Tribune* urged restructuring.").

87. Edelman, *Single Entity, supra* note 7, at 898-99; *see generally* Marc Edelman, *Can Antitrust Law Save the Minnesota Twins: Why Commissioner Selig's Contraction Plan was Never a Sure Deal*, 10 SPORTS L.J. 45, 47 (2003) (discussing the transition of Major League Baseball from organization at the club level to the league level).

88. Edelman, *Single Entity, supra* note 7, at 899.

89. *Id.* at 900.

90. *Id.*

91. SPORTS LAW: CASES AND MATERIALS, *supra* note 80, at 19.

92. Edelman, *Single Entity, supra* note 7, at 900.

93. *Id.*

94. Section 1 of the Sherman Act states, in pertinent part, that "[e]very contract, combination . . . or conspiracy, in the restraint of trade or commerce . . . is declared to be illegal." Sherman Act, 26 Stat. 209 (1890), (codified as amended at 15 U.S.C. §§ 1–7 (2000)). However, the Supreme Court has interpreted § 1 of the Sherman Act to hold illegal only those agreements that unreasonably restrain trade. Standard Oil v. United States, 221 U.S. 1, 51 (1911). Classification as a "single entity" means immunity under § 1 of the Sherman Act because it is impossible for just one entity to collude with itself. Copperweld Corp. v. Independence Tube Corp., 467 U.S. 752, 771 (1984). For this reason, the first single-entity leagues structured themselves in a manner hoping to avoid § 1. *See Panel III, supra* note 83, at 435 (quoting Jeffrey Kessler) ("So why did the MLS owners choose to form a single entity? They did it so that they could claim an exemption from section 1 of the Sherman Act and not have to compete with each other for their players.").

95. *See Copperweld Corp.*, 467 U.S. at 771; *see also* Fraser v. Major League Soccer, 284 F.3d 47, 53 (1st Cir. 2002).

96. Edelman, *Single Entity, supra* note 7, at 900 (citing *Copperweld Corp.*, 467 U.S. at 752); *Panel III, supra* note 83, at 435 (quoting Jeffrey Kessler); Stephen F. Ross & Stefan Szymasnski, *The Law & Economics of Optimal Sports League Design*, 41 TANAKA BUS. SCH. DISCUSSION PAPERS (2005) ("Indeed, one of the principal doctrinal insights to be gleaned from the economic analysis set forth in this Article is that club-run leagues differ significantly from single-entity leagues in the way they are operated").

97. *Panel III, supra* note 83, at 427-28 (quoting Tandy O'Donoghue).

98. *Id.*; *see also* SPORTS LAW: CASES AND MATERIALS, *supra* note 80, at 23 ("Again, the central league motivation to control maverick owners who develop a penchant for cutting their own deals is self-evident.").

99. *See N.F.L. Settles with Cowboys*, N.Y. TIMES, Dec. 14, 1996 at 1-32 (explaining that the NFL filed suit against Dallas Cowboys owner Jerry Jones challenging the signing of Texas Stadium sponsors such as Nike and Pepsi).

100. *See* Sports Ltd. Pship v. NBA, 95 F.3d 593, 595, 599-600 (7th Cir. 1996) (noting that shortly after the Chicago Bulls basketball club began to broadcast its local games on WGN, a super station with broadcast signals extending throughout the entire United States, six years of litigation ensued between the Bulls and the rest of the NBA clubs over the legitimacy of the Bulls' broadcasting practices).

101. *See* Madison Square Garden, L.P. v. NHL, No. 07 Civ. 8455 (LAP), 2007 WL 3254421, slip op. at *1 (S.D.N.Y. Nov. 2, 2007), *affd* 2008 WL 746524 (2d. Cir. Mar. 19, 2008). Recently, the problem of a maverick owner seeking to litigate against a league appeared in the NHL, where the New York Rangers' ownership group filed an antitrust lawsuit against the rest of the league, arguing that the league's plan to collectively share Internet IP rights violated antitrust law. *See id.*; Complaint for Injunctive Relief at ¶ 6, Madison Square Garden, L.P. v. NHL, No. 07 Civ. 8455, 2007 WL 3373461 (S.D.N.Y. 2007). The other NHL clubs have since sought to punish the Rangers by suspending their owners, requiring their owners to sell the team, or even terminating the clubs' league membership. *See In a Letter, NHL Threatens to Kick MSG out of League*, ESPN, *available at* http://sports.espn.go.com/nhl/news/story?id=3452292 (last visited on Apr. 9, 2009). This kind of antagonistic situation would never occur in a single-entity league because, from the very beginning, all property rights are shared equally. Edelman, *Single Entity, supra* note 7, at 922–24.

102. *See* Edelman, *Single Entity*, *supra* note 7, at 901-905 (explaining how the single-entity centrally planned structure morphed into a mixed-mode structure).

103. *See id.* at 902.

104. *See id.*

105. *See Panel III*, *supra* note 83, at 430 (quoting Tandy O'Donoghue) (discussing the greater degree of risk-spreading in centrally planned leagues).

106. *See* Edelman, *Single Entity*, *supra* note 7, at 902 (because of the difficulty initially in finding investors, MLS eventually abandoned its pure common-property structure and turned to a mixed-mode model).

107. *Fraser*, 284 F.3d at 54 ("In return for the services of the operator/investors, MLS pays each of them a 'management fee' that corresponds (in large part) to the performance of their respective team. The management fee equals the sum of one-half of local ticket receipts and concessions; the first $1,125,000 of local broadcast revenues, increasing annually by a percentage rate, plus a 30% share (declining to 10% by 2006) of any amount above the base amount; all revenues from overseas tours; a share of one-half the net revenues from the MLS Championship Game and a share of revenues from other exhibition games.").

108. *Id.* at 58-59 ("To sum up, the present case is not *Copperweld* but presents a more doubtful situation; MLS and its operator/investors comprise a hybrid arrangement, somewhere between a single company (with or without wholly owned subsidiaries) and a cooperative arrangement between existing competitors . . . . The case for expanding *Copperweld* is debatable and, more so, the case for applying the single entity label to MLS.").

109. Edelman, *Single Entity*, *supra* note 7, at 903–05.

110. *See id.* at 903-04; SPORTS LAW: CASES AND MATERIALS, *supra* note 80, at 19.

111. *Id.*

112. Edelman, *Single Entity*, *supra* note 7, at 904.

113. *Id.* at 903-904.

114. *See id.* at 911-924 (discussing the lack of unity of interest among individual club owners).

115. *Id.* at 904-905.

116. *See Madison Square Garden*, 2007 WL 3254421, slip op., at *1; *see also Sports Ltd. P'ship.*, 95 F.3d at 600 (noting a similar argument over television broadcast rights in the NBA during the late 1990s).

117. *See* Edelman, *Single Entity*, *supra* note 7, at 903.

118. SPORTS LAW: CASES AND MATERIALS, *supra* note 80, at 26 ("When new leagues are formed, their organizers hope to learn and benefit from the mistakes and experiences of existing and defunct leagues."); *Panel III*, *supra* note 83, at 435 (quoting Jeffrey Kessler) ("Most of the start-up leagues that have tried a single-entity structure have failed."); *id.* at 444 (quoting Jamin Dershowitz) ("I agree with Jeff that the single-entity structure is not a magic bullet in any way, shape, or form.").

119. *Panel III*, *supra* note 84, at 433 (quoting Jeffrey Kessler); *see also* Jeffrey Kessler Profile, http://www.deweyleboeuf.com/jeffrey_kessler.

120. *See, e.g.*, SPORTS LAW: CASES AND MATERIALS, *supra* note 80, at 22; Andrew Zimbalist, *What Went Wrong with WUSA?* SPORTS BUS. J., Oct. 13, 2003, at 26; *Panel III*, *supra* note 84, at 424 (quoting Kenneth Shropshire); *id.* at 426 (quoting Kenneth Shropshire) ("We have seen some restructuring, particularly with MLS. 'Can we really get funds in by giving owners no kind of Steinbrenner-esque face time?' But they have addressed this and been trying to make it work better."); *see generally id.* at 434 (quoting Jeffrey Kessler) ("The bottom line is that there is a good reason why, up until now, all of the successful sports leagues in this country—and around the world, by the way (this is an international result)—have adopted a model of individual ownership of teams. The reason is that the professional team sports business is basically a local business. You get a local personality who runs it. You want an entrepreneur who will develop it.").

121. *Panel III*, *supra* note 83, at 429 (quoting Tandy O'Donoghue) ("When you are making an effort to appeal to people with a lot of money, and the potentially big egos that go along with that, but you are not willing to offer them that sort of 'individual owner' role in things, you are going to have some difficulty."); *see also* John Wolohan, *Double Setback for Single Entity Leagues*, SPORTS BUS. J., Sept. 8, 2003, at 18.

122. *Panel III*, *supra* note 84, at 424 (quoting Kenneth Shropshire).

123. *See* Wolohan, *supra* note 121, at 18 ("[Y]ou cannot overlook the human ego in explaining why leagues are moving to individual team owners.").

124. *See* Zimbalist, *supra* note 120, at 26 (explaining that WUSA investors lacked sufficient patience and pulled their investment after just three seasons, even though historically new professional sports leagues have taken substantially longer to turn a profit).

125. *See* Kaiser, *supra* note 7, at 11-12.

126. *Id.* ("Citing possible labor unrest and dropping two money-losing franchises, the WNBA decided to allow teams to manage themselves thereby giving them the opportunity to seek more local sponsorship deals . . . a NBA and WNBA owner believed that 'the teams will be accountable where they weren't totally in the past and that accountability will result in better decision and better results.'").

127. *See* Kaiser, *supra* note 7, at 15 (explaining WNBA reasoning for transition away from centrally planned business model); SPORTS LAW: CASES AND MATERIALS, *supra* note 80, at 22.

128. SPORTS LAW: CASES AND MATERIALS, *supra* note 80, at 23.

129. *See* Russell Adams, *Brewers Borrowing Best of What's Around*, SPORTS BUS. J., June 27, 2005, at 7.

130. *Id.*

131. The idea of "think globally, act locally" is the business mantra that focuses on a large consumer market, with a narrowly tailored approach to meet different local constituencies. *See, e.g.*, John Darling et. al., *Enhancing Contemporary Entrepreneurship*: A Focus on Management Leadership, 19 EUROPEAN BUS REV. 14 *available at* 2006 WLNR 22436409 ("Successful transformational entrepreneurial leaders who establish and maintain a high degree of respect from their associates ... think globally and act locally."); *Thailand, Ford, Adopts Fast Forward Strategy*, THAI PRESS REP., Aug. 24, 2006, *available at* 2006 WLNR 14607634 (According to the President of Ford Thailand "[b]eing a global company we can take advantage of resources from all over. Our motto is 'Think globally, act locally.'").

132. Kaiser, *supra* note 7, at 15.

133. *Id.*

134. *Id.*

135. *See Panel III*, *supra* note 83, at 433.

136. SPORTS LAW: CASES AND MATERIALS, *supra* note 80, at 22; *see also* Cain & Haddock, *supra* note 34, at 1130 ("The literature has discussed the benefits of parity extensively—any league's suc-

cess depends on staging games with uncertain outcomes."); Andrew Zimbalist, *May the Best Team Win: Baseball Economics and Public Policy* 37 (Brookings Institute 2004) ("Conventional wisdom has it that a successful sports league must have a healthy dose of competitive balance or parity across its teams. Without such balance, there will not be necessary uncertainty of outcome in individual games and in seasons to maintain fan interest.").

137. *Panel III, supra* note 83, at 433 (quoting Jeffrey Kessler).

138. *Id.* at 435.

139. *See* SPORTS LAW: CASES AND MATERIALS, *supra* note 80, at 27.

140. *See* Marc Edelman, *Single Entity Status Must Pass Legal Test*, SPORTS BUS. J., Apr. 28, 2008, at 24.

141. *See* Edelman, *Single Entity, supra* note 7, at 900 ("Mr. Rothenberg envisioned MLS to serve as a 'single entity' league for purposes of an antitrust advantage. At least in the business sector, this model seemed to meet the Sherman Act's test for 'complete unity of interest.'"); *Fraser*, 284 F.3d at 58-59 (1st Cir. 2002).

142. *See Fraser*, 284 F.3d at 59.

143. *Id.; see generally* SPORTS LAW: CASES AND MATERIALS, *supra* note 80, at 25 (explaining that in the context of the mixed-mode centrally planned leagues 'single entity' response to challenges under Section 1 has received positive reception from a few judges and several law professors, but the precedential decisions have uniformly rejected the defense.").

144. *Fraser*, 284 F.3d at 58-59 ("To sum up, the present case is not *Copperweld* but presents a more doubtful situation; MLS and its operator/investors comprise a hybrid arrangement, somewhere between a single company (with or without wholly owned subsidiaries) and a cooperative arrangement between existing competitors. . . . The case for expanding *Copperweld* is debatable and, more so, the case for applying the single-entity label to MLS.").

145. *Id.* at 56.

146. *Id.* at 57.

. . . .

. 157. *See* Tripp Mickle, *Several Leagues Later, Debate on Single-Entity Model Still Lively*, SPORTS BUS. J., Aug. 4, 2008, at 8 (citing Bob Caporale among others); *see also* SPORTS LAW: CASES AND MATERIALS, *supra* note 80, at 27 ("Beyond the advantages of substantially reduced antitrust exposure and liability, the [common-property] league should yield cost savings associated with reduced competition.... There also may be... cost savings as a result of [the common-property league] being responsible for the business operations of all the teams in the league."); Wolohan, *supra* note 122, at 18 (discussing cost containment).

158. *See, e.g.,* Wolohan, *supra* note 121, at 18 (mentioning WUSA's and WNBA's transition away from the single-entity structure); Kaiser, *supra* note 7, at 11 (mentioning the ABL as a single-entity league that went out of business, and the WNBA and WUSA as leagues that have sought to abandon the structure).

159. *Id.* (citing Sarah Talaly, *WNBA Takes on New Look*, SUN-SENTINEL, May 4, 2003, at 10C).

160. *Id.* at 12.

161. *Id.*

162. *See, e.g.,* Edelman, *Single Entity, supra* note 7, at 903 ("The MISL has proven more successful than the XFL, having just recently signed a multiyear television deal with the Fox Soccer Channel. Only time will tell if the MISL keeps its single-entity structure.").

163. *See* Major Indoor Soccer League Website, http://www.misl.net ("The Management Committee of the Major Indoor Soccer League today announced the MISL ceased operations effective May 31, 2008. The MISL Management Committee has begun formal transition planning and restructuring as they consider moves, which they believe will help lower costs and attract additional owner/operators. A decision on the future structure of the League will be forthcoming in the next couple of weeks.").

164. Terry Lefton & Tripp Mickle, *Dormant MISL Struggles with Next Move*, SPORTS BUS. J., Aug. 4, 2008, at 8.

165. *Panel III, supra* note 83, at 433 (quoting Jeffrey Kessler).

166. *See, e.g.,* Evan Weiner, *Women's Soccer League Faces Tough Obstacles*, THE NEW YORK SUN, Sept. 12, 2007, *available at* http://www.nysun.com/sports/womens-soccer-league-faces-tough-obstacles/62455/ (last visited Apr. 9, 2009) ("American sports customers are just not interested in women's professional sports for some reason. Corporations don't buy huge blocks of club seats and luxury boxes for professional women's sports and fans don't watch it on TV in big numbers."); King, *supra* note 6, at 18 (explaining that data available from Scarborough Research indicates that it is more difficult to develop loyalty in women's professional sports because as fans women do not demonstrate avidity by watching games on television).

167. Guiliano, *supra* note 11 (noting that the 1999 U.S. World Cup was the most watched soccer match in U.S. television history; also noting that in 2001, the U.S. Women's Open singles final between Venus and Serena Williams, which was broadcast in prime time on CBS, even outdrew NBC's broadcast of the historically popular Notre Dame-Nebraska football game); Steve T. Gorches, *Call It the PBA Effect*, MERRILLVILLE POST-TRIBUNE, Sept. 12, 2007, at E-4, *available at* 2007 WLNR 18039570 (noting that women's tennis is actually more popular than men's tennis); Elliot Harris, *Quick Hits with Elliot Harris*, CHIC. TRIB., Nov. 16, 2006, at 114 (noting popularity of women's tennis).

About the Authors

Marc Edelman, Esq. (Marc@MarcEdelman.com), is an Assistant Professor at Barry Law School and a former Visiting Assistant Professor at Rutgers School of Law-Camden. Mr. Edelman earned his B.S. in Economics from the Wharton School (University of Pennsylvania) and his J.D./M.A. (law/sports management) from the University of Michigan.

Mr. Edelman retains all copyrights for this article and the article that appears in Chapter 7 beginning on page 238.

Elizabeth Masterson is a former women's soccer player in the United States' W-League and the Head Soccer Coach at Elmira College. Ms. Masterson earned her B.A. from St. Lawrence University and her M.S. (sports management) from Manhattanville College.

WOMEN'S BASKETBALL

ANALYZING THE WNBA'S MANDATORY AGE/EDUCATION POLICY FROM A LEGAL, CULTURAL, AND ETHICAL PERSPECTIVE: WOMEN, MEN, AND THE PROFESSIONAL SPORTS LANDSCAPE

Marc Edelman and C. Keith Harrison

. . . .

I. SOCIOLOGICAL LANDSCAPE OF WOMEN'S BASKETBALL IN AMERICA

The limited opportunity for women to perform as professional athletes in a male dominated culture is well documented in terms of the resources devoted to, popularity of, and historical discrimination against women's athletics.[11] Until recently, professional athletics were primarily for men.[12] With the late integration of women into professional sports, the role of the female athlete has developed differently. Organizations such as the NCAA have played a major role in promoting the ideology of the well-rounded, traditionally educated female athlete.[13] This ideology contrasts somewhat with the notion of the ruggedly individualistic male athlete.

The relationship between women in sports and their impact on young girls indicates that image is everything.[14] Since the emergence of women's collegiate and professional sports, young girls have begun to participate in athletics at all-time high rates.[15] While Title IX has been a major factor in cultivating women's athletics over the last thirty years, the age/education policy of the WNBA may contribute to a whole new culture of scholarly women that happen to play basketball.[16] For instance, female student-athletes graduate from college at a higher rate than any other student in American higher education.[17]

. . . .

II. THE HISTORY OF PROFESSIONAL WOMEN'S BASKETBALL

Founded in 1996, the WNBA consists of fourteen [*Ed. Note: now twelve*] teams, is more mature in terms of age than the NBA, and has an ethnic makeup of approximately sixty percent African-American and forty percent Caucasian players.[24] Based on WNBA statistics, over ninety percent of the players have earned a bachelor's degree from a four-year institution and twenty percent have earned graduate degrees. This culture of education, which in essence requires WNBA players to earn college degrees, is in stark contrast to the WNBA players' peers in the NBA, National Football League (NFL), Major League Baseball (MLB), and the National Hockey League (NHL).

A. The Early Struggles of Women's Professional Basketball in America

In its early years, American women's professional basketball was filled with various short-lived ventures. After generations of men's professional basketball leagues operating without a female counterpart, two women's professional basketball leagues burst onto the scene in the late 1970s: the Ladies Professional Basketball Association (LPBA) and the Women's Professional Basketball League (WBL).[25] Both leagues were defunct by 1981.[26]

Both the LPBA and the WBL struggled from the very beginning because of their high salaries, low sponsorship revenues, and team owners without significant investment income.[27] Unlike the NBA, neither female professional basketball league had the benefit of a television contract.[28] Without regular television revenues, neither league was able to turn a profit.[29]

By 1981, both the LPBA and WBL had folded, leaving the United States without professional women's basketball.[30] In fact, women's basketball did not return to America for nine years. On March 15, 1990, the Women's Sports Association Professional Basketball League (WSAPBL) presented itself as the first of several small, regional women's basketball leagues to emerge in America.[31] The WSAPBL attempted to control expenses by limiting its host cities to the greater California area.[32] After some initial success, other regional women's leagues followed, such as the Women's World Basketball Association (WWBA) in the Midwest,[33] and the Liberty Basketball Association (LBA) on the East Coast.[34]

Like many small, startup, professional sports leagues, the new, regional women's leagues attempted to draw fan interest by tinkering with the game's traditional rules. For example, the LBA lowered the basket by one foot so women could more easily slam-dunk.[35] Despite such ingenuity, the LBA disbanded within one season due to a recession.[36] The other regional women's basketball leagues also ceased to exist soon thereafter.

B. From Zero Leagues to Two—the Emergence of the ABL and the WNBA

With the failure of regional, women's basketball leagues, sports entrepreneurs in the 1990s decided to re-launch a national women's professional basketball league. As early as the Summer Olympics in 1992, NBA Commissioner David Stern began to consider the possibility of the NBA funding a national, upstart women's basketball league.[37] Even before Stern could propose a business plan, however, California entrepreneur Steve Hams and eleven other investors announced the formation of their own women's basketball league: the American Basketball League (ABL).[38]

Initially an eight-team league, the ABL business plan included teams playing a forty-game season between the months of October and February, overlapping with the first half of the NBA season.[39] The original host cities included Atlanta, Columbus, Denver, Hartford/Springfield, Portland, Richmond, Seattle, and San Jose, where the league headquarters was located.[40] According to this business plan, all ABL teams at least initially would be owned and operated by the ABL as a single entity, and the league would only draft players that had graduated from college.[41]

In November 1995, Hams announced that the ABL had signed nine of the eleven players on the women's United States Olympic team, each to two-year professional contracts with non-compete clauses—a move intended to fortify the league's position as the premier home of women's professional basketball.[42] According to Hams, the league planned to pay each of the U.S. Olympic team players $125,000 a year, maintain a league average salary of $70,000 a year, and institute a league minimum salary of $40,000—all decisions intended to thwart the emergence of a competitor league.[43] Additionally, the ABL secured sponsorship agreements with four major companies: Reebok, First USA Bank, Lady Foot Locker, and basketball manufacturer Baden.[44]

Yet, despite Hams's best efforts to make the ABL the exclusive women's basketball league, on April 24, 1996—almost seven months before the first ABL game—the NBA announced that it, too, was launching a women's professional basketball league (the WNBA), which would begin play in the summer of 1997.[45]

Unlike the ABL, the WNBA planned to compete during a ten-week season in the summer, which did not overlap with the NBA season.[46] Also, the WNBA model enjoyed the immediate advantage of being backed by the NBA—a well-fortified American business with powerful management.[47] On June 28, 1996—a full year before the first WNBA season was to begin—the WNBA entered into a five-year prime-time television contract with the National Broadcasting Company (NBC).[48] In addition, before playing a single game, the WNBA entered into substantial television pacts with ESPN and the Lifetime Network.[49] Meanwhile, ABL television coverage was limited to just twelve Sunday night games on SportsChannel.[50]

The ABL was the first league to begin play, and the early results were positive. In one league-opening game, 5,513 fans witnessed the Colorado Xplosion defeat the Seattle Reign.[51] That same night, 8,767 fans packed the Hartford Civic Center to see the New England Blizzard defeat the Richmond Rage.[52] Throughout the inaugural season, one of the brightest ABL stars was Jackie Joyner-Kersee, the beloved American 1988 Olympic champion in the horizontal jump.[53] Even though 1996 Olympic basketball standouts Sheryl Swoopes and Rebecca Lobo ultimately rejected the ABL,[54] the ABL still hosted most of the 1996 women's basketball Olympians.[55] In the inaugural ABL championships, Valerie Still, a thirty-five-year-old who just four years earlier had been teaching high school, finished the game with 14 points and 13 rebounds to lead the Columbus Quest

to a 77–64 victory over the Virginia Rage before a sellout crowd of 6,313.[56]

The WNBA meanwhile opened its inaugural season on June 21, 1997, with the fanfare of an NBA marketing blitz. The league placed teams in New York, Charlotte, Cleveland, Houston, Los Angeles, Phoenix, Sacramento, and Salt Lake City.[57] Former NBA Vice President Val Ackerman was promoted to the position of the league's first commissioner.[58] Nike, Coca-Cola, and American Express all signed on as premier league sponsors.[59] In the WNBA model, player salaries were kept below the average ABL salary rate, and the WNBA initially implemented a league-wide salary cap on all players' contracts at $50,000.[60]

With heavy fanfare, 14,284 spectators turned out to the Los Angeles Forum to watch the first WNBA game between the Los Angeles Sparks and the New York Liberty.[61] The WNBA also enjoyed opening crowds of 11,455 in Cleveland and 8,915 in Salt Lake City.[62] By season's end, the wildly televised and marketed WNBA drastically exceeded all expectations in fan interest, attracting nearly 9,000 fans per game.[63] From the abyss emerged the Houston Comets's Cynthia Cooper as the league's top-performing player, averaging a league-best 22.2 points per game.[64] The Houston Comets won the league's first championship, 65-51 over the Liberty,[65] and at least in the beginning, it seemed that two professional basketball leagues could co-exist in America: the traditional ABL in the winter, and the hyped, dynamic WNBA in the summer.

C. Survival of the Fittest: How the WNBA Garnered a Monopoly over American Women's Basketball

The two-league women's basketball format in America, which appeared so promising in 1997, however, was not to be. The WNBA had no interest in cooperating with the ABL, and after a few years of fierce competition between the ABL and the WNBA, the deeper-pocketed WBNA emerged as the sole survivor.[66] The first sign of conflict between the ABL and the WNBA was in September 1997, when the ABL's Most Valuable Player, Nikki McCray, jumped ship to the WNBA.[67] Although McCray accepted a pay cut from $150,000 in the ABL to $50,000 in the WNBA (the league maximum), McCray felt that playing in the WNBA would be more profitable in the long run because of the WNBA's premier exposure.[68]

Without national broadcast television, the ABL tried to boost its presence by proposing various joint marketing initiatives with the WNBA, including a proposal for an interleague, all-star game.[69] However, the WNBA rejected all ABL overtures, instead opting to compete directly against the ABL for the women's basketball market.[70] As a result, the ABL was placed in the undesirable position of needing to offer players significantly higher salaries to prevent them from defecting to their more prominent competitor.[71]

Even as the ABL attendance totals increased twenty percent in its second year and the league announced expansion plans into new cities such as Chicago,[72] the ABL was heading into a "no win" situation.[73] Spring 1998 was especially telling for the ABL, as seven of the eight collegiate All-American women's basketball players signed with the WNBA.[74] In an interview with the San Francisco Examiner, Gary Cavelli, CEO and co-founder of the ABL acknowledged, "I think we won Rounds 1 and 2, and they're winning the third round. We're definitely behind at this point."[75]

While WNBA attendance climbed above 10,000 fans-per-game in its second season and ownership moved toward expanding the league,[76] the ABL spent its 1998 summer dissolving its failed Long Beach, California franchise and trying to cope with superstar Dawn Staley's defection to the WNBA.[77] The ABL did catch one huge break in the 1998–99 season, as the NBA players went on strike for the first half of their season and national broadcast television temporarily picked up ABL games as replacement programming.[78] Nevertheless, once the NBA players returned to action, ABL broadcasts ceased, and on Tuesday, December 22, 1998, the ABL folded and filed for bankruptcy.[79]

D.   Transition Game: Changes in the WNBA Structure upon ABL Bankruptcy

Once the WNBA became the only women's game in town, the league began to pursue an expansion strategy, but it was never able to significantly increase its fan base. After averaging an all-time high of 10,869 fans per game in the 1998 season, WNBA attendance began to decline steadily, falling below an average of 10,000 fans per game for the first time in 2000, and then falling below the 9,000 mark in 2003.[80] By 2006, WNBA average per-game attendance fell all the way to 7,490 fans per game.[81] [*Ed. Note: In 2009, average attendance was 8,039.*]

With WNBA attendance and revenues declining, players began to take steps to protect their interests in a declining pie. On November 6, 1998, shortly before the ABL filed for bankruptcy, the WNBA women's basketball players made the first step to change their labor relationship with the WNBA by forming the Women's National Basketball Players Association (WNBPA)—the first labor union ever comprised entirely of professional female athletes.[82] Shortly thereafter, on April 30, 1999, the WNBPA ratified its first league collective bargaining agreement (CBA) with the union.[83] According to the WNBPA website: "The inaugural CBA encompassed significant advances for WNBA players, and represents for all women, an important step toward pay equity and general equality."[84] The CBA established a near seventy-five percent minimum salary increase for WNBA rookies and a one hundred percent minimum salary increase for WNBA veterans beyond the minimums that the WNBA had previously unilaterally imposed.[85] The CBA also provided "year-round health coverage, a retirement plan, guaranteed contracts and a collective share of licensing income."[86] Yet, as compared to the status obtained in collective bargaining by men's professional sports unions,

the WNBPA was relatively powerless. The WNBPA was unable to bargain as aggressively as most men's sports unions because the WNBA teams regularly threatened to either shut down the league or lock out the players if the WNBPA did not agree to certain terms proposed by the league.[87] With the maximum WNBA player salary at the time standing at just $50,000, most WNBA players had not saved enough money to sustain a long lockout.[88]

The first CBA between the parties was ratified on April 30, 1999, and expired on September 15, 2002.[89] On April 25, 2003, the WNBA and WNBPA agreed to a second collective bargaining agreement.[90] [*Ed. Note: The parties agreed to a third collective bargaining agreement in 2008 that continues through the 2013 season.*] . . . According to the WNBPA, advancements in the second CBA include the creation of a free agency system for WNBA players and the return of player group licensing rights to WNBA players.[91] However, the pay for WNBA players, as well as the revenue generated by the WNBA, remained miniscule as compared to that of men's professional basketball players.

Then, in 2003, the WNBA decided to transform its business from a structure including central ownership in the league overall to a structure including independent team ownership as exists in the four premier men's leagues.[92] The impetus for this transition was an important decision handed down by the First Circuit Court of Appeals in *Fraser v. Major League Soccer,* which indicated that the centralized Major League Soccer structure—in many ways similar to the original structure of the WNBA—did not necessarily shield the league from antitrust liability.[93] As a result of the WNBA's structural change to an independent ownership model, WNBA teams began to independently manage their own operations and pursue their own players and sponsorship deals.[94] Nevertheless, this structural change did not affect the coordinated decision-making of the WNBA, which now occurred through the collective bargaining process.

In recent years, many of the top women's basketball players, unhappy with their salary prospects in the WNBA, have started spending their off-seasons playing overseas.[95] A number of American-born players have even indicated their desire to play exclusively overseas.[96] For example, Tina Thompson, a four-time WNBA champion with the Houston Comets, recently indicated she may forego the WNBA altogether because she believes she can triple her WNBA maximum salary by playing exclusively in Moscow, Russia.[97]

E.   The WNBA Education Policy

From their incipient stages, both the WNBA and ABL enforced independent league regulations to prevent their teams from drafting players that still had NCAA college eligibility.[98] When the ABL ceased its operations in 1998, however, prospective women's basketball players lost the leverage of having two separate leagues vying for player services.[99] Without two leagues, the only bargaining chip of a player that did not meet the age/education policy was a threat to play permanently overseas. For some players with young families well-settled in the United States, that was not a viable option.

Once the ABL ceased to exist and the WNBA players unionized, the WNBA took affirmative steps to protect its age/education policy from antitrust scrutiny by adding references to the league's age/education policy into the CBA. . . .

Notes

. . . .

11. Andrew Zimbalist, *Unpaid Professionals: Commercialism & Conflict in Big-Time College Sports* 54 (1999).

12. Jean O'Reilly & Susan K. Cahn, *Women and Sports in the United States: A Documentary Reader* xi (2007).

13. *Id.* at xii.

14. Harrison, *supra* note 10, at 11.

15. O'Reilly & Cahn, *supra* note 12, at xii.

16. Harrison, *supra* note 10, at 11.

17. *See* National Collegiate Athletic Association Home Page, http://www.ncaa.org (last visited Jan. 15, 2008).

. . . .

24. *See generally* Richard E. Lapchick & Kevin J. Matthews, *Racial and Gender Report Card* (2001); *see also* WNBA Home Page, http://www.wnba.com (last visited Jan. 15, 2008).

25. *See* Donna Carter, *Women's Pro Basketball League Planned,* L.A. TIMES, Jan. 26, 1990, at C14. The WBL debuted on December 9, 1978, but disbanded in 1981, whereas the LPBA was launched in 1980 and failed within a few months. *See* Anna Maria Basquez, *Showtime for Shelley,* ROCKY MOUNTAIN NEWS (Denver, CO), July 16, 1996, at 3D.

26. *See* Basquez, *supra* note 25, at 3D.

27. *See* Carter, *supra* note 25, at C14. *See also Idea for NBA: Female League,* ORLANDO SENTINEL, Dec. 26, 1992, at B7.

28. *See* Bill Jauss, *Geraty Digs Up Old Game - Women's League May Sprout Again,* CHI. TRIB., Jan. 17, 1992, at Sports 8.

29. *See id.*

30. *See* Carter, *supra* note 25, at 14.

31. *See id.*

32. *See id.*

33. *See, e.g.,* John Bannon, *Pro's League for Women's Basketball Tries Again,* USA TODAY, July 2, 1991, at 2C.

34. For a more detailed analysis of the LBA, see Jeff Williams, *New Women's Pro League,* NEWSDAY, Dec. 18, 1990, at 131; *see also* Ailene Voisin, *New LBA Hopes to Become NBA for Women,* ATLANTA J. & CONST., Jan. 20, 1991, at H3; Debbie Becker, *New League Hopes Big Things Come from Smaller Packaging,* USA TODAY, Feb. 18, 1991, at 5C. Initially, the LBA showed signs of success, drawing 10,753 fans to their inaugural game in Auburn Hills, MI. *See New League Streamlined for Success,* CHI. TRIB., Feb. 22, 1991, at Sports 4; *see also New Women's Pro Basketball League Rolling,* ST. LOUIS POST-DISPATCH, Feb. 24, 1991, at 9F.

35. *See* Ailene Voisin, *Women's Pro League Plans Comeback,* ATLANTA J. & CONST., Apr. 2, 1993, at E13.

36. *See id.*

37. *See* David Aldridge, *NBA's Stern Defends Dream Team's Quarters,* WASH. POST, Aug. 5, 1992, at F8.

38. *See* Earl Gustkey, *Women Have Two New Incentives this Season,* L.A. TIMES, Nov. 25, 1995, at C9; *see also* Dick Rockne, *Women's Pro Hoops in Seattle? Proposed League Would Feature Some Members of National Team,* SEATTLE TIMES, Nov. 29, 1995, at D2; Rob Oller, *Proposed League Still Trying to Take Flight,* COLUMBUS DISPATCH, Apr. 26, 1996, at 10D; *American Basketball League,* DAILY NEWS (New York, N.Y.), Oct. 6, 1996, at 1C.

39. *See American Basketball League, supra* note 38; *see also* Dick Rockne, *Women's Pro League Takes Shot in Seattle,* SEATTLE TIMES, Feb. 21, 1996, at C1.

40. *See Hartford/Springfield in Women's League,* HARTFORD COURANT, Feb. 21, 1996, at C2.

41. *See* Joey Johnstone, *Playing for Pay,* TAMPA TRIB., Apr. 1, 1996, at Sports 6; Elizabethe Holland, *WNBA Triumphs in Round 3 Against ABL,* ST. LOUIS POST-DISPATCH, May 2, 1998, at Sports 23.

42. *See* Gustkey, *supra* note 38. These players included: Jennifer Azzi, Katy Steding, Lisa Leslie, Sheryl Swoopes, Dawn Staley, Teresa Edwards, Ruthie Bolton, Nikki McCray and Carla McGhee. *See* Tom Flaherty, *Two Other Women's Leagues to Start this Year,* MILWAUKEE J. SENTINEL, May 2, 1996, at Sports 9C; *see also* Liz Robbins, *NBC to Televise the Women's NBA,* CLEVELAND PLAIN DEALER, June 28, 1996, at 2D.

43. *See* Gustkey, *supra* note 38.

44. *See* Celeste E. Whittaker, *American Basketball League Facing Uphill Battle,* ATLANTA J. & CONST., Oct. 16, 1996, at D3.

45. *See* Earl Gustkey, *NBA to Direct a Women's League,* L.A. TIMES, Apr. 25, 1996, at C5.

46. *Id.; see also* Flaherty, *supra* note 42.

47. *See generally* Gustkey, *supra* note 45.

48. *See* Robbins, *supra* note 42. The contract included a promise to broadcast the WNBA on Saturday afternoons. *See* Brian Landman, *One May Be Better than Two,* ST. PETERSBURG TIMES, July 9, 1996, at 1C.

49. *See* Joanne Korth, *Basketball League Channels Energy into TV Deals,* ST. PETERSBURG TIMES, July 21, 1996, at 2C.

50. *See* Tom Flaherty, *Basketball Spotlight Will Shine on the ABL,* MILWAUKEE J. SENTINEL, Oct. 15, 1996, at Sports 12.

51. *See* Glenn Nelson, *Reign Stumbles in First ABL Step,* SEATTLE TIMES, Oct. 19, 1996, at B1.

52. *See Blizzard Opens ABL with Win,* HOUS. CHRON., Oct. 19, 1996, at 15B.

53. *See* Jere Longman, *Jumping to Hoops: Olympian Joyner-Kersee Dribbles Back to Sport of Her Youth for ABL,* DALLAS MORNING NEWS, Oct. 20, 1996, at 17B.

54. Swoopes initially played for the ABL, but began playing for the WNBA in 1997. *See* William C. Rhoden, *Women's N.B.A. Takes First Big Step,* N.Y. TIMES, Oct. 24, 1996, at B20.

55. *See* W.H. Stickney Jr., *Swoopes, Lobo Sign with WNBA,* HOUS. CHRON., Oct. 24, 1996, at 7B; *see also* Stephanie Storm, *Women's League Growing Fast,* ORLANDO SENTINEL, Dec. 15, 1996, at C12.

56. *See* Kathy Orton, *Quest Is Over For Columbus,* WASH. POST, March 12, 1997, at C1.

57. *See* Mark Asher, *WNBA Takes Its Leap Forward,* WASH. POST, Oct. 31, 1996, at C3.

58. *See id.*

59. *See generally* Valerie Lister, *On the Heels of ABL's First Season, Women's NBA Gets Ready to Roll,* USA TODAY, Mar. 13, 1997, at 15C; *see also Marketing v. Heart: WNBA, ABL in a Death Watch,* ORLANDO SENTINEL, Aug. 8, 1997, at C10.

60. *See* Amy Shipley, *With Shrewd Planning, WNBA Ends First Season Leagues Ahead,* WASH. POST, Aug. 31, 1997, at A23.

61. *See* Vic Ziegel, *WNBA States its Case with Well-Attended Debut,* ORLANDO SENTINEL, June 22, 1997, at C4.

62. *See id.*

63. *See generally* David Moore, *WNBA Establishes Itself as Fan Favorite in Rookie Season,* DALLAS MORNING NEWS, Aug. 4, 1997, at 12B.

64. *See* W.H. Stickney Jr., *Cooper's Season One to Remember,* HOUS. CHRON., Aug. 16, 1997, at B8.

65. *See id.*

66. *See* Terry Frei, *New Leagues Don't Follow ABL Lead,* DENVER POST, July 2, 2000, at C4.

67. *See* Valerie Lister, *ABL Says No Bidding War Despite McCray's Jump,* USA TODAY, Sept. 17, 1997, at 10C.

68. *Id.* (noting that McCray would earn additional income from a personal services contract).

69. *See* Stephanie Storm, *Top Official Proposes ABL-WNBA All-Star Game,* ORLANDO SENTINEL, Jan. 18, 1998, at C10.

70. *See ABL-WNBA All-Star Challenge Dunked,* SEATTLE TIMES, Feb. 3, 1998, at C2.

71. *See* Jeff Z. Klein, *Foot Soldiers: The Launch of the WUSA Opens a New Front in Women's Pro Sports,* VILLAGE VOICE, Apr. 24, 2001, at 47 (stating that "the ABL collapsed, largely because of competition from the heavily promoted, heavily bankrolled WNBA"); *see generally* Amy Shipley & Karl Hente, *Women's Pro Hoops Leagues Battle for Position,* ST. LOUIS POST-DISPATCH, May 18, 1997, at 7F (discussing the competition between the ABL and WNBA for players).

72. *See generally* Athelia Knight, *In Its Second Season, ABL Is Above Average: Interest in Sport Helps Attendance Increase in League,* WASH. POST, Jan. 2, 1998, at C7; *see also* Phil Rosenthal, *Can Jackson Be Sold on ABL vs. WNBA?,* CHI. SUN-TIMES, Apr. 8, 1998, at Sports 105; Earl Gustkey, *Women's Basketball: Rumors of Jordan Ownership Keeps the ABL Buzzing,* L.A. TIMES, June 30, 1998, at C8 (discussing a rumor that legendary NBA player Michael Jordan had considered buying a stake in the ABL's Chicago expansion team).

73. *See generally* John Deshazier, *ABL Hasn't Scored Enough Points to Win Ratings Game,* TIMES-PICAYUNE (New Orleans, La.), Feb. 28, 1998, at D1.

74. *See* Holland, *supra* note 41; *UConn's Sales to WNBA,* DAILY NEWS (New York, N.Y.), Apr. 29, 1998, at 71.

75. Holland, *supra* note 41 (quoting Cavelli's interview with the *San Francisco Examiner*).

76. *See* Darrell Williams, *WNBA Keeps Building on a Good Thing,* TIMES-PICAYUNE (New Orleans, La.), Aug. 2, 1998, at C2; *see generally* Tim Povtak, *Disney Makes it Official: Orlando Joins WNBA,* ORLANDO SENTINEL, Aug. 14, 1998, at C1.

77. *See* Susan Slusser, *ABL Season to Start 2 Weeks Later,* S.F. CHRON., Sept. 3, 1998, at D7.

78. *See, e.g.* Athelia Knight, *NBA's Loss Is Gain for ABL: Women's League Hits National TV,* WASH. POST, Nov. 26, 1998, at B14.

79. *See* Melissa Isaacson, *Lights Go Out on the ABL: To No One's Surprise, Boys Club Wins Again,* CHI. TRIB., Dec. 23, 1998, at Sports 1.

80. *See* Kim Callahan, Season By Season WNBA Attendance 1 (2007), http://womensbasketballonline.com/wnba/attendance/sbsatten.pdf (last visited Jan. 12, 2008).

81. *Id.*

82. *See* WNBA Players Association, About the WNBPA, http://www.wnbpa.com/about_wnbpa.php (last visited Jan. 15, 2008).

83. *Id.*

84. *Id.*

85. *See id.*

86. *Id.*

87. *See, e.g.* Bart Hubbuch, *WNBA Labor Deal, Draft Put on Hold,* DALLAS MORNING NEWS, Apr. 23, 1999, at 5B (stating that the WNBA postponed its 1999 draft indefinitely and threatened a lockout unless the players' union consented to the proposed collective bargaining agreement).

88. This is in contrast to professional athletes in the four premier men's sports leagues that, based on their higher salaries, often have more personal reserves. Moreover, in the four premier men's sports leagues, the players' union often keeps a reserve fund to make payments to players in the event of a strike or lockout. For example, one of the reasons why the Major League Baseball Players Association was able to sustain such a long work stoppage in 1994 was because it had reserved $200 million in funds to distribute to players in the event of a work stoppage. See, e.g., Baseball's Last Gasp is Today, PALM BEACH POST, Sept. 14, 1994, at Sports 1C (stating that the union planned to begin making payments to players from its $200 million strike fund).

89. *See* WNBA Players Association, *supra* note 82.

90. *Id.*

91. *Id.*

92. *See* Mel Greenberg, *New-Look WNBA to Open 7th Season: 2 Teams Fold, 3 See Change in Ownership,* CHI. TRIB., May 21, 2003, at Sports 9.

93. *See Fraser v. Major League Soccer, LLC,* 284 F.3d 47, 58-61 (1st Cir. 2002); *see also* Marc Edelman, *Fan Ownership Can Give UFL a Leg Up on Building Brand Loyalty,* STREET & SMITH'S SPORTS BUS. J., Aug. 27–Sept. 7, 2007, at 28 (stating "there are probably lingering perceptions of an antitrust advantage to having 50 percent common ownership amongst teams, even though the decision by the First Circuit Court of Appeals in the 2002 case *Fraser v. Major League Soccer* indicated that any such antitrust advantage is dubious."); Lacie L. Kaiser, *The Flight from Single-Entity Structured Sports Leagues,* 2 DEPAUL J. SPORTS L. & CONTEMP. PROBS. 1, 9–11 (2004).

94. *See generally* Kaiser, *supra* note 93, at 11–13.

95. *See* Oscar Dixon, *More Players Profit from Testing Waters: Overseas Competition Gives League Reason for Concern,* USA TODAY, Aug. 21. 2007, at 10C.

96. *Id.*

97. *Id.*

98. *See* Elizabethe Holland, *Holdsclaw will Stay in College Basketball,* ST. LOUIS POST-DISPATCH, Mar. 30, 1998, at C6.

99. The emergence of a rival professional sports league often impacts whether the dominant league attempts to maintain age/education

policies. For example, the NFL reduced its age/education policy from four to three years after Hall of Fame running back Herschel Walker opted to sign with the New Jersey Generals team in the rival United States Football League after his sophomore year rather than wait the required third and fourth seasons before entering the NFL. *See, e.g.,* PAUL WEILER & GARY ROBERTS, SPORTS AND THE LAW 201 (3d ed. 2004). Initially, the NFL selectively implemented its rule by granting a limited number of special exceptions

to allow superstar collegiate players, including Barry Sanders, to enter the league early. *See* Charean Williams, *Got 'Em – Longhorns Never Seem to Get Burnt by the NFL Draft,* FORT WORTH STAR-TELEGRAM, Apr. 18, 2005, at 1D. Then, in 1990, the NFL rewrote its longstanding eligibility rule to allow NFL entry to all players after their junior year of college or three years after high school. *Id.*

. . . .

XFL

THE INAUGURAL (AND ONLY) SEASON OF THE XTREME FOOTBALL LEAGUE: A CASE STUDY IN SPORTS ENTERTAINMENT

Keith Willoughby and Chad Mancini

INTRODUCTION

. . . .

In 2001, a new professional sports league, the Xtreme Football League (XFL), began play. League developers devoted conscientious effort to avoiding the pitfalls of previous football league failures. In 1974, the World Football League (WFL) was established. It lasted until midway through the 1975 season before ceasing operations. A major factor in the league's demise involved financial difficulties. Created in 1983, the United States Football League (USFL) eventually folded after three seasons. Exorbitant salaries paid to attract collegiate stars, an overly restrictive television contract, and the decision to undertake direct competition with the NFL contributed to the USFL's downfall. Despite the attempt to avoid earlier league mistakes, the XFL failed. This case study analyzes the specific events and particular environment that helped to form the league. We address the developments that occurred during the league's short (12-week) run. We conclude with a discussion of some possible reasons why this new venture proved so disastrous.

THE PRE-GAME: A NEW LEAGUE IS BORN

On February 3, 2000 (a full year prior to the league's first game), plans for the XFL were announced publicly at the World Wrestling Federation (WWF) entertainment complex in New York City's Times Square. Basil DeVito, Jr., league president, proclaimed this sport would be "pro football like you've never experienced it before." (XFL All Access (2001)). Indeed, the notion of combining the entertainment and marketing savvy of the WWF with professional football seemed intriguing. Under the leadership of Vince McMahon, the WWF was a global entertainment leader.

It produced quarterly revenues of around $100 million, with an estimated weekly global viewership of 500 million (www.ww●com).

Less than two months after the league's initial inception, the WWF and the National Broadcasting Company (NBC) announced a strategic partnership to jointly own and operate the league. Regarding this new opportunity, Dick Ebersol, Chairman of NBC Sports, suggested that "we think of ourselves as the 'Xtra Fun League." (XFL All Access (2001)). Certainly, NBC's foray into this sports broadcasting venture was not surprising. It had lost its coveted NFL package after the 1997 season. Moreover, it had recently failed to put together a summer football league with the Turner Broadcasting System. Eventually broadcasting negotiations were completed, and three of the XFL's four weekly games were to be televised: a Saturday evening game on NBC, with Sunday contests featured on up-start cable networks UPN and TNN. To enhance the image of the league's broadcasts, the XFL hired Mike Weisman, a seven-time Super Bowl television executive producer, as its broadcast consultant (McAdams (2000)).

With partnerships formed and television rights obtained, the next step involved determining locations for the league's eight franchises. On June 13, 2000, Chicago was introduced as the league's initial city. League officials were careful to balance the placement of teams. Some were located in cities or areas already home to NFL squads (Chicago, San Francisco and the New York/New Jersey area). Others were positioned in regions without NFL representation (Orlando, Memphis, Las Vegas and Birmingham). The remaining XFL team was situated in Los Angeles, a city without a current NFL team, although it had previously hosted two NFL franchises. In an effort to symbolize the anticipated ferocity and extreme nature of this sport, league officials purposely selected demonstrative team nicknames. These included, among others, Hitmen (New York/New Jersey), Rage (Orlando), Maniax (Memphis) and Enforcers (Chicago).

Any sports league requires credible front-office personnel. For the XFL, such individuals would be needed to bolster the league's reputation and to provide some measure of face validity. In keeping with the expected hard-nosed, "in-your-face" mentality of the XFL, the league made two noteworthy appointments. Dick Butkus, arguably the epitome of football toughness, was hired as Director of Football Competition. He had played nine hard-hitting seasons as middle linebacker with the NFL's Chicago Bears. Drew Pearson, an important player during the Dallas Cowboys' reign as "America's Team", was signed as the inaugural member of the XFL's advisory committee.

Personnel are required to run the league, television stations to broadcast the events, but in the end, players are needed to do the actual running, catching and tackling. Initially, the XFL wanted to conduct pre-season training camps with roughly 70 players per teams (thus, the 8-team league would need 560 players). The original plan was to scour the ranks of mid-level collegiate teams, Arena Football League franchises and semi-professional squads to provide a pool of potential talent. As it turned out, the league was overwhelmed with the submitted number of player applications. Over 50,000 individuals posted their resumes on the league's web site. Roughly 4,000 players sent videotapes of their performances to the league's head offices. Consequently, the XFL had little trouble stocking its rosters.

After months of planning, the new league was set to commence. Various signs pointed to quick and continued future success. A promotional boost was even delivered by Hollywood. On November 13, 2000 (less than 3 months prior to the league's opening match-up), a futuristic movie entitled "The 6th Day" opened on theater screens nationwide. This film featured mega-star Arnold Schwarzenegger and his battles to expose a global human cloning conspiracy. The movie's beginning sequence depicted the XFL championship game involving superstar quarterback Johnny Phoenix, the world's first $300 million professional athlete!

LET THE GAMES BEGIN

The XFL made great strides to separate itself from its professional football competitor, the NFL. To capture its aggressive and cutting-edge flair for players, fans and coaches, the XFL introduced some rule modifications. It did away with video instant replays, a true source of consternation in the NFL. In the XFL, the official's ruling was final—there were no challenges to a referee's call such as one may witness in the NFL. Further, there was no "fair catch" rule protecting the punt returner. This forced the player to receive the ball after it has been kicked. Along with this rule, once the ball has gone more than 25 yards when kicked, either team is allowed to recover it. This marked a definite switch from NFL rules.

Other rules changes sought to bolster offensive production. Teams were not permitted to kick extra points after a touchdown is scored. To receive the extra point, the team scoring the touchdown must either run or pass the ball into the end zone. Moreover, receivers were only required to get one foot in bounds when making a reception instead of the "two feet down" rule that exists in the NFL. Finally, after a play involving any type of clock stoppage, the team with the ball is given only 25 seconds to run the next play.

Perhaps the most intriguing development in XFL rules involved the action at the beginning of a game. In the NFL, a referee flips a coin and a captain from one of the teams calls "heads" or "tails". If the player guesses correctly (thereby "winning the toss"), his team has the option of kicking or receiving the ball, defending a particular end of the field or deferring this choice to the second half. If the player guesses incorrectly, a player on the other team must select between the above options. XFL officials, perhaps sensing that such a process was passe, adopted an alternative method. At the sound of a whistle, a player from each team would race 25 yards towards a football. The first player to retrieve the ball would be given (as above) the choices of kicking/receiving the ball, defending a specific end of the field, or deferring the option to the second half. This modification served to cement the aggressive mentality of the sport.

In an additional effort to distance its product from the NFL, and to make its brand of entertainment more palatable to the "average guy", the XFL established a unique set of salary regulations. The NFL is replete with players earning multi-million dollar contracts; indeed, the league minimum is over $400,000 per year. The XFL wanted nothing of this "prima donna" flamboyance. To wit, XFL players were all paid a base salary depending on their position. All quarterbacks were paid $5,000 each week, kickers received $3,500 a week, and all others earned a $4,000 weekly salary. To enhance the notion that "winning isn't everything—it's the only thing", players on each game's winning squad earned monetary bonuses of $2,500 per player. In the playoffs, the weekly payoff increased to $7,500 for each of the winning team's players. The league championship squad split a $1,000,000 pot amongst its players (roughly $20,000 per player).

The XFL's first games were played on Saturday, February 3, 2001. The specific timing of the season's launch was by no means accidental. It was the consensus of McMahon, DeVito and Ebersol that such a date would provide maximum audience exposure to their brand of football. The NFL's Super Bowl championship is generally held on the final Sunday in January. Up until that time, the American football junkie has been exposed to almost six months of professional and collegiate play. Kicking off XFL action one week after the completion of the NFL season suggests that an upstart league could fill the void of the fan suddenly devoid of their favorite sport.

McMahon's marketing strategy was to obtain advertising support from several big name businesses. In fact, 1-800-CALL-ATT, Burger King, Honda, M&M/Mars and Quaker State/Pennzoil were some of the first companies to advertise during XFL games. XFL officials claimed that simply from these sponsors, half of their TV inventory had already been sold (Lefton [5]). A further element of McMahon's strategy was to develop commercials that showcased the "smash-mouth" nature of his sport. Many of those commercials depicted the game of football involving war-like scenarios, with dirty and bruised players running through mine fields or avoiding cannon fire in potential training camp drills.

When the first league games kicked off in Las Vegas and Orlando, the television audiences were treated to a technological experience unlike anything previously encountered in sports entertainment. Undeniably, a major competitive advantage for the XFL concerned the extent of fan involvement during the televised contests. Extra cameras and microphones were used to bring the fan onto the field, into the locker room, and (perhaps) into the heads of the players and coaches. The use of this uninhibited technology permitted observers to get a glimpse of pre-game pep talks or halftime speeches, something that NFL broadcasts fail to deliver. Further, it was not uncommon to see a camera operator (equipped with a helmet and padding!) on the field behind the huddle. The XFL even developed the "X-Cam", an innovative camera technique, to get a new angle of the game. This camera hung above the field on a pulley system and was able to directly follow game action.

Aggressive rule adjustments, marketing strategies and technological gadgetry produced a national hype for the league's first games. In fact, both of the opening contests were played in front of sold-out crowds. The attendance in Orlando was the largest home-opening crowd of any Orlando professional sports team (Drehs (2001)).

Initial television ratings appeared to support the view that America was prime for this smash-mouth brand of football. NBC was thrilled with their 10.2 Nielsen rating for their Saturday, February 3rd game. (One rating point corresponds to roughly 1,022,000 U.S. households, or 1% of the estimated number of U.S. TV homes). As it turned out, this was more than twice the television ratings expected by NBC officials. For purposes of comparison, the average Saturday night rating for NBC in 2000 was 4.2. Even its National Basketball Association (NBA) Saturday night coverage garnered only a 4.0 rating.

Although NBC and XFL personnel were euphoric over the Saturday night ratings, a further examination of the data revealed a disturbing trend. Television viewership showed a steady decline during each half hour interval. Undoubtedly, the American audience was tuning in to catch an initial glimpse of the action, to see what all this fuss was about. They wanted to witness for themselves the promotional spectacle that was the XFL. Once the novelty factor wore off (and for some viewers, it did not take very long), television ratings nose-dived.

In fact, the weekly ratings underscored the difficulties the XFL was beginning to face across the nation. The ratings for the two games on Sunday, February 4, 2001 did fall to more "ordinary" levels, with UPN's contest between Los Angeles and San Francisco scoring a rating of 4.2. After

the initial hype of week 1, NBC's week 2 television ratings fell by almost 50%. Moreover, the league enraged millions of Americans when NBC's week 2 contest between Chicago and Los Angeles went into double overtime, thereby pushing back the start of "Saturday Night Live" with pop-sensation Jennifer Lopez as guest host. This development motivated the XFL to tinker with its rules by instituting a running clock, ensuring that games would end faster.

During week 3, XFL broadcasts were the 89th ranked television show in the country. To add insult to injury, Honda (one of the league's original sponsors) withdrew its TV ads at the end of this week. In fact, by week 4, the league was providing free air-time for advertisers.

The ratings continued to plummet. The league earned an infamous distinction in week 7 by garnering a 1.6 rating. This was believed to be the lowest prime-time night among NBC, CBS or ABC in Nielsen Media Research history. Ratings in week 8 actually improved, although the 1.8 rating placed the broadcasts 94th overall among shows that week.

The XFL playoff games showed marginal ratings improvement, but nothing like the levels league officials hoped to earn. The first week of playoffs scored a 2.0 rating, while the "Million Dollar Game" on April 22, 2001 achieved a 2.5. In the end, NBC's average XFL rating was 3.3 (although this was bolstered by the huge ratings during the first week of league action). Perhaps more telling than the television ratings was the league attendance, especially at the championship game. A total of 24,153 fans attended this game in the cavernous Los Angeles Coliseum (capacity: 90,000).

THE POST-GAME: WHAT WENT WRONG?

The XFL ceased operations on May 10, 2001, less than three weeks after its championship game. Reportedly, the WWF lost $35 million in this venture, with NBC losing a similar amount. League president DeVito succinctly surmised, "We didn't do everything well out of the gate" (www.espn.com, May, 2001). An analysis of the specific reasons contributing to XFL failure seems to be in order. The XFL failure will be compared to other failed football endeavors in the U.S, and contrasted with other football leagues that have had some measure of success in the United States.

In an effort to be successful, the XFL wanted to avoid the pitfalls of a previous failure, the United States Football League (USFL). The USFL lasted for three complete seasons (1983–1985). Jim Byrne (1987), a former USFL communications director, indicated at least three reasons why the league ceased operations. It had an overly restrictive television contract with the American Broadcasting Company (ABC). Secondly, it paid exorbitant salaries to lure collegiate stars to the new league. Steve Young, Herschel Walker, Doug Flutie and Jim Kelly—each of whom would eventually earn NFL accolades—began their professional careers in the USFL. Finally, prior to the anticipated 1986 season, the USFL announced that it would play its games in the fall (rather than the spring–summer scheduling as was previously done). This move brought some of its franchises into direct competition with NFL teams in their respective cities. Eventually, the USFL filed an antitrust lawsuit against the NFL and, although the new league won the case, it was only awarded $1 in damages!

The XFL observed these challenges and developed a strategy that sought to dodge these difficulties. Unlike the USFL, the XFL had a reasonably good television package with NBC, UPN and TNN. The fact that NBC helped to operate part of the league seemed beneficial. In addition, the XFL avoided lucrative contracts with its relatively modest salary structure. Finally, the XFL purposely opted to play its games during the NFL "down-time", thus steering clear of direct competition with the NFL. The fact that both the USFL and XFL had diametrically opposed strategies, yet each failed, suggests that television packages, salary structures and league timing have little to do with eventual success.

Another failed football venture was the World Football League (WFL). Formed on August 2, 1973, this league played a full season (1974) before folding on October 22, 1975 (part way through its second campaign). Financial difficulties were cited as a major contributing factor in the league's downfall.

The Canadian Football League (CFL) has operated since the late 19th century with some measure of success in Canada. However, beginning in 1993, the league attempted to expand its operations into the U.S. San Antonio, Memphis, Birmingham and Baltimore were some of the cities that featured CFL teams. Ultimately, this move proved disastrous, leading American-based franchises to fold after the 1995 season. These teams had difficulties competing for the sports entertainment dollar with head-to-head competition from collegiate football and the NFL.

. . . .

The analysis of failed and successful professional sports leagues seems to support the conclusion that the over-riding factor for success appears to be one of on-field attractiveness. If this is the extant . . ., then fans will embrace the sport. Inasmuch as it is lacking (witness the USFL and XFL), then such ventures wither. . . . [A]lternative brands may succeed in carving a niche in the sports entertainment industry. Indeed, the final product (in this case, football entertainment) must be viewed as having some semblance of attractiveness.

One additional contributing factor for the XFL's demise was the League officials attempt to "straddle the fence" between two groups of sports and entertainment enthusiasts. The league wavered between football and wrestling, instead of deciding to pursue either a strictly football strategy, or create a league that was more centered on a WWF environment with football as the backdrop. Neal Pilson, former CBS Sports President, felt that the XFL had no promise whatsoever (see Fendrich (2001)). Pilson mentioned "if they had pitched it closer to football, they would have lost the wrestling audience. If they had made a burlesque out of football to conform to the expectations of the wrestling audience, they probably would have lost NBC." By straddling this fence, the XFL created a division in its fan base and left both groups confused and unsatisfied, leaving them no opportunity to give loyal support to the league. Litke (2001) suggested "the XFL was doomed from the start. People were bound to tune in for only so long to see special effects and scantily clad cheerleaders, especially since there are cable channels devoted entirely to those subjects. At some point, there has to be a game." Perhaps this is what McMahon, Ebersol and DeVito failed to realize all along.

In conclusion, some of the lessons learned from the XFL fiasco can be applied to other new sport ventures. Indeed, those attempting to build a new sport entity (whether it be a league, event or property) may appreciate some of these "do's" and "do not's" associated with establishing a new endeavor. In order to be successful, a new venture must have some type of name recognition, whether that involves coaches, athletes or front-office personnel. The XFL's decision to appoint Dick Butkus as its Director of Football Competition did provide the league with some measure of initial credibility. Moreover, any new undertaking must recognize that, in the seemingly crowded world of sports entities, one must articulate—then successfully reach—a specific niche.

The "do not's" involve the attempt to straddle two disparate groups of consumers. As the XFL discovered, adopting such a strategy leads to a product failing to meet any group's needs. Further, sports marketers ought to avoid sensationalized claims of league or event success in the face of competition from an established giant. The XFL's assertion that it would be "pro football like you've never experienced it before", notwithstanding the sheer appeal and magnitude of the NFL, may have struck some football fans as ludicrous. Finally, any new league developers should avoid the inclination to tinker with a particular sport's pre-established set of rules and procedures. The "race for the ball", instead of a simple coin flip at the beginning of a game, may have seemed too bizarre to be real football for the die-hard fan.

. . . .

References

Byrne, J. (1987), *The $1 league: The rise and fall of the USFL,* New York: Simon and Schuster.

Drehs, W. (2001). Target audience revels in XFL's debut. Retrieved February 15, 2001 from ESPN web site, www.espn.com.

Fendrich, H. (2001). 'You can call it the ex-FL'. Associated Press story, May 11.

Lambert, C. (2001). The Dow of professional sports. *Harvard Magazine,* 104(1), 38-45.

Lefton, T. (2000). Spot marks the X. *Brandweek*, 41(33), 4.

Litke, J. (2001). 'It's the game, stupid.' Associated Press story, April 25.

Lowry, T. (2003). The NFL machine. *Business Week*, January 27.

McAdams, D.D. (2000). Leveraging "raw" power. *Broadcasting and Cable*, 130(6), 4.

Noll, R.G., & Zimbalist, A. (1997). Sports, jobs, and taxes. *The Brookings Review*, 15(3), 35–39.

XFL All Access (2001). New York/New Jersey vs. Birmingham game program.

CALLED UP TO THE BIG LEAGUES: AN EXAMINATION OF THE FACTORS AFFECTING THE LOCATION OF MINOR LEAGUE BASEBALL TEAMS

Michael Davis

Between the 2004 and 2005 seasons, the Austin and El Paso franchises in baseball's AA level Texas League moved to Corpus Christi and Springfield, Missouri, respectively. To determine whether such moves make sense, we need to examine a number of different issues. The purpose of this study is to determine the factors that lead to the presence and level of a professional baseball team at a particular location. The results will contribute to the knowledge of which factors affect the demand for professional baseball and will suggest which locations are either under-represented or over-represented in terms of their local baseball teams. Furthermore, the results will suggest which cities should be next in line for a professional baseball team at a particular level if a team relocates or there is expansion.

The organization of the minor leagues presents a clear hierarchy we can exploit to analyze the important factors in locating teams. The minor leagues are set up with the following structure: AAA, AA, High-A, Low-A, Short Season A, and Rookie leagues in descending order. The quality of play will typically be better at AAA than at AA, better in AA than A, and so forth down the list. Also, the season is longer for the higher leagues, with the majors running at least a month longer than all of the minor leagues, and Short Season A and Rookie leagues playing two months less than the other minor leagues. The better quality and greater quantity of baseball at the higher levels suggest that we can assume that the major league teams will be in the best locations, and the AAA teams in the next best locations.

. . . .

We find that a city's population, personal income, and time from the nearest major league city all have a positive impact on whether there is a team in the location. While the results for population and time are expected, the results for per capita personal income are not. Combined with past studies suggesting that personal income does not affect attendance at minor league baseball games, the results support a view that there is a labor–leisure trade off for the wealthy.

MINOR LEAGUE BASEBALL

Wealthier citizens may not be able to take off any more time for recreational activities like watching baseball but expect a higher quality product when they do attend. The presence or absence of alternative sports options appears to have no impact.

INSTITUTIONAL STRUCTURE

The number of teams in particular locations has always been restricted by the agreements between Major League Baseball and minor league baseball. The current locations of teams are influenced by these changing rule structures. Until the 1990s the rule seemed to be that teams had a 15-mile buffer in which they could restrict competition. In the 1990s the rule was extended to a 35-mile buffer area. By 2003 the rules differed between the major and minor league teams. The major league teams were assigned counties from which they could exclude either major or minor league teams. In addition, they had a 15-mile boundary beyond the county borders. According to Jim Ferguson, Director of Media Relations for minor league baseball, the minor league team rules are that a team cannot move into a county that borders another county with a minor league baseball team (CantonRep.com, 2003). These restrictive rules have effectively prevented most of the metropolitan areas that have teams from having additional teams move into them. There are exceptions. Baade and Sanderson (1997) note that the Kane County Cougars located in the far suburbs of Chicago in the 1990s. More recently the Frisco Roughriders moved into the northern edge of the Dallas metropolitan area.

The restrictive practices of the major and affiliated minor leagues, however, have given an opportunity for upstart independent minor league teams to move into under-represented areas. A number of independent minor leagues have come into existence since 1993, the first independent baseball leagues since 1954. Although the independent leagues include teams located in smaller markets not inhabited by any other teams, they consist primarily of teams in markets with major league teams that have used rules to keep out affiliated minor league teams (Cooper, 2004). In 2003, 29 of 179 (16%) affiliated minor league teams were located in metropolitan areas with a major league team, while 21 of 54 (39%) independent league teams were located in similar markets.

In an attempt to find better stadium deals and markets, the affiliated minor leagues have franchises moving almost every year. The number of moves varies from year to year, however. Between 2002 and 2003, seven franchises in the affiliated minor leagues moved; between 2003 and 2004, only three franchises moved. Also many of the franchises are quite stable, having existed in the same location for a long period of time, and Kraus (2003) stated that there has been greater stability in team locations since 1990 than there had been previously.

It is often the case that a city will see a team leave for a different location and then have a team at a different level move into it within a few years. Occasionally the moves will take place in the same year. In 2005, the AA team in Greenville, SC, moved to Jackson, MS. The same year a Low-A team moved from Columbia to Greenville.

The level of stability is much lower in the independent minor leagues than in the affiliated minor leagues. In 2003 there were seven independent minor leagues that began the season. Between 2002 and 2003, one independent league folded (Western Baseball League), one league split into two (the Northern League into the Northern and Northeastern Leagues), one league came into being but did not finish the season (Arizona-Mexico League), and there were four expansion teams as well as six franchise moves or replacement teams for folded teams. Between 2003 and 2004, another league folded (Southeastern), three other teams folded (one of whom was replaced by a traveling team) and one franchise moved. In addition, two teams switched leagues, with Springfield/Ozark moving to the Frontier League from the Central League and Pensacola taking its place in the Central League, moving from the defunct Southeastern League.

LITERATURE REVIEW

Past studies use attendance data for individual teams to investigate the demand for minor league baseball. Siegfried and Eisenberg (1980) estimated the impact of a city's market size, per capita income, ticket prices, and demographic factors on attendance. They find that population and ticket prices are the two main factors affecting the attendance at minor league baseball games. They also find that higher level teams (AAA and AA) have greater attendance than lower level teams (A and Rookie). Branvold, Pan, and Gabert (1997) showed that market size and the success of the team are both important factors, but factors that affect attendance differently depending on the level of the team. Our methodology differs from those studies in that we use the presence of a team, not the attendance, as the dependent variable.

A few studies used data sets similar to the one used in this study. However, most of the analyses assessed the impact minor league teams have on the communities, rather than examining what leads a community to have a team. Baade and Sanderson (1997) found that the presence of a minor league baseball team did little to improve the economic conditions of the area. Colclough, Daellenbach, and Sherony (1994) found only minimal benefits to La Crosse,

WI, in building a stadium for a Class A baseball team. From a survey of local governments that hosted minor league baseball teams, Johnson (1990) found that the leaders of those communities had an unrealistically large perception of the value of the teams to their communities. Contrary to these other findings, Kraus (2003) concluded that there are significant economic and non-economic benefits to a city of hosting a minor league baseball team.

. . . .

FACTORS INFLUENCING THE LOCATIONS OF BASEBALL TEAMS

In describing the benefits to the Frisco Roughriders' new city following their move from Shreveport, the Frisco Roughriders' President stated, "The franchise is now located in one of the fastest growing cities in America and the fan base from the surrounding counties is phenomenal. The team is great, the fans are happy and the ballpark is gorgeous" (Baseball America, 2004). The quote suggests many of the factors that would influence the decision of a baseball team to locate in a particular location: population, population growth, and quality of the ballpark (see **Table 1** and **Table 2**).

The decision to own and locate a team in a particular city is a supply decision; however, the costs will be similar across most cities in the country. There will be some effect of travel costs for cities not located near many other cities, but for the most part there will not be many differences in supply from city to city. The largest cost to an owner of a AAA team will be the opportunity cost of not locating the team in a different city. These opportunity costs will be affected by the differences in demand in different cities. We will examine the differences in factors across cities that affect the demand for baseball.

Siegfried and Eisenberg (1980) and Branvold et al. (1997) suggested factors to include in the model, the most obvious of which is population. A larger population should lead to greater demand for baseball and thus a higher level team in that location. In some cases the metropolitan area may be large enough for multiple teams, but in this study we simply look at the highest level team in a particular location. Another factor that might affect the demand for baseball is the income of the people in the area. Higher income could mean greater disposable income to spend on recreation and therefore greater interest in baseball.

The presence of teams in other sports is a third factor that might affect the presence of baseball teams. However, the presence of professional hockey, football, or basketball teams would likely be determined endogenously with the presence of a baseball team in the city. For example, it is not clear whether Milwaukee does not have a National Hockey League (NHL) team because it already has a Major League Baseball (MLB) team or that it has a MLB team because it

Table 1   Metropolitan Areas with Multiple Teams Including at Least One Major League Team

Metropolitan Area	Total Teams	Breakdown
New York	14	2 Major, 2 AA, 1 Low-A, 4 Short-Season A, 5 Independent
Chicago	8	2 Major, 1 Low-A, 5 Independent
Los Angeles	7	2 Major, 5 High-A
Boston	5	1 Major, 1 Short Season A, 3 Independent
Washington	5	1 Major, 1 AA, 2 High-A, 1 Short Season A
Tampa	4	1 Major, 3 High-A
Cleveland	3	1 Major, 1 AA, 1 Low-A
Dallas	3	1 Major, 1 AA, 1 Independent
Miami	3	1 Major, 2 High-A
San Jose	3	2 Major, 1 High-A
Seattle	3	1 Major, 1 AAA, 1 Short-Season A
St. Louis	3	1 Major, 2 Independent
Cincinnati	2	1 Major, 1 Independent
Kansas City	2	1 Major, 1 Independent
Minneapolis	2	1 Major, 1 Independent
Philadelphia	2	1 Major, 1 Independent
Pittsburgh	2	1 Major, 1 Independent

Source: International Journal of Sport Finance. Used with permission from Fitness Information Technology.

does not have an NHL team. Despite these concerns over endogenicity, we include variables testing whether the presence of football, basketball, or hockey teams affects the presence of a baseball team. The hockey variable indicates the presence of a team in any of the following leagues: NHL, AHL, ECHL, WCHL, CHL, UHL, or ACHL. Any team in the NFL or in one of the three indoor football leagues, AFL, AF2, or NIFL, is indicated by the football variable. Lastly the basketball variable indicates the presence of a team in the NBA, CBA, or NBDL.

One factor that would likely be exogenous to the presence of baseball teams, however, is the presence in the location of a major college sports program. We therefore include in this analysis a dummy variable for whether there is a Bowl Championship Series (BCS) college in the location. The BCS represents the universities with the biggest and best college football programs. It is also likely a good proxy for the universities with the biggest overall college sports programs (see **Table 3**). We hypothesize that this variable or

the professional sports variables should have negative coefficients because they represent alternative sports opportunities for fans (see **Table 4**).

Lastly, the location of the Combined Statistical Area (CSA) relative to other CSAs could be important. The CSAs are combinations of metropolitan areas for cities near one another. For this analysis a simple definition of distance is used. It is assumed that the major league team locations are determined first and are therefore exogenous. For each CSA the time it takes to travel by automobile to the closest major league stadium is used as an explanatory variable. Because there is a realistic limit to how far most people will routinely travel to a sporting event, the time variable is capped at 300 minutes (5 hours). A significant positive coefficient would imply that the fans of a particular team support the major league team nearby and do not need a team of their own. Alternatively we might see a negative coefficient on this variable. All minor league teams have links with major league franchises. If a team is near the city with the major league

Table 2   Metropolitan Areas with Multiple Teams but No Major League Teams

Metropolitan Area	Total Teams	Breakdown
Johnson City, TN	4	4 Rookie
Greensboro	3	1 High-A, 1 Low-A, 1 Rookie
Bluefield, WV	2	2 Rookie
Charlotte	2	1 AAA, 1 Low-A
Columbus	2	1 AAA, 1 Independent
Raleigh	2	1 AAA, 1 AA
Rochester	2	1 AAA, 1 Short-Season A
Salt Lake City	2	1 AAA, 1 Rookie
Syracuse	2	1 AAA, 1 Short-Season A

Source: International Journal of Sport Finance. Used with permission from Fitness Information Technology.

Table 3   Means for Each Baseball Level

Level of Team	Number of Observations	Population	Per Capita Personal Income	Time to Nearest ML Team	With BCS University (%)	With Hockey (%)	With Football (%)	With Basketball (%)
No Team	561	88,981	$24,865	200.1	4%	2%	2%	1%
Independent	28	321,102	$26,975	205.0	11%	43%	25%	7%
Rookie	12	161,541	$25,783	291.3	8%	0%	17%	0%
Short-Season A	12	372,903	$26,628	189.1	17%	17%	8%	17%
Low-A	25	413,487	$27,790	155.8	20%	40%	28%	16%
High-A	17	469,097	$27,784	170.6	6%	24%	24%	6%
AA	24	766,235	$28,770	181.1	17%	67%	42%	17%
AAA	27	1,279,242	$30,348	177.2	22%	67%	56%	19%
Major League	24	5,616,900	$35,376	NA	63%	92%	96%	75%

Source: International Journal of Sport Finance. Used with permission from Fitness Information Technology.
Note: Only highest level team within each CSA is included.
Time to ML Team is truncated so that the maximum allowed is 300 minutes (5 hours).

Table 4   GOLM Estimation Results

	(1) Coefficient	Standard Error	(2) Coefficient	Standard Error
β				
Log Per Capita Personal Income	2.581*	0.891	2.664*	0.892
Log Population	2.362*	0.165	2.330*	0.188
Time	0.005*	0.002	0.005*	0.002
BCS			−0.480	0.359
Hockey			0.883	0.454
γ_2 (SSA/Rook)				
Time	−0.001	0.001	−0.001	0.001
Hockey			−1.147*	0.406
γ_3 (Low-A)				
Time	−0.005*	0.002	−0.005*	0.002
Hockey			−0.766	0.426
γ_4 (High-A)				
Time	−0.002	0.002	−0.002	0.002
Hockey			−0.986*	0.482
γ_5 (AA)				
Time	−0.002	0.003	−0.002	0.003
Hockey			−0.394	0.538
γ_6 (AAA)				
Time	−0.003	0.004	−0.004	0.004
Hockey			−0.800	0.652
α				
α_1	−56.832*	9.160	−57.293*	9.327
α_2	−57.204*	9.169	−57.530*	9.332
α_3	−57.000*	9.164	−57.324*	9.326
α_4	−58.275*	9.177	−58.564*	9.338
α_5	−59.014*	9.194	−59.481*	9.359
α_6	−60.088*	9.219	−60.390*	9.388

Source: International Journal of Sport Finance. Used with permission from Fitness Information Technology.
*Significant at 5% level.
(1) Estimation using generalized ordered logit model of level of team on constant, log of population, log of per capita personal income, and time to nearest major league city.
(2) Estimation using generalized ordered logit model of level of team on constant, log of population, log of per capita personal income, presence of BCS university, presence of a hockey team, and time to nearest major league city.
Both estimations include all CSA/MSAs and micropolitan areas except those with major league teams.

team of which it is a farm team, the fans of the major league team might be willing to visit the minor league team for a chance to see the future prospects of their team. It would also give them a chance to root for a team of the same name as their favorite team but at a cheaper price. One last consideration, as mentioned by Kraus (2003), is that teams such as those in the Eastern League are located where they are in part because nearby major league teams can conveniently call up a replacement from the minors if a starter gets hurt. The benefits of proximity to the major league teams would be limited to AAA and AA teams, as those would have players with sufficient ability to fill in at the major league level.

. . . .

[*Ed. Note: Author's discussion of Data and Methodology are omitted.*]

RESULTS

. . . .

Population is positive and significant as expected. Per capita personal income is positive and significant, suggesting that wealth increases demand. Note that this finding differs from the results of Siegfried and Eisenberg (1980), who found that per capita income did not have a significant positive effect on attendance. The difference in the results could be explained by the difference in methodologies. Because they must sacrifice more income for leisure, wealthier residents might not be interested in attending a greater number of games but have a preference for superior quality games.

The coefficients for time from nearest major league team are positive and significant, but the effect is not the same across all the levels. In particular, as the level goes from

Table 5   Predicted Probabilities of Outcomes

Model	No Team	Independent	Rookie/ SS-A	Low-A	High-A	AA	AAA
All Means	93%	2.6%	2.0%	1.0%	0.68%	0.34%	0.15%
Population							
100,000	92%	3.0%	2.4%	1.2%	0.80%	0.40%	0.18%
200,000	70%	9.6%	9.1%	5.2%	3.8%	2.0%	0.89%
300,000	47%	13%	15%	10%	8.4%	4.7%	2.2%
400,000	31%	12%	17%	14%	13%	8.5%	4.3%
500,000	22%	9.8%	16%	16%	18%	13%	7.0%
750,000	9.8%	5.5%	11%	14%	22%	22%	16%
1,000,000	5.1%	3.1%	6.7%	9.9%	20%	28%	28%
PCPI							
$20,000	96%	1.5%	1.1%	0.55%	0.37%	0.18%	0.08%
$25,000	93%	2.6%	2.0%	1.0%	0.67%	0.33%	0.15%
$30,000	90%	3.9%	3.1%	1.6%	1.1%	0.54%	0.24%
$35,000	85%	5.3%	4.4%	2.3%	1.6%	0.80%	0.36%
Time							
100 min	96%	1.5%	0.55%	1.4%	0.52%	0.25%	0.13%
200 min	93%	2.6%	2.1%	1.0%	0.68%	0.34%	0.15%
300 min	89%	4.4%	4.2%	0.53%	0.89%	0.46%	0.17%
BCS							
0	93%	2.6%	2.1%	1.0%	0.70%	0.35%	0.15%
1	96%	1.7%	1.3%	0.65%	0.44%	0.22%	0.10%
Hockey (Population = mean)							
0	94%	1.9%	2.2%	0.97%	0.72%	0.31%	0.15%
1	86%	10%	0.92%	1.3%	0.31%	0.59%	0.16%
Hockey (Population = 750,000)							
0	11%	4.3%	11%	13%	23%	21%	16%
1	4.7%	14%	5.6%	18%	8.7%	32%	17%

Source: International Journal of Sport Finance. Used with permission from Fitness Information Technology.
Notes: Based on results of estimation from column 2 of Table 4.
All other variables are at means unless otherwise noted.
Population and per capita income estimated and evaluated in log values but displayed in levels.

Short-Season A/Rookie to Low A, the effect of time is negligible. The results suggest that being farther away from a major league location increases the level of the baseball team, as competition from the major league team is less (see **Table 5**).

. . . .

The first conclusion that can be drawn from the data is the overwhelming importance of population. Metropolitan areas with fewer than 100,000 people rarely have teams, while those with more than 750,000 rarely do not. The second conclusion is that the other factors can affect the presence of teams but are of secondary importance. . . .

The presence of a hockey team in a location seems to suggest a higher likelihood for a minor league baseball team. This result is counterintuitive. One explanation is that the presence of a hockey team shows a city's willingness to construct facilities for sports teams, and thus the city is more likely to construct facilities for a baseball team. The other possibility is that there are idiosyncrasies in the locations of hockey leagues. At a higher population level (750,000) the presence of a hockey team reduces the probability of having a team at Rookie/Short-Season A and High-A and increases the probability of having a team in the independent, Low-A, AA, and AAA levels.

Tables 6 and **7** are based on the probabilities suggested from the model results in Table 4, column 2. Table 6 ranks the cities by the probability that they should (by the model) have a team at that level or higher but do not. Table 7 reports the top 10 ranking for cities that do have teams by the lowest probability of having a team at that level or higher. From these tables it appears that either the leagues and team owners are missing a good opportunity or there are factors not accounted for that are determining the locations. Some of these factors are considered below.

The results also suggest that the outliers for the lower level leagues are more severe than for the higher leagues. For example, the top two omissions from the AAA level, San Antonio and Orlando, are the only missing cities that the model suggests should be in the top 15. However, all of the top 10 omissions in High-A would rank in the top 12 most likely locations for teams at that level.

One explanation for there being more omissions in the lower levels is that the geographical locations of the leagues are not included in the model. The two major leagues are both national, having teams throughout the country. The two AAA leagues are not individually national but between them cover the entire country. On the other hand, the three AA leagues (Texas, Southern, and Eastern Leagues) cover only about half the country among them. The same is true of the lower level leagues as well. Grand Rapids and Dayton are deserving of at least AA teams, but geographically the Low-A Midwest League would make more sense for those locations than a higher league that is not as close. . . . One Rookie and one Short-Season A league are located in the western part of the country, where the distances between cities are large and there are few major league teams. The Low-A league with the most teams (Midwestern League) is located in an area with many major league teams.

The study uses 2003 data because that is the most recent available for the population and income statistics. Some of the misallocations identified here have already been corrected by the teams. For instance, Austin now has a AAA team in the Pacific Coast League and Jackson, MS has a team in the AA Southern League. Of course not all of the moves that have taken place would be optimal according to this model, as a AA team in the Texas League, which was ranked 71st in the AA rankings, moved to Springfield, MO, in 2005.

Table 6   Top 10 Cities with Highest Probabilities to Have Team at Particular Level that Do Not Have Team at that Level or Higher

	AAA	AA	High A	Any Team
1	San Antonio (7)	Greensboro (4)	Honolulu (2)	Honolulu (29)
2	Orlando (8)	Grand Rapids (7)	Grand Rapids (3)	Springfield, MA (47)
3	Hartford (17)	Albany (8)	Albany (4)	Anchorage (49)
4	Jacksonville (18)	Dayton (10)	Dayton (5)	Lafayette (57)
5	Greensboro (20)	Honolulu (12)	Allentown (6)	Gulfport (59)
6	Grand Rapids (21)	Springfield, MA (19)	Springfield, MA (8)	Fayetteville, NC (65)
7	Austin (22)	Charleston, SC (20)	Charleston, SC (9)	Reno (69)
8	Albany (24)	Allentown, PA (21)	Baton Rouge (10)	Madison (77)
9	Birmingham (26)	Baton Rouge (22)	Boise (11)	Lancaster, PA (83)
10	Tulsa (27)	Boise (23)	Jackson, MS (12)	Santa Barbara (87)

Source: International Journal of Sport Finance. Used with permission from Fitness Information Technology.
Note: Number in parentheses represents rank for particular level or above excluding teams that have a team at higher rank. The Any Team is rank among all locations. *Example:* Excluding cities with major league teams, Greensboro had the 20th highest probability of having a team at the AAA level, but Greensboro does not have a AAA team. Of the 19 cities in front of Greensboro, 15 of them had AAA teams. Excluding cities with major and AAA teams, Greensboro had the third highest probability of having either a AAA or AA team.

Table 7   Top 10 Cities with Lowest Probabilities to Have Team at Particular Level that Do Have a Team at that Level

	AAA	AA	High A	Any Team
1	Scranton (59)	Altoona (226)	Kinston, NC (336)	Clinton, IA (459)
2	Colorado Springs (53)	Jackson, TN (153)	Vero Beach (114)	Richmond, IN (417)
3	Tucson (46)	Erie (110)	Lynchburg (87)	Oneonta, NY (416)
4	Syracuse (45)	Binghamton (93)	Myrtle Beach (71)	Burlington, IA (410)
5	Des Moines (44)	Norwich (84)	Visalia (68)	Kinston, NC (369)
6	Toledo (38)	Midland (77)	Wilmington, NC (60)	Rome, GA (354)
7	Fresno (35)	Reading, PA (52)	Roanoke, VA (57)	Martinsville, VA (330)
8	Albuquerque (34)	Mobile (40)	Port St. Lucie (52)	Helena, MT (306)
9	Omaha (31)	Huntsville (35)	Modesto, CA (46)	Jamestown, NY (280)
10	Oklahoma City (30)	Chattanooga (33)	Lakeland, FL (36)	Great Falls, MT (279)

Source: International Journal of Sport Finance. Used with permission from Fitness Information Technology.
Note: Number in parentheses represents rank for particular level or above excluding teams that have a team at higher rank. The Any Team is rank among all locations. *Example:* Des Moines has a AAA team; however, according to the model it had only the 44th highest probability of having a AAA team, and there were four cities with lower probabilities that have AAA teams.

The remaining exceptions identified as misallocations could be explained by variables that are impossible to include in the model. Individual tastes in sports could vary from one location to another. Even specific factors that are measurable, such as the extreme distance of Honolulu from the mainland or Greensboro's having three teams instead of one, could explain those cities' rankings. Another possibility could be the willingness or reluctance of a municipality to subsidize stadium construction. The case studies of Johnson (1993), Wessel (1993), and Turner (1993) examined the factors that led to the relocation of minor league franchises, with a key issue in each being that one location gave a better stadium deal than did the other location. Lastly there may be some idiosyncratic decisions made by an individual team owner that cause a team to choose one location over another.

CONCLUSION

We find that population and personal income positively affect the level of minor league baseball in a metropolitan area. Although the population effect is obvious, the personal income finding is more surprising. The driving time to the nearest major league team has a positive effect on the presence of a minor league team, but the presence of a BCS university has no effect. The presence of a major or minor league hockey team generally increases the likelihood of having a team but reduces the probability of having one at some of the levels.

Cities interested in attracting a minor league baseball team should realize from this study that even though the quality of a new ballpark is important, the underlying qualities of the city and surrounding communities are quite important for the locating of minor league baseball teams. In particular, if the population does not appear to be sufficient to support a team of a particular level, it is unlikely that the team will remain there in the long run. The tables listing the outliers that are indicated by the model do not define the only likely locations for long term success at each level, but they are suggestive.

From these results one direction for future study would be to examine the dynamics of team movements over the entire data set of team locations for the past 30 years. For instance, Johnson (1993) asserted that in the early 1990s fundamental changes to the economics of baseball affected the ability of small markets to support minor league baseball teams. Also, a more detailed examination of the location of the leagues themselves, based on population and historical developments, would be an additional possibility for future research.

References

. . . .

Baade, R. A., & Sanderson, A. R. (1997). Minor league teams and communities. In R. G. Noll & A. S. Zimbalist (Eds.), *Sports, Jobs & Taxes* (pp. 452–493). Washington, D.C.: Brookings Institution Press.

. . . .

Baseball America. (2004). *Baseball America Almanac 2004*: Baseball America, Inc.

. . . .

Branvold, S. E., Pan, D. W., & Gabert, T. E. (1997). Effects of winning percentage and market size on attendance in Minor League Baseball. *Sport Marketing Quarterly, 6*(4), 35–42.

. . . .

CantonRep.com (2003). Canton trying to land baseball team. Retrieved July 15, 2006, from http://www.cantonrep.com/index.php?ID=95290&r=0&Categor=11.

. . . .

Colclough, W. G., Daellenbach, L. A., & Sherony, K. R. (1994). Estimating the economic impact of a minor league baseball stadium. *Managerial and Decision Economics, 15*(5), 497–502.

Cooper, J. J. (2004). 2004 Independent League Preview. Retrieved July 15, 2006, from http://www.baseballAmerica.com/today/leagues/independent/040504preview04.html.

. . . .

Johnson, A. T. (1990). Professional baseball at the minor league level: Considerations for cities large and small. *State & Local Government Review, 22,* 90–96.

Johnson, A. T. (1993). *Minor league baseball and local economic development.* Urbana: University of Illinois Press.

Kraus, R. S. (2003). *Minor league baseball community building through hometown sports.* New York: The Haworth Press.

. . . .

Siegfried, J. J., & Eisenberg, J. D. (1980). The demand for minor league baseball. *Atlantic Economic Journal,* 8(2), 59–69.

Turner, R. (1993). Fort Lauderdale, Florida. In A. T. Johnson (Ed.), *Minor league baseball and local economic development* (pp. 164–171). Urbana: University of Illinois Press.

Wessel, H. (1993). Old Orchard Beach, Maine. In A. T. Johnson (Ed.), *Minor league baseball and local economic development* (pp. 144–153). Urbana: University of Illinois Press.

. . . .

Discussion Questions

1. What are the advantages and disadvantages of a single-entity league structure?
2. Does a single-entity structure make sense for an established league? Why or why not? Does it make sense for a start-up league? Why or why not?
3. With the proliferation of cable/internet outlets, was it a smart decision for the Arena Football League to give up so much potential upside in order to get a network TV deal?
4. What obstacles do you see to the growth of the sport of soccer in the United States?
5. What can major league professional sports learn from the minor leagues and start-up leagues?
6. How are the outside forms of competition for major league teams similar to and different from those faced by minor league teams? Explain.
7. How do revenue sources of minor league teams differ from those of major league teams?
8. What ideas can you think of that would have helped failed or struggling leagues such as the AFL, XFL, WUSA, and WNBA?
9. Do you see media entities in the future taking increased equity stakes in the events they televise?
10. Given the risks inherent in new leagues, is it smart for MLS players to challenge the league's single-entity status now? If not, what benchmarks would show sufficient viability to make you believe MLS could survive without its single-entity status?
11. Would a successful challenge to MLS' single-entity status handcuff future leagues from gradually loosening their single-entity rules?
12. If a challenge to the MLS' single-entity status were successful, could MLS abandon the Beckham Rule and return to being a single entity? Would it even want to do so?
13. What is the counterargument to Bezbatchenko's position that MLS is still league directed?
14. For niche sports (which may not have traditional superstars), are the benefits of single-entity status worth sacrificing innovation, investor attraction, natural results, and other benefits that come from a mixed-mode traditional league structure?
15. What was the most important factor in ensuring the WNBA's survival and the ABL's collapse?
16. Which of the five factors for success did the XFL have, going into the inaugural season? What was it missing?
17. Compare and contrast the WNBA/ABL and the XFL.
18. Is there a self-imposed ceiling created by a league or sport that defines itself in opposition to the mainstream?
19. Is there a future in sports that are hyper-targeted; that is, those that do not provide a broad following but are successful because they bring ever more specific demographics to advertisers?
20. What is the value of having a link to a major league team? Is it a necessary condition to success, or are there arguments for staying part of an independent league?
21. Why would a BCS university athletic program located in the same town have no effect with regard to competition for a minor-league baseball franchise?

Revenue Sharing and Competitive Balance

INTRODUCTION

No matter the structure, all professional sports leagues are deeply concerned about the same two basic issues: competitive balance and revenue sharing. With an understanding of the background and structure of leagues provided in the previous chapters, the reader can now give greater attention to revenue sharing policies and competitive balance issues. One way of thinking about revenue sharing is to define it as the amount of revenues earned by members of a professional sports league that are shared by all league teams, regardless of the teams' contributions to the generation of these revenues. Another way to consider revenue sharing is to focus on the amount of money that teams pay each other for the right to play each other.

The history of revenue sharing is interesting. The equalizing of television revenues was first proposed at the MLB owners meetings in 1952 by Bill Veeck (then the owner of the small-revenue St. Louis Browns): "It is my contention that the Browns provide half the cast in every game they play. Therefore, we're entitled to our cut of the TV fees the home club receives for televising our games. Morally, I know I am right, and I plan to fight this thing to the end."[1] To this, Brooklyn Dodgers owner Walter O'Malley responded: "You're a damned communist."[2] Veeck's retort was telling:

> Under this system they want to continue the rich clubs get richer and the poor clubs continue poor. With all that television money they're getting the Yanks can continue to keep outbidding us for talent. They've signed $500,000 worth of bonus players in the last couple of years, paying for 'em out of the TV money we help provide. We poorer clubs are helping cut our own throats. None of us is ever going to catch up with the Yankees at that rate.[3]

Ultimately, Veeck lost this argument, and his proposed 50-50 split of television revenues was voted down by the MLB owners. Nonetheless, an important seed was planted in the mind of baseball executive Branch Rickey that would prove important when he became one of the entrepreneurs behind the contemplated Continental League later in the decade. Rickey proposed using a 33% team–67% league split of television revenues. His guiding philosophy that provided the rationale for revenue sharing was that: "any rule or regulation that removes or tends to remove the power of money to make the difference in playing strength is a good rule."[4]

Although the Continental League was never launched, it, too, was influential in the evolution of revenue sharing, because it provided the basis for sports entrepreneur Lamar Hunt's proposal for the pooling and equal sharing of television revenues in his newly formed American Football League.[5] The AFL ultimately adopted this proposal and sold its pooled television rights in 1960 for $8.5 million over 5 years, which provided each of the 10 teams in the league with $170,000 annually. Comparatively, the television rights in the established, rival NFL were sold by the teams on an individual basis. In 1960, the Baltimore Colts had a $600,000 per year contract with NBC and 9 of the 12 NFL teams had contracts with CBS. The teams acted as competitors in the television marketplace rather than as a unified entity. The New York Giants received $175,000 and the Green Bay Packers only $75,000 from CBS for their broadcasting rights. This is especially relevant given what the startup AFL teams were receiving. This led NFL Commissioner Pete Rozelle to adopt the "League Think" philosophy that became a hallmark of his longtime tenure as commissioner. He successfully persuaded even the largest NFL teams to sacrifice their short-term revenues for long-term growth. This required some teams to forsake—at least in the short-term—hundreds of thousands of dollars in television revenues. He was able to convince them that the strength of the league as a collective entity was more important than the strength of any one team. When legal precedent prevented the NFL from entering into the league-wide television contract that Rozelle envisioned, he successfully lobbied Congress for the passage of the Sports Broadcasting Act of 1961, which allowed for the pooled sale of national television rights by sports leagues. The NFL then entered a 2-year contract with CBS that paid $4.65 million per annum, or $387,500 per team.

The leagues vary in the degree of revenue sharing that they engage in. Further, it is safe to say that there is a fair amount of dispute within each league as to the appropriate level of revenue sharing. The central issues in revenue sharing tend to be the composition of the revenue pool that is shared; that is, which revenues are considered central (paid directly to league) as opposed to local (paid directly to clubs); the local revenue streams that are shared (if any); the amount of sharing (if any) of these local revenues; and the allocation rules used to distribute the shared revenues. This last issue has several alternatives: providing a larger allocation to the teams that have lower local-revenue-generating capabilities; giving an equal allocation to all teams in the league; and making a larger allocation to teams with the highest revenues or the most wins. The latter alternative approaches raw capitalism and is used by the English Premier League, which allocates its national television revenues via a formula that gives the better-performing teams on the field the highest allocations, which increases the absolute revenue differences between clubs. This is a good example of the balance of seeking to equalize revenues while encouraging competition.

Revenue sharing gives rise to moral hazard opportunities. Revenue sharing should reduce opportunistic behavior among profit-maximizing teams by making clubs dependent on each other. However, franchises are not entirely intradependent (even in the NFL), and differing owner motivations means that some are profit maximizing, whereas others are more interested in winning, prestige, ego, and so on. This diversity of owner interests mitigates the effectiveness of revenue sharing in curbing opportunistic behavior by league owners. This opportunistic owner behavior occurs in the form of both "sharking" and "shirking."[6] Sharking is seen in the independent owner action that is initiated to increase the wealth of the individual club at the expense of the overall league welfare. A prime example of this behavior is the undermining of league-wide marketing contracts by teams negotiating their own lucrative marketing agreements, putting compliant teams at a competitive disadvantage. Shirking occurs because revenue sharing creates incentives for a lack of effort among teams, who can free ride the efforts of other teams. Some owners may field uncompetitive teams and undermonetize those club revenues that are shared with other teams. It is difficult to successfully address either form of this opportunistic owner behavior. Getting offending teams

to voluntarily accept the league's governance mechanisms is unlikely, litigation is suboptimal, and increasing the amount of revenue sharing only creates additional shirking opportunities.[7] Leagues have taken divergent paths in attempting to do so.

The NFL has the most aggressive revenue sharing system, a product of historical necessity and the aforementioned foresight and leadership of longtime commissioner Pete Rozelle. The NHL has the least amount of revenue sharing and, at present, the largest number of struggling franchises of any of the leagues. Over the years, various proposals to increase the level of revenue sharing in the NHL have been met derisively by the owners, with the typical response beginning with an owner standing up and saying, "Comrades!" This is in reference to the highly socialistic nature of revenue sharing. Perhaps this underscores the notion that sports leagues are simply different than other types of businesses. Revenue sharing in the NBA and MLB falls between these two extremes, although it is hardly any less controversial. The owners in the NBA and NFL determine the league revenue sharing policy unilaterally, whereas MLB and NHL owners must collectively bargain with the players' union over the terms of their revenue sharing. This is another peculiarity of these sports leagues—the employees have a say in how their employers divide up their revenues. This is because revenue sharing impacts player salaries. All leagues equally divide national media, sponsorship, and licensing revenues among the teams. See **Table 1** for MLB team financial data and **Table 2** for NFL team financial data.

Sharing of gate receipts varies by league. The percentages allocated among the home and visiting teams and league offices have fluctuated over time as well. In the NFL, 66% of gate receipts are retained by the home team and 34% is pooled and shared among the visiting teams. The NBA and NHL are far more capitalistic in their policies, with NBA home teams retaining 94% of the gate receipts (the other 6% is given to the league office) and NHL home teams keeping all of the gate receipts. MLB adopted a radically different revenue sharing system for its local revenues in its 2002 collective bargaining agreement and continued it in its extension covering the 2007–2011 seasons. This is particularly noteworthy given that more than 75% of MLB revenues are local in nature. MLB teams pool 31% of their local revenues after deducting for their stadium-related expenses, including debt service and rent. These net local revenues are then redistributed equally among all 30 teams. This accounts for roughly 65% of the revenue sharing funds. The remaining 35% of the revenue sharing funds is generated by creating a baseline revenue figure for each team that is based on the average of a team's net local revenues in the prior seasons and its projected net local revenues in the future seasons. This is used to create a fixed revenue component for each team that cannot increase or decrease unless a team moves into a new stadium. The team then contributes revenue to the pool based on this figure. This system incentivizes teams to increase their local revenues. Overall, MLB has redistributed between $325 and $450 million each season as a result of its revamped revenue sharing plan.

According to former MLBPA Executive Director Don Fehr, "Revenue sharing in MLB is designed to solve competitive imbalance that could result if it did not occur due to revenue imbalances amongst the clubs."[8] MLB owners and executives believe that the plan has increased the league's competitive balance. After the 2006 Detroit Tigers made the playoffs for the first time since 1987, MLB Commissioner Bud Selig remarked, "I believe that the Tigers are the perfect manifestation of our improved economic climate. I have no doubt that this would not have been attainable a decade ago without our system of revenue sharing."[9]

In MLB, revenue sharing is designed to affect salaries and wages by transferring revenues from wealthy teams that could otherwise be spent on player salaries to poorer teams so as to allow them to increase their spending on player salaries. However, no mechanism is in place to ensure that the latter occurs. Thus, it is believed that several teams use their revenue sharing receipts to engage in profit-taking rather than to improve the club on the field. It also creates perverse incentives, because some clubs will not engage in risk-taking and entrepreneurial behaviors.

Revenue sharing of local revenues besides gate receipts is practiced differently in the NBA, NFL, and NHL than it is in MLB. Local revenue streams such as luxury box premiums, local media contracts, local advertising and sponsorship/signage revenues, and naming rights are generally not shared in these leagues. The home team keeps 100% of these revenue streams. This policy is currently being reviewed by both the NFL and NBA.

A larger amount of revenue sharing was adopted in the NHL as part of the collective bargaining agreement that ended the 2004–2005 lockout. The NHL needed to create a pool of revenue from the largest-grossing clubs and some playoff revenues in order to afford some smaller-revenue teams the ability to spend within the payroll range. The philosophy underlying the NHL's revenue sharing plan is best explained by Deputy Commissioner Bill Daly, who stated, "Our view on revenue sharing has always been that you only need revenue sharing to allow all clubs to afford representative and competitive payrolls, and that's what this revenue sharing does.... The idea is to subsidize clubs on a revenue basis to get them to the point where they can afford to be a quarter of the way up the payroll range. That would be a minimum commitment on revenue sharing."[10] A club in the bottom half in revenue can spend any amount on payroll and still be eligible for partial revenue sharing, but any club spending over the midpoint is not eligible for the entire amount of revenue sharing available to them.

The revenue sharing plan is funded by league-wide revenue, playoff gate receipts, escrow funds, and the top-grossing clubs. This creates an interesting method of maintaining competitive and economic balance. The revenue

sharing also is designed to make sure all clubs maximize local revenue. Mindful of the moral hazard opportunities discussed earlier (read: shirking), Deputy Commissioner Daly remarked, "You don't want a revenue sharing program that doesn't incentivize performance."[11] A team must meet a number of qualifiers in order to receive revenue sharing funds. Clubs such as Chicago, Anaheim, and the New York Islanders that are located in markets with 2.5 million or more television households are ineligible to receive revenue sharing funds, even if they fall in the lower-revenue bracket. Since the completion of the third year of the collective bargaining agreement in 2007–2008, clubs also have to grow revenues faster than the league average and have attendance of 75% of capacity to receive their full revenue sharing allotment. As of the 2008–2009 season, they have to be up to 80% of capacity. Teams not meeting revenue sharing marks receive 25% less the first time that they fail to do so, 40% the second time it occurs, and 50% the third. This qualifier led to the Columbus Blue Jackets being penalized $2.25 million for having flat revenue growth versus the league's 7% growth in 2007–2008. The recipients of the revenue sharing funds tend to be located in the nontraditional hockey markets in the United States. Illustrative of this, the Nashville Predators received a league-high $12 million in revenue sharing in 2008, with contributions from (among others) teams located in hockey-mad Canadian markets: Toronto ($12.0 million), Montreal ($11.5 million), Vancouver ($10.0 million), Calgary ($6.0 million), Ottawa ($1.0 million), and Edmonton ($0.8 million).

Revenue sharing in the NBA is guided by a somewhat different principle. Here, the philosophical question underlying revenue sharing is: "Are there well-managed teams that cannot make a profit due to market factors?" If so, then revenue sharing money should be distributed to them; the revenue sharing pool is funded by part of the escrow and luxury tax payments and in part by teams based on the amount of local revenue generated. In other words, the focus is on profitability rather than revenues and on the limitations faced by some markets in which NBA teams are located. The NBA utilizes a multivariate regression model that determines each team's optimal team business performance levels. Teams that are underperforming their market's potential cannot receive funds. It should be noted that the revenue sharing system is not based on market size; rather, it is based on market performance. The NBA redistributes $49 million to teams (no more than $6 million to any team in 2008–2009 and up to $6.6 million in 2010–2011) that are performing above market potential but are still deemed to be disadvantaged (i.e., losing money). This is an increase from previous seasons, as it distributed $14.8 million in 2005–2006 and $30 million in 2007–2008.

Revenue sharing in the NFL has been particularly challenging for the owners. Given that there is no proven correlation between high revenue teams and winning percentage or between high payroll teams and winning percentage, it is fair to ask whether the revenue sharing system in the NFL is

Table 1   MLB 2001 Team-by-Team Revenues and Expenses Forecast (in Thousands)

Operating Revenue

	Regular-season game receipts	Local TV, radio, and cable	Post-season	All other local operating revenue	Local operating revenue	National revenue	Total operating revenue
Anaheim	$30,208	$10,927	—	$26,195	$67,330	$24,401	$91,731
Arizona	46,509	14,174	13,000	32,970	106,653	18,479	125,132
Atlanta	62,141	19,988	2,629	37,692	122,450	24,401	146,851
Baltimore	53,216	20,994	—	29,691	103,901	24,401	128,302
Boston	89,743	33,353	—	29,485	152,581	24,401	176,982
Chic. Cubs	51,189	23,559	−17	30,642	105,373	24,401	129,774
Chic. White Sox	30,898	30,092	—	26,291	87,281	24,401	111,682
Cincinnati	32,102	7,861	—	6,523	46,486	24,401	70,887
Cleveland	69,470	21,076	2,000	45,295	137,841	24,401	162,242
Colorado	54,015	18,200	—	35,197	107,412	24,401	131,813
Detroit	42,299	19,073	—	21,018	82,390	24,401	106,791
Florida	16,756	15,353	—	4,037	36,146	24,401	60,547
Houston	49,161	13,722	519	36,826	100,228	24,401	124,629
Kansas City	19,520	6,505	—	13,270	39,295	24,401	63,696
Los Angeles	50,764	27,342	—	41,100	119,206	24,401	143,607
Milwaukee	46,021	5,918	—	37,010	88,949	24,401	113,350
Minnesota	17,605	7,273	—	6,987	31,865	24,401	56,266
Montreal	6,405	536	—	2,829	9,770	24,401	34,171
N.Y. Mets	73,971	46,251	−154	38,162	158,230	24,401	182,631
N.Y. Yankees	98,000	56,750	16,000	47,057	217,807	24,401	242,208
Oakland	24,992	9,458	2,686	13,932	51,068	24,401	75,469
Philadelphia	30,435	18,940	—	7,739	57,114	24,401	81,515
Pittsburgh	48,610	9,097	—	26,598	84,305	24,401	108,706
St. Louis	67,084	11,905	1,488	27,581	108,058	24,401	132,459
San Diego	34,381	12,436	—	8,504	55,321	24,401	79,722
San Francisco	67,173	17,197	—	61,524	145,894	24,401	170,295
Seattle	76,570	37,860	7,392	56,211	178,033	24,401	202,434
Tampa Bay	18,193	15,511	—	28,633	62,337	18,258	80,595
Texas	50,664	25,284	—	34,561	110,509	24,401	134,910
Toronto	25,363	14,460	—	14,255	54,078	24,401	78,479
Consolidation	1,383,458	571,095	45,543	827,815	2,827,911	719,965	3,547,876

Operating Expenses

Player compensation and benefit plan	National and other local expenses	Total operating expenses	Income (loss) from baseball operations	2001 revenue sharing	Income (loss) from baseball operations after revenue sharing	Income (loss) from baseball operations after interest
$52,239	$49,061	$101,300	–$9,569	$9,594	$25	$4,953
99,434	57,850	157,284	–32,152	–4,432	–36,584	–44,358
99,671	61,540	161,211	–14,360	–10,647	–25,007	–23,868
79,783	47,059	126,842	1,460	–6,807	–5,347	–13,732
118,471	55,799	174,270	2,712	–16,438	–13,726	–13,675
78,091	46,886	124,977	4,797	–6,568	–1,771	2,894
66,721	50,648	117,369	–5,687	–4,201	–9,888	–7,625
45,410	36,533	81,943	–11,056	13,404	2,348	–285
102,491	57,870	160,361	1,881	–13,254	–11,373	–14,242
69,983	65,245	135,228	–3,415	–6,029	–9,444	–11,522
57,184	49,074	106,258	533	5,127	5,660	–10,694
42,084	46,204	88,288	–27,741	18,561	–9,180	–10,820
71,577	54,266	125,843	–1,214	–5,185	–6,399	–9,455
42,704	37,126	79,830	–16,134	15,997	–137	1,474
116,077	72,873	188,950	–45,343	–9,107	–54,450	–68,887
51,164	47,801	98,965	14,385	1,744	16,129	9,001
30,494	44,305	74,799	–18,533	19,089	536	–3,791
37,676	35,014	72,690	–38,519	28,517	–10,002	–12,837
99,144	75,195	174,339	8,292	–15,669	–7,337	–5,225
117,936	83,413	201,349	40,859	–26,540	14,319	8,230
43,821	38,761	82,582	–7,113	10,520	3,407	–532
49,384	52,996	102,380	–20,865	11,752	–9,113	–9,352
53,227	58,463	111,690	–2,984	1,782	–1,202	–5,879
80,148	50,442	130,590	1,869	–8,229	–6,360	–7,322
46,089	49,784	95,873	–16,151	8,668	–7,483	–10,298
72,185	79,110	151,295	19,000	–6,308	12,692	–139
83,946	84,222	168,168	34,266	–18,791	15,475	14,793
57,000	46,438	103,438	–22,843	12,384	–10,459	–17,880
92,793	57,806	150,599	–15,689	–8,744	–24,433	–31,248
83,801	47,605	131,406	–52,927	9,830	–43,097	–42,504
2,140,728	1,639,389	3,780,117	–232,241	—	–232,241	–344,732

Source: MLB Updated Supplement to *The Report of the Independent Members of the Commissioner's Blue Ribbon Panel.*

Note: Player compensation includes 40-man roster costs and termination pay.

The consolidated loss, when $174,234,000 of nonoperational charges such as amortization of debt are added in, comes to $518,966,000.

suboptimal. The answer depends on who one is talking to—an owner from previous generations or the new generation, or an owner from a smaller-revenue club or a larger-revenue club. When asked if it was problematic, Dan Rooney, the legendary owner of the Pittsburgh Steelers, replied, "We're not there yet. Any team can win and does win. But we might reach a point somewhere down the line where that's not the case anymore."[12] Although the NFL considered a number of different options to varying degrees in the prelude to the 2006 collective bargaining negotiations, including sharing all team revenues equally, forcing teams to cover the full labor cost impact of their own local deals, and expanding the local revenue shared to encompass more revenue streams beyond gate receipts, it ultimately chose what many observers contend is a temporary solution—increasing the supplemental revenue sharing pool in March 2007. The owners replaced the previous supplemental pool of $30 to $40 million per year with a system that requires the 15 highest revenue generating teams to create a pool of $430 million from the 2006–2009 seasons to subsidize the 15 lowest revenue generating clubs. The agreement redistributed $100 million in 2006 and $110 million per year for 2007–2009. The owners also established qualifiers that a team must meet in order to receive these supplemental funds: actual player costs higher than 65% of team revenues, gate receipts of at least 90% of the league average (or it faces a deduction off of their share), and ineligibility after a move into a new or renovated stadium costing more than $150 million and for any new owners. This temporary agreement is certainly suboptimal and is largely a product of the league's politics. Any revenue sharing plan must be approved by three-quarters of the league owners. In other words, a bloc of nine owners can reject any plan that they deem unsuitable. With significant differences between league owners based on the longevity of their ownership and the markets in which their teams are located, it is not difficult for a voting bloc of nine to emerge and unite against any one revenue sharing plan.

The issue of competitive balance is similarly vexing to sports leagues.[13] Perhaps the best way to think about competitive balance is in its alternative—competitive imbalance. Competitive imbalance can take several different forms, all of which are arguably bad for the league as a collective. The first is if one team dominates the top position in a league over an extended period of time (i.e., dynasties).[14] This is bad for the league, because although casual fans may be drawn to the league because of the excellence of the one team, this interest will wane over time because there is little uncertainty of outcome. In addition, fans of the other teams in the league may unite for a period of time to rally against the dynasty, but their interest will wane if their team does not have a realistic chance of winning a championship over a prolonged period of time. A predictable league ultimately becomes of little interest to its followers.

Closely related to this is the second form of competitive imbalance: domination of the top of a league by the same teams over an extended period.[15] For example, Celtic or Rangers have won the Scottish Premier League title every year since 1986. Again, there is little uncertainty of outcome, and fans of other teams will ultimately lose interest.

A final form of competitive imbalance is the domination of the bottom of a league by the same teams over an extended period.[16] This is bad for a league, because fans of those teams will lose interest in the team and sport, and bringing them back into the fold will require a substantial on-field improvement; that is, contending for a championship. Habitually losing teams also impose costs on the rest of the teams in the league in that their contests against the weaker teams are less attractive and thus typically prevent them from maximizing their revenues in these games.

Leagues use a number of mechanisms to promote competitive balance, including a reverse-order draft in which the worst teams are given an increased opportunity to select the best incoming talent in the league's entry draft; salary caps and floors, which are designed to compress the range of team

Table 2   2009 NFL Operating Income by Team

Bank/NFL Team	Operating Income (in Millions)
1. Washington Redskins	90.3
2. New England Patriots	70.9
3. Tampa Bay Buccaneers	68.9
4. Indianapolis Colts	55.9
5. Kansas City Chiefs	52.4
6. Philadelphia Eagles	48.8
7. Baltimore Ravens	44.3
8. Chicago Bears	41.6
9. San Diego Chargers	41.6
10. Houston Texans	41.5
11. Denver Broncos	39.9
12. Buffalo Bills	39.5
13. Cincinnati Bengals	34.9
14. New Orleans Saints	30.7
15. Atlanta Falcons	28.2
16. Jacksonville Jaguars	26.9
17. Miami Dolphins	26.6
18. New York Giants	26.1
19. Tennessee Titans	24.4
20. New York Jets	24.3
21. Arizona Cardinals	23.9
22. Carolina Panthers	22.9
23. St. Louis Rams	22.3
24. San Francisco 49ers	20.8
25. Cleveland Browns	20.2
26. Green Bay Packers	20.1
27. Detroit Lions	18.5
28. Pittsburgh Steelers	17.8
29. Dallas Cowboys	9.2
30. Minnesota Vikings	8.2
31. Seattle Seahawks	−2.4
32. Oakland Raiders	−5.7

Source: Forbes 2009 NFL Team Valuations.

spending on playing talent such that all teams are spending relatively close to one another on their athletes; luxury taxes, which penalize teams that spend beyond a proscribed threshold on player salaries in an effort to rein in teams inclined to spend excessively; relegation and promotion, which incentivize teams to win championships so that they may be promoted to a higher level of competition and reap the financial rewards and disincentivize losing contests to prevent the financial harms associated with demotion to a lower level of competition; and revenue sharing, which theoretically provides teams with an increased ability to spend more on player salaries and thus remain more competitive than they would be in the absence of the receipt of these revenues.[17]

In the first selection, Richard Sheehan examines the revenue sharing practices that have been adopted by professional sports leagues, as well as the economic principles upon which these profit-maximizing endeavors are based. The author proposes a two-part tax on a franchise's costs and its win–loss record to enhance the effectiveness of these revenue sharing models.

After Sheehan's passage, the competitive balance issues facing sports leagues are addressed by economists Allen Sanderson and John Siegfried. In their article, "Thinking About Competitive Balance," they consider various aspects of this often thorny topic. Next, the broad revenue sharing model adopted by the NFL is considered by Clay Moorhead. The development of the NFL's revenue sharing system is instructive for current sports business leaders because, as previously noted, the league's revenue sharing plan is considered a significant part of why the NFL is currently considered to be the most successful of the professional sports leagues. Despite this success, problems remain in the system, including threats posed by opportunistic owner behavior. In recent years, there have been increasing complaints by owners in some markets complaining that the revenue sharing model is not as successful as it used to be and should be revamped. This is often raised in the context of collective bargaining and the need for greater revenues to be retained and shared by the owners rather than passed on to the players.

Finally, Stefan Kesenne investigates the intersection of revenue sharing and competitive balance in his aptly titled article, "Competitive Balance in Team Sports and the Impact of Revenue Sharing."

Notes

1. Michael MacCambridge (quoting Branch Rickey), "A Light Bulb Came On," *America's Game,* Anchor.

2. Michael MacCambridge (quoting Walter O'Malley), "A Light Bulb Came On," *America's Game,* Anchor.

3. Michael MacCambridge (quoting Bill Veeck), "A Light Bulb Came On," *America's Game,* Anchor.

4. Id.

5. Id.

6. Daniel S. Mason, Revenue Sharing and Agency Problems in Professional Team Sport: The Case of the National Football League. *Journal of Sport Management,* Volume 11, Issue 3 (July 1997).

7. Id.

8. Don Fehr, Remarks at the Executive Directors' Panel at the 2005 Annual Conference of the Sports Lawyers Association, May 21, 2005.

9. Eric Fisher (quoting Bud Selig), "A Difficult March into a Golden Era," *Sports Business Journal,* October 4, 2006.

10. Andy Bernstein, Inside the Complex NHL Deal, *Sports Business Journal,* August 1, 2005, at p. 01, http://www.sportsbusinessjournal.com/article/46287.

11. Id.

12. Mark Maske and Thomas Heath (quoting Dan Rooney), "NFL's Economic Model Shows Signs of Strain," *The Washington Post,* January 8, 2005.

13. Id.

14. George Foster, Stephen A. Greyser & Bill Walsh, *The Business of Sports: Cases and Text on Strategy and Management.* South-Western College Pub 29 (2005).

15. Id.

16. Id.

17. Id. at 30–32.

INTRADEPENDENCE: REVENUE SHARING AMONG CLUBS

KEEPING SCORE: THE ECONOMICS OF BIG-TIME SPORTS

Richard G. Sheehan

First, all four leagues on average have been and remain very profitable. The average return to major league professional franchises has been greater than the average return to stocks. Second, profits are not evenly distributed. In each league, some franchises earn substantial profits while other franchises barely break even or lose money. . . . Third, owners have different motives for buying and owning a professional sports franchise. Some are in it primarily for the money while others are in it primarily for wins or ego or civic pride. And fourth, not all major league franchises are competently managed. Some franchises . . . have not been well run, assuming that the objective is to make money or to win games.

The conclusions that each league makes a substantial profit but that the profit is unevenly distributed suggests that some revenue sharing may be appropriate. When a league has an average profit rate over 15 percent but some teams are losing money, there might be a problem in the distribution of league profits, and some mechanism to share league revenues might be appropriate. In fact, each league already has some revenue sharing. For example, all leagues equally divide national television revenues, regardless of a team's number of TV appearances, record, or drawing power. Another example is a league's centralization of the licensing process. . .

This chapter considers three questions on revenue sharing. First, how much revenue has been shared in each league. Second, why should any revenue be shared? That is, is there an economic justification underlying revenue sharing and how can the problems associated with revenue sharing be overcome? And third, is there a specific proposal for revenue sharing that begins to address two of the most important problems facing professional sports: (1) How can revenues be split between rich franchises and poor without destroying the incentives for the rich to keep generating prolific revenues? (2) And how can anyone reconcile the split among owners where some focus primarily on the bottom line and others focus primarily on winning? . . .

CURRENT-REVENUE SHARING ARRANGEMENTS

What revenues currently are shared? For all leagues, the ground rules are strikingly alike. National media money is shared while local media money generally is not; licensing money accrues to the league and is shared while any local advertising money is not; sharing of gate receipts varies by league while luxury box income generally is not shared. NFL gate receipts are split 60-40, with the home team receiving a greater amount justified on the basis of the costs of putting on the game. At the other extreme, the NHL home team retains the entire gate. In the NBA the home team keeps 94 percent of the gate while the league receives the other 6 percent.

. . . .

In terms of total revenue generated per franchise, the NFL leads all leagues . . . Major League Baseball (MLB) is second in revenues. . . . Gate receipts are the largest component of MLB receipts . . . followed by other revenues (primarily stadium revenues) . . . and local media. . . . The NBA's two largest income sources are gate revenues . . . and national media. . . . The NHL relies most heavily on gate revenues . . . and other revenues (again, primarily stadium revenues) . . . .

Comparing the leagues, the advantage of the NFL clearly lies in its television contracts. . . . Based on national media revenues, MLB is no longer the national pastime and is not even number two. The NBA now has that honor. . . . Where baseball is still the most popular is in terms of attendance and gate receipts, where it easily outdistances all other leagues. Perhaps the surprises here are that the NHL has the second highest gate receipts, surpassing the NBA, and that the NFL with so few games still has close to the same gate receipts as other leagues.

In the NFL, the two largest revenue categories, TV money and gate receipts, are split relatively equally. Thus, the NFL has the greatest degree of revenue sharing. . . . In contrast, the NHL has the smallest national media revenues, the smallest licensing revenues, and no split of gate revenues. Thus NHL revenue sharing was the lowest . . . MLB and the NBA fall between these two extremes. . . . In the NBA, the percentage sharing of the gate is relatively small, but national media money is shared and is relatively more important for NBA franchises than for MLB franchises.

Another perspective on the distribution of revenues is given by the range of revenues in a league. How do the revenues of the richest and poorest franchises compare? . . . The results indicate a wide range for all four leagues, smallest in the NFL. . . . Given the importance of TV money to the NFL, this result should not be a surprise. Regardless of how a franchise is run, TV money gives all NFL teams a solid revenue base.

. . . .

What may be most noteworthy about the maximum and minimum revenue numbers is the observation that New York City teams lead in all leagues except the NFL, the league with the most revenue sharing. New York City teams have natural revenue advantages over . . . Buffalo and Salt Lake City. However . . . this revenue advantage has not led to more victories and has led to only marginally greater financial success. New York City teams have both higher revenues and higher costs. . . . Market size may play a minor role, but it is a long way from the whole explanation of profits, wins, or anything else. Whether a team wins and whether it is well run both contribute more to financial success.

THE ECONOMIC LOGIC UNDERLYING REVENUE SHARING

Should there be revenue sharing? Is there any economic justification underlying revenue sharing? For an economist the answer is simple. In MLB, for example, the Yankees and the Brewers take the field to play a game. They create a win, a loss, and entertainment. It is a classic example of a joint product. The fans and the media pay for the entertainment while one of the teams ends up with a win and the other gets a loss. The product obviously is shared, and since the Yankees and Brewers must cooperate to produce it—in terms of agreeing on ground rules—the financial rewards are appropriately shared. But how are the Yankees and Brewers to split the revenues?

Three issues underlie this apparently simple question. First, you have a set of accounting issues: do you split gross revenues or net and how do you define the revenues to be shared? . . .

Second, there are equity concerns. What is a "fair" split of the revenues between the Yankees and the Brewers? . . . Efficiency arguments made below weigh heavily against an equal split of local revenues. Before considering efficiency, however, there is an equity argument against equally splitting local revenues. In any league we should expect the first franchises to be located in the most profitable cities. New York, Chicago, and Los Angeles have franchises in all leagues (temporarily except the NFL) and sometimes multiple franchises. Detroit, Boston, Philadelphia, and San Francisco also have franchises in all leagues. When you buy an expansion franchise, you should know that it is unlikely to generate the revenue stream of many "old guard" franchises. Thus, it would be disingenuous in MLB for expansion franchises in Colorado or Florida to argue that they deserve a share of Yankees' or Dodgers' revenues when the new owners should have known at the outset that they would be among the marginal franchises in the league. . . .

Third and most importantly, how can you undertake revenue sharing while not destroying economic incentives? How can you undertake revenue sharing and give owners or potential owners a greater incentive to pursue profits, victories, and the long-run economic health of the league? From an economic perspective, the interesting question about revenue sharing is its efficiency implications. The simplest way of viewing revenue sharing is to think of it as a tax. The general rule in economics is that any tax will distort economic incentives. In this case, we can put the distorting effects of taxes to an advantage. Many things could be taxed, for example, total costs, total revenues, player payrolls (the owners' favorite), or even wins and losses. What is taxed will effect how owners will react to the tax and will impact how owners, players, and fans will fare.

. . . .

There are fixed costs associated with running a franchise. For example, a MLB franchise has a minimum payroll of $2.5 million [*Ed. Note: the 2010 minimum was $10.0 million*] given the roster size and the minimum salary. Taxing this amount or any fixed cost has no impact on a franchise's operations and is incompatible with revenue sharing. A tax on anything other than incremental costs or revenues is simply bad economics as far as changing incentives is concerned.

A second example of how not to tax has been proposed by some small-market MLB owners. This tax would split all local media money equally among all franchises. . . . More problematic is the question of incentives. What would happen the next time the New York Yankees' media contract is up for renegotiations? How much incentive do the Yankees have to bargain aggressively for a higher fee . . . ? The moral: equally splitting local revenues would likely have devastating long-run impacts on those revenues. Thus this tax also is bad economics.

ECONOMICALLY JUSTIFIED TAXES TO IMPLEMENT REVENUE SHARING

So how can we set a tax that would be good economics? Let me state the requirements for a good tax system, given the problems facing all leagues. (1) Profits are healthy but are unevenly distributed. Implication: some revenue sharing is necessary, and a tax must fall more heavily on profitable franchises. (2) Owners have different goals; some focus more on wins and others on profits. Implication: two types of taxes are necessary, one on those seeking victory and another on those seeking profits. (3) Taxing revenue will make owners reluctant to take steps to "grow" revenues coming into the league. Implication: avoid taxing revenues; where possible, tax costs instead. (4) Taxes should allow markets to operate without introducing additional distortions. Implication: when players' salaries are determined in a competitive market, there is no need to separately tax this component of costs.

With these suggestions, let us consider a two-part tax, on a franchise's total costs and on its win–loss record. First, consider the "cost" tax and three fundamental questions. Why tax costs rather than revenues? What costs should be taxed? And how high a tax rate is appropriate?

Revenue sharing could be undertaken either by taxing a franchise's revenues or its costs. To date, revenue sharing in all leagues has been done by taxing revenues. . . . Taxing a franchise's revenues ultimately depresses the league's revenues and both owners and players suffer in the long run. In contrast, taxing costs strengthens owners' existing desires to control costs and to increase profitability. Owners will be better off even if players are not.

What costs should be taxed? Any tax would appear appropriately levied with respect to all costs and not just player salaries, assuming owners are serious about getting a handle on costs and are not simply out to break a union. . . . While the focus is on all costs, the tax itself should be levied only on incremental costs. For example, if the average costs in a league were $50 million, it would make sense to tax a franchise only on its costs in excess of $50 million, or on its incremental or marginal costs. The goal of the tax is to provide an incentive to keep expenditures below some level.

Now the focus on incremental costs requires some additional explanation, and that explanation is related to how high the tax rate should be and what is the need for revenue sharing in the first place. The tax rate cannot be too high or it will have ugly incentive effects. With a high enough tax rate we could have all franchises fielding a whole new team of rookies each year. But we do not need a tax rate all that high to obtain the desired effect of restricting costs. The main point underlying revenue sharing is that a game creates both a win and a loss and the winner receives more revenues than the loser. Thus, the winner imposes an economic cost on the loser. What is that cost? The answer varies by sport and even by team within [a] sport. . . .

There is some question on what costs should be taxed. The argument made earlier emphasized placing the tax on all costs rather than just on players' salaries. There remains a question of whether this tax should be placed only on costs above some threshold, a so-called "luxury tax" or whether it should be placed on all costs. . . . For simplicity assume all clubs spend the same amount and are equally competitive. Then one owner attempted to buy a championship by increasing spending. His additional expenditures make his team more competitive and presumably cost other owners money. Those incremental expenditures should be subject to a tax. There is no reason why only expenditures, say, 30 percent above the average impose costs on other franchises.

. . . . Two numbers are important. First, how much does it cost to win one more game? . . . Second, how much revenue does a franchise lose when the team loses one more game? . . . The appropriate tax rate is simply the ratio of the revenue sacrificed with one additional loss divided by the cost of winning one more game, or how much one owner's incremental expenditures cost another in lost revenues.

. . . .

Perhaps the most important feature of this type of tax is that it begins to address one of the major problems underlying much economic strife in sports: the problem of differing owner desires. Some owners primarily want profits and some victories. How does this tax address that? Owners that want victories and championships will still choose to spend more. . . . As they spend more and perhaps win more they also impose costs on other owners that place a higher value on profits. Presumably the money from the tax on costs will be used to reimburse those owners who choose not to increase spending and who end up losing more frequently. Owners that want championships can still attempt to buy them if they wish, but only to the extent that they compensate other owners for the costs of losing.

Now this "cost" tax by itself is not the entire solution. Of course, all owners want both wins and profits, but the relative importance placed on each may differ dramatically. The tax above is on those that want to win and are spending freely to do it. They have to pay a penalty for the costs they are imposing on those that want profits. Those who want to win can still spend as freely as they want, but they must internalize the costs they impose on other owners. But owners who primarily want profits also impose costs on other owners. Why? They have little incentive to field a competitive team unless profits are at stake. . . .

League revenues will be higher in the long run when the games and the races are tight, although any one team might be able to reduce short-term expenditures and lose games but gain profits. What can be done to reduce this incentive? One suggestion: tax less-successful franchises. Give owners who focus only on profits a greater incentive to win. In some cases, franchises have effectively stopped trying to field a competitive team. . . . Taxing their losses would likely stimulate more interest in winning and may increase league profitability.

The first tax takes the Steinbrenners . . . and taxes them for their free-spending ways. The second takes the Bill Bidwells (owner of the Arizona Cardinals) and Tom Werners (Chairman of the Boston Red Sox and former owner of the Padres) and says field a competitive team or pay a price. The former says of the win-at-all-cost owners pay attention to those concerned with profits. The second says of the only-profits-count owners that you must also be concerned with the on-the-field competition. Thus both sets of owners must move closer to a common middle ground that explicitly gives weight to both controlling costs and fielding a competitive team. Both types of owners may continue with their original focus, but the economic incentives push them toward a compromise. Furthermore, a compromise between the owners is a prerequisite for an agreement with the players.

. . . .

What is to be done with this revenue? Given that all leagues face a problem not of insufficient profits but of an unequal distribution of profits, it would seem reasonable to take the revenue raised and return it to franchises with revenue below the league average. What mechanism you employ should not seriously weaken poorer franchises' incentives to generate their own revenues. Consider a mechanism that returns taxes proportionately to all franchises with revenues less than the league average. . . . These franchises have experienced real financial difficulties. This system of taxes and revenue sharing would help them all. It would not guarantee them profits, however.

. . . .

The nature of these taxes is to subsidize teams that are well run and yet still have difficulty making ends meet. . . . This tax system, with low tax rates and a carefully selected base, cannot bail out a club . . . that is awash in red ink. It can do two things, however. It can and does reward those clubs that are "doing things right" or fielding a competitive team at a relatively low cost. It also provides an even greater incentive for owners to be financially prudent and exercise appropriate oversight over fielding competitive teams. In a word, this set of taxes cannot give all owners the same set of incentives. However, it does bridge the current chasm between those in the league primarily as a business and those in it primarily as a hobby.

. . . .

REVENUE SHARING IN THE NFL

Virtually all NFL franchises have been quite profitable. One can make the argument that the NFL's success is rooted in their revenue sharing, even as different owners appear to have very different objectives. With the NFL's current revenue sharing arrangements, there is little reason or justification for additional revenue sharing. There is, however, a strong case against allowing owners like Jerry Jones to cut their own deals with whomever they choose. Ultimately, Jones' deals with Nike and Pepsi, for example, reduce the value of the league's deals with Reebok and Coke. When the league's deals through its marketing arm, NFL Properties, come up for renewal they will be negotiated downward and total league revenue may fall.

. . . .

Jerry Jones quite likely can make more money marketing the Cowboys on his own than he will receive from the Cowboys' share of NFL Properties income. Jones may well have the panache to run NFL Properties substantially better than it currently is being run. Jones, however, is totally off base when he says that the average franchise is better off doing its own marketing than going through NFL Properties. With 32 franchises each doing its own marketing, the competition for deals with prime sponsors like Nike will likely drive the value of those deals down for most teams. Teams like the Cowboys and 49ers may be better off but most teams will lose, and many smaller-market teams could lose dramatically. Is the average NFL owner better off with a marketing monopoly and shared profits or with 32 marketing competitors? With apologies to Ben Franklin, NFL owners had better hang together or else competitive markets will hang them all separately.

CONCLUSIONS

What is the bottom line on revenue sharing? Revenue sharing can be simply an out-and-out attempt by small-market franchises to expropriate the wealth of richer teams. . . . If that is the case, for most of us it may be interesting theater but it is not interesting from either a finance or a sports perspective.

Revenue sharing does have a strong economic justification based upon the cooperation required between teams to generate league revenues. Since the game is a joint effort, economic theory can be employed to suggest how revenues can be split to provide positive rather than negative incentives. . . .

The system of taxes and revenue sharing presented here addresses a fundamental problem of sports: that owners are in it both as a business and as a hobby and the weights that different owners place on these two goals sometimes differ dramatically. Taxing both excess costs and excess losses should move owners to roughly the same page in the playbook and should reduce losses at competently managed small-market franchises. This system of taxes also has the potential to reduce tensions between players and owners. Owners would have an incentive to more carefully monitor all costs, including player payroll, because of the cost tax. But owners also would have an incentive to make sure they field a competitive team because of the loss tax.

COMPETITIVE BALANCE

THINKING ABOUT COMPETITIVE BALANCE

Allen R. Sanderson and John J. Siegfried

In an era in which inequalities of wealth and opportunity are constantly at the forefront of public policy discussions in the United States, in the world of professional sports, many high-profile economic events also seem to turn on issues of inequality: between owners and players over the distribution of economic rents; among owners over the distribution of gate receipts, broadcast revenues, and talent; and among mayors, taxpayers, owners, and league officials over figurative level playing fields with regard to the provision of state-of-the-art venues.

. . . .

Simon Rottenberg (1956) long ago noted that "the nature of the industry is such that competitors must be of approximately equal 'size' if any are to be successful; this seems to be a unique attribute of professional competitive sports" (p. 242; see also Rottenberg, 2000). Although the absolute quality of play influences demand and absolute investments in training are socially efficient (Lazear & Rosen, 1981), the relative aspects of demand and quality of competition also loom large in sports. In cases when consumer demand depends, to a large extent, on interteam competition and rivalry, the necessary interactions across "firms" (i.e., teams) define the special nature of sports. Contests between poorly matched competitors would eventually cause fan interest to wane and industry revenues to fall. But potential *arms races*—or *rat races*—are possible and maybe even inevitable (Akerlof, 1976; see also Whitney, 1993).

In the 1990s and early 21st century, while some social scientists wrung their hands over apparent widening inequality of income in the United States and between developed and third-world nations, sports economists, commentators, fans, and owners (at least among the also-rans) lamented the perceived widening inequality of wealth and championships among teams, especially the large-market, high-revenue, and/or high-payroll teams versus their country-cousin kin in baseball.[1] The distribution of playing talent, team revenues and salary expenditures, and competitive balance dominate sports and sports-business conversations whenever a team with the highest payroll (or an owner with the deepest pockets or a decidedly different utility function) wins a championship, whenever a franchise extracts a new publicly funded ballpark from its community on the threat of relocating, or whenever an apparent dynasty emerges. . .

. . . .

Also in 1999, Baseball Commissioner Allan H. "Bud" Selig convened a panel of well-known individuals to study the impact of revenue disparities on competitive balance. It produced a lengthy report, "The Commissioner's Blue Ribbon Report on Baseball Economics" (BRR) (Levin, Mitchell, Volcker, & Will, 2000), that noted large and growing revenue disparities, which, in turn, affected balance.[5] In addition to more quantitative theoretical and empirical measures of competitive balance (see below), the Blue Ribbon panel also defined competitive balance qualitatively: In the context of baseball, proper competitive balance should be understood to exist when there are no clubs chronically weak because of MLB's financial structural features. Proper competitive balance will not exist until every well-run club has a *regularly recurring hope of reaching postseason play.* (Levin et al., 2000, p. 5)

Broadcaster Bob Costas (2000) chimed in with similar laments. MLB conducted a national poll of 1,000 fans in late 2001 that purported to indicate that competitive imbalance was a serious problem in the minds of 75% of respondents; 42% of them indicated they would lose interest in the game were more teams not to have a realistic chance of winning. Summarizing the results, Sandy Alderson, MLB's executive vice president, said, "We have a competitive-balance problem. This is something the average fan cares about. They don't care if owners are losing money. They do care if it translates into negative consequences for their teams" (Rogers, 2001, p. 1).

Although certainly not unique to this particular period or sport, the complaint of woeful imbalance has become more common in the last few years with the lack of significant revenue sharing or a firm payroll cap in MLB relative to the National Football League (NFL), identified as the culprit. Increased player freedom, through which an owner could hire the best players and, at least in the short run, buy a championship, is seen as an accomplice. Apart from the obvious owners' interest in limiting bidding for players and the equally obvious interest among players in that not being allowed to occur, payroll caps, salary caps, luxury taxes, increased revenue sharing, and restructured draft systems are touted as ways to constrain competition and thus improve competitive balance among teams.[6] League restrictions on both the geographical relocations of teams and the mobility of players across teams, in addition to having more self-serving purposes, also affect balance. . . .

In the sections below we attempt to lay out what one might mean by competitive balance, review the theoretical and empirical scholarship and popular contributions with regard to its various dimensions, and describe the natural forces and considerations as well as institutional rules and regulations that contribute to observed distributions of playing performances. We also compare, at various junctures, the situation in baseball versus other sports leagues including college athletics and individual sports.

COMPETITIVE BALANCE IN THEORY AND PRACTICE

Every sport and sports league has had to confront the fundamental issue of relative strengths among competitors. There has not been a uniform, one-size-fits-all approach or set of rules to resolve this problem. Inasmuch as uncertainty of outcome is a key component of fan demand, wide disparities in inputs and, thus, in likely outcomes are seen as inimical to the long-term health and financial viability of the individual enterprise. How to handle weak teams or inferior opponents—to prevent lower quality competitors from free-riding on higher quality rivals—can be as much or more of a problem as dealing with perennially strong ones, because there is at least some interest in seeing the very best individual performers and teams.[7]

Boxing segments fighters into weight classes and employs rankings and ladders to create bouts with equally matched opponents. Auto racing, track competitions, and swimming use qualifying times to ensure competitive fields. Tennis produces seedings based on previous performances in the expectation that the strong will play the strong in later round matches. Claiming races in thoroughbred racing is a mechanism designed to have horses of approximately equal ability entered into the same event. Except for the occasional novelty or promotion, women do not compete against men. Periodic structural changes or modifications in the rules of play, such as elimination of the center-jump and adoption of a shot clock in basketball and altering the height of the mound or changing the effective strike zone in baseball, have been used to tilt the playing field to achieve a certain objective and to prevent some competitors from exploiting particular advantages or decreasing fan interest in the contests. Another example is restrictions on athletes' use of performance-enhancing substances.

. . . .

For English soccer, Szymanski (2001) has shown that the growing financial disparity between clubs has had no impact on imbalance. How closely payroll and market size correlate with winning—including, of course, the determination of the causal relationship— is arguably one of the most important questions about competitive balance. It is also essential to evaluate the relationship between market size and team payroll, which is often inaccurately assumed to be tight.

. . . .

THE NATURAL DEMAND FOR AND SUPPLY OF BALANCE (AND IMBALANCE)

Apart from the constraints leagues place on competition to ensure balance (factors discussed later), which may have the complementary effect of increasing and/or redistributing revenues, there are also natural forces that influence the distribution of outcomes. One obstacle to reducing inequality in sports leagues could be, paraphrasing Pogo, that we may not only be content with the current imbalance but also actually prefer it to the alternatives. Or, at a minimum, we are conflicted and willing to let natural (and unnatural) forces and inertia, rather than explicit interventions, determine outcomes. In economic and sporting walks of life, we have a preference for a positive correlation between effort and reward. To reward the statistically better individual or team for its prior achievements, we tip some balances in its favor— playing more games at home, higher seeds or a better lane, an extended playoff series rather than a single winner-take-all contest. The more evenly matched two opponents are, the higher the probability that a random element—a poor call by an official, a bad bounce, a key injury, or pure luck—will determine the outcome.[12] Thus, the premise that the demand for games is greater, *ceteris paribus*, the greater the degree of uncertainty conflicts with our sense of justice that the better team win. Luck is the way we account for the success of people and teams we do not like, but it is not a factor that we generally want to determine our income distributions in society or our champions in sporting contests.

On the other hand, we have strong identifications with and sympathies for the true underdog. We want David to knock off Goliath, at least on occasion (unless, of course, Goliath plays for us—Chicago was quite content with the Bulls's domination in the 1990s, and Yankee fans have few quibbles with the alleged imbalance in baseball). Nowhere is this better exemplified than in popular sports movies that feed off imbalance. Films such as *Rocky*, *Hoosiers*, *The Mighty Ducks*, and *Major League* cater to these instincts. (And, after all, the play was called *Damn Yankees*, not *Damn Cubs*.) As much as one may loathe a bully, selling tickets to an event in which he has some chance of being upset is marketable. Dynasties and storied franchises, such as the Yankees, Celtics, Packers, and Red Wings, are not without their advantages in terms of fan interest.

The world is replete with examples of healthy inequality more extreme than the current levels in baseball. State lotteries are popular despite daunting odds. Although just 25 of the nation's 400 graduate schools grant a third of all new Ph.D.s each year, the industry maintains diversity and vitality while competing implicitly head to head. Other comparable concentrations and inequalities abound: Live theater, world-class symphonies, and first-rate art museums are not evenly distributed across the landscape.

In sports, virtually all teams win at least a fourth of their games and few win more than two thirds of the time. Victories—and losses—are not inevitable. In leagues with 30 teams, the probability of winning the ultimate prize—a World Series or Super Bowl—with equal distributions of talent in any given year is .033; thus, a team or city could expect to garner a championship about once a generation. The difference between that periodicity and a dynasty can be as little as a factor of three in that, in the latter instance, a team may win a championship once a decade instead of once per generation.

Sports fans' memories are selective and the rate at which they fade appears to be small. That a team last won a Super Bowl or World Series more than a decade ago may seem like yesterday. (Many Chicago fans think of the Bears as a championship team, even though their only Super Bowl win occurred in 1986.) Stadiums and arenas are replete with banners from past conquests—in most cases many years removed. Fans don sweatshirts and caps that evoke past memories as much as current realities. That, coupled with our basic hope-springs-eternal (or wait-until-next-year) spirit, fueled with optimism about the most recent draft choice or free agent acquisition, buoys the soul—and ticket sales. Scully's (1995) empirical validation of serial correlation in sports and his admonition that fans should be patient reinforces our natural instincts and outlooks. In a society that confronts substantial inequality in its daily experiences, the current level of imbalance in baseball may not be intolerable.

In addition to these many factors contributing to the observed inequality of outcomes, whatever the metric, there are several other possible explanations for competitive team imbalance. The following examples are but a few such considerations.

Differences in Population and Preferences

The demand for beachwear in Ft. Lauderdale dramatically exceeds the demand for swimsuits in Buffalo and also in St. Augustine, yet no one seems to worry about bikini imbalances. Indeed, we would probably be puzzled if such sales in Ft. Lauderdale did not exceed combined receipts in Buffalo and St. Augustine by a large margin. Although the populations of Buffalo and Ft. Lauderdale are similar, the per capita demand for bathing suits is greater in Florida than in upstate New York presumably because of greater utility in use. And, although St. Augustine and Ft. Lauderdale share the same climate and accessibility to beaches, the population of Ft. Lauderdale is many times larger than that of St. Augustine. Geographic differences and preferences exist with regard to types of foodstuffs consumed, automobiles driven, and television programs watched.

So, too, is this true for winning sporting contests. Residents in some locations may be willing to pay more to have a more successful local team (e.g., per capita willingness and ability to support a winning ice hockey team is undoubtedly greater in Ontario than in Florida), especially if there are few other recreational, entertainment, and/or cultural amenities close at hand. Population disparities between areas hosting teams can create differences in aggregate willingness and ability to pay even when individual customers in the various host cities have identical tastes.

These differences could be equalized if teams in sports leagues were free to move to areas where the marginal revenue per win is higher than in their initial location. The resulting competition between teams in the same league within a metropolitan area would dilute the incremental revenues earned by the original incumbent and reduce financial disparities among the teams. The collection of Australian rules football teams in Melbourne, the concentration of baseball teams in Tokyo, and the density of premier-league soccer teams in London illustrates the possibility.

Team movements that would help to equalize marginal revenues do not occur, however, because each of the professional men's team sports leagues in North America exercises a form of collective control over member team movements. Incumbents in the larger cities or those cities where fans are willing to pay more for winning are loath to share their revenues with immigrants from smaller communities or from locations where success on the playing field is less important to the residents. They are protected from incursions either by league constitutional provisions protecting their home territory or by their ability to form coalitions sufficient to prevent other teams from moving into their host community. In short, the competitive imbalance that emanates from the monopoly control of home territories by incumbents arises from the conduct of the leagues' member teams themselves, because they are unwilling or unable to introduce competition into areas where favored incumbent teams earn considerable economic rents. . . .

These disparities, and even the large market versus small market distinction, would disappear if expansion occurred within an existing cartel league, a rival league formed, and/or some judicial action broke up the cartel (as the resulting smaller leagues, in search of new markets, spawned new franchises).[14] New York City is considered a large market and Kansas City a small one, in part, because the ratio of teams to population is so dissimilar. Migration of existing franchises and/or the creation of new ones located in larger metropolitan areas would equalize these ratios in sports leagues much as retail establishments and other social amenities equalize in more traditional, competitive markets, such as fast-food outlets and swimsuit retailing.

Willingness to Act on Differences in Fan Tastes

In addition to different preferences for winning, fans who live in different areas may differ in their willingness to act on those preferences (Porter, 1992). The more fickle are fans, the more their willingness to buy tickets depends on the local team's on-field success, the greater is the marginal revenue from the local team's winning additional contests, and the greater is the incentive for a team to expend resources to secure more highly skilled players. A profit-maximizing league could exploit fickleness by strengthening teams located where fans are less loyal and, in turn, weakening teams where fans will turn out regardless of the success of the local franchise. This would not bode well for the Cubs and Steelers. If a league did this, however, the distribution of playing talent could be inefficient because it is configured in response to fans' willingness to act on their preferences rather than on the basis of the preferences themselves.

Moreover, in addition to caring about the on-field success of the home team, fans often have preferences regarding dominance that are independent of which team dominates. That is, the competitive balance distribution itself is a public good. Everyone must live with the same overall distribution, and individuals may have strong preferences about the shape of that distribution. Some may prefer imbalance—even sufficient to create dynasties whether they love them or love to hate them. Others may prefer a league in which almost all teams win about half of their contests.

Although fans may have views on what the general distribution of competitive balance should look like, these views may fluctuate over time. As the real income levels of sports consumers have risen over the second half of the 20th century (Siegfried & Peterson, 2000) and the typical fan has moved further up an increasingly dispersive income distribution, fan preferences toward the overall distribution of competitive balance could migrate toward more imbalance in game outcomes, as well.

Differences in Player Tastes

Differences in team playing skills can arise even if there are no differences in the population base of team territories, in fan fickleness, or in fan preferences toward home-team winning or dynasties, because players also have preferences. Players may have a preference for living in certain areas (e.g., Florida or Southern California) and may be willing to sacrifice part of their salary to do so. Or they may see more lucrative endorsement opportunities in areas with relatively stronger media markets. . . .

Network economies can also affect the distribution of playing talent. Players may accept a lower salary to be on a team with greater odds of winning a championship thereby further enhancing the talent of the contender. . . .

Consider, in the extreme, how players might distribute themselves across teams if their salaries were zero. Would they join teams to balance playing talent? College football and basketball may provide some guidance as to what might happen because players' compensation is relatively constant across universities. There, the attractive new prospects gravitate toward perennial winners to enjoy greater prospects for on-field success, to play with more talented teammates, and to gain more media exposure.

The Trade-Off Between Winning and Uncertainty

Competitive balance is thought to affect attendance of fans through its influence on winning and fans' response to winning. It is well established that home attendance rises when a team wins more games or matches and declines when it loses.[16] Winning teams also attract more fans when they play on the road. The Yankees attract a crowd when they visit other American League cities whether it is because fans love to hate a winner, wish to see marquee players, or the Yankees have a following in other locations. As the mobility of our population has increased in the post-World War II years, fans of particular teams more frequently reside outside their home territory. Similarly, superstation broadcasts have created national Braves and Cubs fans. Although that phenomenon does not affect home attendance much, it can affect away attendance and television ratings. The extent to which owners of stronger teams take these factors into account depends on league rules for sharing gate and television revenues. The Detroit Red Wings draw huge crowds on the road because they are an elite team of established (read: older), talented players and because former residents of Detroit maintain their affinity for the team and attend games that the Red Wings play on the road. This generates incremental revenue for other National Hockey League (NHL) teams but does not affect incentives facing the Red Wings management, because, in the NHL, visiting teams do not share in gate receipts and there is little national television revenue.

Competitive balance may also affect attendance negatively at games of teams that are relatively weak, because fans view them as out of the running for a championship (as opposed to any individual contest on any given day). If this occurs when the revenue sharing rules are confined largely to home and visiting teams, the owners of the higher revenue teams may ignore the external impact of imbalance on the league's overall revenues until it reaches the point where the integrity of the overall competition is called into question and fans abandon the sport altogether. The addition of wild-card teams and smaller divisions or conferences, which both increase the number of teams eligible for the playoffs, are innovations designed to retain fans across more cities longer in the regular season by increasing the uncertainty of ultimate outcomes.

Character of the Events Themselves

In the 1980s and 1990s, responding to fan demand driven in part by higher incomes, professional sports franchises repositioned their product by increasing the emphasis on complementary noncontest services and amenities to blur further the distinction between sports and entertainment. (The short-lived Xtreme Football League [XFL] may have overshot that moving target.) Although the Dallas Cowboys Cheerleaders predate the 1980s, they are a vivid representation of the movement. New stadiums that include upscale restaurants, batting cages and other amusements for children, museums, Jumbotron scoreboards with instant replay and promotions, fireworks, and even a swimming pool (in Phoenix) reduce the relative importance of the game in the overall recreational package. Intermission entertainment at basketball, ice hockey, and football games is now standard fare including contests for fans, minishows by well-known musical artists, trampoline groups, and scoreboard video clips. . . . Luxury boxes and exclusive access areas increase the value of being seen at the game relative to seeing the game.

As the relative importance of the game itself diminishes in the entertainment package, competitive balance becomes a less important determinant of demand. So long as the tendency to broaden the entertainment experience is similar across locations of differing revenue potential, however, this phenomenon, like revenue sharing, should not have more than a modest effect on competitive balance.

Complementary Economic Theory

Traditional economic arguments for what prevents one owner from amassing an all-star line-up in an effort to win every contest and the championship turn on notions of self-interest and the inevitable diminishing marginal returns to, and the increasing marginal cost of, victories. Hence, some natural mechanisms constrain the extent of imbalance in most leagues. That assumes, however, that there are both effective ways to blunt possible negative externalities and that owners, deep down, are profit maximizers.

Common practices within sports leagues to ensure some semblance of a level playing field with regard to the distribution of talent across teams—reverse-order draft systems, various attempts to constrain players' salaries, revenue sharing—are also at odds with how economic theory generally views peer effects and the optimal sorting of workers. Where spillovers are significant, high-ability workers are more valuable to other high-quality workers, and workers should be more homogeneously sorted.[17] The assignment problem involves how to sort heterogeneous units into groups so that output is maximized (see Becker, 1973; Guryan, 2001; Koopmans & Beckman, 1957; Kremer, 1993; Saint-Paul, 2001). Whether in general production processes, law firms, or marriages, higher ability workers, colleagues, or spouses are more productive when grouped with other high-ability people. Because similar quality workers are more productive when sorted into the same firm, a firm with higher quality workers may not be willing to employ lower quality workers even if those workers would work for less pay.

The general application of this sorting principle in sports implies, for example, that an all-star shortstop's productivity is higher if he is paired with an all-star second baseman. Moreover, on-the-field traits carry over into the clubhouse and social settings where discipline, motivation, attitude, and joint monitoring can be important, as well. If this proposition is true, when practiced in sports, it should lead to inequality in the distribution of talent—some teams should have good players, other teams poor ones, and competitive imbalance should emerge. (Within baseball organizations, the farm system may serve as a sorting mechanism, and across-team trades and free-agent signings may represent, in part, attempts to capture potential peer-effect gains.) In some sense, then, sports leagues may be fighting an uphill battle in trying to stem the tide of nature and market forces pushing toward imbalance.

INSTITUTIONAL ARRANGEMENTS AND COMPETITIVE BALANCE

Many institutions or off-the-field rules of the game are negotiated every time a collective bargaining agreement (CBA) is renewed. These changes may affect the degree of competitive balance in any professional sports league.

Payroll Caps and Luxury Taxes

Payroll caps and so-called *luxury taxes* on payrolls create an incentive for owners of teams in higher revenue locations to hire less talent than they would in the absence of these constraints. In the extreme, a binding ceiling on total payroll limits the amount of talent a high-revenue team can accumulate. As a by-product, a firm payroll cap also increases the profits of high-revenue teams. Its impact on competitive balance depends on the extent to which the cap is below the free-market payroll level of the highest payroll team that also dominates on the field (read: Yankees).

One danger of payroll caps is that they may be porous (e.g., the NBA cap that includes a well-known loophole— the Larry Bird exemption—designed to preserve team unity, or the NFL, in which, for 2002, accounting conventions permitted virtually every team in the league to be over the cap), and they create a temptation for violating the rules (e.g., the Minnesota Timberwolves paid a large fine for paying Joe Smith off the books in excess of the cap). A system in which cheaters are more successful than those who play by the rules may be even less inviting than one in which teams fortunate enough to own rights to high-revenue areas are more successful. Moreover, payroll (and salary) caps do not extend to complementary inputs, so successful coaches . . . can command a sizable sum for managing a team on which the total payroll, and even individual salaries, may be frozen.

A less drastic version of the payroll cap is what has come to be known in professional sports as a luxury tax on payrolls. . . . The rationale is that fielding a highly paid team is a luxury for one owner that imposes negative externalities on other franchises. This makes sense if the tax becomes effective at the point where incremental talent on the high-revenue team creates a league-wide net negative impact that might be ignored by the owner of the high-revenue team, because, under league revenue sharing rules, he or she bears little of the cost of an over accumulation of talent. If the tax rate accurately reflects this internal externality, it creates an incentive for the high-revenue team owner to balance his or her gain against the cost to third parties. The trick, of course, is to impose the tax rate at the proper payroll level and to fix the rate such that it internalizes the externality.

To be accepted as fair, luxury tax revenues usually compensate those who bear the burden of the externality. This tax in MLB is, indeed, structured properly to achieve these goals, although no one knows whether the threshold payroll, the tax rate, and the beneficiaries of the redistribution are properly identified.

Salary Caps

The NBA [*Ed. Note: and the NHL as well*] is the only U.S. men's professional sports league currently using individual player salary caps to control team expenditures. Maximum salaries are based on seniority in the league. Salary caps emerged from the NBA's collective bargaining with the players' union in 1998 and early 1999 at least partly in reaction to the league's leaky team payroll cap.

Individual salary caps limit a team's payroll to the product of the roster size times the cap for the most senior players—not a significant constraint. Individual salary caps based on seniority are unlikely to have much of an impact on competitive balance because a high-revenue team can sign a complete team at the highest allowed salary thereby accumulating an entire team of the most desirable players in the league. This is not likely to happen, however, because the most expensive team one can buy is also an old team. A team can assemble a more competitive roster paying less than the maximum.

If league rules constrain salaries, free agent players' choices of which team to join will turn more on their personal preferences including desirable places to live and prospects for endorsements and a championship. Individual salary caps are likely to increase competitive imbalance because they encourage players to rely more on their preference for joining a winning team than on differences between salary offers. Salary caps will, however, limit the payroll of the high revenue teams, because they are the teams that would have bid above-cap salaries to acquire the more talented players. Individual player salary caps probably help the highest revenue teams increase both their profits and their playing talent.

Revenue Sharing

Revenue sharing (see Marburger, 1997) reduces the financial incentive of each franchise to acquire more talent, because the payoff to winning is constrained by the share paid to other franchises. Sharing revenues that are sensitive to playing success blunts the incentive to win for all franchises—those in low-revenue potential locations as well as those in New York.

Because the demand for winning may vary across communities with the intensity of competition for playing talent (fans in some communities find it more satisfying to win when there is a dogfight for talented players), revenue sharing can affect competitive balance. If fans in high revenue-potential locations are relatively more sensitive to winning when competition for players (from all teams) is more intense, then increased revenue sharing will improve competitive balance, because the incentive to acquire better players will be muted further for high revenue-potential teams. Of course, if the fans in high revenue-potential locations are less sensitive to winning when competition for players is more intense, then expanded revenue sharing will exacerbate competitive imbalance. Contrary to popular belief, the effect of revenue sharing on competitive balance, although likely modest, could go in either direction.

If revenue sharing blunts the incentive for all teams to bid aggressively for talented players thereby muting salary differentials between more and less talented players, nonpecuniary considerations will loom larger in free agents' decisions between competing offers. If players value the opportunity to play on championship contenders for reasons beyond financial rewards, increased revenue sharing could thus lead to greater competitive imbalance—a result likely to surprise many people.

The premier men's professional team sports leagues engage in a variety of revenue sharing arrangements. The NFL is the most socialistic, sharing revenues from its huge national television contract and merchandise sales (almost) equally and gate receipts 66/34 to the home and visiting teams, respectively.

The two baseball leagues modestly share local revenues. Ice hockey and basketball share the fewest revenues; in both the NHL and the NBA, the home team retains all gate receipts. A relatively new wrinkle in baseball is *dynamic pricing* (called *variable pricing* in the press)—long a feature in other industries, including airlines and hotels, through which ticket prices vary not only by quality of the seat location but also by day of the week, month, and, now, opponent. . . . To the extent that Kansas City can charge fans more for a popular opponent like the Yankees, this represents implicit revenue sharing that narrows inequality in team revenues across a league and thereby promotes more competitive balance.

Number of Teams and Relocation Restrictions

. . . [T]he core of the competitive imbalance problem is the differences in population and tastes for sports among metropolitan areas coupled with each league's artificial restriction on team movements. Let the teams move to wherever they like and the differences in revenue potential will dissipate and competitive balance will improve.[19] Yes, high revenue-potential teams will be less profitable, but if protecting the profits of teams fortunate enough to have the largest demand for their local monopoly is the goal, then explain the contraction on that basis.

To the extent that a competitive balance-targeted policy also affects profitability by restraining team payrolls, it may also affect the number of teams. Limitations on team payrolls make lower revenue-potential locations viable prospects for joining the league and, in turn, tempt owners who pocket league initiation fees to expand the number of marginal franchises and, thus, by their own conduct, reduce competitive balance.

Reverse-Order Player Drafts[20]

. . . .

To the extent that teams are free to transfer player contracts, the initial allocation of property rights—whether to the worst team in the league or the best team in the league—implies no difference in the ultimate allocation of player resources and, hence, competitive balance. Unless there are constraints on player sales, a player new to the league who is expected to generate a greater marginal revenue product at a franchise with high revenue potential than at one with low revenue potential will end up playing for the high revenue-potential franchise, either by initially signing with it or because the lower revenue-potential franchise sells his contract to the high revenue-potential franchise.

. . . .

Other Revenue Enhancements

Luxury box revenues, stadium naming rights, field advertising, and other local revenue sources can affect competitive balance if they are not proportional to other revenues between teams. If stadium naming rights and luxury box revenues, for example, constitute a higher ratio to gate receipts for higher revenue-potential teams, these added revenues will increase the disparity between teams and may exacerbate competitive imbalance. On the other hand, naming rights and luxury box revenue are not likely to be sensitive to team performance. Although a team in a high revenue-potential location may enjoy more of these peripheral revenues than one in a lower revenue-potential area, unless the revenue is linked to improved team performance on the field, there is no incentive for the team to spend the revenue enhancement on improving its talent level.

Structure of the Competition

Much in the same way that financial arrangements can affect balance between competitors, so, too, can the nature and structure of the contests themselves.[22] How pole positions in auto racing, lane assignments in swimming, brackets in tennis tournaments, or starting gates in thoroughbred races are determined can influence outcomes. In team sports, comparable issues turn on how home field, court, or ice is established for contests and the length of the series.

Lengthening a series reduces the probability that the weaker opponent will win; increasing the number of playoff rounds and the percentage of teams eligible for a championship reduces the chances that the best team will capture the championship (Sanderson, 2002). . . . Reducing the number of playoff teams—say, by reverting to only one American League and one National League division in baseball—with the winner of each league meeting in the World Series would ensure that the teams with the best regular-season record met for the championship, but this would entail serious trade-offs—for example, a loss of excitement late in the season and forgone playoff revenues.

. . . .

A final "macro" structural change that would replace the weakest teams with stronger ones, long familiar in soccer (European football), is the operation of open leagues with promotion and relegation. Closed leagues, when combined with reverse-order drafts and revenue sharing, tend to reward failure and punish success, whereas open leagues reward success and punish failure (see Dobson & Goddard, 2001; Noll, 2002; Rosen & Sanderson, 2001.)

. . . .

Notes

1. Protests of the New York Yankees's payroll in 1999 included Kansas City fans turning their backs when the Yankees came up to bat and then filing out of Kauffman Stadium in the third inning. Similar greetings accompanied the high-salaried Alex Rodriguez in 2001 when he returned to Seattle now as a member of the Texas Rangers.

. . . .

5. Comments on and criticism of the Blue Ribbon Report (BRR) and its conclusions include articles by Ross (2002), Eckard (2001a), and Schmidt and Berri (2002).

6. A century ago, of course, the reserve clause was the principal mechanism employed by owners—allegedly to ensure balance: Outright collusion that restrained bidding for free agents was the tool of choice in baseball 20 years ago. Organizing new leagues, such as Major League Soccer (MLS) and the Women's National Basketball Association, as *single entity* structures is a more recent manifestation of similar goals. Limits on roster size are often thought to enhance competitive balance by preventing some teams from stockpiling talent; however, there is little literature on this subject and scant empirical support for that contention.

. . . .

12. Questionable officiating during the National Football League (NFL) playoffs arguably determined Super Bowl opponents in both 2002 and 2003.

. . . .

14. See Ross (1989) and Baade and Sanderson (1997) for arguments and proposals for breaking up existing leagues into smaller entities.

. . . .

16. Syzmanski's review of the literature (in press) showed that empirical support for the correlation between winning and demand exists but that it is weaker than usually assumed. In his 2001 *Economic Journal* article on English soccer, Syzmanski (2001) found that match attendance appears to be unrelated to competitive balance.

17. The authors are indebted to Todd Kendall for pointing out this literature and complementary arguments.

. . . .

19. Of course, the purchased right to operate in exclusive territories is commonplace and expected in franchise operations and many other commercial areas and, generally, may serve efficiency purposes not just in professional sports.

20. Additional draft dimensions include supplemental drafts, similar to expansion drafts, at the conclusion of regular seasons and, for MLB, the inclusion of non–U.S. players in the annual amateur draft. We do not treat either of these variations in our article.

. . . .

References

Akerlof, G. (1976). The economics of caste and of the rat race and other woeful tales. *Quarterly Journal of Economics*, *90*(4), 599–617.

Baade, R. A., & Sanderson, A. R. (1997). Cities under siege. In W. Hendricks (Ed.), *Advances in the economics of sport, Vol. 2* (pp. 77–114). Stamford, CT: JAI Press.

Becker, G. S. (1973). A theory of marriage. *Journal of Political Economy, Part I, 81*, 813–846.

Costas, B. (2000). *Fair ball: A fan's case for baseball.* New York: Broadway Books.

Dobson, S., & Goddard, J. (2001). *The economics of football.* New York: Cambridge University Press.

Eckard, E. W. (2001a). Baseball's Blue Ribbon Report: Solutions in search of a problem. *Journal of Sports Economics, 2*(3), 213–227.

Guryan, J. (2001). *Estimating peer effects in the workplace: Evidence from random pairings in professional golf tournaments.* Manuscript in preparation.

Koopmans, T. C., & Beckman, M. (1957). Assignment problems and the location of economic activities. *Econometrica, 25*, 53–76.

Kremer, M. (1993). The O-ring theory of economic development. *Quarterly Journal of Economics, 108*, 551–575.

Lazear, E., & Rosen, S. (1981). Rank-order tournaments as optimum labor contracts. *Journal of Political Economy, 89*, 841–864.

Levin, R. C., Mitchell, G. J., Volcker, P. A., & Will, G. F. (2000). *The report of the Independent Members of the Commissioner's Blue Ribbon Panel on baseball economics.* New York: Major League Baseball.

Marburger, D. (1997). Gate revenue sharing and luxury taxes in professional sports. *Contemporary Economic Policy, XV*(2), 114–123.

Noll, R. G. (2002). The economics of promotion and relegation in sports leagues. *Journal of Sports Economics, 3*(2), 169–203.

Porter, P. K. (1992). The role of the fan in professional baseball. In P. M. Sommers (Ed.), *Diamonds are forever: The business of baseball* (pp. 63–76). Washington, DC: The Brookings Institution Press.

Rogers, P. (2001, December 18). Baseball's flaw: Lack of competitive balance. *Chicago Tribune*, pp. 1, 6.

Rosen, S., & Sanderson, A. (2001). Labour markets in professional sports. *The Economic Journal, 111*(469), F47–F68.

Ross, S. F. (1989). Monopoly sports leagues. *Minnesota Law Review, 73*(3), 643–761.

Ross, S. F. (2002). Light, less-filling, it's blue-ribbon. *Cardozo Law Review*, *23*(5), 1675–1704.

Rottenberg, S. (1956). The baseball players' labor market. *Journal of Political Economy*, *64*, 242–258.

Rottenberg, S. (2000). Resource allocation and income distribution in professional team sports. *Journal of Sports Economics*, *1*(1), 11–20.

Saint-Paul, G. (2001). On the distribution of income and worker assignment under intrafirm spillovers, with an application to ideals and networks. *Journal of Political Economy*, *109*, 1–35.

Sanderson, A. R. (2002). The many dimensions of competitive balance. *Journal of Sports Economics*, *3*(2), 204–228.

Schmidt, M. B., & Berri, D. J. (2001). Competitive balance and attendance: The case of Major League Baseball. *Journal of Sports Economics*, *2*(2), 145–167.

Scully, G. W. (1995). *The market structure of sports*. Chicago: The University of Chicago Press.

Siegfried, J. J., & Peterson, T. (2000). Who is sitting in the stands? The income levels of sports fans. In W. S. Kern (Ed.), *The economics of sports* (chap. 3, pp. 51–73). Kalamazoo, MI: UpJohn.

Szymanski, S. (2001). Income inequality, competitive balance, and the attractiveness of team sports: Some evidence and a natural experiment from English soccer. *The Economic Journal*, *111*(469), F69–F84.

Szymanski, S. (in press). The economic design of sporting contests: A review. *Journal of Economic Literature*.

Whitney, J. D. (1993). Bidding till bankrupt: Destructive competition in professional team sports. *Economic Inquiry*, *XXXI*, 100–115.

REVENUE SHARING IN THE NFL

REVENUE SHARING AND THE SALARY CAP IN THE NFL: PERFECTING THE BALANCE BETWEEN NFL SOCIALISM AND UNRESTRAINED FREE-TRADE

Clay Moorhead

I. THE PRE-GAME SHOW: AN INTRODUCTION

Since its inception in 1961, the revenue sharing system utilized by The National Football League ("NFL") has been instrumental in propelling the League to the forefront of professional sports in America.[1] In the early 1960s, Commissioner Pete Rozelle ushered in an era of collectivism among the individual team owners that came to define the NFL's economic approach for the next four decades. Relying on the collective outlook that became known as the "League Think" philosophy, Rozelle convinced the individual owners that by pooling their resources and sharing their profits, they would be able to provide a product that, as a whole, was much more valuable than the sum of its parts.[2]

The idea took off in 1961 when Rozelle successfully persuaded the individual owners to give up their local television broadcasting rights and instead sell all broadcasting rights together as a national package; the proceeds were then split evenly among each NFL team.[3] From 1961 onward, the League's continued commitment to the equal sharing of television revenues has remained the foundation of the NFL's revenue sharing system.[4] Furthermore, the financial parity that resulted from this collective philosophy enhanced the competitiveness of the League as a whole, thereby fostering the massive popularity still enjoyed by the League today.[5]

For nearly forty years, the NFL's revenue sharing system remained largely unchanged as NFL owners were content to rely on the success that revenue sharing brought to the League as a whole.[6] During this period, the individual owners were completely satisfied with the revenue they received under the revenue sharing system, and they were largely unconcerned with trying to garner any type of competitive financial advantage over their fellow owners.[7] In recent years, however, there has been a significant erosion in the NFL's collective mentality largely due to the development of sources of unshared revenue, known as "local revenue," which enables certain teams to gain a competitive advantage by utilizing this unshared revenue that is unavailable to some of their less fortunate counterparts.[8]

Although the NFL and its member-clubs shared more than eighty percent of the roughly $5.5 billion in total League revenue generated during the 2004 season [*Ed. Note: league revenues were approximately $8.5 billion in 2009*], there has recently been a dramatic increase in unshared local revenue, which is threatening the future financial parity of the League.[9] Furthermore, because most sources of local revenue are directly tied to a team's stadium ownership and its market size, the League's current revenue sharing system has created an environment in which the most profitable teams are better situated to capitalize on unshared local revenue, thereby exacerbating a widening revenue gap between those teams at the top and those at the bottom.

The current revenue sharing system utilizes a two pronged approach to distribute League revenue, but it also carves out an exception for sources of unshared local revenue. The two prongs of the revenue sharing system can be distinguished by the source of revenue and amount shared under each category, as well as the various documents that govern their existence. The first category comprises the sharing of revenue generated by licensing and sponsorship agreements, and this category is governed by a recently approved accord among NFL owners known as the "Master Agreement."[10] The second category covers the sharing of all revenue that is generated by the actual playing of games on the field, and this category is governed by a combination of provisions in the Collective Bargaining Agreement ("CBA") and the NFL Constitution and Bylaws ("NFL Constitution").[11] This second category, which includes television broadcasting deals and gate receipts from stadium attendance, is responsible for a strong majority of the total revenue shared between the League and its individual franchises.[12]

Furthermore, while these categories can be viewed as two components in a greater revenue sharing system, it is important to note that they were not developed together, but instead are separate outgrowths of the NFL's greater collective mentality. As a result, the system does not necessarily fit flawlessly together, which makes any comprehensive analysis of the overall system a somewhat difficult task. Nevertheless, under their respective governing documents, both categories treat League revenue in a similar fashion by distinguishing those revenue sources that are subject to sharing from those local revenue sources that remain unshared. . . .

. . . .

This note argues that the League must reform the current revenue sharing model in order to correct the widening revenue gap between the lowest and highest revenue teams, which if not adequately addressed soon could severely impair the future popularity and success of the NFL. Part II describes the emergence of revenue sharing in the NFL; its evolution due to past challenges initiated by profit-oriented owners; and the details of the current revenue sharing system in place today. Part III establishes how the emergence of unshared "local revenue" has eroded the NFL's collective mentality, thereby causing a variety of problems for the League. Part IV proposes a solution intended to effectively alleviate the League's growing financial inequalities while at the same time maintaining the important incentives created by a reasonable amount of unshared revenue. In particular, this section proposes a redistributive formula that allows for a healthy level of unshared local revenue, but simultaneously prevents extreme financial inequalities by redistributing excessive local revenue to those teams most in need.

On March 8, 2006 . . . the NFL owners and the NFLPA reached a last-minute labor agreement, which included significant reforms to the revenue sharing system. . . .

With their backs against the wall, the owners were forced to postpone the official start of the 2006 season and extend the March 3rd free agency deadline in order to find a way to reach an agreement that now preserves the current salary cap system, which would have otherwise expired at the official start of the 2006 season.[18] Largely surrendering to the demands of the players union, the owners not only approved a six-year collective bargaining agreement, but they also reached a corresponding revenue sharing deal, which the NFLPA had astutely required as a condition of its final offer for reaching a new labor pact.[19]

. . . [T]he League's newly adopted plan appears to be somewhat of a quick-fix, which will still face many of the same issues raised in this note, and has already garnered criticism from both ends of the revenue sharing debate.[21] Finally, it is worth noting that the new guard of profit-oriented owners, who strongly opposed the idea of increased revenue sharing, appear to have reluctantly embraced the "League Think" philosophy by putting the League ahead of themselves, and recognizing that the value of their individual franchise is directly tied to the overall health of the League.

II. FIRST AND TEN: THE EVOLUTION OF REVENUE SHARING IN THE NFL—FROM ITS ORIGINS TO THE LEAGUE'S CURRENT SYSTEM

A. The Emergence of the "League Think" Philosophy

The NFL's collective "League Think" philosophy emerged in the early 1960's as the brain child of then Commissioner, Pete Rozelle.[22] Rozelle convinced the League's founding owners, such as George Halas of the Chicago Bears and Wellington Mara[23] of the New York Giants, to relinquish their control over local television broadcasting rights, and instead combine these rights into a national package.[24] According to Rozelle's plan, the League would then sell this national package to the television networks, and the proceeds of the sale would be split evenly among each NFL franchise.[25] Rozelle argued that by pooling resources and sharing revenue, the "League Think" philosophy would stabilize the competitive balance within the League, thereby making its product more marketable over the long run; and as a result, ensuring the viability of the League as a whole.[26] Explaining that the profitability of each individual team was necessarily tied to the success of the League as a whole, Rozelle convinced the owners that their individual profits would increase by putting the interests of the League ahead of their own.[27]

The NFL owners ultimately agreed to sell their television rights to CBS as a national package, but the resulting contract between the NFL and CBS was voided by a 1961 federal circuit court decision finding that the contract violated antitrust laws.[28] Responding to the circuit court's decision, seventy-two days later Congress passed the Sports Broadcasting Act, which enabled professional sports leagues to negotiate television deals as single units, thereby creating an antitrust exemption that has revolutionized the sports industry.[29] In 1962, armed with the recently enacted antitrust exemption, the NFL and CBS entered into a contract whereby CBS paid the NFL $4.65 million per year for two years in exchange for the exclusive rights to broadcast all NFL games played during that period.[30] As a result, the popularity of the league exploded with television ratings soaring fifty percent in the second year of the contract.[31] Furthermore, the NFL's next contract with CBS reflected the League's rapidly growing popularity through a payout of $14.1 million per year, more than triple its previous contract.[32]

Over the next two decades, the NFL continued to grow, especially with the 1970 merger of the NFL and its upstart rival, the American Football League ("AFL").[33] Despite the League's continued growth, however, the NFL's business model and that of the individual teams changed very little.[34] Throughout the 1980s, the NFL owners were content to sit back and collect their ever-increasing, equal shares of the national television deals,[35] while also sharing the gate receipts generated by crowded stadiums.[36] The profits accumulated by the individual teams were heavily dependent on the revenue generated by the league as a whole, and the individual owners were not overly concerned with gaining a competitive advantage by increasing their own team's relative revenues.[37] According to current Baltimore Ravens President Dick Cass, "'There were not as many revenue opportunities . . . .' Most owners "didn't control the stadiums, they didn't control concessions, they didn't control parking. Sports sponsorships weren't a big deal.'"[38] Under this business model, the opportunities for teams to generate their own revenue were virtually nonexistent, and the only way for teams to maximize their profitability relative to other teams was to cut costs—namely, player salaries.[39]

B.   The Evolution of the Revenue Sharing System: Historical Challenges

While the general structure of the NFL's cooperative approach remains an integral part of the League today, challenges to the League's collective mentality, which began in the 1990s, have revolutionized the predominant business model currently utilized by the NFL and its owners. As former NFL Commissioner Paul Tagliabue explains, the NFL remains committed to maintaining its cooperative structure because "clearly, the attractiveness of the league is not dependent on any one team or small group of teams. . . . It's a total league. That was the philosophy from the early '60s onward, and it's continued."[40] The business model followed by the NFL owners, on the other hand, has drastically evolved in recent years due largely to an emerging faction of owners who believe that teams should be given greater control over their revenue in order to better market themselves.[41]

One of the first and most influential owners to challenge the NFL's "League Think" philosophy was Jerry Jones, an oil and gas tycoon who paid $140 million for the Dallas Cowboys franchise in 1989.[42] Initially, Jones focused his confrontations with the League over the issue of national sponsorship and marketing deals, which at that time were exclusively controlled by the League's profitable arm, NFL Properties.[43] Jones criticized his take from the national sponsorship deals as inadequate for the marketing power of his particular franchise.[44] Jones basically felt that he could do a better job of marketing his team by negotiating local deals, instead of relying on the League to market his team as part of the total package of the League.[45]

In 1995, Jones directly challenged the League by entering into local sponsorship deals with Pepsi and Nike, despite the League's supposedly exclusive deals with Coke and Players Inc., the licensing arm of the NFLPA.[46] The brash move by Jones prompted the NFL to file a lawsuit against the Cowboys for $300 million.[47] The League labeled Jones's conduct as "ambush marketing deals" and sought a ruling that would enjoin the Cowboys from violating their agreements with NFL Properties regarding the NFL's exclusive control over team logos.[48] Jones responded by filing a $700 million counterclaim against the League, accusing the NFL of preventing teams from marketing themselves.[49] In late 1996, the two sides ultimately reached a settlement that allowed the Cowboys to keep their new sponsorship deals. More importantly, it opened the door for other NFL teams to secure their own local sponsorship deals.[50]

Jones's ability to successfully challenge the League in the area of local sponsorship not only created a new source of unshared revenue for individual teams, but more significantly, it marked the beginning of an erosion in the collective mentality that has dominated the League for so many years.[51] The current ramifications of this settlement between Jones and the NFL are illustrated by the co-existing marketing deals currently held by both individual teams and the League as a whole. For example, Pepsi and Coors are now the "official" soft drink and beer of the NFL, giving each company the right to use the NFL logo and the logos of the 32 individual franchises in national advertising.[52] Individual teams, however, now may arrange their own local deals with other vendors, such as Coke and Budweiser.[53] While Jones's victory over the NFL was limited to the area of sponsorship and marketing deals, his incentive-based arguments have gained some support from a few of the other owners, and the League has ultimately been forced to re-evaluate the two-prong current revenue sharing system.

C.   The Current Revenue Sharing System in the NFL

The current revenue sharing system in place in the NFL today can be separated into two basic subsections or categories. The first category comprises the sharing of revenue generated by licensing agreements such as sponsorships and marketing deals, as well as League merchandise sales. This licensing element is governed by the recently enacted "Master Agreement," which is an extension of the "NFL Trust," an agreement between owners with origins dating back to the collective mentality that emerged in the 1960s.[54] Under the Master Agreement, the NFL retains most of its control over the team logos used by the 32 individual franchises, and the League has reserved some of its power to determine how each individual franchise can use its own logo.[55] The new agreement, however, does not simply preserve the status quo regarding local sponsorship deals, but instead also gives individual teams greater freedom to control their own local marketing revenue.[56] Nevertheless, because the Master

Agreement was not unanimously approved by all the team owners, there is some uncertainty about whether the agreement will be binding on those owners who voted against it.[57]

The second more commonly known category of the revenue sharing system is comprised of all the revenue that is generated by the actual playing of the games on the field.[58] Unlike the Master Agreement, this category is not governed by a single document, but instead by a combination of provisions from both the NFL Constitution and the CBA. This second category, which includes the television deals covering the rights to broadcast NFL games as well as the gate receipts generated by stadium attendance, comprises the strong majority of the total revenue shared among individual NFL franchises.[59]

Although this second category generates the vast majority of the revenue shared by NFL teams, both aspects of the revenue sharing system represent the collective "League Think" philosophy that has played such a central role in the success of the NFL.[60] Despite their common goal, however, the monetary disparity between these two categories cannot be ignored. For example, under the system in place at the end of the 2004 season, the licensing element only generated between $4 and $5 million for each team, whereas the national television deals alone generated $80 million per team.[61] Notwithstanding the actual disparity in the contribution that each category makes to the overall revenue shared by the individual NFL teams, it is important that they be recognized as part of the same general system because they are inseparably connected by the League's greater collective mentality. Furthermore, as a number of owners noted when voting in favor of the Master Agreement, its approval was a significant gesture in reaffirming the importance placed upon the League's commitment to revenue sharing.[62]

1.   The Master Agreement's Contribution to the Revenue Sharing System

The new Master Agreement determines which categories of licensing are exclusively controlled by the League and conversely, how individual franchises can supplement their income with unshared licensing and sponsorship agreements.[63] Under the Master Agreement, the most significant sponsorship category exclusively controlled by the League is on-field sponsorship deals.[64] The NFL currently has on-field deals with Gatorade, the Pepsi-owned sports drink, [*Reebok*] and Motorola Inc., which supplies headsets worn by NFL coaches.[65] These . . . companies are the only corporate sponsors whose brands are allowed on NFL sidelines.[66]

While the Master Agreement clearly restricts the ability of individual owners to enter into sponsorship deals that might conflict with League-wide sponsors, the agreement also recognizes the victory Jerry Jones achieved in 1996 by providing some flexibility for individual teams to negotiate their own local sponsorship deals.[67] These local sponsorship deals serve as an important source of unshared revenue, which has increasingly drawn the attention of team owners

seeking to obtain a competitive advantage over the rest of the League. According to the Master Agreement, the League can sell the rights to use the 32 team logos collectively only within an exclusively League-controlled sponsorship area.[68] Otherwise, the individual teams legally own their own logos and are free to negotiate their own local marketing deals using their logos.[69] Furthermore, teams can establish their own retail shops to sell team apparel, and unlike the massive quantity of merchandise sold by the League itself, any apparel sold at team stores generates unshared revenue streams.[70] Therefore, teams that create their own retail shops can take advantage of their marketability by keeping all of the revenue generated by these stores.

Under the Master Agreement, the individual franchises and the NFL itself equally share all the revenue that is generated by League merchandise sales and exclusive League-wide sponsorship deals.[71] In recent years, the individual teams received between four and five million dollars a year, but that figure is expected to at least double under contracts already signed by the League.[72] The NFL agreed to extend its sponsorship agreement with Pepsi in 2002, under which Pepsi is obligated to pay $440 million in rights, fees, advertising, and marketing through 2011.[73] Pepsi will pay the League an average of sixteen million dollars a year, which is about one-third more than under its previous contract; other advertising obligations could push the total value of the deal over $550 million.[74] Furthermore, the League also recently extended its sponsorship deals with Gatorade and Visa, which should further contribute to the increasing amount of shared licensing revenue.[75]

Despite mounting concern that there should have been an overhaul of the entire revenue sharing system before proceeding with the Master Agreement, in the spring of 2004 the owners passed the fifteen year-long agreement by a vote of twenty-six to three (with three abstentions).[76] Prior to the vote, the Raiders, Redskins and Cowboys, which at the time were the three teams expected to vote against the agreement, all expressed their belief that they would be bound only if they voted in favor of the agreement.[77]

Following the vote, however, the question still remains whether the agreement is binding on those owners who voted against it. Jerry Jones has publicly maintained that he is not bound by the Master Agreement because he voted against it.[78] The League, on the other hand, expressed the converse view that any vote on matters of League policy requires a three-quarters majority, or twenty-four team owners, at which point the policy takes effect and becomes binding on all NFL teams.[79] Other team owners have supported the League's position. As Cleveland Browns President Carmen Policy explained, "anybody who feels a league, a partnership, cannot bind itself by a three-fourths vote is calling for anarchy."[80]

Furthermore, the League specifically structured the Master Agreement to inoculate its ultimate approval from any legal challenges by owners like Jerry Jones.[81] In particular, the

Master Agreement gives individual franchises ownership of their own logos, and teams no longer need League approval before entering local sponsorship deals.[82] Additionally, the League also tried to placate owners like Jones by expanding the geographic constraints placed on each team's marketing territory, an area within which a given team is free to enter into their own local sponsorship deals.[83] Previously, teams were prevented from marketing beyond a seventy-five mile radius around their home city, but the Master Agreement now allows teams to market throughout their entire state, provided they do not reach within a seventy-five mile radius around an in-state competitor's city.[84] When considering these characteristics of the Master Agreement, it would seem that there is not an especially great probability of an owner challenging the Agreement. It is impossible, however, to predict whether an owner like Jerry Jones might be offered a deal attractive enough to entice him into challenging the Master Agreement.

In the end, the question of whether the Master Agreement is binding on those owners who voted against it remains unanswered, but if the conflict were to come to a head, there could be major ramifications throughout the League. The likelihood that Jones would prevail on such a challenge is relatively slim because the argument articulated by the League and owners like Policy has plenty of merit. Furthermore, there are policy reasons why Jones' argument should fail, such as preventing an increase in significant economic inequalities, which threaten the competitive balance that has been so instrumental to the NFL's success.[85]

Although there is no clear answer regarding what would happen if Jones challenges the Master Agreement, League sources have speculated that Jones might initiate a challenge by seeking a Cowboys sponsor which conflicts with an exclusive category reserved for League-wide action under the Master Agreement.[86] A likely scenario would be for Jones to negotiate a local on-field sponsor that conflicts with the League-wide on-field sponsorship deals already negotiated with companies like Gatorade and Motorola.[87] If Jones indeed decides to challenge the Master Agreement, the League would most likely respond by filing a lawsuit against Jones for violating the terms of the Agreement. The question would then become whether a three-quarters vote by the team owners is in fact binding on every team regardless of whether a specific team voted against the Master Agreement. Finally, in the event that Jones successfully challenges the limitations of the Master Agreement, there would not only be a substantial monetary loss for the NFL's revenue sharing system, but more importantly, it would create a symbolic rift in the foundation of the League's revenue sharing philosophy.

2. The Second Category of the Revenue Sharing System: Television Revenue and Gate Receipts

The second category of the revenue sharing system, which comprises the vast majority of the total amount of revenue shared each year, consists of all the revenue generated by the actual games on the field. This general subsection of the revenue sharing system is governed by a series of provisions in both the CBA and the NFL Constitution. . . .

The two major revenue sources . . . are: (1) the proceeds from the sale of television broadcasting rights and (2) "gate receipts . . . including ticket revenue from "luxury boxes, suites[,] and premium seating subject to gate receipt sharing among NFL Teams."[91]

While the equal sharing of television broadcasting rights is relatively straightforward, the sharing of gate receipts is more complex and deserves further explanation. First, it is imperative to distinguish between "ticket revenue" from luxury boxes, which is "subject to gate receipt sharing among NFL teams," and non-ticket luxury box revenue, which is not subject to revenue sharing, and is therefore coveted by owners as a source of supplemental unshared revenue.[92] This distinction is based on the idea that luxury boxes can be sold in such a way that they are not considered part of normal ticket sales, and thus are not considered gate receipts subject to revenue sharing.[93]

Next, it is important to establish the precise manner in which gate receipts subject to revenue sharing are actually shared among the individual franchises. The NFL Constitution provides, "The home club shall deliver to the League office the greater of $30,000 for each regular season and pre-season game, or [forty percent] of the gross receipts after the following deductions. . . ."[94] While this provision establishes a floor of $30,000 that must be shared by the home team for every game, in today's market, forty percent of gross receipts will invariably exceed $30,000, thereby automatically triggering the forty percent option.[95] Under the old system of gate receipt sharing, the ticket revenue for a particular game was shared roughly sixty-forty between the home and visiting team respectively with none of the ticket revenue reaching beyond the two teams participating in that particular game.[96]

Although it would appear that gate receipts should be shared according to the sixty-forty split, certain deductions afforded to the home team cause the visiting team's share to diminish to thirty-four percent of gross receipts. The NFL Constitution establishes that in addition to deductions for federal, state, and municipal taxes on ticket sales, the home team is allowed a significant deduction for "stadium rental allowance equal to fifteen percent (15%) of the gross receipts after deducting the taxes."[97] As a result of these deductions, the home team ends up giving the League thirty-four percent of the gross receipts for each home game (forty percent of the eighty-five percent remaining after the deduction for the stadium rental allowance).[98] Under the old system of gate receipt sharing, which was in place through the 2001 season, the League would then remit the thirty-four percent directly to the visiting team that played in that particular game.[99]

In 2001, however, the NFL adopted a resolution amending its Constitution with the following language, "beginning with the 2002 NFL season, all regular season and preseason game visiting team shares shall be pooled and shared equally among the 32 Member Clubs."[100] This amendment to the revenue sharing of gate receipts should increase the redistributive effect of the League's revenue sharing system, and serves as a further indication of the NFL's commitment to the "League Think" philosophy. Under the old system, a popular team like the Dallas Cowboys could take advantage of the sellout crowds that it helped draw to opposing stadiums by keeping the entire thirty-four percent of gate receipts for itself. Conversely, perennial cellar-dwellers like the Arizona Cardinals, who drew far smaller crowds while on the road, experienced a competitive disadvantage because their visiting team share ("VTS") was undoubtedly smaller than that of the Cowboys. By pooling each team's VTS, and then redistributing the total amount equally among the individual franchises, the 2001 modification of gate receipt revenue sharing should help ensure greater financial equality throughout the league.

In opposition to this redistributive effect, financially-minded owners like Jerry Jones would argue that individual teams should be able to take advantage of their marketability, and should not be forced to carry the burden of less marketable teams. Despite the apparent justification for such an argument, the redistribution of revenue from teams at the top to teams at the bottom has become necessary for the continued economic success of the League; especially because the current economic inequality in the NFL has reached such critical levels that the future viability of lower-revenue teams is in serious doubt.[101]

3.   Television Revenue: The Foundation of the NFL Revenue Sharing System

The two major revenue sources . . . television revenue and gate receipts, compose the entire second category of the revenue sharing system. As previously noted, these two revenue streams generate the vast majority of the League's shared revenue, which amounted to a total sharing of more than eighty percent of the approximately $5.5 billion in total League revenue from the 2004 season.[102] [*Ed. Note: The NFL reported $8.5 billion in revenue in 2009.*] While gate receipts undoubtedly play a critical role in the League's revenue sharing system, it is the national television deals that operate as the heart and soul of revenue sharing in the NFL.

From the first equally shared national television deal arranged in 1961 to the current national television package, the equally shared proceeds generated by the NFL's television broadcasting rights have always been the single largest contributor to the League's revenue sharing system.[103] Furthermore, the League's television revenue has grown exponentially over the years, starting at $4.6 million for the two year contract signed in 1961, and climbing all the way to $17.6 billion for the recent eight year package that expired after the 2005 season.[104] [*Ed. Note: The NFL subsequently signed television deals with CBS, Fox, NBC, ESPN,*

and DirecTV through 2013 for an average of $3.7 billion per year.] This tremendous growth in the NFL's equally shared television revenue represents a self perpetuating indication of the League's success as a whole. The competitive parity resulting from the League's revenue sharing system in general has unquestionably bolstered the success and popularity of the NFL by ensuring that in any given year almost every team has a chance to make the playoffs.[105] As a result of the League's immense popularity, television networks have been willing to pay endlessly increasing sums of money to secure NFL broadcasting rights, which in turn has ensured the sustainability of the League's revenue sharing system, and thereby the continued success of the League as a whole.

The equal sharing of television revenue has become a symbol of the League's unparalleled success, and its commitment to the "League Think" philosophy. . . . In contrast to the extreme financial and competitive inequalities that have plagued other professional sports leagues like Major League Baseball, the NFL's ability to maintain its unmatched popularity has largely been the result of the League's commitment to revenue sharing.[107] The recent emergence of new sources of unshared revenue, on the other hand . . . have completely transformed the financial realities of the League by enabling individual franchises to gain a competitive advantage through the exploitation of unshared revenue.[108] Furthermore, the drastic increase of these sources of unshared revenue has led to extreme levels of financial inequality throughout the League, which now threaten the continued viability of the NFL's current economic system.

III.   THIRD AND LONG: THE HARMFUL EFFECTS OF "LOCAL REVENUE" AND THE DESPERATE NEED FOR REVENUE SHARING REFORMS

A.   Unshared "Local Revenue" and the Erosion of the NFL's Collective Mentality

The advent of these unshared revenue sources . . . not only drastically altered the landscape of the revenue sharing system in the NFL, but has also revolutionized the business model followed by team owners throughout the League.[109] Abandoning the old passive business model where owners promoted equality and were content to rely on revenue sharing as their primary source of income, teams have increasingly sought to maximize their competitive advantage by exploiting as many sources of unshared revenue as possible. Art Modell, who joined the League in 1961 as the majority owner of the Cleveland Browns and left . . . after selling his share of the Baltimore Ravens, articulated this change in the League's mentality when he said, "The values have changed. We were comrades in arms. We were partners. That doesn't happen now. Everything is revenues and profits."[110]

With the growing emphasis on profits, teams have increasingly turned to . . . the following list of unshared revenue sources: "revenues derived from concessions, parking, local advertising and promotion, signage, magazine advertising, local sponsorship agreements, stadium clubs, luxury box income other than that included in subsection 1(a)(i)(1)."[111] Aptly labeled "local revenue," these unshared revenue sources have been harnessed by expedient owners to supplement their income, and they have had a profound impact on multiple facets of the NFL with mixed results for the League as a whole. While the incentives created by these sources of unshared revenue have helped the League grow by promoting the construction of new stadiums, the drastically increasing nature of local revenue, which is generally more easily utilized by larger market teams, has led to a widening revenue gap between the League's rich and poor teams.[112]

Following the lead of business-driven owners like Jerry Jones, owners throughout the league have recognized that most of the major sources of local revenue stem directly from the ability of individual franchises to gain control over the stadiums in which they play.[113] With owners drooling over the unshared revenue streams generated by controlling stadium parking, concessions, signage, and luxury box income, the League has experienced a significant trend with regard to the construction of new stadiums and the renovation of old ones.[114] . . .

In their relentless pursuit of local revenue, profit-hungry owners have discovered creative ways to not only help finance stadium projects, but to make the completed stadiums even more lucrative with regard to unshared local revenue. It is in this context that the distinction between luxury box "ticket revenue" and non-ticket revenue becomes extremely significant. Luxury boxes, which provide first class amenities like catering and a private bar, are usually leased to a corporate customer for extended periods of time (usually at least an entire season), typically giving the lessee access to the luxury box for all stadium events including those performances unrelated to the NFL, such as rock concerts or other professional sporting events.[117] Therefore, any franchise that owns its own stadium can keep most of the substantial revenue generated by these expensive luxury box lease arrangements.[118] Conversely, teams that have unfavorable leases with a municipality or other entity that owns the stadium are at a competitive disadvantage because they are missing out on enormous streams of unshared revenue.[119]

. . . .

Jerry Jones is quick to proffer his view that these stadium-related sources of unshared revenue are good for the League. Stressing his incentive based arguments, Jones explained, "If you don't have some unshared revenues, those stadiums never get built because of all the debt. You think people are going to build those stadiums if they were sharing the revenue 32 ways? No. Why did they get built? Because of the incentive."[125] While it is hard to argue that unshared local revenue has not had some positive effects

on the current state of the NFL, it is important to weigh the positives and negatives associated with unshared revenue in determining what is best for the future of the League. There is no doubt that in today's economy there is a need for some unshared revenue in order to provide incentives for teams to market themselves and to help generate beneficial externalities like stadium construction. Too much unshared revenue, on the other hand, is detrimental to the League because it will inevitably lead to a widening gap between revenue-rich teams with favorable stadium situations and revenue-poor teams with unfavorable stadium situations.

1. "Local Revenue" as the Cause of "Franchise Free Agency"

At first glance, all this additional revenue and all these new stadiums might appear to be nothing but a good thing for the League, but upon closer inspection it becomes clear that there are some significant concerns lurking just behind the glare of the bright new stadium lights. The incessant quest for unshared revenue by NFL owners has been largely responsible for a phenomenon known as "Franchise Free Agency."[126] This phenomenon, which is characterized by the recent relocation of numerous franchises seeking more lucrative stadiums in which to play, has not only drawn the attention of significant scholarly analysis, but has also prompted Congress to propose numerous bills attempting to prevent franchises from arbitrarily abandoning their home city simply to secure a more profitable venue.[127]

. . . .

Despite Congress' inability to enact any of these bills into law, the prevalence of the proposed legislation indicates that "Franchise Free Agency" is a legitimate concern for the nation as a whole. Furthermore, the large scale of this political response is undoubtedly driven by significant unrest among NFL fans, which poses a direct threat to the future popularity and success of the League.

In addition to the negative reaction that franchise relocation has on the NFL's fan base, the lure of unshared local revenue generated by favorable stadium deals has eroded the NFL's "League Think" philosophy, and, in certain circumstances, has hurt the League as a whole. The relocation of the Rams from Los Angeles to St. Louis serves as a perfect example of the detrimental effect that an individual team's pursuit of local revenue can have on the League.[137] The advent of unshared local revenue has created a situation where an individual owner's best interests are no longer necessarily aligned with the best interests of the League. In the case of the Rams, the franchise moved from the much larger market of Los Angeles to the much smaller market of St. Louis mainly because St. Louis offered a better stadium situation that would generate more unshared local revenue for the team.[138] While the team itself benefited from the move, the League as a whole suffered because St. Louis's smaller market means that fewer people watch the Rams on television, and this reduced audience thereby generates smaller television ratings when compared to the ratings that could have been achieved had the Rams remained in Los Angeles.[139]

Since the Rams only absorbed a small portion of that decrease due to the revenue sharing system, the increase in local revenue made the move worthwhile for the team, but the aggregate effect for the rest of the owners made the move more costly for the League as a whole.[140] Consequently, the emergence of local revenue has indirectly prevented the League from capitalizing on the Los Angeles area fan base and the enormous revenue opportunities presented by the nation's second largest market. As a result, the League cannot maximize its evenly shared television revenues, which thereby hurts the revenue sharing system, and more importantly the League as a whole.[141]

B. The Widening Revenue Gap and the Salary Cap System

The most detrimental consequence resulting from the emergence of unshared local revenue has been the widening gap between the League's revenue-rich teams and its less prosperous counterparts.[142] . . . .

The major source of this widening revenue gap, much like "Franchise Free Agency," is the increasing need for owners to secure beneficial stadium deals in order to capitalize on unshared local revenue.[145] As in the case of the New York Giants [Ed. Note: *before moving into a new stadium in 2010*], teams that are stuck in unfavorable stadium arrangements cannot take advantage of local revenue, and therefore experience a significant competitive disadvantage.[146]

. . . By comparing the enormous local revenue opportunities of a larger market team like the Redskins, who own their own stadium, and the limited local revenue possibilities for a smaller market team . . . who do not control their stadium, the source of the NFL's current revenue gap becomes readily apparent.

Although the increasing economic inequalities in the NFL seem relatively clear, it is also important to recognize some of the arguments against revenue sharing made by those owners who have financed some or all of their stadium acquisitions through private debt. These owners argue that one must think in terms of net profits, not total annual revenue, because the large amount of debt incurred to buy the stadium initially negates much of the apparent advantage.[153] For example, the Philadelphia Eagles, who in 2003 moved into a new $512 million stadium, must allocate more than thirty million dollars a year to service their debt.[154] This argument criticizing too much revenue sharing is adeptly characterized by a statement attributed to Daniel Snyder of the Redskins. Snyder reportedly said, "I'll share my revenue whenever they're ready to share my debt."[155] Owners like Snyder, who has roughly $300 million in debt left from his $800 million acquisition of the Redskins and their stadium in 1999, argue that since they were the ones who put up the initial capital, they are entitled to reap the benefits of stadium ownership.[156]

While there is undoubtedly some merit to these arguments, it is important to note that in the context of acquiring a large market NFL stadium or franchise, there is little in the way of the risk that would normally be associated with a leveraged investment, largely because of the current economic state of the League as a whole. In 2003, every single franchise experienced a net profit; furthermore, the revenue of the League as a whole has increased by a factor of greater than five over the past fifteen years.[157] The strength of the League's current economic outlook is illustrated by the fact that traffic on the NFL's Internet site surpasses that of other pro leagues, its television broadcasts outpace prime-time averages, and its especially devoted fans buy more than ninety percent of available tickets.[158] Furthermore, the League generated . . . the most income produced by any of the four major U.S. professional sports leagues.[159]

When one considers these astounding statistics in relation to the structural reality of the League, it is impossible to ignore that the value of an individual franchise is completely dependent on the success of the League as a whole because without the League, each individual franchise would be worthless. Although the owners who financed their own stadiums would argue that they deserve greater returns because they bore the risk of their leveraged investment, this argument is largely mitigated by considering the minimal amount of risk actually incurred. Therefore, since an individual owner does not bear much financial risk when his franchise leverages its investment in stadium infrastructure, asking the more profitable teams to share a small portion of local revenue with their less prosperous counterparts is not an unreasonable request, especially because the value of an individual franchise is necessarily tied to the success of the League as a whole.

1. The Failure of the Salary Cap System and the Resulting Competitive Inequalities on the Field

While the competitive advantage gained through stadium ownership serves as the largest catalyst for the widening revenue gap, the economic disparities that exist between the individual teams also adversely affect the ability of lower-revenue teams to remain competitive on the field. . . . The discrepancy in the percentage of income that a given team can spend on player salaries has a huge impact on the ability of lower-revenue teams to compete with higher revenue teams in the high-priced free agent market.[161]

. . . Owners critical of too much revenue sharing have been quick to point out that those teams in a superior financial position have not necessarily experienced a competitive advantage on the field. . . .[164] Notwithstanding the inability of the Cowboys to "buy" their success, it would be completely ridiculous to argue with the statement made by Atlanta Falcons owner Arthur Blank, that "at some point there is a correlation between what you're paying your players and your ability to compete."[165]

. . . .

C.   The NFL's Current Reaction to the Problems Posed by "Local Revenue" and the Widening Revenue Gap

The widening revenue gap created by both the emergence of local revenue and the salary cap system has sparked considerable debate amongst the NFL owners. The owners of lower-revenue teams . . . have expressed their belief that under the League's current economic model these less prosperous teams cannot compete with their revenue-rich counterparts who are better equipped to capitalize on the local revenue opportunities created by stadium ownership.[175] According to lower-revenue teams, the revenue gap is reaching such a critical level that their future economic viability will soon be in serious doubt, and therefore the League must find a way to better redistribute some of the local revenue that has created this economic discrepancy.[176]

Conversely, the owners of high-revenue teams like the Redskins and Cowboys argue that if teams are forced to include their local revenue in the total amount of revenue shared by the League, it will eliminate any incentive for less prosperous teams to market themselves.[177] As Cowboys owner Jerry Jones explains, "The big concern I have is not how to equalize the disparity in revenue[,] but how to get the clubs that are not generating the revenue to see the light."[178]

There is some merit to Jones's argument since poor management decisions by lower-revenue teams might be partially to blame for their inferior economic position. However, in deciding whether to reform the current revenue sharing system, the NFL must also consider some of the economic factors that are beyond the control of the lower-revenue owners, such as stadium ownership and market size. Since a team's potential marketability is directly tied to the size of its local market, teams like the Cowboys and Redskins can take advantage of their larger markets to increase their unshared local revenue through both local sponsorship deals and local stadium revenue.[179] At the same time, playing in a large market does not necessarily guarantee that a team will be able to capitalize on sources of local revenue, because that team might be stuck in an unfavorable stadium situation. . . .[180] Therefore, when evaluating the need for revenue sharing reforms, the NFL should not only consider the inherent economic disparities that exist between small and large market teams; it must also factor in the realities surrounding every team's ability to secure a beneficial stadium deal.

The NFL has taken a variety of steps to help address some of the problems that have been created by the emergence of local revenue and the resulting increase in the revenue gap. Some of these League initiatives are specifically designed to combat the increasing economic inequalities within the NFL, while others focus more on addressing some of the indirect effects of local revenue, such as "Franchise Free Agency." In order to facilitate the construction of new stadiums, the League adopted a program set forth in Resolution G-3 of 1999 ("G-3 Program"), which has loaned $650 million in League money to help eight different stadium projects, all of which were funded by a combination of public and private financing.[181] [*Ed. Note: The NFL loaned nearly $1.4 billion to help finance 11 stadium projects through 2008.*] This G-3 Program is meant to promote stadium construction, which could potentially benefit lower-revenue teams by enabling them to build new stadiums and thereby better capitalize on local revenue. Although the program does seek to eliminate some of the local revenue-related incentives that contributed to the emergence of "Franchise Free Agency," this program may actually reduce the overall amount of shared revenue, and is therefore not well suited to address the overarching problems created by the widening revenue gap.

In order to qualify for G-3 financial assistance from the League, a stadium project must be financed by public–private funding, and the amount that the League will contribute is directly tied to the amount of the individual franchise's private contribution ("Private Contribution") to its own stadium project.[182] The allocation of League funds to the financing of a G-3 stadium is technically in the form of a loan, but it is repaid directly out of the visiting team's share ("VTS") of the luxury box and club seat revenue.[183] Similarly, in the context of a non-G-3 stadium, luxury box and club seat revenue can also be exempted from VTS, provided it is used for the direct financing of the non-G-3 stadium's construction.[184] However, notwithstanding this similar treatment of certain luxury box revenues, there are additional benefits that accrue to those owners who qualify for the G-3 Program. In particular, the G-3 Program should reduce a team's cost of capital by eliminating some of the transaction costs that would otherwise be required to secure financing from a private institution. Therefore, under the G-3 Program, the League is in essence simply making private loans easier for the individual owners to obtain by exempting ticket revenue that would otherwise be shared with the visiting club, and instead using that revenue to pay off the loan. This arrangement promotes stadium construction because owners can partially finance the building of their new stadium with revenue that they otherwise would have been forced to share with the visiting teams had they remained in their old stadium.[185]

One of the principal intentions of the NFL's G-3 Program is to encourage large market teams to stay in their home city (instead of moving to a smaller market) by offering favorable loans that help the teams finance their public-private stadium projects.[186] This is implied by the language establishing the precise amounts that the League will loan to a participating franchise under the G-3 Program. The exact provision is enumerated in the subsequent Resolution JC-1 adopted in 2003, which extended the life of the G-3 Program, and provides in part:

> *That the amount of such League loan shall be either 34% or 50% of the Private Contribution, determined by the size of the television market in which the stadium involved is being constructed, with League loans at the 50% level to be made available to facilitate stadium construction projects for NFL clubs currently operating in the six largest national television markets, and with the League loans in all other television markets limited to 34% of the Private Contribution.*[187]

While the G-3 Program helps both small and large market teams finance public-private stadium construction, the program favors large market teams by providing them with much larger loans. This favorable treatment given to the largest market teams is meant to provide incentives for those teams to remain in their home cities, which benefits the entire NFL by enabling the League to capitalize on the increased television revenue generated by these larger markets.

The G-3 Program undoubtedly provides universal benefits that help all franchises looking to utilize public–private financing in the construction of a new stadium. Furthermore, by encouraging teams to remain in the largest markets, this program should help to increase the League's television revenue, which is shared equally, and therefore should benefit the League as a whole. However, an increase in equally shared television revenue confers the same benefit upon every team notwithstanding their relative financial positions. This program therefore does not help to alleviate any of the inherent economic inequalities that exist in smaller market cities. In fact, this program might actually exacerbate the economic disparities that currently exist in the League today by helping large market teams better capitalize on local revenue at the expense of smaller market teams who, under this program, do not enjoy the same level of League subsidies. Instead of redistributing some of the advantages enjoyed by large market teams that can more easily utilize their marketability to generate more local revenue, the G-3 Program actually has the effect of giving the large market teams an additional leg up on their smaller market counterparts.

In addition to the G-3 Program, the NFL has also created a "supplemental" revenue sharing pool, which would appear far better suited to combat the widening revenue gap that threatens the League's current competitive balance. The so-called "supplemental" revenue sharing pool, created under the salary cap system, redistributes roughly forty million dollars a year in local revenue to a small number of lower-revenue teams.[188] Typically, each year six to nine teams draw from the "supplemental" pool, which has grown from eighteen million dollars to its current mark of forty million dollars.[189] [*Ed. Note: In 2006, the NFL increased the amount of supplemental revenue sharing to $110 million

each year that is distributed to 15 teams.] Despite its potential to help alleviate the League's widening revenue gap, the "supplemental" revenue sharing pool has proven insufficient to keep pace with the dramatically increasing nature of the economic disparities in the NFL.[190] . . . Moreover, when this figure is considered in relation to the gap in annual revenue between the NFL's richest and poorest teams, which has well exceeded the $100 million mark, the "supplemental" pool's inadequacy in dealing with the exponentially increasing economic disparity becomes apparent.[192]

Notwithstanding the League's marginal attempts to counteract the various harmful effects that stem from the recent growth in local revenue, these emerging unshared revenue streams no longer simply threaten to bend the rules of the NFL's collective philosophy. Instead, the revenue sharing system itself appears to be on the brink of a complete fracture.

. . . .

IV. FOURTH AND GOAL: SUPPLEMENTAL REDISTRIBUTION—A PROPOSED REFORM TO THE NFL'S REVENUE SHARING SYSTEM

On the one hand, there is no doubt that the NFL's collective approach to its revenue sharing system played an integral part in the continually growing success and popularity of the League as a whole. On the other hand, the existence of some unshared revenue is also undeniably important in today's economy because it provides incentives for teams to market themselves. Forcing the individual teams to share all of their local revenue would not be beneficial for the League as a whole because it would completely eliminate any incentive for teams to seek a competitive advantage, thereby enabling some teams to simply coast on the coattails of their more committed brethren.

Maintaining the status quo, however, is also not an option because the extreme economic disparities that exist between high and low revenue teams will soon render the future economic viability of the lowest-revenue teams untenable. Furthermore, the owners cannot avoid reforming the current revenue sharing system because the NFLPA demands a portion of unshared revenues. . . . Therefore, in order to maintain the incentives provided by unshared local revenue while at the same time preserving the basic revenue sharing structure that has so adequately proved the test of time, the NFL and its owners should consider an economic formula that redistributes some portion of the unshared local revenue from those teams on top to those at the bottom.

Although the League has been largely unsuccessful in the few attempts that it has made to neutralize some of the harmful effects associated with the growth in unshared local revenue, it is important to carefully consider the limited action that the NFL has taken because it is helpful in providing guidelines for a more comprehensive reform of the revenue sharing system as a whole. First, it is important to identify the two major competing interests that must be balanced by any attempt at reform, namely: (1) the need for some unshared revenue to provide incentives for teams to market themselves; and (2) the need to preserve the basic revenue sharing structure that has fostered the success and popularity of the League by ensuring enough parity to establish the correct competitive balance among the individual NFL teams.

. . . .

V.   THE POST-GAME SHOW: A CONCLUDING SUMMARY

For over forty years, the NFL's collective "League Think" philosophy has played a central role in establishing and maintaining the competitive balance that fostered the massive popularity and success still enjoyed by the League today. In particular, the League's two-pronged revenue sharing system has proven the test of time by adapting to the prevailing economic forces that have helped shape the course of the NFL's financial model. While the emergence of too much unshared local revenue currently poses a variety of threats to the League's continued financial and competitive stability, local revenue is not by nature a corrosive force. If properly harnessed, local revenue can help the League's financial model evolve by incorporating the increased incentives that should enhance the League's overall product as individual owners strive to improve the marketability of each individual franchise. However, when unchecked, the lure of unshared local revenue can entice an individual owner to maximize his own benefits at the expense of the League as a whole. Under these circumstances, the individual owners benefiting from local revenue are often blinded by their own success, and they fail to recognize that the success of their individual franchise necessarily depends on the success of the League as a whole.

The League's revenue sharing system was originally designed to ensure that the League's success always came before that of an individual franchise. However, when the development of new economic forces threatened the sustainability of this collective principle, the League's financial system was forced to evolve. For example, the salary cap was adopted in 1994 to help sustain the competitiveness of the League's overall product by combating market inequalities that revenue sharing alone could no longer control. Similarly, the NFL's current financial system, which includes both revenue sharing and the salary cap, is not adequately suited to address the threats posed by the excessive growth of local revenue. This enormous growth of local revenue has now combined with natural market inequalities like market size and stadium ownership to create a widening revenue gap between the richest and poorest teams. The expanding nature of this revenue gap now threatens the competitive balance that has previously

ensured the sustained success of the League's overall product, and must therefore be addressed before inflicting irreparable harm upon the popularity and success of the League. In order to adequately address these growing revenue disparities, the League's financial system must once again evolve by incorporating a redistributive formula that maintains a proper level of unshared local revenue, and redistributes excessive local revenue to those teams most in need. Much like the creation of the salary cap, the adoption of this formula will help the NFL's financial system improve by simultaneously capturing the positive incentives associated with a healthy level of local revenue, while also preventing the corrosive effects of excessive local revenue.

Notes

1. Sanjay Jose Mullick, *Browns to Baltimore: Franchise Free Agency and the New Economics of the NFL,* 7 MARQ. SPORTS L.J. 1, 1 (1996).

2. *Id.*

3. *Id.*

4. *See* Stefan Fatsis, *Can Socialism Survive? The All-For-One, One-For-All Ethos of Pro Football Has Made It the Envy of Other Sports; The NFL Is Fighting To Make Sure It Stays That Way,* WALL ST. J., Sept. 20, 2004, at R1 [hereinafter Fatsis, *Can Socialism Survive?*].

5. Mullick, *supra* note 1, at 12.

6. Fatsis, *Can Socialism Survive?, supra* note 4.

7. *Id.*

8. *Id.*

9. *Id.*; Mullick, *supra* note 1, at 1.

10. The Master Agreement is basically an extension of the NFL Trust, which was a virtually identical agreement among owners regarding the sharing of licensing revenue with origins dating back to the emergence of the "League Think" philosophy in the 1960s. *See* Stefan Fatsis, *Dallas Owner Again Challenges NFL's Licensing,* WALL ST. J, Apr. 2, 2004, at B3 [hereinafter Fatsis, *Dallas Owner*]. *Cf.* Daniel Kaplan, *Tagliabue: NFL Trust Survival "a Done Deal,"* STREET & SMITH'S SPORTS BUSINESS JOURNAL, Mar. 29, 2004, at 1 [hereinafter Kaplan, *Tagliabue*].

11. *See* NFL CONST. art. 10.3; *see also* NFL, NFL COLLECTIVE BARGAINING AGREEMENT 2002–2008 art. XXIV, 1-4, *available at* http://www.nflpa.org/Agents/main.asp?subPage=CBA+Complete [hereinafter CBA]; Fatsis, *Can Socialism Survive?, supra* note 4, at R2; Ira Miller, *Revenue-sharing Rates as a Hot Topic,* S.F. CHRONICLE, Mar. 28, 2004 at, C2 [hereinafter Miller, *Revenue-sharing Rates*].

12. Miller, *Revenue-Sharing Rates, supra* note 11, at C2.

. . . .

18. Before the new labor agreement was approved, the now-defunct CBA would have lasted through the 2007 season, but the current 2006 season would have been the last one subject to the salary cap, which would have therefore expired along with the start of the 2006 season.

19. Kaplan, *NFL Owners, supra* note 17, at 1; Kaplan, *Chaos and Compromise, supra* note 17, at 1; Mullen, *Winding Road, supra* note 17, at 1.

. . . .

21. *See* Kaplan, *NFL Owners, supra* note 17; Kaplan, *Chaos and Compromise, supra* note 17 (discussing unhappy owners, who are already expressing various criticisms of this new plan, including some of the lowest-revenue owners who have criticized its failure to include all local revenue within the revenue shared between teams).

22. *See* Fatsis, *Can Socialism Survive?, supra* note 4, at R3; Mullick, *supra* note 1, at 1.

23. The author would like to pay his respect to the family of the late Giants owner Wellington Mara, who passed away on October 25, 2005 at the age of 89. In addition to being a wonderful person, Mara has been widely recognized as one of the NFL's most influential and beloved owners, whose foresight helped pave the way for the League's revenue sharing system and the resulting success still enjoyed by the NFL today. *See* Daniel Kaplan, *Pro Football Loses a Giant Leader,* STREET & SMITH'S SPORTS BUSINESS JOURNAL, Oct. 31, 2005, at 4 [hereinafter Kaplan, *Pro Football Loses*].

24. Fatsis, *Can Socialism Survive?, supra* note 4, at R3.

25. *Id.*

26. Mullick, *supra* note 1, at 1.

27. *Id.* at 1-2.

28. *See* United States v. NFL, 196 F. Supp. 445, 446-47 (E.D. Pa. 1961); Fatsis, *supra* note 4, at R3; *see also* WTWV, Inc. v. NFL, 678 F.2d 142, 144 (11th Cir. 1982) (describing the history behind the decision in U.S. v. NFL and stating that the contract with CBS was actually meant to mimic a similar broadcasting agreement already arranged by the NFL's upstart competitor, the American Football League ("AFL")).

29. *WTWV,* 678 F.2d at 144; Fatsis, *Can Socialism Survive?, supra* note 4, at R3.

30. Fatsis, *Can Socialism Survive?, supra* note 4, at R3.

31. *Id.*

32. *Id.*

33. *Id.*

34. *Id.*

35. In 1982, the NFL signed national TV deals with CBS, NBC, and ABC, which when combined generated a total of $1.89 billion in revenue for the NFL through the 1986 season. *NFL TV Rights: The Escalation of Television Rights Fees for the NFL:*, SPORTS ILLUSTRATED.COM, Nov. 8, 2004, http://sportsillustrated .cnn.com/2004/football/nfl/wires/11/08/2024.ap.fbn.nfl.tv.rights .chart.0268 (on file with author).

36. Fatsis, *Can Socialism Survive?, supra* note 4, at R3.

37. *See* Mullick, *supra* note 1, at 12-13.

38. Fatsis, *Can Socialism Survive?, supra* note 4, at R3.

39. Mullick, *supra* note 1, at 13.

40. Fatsis, *Can Socialism Survive?, supra* note 4, at R3.

41. *See id.* at 3-6.

42. *Id.* at 3.

43. *See* Miller, *Revenue-sharing Rates, supra* note 11, at C2.

44. *See* Fatsis, *Can Socialism Survive?, supra* note 4, at R3-R4; Miller, *Revenue-sharing Rates, supra* note 11, at C2.

45. Sam Farmer, *NFL Reviews Matter of Trust,* L.A. TIMES, Mar. 28, 2004, at D1.

46. *Id.*

47. *Id.*

48. *Id.*

49. *Id.*

50. *Id.*

51. Fatsis, *Can Socialism Survive?, supra* note 4, at R4.

52. *Id.*; see Fatsis, *Dallas Owner, supra* note 10, at B3.

53. Fatsis, *Can Socialism Survive?, supra* note 4, at R4; Fatsis, *Dallas Owner, supra* note 10, at B3 (stating that Coke is poured in 19 NFL stadiums whereas Pepsi is only poured in 12 stadiums).

54. *See* Fatsis, *Dallas Owner, supra* note 10, at B3.

55. *Id.* Under the NFL Trust, the League actually owned each team's logo, and teams had to get League permission before entering into their own sponsorship deals. Kaplan, *Tagliabue, supra* note 10, at 1. Under the newly enacted Master Agreement, teams now legally own their own logo, which was intended to insulate the Master Agreement from any legal challenges by those owners who voted against it. *Id. See, e.g., infra* text accompanying notes 81-84.

56. *See id.*

57. *See* Farmer, *supra* note 45, at D1; Fatsis, *Can Socialism Survive?, supra* note 4, at R1.

58. *See* CBA, *supra* note 11, art. XXIV, 1(a)(i)(1).

59. *See* Miller, *Revenue-sharing Rates, supra* note 11, at C2.

60. *Id.*

61. Farmer, *supra* note 45, at D1; Miller, *Revenue-sharing Rates, supra* note 11, at C2.

62. *See* Miller, *Revenue-sharing Rates, supra* note 11, at C2.

63. *See* Fatsis, *Dallas Owner, supra* note 10, at B3; Kaplan, *Tagliabue, supra* note 10, at 1.

64. Fatsis, *Dallas Owner, supra* note 10, at B3.

65. *Id.*

66. *Id.*

67. *Id.*

68. *See id.*

69. *See id.* As further explored below, this is a somewhat significant difference between the Master Agreement and its predecessor, the NFL Trust. *See, e.g., infra* text accompanying notes 81-84.

70. *See* Daniel Kaplan, *Divide on Revenue Sharing Persists in NFL Trust Debate,* STREET & SMITH'S SPORTS BUSINESS JOURNAL, Feb. 23, 2004, at 1 [hereinafter Kaplan, *Divide on Revenue Sharing*]; Farmer, *supra* note 45, at D1 (stating that New England, Washington, Dallas, and Tampa Bay have all established retail shops to sell team gear).

71. Kaplan, *Divide on Revenue Sharing, supra* note 70, at 1; Kaplan, *Tagliabue, supra* note 10, at 1.

72. Miller, *Revenue-sharing Rates, supra* note 11, at C3; see Jeff Duncan, *Licensing Deal to Continue As Is,* TIMES-PICAYUNE, Mar. 31, 2004, at 2. The statistics used above to illustrate the monetary value of licensing revenue shared in recent years were calculated under the NFL Trust not the Master Agreement, but overall numbers should not be significantly different under the Master Agreement.

73. Fatsis, *Dallas Owner, supra* note 10, at B3.

74. *Id.*

75. *Id.*

76. *Id.*; see Miller, *Revenue-sharing Rates, supra* note 11, at C2.

77. Miller, *Revenue-sharing Rates, supra* note 11, at C2. Oakland Raiders President Amy Trask articulated the Raiders' position when she said, "our general counsel has advised the league that on April 1 [2004] the right to our marks and logos reverts to us." Kaplan, *Tagliabue, supra* note 10, at 1.

78. Fatsis, *Dallas Owner, supra* note 10, at B3 (mentioning that Jones said that turning over marketing rights to the League has been an individual club decision in the past, and quoting Jones as saying, "[league-wide deals] are well and good as long as each club, of its own volition, participates in those deals . . . . I'm saying I have my logos and marks and can do what I want with them.").

79. *Id.*

80. Miller, *Revenue-sharing Rates, supra* note 11, at C2.

81. Kaplan, *Tagliabue, supra* note 10, at 1.

82. *Id.*

83. *Id.*; Daniel Kaplan, *Texans Lead The NFL in Marketing Statewide*, STREET & SMITH'S SPORTS BUSINESS JOURNAL, Sept. 13, 2004, at 3 [hereinafter Kaplan, *Texans Lead*].

84. Kaplan, *Tagliabue, supra* note 10, at 1; Kaplan, *Texans Lead, supra* note 83, at 3.

85. *See* discussion *infra* Part III.B for a description of the widening revenue gap in the NFL and its potential consequences for the success of the League.

86. Fatsis, *Dallas Owner, supra* note 10, at B3.

87. *Id.*

. . . .

91. CBA, *supra* note 11, art. XXIV, 1(a)(i)(1)-(2) (emphasis added); see NFL CONST. art. 10.3 (stating, "all regular season (and preseason network) television income will be divided equally among all member clubs of the League"); Fatsis, *Can Socialism Survive?, supra* note 4, at R2.

92. *See* CBA, *supra* note 11, art. XXIV, 1(a)(i), (iii); Mullick, *supra* note 1, at 15-17.

93. *See* discussion *infra* Part III.A explaining the role that unshared non-ticket luxury box revenue plays in the revenue sharing system.

94. NFL CONST. art. 19.1(A).

95. *See* Alan Ostfield, *Seat License Revenue in the National Football League: Shareable or Not?*, 5 SETON HALL J. SPORT L. 599, 604 n.22 (1995) (stating that for the $30,000 option to kick in, gross receipts would have to be less than approximately $89,000, which is extremely unlikely considering that the average gross receipts for 1990–1995 was around $1.5 million).

96. *Id.* at 603-04.

97. NFL CONST. art. 19.1(A)(1)-(2).

98. *See* Ostfield, *supra* note 95, at 603-04.

99. *Id.*

100. NFL, NFL Res. G-1 (2001) (stating that "the term 'visiting team share' shall mean the portion of gross receipts currently required (in the absence of a waiver) to be paid to visiting clubs under Article 19.1(A) of the NFL Constitution and By-Laws in respect of regular season games").

101. *See* discussion *infra* Part III.B for a detailed analysis of the NFL's current economic inequality.

102. Fatsis, *Can Socialism Survive?, supra* note 4, at R1.

103. Farmer, *supra* note 45, at D1; Miller, *Revenue-Sharing Rates, supra* note 11, at C3; Mullick, *supra* note 1, at 12.

104. Jarrett Bell, *NFL Tug-of-War, supra* note 14, at C1.

105. Fatsis, *Can Socialism Survive?, supra* note 4, at R1.

. . . .

107. Mullick, *supra* note 1, at 12.

108. *See* Fatsis, *Can Socialism Survive?, supra* note 4, at R1-R2.

109. *See* Mullick, *supra* note 1, at 14-18.

110. Fatsis, *Can Socialism Survive?, supra* note 4, at R2.

111. CBA, *supra* note 11, art. XXIV, 1(a)(iii). The language "other than that included in subsection 1(a)(i)(1)" is referring to "ticket revenue from 'luxury boxes' . . . subject to gate receipt sharing." *Id.*

112. *See* discussion *infra* Part III.B explaining that unshared local revenue has been a major cause of the widening revenue gap.

113. *See* Fatsis, *Can Socialism Survive?, supra* note 4, at R6-7; Mullick, *supra* note 1, at 14-18.

114. *See* Fatsis, *Can Socialism Survive?, supra* note 4, at R4; Mullick, *supra* note 1, at 14-18. *See* discussion *infra* Part III.C describing the League's efforts to facilitate the construction of new stadiums.

. . . .

117. *See* Gavin Power, *Luxury Boxes Do Score Big*, S.F. CHRONICLE, June 24, 1995, at D1.

118. *See* Mullick, *supra* note 1, at 16-17.

119. *See Giants Want A Stadium That Says 'Amenities,'* N.Y. TIMES, Feb. 13, 2005, 8, at 1 [hereinafter *Amenities*, N.Y. TIMES].

. . . .

125. Bell, *NFL Tug-of-War, supra* note 14, at 2-3C.

126. *See* Mullick, *supra* note 1.

127. Don Nottingham, *Keeping the Home Team at Home: Antitrust and Trademark Law as Weapons in the Fight Against Professional Sports Franchise Relocation*, 75 U. COLO. L. REV. 1065, 1078–79 (2004).

. . . .

137. *See id.* at 1070.

138. *Id.*

139. *Id.*

140. *Id.*

141. From speaking with Steve Underwood, the Executive Vice President, General Counsel and Executive Assistant to the Owner of the Tennessee Titans, the author has gained firsthand knowledge of the significance that NFL insiders place on the current financial void left by the League's inability to place a franchise in the nation's second largest market, Los Angeles.

142. Fatsis, *Can Socialism Survive?, supra* note 4, at R2.

. . . .

145. Bell, *NFL Tug-of-War, supra* note 14, at 1C

146. *Id.* at 3C. For a detailed discussion of the Giants stadium situation *see supra* text accompanying notes 120–121.

. . . .

153. *See* Fatsis, *Can Socialism Survive?, supra* note 4, at R6; Bell, *NFL Tug-of-War, supra* note 14, at 4C.

154. Fatsis, *Can Socialism Survive?, supra* note 4, at R6.

155. *Id.*

156. *Id.*

157. *Id.* at R1-R3.

158. *Id.* at R3.

159. *Id.* at R1. The four major leagues are baseball, basketball, football, and hockey.

. . . .

161. *See* Fatsis, *Can Socialism Survive?, supra* note 4, at R5; Bell, *NFL Tug-of-War, supra* note 14, at 1C-2C.

. . . .

164. *Id.* [Fatsis, *Can Socialism Survive?,*] at R6.

165. Bell, *NFL Tug-of-War, supra* 14, at 4C.

. . . .

. . . .

175. *See* discussion *supra* Part III.B.1.

176. *See* Miller, *Revenue-Sharing Rates, supra* note 11, at C2. As Colts owner, Jim Irsay argued, "There are many teams that realize they cannot go forward like this. It's become that big of an issue." Fatsis, *Can Socialism Survive?, supra* note 4, at R2-R3.

177. Fatsis, *Can Socialism Survive?, supra* note 4, at R6.

178. *Id.*

179. *See* discussion *supra* Part III.B.

180. *See supra* text accompanying notes 121–122.

181. NFL, NFL Res. G-3 (1999) [hereinafter NFL Res. G-3]; Fatsis, *Can Socialism Survive?, supra* note 4, at R4; Glenn Dickey, *Mayor Sets Stadium Deadline,* S.F. CHRONICLE, Oct. 24, 2004, at C1. The original G-3 plan established in Res. G-3 was set to expire after the 2002 NFL season, but the League extended and reaffirmed the G-3 Program in NFL Res. JC-1 (2003) retaining all of the original principal parameters set forth in Res. G-3.

182. NFL Res. G-3, *supra* note 181; NFL Res. JC-1 (1) (2003) [hereinafter NFL Res. JC-1] (stating "the League shall make a loan to the affected Club to support such project based on the amount that the affected Club has committed to such project as a private contribution (the 'Private Contribution')").

183. NFL Res. G-3, *supra* note 181; NFL Res. JC-1, *supra* note 182; Dickey, *supra* note 181, at C1.

184. NFL Res. G-3, *supra* note 181; NFL Res. JC-1, *supra* note 182; Dickey, *supra* note 181, at C1.

185. This arrangement provides the incentives for stadium construction at the expense of the revenue sharing system by funneling revenue away from the sharing system, and into the pockets of individual clubs.

186. NFL Res. G-3, *supra* note 181; NFL Res. JC-1, *supra* note 182; Dickey, *supra* note 181, at C1.

187. NFL Res. JC-1, *supra* note 182 (emphasis added).

188. Bell, *NFL Tug-of-War, supra* note 14, at 4C; Fatsis, *Can Socialism Survive?, supra* note 4, at R6; Miller, *Revenue-Sharing Rates, supra* note 11, at C2.

189. These statistics are derived from the observations of Harold Henderson, who is the NFL's Executive Vice President for Labor Relations. *See* Bell, *NFL Tug-of-War, supra* note 14, at 4C.

190. *Id.* Since 1990, the size of the revenue gap has increased by a factor of about twelve. Fatsis, *Can Socialism Survive?, supra* note 4, at R6.

192. Bell, *NFL Tug-of-War, supra* note 14, at 4C.

IMPACT OF REVENUE SHARING ON COMPETITIVE BALANCE

COMPETITIVE BALANCE IN TEAM SPORTS AND THE IMPACT OF REVENUE SHARING

Stefan Kesenne

One of the major concerns of league administrators in the professional team sports industry on both sides of the Atlantic has always been the competitive balance in the league. Although the empirical research does not always confirm the importance of a balanced competition (see Borland and MacDonald, 2003), it is generally accepted that an excessive imbalance in sports competitions will have a negative impact on spectator interest. In the literature, different measures have been proposed to improve the competitive balance. Among these regulations, revenue sharing has been the most controversial one. The proposition that revenue sharing does not affect the distribution of playing talent among profit maximizing teams, has been challenged by many sports economists since the article of Rottenberg (1956) and the formal proof of the proposition by Quirk and El Hodiri (1974).

In dealing with the impact of revenue sharing on competitive balance, it is important to realize that there are important structural differences between the US major leagues and the EU national leagues. The US leagues are closed monopoly leagues with no possibility of relegation or promotion and with a more or less constant supply of talent at a give[n] moment of time. US teams are playing more than just one home and one away game against other teams. Most US major leagues organize play-offs after the regular season. North America does not organize international championships for the winners of the national league championships, such as the Champions League or the UEFA cup *[now known as the Europa League]* in European soccer. Also, Europe does not have any kind of rookie draft system. Nevertheless, the analysis in this review applies to both league structures if a few important differences are taken into account as will be discussed below.

The aim of this paper is to present an overview of the main findings from economic theory regarding the competitive balance in a league and the impact of revenue sharing. No discussion of the empirical evidence is included. In the next sections, we start with the basic model specification. In the following sections, the main determinants of competitive balance and the impact of revenue sharing are analysed and some policy implications are discussed. The last section concludes.

MODEL SPECIFICATION

The model describes a single monopoly league in professional team sports. The clubs are located in large or small markets, where they hold a local monopoly position. Relocation is excluded. Clubs are wage takers on a competitive player market. The season revenue of each club depends on three important variables: the size of the market, which affects the drawing potential of the club for supporters and players, the winning percentage of the team, because supporters prefer to watch a winning team, and the uncertainty of outcome. Spectators' interest and match attendance are assumed to fade if the winning percentage of a team becomes too high so that there is not enough uncertainty of outcome. The winning percentage of a team depends on its relative playing strength, which is a function of the number of playing talents of the team compared with the other teams in the league. On the cost side, the total season cost of a club consists of the cost of capital and the cost of playing talent.

. . . .

[I]nitially, the winning percentage has a positive but decreasing marginal effect on club revenue, but that the effect can turn negative in case of an excessive competitive imbalance.

. . . .

COMPETITIVE BALANCE AND REVENUE SHARING

The most important factor that affects the competitive balance in a league is the difference in the size of the market where the clubs are located. The larger the market, in terms of population size and density, the larger a team's drawing potential for spectators and players. However, it is obvious that many other factors affect the competitive balance in a league, and the impact of revenue sharing. . . . Four major factors will be discussed:

- the objectives of the clubs
- the spectator preferences
- the specifics of the sharing arrangement
- the hiring strategies of clubs

The Objectives of the Clubs

In the US literature, the usual assumption is that all clubs are profit maximizers, meaning that they are trying to maximize the difference between total season revenue and total season cost (see Noll, 1974; Scully, 1989; Fort and Quirk, 1995) . . . However, some European sports economists assert that professional soccer clubs are utility maximizers (see Sloane, 1971). A more operational variant of the utility maximization assumption is called win maximization. Kesenne (1996, 2000) argues that clubs are trying to maximize their winning percentage under the breakeven constraint or a given profit or loss rate. A club can be profitable without being a profit maximizer. The only way to maximize the winning percentage is to maximize the playing talent of the team. . . .

In addition, economists in the US have their doubts about the profit maximizing assumption in the major leagues (see Zimbalist, 2003). Rascher (1997) introduced a model assuming that professional sports clubs are maximizing a linear combination of profits and wins. . . . In addition, this utility maximization model allows a club to be profitable without being a profit maximizer.

These different club objectives have an important impact on the competitive balance in a league. To show this, we will consider only the two extreme cases of profit maximization and win maximization . . . assuming that clubs only differ in the objectives of the owners, one can derive that the distribution of talent is more unequal if all clubs are win maximizers, compared with a league where all clubs are profit maximizers.

. . . .

If clubs are profit maximizers, the linear demand curves for talent are given by the marginal revenue (MR). The marginal revenue is the extra revenue of one more talent in the team; profit maximizing clubs are only interested in hiring more talent if the extra revenue is higher than the unit cost of talent. . . .

The linear demand functions of a win maximizing club are given by average revenue (AR). The average revenue is the revenue per unit of talent. If clubs are win maximizers under the breakeven condition, they will hire talent until the average revenue equals the unit cost of talent. . . . The distribution of talent . . . in a win maximization league is more unequal than in a profit maximizing league. It follows that regulations to cure the imbalance are more needed in a win maximization league. Moreover, it can be shown that, in a win maximization league, also total league revenue is lower than in a profit maximization league, where playing talent is more efficiently allocated. The distribution of playing talent in a win maximization league is causing a welfare loss. Players are employed in the team where their productivity is not at the highest possible level (see Kesenne, 2000). Another consequence of win maximization is that the unit cost of playing talent is higher . . . because win maximizing clubs spend all their revenue on talent so that the market demand for talent in higher.

. . . [T]he distribution of playing talent is different if one club is a profit maximizer and the other is a win maximizer. If the small market club is a win maximizer and the large market club is a profit maximizer, the competition will be more balanced. . .

The next question is how revenue sharing changes the distribution of talent. . . . It can be shown that, in a profit maximization league, gate revenue sharing does not affect the competitive balance (Rottenberg, 1956; Quirk and El Hodiri, 1974; Fort and Quirk, 1995). All clubs equally reduce their demand for talent, because they all have to share the extra match revenue from an extra talent with each visiting club. Consequently, also the unit cost of talent goes down. . . .

In a win maximization league, however, it can be easily seen that revenue sharing improves the competitive balance. Given the breakeven constraint, the small market club will increase its demand for talent as long as it benefits from the sharing arrangement, while the large market club lowers its talent demand. The impact of revenue sharing on the equilibrium unit cost of talent in a win maximization league is less obvious. Because the large market club reduces its demand for talent and the small market club increases its demand for talent, the outcome depends on the relative size of the demand shifts. Because the downward shift of the demand curve of the large market club is smaller than the upward shift in the small market club, the unit cost of talent will go up. The reason is that revenue sharing moves the distribution of talent in the direction of the profit maximization equilibrium, where total league revenue is at its maximum level given the efficient allocation of talent. An alternative explanation is that the large market club has more talent.

. . . .

The Spectator Preferences

When clubs only differ in market size, the large market club dominates the small club in terms of talent. However, clubs can also differ in the preferences of their supporters for a more balanced competition. . . . it is possible that the small market club dominates the large market club. An important implication of this situation is that, if the small market team dominates, the distribution of playing talent in a profit maximization league is more unequal than in a win maximization league (see Kesenne, 2004a).

. . . .

This situation has consequences for the impact of gate revenue sharing. In a profit maximization league, the proposition still holds that revenue sharing does not change the distribution of talent. In a win maximization league, gate revenue sharing still improves the competitive balance but,

in this situation, now the ill-performing large market club profits from the sharing arrangement to the disadvantage of the well-performing small market club. The reason is that the small market club has the largest budget if it dominates the large market club. Moreover, in this scenario, gate revenue sharing implies a loss of total league revenue, because the distribution of talent is moving away from the most efficient allocation of talent.

. . . . the interest of spectators can also be influenced by the absolute quality of the teams (see Marburger, 1997) or by the winning percentage of the visiting team. Certainly in the small European countries, where many supporters travel with their team to watch the away games, the winning percentage of the visiting team can be an important determinant of club revenue. . . .

The Specifics of the Sharing Arrangement

The two most important sharing arrangements, gate sharing and pool sharing, can have a different impact on competitive balance. A gate sharing arrangement implies that the revenues from the ticket sales of every single match are shared between the home and the visiting club. . . . The 60/40 gate sharing in NFL (the National Football League in the US) is the best example of this kind of arrangement.

In a simplified pool sharing system, all clubs contribute a certain percentage of their total season revenue in a pool, which is managed by the league and equally distributed among all clubs. . . .

The sharing of broadcasting rights in the North American major leagues and in most European national soccer leagues are examples of this sharing arrangement. However, both sharing systems are identical, apart from the value of the share parameter, if there are only 2 clubs in the league, but they clearly differ in the realistic case of more than 2 teams. It is also possible that some club revenues are not shared. Fort and Quirk (1995) have shown that . . . gate sharing can also worsen the competitive balance if some club revenues, such as local broadcasting rights, are not shared. Kesenne (2001) has shown that . . . gate sharing improves the competitive balance in a profit maximization league, whereas pool sharing does not change the balance.

In a win maximization league, revenue sharing always improves the competitive balance, whatever the specifics of the sharing arrangement. Nevertheless, if an imbalance shows up where the small market club dominates the large market club, revenue sharing punishes the well-performing small market team and lowers total league revenue. Therefore, one might consider another sharing system, which is not based on the size of the budget, but on the size of the market. . . . In this case, money is taken away from the large market club and given to the small market club. This sharing arrangement not only has the advantage of establishing a more balanced competition in the scenario where the large club dominates the small market clubs, it also avoids the disadvantage that the small market club is punished for performing better than the large market club. Moreover, this sharing arrangement always increases total league revenue by reducing the welfare loss, because it moves the win maximization equilibrium closer to the profit maximization equilibrium. . . .

The Hiring Strategies of Clubs

In most studies, to the best of our knowledge, the explicit or implicit assumption is made that the supply of talent is constant (Quirk and El-Hodiri, 1974; Fort and Quirk, 1995; Vrooman, 1995). Moreover, it is assumed that team managers also take the constant supply into account when hiring new talent, because they know that one extra talent not only strengthens the own team, but also weakens another team in the league. . . .

In a recent paper, however, Szymanski and Kesenne (2004) argue that the constant-supply approach is not a realistic option in Europe with its many open national soccer leagues, certainly after the Bosman verdict of 1995 by the European Court of Justice in Luxemburg, which established a free move of players between the countries of the European Union. Given the increased international player mobility in Europe, the supply of talent in each national league is variable. But even if the supply is constant, it is questionable if it can or will be fully internalized in the hiring decisions of the owners. Moreover, it is more realistic to assume that the hiring strategy of one team depends on the strategy of the other teams, which is a scenario that should be approached by game theory. . . . The explanation can be found in the negative external effects that clubs cause on each other when hiring new talent. In the competitive equilibrium approach, it is implicitly assumed that these external effects are fully internalized, that is, they are taken into account in the hiring decisions of the clubs, so that they are neutralized. In the game theoretic approach, these externalities are not internalized. Because the large club has a higher marginal revenue, the negative external effect that the small club causes on the large club is larger than the external effect that the large club causes on the small club, so that the small club is better off in the game theoretic approach.

. . . .

[O]ne can see that the win maximization league shows a more unbalanced competition than the profit maximization league.

. . . Szymanski (2003) has also shown that revenue sharing improves the competitive balance if the sharing arrangement is such that a fixed sum is contributed to a prize fund awarded to the winning team. Again, revenue sharing improves the competitive balance if clubs are win maximizers. As long as the sharing arrangement implies that money is transferred from the large budget club to the small budget club, it causes an upward shift of the small club's average revenue curve and a downward shift of the large club's average revenue curve.

DISCUSSION AND POLICY IMPLICATIONS

If a reasonable degree of competitive balance is important for spectators, what can league administrators conclude from the findings of economic theory regarding the impact of revenue sharing? One of the first things to find out is if clubs are profit or win maximizers. So far, the empirical tests have not been of great help. All tests, based on the ticket pricing rule or the size of the price elasticity, do not reject the hypothesis of profit maximization, but they do not reject the win maximization hypothesis either, because the pricing rules turn out to be the same in both scenarios (Kesenne, 2002).

In general, the case for revenue sharing in a profit maximization league is not very strong. In the benchmark scenario of Rothenberg (1956) and Quirk and El Hodiri (1974), revenue sharing does not affect the competitive balance. Moreover, the distribution of talent is optimal if clubs are profit maximizers, so that revenue sharing, which leads to a less efficient allocation of talent, is not needed. So far, to the best of our knowledge, the impact of revenue sharing in the most realistic scenario has not been analysed. This scenario should include a league with more than 2 clubs, where club revenue is affected by both the winning percentage of the home and the visiting team, where the revenue sharing system is based on the sharing of gate receipts, the pool sharing of broadcasting rights and the non-sharing of some other revenue, and where the talent supply can be fixed or flexible, but analysed in an appropriate game theoretic setting. Some partial results, taking onto account deviations from the benchmark case, show that revenue sharing can improve or worsen the competitive balance, which leads to the general conclusion that the impact of revenue sharing on the competitive balance can be expected to be rather limited in the profit maximization scenario.

According to most American economists, this scenario seems to apply to the North American major leagues, where clubs are assumed to be profit maximizers, and the supply of talent is constant and internalized into the hiring strategy of the owners. Some club revenues are shared, like gate receipts in NFL (National Football League) and MLB (Major League Baseball). Also federal broadcasting rights are pooled and redistributed, while local television rights are not shared.

If all clubs are win maximizers, the theory shows that revenue sharing is effective in establishing a more balanced distribution of talent among large and small market clubs. Moreover, it can be expected that, without any sharing, the distribution of talent in a win maximization league is more unequal than in a profit maximization league. Also, the distribution of talent without sharing is suboptimal in terms of total league revenue, because of the inefficient allocation of talent among clubs. In the national soccer leagues in Europe, where clubs are assumed to behave more like win maximizers, revenue sharing will be even more appropriate after the abolition of the transfer system by the Bosman verdict. The small market clubs, being net-sellers of talent on the transfer market, complain about a dramatic loss of revenue. If the transfer market has partially functioned as a redistribution system between large and small market clubs, revenue sharing might remedy the weak financial position of the small market clubs. However, in European football, the combination of national leagues and the European Champions League is a serious obstacle to any revenue sharing arrangement on the national level. In the small football countries, like Holland or Belgium, the big clubs are not willing to share revenue with the small clubs, because this will further weaken their position in the Champions League where they have to face the rich clubs of the Big Five (England, Spain, Italy, Germany and France). The growing gap between the Big Five and the other European countries, on the one hand, and the growing gap between the bigger and the smaller clubs in the national leagues, on the other hand, is a serious threat to the competitive balance and the health of European football.

CONCLUSION

The competitive balance in a league, which mainly depends on the distribution of playing talent among clubs, has been a central issue in the economics of professional team sports. It turns out that the size of the market is the most important, but not the only factor affecting the talent distribution. Also the objectives of the clubs, the supporters' preferences, the talent supply conditions and the specific sharing arrangements can affect the competitive balance and the impact of revenue sharing. A survey of the economic theory suggests that revenue sharing in a profit maximization league can be expected to have only a minor impact on competitive balance, whereas revenue sharing in a win maximization league clearly improves the competitive balance.

References

. . . .

Borland J., & Macdonald R., (2003), Demand for Sport, *Oxford Review of Economic Policy*, 19(4), 478–502.

Fort R., & Quirk J. (1995), Cross-subsidization, incentives and outcomes in Professional Team Sports Leagues, *Journal of Economic Literature* XXXIII, 1265–1299.

. . . .

Kesenne S., (1996), League Management in Professional Team Sports with Win Maximizing clubs, *European Journal for Sport Management*, 2(2), 14–22.

Kesenne S., (2000), Revenue Sharing and Competitive Balance in Professional Team Sports, *Journal of Sports Economics*, 1(1), 56–65.

Kesenne S., (2001), The different impact of different sharing systems on the competitive balance in professional team sports, *European Sports Management Quarterly*, 1(3), 210–218.

Kesenne S., (2002), Club *Objectives and Ticket Pricing in Professional Team Sports*, Research Paper 2002-018, Economics Department, University of Antwerp.

Kesenne S., (2004a), Competitive Balance and Revenue Sharing when rich clubs have poor teams, *Journal of Sports Economics*, 5(2), 206–212.

. . . .

Marburger D., (1997), Gate Revenue Sharing and Luxury Taxes in Professional Sports, *Contemporary Economic Policy*, XV(2), 114–132.

Noll R., (ed), (1974), *Government and the Sports Business*, Washington DC: Brookings Institution.

Quirk J., & El Hodiri M., (1974), 'The Economic Theory of a Professional Sports League', in: Noll, R. Editor, *Government and the Sport Business* (pp. 33–88). Washington DC: Brookings Institution.

Rascher D., (1997), A Model of a Professional Sports League, in: Hendricks, W. Editor, *Advances in the Economics of Sport, vol. 2,* (pp. 27–76), London: Jai Press Inc.

Rottenberg S., (1956), The Baseball Players' Labor Market, *Journal of Political Economy*, 64(3), 242–258.

Sloane P., (1971), The Economics of Professional Football, the Football Club as a Utility Maximiser, *Scottish Journal of Political Economy*, 17(2), 121–146.

Scully G., (1989), *The Business of Major League Baseball*, Chicago: University of Chicago Press.

Szymanski, S., (2003), The Economic Design of Sporting Contests, *Journal of Economic Literature*, XLI (December), 1137–1187.

Szymanski S., & Kesenne S. (2004), Competitive balance and gate revenue sharing in team sports, *Journal of Industrial Economics*, LII(1), 165–177.

. . . .

Vrooman J, (1995), A general theory of professional sports leagues, *Southern Economic Journal*, 61(4), 971–990.

Zimbalist, A. (2003), Sport as Business, *Oxford Review of Economic Policy*, 19(4), 503–511.

Discussion Questions

1. Describe the revenue sharing agreements in each of the four major professional sports leagues.
2. Are the current revenue sharing arrangements in each league optimal or suboptimal? Explain.
3. What is the ideal amount of revenue sharing for a league to engage in? Explain.
4. Why do owners seek to undermine league welfare by not complying with league policies?
5. How much revenue is shared in each league?
6. Why should revenue be shared among the teams in a league?
7. Is there an economic justification underlying revenue sharing? How can the problems associated with revenue sharing be overcome?
8. Sheehan's tax plan calls for the taxing of those teams that are not competitive. What are the reasons for doing this? Would this be effective? Why or why not?

9. How did Commissioner Rozelle ensure a stable ownership of NFL franchises? Is this still effective today? Why or why not?

10. In each professional sports league, where does the majority of team revenue come from? Will revenue continue to grow? Why or why not?

11. What are some of the differences in how American and European leagues handle issues of competitive balance?

12. What are some ways that leagues can protect against free-riding, "profit-taking" owners who would threaten competitive balance?

13. If you were starting up a new league, which revenue streams would you share? Which would you leave to the individual clubs? What incentives would motivate your decisions?

14. When determining who should get revenue sharing funds, should leagues focus on teams' total revenues (NHL model) or profitability (NBA)? What incentives does each plan create?

15. What are the financial interests of a rich team subsidizing one or more of its poor brethren in a league?

16. Open leagues can rely on carrots (revenue sharing) and sticks (relegation) to promote competition. Is this a more effective way of ensuring competitive balance? Why or why not?

17. Does Richard's Sheehan's "loser tax" fix the free-rider problem in league revenue sharing, or does it take tax money from a rich team's right pocket and transfer it to its left pocket?

18. As teams and leagues find additional revenue streams, how should those streams be treated for purposes of revenue sharing? Should leagues try to find a common standard for all future revenue streams, or deal with each new one as it arises?

19. Now that the NFL is a multibillion-dollar industry, is it still reasonable to ask big-market clubs to share lucrative revenue streams for the good of "League Think"? If not, how would you incentivize these owners to continue to act for the good of the league?

20. If a team/city has a rabid fan base that will pay more for a good team, should its teams have more money to spend in order to reward that support?

21. If NFL teams share revenues, should they also share debt (particularly from new stadium construction that increases team revenues)? Is the G-3 program a sufficient sharing mechanism in this way?

22. Does equitable distribution of revenues necessarily lead to equitable distribution of talent?

23. What other factors besides revenue sharing can affect competitive balance?

24. How can revenue sharing solve competitive imbalance if, in Kesenne's words, some teams are "profit maximizers" and others are "win maximizers"?

25. How can you determine if an owner is a profit maximizer, a win maximizer, or some combination of the two?

26. How are revenue sharing decisions in international sports (such as soccer) affected when multiple leagues compete against each other for talent?

Teams

INTRODUCTION

Hundreds of teams are competing in sports leagues throughout the United States, and thousands more are competing globally. Revenues generated by sports leagues can be divided into two very broad categories: (1) national (and global) revenues that are shared equally by all of the teams in the league and (2) local revenues generated by each individual team that are retained, in large part, by that individual team.

Like franchises in many other industries, professional sports franchises are typically granted an exclusive geographic territory by the league in which they play that is theirs to exploit. These home territories range from a 50-mile radius from the home city in the NHL to a 75-mile radius from the home playing facility in the NFL, NBA, and MLB.

The market in which a team plays obviously has an enormous impact on its local revenue-generating capability. Every city is different, and this is manifested in the team's ability to monetize the local market. As one travels to various cities across the United States, the differences are readily apparent. New York, Green Bay, San Diego, and Detroit are all very different places, yet their teams compete against one another and they are allowed to generate revenues in their local marketplaces. The size of the market and fan avidity in those marketplaces varies greatly.

Like all businesses, professional sports teams are always attempting to increase their revenues. But the fact that teams come together in the context of a league makes for an interesting dynamic. Teams with a larger revenue-generating potential sacrifice some of their upside for the betterment of the league as a whole. This is effectuated by the presence of league-wide agreements in a variety of areas, from the creation of defined home territories to revenue-sharing programs. Thus, a fundamental tension exists between the

teams that try to push the envelope of league rules as far as possible (and sometimes even break them), and the league offices, which attempt to control these aggressive behaviors. The first article by Jack Williams discusses potential revenue streams for professional teams.

These local revenues are extremely important to the financial fortunes of each team. Sports fans are tribal in nature and are passionate about their teams. Fans disproportionately support their hometown teams over out-of-market teams, and fan avidity is strongest in the local market. In short, fans "root, root, root for the home team." Teams monetize this passion in their local market through a number of different means. Local revenues are typically generated through ticket sales; stadium-related revenues, such as luxury and club seating premiums, stadium club fees, and facility naming rights fees; concessions and parking revenues and other revenues derived from the facility on game and nongame days; local media rights deals with local cable and broadcast television outlets and radio stations; local advertising and sponsorship sales; and sales of novelties, programs, and merchandise sold in the stadium and at team-owned stores. National revenues are generated through league-wide media rights deals with national broadcast, cable, satellite, and radio companies; revenues generated by league-owned sports networks; digital media revenues realized through league and team Web sites; league-wide sponsorship deals; consumer products and licensing; league events and the hospitality surrounding them; and all international revenues generated by the league and its teams.

Extrapolating from the Green Bay Packers 2008 annual report, distribution of non-media-related national revenues in the NFL in 2007 totaled nearly $1.1 billion. Distribution of media-related national revenues was $2.8 billion. (See **Table 1** for an overview of the Green Bay Packers' finances.) The importance of each revenue source varies both by league and by team, as does the relative importance

Table 1   Green Bay Packers Financials, 2007

Revenues Source	Amount
National TV revenue	$87.5 million
Road-game share	15.1 million
Other national NFL revenue	32.9 million
Local revenue	105.8 million
Total Revenue	**$241.3 million**
Expenses	
Operating expenses	219.9 million
Player Expenses	124.7 million
Operating Profit	**$21.4 million**

Source: Green Bay Packers 2008 Annual Report.

of local revenues in the overall league revenue mix. For example, local revenues comprise over three-quarters of MLB revenues due to the large number of games played; at the same time, they comprise less than half of NFL revenues because of the size of the national media contracts held by the league (a consequence of the league's popularity, the relatively small number of games played, and the fact that all games are broadcast nationally). NHL teams generated a combined $1.12 billion from regular season gate receipts alone in 2007–2008, a season in which the league generated a total of $2.56 billion. Ticket sales are the lifeblood of NHL franchises, because its national revenues, especially those from its national television contracts, are relatively low compared to other leagues. See **Table 2** for NHL team ticket revenues in 2006–2007 and 2007–2008. This chapter focuses on the primary revenue opportunities available to each team in the local market, its primary expenses, and the accounting issues faced by professional sports franchises.

As noted earlier, gate receipts are a key revenue driver for sports franchises. *Team Marketing Report* issues a seasonal report for each league that documents ticket prices across the league. According to its most recent reports, the average ticket price in the NFL in 2009 was $74.99, with the average for each team ranging from $160 for the Dallas Cowboys to $51 for the Buffalo Bills. The average ticket price in MLB in 2009 was $26.64, from the high of $73 charged for the average ticket to a New York Yankees game in their new stadium to a low of $14 charged by the Arizona Diamondbacks. In the NBA, the average ticket price was $49.47 in 2008–2009, with a high of $93 for the Los Angeles Lakers to a low of $24 for the Memphis Grizzlies. Finally, the average ticket to an NHL game cost $49.66 in 2008–2009, ranging from $76.15 for Toronto Maple Leafs tickets to $29.94 for the St. Louis Blues.[1] This highlights the difference in demand for the tickets for teams even within the same league. It is not surprising that very popular teams in markets where fan avidity is strong, such as New York, Dallas, and Toronto, can charge more for tickets than those less popular teams located in Phoenix, Memphis, and

Buffalo. Season tickets are immensely important for teams, because they provide annual upfront revenue that is guaranteed regardless of team performance and a myriad of other factors. Individual game sales and group sales comprise the remaining ticket sales. Demand for tickets to any one game is a function of a number of different factors—the won–loss record of the home team, team tradition, the presence of a superstar player, the quality of the visiting team, promotional giveaways, day of the week, weather, and perceived value. The article by Berri, Schmidt, and Brook examines the impact of star players on gate receipts in the NBA; the excerpt that follows by Lawson, Sheehan, and Stephenson looks specifically at the impact that David Beckham's arrival had on MLS ticket sales.

In order to drive attendance and increase revenues to lower-demand games, teams began to widely adopt variable ticket pricing schemes in the early 2000s. These pricing policies can be based on any number of different factors, including many of those that have already been noted. Beyond the

Table 2   NHL Ticket Revenue per Game

Team	2006–2007	2007–2008	% Change
Toronto	$1.5 million	$1.9 million	26.7
Montreal	1.3 million	1.7 million	30.8
Vancouver	1.1 million	1.4 million	27.2
Calgary	1 million	1.3 million	30
N.Y. Rangers	1.1 million	1.3 million	18.2
Ottawa	950,000	1.2 million	26.3
Edmonton	1 million	1.2 million	20
Minnesota	1 million	1.1 million	10
Colorado	1.05 million	1 million	−4.8
Detroit	1.1 million	1 million	−10
Philadelphia	1 million	1 million	0
Dallas	1 million	950,000	−0.5
San Jose	850,000	950,000	11.8
Anaheim	800,000	900,000	12.5
New Jersey	600,000	850,000	41.6
Columbus	850,000	800,000	−5.9
Pittsburgh	600,000	800,000	33.3
Tampa Bay	800,000	800,000	0
Boston	800,000	800,000	0
Buffalo	650,000	750,000	15.4
Carolina	700,000	700,000	0
Los Angeles	700,000	650,000	−7.1
St. Louis	450,000	600,000	33.3
Nashville	550,000	600,000	9
Washington	500,000	550,000	10
Atlanta	500,000	550,000	10
N.Y. Islanders	500,000	550,000	10
Chicago	350,000	500,000	42.8
Florida	500,000	500,000	0
Phoenix	550,000	450,000	−18.2
Total	**$24.8 million**	**$27.3 million**	**9.90%**

Source: Toronto Star graphic from NHL data. Reprinted with permission–Torstar Syndication Services.

primary ticket market composed of season, individual, and group sales, teams are attempting in varying degrees to monetize the secondary ticket market. Traditionally the prerogative of ticket scalpers and licensed ticket brokers, technological innovations and entrepreneurial endeavors have led to the creation of more transparent, and thus legitimate, secondary ticket markets. Teams and leagues have established their own secondary ticket markets and have struck marketing deals with established market leaders such as StubHub. In addition, recognizing that they have sacrificed millions of dollars in ticket revenues to suboptimal pricing models, savvy teams have used these secondary markets to gauge the inefficiencies in their pricing models and make the appropriate modifications in their pricing in subsequent seasons. The article by Rascher, McEvoy, Nagel, and Brown takes a deeper look at variable ticket pricing strategies in MLB.

Beyond gate receipts, teams can generate substantial revenues from their playing facilities. The recognition of these potential revenues leads to periodic facility-building booms across professional sports, including one that is currently approaching its end. Seeking to fully monetize their home contests, teams have sought to build stadiums and arenas funded as much as possible from public sources. The construction of a new facility is a transformational moment for a professional sports franchise, because it creates a host of new revenue streams. Beyond providing teams with the ability to substantially increase ticket prices, new revenues can be generated from the sale of naming rights to the facility; multiple-season leasing of luxury seating and other premium seating areas; seat licensing fees; the creation of lucrative marketing partnerships; the establishment of new concessions agreements with one of the dominant concessions companies and new parking arrangements with the appropriate body; and the possibility of hosting events at the facility on nongame days. **Table 3** examines the local revenues generated by the New Orleans/Oklahoma City Hornets during the 2006–2007 season.

Sports venue concessions in the United States are dominated by a handful of providers. Sports franchises that control the concessions environment in their facility either through ownership or by the terms of their lease typically outsource this function in order to focus on their core competencies. Aramark (31% market share), Levy Restaurants (19%), Centerplate (16%), and SportService (16%) dominate the marketplace, with the remainder divided among a number of smaller firms (9%) and teams that handle concessions in-house (9%).[2] Facility operators enter into long-term contracts with concessions companies that are granted the exclusive right to provide their products and services at the venue. The most common types of vendor contracts are profit-and-loss agreements, whereby the concessionaire receives all of the net sales and bears all of the expenses from providing its services at the facility; profit-sharing agreements, whereby the venue is paid a commission based on the concessionaire's profits at the venue; and management

Table 3 Oklahoma City/New Orleans Hornets Local Revenue, 2006–2007

Revenue Source	Amount
Season tickets	$28.7 million
Single-game and group tickets	1.5 million
Sponsorship/advertising	9.35 million
Suite sales	3.9 million
Club seats	1.35 million
Concessions	921,000
Merchandise	132,000
Parking	198,000
Other	6,000
Total Local Revenue	**$46.1 million (in OKC, $40.6 m; NO, $5.5 m)**

Source: New Orleans/Oklahoma City Hornets 2006–2007 statement of local revenue.
Note: 35 regular season games and 2 preseason games in Oklahoma City, 6 games in New Orleans.

fee agreements, whereby the concessionaire is paid a management fee for its services. In most of these contracts, the concessionaire pays the facility a significant upfront payment and agrees to upgrade the facility's concessions infrastructure. This can provide the franchise quite a windfall if it controls the concessions at the facility. The excerpt from Coates and Humphreys examines the relationship between the demand for attendance at MLB games and the prices of tickets and concessions.

A recent trend in stadium construction that teams are attempting to monetize whenever possible is to incorporate the facility into a larger real estate opportunity. The modern sports facility is typically part of a larger mixed-use project that incorporates residential housing, hotels, retail stores, restaurants, movie and music theaters, and bars into an entertainment zone that the team will participate in developing. Examples of this include the Staples Center in the AEG Live project in Los Angeles; Gillette Stadium in the Patriot Place development in Foxboro, Massachusetts; and proposed projects in Brooklyn (Atlantic Yards), Philadelphia, and St. Louis. The financing of each new stadium project is idiosyncratic; some locales are willing to provide a substantial amount of the funding for the project, whereas others are unwilling to provide anything beyond infrastructure. If such a thing exists, the typical deal of late involves a public–private partnership, with the project funded by both public and private financing. Chapter 7 explains stadium revenues and funding in great detail.

In addition to stadium-related revenues, the national and local sale of broadcast, cable, satellite, radio, and Internet rights can provide teams with vast amounts of revenue. (Chapter 8, which focuses on media, provides a wealth of information on this topic.) In the United States, the sale of national television rights through each league's current long-term deals provides the NFL with an average of $3.7

billion annually through 2013; the NBA with an average of $930 million per year through 2016; MLB with an annual average of $783 million through 2013; NASCAR with an average of $560 million until 2014; and the NHL with $72.5 million per annum through 2011. Thus, each NFL team receives an average of $115.6 million per year from the current national television deal; each NBA team receives $31 million; each MLB club gets $26.1 million; and each NHL team nets $2.4 million.

The media revenues available at the local level vary by team and league. NFL teams are generally limited in their ability to monetize local media, because the presence of the overarching national media deals leaves them with a limited inventory of local media opportunities, consisting of preseason television rights, regular season radio rights, and shoulder programming, such as pre- and post-game shows, coaches' shows, and youth-focused shows. MLB teams, in contrast, have substantial local media opportunities. *Forbes* estimated that in 2008 MLB teams earned a combined $690 million from local cable deals—an average of $23 million per team.[3] The revenues are top-heavy, with the top 10 teams generating $379 million. See **Table 4** for information on MLB's largest local media deals.

A number of teams own part or all of their regional sports networks, which offers tremendous revenue potential, because teams can receive part of the advertising dollars and subscriber fees that drive these businesses. For the Boston Red Sox, New York Yankees, Toronto Blue Jays, Cleveland Indians, Chicago Cubs, Chicago White Sox, Washington Nationals, Baltimore Orioles, San Francisco Giants, and New York Mets, this ownership is a windfall. Other teams receive a guaranteed rights fee for the sale of

their games, including the Los Angeles Angels of Anaheim, who receive an average of $40 million per year as part of their long term deal with FSN West.[4] The revenue disparity among MLB clubs in their local media deals is noteworthy, with teams in the lower third of the scale receiving a fraction of those in the top third.

The popularity of NBA and NHL teams allows them to similarly monetize their local media rights, though typically not nearly to the same degree as their MLB brethren. This is a function of the ratings generated (which, in turn, is a function of the popularity of the team in the local market) and there being half as many games played in each league (162 in MLB vs. 82 in the NBA and NHL).

Teams and leagues generate revenue through the sale of sponsorships at both the national and local levels. Sponsoring companies use the association, exposure, and ability to leverage their relationships with the team or league to achieve their marketing goals.[5] The sponsorship may entail a number of different elements, including advertising, grassroots marketing, hospitality, cause-related marketing, sales promotion, and public relations.[6] With various levels of sponsorships sold by leagues at the national level and by teams at the local level, there is ongoing debate about which categories of sponsorship, if any, should be reserved exclusively for either the teams or the leagues. Another issue is the degree of category exclusivity that should be provided at each level. Broad category exclusivity can be of great value to the sponsor. The NFL example is instructive. The league has a large number of sponsors at the league level, as seen in **Table 5**. Although the benefits of these deals vary, sponsors typically receive category exclusivity, the ability to use league marks in advertising and promotions, signage at league events, media exposure, and hospitality benefits. The NFL's sponsorships with Gatorade (isotonic beverage), Motorola (wireless telecommunications equipment), and Reebok (on-field apparel)—all of which appear on the playing field and/or sidelines—are exclusive to the league; that is, no team may sell sponsorships in any of these categories. These deals are quite lucrative: Gatorade pays the league a reported $45 million annually through 2011 for the sponsorship, Reebok pays over $30 million annually through 2012, and Motorola pays $50 million annually through 2011 to showcase a product that it does not even sell at retail—coaches' headsets! In the other categories, teams may sell sponsorships in their local markets alongside the league's national deals. In the most lucrative of these nonexclusive league deals, Anheuser-Busch pays a reported $200 million per year (including up to $50 million in cash rights fees and an additional $150 million in marketing, media, and team spending commitments) for its Bud Light brand to be the league's official beer from 2011–2016. This deal replaces the NFL's previous beer sponsorship with MillerCoors that paid a reported $100 million annually. At the team level, the sale of sponsorships similarly can be exclusive or nonexclusive. For example, in

Table 4 Baseball's 10 Largest Local Cable Deals

Team	Cable Deal Per Year	Cable Network
New York Yankees	$80 million	YES
New York Mets	52 million	SNY
Los Angeles Angels of Anaheim	40 million	FSN West
Detroit Tigers	33 million	FSN Detroit
Los Angeles Dodgers	31 million	Prime Ticket
San Francisco Giants	30 million	CSN Bay Area
Seattle Mariners	29 million	FSN Northwest
Arizona Diamondbacks	28 million	FSN Arizona
Baltimore Orioles	28 million	Mid-Atlantic Sports Network (MASN)
Washington Nationals	28 million	Mid-Atlantic Sports Network (MASN)

Source: Christina Settimi, "Baseball's Cable Kings," *Forbes*, April 22, 2009.

Table 5   NFL Sponsorships, 2009

Sponsor	Product or Service	Year Sponsorship Began
Bank of America	Team identified credit cards, official bank; NFL affinity credit cards	2007
Bridgestone	Automotive tires	2008
Campbell Soup	Soup, canned pasta, tomato food sauces, salsa, chili	1998
Canon USA	Cameras and equipment, binoculars and field glasses, photo printers, camcorders	1984
FedEx	Worldwide package delivery service	2000
Frito-Lay	Salted snacks, popcorn, peanuts and peanut products, salsa, dips	2000
Gatorade	Isotonic beverage	1983
General Motors	Passenger cars, passenger trucks	2001
IBM	Computer hardware and software, IT services	2003
Mars Snackfood	Chocolate and non-chocolate candy products	2002
MillerCoors	Beer	2002
Monster.com	Career services	2008
Motorola	Wireless telecommunications equipment	1999
National Dairy Council	Milk products	2003
National Guard	NFL High School Player Development	2009
News America	Super Bowl insert	1979
Pepsi	Soft drink	2002
Procter & Gamble (Prilosec OTC)	Over-the-counter heartburn medication, locker room products	2005
Samsung	Televisions, stereo and speaker components, DVD players and recorders	2005
Sprint	Wireless telecommunications services	2005
Ticketmaster	Online ticket exchange provider	2008
Tropicana	Juice	2002
Visa	Payment systems services	1995

Source: "NFL close to IBM renewal; Visa up next," *SportsBusiness Journal*, September 14, 2009. Used with permission of the National Football League.

2009 the Philadelphia Eagles had beer sponsorships with Miller Lite, Budweiser, and Heineken. Overall, the team had 45 sponsors at multiple levels in a number of different categories.

In addition to revenues generated directly from the aforementioned sources, professional sports franchises, leagues, and other sports properties realize significant monies through the sale of officially licensed products bearing their names, logos, and marks. In 2001, the NFL sold $2.5 billion of licensed products. MLB had sales of $2.3 billion, and NASCAR's sales were $1.2 billion. The NBA generated $1.0 billion, and the NHL sold $900 million of its goods. Collectively, the sale of sports-related products represented 14.9% of all licensed goods sold in the United States in 2001. This figure actually represents a decrease from previous years in the overall sales of sports-related licensed goods, which is likely attributable to both a shift in fashion trends and a downturn in the economy. The fickle nature of fashion can cause revenues to fluctuate, presenting a problem to professional sports leagues and franchises in that the uncertainty in the revenue stream can dissuade the entity from relying on the sale of licensed products in its budgeting process.

Licensees—the manufacturers of these products—typically pay the sports property a royalty fee ranging from 4 to 10% of the wholesale selling price of the goods (depending on the product) in exchange for the right to sell products containing league and team names, logos, and marks. These monies are paid by the licensees to each league's properties division. The respective properties division then pools the funds and distributes them equally across all league teams, similar to the manner in which revenues generated from the sale of national media rights are apportioned. So, although all teams benefit from the increased royalties generated from an increase in the sales of licensed products, there appears to be little incentive for an individual club to incur a significant amount of the cost of doing so, while reaping little of the benefit in the form of increased revenue. To overcome this obstacle, leagues have carved out exceptions to this general revenue sharing rule and typically allow teams to keep a disproportionate share of the proceeds generated from the sale of their licensed products where they also serve as the retailer, such as when selling in their playing facilities and at team-owned stores or when the sale occurs within a specific mile radius of this facility. See **Table 6** for the top-selling NFL player jerseys and **Table 7** for the top-selling NBA jerseys.

Despite these efforts, the general sentiment among popular clubs with strong licensed product sales, such as the Dallas Cowboys, is that they should not be forced to share the value of their brands with other, less popular clubs that

Table 6   Top-Selling NFL Player Jerseys, 2008

2008 Rank	Player	2008 Rank	Player
1	Jets QB Brett Favre	14	Bears LB Brian Urlacher
2	Cowboys QB Tony Romo	15	Falcons QB Matt Ryan
3	Giants QB Eli Manning	16	Giants RB Brandon Jacobs
4	Steelers S Troy Polamalu	17	Broncos QB Jay Cutler
5	Vikings RB Adrian Peterson	18	Steelers WR Hines Ward
6	Colts QB Peyton Manning	19	Bears WR Devin Hester
7	Cowboys RB Marion Barber	20	Cowboys LB DeMarcus Ware
8	Cowboys TE Jason Witten	21	Patriots WR Randy Moss
9	Chargers RB LaDainian Tomlinson	22	Redskins TE Chris Cooley
10	Steelers QB Ben Roethlisberger	23	Ravens QB Joe Flacco
11	Eagles RB Brian Westbrook	24	Bears RB Matt Forte
12	Patriots QB Tom Brady	25	Saints QB Drew Brees
13	Cowboys WR Terrell Owens		

Source: "Cowboys Rank as Top-Selling NFL Team; Favre Leads in Jersey Sales," *SportsBusiness Daily*, January 8, 2009. Used with permission of the National Football League.

have lower brand value. Thus, the manner in which revenues from licensed products are allocated is likely to remain a matter of intraleague dispute. Although the net revenues received by each club from the sale of licensed products are approximated to be only several million dollars per year, the resolution of this debate is an important indicator of the future of revenue sharing in each league. (See **Tables 8** and **9** for a list of top merchandise sales by team in the NFL and NBA, respectively.)

On a percentage basis, team expenses are generally consistent across professional sports leagues. Player compensation is the biggest expense for every team in the NFL, NBA, NHL, and MLB. An extensive discussion of athlete compensation is found in Chapter 10. The second

largest expense for most teams is staff compensation. Head coaches' salaries have increased dramatically in the past two decades, as has the compensation (and quantity) of assistant coaches. Front office staffs have grown in size as teams have become much more complex organizations, and, although salaries are still much smaller than those of the coaches and players, they represent a sizable expense for most teams.

Every franchise has team and game-related expenses; that is, those expenses that are associated with team travel to away games and the cost of putting on home games. And, like every business, sports franchises have general and administrative expenses that arise. Teams also have marketing expenses that arise out of their marketing efforts, including the servicing of their numerous corporate partners.

Similar to many other businesses, sports franchises also have a research and development (R&D) expense. Here, the R&D function is called player development. Teams must scout amateur and professional players and pay for the salaries of the players and coaches in its minor league system.

Table 7   Top NBA Jersey Sales, 2008–2009

Rank	Player
1	Kobe Bryant (L.A. Lakers)
2	LeBron James (Cleveland Cavaliers)
3	Chris Paul (New Orleans Hornets)
4	Kevin Garnett (Boston Celtics)
5	Allen Iverson (Detroit Pistons)
6	Dwyane Wade (Miami Heat)
7	Paul Pierce (Boston Celtics)
8	Nate Robinson (New York Knicks)
9	Pau Gasol (L.A. Lakers)
10	Dwight Howard (Orlando Magic)
11	Derrick Rose (Chicago Bulls)
12	Ray Allen (Boston Celtics)
13	Steve Nash (Phoenix Suns)
14	Shaquille O'Neal (Phoenix Suns)
15	Carmelo Anthony (Denver Nuggets)

Source: NBA.com. Figure used with permission from NBA Properties, Inc. All Rights Reserved.

Table 8   Top Selling NFL Team Merchandise, 2008

2008 Rank	2007 Rank	Team
1	1	Cowboys
2	7	Giants
3	3	Steelers
4	N/A	Jets
5	4	Bears
6	2	Patriots
7	8	Redskins
8	9	Eagles
9	5	Packers
10	6	Colts

Source: "Cowboys Rank as Top-Selling NFL Team; Favre Leads in Jersey Sales," *SportsBusiness Daily*, January 8, 2009. Used with permission of the National Football League.

Table 9   Top NBA Team Merchandise Sales, 2008–2009

Rank	Team
1	Los Angeles Lakers
2	Boston Celtics
3	New York Knicks
4	Cleveland Cavaliers
5	Chicago Bulls
6	New Orleans Hornets
7	Phoenix Suns
8	Miami Heat
9	Detroit Pistons
10	San Antonio Spurs

Source: NBA.com. Figure used with permission from NBA Properties, Inc. All Rights Reserved.

Although college basketball and football programs serve as a no-cost player development system in the NBA and NFL, MLB and NHL teams have farm systems that require them to spend considerable sums on player development annually. NBA teams do subsidize their NBDL affiliates, and most NHL teams have one minor league affiliate (and some have two). However, most MLB teams have six minor league affiliates. MLB teams spend approximately $20 million on player development annually.[7]

Teams also have facility-related expenses. Rent payments, stadium upkeep and renovations, utility bills, and seating reconfigurations can all be part of the team's responsibility as a tenant. The amount depends entirely on the lease deal that the team has entered into. Teams that paid for part or all of their playing facility must service the debt on the facility, which can be onerous, depending on the amount and terms of the financing. More details on facility financing and expenses can be found in Chapter 7.

Facility construction and the purchase agreement are the two largest sources of debt for professional sports franchises. The acquisition of most teams is financed by debt. In 2008, NFL teams carried a combined $9 billion of debt, and MLB clubs carried over $5 billion in debt obligations. Although leagues have facilitated the debt financing process by establishing credit facilities that teams can borrow from, the leagues are wary of teams being weighed down by this debt. To that end, the leagues have enacted rules that restrict the amount of debt that teams can carry. MLB teams must have a 60–40 debt–value ratio (although there are some exceptions for teams in new stadiums), NBA teams are each limited to $175 million in debt, and NHL teams can carry debt up to 50% of the team's value. The article by Hill and Vincent takes a deep dive into the business of Manchester United, perhaps the top sports brand globally.

Like many other industries, the operations and financial results of professional sports franchises are highly seasonal in nature. Likewise, sports organizations are entities with inventories, production functions, research and development functions, and very high fixed costs that require significant capital. However, unlike other industries, the accounting practices of professional sports franchises vary significantly.

One common accounting issue for professional sports franchises involves the use of related-party transactions. The ownership of sports franchises by non-sports-related businesses and the nature of the sports industry have created numerous opportunities for these types of transactions. Typically, the presence of the nonsports business is used to lower the apparent profitability of the sports franchise in favor of improving the situation of the other, related businesses. This is problematic in that the tax liability of the sports franchise is lowered, and the team's financial outlook is distorted. A professional sports franchise with an operating profit may be able to claim a book loss. Paul Beeston, a Toronto Blue Jays executive, summed up how the use of related-party transactions can dramatically affect the book profits of a professional sports franchise: "Anyone who quotes profits of a baseball club is missing the point. Under generally accepted accounting principles, I can turn a $4 million profit into a $2 million loss and get every national accounting firm to agree with me."[8] This distortion has been the cause of much controversy, because the misleading financial picture has been relied upon by professional sports franchises in pursuit of new, publicly funded stadia and by professional sports leagues when negotiating collective bargaining agreements with athletes. Teams and leagues have argued that their dire financial status requires that other stakeholders make significant concessions in negotiations.

Although the use of related-party transactions is not an illegal practice per se, it has created animosity and mistrust and, consequently, has harmed the long-term relationships between the negotiating parties. As a result, the perception among many stakeholders is that the financial statements of sports franchises cannot be relied upon whether related-party transactions are being used or not. Given the recent spate of accounting scandals in the United States that have depleted consumer and investor confidence in big businesses across numerous sectors of the economy, it is imperative that the sports industry avoid a similar fate.

Excerpts from the SEC filing made by the publicly held parent company of the New Jersey Nets upon the announcement of its sale to Russian oligarch Mikhail Prokhorov provide a rare glimpse into the finances of an NBA franchise. The filing indicates a franchise in some financial distress. The Nets' gross revenues dropped nearly 20% from 2007 to 2009 due to the team's poor on-court performance and the recession. Although operating expenses also decreased during this period, the team suffered annual operating losses of $68.5 million and $68 million in the two most recent years.

Despite the relative financial strength of the professional sports industry compared to other industries, the financial failures of several franchises and leagues has led those entities to seek financial reorganizations. The Phoenix Coyotes filed for bankruptcy protection under Chapter 11 in

Table 10   Major Sports Team Bankruptcies Since 1969

Year	Team
2009	Phoenix Coyotes (Hockey)
2003	Buffalo Sabres (Hockey)
2003	Ottawa Senators (Hockey)
1998	Pittsburgh Penguins (Hockey)
1995	Los Angeles Kings (Hockey)
1993	Baltimore Orioles (Baseball)
1975	Pittsburgh Penguins (Hockey)
1970	Seattle Pilots (Baseball)
1969	Philadelphia Eagles (Football)

Sources: CNNmoney and East Valley Tribune.

2009 after incurring nearly $270 million in operating losses from 2004 to 2008. (See **Table 10** for a list of bankruptcies.) Such reorganization can be done either privately between the franchise and its creditors or publicly through Chapter 11 of the Bankruptcy Code. Although hardly a desirable outcome, it is important for sports industry leaders to understand the process of financial reorganization. In a selection found in the supplementary online materials, Timothy Cedrone gives a comprehensive explanation of this process in both England and the United States.

Notes

1. *Team Marketing Report,* "Fan Cost Index." Available at *http://www.teammarketing.com/fancost/* (accessed June 2009).

2. *ESPN The Magazine,* July 13, 2009, at 34.

3. Christina Settimi, "Baseball's Cable Kings," *Forbes,* April 22, 2009.

4. *Id.*

5. Steven M. McKelvey, "Sport Sponsorship," in Lisa Masteralexis and Carol Barr (eds.), *Principles and Practice of Sport Management* (3rd ed.). Sudbury, MA: Jones & Bartlett, 2008, at 338.

6. *Id.*

7. Andrew Zimbalist, "There's More than Meets the Eye in Determining Players' Salary Shares," *Sports Business Journal,* March 10, 2008, at A4.

8. Larry Millson, *Ballpark Figures: The Blue Jays and the Business of Baseball.* Toronto: McClelland & Stewart, 1987, at 137.

THE COMING REVENUE REVOLUTION IN SPORTS

Jack F. Williams

> *Along with the U.S. population, [sports'] fanbase has grown enormously in the last half century, as new professional leagues sprouted, media mushroomed, and professional sports became thoroughly assimilated into the entertainment industry. Fans are the geese who have laid the golden eggs for pro athletes, team owners, sports broadcasters. Meanwhile, that same flow of cash has altered the relationship between spectators and the contests. A newfound distance, which can verge on alienation, separates the audience from athletes and teams. Choices made within the sports and political establishments over the next few years may determine whether pro sports' dizzy growth continues, or if those golden orbs will turn into goose eggs.[1]*

Sports as a business has matured at an accelerating pace in the past two decades.[2] During this time period, participants in the business of sports have aggressively pursued alternative sources of revenue in an effort to drive earnings. These new sources are sought both to grow and stabilize revenue.[3] In large part, technology has been at the vanguard of the revenue revolution, allowing a level of fan interaction that has changed how we think about sports and the successful sports business plan. Traditionally, the sports

OVERVIEW

market consists of gate revenues for live sporting events; rights fees paid by broadcast and cable television networks and TV stations to cover those events; merchandising, which includes the selling of products with team or player logos; sponsorships, which include naming rights and payments to have a product associated with a team or league; and concessions. Currently, other revenue streams such as internet, satellite, or mobile phone subscriptions to sports events or programming are transforming sports into programming content designed as a means to secure greater revenue. These new sources bring with them a host of legal, financial, and business issues that will challenge our understanding about fundamental aspects of property law, privacy, publicity, and value. This paper will discuss both traditional and non-traditional revenue sources, the legal and business implications they create, and the need for a new business paradigm to address these issues and harness the new synergies the leveraging of existing and future technologies present.

I.   STATE OF THE BUSINESS OF SPORTS

Sports is big business.[4] Its present structures and attributes are well known.[5] . . . The focus in this article is on the sports entertainment sector. That sector includes professional and amateur sports teams and tournament sports. . . . The sports entertainment sector is comprised of various firms (i.e., clubs) that join together in leagues to provide similar, well-defined products and services (i.e., some form of competition, media, merchandise, etc.) through similar production methods (i.e., play the game).[6]

. . . .

II. TRADITIONAL SOURCES OF REVENUE

Traditionally, revenue platforms in the sports sector consist of: (1) gate revenues for live sporting events; (2) rights fees paid by broadcast and cable television networks and TV stations to cover those events; (3) merchandising, which includes the selling of products with team or player logos; (4) sponsorships, which include naming rights and payments to have a product associated with a team or league; (5) actual team ownership; and (6) concessions.[14] Following is a discussion of how those revenue platforms play out in the context of three professional sports leagues—the National Football League, Major League Baseball, and the National Basketball Association.

A. National Football League (NFL)[15]

Established in 1920, the National Football League (NFL) has emerged as the most stable of professional sports when it comes to controlled growth, revenue, and financial success.[16] . . .

. . . .

Unlike other industries, sports require the cooperation of all firms through the league and competition on the field of play. Although General Motors Corporation does not need Ford Motor Company to produce automobiles, the Atlanta Falcons need the Dallas Cowboys to produce football games. In an effort to theoretically bring greater competition to the field, the sports entertainment sector has sought various revenue models. The NFL has adopted a sourced approach to revenues: (1) retained revenues and (2) shared revenues.[26]

Retained revenues are generated and kept by each team; thus, retained revenues are not shared among teams in the NFL. . . . Retained revenues include the following:

• Sixty percent of the gate receipts from home games,[28]

• Naming rights,

• Sponsorships,

• Luxury suite revenue,

• Concessions, and

• Local broadcast rights.[29]

Shared revenues are allocated and shared across the teams in the NFL. . . . The primary sources of shared revenue include:

• National broadcast rights fees,[31]

• Forty percent of away game ticket sales,[32] and

• Licensing.[33]

NFL Properties, Inc., the marketing arm of the NFL, is also a major revenue source. . . . Revenue from NFL Properties activities is shared equally among all thirty-two teams, the league office, and NFL Charities.[35] Experts, however, have observed that this particular revenue stream may be stabilizing or possibly decreasing because of competition from other sports and consolidation among vendors that deal with NFL Properties.[36]

Finally, franchise values in the NFL have accelerated at an accelerating rate over the past three decades.

. . . .

B. Major League Baseball (MLB)[45]

The beginnings of baseball in America are shrouded in some mystery and considerable controversy.[46] Although most experts agree that baseball began in the United States in the mid-1800's, some trace the game back to American Indian stickball and some to the English game of rounders. Many wrongly trace the "invention" of baseball to Abner Doubleday. The legend goes that General Doubleday, Civil War hero, invented baseball in 1839 in Cooperstown, New York. However, in 1839, Doubleday was a cadet at West Point, living a very busy day with hardly the opportunity to play let alone invent a new game. Moreover, General Doubleday never took credit or even mentioned the game of baseball in his many personal journals.[47]

All early baseball players were amateurs. In 1869, that changed, and with it, the face of the game.[48] In that year, the Cincinnati Red Stockings paid its players becoming the first professional baseball team to publicly acknowledge that they actually paid their players, a practice that had existed surreptitiously for some time. By 1876, eight professional teams formed the National League. In 1900, eight teams formed the American League.[49] Although the Leagues increased the number of games per season over time, in 1961, the American League increased the number of games played each season by each team from 154 to 162.

. . . .

The attendance at MLB games has steadily increased along with ticket prices. . . . Each team in MLB generates its operating revenue through several sources.[57] These sources include the following:

• Regular season game receipts,

• Local television, radio, and cable contracts,

• Post Season (for those teams that qualify),

• Local operating revenue, and

• National revenue.[58]

. . . Presently, MLB teams are participating in a revenue sharing program. In accordance with the program, each team invests thirty-four [*now 31%*] percent of net local revenues into a pool. The pool is then divided among the teams.

Some teams are net contributors, that is, revenue sharing is a net liability, whereas, some teams are net recipients, that is, revenue sharing is a net asset.[60]

In MLB, when it comes to revenue sources, the gate is still king. Approximately forty percent to fifty percent of total revenue is traced to game receipts.[61] When one also considers other local revenues, including concessions, suites, and other game-day in-park revenue, the number increases to as much as sixty percent.[62] The gate receipts are shared with approximately eighty to ninety percent retained by the home team and the remaining ten to twenty percent going to the visiting team.[63]

. . . .

C.   National Basketball Association (NBA)[68]

. . . .

NBA attendance has grown steadily over the past decade. . . .

Unlike the other sports leagues considered in this article, NBA teams keep all home gate receipts and do not share with the visiting teams.[77] NBA television contracts also generate substantial revenues.[78] . . .

The NBA has also focused attention on licensing fees.

. . . .

D.   Other Revenue Sources

Smart financial and legal minds hover all around sports. Notwithstanding some notable setbacks, failures, and false starts, those folks that toil in these fertile fields have invented and developed several interesting revenue growth models. Most of these models build on traditional revenue sources, using those traditional sources as a platform from which to spring new growth models. The following section explores just a few of these revenue growth models.

1.   Architecture

Our first revenue source is a subtle but effective variant of the adage that "gate is king." Architects have captured something that we fans have known intuitively for some time. If you build a nice stadium, specifically designed and suited for the game at hand, the fan experience is more gratifying. Build a baseball field, construct a football stadium, erect a basketball arena, and watch the fan base grow. Multipurpose sports facilities are out, kind of ugly, and bad for revenue growth. A well-suited facility breeds fan gratification. That gratification translates into more at the gate - both in increased attendance and higher ticket prices.[88] What the architects and financial experts have also uncovered, not so intuitive to us fans, is that the smaller the stadium (within reason), the greater the gate.[89] The data suggest that the smaller the stadium, the smaller the number of seats; the smaller the number of seats, the more scare tickets become;

the more scare tickets become, the more a team can charge for those tickets.[90] Under the watchful eye of MLB, architects are working to get the supply-and-demand of stadium design at perfect balance.[91] Other sports should also consider this formula; bigger is not always better, at least from a revenue growth perspective.

2.   Luxury Suites and Club Seats

Our second revenue source simply seeks to retrofit existing stadiums or incorporate by design in new stadiums a new look and feel to the game that is business and corporate user-friendly. Luxury suites and club seats present a lucrative opportunity for increasing revenues.[92] According to some experts, these products represent one of the fastest growing revenue sources in sports.[93] New stadiums. . . are incorporating luxury seats in their design and construction.[94] Older stadiums are re-designing and retrofitting their present seats in an effort to convert them to luxury seats.[95]

Luxury suites, also known as luxury boxes, sky boxes, or executive suites, are private to semi-private rooms that ring the stadium and allow groups to mingle, schmooze, and at least occasionally watch the game either through the large window or balcony or on closed-circuit television. As mentioned these suites are lucrative, allow the team to increase revenue per seat, and hook corporate sponsors.[96] Club seats, also referred to as premium seats, do not offer the privacy or most of the amenities of the luxury suite, but are usually more comfortable, often come with service at your seat, and usually have some of the best sight lines in the stadium.[97]

. . . It is not unusual for a team to offer several grades of luxury suites based on size, location, and amenities, in order to capture even greater premiums. . . .

3.   Pay-Per-View

Professional sports franchises are adding to their revenue through pay-per-view (PPV) contracts with local networks and cable companies.[103] Revenues from PPV have increased dramatically from a humble $435 million in 1991 to $3 billion in 2000.[104] This is, by all accounts, a virtually untapped revenue resource.

An extension of the PPV platform is to offer the Super Bowl and World Series on PPV in addition to those marquee sports events' regular network broadcasting. The PPV version could offer different angles, additional content, trivia contests, on-field sound, and the like.

4.   Satellite Radio

Professional sports have found a new home on satellite radio. These satellite broadcast providers look to sports to provide content that attracts listeners and advertisers. Fans love satellite broadcast. It allows them the opportunity to follow their home teams even when their employment requires that they change "homes." This revenue platform is also relatively untapped. Watch for professional sports leagues to enter into the market with a greater presence. Also, watch for the possibility that a professional sports league or combination of leagues explore or consider purchasing their own satellite broadcast company. Imagine the NFL, MLB, and NBA entering into a joint agreement in order to reduce start-up costs and tap an even greater audience with greater league control. Armed with ready-made content, we may witness the revenue race thrusting back to the future when it comes to satellite broadcasts.

5.   Personal Seat Licensing

In 1997, personal seat licensing (PSL) was estimated to raise $500,000 in one time fees.[105] That number appears to have increased. The PSL is a "cheap" way in which to raise one-time revenue. However, as a revenue generating product, it lacks strategic legs.

6.   Media Access Charges

The Media Access Charge (MAC) is a rent based on gross receipts. The MAC operates in a way similar to a percentage rent term between a tenant and a shopping mall. For example, according to the Minnesota Legislature Study on Sources of Revenues, fees from use of the broadcast facility at a stadium, at rates of $10,000 per game for television/cable and $5,000 per game for radio broadcast, would raise an estimated $2.16 million per year from MLB and $215,000 per year from NFL broadcasts.[106]

7.   Naming Rights

. . . . Although quite cumbersome and the butt of many sports commentators' jokes, there seems to be no letting up on the name game.

8.   Sport as Entertainment

In the arena of sports as entertainment, the NBA is unequivocally "best in show." Both the NBA and the National Basketball Players Association (NBPA) emphatically recognize that the sports industry, properly understood, is a sector of the entertainment industry. The NBA not only competes with the NFL and MLB, but also competes for the entertainment dollar with movies, recordings, videos, and the like.

The NBA has been aggressive in blurring the distinction between sport and entertainment, exploiting the bleed over of one form of entertainment into the other. Among products that the NBA has developed are the commissioning of a recording that captures the "NBA spirit" and video games that take the video experience to another level of entertainment. For example, the soundtrack for EA sports "NBA Live 2003" was certified a platinum album with over 1 million recordings sold, the first ever video game soundtrack to reach that recording milestone.[109]

Although both the NFL and MLB have joined the NBA in recognizing that the sports sector is a part of a much bigger picture, the three professional sports leagues have so much unrealized potential that one should not be surprised to see more attempts at exploiting the natural fit between sports and other forms of entertainment. Some may argue that such an alliance is a pact with the devil in that it taints the game, making it too glitzy, too "Hollywood"; that view, however, is quaint and shortsighted.

9.   International Expansion

One way in which to increase revenue is to increase the geographic pie. Historically, the NFL, MLB, and the NBA looked exclusively to the United States for their fan base and revenue growth. That has changed. Recognizing that the three professional leagues operate in a mature domestic environment, international expansion is a logical and rational next step to revenue growth. The sports industry is not immune from globalization. For some time, MLB has operated in an international market through exhibition games and the like. It also has successfully discovered and cultivated players from Mexico, the West Indies, Central America, and South America for decades. More recently, player scouting has included other countries like Australia and Canada. In 2006, the World Baseball Classic, a tournament of national teams featuring MLB players on the rosters of the United States and foreign teams, brought baseball to the world in a more formal sense. If not a domestic success, the Classic was certainly an international one. Surprisingly, however, MLB has been slow in moving outside the continental United States.

. . . .

The NBA is also considering international expansion. With the popularity of basketball in Europe, that continent appears to be the likely start for the NBA. The presently existing professional league structure in countries like Italy, France, Spain, and Israel suggests an interesting possibility. Would the NBA consider a merger or alliance with an existing European league? Experts appear to think not; the NBA's brand is worldwide and already strong in Europe.[112] For example, approximately twenty percent of all NBA merchandise (about $430 million) is sold internationally.[113] Moreover, over fifteen percent of the $900 million in annual television revenue (excluding local broadcasts) comes from 148 non-U.S. television partners in 212 countries.[114] The NBA has also determined that approximately forty percent of its visitors to www.nba.com access the website from locations outside of the United States.[115] More promisingly, it appears that almost fifty percent of NBA fans said that the "influx of international players has increased their interest."[116]

III.   NONTRADITIONAL REVENUE SOURCES

Professional sports leagues are competing in a vicious arena, and one that is not on the playing field. With the heavy competition for the entertainment dollar coming from many different angles, every revenue dollar is precious. However, any professional sports league or organization that sets its eye on the quick buck will someday realize just how much potential revenue slipped through its collective hands.

Professional sports leagues are leaving revenue on the table. Extending existing revenue platforms are necessary but not sufficient in order to maximize revenue. With operating costs increasing, driven largely by player salaries, and with competition being launched from other entertainment sectors that are competing for the same seats and eyes, a new revenue paradigm is necessary. . . .

The key is to find efficient and effective techniques in order to mine such revenue. This emerging revenue paradigm will embrace existing and new technologies. These new technologies will change the fan experience, allowing more interaction and greater fan control over his or her experience. These new technologies will also permit the fan to customize his or her experience, developing a cozy and personalized interface with the game.

Another example may help demonstrate what I am suggesting. NFL future revenue trends necessarily include internet and broadband media rights. . . . Leveraging the new technologies with these and other relationships is precisely what the NFL must do to compete effectively.

Any revenue paradigm shift would not leave behind existing revenue sources. In fact, a new paradigm would continue to build on and expand such sources. What the new paradigm offers, however, that the old revenue thought experiments did not, is a new perspective. This new perspective is fueled by an understanding that professional sports is not about the game, it is about the way in which we as fans experience the game.

Following are some suggestions for reaping revenue:

1.   Housing Related to the Sports Complex

NASCAR has moved into the housing market with luxury suites at the Atlanta Motor Speedway, for example. These houses are selling for more than $1 million. A variety of housing options could be crafted, depending on the venue, to suit a range of budgets. For example, in more rural or suburban areas, a league or team within the league might design and market communities based on their proximity to the venue, with prices descending the farther away one's home rested.

In urban markets, with land at a premium, it might make more sense to design arenas to incorporate mixed use luxury condo and hotel units into the existing structure. Because major sports complexes frequently host a wide range of activities from massive religious revivals to tractor pulls and from large concerts and conventions to traditional sporting events, the demand for permanent housing to experience the full range of these events might be limited. Nonetheless, hotels allowing customers to self-select the events they wish to see, and rent suites accordingly, might be a viable option.

2.   Computers at Your Seat

It is undeniable that every game in every sport faces some down time. Why not offer fans the ability to use a computer while sitting at their seat? Initially, I thought renting a portable device would be the most effective way to go. For example, a Tough Book is a laptop computer designed by Panasonic to take a beating. However, almost immediately, the flaws in this idea become apparent. A laptop is a cumbersome device for someone sitting in cramped stadium seating; if a baseball is flying towards you and you jump up to catch it, your ToughBook is going to go flying. Moreover, because they are portable, the notebook computer would also be easy to steal. Additionally, if you are sitting in an upper deck and you dropped or threw one of those devices, it could kill someone. That is a bad thing.

Yet, still the basic idea has some merit. What if the device was small and folded up, attached to your armrest? It could have a small LCD screen and a place to swipe a credit card. You could order drinks or food from your seat and perhaps check your email. You could allow patrons to surf the web set to your website, of course. Of course, with advances in cell phones and PDAs, it seems unlikely that folks would pay for what they may be able to already do on their own devices. However, beyond ordering food and drinks and surfing the web, what if you offered up the fan the ability to cycle through the various camera signals in the facility. A fan could use the device to access the TV coverage of the game, the camera shots not on the air, and perhaps additional camera feeds (for example, in the locker room, tunnel, dug out, etc.) not available anywhere else. Advertisements could also be mixed in with this programming either in the form of logos appearing on live camera feeds or traditional commercials during breaks.

3.   Projected Ads on Field/Court/Ice

Because soccer games do not take commercial breaks, other than at half time, professional soccer was forced to come up with alternative ways of selling advertisements. One revenue source has been to place advertisements around the stadium along the walls surrounding the field. Most professional sports already sell similar advertising. Check out the ads around the ring of a stadium next time you take in a game. Another creative way professional leagues have made up for the lost opportunity for commercials is by selling time for companies to either attach their logo to the bug on the screen or by superimposing their logo directly onto the field of play. When MLB attempted to promote the film Spiderman II by placing the movie's logo on the bases during one game, MLB was widely criticized for defiling the game.[122] Superimposing a logo on the field of play would only be seen by television viewers, and, thus, it might be less controversial. The right to sell those images might be retained by the professional sports teams when negotiating their broadcast licenses.

. . . .

5.   Headsets that Would Connect the Fan to the Field

Technology drives new fan experiences. The use of multiple camera angles, helmet cameras, live microphones, sideline interviews, slow motion, instant replay, superimposed first down lines, and the like are designed to bring a new and fresh experience to the fan. A new fan experience that would extend that logic could include headsets that would connect the fan to the field of play by allowing fans to listen to the interaction among coaches or between a coach and his players. Obviously, teams would need to be certain that providing radio content did not violate any exclusivity rights offered to their broadcasters. This could be done either by renting/selling cheap headsets that could pick up a low frequency radio signal or by simply providing the signal and allowing fans to bring their own radios. It is not unusual for fans to watch a game, in person or on TV, with the sound turned down, while simultaneously listening to the play-by-play on the radio. Fans could choose to do this in most arenas already by simply tuning into their local radio station that is broadcasting the game. In addition, what if fans were given access to radio feeds that picked up sideline/on-the-field conversations or picked up signals from up in the booth? This could be offered for free with commercials or offered for a service fee with or without commercials.

. . . .

7.   Interactive TV

Interactive Television or iTV is touted as a technology that will change the way a fan interacts with the sports broadcasting. By providing greater access to content including statistics, live games, commentary, and perhaps linking content to a fan's fantasy team, the iTV promise is to generate greater interaction between a fan and the sport and to retain viewership.[125] Additionally, broadcasters could offer viewers the ability to cycle through alternative camera angles for a single game or display multiple games simultaneously.[126]

8.   Broadcast License for Trains and Airlines

Professional sports, assuming this would not violate their contracts with TV broadcasters, might license train and airline companies to provide live coverage of their games or, perhaps, video of past "classic" games. This could be either by pay-per-view with a customer swiping a credit card through the monitor on the seat back in front of him or by a licensing agreement with the carrier.

9.   Fan Blogs (with Advertising)

Blogs (Web Logs or journals) are becoming ubiquitous on the internet. Although the bane of some in the sports industries, they have become a fixture in the sports landscape.[127] They are a way for fans to express their opinions on a forum of their peers. Presently, various fans may have their own blogs where they can rant about every possible bit of minutia involving their team. Why not channel this by providing fans with the opportunity to post their thoughts on the team's webpage? It would have to be a relatively open forum allowing fans to be critical of owners, players, and management alike. The owner, manager and players might occasionally post their own thoughts on this blog, thus encouraging fans to frequently check in to see who is saying what. By channeling fans onto the team's own, free blog, the team could then sell advertisements and merchandise on its blog page.

10.   Gaming

Professional sports and gaming present a paradox. On one hand, professional sports benefit indirectly from gaming in that placing wagers on outcomes of games and other events increases brand awareness and fan interest. On the other hand, direct involvement between the leagues and gaming establishments may call into question the integrity of the game, price shaving, throwing a competition, etc. From a revenue generating perspective, however, gaming is the proverbial "elephant in the room." Gaming must be addressed in a careful, deliberate manner, eschewing hyperbole and "parades of horribles." There are many ways in which both the integrity of the game may be preserved and revenues from gaming enjoyed by professional sports teams. It really is just a matter of time.

A common approach may be the simple raffle. A team could raffle off choice sideline seating, a court or dugout presence, ride a team flight or bus, or toward an even bolder step, a chance to call a play. To be sure, there would be substantial push back. But there is with any innovation.

. . . .

A professional sports league could run the same program, partnering with a state, an Indian tribe, or the federal government through a national lottery. It could even earmark a large percentage of revenue to its charitable foundations. Thus, there are ways by which a league could limit its operational involvement in the gaming activity. Ultimately, gaming provides new opportunities for revenue growth, expansion of the fan base, content for advertising, and a new way by which fans may experience a game.

[*Ed. Note: Author's discussion of fantasy leagues is omitted.*]

. . . .

V.   OBSERVATIONS

. . . .

The coming revolution in revenue is like the runners at second and third—ducks on the pond, golden opportunities if one acts thoughtfully and boldly. The real question is whether the leagues pick up the runners. If they execute properly, we can all come out winners; if not, they will continue a revenue slide as other forms of entertainment compete for our dollar. The key is an understanding of two fundamental drivers: (1) content is everything, and (2) technology (including, but not limited to the Internet) delivers content. Those that can develop a revenue model that integrates both drivers will succeed.

Only the most naive would reject the notion that new technologies have changed the game and the way fans experience the game. The Internet, just one ubiquitous example of the new technologies saddling up to the sports industry, has done more than change sports—it has transformed sports. Not only is the Internet a vehicle for online retailing of merchandise and a stage for advertising, it is also one's own highlight vault and mirror into the experience of professional sports. With the advent of the Internet and its accessibility through the worldwide web, the sports industry has mutated. Sports are no longer sports plus the Internet; they are a whole new industry—"new, interactive sports." Those business competitors that recognize this seismic shift will be able to position their teams, league, or organization to reap the advantages of the new technologies and the new markets. Those that do not, will fail. Ducks on the pond, indeed.

Notes

1. Craig Lambert, *Has Winning on the Field Become Simply a Corporate Triumph?*, HARV. MAG., Oct. 2001, *available at* http://www.harvardmagazine.com/on-line/09014.html.

2. *Id.* The reader will notice that in this article, the National Hockey League (NHL) has been left out . . .

3. Sports teams also provide an opportunity for state and local taxing authorities to grow their respective tax bases. For example, in a financial report prepared for the Minnesota State Legislature on sports activity conducted at the Metrodome (NFL Minnesota Vikings, MLB Minnesota Twins, and Big Ten University of Minnesota Gophers football), the following taxes are collected: (1) sales tax on food and alcohol; (2) 10% ticket tax (including complimentary tickets) and 6.5% state sales tax on tickets (in addition to the 10% ticket tax); (3) 6.5% gross receipts tax on merchandise licensed by professional and collegiate sports teams; (4) personal income tax paid by visiting teams; (5) lottery games with a sports theme; and (6) tax on rental vehicles in the Metro area. See Paul Wilson & Mary Jane Hedstrom, *Appendix C: Summary of Revenue Sources*, Minn. Leg. (January 31, 2002) (on file with author). *See also I.R.S., Sports Franchises, Market Segment Specialization Program Training* 3123-005 (8-99); TPDS No. 839831 (on file with author).

4. Sports is big business in the United States and internationally. *The Sports Industry,* Bus. & Econ. Research Advisor (BERA) (2005), http://www.loc.gov/rr/business/BERA/issue3/issue3_main.html.

5. To say that the sector is well known is not to suggest that the sector is static. On the contrary, the sports sector is dynamic. For an excellent book on the evolution of the modern sports industry that includes discussions on sponsorships, franchise relocation, radio and television, stadium issues, and endorsements, *see* PHIL SCHAAF, SPORTS, INC.: 100 YEARS OF SPORTS BUSINESS (2004). *See also* THE ECONOMICS OF SPORT VOLUME I (Andrew Zimbalist ed., 2001) (covering many aspects of the business of sports).

6. *See generally* WILKOFSKEY GRUEN ASSOC., GLOBAL ENTERTAINMENT AND MEDIA OUTLOOK: 2005–2009: FORECASTS AND ANALYSIS OF 14 INDUSTRY SEGMENTS (6th ed. 2005).

. . . .

14. I.R.S., *supra* note 3.

15. *See* National Football League website, www.nfl.com (last visited May 31, 2006).

16. *The Business of Professional Football,* Bus. & Econ. Research Advisor (BERA) (2005), http://www.loc.gov/rr/business/issue3/football.html.

. . . .

26. *The Business of Professional Football, supra* note 16.

. . . .

28. *See* Soonhwan Lee & Hyosung Chun, *Economic Values of Professional Sports Franchises in the United States,* 5 SPORTS JOURNAL (2002), *available at* http://thesportsjournal.org/2002Journal/Vol5-No3/economic-values.htm.

29. *The Business of Professional Football, supra* note 16.

. . . .

31. The current agreement with the NFL is an eight-year contract that totals $17.6 billion. Kagan, *supra* note 25, at 45. About 65% of all revenues of NFL teams are from television rights licensing. Lee & Chun, *supra* note 28.

32. Lee & Chun, *supra* note 28.

33. *The Business of Professional Football, supra* note 16.

. . . .

35. Kagan, *supra* note 25, at 64.

36. *The Business of Professional Football, supra* note 16.

. . . .

45. Major League Baseball, www.mlb.com (last visited June 5, 2006).

46. . . . For interesting treatments of the business of baseball, see Andrew Zimbalist, *May the Best Team Win: Baseball Economics and Public Policy* (2003); Fred Claire with Steve Springer, *My 30 Years in Dodger Blue* (2004); Charles P. Korr, *The End of Baseball as We Knew It: The Players Union, 1960-81* (2004); Fay Vincent, *The Last Commissioner: A Baseball Valentine* (2002); Marvin Miller, *A Whole Different Ball Game: The Inside Story of the Baseball Revolution* (2004); John Helyar, *Lords of the Realm* (1995); Stefan Szymanski & Andrew Zimbalist, *National Pastime: How Americans Play Baseball and the Rest of the World Plays Soccer* (2005).

47. Abner Doubleday, BaseballLibrary.com, http://www.baseballlibrary.com/baseballlibrary/ballplayers/D/Doubleday_Abner.stm (last visited July 25, 2006).

48. Reds Timeline History Highlights, http://mlb.mlb.com/NASApp/mlb/cin/history/timeline1.jsp (last visited July 25, 2006).

49. National League, http://www.ringsurf.com/info/Sports/Baseball/National_League/ (last visited July 25, 2006).

. . . .

57. See generally Richard C. Levin et al., THE REPORT OF THE INDEPENDENT MEMBERS OF THE COMMISSIONER'S BLUE RIBBON PANEL ON BASEBALL ECONOMICS (July 2000).

58. Baseball, USA Today Baseball Weekly.com, Dec. 5, 2001, http://www.usatoday.com/sports/baseball/stories/2001-12-05-focusexpenses.htm.

. . . .

60. Tim Reason, Squeeze Play, CFO.com, Apr. 1, 2004, http://www.cfo.com/article.cfm/3012785?f=search Baseball, USA Today Baseball Weekly.com, http://www.usatoday.com/sports/baseball/stories/2001-12-05-focusexpenses.htm.

61. *Id.*

62. *Id.*

63. Lee & Chun, *supra* note 28.

. . . .

68. National Basketball Association, www.nba.com (last visited July 28, 2006).

. . . .

77. Lee & Chun, *supra* note 28.

78. Kagan, *supra* note 76, Executive Summary.

. . . .

88. *See* Reason, *supra* note 60.

89. *Id.*

90. *Id.*

91. *Id.*

92. For an interesting take on luxury suites, *see* Lambert, *supra* note 1.

93. Lee & Chun, *supra* note 28.

94. *Id.*

95. *Id.*

96. *Id.*

97. *Id.*

. . . .

103. Lee & Chun, *supra* note 28.

104. *Id.*

105. Wilson & Hedstrom, *supra* note 3.

106. *Id.*

. . . .

109. Horrow, *supra* note 81.

. . . .

112. Horrow, *supra* note 81.

113. *Id.*

114. *Id.*

115. *Id.*

116. *Id.*

. . . .

122. See Darren Rovell, The Tangled Web of Sports and Advertising, Espn.com, May 6, 2004, http://sports.espn.go.com/espn/sportsbusiness/news/story?id=1795742; Spiderman Bases Shot Down, USAToday.com, May 6, 2004, http://www.usatoday.com/sports/baseball/2004-05-06-spider-man-plan-dropped_x.htm.

. . . .

125. See Interactive TV: The Opportunities for Sport, available at http://www.sportbusinessassociates.com/sports_reports/interactive_tv.htm (last visited June 6, 2006).

126. Global Interactive Sports TV Revenues to Increase, Indiantelevision.com, http://www.indiantelevision.com/headlines/y2k3/mar/mar92.htm (last visited June 6, 2006).

127. See, e.g., Sports Illustrated, Blog Central, http://sportsillustrated.cnn.com (last visited June 6, 2006).

. . . .

IMPACT OF STAR PLAYERS ON GATE RECEIPTS

STARS AT THE GATE: THE IMPACT OF STAR POWER ON NBA GATE REVENUES

David J. Berri, Martin B. Schmidt, and Stacey L. Brook

Competitive balance in professional team sports has been the subject of numerous theoretical and empirical publications. The theoretical literature argues competitive imbalance, or the on-field domination of one or a small number of organizations, reduces the level of uncertainty of outcome and consequently reduces the level of consumer demand.[1] The empirical literature, whether examining game day attendance[2] or aggregate season attendance,[3] has also generally confirmed a relationship between uncertainty of outcome or competitive balance and demand for tickets to sporting events.

Decision makers in the professional sports industry have not needed economists to understand this basic relationship. Virtually from the inception of organized sports in North America, leagues have enacted various institutions to promote competitive balance.[4] Such institutions include the reserve clause, the rookie draft, payroll caps, salary caps, revenue sharing, and luxury taxes. Despite the similarity of effort, professional team sports leagues continue to have varying degrees of competitive balance.

The variability of competitive balance across professional team sports was illustrated by Quirk and Fort (1992). One of the findings of this seminal work, extended by Berri and Vicente-Mayoral (2001) and Berri (in press), was the relative lack of competitive balance in the National Basketball Association (NBA). The relative imbalance continued in spite of the NBA's institution of a rookie draft, payroll caps, revenue sharing, free agency, and, at times, a reserve clause. By virtually any measure, the NBA has been unable to achieve the level of competitive balance observed in the other North American professional sports leagues.

The purpose of this article is not to examine why the NBA is competitively imbalanced but rather to examine the impact competitive imbalance has on consumer demand for the NBA product. The works of Knowles, Sherony, and Haupert (1992) and Rascher (1999) found that Major League Baseball attendance was maximized when the probability of the home team winning was approximately .6.[5] These studies suggest that consumers prefer to see the home team win but do not wish to be completely certain this will occur prior to the game being played. For fans of NBA teams located near the bottom of the league rankings, though, the opposite is often true. Not only is their team not likely to win, but often the fan is quite certain of this negative outcome. The question is therefore "How do these NBA teams still maintain demand in the face of the certainty of an unwelcomed outcome?"

One possible strategy is for teams to shift their focus from the promotion of team performance to the promotion of individual stars. Hausman and Leonard (1997) found the presence of stars had a substantial affect on television ratings, even after controlling for team quality. Although this work also considered the effect stars had on team attendance, the inquiry into team attendance was "less formal" (p. 609). In essence, these authors only looked at how attendance changed when a team either added or played one of the stars these authors identified.

An objective of the present work is to extend the work of Hausman and Leonard (1997) in a more comprehensive study of the relationship between team attendance and both team performance and the team's employment of star players. The structure of the study is as follows: The following section details the empirical model we will utilize to examine the demand for professional basketball. This discussion is followed by a review of the econometric estimation of the aforementioned model. The final section offers concluding observations.

THE DATA TO BE EMPLOYED

Given rudimentary consumer theory, demand is primarily determined by three factors: team performance, franchise characteristics, and market characteristics. The literature on attendance in professional sports has turned to a variety of factors designed to capture these primary determinants of demand. **Table 11** lists our choice of dependent and independent variables. In addition to listing the variables and the nomenclature we employ, we report the hypothesized effect of the independent variables and corresponding descriptive statistics. We follow with a brief review of the theoretical reasoning behind this chosen list of factors.

Consumer Demand

The data utilized to tabulate the variables listed in Table 11 comes from four seasons, beginning with the 1992–1993 campaign and concluding with the 1995–1996 season.[6] A common practice within the professional team sports literature is to utilize aggregate attendance data as the dependent variable in a study of consumer demand. Over the period our study highlights, though, such a choice is problematic. Specifically, if one compares the reported attendance figures to the maximum attendance the stadium capacity of these teams would allow, one would note that of the 108 teams considered, 43 teams, or 40%, sold out every single home game. Given the divergence between attendance and demand, we employ gate revenue[7] as a proxy for the level of consumer attraction to professional basketball.[8] The use of gate revenue incorporates price adjustments and therefore allows for full variation in the dependent variable.[9]

Team Performance

The most common measure of team performance is regular season wins. Team performance can also be captured via playoff wins, lagged values of both regular season and playoff victories, and past championships won. Following Berri and Brook (1999), the effect of past championships is estimated via... calculation involved assigning a value to a team for each championship won in the past 20 years. This value was 20 if the team captured a championship during the prior season, 19 if the championship was won two seasons past, and so forth.[10]

In addition to these measures, we also consider the impact of a team's star attractions. The relationship between demand and stars has been considered by Scott, Long, and Sompii (1985), Brown, Spiro, and Keenan (1991), and Burdekin and Idson (1991), as well as the aforementioned work of Hausman and Leonard (1997). Of these studies, only Brown et al. (1991) was able to find a statistically significant relationship between a measure of consumer demand and a team's star attractions.

Each of these studies employed a different definition of star attraction. Scott et al. (1985) defined a superstar as "a player who has made the All-Pro team five times or, if he has only played a few years, dominates his position" (p. 53). Brown et al. (1991) defined a superstar as "a player who has played in the NBA All-Star Game for at least 50% of his years in the league" (p. 338). Finally, Burdekin and Idson (1991) considered a player a star if he was voted by the media to either the first or second All-NBA teams.

Given our focus on consumer demand, we sought a measure that would directly incorporate fan preference. We therefore introduced All-Star Game votes as our measure. Specifically, the starters for the midseason All-Star Game are chosen via balloting by the fans. We were able to obtain the number of votes received by the top 10 players at guard,

Table 11   Dependent and Independent Variables Sample: 1992–1993 through 1995–1996

Item	Label	M	Maximum	Minimum	SD
Dependent variable					
Gate revenue (in $ millions)	GATE	20.13	41.20	9.90	7.67
Independent variables					
Team performance characteristics					
Regular season wins	WINS	41.43	72.00	11.00	13.28
Playoff wins	WPLAY	2.72	15.00	.00	4.20
Lagged playoff wins	WPLAY(−1)	2.77	15.00	.00	4.22
Championships won, weighted	WCHM20	7.76	67.00	.00	16.10
All-Star votes received	STARVOT	894,482.33	3,176,443.00	.00	813,666.48
Franchise characteristics					
Stadium capacity	SCAP	17,953.86	24,042.00	12,888.00	2,382.28
Teams at capacity	DCAP	.343	1.000	.000	.477
Age of stadium	OLD	16.472	66.000	.000	14.975
Expansion team, dummy	DEXP5	.06	1.00	.00	.23
Roster stability	RSTAB	.71	.97	.40	.13
White ratio (WHITEMIN/ WHITEPOP)	WHITERATIO	.20	.68	1.00	.14
Team attendance	ATTEND	677,196	985,722	414,560	126,079
Market characteristics					
Competitive balance in conference	CB	2.944	3.335	2.344	.310
Competing teams	COMPTM	2.602	8.000	.000	2.230
Real per-capita income	RYCAP	167.92	247.37	111.97	25.62
Population	POP	5,361,974.97	18,204,047.00	1,159,845.00	5,165,118.64
Racial variables					
Percentage of White minutes	WHITEMIN	.16	.47	.00	.11
Percentage of Whites in population	WHITEPOP	.82	.95	.69	.07

Source: Journal of Sports Economics. Used with permission.

forward, and center.[11] For each team, we summed the number of votes received by the players employed. In addition, following Hausman and Leonard (1997), we also considered dummy variables for four superstars: Michael Jordan, Shaquille O'Neal, Grant Hill, and Charles Barkley. Each of these players was either explicitly noted by Hausman and Leonard (Jordan, O'Neal) or led the league in All-Star votes received in one of the years examined in the study (Jordan, Barkley, Hill).

Franchise Characteristics

In general, the variables utilized to capture the characteristics of the franchise follow convention. Both stadium capacity and being an expansion team are expected to have a positive affect on both team attendance and team revenue. Along similar lines, the age of a stadium is expected to decrease demand. . . .

As noted, the data set contains a number of teams that consistently sell out their venue. Shmanske (1998), in a study of golf courses, noted that an increase in demand would elicit different responses from courses at capacity relative to those that still were capable of serving additional

customers. Specifically, a course with excess capacity could increase both quantity and price in response to an increase in demand. Courses at capacity, though, could only increase price. Therefore, as Shmanske argued, the estimated parameters in the demand function may differ depending on whether an organization is at capacity. . . .

In addition to these factors, we consider a factor suggested by Blass (1992) and Kahane and Shmanske (1997). Each of these authors considered the effect that roster stability or, conversely, turnover has on team attendance. Although Blass failed to find a relationship between team attendance and player tenure with the team, Kahane and Shmanske presented evidence that a negative relationship existed between roster turnover and team attendance. In other words, the more stability a roster exhibits from year to year, the greater the level of consumer demand. To the best of our knowledge, this study is the first to consider the affect of this variable on consumer demand in the NBA. Roster stability was measured by examining the minutes played by returning players over both the current and prior seasons. We then averaged the percentage of minutes played by these players for both of these campaigns.[14]

Market Characteristics

This exposition began by noting the lack of competitive balance in the NBA. Previously, Schmidt and Berri (2001) found that the level of competitive balance affected consumer demand in Major League Baseball. To ascertain if such a relationship exists for the NBA, a measure of competitive balance is required. Following the lead of Quirk and Fort (1992), who in turn built on the writings of Noll (1988) and Scully (1989), competitive balance can be measured by comparing

> the actual performance of a league to the performance that would have occurred if the league had the maximum degree of competitive balance in the sense that all teams were equal in playing strengths. The less the deviation of actual league performance from that of the ideal league, the greater is the degree of competitive balance. (Quirk & Fort, 1992, p. 244)

. . . .

As noted by Quirk and Fort (1992), the idealized standard deviation represents the standard deviation of winning percentage if each team in a league has an equal probability to win each game. The greater the actual standard deviation is relative to the ideal, the less balance exists within the professional sports league. The measure of competitive balance . . . was calculated for each conference, Eastern and Western, and each year, examined by this study.

The remaining market characteristics utilized follow the standard list employed in the literature. The number of competing teams is simply the number of teams from each of the four major North American professional team sports located in each franchise's city. This is expected to have a negative effect on consumer demand. In contrast, population and per-capita income should each increase team revenue. Population is measured for each team's standard metropolitan area. We also consider per-capita income in real terms, which we ascertained by adjusting nominal income for each city's cost of living.[15]

The final independent variables listed in Table 11 are associated with measuring the effect the racial composition of the team has on NBA demand. Following the lead of Hoang and Rascher (1999), we employed the ratio of the percentage of minutes on the team allocated to White players (WHITEMIN) to the percentage of White persons in the population of the city (WHITEPOP). If this variable increases in size, the racial match between the team and the city improves. Consequently, we would expect WHITERATIO to have a positive sign if people within the market prefer a team that represents the racial mix of the city.[16]

. . . .

Econometric Issues and Estimation

. . . .

The Estimation of the Model

. . . .

The stated focus of this article is the effect two measures of team performance, wins and the star attraction, have on team revenue. The choice of functional form does not appear to dramatically effect the estimation of the relationship between measures of team wins and revenue. With respect to either functional form, a statistically significant relationship for regular season wins, playoff wins, and championships won is found. Furthermore, the reported relationships conform to the expected signs. The effect of star votes, though, does differ substantially across the two models. According to the linear model, the functional form frequently utilized in the literature, no relationship exists between a team's accumulation of star votes and gate revenue.

. . . .

Consistency in results was found with respect to the other variables considered. For example, all of the other variables designed to capture team performance were statistically significant. In addition, stadium capacity was found to have a significantly positive affect on gate revenue. In other words, with respect to a team's arena, bigger does appear to be better. Finally, of the specific players we examined, only DHILL was found to be statistically significant. The sign, though, was negative, indicating that the presence of Grant Hill actually diminished gate revenues in Detroit. Given the failure of the Pistons to win a playoff game in Hill's first two seasons, though, a more plausible explanation is that the Pistons' failures on the floor led to declines at the gate that the star power of Hill could not overcome. Unlike Hausman and Leonard (1997), none of the other players we examined were found to have a statistically significant effect on gate revenue. Such a result suggests that individual players do not have a significant effect on revenue beyond their contribution to team wins.[23]

In addition. . . a number of variables were found to not statistically affect gate revenue. This list includes the level of roster stability on the team, per-capita income in the market, the measure of racial matching, and the level of competitive balance in the conference. The latter result is inconsistent with the work of Schmidt and Berri (2001), who found competitive balance to significantly affect Major League Baseball attendance. One should note that the previous work of Schmidt and Berri considered a much longer time period than that which was considered for this study. However, such results do suggest that NBA fans do not respond as baseball fans do to the level of competitive balance in the sport.

The Effect of Wins and the Star Attractions

With the choice of models made and subsequently estimated, what is the answer to the question posed by this inquiry? To answer this question, we turn to an examination of the economic significance of both wins and star votes.

. . . .

In terms of elasticities, revenue is the least responsive to the star attraction. The relative effect of wins and star power is also revealed in an examination of the marginal values. An additional win produces $83,037 in GATE revenue, on average. Given that one All-Star vote generates, on average, $.22, the players on a team would need to receive nearly 370,000 votes to generate the revenue a team receives from one win. To equal the revenue generated by 41 wins, or the average number of regular season victories, a team would need to receive approximately 15.1 million votes. Such a total represents nearly 5 times the maximum number of votes any team received in the sample. These results suggest that it is performance on the court, not star power, that attracts the fans in the NBA.

How does the value of a win differ between large- and small-market teams? . . . one can see that increases in population will increase gate revenue. Specifically, one additional person is worth, on average, $.40. Given this result, moving to a city with an additional million persons is worth $399,503. Such an increase in revenue would increase the value of a win by $1,648. Again, consistent with the work of Rottenberg (1956), additional persons in the population enhance the monetary value of on-court performance.

One final extension is the issue of pricing strategies of NBA teams.[24] Past studies (see Burdekin & Idson, 1991; Demmert, 1973; Fort, in press; Fort & Quirk, 1995, 1996; Heilmann & Wendling, 1976; Jennett, 1984; Medoff, 1986; Noll, 1974; Scully, 1989) have presented both empirical evidence and theoretical arguments that teams in professional sports may price in the inelastic portion of the demand curve. We therefore included attendance as an additional regressor. If the coefficient on attendance is negative, one may infer that the teams are posting inelastic prices.

. . . Such results suggest that NBA teams do not set prices in the inelastic range. Given the capacity constraints noted above, such a finding should not surprise. One caveat to this result is that NBA teams may benefit from additional revenue from parking and concessions by lowering prices and hence attracting additional fans. The size of NBA facilities, though, limits this strategy option. These results are available from the authors on request.

CONCLUDING OBSERVATIONS

The lack of competitive balance in professional basketball leads one to question how one can best generate demand for this sport. Hausman and Leonard (1997) suggested that it is star power, rather than on-court productivity, that

attracts the fans. Although star power was found to be statistically significant in this present study, the ability of a team to generate wins appears to be the engine that drives consumer demand.

The propensity of NBA teams to sell out each and every contest shifted the focus of this study from attendance to gate revenue. . . .

One final question remains: Do the reported results suggest that stars are not important in the NBA? The true power of star power may lie in the revenue received by the star's opponent.[25] In other words, the true power of the star may lie in his ability to enhance attendance on the road. . . .

Notes

1. See Rottenberg (1956), Neale (1964), El-Hodiri and Quirk (1971), and Quirk and Fort (1992).

2. See Jennett (1984), Peel and Thomas (1988), Borland and Lye (1992), Knowles et al. (1992), and Rascher (1999).

3. See Schmidt and Berri (2001).

4. We are focusing on the stated objective of these institutions. As noted first by Rottenberg (1956), if transaction costs are low, the reserve clause would not likely affect competitive balance. Rather, its primary affect would be on the profit potential of the individual teams. A similar story could be told with respect to the rookie draft.

5. Knowles et al. (1992), in their study of the 1988 Major League Baseball season, found that balance is achieved (i.e., attendance is maximized) when the probability of the home team winning was .6. Rascher (1999) offered an examination of the 1996 Major League Baseball season that examined a larger sample of games and a greater number of independent variables.

   Rascher's study demonstrated that fans prefer to see the home team win, and consistent with the work of Knowles et al., fan attendance is maximized when the home team's probability of winning equals .66. Each of these studies suggested that a home team with a high probability of winning the contest will see a decline in fan attendance, indicating that uncertainty of outcome is a significant determinant of demand.

6. For the first 3 years considered, the population of NBA teams equaled 27. For the 1995–1996 season, 2 teams were added in Vancouver and Toronto. The model we employ, though, utilizes lagged values of several independent variables. Consequently, data from these 2 teams could not be utilized, and the final number of observations employed was 108.

7. Data on gate revenue were reported in various issues of *Financial World* (Atre et al., 1996; Badenhausen, Nikolov, Alkin, & Ozanian, 1997; Ozanian, Atre et al., 1995; Ozanian, Fink, et al., 1994). The last season this periodical reported such information was the 1995–1996 campaign. To the best of our knowledge, such information was not reported for the 1996–1997 campaign. Data on revenue are reported for more recent years by *Forbes* magazine, although *Forbes* does not report data specifically on gate revenue. Rather, a team's media revenues, stadium revenues, and gate are aggregated and simply reported as total revenue in *Forbes*. This change in reporting prevents us from examining seasons after 1995–1996.

8. The examination of team revenue was initially conducted by Scully (1974) in his seminal examination of marginal revenue product. A list of additional studies that have examined revenue would include Medoff (1976), Scott et al. (1985), Zimbalist (1992), and Berri and Brook (1999).

9. We would like to thank an anonymous referee for noting the potential link between gate revenue and other revenue streams. For example, if stadium revenues (concessions, parking, and so forth) are high, the firm has an incentive to lower ticket prices so that more people are admitted to take advantage of this revenue stream. In addition, one might expect a link between gate and media revenues. Again, as the referee notes, a sold-out stadium may enhance TV ratings, hence enhancing media revenues. One possible solution is to include stadium and media revenues as additional regressors in the model. However, because such revenue streams would be related independent of causal factors, such a solution is not attractive econometrically. Indeed, when such a model was estimated, both stadium and media revenues were found to be positively related to gate revenue. Furthermore, the remaining regressors are largely unaffected by the inclusion of these two variables. Therefore, we have chosen to omit the results with these two regressors. Such results are available from the authors on request.

10. Data on regular season wins, playoff wins, and championships won were obtained from various issues of *The Sporting News: Official NBA Guide* (1993–1996).

11. These data were obtained from various daily newspapers. The top finishers at each position are chosen as starters for the midseason classic. In addition, the guard and forward receiving the second most votes at these positions are also named as starters. Because only one center is chosen, the above analysis only considered the top five recipients of votes at this position.

. . . .

14. An example may help illustrate the method employed to measure roster stability. During the 1994–1995 season, George McCloud's NBA career was resurrected by the Dallas Mavericks, who employed him for 802 minutes. The following year, McCloud's minutes increased more than threefold to 2,846. If we only consider McCloud's minutes during the 1995–1996 season, we would be overstating the level of roster stability because McCloud was not an integral part of the Mavericks in 1994–1995. Consequently, in measuring roster stability, we consider more than just how many minutes a player played during the current season but also the number of minutes the team allocated to the player during the prior campaign. We wish to acknowledge the assistance of Dean Oliver, who argued that a better label for this measure is roster stability, as opposed to roster turnover. Data on minutes played, utilized to construct the roster stability variable, were obtained from various issues of *The Sporting News: Official NBA Guide* (1993–1996).

15. Data on metropolitan statistics area (MSA) population was taken from Missouri State Census Data Center (2001). Personal income came from U.S. Bureau of Economic Analysis (1992–1996), whereas MSA Consumer Price Indexes came from U.S. Bureau of Labor Statistics (1992–1996).

16. An anonymous referee noted that WHITERATIO only implies an improvement in racial match if it does not exceed 1. If the value of the ratio exceeds 1, then further increases actually imply a worsening of the racial match. Although this is true theoretically, in the sample, the value of this variable was below 1 for every team. Data on the size of the White population in each city was obtained from Missouri State Census Data Center (2001). For the racial mix of the team, we consulted both *The Sporting News: Official NBA Guide* (1993–1996) and the pictures of the players offered in *The Sporting News NBA Register* (1993–1996).

. . . .

23. In a previous version of this article, we estimated the double-logged model without DCAP, CB, and the year fixed effects. The results with respect to the remaining independent variables were quite similar. The lone exceptions were the star dummy variables. In the previous estimation, DSHAQ was positive and significant, and the remaining dummies were statistically insignificant. As noted, in the current formulation, DSHAQ is now statistically insignificant whereas DHILL has become statistically significant. Such variation in results cast suspicion on the validity of these dummy variables.

24. We wish to thank an anonymous referee for raising this issue.

25. We wish to thank an anonymous referee for raising this issue.

References

. . . .

Berri, D. J. (In press). Is there a short supply of tall people in the college game. In J. Fizel & R. Fort (Eds.), *Economics of collegiate sports*. New York: Praeger.

Berri, D. J., & Brook, S. L. (1999). Trading players in the NBA: For better or worse. In J. L. Fizel, E. Gustafson, & L. Hadley (Eds.), *Sports economics: Current research*. New York: Praeger.

Berri, D. J., & Vicente-Mayoral, R. (2001). *The short supply of tall people: Explaining competitive imbalance in the National Basketball Association*. Unpublished manuscript.

Blass, A. A. (1992). Does the baseball labor market contradict the human capital model of investment? *Review of Economics and Statistics, 74,* 261–268.

. . . .

Brown, E., Spiro, R., & Keenan, D. (1991, July). Wage and non-wage discrimination in professional basketball: Do fans affect it? *American Journal of Economics and Sociology, 50*(3), 333–345.

Burdekin, R. C., & Idson, T. L. (1991). Customer preferences, attendance and the racial structure of professional basketball teams. *Applied Economics, 23,* 179–186.

. . . .

Demmert, H. (1973). *The economics of professional team sports*. Lexington, MA: Lexington Books.

. . . .

Fort, R. (In press). Inelastic sports pricing. *Managerial and Decision Economics*.

Fort, R., & Quirk, J. (1995, September). Cross-subsidization, incentives, and outcomes in professional team sports. *Journal of Economic Literature, 33,* 1265–1299.

Fort, R., & Quirk, J. (1996). Over-stated exploitation: Monopsony versus revenue sharing in sports leagues. In J. Fizel, E. Gustafson, & L. Hadley (Eds.), *Baseball economics: Current research*. New York: Praeger.

Hausman, J. A., & Leonard, G. K. (1997). Superstars in the National Basketball Association: Economic value and policy. *Journal of Labor Economics, 15*(4), 586-624.

Heilmann, R. L., & Wendling, W.R. (1976). A note on optimum pricing strategies for sports events. In R. E. Machol, S. P. Ladany, & D. G. Morrison (Eds.), *Management science in sports*. Amsterdam: North-Holland.

Hoang, H., & Rascher, D. (1999, January). The NBA, exit discrimination, and career earning. *Industrial Relations, 38*(1), 69–91.

Jennett, N. I. (1984). Attendance, uncertainty of outcome and policy in Scottish League Football. *Scottish Journal of Political Economy, 31*(2), 176–198.

Kahane, L., & Shmanske, S. (1997, April). Team roster turnover and attendance in Major League Baseball. *Applied Economics*, 29(4), 425–431.

Knowles, G., Sherony, K., & Haupert, M. (1992, fall). The demand for Major League Baseball: A test of the uncertainty of outcome hypothesis. *The American Economist*, 36(2), 72–80.

Medoff, M. (1986). Baseball attendance and fan discrimination. *Journal of Behavioral Economics*, 15, 149–155.

. . . .

Noll, R. (1974). Attendance and price setting. In R. Noll (Ed.), *Government and the sports business*. Washington, DC: Brookings Institution.

Noll, R. (1988). *Professional basketball* (Working Paper No. 144). Palo Alto, CA: Stanford University.

. . . .

Quirk, J., & Fort, R. (1992). *Pay dirt: The business of professional team sports*. Princeton, NJ: Princeton University Press.

Rascher, D. (1999). A test of the optimal positive production network externality in Major League Baseball. In J. Fizel, E. Gustafson, & L.

Hadley (Eds.), *Sports economics: Current research* (pp. 27–45). New York: Praeger.

Rottenberg, S. (1956, June). The baseball player's labor market. *Journal of Political Economy*, pp. 242–258.

Schmidt, M. B., & Berri, D. J. (2001). Competition and attendance: The case of Major League Baseball. *Journal of Sports Economics*, 2(2), 147–167.

Scott, F., Jr., Long, J., & Sompii, K. (1985). Salary vs. marginal revenue product under monopsony and competition: The case of professional basketball. *Atlantic Economic Journal*, 13(3), 50–59.

Scully, G. (1989). *The business of Major League Baseball*. Chicago: University of Chicago Press.

Scully, G. W. (1974). Pay and performance in Major League Baseball. *American Economic Review*, 64, 917–930.

Shmanske, S. (1998, July). Price discrimination at the links. *Contemporary Economic Policy*, 16, 368–378.

. . . .

VEND IT LIKE BECKHAM: DAVID BECKHAM'S EFFECT ON MLS TICKET SALES

Robert Lawson, Kathleen Sheehan, and E. Frank Stephenson

In January 2007, Major League Soccer (MLS) announced that international soccer sensation David Beckham would be joining the league. Beckham was signed to a large five-year contract with the Los Angeles Galaxy, with both the MLS and LA Galaxy sharing the cost of his contract. Beckham thus became the first player signed under MLS's new Designated Player Rule, which allows teams to sign one player outside of the salary cap with the league paying $400,000 [*Ed. Note: now $335,000*] of the player's contract. Although the exact terms of Beckham's contract have not been revealed, ESPN.com (2007) and other media sources have reported a figure of around $250 million for the entire five-year package, including various commercial endorsements. Presumably, MLS and its sponsors hope that the addition of Beckham will increase revenues from ticket, merchandise, advertising, and sponsored product sales.

Examining the NBA, Hausman and Leonard (1997), Berri et al. (2004), and Berri and Schmidt (2006) found that star players create positive externalities. When superstars such as Michael Jordan and Larry Bird play on the road, home teams experience an increase in attendance and revenue even though they do not contribute to the cost of the superstar's contract. Conversely, teams signing superstars do not receive the full marginal revenue product of the

superstar. Hence, the MLS Designated Player Rule may be an attempt to better align the costs and benefits of superstars by having the league pay a portion of star players' salaries. The rule is probably also an acknowledgment that a superstar such as Beckham may be necessary to firmly establish a league that has had mixed success in attracting fans since its inaugural season in 1996.

This paper examines Beckham's participation in MLS soccer and how it affected ticket sales for the 2007 season. Beckham's contract start date was July 1, which is about midway through the season. Because of injury, he did not play his first official game for the Galaxy until August 15. Injuries continued to plague him through the remainder of the season, and of the 17 games (out of the 30-game season) for which he was on the roster, Beckham played in just five games (two at home and three on the road). However, fans may have already purchased tickets to the games he had been expected to play. Our analysis captures both the effect of Beckham's being expected to play and the effect of his actually playing on ticket sales. This paper also allows for the possibility of other star players increasing attendance by including United States men's national team players as an explanatory variable.

DATA AND EMPIRICAL MODEL

An informal look at the data shows that David Beckham did indeed increase ticket sales. Average sales for all MLS games during the 2007 season were 16,758. Average ticket sales for games for which Beckham was on the roster were 29,694, a dramatic increase. For games in which Beckham actually played, ticket sales more than doubled to an average of 37,659. These findings show that Beckham did appear to increase attendance. However, because other influences may affect ticket sales, isolating Beckham's effect on attendance requires multivariate regression analysis.

The regression analysis uses match level data from the 2007 season. There were 13 teams in the league, and each team played 15 home games; thus there are 195 observations.

Attendance as a percentage of stadium capacity (AT-TENDPCT) is the dependent variable. Specifying attendance as a percentage of capacity is necessary because stadiums have different capacities and because capacity constraints are binding for 10 games in our sample (including three of the five Beckham played). Attendance data are obtained from mlsnet.com and, to the best of our knowledge, reflect tickets sold rather than game attendance. Stadium capacity data are obtained from team websites and from team or stadium Wikipedia entries. Capacity varies greatly across teams; some teams play in modern soccer-specific venues seating around 20,000, while other teams play in NFL stadiums seating up to roughly 80,000. Descriptive statistics for ATTENDPCT and other variables can be found in **Table 12**.

The explanatory variables of interest are BECK-HAMROSTER and BECKHAMPLAYED, dummy variables taking a value of one for games for which David Beckham was on the LA Galaxy's active roster and games in which David Beckham actually played, respectively. Hence, our specification captures both increases in advance ticket sales and increases in match day sales.

We take two approaches to control for city specific factors affecting attendance. In one approach, following from Jewell and Molina (2005), we include several variables for various attributes of the home team's market. These include population (in millions), income per capita (in thousands), Hispanics as a share of the population, blacks as a percentage of the local population, home team points from the previous season (more points indicates a better quality team), and dummies for other sports franchises in the same market

(NBA, NFL, MLB, NHL, and dummy if a city has a team in all four major sports leagues). In the other approach, we include team specific dummy variables in the model in lieu of these home market variables. (FC Dallas is the omitted team.) Because the home team market variables such as population, income, and the minority population shares do not vary over the season, we cannot use these measures and the city dummies simultaneously without having perfect multicollinearity.

As for other right-hand side variables, evidence (Bruggink & Eaton, 1996; Garcia & Rodríguez, 2002; Chupp et al., 2007) indicates that precipitation depresses sporting event attendance, so the number of inches of precipitation on the day of the match is included as a regressor. Our model also includes a dummy variable for each team's first home match of the season and a dummy variable for matches featuring one or more players who were members of the 2006 U.S. World Cup team. National team players are looked to be the best United States players and the players with the most name recognition, so fans may be excited to see them play. Because fans may be attracted to better quality play, we also include the opposing team's points from the previous season.

Lastly, we estimate the model both with and without dummy variables for day-of-week effects, month-of-season effects, and matches played on holidays.

We should note two limitations of our model. First, we do not include a price variable, because consistent data on pricing across teams is not available. (Jewell and Molina, 2005, also omit a price variable from their model.) Second, the model does not include a measure of promotions (e.g., giveaways or entertainment acts) as an independent variable. Promotions have been shown to be important in minor league baseball and to have a positive effect on attendance (Hixson, 2005; Chupp et al., 2007). However, information regarding promotions for MLS is not readily available. Moreover, the omission of promotions variables from soccer attendance studies by Garcia and Rodríguez (2002) and Jewell and Molina (2005) suggests that promotions are not commonly used to increase soccer match attendance.

ESTIMATION RESULTS

. . . The coefficients on both Beckham variables are large and statistically significant; Beckham's being on the roster increased ticket sales by 32.7 percentage points of stadium capacity and his actually playing increased ticket sales by an additional 24.3 percentage points of stadium capacity. Hence, Beckham's playing essentially doubled ticket sales, because the typical match for which Beckham was neither playing nor on the roster was played in a half-full stadium (mean = 52%, median = 45%).

All of the home team market variables except for the dummy for cities having franchises in all four major sports leagues are significantly different from zero; however,

Table 12   Descriptive Statistics

Variable	Mean	SD	Max.	Min.
AttendPct	55.044	30.041	100.000	8.650
Beckham Roster	0.088	0.283	1	0
Beckham Played	0.026	0.159	1	0
Precip	0.085	0.510	6.760	0
OppPoints2006	41.923	7.670	55.000	25.000
HomePts2006	41.923	7.670	55.000	25.000
OpeningDay	0.067	0.250	1	0
National	0.795	0.405	1	0
Pop	6.754	5.138	18.819	1.068
PerCapInc	38.178	6.870	48.697	21.100
PctHisp	19.603	13.676	43.970	1.960
PctBlack	12.349	6.729	26.860	1.500

Source: International Journal of Sport Finance. Used with permission from Fitness Information Technology.

several of them have signs at odds with *a priori* expectations. As might be expected because of their nearly identical seasons, teams playing in cities with MLB franchises have lower attendance; sharing a city with an MLB franchise is estimated to reduce attendance by (a surprisingly large) 16 percentage points of stadium capacity. By contrast, teams located in cities with NFL, NBA, or NHL teams are estimated to have higher ticket sales. Given the popularity of soccer in Latin America, it is not surprising that we find a positive relationship between the Hispanic population share and attendance; a one percentage point increase in the Hispanic population share is associated with a 1.75 percentage point increase in tickets. The positive relationship between the Hispanic population share and ticket sales differs from that of Jewell and Molina (2005).

As for the results at odds with prior expectations, population, income, and home team points from 2006 are all found to be negatively related to attendance as a share of stadium capacity, and the black population share has a positive effect. These findings, however, may be artifacts of some teams playing in stadiums with large capacities and having, *ceteris paribus,* lower attendance as a share of capacity. For example, Washington is a relatively wealthy city and has the largest black population share; DC United plays in the 56,000 seat RFK Stadium. The New England Revolution plays in 60,000-seat Gillette Stadium; Boston is also a wealthy city with a large population. Moreover, DC and New England had the highest point totals in 2006.

As for the other explanatory variables, opening day attendance is estimated to be about seven percentage points higher than other games and is statistically significant. Rain dampens attendance somewhat (one inch reduces ticket sales by three percentage points) but is not statistically significant. Neither national team players nor opponent points in 2006 are meaningful in magnitude or statistical significance.

. . . .

As before, the Beckham effects are large and statistically significant; Beckham is estimated to increase attendance by approximately 55 percentage points of stadium capacity. As for the other regressors, the signs on precipitation, opposing team points, and national team players are consistent with *a priori* expectations; however, their marginal effects are modest in magnitude and are not statistically significant. . . . the inclusion of the day, month, and holiday variables has little effect on the other variables. . .

The estimated coefficients on the team dummy variables are consistent with the previous discussion of the negative findings for population and income per capita . . . in columns (1) and (2). Teams such as Kansas City, New England, New York, and Washington that play in large capacity stadiums all have large negative coefficients. Although estimating the relationship between city attributes such as population and income may be difficult using a single season of data, the important finding for our purposes is the consistency of

Beckham's estimated effect regardless of specification. It should also be noted that, to the extent that teams required fans wanting to see Beckham play to purchase multi-game ticket packages or season tickets, the estimated effect of Beckham on ticket sales is understated.

CONCLUSION

As with the findings of superstar externalities associated with NBA players such as Michael Jordan and Larry Bird, we find that David Beckham has a large effect on MLS attendance. Our estimates also allow us to make a rough assessment about whether the additional ticket sales from signing Beckham cover the $400,000 league contribution to his salary. The median MLS stadium seats 27,000 fans, so . . . a 55 percentage point increase in attendance as a share of stadium capacity implies an additional 14,850 tickets sold. If each additional ticket sold generates an additional $27 in revenue, a conservative assumption based on MLS prices for 2007, then Beckham generates enough additional revenue in each game played to cover the entire $400,000 league contribution to his salary (14,850 × $27 = $400,950). Because each team plays 15 road games, our estimate of the Beckham effect implies that the MLS's Designated Player Rule should allow the league to pay up to $6,000,000 (= $400,000 × 15) of Beckham's salary in order to fully internalize the superstar externality.

Turning to Beckham's value to the LA Galaxy, McNulty (2007) reported that the Galaxy pays Beckham approximately $9.6 million per year. (This figure implies that about $40 million per year of Beckham's contract would come from commercial endorsements.) If this report is correct, then our estimates suggest that signing Beckham looks to have been a shrewd deal for the Galaxy. If each ticket sold because of Beckham yields $100 of revenue—a distinct possibility since the Galaxy are selling (in 2008) one zone of tickets for $275 and another section for $150—signing Beckham would mean more than $20 million of additional revenue per year for the team. This would make Beckham's marginal revenue product for the team at least twice as large as his annual salary.

References

Berri, D. J., Schmidt, M. B., & Brook, S. L. (2004). Stars at the gate: The impact of star power on NBA gate revenues. *Journal of Sports Economics, 5*(1), 33–50.

Berri, D. J., & Schmidt, M. B. (2006). On the road with the National Basketball Association's superstar externality. *Journal of Sports Economics, 7*(4), 347–358.

Bruggink, T. H., & Eaton, J. W. (1996). Rebuilding attendance in Major League Baseball: The demand for individual games. In J. Fizel, E. Gustafson, & L. Hadley (Eds.), *Baseball economics: Current research* (pp. 9–31). Westport, CT: Prague.

Campbell, M. (2007). Vend it like Beckham. *Toronto Star,* January 12, D1.

Chupp, A., Stephenson, E. F., & Taylor, R. (2007). Stadium alcohol availability and baseball attendance: Evidence from a natural experiment. *International Journal of Sport Finance, 2*(1), 36–44.

ESPN.com (2007, January 11). Coming to America: Beckham to sign with Galaxy. Retrieved March 10, 2008, from http://soccernet.espn.go.com/news/story?id=399465&cc=5901

Garcia, J., & Rodríguez, P. (2002). The determinants of football match attendance revisited: Empirical evidence from the Spanish Football League. *Journal of Sports Economics*, 3(1), 18–38.

Hausman, J. A., & Leonard, G. K. (1997) Superstars in the National Basketball Association: Economic value and policy. *Journal of Labor Economics*, 15(4), 586–624.

Hixson, T. K. (2005) Price and non-price promotions in minor league baseball and the watering down effect. *The Sport Journal*, 8(4).

Jewell, R. T., & Molina, D. J. (2005) An evaluation of the relationship between Hispanics and Major League Soccer. *Journal of Sports Economics*, 6(2), 160–177.

McNulty, D. (2007, April 13) For MLS, Becks is worth the bucks. *Toronto Sun*, S11.

TICKET PRICING

TICKET PRICES, CONCESSIONS AND ATTENDANCE AT PROFESSIONAL SPORTING EVENTS

Dennis Coates and Brad R. Humphreys

INTRODUCTION AND MOTIVATION

The demand for attendance at major league sporting events has been the subject of a great deal of empirical research over the years. An important barrier to much of this research has been the lack of a long time series of ticket price data, especially for professional football and basketball. Since the early 1990s, Team Marketing Report has published a Fan Cost Index. As part of this index, they collect data on tickets, but also on concessions and parking so that the index measures the full dollar cost of attending a game. The index and its components are available for each of the NFL, NBA, and MLB franchises over the period.

These data make it possible to estimate empirical demand models for the NFL, NBA, and MLB, something that has been difficult since Noll's (1974) seminal paper. Moreover, the Fan Cost Index data makes it possible to assess the effect of the prices of complementary goods like concessions, parking, and programs on attendance. The Fan Cost Index attempts to paint a complete picture of the cost of attending a sporting event. The addition of the prices of the ancillary purchases related to attendance enables researchers to assess the role of these other prices in the determination of attendance.

Knowing the effects of these other prices is quite important for public policy reasons. Fort (2004) has argued that many researchers find inelastic demand for attendance in professional baseball, despite franchise monopolies, because multiple products—most notably, local TV broadcasts—are being sold. Once the multiple product nature of the franchises is correctly addressed through fuller specification of the revenue functions, then inelastic ticket pricing is implied by profit maximization.

The problem for empirical work is that time-series data sets of local television contract revenues covering many years is not available in any of the sports. Indeed, for the NFL, teams are not able to individually negotiate television contracts. However, with the Fan Cost Index data on concession, parking, and program prices, the analysis of demand can occur while accounting for greater richness in the revenue function of the franchises in all three sports.

This paper uses the Fan Cost Index, and the ticket price component of this index, to estimate the demand for attendance at professional baseball, basketball, and football games from 1991 through 2001. We analyze demand in each of these sports at the franchise level using a time series cross section data set. Price and income elasticities are estimated for each sport, controlling for demand shifters such as the age of the facility in which the franchise plays, the length of time the franchise has been in the city, the size of the city, and the success of the franchise on the field. . . .

The results confirm findings in the literature that demand for tickets is inelastic with respect to price. However, there are differences between sports. For example, while demand is inelastic in both the NBA and MLB, the ticket price elasticities are not generally the same size. The evidence here is that demand for tickets to NFL games is quite unlike demand for tickets to baseball or basketball games. The instruments used to identify the endogenous variables in the MLB and NBA demand equations are not found to be valid in the NFL equations. Coefficient estimates from the NFL equations are, generally, much less likely to accord with demand theory than are the estimates from the MLB and NBA equations. This can be partially attributed to differences in the likelihood of a contest selling out all the seats in the stadium. Sellouts are much less frequent in baseball and basketball than in football.

Using the Fan Cost Index, which includes prices of concessions and other ancillaries like parking, the analysis also provides some insight into the profit-maximizing behavior of the franchises. For example, based on a simple model of revenue maximization presented below, we show that the difference in the ticket price elasticity and the Fan Cost Index elasticity is consistent with concession price being set at the concession-revenue maximizing level. The finding that attendance is in the inelastic portion of the demand is, according to the theory, consistent with concession demand falling as ticket prices rise. This also supports the implication that franchises set ticket prices to maximize concessions' revenues.

THE ATTENDANCE DEMAND LITERATURE

. . . .

A general finding in these studies is that attendance demand is price inelastic. Fort (2004) shows that this is not inconsistent with the idea that professional sports franchises are monopolies, so long as the franchises have other sources of revenue. . . .

Finally, some recent literature examines the relationship between concessions and attendance at professional sports. Krautmann and Berri (2007) develop a model of ticket pricing, concession pricing, broadcasting revenue, and revenue sharing in a professional sports league. They use this model to motivate an unconditional analysis of ticket and concession prices that supports the idea that revenue maximizing teams price tickets in the inelastic portion of the demand curve in order to maximize total revenues by increasing revenues from other sources like concessions.

. . . .

A MODEL OF MONOPOLY PRICE DETERMINATION

Consider a monopoly sports franchise that is able to set prices for tickets and ancillary goods and services like concessions and parking. Suppose that costs to the franchise are independent of attendance and sales of these ancillaries. In these circumstances the objective of the franchises is to set ticket and concession prices to maximize revenues, given the constraint that attendance is limited by the seating capacity of the stadium or arena. Subject to these circumstances, this section derives implications for the attendance demand equation.

. . . .

Above, we suggested that the cross-price elasticities between concession prices and ticket demand would likely be negative, indicating that concessions and tickets are gross complements. If tickets and concessions are, in fact, complements, then the model predicts that a revenue maximizing franchise with monopoly power will set both ticket and concession prices in the inelastic portion of the respective demand curves. . . . Additionally, note that the stronger the degree of complementarity between concessions and tickets,

the lower the own-price elasticity of demand for tickets. . . . In other words, if high ticket prices have a strong negative effect on concessions purchases, a revenue maximizing franchise will price tickets in the inelastic portion of the demand curve—and forego some revenue from ticket sales—but make up for it in increased revenues from concession sales.

. . . In other words, the model predicts that franchises set concessions prices at their revenue maximizing levels—in the elastic portion of the demand curve—when facilities have excess capacity.

. . . .

Consider the situation when the capacity constraint is binding with no excess demand for tickets. In this case, in order to raise revenues by selling an additional ticket, and assuming capacity expands, the ticket price must be reduced. This is because we have assumed that at the existing price, the tickets demanded exactly equal the stadium capacity; if there were an additional seat, it would not sell at the current price. . . . .

. . . However, with the stadium sold out, a stronger relationship between concession prices and ticket demand may still be nearly consistent with revenue maximizing prices of concessions. . . . In other words, concession prices may be set near to the revenue maximizing level despite the dampening effect of those prices on ticket demand.

The model of price determination by a monopoly sports franchise developed in this section contains a number of empirically testable predictions about the own- and cross-price elasticities of ticket demand. First, if the attendance demand is inelastic with respect to ticket prices, then an increase in ticket prices reduces demand for concessions. Second, concession prices that do not affect ticket demand imply concession prices are set at revenue maximizing levels. Third, clubs whose attendance is constrained by stadium capacity or that have waiting lists for tickets may be able to approximate the concessions' revenue maximizing prices even if increased concession prices reduce attendance.

[*Ed. Note: Authors' discussion of the empirical approach is omitted.*]

. . . .

DATA DESCRIPTION

. . . .

The mean values are what one would expect for these three sports. Average attendance is largest at NFL games, and smallest at NBA games. The FCI is highest for NFL games and lowest for MLB games. More NBA teams make the playoffs than do NFL or MLB teams. NFL franchises are located in smaller cities, on average, while NBA and MLB franchises are located in larger cities. The stadium and franchise age variable means are also as expected. MLB teams are older and play in older stadiums. NBA teams play in newer facilities. MLB teams play in cities with higher income per capita. NFL teams, because of the greater revenue sharing and revenues from national television broadcasting contracts in that league, play in smaller cities and in cities with lower income per capita.

EMPIRICAL RESULTS

. . . .

The ticket price variable is significant for both the NBA and MLB; the Fan Cost Index variable is significant in the NBA and nearly significant in MLB. The signs on these variables are negative, as expected, indicating that higher prices are associated with lower attendance, all else equal. . . . the evidence suggests that teams set prices in the inelastic portion of the demand curves in the NBA and MLB.

In both baseball and basketball, the ticket price elasticity is smaller than the Fan Cost Index price elasticity. The Fan Cost Index contains ticket, concession, and other related good prices. Because the FCI elasticity is higher than the ticket price elasticity, the elasticity of the nonticket components of the FCI may be larger than the ticket price elasticity. This result is consistent with the prediction that emerges from the model developed above, when attendance is less than capacity. It implies that revenue maximizing teams price concessions and other goods closer to the revenue maximizing elastic portion of the demand curve and trade off these revenues by pricing tickets in the inelastic portion of the demand curve. This result is consistent with the unconditional results reported by Krautmann and Berri (2007).

The team's winning percentage and the previous year's attendance in the metropolitan area in which the team plays are both significant at the 5% level and correctly signed in all model specifications. The population of the metropolitan area is significant and positive for MLB and NBA teams, but not for the NFL. All specifications explain between 70% and 80% of the observed variation in attendance in the sample. In the NBA, aging arenas reduce attendance, perhaps explaining why NBA teams replace their facilities so frequently. Each 10% increase in the age of a basketball arena reduces attendance by about 0.5%, based on these estimates.

The results for the National Football League are quite different from those for MLB and the NBA. The price and Fan Cost Index variables are not significant, suggesting that attendance at NFL games is not very sensitive to changes in the FCI or the ticket price. Of the other explanatory variables, only the lagged attendance and current winning percentage variables are significant in the NFL models. Average attendance at NFL games is typically much closer to the capacity of the facility than in MLB or the NBA. Many NFL teams have average attendance near stadium capacity in every season. This result is also consistent with the predictions of the revenue maximization model developed above, when the capacity constraint is binding.

. . . .

If one splits the Fan Cost Index into its components, it is possible to estimate the attendance demand equations including the prices of other goods. . . . We estimated attendance equations for each league using the ticket price as well as the prices of hot dogs, beers, sodas, programs, and parking. . . .

The weakness of these results makes drawing inferences from them suspect. Nonetheless, the lack of significance of concessions prices in the attendance demand equation strikes us as intuitively plausible. More interesting is the lack of significance these prices have in determining attendance, which is consistent with the implications . . . that hold concession prices are set to maximize concessions' revenue.

DISCUSSION AND CONCLUSIONS

The evidence here suggests that demand for attendance at professional sporting events is quite inelastic with respect to the ticket price. This evidence appears to be at odds with the common idea that professional sports franchises are monopolists whose pricing behavior should be to set prices in the elastic portion of the demand. Following Fort (2004), who built on earlier analysis, we devise a simple model of a multiproduct sports franchise and derive implications for the pricing of each of the products of the team. The precise predictions depend upon whether the team sells out its entire stadium or whether there is excess capacity. In the latter case, the profit maximization conditions imply that when concessions prices do not affect ticket demand, concession prices are set to maximize concessions' revenue. We find weak evidence that this is the case.

The results also indicate that demand for professional football differs fundamentally from that of basketball and baseball. Football far more frequently sells out its games, and the theory section shows that the comparative static effects of sell outs are more complicated than those of non-sell outs. Moreover, the football equations are not well-estimated in that they reject the validity of the instruments and few coefficients are significantly different from 0. Indeed, the price variable frequently has the wrong sign for the NFL, although the estimated parameters are not different from 0. Because the capacity constraint may be binding for the NFL, while it clearly does not bind for MLB and the NBA, the pattern of estimated parameters for the NFL may reflect this constraint.

The results in this paper support the idea that ticket price elasticities in the inelastic portion of the demand curve reported in the literature are due to the inter-related pricing decision on tickets, concessions, and other related goods made by revenue maximizing monopolists in the NBA and

MLB. . . . We also find that the determinants of demand for NFL tickets differ significantly from the determinants of NBA and MLB tickets.

. . . .

References

. . . .

Fort, R. (2004). Inelastic sports pricing. *Managerial and Decision Economics 25*, 87–94.

. . . .

Krautmann, A. C., & Berri, S. B. (2007). Can we find it at the concessions? Understanding price elasticity in professional sports. *Journal of Sports Economics, 8*(2), 183–191.

Noll, R. G. (1974). *Attendance and price setting, in government and the sports business.* Washington, DC: The Brookings Institution.

Noll, R. G. (1974). *Government and the sports business.* Washington, DC: The Brookings Institution.

. . . .

VARIABLE TICKET PRICING IN MAJOR LEAGUE BASEBALL

Daniel A. Rascher, Chad D. McEvoy, Mark S. Nagel, and Matthew T. Brown

Variable ticket pricing (VTP) has recently been a much-discussed topic in the business of sport, especially as it relates to professional baseball, professional hockey, and college football (King, 2003; Rovell, 2002a). VTP refers to changing the price of a sporting-event ticket based on the expected demand for that event. For example, Major League Baseball's (MLB) Colorado Rockies had four different price levels for the same seat throughout the season (Cameron, 2002). The different price levels were based primarily on the time of the year (summer versus spring or fall), day of the week (weekends versus weekdays), holidays (Memorial Day, Independence Day, etc.), the quality of the Rockies' opponent, or their opponents' star players (e.g., Barry Bonds). The same seat in the outfield pavilion section of Coors Field, the Rockies' home stadium, ranged in price in 2004 from a high of $21 for what the Rockies labeled as "marquee" games to a low of $11 for what were considered "value" games. MLB teams who used VTP in 2004 are detailed in **Table 13**. Other sport organizations besides MLB franchises use VTP, as well. Several National Hockey League (NHL) teams use VTP strategies, as do a number of intercollegiate athletics programs (Rooney, 2003; Rovell, 2002a).

Some MLB teams have concluded that their 81 home games are not 81 units of the same product, but rather, based on the aforementioned characteristics such as the day of the week and quality of the opponent, are 81 unique products. As such, the 81 unique products should each be priced according to their own characteristics that make them more or less attractive to the potential consumer. MLB attendance studies support this notion. For example, in a study including more than 50 independent variables in explaining MLB game attendance, McDonald and Rascher (2000) found variables such as day of the week, home and visiting teams' winning percentages, and weather, among many others, to be statistically significant predictors of game attendance. Clearly, a variety of factors make some games

Table 13   2004 MLB Variable Ticket Pricing Programs

Team	Number of Levels	Levels (price for typical outfield bleacher seats)
Arizona Diamondbacks	3	premier ($18), weekend ($15), weekday ($13)
Atlanta Braves	2	premium ($21), regular ($18)
Chicago Cubs	3	prime ($35), regular ($26), value ($15)
Chicago White Sox	2	weekend ($26), weekday ($22)
Colorado Rockies	4	marquee ($21), classic ($19), premium ($17), value ($11)
New York Mets	4	gold ($16), silver ($14), bronze ($12), value ($5)
San Francisco Giants	2	Friday–Sunday ($21), Monday–Thursday ($16)
Tampa Bay Devil Rays	3	prime ($20), regular ($17), value ($10)
Toronto Blue Jays	3	premium ($26), regular ($23), value ($15)

Source: Journal of Sport Management. Used with permission.

Note: Different seating configurations of each stadium make comparing like seats difficult; however, this attempt was made to provide the reader with an idea of the range of price levels used by each team for similar seats.

more appealing and others less appealing to consumers. It seems quite logical to price tickets to these games at different levels, especially with teams constantly searching for revenue sources to compete with their opponents for players (Howard & Crompton, 2004; Zimbalist, 2003).

The varying quality of games throughout a season often creates a secondary market because demand for the most popular games might exceed available supply. Independent ticket agents, or scalpers, broker tickets obtained from various sources to fans unable or unwilling to purchase tickets from a team's ticket office or licensed ticket agency (Caple 2001; Reese, 2004). Ticket scalpers respond to market demands (often in violation of city ordinances or state laws), but the team initially selling the ticket does not realize any increased revenue during a scalper's transaction ("History of Ticket Scalping," n.d.). For this reason, the Chicago Cubs have recently permitted ticket holders to auction their Wrigley Field tickets on a Cubs affiliated Web site, with a fee being paid to the Cubs for this service (Rovell, 2002b; see also www.buycubstickets.com). It is believed that instituting a comprehensive VTP policy would diminish the influence of scalpers and permit greater revenue to be generated by the team for games in high demand.

Many industries have previously embraced the variable pricing concept as a method for increasing revenue and providing more efficient service to consumers (Bruel, 2003; Rovell, 2002a). Airline flights are typically more expensive for selected days of the week (Monday, Friday), times of the day (morning, late afternoon), and days of the year (holidays) when travel demand is higher. The airlines also use variable pricing to encourage passengers to book their flights early (typically a purchase at least 10–14 days in advance results in a lower fare) or, in some cases, at the last minute ("Travel Tips," 2004). Hotel pricing characteristically reflects expected demand, even though the actual physical product does not change, because rooms for weekends or holidays are usually priced higher than for weekdays or off-season visits. In fact, sometimes variable pricing even relates to major sporting events like the Super Bowl. Many hotels substantially raise room rates during Super Bowl week (Baade & Matheson, n.d.). Other industries such as transportation use variable pricing; some toll roads now charge higher toll rates during peak times and lower rates during off-peak times ("Group Commends," 2001). The arts use variable pricing; matinee movie pricing is one example (Riley, 2002).

Sports franchises are moving forward with VTP strategies before sufficient research has been done to empirically evaluate its specific merits to the industry. This article provides a straightforward assessment of optimal VTP. First, a review of the literature reveals difficulties in estimating the nature of demand functions in sports. Specifically, optimal pricing is partially determined by price elasticities of demand, yet it is difficult to estimate ticket-price elasticities that are consistent over time. Next, a theory of complementary demand is explained that will account for nonticket products

and services and the effect that ticket prices have on the demand for these products and services. Then, using individual game data from the 1996 MLB season, ticket prices and corresponding quantities are estimated that would have maximized ticket revenue. These are compared with actual prices and revenue to determine the yield from initiating a VTP policy. The final section contains a discussion of the implications of the results. In summary, this article shows that there are financial benefits to be gained from implementing VTP, details how much can be gained from a general VTP policy, and provides strategies for implementing VTP.

. . . .

TICKET PRICING ISSUES

It has been difficult for researchers to show profit-maximizing ticket pricing by sports teams. There are a number of reasons for this besides the inclusion of other revenue streams. First, most pricing data is a simple average of prices that are available for various seats for each team each season. Currently, Team Marketing Report (TMR) collects pricing data that some researchers have used (e.g., Rishe & Mondello, 2004; Rascher, 1999). Although it is likely an improvement over previously collected pricing data, it has lacked consistency across teams and over time. Numerous discussions by the authors and TMR have revealed that TMR is able to separate out the luxury-suite ticket prices. TMR has also separated out club-seating prices for some, but not all, teams. Furthermore, this varies across seasons. TMR relies on the teams to self-report. Because of the prominence of the TMR Fan Cost Index, some teams potentially manipulate their reported prices to appear relatively inexpensive. Moreover, the number of seats available at each price level does not typically weight these prices. In addition, the number of seats sold is generally known in aggregate, not separated by seat price. Second, Demmert (1973) noted that there is a correlation between population and ticket price across many seasons (likely based on the connection to income in which more highly populated areas are associated with higher incomes, increasing demand and, therefore, prices). This multicollinearity can cloud the interpretation of coefficients on price. Third, as Salant (1992) pointed out, the long-term price of tickets might be optimal (adjusting for risk), but in the short term a team might be over- or underpricing in order to maintain consistency. This is a form of insurance in which the team bears the risk. Fourth, similar to Fort's (2004) findings, ticket prices might be kept relatively low in order to increase the number of attendees at an event who are likely to spend more money on parking, concessions, and merchandise and who will drive up sponsorship revenue for the team, thus maximizing overall revenues, rather than simply ticket revenues.

DeSerpa (1994) discussed the rationality of apparently low season-ticket prices. Even though many games sell out in the National Basketball Association and National Football League (focal sports in his study), it is rational for the seller to price below the myopic short-term demand price in order to give a fan a reason to purchase season tickets. In fact, DeSerpa discussed the possibility, but unlikeliness, of charging different prices for each event based on its demand. He surmised that it was administratively expensive and subject to potential negative fan reaction.

DeSerpa (1994) also noted that it is optimal to underprice season tickets if fans will likely want to attend only some of the games and resell the tickets for the remaining contests. The season ticket must be priced low enough for holders to be able to at least recoup their initial investment after assuming the transaction costs of resale (e.g., time, effort, search costs, and actual costs such as postage and advertising). Lower priced season tickets also potentially created a home-field advantage for teams. Each argument or concern DeSerpa proffered can be addressed in a VTP system.

. . . .

THEORETICAL FOUNDATIONS

The demand for baseball games changes from game to game, partly because of the varying quality and perception of quality of the home and visiting teams and partly because of nonperformance factors such as day of the week or month. For a given price, **Table 14** (columns 2 and 3) shows that attendance varies greatly across games. The average deviation from the mean is nearly 23%. . . .

In general, many organizations are trying to minimize the effect of team performance, which is one of the key

Table 14   Summary of Effects of Variable Ticket Pricing (No Capacity or Nonticket-Revenue Adjustment)

	1	2	3	4	5	6	7	8	9	10	11	12
Atlanta	35,793	5832	16.3	13.06	8.1	467,458	471,825	4367	37,864,102	38,217,807	353,706	0.9
Baltimore	45,475	1930	4.2	13.14	2.1	597,539	597,909	371	48,400,634	48,430,660	30,026	0.1
Boston	28,687	3847	13.4	15.43	6.7	442,643	445,436	2794	35,854,064	36,080,352	226,288	0.6
California	22,476	4899	21.8	8.44	10.9	189,697	193,539	3842	15,365,441	15,676,653	311,212	2.0
Chicago (AL)	21,115	4530	21.5	14.11	10.7	297,927	303,781	5854	24,132,054	24,606,230	474,176	2.0
Chicago (NL)	28,606	6854	24.0	13.12	12.0	375,309	382,932	7622	30,400,069	31,017,468	617,399	2.0
Cincinnati	24,097	4492	18.6	7.95	9.3	191,568	194,618	3049	15,517,036	15,764,032	246,996	1.6
Cleveland	41,983	512	1.2	14.52	0.6	609,592	609,629	37	49,376,968	49,379,960	2992	0.0
Colorado	48,037	80	0.2	10.61	0.1	509,675	509,679	4	41,283,673	41,284,030	357	0.0
Detroit	14,464	5018	34.7	10.60	17.3	153,322	162,531	9209	12,419,066	13,165,021	745,954	6.0
Florida	21,839	4541	20.8	10.37	10.4	226,469	230,737	4268	18,343,988	18,689,707	345,720	1.9
Houston	24,394	7362	30.2	10.65	15.1	259,793	268,433	8640	21,043,206	21,743,062	699,856	3.3
Kansas City	17,949	4013	22.4	9.74	11.2	174,828	178,510	3682	14,161,039	14,459,292	298,253	2.1
Los Angeles	39,364	7038	17.9	9.94	8.9	391,274	395,669	4394	31,693,231	32,049,165	355,934	1.1
Milwaukee	16,847	5594	33.2	9.37	16.6	157,853	165,387	7535	12,786,054	13,396,356	610,302	4.8
Minnesota	17,930	4899	27.3	10.16	13.7	182,170	188,905	6735	14,755,746	15,301,288	545,542	3.7
Montreal	19,982	7149	35.8	9.07	17.9	181,240	190,229	8989	14,680,457	15,408,584	728,127	5.0
New York (AL)	28,371	8999	31.7	14.58	15.9	413,655	428,965	15,310	33,506,040	34,746,176	1,240,136	3.7
New York (NL)	20,260	4610	22.8	11.83	11.4	239,676	245,833	6157	19,413,778	19,912,512	498,734	2.6
Oakland	14,339	5183	36.1	11.34	18.1	162,607	171,942	9335	13,171,166	13,927,263	756,097	5.7
Philadelphia	23,077	4679	20.3	11.01	10.1	254,072	258,556	4483	20,579,872	20,943,035	363,163	1.8
Pittsburgh	17,039	5914	34.7	10.09	17.4	171,919	179,698	7779	13,925,450	14,555,555	630,106	4.5
San Diego	27,258	10,474	38.4	9.88	19.2	269,311	284,010	14,698	21,814,230	23,004,773	1,190,543	5.5
San Francisco	17,548	6898	39.3	10.61	19.7	186,182	198,697	12,515	15,080,772	16,094,448	1,013,676	6.7
Seattle	33,593	9398	28.0	11.59	14.0	389,349	400,760	11,411	31,537,236	32,461,526	924,289	2.9
St. Louis	32,912	6038	18.3	9.91	9.2	326,153	330,616	4463	26,418,415	26,779,886	361,472	1.4
Texas	36,111	6664	18.5	11.96	9.2	431,888	437,077	5189	34,982,929	35,403,253	420,324	1.2
Toronto	31,600	2718	8.6	13.93	4.3	440,190	441,845	1655	35,655,410	35,789,472	134,063	0.4
Average	26,827	5363	22.9	11.32	11.4	310,477	316,705	6228	25,148,647	25,653,127	504,480	2.62

Source: Journal of Sport Management. Used with permission.
Note: The total change in ticket revenue accounting for variable ticket pricing across Major League Baseball is $14.1 million. 1 = average attendance; 2 = average absolute change; 3 = average deviation from the mean (%); 4 = average ticket price ($); 5 = average absolute change in price (%); 6 = average actual ticket revenue ($); 7 = average variation-pricing ticket revenue ($); 8 = average change in ticket revenue ($); 9 = total actual ticket revenue ($); 10 = total variation-pricing ticket revenue ($); 11 = total change in ticket revenue ($); 12 = change in revenue (%).

factors in the changing demand from game to game (Brock-inton, 2003; George, 2003). As shown in the literature, team performance is one of the most significant demand factors that can be affected by an owner. For example, Bruggink and Eaton (1996) and Rascher (1999) analyzed game-by-game attendance and the importance of team performance. Using annual data, Alexander (2001) showed that the variable with the highest statistical significance is the number of games behind the leader, a measure of team performance. Teams are building new stadiums, improving concessions and restaurants, and creating areas where kids and adults can enjoy themselves but not necessarily watch the game (George, 2003). These improvements not only increase demand but also lessen the importance that team performance uncertainty has on expected revenues.

At the same time, teams are beginning to use variable pricing in an attempt to manage shifting demand from game to game, given that they are unable to completely remove the variation. The theory on which this analysis is based is simply short-term revenue maximization with two goods that are complementary. Tickets and concessions are complementary goods. The demand for tickets is higher if concessions prices are lower because the overall cost of enjoying the game would be lower (Marburger, 1997; Fort, 2004). Similarly, the demand for concessions is higher if ticket prices are lower. The model consists of demand for tickets and a separate aggregate demand for nonticket products and services (hereafter referred to as concessions) that is affected by ticket price. This is where the complementarity between the two demand functions occurs.

. . . .

To be clear, these models do not assume profit maximization, win maximization, or something else; they only assume that a team's objectives are consistent throughout the season. For example, if a team is focused primarily on profits, it will set ticket and concessions prices in order to maximize the sum of both revenues. In a similar way, if a team is attempting to maximize wins, it will still want to price as a profit maximizer because its relevant costs are not variable. Such a team would likely spend more on players in order to improve winning than a profit-maximizing team would. The team would still want to set prices in order to maximize revenues from tickets and concessions, however, just as a profit-maximizing team would. An exception to this argument is if a win-maximizing owner chose to price below profit-maximizing levels in order to raise attendance (even though it is lowering revenues) to increase the impact of home-field advantage, which would increase the likelihood of winning more games and, therefore, satisfy his or her objectives.

The models also do not need to assume linear demand functions. Linear demand is chosen for simplicity. As described in the next section, nonlinear demand changes the magnitudes of the findings. Using linear demand generates

more conservative findings—the gains from variable pricing are lower. The empirical analysis operationalizes this by noting that regardless of an owner's objectives (winning, profits, or a combination of the two), it is assumed that prices are set to maximize those objectives. For a particular game it might be that prices are too low or too high given demand, but because one price is charged for the entire season, it is objective maximizing on average.

One hypothesis stemming from these models is that adoption of VTP would improve revenues for MLB teams. Another hypothesis is that for those teams who are adjusting prices, the amount of adjustment is correct. For instance, the Cardinals had only raised their prices for VTP games by $2 for 2002. In contrast, the Rockies have had prices for particular seats that varied by as much as $6 (Rovell, 2002b). This analysis will provide a benchmark for how much teams should be adjusting their prices.

It is important to note that there are public relations issues that play a role in VTP. For example, the Nashville Predators have been thinking about incorporating VTP but fear a negative fan backlash at a time when they are trying to build a loyal fan base (Cameron, 2002). A team might therefore opt to raise its prices only nominally to see if there is a backlash in which fans react with an emotional response that actually shifts demand (not slides along demand, as price changes are expected to do). This analysis ignores any public relations issues.

[*Ed. Note: Authors' discussion of method is omitted.*]

. . . .

RESULTS

. . . .

Variable pricing would have yielded an average of approximately $504,000 per year in additional revenue for each MLB team, ceteris paribus, or over $14 million for the league as a whole. This amounts to only about a 2.6% increase above what occurs when prices are not varied, as shown in Table 14. The amount of variation in ticket prices is just over 11% on average. The fact that such a large price swing only yields a revenue swing four times smaller is simply based on the large change in attendance that occurs when prices are varied. This occurs with all downward sloping demand curves and is not unique to baseball. For the 1996 season, the largest revenue gain would have been for the New York Yankees, which would have generated an extra $1.24 million in ticket revenue, or a 3.7% increase. The largest percentage revenue gain would have been for the San Francisco Giants. The Giants would have seen an estimated 6.7% increase in revenue, or $1.01 million, if they had used optimal VTP. The smallest amount of impact would have been for the Colorado Rockies, which averaged only plus or minus 80 patrons in absolute deviation from the mean attendance per game throughout the 1996 season. In fact, teams with the lowest average attendance benefit the most from variable pricing. This is not surprising because those teams tend to have the highest variation in attendance, allowing them to gain from dynamic pricing.

The Rockies would gain the least from VTP because they had many sellouts in 1996. As described in the Method section, a censored regression is carried out in order to forecast the true demand above the capacity constraint. Although there are many more factors that affect game-by-game attendance than those used here, this analysis used only those factors known before ticket-price setting occurred. Thus, only factors known before the beginning of the season are used in order to be consistent with what would be known by team management when setting prices. . . . As explained, performance-specific factors that are only known to price setters once the season has begun, such as the home pitcher's earned-run average at that point in the season, were omitted.. . .

Overall, adjusting for demand beyond stadium capacity raises the increased revenue from VTP policies from $14.1 million to $16.5 million for the league as a whole.

The final analysis addressed . . . accounting for nonticket revenues such as concessions, merchandise, and parking. . . . the average team would have gained $911,000 in ticket and nonticket revenue by adopting a VTP policy while accounting for nonticket prices. The league overall would have gained $25.5 million. The Cleveland Indians would have earned the most, over $2.2 million, from such a policy.

DISCUSSION

This analysis has shown that MLB could have increased ticket revenues by approximately 2.8%, or $16.5 million, and total stadium revenues by about $25.5 million for the 1996 season if teams used VTP. Total revenues in MLB are estimated to have grown from $1.78 billion in 1996 to approximately $4.3 billion in 2003, or 250%. Similar changes in the effect of VTP strategies, as discovered in this study, would yield nearly $40 million in ticket revenue and over $60 million in ticket plus nonticket revenue for MLB. Therefore, it behooves team owners and the league office to consider and implement VTP strategies, especially because teams and the league are constantly searching for ways to increase revenues.

The San Francisco Giants would have seen an estimated 6.7% increase in ticket revenue, or $1.01 million, if they had used optimal VTP in 1996. It is interesting that the Giants had considered using VTP since the 1996 season because they had noticed a huge variation in attendance patterns at Candlestick Park, the team's then-home facility (King, 2002a). In addition to weather issues (pleasant for day games but frigid for night) in their facility, the Giants of the mid-1990s occasionally fielded teams of lower quality. The results of this study would strongly suggest that teams in similar facility or on-the-field talent situations maximize their revenues through VTP.

The results of this study support the use of VTP both to increase and decrease prices from average seasonal levels. The data showed fewer games with excess demand than those with diminished demand. The selected games with excess demand deviated, however, from the mean at a greater rate than those with decreased demand. Currently, most MLB teams have focused their VTP strategies on the revenue potential of increased prices from highly demanded games (King, 2002a). It appears that some teams, however, have begun to realize the potential benefit of attracting fans to less desirable contests by lowering prices (King, 2002b). The New York Yankees sold $5 tickets in certain sections of Yankee Stadium on Mondays, Tuesdays, and Thursdays in 2003 (King, 2003).

Lowering ticket prices for less desirable games would potentially create more positive relationships between teams and local municipalities. MLB teams have often been chastised for seeking subsidies for new revenue generating facilities that are financially inaccessible to many taxpayers (Pappas, 2002; O'Keefe, 2004). Given the number of games in a typical season for which demand is below the yearly average . . ., lowering prices creates an opportunity for teams to potentially attract new or disenfranchised fans and presents local governments with a more favorable reaction to their public-policy decisions supporting the local franchise. Marketing less desirable games with lower ticket prices as "value" games, as the Chicago Cubs, Colorado Rockies, New York Mets, Tampa Bay Devil Rays, and Toronto Blue Jays did in 2004, allows teams to reach market segments perhaps otherwise unreachable because of pricing/income issues, in addition to the aforementioned public relations benefits.

Currently, teams might not want to implement multiple price points for each game. . . . As discussed by Levy, Dutta, Bergen, and Venable (1997), menu costs affect the frequency and desire to change prices to reflect changes in demand or supply. *Menu costs* are costs associated with physically changing prices on products, having to look up prices to tell a customer the price for a particular game, or, more generally, any costs associated with having more than one price for a product or service. In addition, asymmetric information, search costs, and simple confusion for customers regarding the price for different games might cause franchises to have fewer prices for a particular seat throughout the season than variable pricing predicts. For this reason, many teams have only used a minimal number of ticket-pricing tiers, usually two to four, in their VTP system (Rovell, 2002b).

Confusion and the additional costs associated with changing ticket prices might already be in the process of being eliminated. Kevin Fenton, Colorado Rockies senior director of ticket operations, noted that once the initial confusion regarding multiple price points for games is overcome, patrons realize that tickets can be priced like other industries (Rovell, 2002b). In the near future, the negative fan reaction to changing ticket price will likely be alleviated if not eliminated (Adams, 2003). Ticket offices are also now better equipped to handle menu costs issues. Although ticket offices were not prepared to handle extensive VTP in the 1990s, recent technological advances have allowed most American professional sport teams to implement new ticket policies such as bar-coded and print-at-home tickets to prepare for extensive VTP in the future (Zoltak, 2002).

An initial VTP recommendation is that for every 10% increase in attendance (or specifically, expected attendance) above the average, teams should raise ticket prices by 5% and receive a gain of 1.2% in ticket revenue. The practical use of variable pricing, however, would entail creating, at most, five different prices for each seat in a stadium throughout the season, not a different price for each game. High-demand games or series should be priced accordingly, but teams should not forget the potential benefits of lowering prices for less desired games. The present findings reinforce previous research identifying factors such as day of the week or a rivalry game as affecting demand for MLB tickets.

. . . .

The hypothesis that the few teams administering VTP are doing so properly is consistent with the findings. In fact, the present analysis shows that optimal VTP is managed by small changes in ticket prices. The Giants expected to gain an additional $1 million from VTP in 2002 (Isidore, 2002; Rovell, 2002b). The Giants VTP strategy in 2002 affected only 39 of their 81 home games (all weekend dates). The present analysis shows a gain of about $1 million for the 1996 season if optimal pricing were used by the Giants.

. . . .

References

Adams, R. (2003, January 6). Variable price ticket policy wins converts. *Sports Business Journal*, p. 14.

Alexander, D.L. (2001). Major League Baseball: Monopoly pricing and profit-maximizing behavior. *Journal of Sports Economics, 2*, 341–355.

Baade, R., & Matheson, V. (n.d.). Super Bowl or super (hyper)bole? The economic impact of the Super Bowl on host communities. Unpublished manuscript.

. . . .

Brockinton, L. (2003, May 26). New NFL digs offer more revenue possibilities. *Sports Business Journal*, p. 25.

Bruel, J.S. (2003, January 27). Finding hidden revenue under the seat cushions. *Sports Business Journal*, p. 23.

Bruggink, T.H., & Eaton, J.W. (1996). Rebuilding attendance in Major League Baseball: The demand for individual games. In J. Fizel, E. Gustafson, & L. Hadley (Eds.), *Baseball economics: Current research* (pp. 9–31). Westport, CT: Praeger.

Cameron, S. (2002, May 27). Bruins to set prices hourly. *Sports Business Journal*, pp. 1, 50.

Caple, J. (2001, August 21). All hail ticket scalpers! *ESPN Page 2*. Retrieved April 16, 2003, from http://espn.go.com/page2/s/caple/010821.html

. . . .

Demmert, H.G. (1973). *The economics of professional team sports*. Lexington, MA: Lexington Books.

DeSerpa, A.C. (1994). To err is rational: A theory of excess demand for tickets. *Managerial and Decision Economics, 15*, 511–518.

Fort, R.D. (2004). Inelastic sports pricing. *Managerial and Decision Economics, 25*, 87–94.

George, J. (2003, May 26). Phillies go big with entertaining Ashburn Alley. *Sports Business Journal*, p. 24.

Group commends port authority for variably priced tolls. (2001). Retrieved July 19, 2004, from http://www.tstc.org/press/322_PAtolls.html

. . . .

History of ticket scalping. (n.d.). Retrieved July 16, 2004, from http://metg.fateback.com/ metghistory.html

Howard, D.R., & Crompton, J.L. (2004). *Financing sport* (2nd ed.). Morgantown, WV: Fitness Information Technologies.

Isidore, C. (2002, December 27). Fans to pay the price(s). *CNN/Money*. Retrieved July 23, 2004, from http://money.cnn.com/2002/12/27/commentary/column_sportsbiz/ ticket_prices/

King, B. (2002a, April 1). Baseball tries variable pricing. *Sports Business Journal*, pp. 1, 49.

King, B. (2002b, December 9). MLB varied ticket pricing a boon. *Sports Business Journal*, p. 23.

King, B. (2003, December 1). More teams catch on to variable ticket pricing. *Sports Business Journal*, p. 16.

Levy, D., Dutta, S., Bergen, M., & Venable, R. (1997). The magnitude of menu costs: Direct evidence from large U.S. supermarket chains. *Quarterly Journal of Economics, 112*, 791–825.

Marburger, D.R. (1997). Optimal ticket pricing for performance goods. *Managerial and Decision Economics, 18*, 375–381.

McDonald, M., & Rascher, D.A. (2000). Does bat day make sense?: The effect of promotions on the demand for Major League Baseball. *Journal of Sport Management, 14*, 8–27.

. . . .

O'Keefe, B. (2004, March 29). Pro baseball franchise hit with unusual state audit. *Stateline.org*. Retrieved July 24, 2004, from www.stateline.org/stateline/?pa=story&sa=showStoryInfo&print=1&id=360450

Pappas, D. (2002). The numbers (part three; part five). *Baseball prospectus*. Retrieved June 20, 2004, from www.baseballprospectus.com/article.php?articleid=1305

Rascher, D.A. (1999). The optimal distribution of talent in Major League Baseball. In L. Hadley, E. Gustafson, & J. Fizel (Eds.), *Sports economics: Current research* (pp. 27–45). Westport, CT: Praeger.

Reese, J.T. (2004). Ticket operations. In U. McMahon-Beattie & I. Yeoman (Eds.), *Sport and leisure operations management* (pp. 167–179). London: Continuum.

Riley, D.F. (2002). Ticket pricing: Concepts, methods, practices, and guidelines for performing arts events. *Culture Work, 2*(6). Retrieved July 19, 2004, from http://aad.uoregon. edu/culturework/culturework20.html

Rishe, P., & Mondello, M. (2004). Ticket price determination in professional sports: An empirical analysis of the NBA, NFL, NHL, and Major League Baseball. *Sport Marketing Quarterly, 13*, 104–112.

Rooney, T. (2003, January). *The pros and cons of variable ticket pricing*. Paper presented at the 2003 National Sports Forum, Pittsburgh, PA.

Rovell, D. (2002a, December 31). Forecasting the sport business future. *ESPN.com*. Retrieved July 12, 2004, from http://espn.go.com/sportsbusiness/s/2002/1230/1484284.html

Rovell, D. (2002b, June 21). Sports fans feel pinch in seat (prices). *ESPN. com*. Retrieved July 20, 2004, from http://espn.go.com/sportsbusines s/s/2002/0621/1397693.html

Salant, D. (1992). Price setting in professional team sports. In P. Sommers (Ed.), *Diamonds are forever* (pp. 77–90). Washington, DC: The Brookings Institution.

. . . .

Travel tips. (2004). Retrieved July 20, 2004, from http://clarkhoward.com/travel/tips/todays_tip.html

Whitney, J.D. (1988). Winning games versus winning championships: The economics of fan interest and team performance. *Economic Inquiry, 26*, 703–724.

Zimbalist, A. (2003). *May the best team win: Baseball economics and public policy*. Washington DC: The Brookings Institution.

Zoltak, J. (2002, July). Tickets and technology: Perfect together. *Venues Today*, pp. 1, 20.

MICROPERSPECTIVES

GLOBALISATION AND SPORTS BRANDING: THE CASE OF MANCHESTER UNITED

John S. Hill and John Vincent

INTRODUCTION

May 2005 will go down as a watershed moment in the storied history of Manchester United, when US businessman Malcolm Glazer bought financial control of the fabled English football club. While it is not the intention of this article to argue the pros and cons of this move, it is noteworthy that Glazer's move was premised on Manchester United's position as one of the most prominent global brands in a sport that has proven worldwide appeal.

In this article we examine how Manchester United evolved out of its position as one of two provincial football teams in the city of Manchester to its current status among the best known brands in sport. Our conceptual centrepiece is Aaker's (1996) brand identity model that culls the major resource factors that contribute to strong marketplace brands. Complementing this model, to add depth and a more complete analysis, we evaluate two structural factors relevant to corporate strategy-making—global and industry environments. This follows Gerrard's (2003) assertion that strategic analyses in the sports arena should include both structural and resource-based factors for a balanced view.

. . . .

STRUCTURAL FACTORS: GLOBALISATION, GLOBAL SPORTS AND GLOBAL BRANDING

Effective strategies take account of marketplace developments, and as the 21st century got underway, the trend of globalisation was very much apparent in the world economy. Defined by Aninat (2002, p.4) as "the process through which an increasingly free flow of ideas, peoples, goods and services and capital leads to the integration of economies and societies", globalisation has resulted in nation states forging links through trade, investments and the activities of international companies participating in the world economy. . . . The end of the Cold War in the late 1980s and early 1990s decreased world political tensions, and the meteoric rise of the internet and of global communications caused an unprecedented acceleration in commercial activities outside domestic markets, increasing the variety of goods and services available in the world marketplace (Hill & Holloway, 2001). The integration of world economies has led to increasing competition in many industries (Porter, 1986). In the field of sport, globalisation has added impetus to international rivalries that date in the modern era from the 1896 Olympic Games. Since that time, many sports have benefited as their international media exposure has increased from quadrennial appearances in the Olympics. Sports such as tennis and golf have been global for decades; as have the British and colonies-based sports of cricket, rugby, squash and badminton. Equestrian, motorsport, table tennis (ping-pong), boxing, hockey, ice hockey and lacrosse have all benefited from international exposure. US sports such as basketball, American football and baseball have established footholds in foreign markets as global media has broadened their appeal beyond domestic markets. But no single sport has benefited from its global exposures as much as soccer (Giulianotti, 2002). Since its first appearance in the 1908 Olympics, the sport has attracted increasing international attention. The first World Cup was organised in 1930 by Jules Rimet in Uruguay. Since then, soccer has consistently drawn more support worldwide than any other pastime. As globalisation trends accelerated after the 1980s, increasing numbers of professional soccer clubs sought to capitalise on the sport's global appeal, but only two clubs, Manchester United and Real Madrid, emerged as global brands. Although Real Madrid has a very high global awareness and recently overtook Manchester United as the club with the highest turnover, many observers consider that Manchester United's innovative branding and marketing strategies were at the leading edge of the contemporary trend in sport globalisation. . . .

The club's pre-eminent position was noted in its 2003 annual report (p. iii): "Manchester United is one of the leading clubs in world football, with a global brand and following that embodies the passion and excitement of the world's most popular sport." The report reaffirmed the need to convert more of its 75 million global fans into paying customers. In implementing its international strategy, Manchester United has been the pathfinder for many other sports and clubs seeking to establish global identities in the international marketplace.

STRUCTURAL FACTORS: INDUSTRY ENVIRONMENT

The forming of the English Premier League (EPL—also known as The Premiership) in 1992–93 signaled an era of heightened competitiveness. We analysed additional pressures on soccer using frameworks developed by Porter (1980) and Lonsdale (2004).

Upstream Pressures—Player Scarcity Effects

The forming of the EPL in 1992 added pressures to clubs as they competed among a limited supply of talented players. This competition for players intensified further following the Bosman Ruling, instituted in 1995 by the European Court of Justice that decreed that professional soccer players could become free agents following expiry of their contracts. The ruling also removed the 'maximum of three foreigners rule' observed in British soccer clubs. Together, these changes gave European-born players the right to move freely to any club within the European Union (Boyle & Haynes, 2000). As competition for talent escalated, club costs rocketed under the impetus of player salary increases, while attendance receipts and existing television deals were levelling out (Crispin, 2004a). Both the Football Association and individual clubs looked for additional revenue streams to bolster finances and attract star players in inflation-affected transfer markets. These were realised in the widening of soccer's downstream appeal to spectators, sponsors, sports merchandisers and television viewers, both domestic and global.

Downstream Pressures—Broadening Spectator Appeal

Recognising the need for increased gate receipts, in 2004 the English Football League set a goal to increase game attendances from 16 to 21 million by 2010 (Sweney, 2004). This was deemed feasible given a League directive that stadia were to be all-seater, following the 1989 Hillsborough disaster, where 95 people were killed in an FA Cup semi-final between Liverpool and Nottingham Forest, played at Hillsborough, Sheffield (Lonsdale, 2004). Although the mandated trend towards creating all-seater stadia initially reduced stadium capacity for some clubs, many made significant investments to expand their stadia capacity. All seater stadia also became more family-friendly, which broadened the game's appeal among the middle classes (Miller, 2004).

Manchester United followed this trend. The current Old Trafford stadium is the largest club facility in England, and is being expanded by a further 7900 seats to give it a capacity of nearly 76,000 by the 2006–07 season. [*Ed. Note: This expansion has been completed.*] Included in the plans are executive suites to accommodate a further 2400 corporate customers. The club's emphasis on heightening the matchday experience includes the Old Trafford Chef's Table dining facility, in-stadium and online betting (courtesy of platinum sponsor Ladbrokes), the club museum (and tour), the Red Cafe, a megastore and LED perimeter advertising displays. The stadium also houses the MU Finance Advisory Centre and MUTV studios (Manchester United Annual Report, 2004).

. . . .

Downstream Pressures—Adding Merchandising Deals

Between 10 and 15 years ago, sponsorships and merchandising deals were viewed as minor appendages to club activities (Sport's Premiers, 2003). Today they are big business. . . .

Downstream Pressures—Competing for TV Viewers

A key event for English soccer occurred as Rupert Murdoch's media empire sought to enter the UK television market in the late 1980s. Murdoch's BSkyB satellite channel offered £304 million—five times ITV's 1988 deal—to broadcast top-tier games. The four-year follow-on contract to 1997 was worth £670 million, and the two follow-on arrangements were both in excess of £1,000 million (Timeline, 2003).

Manchester United supplemented this package when in 1999 it launched its own dedicated television network, MUTV, in conjunction with Granada Media and BSkyB. MUTV had the rights to club games after their airing on the Sky network (Granada, 1999). MUTV also negotiated rights to show archive footage of Manchester United's UEFA Champions League matches; through its broadband service (MU.tv available through subscription), classic games can be viewed. Under current consideration, and taking advantage of the latest technologies, is the proposal to promote club products and services through MU Interactive, MU Mobile and MU Picture facilities (Manchester United Annual Report, 2004).

Downstream Pressures—Competing for Global Audiences

The BSkyB contract added both benefits and pressures through its international connections as EPL clubs were given global exposure. Murdoch's ownership of Fox Sports gave the EPL global coverage through its Fox Sports World channel. In the US, Murdoch's 2004 takeover of DirecTV consolidated this hold in the important North American market, while his agreement with ESPN Star Sports in Asia upped regional audiences of Premiership matches by 150 million households (Crispin, 2004b). Today the EPL reaches an audience of about 1 billion viewers in over 170 countries (Brand Strategy, 2003), giving the league the worldwide marketing platform to reach new fans and to sell its wares to broader consumer bases. These measures—increased ticket, advertising and merchandising revenues—increased turnover for the top 20 English clubs. . . . They also provided new opportunities for clubs to build their brand profiles and promote themselves to broader audiences; but it was Manchester United that seized the moment to capitalise on its reputation and establish itself as a global brand and sports icon.

BUILDING BRAND IDENTITY

The resource-based view (RBV) of competitive advantage posits that corporate resources—including intangible assets such as brand identities—are key factors in sport (Amis, 2003). A brand identity provides direction, purpose and meaning for the brand—its core values are how it is perceived, what traits it projects and the relationships it engenders (Aaker 1996, p.68). Brand identities comprise the core identity that Aaker defined (p. 85) as "the timeless essence of the brand"—that which makes it unique and valuable. The brand's extended identity includes those elements that provide "texture and completeness". In essence, one or more of the extended brand identity characteristics are so dominant that singly, or in concert, they become its core identity. We used Aaker's brand identity structure concepts to delineate the distinctive features of the Manchester United brand. . . . Not all components are relevant for individual brands. Our discussion focuses on 10 of the 12 components under four headings: the brand as product, the brand as organisation, the brand as person and the brand as symbol.

. . . .

The Brand as Product

All brands are parts of broader product classes whose characteristics define the parameters within which the brand operates.

Product Scope

Product scope defines the broad industry environment in which the brand operates—in this case, the game of soccer. The global appeal of soccer is based on its history—the fact that many nations and cultures have been playing the sport (or some version of it) for thousands of years.

. . . .

The early organisation of British football established a blueprint that laid the foundation for the sport. The club-based template quickly took root in Europe and through colonisation the organised game spread to Latin America, Africa and Asia.

Product Attributes

In contrast to some sports, soccer has many attractive features that contribute to its current 300-million player following and a fan base that is measured in the billions worldwide (Blatter, 1999). It is action-oriented. It builds stamina and aerobic conditioning. There are few physical size or age limitations. Its rules are relatively simple to understand. It requires minimal equipment (appropriate footwear, shinguards and uniforms for organised play) and facilities. Soccer is very team-oriented, with many players usually participating in moving the ball up the field. It can be played in many climates; and in contrast to many US sports, on-field strategies are largely player-created.

Quality/Value

For a brand to be successful, it must be part of a product group that is perceived to be quality-laden and that provides value for money. In the automobile industry, for example, Mercedes has this image. In football, Manchester United is part of the EPL, widely touted as the most competitive in the world. The reasons for this reputation are rooted in Porter's (1990) Competitive Advantage of Nations theory of international competitiveness, which posits that within specific industries, clusters of expertise result from highly competitive national environments. This expertise enables them to become extremely competitive in the global marketplace. The strong rivalries within the British club system, from local leagues all the way up to the Premier League, have resulted in a consistent ratcheting up of performance levels in the modern era.

Over the past decade, on-field performance has been bolstered through a global commitment to excellence—obtaining the best players and managers regardless of national origin. . . . As a result, to maintain leadership positions, top clubs such as Manchester United must consistently perform to high standards over long periods. This makes them attractive propositions in the international marketplace.

Country of Origin

While the sport of soccer is global, British (and English) football has specific advantages over that of other countries and these have contributed to the global appeal of its clubs. One of these is its history as the home of the modern organised game. International marketers (e.g. Roth & Romeo, 1992) have noted that country-of-origin advantages accrue when countries become associated with specific industries, products or services. French champagne, German engineering and cars (Mercedes, Porsche, BMW), Japanese electronics (Sony, Panasonic) and US computers and software (IBM, Microsoft) have all benefited from being centres of excellence for their specific industry sectors. While the sport of soccer did not originate in Britain, British clubs have benefited from being the birthplace of the modern organised game. Many clubs in the UK have been established for more than 100 years and their solid geographic franchises have resulted in strong local fan bases. Manchester United celebrated its centenary in 2002.

The Brand as Organisation

Brand identities are often associated with the activities of the parent organisation: its people, culture and values; its organisational attributes, such as innovation and quality; and its outlook (local or global).

Organisational Attributes

The Manchester United organisation has garnered a reputation as one of the best organisations in sport and football management, known for:

Traditional Club Values

The arrival of manager Alex Ferguson in 1986 revived the traditional club values established by Matt Busby in the 1950s to 1970. The traditional value of developing the best local talent was continued as the bulk of the side, including Ryan Giggs, Paul Scholes, the Neville brothers and David Beckham, moved up through the club's youth system. Over the championship-laden 1992-2003 period, Manchester United topped the EPL in starting appearances for home-grown talent (Gerrard, 2004).

The Quest for Soccer Excellence

Increasing competition in the EPL and Ferguson's perpetual search for the very best talent has resulted in many players being brought in from outside. The current team roster has a number of players bought for substantial sums. . . .

Attacking Soccer

The club's potent combination of home-grown and imported talent resulted in an attacking style of football that attracts fans worldwide. . . .

Organisational Outlook—Local Versus Global

Manchester United has always been one of the more cosmopolitan teams. In the 1950s it was the first British club to participate in European competition (against the best advice of the English Football League at the time). In 1968, it was the first English club to win the European UEFA club championship (the competition which preceded the Champions League). Scotland's Celtic had won the trophy the previous season to become the first British winner. As soccer became global during the 1990s, the club toured frequently in Asia and North America, as well as being a frequent competitor in Europe. In recent years, the club has signed players from Latin America, Africa, the US and Asia, as well as Europe.

The Brand as Person

Brands, like people, take on personal attributes that distinguish them from key competitors. These include personality attributes such as:

Youthfulness

Matt Busby started Manchester United's youth orientation in 1953, when he fielded a side with seven teenagers against Huddersfield (Wagg, 2004). This policy was continued over the years, especially during the 1990s, when many of the club's star players (Ryan Giggs, Gary and Phillip Neville, Paul Scholes, Nicky Butt and David Beckham) emerged from the youth side to play key roles in the club's phenomenal success. Seven of the 2004–05 first team squad were products of the club's highly successful youth academy, and the youth orientation was maintained with the signings of Christiano Ronaldo and Wayne Rooney. The club has augmented its youth talent pipeline through alliances with other European clubs—Bromma, Shelbourne, Nantes, Royal Antwerp and Sporting Lisbon (Manchester United Annual Report, 2004).

Excitement

While the Manchester United tradition of playing stylish, attacking football has brought in many new fans worldwide, its players have also generated excitement off the field. Just as individual brands add sparks to corporate brand lines [e.g. the 'silver bullet' effect of the Mazda RX7 on Mazda's corporate image (Aaker 1996, Barwise & Robertson, 1992)], so player personalities add excitement to club images. In the 1950s it was teenager Duncan Edwards; in the 1960s, George Best, ably supported by Bobby Charlton and Denis Law, generated on- and off-the-field media coverage to maintain Manchester United's high news profile. In the 1990s, the charismatic Eric Cantona provided headline sports news, until the crop of more recent stars, including media celebrity icon David Beckham, came on stream. Such talents exemplified and magnified the aura of the club.

Competence

Delivering on-field success over long periods is a challenge for any team. In this area, Manchester United has few equals.

In the modern era, . . .[t]his consistency in excellence has earned Manchester United a coveted place in English and European football annals, matched perhaps only by Spanish club Real Madrid.

Building Customer Relationships

Manchester United has been an active relationship-builder throughout much of the post-1945 era. Today, the club maintains a fan base of nearly 200,000 with its One United Membership Scheme in the UK and up to 75 million fans worldwide.

Ironically, it was a tragedy that first triggered emotional ties among football fans toward the club. In 1958, eight players were killed in Munich, Germany, as the team aeroplane crashed. A surviving player, Bobby Charlton, noted (Dunphy, 1991, p. 249): "Before Munich, it was Manchester's club, afterwards, everyone felt they owned a little bit of it." Since that time, the club has devoted considerable time and expense to nurturing and developing its fan base, both in the UK and outside.

Commercial Relationships with Fans

Manchester United was among the first football clubs to track fan needs through research and cement ties through opportunities to purchase club-branded products and services. As the Premiership got underway in the early 1990s, Manchester United capitalised on its success to launch a stream of non-football-related products and services. Its Champs Cola was launched in 1993 (Manchester United aims to score, 1993). In the mid-1990s, Manchester United added branded wines, lagers and a champagne to the list (Manchester United tries branded champagne, 1997). Financial services (insurance, loans, credit cards) were added under the MU Finance brand. The club joined with Vodafone to launch MU Mobile, and with Travelcare to provide travel services under the MU Travel brand. In 2003, the Red Cinema Complex was opened in the Salford suburb of Manchester.

. . . .

Building Relationships with Other Global Brands

Being associated with other international brand names lends global auras to brands as they go worldwide. Rossaaen & Amis (2004) noted that both Manchester United and Nike gained in global stature after the announcement of their global tie-in. In recent years Manchester United has formed commercial alliances with a number of global players in other industries: Vodafone, Pepsi, Budweiser and Fuji were all added to the club's sponsorship list. Under these arrangements the club gains from sponsors' international reputations and sponsors gain from their association with a marquee sports brand.

Building Relationships with Foreign Fans

In the home market, British clubs can build relationships with fans from being a part of the national local sports scenes over decades and through week-to-week media exposure during the soccer season (August to May). Taking the Manchester United image and brand into foreign markets poses the challenge of building emotional ties with fans less familiar with the club's history or who have not witnessed at first hand the excitement of the 'Theatre of Dreams' atmosphere at the Old Trafford stadium. Televised broadcasts and print exposures are the entrees, but the all-important follow-ups are where club–fan relationships are built and fans are converted into consumers.

Building brand relationships with global consumers works best when not done through conventional mass media. Joachimsthaler & Aaker (1997) noted that the most successful brands are built through experiences in unconventional settings—sponsorships (such as Hugo Boss with Formula One racing, art exhibitions, golf); publicity (Benetton's controversial non-product-related AIDS campaigns); or the Cadbury's Chocolate theme park, Cadbury World, in Bournville, UK. All have one thing in common: customer involvement in the brand-building experience. The involvement factor has been critical to Manchester United's brand-building efforts in Asia and North America.

The Asian Strategy

Manchester United estimates that it has about 40 million fans in Asia. Much of this support has resulted from the increased popularity of the sport within the region. While soccer has been around in Asia for a long time, demand for the sport has been revitalised through: (a) English teams that have periodically visited the region since the 1980s; (b) China qualifying for the 2002 World Cup that was hosted in South Korea and Japan; (c) Asian players signed by Manchester United (Dong Fangzhou and Park Ji-sung), Everton (Li Tie), Crystal Palace (Fan Zhiyi), Manchester City (Sun Jihai) and Tottenham Hotspur (Kazuyuki Toda); (d) live broadcasts through ESS (ESPN Star Sports); and (e) the prospect of Beijing hosting the 2008 Olympic Games (Bowman, 2003; Crispin, 2004b). Manchester United has capitalised on this interest through:

- South-east Asia tour 2001 in which the club played exhibition games in Malaysia, Singapore and Thailand to connect with their Asian fan base and promote their branded products and services. This was followed by a pre-season tour in 2005 comprising four matches in China, Hong Kong and Japan. During this tour, the club signed a sponsorship deal with Malaysia-based budget airline AirAsia, which included plane liveries using Manchester United branding.

- Establishment of foreign outlets—a Theatre of Dreams branded leisure complex in Hong Kong, which houses a museum, interactive games and a cafe, as well as selling club merchandise (Bawden, 1999). In 2004, the club opened a theme restaurant in the Chinese city of Chengdu. Another 100 outlets are planned for Asia (Crispin, 2004b).

- Club merchandise—in 2002, Manchester United granted Thailand's Central Marketing Group rights to produce sporting casual wear, stationery, bags, car accessories and souvenirs for distribution in department stores, stand-alone outlets and megastores. This arrangement complements similar deals signed in Malaysia, the Philippines and Hong Kong. These producers were to service third-party markets in Asia and Europe (Jitpleecheep, 2002).

- Website promotions—the club, in conjunction with website specialist Lycos, launched a Chinese language website. Sponsored by Vodafone and listed at manunited.com.cn, the website attracts over 25 million page views per month and aids the club's sponsorship, e-commerce and betting businesses (Manchester United Annual Report, 2003).

- Soccer schools—To further the club's youth development policy, the first of its Asian soccer academies was opened in 2004 in Hong Kong. In the same year the club opened a soccer school in Disneyland, Paris, and this was followed in 2005 by the opening of a facility in Dubai Sports City in the United Arab Emirates.

The North American Strategy

Manchester United has about 5 million fans in North America, a following enhanced through Rupert Murdoch's marketing of his Fox Sports World TV channel (now Fox Soccer Channel) in the US.

- In 2002, the club formed an alliance with baseball's New York Yankees to extend television coverage over the Yankee network and to establish distribution for club merchandise through Yankee outlets.

- In 2004, the club teamed with Master Card International to launch a Manchester United credit card.

- In 2004, the club joined eight other famous European clubs for a series of games to promote the sport throughout the US—a move dubbed the "Manchester United Global Brand Enhancement Tour" (Saporito, 2004). This followed a 2003 tour, sponsored by Budweiser and Pepsi, that attracted over 250,000 fans.

- In 2003, the club piloted summer soccer schools in Seattle, Washington, a move that has since evolved into year-round youth development programmes (Manchester United Annual Report, 2003).

THE BRAND AS SYMBOL

Visual imagery and brand heritage become symbolic when they are uniquely associated with a product or service. McDonald's Golden Arches and the Levi Strauss storied jean history are testaments to the powers of brand symbolism and heritage. For Manchester United, the Red Devil nickname is well known throughout the soccer world, along with the club crest. But it is the club's history that has always had popular appeal for soccer fans everywhere.

Brand Heritage, History and Development of a Distinctive Manchester United Culture

The club now known as Manchester United was originally formed in 1878 as the Newton Heath Lancashire and Yorkshire Football Club. Financial problems followed and the club was reformed under its present name in 1902. The club moved to its Old Trafford ground in 1910 (Manchester United official website, 2005b). Its move towards national and international prominence can be traced back to the appointment of Matt Busby as manager in 1945. It was Busby who established the traditional corporate culture that characterises the club today (Rossaaen & Amis, 2004). Wagg (2004) noted that Busby's soccer philosophy established club precedents in many key areas. He established the youth orientation (the 'Busby Babes'). Busby's quest for soccer excellence extended nationally as he scoured the country in search of soccer talent. He promoted individuality and flair on the field but encouraged a club-oriented 'one for all' camaraderie off the field. He enhanced team unity by arranging off-the-field perks for all players, including golf memberships, local cinema passes and concessions at resort hotels. In 1956, he took the club into Europe in defiance of the English Football League. The Busby corporate culture legacy imbued Manchester United with a reputation for youth, talent development, attacking football and individual excellence, all within the framework of a club steeped in traditional values and atmosphere.

During the 1960s and 1970s, the club took advantage of the era's Beatles, James Bond and Anglophile tendencies (including England's 1966 World Cup win) to enhance its reputation, garnering the European Cup in 1968 with charismatic Irishman George Best being voted European Player of the Year. The club languished during the 1970s and 1980s as first Leeds United and then Nottingham Forest and, most notably, Liverpool superseded them as England's leading club, although Manchester United was still the best supported (Rossaaen & Amis, 2004).

The hiring of Alex Ferguson in 1986 heralded a return to traditional club values and a revival in the club's fortunes, with Manchester United dominating English football through the 1990s, winning the League title eight times over 1992–2003, and being crowned European champions in 1999. As Farred (2004, p. 222) noted: "It was a good decade to dominate English football. . . The Premier League was formed in 1992. . . a move that saw television revenues skyrocket and it made the clubs and players. . . wealthier. With the proliferation of satellite, cable and digital TV the beautiful game became. . . the truly global game."

DISCUSSION

Key Success Factors for Global Sports Branding

Soccer is a global sport by virtue of its simplicity and its benefits as a player- and team-oriented form of physical exercise. It appeals to both collective and individual instincts that are essential aspects of the human existence (Hofstede, 1980). Its diffusion worldwide can be traced back to European colonial influences of the 19th and 20th centuries. This worldwide appeal is the basis for branding strategies put into motion by a number of European clubs.

English football clubs have capitalised on their national birthrights as organisers of the modern game, and on their first mover advantages in establishing competitive leagues to raise national standards of play. In making these moves, the EPL has attracted much media attention that has broadened its appeal both nationally and internationally as global media developments have taken clubs 100 years old and more into worldwide markets. In particular, the Murdoch media empire tie-ups have been instrumental in taking EPL and European soccer into over 100 national markets. The League's August to May season has ensured that its activities are rarely out of the public eye.

But why has Manchester United, rather than Liverpool, Real Madrid, or Bayern Munich, become the best known soccer club in the world? All clubs, both in the EPL and worldwide, have been subject to the same industry pressures as Manchester United. . . . But the timing of its successes in both the 1960s and the 1990s has been critical. They occurred in eras which saw huge developments in the media industry. In 1968 television had only recently become available on a mass basis. In the 1990s, global communications and media came on stream as part of the globalisation push. Manchester United capitalised on an English football heritage that included tragedy (the Munich disaster), a football culture that emphasised youth, talent development and an attacking style of play, and a number of charismatic, talented players who attracted fans as much with their off-the-field activities as their matchday performances.

A Resource-Based Viewpoint (RBV) on Manchester United's Success

If many other clubs were exposed to the same industry pressures as Manchester United, why was the Old Trafford club the first to translate sporting success first into national brand-building activities and then into a global reputation? The answer is a critical resource: management. Manchester United executives were the first in the industry to build and leverage their brand marketing capabilities. As Real Madrid president Florentino Perez noted in 2004: "In past years, Manchester United has become the best known club in the world because its marketing policies were ten years ahead of their time." (Liga Futbol, 2004) Key management additions that gave the club its global impetus were Martin Edwards, who became club chairman in 1980, the recruitment of Umbro's Peter Kenyon as director of international marketing in 1997, and the appointment of Peter Draper, also from Umbro, as director of marketing.

The appropriate organisational structures were created. Kenyon put into place a new affiliate, MU International, in 1998 to replicate the Old Trafford experience in international markets. In 2000, advertising agency Cheetham Bell was charged with the creation of a global brand awareness campaign; and in 2003, One United was launched as the club's global brand initiative.

Professionalism in soccer club management is not new—Liverpool was renowned for it from the 1970s, when it enjoyed its greatest success (Taylor & Ward, 1997)—but Manchester United was the first to bring a true marketing-oriented focus to football to capitalise on its reputation as one of England's premier clubs. In this instance, it was an alert management that initiated strategies to take advantage of the club's 'first mover' advantages in the world game and establish itself in the minds of soccer fans worldwide.

Lessons from the Manchester United Model

Few sporting endeavors can become a Manchester United, but there are lessons to be gleaned.

- Creating and maintaining global brands requires constant exposure to maintain a worldwide profile. The EPL's long season and the north–south hemispheric split are major advantages in sustaining enthusiasm among soccer fans worldwide, and in making club–fan connections worthwhile. This gives merchandise year-long sales appeal. Such advantages accrue less easily to sports such as American football with its four-month season, or baseball with its six-month season.

- Nothing succeeds like success, and success over significant periods has given rise to a Manchester United brand heritage that few can match in commerce or sports. Most of the world's global brands have been successful for decades—Exxon, Coca-Cola, Marlboro, McDonald's (Aaker, 1996). Success in the sports arena by comparison can be ephemeral (e.g. Olympic success), especially for individual athletes, who can rarely sustain sporting excellence over long periods. Athletes and their managers must therefore be alert in taking advantage of limited timeframes of opportunity.

- In contrast, sports teams that demonstrate success over long periods tend to be those that have established corporate cultures, with 'club above all' mentalities, while encouraging individuality within the team. Sports teams offer superior opportunities for brand development because of their longevity and their abilities to renew the excitement quotient through player development and acquisitions.

- Technology, especially the internet, gives fans and followers access to club and team activities. It is inexpensive. In almost any sport, youth, local and regional clubs can maintain website connections for information and merchandising purposes. Just as Manchester United creates opportunities for faraway fans to participate in the Theatre of Dreams, so sports club enthusiasts can follow their teams no matter where they are in the world. As webcast technologies develop, opportunities exist for sports fans anywhere to follow their favourite teams, be they local, regional, national or international. Such is the power of technology. With these renewals of club–player–fan relationships come opportunities for sales and commercial development.

- A theme evident both on- and off-the-field at Manchester United is the commitment to excellence. While this may be expected for on-the-field performances, the club's expectations of excellence extend to management in providing resources to support club activities. As Gerrard (2004) noted, while other soccer clubs flinch under the onslaught of player wage inflation, Manchester United has maintained a star-studded roster while having one of the lowest wages to revenues ratios in the EPL. Professional management of the club–fan interface is integral for two reasons. First, it cements relationships with fans who can tangibly demonstrate their loyalties through merchandise sales and TV audience participation. Second, additional revenues allow clubs to make key reinvestments in player resources and fan facilities. Excellence in club reputation and image management has become a cornerstone for future survival and on-field performance.

- Within the academic field, the soccer fan–club interface in particular presents significant potential for research in at least three areas. First, as laid out by Morgan and Hunt (1994), relationship marketing and the forming of major emotional bonds between firms and customers is a fertile area for research. In few industries are the relationships between fans/customers and clubs as deep as in soccer and sports, generally. Belk, Wallendorf & Sherry (1989) have advocated the notion of 'consumer devotion' as extreme forms of brand loyalty. Hunt, Bristol & Bashaw (1999) have noted sports fans as logical extensions of the consumer devotion concept. Its further investigation in the sports or soccer arena would appear inevitable. Second, Manchester United already tracks customer needs in ways similar to many major corporations, but as the stakes rise in professional sports, academics and consumer behaviourists in particular have much to probe as soccer's appeal broadens from its traditional audience to attract broader fan bases. Third, the depth of fan allegiances should be ideal subject matter for consumer psychologists as a baseline for future market segmentation strategies.

- As more athletes and clubs seek to leverage their personal or club reputations in the marketplace, the need is to develop a cadre of professional managers with distinctive expertise in sport. Manchester United is a testament to the difference competent management makes in professional sports. Additionally, with the advent of globalisation, future managers of sports should be fully prepared to deal with the international aspects of their activities. As the Glazer takeover starts a new chapter in the Manchester United history, uncertainty prevails. The club's success has been founded on solid stakeholder principles, with commitments to players, fans, man-

agement and the soccer community generally. Taking the club public in 1991 brought shareholders into the equation. As Glazer pulled the club back into private ownership, there were opportunities to maintain and revitalise the traditional values that made the club famous. Whether this course is taken—or another that places the primary emphasis on profiteering—remains to be seen.

The club also faces uncertainty from an unexpected source. Roman Abramovich's huge investment in Chelsea means that despite having the largest turnover and profit in English football, Manchester United can no longer guarantee to have the largest transfer and wage funding. In 2004–05 Chelsea broke the Manchester United/Arsenal stranglehold on the English Premiership and Manchester United finished the season without a trophy. In 2005–06 it would appear that Manchester United will have to be content with football's equivalent of the wooden spoon—the Carling Cup, having failed in the Champions League and FA Cup earlier than its main competitors and seen Chelsea develop a commanding lead in the Premiership.

Similarly, Arsenal's resurgence on the pitch through the recruitment of promising young players and its move to a new stadium with higher ticket prices than Manchester United could see it compete strongly with Manchester United financially.

On the commercial front, Manchester United has successfully replaced Vodafone as its primary shirt sponsor with United States financial services company AIG. [*Ed. Note: In the face of mounting financial losses and a bailout by the United States government, AIG terminated its deal with Manchester United in 2009. The club subsequently announced that it will replace AIG with U.S.–based insurance broker Aon Corp. beginning in the 2010–11 season for a reported $131.2 million over 4 years.*] Although this also offers potential in leveraging cash from supporters buying AIG products, it is arguable whether it provides the opportunities Vodafone delivered to develop the club brand. Being a global communications company, Vodafone helped to promote the club to tens of millions of people and was able to offer incremental revenue streams such as selling subscription mobile services and merchandise. On top of its sponsorship fee, these extra benefits have been worth millions to the club.

The success the club has had in recruiting fans on a global basis, however, has so far failed to deliver significant revenue benefits with estimates that only 2% of the club's earnings are derived from overseas markets. In the Far East, club merchandise has to compete with the well established counterfeit industry, which can undercut official product prices by considerable margins.

The big challenge for the club, therefore, will be to realise its potential through digital media, in particular through subscription media revenues. There are two issues that could stand in the way. First, will the future on-field performance be strong enough to see fans with arguably only loose ties to the club pay large amounts for subscription access to live match footage? Second, the club will have to see the English Premiership break its collective selling of overseas media rights to be able to cash in on this fully. Professional football changed enormously in the 1990s as vast amounts of money flooded into the game from subscription television, gate receipts, merchandise and hospitality. It is set to undergo further massive change as it enters the unpredictable territory of the global digital revolution. The potential for development for a club such as Manchester United is enormous, but as in any period of major change, those at the forefront at the start are not necessarily those that will emerge as winners.

References

Aaker, D.A. (1996) *Building strong brands.* New York: The Free Press.

Amis, J. (2003) 'Good things come to those who wait: the strategic management of image and reputation at Guinness', *European Sport Management Quarterly, 3,* 189–214.

Aninat, E. (2002) 'Surmounting the challenges of globalization', *Finance & Development, 39* (1), 4–7.

. . . .

Barwise, P. & Robertson, T. (1992) 'Brand portfolios', *European Management Journal, 10* (3) 277-286.

Bawden, T. (6 May 1999) 'Man Utd. aims brand at Asian goal', *Marketing Week,* 6.

Belk, R.W., Wallendorf, M. & Sherry, J.F. (1989) 'The sacred and the profane in consumer behavior: theodicy on the odyssey', *Journal of Consumer Research,* 16, 1–38.

Blatter, J. (1999) 'The global game', *Harvard International Review, 21* (3) 86–89.

Bowman, J. (2003, July 25) 'ESS rides on China sports interest to make new inroads', *Media,* 16.

Boyle, R. & Haynes, R. (2000) *Power play: sport, the media and popular culture.* Harlow: Pearson Education.

Brand Strategy. (2003) Brand Papers: Sponsorship with a strategy. October p. 32.

. . . .

Crispin, S.W. (2004a, June 9) 'European soccer rolls over Asia, as Asian investors look to buy in', *Wall Street Journal,* 1.

Crispin, S.W. (2004b, June 19) 'Moving the goalposts', *Far Eastern Economic Review,* 50–53.

. . . .

Dunphy, E. (1991) *A strange kind of glory—Sir Matt Busby and Manchester United.* London: William Heinemann.

Farred, G. (2004) Anfield envy. In D.L. Andrews (ed.), *Manchester United: A Thematic Study* 222–238, London: Routledge.

. . . .

Gerrard, B. (2003) 'What does the resource-based view bring to the table in sport management research?', *European Sport Management Quarterly, 3,* 139–144.

Gerrard, B. (2004) 'Why does Manchester United keep on winning on and off the field?' in Andrews, D.L. (ed.), *Manchester United: A thematic study* 65–86, London: Routledge.

Giulianotti, R. (2002, July–August) 'Soccer goes global', Foreign Policy, 82–83.

Granada to strike MUTV overseas deal. 11 February 1999, *Marketing Week,* 14.

Hill, J.S. & Holloway, B.B. (2001) 'Multi-market branding strategies in the new millennium', Proceedings 10th World Business Congress, Zagreb Croatia: 252–259.

Hofstede, G. (1980) *Culture's consequences: International differences in work-related values.* Beverly Hills, CA: Sage Publications.

Hunt, K.A., Bristol, T. & Bashaw, R.E. (1999) 'A conceptual approach to classifying sports fans', *Journal of Services Marketing, 13* (6) 439–452.

Jitpleecheep, S. (6 September 2002) 'Thai company to make Manchester United products', Knight Ridder Tribune Business News, 1.

Joachimsthaler, E. & Aaker, D.A. (January–February 1997) 'Building brands without mass media', *Harvard Business Review,* 39–50.

. . . .

Liga Futbol (July 19 2004) 1.

Lonsdale, C. (2004) 'Player power: capturing value in the English football supply network', *Supply Chain Management: An International Journal 9* (5) 383–391.

'Manchester United aims to score with cola brand', (September 30 1993) *Marketing,* 1.

Manchester United official website. (2005a) Retrieved from: http://www.manutd.com/history/default.sps?itype=814&icustompageid=1029&teamid=458&compid=7

Manchester United official website. (2005b) Retrieved from: http://www.manutd.com/history/heritage.sps?iType=489&icustompageid=944

Manchester United PLC Annual Report. (2003) Manchester, England: Manchester United plc.

Manchester United PLC Annual Report. (2004) Manchester, England: Manchester United plc.

Manchester United tries branded champagne. (July 10 1997) *Marketing Week,* 8.

Miller, T. (2004) Manchester USA? In Andrews, D.L. (ed.), *Manchester United: A thematic study,* 241–264, London: Routledge.

. . . .

Morgan, R.M. & Hunt, S.D. (July 1994) 'The commitment–trust theory of relationship marketing', *Journal of Marketing, 58* (3) 20–39.

Porter, M.E. (1980) *Competitive strategy: Techniques for analyzing industries and competitors.* New York: Free Press.

Porter, M.E. (1986) *Competition in global industries.* Cambridge MA: Harvard Business School Press.

Porter, M.E. (1990) *The competitive advantage of nations.* New York: Free Press.

Rossaaen, K. & Amis J. (2004) 'From the Busby Babes to the Theatre of Dreams', in Andrews, D.L. (ed.), *Manchester United: a thematic study,* 43–62, London: Routledge.

Roth, M. & Romeo, M.B. (1992) 'Matching product category and country image perceptions: a framework for managing country-of-origin effects', *Journal of International Business Studies, 23* (3) 477–497.

Saporito, B. (9 August 2004) 'Will Americans love Glasgow Celtic?', *Time,* 22.

Sport's premiers. (18 September 2003) *Marketing Week,* 22.

Sweney, M. (4 August 2004) 'New season, added fizz', *Marketing,* 16.

Taylor, R. & Ward, A. (1997, August 7) 'The people's game', *People Management,* 22–28.

Timeline: 'A history of TV football rights', (25 February 2003) *The Guardian,* 9.

Wagg, S. (2004) 'The team that wouldn't die: on the mystique of Matt Busby and Manchester United', in Andrews, D.L. (ed.), *Manchester United: a thematic study,* 13–27, London: Routledge.

CONSOLIDATED BALANCE SHEETS AT JUNE 30, 2009 AND 2008, AND CONSOLIDATED STATEMENTS OF OPERATIONS, CONSOLIDATED STATEMENTS OF MEMBERS' EQUITY (DEFICIT), AND CONSOLIDATED STATEMENTS OF CASH FLOWS FOR THE FISCAL YEARS ENDED JUNE 30, 2009, 2008 AND 2007, INCLUDING THE NOTES THERETO.

Forest City Enterprises, Inc., Nets Sports and Entertainment, LLC and Subsidiaries

Nets Sports and Entertainment, LLC and Subsidiaries Consolidated Balance Sheets

Assets	June 30, 2009	2008 (Unaudited)
Current assets		
Cash and cash equivalents	$7,667,350	$1,371,197
Accounts receivable, net	12,167,573	14,213,491
Prepaid expenses and other current assets	2,393,399	1,351,451
Total current assets	22,228,322	16,936,139
Arena land and related costs	183,858,993	137,922,470
Intangible assets, net	165,484,127	198,863,261
Property and equipment, net	5,512,121	6,565,630
Deferred loan costs, net	1,506,152	929,226
Investments in NBA-related entities	7,980,000	6,760,333
Other assets	747,046	973,542
	365,088,439	352,014,462
Total assets	387,316,761	368,950,601
Liabilities and Members' Deficit		
Current liabilities		
Accounts payable and accrued expenses	33,053,050	16,178,565
Due to affiliates	83,419,347	85,326,346
Deferred revenue	4,735,994	13,563,560
Deferred compensation	507,952	1,007,952
Total current liabilities	121,716,343	116,076,423
Long-term liabilities		
Senior notes and credit facility	207,157,400	205,618,400
Land loans	18,617,533	20,342,510
Member loans	37,145,448	10,884,906
Land sale—deposit payable	85,000,000	40,000,000
Deferred compensation, long-term	1,489,531	1,657,114
Deferred revenue, long-term	1,301,239	1,461,143
Total long-term liabilities	350,711,151	279,964,073
Total liabilities	472,427,494	396,040,496
Commitments and contingencies	—	—
Members' deficit		
Member units		
Class B-1	60,000,000	60,000,000
Class B-2	38,594,984	37,124,051
Class A and C	203,235,026	183,953,326
Accumulated deficit	(386,940,743)	(308,167,272)
Total members' deficit	(85,110,733)	(27,089,895)
Total liabilities and members' deficit	387,316,761	368,950,601

Nets Sports and Entertainment, LLC and Subsidiaries Consolidated Statements of Operations

	Years Ended June 30		
	2009	**2008 (Unaudited)**	**2007 (Unaudited)**
Operating income			
Ticket sales, net of admission taxes and league gate share	$25,921,191	$37,424,537	$39,974,789
Television broadcast revenues	32,534,913	30,628,610	29,993,323
Sponsorship and promotional revenues	13,170,278	14,699,146	13,458,759
Game day and other revenues	7,157,295	11,205,004	8,636,456
Playoff revenue	—	—	4,967,564
Total operating income	78,783,677	93,957,297	97,030,891
Operating expenses			
Player and team staff salaries	66,188,454	71,098,848	70,271,544
Team costs	12,592,534	14,333,539	13,789,142
General and administrative	12,341,736	12,190,123	12,243,291
Marketing	8,736,771	10,278,978	10,666,302
Ticket sales and operations	6,754,624	7,597,695	6,963,741
Game presentation costs	3,742,314	3,864,848	3,588,850
Scouting and public relations	1,562,768	1,581,427	1,479,088
Playoff expenses	—	—	2,528,603
Depreciation	2,041,611	1,008,747	894,033
Amortization of intangible assets	33,379,134	40,006,132	40,606,133
Total operating expenses	147,339,946	161,960,337	163,030,727
Operating loss	(68,556,269)	(68,003,040)	(65,999,836)
Other income (expenses)			
Equity in income of NBA-related entities	4,742,066	4,474,633	5,180,517
Interest expense	(13,412,981)	(12,891,336)	(16,211,203)
Net loss	$(77,227,184)	$(76,419,743)	$(77,030,522)

Source: Courtesy of EDGAR and the U.S. Securities and Exchange Commission.

Nets Sports and Entertainment, LLC and Subsidiaries Consolidated Statements of Cash Flows

	Years Ended June 30		
	2009	**2008** **(Unaudited)**	**2007** **(Unaudited)**
Cash flows from operating activities			
Net loss	$(77,227,184)	$(76,419,743)	$(77,030,522)
Adjustments to reconcile net loss to net cash flows used in operating activities			
Depreciation	2,041,611	1,008,747	894,033
Amortization of intangible assets	33,379,134	40,006,132	40,606,133
Amortization of deferred loan costs	675,577	337,223	1,693,492
Bad debt expense	492,500	247,179	329,307
Equity in income of NBA-related entities	(4,742,066)	(4,474,633)	(5,180,517)
Cash distributions from NBA-related entities	3,522,399	4,997,300	5,208,517
	2009	**2008** **(Unaudited)**	**2007** **(Unaudited)**
Changes in operating assets and liabilities			
Accounts receivable	1,553,418	(4,212,430)	2,416,961
Prepaid expenses and other current assets	(1,041,948)	855,424	(215,378)
Other assets	(24,818)	406,249	(333,014)
Accounts payable and accrued expenses	6,690,727	1,494,107	(7,742,88)
Deferred revenue	(8,987,470)	(3,059,580)	(1,597,286)
Deferred compensation	(667,583)	(599,364)	(540,252)
Accrued interest on member loans	1,660,542	749,061	135,845
Net cash flows used in operating activities	(42,675,161)	(38,664,328)	(41,355,561)
Cash flows from investing activities			
Arena land and related costs	(36,318,615)	(56,774,369)	(11,721,991)
Intangible assets—syndication costs	—	—	(76,234)
Additions of property and equipment	(988,102)	(5,522,805)	(756,734)
Decrease (increase) in restricted cash	251,314	(103,523)	20,447
Land sale—deposit payable	45,000,000	40,000,000	—
Net cash flows provided by (used in) investing activities	7,944,597	(22,400,697)	(12,534,512)
Cash flows from financing activities			
Advances (to) from affiliates, net	(1,299,998)	18,436,557	16,168,538
Deferred loan costs	(1,293,654)	(253,126)	(304,892)
Proceeds from senior notes and credit facility	63,452,333	74,000,000	97,618,400
Payments of senior notes and credit facility	(61,913,333)	(54,000,000)	(100,618,400)
Proceeds from member loans	24,600,000	—	10,000,000
Proceeds from land loans	—	4,235,565	829,881
Payments of land loans	(1,724,977)	—	—
Capital contributions	20,752,633	19,708,333	40,510,260
Capital distributions—preferred units	(1,546,287)	(6,414,464)	(6,575,399)
Net cash flows provided by financing activities	41,026,717	55,712,865	57,628,388
Net increase (decrease) in cash and cash equivalents	6,296,153	(5,352,160)	3,738,315
Cash and cash equivalents			
Beginning of the period	1,371,197	6,723,357	2,985,042
End of the period	$7,667,350	$1,371,197	$6,723,357
Supplemental cash flow information and noncash transactions			
Cash paid for interest, net of capitalized interest	$9,360,106	$11,968,925	$15,381,181
Conversion of revolving credit facility to term loan	—	—	$25,000,000
Change in construction payables included in accounts payable and accrued expenses and due to affiliates related to arena land and related costs	$9,576,757	$ (12,329,349)	$20,405,100

Source: Courtesy of EDGAR and the U.S. Securities and Exchange Commission.

NETS SPORTS AND ENTERTAINMENT, LLC AND SUBSIDIARIES

Notes to Consolidated Financial Statements

June 30, 2009, 2008, and 2007

1. NATURE OF THE BUSINESS AND SUMMARY OF SIGNIFICANT ACCOUNTING POLICIES

Nature of the Business

Nets Sports and Entertainment, LLC ("NS&E"), a Delaware limited liability company, was formed for the purpose of acquiring 100% membership interests in Brooklyn Arena, LLC ("Brooklyn Arena") and Brooklyn Basketball, LLC ("Brooklyn Basketball").

Brooklyn Arena, a Delaware limited liability company, was formed for the purpose of developing and operating a proposed sports and entertainment arena in Brooklyn, New York (the "Arena").

Brooklyn Basketball, a Delaware limited liability company, was formed to acquire 100% of the membership interests in New Jersey Basketball, LLC ("Basketball"). Basketball, a New Jersey limited liability company, primarily operates as a professional basketball team in New Jersey under the name of the New Jersey Nets (the "Nets") and is a member of the National Basketball Association ("NBA") through its execution of the NBA's joint venture agreement.

Basis of Presentation

The accompanying financial statements have been prepared on a consolidated basis and include NS&E and its wholly-owned subsidiaries, Brooklyn Arena and Brooklyn Basketball (collectively, the "Company").

The Company is an equity method investment of Forest City Enterprises, Inc. ("FCE"), a publicly traded company, and was deemed to be a significant subsidiary of FCE for its fiscal year ended January 31, 2009. As a result, audited financial statements for the Company are required to be filed with the Securities and Exchange Commission in accordance with Rule 3-09 of Regulation S-X, as of and for the year ended June 30, 2009.

. . . .

Deferred Loan Costs

Costs incurred in connection with obtaining the revolving credit facility, term loan and senior notes (see Note 6) are capitalized and amortized over the term of the related financing. Costs incurred in connection with obtaining land loans are capitalized as deferred loan costs and the related amortization is capitalized as part of arena land and related costs in the accompanying Consolidated Balance Sheets. Amortization expense, net of capitalized amounts of $675,577,

$337,223 and $1,693,492 for the years ended June 30, 2009, 2008 and 2007, respectively, is included in interest expense in the accompanying Consolidated Statements of Operations. The amount for 2009 and 2007 includes $127,898 and $1,271,992, respectively, of previously unamortized loan costs that were written off upon refinancing.

Investments in NBA-Related Entities

Investments in NBA-related entities are reported on the equity method. The Company's allocable portion of the operating results of the NBA-related entities totaled $4,742,066, $4,474,633 and $5,180,517 for the years ended June 30, 2009, 2008 and 2007, respectively. Losses greater than the Company's investment are not recorded as the Company is not required to provide funding for the operations of the NBA-related entities. The Company also received distributions of $3,522,399, $4,997,300 and $5,208,517 from the NBA-related entities during the years ended June 30, 2009, 2008 and 2007, respectively.

Membership Units

The capital structure of NS&E is comprised of four classes of membership units ("Units"), each having different priorities in distribution and differing capital funding requirements. The senior preferred units are entitled to distributions payable quarterly at a rate equal to the lesser of six-month London InterBank Offered Rate ("LIBOR") plus 200 basis points or 6.5%. The junior preferred units are entitled to distributions payable quarterly at a rate of 8% per annum subject to an increase of 15% if distributions are not paid for two consecutive quarters. Undeclared preferred distributions have liquidation priority over common units.

NS&E made distributions on its two preferred classes of Units of $1,546,287, $6,414,464 and $6,575,399 for the years ended June 30, 2009, 2008 and 2007, respectively. No distributions have been declared since September 30, 2008.

Revenue and Expense Recognition

Ticket sales, television broadcasting and sponsorship and promotional revenues are recorded on a game-by-game basis over the playing season. Team expenses, principally player compensation and game expenses, are recorded as expense on the same basis, except for early contract terminations that are expensed upon termination. Accordingly, advance ticket sales for games not played yet are recorded as deferred revenue until the associated game is played or credit is applied for a subsequent game played. General and administrative expenses, as well as advertising and promotional expenses, are charged to operations as incurred. NBA expansion and relocation fees are recognized on an as-received basis as the NBA controls allocation and disposition of these funds until payments are made to the teams.

. . . .

5.   INTANGIBLE ASSETS, NET

Intangible assets, net consists of the following at June 30, 2009 and 2008 [see **Table 15**]:

Intangible assets are amortized over their estimated useful lives on a straight-line basis over the playing season each year, with the exception of the franchise asset and syndication costs. Player contracts, arena lease, management contracts, season ticket holder list and sponsorship contracts are amortized on a straight-line basis generally over five, four, three, six and two years, respectively. The franchise asset and syndication costs are not amortized as they have been categorized as indefinite-lived intangible assets. Syndication costs incurred are in connection with the sale of member interests. Amortization of the intangible assets for the years ended June 30, 2009, 2008 and 2007 was $33,379,134, $40,006,132 and $40,606,133, respectively.

6.   DEBT

. . . .

Senior Notes

. . . .

Pursuant to rules applicable to all teams participating in the League Wide Credit Facility, mandatory redemption is triggered when Basketball's current exposure (reflecting, in part, the principal amount outstanding under the Senior Notes) exceeds a percentage of the average NBA membership value or when such exposure exceeds a multiple of its allocated television broadcast revenues, as defined. The maximum available outstanding debt amount for any team participating in the League Wide Credit Facility cannot exceed 60% of the average value of an NBA membership value, as defined. Also, a participating team's outstanding debt may not exceed 4.5 times the sum of (i) its pro forma annual allocated national television broadcast revenues, as defined, and (ii) certain other pro forma contractually obligated income streams, as defined. Otherwise, on or before the first anniversary of the existence of any such excess, the team is required to offer to prepay its outstanding Senior Notes in an amount equal to such excess.

. . . .

Credit Facility

On September 12, 2006, NS&E entered into a credit facility of $59,618,400 that matures on September 12, 2011. The interest rate on the credit facility is LIBOR (subject to a floor of 2.75%) plus 2.75%, or the alternate base rate, as defined in the credit facility agreement, plus 1.75% per annum and has no prepayment penalties. Borrowings will bear interest at the alternate base rate only when no reasonable means exists to ascertain the LIBOR rate or when the LIBOR rate for such interest period does not accurately reflect the cost to the lenders for maintaining their loans. This facility is subordinate to the below mentioned revolving credit facility and term loan. Interest expense on the credit facility totaled $3,420,274, $4,214,207 and $5,274,543 for the years ended June 30, 2009, 2008 and 2007, respectively.

. . . .

10.   LICENSE AGREEMENT

For its home basketball games, Basketball leases its playing facility ("IZOD Center") from the New Jersey Sports and Exposition Authority ("NJSEA") under a license agreement, which in November 2006 was extended by amendment to run through the 2012–2013 Nets season. Lease payments for the 2008–2009 Nets season were $51,840 per game. This per-game rent increases 3% per NBA season. The license agreement also defines the arena revenue sharing of sponsorship revenue, parking receipts, concession revenue and suite revenue. Basketball has the right to terminate the license agreement on an annual basis prior to the 2012–13 Nets season, without the payment of a penalty, as specified in the license agreement.

11.   SIGNIFICANT MEDIA CONTRACTS

Basketball is entitled to receive future media revenues resulting from contracts it has entered into, as well as from contracts entered into by the NBA. The most significant of these are for national broadcast television and local and national cable television broadcasts. The current NBA national broadcast and national cable contracts took effect

Table 15   Amortization of Intangible Assets

	Franchise Asset	Player Contracts	Arena Lease	Management Contracts	Ticket-Holder List	Sponsorship Contracts	Syndication Costs	Total
Cost	$161,111,561	$173,500,000	$22,600,000	$1,800,000	$1,600,000	$500,000	$76,234	$361,187,795
Accumulated amortization	—	(169,470,336)	(22,600,000)	(1,800,000)	(1,333,332)	(500,000)	—	(195,703,668)
	$161,111,561	$4,029,664	—	—	$266,668	—	$76,234	$165,484,127

Source: Courtesy of EDGAR and the U.S. Securities and Exchange Commission.

beginning with the 2008–2009 NBA season and currently run through the 2015–2016 NBA season. Basketball's local media rights agreement with Yankees Entertainment and Sports Network, LLC ("YES Network") began in the 2002–2003 NBA season and runs through the conclusion of the 2021–2022 NBA season, which includes certain market reset provisions and is subject to certain early termination provisions.

Certain members of the Company have a minority ownership interest in the YES Network. Basketball earned gross broadcast revenue as a result of their contract with YES Network for local cable television broadcasts. These revenues are included in Television broadcast revenues in the accompanying Consolidated Statements of Operations.

In June 1976, the NBA and four teams from the American Basketball Association ("ABA"), including the Nets, the Denver Nuggets, the Indiana Pacers, and the San Antonio Spurs (the "Expansion Teams") reached an agreement with the NBA to become members of the NBA, but no agreement was reached with the Spirits of St. Louis Basketball Club, L.P. (the "Spirits"), another former ABA team. Instead, a settlement was reached among the Spirits, the Expansion Teams and the NBA (the "1976 Settlement") calling for the Spirits to receive approximately 1/7th of certain television revenues of Basketball earned by the NBA (calculated on the basis of 28 teams). Accordingly, Basketball receives net, approximately 85% of its share of NBA national television contract distributions.

Basketball's net share of season television revenue for contracts in effect for the years ended June 30, 2009, 2008 and 2007 are shown in **Table 16**.

Revenue sharing earned on the NBA's national television and national cable contracts are prorated by the NBA equally among the NBA's 30 teams.

. . . .

Table 16   Television Revenues

	Year Ended June 30		
	2009	2008	2007
National broadcast and cable television	$22,862,814	$21,328,516	$21,050,924
Local cable television	9,672,099	9,300,094	8,942,399
Total Television broadcast revenues	$32,534,913	$30,628,610	$29,993,323

Source: Courtesy of EDGAR and the U.S. Securities and Exchange Commission.

12.   RELATED PARTY TRANSACTIONS

Arena Development Agreement

Brooklyn Arena entered into a Development Agreement with an affiliate of a member (the "Developer"), pursuant to which it hired the Developer to plan, develop and oversee construction of the Arena for a fee not to exceed 5% of the total project cost at completion. Through June 30, 2009 and 2008, approximately $28 million and $21 million, respectively, of development fees were incurred.

Arena Land and Related Costs

The Company has borrowed from affiliates for Arena-related costs not financed through land loans. At June 30, 2009 and 2008, approximately $83.4 million and $85.3 million of loans from affiliates were outstanding, respectively and are included in Due to Affiliates in the accompanying Consolidated Balance Sheets. The loans accrue interest at the affiliates' weighted average cost of capital, as defined, which averaged approximately 8% for the years ended June 30, 2009 and 2008. For the years ended June 30, 2009 and 2008, interest expense totaled $6.2 million and $6.8 million, respectively, and was all capitalized.

Member Loans

NS&E obtained member loans on various dates from January 2007 to June 2009 totaling $34,600,000 and in July and August 2009 obtained additional member loans totaling $24,200,000 to fund the operations of the team for the 2009-2010 season ending June 30, 2010, with the balance, if any, to be funded by the various means available to the Company. The loans mature at various dates from December 2011 to August 2013 and bear interest at various rates ranging from 5.5% to 20%. Member loans including accrued interest totaled $37,145,448 and $10,884,906 for the years ended June 30, 2009 and 2008. Interest expense incurred on loans totaled approximately $2,000,000, $749,000 and $136,000 for the years ended June 30, 2009, 2008 and 2007, respectively.

13.   COMMITMENTS, CONTINGENCIES AND LITIGATION

. . . .

NBA Fees

Basketball is required under NBA rules and regulations, among other things, to contribute to the NBA certain amounts, as defined, to be used by the NBA for operating expenses. For the years ended June 30, 2009, 2008 and 2007, Basketball contributed a fixed payment of approximately $28,000, $32,000 and $70,000, respectively, allocable from suite revenue and contributed approximately $1,707,000, $2,389,000 and $5,353,000, respectively, from regular season and playoff ticket sales based on each game's ticket sales, as defined, according to a formula specified by the NBA. These NBA gate share fees are netted in Ticket sales, net of admission taxes and league gate share in the accompanying Consolidated Statements of Operations.

Pension Plans

Basketball participates in the NBA Players' Pension Plan, NBA General Managers Pension Plan and the NBA Coaches, Assistant Coaches and Trainers Pension Plan, all of which are multiemployer defined benefit plans administered by the NBA. Contributions charged to pension costs totaled approximately $2,119,000, $1,790,000 and $1,280,000 for the years ended June 30, 2009, 2008 and 2007, respectively, and are included in Team costs in the accompanying Consolidated Statements of Operations. As of June 30, 2009 and 2008, there are accrued pension costs of approximately $1,948,000 and $1,637,000, respectively, which are included in Accounts payable and accrued expenses in the accompanying Consolidated Balance Sheets.

. . . .

Naming Rights

On January 17, 2007, Brooklyn Arena and Basketball (collectively, the "Brooklyn Parties") entered into a Naming Rights Agreement (the "NR Agreement") with Barclays Services Corporation ("Barclays"), where, in exchange for certain fees and other considerations, the Arena will be named Barclays Center, and Barclays will be entitled to certain additional sponsorship, branding, promotional, media, hospitality, and other rights and entitlements in association with the Arena, Basketball and the Atlantic Yards Project. The NR Agreement expires on June 30 following the twentieth anniversary of the opening date of the Arena, subject to certain extension rights as defined in the NR Agreement. The NR Agreement also contains certain Arena construction commencement and Arena opening deadlines, as defined in the NR Agreement. If Brooklyn Arena fails to achieve these deadlines, Barclays is entitled to termination and other rights, as defined in the NR Agreement.

Suite License Agreements

As of June 30, 2009, Brooklyn Arena entered into suite license agreements with various companies and, in addition, granted a suite license as an entitlement to certain sponsors of the Arena within sponsorship agreements entered into by the Brooklyn Parties with such sponsors. Each suite license entitles the licensee the use of a luxury suite in the Arena, with most such luxury suites containing seats for viewing most events at the Arena (although one such suite license agreement applies only to Nets games at the Arena). The suite license agreements commence on the first date when the Arena is open to the general public and expire at various terms ranging from one to 20 years (i.e., for a suite license granted within the confines of a sponsorship agreement, the term of the suite license agreement will be coterminous with the term of the sponsorship agreement). As of June 30, 2009, NS&E has received advance deposits on suite license agreements of $375,600, which is included in Deferred revenue, long term in the accompanying Consolidated Balance Sheets.

Also, the suite license agreements call for the payment of the first license year fee to be made in advance of the opening of the Arena. Suite contracts currently have no impact on Basketball's revenues, as deposits received for suites are accounted for as deferred revenue. These deposits are refundable, contingent upon the construction of the Arena.

Sponsorship and Product Availability Agreements

As of June 30, 2009, the Brooklyn Parties entered into sponsorship and product availability agreements ("Agreements") with various entities, primarily with respect to the Arena and Basketball (after its planned relocation to the Arena). These Agreements entitle such sponsors to certain sponsorship, promotional, media, hospitality and other rights and entitlements in association with the Arena and Basketball, and expire at various terms ranging from three to ten years from the Opening Date of the Arena, as defined in each such Agreement. These Agreements may be terminated, without penalty, based on a failure to construct and open the Arena.

In addition, Basketball has entered into several sponsorship agreements relating to the Nets and its play of NBA games at the IZOD Center. These agreements have terms ranging from one year to a term that is coterminous with the Nets' final season of play at the IZOD Center.

. . . .

14.   SUBSEQUENT EVENT

On September 23, 2009, NS&E and an affiliate signed a letter of intent with an affiliate of an international private investment fund ("Newco") to create a strategic partnership for the development of the Atlantic Yards Project, a 22-acre residential and commercial real estate project in Brooklyn, and the Barclays Center, the future home for the Nets.

In accordance with the agreement, Newco will invest $200,000,000 and make certain other contingent funding commitments to acquire through the issuance of newly-issued units a 45% interest in Brooklyn Arena and 80% interest in Brooklyn Basketball, and the right to purchase up to 20% of the Atlantic Yards Development Company, which will develop the non-arena real estate. Following the completion of the transaction, NS&E would own a 55% interest in Brooklyn Arena and 20% interest in Brooklyn Basketball.

Discussion Questions

1. Discuss the relationship of team heritage/tradition to team value. Why does a team's heritage become a driver of value?

2. How can younger franchises or expansion franchises develop the heritage that you would find in a traditional professional sports town like New York, Boston, Chicago, etc.?

3. Discuss the specific proposals set forth by Jack Williams. Are there any that threaten fan alienation by abandoning traditions of the games? Are there any that could threaten competition on the field? How should a team roll out similar reforms to ensure that they will be accepted by fans?

4. Should sports leagues try to realize revenues from gambling, or are the threats to the integrity of competition too great?

5. Is the fantasy sports boom an example of leagues benefiting from gambling without getting their hands dirty?

6. Given the study claiming that "it is performance on the court, not star power, that attracts fans," in the NBA, are teams wrong to market their teams around star players?

7. Would teams be better off explicitly tying star player compensation to revenues generated through ticket sales, merchandising, etc.?

8. In 2007, Coates and Humphreys said that attendance demand for concessions was generally price elastic. Do you think a similar study would find different results after the economic downturn of 2008 and 2009?

9. Would it be better to reduce ticket prices in order to maximize attendance, and then concessions, parking, etc.? Explain how the answer may vary by sport.

10. In what scenarios should teams consider moving their ticket sales to an auction model?

11. What are the justifications for underpricing season tickets?

12. In what other areas of team revenue (other than ticket sales) could variable pricing be used effectively?

13. What lessons can American teams take from Manchester United's rise as a global brand? What can they reasonably emulate, and what factors are specific to Manchester United?

14. What factors are necessary to create an effective marketing alliance of American and European teams?

CHAPTER SEVEN 7

Stadiums and Arenas

INTRODUCTION

A major income generator for sports enterprises is the facility where teams play or events are held. This is also often a revenue source for the municipalities in which these teams play. It can also be a huge expenditure for the parties involved. The importance of a quality facility to the financial success of a sports franchise is now clearly appreciated by all parties involved. The opening of a new or heavily renovated facility is a transformational moment in the business of a sports franchise. This moment has already occurred for the majority of professional sports franchises, with approximately 80% of MLB, NBA, NHL and NFL teams doing so since 1990. Although the building boom for the current generation of facilities is largely over, and franchise owners have turned to the creation and exploitation of other revenue streams, there can be no doubt that what is past is prologue and that a construction era will begin anew when the current generation's state-of-the-art facilities are deemed obsolete at some point in the future. The most recent trend is for teams to try to make the facility part of a larger real estate play, with a mixed-use sports, commercial, residential, and entertainment development incorporating the playing facility, retail stores, hotel and residential housing, restaurants, and other entertainment options. AEG's L.A. LIVE in Los Angeles is the best example of this to date. More on this is discussed in Chapter 6, "Teams," and Chapter 11, "Sports Franchise Valuation." The focus here is on the major sources of revenue and the major political issues associated with sports facilities.

From a leadership perspective, the broad scope of the successful sports venue is not complex. The first priority is to ensure that the facilities generate revenues; the second is to ensure that a substantial portion of that revenue stream goes to the sports owner or promoter—that is, of course, unless you represent the municipality. The direction of rev-

enue streams is the main focus of the complex negotiations between teams and the venue owners.

The understanding of this formula has evolved as the burden of the construction of facilities has shifted from initially being a largely private task, to a predominantly public expenditure, to the current mix that exists in most instances today with various forms of public and private partnerships. Public contributions are much harder to come by today than they were in the earlier phase of the most recent building boom. The taxpayers in the cities where a public contribution towards the facility construction is sought are now seeking a clearer understanding of the return they receive on their sports facility investments. This has led to an increase in the aforementioned public–private partnerships, with the teams paying for an increasingly substantial part of the facility construction costs—an obligation that causes them to incur significant debt. The ever-escalating facility construction costs have made these public–private partnerships more of a necessity. The cost is simply too high for most parties to take on entirely on their own. The municipality has higher-order priorities, and many of the teams do not have the necessary funds. Interestingly, in the NFL, a league-funded initiative (the G-3 stadium plan) typically contributes to the team's share of the construction costs, up to $150 million. (See **Table 1** for recent stadium costs and Chapter 5 for a more elaborate discussion of the G-3 stadium plan.)

Franchises often pursue new facilities or renegotiate leases in pursuit of additional revenues. The revenues that have increased most dramatically in importance are those that are not shared with other teams via league-wide revenue-sharing plans. These important revenue sources include luxury boxes, naming rights, and signage.

The excerpts from *The Stadium Game* lay out the major revenue-generating streams these facilities create. Here we highlight some of the major sources. The distribution of the various revenue streams between the tenant team(s) and

Table 1   Selected Recent Stadium Construction

City	Sport	Year/Opened	Total Cost	Government Funding
New York	Baseball	2009	$850 million	$264 million
New York	Baseball	2009	1300 million	507 million
Indianapolis	Football	2008	720 million	620 million
Washington D.C.	Baseball	2008	611 million	611 million
Newark, NJ	Hockey	2007	468 million	312 million
Glendale, AZ	Football	2006	455 million	9.5 million
St. Louis	Baseball	2006	346 million	0
Charlotte	Basketball	2005	265 million	265 million
Memphis	Basketball	2004	250 million	250 million
Philadelphia	Baseball	2004	346 million	173 million
San Diego	Baseball	2004	411 million	287.7 million
Houston	Basketball	2003	202 million	202 million
Philadelphia	Football	2003	512 million	180 million

landlord municipality are the subject of the stadium lease negotiations previously noted. "The Name is the Game in Facility Naming Rights" focuses on one of the most important revenue streams—facility naming rights deals. We highlight this source separately because of the dominant role it plays. Facilities with names such as Enron, Adelphia, CMGI, PSINET, and TWA—companies that no longer exist or toil in bankruptcy—add an additional element that both sports and corporate leadership should be aware of in marrying the two sectors. This was highlighted even further during the 2009 economic downturn when corporations were left to justify sponsorship investments, including sports facility naming rights. The prime example of this dilemma was Citi Field in New York, a naming rights obligation of $400 million over 20 years for a corporation receiving hundreds of billions of dollars in a government bailout. This left many taxpayers wondering if their dollars should be used for sports sponsorship.

The chapter closes with three pieces that focus on the policy dilemma stakeholders confront in the "who should pay for it" decision-making process. The first, by Marc Edelman, "Sports and the City: How to Curb Professional Sports Teams' Demands For Free Public Stadiums," provides an in-depth history of this subsidy issue. This is followed by two pieces of Congressional testimony, one by Neil Demause, a long-time follower of this issue, and the other by Professor Brad Humphreys.

FINANCING AND ECONOMIC BACKGROUND

THE STADIUM GAME

Martin J. Greenberg

FINANCING OVERVIEW

The financing of sports facilities has recently garnered considerable attention. Sports facilities have become increasingly important components in the public finance marketplace with many state and local governments aggressively trying to keep or lure sports franchises into their communities. . . . there has been an explosion in the number of financing projects for stadiums and arenas, as communities have made plans to build state-of-the-art facilities to attract and retain professional franchises and draw major sporting events.

Fueling this development explosion is league expansion, facility obsolescence and a demand for increased franchise revenue. Since 1990, there have been seventy-seven major league facility lease re-negotiations, stadium renovations, or new venues built for professional football, baseball, basketball, and hockey at an approximate cost of $12 billion.

. . . .

Since 1990, thirty-seven new stadiums and arenas—worth more than $6.5 billion in construction costs—have opened. By 2000, more than half of the country's major professional sports franchises were either getting new or renovated facilities, or had requested them. [*Ed. Note: As of 2010, approximately 80% of the teams in the NBA, NFL, NHL, and MLB were playing in facilities that have been either constructed or heavily renovated since 1990.*] This increase in sports facility construction is expected to continue throughout the decade *[2000s]* as league expansion and the underlying economics of the sports industry evolve.

The evolution of stadium and arena financing can be divided into four distinct periods: the Prehistoric Era dating back before 1965; the Renaissance Era carrying through 1983; the Revolution Era occurring between 1984 and 1986; and finally the New Frontier Era, from 1987 until today. . . .

The Prehistoric Era: Prior to 1965, the sports industry was not quite the big business that it is today. Government financing was the only source of funding. The most common funding instrument was general obligation bonds. [*Ed. Note: Wholly privately financed stadiums can be found in this era as well.*]

The Renaissance Era: From 1966 to 1983, the popularity of professional sports grew tremendously in terms of both live attendance and television viewership. Franchise owners saw the values of their sports investments grow dramatically. The financial performance of arenas and stadiums improved through increased utilization by other events, such as concerts and family shows. Financing for the facilities continued to be dominated by the public sector.

During this era, bonds secured by taxes were the most traditional approach to stadium and arena financing taken by the public sector. In this situation, the municipality (city, county, state, or other government entity) backs a bond issue with a general obligation pledge, annual appropriations, or the revenues from a specific tax.

The Revolution Era: The Deficit Reduction Act of 1984 and the Tax Reform Act of 1986 both had large implications on stadium and arena financing. Many of today's older facilities were financed on a tax-exempt basis prior to the Tax Reform Act of 1986.

The Deficit Reduction Act lowered the priority of constructing public assembly facilities using funds from the public sector in light of the need to lower the national deficit. The Tax Reform Act made it much more difficult to finance stadiums and arenas with tax-exempt bonds. As a result, financing structures became more complex as revenue streams are often segregated to support multiple issues of debt in both taxable and tax-exempt markets.

New Frontier Era: Since 1987, stadium and arena financing has embarked upon a fascinating new path. The days of "vanilla" financings are over, giving way to greater complexity in financing arrangements. In addition, the planning and construction period has been stretched to a five to ten year time horizon. "Typical" construction risks, voter approval, and political "red tape" associated with the public's participation in stadium and arena financing projects have caused significant delays and have put the financial feasibility of some new facilities in doubt.

Most deals now involve partnerships between multiple parties from the public and private sectors. These mutually beneficial public/private partnerships are dictated by what each party can bring to the table. The public sector may be able to provide any combination of land, public capital/ revenue streams, condemnation, infrastructure improvements, and tax abatement. The private sector may likewise provide any or all of the following: land, investment capital in the form of debt or equity, acceptance of risk, operating knowledge, and tenants.

Private sector participation in financing structures has typically been through taxable debt secured by the facility's operations and/or corporate guarantees. This is a relatively expensive source of funding that has generally required a higher debt coverage ratio and significant equity contributions. Thus, the private sector has sought other nontraditional sources. Those can include luxury suites, club seats, personal seat licenses (PSLs), concessionaire fees, and naming rights, among others.

The unique background and political environment surrounding the financing and construction of professional sports facilities plays a critical role in shaping the appropriate financing structure. The changing economics of professional sports has led franchises to demand a greater share of facility-generated revenue. As a result, reliance solely on public bond financing has become increasingly difficult and a combination of both public and private participation is often the cornerstone of current financing structures.

FINANCING INSTRUMENTS

Stadiums and arenas have been financed through a variety of public and private financial instruments. Because sports facilities represent a significant capital investment and provide benefits, both economic and social, to the public, financing structures typically rely on a combination of public and private financing instruments. These structures can become complex, particularly when traditional landlords and tenants form partnerships to provide capital for the facility. The appropriate financial instruments depend significantly on the unique circumstances surrounding the particular project.

Defined Instruments

Municipal notes and bonds are publicly traded securities. Congress exempted municipal securities from the registration requirements of the Securities Act of 1933 and the reporting requirements of the Securities Exchange Act of 1934. However, anti-fraud provisions remain in effect for any offering circulars issued to prospective investors.

Congress has not regulated issuers of municipal securities nor required that they issue a registration statement for several reasons. Among these reasons are the desire for government comity, the absence of recurrent abuses, the greater level of sophistication of marketplace investors, and few defaults. Municipal bonds are often analyzed by rating agencies such as Fitch, Moody's, and Standard & Poors. The key factors considered by rating agencies, credit enhancers, and investors in analyzing tax-secured debt include:

- Level of coverage;
- Broadness, stability, and reliability of tax base;
- Historic performance of revenue stream;
- Appropriation risk;
- Underlying economic strength;
- Political risk; [and]
- Financial viability of the project.

[*Ed. Note: See Chapter 11 for further discussion of the credit-rating process.*]

The following are descriptions of common financial instruments used to fund sports facilities.

General Obligation Bonds: General obligation (G.O.) bonds are secured by the general taxing power of the issuer and are called *full faith and credit obligations.* States, counties, and cities are common issuers of this form of debt. Repayment of the debt comes from the entity's general fund revenue, which typically includes property, income, profits, capital gains, sales, and use taxes. The full faith and credit pledge is typically supported by a commitment from the government issuer to repay the principal and interest through whatever means necessary, including levying additional taxes. In addition, double-barreled bonds are issued and secured not only by taxing power, but also by fee income that is outside the issuer's general fund. G.O. bonds secured by limited revenue sources such as property taxes alone are called *limited-tax general obligation bonds.* This type of bond typically requires legislative or voter approval.

Since G.O. bonds are backed by the general revenue fund of the issuing instrumentality, they usually represent the issuer's lowest cost of capital. General obligation bonds, however, are becoming increasingly difficult to issue for sports facilities with a growing demand on government for other capital projects and services.

Special Tax Bonds: These bonds are payable from a specifically pledged source of revenue—such as a specific tax—rather than from the full faith and credit of the municipality or state. *Tax and Revenue Anticipation Notes* (TRANs) are issued for periods from three months to three years in anticipation of the collection of tax or other revenue. Similarly, TRANs are issued in anticipation of a bond issue. *Tax-exempt commercial paper* is issued for thirty to 270 days, and typically is backed by a letter of credit from a bank or a bank line of credit. These are all used to even out cash flows when revenues will soon be forthcoming from taxes, revenues, or bond sales.

Revenue Bonds: Revenue bonds are more complex and less secure than general obligation bonds. Revenue bonds are typically project specific and are secured by the project's revenue, income, and one or more other defined revenue sources, such as hotel occupancy taxes, sales taxes, admission taxes, or other public/private revenue streams. The debt service (principal and interest) is paid for with dedicated revenue.

Since revenue bonds limit the financial risk to the municipality, they typically have a lower credit rating. The more stable and predictable the source of revenue, the more creditworthy the bond issue. Naturally, revenue sources with an existing collection history are preferable to underwriters and rating agencies, but revenue bonds do not offer that predictability.

Lease-Backed Financing (Lease Revenue Bonds): This financial instrument still benefits from the credit strength of a state or local government. An "authority" typically issues bonds with a facility lease arrangement with the governmental entity. The government leases the facility from the authority and leases the facility back to the authority pursuant to a sublease. The lease typically requires the government to make annual rental payments sufficient to allow payment of the debt service on the authority's bonds. There are several related lease structures including Sale/Leaseback and True Lease arrangements.

Certificate of Participation: Certificates of Participation (COPs) have become an increasingly common financial instrument used to finance sports facilities. COP holders are repaid through an annual lease appropriation by a sponsoring government agency. COPs do not legally commit the governmental entity to repay the COP holder, and therefore generally do not require voter approval. In addition, COPs are not subject to many of the limitations and restrictions associated with bonds.

Although COPs offer the issuing authority less financial risk and more flexibility, they tend to be more cumbersome due to the reliance on the trustee. In addition, COPs carry a higher coupon rate relative to traditional revenue bonds.

[*Ed. Note: The author's examples of applications of the financial instruments described are omitted.*]

. . . .

Economic Generators

The creation and expansion of sports facility revenue generators has been one of the driving forces behind the sports facility boom in the 1990s. These new revenue generators are joining traditional income sources such as concessions, parking, and advertising in determining whether the lessor or the lessee will earn a profit at the facility. Thus, the allocation of revenues derived from items such as club seats, seat licenses, corporate naming rights, restaurants, luxury suites, and retail stores is quickly becoming an important part of every sports facility lease agreement.

This . . . is an examination of the primary revenue generators and how these items are currently being addressed in major and minor league sports facility lease agreements.

Club Seats

Club seats were the invention of former Miami Dolphins' owner Joe Robbie who created a new level of premium seating in hopes of securing enough funding to privately finance a new home for the Dolphins. Robbie placed 10,214 wide, contour-backed seats in the middle tier of the three-tiered facility and dubbed them, "individual club seats." The seats, which cost from $600 to $1,400 annually, had to be leased on a ten-year basis. In return, club seat patrons received twenty-one-inch-wide seats, overhead blowers puffing cool air on them during hot days or nights, and access to an exclusive series of lounge areas that were finely decorated and serviced by wait-staff ready to handle the patrons' concessionary needs. With the guaranteed revenues from the ten-year leases for the club seats and luxury suites in hand, Robbie was able to secure the financing necessary to build the facility that was later named in his honor and assumed a place in the stadium financing annals.

Since its inception in the mid-1980s, club seating has become one of the largest revenue producers for stadiums. And since 1991, the number of leased club seats has risen by more than 500 percent, producing a significant and steady revenue stream for the four major league professional sports teams. . . .

Luxury Suites

In 1883, Albert Spalding's new baseball stadium for the Chicago White Stockings catered to the upscale fan by offering eighteen private boxes furnished with drapes and armchairs. Since then, professional sports franchises have continued their race to install luxury suites in their playing facilities.

Luxury suites have entrenched themselves as the second-most important revenue stream for professional sports franchises behind television revenues.

. . . .

Personal Seat Licenses

In Tampa Bay, Buccaneers owners used it to finance the National Football League team's sparkling new stadium. On campus at the University of Wisconsin, Badgers' officials are using it to help fund the school's athletics program. . . . . . [*Ed. Note: The Philadelphia Eagles, Houston Texans, and the New York Giants and Jets have used them more recently.*] and thereby join ten other NFL teams (Baltimore, Carolina, Cincinnati, Cleveland, Dallas, Oakland, Pittsburgh, St. Louis, Tampa Bay, and Tennessee) that have variations of them.

It is a personal seat license, or PSL, one of the most important—and often misunderstood—of the legal and financial vehicles available for sports stadium funding.

Although there has been a greater increase in private sector contributions to sports stadium and arena development, teams and communities continue to seek new ways to finance stadiums. Personal seat licenses have provided, at least in some instances, another means of contributing to the private equation in the facilities partnership formed between private financiers and public funding.

In addition to providing private sector funds for the construction of sports facilities, personal seat licenses also have generated season ticket sales and facility revenues, and have been used as a means to attract teams contemplating relocation.

The expanded use of seat licenses seems beneficial for all parties involved [in the] financing process of sports facilities. Teams receive upgraded facilities and guaranteed ticket bases, which should allow them to remain competitive on and off the field for many years. Fans receive property rights in their personal seat licenses, which can become valuable items on the open market. And governmental entities receive the benefits of upgraded or new sports facilities at reduced costs to taxpayers, theoretically allowing these entities to allocate tax monies for essential governmental services.

The stadium financing effort in the Carolinas for the home of the Carolina Panthers is an example of the interaction between seat licensing revenues and governmental interests. Ericsson Stadium, the $248-million home for the NFL's expansion Carolina Panthers opened in 1996, was built at a cost to taxpayers of $55 million, while the rest of the financing for the facility was derived from seat license revenues. The Panthers were projected to have a $200- to $300-million impact on the Carolina economy, easily generating enough of a return to cover the initial taxpayer investment.

. . . .

Funds for the bulk of the Panthers' development costs—$162 million (about $100 million after taxes)—came from private seat licenses priced from $700 to $5,400 for season tickets and club seats. Nearly 62,000 private seat licenses were sold by the time the stadium opened, including 49,724 seat licenses and 104 suites (valued at nearly $113 million) a month before the franchise was awarded. Today, 156 of 158 suites (price: $50,000 to $296,000) are leased for six- to 10-year periods.

. . . .

Understanding the PSL

A personal seat license is defined as a contractual agreement between a team (the PSL licensor) and the purchaser (the PSL licensee) in which the licensee pays the team a fee in exchange for the team guaranteeing the licensee a right to purchase season tickets at a specified seat location for a designated period of time (such as five years, ten years, or even the life of the facility) as long as the license holder does not violate the terms of the license agreement. Should the licensee violate these terms, the team automatically gets the personal seat license back, or has the ability to exercise a right to buy back the license at the original selling price and then resell it on the open market.

A personal seat license, which can be resold on the open market, generally offers the purchaser no guarantee of a return on the initial investment—none, of course, except for the benefits of enjoying use of a seat at a game. The main variables in legal constructions of modern personal seat licenses—which also have been called permanent seat licenses—are (1) the cost and (2) the time period of the license.

Variations on the Personal Seat License Theme

Tampa Bay employed a variation of the personal seat license to raise money for constructing Raymond James Stadium, home of the Buccaneers. Fans were asked to pay a deposit for the right to buy tickets for the next ten years. The deposit, which was equal to the price of a season ticket for one year, is to be refunded at the rate of 5 percent per year for nine years, with the balance paid at the 10th season.

The Kohl Center—home of University of Wisconsin hockey and the men's and women's basketball teams—has a plan called the Annual Scholarship Seating Program. It calls for season ticket holders to donate to the University Scholarship Fund in exchange for the right to purchase prime seats.

Recently, the Green Bay Packers announced a $295 million plan to renovate Lambeau Field, which would be paid for through a public/private split of 57/43 percent. The team, through a one-time user fee on paid season ticket holders, would raise a total of $92.5 million. Lambeau Field season ticketholders would pay $1,400 per seat and Milwaukee package season ticket holders would be asked to pay $600 per seat. [*Ed. Note: The renovation has been completed.*]

A one-time user fee differs from a PSL. In Green Bay, the fee paid only entitles the season ticket holder to obtain tickets to renovated Lambeau Field. It does not guarantee the season ticket seat beyond the first season in renovated Lambeau, nor is the right transferable. The Packers are discussing, however, implementing a policy that, if season ticketholders ever surrendered their tickets, the next person on the team's waiting list would be required to reimburse the user fee to the original ticket holder before any tickets actually changed hands.

In December of 1999, Robert McNair's Houston NFL Holdings, Inc. unveiled its plan to sell fewer personal seat licenses at a lower price than has been fashionable recently in financing new NFL stadiums. Its goal is to attract a broader demographic to games.

. . . .

Comparatively, 80 percent of the seats in Cleveland Browns Stadium and 85 percent of the seats at Adelphia Coliseum, home of the Tennessee Titans, were subject to licenses. The Steelers sold 50,000 PSLs for Pittsburgh's new 64,000-seat stadium.

. . . .

Naming Rights

[*Ed. Note: For a more extensive discussion of naming rights, see the reading "The Name Is the Game in Facility Naming Rights."*]

One of the most recent additions—and the most lucrative—to the list of stadium revenue generators is the selling of naming rights. Naming rights are currently sold for not only the right to rename an entire stadium, but also to name entryways into the stadium, the field, breezeways, etc.

In 1987, the Los Angeles Forum, then home to the Lakers and Kings, became the Great Western Forum when Great Western Bank became the first corporation to purchase the rights to name any professional sports facility. Since then, it has become the rule rather than the exception for a facility to bear the name of a company.

Historically, stadiums and arenas have been named either for a geographic region (Milwaukee County Stadium), in honor of a renowned individual (RFK Stadium), or after the name of the home team (Giants Stadium). Today, the increasing need for capital has resulted in most new facilities bearing the name of an individual company. In fact, the naming rights deals have grown so lucrative, that even storied stadiums such as Lambeau Field in Green Bay are considering the sale of its naming rights in some fashion or another.

The selling of naming rights is a trend that will continue because as time goes on, the revenue it produces is vital to financing venue development and renovations. Jerry Colangelo, *[former]* owner of the Arizona Diamondbacks and Phoenix Suns, has stated that, "I think you're going to see more and more corporate involvement in terms of naming rights and major involvements with large companies. In order to deliver that product, the game itself, you need to build venues that have the opportunity to pay for it. Our group is indicative of that trend."[74]

. . . .

Beyond Stadium Naming Rights

There are times when a facility chooses not to sell the name of [the] facility itself, but rather sell the rights to name the field, breezeways, or portals into the stadium. This is a very new concept that began in 1999 when the Cleveland Browns christened its new stadium without a corporate naming rights sponsor—by choice. The club chose instead to sell only the rights to name the stadium's portals at $2 million a year for ten years.

One such company is National City Bank, who receives other benefits with their deal, including:

- The right to call themselves the "Official Bank of the Cleveland Browns" for five years while serving as the team's sole bank provider;

- The right to use the Cleveland Browns logo in conjunction with various advertising and promotional activities;

- Maintain the right for product merchandising for several unnamed existing products, as well as several new products;

- Name identification in the southeast quadrant (presumably the gate with the most public exposure) of the new stadium, including logos on all turnstiles, entranceways, directional signage, tickets, and seat cup holders;

- A permanent presence in the west end zone scoreboard; [and]

- Numerous other signage rights throughout the stadium.

. . . In the case of Soldier Field, selling naming rights to auxiliary areas will be the only option to generate this type of revenue because the overall naming rights of the stadium are not for sale. Chicago Mayor Richard Daley recently stated publicly, "(The stadium) will always be known as Soldier's Field. That is dedicated to the veterans here in Chicago. It will always be that."[165]

But selling the rights to the auxiliary facility areas is not limited only to those facilities that choose not to sell their overall naming rights. When the Patriots sold the naming rights to their new field for $114 million-plus over fifteen years to CMGI—an Internet holding company with affiliations and financial interests with 70 Internet companies—the Patriots reserved the right to additionally sell the rights to the stadium's entrances, which is expected to earn the team millions more on an annual basis, based on the Cleveland deal.

These auxiliary areas can even include seating sections. At Bank One Ballpark [now Chase Field], for example, Nissan struck a deal with the Arizona Diamondbacks to name the premium seating level the Infiniti Level. Nissan's annual price tag for that right actually exceeds the $2.3 million paid annually by Bank One for the facility's naming rights deal, although Bank One's deal included several other options bringing its annual commitment to $4.6 million per year.

And naming rights are not limited to the game-day field only. The Indianapolis Colts recently announced that they sold the rights to their practice facility to Union Federal Bank. The venue will be known as Union Federal Football Center. Although no price was announced, team officials said it was the largest sponsorship deal in the team's history. The package includes radio spots, sponsorship of the team's fan club, signage in the RCA Dome, and print advertising.

. . . .

In the most recent Houston deal with Reliant Energy, the deal also called for Reliant to maintain the naming rights to the Astrodome Complex, which includes the Astrodome, the AstroArena, and a new convention center.

Parking

Of the main economic generators discussed . . . parking revenue continues to remain the smallest revenue generator of this group. As a result, parking—in a strictly financial sense—is not usually the most significant issue during lease negotiations between teams and sports facilities.

. . . .

Advertising

It may appear as though sports teams have a new interest in advertisements and sponsorships. . . . years ago, nearly all stadiums bore the names of famous people or cities. These days all but a handful carry the names of companies willing to pay millions to have a corporate logo identified with a team and its hometown stadium.

It is not so much that it is a new revenue source, however. Instead, it is the ability of teams to keep this revenue that is making advertising the goose that laid the golden egg. In the NFL, for instance, advertising and signage revenue is exempt from the league's revenue-sharing program.

The demand for advertising has turned every square inch of a sports facility into a potential source of advertising income. Advertising consists of everything from signage on the outside of arenas to sleeves that cover the turnstiles to posters above the urinal.

For the Washington Wizards, the . . . MCI [now Verizon] Center will earn more than $6 million from signs alone, a 100 percent increase over US Airways Arena. The Washington Redskins earned approximately $250,000 in advertising income during the team's final season at RFK Stadium, a figure ranked near the bottom of the NFL. When the team moved in to Jack Kent Cooke Stadium, the new home of the Redskins, advertising industry specialists believe advertising revenue climbed to between $6 million and $8 million a year from sponsorships alone.[222] That number grew even larger when new owner Daniel Snyder sold the naming rights for the stadium to Federal Express.

These examples of the boost advertising can give to team revenue are not uncommon. Generating revenue that a team can keep for itself has become a necessity for teams to keep up with climbing player salaries.

Stadium advertising has become necessary to maintain a profitable franchise.

. . . .

Concessions

Concession rights are rights transferred to a concessionaire for the sale and dispensing of food, snacks, refreshments, alcoholic and nonalcoholic beverages, merchandise, souvenirs, clothing, novelties, publications, and other articles in the stadium or arena, pursuant to a concession agreement. The concession agreements set aside sales spaces which include concession stands, condiment areas, vending machines, hawker's station, the press room, the stadium club, cafeterias, executive clubs, executive suites, food courts, outdoor cafés, and waitress service for club seats, among others. Either a team or facility owner hires the concessionaire. The concession agreement will normally grant a concessionaire the exclusive right to exercise concession rights in concession spaces throughout a facility.

Wes Westley, President and CEO of SMG, has said:

"In the past, facilities relied solely on the success of concession stands. With 'state of the art' arenas and stadiums being built, emphasis is now placed on luxury box and club seating, catering, restaurants, hospitality suites, and other nontraditional concessionaire sales. In addition, branded foods and franchising has also impacted the amount of gross sales being generated. Simply stated, there's now a much greater pie of revenue to share."[388]

This shift has dramatically increased total gross sales at all new venues. Today's concession contracts include commission payments on specific types of sales rather than on total sales. New contracts may have as many as 15 different sales categories in which various commission rates are paid.

. . . .

Other Economic Generator Provisions

At a time when sports teams are looking to meet the demands of increasing player salaries and still provide a growing income stream to owners, alternative sources of revenue are becoming increasingly important and popular.

Everything from restaurant operations to sports amusement parks are developed to create excitement about the team and generate revenue in the process. While stadium tours and team retail stores may only provide a few thousand dollars to the annual income statement, they often go a lot further in keeping teams at the top of the mind of fans.

The more interesting development is that there appears to be little or no uniformity among how these programs are developed or how they are implemented. While most restaurants, for instance, are operated by a concessionaire, some leases send the revenue to the team, while others give it to the district.

The same is true of tours. Some new stadiums are offering them and raking in revenue, while others never even opened the doors to paying tour groups. And then there is the Grand Dame of stadiums, The Louisiana Superdome, which is expanding its tours even though it is more than two decades old.

What is clear, however, is that ancillary revenue is increasingly important, whether it goes to the teams or the stadium districts.

Restaurants

Restaurants are becoming an important part of making stadiums a constant attraction, even when there are no games scheduled. The Southeast Wisconsin Professional Baseball Park District proved this when it allowed for the completion of the Klements Sausage Haus, a freestanding restaurant, even

after the opening of Miller Park for the Milwaukee Brewers was delayed for a year because of a construction accident.

The Milwaukee Brewers have started using the Sausage Haus, which is currently open during games, for press events. The team, for instance, introduced its new skipper at the restaurant. The restaurant stands adjacent to Miller Park.

The District's lease agreement with the Brewers calls for the facility to be operated by an outside vendor, with revenue from the restaurant to go to the Brewers.[445]

Like many new stadiums, the Brewers' Miller Park also features several restaurants, all of which will be operated by SportService, Inc.

In addition to the Klements Sausage Haus, Miller Park will have a sports bar and restaurant, which is scheduled to be open all year. It will also have a high-end restaurant near the luxury boxes, which will be open only during games and for special events.

The goal is to allow fans to use baseball games for all sorts of entertaining. The restaurant facilities are capable of hosting everything from a business meeting to a birthday party.

The Brewers retain all of the revenue from the restaurants.

The St. Louis Rams also collect all of the revenue from the restaurant at the TransWorld Dome [*Ed. Note: now known as the Edward Jones Dome*.].[448] The only time the Rams do not collect the revenue from the restaurant is when the St. Louis Convention and Visitors Commission, which operates the . . . Dome, hosts an event at the restaurant. That money goes to the commission.

The Rams, however, are also responsible for all the costs associated with the restaurant.

The Miami Heat have yet another arrangement. The team gets all revenue from the restaurants during its games and 47.5 percent of the revenue from all other concessionaires operated during Heat games.

The Colorado Rockies' lease gives the team 97 percent of year round bar and restaurant revenue if the team uses the facility's approved concessionaire. If the team chooses another operator, its percentage drops to 95 percent.[450] The District collects the remainder of the revenue.

Revenue, however, is not the only concern of a team when it comes to food served at stadiums. Teams have started specializing in regional delicacies in an effort to make the food more interesting and thus increase sales.

The Baltimore Ravens offer Maryland's famous crab cakes, Latin food is common . . . in Miami, and sushi is a regular offering in San Francisco at Pacific Bell [*Ed. Note: now AT&T*] Park.

The theory is that improved gastronomy will increase the amount of money spent at the ballpark. . .[451]

Along with local specialties, however, some ballparks are favoring national chains that will bring in diners all year. Both Bank One [*now Chase Field*] Ballpark, home of the Arizona Diamondbacks, and the Texas Rangers' Arlington ballpark are home to TGI Friday's restaurants.

Reservations at the Rangers' Friday's restaurant include the price of a ticket to the game and offers seating on three levels, with pool tables and darts serving as a diversion from the baseball game.

Freestanding restaurants, whether as part of a national chain or with a local flair, are almost a requirement for a new ballpark intended to keep the interest of fans, according to Stan Kasten, [*then*] chairman of Philips Arena in Atlanta.

Facility Tours

Enron Field [*Ed. Note: the former name of Minute Maid Park*], the home of the Houston Astros, has a fancy coal-fired train, but no tours. Neither does the shiny new Cleveland Browns Stadium. In San Francisco, however, Pacific Bell [*AT&T*] Park charges $10 a head for tours. The revenue from the tours goes to the team.

The two stalwart stadiums of the NFL still lead the league in tour revenue.

Lambeau Field, which only offers tours from June to August, takes an average of 12,500 fans from the press box to the field each summer. The tours begin at the Packers Hall of Fame on the same grounds as the stadium and take upwards of 90 minutes. Brown County operates the tours and collects about $6 per person. The Green Bay Packers collect the revenue, according to the team.

The Louisiana Superdome collects $7.50 per person for tours and all of the revenue goes to the stadium district. The Superdome, however, developed a special tour of the engineering marvels of the stadium in 1999. Those tours are only offered for groups and prices vary depending on the size of the group and the amount of interest the group has in seeing the underbelly of the stadium.

The Maricopa County Stadium District collects all of the revenue from tours . . . in Phoenix. Tickets to the . . . tours are $7.50.

What makes the Superdome and Lambeau Field unique, however, is that most stadium districts find enough demand to justify having a tour staff for up to five years. After that, few fans are interested in touring the stadiums. It is the uniqueness and history of these two facilities that continue to draw the interest of fans.

While younger facilities eventually lose the allure that makes a tour operation successful, older teams continue to look for new ways to generate both revenue and fan interest.

The Green Bay Packers, with the help of the Brown County Convention & Visitors Bureau, created the Packers Experience, which it runs from June to August. The Packers Experience allows fans to get involved in every facet of the game, mimicking the now familiar Lambeau Leap and practicing the punt, pass, and kick.

Fun and Games

The facility is open during the training camp season and serves, along with the Green Bay Packers Hall of Fame, as part of a destination package for football fanatics.

The revenue for the Packers Experience is divided evenly between the team and the Brown County Convention & Visitors Bureau. The indoor amusement park drew an average of 65,000 visitors each summer in the first two years it was open.

After its first year, attendance at The Packers Experience dropped from 73,000 to 54,000. All of the revenue from the Packers Hall of Fame goes to the Packers. It is open year round and takes in as many as 75,000 visitors a year.

In Denver, the Colorado Rockies and Denver Metropolitan Major League Baseball Stadium District split the revenue equally from the baseball museum at Coors Field. The District gives its portion of the revenue from the museum to the Rockies Youth Foundation.

The real fun, however, is coming from the newest stadiums.

For $4,000, fans can watch a game at Phoenix's . . . [*Chase Field*] from the outfield swimming pool.

The Texas Rangers have a running track, Six Flags water park, children's center, and baseball museum, all of which are busier when there is no game at the ballpark than when the Rangers are in town.

Perhaps the most controversial of the entertainment venues is the Coca-Cola-sponsored playground at . . . Pacific Bell Park in San Francisco, shaped like a Coke bottle. Some argue it is a symbol of commercialism finally going too far.

Baseball purists worry that the game is being overwhelmed by all the other attractions at the stadiums, but teams counter that they are only giving fans what they want: a destination rather than just a ball game.

Retail Stores

While teams have always sold their merchandise and retained the revenue from it—t-shirts, puffy fingers, and the like—many teams are now negotiating for retail stores that are open year round at the stadiums. This is all part of making the venue a constant tourist destination.

The Baltimore Orioles, Anaheim Ducks, and St. Louis Rams all have exclusive rights to revenue from their retail stores. The management company that operates The Pond gives the Ducks retail space. The team is allowed to retain 100 percent of the revenue from the sale of merchandise at the store.

The Orioles are one of the teams that have their retail store open all year, even when the team is not playing at Camden Yards, or when it is not baseball season. Like the Ducks, the Orioles retain all revenue from the store.

The Tampa Bay Devil Rays embarked on the most aggressive retail strategy in professional sports when the team designed a full-scale mall with several restaurants into the renovated Tropicana Field in 1997.[467]

The team paid a portion of the costs for the $85 million renovation, which also included a reconfiguration of the ball field. In return, the Devil Rays collect the revenue from the shopping and dining center.

The mall remains open year round, providing a constant revenue stream for the Devil Rays. The team designed the park so that fans would treat Tropicana Field as a place to spend a day or a weekend, rather than just a game-time destination.

The granddaddy of this concept, of course, is Toronto's Skydome, which was built more as a destination than a ballpark.

The stadium features a 350-room hotel, the largest McDonald's in North America, a Hard Rock Café, a health club, movie theater, meeting rooms, and shopping mall.[469]

. . . Revenue from the various businesses associated with Skydome is divided between the team and the stadium district. The profits are divided at different rates depending on which venture is contributing to the revenue stream.

CONCLUSION

What has become obvious through alternate forms of revenue generation is that teams are seeking ways to get fans to the stadium as much as they are seeking outside forms of revenue.

Few teams, if any, will say that revenue from restaurants, museums, retail stores, and the like, have saved their budget. What teams are likely to say, however, is that the additional revenue from these ventures allows the team to capture a larger portion of the fan's wallet. That is what makes sports good business.

References

74. Don Ketchum, "D-Backs Go to the Bank (One) for Stadium Name: 30-Year Deal Continues Trend to Sponsorship," *Phoenix Gazette,* April 6, 1995, at C1, and Eric Miller, "Million-Dollar Name: Bank One Ballpark," *Arizona Republic,* April 6, 1995, at A1.

165. Mark J. Konkol, "Daley Says Soldier Field Has Right Ring," *Daily Southtown,* June 16, 2000.

222. "Clear and Visible Signs of the Times," *The Washington Post,* Aug. 24, 1997.

388. Presentation, National Sports Law Institute, "Stadium Revenues, Venues and Values," October 1995.

445. Southeast Wisconsin Professional Baseball Park lease, p. 12.

448. Amended and restated St. Louis NFL lease by and among the Los Angeles Rams Football Club, the Regional Convention and Visitors Commission, and the St. Louis NFL Corp., Jan 17, 1995, Annex 3, at O.

450. Amended and restated lease and management agreement by and between the Denver Metropolitan Major League Baseball Stadium District and Colorado Rockies Baseball Club Ltd., March 30, 1995, at 18,19.

451. Alexander F. Grau, "Where Have You Gone, Joe DiMaggio? And Where Are the Stadiums You Played In?" *Georgetown Science, Technology & International Affairs,* Fall 1998, p. 5.

467. Tampa Bay Devil Ray Internet site: http://www.devilrays.com/thetrop/thetrop.php3.

469. Grau, p. 4.

SPORTS AND THE CITY: HOW TO CURB PROFESSIONAL SPORTS TEAMS' DEMANDS FOR FREE PUBLIC STADIUMS

Marc Edelman

I.   THE HISTORY OF PROFESSIONAL SPORTS SUBSIDIES

American communities have not always subsidized the professional sports industry.[10] To the contrary, for the first seventy-five years of professional sports, most team owners built their own facilities and covered their own costs.[11] By the end of World War II, however, changing demographics led to the start of communities subsidizing professional sports teams.[12]

A.   The Emergence of Public Subsidies

The era of publicly funded sports facilities that continues into today began in 1950 when the city of Milwaukee, unable to secure a Major League Baseball ("Baseball")

expansion franchise, decided to lure an existing team by building a public stadium.[13]

Enticed by the offer to play in a new, publicly funded stadium, on March 18, 1953 Lou Perini, then the owner of MLB's Boston Braves, decided to move his team to Milwaukee.[14] This move marked the first time since the signing of Baseball's Major League Agreement in 1903 that a MLB team switched host cities.[15]

As it turned out, the Braves' move to Milwaukee greatly improved Perini's bottom line.[16] In addition to a new stadium, Perini inherited a larger fan base that purchased 1.8 million tickets in 1953—more than six times as many tickets as Braves fans bought during the team's final season in Boston.[17]

Over the next two years, two other MLB teams, the St. Louis Browns and Philadelphia Athletics, decided to similarly leave shared markets and private stadiums in favor of solo markets and public stadiums.[18] The Browns left St. Louis, a market they shared with the Cardinals, in favor of Baltimore's Memorial Stadium, where they became known as the Baltimore Orioles.[19] Meanwhile, the Athletics, a team which shared the Philadelphia market, moved to Kansas City to play in Municipal Stadium.[20]

In 1958, Brooklyn Dodgers owner Walter O'Malley continued this trend—moving his beloved Dodgers out of Brooklyn and to Los Angeles, another city that had been long trying to land a MLB franchise.[21] Unlike the earlier teams that had moved—the Braves, Athletics, and Browns—the Dodgers had regularly drawn large crowds and maintained a loyal fan base while playing in Brooklyn.[22] However, by moving the Dodgers to Los Angeles, O'Malley became the beneficiary of a prime chunk of real estate.[23]

B. The 1960s: A Rollercoaster Ride for Stadium Subsidies

Once O'Malley moved the Dodgers to Los Angeles, MLB owners became cognizant of a basic tenet in economics: the law of supply and demand.[24] As long as there were more cities that wanted to capture the essence of professional sports than there were MLB teams available, existing team owners could levy heavy stadium demands on cities, which would often pay the price.[25] By keeping a limited supply of professional baseball teams, the public share of new stadium financing by the end of the 1950s reached close to 100%.[26]

Shortly thereafter, MLB club owners learned the flip side of this rule, when, in November 1958, New York lawyer William Shea and former Dodgers general manager Branch Rickey announced plans to launch a rival professional baseball league, the Continental League.[27] In fear that the planned rival league would begin to gain a presence for itself in untapped MLB markets, MLB owners quickly announced that they would expand into most of the territories that the Continental League sought to enter.[28] From 1962 through 1969, MLB expanded from sixteen to twenty-four teams, temporarily returning the supply of baseball teams back into equilibrium with demand.[29] As a result, the rate of stadium subsidies fell during the early part of the 1960s from nearly 100% to just above 60%.[30]

This counterbalance, however, was short-lived. On August 2, 1960, the Continental League ceased its plans to launch a rival league, and thereafter no other investor group seriously proposed doing the same.[31] As a result, once the next wave of communities interested in investing in professional sports emerged, MLB clubs again had an opportunity to increase their subsidy demands.[32]

C. Stadium Subsidies Today

Since the 1970s, most local communities have paid between seventy percent and eighty percent of new stadium building costs.[33] Today, these subsidies are paid to MLB teams, as well as to teams in the National Football League ("NFL"), National Basketball Association ("NBA") and National Hockey League ("NHL").[34] Although the modern subsidy rate remains below that of the late 1950s, most teams exert more power over local communities today than ever before.[35] This is seen in three ways.

First, local communities today are paying more than ever before to build sports facilities.[36] For instance, the Astrodome, which was the most expensive sports facility built or refurbished prior to 1968, cost $35 million.[37] By contrast, the Skydome, which opened in Toronto, Ontario in 1989, cost $532 million.[38] In addition, the new publicly funded baseball stadium in Washington, D.C., which opened in April 2008, cost $611 million,[39] and Indianapolis's new football and NCAA basketball stadium, which opened in August 2008, cost $720 million.[40] . . . .

In addition, the number of new facilities that sports teams are demanding is also rising.[42] From 1950 to 1959, sports teams moved into only seven new sports facilities, as compared to twenty-one from 1960 to 1969, twenty-five from 1970 to 1979, fourteen from 1980 to 1989, thirty-two from 1990 to 1998, and already more than forty since 1999.[43] A significant percentage of the increase in new stadiums built over the past decade is attributable to baseball and football teams, which once shared community stadiums, beginning to demand their own separate facilities.[44] Another component of the increase is based on teams with greater frequency declaring their facilities obsolete.[45] For example, in 2002, owners of the Spurs basketball team demanded that the city of San Antonio build them a new public arena, even though their current arena was just ten years old.[46]

Finally, in recent years, teams have even begun to negotiate the right to keep sports facilities' non-sports related revenues.[47] For instance, when the State of Maryland in 1998 built its new state-of-the art football stadium for the Baltimore Ravens, Maryland agreed to provide the Ravens' ownership with rights to all of the stadium's revenues, including those derived from rock concerts held during the NFL off-season.[48] Similarly, in Miami-Dade County's recent stadium agreement with Marlins ownership, the county agreed to provide the Marlins owners with 100% of all non-baseball related revenues, including revenues from rock concerts, other sporting events, and even the sale of the stadium's naming rights.[49]

In sum, these three trends have created "such a confusion of interests [that] ordinary tax payers are now expected to subsidize the already immense wealth of . . . an indescribably small number of owners."[50] In other words, subsidized sports stadiums have gone from being an exception in the world of professional sports to something far closer to the rule.[51]

D. Today's Sports Teams Do Not Need Subsidies to Turn a Profit

Despite the trend toward subsidizing professional sports stadiums, most professional team owners do not need government aid to profit.[52] This is because, in addition to earning a high rate of return on the team's resale,[53] most team owners have recently learned to capitalize on two important stadium-related revenue streams: stadium naming rights and personal seat licenses.[54]

Stadium naming rights are the rights of corporations to place their name on major sports stadiums.[55] Although the first reputed naming-rights agreement goes back to 1971, when Schaefer Brewing Company paid $150,000 to name the Patriots' stadium Schaefer Field, sports teams did not begin to recognize the full power of selling naming rights until recently.[56] In recent years, teams in large markets such as the New York Mets have sold stadium naming rights for as much as $400 million (20 year rights at $20 million per year).[57] Meanwhile, teams that play in less traditional sports markets such as the Houston Texans have sold their stadium naming rights for as much as $300 million (30 year rights at $10 million per year).[58] Although many teams that have obtained lucrative naming rights agreements have chosen to build expensive sports facilities, these kind of naming rights agreements could conceivably cover the entire cost of building a more affordable stadium or arena.[59]

Personal seat licenses ("PSLs"), meanwhile, are advance payments to purchase the right to secure a particular seat in a given venue.[60] Although the Dallas Cowboys football team sold a limited number of "seat options" back in 1968,[61] the NFL's Carolina Panthers in 1993 became the first team to extensively use the concept of PSLs when they privately financed their new facility, Bank of America Stadium (formerly known as Ericsson Stadium).[62] By selling PSLs before beginning stadium construction, Carolina Panthers ownership raised $180 million in upfront capital.[63] Since then, several other sports teams including the Baltimore Ravens, St. Louis Rams, and Chicago Bears have copied this strategy, similarly raising substantial amounts of money.[64]

II. WHY AMERICAN COMMUNITIES SUBSIDIZE PROFESSIONAL SPORTS

Although professional sports teams rarely need subsidies to profit, most American communities continue to subsidize their professional sports teams because they fear their teams would otherwise move to other communities.[65] As explained by sports economist Rodney Fort, "[l]eaving some viable locations without teams enhances the bargaining power of existing owners with their current host cities."[66] Some examples of viable locations without teams in each of the four premier sports leagues include: Los Angeles (no NFL team), Houston (no NHL team), Seattle (no NBA or NHL team), Cleveland (no NHL team), San Diego (no NBA or NHL team), St. Louis (no NBA team), Pittsburgh (no NBA team) and Baltimore (no NBA or NHL team).[67]

In a perfectly competitive market, new premier leagues such as Shea and Rickey's Continental League would periodically emerge to meet communities' demand for sports teams, and existing leagues would in turn have an incentive to expand into on-hold cities.[68] However, in practice, the four premier sports leagues rarely face competition from any new league because sports markets have high barriers to entry.[69] Indeed, competitor leagues are rarely able to compete against MLB or the NBA, NFL and NHL because these leagues enjoy an almost insurmountable lead in building

a fan base, signing superstar players, acquiring television broadcast contracts,[70] and obtaining playing facilities.[71] For this reason, some liken a sports league's tight control on its number of franchises to a form of blackmail or extortion.[72]

According to former Washington, D.C. mayor Sharon Pratt Kelly, the limited number of franchises in professional sports forces American communities to deal with "a prisoner's dilemma of sorts."[73] The dilemma is that "if no mayor succumbs to the demands of a franchise shopping for a new home, then the team will stay where they are."[74] However, this outcome is unlikely because "if Mayor A is not willing to pay the price, Mayor B may think it is advantageous to open up the city's wallet. Then to protect his or her interest, Mayor A often ends up paying the demanded price."[75]

[*Ed. Note: The author's discussion on the propriety of subsidies and specific business and legal cases is omitted. Marc Edelman's biography can be found on page 122.*]

Notes

. . . .

10. *See* Edelman, *Bargaining Power, supra* note 8, at 284 (describing the "glory era" of professional sports).

11. *See id.* at 284 (citing Lee Geige, *Cheering for the Home Team: An Analysis of Public Funding of Professional Sports Stadia in Cincinnati, Ohio,* 30 U. TOL. L. REV. 459, 461 (1999)); FORT, SPORTS ECONOMICS, *supra* note 7, at 338. Indeed, until 1950, there were just three publicly funded stadiums used by professional sports teams: the Los Angeles Coliseum (built in 1923), Chicago's Soldier Field (built in 1929) and Cleveland's Municipal Stadium (built in 1931). Edelman, *Bargaining Power, supra* note 8, at 285; *see also* John Siegfried & Andrew Zimbalist, *The Economics of Sports Facilities and Their Communities,* 14 J. ECON. PERSP. 95, 95–96 (2000).

12. *See* Edelman, *Bargaining Power, supra* note 8, at 285 ("With new metropolitan markets in the western United States opened by jet travel, the growth of in-home television, and the baby boomers coming of age, professional sports leagues for the first time encountered significant growth opportunities. Major League Baseball ('MLB'), however, chose not to expand to meet these opportunities.").

13. *See* Siegfried & Zimbalist, *supra* note 11, at 96; JAMES QUIRK & RODNEY FORT, HARD BALL: THE ABUSE OF POWER IN PRO TEAM SPORTS 15 (1999) [hereinafter QUIRK & FORT, HARD BALL].

14. *See* Siegfried & Zimbalist, *supra* note 11, at 96; QUIRK & FORT, HARD BALL, *supra* note 13, at 15; A Fan Site Dedicated to Preserving The Memory of Wisconsin's Lost Treasure, http://www.milwaukeebraves.info (last visited Nov.12, 2008).

15. *See* JAMES EDWARD MILLER, THE BASEBALL BUSINESS: PURSUING PENNANTS AND PROFITS IN BALTIMORE 31–32 (1990); JEROLD J. DUQUETTE, REGULATING THE NATIONAL PASTIME: BASEBALL AND ANTITRUST 5, 8 (1999); *see generally* Marc Edelman, *Can Antitrust Law Save the Minnesota Twins? Why Commissioner Selig's Contraction Plan was Never a Sure Deal,* 10 SPORTS L.J. 45, 47 (2003) (discussing the merger of the National and American leagues under the Major League Agreement).

16. *See* MILLER, *supra* note 15, at 31; JAMES QUIRK & RODNEY D. FORT, PAY DIRT: THE BUSINESS OF PROFESSIONAL TEAM

SPORTS 480 (1992) [hereinafter QUIRK & FORT: PAY DIRT] (Table: Attendance Records: Baseball, National League).

17. *See* MILLER, *supra* note 15, at 31; QUIRK & FORT, PAY DIRT, *supra* note 16, at 480 (compiling attendance records for Major League Baseball's National League).

18. *See* MILLER, *supra* note 15, at 79 and accompanying text; QUIRK & FORT, HARD BALL, *supra* note 13, at 15.

19. *See* MILLER, *supra* note 15, at 79; QUIRK & FORT, HARD BALL, *supra* note 13, at 15.

20. *Id.*

21. *See* JOANNA CAGAN & NEIL DEMAUSE, FIELD OF SCHEMES: HOW THE GREAT STADIUM SWINDLE TURNS PUBLIC MONEY INTO PRIVATE PROFIT 186 (1998); QUIRK & FORT, HARD BALL, *supra* note 13, at 16.

22. *Hearings*, *supra* note 9, at 55 (testimony of Sen. Charles E. Schumer of New York) ("I am one who believes in what Pete Hamill has written[,] that the three most evil men of the 20th century were Hitler, Stalin and Walter O'Malley, Sr.").

23. *See* CAGAN & DEMAUSE, *supra* note 21, at 186; QUIRK & FORT, HARD BALL, *supra* note 13, at 16. Shortly after O'Malley moved the Dodgers to Los Angeles, New York Giants owner Horace Stoneham followed by moving his Giants from Manhattan to San Francisco. The Giants' move, however, was different from the one made by the Dodgers in that the Giants were struggling with attendance before heading to California. *See* MILLER, *supra* note 15, at 79–80; QUIRK & FORT, PAY DIRT, *supra* note 16, at 480.

24. *See* E. THOMAS SULLIVAN & JEFFREY L. HARRISON, UNDERSTANDING ANTITRUST AND ITS ECONOMIC IMPLICATIONS 112–22 (3d ed. 1998) (discussing the law of supply and demand).

25. *See* FORT, SPORTS ECONOMICS, *supra* note 7, at 140. At the same time, the law of supply and demand has allowed existing team owners to charge huge entry fees to prospective new entrants. *See* Fort, *Direct Democracy*, *supra* note 7, at 7 tbl.1.3 (showing rapidly increasing expansion franchise rights fees).

26. *See* Siegfried & Zimbalist, *supra* note 11, at 96; QUIRK & FORT, HARD BALL, *supra* note 13, at 19–20.

27. DUQUETTE, *supra* note 15, at 52–53; *see also* FORT, SPORTS ECONOMICS, *supra* note 7, at 134.

28. *See* DUQUETTE, *supra* note 15, at 53–54; QUIRK & FORT, PAY DIRT, *supra* note 16, at 479–87 (Major League Baseball added eight new teams in the years from 1962–69, with new teams beginning play in New York City, Houston, San Diego, Montreal, Los Angeles, Washington, Seattle and Kansas City); FORT, SPORTS ECONOMICS, *supra* note 7, at 134, 141 ("[E]xpansion and relocation also protect existing owners from outside competition."); *id.* at 148 (discussing how leaving viable locations without teams increases the risk of new leagues forming).

29. *See generally* DUQUETTE, *supra* note 15.

30. Siegfried & Zimbalist, *supra* note 11, at 96.

31. *See* FORT, SPORTS ECONOMICS, *supra* note 7, at 134; *see also* Wikipedia, Continental League, http://en.wikipedia.org/wiki/Continental_League (last visited Nov. 12, 2008).

32. *See generally* CAGAN & DEMAUSE, *supra* note 21, at 28–29 ("North America is in the midst of a remarkable stadium and sports arena building boom unlike any other in its history . . . . Between 1980 and 1990, U.S. cities spent some $750 million on building or renovating sports arenas and stadiums. The bill for the '90s is expected to total anywhere between $8 billion and $11 billion, the bulk of it paid by taxpayers—and hidden subsidies could amount to billions more.").

33. *See, e.g.*, Michael Cunningham, *Stadium Deal Just Doesn't Make Sense: Money Could Be Used on Much More Important Priorities*, SOUTH FLA. SUN SENTINEL, Feb. 22, 2008, at 1C (evaluating stadium subsidy percentages since 1992). Cunningham notes that: There are 20 baseball parks built or that are currently under construction since 1992, when Baltimore's Oriole Park at Camden Yards sparked a building boom. The median public contribution for those parks was 73 percent of costs, according to information compiled by the National Sports Law Institute of Marquette University Law School. *Id.*; *see also* Siegfried & Zimbalist, *supra* note 11, at 96 tbl.1 (detailing Expenditures on New Sports Facilities for Professional Teams by Decade); FORT, SPORTS ECONOMICS, *supra* note 7, at 338 (finding, from the period of 2000–06, the median public contribution was just sixty-three percent. Yet, this figure is skewed downward because it includes the San Francisco Giants' entirely privately financed stadium, built in the year 2000).

34. See Edelman, *Bargaining Power*, *supra* note 8, at 288.

35. *See infra* notes 36–49 and accompanying text.

36. *See infra* notes 37–41 and accompanying text.

37. *See* QUIRK & FORT, PAY DIRT, *supra* note 16, at 161–63.

38. *See* QUIRK & FORT, PAY DIRT, *supra* note 16, at 161–63.

39. *See* Eric Fisher, *In D.C., Baseball Hits a Crossroads at New Park*, STREET & SMITH'S SPORTS BUS. J., Mar. 10, 2008, at 18.

40. *See* Don Muret, *Opening in 2008*, STREET AND SMITH'S SPORTS BUS. J. (Jan. 21, 2008), at 15; Don Muret, *Indy's Showplace is also a Showroom*, STREET AND SMITH'S SPORTS BUS. J. (Sept. 15, 2008), at 1 [hereinafter Muret, *Indy's Showplace*].

. . . .

42. *See infra* note 43 and accompanying text.

43. *See* Siegfried & Zimbalist, *supra* note 11, at 96; *see also* FORT, SPORTS ECONOMICS, *supra* note 7, at 340 tbl.10.1 (describing Recent and Upcoming Stadium and Arena Openings as of 2004). 44 *See* Editorial, *Take Us Out*, RICHMOND TIMES DISPATCH, Apr. 29, 2008, at A10 ("Orioles Park at Camden Yards started the trend away from multipurpose stadiums shaped like doughnuts and toward baseball-only stadiums with so-called throwback designs."); *see also* David Armstrong, *49ers on the Move? Economics, Football-Only Stadiums Rarely Pay Off for Cities, Experts Say*, SAN FRANCISCO CHRONICLE, Nov. 10, 2006, at B4; *Bengals have Sold 20 Percent of Seat Licenses in Three Weeks*, COLUMBUS DISPATCH (Ohio), Jan. 9, 1997, at 4D (discussing the city of Cincinnati's building of separate ballparks for the Reds and Bengals); *Hearings*, *supra* note 9, at 14 (testimony of Sen. Arlen Specter of Pennsylvania) ("[Pennsylvania is] looking at four new [publicly funded] stadiums. Two are under construction now in western Pennsylvania for the Steelers and the Pirates, and two are in the immediate offering for the Phillies and the Eagles.").

44. *See* Editorial, *Take Us Out*, RICHMOND TIMES DISPATCH, Apr. 29, 2008, at A10 ("Orioles Park at Camden Yards started the trend away from multipurpose stadiums shaped like doughnuts and toward baseball-only stadiums with so-called throwback designs."); *see also* David Armstrong, *49ers on the Move? Economics, Football-Only Stadiums Rarely Pay Off for Cities, Experts Say*, SAN FRANCISCO CHRONICLE, Nov. 10, 2006, at B4; *Bengals Have Sold 20 Percent of Seat Licenses in Three Weeks*, COLUMBUS DISPATCH (Ohio), Jan. 9, 1997, at 4D (discussing the city of Cincinnati's building of separate ballparks for the Reds and Bengals); *Hearings*, *supra* note

9, at 14 (testimony of Sen. Arlen Specter of Pennsylvania) ("[Pennsylvania is] looking at four new [publicly funded] stadiums. Two are under construction now in western Pennsylvania for the Steelers and the Pirates, and two are in the immediate offering for the Phillies and the Eagles.").

45. *See, e.g.*, Siegfried & Zimbalist, *supra* note 11, at 96; David McLemore, *Functioning in a New Arena; San Antonio's Alamodome Alive despite SBC Center*, DALLAS MORNING NEWS, Dec. 1, 2002, at 43A.

46. *See* McLemore, *supra* note 45.

47. *See infra* notes 48–49 and accompanying text.

48. *Hearings*, *supra* note 9, at 31 (testimony of Jean B. Cryor, former Member, Maryland House of Delegates).

49. *See* Benn, Rabin & Vasquez, *supra* note 5.

50. *Hearings*, *supra* note 9, at 13 (testimony of Thomas Finneran, former Speaker of the Massachusetts House of Representatives).

51. *See supra* notes 11–34 and accompanying text.

52. This argument is supported by building a mathematical model for sports team profitability, which estimates net operating income and annual expected return on investment by team. *See generally* QUIRK & FORT, HARD BALL, *supra* note 13, at 206, 212. The model considers the additional costs of constructing a new stadium and factors in revenue streams that are created by building a new stadium. *See generally id.*

53. *See, e.g.*, FORT, SPORTS ECONOMICS, *supra* note 7, at 1–2 (showing that, since 1915, ownership of a sports team such as the New York Yankees has provided twice as large a rate of return as owning a diversified investment portfolio); *id.* at 9 ("Professional team sports generated revenues of about $13.9 billion in 2002–03.").

54. *See* Zimmerman, *infra* note 79, and accompanying text.

55. *See* HOWARD & CROMPTON, *supra* note 3, at 272.

56. *See id.*

57. *See* Edelman, *"Single Entity" Defense*, *supra* note 3, at 914; *see also* Terry Lefton, *CAA Hired to Land Sponsors for the Yankees*, STREET & SMITH'S SPORTS BUS. J., Oct. 1, 2007, at 1; John Lombardo, *Barclays-Nets: A Brand Grows in Brooklyn*, STREET & SMITH'S SPORTS BUS. J., Jan. 22, 2007, at 1.

58. *See* HOWARD & CROMPTON, *supra* note 3, at 275 tbl.7–5 (compiling the largest sports venue naming rights agreements); *see also* FORT, SPORTS ECONOMICS, *supra* note 7, at 79 tbl. 3.8 (noting recent naming rights agreements). Among the newest stadium naming rights agreements, the Indiana Stadium and Convention Building Authority recently sold naming rights to their luxurious, new $720 million facility to Lucas Oil for $120 million over a 22 year period. *See* Muret, *Indy's Showplace*, *supra* note 40, at 1. The Dallas Mavericks sold their naming rights for $195 million (30 years at $6.5 million per year), and the Atlanta Hawks and Thrashers sold naming rights for a combined $185 million (20 years at $9.3 million per year). *See* HOWARD & CROMPTON, *supra* note 3, at 275 tbl.7–5.

59. For one example of a more affordably built professional sports stadium, Miller Field in Milwaukee, Wisconsin was constructed in time for opening day of the 2001 season at a cost of just $313 million. *See* Edelman, *Bargaining Power*, *supra* note 8, at 288 (citing Don Walker, *Auditors Blame 'Enron-Style Accounting' for Ballpark Cost Dispute; Stadium District Relied on Future Revenue, Memo Says*, MILWAUKEE J. SENTINEL, May 22, 2002, at 1A). As another example, the San Francisco Giants privately financed their ballpark, which opened in 2000, for the total cost of $319 million. *Id.* at 289 (citing Richard Alm, *Nosebleed Prices: Cost of a Day of Baseball Has Soared at New Arenas*, DALLAS MORNING NEWS, Jul. 11,

2000, at 1D). Meanwhile, the Cincinnati Reds new ballpark, which opened in 2003, cost just $288 million to build. FORT, SPORTS ECONOMICS, *supra* note 7, at 340.

60. *See Hearings*, *supra* note 9, at 63 (statement of Jerry Richardson, Owner and Founder, Carolina Panthers); *see also Hearings*, *supra* note 9, at 104 (testimony of Paul Tagliabue, former Commissioner, National Football League); FORT, SPORTS ECONOMICS, *supra* note 7, at 42 (discussing the economics behind PSLs).

61. *See* HOWARD & CROMPTON, *supra* note 3, at 288.

62. *Hearings*, *supra* note 9, at 63 (statement of Jerry Richardson, Owner and Founder, Carolina Panthers); *see also* HOWARD & CROMPTON, *supra* note 3, at 288.

63. *See Hearings*, *supra* note 9, at 63 (statement of Jerry Richardson, Owner and Founder, Carolina Panthers).

64. *See* HOWARD & CROMPTON, *supra* note 3, at 288 tbl. 7–7 (compiling statistics on the size, price, and economic magnitude of current PSL programs).

65. *See* Fort, *Direct Democracy*, *supra* note 7, at 149–50; FORT, SPORTS ECONOMICS, *supra* note 7, at 140 ("Owners acting through their leagues limit the number of teams in their league by choice rather than through the forces of competition. There are two important indicators that the number of teams is smaller than a more economically competitive sports world would give to fans. First, rival leagues do form occasionally . . . . Second, every time a league announces that it plans to expand, a long line of candidate-owners forms in hope of becoming the newest addition to the league.").

66. FORT, SPORTS ECONOMICS, *supra* note 7, at 141.

67. *See* LEEDS & VON ALLMEN, *supra* note 7, at 100 tbl.3.7 (listing the fifteen most populous metropolitan areas and their respective sports teams).

68. *See generally* DUQUETTE, *supra* note 15, at 52–53; FORT, SPORTS ECONOMICS, *supra* note 7, at 140.

69. See Edelman, *Bargaining Power*, *supra* note 8, at 291. Almost all attempts to form rival, premier professional sports leagues in the four major sports over the past forty years have failed. For example, in football, the World Football League emerged in the 1960s and almost from its first games exhibited dire financial trouble; missed payrolls were common and the league folded during its second season. *See* ROBERT BERRY ET AL., LABOR RELATIONS IN PROFESSIONAL SPORTS 93 (1986). The United States Football League then emerged in 1983 with a differentiated strategy of playing football during the spring; the USFL quickly found itself in a bidding war for players with the NFL, and in November of 1986, it too filed for bankruptcy. *See id.* at 95–96. In basketball, Harlem Globetrotters owner Abe Saperstein launched the American Basketball League in 1961, but the league folded in its second season. *See id.* at 155. Its successor, the American Basketball Association, which started in 1967–68, performed slightly better; however, it too was heading toward bankruptcy in 1976 when the league disbanded and four existing teams joined the NBA. *Id.* at 156–57. In hockey, the World Hockey Association was founded by entrepreneurs Gary Davidson and Dennis Murphy in 1972, but by 1979, most of its teams were bankrupt; the four remaining franchises were acquired by the NHL. *Id.* at 213–14.

70. *See* LEEDS & VON ALLMEN, *supra* note 7, at 124–25.

71. *See* QUIRK & FORT, HARD BALL, *supra* note 13, at 135.

72. *See, e.g., id.* at 6; *Hearings*, *supra* note 9, at 11 (testimony of Sen. Arlen Specter of Pennsylvania).

73. Fort, *Direct Democracy*, *supra* note 7, at 150.

74. *Id.*

75. *Id.*

THE NAME IS THE GAME IN FACILITY NAMING RIGHTS

Martin J. Greenberg and April R. Anderson

WHY THE BOOM?

The growth of naming rights deals did not occur in a vacuum; rather, they increased in tandem with the recent boom of new sports venues. The bottom line, of course, has been money. Corporate naming of stadia and arenas provides significant revenue for sports facilities and a positive attempt to defray public sector building costs.

It has really only been in the last decade when the use of corporate names for sports venues has gained widespread acceptance. The first corporate naming rights agreement was negotiated in 1973 between Rich Products Corporation and the County of Erie, New York, under which the new stadium for the NFL's Buffalo Bills would be called Rich Stadium at a cost of $1.5 million over 25 years. Fourteen years later, in 1987, the contemporary use of corporate naming rights began in earnest when the naming rights to the Los Angeles Forum were purchased by Great Western Bank. Prior to 1990, only two of the NBA's twenty-seven teams (7.4%) had sold naming rights. . . . [*Ed. Note: As of June 2010, 25 of 30 NBA teams had sold naming rights to their playing facilities. Overall, 91 of 122 teams in the NBA, NFL, NHL, and MLB have sold naming rights to their facilities.*]

Since that time, corporate naming rights for stadia and arenas have become the norm. This has occurred for two reasons. First, as more facilities take on corporate names, the public acceptance for such a practice has grown. Whatever initial reluctance there may have been toward what some experts have called the "corporatization" of stadia and arenas has largely dissipated to the point where naming rights deals are now status quo; an expectation that comes with obtaining a new facility.

Second, the increasing costs of building these facilities and the reluctance of public officials to raise taxes in order to fund them, make it necessary to maximize facility revenues. Thus, the selling of corporate naming rights creates an additional funding vehicle to recover, or reduce, initial sports facility costs and debt payments, which would otherwise be subsidized by taxpayers. As the trend toward building new facilities continues, so too will the use of naming rights, especially in light of the fact that if a new facility is to be built, it must carry with it some opportunity to pay for itself.

WHY CORPORATE AMERICA BUYS NAMING RIGHTS

A variety of corporations, representing a myriad of industries, purchase stadium naming rights. Airlines, automobile manufacturers, beverage producers, telecommunication companies, financial services, computer manufacturers, and consumer product producers all are currently represented by facilities bearing their names.

Corporate entities generally purchase the naming rights of sports facilities for seven reasons.

First, buying an arena's naming rights is a highly cost effective way for companies to advertise. Television, radio, and the media all use the company name when reporting on events held at the facility, while visibility is also attained by the signage on the facility itself. Consider the following examples: In 1991, America West Airlines purchased the naming rights for the new arena being built for the Phoenix Suns at a cost of $550,000 for the first year with a three percent annual increase to this initial fee. During the 1993 NBA Finals, when the Suns hosted the Chicago Bulls, one thirty-second television commercial spot on NBC cost $300,000. Because the company purchased the naming rights to the facility, America West's name and logo were seen countless times throughout the series at a mere cost of $583,495—less than a single one-minute television commercial.

Meanwhile, 3Com, a computer company in Santa Clara, California, paid $500,000 for the naming rights to San Francisco's Candlestick Park for a six month period. Company spokesmen have publicly stated that 3Com has been featured in at least 180 articles, that the company has received forty percent more resumes since the naming, and that the volume of trading on the company's stock has increased dramatically in that time.

This cost-effectiveness theory was recently buttressed by a study conducted by Joyce Julius and Associates of Ann Arbor, Michigan, which determined the gross value of "impressions" generated by naming rights deals. By studying twelve sports venues (in markets averaging 2.16 million television households), and counting the number of impressions made on the site itself, print media, and national, regional, and local television and radio, analysts were able to calculate the financial impact of the impressions and the amount that it would have cost the companies to generate the same degree of impressions through traditional national and local television advertising. The results were quite impressive. Stadium naming right packages generated an average of $31.7 million worth of "impressions" in 1997, and arena naming rights packages generated an average of $69.9 million of "impressions." Had the sponsors of those sports facilities purchased the same degree of traditional media advertising, the costs would have been ten times those amounts.

Second, the purchase of corporate naming rights represents a unique opportunity for corporate entities. Sports facilities are relatively few in number, making imitation or duplication by competitors nearly impossible. The exclusivity in purchasing external signage that cannot be used by anyone else is extraordinarily valuable.

Third, the purchase of naming rights allows a company to project a positive image and create goodwill into the community in which the facility is located. For example, General

Motors of Canada and Fleet Financial Group, purchasers of naming rights to sports facilities in Vancouver and Boston, respectively, have announced new community service programs coinciding with the purchase of those arena naming rights.

Fourth, companies may use naming rights to establish a presence in regions where they may not have previously conducted business, or in areas where they are seeking to expand operations. Key Bank adopted this approach when it purchased the naming rights to the newly refurbished Seattle Coliseum. The bank had recently purchased new branches in Washington and wanted to expand its name recognition throughout the state.

Fifth, naming rights agreements usually allow for cross-promotion through on-site product tie-ins. For instance, sports facilities in Boston, Seattle, and Grand Rapids, Michigan have automated teller machines placed by the banks which have purchased the naming rights to those buildings. Arenas in Chicago and Phoenix have ticket booths for their airline namesakes. General Motors plans on capitalizing on its purchase of naming rights to the . . . home of the Canucks . . . in Vancouver by tying in vehicle promotions with events at the stadium. Finally, Anaheim Arena suites and concession stands offer bottled water from Arrowhead Water Company, the corporation which purchased the naming rights to the home of the Anaheim Ducks.

Sixth, corporate entities usually receive, or purchase, a skybox or suite at the facility as a part of the naming rights contract. Bringing prospective clients or sought-after prospective employees to a sports facility with the company name on the building offers considerable corporate prestige.

Finally, there may be tax advantages associated with purchasing naming rights to a sports facility, in that such expenditures may be taken as a business expense deduction pursuant to the Internal Revenue Code. . . .

ANATOMY OF THE DEAL

Any naming rights agreement is comprised of important contractual provisions, such as ownership rights, cost, time payments and escalators, term and renewal options, exclusive rights and non-compete covenants, first options and rights of first refusal, and intellectual property related clauses. All of these issues may become a part of the contract and may ultimately impact the value of the deal to the corporate sponsor.

Generally, naming rights are achieved by making an initial, up-front payment, followed by annual payments for a specified term, typically 15 to 30 years. Additionally, the corporate sponsor may be permitted to extend the term of the agreement by holding an option to renew, a right of first option to negotiate, or a right of first refusal. . . .

Naming rights agreements, like other contracts, also include other contractual concerns such as trademark ownership rights and termination, indemnification, default, and force majeure clauses.

While the phrase "naming rights deal" often connotes merely signage, the total deal package actually is often much more extensive. Understanding the extent of amenities to be included in the package is a significant consideration in the economic valuation of the deal. In addition to the corporate signage associated with the facility, purchasers of naming rights also tend to negotiate deals related to luxury box suites, television and radio advertising, uniforms for facility personnel, use of the facility, and the incorporation of the sponsor's product as a part of the total package.

[*Ed. Note: The authors' discussion of the Indianapolis Colts deal with RCA and Thomson Consumer Electronics is omitted.*]

. . . .

VIABILITY AND PRICING

The viability and pricing of sports facility naming rights agreements are determined by four factors. The first factor is the number of events to be held at the facility. The presence of a professional or collegiate team playing its home games at the facility is a basic requirement for a naming rights agreement because it guarantees a minimum number of dates that a particular facility will be in operation.

The presence of an anchor tenant team also can lead to a facility's hosting of other sports related events, such as All-Star and championship games, bowl games, league meetings, and camps. Camps can range from the RCA Dome's hosting of the NFL's annual February prospect combine to fantasy camps allowing fans to compete with their childhood heroes. Concerts, conventions, conferences, or other community events also can generate considerable exposure. For instance, Chicago's United Center hosted the Democratic National Convention in 1996. By combining sports and non-sports related events, a facility can generate the number of events necessary to make naming rights attractive to potential buyers.

The second factor is the type of events that take place at the facility. The presence of a professional or amateur team again is a basic requirement because teams usually generate the high-profile exposure events necessary to satisfy the needs of naming rights purchasers. The hosting of special events at the facility—such as the Super Bowl, the NCAA Final Four, college bowl games, All-Star games, or political conventions—also increases the facility's visibility, creating more demand for that arena's naming rights.

The third factor determining the viability and pricing of naming rights agreements is the presence of corporate entities in the city or region where the facility is located. Because companies usually are more willing to buy naming rights for facilities in their home cities or regions, stadia and arenas in cities or regions with a concentration of corporate entities are likely to have an easier time selling their rights.

Keep in mind that the final factor affecting viability and pricing of naming rights is the composition of the package purchased by the company from the facility. As indicated earlier, the trend in this area is towards the purchase of naming rights as part of a larger, more extensive package, which also may include items such as team sponsorship or media rights.

TRENDS FOR THE FUTURE

The one certainty in this area is that highly lucrative naming rights deals will continue to proliferate. . . .

First, the terms of the deals are becoming shorter in length. As previously noted, naming rights deals typically run for a term of 15 to 30 years. Recently, however, deals with terms of ten years or less are becoming popular. . . .

Second, smaller markets, which are typically home to minor league or collegiate teams, also are selling naming rights in order to reduce costs and increase revenues. For example, Knickerbocker Arena in Albany, New York, which is home to the American Hockey League's River Rats, the Arena Football League's Firebirds, and the Siena College men's basketball team, was renamed Pepsi Arena. Additionally, Oldsmobile Park in Lansing, Michigan is the new home for the Class A minor league baseball Lugnuts. What was once a phenomenon reserved for elite leagues in major cities has filtered down to lower tiers, allowing smaller markets to benefit.

Third, naming rights deals are emerging for nonsports related facilities such as convention centers and amphitheaters. In Milwaukee, Wisconsin, for example, Midwest Express Airlines entered into a 15-year, $9.25 million deal to purchase the naming rights to the city's downtown convention center. Other examples include the Nissan Pavilion in Stone Ridge, Virginia, and the PNC Arts Center in Holmdel, New Jersey.

Finally, consulting organizations are continually reassessing how naming rights deals can be better structured to effectively benefit both parties. Such analysis includes, for example, exploring the tax ramifications of such deals. As a result, some experts agree that it is likely that future deals may routinely involve loans or equity partnerships instead of standard annual payments, which may be taxable to the recipient as ordinary income.

The cost of sports venues continues to increase as demand for state-of-the-art sports and entertainment facilities proliferates. To help meet these construction needs in tenuous economic climates, corporate America has again demonstrated its ingenuity by providing relief to taxpayers and facility owners alike through the purchase of naming rights. And with deals such as Staples' $100 million Los Angeles arena naming rights agreement hovering over the industry, it appears certain that the days of naming a facility for an honored individual or government locality are long past. The name is the game, and it is one that only corporations can afford to play. [*Ed. Note: See* **Table 2** *for selected naming rights deals.*]

Table 2   Naming Rights Deals at Major League Facilities

Stadium Name	Sponsor	City	Average per Year	Expires
Air Canada Centre	ACE Aviation Holdings Inc.	Toronto	$1.52 million	2019
American Airlines Arena	AMR Corp. (American Airlines)	Miami	2.1 million	2019
American Airlines Center	AMR Corp. (American Airlines)	Dallas	6.5 million	2030
Amway Arena	Amway Corp.	Orlando	4.0 million	2020
Arco Arena	Atlantic Richfield Co.	Sacramento	750,000	N/A
AT&T Center	AT&T Inc.	San Antonio	2.05 million	2022
AT&T Park	AT&T Inc.	San Francisco	2.08 million	2024
Auto Club Speedway	Auto Club of Southern California	Fontana, CA	N/A	2017
Bank of America Stadium	Bank of America	Charlotte	7.0 million	2023
BankAtlantic Center	BankAtlantic Bancorp	Sunrise, FL	2.7 million	2015
Barclays Center (a)	Barclays PLC	Brooklyn, NY	20.0 million	2029
Bell Centre	BCE Inc.	Montreal	3.2 million	2023
BMO Field	Bank of Montreal	Toronto	2.28 million	2016
Busch Stadium	Anheuser-Busch Cos.	St. Louis	N/A	2025
Chase Field	JPMorgan Chase & Co.	Phoenix	2.21 million	2028
Cisco Field (a)	Cisco Systems Inc.	Fremont, CA	4.0 million	N/A
Citi Field	Citibank N.A.	Queens, NY	20.0 million	2028
Citizens Bank Park	Citizens Financial Services	Philadelphia	3.8 million	2029
Comerica Park	Comerica Bank	Detroit	2.2 million	2030
Conseco Fieldhouse	Conseco Inc.	Indianapolis	2.0 million	2019
Coors Field	Molson Coors Brewing Co.	Denver	(15 million overall)	Indefinite

(continued)

Table 2 *(Continued)*

Stadium Name	Sponsor	City	Average per Year	Expires
Dick's Sporting Goods Park	Dick's Sporting Goods	Commerce City, CO	$2.0 million	2021
Edward Jones Dome	The Jones Financial Cos.	St. Louis	2.65 million	2012
EnergySolutions Arena	EnergySolutions	Salt Lake City	N/A	2016
FedEx Field	FedEx Corp.	Landover, MD	7.59 million	2025
FedEx Forum	FedEx Corp.	Memphis	4.09 million	2024
Ford Field	Ford Motor Co.	Detroit	2.27 million	2026
General Motors Place	General Motors Corp.	Vancouver	844,366	2015
Gillette Stadium	Global Gillette	Foxboro, MA	8.0 million	2016
Great American Ball Park	Great American Insurance Co.	Cincinnati	2.5 million	2032
Heinz Field	H.J. Heinz Co.	Pittsburgh	2.85 million	2021
Home Depot Center	The Home Depot Inc.	Carson, CA	7.0 million	2013
Honda Center	American Honda Motor Co.	Anaheim	4.03 million	2020
HP Pavilion at San Jose	Hewlett-Packard Co.	San Jose	3.13 million	2016
HSBC Arena	HSBC USA Inc.	Buffalo	750,000	2026
Infineon Raceway	Infineon Technologies AG	Sonoma, CA	3.46 million	2011
Invesco Field at Mile High	Invesco Institutional NA	Denver	6.0 million	2021
Izod Center	Phillips-Van Heusen Corp.	East Rutherford, NJ	1.4 million	2012
Jobing.com Arena	Jobing.com	Glendale, AZ	3.0 million	2016
Key Arena	Key Corp.	Seattle	1.01 million	2010
Lincoln Financial Field	Lincoln National Corp.	Philadelphia	6.98 million	2022
Lowe's Motor Speedway	Lowe's Cos.	Concord, NC	3.5 million	2009
LP Field	Louisiana-Pacific Corp.	Nashville	3.0 million	2016
Lucas Oil Stadium	Lucas Oil Products	Indianapolis	6.07 million	2027
M&T Bank Field	M&T Bank Corp.	Baltimore	5.0 million	2017
Mellon Arena	Bank of New York Mellon Corp.	Pittsburgh	1.8 million	2009
Miller Park	Miller Brewing Co.	Milwaukee	2.06 million	2020
Minute Maid Park	The Coca-Cola Co.	Houston	6.36 million	2029
Nationwide Arena	Nationwide Financial Services	Columbus	N/A	Indefinite
Oracle Arena	Oracle Corp.	Oakland	3.0 million	2016
Pengrowth Saddledome	Pengrowth Management Ltd.	Calgary	1.0 million	2016
Pepsi Center	PepsiCo	Denver	3.4 million	2019
Petco Park	Petco Animal Supplies Inc.	San Diego	2.73 million	2025
Philips Arena	Royal Philips Electronics N.V.	Atlanta	9.25 million	2019
Pizza Hut Park	Pizza Hut Inc.	Frisco, TX	1.5 million	2025
PNC Park	PNC Financial Services Group Inc.	Pittsburgh	2.0 million	2021
Progressive Field	Progressive Corp.	Cleveland	3.6 million	2023
Prudential Center	Prudential Financial Inc.	Newark, NJ	5.26 million	2027
Qualcomm Stadium	Qualcomm Inc.	San Diego	900,000	2017
Quicken Loans Arena	Quicken Loans	Cleveland	N/A	N/A
Qwest Field	Qwest Communications Intl.	Seattle	4.0–5.0 million	2019–2024
Raymond James Stadium	Raymond James Financial Inc.	Tampa	2.53 million	2016
RBC Center	RBC Centura Banks Inc.	Raleigh	4.0 million	2022
Red Bull Arena	Red Bull GmbH	Harrison, NJ	(30 million overall)	NA
Reliant Stadium	Reliant Energy Inc.	Houston	10.0 million	2032
Rexall Place	Katz Group	Edmonton	N/A	2013
Rogers Centre	Rogers Communications	Toronto	1.77 million	2014
Safeco Field	Safeco Corp.	Seattle	2.0 million	2019
Scotiabank Place	Scotiabank	Kanata, Ontario	1.17 million	2016
Scottrade Center	Scottrade Inc.	St. Louis	2.0–3.0 million	NA
Sprint Center	Sprint Corp.	Kansas City	2.5 million	2031
St. Pete Times Forum	St. Petersburg Times	Tampa	2.5 million	2014
Staples Center	Staples Inc.	Los Angeles	5.8 million	2019
Target Center	Target Corp.	Minneapolis	1.25 million	2010
Target Field	Target Corp.	Minneapolis	N/A	2034
TD Banknorth Garden	TD Banknorth, Inc.	Boston	5.95 million	2025
Time Warner Cable Arena	Time Warner Cable	Charlotte	N/A	N/A
Toyota Center	Toyota Motor Sales USA Inc.	Houston	4.75 million	2023
Toyota Park	Toyota Motor Sales USA Inc.	Bridgeview, IL	750,000	2015
Tropicana Field	Tropicana Products Inc.	St. Petersburg, FL	1.53 million	2026

Stadium Name	Sponsor	City	Average per Year	Expires
U.S. Cellular Field	U.S. Cellular Corp.	Chicago	$2.96 million	2025
United Center	UAL Corp. (United Airlines)	Chicago	1.8 million	2014
University of Phoenix Stadium	Apollo Group Inc.	Glendale, AZ	7.72 million	2025
US Airways Center	US Airways	Phoenix	2.0 million	2015
Verizon Center	Verizon Communications, Inc.	Washington, D.C.	2.2 million	2017
Wachovia Center	Wachovia Corp.	Philadelphia	1.38 million	2023
Xcel Energy Center	Xcel Energy Inc.	St. Paul	3.0 million	2024

(a) Facility is under construction or in late stages of development.

Source: SportsBusiness Resource Guide and Fact Book 2009. Used with permission.

TESTIMONY OF BRAD R. HUMPHREYS, ASSOCIATE PROFESSOR, UNIVERSITY OF ILLINOIS AT URBANA-CHAMPAIGN, ON PUBLIC FINANCING FOR CONSTRUCTION AND OPERATION OF SPORTS STADIUMS AND ECONOMIC REVITALIZATION AND DEVELOPMENT IN URBAN AMERICA BEFORE THE ONE HUNDRED TENTH CONGRESS OF THE UNITED STATES HOUSE OF REPRESENTATIVES, COMMITTEE ON OVERSIGHT AND GOVERNMENT REFORM SUBCOMMITTEE ON DOMESTIC POLICY, THURSDAY, MARCH 29, 2007

Local, state, and federal government has historically provided large subsidies for the construction and operation of professional sports facilities in the United States. These subsidies take the form of direct monetary support for land acquisition and physical plant construction, direct monetary support for physical plant operation and maintenance, in-kind donations of land, construction of infrastructure like roads, sewerage, and public transportation facilities, indirect subsidies in the form of special tax treatment for property, operating income, special tax treatment for bonds used to finance facility construction and other subsidies. Since 1990, the total value of the subsidies for construction of sports facilities alone in the United States has been about fifteen billion dollars in inflation adjusted terms. There are currently a large number of proposed new sports facilities in the planning phase around the country. The most common justification for these subsidies is that professional sports facilities and franchises generate significant, tangible economic benefits in the form of higher income, earnings, employment and tax revenues, for the local economy thus contributing to the revitalization of American cities.

DO PROFESSIONAL SPORTS GENERATE TANGIBLE ECONOMIC BENEFITS IN AMERICAN CITIES?

It is often said that economists cannot reach a consensus on matters of economic policy. While this might be accurate in areas like tax policy or international trade policy, it is clearly not the case when assessing the economic impact of professional sports facilities. There currently exists a large body of evidence published in peer-reviewed academic journals concluding that professional sports facilities and franchises have no positive tangible economic impact on income, earnings, employment, and tax revenues in American cities. This literature has examined regular season and postseason sporting events in all of the major North American professional sports leagues, as well as special events like All-star games and the Super Bowl.

The research supporting this consensus examined economic performance in every U.S. city that hosted a professional sports team over the past thirty years. This research uses economic and statistical modeling to explain the overall performance of local economies, in terms of income, employment, and other economic indicators in metropolitan areas. The basic approach assesses how much of the variation in local income and employment, as well as earnings and employment in specific sectors of the local economy like hotels, restaurants and bars, can be explained by variation in sports-related variables as well as by variation in other factors that economic theory predicts help determine the state of the local economy.

Again, the consensus from this substantial, carefully conducted, peer-reviewed body of academic research strongly supports the conclusion that professional sports facilities and franchises do not produce tangible economic benefits in the surrounding local economy. Based on the economic performance in every U.S. city with a professional sports team over the past thirty years, professional sports facilities and franchises were not associated with higher levels of local income; they were not associated with greater employment in any sector of the local economy except the small sector containing sports enterprises; they were not associated with higher tax revenues; they were not associated with faster growth rates of local income or employment. Professional sports facilities and franchises cannot be used to revitalize the economy in American cities. Subsidies for the construction and operation of professional sports facilities cannot be viewed as a viable economic revitalization strategy for our cities. Dozens of papers published in peer-reviewed academic journals support this consensus conclusion.

Some astute observers might question this conclusion. After all, millions of Americans attend professional sporting events each year, and there is clearly a great deal of economic activity going on in and around sports facilities. Bars and restaurants near ballparks, stadiums, and arenas are packed on game day. Parking lots near these facilities are full. Vendors outside and inside the facilities do a brisk business and many facilities operate at or near capacity. Any person attending a sporting event can see this with her own eyes. Clearly, this economic activity must have some affect on the local economy.

And it does, of course. But the economy in an American city is much larger, more varied, and more complex, than a spectator at a sporting event can observe. The economic activity that takes place in and around a modern professional sports venue does not translate into additional new economic activity in cities because most of the spectators are residents of the metropolitan area and all consumers face a limited budget to spend on necessities like food, clothing, and shelter as well as on other factors like entertainment. All household spending, including spending on entertainment like professional sporting events, is constrained by available household income.

Money spent on tickets, parking, and concessions in and around a sports facility represents money not spent on other entertainment activities elsewhere in the metropolitan area. Nearly all the economic activity observed taking place in and around professional sports facilities would have taken place somewhere else in the metropolitan area at some other point in time.

Professional sporting events concentrate economic activity at a specific location at a particular point in time. This fact is easily observable to the casual observer attending a sporting event. But sporting events only concentrate spending, they can not generate new spending. The casual observer taking in a ball game does not observe economic activity that might take place in other parts of the city at other times. And the economic activity that takes place in and around a stadium represents lost revenues to other entertainment industry businesses located in other parts of metropolitan areas. The casual observer cannot observe the transactions that do not take place because of the presence

of a professional sport team, but the existence of household budget constraints strongly implies that this occurs.

Economic research on the impact of professional sport on the local economy does not count attendance at sporting events or survey consumer spending at these events. Economic theory predicts that money spent at a sporting event would alternatively be spent somewhere else in the local economy, at some other point in time, even if the city did not use taxpayer money to build a new sports facility. A substantial body of research carried out over decades supports this prediction.

Clearly, to the extent that a professional sports facility and franchise attracts out of town visitors to a city for the express purpose of attending a sporting event, the local economy will benefit from the spending by these visitors, and this spending will ripple throughout the local economy creating additional economic benefits. But most spectators at professional sporting events are residents of the metropolitan area. From a national perspective there can be no net economic benefit from this spending, because a hundred dollars spent on baseball in Baltimore and a hundred dollars spent on baseball in Washington DC make an identical contribution to the nation's Gross Domestic Product. Why should billions of tax dollars subsidize an activity that reallocates a small amount of consumer spending from one city to another?

CATEGORIES OF EVIDENCE ON ECONOMIC IMPACT AND THE IMPORTANCE OF THE PEER REVIEW PROCESS

Evidence about the economic impact of professional sports comes from two sources: academic research, and "promotional" economic impact studies sponsored by professional sports teams, leagues, and other entities interested in obtaining government subsidies for professional sports. These two categories of evidence use widely different methodologies, undergo different levels of scrutiny, and reach strikingly different conclusions.

"Promotional" studies, primarily carried out by consultants hired by professional sports teams or their boosters, always conclude that building a new sports facility will add substantial sums to local income, often hundreds of millions of dollars each year, and will create many new jobs in the local economy. Sometimes the forecasted jobs created run into the thousands. Of course, all this additional income and employment is forecasted to substantially raise state and local tax revenues. Academic research on the economic impact of professional sports concludes that new facilities and franchises have either no measurable impact on local income and employment, or in some cases a small but negative impact on the local economy.

"Promotional" studies are economic forecasts. They predict how much local income or employment will rise in the future, after a new facility is built, and perhaps a new team attracted to the city. These studies forecast the number of spectators that will attend games in the new facility, and use multipliers to further estimate the wider impact of spectators' spending on the local economy. In economic jargon, they make use of "input–output" models to predict the total economic impact flowing from a sporting event. Put simply, they apply a multiplier—a scaling factor greater than one—to increase the forecasted direct economic activity associated with a sporting event to a larger number reflecting the forecasted total effect on the entire metropolitan economy. Since "promotional" economic impact studies are forecasts, they have the same inherent weaknesses as any other economic forecast, like a forecast of the growth rate of GDP over the next five years. But "promotional" economic impact studies always project a high degree of precision. Rather than being stated in terms of a predicted value plus or minus some margin of error, the forecasts in these studies are always a single number, implying a higher degree of precision than other economic forecasts, even though there is no evidence that they are more precise.

Academic research on the economic impact of professional sports is retrospective. Researchers begin with the historic performance of metropolitan economies, in terms of economic indicators like income, earnings, and employment, and use statistical methods to understand why the local economy performed the way that it did. Although this approach is not experimental in nature, there has been a tremendous amount of variation in the professional sports environment in metropolitan areas over the past thirty years which resembles the variation that an experiment might generate. Franchises moved; old facilities were torn down and new ones built; labor disputes resulted in the cancellation of large numbers of games, or even entire seasons in professional sports leagues. Academic research exploits this variation in the sports environment over time to understand the overall economic impact of professional sports on metropolitan economies.

Unlike sports team owners and others with a vested interest in the sports industry, academic researchers do not stand to benefit financially from research on the economic impact of professional sports. The owner of a professional sports team could see the value of his franchise increase by hundreds of millions of dollars if the local government builds him a new facility using public funds. Local businesses near the new facility will see increases in their business. Local media companies may see increases in revenues due to increased interest in the new team in town. Local financial institutions that underwrite the bond issue used to finance construction earn millions in fees. All stand to profit from a new publicly financed sports facility and all are interested in justifying these subsidies on the grounds of the tangible economic benefits created by sport. In contrast, journals that publish academic research on the economic impact of professional sports

charge researchers submission fees to consider their papers for publication. They do not pay royalties to researchers who write the papers they publish. A researcher in this area has no personal financial stake in the outcome of the research.

The most important difference between evidence from academic research and evidence from "promotional" economic impact studies is the degree of scrutiny they undergo. "Promotional" studies are typically carried out by consultants. They are released with great fanfare in the local media, and typically get widespread coverage for a brief time. The press releases and sound bites associated with these studies are typically short on details and long on large round numbers. Very few people ever read the entire reports. The vast majority of these "promotional" studies disappear within a few days of their release. The methodology used in "promotional" studies, and the results, are not reviewed or evaluated in any way. I do not know of a single instance where the predicted outcomes from a "promotional" economic impact study have been systematically evaluated for accuracy after a sports facility was completed.

In stark contrast, academic research on the economic impact of professional sport published in scholarly journals goes through a rigorous peer review process. In this process, the papers are distributed to other experts in the field, often stripped of identifying information about authorship, who are asked to anonymously evaluate the quality of the research. Academic economic impact studies judged as flawed or incompetently executed are not published. In some instances flaws judged as serious are removed from the paper or revised to correct the deficiency. The peer-review process provides important oversight for research in this area, as other experts in the field have examined the methodology, data, and results in detail and found it to be credible.

It is imperative that those who make decisions on sports subsidies understand this important difference in the evidence about the economic impact of professional sports. Results that have been through the peer-review process should be given much more credence by decision makers than "promotional" economic impact studies. We do not make health policy decisions based solely on the claims of pharmaceutical companies, and we should not make decisions on subsidies for professional sports based solely on the claims made by professional sports team owners and other proponents of these subsidies.

The consensus conclusion that emerges from peer reviewed research on the economic impact of professional sports facilities and franchises on the urban economy is clear: professional sports are not an engine of economic growth. The contribution of professional sports to the economic wellbeing of American cities is negligible. Using sports subsidies to revitalize the economy in urban America is not sound economic policy. When cities decide to spend hundreds of millions of dollars of taxpayers' money to build new sports facilities for billionaire sports team owners and millionaire professional athletes, they are making poor economic policy decisions. This money would be better spent on activities with a higher overall return, like education, public health and safety, or infrastructure.

However, professional sports clearly provide important non-economic benefits to urban America. The presence of a professional sports team is often said to bestow "big league" status on a metropolitan area. The residents of American cities derive a great deal of civic pride and sense of community from the presence of home town professional sports teams. Rooting for the local team provides an important touchstone to the residents of American cities and brings together society in ways that few other civic institutions can. These factors are all important to American cities. To the extent that civic pride, "big league" status, and sense of community are important and valuable to the residents of American cities, the large public subsidies for the construction and operation of professional sports facilities may be justified.

Although professional sports cannot revitalize the economies in American cities, they may be able to revitalize the residents of American cities, and improve the quality of life in urban America. However, valuing "big league" status and professional sports' contribution to the sense of community in urban America is difficult to value, in monetary terms. The limited amount of existing academic research on valuing the non-monetary benefits generated by professional sports suggests that the value placed on these intangibles by the residents of American cities is not as large as the subsidies, but more research is clearly needed in this area.

Professional sports facilities and franchises may generate one specific type of non-traded economic benefit. Evidence from recent economic research, some of it not yet peer-reviewed, suggests that residential property values may be higher in cities with professional sports teams. If this turns out to be the case—and at this point the evidence is both mixed and preliminary—then some subsidies for the construction and operation of professional sports facilities may be justified on economic ground. However, the overall effect of higher residential property values on social welfare, particularly on the social welfare of lower income groups, is unclear, even if sports facilities can raise property tax revenues.

WHY DO WE CONTINUE TO SUBSIDIZE PROFESSIONAL SPORTS FACILITY CONSTRUCTION AND OPERATION?

The process of determining how much to subsidize the construction and operation of professional sports facilities involves a complex negotiation between many different groups: team owners, state and local politicians, local businesses, and taxpayers, including team fans. Sometimes the process includes one or more referendums on these subsidies, but the referendum process is not a perfect vehicle for the determination of subsidies.

No matter how they are determined, cities have shown a willingness to provide these subsidies in the past, and continue to provide them today. Why does this continue to happen? Cities may continue to subsidize sports facility construction because the non-pecuniary benefits outweigh the costs in taxpayers' minds. They may continue because proponents of these subsidies are more successful in publicizing the results of their "promotional" economic impact studies than academics are in publicizing their research, leading taxpayers and other decision makers to make ill-informed choices. Local politicians and other elites may derive more private benefits from professional sports than the cost to taxpayers and take action to force them on unwilling taxpayers.

Whatever the reason, it is important to realize that government policies, including government economic policies, have an important impact on the relative amount of influence that each of these groups is able to bring to bear during the negotiation over subsidies for sports facility construction and operation. In particular, the anti-trust protection that this Congress has extended to professional sports leagues provides the owners of professional sports teams with a clear upper hand in these negotiations, and clearly increases the size of the subsidies that professional sports are able to extract from state and local government.

The anti-trust protection extended to professional sports leagues by the Congress allows sports leagues to operate as effective monopolies, or cartels in economic terms. Sports leagues behave exactly like economic theory predicts that cartels will behave: they restrict output in order to earn profits above the level that would prevail if there were competition in the market for professional sports franchises. Restricting the number of franchises means that cities that could support a professional sports team cannot have one. It also implies a loss of social welfare for the residents of cities that want a professional sports team but cannot get one because of leagues' monopoly power. This explains why Los Angeles has been without a National Football League team for over a decade. It also explains why the London, England metropolitan area, with a population of 7.5 million in 2005, can support nine professional soccer teams at the top level, and scores more professional soccer teams at lower levels of competition, while the metropolitan New York area, population 18.7 million in 2005, is home to only nine top-level North American professional sports teams. Professional soccer in the U.K. operates under a promotion and relegation system that allows freedom of entry into the professional sports team market.

American professional sports leagues do not. Professional sports leagues in the U.S. operate as cartels, thanks to the special anti-trust protection provided to these leagues by Congress. The artificial scarcity of professional sports teams generated by this anti-trust protection means that the owner of any professional sports team will always have a viable alternative city to threaten to move to when negotiating for a new publicly financed stadium or arena. The possibility of a team moving to another city provides sports team owners with a huge advantage when negotiating for sports facility construction subsidies, and allows team owners to continue to extract subsidies, even though they are not justified on the basis of tangible economic returns to the taxpayers who provide them.

TESTIMONY OF NEIL DEMAUSE, SUBCOMMITTEE ON DOMESTIC POLICY, COMMITTEE ON OVERSIGHT AND GOVERNMENT REFORM, MARCH 29, 2007

Advocates of sports stadium subsidies say that there are valid reasons why they're a good use of public money, even as schools, transportation, and other public necessities go underfunded. Let's run through the proponents' arguments, one at a time:

ECONOMIC BENEFITS

Stadium boosters claim that publicly subsidized facilities are worth spending taxpayer money on because they provide a shot in the arm to local economies. In my time researching this issue, I have yet to find any independent economists—that is, ones not on the payroll of pro sports teams—who believe there is any significant positive impact to local economies from sports stadiums and arenas. One study, by Lake Forest College economist Robert Baade, looked at 30 cities that had built new stadiums and arenas over a 30-year period, and found that in 27 cases, there was no measurable effect on the per-capita income; in the other three cities, the stadium appeared to have hurt the local economy.[1] And in terms of job creation, where good job-development programs can cost about $10,000 for each new job created, sports facilities typically come in at as much as $250,000 in public cost for each new job—a worse ratio than some of the most infamous corporate giveaways in history.

As for revitalizing urban neighborhoods, this is likewise a myth: While stadiums are often built to take advantage of already-rebounding districts like Denver's LoDo or Baltimore's Inner Harbor, there is no evidence that they can create significant new development by themselves . . . walk a block or two away from Jacobs Field in Cleveland and you will find the same shuttered stores that were there before the sports complex. This is especially true for baseball and football stadiums, which can't be used year-round like arenas can—no self-respecting businessperson is going to open a restaurant around the corner from a building that is dark most of the year.

. . . .

MOVE THREATS

Sports team owners almost always threaten that they will move their team out of town if their stadium demands are not met. But while teams do sometimes move, far more often owners are just crying wolf to shake a few more dollars loose from local governments. Most recently, we saw how during talks over a new Pittsburgh Penguins arena, the team's owners would jet off to Kansas City or Las Vegas every time negotiations seemed to be bogging down; in the end, the team got millions of dollars worth of concessions from the state as a result of their veiled threats. And both the Chicago White Sox' threatened move to St. Petersburg, Florida in the 1980s and the Minnesota Twins' threatened move to North Carolina in the 1990s turned out to have been ideas hatched in the Illinois and Minnesota governors' offices, to scare locals into coughing up funds for new stadiums at home. As White Sox owner Jerry Reinsdorf later explained, he had no intention of abandoning the nation's third-largest media market for one of the smallest, but "a savvy negotiator creates leverage."

This problem is only made worse by cities that build sports facilities "on spec," with no team to play in them. The White Sox were one of seven baseball teams that hinted at moving to St. Petersburg after that city built its domed stadium in the 1980s; all stayed put, usually after using the threat of a move to extract stadium subsidies from their current homes, and it took a threatened antitrust suit by the state of Florida to get Major League Baseball to grant the city of Tampa Bay the Devil Rays as an expansion team. More recently, after Oklahoma City built an arena without any idea of who would play in it, the city ended up giving the New Orleans Hornets an incredible sweetheart lease—with free rent and guaranteed profits—just to play in their new building temporarily for two years during repair operations following Hurricane Katrina.

Remarkably, though, even without a viable move threat, we still see cities bidding against themselves for the right to throw money at their local sports franchise. One argument the New York Yankees made for the city to approve a new stadium was that they would be forced to leave town otherwise—even though the entire value of the franchise is wrapped up in the fact that it plays in the nation's number-one media market. . . . in Washington, D.C., meanwhile, the city's offer of $440 million to the Montreal Expos to move here and become the Nationals—an offer ultimately raised to $611 million once the inevitable cost overruns were tallied—was even more incredible considering that no other city had made a viable offer to build a stadium for the team.

OBSOLESCENCE

Team owners continue to say that their current homes are "obsolete" and in need of replacement. When pressed, they will admit that it's not that their current homes are in danger of falling down, but rather because they are "economically obsolete"—in other words, the team could make more money with a new one, so long as they didn't have to pay to build it. We now see buildings as young as 10 or 15 years old declared "obsolete" because they have too few ad boards or the club seats aren't cushy enough. In proposing a new stadium for the New York Yankees the same year that the team was setting attendance records, Mayor Michael Bloomberg explained that the problem with the House That Ruth Built was that it "fail[ed] to reflect the glamour of the club."

New stadiums are certainly glamorous: They feature state-of-the-art scoreboards, massive food courts, and other amenities that are as dazzling as they are lucrative to the teams that run them. As places to watch sporting events, though, they're often worse than the old "obsolete" buildings that they replaced. Contrary to claims of "intimacy," cheap seats are both fewer and farther from the action, thanks to all those corporate seats pushing upper decks skywards—the New York Mets' new stadium may have elements modeled after Ebbets Field, but it will be twice as tall and take up double the acreage of that genuine old-time ballpark. And fans can expect to pay more for the privilege of watching from the rafters: Baseball teams moving into new parks raised ticket prices by an average of 41% in their first year in their new homes, with some teams as much as doubling prices.

These are the standards of the stadium playbook, but new tactics are being added all the time as citizens and their elected representatives grow increasingly leery of handing over tax money to sports franchises. "State-of-the-art" lease clauses require cities to spend more and more to make sure that their stadiums keep up with those down the block; the Cincinnati Bengals' lease specified such necessary items as "smart seats," "stadium self-cleaning machines," and a "holographic replay system." Building "ballpark villages" of housing and retail development alongside stadiums muddies the economic waters, allowing boosters to counter charges that stadiums are bad investments by saying, "it's not just a stadium." Sports teams are also increasingly looking to avail themselves of "tax increment financing," or TIFs, where instead of paying property taxes like other landholders, they get them kicked back to pay their own construction costs.

Perhaps the most widespread trend is for complicated financing plans involving free rent, tax breaks, "infrastructure" expenses, and other hidden subsidies. Two summers ago, New York City Mayor Michael Bloomberg declared that a new Yankees stadium could be built with "the state helping the way, but George footing the bill—it doesn't get any better than that." Added Yankee executive Steve Swindal, George Steinbrenner's son-in-law: "There will be no public subsidies."

In fact, research by myself and by other journalists and city budget watchdogs, most notably Good Jobs New York, found that after all the hidden subsidies, the city would be subsidizing the new Yankees stadium to the tune of about $280 million, with an additional $100 million from the state and $44 million from the federal government; nearly another $400 million would go to subsidize a similar stadium for the Mets. . . . In each case, the public subsidy was actually *more* than the teams would end up spending on these "privately financed" stadiums. The teams, meanwhile, will reap all the revenues from the new facilities: The Mets, for example, will be able to recoup most of their expense via a $400 million naming-rights deal with CitiGroup—none of which will go to city taxpayers, even though the city will own the building.

This split—the public pays the costs, the teams get all the revenues—is a relatively new phenomenon. When the city of Minneapolis spent $84 million to build the Metrodome in 1982, the Twins and Vikings agreed to pay rent and share ticket, concessions, and ad revenues with the city, enabling taxpayers to recoup their investment. In the new Twins stadium . . ., by contrast, taxpayers . . . put up almost $400 million—and receive no rent or stadium revenues. Harvard researcher Judith Grant Long, who has laboriously investigated every lease agreement covering the four major sports, has found that once hidden tax breaks and lease kickbacks are accounted for, the average stadium costs 40% more than is publicly reported—and that figure is on the rise.

As someone who writes critically about public spending on sports facilities, I'm often asked, "Do you hate *all* stadium deals? Aren't there any that you think worked out well for the public?"

There are certainly a few that come to mind—the new Giants' ballpark, which currently bears the name of whatever the Bay Area's telephone company is called this week, is one, where the team put up most of the funds for construction, though public tax breaks and land subsidies did cover about 14% of the costs. That is a rare exception, however, one made possible by the fact that the booming tech economy of the 1990s allowed the Giants to defray their private costs by raising large sums of money from the sale of high-priced seat licenses, something not available to most other teams.

This is, in fact, the sports industry's dirty little secret: *New stadiums don't make money.* While teams are quick to paint new buildings as cash cows, in the vast majority of cases, the new revenues from a stadium or arena simply aren't enough to pay for all of the land and construction costs without subsidies. Teams don't want new stadiums because they make money; they want new stadiums because of the public subsidies that come with them.

WHAT CONGRESS CAN DO

The battle over sports subsidies has now touched most every city and town in the nation, as even sports like soccer and minor-league baseball and hockey teams seek their share of the boodle. It's a trend, of course, that is not limited to the sports industry. The $2 billion a year that taxpayers spend on stadiums is just a small slice of the hundreds of billions that go to subsidize other industries, in what Minneapolis Federal Reserve vice-president Arthur Rolnick has called the new "War Between the States." But sports facilities are, on a dollar for dollar basis, among the worst investments that cities and states can make, as well as being high-profile, as debates over a new computer-chip plant seldom make it onto the front page. And since local governments have proven unwilling to unilaterally call an end to the hostilities, Congress is in the best position to end the worst of these giveaways.

Some of the most immediate ways that Congress can act:

First off, close the loophole that allows teams to use federally subsidized tax-exempt bonds for private sports stadiums. In 1986, Congress tried to bar the use of tax-exempt bonds for "private activities," but teams have been finding ways around this restriction ever since. Most recently, the New York Mets and Yankees blew a hole in the limitations by disguising their private stadium expenses as public "payments in lieu of taxes" in order to use tax-exempt bonds. Kansas City Royals fans would no doubt not be pleased to learn that their tax dollars are going to help make the New York Yankees and Mets even richer.

Second, drastically restrict the business-entertainment deduction for luxury box and club seat purchases, which would reduce team owners' incentive to shake down cities for new buildings. Much of the reason why existing stadiums are considered "obsolete" is because they lack enough high-priced corporate seating; take away the tax subsidies for businesses to buy tickets to sporting events, and you'll reduce the demand for new stadiums—and, as a side benefit, leave more tickets available for the average fan who can't take a tax deduction on spending a day at the ballpark.

Finally, Congress has the power, if it so chooses, to put on the brakes for not just sports teams, but all industries, holding cities hostage for tax subsidies. The simplest solution presented so far was the Distorting Subsidies Limitation Act proposed by your former colleague David Minge, which would have taxed all direct and indirect subsidies to corporations, including land and infrastructure, as income. A team owner asking for a $500 million stadium subsidy might think twice if he was going to face a $150 million IRS bill as a result.

The rush to build new sports stadiums has had many casualties: We have lost historic ballparks such as Tiger Stadium and . . . Yankee Stadium; we have seen public parks destroyed and thriving neighborhoods disrupted; we have hastened the transformation of sports fandom from an experience that brought together people of all walks of life into one that is affordable only to the well-heeled; and we have cost local, state, and federal governments billions of dollars. In both polls and referendums, voters across the political spectrum are consistently opposed to spending sorely needed tax dollars just to make rich sports team owners even richer. All that's needed is for our elected officials to step up to the plate and say "the bucks stop here."

. . . .

Note

1. Robert A. Baade, "Stadiums, Professional Sports, and Economic Development: Assessing the Reality." *A Heartland Policy Study,* April 4, 1994.

Discussion Questions

1. What is the relationship between player salaries and new stadium construction?
2. What are the limits of personal seat license (PSL) property rights?
3. What are the differences between the rights granted by PSLs and season tickets?
4. What are some unrecognized areas where teams could sell naming rights?
5. What types of business enterprises are most likely to enter into naming rights deals?
6. What are the seven reasons companies enter into naming rights deals?
7. Describe the basic structure of a naming rights deal.
8. What are the most important lease provisions related to stadium revenue generation?
9. What role do lease provisions play in sports franchise relocations? What role do they play in demands for new facilities?
10. Describe luxury suites, personal seat licenses, and club seats.
11. Should revenue streams recognized within stadiums and arenas (not including ticket sales) be subject to revenue sharing? At what rate?
12. How can teams increase revenue from their facilities when the teams are not playing?

13. Given that PSLs and naming rights have been introduced as *de facto* private loan guarantors, are we less likely to see large-scale public funding of stadiums and arenas?

14. Are there any ways that cities could combat the "prisoner's dilemma," in which owners play one city off another to get increased public subsidies?

15. Given the growing saturation of sponsorship in the sports segment, are naming rights still a good buy for companies?

16. If stadiums provide no significant economic benefit, why approve public funds for such a project?

Media

INTRODUCTION

In most industries, a revenue stream periodically appears that ultimately leads to a fundamental change in the way that the industry conducts its business. The sports industry is no exception. Revenue sources for sports franchises have evolved over time, with owners continuously searching for new ways to profit from their investments. In sports, the sea change was fueled by television. Sports teams found that they were able to generate significant amounts of revenue from the sale of the rights to televise their games to broadcasters. Broadcasters found that sports could attract an audience with significant buying power that was otherwise hard to reach in large numbers because of its inconsistent viewing habits—young male viewers in their 20s and 30s. This demographically strong audience was quite attractive to companies searching for an effective medium through which they could advertise their products to their intended buyers. With this demographic in place, broadcasters were able to sell advertising spots on sports programs for a higher rate than on other programs. Thus was born the symbiotic relationship between sports, television, and advertisers that endures to this day. Although the relationships among these stakeholders have become increasingly complex with the passage of time and the introduction of both new broadcasting mediums and methods of distribution, today nearly all sports' business models include television as a main financial driver. Whether a single pay-per-view event or a multiyear broadcasting contract, few structural decisions are made without first considering the impact on broadcast revenues.

However, this was not always the case. When television emerged as a role player in sports in the 1950s, the initial concern was the negative impact broadcasting an event would have on live attendance at the gate. The logic of the owners of the day made sense. Why would fans pay to see a game in person when television would allow them to see the game for free? Those concerns were short-lived, because the experiment with television proved to be both a financial engine and a fan-base builder. Rather than causing declines in attendance, television led to the creation of new fans who ultimately attended the games. In the 1960s, television started to become the financial engine that it is today. Many of the early concerns about the effect of television on gate attendance were addressed by establishing home game local broadcast and blackout rules. With the evolution of cable, satellite, pay-per-view, and the Internet, the effect of television on the local gate has become even less of a concern to many teams. However, there is a growing concern that the home viewing experience has become so comfortable and robust that fans will increasingly choose to watch games from the convenience of their own living rooms on large flat-screen televisions rather than attend games.

Broadcasting of league games occurs at both the national and regional levels. All sports leagues collectively pool and sell their television rights on a league-wide level, with the resulting rights fee divided equally among all of the teams. These national television contracts are considered to be essential for the long-term success of a sports league, because they provide the league with the broad exposure that is necessary to build spectator interest in the sport as well as the revenues that are required for survival.

Traditionally, national television contracts have been executed with networks that are available on free television nationwide. Until the 1990s, there were only three bona fide networks in the United States; today there are five: ABC, CBS, NBC, Fox, and the relative newcomer CW. In addition to the free networks, approximately 85% of U.S. homes currently pay a monthly fee to subscribe to cable or satellite television. Technological innovations have led to the creation of hundreds of channels that are broadcast on cable television. Beginning with the advent of ESPN in 1979, a number of these cable channels broadcast sports programming, because of its aforementioned appeal. In 2009, approximately 43,700 hours of sports programming was broadcast in the United States.

Skyrocketing rights fees have increased the threshold requirement for profitability for the networks. (See **Table 1** for recent television rights deals for the major North American sports leagues and **Table 2** for information on the NFL's television rights fees from 1962–2013.) The networks need to increase their advertising revenues in order to recoup this increased investment. Because advertising rates are based on program ratings, the networks had hoped that increased ratings would lead to increased advertising dollars. However, the days of ratings increases for networks are all but over. Prime time ratings for CBS, ABC, NBC, and Fox fell a combined 29% from 1996–1997 to 2006–2007, from a combined 37 ratings points to 26.4. This drop in ratings is likely attributable to the technological innovations that have led to the development and ubiquity of the Internet and digital cable, both of which compete with broadcast networks

for the individual's attention. People—especially younger demographics—are spending more time online and less time watching television than in the past.

The advent of digital cable has led to a proliferation of cable networks serving a variety of general and sports-related programming niches (see **Tables 3** and **4**). There seems to be a channel for every interest. This proliferation of programming outlets has led to fragmentation of the viewing audience. All is not lost for sports programming, however. Fragmentation has led to the increased importance of coveted demographic groups who no longer watch any one type of programming in the same numbers as in the past—specifically the 18- to 34-year-old males that sports programming attracts.

Sports ratings vary based on the teams or athletes involved, the existence of any compelling storylines, the presence of certain superstar athletes, the broadcast window in which the game is shown, the programming that airs immediately before and after an event, and the competitiveness

Table 1   Recent Television Rights Deals

League	Contract Period	Rights Holder(s)	Total Rights Fee	Avg. Annual Value/League
NFL	1994–1997	ABC, Fox, NBC, ESPN/TNT	$4.3 billion	$1.1 billion
	1998–2005	ABC, Fox, CBS, ESPN	17.6 billion	2.2 billion
	2006–2013	CBS, NBC, Fox, ESPN, DirecTV, NFL Network	29.6 billion	3.7 billion
MLB	1996–2000	Fox, NBC, ESPN	1.7 billion	340 million
	2000–2005*	ESPN	851 million	141.8 million
	2001–2006	Fox	2.5 billion	416.7 million
	2006–2013	ESPN	2.37 billion	296 million
	2007–2013	Fox, Turner, DirecTV, iN DEMAND	3.26 billion	466 million
NBA	1994–1998	NBC, TNT	1.1 billion	275 million
	1998–2002	NBC, TNT/TBS	2.64 billion	600 million
	2002–2008	ABC/ESPN, AOL Time Warner	4.6 billion	766.7 million
	2008–2016	ABC/ESPN, TNT, NBA TV	8.37 billion	930 million
NHL	1994–1999	Fox	155 million	31 million
	1999–2004	ABC/ESPN	600 million	120 million
	2005–2007	Versus	135 million	67.5 million
	2005–2007	NBC	Revenue sharing	Revenue sharing
	2008	Versus	72.5 million	72.5 million
	2008–2010	NBC, Versus	Revenue sharing	Revenue sharing
	2008–2013	CBC, TSN (Canada)	810 million	135 million
	2009–2010	NASN/ESPN America (Europe)	11.25 million	11.25 million
NASCAR	2001–2008**	Fox/NBC, Turner	2.4 billion	400 million
	2007–2014	Fox/Speed, ABC/ESPN, Turner	4.48 billion	560 million
MLS	2007–2014	ESPN/ABC, Univision	135.5 million	17 million
	2007–2017	FOX Soccer Channel	24.2 million	2.2 million
	2007–2009	HDNet	7.5 million	2.5 million

*Terms of the deal replaced the terms of the previous MLB deal for ESPN for the 2000 season.
**Represents a 6-year, $2.4 billion deal, plus 2 additional years for Fox. Under the terms of NASCAR's previous television contract, individual tracks made their own TV deals and Winston Cup races were spread across CBS, ABC, ESPN, TNN, TBS, and NBC for about $100 million in total rights fees paid.
Sources: Street & Smith's SportsBusiness Journal research, Gould Media, NFLPA.

Table 2   NFL National Television Rights Fees, 1962–2013

Contract Period	Rights Holder(s)	Total Rights Fee	Average Annual Value
1962–1963	CBS	$9.3 million	$4.65 million
1964–1965	CBS	28.2 million	14.1 million
1966–1969	CBS	75.2 million	18.8 million
1970–1973	CBS, ABC, NBC	185.6 million	46.4 million
1974–1977	CBS, ABC, NBC	269 million	67.25 million
1978–1981	CBS, ABC, NBC	646 million	161.5 million
1982–1986	CBS, ABC, NBC	2 billion	402 million
1987–1989	CBS, ABC, NBC, ESPN	1.4 billion	471 million
1990–1993	CBS, ABC, NBC, ESPN, TNT	3.6 billion	904 million
1994–1997	ABC, FOX, NBC, ESPN, TNT	4.3 billion	1.1 billion
1998–2005	ABC, FOX, CBS, ESPN	17.6 billion	2.2 billion
2006–2013	CBS, NBC, FOX, ESPN, DirecTV, NFL Network	29.6 billion	3.7 billion

Source: Data on file from authors.

of the event. Consider the following sporting events that occurred in 2008 (see also **Table 5**):

- The most-watched Super Bowl ever was an incredibly close game between the large-market New York Giants and the New England Patriots, a team attempting to complete a perfect season.

- The most-watched cable broadcast ever was a Monday Night Football divisional rivalry game between the very popular Dallas Cowboys and the large-market Philadelphia Eagles.

- The most-watched cable golf event ever was a Monday afternoon playoff in the U.S. Open involving Tiger Woods, the transcendent athlete of his generation, competing with a severely injured knee against a journeyman golfer, Rocco Mediate, who was easy to identify with.

- The most-watched Wimbledon final in 8 years featured an amazing five-set match between the world's two best players, Roger Federer and Rafael Nadal. Some have called it the greatest tennis match of all time.

- The most-watched NBA and NHL Finals in 5 years included a matchup between two historic rivals and leading brands, the Los Angeles Lakers and Boston Celtics, and the latter a matchup of a historically strong franchise and a team featuring young stars.

Ratings for televised sports are relatively strong in comparison to general entertainment programming. In addition, sports programming is considered to be advertising-friendly because it is "DVR proof"; that is, it is still primarily consumed in real time, unlike other programming that is increasingly being recorded and watched at a later time, with the viewer presumably skipping through the commercials instead of watching them.

Nonetheless, networks have lost significant amounts of money on their sports programming due to the enormous rights fees that they have paid and their inability to recoup their investment through advertising sales. Morgan Stanley estimated that total losses from sports broadcasting from 2000–2006 were over $6.6 billion.[1] Despite this, the networks are still interested in sports programming because of the ancillary benefits that it provides, namely,

Table 3   Types of Sports-Related Cable Networks

Category	Networks
General with sports programming	TNT, TBS, etc.
General sports networks	ESPN, ESPN2, ESPN Classic, ESPN News, Versus, etc.
Sport-specific networks	Golf Channel, Tennis Channel, Fuse, ESPN U, CBS College Sports Network (CTV), Fox Soccer Channel, etc.
Media-owned regional sports networks (RSNs)	Fox Regional Cable Sports Nets, Comcast SportsNet (Philadelphia, Chicago, Baltimore-Washington D.C., Sacramento, etc.), Cox Channel 4 (San Diego), etc.
Team-owned RSNs	NESN, YES, SNY, etc.
League-owned networks	NBA TV (1999), NFL Network (2003), The MTN. (2006), Big Ten (2007), NHL Network (2007), MLB Network (2009)

Source: Data on file from authors.

Table 4   Top Cable Network Universes (12/09) (# Households)

Network	Universe Estimate (millions)	Coverage (%)	Rank
TBS Network	$100,146	87.16	1
Discovery Channel	99,837	86.89	2
The Weather Channel	99,787	86.85	3
Nick-At-Nite	99,590	86.68	4
Nickelodeon	99,590	86.68	4
Cable News Network	99,299	86.42	6
Headline News	99,295	86.42	7
Food Network	99,243	86.37	8
USA Network	99,174	86.31	9
Turner Network Television (TNT)	99,143	86.29	10
ESPN	99,065	86.22	11
A&E	98,919	86.09	12
TLC	98,837	86.02	13
Lifetime Television	98,804	85.99	14
Spike TV	98,772	85.96	15
ESPN2	98,770	85.96	16
HGTV	98,708	85.91	17
Disney Channel	98,617	85.83	18
MTV: Music Television	98,454	85.69	19
ABC Family	98,416	85.65	20
Adult Swim	98,276	85.53	21
The Cartoon Network	98,276	85.53	21
History Channel	98,173	85.44	23
Comedy Central	98,109	85.39	24
Fox News Channel	98,044	85.33	25
VH1	97,858	85.17	26
CNBC	97,591	84.94	27
TV Land	97,225	84.62	28
E! Entertainment TV	96,991	84.41	29
Sci-Fi Channel	96,379	83.88	30
Animal Planet	96,292	83.81	31
FX	95,845	83.42	32
AMC	95,188	82.84	33
Travel Channel	95,131	82.79	34
MSNBC	92,996	80.94	35
Bravo	92,321	80.35	36
truTV (formerly Court TV)	92,221	80.26	37
CMT	89,910	78.25	38
Black Entertainment TV	89,588	77.97	39
Hallmark Channel	88,320	76.87	40
Golf Channel	81,786	71.18	41
TV Guide Network	80,885	70.40	42
MTV2	76,925	66.95	43
Oxygen Media	75,783	65.96	44
WE: Women's Entertainment	74,941	65.22	45
Speed	74,667	64.98	46
Lifetime Movie Network	74,582	64.91	47
Disney XD (formerly Toon Disney)	74,573	64.90	48
Discovery Health	74,266	64.64	49
Soapnet	73,232	63.74	50
WGN America (formerly Superstation WGN)	72,309	62.93	51
Nick Jr (formerly Noggin)	71,061	61.85	52
ESPN News	70,818	61.63	53
GSN	70,139	61.04	54
National Geographic Channel	69,595	60.57	55
Teennick (formerly The N)	68,560	59.67	56

Table 4 *(Continued)*

Network	Universe Estimate (millions)	Coverage (%)	Rank
G4	$66,762	58.10	57
Fuse	65,802	57.27	58
ESPNU	65,788	57.26	59
BBC-America	65,593	57.09	60
Style	65,573	57.07	61
Versus	63,379	55.16	62
ESPN Classic	60,580	52.72	63
Science Channel	58,490	50.91	64
Great American Country	58,482	50.90	65
Biography Channel	56,640	49.30	66
Fine Living	55,933	48.68	67
Galavision	55,783	48.55	68
History International	55,762	48.53	69
VH1 Classic	55,563	48.36	70
Military Channel	55,442	48.25	71
Nicktoons	55,386	48.20	72
NFL Network	54,722	47.63	73
Investigation Discovery (Was Disc Times)	54,714	47.62	74
DIY Network	52,629	45.80	75
Fox Business Network	51,567	44.88	76
TV One	48,946	42.60	77
Fox Reality	48,316	42.05	78
Reelzchannel	46,867	40.79	79
Gospel Music Channel	45,470	39.57	80
RFD-TV	36,687	31.93	81
Fox Soccer Channel	35,532	30.92	82
Encore	34,662	30.17	83
Outdoor Channel	34,055	29.64	84
Encore Primary	33,641	29.28	85
mun2 Cable	33,264	28.95	86
HBO—The Works	32,072	27.91	87
HBO Prime	31,917	27.78	88
Showtime	22,521	19.60	89
Showtime Prime	22,362	19.46	90
Starz	21,907	19.07	91
Starz Primary	21,740	18.92	92
Multimax	16,852	14.67	93
Maxprime	16,740	14.57	94
Total Cable Plus	103,974	90.49	
Total wired cable	71,005	61.80	
Cable Plus w/Pay-per-view	59,071	51.41	
Wired cable w/Pay-per-view	41,041	35.72	
Ads	33,902	29.51	
Broadcast only	10,926	9.51	
Total U.S. TV Households	114,900	100.00	

Source: The Nielsen Company. Copyrighted information of The Nielsen Company, licensed for use herein.

the promotional opportunities that it offers to its other, non-sports shows, and the larger branding opportunity. Leslie Moonves, the president of CBS Television, stated, "Broadcast networks must look at sports as a piece of a much larger puzzle and not focus on the specific profits and losses of sports divisions. You can't remove sports from the other parts of the networks. If you did, it would look as bad as some others make it out to be."[2] Though the evidence of such benefits appears to be anecdotal in nature, it is driving many network decisions. The promotion of a network's prime-time lineup during its sports programming exposes this programming to an audience that would not otherwise

Table 5   2008 Top Rated TV Sports Events

Rank	Program	Network	Match-Up	Viewers (2+ years)
1	Super Bowl XLII	FOX	NY Giants vs. New England	97,563,000
2	NFC Championship	FOX	NY Giants at Green Bay	54,005,000
3	AFC Championship	CBS	San Diego at New England	44,850,000
4	NFC Playoff-Sunday	FOX	NY Giants at Dallas	40,094,000
5	Summer Olympics Tuesday Prime 1	NBC	N/A	34,586,000
6	Summer Olympics Sunday Prime 1	NBC	N/A	32,679,000
7	Summer Olympics Saturday Prime 2	NBC	N/A	31,890,000
8	AFC Divisional Playoff—Sunday	CBS	San Diego at Indianapolis	31,598,000
9	AFC Divisional Playoff—Saturday	CBS	Jacksonville at New England	30,932,000
10	Summer Olympics Monday Prime 1	NBC	N/A	30,579,000

Source: The Nielsen Company. Used with permission.

be as likely to be aware of it. If this increased awareness leads some of the sports audience to watch these other offerings, then the network could see a ratings increase in its other programming and allow it to reap additional advertising revenues as a result. In this way, sports could be seen as an overall ratings driver for the network. In addition, the network's ability to promote its other programming during its sports lineup allows the network to save on the promotional budgets for this programming, because it can reduce the amount of money it spends on promoting these shows in other mediums. For example, NBC received 5 minutes of promotional opportunities during its Super Bowl broadcast in 2009. At the listed advertising rate of $3 million per 30 seconds, NBC received $30 million of free promotions for its prime-time lineup during the game. In theory, then, this allowed the network to spend considerably less in its promotion of these shows via other mediums. (See **Figure 1** for a list of advertising costs for the Super Bowl.)

Year	Price*	Price Adjusted for Inflation**	Network
1998	$1,300,000	$1,621,886	NBC
1999	1,600,000	1,963,990	FOX
2000	2,100,000	2,503,131	ABC
2001	2,050,000	2,357,880	CBS
2002	1,900,000	2,160,721	FOX
2003	2,100,000	2,323,355	ABC
2004	2,250,000	2,445,073	CBS
2005	2,400,000	2,532,392	FOX
2006	2,500,000	2,541,562	ABC
2007	2,600,000	2,600,000	CBS

*Consensus reported price for :30 commercial.
**Adjusted for inflation in 2007 dollars.
Source: Advertising Age. Copyright 2007 by Crain Communications Inc. Reproduced with permission of Crain Communications Inc. in the formats Textbook and Other book via Copyright Clearance Center.

Figure 1   Super Bowl Ad Rates

To a certain degree, networks are willing to view sports programming as a loss leader, because the programming also offers them significant branding opportunities. Fox established itself as a legitimate network when it acquired the broadcasting rights to the NFL and NHL in 1994. The network was able to use its acquisitions to add a number of affiliates in NFL markets that previously had balked at the opportunity to associate themselves with the fledgling network. With the leagues in tow, Fox had instant credibility. Recently, NBC has focused its efforts on key programming, such as the Summer and Winter Olympics and NFL football on Sunday evenings, and then entered into more conservative deals for Notre Dame football and an array of niche sports.

It is likely that each broadcast network will consider certain sports properties to be cornerstones of its programming lineup. They will continue to be willing to pay dramatic rights fee increases in order to retain these "tent pole" properties. However, for other sports properties, the network will take a more conservative approach and only pay rights fees that make financial sense. For example, in addition to the aforementioned approach by NBC, CBS will continue to focus its efforts on four properties—the NCAA men's basketball tournament, SEC football, NFL football and the Masters.

Cable television is likely to increasingly dominate the national broadcasting agreements entered into by major sports properties. As leagues seek out rights fee increases, cable television networks are most able to bear the additional costs of doing so. This is a function of a cable network's revenue model. Major cable system operators, such as Comcast, Time Warner, Cox, Charter, and Cablevision, and satellite operators, such as DirecTV and Dish Network, pay monthly per-subscriber carriage fees to cable networks for the right to distribute their channels to their customers. Thus, whereas broadcast networks receive revenues primarily from advertising, cable television networks have dual revenue streams—advertising revenue and negotiated subscriber fees. This dual-revenue stream will enable cable networks to better afford the high cost of sports programming.

In order to afford the ever-increasing rights fees sought by sports properties, sports programmers are constantly attempting to increase the subscriber fees that it receives from the cable system operator. Although typically the most expensive programming for cable system operators, sports programming is important for them because of subscriber demand for the programming and the need to differentiate themselves from their competitors, including direct-satellite subscription providers such as DirecTV. Sports programming, especially the regional sports networks that carry the majority of the home teams' games, is must-have content for cable system operators, a fact well-known to both the cable networks and the cable system operators. **Tables 6** and **7** provide monthly fees per subscriber for sports and nonsports networks, respectively.

Some cable system operators have negotiated fiercely with cable networks over proposed increases in subscriber fees. They feel that the cable networks must absorb some of the increase rather than pass all of it along to the cable system operator's subscribers, many of whom have no interest in sports and do not want to pay higher cable bills in order to pay for the networks that carry this programming. This has led some cable systems to attempt to place many national

Table 7   Monthly Cable Major Nonsports Network Subscriber Fees (January 2009)

Network	Monthly Fees per Subscriber
TNT	$0.93
USA	0.52
CNN	0.47
TBS	0.46
Nickelodeon	0.45
FOX News Channel	0.42
FX	0.37
MTV	0.32
CNBC	0.27
Discovery Channel	0.26
Lifetime Television	0.25
A&E	0.25
AMC	0.23
History Channel	0.21
MSNBC	0.15
VH1	0.14
The Weather Channel	0.11

Source: Wayne Friedman, "Cable Sports Nets Pay More To Play," February 27, 2009, Media Daily News.

Table 6   Monthly Cable Sports Networks Subscriber Fees (January 2009)

Network	Monthly Fees per Subscriber
ESPN	$3.65
YES	2.15
Comcast Philadelphia	1.97
Comcast Mid-Atlantic	1.95
NESN	1.95
FOX Sports West	1.93
Comcast Chicago	1.90
FOX Sports Florida	1.90
MSG	1.85
FOX Sports New York	1.80
SportsNet N.Y.	1.80
FOX Sports North	1.67
Big Ten Network	1.10
NFL Network	0.83
ESPN 2	0.52
NBA TV	0.35
MLB Network	0.35
Versus	0.27
Golf Channel	0.25
NHL Network	0.21
Speed	0.19
ESPN Classic	0.17

Source: Media Daily News and authors.

and regional sports networks on a pay-tier where subscribers have to pay an additional monthly sum for access to the network instead of on an expanded basic cable package, where all subscribers have access to the channel. However, the sports-tier strategy has seen limited success and is unlikely to endure, especially for established national cable networks such as ESPN and TNT and more popular niche networks.

Despite a difference in penetration between network and cable television of approximately 15% (representing 20 million households) as of January 2009,[3] the line between the two broadcasting universes is becoming increasingly blurred. Popular cable programming garners ratings that are competitive with network shows. Cross-ownership of network and cable broadcasters, such as Disney's ownership and shared production of ABC and ESPN and News Corporation's ownership of Fox and Fox Sports Net, has made the distinction between cable and network even less important. Thus, cable is likely to be the new national rights model for sports programming. This is evidenced by ESPN landing the exclusive rights to the British Open beginning in 2010 and the entire slate of Bowl Championship Series games beginning in 2011, as well as CBS and Turner jointly sharing the NCAA men's basketball tournament from 2011–2024.

Unless they see a significant increase in the amount of the retransmission fees that the broadcast networks receive from cable companies (which are analogous to the aforementioned subscriber fees), it is also fair to consider whether the broadcast network model will be able continue to compete against the cable model in landing sports properties.

This raises a significant transitional issue confronting sports leagues today, as they consider whether they should move away from the original network model and to what degree. The NBA led the way in this thinking by entering into a 6-year, $4.6 billion deal with ESPN, TNT, and ABC in 2002, and continued with its current 8-year, $7.4 billion deal with the same partners. Most analysts have concluded that it is still too early to tell whether this route is more beneficial to the relevant stakeholders than the league's single-network model, but a few differences are clear. Although there are fewer viewers, there is an opportunity for the sports property to receive an increase in its rights fees. The NBA is earning more money over the length of these agreements than in its previous broadcasting contracts with NBC and TNT, but these cable outlets only reach 85% of the households that network television reaches. The remaining 15% is problematic, in that people living in these households are unable to watch most of the league's programming.

In addition to the league-wide national agreements in place with network and cable broadcasters and the emergence of league-owned networks in the major North American professional leagues, sports franchises in the NBA, NHL, and MLB have individual deals in place with broadcasters in their home territories. These deals can be quite important, because the vast majority of each team's games are broadcast on this basis. (Note that in the NFL the rights to all regular and postseason games are controlled by the national broadcast partners, with only preseason games shown on a local basis.) The value of the local broadcasting agreement varies according to a number of factors, the most important being the size of the team's market and the team's popularity within this market. Prior to the advent of cable television, most of the local broadcasting agreements were with independent, over-the-air stations that had limited geographic reach. Cable television created the opportunity for teams to expand their presence on a more regional basis.

The aforementioned proliferation of cable networks included a number of distinct regional sports networks (RSNs) whose programming was built around the home teams. Ultimately, there was a consolidation of many of these RSNs, and Fox Sports Net emerged as the dominant player in the marketplace with its ownership of 19 RSNs nationwide and an affiliation with 5 others. The majority of NBA, NHL, and MLB teams are broadcast partners with Fox Sports Net. Comcast has emerged as another major participant in RSNs, with a hand in 11 of the networks across the country. The ratings for sports programming on RSNs are still strong, reflecting fans' continued interest in their home teams. RSNs capitalize on the much greater appetite that local fans have for their teams than a national audience would have. Recognizing an opportunity to exploit its revenue potential, cable system operators, media companies, individual teams, and leagues have started their own RSNs. In addition, a number of niche channels focusing on a single sport such as soccer, tennis, golf, action sports, auto racing, skiing, and nonrevenue college sports have been launched.

While the programming content on the RSN must be attractive to viewers, the distribution of the RSN to a large number of subscribers at an appropriate monthly subscriber fee is a key to its success. Enough people must have access to the channel for the advertising rates and subscription fees to sustain the RSN. Thus, it is vital for the RSN to be carried by a large number of cable systems in the local market. Without sufficient carriage, the RSN will fail. In addition, the RSN must have sufficient financing to support the substantial startup costs and initial operating losses, as well as an experienced management team that has the ability to negotiate the aforementioned affiliate agreements and rights fee deals.

The RSN concept is still evolving, and thus far has been met with varying degrees of success across the country. It clearly has not been the answer for every team. The Portland Trail Blazers, Charlotte Bobcats, and Minnesota Twins all unsuccessfully attempted to launch a RSN. Notably, Trail Blazers owner and Microsoft cofounder Paul Allen's Action Sports Network lost a reported $25 million when the RSN failed after it could not get sufficient distribution in the Pacific Northwest. Then-Charlotte Bobcats owner and BET founder Bob Johnson's Carolina Sports Entertainment Television (C-SET) shuttered after only one season, because its distribution deals left most of the team's home market without the network. These failures embody the significant risk that teams face when attempting to launch an RSN. Although the potential payoff to sports teams that own their own RSN is huge, it is very difficult to successfully launch an RSN. Carriage and distribution are difficult obstacles to overcome, especially for sports teams that are newcomers to this aspect of the television business. Even Disney was unsuccessful in its attempt to launch ESPNWest, a proposed RSN that would have carried the games of both the Disney-owned Anaheim Angels and Mighty Ducks. This should send a cautionary note to any team attempting to launch its own RSN. It may be that the team is better off using the possibility of starting its own RSN as leverage in negotiating new rights fees deals with the already existing local RSN.

The discussion of media now transcends television and must include the multiplatform world of broadcast, cable, broadband, mobile, online, and print outlets. In October 2008 alone, 75 million people visited sports Web sites. (See **Table 8** for the top five U.S. sports Web sites.) Similar to what has transpired with the advent of "disruptive" technologies such as radio, over-the-air television, and cable and satellite television in previous eras, the creation and continued expansion of the digital world has provided the sports industry with a vibrant revenue opportunity. Sports programming is highly valuable content in the digital world as well, as sports fans clamor for more information and interaction with their favorite athletes, teams and leagues.

Table 8   Top Five U.S. Sports Web Sites: November 2008

Rank	Web Site	Unique Visitors	% Change vs. November 2007
1	Yahoo! Sports	22,788,000	2%
2	ESPN	22,198,000	12%
3	NFL Internet Network	14,072,000	0%
4	FOX Sports on MSN	13,766,000	−10%
5	CBS Sports	12,939,000	−7%
	All U.S. sports Web sites	*78,499,000*	*5%*

Source: The Nielsen Company. Used with permission.

Internet use continues to increase; according to U.S. Census data from 2007, over 60% of U.S. households have broadband access. Mobile phones are nearing ubiquity—nearly 85% of U.S. households have them, and a growing number of people are living in wireless-only homes.

Although the business model continues to evolve, sports properties have thus far monetized the digital world via two somewhat distinct strategies: a subscription-based model where individuals pay a fee to view the content and an advertising-supported model where the viewership is free and advertising is sold on the site. Although each strategy has its advocates, it is likely that content that appeals to a smaller but dedicated core audience is better suited for a subscription-based model; the advertising dollars that the content can generate is relatively small due to the limited number of unique visitors to the site, but the fan base's loyalty is high enough that it will be willing to pay to view the content. An example of this is the ATP World Tour and Sony Ericsson WTA Tour's streaming of 37 of its 2009 tournaments via TennisTV.com, the official video Web site of each tour. Individuals could subscribe to a variety of packages ranging in price from $130 for annual access to $20 for a single tournament. At the league level, the NBA, NHL, and MLB offer their subscription-based out-of-market packages via broadband as well as on television.

An advertising-supported model works best for content that is attractive to a mass audience; here the audience size is large enough to command significant advertising fees. The most successful example of this model to-date has been CBSSports.com's March Madness on Demand (MMOD) product, the online streaming video of the NCAA Division I Men's basketball tournament. MMOD operated on a subscription basis, costing an average of $15 from its launch in 2003 through 2005, when approximately 20,000 users bought it. It converted to a free, advertising-supported model in 2006, and over 1.3 million viewed it; this model endures and the product has seen tremendous growth. The 63-game event drew over 7.5 million unique visitors to the MMOD video player in 2009 (58% higher than in 2008), with 8.6 million total hours watched (a 75% increase from

2008).[4] In 2009, CBSSports.com generated over $30 million in advertising revenues from MMOD. Other examples of successful live-streaming on a free, ad-supported basis include CBSSports.com's showing of the 2008 U.S. Open men's tennis final between Roger Federer and Andy Murray, which reached 300,000 unique visitors who watched a combined 243,000 hours (an average of 49 minutes per user), and NBCOlympics.com's live-streaming of 2,000 hours during the 2008 Beijing Olympics. Although the technology exists to allow teams to stream their games live in their home territories, in-market streaming has a number of operational and financial obstacles that must be overcome. However, the revenue potential of in-market streaming to mobile devices makes it inevitable; there is simply too much money to be made for a reasonable solution not to appear.

In 2009, MLBAM, the digital arm of MLB and a long-time leader in the digital space, began offering a mobile version of its MLB.TV Premium subscription-based out-of-market broadband video package to subscribers of its $9.99 MLB.com at Bat application on the iPhone and iPod Touch. It is likely that the other leagues will follow in due course, giving fans near-constant access to their favorite sports, teams, and athletes. Today's blogs, message boards, and social networking applications enable sports properties to deepen their relationship with their fans. Tomorrow's technologies will allow for even more of the same. Although exactly how sports and digital media will intersect going forward is unknown, the passion and loyalty of sports fans and their seemingly insatiable appetite for content related to the object of these desires should allow the industry to monetize this opportunity.

In the first article, "Panel I: The Future of Sports Television," a panel of sports experts discuss the future of sports television in a wide-ranging conversation, providing a good starting point for the analysis that follows. In the second selection, John Fortunato examines the business of one league's television programming—the highly rated NFL. Although ratings for NHL programming are low in the United States, hockey games are quite popular among Canadian television viewers, a topic that is examined by O'Reilly and Rahinel in the third selection. In the fourth selection, Diana Moss details the business of RSNs.

Sports properties have exerted considerable efforts to find other revenue streams beyond television. The "new media" certainly encompasses analog and digital cable, satellite, high definition television (HDTV), and other broadcast vehicles. The largest focus in this new media realm, however, has been the Internet. There is not a sector in the sports business that has not dabbled in some way in cyberspace seeking to find a way to add the Internet to its business model. Thus, the chapter concludes with predictions about the future of sports media in an article by Rein, Kotler and Shields.

Notes

1. Andy Bernstein, "Moonves: Sports Worth More Than Money," *The Sports Business Journal,* March 17, 2003.

2. Alan Miles, "Digital TV Transition: 2009," Barclays Capital Equity Research, December 12, 2008.

3. Richard K. Miller and Associates, "Sports Television Broadcasting," *The 2006 Sports Business Marketing Research Yearbook,* July 2005.

4. "Final 2009 NCAA March Madness On Demand Traffic Figures Show All-Time Record," April 10, 2009. Available at: http://www.reuters.com/article/pressRelease/idUS92989+10-Apr-2009+PRN20090410.

OVERVIEW

PANEL I: THE FUTURE OF SPORTS TELEVISION

Ronald A. Cass, Mark Abbott, Irwin Kishner, Brad Ruskin, and Alan Vickery

MR. ABBOTT: . . . I wanted to speak this morning a little bit about the impact that new technologies have had on the television business for sports. . . . Most of what I will talk about are things that I have had direct experience with in the last twelve months. . . .

To de-glamorize sports, which has to be done sometimes, it's about the basic allocation of rights. When you take a look at what we as lawyers in the sports business do, it is often refereeing the fights over how those rights have been allocated. Whether it's an issue between a league and a team over an allocation of a right or between various broadcast partners, a lot of what we have to do is think through how we want to allocate those rights which we have to maximize the overall value for our sports league. We'll talk about that in a moment.

But I wanted to talk, first, about the impact that several new technologies have had on the sports business. I think everybody is generally aware. . . of the great move away from the three broadcast networks to cable and to satellite television and all that that entails.[3]

I think there are really four trends that I've seen, and that we've all seen in the last couple of years, that have really come to the forefront and dramatically changed the business, more so than the previous twenty years had done so.

The first is the growth of digital television. Digital television ("DTV"), if you're not familiar, is the digital transmission rather than through analog. This is done through either a satellite, like DirecTV or Dish Network, or now digital cable which is starting to roll out across the country.[4]

There is no more room for analog channels. . . . The bandwidth is already used up.[5] And so any new channels that you see are digital. That means they can only be broadcast over satellite or broadcast in an area that has digital cable.

This has presented a great opportunity but also a limitation. The new niche channels that you see rising up that people are talking about—NBA TV,[6] or the National Football League ("NFL") . . . channel[7]—they rely upon the rollout of this digital platform.

It has gone a little bit slower than people had anticipated that it might go. It really relies upon cable systems adopting the digital platform for its distribution in order to get your channel distribution.[8] So a lot of these channels have an opportunity to be distributed because there is now bandwidth. . . .

That presents a lot of opportunities for sports leagues. We see it really in two ways that I think have already been alluded to. The first is the single-sports channels which have come up. The second is something which is very popular—what are called out-of-market packages.[9] We have one called MLS Shootout. NFL Sunday Ticket and Major League Baseball Extra Innings are the types of packages that we are talking about,[10] which have become very popular as a result of satellite.

It's a way for a league and teams to more directly connect with its fans all throughout the country, because no longer do you need to have just a national broadcast to reach everybody. If somebody is willing to pay the fees, which are relatively modest actually, to get one of these packages, you can have access to all the games from all the local markets. That is quite a lot of benefit to the fans and it is a great opportunity for professional sports leagues.

The second trend that is really starting to hit right now is high-definition television ("HD" or "HDTV").[11] There has been a lot of talk about high-definition television over the last few years and there has been a lot of talk about the requirements of broadcasters to broadcast in high-definition, but it is really starting to break out now.[12] That is driven by a few things.

One is the development of more content being broadcast in high-definition, which is causing more people to buy high-definition television. High-definition televisions are coming down lower in price.

. . . .

The third trend in technology that is impacting all of television but is a benefit for sports is TiVo and digital video recorders.[16] I think you're probably all familiar with what TiVo is. Basically it's a hard drive that allows you to simply record things off of television. It's much easier to use than a VCR. It's much higher quality. It allows you to very quickly fast-forward through commercials.[17]

. . . .

People in the sports business tend to think that of all broadcast properties, sports is among the most TiVo-proof, and that is because you incorporate with more frequency now broadcast sponsorship and commercial elements within the game itself. So, the classic example is on the sidelines of an NFL game you will see the Gatorade container or the Motorola headset. That is not just there because the team chose they like Motorola. It is there because Motorola paid millions and millions of dollars for that to get that exposure.[20] And you cannot TiVo through that. It is on. When they shoot the coach, you are not TiVo'ing through that. And so TiVo presents sports a really unique opportunity to offer advertisers a way to reach fans that they cannot avoid. I think that is a very important trend and very important for the value of sports broadcast rights going forward.

The fourth trend, which has been going on for a long time—in fact, it had both a boom and bust in the last five years—is obviously new media, and that's the Internet.

. . . .

No one doubts that the Internet is a transformational medium. I saw a very interesting article the other day that compared it to the airline industry, the point of which was that both the airline industry and the Internet have done more to transform the economy than any other industries. That is, by virtue of being able to fly around the country, it has grown our economy, and the Internet allows communication to happen much quicker and access information much quicker. And so it has transformed the economy in very profound ways, yet you cannot make money at either of them.

I think that is one of the debates that is going on in the Internet. There are those who come to speak to sports professionals and say that the economic model is no different than that of the public library; it is just an information access device. I think most people in the sports business vehemently disagree with that and feel that the Internet is a way to more closely connect your product with the fan. It is all about providing the fan access to information that they want in a way that they want to receive it, and people are starting to find ways to monetize that.

When there was a lot of crazy money and it reached a fever pitch, just as the NASDAQ reached a fever pitch in March of 2000,[21] people had raised money from the public markets and the capital markets and were throwing a lot of money at sports rights because, just as sports rights had been used, for example, in Europe by satellite providers to reach homes and to get subscribers, and just as it had been used here by cable companies to get subscribers, the Internet companies were going to use sports content to get eyeballs. The problem was nobody figured out how to monetize those eyeballs once they had them.

There is now a move to subscription-based services, and you will see a lot of this coming. It has happened already, and it is going to come even more this year. People have found that a model that works reasonably well on the Internet is to offer fans—for $9.95 a month—the ability, for example, in baseball to get all the audio broadcasts of all the games nationwide, or to get a package of highlights customized for the teams that you want.[22]

So, I think the story is still not told entirely on where the Internet is going exactly with respect to sports, but there is no question that it is transformational and that sports leagues are all grappling with the best way to deal with it. I think that you are going to see the fan benefit from that as there are going to be more opportunities to follow your favorite team and learn more about it.

That is a brief overview of the impact that technology has. There is a lot more to say about that, but those are the trends that I think are the most currently being discussed in sports leagues and sports teams.

. . . .

MR. KISHNER: . . . . Today I am going to talk about the future of sports television and the emergence of what I term the vertically integrated model, or the regional sports network as it has been called in the press in recent days.[26]

I am going to start off by just giving you a background of what the TV/media rights world looks like today, talk about some of the components that go into it and some of the considerations of forming and organizing a vertically integrated network, and where I see it in the future emerging and in which particular markets.

Television programming of sports events has increased tremendously, almost geometrically, from decade to decade. From 1980 to 1990 television and cable networks went from an average of approximately 4,600 hours of programming to 7,500 hours of sports broadcasting, and from 1990 to 2000 that 7,500 hours increased to over 14,000 hours of sports broadcasts.[27]

The big four broadcasting networks spend over a billion dollars each on sports programming annually. Gross revenues generated by professional and collegiate athletic contests amounted to a $194 billion business in 2001.[28] So clearly there is a tremendous amount of money here, a tremendous amount of value here.

What the regional sports network, with a vertically integrated model, does is it takes one plus one. In other words, combining a sporting event with those broadcasting rights, thereby equaling a greater synergy, greater than one plus one.

The revenue stream from a media contract is one of the primary assets of any sports franchise. It is the means by which a team is able to put product on the field. For example—and I will get to this later—when the Texas Rangers were able to pay $25 million per year for Alex Rodriguez, or $250 million,[29] the reason by which that contract was able to be generated was as a result of Tom Hicks and his creating this regional sports network which was ultimately sold to Fox Sports Net for $500 million,[30] but the point being that this is a tremendous creation of value.

As an aside, while the TV contract is primarily the main generator of revenue for the team, there are other forms of media which also generate revenue, not the least of which is the radio contract. On the TV contract you are talking in the $50-million-plus area on the high side, to—well, for the Expos it was just under a million. But on the radio side you are talking, call it $8, $9, or $10 million a year potentially for the rights.[31]

In forming these vertically integrated models, one of the considerations that you need to take into account are the league rules, because ultimately every league has a different set of rules which you need to navigate through.[32] Ultimately, these deals all need to be blessed by the league and you need to know what the discrepancies are.

Just to cull out one or two of these, there are territorial restrictions. For example, in the National Basketball Association you have the concept of an inner market where each team has by right an ability to broadcast its signal, and you have an external market which you can buy.[33] Actually, by paying to the NBA money, you can broadcast your signal to what is called the outer market.[34]

There are differences in the leagues between a television market and a radio market. Indeed, in Major League Baseball, just to point out one of the anomalies, every TV deal has to have a provision in it which states that if the broadcast signal is put out to in excess of 200,000 households outside of your territory, then you can terminate that contract as a matter of right, if directed by the commissioner.[35] So that is just one of the considerations.

Another consideration is that each league has its own national rights agreement with TV producers, TV companies, and almost always the national rights agreement will preempt the local rights agreement.[36] This is one form, in my opinion, of revenue-sharing. I mean, here you have a league that is taking broadcast opportunity from the individual teams and packaging that. But that is another consideration.

Lastly, one of the major considerations, as Mark had alluded to earlier, is the effect of the Internet on all this. As of today, it still has not been a major issue, but clearly as time evolves, that is something that we are going to need to consider.

The new vertically integrated model can be said to have its basis in other derivative models. What I mean by that is there are definitely vertically integrated media companies today. For example, Cablevision owns the Knicks and the Rangers . . . and there are a couple of other examples.

Actually, you could trace the roots of the vertically integrated model back to CBS, with its purchase of the New York Yankees in the 1960s, although that did not work out too well for CBS at the time. . . .

But in any event, all these models were based on existing media companies trying to find new product to put on the airwaves. The vertically integrated model is different, because here it is ownership of the sports team, either by itself or in alliance with others, creating this new company, if you will, and by doing so creating additional revenue streams as well as creating enhanced value for the company and the franchise—enhanced value, in the sense that for the franchise, because you now have a combined company which, in theory at least, will expand the universe of potential buyers for that product.

Attempts to execute this strategy have met with a fair degree of success. Sometimes it has failed, but most of the models that I have been seeing really have been fairly successful.

As I alluded to earlier, Tom Hicks, the owner of the Dallas Stars and the Texas Rangers, was planning to start a competitive sports network.[42] After doing the initial legwork, he sold the rights for that network for $500 million.[43] Again, he created much more value than he would have had through the traditional means.

Paul Allen, the chairman of Charter Communications, created a regional sports network built around his team, the Portland Trail Blazers.[44] Although that effort ultimately failed, in the end, I believe, he garnered more dollars for his team or for himself than he would have normally.

Also, another good example is the recent sale of the Boston Red Sox, in which an ownership group led by John Henry purchased the Red Sox for $700 million.[45] The reason why that deal was so highly valued was that as part of that deal, the team's stake in the New England Sports Network was included.[46] That $700 million valuation for the sale of the Red Sox shattered the previously high sale of the Cleveland Indians, which was $323 million.[47]

In forming a regional sports network or this vertically integrated model, there are seven major components that everybody needs to consider before you can even begin to undertake the analysis. I just want to hit those before going into what I see as the future of this.

First off, you need year-round programming, or at least marquee programming. That marquee programming is obviously found by the sporting broadcast of the team or teams that you are going to have the rights to. Therefore, if you want year-round programming, you will need to combine baseball and basketball, or baseball and hockey.

Another component is you need filler programming: historical interest stories or human interest stories. You can accomplish this by purchasing a library of rights from others.

Another factor: you need the correct demographics. You need to have the people who can pay and a sufficient population base to support the emergence of the network.

You need the proper economics. . . . That turns out to be based on whether YES should be carried as a basic package product or a premium package product.[48] That translates into the revenue stream that ultimately winds up into the network.

You need to have financing lined up because the start-up costs here are fairly substantial, and to weather the storm through that start-up it is very advisable to have financing in place.

Solid management. You need to have a management team that is able to cut your affiliation agreements in such a way as to know what the market is, what the rights fee should be, etc.

Another very key element in the emergence of these regional sports networks ("RSNs") or the vertically integrated model is that the existing media deal for these teams needs to be expiring or about to expire, because otherwise there are no rights which you can sell.

. . . .

The bottom line on all this is that this model has many uses way beyond just big-market teams. Indeed, I foresee in the not-too-distant future the emergence of specialty sports networks beyond just the major four leagues. For example, NASCAR racing would be ripe for forming a network; championship wrestling; Major League Soccer—all these arenas are ripe for the emergence of this new model.

. . . .

MR. RUSKIN: . . . The two themes that I want to touch upon today are: (1) the special strength and value that sports has, and will continue to have, in the television marketplace; and (2) the extent of migration of sports to various non-broadcast options.

Now, on the one hand. . . sports faces tremendous challenges in the marketplace today. There is certainly a level of pressure on rights fees, on what broadcasters will commit in the first instance to leagues, that I think is greater than it has been probably at any other time over the past decade.

There is certainly among telecasters an increasing desire for low-cost programming. The advertising market is extremely tight, and has been tight for a period of time.

And the market is plagued by, or at least marked by, fragmentation—fragmentation meaning the ever-increasing number of broadcast outlets, of channels—which has the effect of each individual channel being less significant in the marketplace. Now, that trend has been ongoing for many years, but the trend when one looks at it today leads, across all television programming, to ratings for any type of television program that are markedly less than ratings for similar programs five year ago, certainly ten years ago or twenty years ago.

All that said, sports remain special, and they remain special in the marketplace for a number of reasons. The first really goes to the very special nature of sports. What many telecasters are looking for is destination viewing, a common term today. They want programming that viewers will want to make an appointment to see. I think NBC called it "appointment television," the first one to coin it.[56] They want programming that viewers are going to see as somehow special, necessary, and that they will actually at ten o'clock want to be in front of their television set.

Mark mentioned before that sports is viewed as either TiVo-proof or more TiVo-proof than most other forms of content. That is true. He explained one of those reasons, which is the ability to continue to provide advertiser or sponsor message during the content of the sport, be it on ice, be it through showing signage, be it through other forms that he described.[57]

The other reason that it is TiVo-proof, or somewhat TiVo-proof, is that people care about seeing the event live. One of the joys of sports is that you do not know what the outcome is going to be and you want to watch it when you still do not know what the outcome is going to be. . . But nevertheless, and for the joys of ESPN Classic,[58] the fact is sports has that. Very little else does.

I would have said nothing else does. But, interestingly, I think that one of the things that now does is reality television. On the one hand, it is the telecaster's dream because it is low-cost programming. . . .

But it also has the element that people want to see it live. You know, when they're in the office at the water fountain the next day. . .

And so reality television has some of those elements. In fact, as you can see, it has been, and is continuing to be, dominant in the television landscape, and certainly in the over-the-air broadcast landscape.[60] That said, sports is still the dominant flow of content that has that special quality and that allows it to be of great interest to telecasters.

Sports also has a different element, and I think it is an element that is sort of interesting as we face a time of possible war and other things that we face in our lives. Sports creates, probably as much as anything, the ability for a shared common experience. The fact is that sports allows us to connect with people whom we do not otherwise know. I mean, how quickly when one is abroad and meets another American does your conversation somewhere along the way turn to sports as an immediate bond that you know things and your life has been touched in a similar way? I think that shared common experience, for obvious reasons, is always important but becomes ever more important.

It is also why—and I will come to this in a moment—certain big events will always remain on broadcast network, events like the Super Bowl, because those events have an ability to reach a number of people that few things do. That experience remains important, I think, as part of, the American psyche if you will.

So for all those reasons sports have a lot of very special qualities.

You can look at how important sports is, how important it is to television, through many prisms. Looking at ESPN and its growth is extremely telling.[61] As a few people have mentioned, there is a great proliferation of various networks on cable television today. But if you were to ask a question to a cable operator: "You only get one, you only get to pick one network; what's the most important network that you must have?" The answer invariably is ESPN. Not surprisingly, this is why ESPN is able to charge more per subscriber than any other national or cable network.[62] But the fact is it is ESPN that stands tallest among all of the various cable networks.

. . . .

With respect to ratings, while it is true that ratings have moved down across programming, I think it is probably also so that they have gone down less across sports programming than many other forms of programming. I think in the sports world there is a lot of wringing of the hands: "How can it be Major League Baseball used to get a sixteen and now it's getting a four or a five?"[64] You can look at it in a lot of different areas and a lot of different sports. But the fact is "All in the Family" used to get a twenty-seven;[65] today the leading shows are getting approximately half that.[66] It is all the way across television programming that the fragmentation has had its impact.

But sports stays strong, amid many of those decreasing effects. And, if you were to look from 1980 to 1990, it was true that for virtually every sport, there was a significant decrease in its average rating of any of its events, across regular season or across average playoffs, that was market.[67] If you look over the last three or four years, it is much more of an up and down.[68] There has been some flattening out there, and for many of the sports they have been increased on a year-to-year basis. It is really more sport-to-sport and the particular match-ups that they might have over the course of a period of time.

The other thing that makes sports special is technology. Mark was addressing some of the aspects of technology and some of the trends.[69] But what is interesting is the extent to which sports is such a leader in the development of technology as it affects the broader viewing experience.

Again, anyone who watches sports can think among the things that you have seen that have enhanced your viewing experience. . . And we quickly go from being amazed by it to it being an essential part of our viewing.

It was less than ten years ago that Fox created the Fox Box, which in the upper-left-hand corner told you the score and told you how much time was left.[71] It seems like such an essential element of your viewing; it's almost annoying if it isn't there and you tune in and you want the information. Again, a technology developed through sports.

. . . .

You know, think about it. At what other forms of television do you see that level of technology? If you think about sitcoms or dramas, they increase in certain ways, but they do not bring technology to us in those ways to enhance the experience.

I think HDTV will do more of that. It is really a form of distribution. As Mark said, there are real questions as to where the money gets made. Other than that, it will become an essential way of viewing. And for many sports, the promise of HDTV, both because of its clearer picture and also because of the shape that it will bring you, is viewed as a wonderful promise. Hockey, for example, suffers on television because the shape of the rink is different than the shape of your television set. The ability to expand that, to be able to see a greater amount of action, and to be able to see plays forming should be wonderful to the viewing experience. And again, for all those reasons television is special and sports is special on television.

Interactivity is another area. Again, it is difficult to know all the ways in which the Internet will emerge and evolve, but what is certain is that it provides additional opportunities for information exchange, which is a part of sports that brings the fan and the viewer closer to the sport—whether or not people will be watching streaming video in their office, whether or not it is an ability for them to exchange information with people while they are watching something to call the play, try to make decisions, or create their own camera angles in the way that they want to see it. . . .

The other thing I wanted to touch upon is the area of migration. This is a 1994 report by the Federal Communications Commission ("FCC"), a decade ago, commissioned by Congress in 1992, titled "The Inquiry into Sports Programming Migration."[75] Interestingly, as part of the 1992 Cable Act,[76] Congress instructed the FCC to conduct an examination of the carriage of local, national, and regional sports programming by broadcast stations, by cable programmers, and what they described as pay-per-view services, and at that time to analyze the economic causes and the economic and social consequences of migration trends, and to submit legislative or regulatory recommendations.[77]

They defined sports programming migration as "the movement of sports programming from broadcast television to a subscription medium (i.e., one for which viewers pay a fee)."[78] They looked at the period from 1980 through 1994. They concluded at that time, interestingly, that there had not been significant migration of sports programming from broadcast to subscription television. Now, there are a number of things that I find interesting in this.

The first thing that is interesting is the very fact that Congress would commission such a study. It really highlights the uniqueness of sports and how we look at sports in our life.

. . . .

Sports is different in that way. The fact is that with respect to migration, there has been an evolution, not a revolution, but it shows the power of evolution, because the fact is, what was unthinkable not that long ago is now commonplace. The fact is that when one looks at the cable and satellite landscape today, it dominates the sports world. It is really only the NFL that is able to make broadcast television its primary method of distribution.[79] As to each of the other major sports and as to every other sport, cable and satellite is their major mode of distribution, and that means playoff games—something that would have been unthinkable at one point in time.[80] And again, that has happened as cable TV has grown, and it has become really a part of our life in most every way.

The effect of that, I think, has been, on balance, wonderful for the fan, because at the end of the day it has created more opportunity for viewing, it has created the kind of packages that leagues have created, some of which Mark referred to—the satellite packages, or those available on cable through on-demand, and allow super-fans to obtain as many games or obtain every game, if that is what they want. It allows other fans to have all kinds of viewing available to them on cable, and the like.[81]

The ultimate point, the reason that this has happened is that cable creates a dual-income stream, and that dual-income stream—the ability to get money both through advertising and through subscriber bases—is what is attractive and what allows leagues and property owners to ultimately get the value to which they are entitled out of the rights of their product.

So, all that said, the bottom line is sports remains strong, sports remains attractive, and it will continue to exist in a highly competitive world, but sports will continue to be critical to the future of television.

. . . .

MR. VICKERY: . . . .There are two points that I want to address today. . . . One is the whole question of the struggle between vertically integrated cable companies and sports teams for the ownership and the right to exploit the television rights that go with putting on a sports event. The other issue is the future of sports broadcasting in what is called advanced basic, or expanded basic, compared to paying a separate premium price for sports on a tier.[83]

Let me start, first, with the question of the struggle over the right to control. The way in which . . . sports broadcasting has worked in recent years is through vertical integration between the ownership of the teams and the broadcasting of the games to the media. There are really three levels of integration, and he touched on all three: one is the actual ownership of the team that puts on the event; the second is the ownership of the network that programs and packages the sporting events; and then the third level of integration is the distribution, either over-the-air, traditional broadcasting, or through cable distribution, or now through satellite distribution.[84] And I suppose the Internet is yet an additional one, although that has not caught on as much thus far.

The Cablevision model . . . is one in which, at least a number of years ago, Cablevision controlled the distribution to a very large segment of the New York area through its ownership of cable companies. And it integrated into the programming level through Madison Square Garden and Fox Sports New York, in effect, to ensure a supply of programming for its cable distribution.[85] That is particularly important to a cable company, or at least the FCC concluded a number of years ago in its report on the cable industry that sports programming is deemed critical to the success of a cable company in a particular area.[86] Now, that may be a question that is, at least with respect to regional or local sports, up in the air at this juncture, but that is the traditional wisdom.

Cablevision then took it a step further by integrating all the way to the team level, so that by acquiring Madison Square Garden LP, it acquired the Knicks and the Rangers as well as the forum in which they put on the games.[87] So they were integrated at all levels. And for a time, Madison Square Garden Network and Fox Sports New York were the only regional sports networks in the New York area and carried the Yankees under a long-term licensing agreement, the Nets, the Knicks, the Rangers, the Devils, etc.[88] And, in a very true sense, their advertising slogan, "New York is our town," was accurate.[89]

Now, when the long-term rights agreement—I think it was a ten- or twelve-year agreement—between the Yankees and Madison Square Garden came up for renewal, there was a contentious fight and litigation over the continuation of those rights.[90] The licensing agreement, like many sports licensing agreements, had a "right to match" provision in it.[91] What at least the owners of the Yankees recognized was that the middleman—that is, the programming network level—was a new line of business that was potentially quite lucrative. And why should they give it up to somebody else?

So the Yankees and the Nets got together and formed YankeeNets,[92] and they then, in turn, after litigation—there was litigation which resulted in a settlement that allowed the Yankees, in effect, to get back their broadcast rights and then re-market them free of any matching provision.[93] What they did was they ended up joining with other partners to create the YES Network.[94]

YES Network was an independent programming network. It was not affiliated with a cable company or a national media company, which was a new model.[95] But, instead, it was affiliated with the actual teams that were being broadcast. So, in effect, the benefit of the broadcast was now being fully exploited by the owners of the teams rather than by deferring to the cable companies.

It has led to a fight between the cable companies and the owners of the teams because there are some thirty-one regional sports networks across the country,[96] and traditionally they have been controlled by cable companies or other giant media companies, and now the future model seems to be the teams taking over their rights and trying to do the programming themselves.

. . . .

Traditionally, there has been an interdependence between the regionals' programming and the distribution. You can't have a successful regional programming network unless you get to the customers in that region because, in effect, what regional sports programming networks capitalize on is the much greater appetite that local fans have for their teams than a national audience would have. Therefore, there may be twelve major Yankees games broadcast by Major League Baseball over national network television, but there are 150 or 160 games that are broadcast over the local regional sports network to the people in New York who would like to see a lot more games and follow the team much more closely. The traditional model was that the cable company wanted to ensure that it had the control of all those games so that it could guarantee delivery. Now the teams are controlling it, and yet the teams cannot do it without access to the distribution.

. . . .

One of the examples mentioned earlier was Paul Allen's venture out on the West Coast.[105] As I understand it, it did not succeed, and the reason it did not succeed . . . is that they did not have the key piece, that is, the access to the distribution channel, because the cable companies refused to do a deal with them. And so that highlights the power that refusal to carry by the cable company has in determining the success of a regional sports network.

Let me turn to the second point that I wanted to raise, which is an outgrowth of the first, and that is whether the future of sports broadcasting is going to be in broadcast basic or expanded basic, which is what most people pay for when they sign up for either a satellite product or a cable company.[106] In effect, what you do is pay about $40 or $50 a month, and the satellite company or the cable company decides what comes with that price. You typically get CNN,

the History Channel, the network broadcast signals, ESPN, and then. . .you get the local regional sports networks.[107]

As the . . . fight between YES and Cablevision[108] illustrates, Madison Square Garden Network and Fox Sports New York, with some exceptions that I will not get into because it is just too complicated to take up the time right now, are carried in Cablevision's advanced basic offering. Cablevision requires all other cable companies in the area to offer it that way. And that is the way in which regional sports program networks are offered throughout the country.

One of the things that Cablevision is saying—and this again is in the papers—is that YES is too expensive, that subscribers to Cablevision should not be forced to bear the cost of YES if they do not happen to be Yankees fans.[109] Well, what they are saying is a challenge to the entire way in which the cable industry has developed. Everybody who subscribes to cable probably has some channels that they never watch, yet they are still paying for. That is always the problem with bundling. In some sense, it is like a newspaper—you buy the New York Times, you might never read the editorial page, or conversely you might not ever reach the sports page, but you are still paying for it. Expanded basic is essentially the same idea. You've got the Travel Channel, History Channel, cooking channels, sports, news, and you are not asked to pick which ones you want to include in the package.[110]

Now, the idea of picking is what is referred to as "á la carte," and there may be a future in which when you sign up for your cable company, you agree to pay a price, such as $40 a month, and you pick from a Chinese menu of programs, and you get to select ten or fifteen. The problem with that is that it completely redistributes the way in which the revenues and costs would flow, and it is unclear whether a lot of channels would survive, such as the History Channel or a lot of specialties. The sports networks, interestingly enough, would probably be the most vigorous under that model.

But again, the problem in the . . . Cablevision proposal is that trying to do it with just one network isolates it in a way that it would be economically infeasible. And so if the industry is going to move to a model of "á la carte" or "tiering," it has to be done on a broad basis, such as putting all sports, including national sports, on a tier, or putting at least all regional sports on a tier.

. . . .

I will conclude by saying that the outcome of this debate goes well beyond the sports world, but the most obvious effect that it would have in the sports world is if the cable companies prevail and they are able to keep regional sports networks off the air if the price is not what they want to pay, then there is going to be a lot less money for regional sports networks; and if there is a lot less money for regional sports networks, that means a lot less money to pay for the broadcast rights from the local teams. And if there is less money for the broadcast rights, that means there is less money to pay salaries of players.

So, the outcome of the current fight between the cable companies and the teams and the fight between independent regional sports programmers and the cable companies for control will have wide ramifications not only for the immediate companies involved but for ultimately the teams themselves. . . .

Notes

3. *See, e.g.,* J.R. Ball, *Can TFN Find Its Niche?,* GREATER BATON ROUGE BUS. REP., Aug. 5, 2003, at http://www.businessreport.com/pub/21_24/cover/3636-1.html.

4. Digital Television ("DTV") is a type of broadcasting technology by which broadcast television stations and cable providers send their signals out to viewers digitally. *See* Fed. Communications Comm'n [FCC], *Strategic Goals: Media, Digital Television, at* http://www.fcc.gov/dtv/ (last modified Sept. 10, 2003); *Digital Television, What Is Digital Television? Consumer Information Page, at* http://www.digitaltelevision.com/consumer/what.shtml (last visited Feb. 6, 2004).

5. According to the FCC, bandwidth, the range of frequencies over which analog television is broadcast, is scarce. *See* FCC, *Strategic Goals: Spectrum, at* http://www.fcc.gov/spectrum/ (last modified Oct. 6, 2003) ("Because there is a finite amount of spectrum and a growing demand for it, effectively managing the available spectrum is a strategic issue. . . ."). Alternative broadcasting methods, such as digital television, are more efficient and will make the broadcast spectrum available for other uses. *Cf.* KAET-DT, *Glossary of Terms, at* http://www.kaet.asu.edu/dtv/glossary.htm (last visited Feb. 6, 2004) ("Analog television receives one continuous electronic signal. In contrast, DTV works on the same principle as a computer or a digitally recorded compact disk. It uses binary code, a series of ones and zeros, rather than a continuous signal.").

6. NBA TV allows viewers to purchase television packages of live National Basketball Association ("NBA") games on cable, satellite, and digital cable. *See* NBA, *NBA TV, at* http://www.nba.com/video/nbacom_tv.html (last visited Feb. 6, 2004).

7. *See* Ball, *supra* note 3.

8. For the FCC's discussion of the conversion of analog cable systems to digital television, *see* FCC, *FCC Acts to Expedite DTV Transition and Clarify DTV Build-Out Rules, at* http://www.fcc.gov/Bureaus/Mass_Media/News_ Releases/2001/nrmm0114.html (Nov. 8, 2001).

9. Out-of-market packages allow viewers across the country to purchase subscriptions to watch games of a particular sport that take place outside of their local area. *See, e.g.,* DIRECTV Sports, *Subscriptions, at* http://directvsports.com/Subscriptions/ (last visited Feb. 6, 2004).

10. *See id.*

11. *See* Gary Brown, *How HDTV Works,* HowStuffWorks, *at* http://electronics.howstuffworks.com/hdtv.htm (last visited Feb. 6, 2004). High definition is also referred to as "hi-def" or "HD."

12. *See* Gary Merson, *High Definition All the Time: The HDTV Insider Talks With HD Net Founder Mark Cuban,* HDTV INSIDER NEWSLETTER (Jan. 2002), *at* http://hdtvinsider.com/sample.html; *see also Comcast Adds ESPN Programming to Local HDTV Service,* PUGET SOUND BUS. J. (SEATTLE), July 31, 2003, *available at* http://www.bizjournals.com/seattle/stories/2003/07/28/daily40.html (last visited Feb. 6, 2004).

. . . .

16. TiVo is a service that can be programmed to find and digitally record a user's choice of shows. See TiVo, *The TiVo Story, at* http://www.tivo.com/5.1.asp (last visited Feb. 6, 2004).

17. *See id.*

. . . .

20. Motorola is the official wireless communications sponsor of the National Football League ("NFL"). *See* Terry Lefton, *Motorola Renews with NFL for $105M: League Bags a Big One as Sideline Sponsor Returns for 5 Years and Plans to Do Additional Promotions,* STREET & SMITH'S SPORTSBUSINESS J., Nov. 12–18, 2001, at p1.

21. The NASDAQ reached its all-time high on March 10, 2000 when the index closed at 5048.62. *See* K.C. Swanson, *Lessons From the Folly: Opening the March 10, 2000, Time Capsule,* THESTREET .COM (Mar. 8, 2001), *at* http://www.thestreet.com/pf/funds/investing/1335205.html.

22. For an overview of Major League Baseball's subscription services, *see* Major League Baseball, Subscriptions, *at* http://mlb.mlb.com/NASApp/mlb/mlb/subscriptions/index.jsp (last visited Feb. 6, 2004).

. . . .

26. *See, e.g.,* David Barron, *Rockets to Begin Network: Astros to Be Joint Owner If FSN Can't Equal Offer,* HOUSTON CHRON., Mar. 1, 2003, at Sports 1 (discussing the proposed Houston Regional Sports Network), *available at* http://www.chron.com/cs/CDA/ssistory.mpl/sports/bk/bkn/rox/1800212 (last visited Feb. 6, 2004).

27. According to a 1997 poll, cable television provided over 14,000 hours of sports each year, with the four major networks contributing an additional 2,100 hours of televised sports. *See* Soonhwan Lee & Hyosung Chun, *Economic Values of Professional Sport Franchises in the United States,* SPORT J., *at* http://www.thesportjournal.org/2002Journal/Vol5-No3/econimic-values.htm (last visited Feb. 6, 2004).

28. In 2002, the sports industry grossed over $212.53 billion annually. *See* Tim Kroeger, *"Sporting" New Technology, at* http://komar.cs.stthomas.edu/qm425/03s/Kroeger1.htm (last visited Feb. 6, 2004).

29. See USAToday.com, *Baseball, Inside Alex Rodriguez's Record Deal, at* http://www.usatoday.com/sports/baseball/mlbfs41.htm (last updated Dec. 20, 2000).

30. The actual purchase price was $550 million. *See* Barry Horn, *FSN Adds Rangers, Stars over-Air TV Rights,* DALLAS MORNING NEWS, Mar. 23, 2000, at 8B.

31. In 2001, the New York Yankees received over $56 million in combined television and radio contracts, while the Montreal Expos received $536,000. *See* Doug Pappas, *The Numbers (Part Two): Local Media Revenues, at* www.baseballprospectus.com/news/20011212pappas.html (Dec. 12, 2001).

32. For the regional sports networks' blackout regulations of individual sports leagues, *see* Dishnet, *Sports Blackout Information, at* http://www.dishnet.com/images/multisports/blackout.html (last visited Feb. 6, 2004).

33. *See* Staci Kramer, *Sports Nets Get Closer to Home,* CABLEWORLD, Jan. 6, 2003, *available at* http://www.kagan.com/archive/cableworld/2003/01/06/cwd03010607.shtml (last visited Feb. 10, 2004).

34. *Cf.* Comcast SportsNet, *FAQ, at* http://midatlantic.comcastsportsnet.com/faq/faq.asp (last visited Feb. 6, 2004) ("If you live outside of Comcast SportsNet's broadcast territory you may get Comcast SportsNet's Orioles, Wizards and Capitals broadcasts via DirecTV

by ordering the MLB Extra Innings package, the NHL Center Ice package or NBA League Pass or through an outer-market package which your cable system may offer.").

35. *See generally* Jeff Friedman, *The Impact of Major League Baseball's Local Television Contracts,* 10 SPORTS LAW. J. 1, 3–9 (2003).

36. *See, e.g.,* FindLaw, *Corporate Counsel Center, Purchase of NBC TV Advertising Inventory, at* http://contracts.corporate.findlaw.com/ agreements/net2phone/nbc.ad.1999.06.25.html (last visited Feb. 8, 2004).

. . . .

42. *See supra* note 30 and accompanying text.

43. *See id.*

44. Paul Allen, owner of the Portland Trailblazers, launched the Action Sports Cable Network in July 2001. *See* Andrew Seligman, *Commentary: ASCN Folds, and That's a Good Thing for Trail Blazers,* COLUMBIAN (VANCOUVER, WASH.), Nov. 8, 2002, at b1. The network went out of business in the fall of 2002. See *id.*

45. *See Done Deal: Red Sox Sold to Henry Group; Duquette's Days Numbered, SI.com, at* http://www.cnnsi.com/baseball/ news/2002/02/27/redsox_sold_ ap/ (Feb. 27, 2002). The reported value of the deal was $660 million. *See id.*

46. *See id.*

47. *See id.*

48. *See* Len Maniace, *YES-Cablevision Dispute Settled,* JOURNAL NEWS (WHITE PLAINS, N.Y.), Mar. 13, 2003, *available at* http://www .thejournalnews.com/print_newsroom/031303/a01p13yes.html (last visited Feb. 10, 2004).

. . . .

56. *See* NBC Cable Networks, *NBC Olympics & Clear Channel Advantage in Joint Marketing Alliance, at* http://www.nbccableinfo.com/ insidenbccable/networks/Olympics/resources/inthenews/081303.htm (last visited Feb. 8, 2004).

57. *See supra* note 20 and accompanying text.

58. ESPN Classic, which launched in May 1995, "is a 24-hour, all-sports network featuring the greatest games, stories, heroes and memories in the history of sports." *See* ESPN ABC Sports, *Customer Marketing and Sales, at* http://www.espnabcsportscms .com/adsales/portfolio/index.jsp?content=general_portfolio _expanded.html#classic (last visited Feb. 8, 2004).

. . . .

60. *See* Nadine Sack, *Reality Programs Dominate TV, Red & Black,* Feb. 28, 2003, *available at* http:// www.redandblack.com/vnews/ display.v/ART/2003/02/28/3e5f8e32bc-590?in_ archive =1 (last visited Feb. 10, 2004).

61. ESPN/ABC Sports currently operates several media outlets, including ESPN, ESPN2, ESPN Classic, ESPN Radio, ESPN News, and ESPN.com. *See* ESPN ABC Sports, Customer Marketing and Sales, *The ESPN ABC Sports Media Mix, at* http://www .espnabcsportscms.com/adsales/portfolio/index.jsp?content =portfolio.jsp?category=PORTFOLIO (last visited Feb. 10, 2004).

62. *See* Jon Lafayette, *ESPN Sweetens Bitter Pill of Next Rate Hike: Execs Say Extreme Sports SVOD-broadcast Service Adds Value,* CABLEWORLD, Apr. 29, 2002 (noting that ESPN is the most expensive national basic cable service at $2 per subscriber), *available at* http://www.kagan.com/archive/cableworld/2002/04/29/cwd141722 .shtml (last visited Feb. 10, 2004).

. . . .

64. *See generally* Charles P. Pierce, *The Decline (and Fall) of Baseball,* BOSTON GLOBE MAG., June 23, 2002, at 12 (discussing the problems facing baseball, including its declining popularity).

65. Nielsen Media Research bases its ratings on its "National People Meter Sample." According to Nielsen's Web site, "[a] single national household ratings point represents 1%, or 1,084,000 households." Nielsen Media Research, Inc., *Top Ten Primetime Broadcast TV Programs, at* http://www.nielsenmedia.com/ratings/broadcast _programs.html (last visited Feb. 8, 2004). "All in the Family" aired on CBS from January 12, 1971, until September 1983. See Tim's TV Showcase, *All in the Family, at* http://timstvshowcase .com/aif.html (last visited Feb. 8, 2004). It was the most popular show of the 1978–1979 season, averaging a 30.5 household rating. *See R.D. Heldenfels, *Stand-Up Comic Gets Different Kind of Show: 'Big Time' Variety Program Will Allow Audience to Discover 'Real' Steve Harvey,* AKRON BEACON J., July 14, 2003.

66. For more information about the weekly Nielsen ratings, *see* Nielsen, *supra* note 65. The ratings information is updated weekly.

67. *See generally* Museum of Broadcast Communications, *Sports and Television, at* http://www.museum.tv/archives/etv/s/htmlS/ sportsandte/sportsandte.htm (last visited Feb. 8, 2004) (discussing the relationship between sports and television as well as the viewership of televised sports over several decades).

68. *See* Richard Sandomir, *The Decline and Fall of Sports Ratings,* N.Y. TIMES, Sept. 10, 2003, at D1 (explaining that a "confluence of factors" in 2003, ranging from the war in Iraq to rain delays, put "a larger-than-usual dent in the viewership" of major sporting events, but that viewership for some sporting events, such as the World Series, are stronger than ever).

69. *See supra* notes 3–22 and accompanying text.

. . . .

71. In 1994, Fox debuted the Fox Box. *See* John Levesque, *A Perilous Evening in the Fox Box,* SEATTLE POST-INTELLIGENCER, July 11, 2001, at D3.

. . . .

75. In the Matter of Implementation of Section 26 of the Cable Television Consumer Prot. & Competition Act of 1992; Inquiry into Sports Programming Migration, 9 FCC Rcd. 3440 (1994) (final report) [hereinafter Inquiry].

76. Cable Television Consumer Prot. and Competition Act of 1992, 47 U.S.C. § 521 (1992).

77. *See id.*

78. Inquiry, *supra* note 75, at 3442.

79. *See* Stefan Fatsis, *What Price Touchdowns?,* WALL ST. J., Jan. 3, 2003, at A7.

80. The NBA has entered into multi-year distribution deals with three cable providers. *See, e.g., NBA Enters Deal with Cable Systems,* SI.com, *at* http://sportsillustrated.cnn.com/2003/basketball/ nba/09/29/bc.bkn.nbatv.distributi.ap/index.xml (Sept. 29, 2003).

81. *See supra* notes 9–10 and accompanying text.

82. *See supra* notes 23–25 and accompanying text.

83. *See, e.g.,* Frank Angst, *A Guide to Keeping Your Eye on Junior,* CHARLESTON GAZETTE (W. VA.), Mar. 26, 2000, at P4D.

84. *See generally* Wikipedia, *Satellite Television, at* http://en.wikipedia
.org/w/wiki.phtml?title=Satellite_television&printable=yes
(last modified Oct. 25, 2003).

85. *See generally* Bob Raissman, *Giving Hockey Cold Shoulder,* DAILY
NEWS (N.Y.), Apr. 11, 2003, at 98.

86. *Cf.* Elizabeth L. Warren-Mikes, Note, *December Madness: The Seventh Circuit's Creation of Dual Use* in Illinois High School Association v. GTE Vantage, 93 Nw. U. L. REV. 1009 (1999) ("Any event,
particularly a sports event, enjoys a symbiotic relationship with the
networks or cable stations that broadcast it. . . . [T]he media depend
upon the advertising as well as the ratings boost that occurs when it
is granted the right to televise a major event. . . .").

87. *See* Cablevision, Corporate Information, *Sports & Entertainment, at*
http://www.cablevision.com/index.jhtml?pageType=entertainment
(last visited Feb. 9, 2004) (describing Cablevision's properties,
which include Madison Square Garden).

88. *See* Brad Rock, *A Utahn Makes It Big in N.Y.,* DESERET NEWS, Sept.
27, 2002 (providing that until recently, Madison Square Garden
Network ("MSG Network") and Fox Sports New York had broadcast
rights to eight of ten major professional sports teams in New York:
the Knicks, Nets, Islanders, Rangers, Devils, Yankees, Mets, and
Liberty).

89. This is the slogan for the MSG Network. *See* MSGNETWORK.COM,
at http://www.msgnetwork.com/index.jsp (last visited Feb. 9, 2004).

90. *See* Nate Allen, *MSG Matches Yankees' IMG TV Deal: Dispute Likely to Continue Over Deal,* MARK'S SPORTSLAW NEWS,
at http://www.sportslawnews.com/archive/Articles%202000/
Yankeesoneyeardeal.htm (Nov. 17, 2000).

91. *See id.*

92. YankeeNets LLC was formed in June 2001, when the Yankees broke
away from the Cablevision Systems Corp.-owned MSG Network.
See R. Thomas Umstead, *Yankees Go Home, Form Own Net,* MULTI-

CHANNEL NEWS, *at* http:// www.multichannel.com/article/CA90559?
display=Search+Results&text=yankees+go+home%2C+form+
own+net (June 25, 2001).

93. *See* Richard Sandomir, *Yanks Pay $30 Million to End Deal with
MSG,* N.Y. TIMES, June 21, 2002, at D2.

94. *See* Rudy Martzke, *Yank' TV Could Bring in $100M,* USA TODAY,
Sept. 11, 2001, *at* 1C.

95. *Cf. id.*

96. *See, e.g., DirecTV Regional Sports Networks, at* http://www
.satisfied-mind.com/directv/regsports.htm (listing DirecTV Regional
Sports Networks) (last visited Feb. 9, 2004).

. . . .

105. *See supra* note 44 and accompanying text; *see also* Gilbert Chan,
Seeking Deal Fit for Kings, SACRAMENTO BEE, Apr. 28, 2003, *available at* http:// www.sacbee.com/content/sports/basketball/kings/
story/6531885p-7482561c.html (last visited Feb. 9, 2004).

106. *See supra* note 83 and accompanying text.

107. For packages and monthly rates, *see* Cablevision, *Products & Services, Pricing and Packages, at* http://www.cablevision.com/index
.jhtml?pageType=ratecard&zCode=10583&serviceType=io (last
visited Feb. 9, 2004).

108. *See generally* Yankees Entm't & Sports Network v. Cablevision Sys.
Corp., 224 F. Supp. 2d 657 (S.D.N.Y. 2002).

109. *See, e.g., YES Sports Channel Files Antitrust Suit Against Cablevision,* WALL ST. J., Apr. 30, 2003, *available at* 2002 WL-WSJ
3393318.

110. *See* Cablevision, *supra* note 107.

. . . .

LEAGUE PERSPECTIVES

THE NFL PROGRAMMING SCHEDULE: A STUDY OF AGENDA-SETTING

John A. Fortunato

In 2006 the National Football League (NFL) began televising its games under the contractual parameters of broadcast agreements with CBS, Fox, NBC, ESPN, and DirecTV. These networks pay the NFL revenue totaling over $3.75 billion per season. (The previous contract from 1998–2005 had generated an average of $2.2 billion annually for the NFL.) In addition to being the NFL's greatest revenue source, television networks are the league's greatest source of exposure. Once a broadcast contract is signed a partnership is formed with the objective of creating a television programming schedule that attracts the most viewers for NFL games. The creation of the television programming schedule includes the strategic placement of games and the selection of the teams playing in those games.

The broadcast agreements for the 2006 season brought about substantial changes in the NFL television programming schedule. *Monday Night Football* moved from ABC to ESPN. NBC became the NFL's primetime, over-the-air network televising games on Sunday night. NBC was also granted a flexible schedule component that allowed the network to broadcast a more meaningful game late in the season. Finally, eight games would be televised on the NFL Network in the final six weeks of the regular season on either Thursday or Saturday night. The result of these programming schedule changes was that there was an increase in audience viewership of NFL games in 2006 for all television network partners.

The agenda-setting model provides a theoretical explanation for the NFL's television programming schedule strategy. Transfer of topic salience from the media to the

public is always at the core of agenda-setting studies. Organizations, such as the NFL, examine the use of the media to help achieve this transfer. Agenda setting research claims that media exposure of a topic increases the public salience of that topic. The theory also suggests that the emphasis of certain attributes of the topic can increase the public salience of those attributes. Therefore agenda-setting researchers claim that the media can influence what topics the audience will think about and how they will think about those topics. For a sports league its attributes are its teams and players. Creating a format that allows the audience to see games with the best teams and the best players and placing these games in a proper location in the programming schedule allows a league to communicate and promote its best attributes. In sports the proper programming schedule can do more than transfer topic salience; in fact, it can help influence the behavior of audience viewing that translates into revenue for the networks and the sports league.

. . . .

THE BUSINESS MODEL OF SPORTS AND TELEVISION

Applying agenda-setting to sports is unique because leagues and television networks sign broadcast rights contracts. In a broadcast rights contract the network agrees to pay a sports league a certain dollar amount for a certain number of years for the rights to televise that league's games (e.g., Fortunato, 2001; Wenner, 1989). While some agenda-setting researchers have examined how media agendas are constructed (e.g., Kiousis, et. al., 2006; Kosicki, 1993; Roberts, 1997), once sports leagues and networks sign a broadcast rights agreement the topic is clearly placed on the media agenda.

The system of selling broadcast rights to television networks was legally established in the Sports Broadcasting Act passed by the United States Congress in September of 1961. The law provides sports leagues with an antitrust exemption that allows them to collectively pool the broadcast rights to all of their teams' games and sell them to the highest bidding television network (e.g., Fortunato, 2001; Scully, 2004). In what Congress termed as "special interest legislation" for this single industry of sports leagues, an economic system that provides the NFL with its greatest revenue source was established.

In addition to being their greatest revenue source, television networks provide sports leagues with their greatest source of exposure (e.g., Fortunato, 2001). Exposure is ascertained through the league's placement in the television programming schedule (day and time that the game is played). The signing of a broadcast contract creates a partnership between a sports league and a television network where both now have a vested interest in increasing the audience watching the games. In addition to game

placement, determining which teams will play in these nationally televised games is very much a part of a league's exposure strategy. The selection of which teams will appear on nationally televised games is the first step in setting up the entire schedule of games for a league (e.g., Fortunato, 2001). The general objective is to provide the audience with games involving the best teams and players at the best placement within the programming schedule. In relating sports to agenda-setting the proper programming schedule can do more than transfer topic salience, and in fact, help influence the behavior of audience viewing that translates into revenue for the networks and the sports league. Offering the games with the best teams and players at the best placement in the programming schedule provides the opportunity for higher audience viewership.

While the league receives its money from the networks, these networks that made the investment in the sports league are selling commercial time during these games to advertisers. Wenner (1989) contends that sports programming is a good proposition because this type of programming offers the desirable, and relatively hard-to-reach, male audience between the ages of 18 and 49. He claims the sports programming demographic tends to be well-educated with considerable disposable income and "advertisers are willing to pay top dollar for this audience because they tend to make purchase decisions about big-ticket items such as automobiles and computers" (p. 14). Bellamy (1998) adds that "with a seemingly endless proliferation of television channels, sport is seen as the programming that can best break through the clutter of channels and advertising and consistently produce a desirable audience for sale to advertisers" (p. 73). Fortunato (2001) summarizes the business relationship between sports leagues, television networks, and advertisers where "the proper exposure and positioning in the program schedule and offering the best product to viewers in the form of teams, players, and matchups are essential to achieve the best television rating, and subsequently to earn the greatest advertising revenue, which would initially benefit the network—and eventually the league—when negotiating its next broadcast rights contract" (p. 73).

TELEVISION PROGRAMMING AND AUDIENCE VIEWERSHIP

Understanding some general perspectives of media use behavior helps to better explain how to possibly achieve the programming schedule objective of high audience viewership. Rubin (1984, 2002) identifies two media-use orientations toward a medium and its content that are based on audience motives, attitudes, and behaviors: (1) ritualized media use and (2) instrumental media use. Ritualized media use focuses on a particular medium, rather than on content. It indicates how people use their leisure time and which medium they attend to when all of these media options are available. In ritualized media use the tendency is to use the medium regardless of the content. Rubin (2002) explains that ritualized use is about participating in a medium more out of habit to consume time as it is the medium that the person enjoys. In ritualized media use people are turning on the television and randomly going through different channels during their leisure time attempting to find a program worthy of taking the time to view, as "watching" is the ritual activity.

Instrumental media use focuses on purposive exposure to specific content and is more intentional and selective on the part of the individual audience member (e.g., Rubin, 1984, 2002; Rubin & Perse, 1987). It is the content available through a particular medium at a particular time that is dictating the media use behavior. In an instrumental media use orientation people are purposely turning on NBC on Sunday night because they want to watch the football game. This instrumental mass media use can be a factor in a person organizing his or her day so as to be done with any other activities and be available to participate in the mass media content at the time it is available.

Television networks attempt to tap into both the ritualized and instrumental media use orientations by aligning certain programming with the leisure time of their desired audience (e.g., Fortunato, 2001). Understanding that television viewing can be based on the audience's leisure time, the NFL and its television partners will try to create a placement programming schedule that capitalizes on the ritualized nature of television viewing. However, NFL personnel and the television networks that invested in this programming would like to believe they have content whose audience participates in instrumental viewing, watching television to specifically view an NFL game. Having the best teams and the best players participating in the game is the attempt to increase instrumental viewing. This strategy of executing both programming schedule components, placement of games (agenda-setting through exposure) and having the best teams and players participating in those games (agenda-setting through selection of attributes) gives the league and the networks the best opportunity for one or both media-use orientations to be exercised by the audience.

SPORTS AUDIENCE

Understanding some general characteristics of the sports audience also contributes to developing the proper television programming schedule. The sports audience has been described as very loyal and watching sports has been found to satisfy emotional needs (e.g., Madrigal, 2000; Mullin, Hardy, & Sutton, 2000; Sutton, McDonald, Milne, & Cimperman, 1997; Tutko, 1989; Underwood, Bond, & Baer, 2001). Funk and James (2001) indicate that the emotional and loyalty characteristics of the sports fan can result in consistent and enduring behaviors, including attendance and watching games on television. With only a small number of

fans having access to tickets to games, watching the NFL on television remains a necessary condition to visually experience the sport live (e.g., Lever & Wheeler, 1993; Wenner, 1989). The emotion and loyalty of the audience combining with the need for television on the part of the audience to experience sports games helps to maintain consistent audience viewership and keep a steady stream of advertisers.

Still, certain game matchups attract larger audiences. Sports fans are obviously most interested in games where their favorite team is playing (e.g., Wann, Schrader, & Wilson, 1999). The opportunity to see a favorite team win has been identified as the number one fan motivation for watching sports (e.g., Gantz, 1981; Wenner & Gantz, 1998; Zillmann, Bryant, & Sapolsky, 1989). Fans also have a strong interest in games where their favorite team is not playing, but the outcome of the game between the two teams that are playing has an impact on their favorite team in the standings and their opportunity to qualify for the playoffs (e.g., Fortunato, 2004; Zillmann et. al., 1989). Therefore, selecting games whose outcome is of interest to many fans is a scheduling objective.

METHOD

The purpose of this paper was to describe the NFL's television programming schedule and demonstrate how the agenda-setting model helps provide a rationale for this strategy. By following the agenda-setting theoretical claims that transfer of topic salience is through both media exposure of the topic and selection of certain topic attributes, an understanding of what the NFL hopes to attain through its television agreements is provided. To demonstrate how the agenda-setting theoretical model can be applied to the NFL programming strategy, the 2006 season is examined. The NFL is selected because it is the league that generates the highest broadcast rights fees and the largest viewing audiences. The 2006 season's programming schedule is important to explain because it is the first year of television agreements for the NFL with CBS, Fox, NBC, ESPN, and DirecTV and these broadcast contract parameters will remain in place until at least 2011 [*Ed. Note: now 2013*].

The results section begins by describing the current financial status of the NFL's television agreements with all of its broadcast partners. It then explains the exposure changes in the programming schedule that were brought about by the broadcast rights agreements that began in 2006. In particular, the most notable change of a flexible schedule given to NBC for games at the end of the regular season will be explained.

Finally, the viewership of NFL games in 2006 for each broadcast partner is provided. The result of audience viewership is important because that is the objective of the programming schedule strategies and is still the most important audience feedback measure for the networks and the NFL (e.g., Fortunato, 2001). Ratings and viewership data are vital because these numbers have such a tremendous impact on the economics of a television network. Webster and Lichty (1991) describe ratings as "a fact of life for virtually everyone connected with the electronic media. They are the tools used by advertisers and broadcasters to buy and sell audiences" (p. 3). Whether correctly or not, network personnel, advertisers, and to a large extent sports leagues treat ratings as the ultimate audience feedback measure. These ratings numbers are so accepted in the practical industry that they are often the basis for content decision-making on the part of a television network and advertisers. The ratings and viewership data presented here are provided by Nielsen Media Research and ascertained through NFL and network press releases.

RESULTS

In April 2005, the NFL announced broadcast rights contracts that would begin in the 2006 season and change the parameters of the league's revenue and exposure on television. Under these agreements the NFL would receive television revenue totaling over $3.75 billion per season paid by CBS, Fox, NBC, ESPN, and DirecTV (*"Street & Smith's,"* 2005). CBS and Fox remained as the Sunday afternoon rights holders paying a total of $3.73 billion and $4.27 billion respectively to broadcast the NFL through 2011. In the agreements each network received the rights to televise two Super Bowls. NBC replaced ABC as the NFL's primetime, over-the-air network in a deal that would pay the league a total of $3.6 billion through 2011. Similar to the agreement with ABC, NBC would also receive the rights to televise two Super Bowls, two playoff games on Wild Card Weekend, and the Thursday night season opening game. The network that televises the Super Bowl in a given year would also televise the Pro Bowl in that year. ESPN remained as the NFL's cable partner agreeing to broadcast *Monday Night Football* at a price totaling $8.8 billion through 2013. ESPN had previously televised NFL games on Sunday night. DirecTV continued to be the NFL's exclusive satellite television partner, paying the league a total of $3.5 billion through 2010. The DirecTV NFL Sunday Ticket allows fans to receive all out-of-market games on Sunday afternoon.

These broadcast agreements brought about significant changes in the NFL television programming schedule. The primetime, over-the-air network game would shift from Monday night, where it had been since ABC began televising *Monday Night Football* in 1970, to Sunday night. In addition to changing the day of the week from Monday to Sunday for the NFL to showcase its premier primetime matchup, the primetime shift featured NBC being awarded a flexible schedule for the final seven weeks of the regular season. There would also be an earlier start time for the primetime games with the Sunday games on NBC beginning at 8:15 ET and the Monday night games on ESPN beginning

at 8:40 ET. Finally, eight games would be televised on the NFL Network in the final six weeks of the regular season on either Thursday or Saturday night.

Determining which teams play in these primetime games is more complicated for the NFL than other sports leagues because the NFL does have multiple network broadcast partners. (The NBA, NHL, and Major League Baseball have only one over-the air network partner, although all leagues do have cable partners.) CBS is the primary rights holder to the American Football Conference (AFC), while Fox is the primary rights holder to the National Football Conference (NFC). CBS initially receives all of the AFC intra-conference matchups as well as the games when an AFC team plays an NFC team in the NFC city (i.e., if the New England Patriots played the Bears in Chicago the game would be televised on CBS). Fox initially receives all of the NFC intra-conference matchups as well as the games when an NFC team plays an AFC team in the AFC city (i.e., if the Chicago Bears played the Patriots in New England the game would be televised on Fox). Games must still be allocated to NBC and ESPN, as well as the eight games being televised on the NFL Network. Obviously all networks would like to have the most attractive games televised on their network so they can generate the larger viewership and advertising revenues. The challenge for the NFL is to satisfy all of these networks and generate the highest overall viewership through all of its programming schedule segments.

The flexible schedule given to NBC was the programming schedule change that had the most impact for the NFL's other broadcast partners. The NFL decided to offer flexible scheduling to its primetime rights holder as an incentive for a network to increase its bid. The need for the flexible schedule stemmed from the difficulty to predict in the spring, when the programming schedule was formulated, which teams would be good in November and December. Whereas Fox or CBS could easily decide which of their many games would be broadcast to the majority of the country, for the primetime network rights holder it did not have this option to switch games and could easily get stuck with ones not featuring the best teams. The most glaring example was that in the 1999, 2000, and 2001 seasons, the Super Bowl champion St. Louis Rams, Baltimore Ravens, and New England Patriots were not part of the *Monday Night Football* schedule. Therefore to remedy that problem, at the next opportunity to negotiate its broadcast contracts the NFL offered a flexible schedule component to its primetime rights holder.

NBC was awarded flexible scheduling for Weeks Ten through Fifteen, and Week Seventeen in 2006. Week Sixteen did not feature flexible scheduling in 2006 because it was a holiday weekend so that game was determined prior to the season. In flexible scheduling a game would simply be moved from Sunday afternoon to Sunday evening. Games that are originally scheduled for Monday, Thursday, or Saturday are not eligible to be shifted. Teams would be notified twelve days in advance of the switch in Weeks Ten through Fifteen and on six days notice prior to Week Seventeen.

The NFL is also allowed to shift games on Sunday afternoon between the 1:00 ET and the 4:00 ET time periods. Moving games on Sunday afternoon is a common practice of the league and the networks, having occurred eight times during the 2005 season. During the seven-week flexible schedule period CBS and Fox are each able to protect a total of five games, but could not protect more than one game in any week. CBS and Fox did, however, have to make the selections of the games they were going to protect in Week Four (e.g., Hiestand, 2006). All games not protected by CBS and Fox were eligible to be shifted to Sunday night. NBC would make a request for a particular game, but the final decision as to which game gets switched is still at the discretion of the NFL. According to Dick Ebersol, NBC Sports chairman, "We're able to say to the league, 'here is a game we would like to have, and here are reasons why we think this is a compelling game.' And then the league's television department and the commissioner make the final decision" (Stewart, 2006a). The NFL described flexible scheduling as a strategy that "will ensure quality matchups on Sunday night in those weeks and give surprise teams a chance to play their way onto primetime" ("Flexible scheduling," 2007).

The flexible schedule could also help preview and promote the teams that figured to appear in the playoffs. In the seven games that were part of the flexible schedule on NBC in 2006, of the fourteen teams playing in those games eleven would qualify for the NFL playoffs. Of the flexible schedule matchups, only the Denver Broncos and the Green Bay Packers did not qualify for the NFL playoffs. The Broncos appeared twice in the NBC schedule during the flexible period, but were eliminated from the playoffs by losing their final regular season game, being upset at home by the San Francisco 49ers. The Green Bay Packers appeared in the Week Seventeen flexible schedule game played on New Year's Eve against the Chicago Bears amid speculation it would be future Hall-of-Fame quarterback Brett Favre's final game. The Bears also had the second-best record in the NFL in 2006.

In comparison to previous seasons only six of the fourteen teams playing in the Monday Night game in the final seven weeks of the 2003 season qualified for the playoffs. In 2004 eight of the fourteen teams playing in the Monday Night game in the final seven weeks would reach the playoffs, and in the 2005 season only four of the fourteen teams playing in the Monday Night game reached the playoffs. Also, from 2003 to 2005 in the final seven games of the regular season, there were only a total of four games out of twenty-one in which the game featured teams that would both qualify for the playoffs in that season. Eight of the twenty-one games over that three-year period had matchups where neither team qualified for the playoffs. With the flexible schedule there were four games in 2006 that featured both teams that would qualify for the playoffs and every game had at least one team that qualified for the 2006 playoffs.

The flexible schedule is another example of the partnership that is formed between the NFL and the television networks. The NFL has consistently demonstrated a willingness to work with its broadcast partners and shift its programming schedule. The implementation of the bye-week, a week where the team does not have a game scheduled, was a way to turn a sixteen-week regular season into a seventeen-week regular season, giving the networks an extra week of valuable NFL programming that no doubt helped increase the rights fees they paid to the NFL. Other programming schedule strategies have also been implemented to increase ratings. To illustrate how a seemingly small shift in the program schedule can impact the ratings, when the NFL pushed back the starting times of divisional and wild-card playoff games in the 2001 and 2002 seasons, the result was a 9% ratings increase (Martzke, 2003). After the meaningless final regular season Monday Night game of the 2002 season between the St. Louis Rams and the San Francisco 49ers produced what was at the time the lowest rated game (8.7) in the history of *Monday Night Football*, the NFL and ABC agreed to not have a *Monday Night Football* game the last week of the season. Instead in 2003 ABC would inherit the opening game of the NFL regular season with a Thursday evening telecast as part of the NFL's "Kickoff Weekend." The season-opening Thursday night game telecast remains a staple in the NFL programming schedule. Again, though, providing one network with a programming asset in the NFL means denying another broadcast partner of televising that game.

AUDIENCE VIEWERSHIP—NFL 2006 SEASON

The result in 2006 for the NFL with its flexible schedule strategy was a 7% increase (1.2 million viewers) in NBC's viewership compared to *Monday Night Football* on ABC in 2005. The average of 17.5 million viewers was the best viewership the NFL had received in primetime since 2000 when ABC averaged 18.5 million viewers. NBC also saw a dramatic increase in comparison to the Sunday night programming it aired in 2005, averaging 73% more viewers in the time period of the football game.

There was certainly concern that the flexible schedule would benefit only NBC, hurting both CBS and Fox by denying them the better games. The ultimate result for the NFL and its broadcast partners, however, was that each network had an increase in viewership in 2006 in comparison to the previous year (see **Table 9**). Dick Ebersol, NBC Sports Chairman, commented, "What is really amazing is that in a backdrop of eroding ratings on broadcast television, that doesn't seem to be happening with the NFL. It is rare when one entity can keep all its television partners happy, but that's what the NFL has done" (e.g., Stewart, 2006b).

Table 9   Audience Viewership by Television Network—NFL 2006

Network	Average Viewers	Increase from 2005
CBS	15.2 million	+1%
Fox	16.6 million	+5%
NBC	17.5 million	+7%*
ESPN	12.3 million	+41%**

*Compared to ABC Monday Night Football in 2005.
**Compared to ESPN Sunday Night Football in 2005.

Sources: NFL, Nielsen Media Research. Previously published in *Journal of Sports Media.* Used with permission.

In 2006 each network televising the NFL had its own audience viewership successes. Fox's national game in the late Sunday afternoon programming schedule segment had an average rating of 13.8, 21.8 million viewers, giving it a larger audience than any primetime show during the autumn of 2006 (e.g., Lemke, 2007). Fox also had the three most watched regular season game programming schedule segments of the year, with two of them coming during the flexible schedule period: the late Sunday afternoon segment in Week Thirteen, with most of the country seeing the Dallas Cowboys play the New York Giants, attracted 27.6 million viewers and the late Sunday afternoon segment in Week Twelve, with most of the country seeing the New England Patriots play the Chicago Bears, attracted 24.2 million viewers. Fox's game on Thanksgiving Day between the Cowboys and the Tampa Bay Buccaneers was the third most watched regular season game of 2006 with 23.8 million viewers. . . The late Sunday afternoon segment featuring the game between the Cowboys and the Giants was the most-watched NFL regular-season game since the 1999 Thanksgiving Day game between the Cowboys and the Miami Dolphins on CBS.

CBS has the rights to the AFC, which features some teams in smaller television markets than the NFC (i.e., Indianapolis, Jacksonville, Kansas City, Nashville, compared to Fox which has Chicago, Philadelphia, San Francisco, Washington D.C., and also the initial rights to televise the very popular Dallas Cowboys). CBS had two of the top ten programming schedule segments. The late Sunday afternoon segment in Week Eight, with most of the country seeing the Indianapolis Colts play the Denver Broncos, was the most watched television program for that week, including all primetime programming. On five other occasions the CBS national game was one of the top five most watched television programs for that particular week.

In televising *Monday Night Football* ESPN had the most-watched series in cable television history in 2006. After the 2006 season, excluding breaking news, ESPN's *Monday Night Football* occupied nine of the top ten spots on the list of cable's biggest household audiences ever, including at the time the most watched program in cable television history being the October 23 game between the Dallas Cowboys and the New York Giants with viewership in 11,807,000 homes. (The game was eclipsed by the Disney Channel premiere of *High School Musical 2* on August 17, 2007, which had 17.2 million viewers [Levin, 2007]). ESPN also led all networks, cable or over-the-air, in the male demographics of 18–34, 18–49, and 25–54 on Monday night, and on four occasions ESPN was the most watched network, cable or over-the-air, in primetime on Monday night in the autumn of 2006. For ESPN the switch from Sunday night to Monday night produced an average rating jump from 5.8 in 2005 to an 8.2 in 2006 with the games averaging 12.3 million viewers, 3.6 million more than the previous year. George Bodenheimer, president of ESPN and ABC Sports, commented, "ESPN's *Monday Night Football* greatly exceeded all expectations. Our commitment to present *MNF* as never before served our fans and lifted every aspect of ESPN's business" ("ESPN Mediazone," 2006).

Finally, the NFL placed games on the NFL Network for the first time, with eight games played on Thursday and Saturday nights over the final six weeks of the season beginning on Thanksgiving evening. The eight games on the NFL Network averaged 4.1 million viewers. At the time the NFL Network was only in 40 million homes, with several cable companies balking at the NFL's asking price of 70 cents per subscriber per month. In November of 2006 the NFL Network was available to all DirecTV and Dish Network subscribers, but provided only by Cox and Comcast cable companies to customers as part of their higher-priced digital sports tiers, while Time Warner and Charter did not carry the NFL Network at all (e.g., Lemke, 2006). The NFL did undertake an advertising effort asking customers to call their cable provider to urge it to make the NFL Network available on its service. By putting games on its own network the NFL simply now has a communication vehicle to promote its own agenda as well as an asset that fans desire, increasing the long-term profitability of the network. The NFL Network has committed to broadcasting games for four years, with Pat Bowlen, owner of the Denver Broncos and chairman of the NFL's broadcast committee, saying, "As far as I'm concerned, it's pretty much going to remain a staple of what we do" (e.g., Maske, 2006). It should be pointed out that games on either the NFL Network or ESPN are still available in the home markets of the two teams playing in the game on an over-the-air channel, a policy the NFL instituted when it started placing games on cable television in 1987. The NFL remains the only league that requires games carried by a cable network to be televised on an over-the-air television station into the home markets of the teams that are playing.

DISCUSSION

It is clear that the changes made by the NFL in the television programming schedule are designed for the league to increase its revenue and exposure. Through its broadcast partners the NFL is trying to create a programming schedule that capitalizes on two vital components: the placement of the games and the selection of the teams and players participating in those games. The programming schedule objective is to attract the most viewers for the games that generate greater advertising revenues for the networks and eventually higher broadcast rights fees paid to the NFL. For the NFL, selecting which teams will appear in the primetime games is difficult because to place a game on one network is to deny another network of that asset. When the NFL awarded NBC its Sunday night television package with a flexible schedule component, it guaranteed the network a quality game in primetime, however, CBS and Fox were each certain to lose some games they would have liked to have on their air. As its greatest revenue source the flexible schedule also reiterates that the needs and desires of the television networks and the interests of the television audience are more important than the fans attending the stadium, with fans being told the change of a game time possibly only twelve days in advance (six days for the final week of the season) and perhaps having to alter travel schedules to still attend the game.

Applying agenda-setting to the NFL's exposure strategy is an example of a theory lending insight into a practical situation. The agenda-setting theoretical model illustrates the importance and provides a theoretical rationale for the NFL's television programming schedule strategy. This strategy of developing both programming schedule components, placement of games (agenda setting through exposure) and having the best teams and players participating in those games (agenda-setting through selection of attributes) gives the league and the networks the best opportunity to transfer the salience of the NFL to the public and produce an agenda-setting effect. In this example of agenda-setting being applied to the NFL, the proper exposure in the programming schedule and showing better teams in these games not only transferred the topic salience, but increased the behavior toward that topic, an increase in watching NFL games on television. The ultimate agenda-setting result for the NFL of these programming schedule changes was that there was an increase in audience viewership in 2006 for all networks televising NFL games.

References

Bellamy, R. V., Jr. (1998). The evolving television sports marketplace. In L.A. Wenner (Ed.), *Mediasport* (pp. 73–87). London: Routledge.

. . . .

ESPN mediazone. (2006, December 6). Retrieved December 11, 2006 from: http://media.espn.com/ESPNTODAY/2006/Dec_06/MNF mostviewed .htm.

Flexible scheduling. (2007). *National Football League*. Retrieved February 11, 2007 from: http://www.nfl.com/schedules/tv/flexible.

Fortunato, J. A. (2001). *The ultimate assist: The relationship and broadcast strategies of the NBA and television networks*. Cresskill, NJ: Hampton Press.

Fortunato, J. A. (2004). The rival concept: An analysis of the 2002 Monday Night Football Season. *Journal of Sport Management, 18*(4), 383–397.

Funk, D., & James, J. (2001). The psychological continuum model: A conceptual framework for understanding an individual's psychological connection to sport. *Sport Management Review, 4*(2), 119–150.

. . . .

Gantz, W. (1981). An exploration of viewing motives and behaviors associated with television sports. *Journal of Broadcasting & Electronic Media, 25*(3), 263–275.

. . . .

Hiestand, M. (2006, October 25). Flex concept looking like sweet deal for NBC. *USA Today*, p. 6C.

. . . .

Kiousis, S., Mitrook, M., Wu, X., & Seltzer, T. (2006). First- and second-level agenda-building and agenda-setting effects: Exploring the linkages among candidate news releases, media coverage, and public opinion during the 2002 Florida Gubernatorial Election. *Journal of Public Relations Research, 18*(3), 265–285.

Kosicki, G. M. (1993). Problems and opportunities in agenda-setting research. *Journal of Communication, 43*(2), 100–127.

. . . .

Lemke, T. (2006, November 18). NFL Network to air games, differences. *Washington Post*, p. C3.

Lever, J., & Wheeler, S. (1993). Mass media and the experience of sport. *Communication Research, 20*(1), 125–143.

Levin, G. (2007, April 22). High marks for 'Musical 2,' *USA Today*, p. 4D.

Madrigal, R. (2000). The influence of social alliances with sports teams on intentions to purchase corporate sponsors' products. *Journal of Advertising, 29*(4), 13–24.

Martzke, R. (2003, January 15). Later starting times help boost NFL's playoff ratings. *USA Today*, p. 2C.

Maske, M. (2006, December 28). So far, owners happy with NFL Network. *Washington Post*, p. E4.

. . . .

Mullin, B. J., Hardy, S., & Sutton, W. A. (2000). *Sport marketing,* 2nd ed. Champaign, IL: Human Kinetics.

. . . .

Roberts, M. (1997). Political advertising's influence on news, the public and their behavior. In M. E. McCombs, D. L. Shaw & D. Weaver (Eds.), *Communication and democracy: Exploring the intellectual frontiers in agenda-setting theory* (pp. 85–96). Mahwah, NJ: Lawrence Erlbaum Associates.

Rubin, A. M. (1984). Ritualized and instrumental television viewing. *Journal of Communication, 34*(3), 67–77.

Rubin, A. M. (2002). The uses-and-gratifications perspective of media effects. In J. Bryant & D. Zillmann (Eds.), *Media effects: Advances in theory and research,* 2nd ed. (pp. 525–548). Mahwah, NJ: Lawrence Erlbaum Associates.

Rubin, A. M., & Perse, E. M. (1987). Audience activity and television news gratifications. *Communication Research, 14*(1), 58–84.

Scully, G. W. (2004). The market structure of sports. In S. R. Rosner & K. L. Shropshire (Eds.), *The business of sports* (pp. 26–33). Sudbury, MA: Jones and Bartlett Publishers.

. . . .

Stewart, L. (2006a, October 25). Bears–Giants moved under flex schedule. *Los Angeles Times*, p. D5.

Stewart, L. (2006b, December 15). NFL scoring big in the ratings. *Los Angeles Times*, p. D12.

Street & Smith's Sports Business Journal (2005, November 7–13). In-depth: Sports media, p. 22.

Sutton, W., McDonald, M., Milne, G., & Cimperman, J. (1997). Creating and fostering fan identification in professional sports. *Sport Marketing Quarterly*, 6(1), 15–22.

. . . .

Tutko, T. A. (1989). Personality change in the American sport scene. In J. H. Goldstein (Ed.), *Sports, games, and play: Social and psychological viewpoints* (pp. 111–127). Hillsdale, NJ: Erlbaum.

Underwood, R., Bond, E., & Baer, R. (2001). Building service brands via social identity: Lessons from the sports marketplace. *Journal of Marketing Theory & Practice*, 1–13.

Wann, D. L., Schrader, M. P., & Wilson, A. M. (1999). Sport fan motivation: Questionnaire validation, comparisons by sport, and relationship to athletic motivation. *Journal of Sport Behavior*, 22(1), 114–139.

. . . .

Webster, J. G., & Lichty, L. W. (1991). *Ratings analysis: Theory and practice*. Hillside, NJ: Erlbaum.

Wenner, L. A. (1989). Media, sports, and society: The research agenda. In L. A. Wenner (Ed.), *Media, sports, and society* (pp. 13–48). Newbury Park: Sage.

Wenner, L. A., & Gantz, W. (1998). Watching sports on television: Audience experience, gender, fanship, and marriage. In L.A. Wenner (Ed.), *Mediasport* (pp. 233–251). London: Routledge.

. . . .

Zillmann, D., Bryant, J., & Sapolsky, B.S. (1989). Enjoyment from sports spectatorship. In J.H. Goldstein (Ed.), *Sports, games, and play: Social and psychological viewpoints* (pp. 241–278). Hillsdale, NJ: Lawrence Erlbaum.

FORECASTING THE IMPORTANCE OF MEDIA TECHNOLOGY IN SPORT: THE CASE OF THE TELEVISED ICE HOCKEY PRODUCT IN CANADA

Norm O'Reilly and Ryan Rahinel

BACKGROUND

The concept of bringing enhanced technology into sport is flush with optimism (Silk et al, 2000). With regard to media technology research, the realisation that sports marketing encompasses the duality of the sports industry (see Mullin et al, 2000; Shank, 2002) is important, as media technologies enable and enhance both the direct exchange of sports products to sports consumers (e.g. watching a game on HDTV) and the indirect marketing of non-sports products through sport (e.g. a beer company's corporate sponsorship of a professional sports franchise enhanced by iTV). Sports management researchers have devoted attention to technology's use in live situations (Siegel, 2000; Moore et al, 1999) and in the indirect marketing of non-sports products through sport (Moore et al, 1999; Mendez, 1999). Yet practitioners are also keen on learning how decisions can be made regarding the implementation of technology in the direct exchange of sport products. This decision is not easy for the following reasons:

1. revenues from new technologies may simply be cannibalizing those from old or existing ones

2. senior management may view media as a secondary concern

3. forecasting consumer adoption is difficult when many overlapping variables must be considered (see Boyd & Mason, 1999)

4. adoption may be required from other stakeholders

5. data on which to base a decision may be difficult to acquire.

This paper demonstrates how qualitative research can be used to aid in media technology selection decisions in sport by examining the case of ice hockey, specifically, the NHL in Canada.

WHY ICE HOCKEY AND THE TELEVISED NHL?

Ice hockey plays an important role in Canada's identity, society, economy and culture (Whitson et al, 2000; Gruneau & Whitson, 1993). It is broadcast by four national networks, its games are among the most watched programmes in Canadian television history (Canadian Broadcasting Corporation, 2002; Hockey Canada, 2004), and its leagues and tournaments (in the professional, junior and international realms) garner widespread public interest.

The NHL is ice hockey's most commercialised media property. It had revenues of $1.996 billion in the 2002–03 season (Levitt, 2004), including a five-year, $600 million television rights contract in the United States with ABC/ESPN that expired after the 2003–04 season (*Street & Smith's Sports Business Journal,* 2005). In Canada, television revenues are lower and from a number of networks (e.g. CTV, Rogers Sportsnet, TSN and CBC). Once content rights to broadcast an event have been purchased, the broadcaster sells advertising to cover the costs of rights. Thus the ability to attract desirable and sizeable audience segments is essential for selling the advertising time around telecasts (Chalip et al, 2000; Shoham & Kahle, 1996). Ratings, measured as a percentage by Nielsen Media Research, are used to assess audience size in Canada and the United States. The higher the ratings, the higher the revenue a broadcaster can earn from the sport (Chalip et al, 2000).

In examining trends in rights fees and ratings, a surprising result emerges. While rights fees have increased, television ratings for all the major professional sports leagues in North America, including the NHL, have declined noticeably over the past decade (Sandomir, 2004).

Over the course of the NHL's recent six-year TV deal with ABC/ESPN (1999–2004), regular-season cable ratings decreased 31% on ESPN and 38% on ESPN2, with network broadcast ratings on ABC also slipping 21% over that period (The Sports Network, 2005). Furthermore, the ratings demonstrate that the National Basketball Association (NBA) and professional basketball have been and are clearly outperforming the NHL and professional ice hockey. In 2002–03 the NBA had ratings of 1.2 (ESPN), 2.6 (ABC) and 6.5 (NBA Finals) as compared to the NHL with 0.46 (ESPN regular season), 1.1 (ABC) and 2.9 (NHL Finals). In all three cases, the NBA drew at least double the viewership of the NHL (Sandomir, 2004). In recent years, this gap has continued to widen (The Sports Network, 2005; Soloman, 2005).

The comparison to the NBA is important for the NHL, as the NBA is often considered its closest competitor—they are of similar size and scope, have similar schedules at the same time of year and have experienced similar growth patterns. Therefore, it could be said that the NHL is underperforming in the televised media.

A nascent issue here is the impact of digital technology. Digitisation enables the combination of computing and broadcasting technologies and has been posited to be well suited to sport (Chalaby & Segell, 1999; Barnard, 1996; Wolfe et al, 1998). For example, horse-racing (Kruse, 2002), basketball (Silver & Sutton, 2000) and Formula One (Dransfeld et al, 1999) have all dabbled in some form of digital web-enabled television, a delivery paradigm that is forecast to be important to sport for years to come (Turner, 1999). Stakeholders in the ice hockey industry also understand the importance of new media, as shown by the Shanahan Summit (2004), where players, coaches, administrators and broadcasters made recommendations for the future of ice hockey, including those related to television. Indeed, careful consideration by any sporting organisation is needed when deciding upon new technologies, as these opportunities are extended with increasingly incalculable risks (Chalaby & Segell, 1999).

OVERVIEW OF KEY MEDIA TECHNOLOGIES

Preliminary consultation with experts (Peddie, 2004; Anselmi, 2004) and the literature revealed five major media technologies with the potential to impact upon televised sport: VOD, PVRs, MMDs, iTV and HDTV.

Video on Demand (VOD)

Ling et al (1999) describe VOD as "a technology through which video material can be ordered and retrieved over the traditional telephone lines from a central server". In essence, the viewer determines the viewing schedule, deciding which programmes ("televised products") should be broadcast at any given time. The benefits of VOD are accrued by broadcasters, who can charge premium fees from advertisers privy to a targeted and distinct market, independent of time constraints.

For televised ice hockey, the impacts of VOD are debatable. First, the marginal targeting implications of VOD are quite small compared to other televised properties, as it is already widely known that the majority of ice hockey viewers are adult males (McDaniel, 2005) and the majority of ice hockey broadcasts are in prime time. Second, and more importantly from a revenue-generation standpoint, VOD customers may disapprove of commercials during programming that they have paid a premium to view during specified timeslots.

Personal Video Recorders (PVRs)

PVRs are an intermediary between the cable signal and the TV that store televised content on hard drives capable of holding anywhere from 10 to 30 hours of programming. One of the features of PVR is the ability for viewers to bypass advertising by "zipping" through the commercial using the fast-forward button (Elphers et al, 2003) or by evading entire commercial sections using an auto-skip feature that automatically records content commercial-free (Williamson, 2001). Poniewozik (1999) cites three additional viewer-centric benefits to PVRs, namely: (i) the ability to choose shows by name rather than channel or time (similar to VOD); (ii) the ability to rewind/replay/pause while recording; and (iii) the absence of a videotape-like storage medium (as compared to traditional VCRs).

Mobile Multimedia Devices (MMDs)

MMDs are a new breed of consumer information and entertainment platforms, which include personal digital assistants (PDAs) and cellular phones. Coined by Apple, PDAs were originally used to support clerical tasks such as note-taking, contact list maintenance and diary-keeping (Daniels, 1994) but they are now evolving into multimedia-oriented devices. Although TV is not widely consumed on PDAs, recent developments in the field may allow for digital TV to be broadcast on these small devices (see Royal Philips Electronics, 2005). Conversely, a more rapid convergence with TV has taken place in the cellular industry. Many common televised products such as news, sports clips and weather forecasts can be broadcast to a customer anywhere. Broadcast partners in this service include ESPN, CNN, Fox Sports, the Weather Channel and NBC. Recently, Bell Canada and Rogers Wireless advertised their mobile video coverage of the 2006 NHL Stanley Cup playoffs and the 2006 FIFA World Cup respectively. Worldwide revenues for FIFA in the latter case were in the tens of millions and distribution spanned 100 countries (Masters, 2006). . . .

Interactive Television (iTV)

The Canadian Radio-Television and Telecommunications Commission (2002b) describes iTV as: "services [that] require two-way communication between the viewer and the distributor or content provider. This two-way communication is composed of a traditional 'downstream' signal from the distributor or content provider and 'upstream' or 'return-path' information from the viewer to the distributor or content provider." Broadcasters are interested in this two-way transaction because it allows for highly personalised interactions and appeals (Gladden et al, 2001; Dransfeld et al, 1999) that might lead to emotional loyalty (Rozanski et al, 1999). To date, there is no real consensus on the benefits of iTV to sport. Bernie Ecclestone, sole owner of the rights to promote Formula One, indicated that he was convinced viewers would pay significant sums of money to be able to call up statistics, choose camera views in real-time and play interactive games (Dransfeld et al, 1999). In contrast, some literature suggests that the upward communication capabilities of iTV are still somewhat lacking, and escaping these limitations still requires interaction with one's computer or mobile phone (Puijk, 2004).

High Definition Television (HDTV)

For the past 40 years, television signals in North America have ascribed to the North American Television Systems Committee (NTSC) standard, which uses analogue signals for production, transmission and display. **Table 10** highlights the technological differences between NTSC and the newer standard of HDTV.

As Table 10 outlines, transmission signals can be scanned either interlaced (i) or progressive (p). Conventional analogue televisions use the interlaced method, which paints every other line in one pass and all other lines in the following pass. Each frame is sent as two fields; one with odd-numbered scanning lines (A) and the other with even-numbered lines (B). In a progressive scanning system, all lines of the frame are scanned sequentially and sent as a single frame, all of which is completed in the same time that interlaced scanning requires to send only one field (A or B). HDTV allows for both methods, while NTSC only allows for interlaced scanning. In addition, for each pixel in a

conventional television, HDTV has 4.5, resulting in superior picture clarity, notable especially in televised products with small objects or subjects apt to blurriness. HDTV is also endowed with Dolby Digital surround-sound to provide vibrant and realistic acoustics that account for the foreground and background in addition to left and right partitions.

Table 11 summarises the five technologies reviewed.

DIFFUSION OF INNOVATION

In general, an organisation's decision to adopt a media technology relies not only on the functional characteristics of that technology but also on target consumers' current and forecast purchases of related products. Functional superiority and consumer adoption are usually correlated, but not always. From a consumer perspective, the process of innovation adoption is asymmetric (Rogers, 1995). Different consumers will purchase new products at different times relative to the product's initial release into the market and consistent with their personal frame of reference (Kirton, 1976; Goldsmith & Hofacker, 1991; Rogers, 1995). A foundational model to explain such phenomena is offered by Bass (1969). In this model, cumulative adoption is plotted against time, where adoption is explained partially by internal influence (word of mouth) and external influence (mass media communication). The result is a logistic function that profiles diffusion as beginning slowly and growing at an increasing rate, followed by increased growth at a decreasing rate, and then finally by a peak and then recession (Lekvall & Wahlbin, 1973; Bass, 1969). In empirical demonstrations (including black and white television sets), the rigour of the Bass (1969) model has been established and is used later in this case to forecast consumer adoption.

OBJECTIVE

The objective of this case study is to demonstrate the importance of forecasting media technologies to managers and marketers in sport and, in turn, to provide them with direction in their media technology decisions.

. . . .

Table 10   NTSC and HDTV Specifications for Broadcast

	Transmission	Lines	Frames per Second	Aspect Ratio	Audio
NTSC	Analog	480 visible lines, 525 total– interlaced only	30 frames per second	4:3	2 channels (left/right) analogue
HDTV	Digital	1080—interlaced or progressive, 720– progressive	24, 30, or 60 frames per second	16:9	Dolby Digital 5.1 (5 channels plus subwoofer)

Source: International Journal of Sports Marketing and Sponsorship. Used with permission.

Table 11   Comparison of Five Media Technologies

Media Technology	Key Viewing Characteristics	Potential Impact on Televised Sports Products
Video on Demand (VOD)	Viewing convenience (time)	Targeted advertising, relaxed competition for timeslots, pay-per-view payment model
Personal Video Recorders (PVRs)	Viewing convenience (time, advertising bypass, replay)	Advertisement disputes, relaxed competition for timeslots
High Definition Television (HDTV)	Sharper image, wider screen, built-in surround sound	Increased sports visibility with higher resolution, less panning—easier to follow action, product enhancing—sharper image/better sound
Mobile Multimedia Devices (MMDs)	Viewing convenience (geography), small size, motion quality	Highlights and box scores available on demand, additional decreased sharpness and content rights revenues
Interactive Television (ITV)	Viewer participation, viewing customisation	Player statistics available on demand during game, personalized interactions, customized camera angles

Source: International Journal of Sports Marketing and Sponsorship. Used with permission.

RESULTS

'Hockey Night in Canada': Review of Televised Hockey Diffusion in Canada

During February 2004, 187 NHL games were played (approximately 6.45 games per day); 65 were broadcast nationally and 205 regionally. Interestingly, only 43% of the nationally broadcast games involved at least one Canadian-based NHL team (n = 26 games). Of the 187 games, 150 were broadcast on major networks. . . .

[A]s a percentage of total broadcasts, CBC broadcasts the most games involving Canadian teams (100% of its total broadcasts). Furthermore, . . . 32% of the major broadcasts (including national and regional broadcasts) involved Canadian teams. This suggests that it may be profitable for major networks to engage in the broadcasting of non-regional teams as demand may transcend regional barriers.

'Flooding the Ice': The Ice Hockey Environment and Media Technologies

Underlying the drive for technology examination in sport is the immense demand for the ice hockey product in Canada. Although Anselmi (2005) disagreed with hockey being the most consumed product in Canada by noting "there are probably 20 million cans of Coke [consumed] every day", both Peddie (2005) and Hendren (2005) focused on the importance of ice hockey consumption, referring to the ice hockey product as the "undisputed emotional leader" and "part of the Canadian fabrique". One can infer that in assessing the impacts of technology, both unit consumption and the significance of each unit consumed should be taken into account (especially when drawing comparisons between asymmetric product classes).

An early emergent theme in the interview sessions was the reciprocal relationship between media technology and professional ice hockey. That is, ice hockey viewership is a driving force behind media technology adoption in general (Peddie, 2005; Anselmi, 2005; Hendren, 2005; Shannon, 2005) and media technologies affect the way ice hockey can be, and is, consumed (Peddie, 2005; Anselmi, 2005; Hendren, 2005; McEwen, 2005; Shannon, 2005). Further to this point, each of the sports management experts commented specifically on this latter relationship with reference to television, suggesting a 'first to mind' association between media technology and the television medium. For example, Anselmi (2005) describes the relationship between ice hockey and television as enabling the distribution of the ice hockey product "outside the shell" of the arena, which he in turn related to the ability for growth demanded by shareholders.

Peddie (2005) supported this by noting: "Just the numbers will speak to that. We'll get 19,000 to 20,000 [at the arena] sold out every night and at home we're getting 350,000 locally and 1,300,000 plus [nationally] going to three million for the Stanley Cup. So you just touch more people [with TV]."

Hendren (2005) alluded to speciality channels and specifically to the current near-saturation status of sport channels. If this holds, then further addition, and therefore, fragmentation, of sports channels will yield only minimal returns, necessitating other means if sport organisations are seeking to grow through technology or its applications.

An important note is that in all of the general questions posed regarding media technology, sports management experts alluded only once to a non-television technology; ironically this was the website for Canada's subscription sports channel (TSN—www.tsn.ca). This lends support to the selection of the five media technologies in question, as they are concerned with the visual aspects of ice hockey delivery versus the primarily audio and informational mediums such as satellite radio and the World Wide Web. In selecting one of the five media technologies, experts were unanimous in their assertions that HDTV would be the most influential (Peddie, 2005; Anselmi, 2005; Hendren, 2005; McEwen,

2005; Shannon, 2005; Hearty, 2005). Here, the experts specifically noted that while economic factors limited the initial adoption of HDTV, production and viewer-centric factors are becoming paramount in its rapidly increasing market adoption.

'Cycling the Puck': Market Forces and HDTV Adoption

The unanimity among experts was somewhat perplexing given that HDTV technology had been around for quite some time and that its adoption had been sluggish. When pressed further on their position, technology experts attributed this to the fact that the Canadian broadcast community continues to lag behind the United States (Hearty, 2005; McEwen, 2005) since, in the early days of HDTV, the Canadian Radio and Telecommunications Commission decided to allow market forces to determine when broadcasters should commence delivery of HDTV signals in Canada (Canadian Radio-Television and Telecommunications Commission, 2002a; Hearty, 2005; McEwen, 2005). By contrast, the Federal Communications Commission in the United States set a mandate that all U.S. broadcasters must use digital feeds by 2006, and subsequently, all televisions on the U.S. market must be capable of receiving these feeds by 2007 (Federal Communications Commission, 2002; Hearty, 2005; McEwen, 2005).

The impact of this decision on the HDTV landscape was a Canadian HDTV content void, as Hearty (2005) notes: "From an equipment perspective there is a twenty per cent increase in costs if using HD . . . the costs of talent are the same. HD will cost more for bandwidth so there is an incremental cost of carriage. Depending on quality standards of SD, the HD could be in the order of three to six times the cost."

Without forced transition, Canadian content producers were reluctant to invest in the extra equipment, talent and bandwidth required for HDTV. This resulted in a Canadian content void such that the switch to HDTV will necessitate the importing of content from the United States or a radical shift towards producing Canadian HDTV content (Hearty, 2005).

From a demand perspective, Shannon (2005) noted the following with regards to the slow consumer adoption of HDTV: ". . . the viewer is not necessarily akin to change as much as we think. They are much more conservative in what they like than the people that create the entertainment . . . I'm not changing until I get tons of programming and I know the price is reasonable and won't take my family vacation away".

Indeed, Shannon asserts that the historic adoption of HDTV was equally hindered by the high initial price-point for related purchases (i.e. HDTV feed and HD-ready television). Combined with a long purchase cycle (Hendren, 2005), viewers chose to ride out high prices from HDTV equipment manufacturers and service providers that may perhaps have been enacted to cover the increase in production costs noted by Hearty (2005) and to tap into the lack of price sensitivity among innovative customers.

In summary, the technology experts reveal that a clearly superior core technology was jockeyed out of its market potential due to the circular requisites of broadcasters, producers and consumers (Shannon, 2005; Hearty, 2005; McEwen, 2005). On the one hand, relatively little content was being produced because of the lack of HDTV feeds and HDTVs purchased, while on the other hand, consumers were waiting for HDTV content prior to purchasing. Coupled with other extraneous factors such as a long purchase cycle and high costs of production, consumers were impervious to HDTV despite its clear dominance as a media technology. Thus the experts maintain their position that HDTV will be the most influential media technology for the ice hockey product.

They provided further support for this position by indicating that current markets are now shifting. We sought to explore this further since we know that current adoption of HDTV in Canada is approximately 1 million households (McKay, 2005). In the absence of readily available data for future adoption in Canada, we can adopt comparable data and forecasts from the US market which reveal dramatic HDTV sales increases in 2004, 2005 and 2006 (Yankee Group, 2004; Consumers Electronics Association, 2004; TWICE, 1999). From this data, a Bass model forecast was carried out, which determined that the Canadian market would peak sometime in 2007 at anywhere between 3 million and 5 million units. The experts generally supported this forecast, with only Hendren (2005) noting that it could be "a little longer". Also, Peddie (2005) underlined the importance of the impact of dropping prices.

'Power-Play': Production-Centric and Viewer-Centric Advantages of HDTV in Ice Hockey

Ice hockey coverage is distinct from other sports for a variety of reasons, many of which broadcasters have struggled with, as Shannon (2005) describes:

> *"Of the big four [North American professional sports], you could create a graph of the live experience versus TV experience. The biggest gap in the ratio is hockey, as we don't do as good a job with the sound of the game as we should [and] we do a terrible job with the speed of the game . . . and that is where we need to improve our focus—on telling the stories of the game. NBA does the best and there is no coincidence that basketball has the smallest playing surface. Hockey is the only sport with a physical barrier between cameras and the game . . . NBA puts camera positions ahead of seats, NHL does not."*

Unprompted, Shannon (2005) confirms the appropriateness of our comparison between the NHL and NBA, duly noting that the NBA is clearly outperforming the NHL because of the NBA focus on "telling the stories of the game".

Shannon (2005) further asserts two shortcomings of current NHL coverage in order of increasing deviation from the live experience: sound and speed; both were supported by other experts as areas that will benefit considerably from HDTV (Hearty, 2005; Anselmi, 2005; Peddie, 2005; McEwen, 2005). Specific to the issue of sound, HDTV surround-sound is able to provide viewers with a "true auditory experience of sitting in the stands with commentary and game sounds in the fore and arena clamor in the background" (McEwen, 2005). Although the issue of speed is likely to go unnoticed by avid fans and viewers (Peddie, 2005), it does play an important role in attracting new viewers. In this regard, Anselmi (2005) noted that speed was the primary complaint communicated by novice fans in non-hockey intensive markets: ". . . we don't necessarily understand the game, we can't really anticipate where the play is going to go next, we have trouble seeing the puck". While the increased clarity of HDTV can partially remedy this through the decreased blurring of images (Mc-Ewen, 2005; Hearty, 2005), the wide aspect ratio allows for the reduction of several filming techniques that have made it difficult to follow televised ice hockey, as Hearty (2005) described: "Think about production values with sports for SDTV. SDTV is low resolution; you have to get in close—use long lenses and zoom in. Recognise it moves very fast in cases, so you are challenged, the more you move in the smaller the field you can capture. Cut, cut, cut or pan and zoom. Both techniques are used due to lack of resolution. . . . With HD you can pull back because of additional resolution, you don't have to move the camera as much and don't have to cut as much."

In short, experts indicate that HDTV allows for decreased camera movement and switching commonly found in current NHL coverage, enabling the viewer to follow the puck in the same field of view more than in SDTV. Additionally, it allows viewers to see up-ice and follow players without the puck as plays materialise (Anselmi, 2005). Collectively, these improvements will allow the novice fan to follow the game more competently and the experienced fan to enjoy it more comfortably (Peddie, 2005; Anselmi, 2005).

'Know Your Opponent': HDTV against the Competition

In addressing HDTV in the context of the alternative media technologies, some experts commented on the projected behaviour of ice hockey viewers. In referring to Table 11, one might classify the five media technologies into two groups—those that allow for convenience (PVRs, VOD, MMDs) and those that directly affect the core viewing experience (iTV, HDTV). Experts noted the latter were more relevant to this analysis of the televised hockey product (Hendren, 2005; Anselmi, 2005). We agreed, as the legal aspects of PVRs (see Paramount Pictures Corporation vs. ReplayTV, Inc. & SonicBlue, Inc., 2001; Anselmi, 2005), the difficulties of a pay-per-view model as implicated by VOD and the degraded viewing quality of MMDs all

pose barriers to adoption in the sport industry. Of the two remaining technologies, HDTV is an improvement (i.e. sound, aspect ratio, resolution) of a previously adopted viewing technology—NTSC, whereas iTV is essentially a convergence between television and the internet, which is not currently adopted in television viewing behaviours. Anselmi (2005) describes this divide:

"Over the last several years you've heard a lot about 'interactive'—you know, it's one of those buzzwords of the 90s that you get sick of. And I'm still not entirely convinced that people want to do that—generally . . . because I think people who watch TV are still kind of passive consumers. I mean, do you want to sit there and [interact] while watching a game? I don't want to. If I really want the stats . . . I can go to leafs.com and figure out anything I want. It's all there you know so do you really need to do that as part of the broadcast?"

This finding is consistent with previous diffusion studies, which found higher diffusion rates among technologies that were functionally similar to previously adopted technologies (e.g. Ettema, 1984) and, more specifically, projected sports as a driver of HDTV diffusion (e.g. Dupagne, 1999).

CONCLUSION

This case study demonstrates the importance of adopting expert consultation and forecasting techniques to assessing future impacts of media technologies on sport. Both practitioners and researchers must forecast and be cognisant of media technologies and related happenings in the marketplace. Importantly, this case reveals a six-stage procedure for this:

1. expert identification of potentially important technologies

2. background research and expert consultation to narrow the consideration set to the key technology (or two)

3. use of industry data to forecast the growth of that technology

4. expert understanding of that technology vis-a-vis market forces

5. expert identification of the advantages of that technology to the sport or interest, both for production and consumption

6. expert consultation to ensure that these advantages are sustainable through comparison to other competing technologies.

HDTV is identified as the most influential future media technology for the televised hockey product in Canada. This finding provides important direction to practitioners involved in ice hockey. Pertinent information for the future of ice hockey is also hypothesised for all five media technologies, with particular emphasis on HDTV. Practitioners need to understand all five technologies and support and plan for the adoption and diffusion of HDTV as a common technology in the mass market, as both the literature and the experts believe that all five are potentially impactful and that HDTV will provide greater benefit to the televised hockey product over other televised products. This is an important contribution as it suggests HDTV as a potential source of competitive advantage. In this regard, practitioners must not overlook two other findings: the potential impact of the certain arrival of iTV and HDTV convergence and our forecast that HDTV market adoption will pass the 25% benchmark in late 2007, at which point more than a quarter of all Canadian televisions will be HDTV. The latter is especially pressing as it provides a managerial deadline for adoption after which competitive advantage through adoption might dwindle.

References

Anselmi, T. (2004) Personal Communication, Toronto, Canada, 8 November.

Anselmi, T. (2005) Personal Communications, Toronto, Canada, 3 January.

Barnard, P. (1996) Danger of a shotgun marriage, *The Times,* 12 June, 1–3.

Bass, F. M. (1969) A new product growth for model consumer durables, *Management Science 15* (5), 215–227.

Boyd, T. C. & Mason, C. H. (1999) The link between effectiveness of 'extrabrand' attributes and the adoption of innovations, *Journal of the Academy of Marketing Science 27,* 306–319.

Canadian Broadcasting Corporation (2002) Olympic Hockey Ratings. Retrieved 10 April from: www.cbc.ca.

Canadian Cable Television Association (2001) Re: public notice CRTC 2001-62, call for comments on a proposed policy to oversee the transition from analogue to digital over-the-air television broadcasting. Retrieved 3 July from: www.ccta.com.

Canadian Radio-Television and Telecommunications Commission (2002) Broadcasting Public Notice CRTC2002-31. Retrieved 3 July 2005 from: http://www.crtc.gc.ca.

Canadian Radio-Television and Telecommunications Commission (2002b) Report on Interactive Television Services. Retrieved 30 March from: http://www.crtc.gc.ca.

Chalaby, J. & Segell, G. (1999) The broadcasting media in the age of risk, *New Media and Society 1* (3), 351–368.

Chalip, L. & Leyns, A. (2002) Local business leveraging of a sport event: managing an event for economic benefit, *Journal of Sport Management 16* (2), 132–158.

Chalip, L., Green, B. C. & Vander Velden, L. (2000) The effects of polysemic structures on Olympic viewing, *International Journal of Sports Marketing & Sponsorship 2* (1), 39–57.

. . . .

Consumers Electronics Association (2004) Digital cable ready HDTV sales to hit 1 million, *TWICE 19* (13), 16.

Daniels, S. (1994) Personal digital assistants, *Work Study 43* (2), 22–23.

Dransfeld, H., Jacobs, G. & Dowsland, W. (1999) Interactive TV and Formula One: a strategic issue for engine suppliers, *European Business Review 99* (5), 292–299.

Dupagne, M. (1999) Exploring the characteristics of potential High Definition television adopters, *Journal of Media Economics 12* (1), 35–50.

. . . .

Elphers, J. L. C. M., Wedel, M. & Pieters, R. G. M. (2003) Why do consumers stop viewing television commercials? Two experiments on the influence of moment-to-moment entertainment and information value, *Journal of Marketing Research 40* (4), 437–453.

Ettema, J. S. (1984) Three phases in the creation of information inequities: an empirical assessment of a prototype videotext system, *Journal of Broadcasting 28* (4), 383–395.

Federal Communications Commission (2002) Review of the Commission's rules and policies affecting the conversion to digital television. Retrieved 3 July 2005 from: http://www.fcc.gov/.

Gladden, J., Irwin, R. & Sutton, W. (2001) Managing North American major professional sport teams in the new millennium: a focus on building brand equity, *Journal of Sport Management 15* (4), 297–317.

Goldsmith, R. E. & Hofacker, C. F. (1991) Measuring customer innovativeness, *Journal of the Academy of Marketing Science 19* (3), 209–222.

Gruneau, R. & Whitson, D. (1993) *Hockey night in Canada: sport, identities, and cultural politics.* Toronto: Garamond Press.

Hearty, P. (2005) Personal Communication, Toronto, Canada, 26 January.

Hendren, G. (2005) Personal Communication, Toronto, Canada, 13 January.

Hockey Canada (2004) TV Ratings for Hockey Canada events in Dec/Jan, press release, 7 January.

. . . .

Kirton, M. (1976) Adaptors and innovators: a description and measure, *Journal of Applied Psychology 61* (5), 622–629.

Kruse, H. (2002) Narrowcast technology, interactivity, and the economic relations of space: the case of horse race simulcasting, *New Media and Society 4* (3), 385–404.

. . . .

Lekvall, P. & Wahlbin, C. (1973) A study of some assumptions underlying innovation diffusion functions, *Swedish Journal of Economics 75,* 362–377.

Levitt, A. (2004) Independent review of the combined financial results of the National Hockey League 2002–2003 season, report commissioned by the National Hockey League under the retention of the NHL legal counsel, published 5 February.

Ling, R., Nilsen, R. & Granhuag, S. (1999) The domestication of video on demand: folk understanding of a new technology, *New Media and Society 1* (1), 83–100.

Masters, C. (2006) World cup kicking off with mobile video content. Retrieved 2 July 2006 from: http://www.hollywoodreporter.com/thr/international/article_display.jsp?vnu_content_id=1002613791.

McDaniel, S. R. (2005) Reconsidering the relationship between sensation seeking and audience preferences for viewing televised sports, *Journal of Sport Management 17* (1), 13–36.

McEwen, M. (2005) Personal Communication, Toronto, Canada, 2 August.

McKay, J. (2005) Canada lagging US in HDTV, Canadian Press, 7 March.

Mendez, H. Y. (1999) Virtual Signage: The pitfalls of 'Now you see it, now you don't', *Sports Marketing Quarterly 8* (4), 15–21.

Moore, J. N., Pickett, G. M. & Grove, S. J. (1999) The impact of a video screen and rotational signage systems on satisfaction and advertising recognition, *Journal of Services Marketing 13* (6), 453–468.

Mullin, B. J., Hardy, S. & Sutton, W.A. (2000) Sports marketing. Champaign: Human Kinetics Publishers.

Paramount Pictures Corporation vs. Replay TV, Inc. & SonicBlue, Inc. (2001) United States District Court—Central District of California. Retrieved July 2, 2005 from: http://www.eff.org/IP/Video/Paramount_v_ReplayTV/20011031_complaint.html.

Peddie, R. (2004) Personal Communication, Toronto, Canada, 8 November.

Peddie, R. (2005) Personal Communication, Toronto, Canada, 3 January.

Puijk, R. (2004) Television sport on the web: the case of Norwegian public service television, Media, Culture & Society 26 (6), 883–892.

Poniewozik, J. (1999) Here come PVRs, *Time Canada, 154* (13), 50–52.

Rogers, E. M. (1995) *Diffusion of innovations* (4th ed.). New York: The Free Press.

Royal Philips Electronics (2005) New Philips technology allows watching digital TV on small portable devices, press release. Retrieved 2 July from: www.philips.com/newscenter.

Rozanski, H. D., Baum, A. G. & Wolfsen, B. T. (1999) Brand zealots: realizing the full value of emotional brand loyalty, *Strategy-Business* (Booz Allen Hamilton) 17 (Fourth Quarter).

Sandomir, R. (2004) TV SPORTS; Ratings and Labor Woes Cloud NHL's TV Talks, *The New York Times,* 24 February, D5.

Shanahan Summit (2004) Shanahan Summit Recommendations, press release, 8 December.

Shank, M. D. (2002) *Sports marketing: a strategic perspective.* Upper Saddle River: Prentice Hall.

Shannon, J. (2005) Personal Communication, Toronto, Canada, 5 January.

Shoham, A. & Kahle, L. R. (1996) Spectators, viewers, readers: communication and consumption communities in sports marketing, *Sports Marketing Quarterly* 5 (1), 11–19.

Silk, M., Slack, T. & Amis, J. (2000) Bread, butter, and gravy: an institutional approach to televised sport production, *Culture, Sport, Society* 3 (1), 1–21.

Silver, A. & Sutton, W. (2000) An interview with Adam Silver, President and Chief Operating Officer, NBA Entertainment, *International Journal of Sports Marketing & Sponsorship 2* (2), 101–110.

Soloman, G. (2005) The NHL could learn a few things from the NBA, *The Washington Post,* 26 June, E02.

Street & Smith's Sports Business Journal (2003) Year of the Rights Deal, 7 February.

The Sports Network (2005) The NHL has lost its only remaining U.S. cable TV rights holder, press release, 1 June.

Turner, P. (1999) Television and the Internet convergence: Implications for sports broadcasting, *Sports Marketing Quarterly 8* (2), 43–51.

TWICE (1999) HDTV Sales are seen at 2M by 2005, *TWICE 14* (22), 4–5.

Whitson, D., Harvey, J. & Lavoie, M. (2000) The Mills Report, the Manley Subsidy Proposals, and the business of major league sport, Canadian Public Administration 43 (2), 127–156.

Williamson, R. (2001) Content cutbacks endanger broadband growth. Retrieved July 2, 2005 from: http://www.eweek.com/print_article2/0,1217,a=17828,00.asp.

Wolfe, R., Meenaghan, T. & O'Sullivan, P. (1998) Sport, media and sponsor—The shifting balance of power in the sports network, *Irish Marketing Review 10* (2), 53–66.

Yankee Group (2004) Sales of high-definition TV sets expected to grow rapidly this year, industry report, 16 March.

REGIONAL SPORTS NETWORKS

REGIONAL SPORTS NETWORKS, COMPETITION, AND THE CONSUMER

Diana Moss

I. INTRODUCTION

In an economy increasingly characterized by complex business relationships, Regional Sports Networks (RSNs) are no novelty. There are now about 40 such entities in the U.S., the oldest of which is the Madison Square Garden Sports Network (MSG). Launched in 1969, MSG offers programming for the New York Knicks (NBA), New York Rangers and Buffalo Sabres (NHL), New York Liberty (WNBA), and New York Red Bulls (MLS).[1] Arguably, the centerpieces of the RSN industry in the U.S. are the two large, rival families of RSNs controlled by Comcast SportsNet (CSN) and Fox Sports Net (FSN).[2] CSN operates eight [*now 11*] RSNs while FSN controls almost 18 [*now 19*] networks that offer sports programming for a variety of individual U.S. cities and regions.

The prominent role of media in sports likely accounts for the ownership interests of multi-channel video programming distributors (MVPDs) in many RSNs. MVPDs include cable and Direct Broadcast Satellite (DBS) providers. RSNs are hugely profitable, with margins estimated at 30 to 40 percent and average fees of $2 per subscriber, second only to the Entertainment and Sports Programming Network's (ESPN) fees of $2.50 per subscriber [*and currently approximately $4.00*].[3] In the recent acquisition of Adelphia cable assets by Time Warner and Comcast, Federal Trade Commission Commissioners Leibowitz and Jones Harbor noted that "RSN programming. . . is a unique product, of tremendous value to a certain segment of consumers, and thus access to it is crucial to cable and satellite providers' ability to remain competitive."[4]

Comcast and Fox have aggressively pursued the formation of RSNs around the country, often vying with each other for control of key markets. For example, Fox has recently ceded RSN markets in Chicago, the Bay Area, New England, and New York to CSN and entered other markets in Southern California, Arizona, Houston, Indiana, and Kansas. Both CSN and FSN have purchased a number of formerly independent RSNs. Strategic competition also appears to play a large role in the RSN industry. For example, News Corporation, parent of FSN West, purchased the Los Angeles Dodgers (MLB) in 1998 with the alleged purpose of discouraging Disney (which then owned ESPN and the Anaheim Angels (MLB)) from launching its own RSN—ESPN West.[5]

Competition between RSNs in bidding for team media rights and in negotiating with MVPDs for distribution is often quite fierce. A number of independent RSNs have been outbid by the larger incumbents, CSN and FSN, in their attempts to purchase the media rights to specific teams. The Grizzlies Regional Sports Network, for example, was formed to carry the programming for the Memphis Grizzlies (NBA) but folded before its first scheduled game because the team re-signed with FSN South.[6] And the Victory Sports channel, owned by the Minnesota Twins (MLB), collapsed in 2004 after less than six months on the air because the Twins failed to negotiate deals with local area cable or DBS distributors.[7] Twins programming returned to the local FSN network.

Vertical relationships involving sports-related multi-video programming (MVP) link up the media rights holders (i.e., the teams) with the RSN, which purchases the rights to transmit the events. The RSN then coordinates with and jointly markets the programming to MVPDs who offer it in turn to subscribers in the form of sports channels and other premium sports packages. These relationships can range from ownership through merger or acquisition, to contractual agreements with exclusive terms and conditions, to simple buyer-seller relationships.

Partial ownership structures are common for RSNs. For example, Comcast has a 20 percent ownership interest in SportsNet Chicago (which replaced the defunct FSN Chicago), along with Cubs (MLB) owner the Tribune Company (20 percent share) [*Ed. Note: now Tom Ricketts, who owns a 25 percent share*] and the White Sox (MLB) and Bulls (NBA) owner, Jerry Reinsdorf (40 percent share). The CSN Bay Area is jointly owned by Comcast (45 percent), Fox (30 percent), and the San Francisco Giants (25 percent). Other RSNs are joint ventures that do not include MVPD ownership. The New England Sports Network (NESN), for example, is a joint venture between the Boston Bruins (NHL) and Red Sox (MLB). . . .

RSNs raise threshold competition policy issues because of the unique structure of the markets involved. Rivalry at one or more levels in the chain of vertical integration involving sports teams, RSNs, and MVPDs is often limited, if not nonexistent. Under these circumstances, changes in control that create or strengthen vertically-integrated content/distribution platforms warrant a rigorous level of scrutiny by antitrust and regulatory agencies.

This article sets forth the various scenarios for vertical arrangements involving RSNs that potentially raise competitive and consumer problems. Central to the analysis are the unique issues surrounding the demand for sports programming and market definition surrounding those markets. This article also notes that while there are no antitrust exemptions involving relationships between professional league sports and MVPDs, other sports-related immunities might be argued to apply to RSNs.

Fact situations in RSN markets can vary substantially, so there are no simple answers to the foregoing questions. But it is possible to frame the major questions they raise for competition policy. The article proceeds in Section II with some brief background material on markets for sports MVP. Section III then discusses potential horizontal and vertical competitive issues that may arise in such markets. Section IV considers important questions that are specific to markets for sports MVP that can bear on antitrust analysis. Set forth in section V is a discussion of the applicability of certain sports-related immunities to RSNs and MVPDs. The article concludes with a discussion of the implications that competitive issues surrounding sports MVP markets have on antitrust and regulatory policy.

MARKETS FOR SPORTS MVP

There are a number of possible scenarios involving markets for local sports programming. Two scenarios, however, are most likely to be encountered. One scenario is a single, unintegrated RSN in the upstream media rights market and competing cable and/or satellite providers in the downstream MVPD market (**Figure 2**). A second scenario (**Figure 3**) involves multiple, unintegrated upstream RSNs and competing downstream MVPDs. Figures 2 and 3 indicate the relationship between the RSN and MVPDs in the downstream market and the individual teams and the RSN in the upstream market. In either case, an unintegrated RSN markets

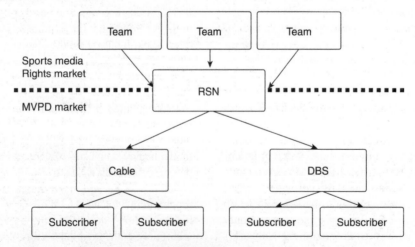

Figure 2   Single RSN and Rival MVPDs
Source: Loyola Consumer Law Review. Used with permission.

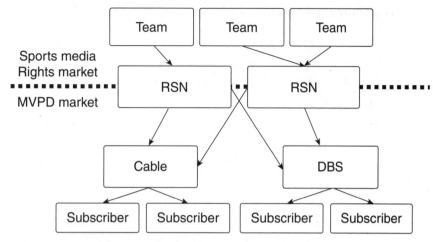

Figure 3   Rival RSNs and MVPDs
Source: Loyola Consumer Law Review. Used with permission.

programming to both the local cable and DBS providers, although it could have an exclusive arrangement to market programming to only one MVPD.[9] Also note that the figures assume that consumers choose one mode of MVP distribution, but nothing precludes sports enthusiasts from subscribing to both cable and DBS services, if they are available.

As for the relationships in the upstream market, Figure 2 indicates that an RSN purchases the media rights for one or more local professional teams. This relationship best describes, for example, CSN Chicago, which handles programming for the White Sox, Cubs, Bears (NFL), Bulls (NBA), Blackhawks (NHL), and Fire (MLS). The FSN West and FSN Prime Ticket serve the Southern California market, collectively covering a vast array of teams, including: the Clippers (NBA), Lakers (NBA), Angels (MLB), Dodgers (MLB), Ducks (NHL), Sparks (WNBA), Kings (NHL), Chivas (MLS), and Galaxy (MLS).

Figure 3 shows the scenario involving multiple RSNs that market programming for different combinations of teams or sports in the same geographic area.[10] For example, the Rocky Mountain region hosts both the Altitude Sports and Entertainment Network (ASE), which carries programming for the Nuggets (NBA), Avalanche (NHL), Rapids (MLS), and Mammoth (NLL). Rival FSN Rocky Mountain carries the Broncos (NFL), Rockies (MLB), and Mammoth.

The scenario shown in Figure 3 prompts a number of questions. One is the extent to which consumers have access to both cable and DBS modes of MVPD, since different RSN programming can be carried on rival MVPD providers. The ability of consumers to switch MVPD providers in response to programming prices, content, and quality is an important feature in markets with multiple RSNs. DBS continues to be slightly less available in certain markets that are served by cable. In 2002 the Federal Communications Commission estimated that 88 percent of cable subscribers also had access to DBS, up by 12 percent from 2001.[11] Cable

penetration rates, however, have declined over time—falling to a 17 year low of about 61 percent in February 2007.[12] Most of this share was given up to DBS. Between 2004 and 2005, for example, DBS subscribership increased by almost 13 percent.[13] In 2005, DBS accounted for about 28 percent of all U.S. MVP subscriptions.[14]

Another question is the extent of competition in the upstream market for sports media rights, which arguably influences the number of RSNs that potentially operate in any given region. **Table 12** lists U.S. RSNs that carry programming for professional sports and the regions they cover as of the writing of this article. There are a total of 15 RSNs nationwide, serving 28 regional markets. Seven markets contain two or more RSNs, including: New York City (three), Kansas City (two), the Mid-Atlantic region (two), Ohio (three), New England (two), the Rocky Mountain region (two), and the Northwest (two). The remaining 21 markets contain only one RSN.[15]

Potential "overlaps" in RSN programming are greater in large cities that can support more than one same-sport team or that contain a large enough number of professional sports teams to support multiple RSNs. For example, New York City hosts both the Yankees Entertainment and Sports Network (YESN) that covers the Yankees (MLB) and SportsNet New York (SNY), which carries the rival Mets. The Mid-Atlantic region also hosts multiple RSNs. The Mid-Atlantic Sports Network (MASN) carries programming for rival MLB teams the Orioles and Nationals as well as the Ravens (NFL). The CSN Mid-Atlantic carries the Redskins (NFL), Wizards (NBA), Capital (NHL), D.C. United (MLS), Bayhawks (NLL), and Mystics (WNBA).

Because the demand for sports programming is driven in large part by fan loyalty, however, it is not clear to what extent RSN packages actually compete, despite the apparent choices in programming that are evident in many of the markets served by multiple RSNs.

Table 12   Regional Sports Networks (RSNs) in the United States

Geographic Region	FSN	CSN	MSG	NESN	YESN	ASEN	4SD	MASN	MS	COX	STO	C47	CoSN	TWS26	SNY
Arizona	•														
Chicago		•													
Detroit	•														
Florida	•														
Houston	•														
Indiana	•														
Kansas City	•								•						
Mid Atlantic		•						•							
Midwest	•														
New England		•		•											
New Orleans										•					
New York														•	
New York City			•		•										•
North	•														
Northern California†		•													
Northwest	•	•													
Ohio	•										•		•		
Philadelphia		•													
Pittsburgh	•														
Prime Ticket	•														
Rocky Mtn.	•					•									
San Diego							•								
South	•														
Southern California‡	•														
Southeast		•													
Southwest	•														
Tampa												•			
Wisconsin	•														

Key to Abbreviations:

FSN = Fox Sports Net; CSN = Comcast Sports Net; MSG = Madison Square Garden Network; NESN = New England Sports Network; YESN = Yankees Entertainment and Sports Network; ASEN = Altitude Sports and Entertainment; 4SD = Channel 4 San Diego; MASN = Mid-Atlantic Sports Network; MS = Metro Sports; COX = Cox Sports; STO = SportsTime Ohio; C47 = Catch 47; CoSN = Columbus Sports Network; TWS26 = Time Warner Sports 26; SNY = SportsNet New York.

†Includes CSN West and CSN Bay Area Networks

‡Includes FSN West and FSN Prime Ticket

Source: Loyola Consumer Law Review. Used with permission.

Note: ESPN is not included in the table because it is a national sports network.

COMPETITIVE ISSUES INVOLVING RSNS AND MVPDS

Mergers or contractual agreements involving RSNs and MVPDs can fundamentally alter the incentives and abilities of market participants, potentially affecting prices, output, choice, and innovation in both programming and distribution. While the focus here is primarily on vertical arrangements, it is helpful to review the horizontal issues that can arise in RSN and MVPD markets.[16] For example, does the aggregation, coordination, and joint marketing function performed by a single RSN eliminate competition in the upstream media rights market? If it does, then the RSN could restrict programming output and raise prices to MVPDs. The answer to this query, of course, largely depends on whether individual team programming competes for the viewership of local fans or, in the alternative, whether the RSN performs a valuable economic integration function for a series of individual team "monopolies," each with no good substitutes.

Mergers of either MVPDs or RSNs also have horizontal effects. In Figure 3, for example, the merger of two independent RSNs could produce a more powerful entity with a greater ability to make demands on downstream MVPDs. This includes placement on an MVPD's standard tier and/or a per customer charge that would be passed on to subscribers. The rumored combination of the YESN and NESN in 2004 potentially raised this issue.[17] A merger of unintegrated local cable providers that creates significant market share, on the other hand, might enhance buyer market power. The likely competitive effects of these scenarios depend on a variety of factors, including the structure of upstream and downstream markets, the degree of vertical integration, consumer preferences, and any relevant efficiencies. The preponderance of vertical integration involving RSNs (e.g., joint-ownership by teams and MVPDs), however, bears strongly on competitive judgments involving horizontal integration such as the merger of two cable companies.

Vertical integration or contractual arrangements that mimic a merger between RSNs and MVPDs pose the classic double-edged sword for competition and consumers—the balancing of efficiencies against potentially restricted output, higher prices, reduced choice, and less innovation resulting from the exercise of market power. There are three potential categories of economies that might result from such integration. One is lower transactions costs for the merged firm due, for example, to: (1) eliminating price negotiations for certain services and (2) avoiding the haggling between stakeholders about how to divide the proceeds of sports media productions. A second source of savings is investment in equipment that can be used in joint production of sports and non-sports programming. Finally, integration can eliminate double margins (i.e., successive markups)

associated with imperfectly competitive up and downstream markets.

At the same time, consolidation that creates a vertically-integrated content/distribution platform or exclusive agreements involving an unintegrated RSN and MVPD can have potentially anticompetitive effects.[18] For example, consider a merger between the RSN and cable provider in Figure 2. Such a combination potentially creates the ability and incentive for the firm to adversely affect market outcomes by foreclosing the rival DBS supplier from access to RSN programming (i.e., input foreclosure) or to engage in conduct that would otherwise raise its rival's costs by charging more for programming or lowering the quality of such programming in a way that could inhibit the MVPD's ability to compete.[19] A merger or exclusive agreement between an RSN and DBS supplier in Figure 3 poses the additional possibility that the merged entity could deny or frustrate the rival RSN access to placing programming on its MVP system (i.e., customer foreclosure).

The foregoing types of input and customer foreclosure or raising rivals' costs strategies are typically considered in vertical arrangements involving upstream input and downstream output suppliers.[20] The integrated firm's ability to foreclose or raise rivals' costs stems from the control of RSN programming. Incentive turns on whether frustrating or denying access is a profitable strategy. For example, the integrated or contractually-related firm must offset the lost programming revenue from rival MVPDs with a revenue gain from its own sales of sports programming at supra-competitive prices. This cost/benefit analysis depends on the structure (i.e., market shares and concentration) in upstream and downstream markets.

Consider now a merger of the two cable providers (one with an existing interest in an RSN) in **Figure 4**. Such a combination might increase the firm's incentive to adversely

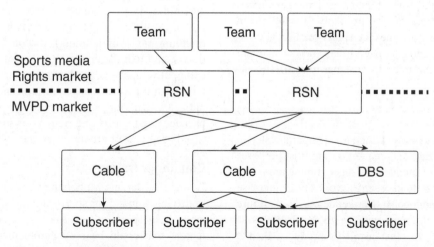

Figure 4   **Rivals RSNs and Multiple, Rival MVPDs**
Source: Loyola Consumer Law Review. Used with permission.

affect market outcomes. With a greater share of the downstream MVPD market, the merged company might find it profitable to deny or frustrate the rival DBS supplier's access to the programming of its integrated RSN affiliate or otherwise raise its costs, thus impairing the firm's ability to compete in the downstream market. Alternatively, the larger post-merger MVPD might have more incentive to foreclose the competing RSN from access to the merged company's MVPD as a customer.

Likewise, the merger of the two competing RSNs in Figure 4 (one with an existing interest in a MVPD) could increase the ability of the merged entity to adversely affect market outcomes. With a control over all RSN programming in the market, foreclosure of the rival MVPD is more viable.

The exclusionary conduct embodied in foreclosure is problematic because it narrows the field of options for rivals in their respective markets. Depending on the type of foreclosure, such diminished competition can increase the prices at which RSN programming is sold to MVPDs and/or those charged to subscribers of MVP services.

Consumers' ability to switch to competing MVPDs to avoid subscription price increases or degradation in programming quality is a key factor in determining whether mergers or exclusive agreements involving RSNs and MVPDs can harm consumers. These issues have arisen in a number of cases, including the Federal Communication Commission's decision in Fox's proposed acquisition of DirecTV[21] and the Federal Trade Commission's investigation into Comcast and Time Warner Cable's proposed acquisition of the cable assets of Adelphia.[22]

IMPORTANT FACTORS IN EVALUATING COMPETITIVE ISSUES

Competition analysis under both antitrust and regulatory standards typically looks at a number of factors: market definition and structure (i.e., market shares and concentration), competitive effects, the role of entry, and merger-related efficiencies. Two of these factors are likely to stand out in assessing competitive outcomes in sports-related MVP—market definition in upstream media rights and downstream MVPD markets and the role of consumer-related efficiencies.

Market Definition

Market definition is the first and often most important step in antitrust analysis. A "relevant" market for antitrust purposes is the smallest group of products (in a geographic area) that consumers could switch to in order to avoid a price increase by a "hypothetical" monopolist. Market definition therefore asks what products consumers view as good substitutes. If consumers can switch to other available products, then it would be harder for any single seller or group of sellers to profitably increase prices.[23] Applied in the RSN context,

the question of market definition centers on how MVPDs are likely to view programming for different local teams marketed by an RSN.

For example, is programming for the local baseball team a good substitute for local hockey? Is programming for one local baseball team a viable substitute for a rival local baseball team, as in the case of the Yankees and Mets in New York or the Dodgers and Angels in Southern California? If not, then the media rights for each team are effectively individual monopolies and joint marketing would not eliminate competition.[24] Alternatively, if programming for individual teams offered by an RSN does compete for the viewership of local fans, joint marketing through an RSN eliminates such competition and could result in restricted or lower quality programming and higher prices to MVPDs.

Decisions in a number of antitrust cases, including USFL v. NFL, indicated that the most important sports constitute separate markets.[25] Under such circumstances, an RSN such as CSN Chicago that coordinates the rights for multiple different-sports teams may not raise competitive concerns. However, RSNs like MASN and FSN West that jointly market the rights of the rival Orioles and Nationals and the Dodgers and Angels, respectively, may be problematic.

In downstream markets, the relevant antitrust question is how MVP subscribers view RSN products offered through different MVPDs. For example, do consumers consider different RSN channels and packages sold by local cable and satellite providers to be effective substitutes? This may be the case in the larger metropolitan areas that host the multiple RSNs shown in Table 12. And in what instances do sports channels compete with other forms of non-sports premium programming? In downstream markets, the FTC has made both of the foregoing determinations—i.e., that premium sports channels comprise a market and that premium pay television programming comprises the relevant market.[26]

Based on the foregoing, consolidation of RSNs in a "premium sports channel" market could pose competitive problems while under a broader market definition (e.g., all premium pay programming), it would not. Market definition is, and will likely continue to be a controversial part of competitive analysis involving sports-related MVP, particularly with ongoing changes in how sports programming is marketed, with larger numbers of channels offered in basic packages and sports and non-sports programming bundled together as part of premium services.

Consumer Issues

Because of the intense popularity of and role of fan loyalty in driving demand for sports programming, the competitive analysis of sports-related MVP is likely to consider other factors that could bear on enforcement decisions involving integration or contractual relationships. First, MVP subscribers may place a higher value on convenience and quality than they do on price. This characteristic of consumer demand creates tensions for the desirability of certain market structures that would be achieved through mergers or agreements involving RSNs and MVPDs. For example, fans might willingly pay a supracompetitive price to avoid the service interruptions that could occur because of disruptive bargaining. Such problems could arise between rival RSNs over the media rights to individual or groups of teams or between multiple RSNs and MVPDs in a geographic market.[27] Under the foregoing circumstances, arrangements or outcomes that place local sports programming with a single RSN could provide benefits to consumers.

Second, placing RSN's sports programming with an MVPD in an exclusive arrangement could arguably allow the firms to differentiate themselves from a competing sports content/distribution (i.e., RSN/MVPD) platform in the market. This type of "systems" competition could allow rival RSN/MVPD platforms to compete more effectively.[28] Both of these potential pro-consumer scenarios involving vertical relationships between RSNs and MVPDs should, however, be considered in light of the fact-patterns in specific cases. For example, horizontal integration between MVPDs (as in the case of Comcast/Time Warner/Adelphia), if superimposed on exclusive arrangements between unintegrated RSNs and MVPDs may renew or intensify the bargaining over the share of profits that are divided between the various stakeholders. This increases the likelihood of service disruptions that inconveniences fans and viewing audiences.

Multiple offerings between rival RSNs, each with exclusive agreements with cable and DBS providers, could also force consumers to invest in different or additional equipment and pay for bundled packages that include redundant sports programming.[29]

The weight given to the foregoing considerations in antitrust analysis will depend largely on the magnitude of potential competitive harm raised by various transactions. More competition in popular sports channels and packages offered through RSNs is very much in the interest of MVPDs who—given strong viewership for the team-specific programming that is offered by different RSNs—would find ready customers. Moreover, promoting competition at both the RSN and MVPD levels is likely to ensure that prices are low, and that consumers are afforded choice in sports-related programming.

APPLICABILITY OF ANTITRUST EXEMPTIONS RELATING TO PROFESSIONAL LEAGUE SPORTS

There are no specific antitrust exemptions involving professional league sports and MVPDs. Nonetheless, another source of controversy in the RSN debate may be whether antitrust immunity afforded league sports in certain contexts

should apply to RSNs.[30] For example, professional baseball has the benefit of a court-created exemption which extends to franchise relocations and other conduct that is the "business of baseball."[31] Arguments that the provisions of the Sports Broadcasting Act (SBA) of 1961 may exempt RSNs may also surface in the debate. The SBA exempts from antitrust scrutiny any league that "sells or transfers all or part of the (broadcast) rights of the league's member clubs."[32]

While the applicability of the baseball exemption outside the player market is still unresolved by the courts, it is likely that the exemption would not easily be extended to the joint marketing activities of RSNs. Several attempts to apply the baseball exemption to media have failed.[33] The exemption does not cover arrangements that are designed to protect or increase the profits of a particular team owner or when the controlling entity (the RSN) is not a baseball team engaged in the business of baseball.[34] Arguably, the joint marketing of rights through RSNs is no more the business of baseball than is running a parking lot adjacent to the stadium.

The broadcast exemption is also not easily extended to RSNs. Here again, several attempts to expand coverage of the SBA to MVPD have failed.[35] The SBA deals with collective sales of rights or joint contracting by a league, not to sales of individual rights by local team owners or to the resale of rights by a rights purchaser (e.g., an RSN). Moreover, major federal cases have construed the applicability of the SBA to "sponsored telecasting" to apply narrowly to over-the-air television broadcasting. This means it would not affect negotiations with cable or satellite providers by entities controlling the media rights.

Implications for Antitrust and Regulation

The foregoing analysis of competitive issues in sports programming markets highlights two major policy issues. First, MVPD markets have benefited by continued penetration of DBS. But cable mergers that increase incentives to foreclose rival MVPDs from affiliated RSN programming could quickly reverse those gains. Competition will therefore benefit from continued close monitoring and scrutiny of cable consolidation. In problematic cases, divestiture can reduce cable market power. And regulatory policy initiatives and directives that promote the continued penetration of DBS and compel carriage of independent programming should be promoted.

Second, the lack of close substitutes created by fan loyalty to particular local teams can have significant implications for competition in MVPD markets. This unique feature of demand for sports programming will affect whether joint marketing of rights through RSNs creates competitive problems. It also will affect outcomes of vertical relationships between MVPDs and RSNs and mergers or either downstream MVPDs or upstream RSNs in the presence of vertical arrangements. Exclusive agreements that foreclose competing MVPDs from access to RSN programming could impose significant switching or duplication costs on consumers who are forced to invest in multiple services to get the programming they want.

The foregoing issue highlights the growing dichotomy between cable-based and DBS-based MVPD systems. In this case, maintenance of "systems competition" is heavily dependent on robust upstream media rights and downstream MVPD markets and open and unfettered MVPD access to local sports programming. Exclusive agreements or mergers that limit MVPD access to programming undercut the benefits of growing, head-to-head competition between cable and DBS. Vertical relationships therefore require careful monitoring and (when necessary) remedial conditions such as "open access" to programming or divestiture.[36]

Notes

1. Little League Communications Division, *New England Sports Network, Madison Square Garden Network to Televise LLB New England, Mid-Atlantic Region Tournament Games,* Little League Online, April 14, 2008, http://www.littleleague.org/media/newsarchive/2008stories/New_England_Sports_Network_Madison_Square_Garden_Network_to_Televise_LLB_New_England_Mid-Atlantic_Region_Tournament_Games_-_April_14.htm.

2. *See, e.g.,* Ronald Grover et al., *Rumble in Regional Sports,* Bus. Week, November 22, 2004, *available at* http://www.businessweek.com/magazine/content/0447/b3909143mz016.htm.

3. Grover, *supra* note 2; *see also* Frank Ahrens, *Area Baseball Network Must Form Quickly,* Wash. Post, Sept. 30, 2004, at A14.

4. Time Warner/Comcast/Adelphia, Statement of Commissioners Jon Leibowitz and Pamela Jones Harbour (Consurring in Part, Dissenting in Part), January 31, 2006, File No. 051-0151, *available at* http://www.ftc.gov/os/closings/ftc/0510151twadelphialeibowitzharbour.pdf.

5. *See* John Dempsey, *Disney, Fox in NHL Faceoff,* Variety, Aug. 6, 1998, *available at* http://www.variety.com/article/VR1117479211.html?categoryid=18&cs=1.

6. Grover, *supra* note 2.

7. *See* Mike Reynolds & R. Thomas Umstead, *Twins Rights Victory for Fox,* Multichannel News, May 17, 2004, *available at* http://www.allbusiness.com/government/government-bodies-offices-regional-local/6259986-1.html.

. . . .

9. Federal Communications Commission (FCC) program access rules prohibit exclusivity between integrated cable providers and RSNs. Integrated entities are required to charge other MVPDs reasonable and non-discriminatory fees for programming. These rules were extended for five years in September 2007. *See, e.g.,* John Eggerton, *NCTA Pans Program-Access Rules in FCC Filing,* Broadcasting & Cable, Jan. 4, 2008, http://www.broadcastingcable.com/article/CA6517249.html.

10. Some RSNs also cover local collegiate and minor league teams.

11. This issue has arisen in controversial mergers of cable or DBS providers. *See, e.g.,* Richard J. Gilbert and James Tarliff, *Sky Wars: The Attempted Merger of EchoStar and DirecTV, in* The Antitrust Revolution 120 (J. E. Kwoka & L. J. White, eds. 5th ed. 2008) (citing F.C.C., Report on Cable Industry Prices, FCC 03-136, released

July 3, 2003, *available at* http://fjallfoss.fcc.gov/edocspublic/attachmatch/FCC-03-136A1.pdf).

12. Steve Donohue, *Cable Penetration Hits 17-Year Low,* Multichannel News, Mar. 19, 2007, http://www.multichannel.com/article/CA6425963.html.

13. F.C.C., Annual Assessment of the Status of Competition in the Market for the Delivery of Video Programming, 12th Annual Report, released March 3, 2006, at 37, *available at* http://hraunfoss.fcc.gov/edocspublic/attachmatch/FCC-06-11A1.pdf [hereinafter 12th Annual Report]. Note that a more recent report has not yet been released by the FCC. *See, e.g.,* Barbara Esbin & Adam Thierer, *Where is the FCC's Annual Video Competition Report?,* Progress & Freedom Foundation, Apr. 11, 2008, *available at* http://www.pff.org/issues-pubs/ps/2008/ps4.11whereisFCCvidcompreport.html.

14. 12th Annual Report, *supra* note 13.

15. Table 12 does not report RSNs that carry collegiate sports or arena football programming. For the purposes of distinguishing regions by distinct geographic area, Northern and Southern California are divided into two regions. RSNs serving the Portland and Seattle areas (Northwest) are combined, as are those offering programming for teams based in Ohio.

16. The competitive effects of consolidation or agreements on competition and consumers are evaluated under the "no-harm" (to competition) standard employed by the antitrust agencies under Section 7 of the Clayton Act (15 U.S.C. § 18); Section 5 of the Federal Trade Commission Act (as amended, 15 U.S.C. § 45); and the broader public interest standard applied by the FCC in exercising its statutory authority under the Communications Act (410 U.S.C. § 310(d)).

17. *See, e.g., Yanks, Red Sox in TV Merger?,* CNN Money, Aug. 3, 2004, http://money.cnn.com/2004/08/03/news/midcaps/yesnesn/index.htm.

18. The United Kingdom Monopolies and Mergers Commission blocked the take-over of the Manchester United football (soccer) club by Rupert Murdoch's BSkyB—the monopoly supplier of premium sports programming. *See, e.g.,* Martin Cave and Robert W. Crandall, *Sports Rights and the Broadcast Industry,* 111 The Econ. J. 469 (2001) at F4-F26.

19. Note that FCC rules that require integrated cable providers to offer programming on reasonable and non-discriminatory terms can be gamed by setting a high price charged to competing MVPDs. But the same price—charged by the cable provider to "itself"—is effectively a transfer price and arguably does not affect the ability of the firm to compete.

20. *See, e.g.,* Michael H. Riordan and Steven C. Salop, *Evaluating Vertical Mergers: A Post-Chicago Approach,* 63 Antitrust L.J. 513 (1994) and David Waterman, *Vertical Integration and Program Access in the Cable Television Industry,* 47 Fed. Comm. L.J. 511 (1994) at 517-20.

21. *See* F.C.C., General Motors Corp. and Hughes Electronics Corp., Tranferors, and News Corp. Ltd., Transferee, Memorandum Opinion and Order, FCC 03-330, released January 14, 2004, *available at* http://hraunfoss.fcc.gov/edocspublic/attachmatch/FCC-03-330A1.pdf.

22. *See, e.g.,* posting of Shepard Mullin to Antitrust Law Blog, FCC Antitrust Highlights, http://www.antitrustlawblog.com/highlights-153-fcc-antitrust-highlights.html (Aug. 7, 2005); David Lieberman, *FCC Asked to Put Limits on Deal for Adelphia,* USA Today, July 24, 2005, *available at* http://www.usatoday.com/money/media/2005-07-24-adelphia-usatx.htm; F.T.C., FTC's Competition Bureau Closes Investigation into Comcast, Time Warner Cable and Adelphia

Communications Transactions, January 31, 2006, http://www.ftc.gov/opa/2006/01/fyi0609.htm.

23. *See* U.S. D.O.J. and F.T.C, Horizontal Merger Guidelines, 57 FR 41,552 (1992), revised, 4 Trade Reg. Rep. (CCH) P 13,104 (April 8, 1997), Section 1, *available at* http://www.usdoj.gov/atr/public/guidelines/hmg.htm.

24. Most RSNs provide coverage of local or sports teams within or near a major metropolitan area with strong fan loyalty and support. A local MVPD would be unlikely to consider sports-related MVP offered by non-local RSNs a good substitute.

25. *See, e.g.,* USFL v. NFL, 842 F.2d 1335 (1988). For a more detailed discussion, *see* Franklin M. Fisher, Christopher Maxwell, and Evan Sue Schouten, *Sports League Issues: The Relocation of the Los Angeles Rams to St. Louis,* in THE ANTITRUST REVOLUTION at 277 (J. E. Kwoka and L. J. White, eds., 4th ed. 2004).

26. European competition authorities have made similar findings. *See, e.g.,* Office of Fair Trading, The Director General's Review of BSkyB's Position in the Wholesale Pay TV Market, (1996), *available at* http://www.oft.gov.uk/ shared–oft/reports/media/oft179.pdf.

27. Due to asymmetries (i.e., imbalances) in information between buyers and sellers, establishing prices for programming is costly and bargaining can be a disruptive process. One example of this is the negotiations between YESN and Cablevision in NYC. *See, e.g., Echostar's Dish Network is Lone Holdout in Cablevision, YES Network Deal,* LONG ISLAND BUS. NEWS, March 28, 2003, *available at* http://www.allbusiness.com/north-america/united-states-new-york/1147329-1.html.

28. *See, e.g., Sports Programming and Cable Distribution: The Comcast/Time Warner/Adelphia Transaction,* December 7, 2006, Prepared statement of Federal Trade Commission, (Presented by Michael Salinder, Director, Bureau of Economics to Committee on the Judiciary, US Senate), *available at* http://www.ftc.gov/os/testimony/P052103SportsProgrammingandCableDistributionTestimonySenate12062006.pdf.

29. At the same time, mergers or exclusive agreements could also harm consumers by forcing them to purchase multiple and/or incompatible hardware.

30. *See, e.g.,* Stephen F. Ross, *Monopoly Sports Leagues,* 73 MINN. L. REV. 643 (1988). Ross argues that the single-entity argument is flawed as a matter of economics because club-run leagues do not have a unity of economic purpose and lack a residual claimant to organize the league and distribute the proceeds. *See also, e.g.,* Bengt Holmstrom, *Moral Hazard in Teams,* 13 BELL J. OF ECON. 324 (1982) and Michael A. Flynn & Richard J. Gilbert, *The Analysis of Professional Sports Leagues as Joint Ventures,* 111 THE ECON. J. 469 at 27 (2001).

31. *See* Federal Baseball Club vs. National League, 259 U.S. 200 (1922); *see also* Toolson v. New York Yankees, Inc., 346 U.S. 917 (1953) and Flood v. Kuhn, 407 U.S. 258 (1972).

32. 15 U.S.C. § 1291.

33. *See, e.g.,* Henderson Broadcasting Corp. v. Houston Sports Association, Inc., 659 F. Supp. 109 (S.D. Tex. 1987). Here, a district court held that an exclusive agreement between the Houston Astros and a radio station was not exempt because the competition affected was with a rival broadcaster, not a participant in the baseball industry.

34. *See* Stephen F. Ross, *The Baseball Antitrust Exemption Lives, But with Criticism, in the Eleventh Circuit,* American Antitrust Institute, May 28, 2003, http://www.antitrustinstitute.org/Archives/247.ashx.

35. In Shaw v. Dallas Cowboys Football Club, Ltd., 172 F.3d 299 (3d Cir. 1999), the Third Circuit Court of Appeals held that the statute did not protect the NFL's sale of games for satellite programming packages.

36. *See, e.g.,* Thomas A. Piriano, Jr., *A Proposal for the Antitrust Regulation of Professional Sports,* 79 B. U. L. REV. 889 (1999) at 954-55.

THE FUTURE

THE FUTURE OF SPORTS MEDIA

Irving Rein, Philip Kotler, and Ben Shields

There is probably no better place to examine the media landscape in the next decades than the sports arena, especially the first big players in this highly lucrative, multibillion dollar worldwide industry. We are now seeing a massive readjustment in what has historically been a synergistic relationship between the sports leagues and teams and the media. In this transformation, new alliances will be formed, media giants will be sorely pressed to operate, and viewers—i.e., fans or customers— will have unprecedented access to information on numerous and yet-to-be-determined distribution channels.

In the United States, today's sports-media model was pioneered on television by ABC's *Wide World of Sports,* NBC's coverage of the Olympics, and CBS's Sunday afternoon football. This relationship was clear: The sports properties sold their rights to the media, who then sold the sports content to advertisers, who gained audiences and potential customers for their products. The model was primarily built on network television and was largely responsible for turning professional and college sports into multibillion dollar businesses. Over time, this model began to change as cable television networks entered the sports rights fee arena and, because of cable subscriptions revenues, began competing with network television and fragmenting what was once a scarcity-driven market.

The best example of a current winner is ESPN (Entertainment and Sports Programming Network), the synergistic sports-media brand that communicates with its fans through every distribution channel imaginable. From its flagship television network, the company has spawned other networks (ESPN2, ESPNEWS, ESPN Classic, ESPN Deportes), syndicated radio stations (ESPN Radio), a magazine *(ESPN the Magazine),* an interactive Web site with streaming video, audio, insider information, and fantasy games (ESPN.com), . . . and sports-themed restaurants (the ESPN Zone). Throughout most of the cable network's history, if a sport wasn't covered by ESPN, it didn't exist.

In the next stage, sports leagues and teams, because of technological innovations, are beginning to communicate differently with fans. For the first time, the content providers are developing pipelines directly aimed at their fans. A leader in this transformation is Manchester United, the billion-dollar English football (soccer) club, which has adapted and expanded ESPN's blueprint to its own one-city team. It has a television channel (MU TV), radio station (MU Radio), magazine *(United),* mobile phone service (MU Mobile), team-themed restaurants (the Red Cafe), and interactive Web site (Manutd.com) with streaming video, audio, insider information, and a fantasy game. Outdoing ESPN, it even has its own financial services, including car insurance, credit cards, and mortgages; a ManU lottery; and a host of other attractions. As an English football club outside of London, Manchester United has transformed itself into a global lifestyle brand through innovative partnerships and new media communication strategies.

The signals of this future trend are everywhere. Sports properties are becoming their own media companies, interacting directly with their consumers without the filter of traditional media. For example, the most valuable television property in sports is America's National Football League (NFL). For most networks, the NFL is sought after not only for its high ratings but also for the promotional lead-ins to the rest of the network's schedule and as a competitive asset in the television content wars.

Despite their league's television rights monopoly, the NFL has been building its own television channel, the NFL Network, which competed against ESPN with its own NFL draft show and broadcast eight regular season games in the 2006 season. Rather than selling its Thursday and Saturday night television package to other networks, the NFL is investing in its own media brand, using the network as a backup plan for the time when or if television networks won't pay the rights fees. The NFL Network has also bought the rights to several college bowl games, covers the league's teams all year round from the draft to training camps, and builds the legends of the league with its popular NFL Films content. For the traditional sports media, the NFL Network—along with the National Basketball Association's NBATV, the Baseball Network, and other team only channels—is redefining sports television and transforming the once-reliable sports rights infrastructure.

The Internet is another area in sports media where rules are being rewritten and the marketplace is rapidly changing. Major League Baseball (MLB), for example, through its Advanced Media division, has built a substantial Internet infrastructure for streaming live video of baseball games throughout the season. For a one-time subscription fee, fans can watch almost every baseball game of the season on their computer.

The streaming video business has been a substantial revenue generator for the league, and it is defining the ways that leagues and teams broadcast sports on the Internet and make a profit in the process. When the National Collegiate Athletic Association decided to stream the Final Four college basketball tournament, it turned to MLB because it had the capacity and skill to do so. MLB has become one of the benchmarks for integrating new technology into its communication strategies to meet the changing expectations of fans, and MLB's current success only means that other sports properties will begin emulating and reconfiguring their formula.

A final indicator of the changing sports-media relationship is the increasing amount of fan-driven content on the Internet. A good example is Deadspin.com, a sports news Web site that is operated out of the New York City apartment of the site's founder. Deadspin covers sports news like any other newspaper and magazine, provides forums for fans to discuss the latest sports controversies, and is sometimes the first media outlet to break a story. Deadspin's influence has become so important that even members of the traditional media often get their material from the site. That fans have also become the distributors of information demonstrates how the traditional media's role as filter is diminishing, and both sports properties and the fans themselves are increasingly filling the channels.

The radical realignment of sports is the canary in the coal mine for the future of media. It's only a matter of time before the professional sports model becomes the standard in college and high-school sports. The Big Ten Conference, for example, has plans to begin a satellite channel to provide content to its fans. [*Ed. Note: The channel launched in 2007.*] Other entertainments such as film, fashion, and music are also developing their own content and media pipelines to reach targeted fan bases.

It's fair to say that the media landscape over the coming decades will look considerably different than it does now. Moreover, the storytellers and strategists who formerly worked in these media channels will increasingly find employment with the content providers and nontraditional information distributors. If the traditional media pipelines are going to survive, they will have to seek new alliances and look to connect to the content providers in innovative ways. Already we see increased bartering, cost-sharing, and integrated multiplatform distribution strategies. The only certainty about the sports marketplace is that it is adapting, and for the stakeholders, this means constant monitoring of change and a commitment to innovation.

TEXAS HOLD 'EM IN SPORTS TELEVISION

In 1976, the major networks played in their own game and had all the chips. Three decades later, the table is crowded, with more chips and more players.

Major Networks: A fourth major network has been added to the mix, FOX, which has invested heavily in sports programming to build its media brand.

Regional Sports Networks: This group comprises team-owned channels, such as the YES Network and Altitude Sports & Entertainment, and regional cable networks, such as the Comcast Sports Net Chicago or Fox Sports Net Pittsburgh.

Cable Networks: Cable television created new opportunities for sports programming. ESPN was the avatar of the 24-hour sports network and has since been followed by OLN *[now Versus]*. Superstations such as TBS and WGN have also integrated sports into their programming.

Single Sports Channels: Leagues and specific sports have developed dedicated channels to their sports. Examples include the NFL Network, Fuel TV, and the Golf Channel.

Satellite TV: Leagues now offer subscriptions that give the viewer access to almost any game. Examples include NFL Sunday Ticket and Cricket Ticket.

Discussion Questions

1. Why is there an apparent move by leagues away from network television deals to deals led by cable networks?

2. What inherent advantages for advertisers does sports programming have over nonsports programming?

3. What could football Web sites do better?

4. Why are cable companies currently better positioned than broadcast networks to offer large rights fees for sports programming?

5. As a team owner, what factors might affect your decision whether to start your own RSN or use the threat of such a move as leverage in negotiations with existing cable companies in your area?

6. You are CEO of a media company that televises the program "High School Game of the Week," showing the best high school games and brightest future stars in football, basketball and baseball. You want to start streaming those games and related content on your Web site. Do you use an advertising or subscription model? Explain.

7. What are the necessary factors for a successful vertically integrated RSN?

8. Are subscription models better for "mobile media" distribution channels? Why, or why not?

9. What is the difference between the idea of the Internet as an access device versus a place to connect with fans (as described in Mark Abbott's presentation)? Which side do you feel more accurately reflects the state of sports on the Internet today?

10. In his presentation, Brad Ruskin said certain events, such as the Super Bowl, would always be shown on broadcast networks. Can you envision a scenario where that is not the case?

11. How should sports networks respond to leagues and conferences increasingly attempting to vertically integrate their own content (NFL, MLB, Big Ten Network, etc.)?

12. What are some factors keeping leagues, such as the NFL, from abandoning broadcast networks/cable to exclusively distribute their content on their own channels?

13. Sports programming is now available on a multitude of mediums. Are these distribution channels complementary, or is there danger of one cannibalizing the other? What do teams/leagues/media entities need to do to ensure they're not sacrificing "analog dollars for digital dimes?"

CHAPTER NINE

Labor Matters: Unions

INTRODUCTION

Similar to many other industries in which unions represent the collective interests of employees, management and labor in many sports leagues use a collective bargaining agreement (CBA) to set forth the rules regarding how they will conduct business and resolve disputes between one another. Athletes in the NBA, NFL, NHL (and the minor league AHL and ECHL), MLB (and its affiliated minor leagues), MLS, and WNBA are unionized. The CBA creates a system of laws and guidelines that govern the relationship between management and the union. This agreement is hammered out in the collective bargaining process, a negotiation that in sports, as in other industries, is bounded by the economic weapons of a management lockout or union strike, both of which are legally protected by the National Labor Relations Act.

The CBA is particularly important in professional sports leagues for three reasons. First, the cumulative wages earned by all of the members of the union typically represent what is far and away the largest expense for the members of the league. Athletes in the NBA, NHL, NFL, and MLB receive between 50–60% of the revenues generated by the league. This dwarfs the percentage of revenues that unions in other industries receive. In sports, the CBA is the basis for determining the parameters of a number of issues that are fundamental to a league's success. The league's duration (length of season), talent distribution mechanisms (entry draft), salary containment mechanisms (salary cap, luxury tax, and maximum individual player salary limit), salary inflators (free agency, salary arbitration, and minimum player salary limit), employee termination procedures (waivers), workplace integrity and discipline (player suspensions and drug testing policy and procedures), dispute resolution systems (grievance arbitration systems), and even the manner in which the employers redistribute their own wealth (revenue

sharing, in some leagues) are all among the topics included in a CBA.

Having an agreement that makes fiscal sense for management is of utmost importance; in the modern era, this means that a salary cost-containment mechanism is included in most CBAs. It should be noted that the legal framework is important here as well. It is now established precedent that the mandatory subjects of bargaining included in a bona fide agreement between union and management will receive legal protection from the application of the antitrust laws through what is known as the *nonstatutory labor exemption*. (Such mandatory subjects include those concerning wages, hours, and terms and conditions of employment.) For example, sports leagues are monopolies that dictate to employees where they will work and the maximum wages they can earn if they are to work in the league. These are employment conditions that businesses in other industries would find extremely desirable, and they are legal in sports leagues because the parties have collectively bargained to hold a draft and set maximum player salaries and salary caps.

Second, all of the unions in professional sports are composed of employees whose average career is less than 5 years long. Errors in collective bargaining that cannot be corrected until the next agreement can impact an athlete's earning capacity for his entire career. With player salaries relatively low during the early stage of the athlete's career, it is imperative for the players' association to gain free agency rights for its members as early as possible so that the athletes can maximize their earnings during their short careers. Most athletes only get to sign one free-agent contract; this "bite of the apple" can provide the athlete with financial security for the remainder of his or her life if the money earned is handled correctly. The stakes are high for the union.

Nonetheless, the media and public often look unfavorably upon the players' associations during labor strife, a dilemma that results from having high-profile unions populated by a number of multimillionaires. The players' associations in professional sports leagues are among the most powerful in the world, and their memberships have a degree of wealth that is unlike that of any other union. Despite the fact that they are negotiating with a management side that has considerably more wealth, public opinion is usually against the unions.

Third, the "major" leagues in professional sports represent the top level of competition in that sport because of the quality of the athletes that play in the league. Unlike in many other industries, the superior talent of the unionized workforce in these leagues is easily recognizable to even the most casual fans. Without the athletes, there are no games and no league product to speak of—even if management engages in its legally protected right to hire replacement workers during a work stoppage, as occurred in the NFL during the 1987 player strike and MLB in the 1994–1995 strike. The entire industry essentially shuts down during a work stoppage. Players lose a year of salary in their already short careers and management loses a year of revenues and risks damaging its business for several years thereafter as fans slowly return to the sport. The NHL shut down for the entire 2004–2005 season during its lockout. This places an enormous amount of pressure on both union and management; although they rarely agree on most issues that arise, they must decide whether it is worth shutting down an entire industry over their disagreements.

Given this pressure, work stoppages should occur only when one of the parties is seeking a "sea change"; that is, a fundamental change to an important collective bargaining issue (usually related to player salaries) that impacts the league's underlying business model in a dramatic fashion. The most recent work stoppages in each of the major North American professional leagues—the NHL lockout in 2004–2005, the NBA lockout in 1998–1999, the MLB player strike in 1994–1995, and the NFL strike in 1987—were all driven by management's ultimate desire to gain a salary cost-containment mechanism (a salary cap in the NHL, MLB, and NFL and a luxury tax and maximum player salary in the NBA). The settlements in these disputes were typically a trade-off, where management gained the right to contain player salaries across the entire league in exchange for allowing the athletes to increase their salaries as individuals by liberalizing the free agent system, giving them increased access to the lucrative free agent marketplace. Management was engaged in concession bargaining in all of these agreements, as they sought to curtail the gains made by the athletes in prior agreements.

This was a dramatic shift from earlier collective bargaining eras across the leagues. Collective bargaining in professional sports leagues occurred much later than in other industries, with the first CBA reached in 1968 between MLB and the MLBPA. (See **Table 1** for a time line of labor relations in professional sports.) In the first generation of collective bargaining agreements, the unions sought a "sea

Table 1 Time Line of Labor Relations in Professional Sports

MLB	
1885	National Brotherhood of Professional Ball Players founded
1890	Players' League founded
1900	League Protective Players' Association founded
1912	Baseball Players Fraternity founded
1946	American Baseball Guild founded
1954	Major League Baseball Players Association founded
1966	Marvin Miller named executive director of MLBPA
1972	Strike, 13 days
1973	Lockout, 17 days
1976	Lockout, 17 days
1981	Strike, 50 days
1985	Strike, 2 days
1990	Lockout, 32 days
1994–1995	Strike, 232 days

NFL	
1956	NFLPA formed
1968	Strike/lockout, 10 days
1971	Strike/lockout, 20 days
1974	Strike, 42 days
1982	Strike, 57 days
1987	Strike, 24 days
1988	NFLPA decertified
1993	NFLPA recertified

NHL	
1958	NHLPA formed
1992	Strike, 10 days
1994	Lockout, 103 days
2004–2005	Lockout, 310 days

NBA	
1954	NBPA formed
1995	Lockout, 77 days
1998	Lockout, 191 days

change" in their efforts to gain pension plans and grievance arbitration rights, both of which were common in other unionized workplaces. The next generations of agreements focused on the unions seeking salary increases via free agency, with management desiring to maintain the historic status quo in which they had perpetual control over the players' rights, and thus their salaries. Against the backdrop of these eras was a fairly substantial amount of strategic litigation that established the legal framework that would guide the bargaining process. The growth of player salaries that resulted from these gains led to the present era, where management generally has sought concessions and the players have sought to maintain the status quo.

A unique aspect of both the sports and entertainment industries is that the unions allow the individual employees to negotiate their salaries on their own. In contrast to, for example, the United Steelworkers and other unions that establish salaries for all members along with the other collectively negotiated terms and conditions of employment, the salary negotiation in professional sports is typically in the hands of the individual athlete. The CBA establishes a minimum salary floor for negotiations in most sports leagues, and in the case of the NBA and NHL the collective bargaining agreement sets a ceiling as well. Thus, CBAs in professional sports merely set general salary parameters instead of the actual salaries. The next chapter fully explores this compensation issue.

Each of the major North American professional leagues is currently near the end of a long-term CBA that was reached, excepting the NHL, without a work stoppage in the mid-2000s. This stems from a number of factors, not the least of which is the fact that their respective industries were generating record amounts of revenues and that the individual teams generally were generating operating profits and/or appreciating in value, while the athletes, on average, were making substantial amounts of money. An industry where both parties to the CBA are making money is not in need of a "sea change" that leads to work stoppages. The recession that began in 2008 may change that dynamic in future rounds of CBAs, with the owners perhaps seeking to further contain their expenses to compensate for the revenue shortfall that they faced in the latter part of the decade. Current CBAs expire after the 2010 NFL season, the 2011 MLB season, the 2011–2012 NHL season, and the 2010–2011 NBA season. In addition, these will be the first collective bargaining negotiations for the heads of the MLBPA (Michael Weiner), the NFLPA (DeMaurice Smith), and the NHLPA. It will be interesting to see how this affects the collective bargaining dynamic as they lead the unions in negotiations with their respective league counterparts.

The MLBPA is considered by many to be one of the strongest unions in existence in any industry. The articles by Andrew Hanson and Andrew Zimbalist provide a good overview of the MLBPA and set forth the framework for collective bargaining in MLB. The article by Ryan Dryer continues the discussion by taking a broader view of collective bargaining across all of the major sports leagues. The chapter concludes with a selection by Paul Staudohar that focuses on the NHL lockout of 2004–2005 and its resolution. The NHL is the only sports league to-date to have an entire season cancelled by a work stoppage, a dubious distinction.

MICROPERSPECTIVE: THE BASEBALL STORY

THE TREND TOWARD PRINCIPLED NEGOTIATION IN MAJOR LEAGUE BASEBALL COLLECTIVE BARGAINING

Andrew P. Hanson

Americans love baseball. It is a classic form of entertainment highlighted by graceful and powerful athletic prowess. It is also a daily dose of drama. Every morning, fans can open up the sports page, digest the box scores, and learn whether their team triumphed or failed the night before. The drama is not guaranteed, however. It depends on competition.

. . . .

To protect the allure of the game, the parties in charge of making the rules need to establish a framework that is designed to foster an attractive brand of athletic competition. The parties who share that task are the Labor Relations Departments—the negotiators for the owners—and the Major League Baseball Players Association (the Union), which represents the players. These parties seek to foster that attractive brand of athletic competition by engaging in a collective bargaining process every few years to establish the rules for the upcoming seasons.

The rules that are created in the terms of a collective bargaining agreement (CBA) are like the laws of the baseball industry. They govern a certain number of seasons and dictate, inter alia, how many games are played, the minimum salaries for the players, and what rights a player has to use free agency to increase his salary or play for a different team.

Historically, the collective bargaining process in baseball has been fraught with tension and strife.[1] Between 1972 and 1994, every time the owners and the players attempted to negotiate a new contract there was either a union strike or a management lockout.[2] Tension between the two sides reached an all time high in 1994 when the players went on strike and the World Series was canceled for the first time since 1904.[3] In 2002, however, the parties reached an agreement the same day of a scheduled strike, thereby avoiding another work stoppage.[4]

The 2002 agreement appears to have been a turning point in baseball's labor war. In October 2006, the owners and the players agreed to the terms of the newest CBA two months prior to the expiration of the previous agreement.[5]

This type of cooperative outcome had never occurred in baseball. This project is an effort to determine what factors led to this cooperative outcome, and what will need to be done in the future to ensure there is a critical mass of financially stable teams and that baseball's core element of competition continues to be present.

Why were the parties able to negotiate a new collective bargaining agreement in 2006 with such relative ease? It was the result of complex legal, financial, and psychological factors, as well as the parties' negotiating strategies and styles that had led to the 1997 CBA and the 2002 CBA. These variables were inextricably linked, and they combined to determine the substantive outcomes of those two collective bargaining processes. The substantive terms of the 1997 CBA and the 2002 CBA and the bargaining histories that led to those agreements influenced the collective bargaining outcome in 2006. Most importantly, those variables forced the parties to adopt new negotiating strategies and styles prior to their agreement in 2006. This new system of negotiating closely resembles an approach to negotiating espoused by Roger Fisher and William Ury called "principled negotiation."[6]

. . . .

II.   BARGAINING HISTORY OF THE 1997 CBA

After the 1990 CBA expired on December 31, 1993, the MLB owners set out to restructure the game's financial system.[31] What followed was a lengthy, bitter struggle between the owners and the union to establish the terms of the next collective bargaining agreement.

The process began when Bud Selig, the owner of the Milwaukee Brewers and the acting MLB Commissioner, brought the owners together to determine a group strategy. The owners decided that they would be willing to share revenues if the players would agree to a salary cap. The owners made their first proposal of a salary cap on June 14, 1994. The primary problem with this proposal was that the players preferred the "free market system of individually bargained salaries" currently in place.[32] Another problem was that the 1990 CBA had expired more than six months prior to this initial offer.[33] By delaying the start of negotiations with the union, the owners had "squandered potentially valuable months of discussion and subverted any hope of establishing more open and trusting lines of communication."[34] Unfortunately, time ran out on the parties to come to an agreement. The players went on strike on August 12, 1994. On September 14, 1994, Selig announced the cancellation of the rest of the season and the World Series.

How had the parties' conduct created a situation that resulted in the cancellation of the World Series? First, the relationship between the parties was severely strained. The owners had recently colluded to prevent the players from

signing contracts that were commensurate with market value. According to former MLB Commissioner Fay Vincent, this collusion had "so thoroughly polluted the whole relationship between the union and the owners that the impact [was] still being felt."[35] The parties were thus, according to the principled negotiation approach, unable to separate the people from the problem prior to the strike.

Second, the negotiating styles that the parties had employed were the antithesis of principled negotiation. Instead of focusing on interests, the parties chose to concentrate on their positions. According to Lauren Rich, one of the lead negotiators for the union at the time, the prevailing dynamic was power negotiating, meaning that "whoever gave up first lost."[36] The owners were firmly entrenched in their position that the game needed a salary cap in order to "blunt free agent salaries."[37] The players' position was that a free market for salaries should prevail.[38] The parties stuck to these conflicting positions throughout the summer of 1994, and neither side budged. By the time the players were prepared to go on strike, the parties were still advocating completely different frameworks for determining player salaries.[39] This prevented the parties from even engaging in the inferior negotiation method of positional bargaining, where they would make concessions in order to reach a compromise.[40]

Third, by failing to separate the people from the problem and by failing to focus on interests rather than positions, the parties never had an opportunity to start inventing options for mutual gain or insisting on using objective criteria. It was not until after the strike that the parties ever convened with a sincere purpose of engaging in a creative dialogue to advance both parties' interests.[41] The third and fourth components of principled negotiation were thus completely ignored by the parties prior to the strike.[42]

Following the strike, the parties negotiated into December of 1994 with the help of a mediator appointed by President Bill Clinton.[43] Despite the union's offer to agree to a luxury tax on high team payrolls, the owners declared an impasse in bargaining and unilaterally implemented their salary cap proposal.[44] The union responded by filing an unfair labor practice charge with the National Labor Relations Board (NLRB).[45] In February of 1995, the parties returned to the bargaining table and resumed discussions about a luxury tax.[46] The stalemate continued as the owners made additional unilateral changes and refused to participate in an arbitration proceeding.[47] The union filed another unfair labor practice charge with the NLRB.[48] After the NLRB found merit in the union's claims, the union sought an injunction in federal court to force the owners to return to the status quo.[49] The injunction was granted against the owners, and the parties were forced to return to the bargaining table.[50]

The parties realized that after using their economic weapons they had still not gained any advantage in negotiations and neither side had caved.[51] They had done an "incredible job alienating fans," though, and the game had taken a major hit on attendance.[52] League-wide shared revenue that each team received had also plummeted from $19 million per team in 1993 to less than $8 million per team in 1994, due in large part to the new national television contract.[53] Average player salaries had also fallen by almost 10% in 1995, the year following the strike.[54] Collectively, these factors created an impetus for both parties to reach a new deal that would be mutually beneficial.

Now for the first time, when the parties met at the bargaining table, they started focusing on underlying interests, and "there was real communication on the issues."[55] Even with this shift toward principled negotiating, it took more than a year for the parties to come to terms on a new collective bargaining agreement. On October 24, 1996, the two sides reached a tentative agreement, and the owners formally approved the deal on November 26, 1996.[56] The agreement, however, did not reflect the culmination of an efficient negotiation process. Instead, after butting heads for almost three years since the expiration of the 1990 CBA, "labor and management reached an accommodation only when pragmatism combined with exhaustion."[57]

There were three revolutionary components of the 1997 CBA: (1) a luxury tax system, (2) a framework for substantial revenue sharing, and (3) the Industry Growth Fund. For the luxury tax, the parties agreed that up to five teams with a payroll exceeding a certain threshold would pay a 35% tax in 1997 and 1998 and a 34% tax in 1999.[58] This provided the owners with some relief from the existing system by creating a disincentive for the richer teams to increase their payrolls. The players agreed to the tax because it was not an absolute cap on salaries;[59] the union predicted it would not have a substantial negative impact on average salaries.[60] Further, the owners had agreed not to assess a tax in 2000 and gave the union the option to extend the contract into 2001 without a luxury tax.[61]

The revenue sharing plan and the Industry Growth Fund were designed to spur the game's international growth and to create a greater base of revenue for the owners and players to share in the future.[62] These components of the 1997 CBA also revealed a burgeoning level of cooperation between the parties. The stated purpose of the payroll tax, a 2.5% tax on player salaries in 1996 and 1997 to be paid by the players, was "to further the growth and development of the Game and the industry on an individual Club and on an aggregate basis with the view toward advancing the interests of both the Clubs and the Players."[63] The payroll tax was thus the players' pledge to make a sacrifice for the long-term health of the sport. The owners made a similar pledge with their contributions to the revenue sharing plan.[64] The parties then made the combined pledge, via the Industry Growth Fund, "(1) to enhance fan interest in the game; (2) to increase baseball's popularity; and (3) to ensure industry growth into the 21st Century."[65] As it turned out, the game did experience rapid financial growth during the life of the contract, but the parties' historic antagonistic tendencies continued to thwart cooperation in the ensuing rounds of collective bargaining

and continued to interfere with the task of creating a wise agreement efficiently and amicably.

III. BARGAINING HISTORY OF THE 2002 CBA

During the life of the 1997 CBA, baseball's financial landscape underwent a dramatic transformation. Between 1996 and 2001, after deducting player payroll, the owners' yearly revenues increased from $836 million to $1.576 billion.[66] The average franchise value had risen from $111 million in 1994 to $286 million in 2001.[67] The owners had approved a new television deal with Fox worth $2.5 billion over 6 years—a 50% increase in revenue from the previous television deal[68]—and a deal with ESPN for another $851 million.[69] The players' average salaries had also nearly doubled, rising from $1.177 million in 1996 to $2.264 million in 2001.[70]

Despite all this increase in revenue for both the owners and the players, the game had some serious problems. First, there was now a vast revenue disparity between large and small market teams.[71] In 1989, the difference in revenue between the richest and poorest team was approximately $30 million.[72] By 2001, that figure had grown to a staggering $208 million.[73] Not surprisingly, as revenue disparity grew, so did payroll disparity. In 1995, the difference between the highest and lowest payroll for the 25-man roster was $45.1 million.[74] By 2001, that figure had more than doubled to $103.8 million.[75] Payroll disparity affected competitive balance.[76] According to Andrew Zimbalist, a prominent sports economist, "high payrolls greatly increase the probability of strong team performance, while low payrolls greatly lower this probability."[77] Indeed, from 1985 to 1994, the relationship between payroll and winning percentage in major league baseball was never significant at the 1% level; but from 1995 to 2001, the relationship was significant at the 1% level every single year.[78] In other words, the economics of baseball were now playing an extremely important role in determining which teams were successful on the field.

Given the overall economic state of the game, the owners voted on November 6, 2001, to eliminate 2 of the 30 major league teams.[79] The timing of this unprecedented decision could not have been more controversial. Two days earlier, baseball had just treated its fans to a scintillating World Series, culminating in the Arizona Diamondbacks' game seven victory over the New York Yankees.[80] The 1997 CBA was set to expire at midnight the next day, and the parties were not yet engaging in any negotiations, let alone negotiations to contract a franchise.[81] When the owners voted to contract before negotiating the issue with the union, according to former Commissioner Fay Vincent, it was "like bombing someone and then asking him to come to the table and talk about a peace."[82] Andrew Zimbalist referred to the move as a "grenade," because contracting two teams "would mean the reduction of union membership by eighty players; and lowering demand for players by eighty relative to supply would put downward pressure on salaries."[83] Donald Fehr, the executive director of the union, called the announcement to contract "the worst manner in which to begin the process of negotiating a new collective bargaining agreement. We had hoped that we were in a new era, one which would see a much better relationship between players and owners. Today's announcement is a severe blow to such hopes."[84]

As the parties prepared to negotiate the next collective bargaining agreement, they had once again returned to the important hurdle of attempting to separate the people from the problem.[85] They were off to a rocky start. Selig and the owners had not involved the union in the contraction discussions, and in late November 2001, Selig made the powerful yet risky statement: "Will we contract? We will contract."[86] By staking out the owners' position with this type of public commitment, Selig had converted negotiations "into a 'take-it-or-leave-it' game . . . [that could] produce either an agreement or a stalemate."[87]

Before the parties initiated a new round of negotiations, Selig made a dramatic public presentation that revealed why the owners were so pessimistic about the financial state of the game.[88] On December 6, 2001, the Commissioner told the United States House Judiciary Committee that MLB would lose approximately $519 million in 2001.[89] Andrew Zimbalist referred to this figure as "misleading," based on accounting issues such as amortization, depreciation, and interest expense.[90] Zimbalist also observed some "discrepancies between the revenue figures reported by Selig and those reported by the teams."[91] He suggested that individual teams had strong incentives to reduce their reported revenue, such as baseball's revenue sharing system, the attempt to garner public support, and the attempt to lower player salaries by convincing the union that the teams were losing money.[92]

Now with a controversial cloud hanging over the teams' true financial positions, the parties began formal negotiations in January of 2002.[93] The owners crafted their first proposal from the recommendations of a blue-ribbon panel that Selig had created in 1999.[94] The blue-ribbon panel studied baseball's economic system for fifteen months and made recommendations for improvements in a July 2000 report.[95] Selig had failed to include the union in the project,[96] however, and chose to rely only on four experts and twelve owners.[97] The panel suggested that baseball set the luxury tax threshold at $84 million with a 50% tax rate, increase revenue sharing to between 40 and 50% of net local revenue, and withhold revenue sharing from teams unless they spent around $40 million or more on team payroll.[98] The panel also predicted that if the parties agreed on those terms, baseball would not need to contract.[99]

By beginning negotiations with this proposal, the owners had set the stage for another classic battle with the union over conflicting positions. In mid-January however, Selig made the first of a series of cooperative gestures aimed at improving the parties' relationships—he invited Donald Fehr to speak to the owners. In the thirty-five-year history of the union, "no union official had ever been invited to speak to the owners."[100] Not surprisingly, Fehr admitted, "I don't know many of the owners very well and they don't know me very well. Better knowledge of one another is probably to be preferred."[101] Selig deserves credit for finally taking this obvious step toward improving the parties' working relationship, an essential component of principled negotiation.[102] Similarly, Fehr deserves credit for opening the lines of communication by offering the owners "to dance as long as we're partners" and asking them to "look at things from my point of view as well as your own."[103]

By mid-March 2002, the parties were in the midst of examining their respective points of views and interests. The owners had indicated that they considered three elements essential in a new collective bargaining agreement: an increase in revenue sharing, a luxury tax, and a worldwide draft.[104] The players also knew that Selig wanted to deal with baseball's competitive balance problem[105] by significantly increasing the revenue sharing and luxury tax money transfers.[106] The union was willing to agree to a slight increase in revenue sharing, but it was still opposed to another luxury tax provision, and it preferred to address competitive balance issues by redistributing players instead of money.[107]

Two months later, negotiations had begun to stagnate, and the union started to discuss setting a strike date.[108] As the All-Star Game approached, Selig removed the threat of a $1 million fine on owners who spoke publicly about the labor negotiations, and the parties began jockeying for public appeal and accusing each other of using stalling techniques.[109] Selig himself continued to discuss the negative aspects of baseball's financial landscape, and some union enthusiasts considered this "doom-and-gloom talk" as deliberately aimed at increasing the owners' bargaining leverage.[110]

By the end of July the parties had made strides in communicating their underlying interests,[111] and the owners' negotiators claimed to be working on a proposal that "accomplishes the philosophical goals of both sides."[112] In early August, the parties built momentum by coming to terms on minor issues such as minimum salaries and the player benefit plan.[113] On August 16, however, with the parties struggling to agree on a luxury tax provision,[114] the union set August 30 as a strike date.[115] The players set the strike date because they feared that if the season ended without an agreement, "the owners would declare an impasse and put a new economic system in place after the World Series."[116]

In the final week of negotiations leading up to the strike deadline, the parties met regularly, sometimes as many as five bargaining sessions a day, and exchanged dozens of ideas on revenue sharing and the luxury tax threshold, rate and duration.[117] Selig and Fehr, the two men with ultimate authority for their constituencies, were now at the forefront.

Selig had begun to accept responsibility for baseball's precarious position and admitted that "we've come to a moment in history where we" have to solve the problems.[118] On Friday morning, August 30, 2002, the parties met at the commissioner's office. Selig and Fehr joined the negotiations, and they finally reached a deal a few hours short of the scheduled strike. Selig was "euphoric," because the "two parties [had] come together, [made] a very meaningful deal and [done] it without one game of work stoppage."[119]

Selig was perhaps the most influential figure in ensuring that the games went on as scheduled. During the collective bargaining process leading up to the 2002 CBA, Selig had not always acted publicly in a way to build cohesion among the owners and the union. Behind the scenes, however, the positive impact that Bud Selig's personality and negotiating style had had on the collective bargaining process was remarkable. Before 2002, Selig had always been adept at "identifying the owners' common problems and interests" and "creating a common denominator for ownership cohesion."[120] According to Jerry Reinsdorf, owner of the Chicago White Sox, when Selig became acting commissioner in 1992, he was the only owner "who [could] get votes out of the other owners . . . because he's such a nice guy, and he works at staying in touch with the rest of us."[121] Selig wanted to work through issues by "consensus rather than confrontation."[122] As he put it, this "is the approach I would like to take to each and every problem confronting the game today."[123]

By employing a consensus building approach during his communications with the owners and the owners' negotiations with the union, Selig had departed from the approaches used by his predecessor commissioners. Bowie Kuhn, who served as the commissioner of Major League Baseball from February 4, 1969, to September 30, 1984, did not foster "constructive and cooperative relations" between the owners and the players.[124] Instead, according to then union head and Kuhn's chief adversary, Marvin Miller, Kuhn's "attempts at leadership created divisions," and he exhibited a "lack of concern for the rights of players . . . and even of the stray, unpopular owner."[125] Due in part to Kuhn's poor leadership, the first players' strike occurred in 1972.[126] The advent of free agency also occurred during Kuhn's tenure as commissioner when, according to Miller, Kuhn was "so hostile to the players that he motivated them for the struggle."[127]

Following Kuhn, Peter Ueberroth served as commissioner from October 1, 1984, to March 31, 1989.[128] Ueberroth increased the tension between the owners and players by announcing that the parties had reached an agreement to end the 1985 strike before the agreement had been approved by the owners.[129] More importantly, however, Ueberroth was the "ringleader of ownership collusion during 1986–1988 that ultimately cost the owners $280 million in damages and a deepening distrust in their relations with the players."[130]

Another commissioner who struggled to improve the relationships among and between the bargaining parties was Fay Vincent, who served from September 13, 1989, to September 7, 1992.[131] After the owners voted to lock the players out of spring training in 1990, Vincent stepped into negotiations and persuaded the Player Relations Committee, which was bargaining on behalf of the owners, to reach a deal with the union.[132] Some of the owners resented Vincent's impact on the bargaining process.[133] They thought Vincent had weakened their position with his direct involvement and with the hiring of Steve Greenberg, a critical member of the negotiating process who had a "conciliatory attitude" toward the union.[134] Despite Vincent's efforts to improve baseball's labor relations, he was "not able to build consensus among owners."[135] The owners were so dissatisfied with Vincent's leadership that they passed a no-confidence vote against him that led to his resignation.[136]

Unlike Kuhn, Ueberroth, and Vincent, Bart Giamatti did exhibit a personality and negotiating style similar to Selig when he served as commissioner from April 1, 1989, to September 1, 1989. According to Leonard Koppett, Giamatti had "persuasive powers, people skills, the ability to establish positive relationships, and certainly the intelligence to deal with the real difficulties. . . . He might have become the best of all the commissioners."[137] Giamatti only served for five months, however, due to a fatal heart attack. Thus, baseball lost the opportunity to benefit from Giamatti's leadership.

Selig, however, has provided baseball with the opportunity to benefit from a positive leader. Since 1970, when Selig appeared on the baseball scene as owner of the Milwaukee Brewers, he has cultivated relationships among the owners.[138] When he took over as the permanent commissioner on August 1, 1998, he told the owners that reducing acrimony in their ranks was "the most important thing I have ahead of me. My father was a great peacemaker, and obviously I've inherited that."[139] To earn the owners' trust, Selig often spent a great deal of his day on the phone speaking with owners, listening to their needs.[140] Then he would work like "a master politician," according to Larry Lucchino, trying to enhance the game and improve the economic status of the owners.[141] By August 2002, when the future of the game was hanging in the balance, Selig had earned the trust of the owners, "because he was one of them, knew their needs and served as the consensus commissioner."[142] As a result, Selig was instrumental in engineering agreement on the 2002 CBA.[143]

As with the 1997 CBA, the two biggest sources of contention during the negotiation of the 2002 CBA were the luxury tax and revenue sharing. In the last few weeks prior to the union's strike deadline, the parties inched toward agreement by making slight adjustments to their positions on the luxury tax thresholds, the applicable tax rates, and the total amount of revenue sharing. This type of "haggling,"[144] which runs afoul of principled negotiation, allowed the parties to narrow the gaps between their positions enough to come to terms.

There were some signs, however, that the parties focused on their respective underlying interests to make bargaining headway. First, on August 5, 2002, Fehr conditioned a discussion regarding a luxury tax on the owners' agreement to table the issue of contraction until 2007.[145] This move opened up discussions on the luxury tax, allowed the union to save 80 jobs in the short-term, and allowed the owners to retain the right to contract in the future if economically necessary.[146] Then, while negotiating the luxury tax, the parties hit a snag with respect to its application in the fourth year of the contract.[147] They overcame this problem when the union agreed to accept a luxury tax in the fourth year as long as it did not apply to first time offenders.[148] Finally, the union had wanted a phase-in where full revenue sharing would not occur until the fourth year of the contract.[149] The owners wanted no phase-in, but the parties were able to agree on a partial phase-in with full revenue sharing occurring in the last two years of the deal.[150]

Although these trade-offs with respect to the parties' underlying interests helped produce agreement on the 2002 CBA, the terms of the deal did not guarantee that the owners would realize their goals of "retarding the escalation of salaries, reducing payroll disparity and restoring competitive balance."[151] With the benefit of hindsight, the agreement did yield "some important gains that supported baseball's economic health, [but] it was also highly flawed."[152] According to Zimbalist, the 2002 CBA was flawed because it "had no minimum payroll at all; nor did it have any other effective incentives for revenue-receiving teams to spend the transfers on their players."[153] In fact, the structure of the contract created a disincentive for low-revenue teams to invest in players, because the "revenue-sharing system imposed what amounted to a marginal tax rate of roughly 39 percent on the top half of teams and 47 percent on the bottom half."[154]

Right from the outset, the contract's deficiencies were manifested. First, in 2003, five of the seven lowest-payroll teams collectively lowered their payrolls by $62.6 million, despite receiving $63.1 million in revenue sharing.[155] Second, the standard deviation of payroll disparity increased by 11.8% in 2003, 17.8% in 2004, and 5.1% in 2005.[156] Finally, the average player salary on opening day increased by at least 5% in every year except one.[157] Perhaps if the parties had left themselves more time to brainstorm, focus on using objective criteria, and analyze the potential impacts of their decisions, they would have been able to find more joint gains.

IV. BARGAINING HISTORY OF THE 2007 CBA

Although the impact of the 2002 CBA had not been ideal, as the parties prepared to negotiate a new collective bargaining agreement in 2006, the overall economic climate of the game provided them with a strong incentive to forge another deal without a work stoppage.[158] Attendance was at an all-time high,[159] industry revenue had risen to $4.7 billion in 2005,[160] and average player salaries were approaching $3

million per season.[161] The parties appeared poised to take the next step in their labor relationship: to come to terms ahead of schedule without a work stoppage or even the threat of a work stoppage.

The foundation for cooperation had been established back in 2002. When it came time to announce that the parties had reached agreement on the 2002 CBA, Selig and Fehr held a joint press conference, standing side by side and taking turns speaking at the microphone.[162] This symbolic gesture, a key component of principled negotiation,[163] signaled that the parties were finally ready to separate the people from the problem and to attack their mutual problems, not each other.[164]

The parties demonstrated this new approach when they worked together to address the issue of steroid use in baseball. In January of 2005, the union agreed to reopen the 2002 CBA in order to revise the drug testing policy.[165] Then in May 2005, Selig wrote a letter to Fehr asking him to "demonstrate once again to America that our relationship has improved to the point that we can quickly and effectively deal with matters affecting the interest of our sport."[166] In November 2005, the Union agreed to adjust the steroid testing policy for a second time, and Selig avoided the opportunity to boast about convincing the union to reopen the negotiations again.[167] Selig stated that there had not been "a question of putting [the union] in a corner. It was an integrity issue facing our sport."[168] This was a helpful public spin for the relationship, and it kept attention on the parties' shared interests.

The parties also had the key cooperative experience of organizing the World Baseball Classic (WBC).[169] In December 2005, agent Tommy Tanzer noted that the parties were "selling the international baseball thing so hard. They're enthusiastic about it. I just don't believe there will be a work stoppage. I don't see it this time."[170] While the WBC gave the owners a new forum for global marketing of Major League Baseball's brightest stars, those stars were also able to participate in a new forum of intense competition. Indeed, MLB superstar Ichiro Suzuki explained, "I didn't really care if I would get injured in this game. That's how much I really wanted to win this one."[171]

Shortly after the WBC was played, by early April 2006, the parties were in an ideal position regarding the forthcoming negotiations. The 2002 CBA was set to expire in eight months, and the parties had already conducted background talks on the next CBA.[172] They had thus given themselves a head start, unlike in 1994 and 2002 when they waited until after the expiration of the previous contract to begin negotiating. Their relationship was also as amicable as ever, and Fehr indicated that he would "like to believe the atmosphere of lower levels of public dispute is going to be maintained."[173] Selig continued to do his part to keep negotiations civil by increasing the possible owners' fine from $1 million to $2 million if they spoke to the union or the news media about the labor talks.[174]

According to Michael Weiner, a lead negotiator for the union, one factor that helped the parties make progress toward a new deal in 2006 was that the owners were willing to negotiate within the same framework as the 2002 CBA.[175] Given this, the parties knew that they would not be able to effectuate a major change in the economic structure of the game without resorting to the threat of a work stoppage.[176] However, in order to avoid the pitfalls of another protracted labor dispute, both sides wanted to get a deal done before the World Series.[177] The owners also had the incentive to work something out, because if they failed, 2007 would be played without a luxury tax.[178] The parties met consistently throughout the season, and by October they were approaching an agreement by meeting daily and by refraining from discussing the bargaining sessions publicly.[179] On October 24, 2006, the parties announced that they had reached a new agreement that would run through the 2011 season.[180] . . .

V. THE FUTURE OF COLLECTIVE BARGAINING IN BASEBALL

With attendance and revenues at all-time highs . . ., the future looks bright for baseball. There is even evidence that the owners' attempt to reduce payroll disparity is coming to fruition.[182] In 2006, the standard deviation of payrolls fell by 5.7%, the first year-over-year tightening in team payrolls since 1994.[183] Furthermore, during the life of the 2002 CBA, only three teams spent enough on salaries to be forced to pay a luxury tax.[184]

The ultimate question, however, is what impact collective bargaining has had and will have on competitive balance—the "prerequisite for a successful team sports league in the long run."[185] After the parties agreed to the 2002 CBA, David Leonhardt of the New York Times predicted that for most fans, "the only true test of the new agreement will be whether it does a better job than the previous one of providing competitive balance and [allowing] teams to hold onto their star players."[186] The debate hinges on how one defines competitive balance. Selig's blue-ribbon panel opined that "proper competitive balance will not exist until every well-run club has a regularly recurring hope of reaching postseason play."[187] In late September of 2006, there were fourteen teams within five games of a playoff berth, prompting Selig to conclude that "we do have competitive balance."[188]

Others, however, disagree. Billy Beane, the General Manager of the Oakland Athletics, thinks "we're still a long way off from saying there's parity"[189] even though his low-revenue team recently made the playoffs. Instead, Beane believes the wild card[190] "gives people the impression of parity."[191] Since the wild card was added in 1995, there have been 96 playoff berths, but 7 of the 30 teams have failed to capture even one of them.[192] The lack of incentives to increase payroll appears to be the most significant factor. According to Zimbalist, the "present system rewards failure and encourages teams to take a free ride. . . . With

higher marginal tax rates on the bottom teams and with the commissioner not enforcing the CBA provision requiring revenue transfers to be spent on improving team quality, the current scheme does not promote competitive balance."[193]

. . . .

The owners and the players have started to develop a "different kind of bargaining history."[204] That bargaining history places a premium on reaching agreement without a work stoppage, and it also resembles principled negotiation more than ever. The parties have become more adept at focusing on their shared interests rather than their individual positions, and they are doing so in a much more cooperative working environment. If the parties continue to strengthen their resolve for mutual growth and satisfaction, America's pastime will thrive like never before as an unparalleled brand of athletic competition.

Notes

1. See Players' Union Sets Aug. 30 Strike Date, SI.com, Aug. 18, 2002, http://sportsillustrated.cnn.com/baseball/news/2002/08/16/strike_date_ap/.

2. Id.

3. Roger I. Abrams, Legal Bases: Baseball and the Law 185–86 (1998).

4. Murray Chass, Last-Minute Deal in Baseball Talks Prevents a Strike, N.Y. Times, Aug. 31, 2002, at A1, available at 2002 WL 4088944.

5. Id.

6. Roger Fisher & William Ury, Getting to Yes: Negotiating Agreement Without Giving In 11 (Bruce Patton ed., Penguin Books 1991) (1981).

. . . .

31. Abrams, supra note 3, at 180.

32. Id. at 183.

33. Andrew Zimbalist, May the Best Team Win: Baseball Economics and Public Policy 88 (2003).

34. Id.

35. Id. at 85.

36. Telephone Interview with Lauren Rich, NLRB, in Atlanta, Ga. (Apr. 30, 2007).

37. Id.

38. Id.

39. Id.

40. Fisher & Ury, supra note 6, at 3.

41. Interview with Lauren Rich, supra note 36.

42. See Fisher & Ury, supra note 6, at 66, 82-83.

43. Abrams, supra note 3, at 187.

44. A luxury tax allows teams to set their own payrolls, subject to a tax on combined player salaries that exceed a certain threshold. A salary cap does not allow teams to set their payrolls above a certain threshold. The owners prefer the salary cap because it forces them to limit their spending, which theoretically results in lower costs and a more level playing field among the clubs.

45. Abrams, supra note 3, at 187.

46. Id.

47. Id.

48. Id.

49. Id. at 190.

50. Id. at 194.

51. See generally id. at 195-98.

52. Interview with Lauren Rich, supra note 36.

53. Zimbalist, supra note 34, at 46.

54. Average MLB Player Salary Chart, http://sportsline.com/mlb /salaries/avgsalaries (last visited Sept. 22, 2007).

55. Interview with Lauren Rich, supra note 36.

56. For an in-depth discussion of the negotiation timeline from 1994 to 1996, see Abrams, supra note 31, at 175-200.

57. Id. at 201.

58. MLB Basic Agreement 1997–2000 art. XXIII.

59. Interview with Lauren Rich, supra note 36.

60. Id.

61. Id.

62. Id.

63. MLB Basic Agreement 1997–2000 art. XXIV.

64. The intricacies of the revenue sharing plan are beyond the scope of this Article. The stated intent of the plan, however, was to "effect a net transfer of Net Local Revenue among Participating Clubs of $70 million at 100% implementation." Id. art. XXV(B)(1)(a) (2001).

65. Id. art. XXVI.

66. Zimbalist, supra note 34, at 71.

67. Michael J. Haupert, The Economic History of Major League Baseball, http://eh.net/encyclopedia/article/haupert.mlb (last visited Jan. 21, 2008).

68. Murray Chass, ROUNDUP; Piniella Stays in Seattle, N.Y. Times, Nov. 1, 2000, at D7, available at 2000 WLNR 3295459.

69. Zimbalist, supra note 34, at 1.

70. Average MLB Player Salary Chart, supra note 54.

71. Zimbalist, supra note 34, at 46.

72. Id.

73. Id.

74. Id. at 47.

75. Id.

76. Id. at 45.

77. Id.

78. Id. at 43.

79. Murray Chass, Back to Business: Baseball Votes to Drop 2 Teams, N.Y. Times, Nov. 7, 2001, at A1, available at 2001 WLNR 3399574.

80. 2001 Major League Baseball Playoffs, http://sportsillustrated.cnn .com/baseball/mlb/ml/recaps/2001/11/04/diamondbacks_yankees (last visited Jan. 21, 2008).

81. Chass, supra note 79.

82. Outside the Lines: Contraction—Is Less More?, http://www.espn .go.com/page2/tvlistings/show85transcript.html (last visited Sept. 22, 2007).

83. Zimbalist, supra note 34, at 95.

84. Chass, supra note 79.

85. Fisher & Ury, supra note 6, at 17.

86. Murray Chass, Selig Offers His Forecast for the Game, N.Y. Times, Nov. 28, 2001, at S1, available at 2001 WLNR 3417621.

87. Roger I. Abrams, The Money Pitch: Baseball Free Agency and Salary Arbitration 59 (2000).

88. Zimbalist, supra note 34, at 57.

89. Id. at 57. For a complete look at the accounting figures that Selig presented to Congress, see a table illustrating the 2001 team-by-team revenues and expenses forecast for MLB franchises, available at http://www.usatoday.com/sports/baseball/stories/2001-12-05 -focus-expenses.htm (last visited Sept. 22, 2007).

90. Zimbalist, supra note 34, at 57.

91. Id. at 60.

92. Id. at 62.

93. Id. at 1. There had been three months of secret talks between the parties in the spring of 2001 that insiders believe could have produced a deal before the All-Star Game, but Selig abruptly called a halt to those talks in late June. Chass, supra note 86.

94. For a discussion on the differences between the panel's recommendations and the owners' first proposal, see Zimbalist, supra note 34, at 93-95.

95. Id. at 93.

96. By doing so, Selig failed to abide by one of the tenets of principled negotiation; namely, he failed to give each party "a stake in the outcome by making sure they participate in the process." Fisher & Ury, supra note 6, at 27.

97. Zimbalist, supra note 34, at 93.

98. Id. at 94.

99. Id.

100. Murray Chass, Players Union Chief Talks to Owners, N.Y. Times, Jan. 18, 2002, at D2, available at 2002 WLNR 4084764.

101. Id.

102. Fisher & Ury, supra note 6, at 37.

103. Chass, supra note 100.

104. Murray Chass, Players Offer Their View of a Contract They'd Like, N.Y. Times, Mar. 15, 2002, at D2, available at 2002 WLNR 4045869.

105. In January 2000, the owners unanimously passed a resolution directing Selig to do "whatever he could to restore competitive balance to baseball." Murray Chass, Owners Can Talk Publicly on Issues, N.Y. Times, July 4, 2002, at D3, available at 2002 WLNR 4034934.

106. Chass, supra note 104.

107. Id.

108. Murray Chass, A Strike Date Is Discussed as Talks Lag in Baseball, N.Y. Times, May 15, 2002, at D1, available at 2002 WLNR 4079065.

109. Chass, supra note 105.

110. Murray Chass, Both Sides Say Talk About Baseball's Problems Is One, N.Y. Times, July 13, 2002, at D1, available at 2002 WLNR 4062465.

111. For a detailed discussion of the parties' competing interests, see Murray Chass, Union Puts Off Strike Date To Pursue Talks, N.Y. Times, Aug. 13, 2002, at D1, available at 2002 WLNR 4070063.

112. Murray Chass, Little Progress Made on Revenue Sharing, N.Y. Times, July 27, 2002, at D4, available at 2002 WLNR 4093309.

113. Murray Chass, Union Prepared To Set Strike Date on Monday, N.Y. Times, Aug. 9, 2002, at D3, available at 2002 WLNR 4031542.

114. The union opposed a luxury tax because it felt that it would decrease league-wide spending on salaries. The owners supported the tax as a method of reducing payroll disparity without reducing total industry payroll. Murray Chass, Baseball Sees Progress in Talks, but the Union Isn't So Sure, N.Y. Times, July 26, 2002, at D1, available at 2002 WLNR 4072832.

115. Murray Chass, Union, Still Talking, Sets a Strike Date of Aug. 30, N.Y. Times, Aug. 17, 2002, at A1, available at 2002 WLNR 4092464.

116. Chass, supra note 4.

117. Murray Chass, Talks Are Feverish with Strike Due Tomorrow, N.Y. Times, Aug. 29, 2002, at D1, available at 2002 WLNR 4060526.

118. Murray Chass, Baseball Commissioner and Consensus Builder, N.Y. Times, Aug. 28, 2002, at D1, available at 2002 WLNR 4020755.

119. Chass, supra note 4.

120. Andrew Zimbalist, In the Best Interests of Baseball?: The Revolutionary Reign of Bud Selig 127 (2006).

121. Id. at 135.

122. Id.

123. Id.

124. Id. at 83.

125. Id. at 82.

126. Id. (Former MLB Union Head, Marvin Miller, was discussing Kuhn's lack of leadership as commissioner).

127. Id.

128. Id. at 93.

129. Id.

130. Id. at 94.

131. Id. at 102.

132. Id. at 104.

133. Id.

134. Id.

135. Id. at 109.

136. Id.

137. Id. at 100.

138. Id. at 125.

139. Id. at 159.

140. See id. at 125-26.

141. Chass, supra note 118.

142. Id.

143. See id.

144. Fisher & Ury, supra note 6, at 3.

145. Murray Chass, Luxury Tax on Clubs: Less Than Meets Eye, N.Y. Times, Sept. 8, 2002, at 87, available at 2002 WLNR 4024221.

146. Id.

147. Id.

148. Id.

149. Chass, supra note 4.

150. Id.

151. Chass, supra note 145.

152. Zimbalist, supra note 120, at 164.

153. Id. at 105.

154. Id. at 164.

155. Id. at 166.

156. Chris Isidore, Baseball's Flatter Playing Field, http://money.cnn.com/2006/10/06/commentary/sportsbiz_baseball/index.htm (last visited Sept. 22, 2007).

157. Average MLB Player Salary Chart, supra note 54.

158. Telephone Interview with Michael Weiner, General Counsel, MLB Players Ass'n (May 11, 2007).

159. Allan H. "Bud" Selig, Ninth Commissioner of Baseball, http://mlb.mlb.com/mlb/history/mlb_history_people.jsp?story=com_bio _9 (last visited Sept. 22, 2007).

160. Murray Chass, Labor Talks: Don't Worry, There Must Be Something To Fight Over, N.Y. Times, Apr. 2, 2006, at S10, available at 2006 WLNR 5514660.

161. Average MLB Player Salary Chart, supra note 54.

162. David Leonhardt, Season Is Salvaged, but Baseball Still Has Rich Facing the Poor, N.Y. Times, Sept. 1, 2002, at 11, available at 2002 WLNR 4018027.

163. Fisher & Ury, supra note 6, at 32.

164. Id. at 11.

165. Murray Chass, Congress Nudges Union in Selig's New Lineup, N.Y. Times, Nov. 16, 2005, at D2, available at 2005 WLNR 18488971.

166. Jack Curry et al., Selig Seeks Harder Line on Drugs in Baseball, N.Y. Times, May 1, 2005, at S1, available at 2005 WLNR 6802195.

167. Chass, supra note 165.

168. Id.

169. The WBC was an 18-day tournament from March 3, 2006, to March 20, 2006. Sixteen teams competed, and they were comprised of the world's best players representing their home countries. World Baseball Classic FAQ, http://ww2.worldbaseballclassic.com/2006/about/index.jsp?sid=wbc (last visited Sept. 22, 2007).

170. Murray Chass, Agents Strikingly Optimistic About Labor Situation, N.Y. Times, Dec. 13, 2005, at D2, available at 2005 WLNR 19972339.

171. Murray Chass, The Critics Missed the Cheers Heard Around the World, N.Y. Times, Mar. 22, 2006, at D5, available at 2006 WLNR 4710964.

172. Chass, supra note 160.

173. Id.

174. Murray Chass, At Wrigley Field, It Was the Worst of Times, N.Y. Times, May 21, 2006, at S5, available at 2006 WLNR 8714287.

175. Interview with Michael Weiner, supra note 158.

176. Id.

177. Id.

178. Zimbalist, supra note 34, at 112-13.

179. Murray Chass, Labor Contract May Be Ready Soon, N.Y. Times, Oct. 20, 2006, at D5, available at 2006 WLNR 18221365.

180. Murray Chass, Players Union to Yankees: No New Taxes, N.Y. Times, Oct. 25, 2006, at D1, available at 2006 WLNR 18483270.

. . . .

182. Isidore, supra note 156.

183. Id.

184. Murray Chass, It's Too Early for the Yankees To Celebrate Their Tax Bill, N.Y. Times, Dec. 23, 2006, at D1, available at 2006 WLNR 22415111.

185. Zimbalist, supra note 34, at 151.

186. Leonhardt, supra note 162.

187. Zimbalist, supra note 34, at 35.

188. Murray Chass, Parity on the Field (Maybe), Dollar Disparity (Definitely), N.Y. Times, Sept. 24, 2005, at 82, available at 2006 WLNR 16557924.

189. Id.

190. The wild card system allows one extra team in both the American and the National Leagues to reach the playoffs every year.

191. Chass, supra note 188.

192. Division Series Summary, http://mlb.mlb.com/mlb/history /postseason/mlb_ds.jsp (last visited Sept. 22, 2007).

193. Zimbalist, supra note 120, at 216.

. . . .

204. Interview with Michael Weiner, supra note 158.

LABOR RELATIONS IN MAJOR LEAGUE BASEBALL

Andrew Zimbalist

Mention baseball labor relations to the typical fan and, as sure as Barry Bonds will be walked with a runner on second and two outs, the reaction will be disgust. Some say it is unseemly, if not immoral, for millionaires to fight billionaires in a world riddled with hunger and homelessness. Others personalize the matter and assert that Bud Selig and Don Fehr are both unspeakably despicable, then they state that they will not go to another game until baseball has new leadership.

Of course, if one bothered to ask Don Fehr or Bud Selig what Major League Baseball's (MLB's) labor struggles were all about, one would get sincere proclamations of principle and economic exigency. The players are not really fighting for an extra $100,000 in salary, Fehr might say; they are fighting for principle—the principle of free markets. Players should be paid what they are worth, and there is no fairer test of that than the free market. If the market says Alex Rodriguez is worth $1 million, then so be it. If it says he is worth $25.2 million, then that is okay, too. This principle has served the players well since 1977 and there is little reason for them to abandon it.

The owners, in contrast, have not really articulated a theoretical basis for the case against free markets in team sporting leagues. They simply claim that too many teams are losing too much money and that competitive balance is undermined by free markets. The former argument contains elements of truth but is overstated; the latter is never adequately explained.

It is fundamentally a battle over the degree of freedom in the labor market that has plagued MLB since the mid-1970s. Indeed, each work stoppage since 1976 has been the result of owner efforts to further constrain the operation of free agency and salary arbitration.

. . . [O]n only three occasions (1972, 1981, and 1994–95) were regular season games lost, and the lockout of 1973 affected only the early-arrival spring training. This, of course, is not to deny that baseball's labor relations have been contentious. They have been. The point, rather, is that sometimes fans (and the commissioner) start to feel sorry for themselves and think they have suffered more than the actual numbers suggest.

This article explores some of the roots and processes of this contentiousness. . . .

LABOR RELATIONS PROCESS

Two themes repeat themselves in MLB's collective bargaining history: owners' distrust of owners and players' distrust of owners.

Owners' Distrust of Owners

It has been said that bargaining with baseball's owners is like negotiating with a three-headed monster. In this charming metaphor, the monster's heads represent the high-revenue, the middle-revenue, and the low-revenue teams. Because each group of teams faces a radically different economic reality, each often has radically different ideas about what remedies are needed.

Since 1990, the monster's heads have grown larger and farther apart. In 1989, the revenue spread from the top to the bottom team was approximately $30 million. In 2002—resulting from the explosion of local media contracts and the uneven emergence of new stadiums among other factors—this disparity grew to more than $200 million (Major League Baseball Staff, 2001).

Compounding these reported revenue differentials is the presence of related party transactions (RPTs). RPTs permit a team owner who also owns a related business, such as a local sports channel, to transfer revenue away from the baseball team to the related business or to add costs to the team that originate in the related business. By now, this phenomenon is well known, so I shall cite only one illustration.

According to figures that Bud Selig presented to Congress in December 2001, the Chicago White Sox' income from local TV, radio, and cable was $30.1 million in 2001, and that of the Chicago Cubs was $23.6 million (Major League Baseball Staff, 2001). A curiosity, to say the least. Everyone knows that the Cubs are the more popular team in the Windy City, and TV ratings bear this out: In 2001 the Cubs average ratings were 6.8 on over-the-air broadcasting and 3.8 on cable; the White Sox were 3.6 and 1.9, respectively (McAvoy, 2002). And this does not take account of the fact that the Cubs games are shown on superstation WGN, which reaches more than 55 million homes nationally.

So, what is going on? The Cubs are owned by the Tribune Corporation, which also happens to own WGN. The Tribune Corporation transfers revenue away from the Cubs and correspondingly lowers the costs of WGN. According to *Broadcasting and Cable*, the industry's authoritative source, the Cubs local media earnings were $59 million (McAvoy, 2002). If the Cubs reported this figure instead of $23.6 million, then their reported $1.8 million loss would become a $33.6 million profit in 2001![1] Although the extent of RPTs for the Cubs is unusually large, significant RPTs affect a dozen or more clubs.[2]

Perceptions of baseball's economic reality also differ because franchises have different roles in owners' investment strategies. Often, the team itself is not managed as a profit center but, rather, as a vehicle for promoting the owner's other investments.

Owners can take their investment returns in a number of ways. For instance, George Steinbrenner used his Yankees to create the Yankee Entertainment and Sports (YES) regional sports network in the nation's largest media market. In late 2001, YES had a market value upward of $850 million.[3] Rupert Murdoch recently admitted that his purchase of the Dodgers had already paid off, because it enabled him to prevent Disney from creating a regional sports network in Southern California (Shaikin, 2001). Tom Hicks hopes to use his ownership of the Rangers to develop some 270 acres of commercial and residential real estate around the ballpark in Arlington and to grow his Southwest Sports Group, among other things. Dick Jacobs exploited his ownership of the Indians to promote the value of his downtown Cleveland real estate. To differing degrees, owners exploit their community prominence to establish profitable relationships with politicians and other business executives. Still others derive a handsome consumption return from team ownership.

On top of the growing differences in material circumstance among the owners, owners also diverge in their ideologies and personalities. These differences often produce cliques, and the cliques, in turn, engender rivalries if not animosities. Although fragmentation among the owners was obscured in 2002 by Bud Selig's gag order backed by threat of a $1 million fine, occasional signs of division in the ranks saw the light of day. For instance, one anonymous medium-market club owner told the *Illinois Daily Herald* in late July 2002:

You think this is funny but this is how Bud operates. He tells 30 owners 30 different things and then slaps a gag order on us and threatens us with a million-dollar fine so that the players don't find out we all hate what's going on. We're supposed to be unified? That's laughable. Lift the gag order again, and you'll see how unified. Now, on top of everything else in Montreal, the [former Expos] minority owners have filed racketeering charges against Bud and [Marlins Managing General Partner] Jeff [Loria], and if the books of every team are exposed during that legal fight, you can say goodbye to Bud and any deal with the players. This is more dangerous than you can imagine. Bud is playing with fire here and we're all getting burned. I'm convinced Bud got his contract extension by threatening 10 of us, making promises to the other 10 and loaning money to the last 10. This thing is on the track headed for a disaster, and Bud is right there in the front of the train conducting the whole operation. (Sports Business Daily, 2002a, p. 11)

Alternatively, listen to Selig himself, who, in a moment of public candor, told the Associated Press after the owners voted 29 to 1 to ratify the new labor deal, "I'm not going to suggest to you today that there are not clubs with very different views, but at some point you have to come together" (*Sports Business Daily*, 2002d, p. 13).

At least three problems evolve from this disunity. First, the owners cannot agree on a common vision for the game, let alone a cohesive plan for its future. Their inability to agree on basic demands inevitably leads to long delays before collective bargaining is initiated. Shortly after the owners reopened the 1990 collective bargaining agreement in December 1992, the owners' chief negotiator, Richard Ravitch, told Don Fehr that he wanted to start negotiating right away. Actual bargaining did not begin until March 1994—16 months later.

Selig's unilateral Blue Ribbon Panel produced its report on the state of baseball's economics and its collective bargaining recommendations in July 2000 (Levin, Mitchell, Volcker, &Will, 2000). Then, nearly a year passed before Selig, in the spring of 2001, authorized then MLB COO Paul Beeston to commence discussions with the Players Association (MLBPA). According to Steve Fehr (personal communication, February 20, 2003), a union negotiator, the two sides had 23 meetings between February 28, 2001, and June 20, 2001. When the June 20 meeting adjourned, the MLBPA thought they had an agreement. Beeston had responded favorably to the players' last proposal and said he would get back to them in short order. But the players never heard back. Selig had abruptly terminated the discussions without explanation. The owners did not put their substantive demands on the bargaining table until December 2001—a month after the expiration of the old agreement and 18 months after the Blue Ribbon Panel's report was issued.

A likely explanation for these delays is the disunity among owners. They cannot agree what demands to put on the table, so bargaining is pushed back. Then, when they start preliminary bargaining, a previously dormant ownership clique gets wind of the talks, objects, and the talks are terminated. The end result is that bargaining goes down to the wire and either does not get resolved in time (as in 1994) or is resolved in haste (as in 2002) with a flawed structure resting on compromise.

Second, when the owners finally come to the bargaining table, it is usually based on the lowest common denominator among them: They would like salaries to be lower. Accordingly, rather than producing a coherent, balanced plan for the game's future, the owners' tendency has been to come to the bargaining table with a demand for unilateral sacrifice by the players that restricts free agency rights in one way or another. This sets an adversarial tone to the bargaining process and reinforces the deep-seated distrust that the players have felt toward the owners.

Third, the MLBPA confronts formal ownership demands, but, in practice, it is bargaining with different groups that must be reconciled. It is put in the strange position of triangulating an agreement. This, too, is conducive to inefficient outcomes. For instance, a few owners may find themselves aligning more closely with the players on the issues of revenue sharing and luxury taxes. We know this to be the case at least with George Steinbrenner. As we shall see, this phenomenon leads the majority of owners to seek to penalize owners who break ranks, even if it means deviating from a rational design of collective bargaining institutions.

Players' Distrust of Owners

Distrust between players and owners produces its own set of distortions. In his 2002 book, former commissioner Fay Vincent singles out ownership collusion during 1985 to 1987 as a turning point in baseball's labor relations:

> *The effects of collusion so thoroughly polluted the whole relationship between the union and the owners that the impact is still being felt. . . . Selig and Reinsdorf, two ringleaders of collusion, were the ones who were the most adamant in saying, "We've got to find some way to get around this union, we have to see if we can break them." (pp. 281, 286)*

Collective bargaining in any industry is often characterized by posturing and bluffing. This process in baseball, however, takes on an exaggerated form. Consider, for instance, the maneuvering of Bud Selig during the 2001–02 round of bargaining. In addition to his plan for contraction

(which Selig's own Blue Ribbon Panel explicitly stated would not be necessary if its other ideas were implemented), Selig wanted: (a) the owners' 60/40 rule (see below) ratified in the collective bargaining agreement, (b) the establishment of a fund of $100 million that the commissioner could use at his discretion, (c) the right for owners to release players whose salary arbitration figures were deemed to be too high, and (d) a new pension plan contribution system (Zimbalist, 2003, chap. 5). Let us consider the meaning and weight of these bargaining demands.

Selig's demand for contraction was announced on November 6, 2001, 2 days after the end of the old labor agreement and the most scintillating World Series in recent memory. What a way to initiate negotiations on a new agreement! He might as well have launched a grenade at the 12 East 49th street offices of the Players Association. Cutting two teams would mean eliminating 80 union members and reducing the demand for players by 80 as the supply of players stayed the same.

Then Selig announced in late March 2002 that he was going to dust off the long dormant 60/40 rule and begin its implementation during the 2002 season. This rule, first introduced by the owners in December 1982, required teams to maintain a ratio between assets and liabilities of at least 60 to 40. At the time, the players filed a grievance that this rule would affect salaries and, hence, was a mandatory subject for collective bargaining. In his ruling of January 1985, arbitrator Richard Bloch upheld the owners' right to implement the rule unilaterally by arguing that it was a matter of fiscal responsibility and management prerogative.

When Selig announced that the owners would have to comply with the 60/40 rule by June 2002, he stipulated new implementation guidelines. According to press reports and a legal complaint filed by former Mets co-owner Nelson Doubleday, among these guidelines were the franchise valuation rule that a team's value equaled only two times its (trailing) annual revenue and the liability instruction that long-term player contracts would count as debt.[4] Selig threatened noncompliers with fines, loss of payments from the central fund, or being put into trusteeship. On the surface, the implementation of 60/40 smacked of financial prudence, but the reality was otherwise.

Under the liability accounting instruction, long-term player contracts count as debt. This makes no economic sense.[5] As of June 2002 when the rule was to kick in, the Boston Red Sox, for instance, had a remaining obligation to Manny Ramirez of roughly $120 million. For the rest of the squad, the Sox had approximately another $70 million in long-term obligations. So the team's total long-term contract obligations alone were roughly $190 million; that is, they were already $60 million-plus over their debt limit without counting the $40 million of preexisting debt the new owners inherited or the $200 million they had borrowed from Fleet Bank to buy the team. Thus, the Sox would have had to do some massive payroll cutting to avoid violating the 60/40 rule.

Nor are the Red Sox an aberration. According to Selig, at the end of 2001, MLB teams had more than $3 billion in debt, or more than $100 million per team. Using Selig's unreasonably low 2 × revenue multiple to value teams and his figure of $112.1 million average team revenues in 2001 (also low because of RPTs), the average franchise would be worth $224.2 million. With an average debt of $100 million-plus (and this is before long-term player contracts), the average team was already in violation of the rule with a 55.4/44.6 asset/debt ratio.

Whatever Bloch may have believed back in 1985, it is clear that the 60/40 rule would function as a backdoor salary cap in 2002. Selig was supposedly implementing the rule in 2002 under the authority of Bloch's ruling. Apparently recognizing its vulnerability, he put it on the bargaining table for labor ratification. The effects of the rule, however, were too draconian to be acceptable to the Players Association.

Why, then, did Selig put it on the table? Is he so out of touch with what is in the realm of possibility? Not likely. More likely, he put it on the table as a bargaining chip to loosen the players' position on other issues. This is part of the bargaining game played by both sides.

The demand for a commissioner's discretionary fund of $100 million (later reduced to $85 million) was only a little more benign. The discretionary fund could have been used by the commissioner to reward teams that toed the commissioner's line. The Players Association believed that this would provide a further drag on salaries. If a substantial fund were needed to help financially distressed franchises, then the players surely wanted it to operate according to set rules or be coadministered much like the Industry Growth Fund from the 1996 accord.

The right for owners to cut loose players who ask for high salary arbitration awards would undermine the value of the longstanding arbitration system to the players. Unless the owners were willing to substitute an equally effective mechanism, such as earlier free agency, it was not conceivable that the players would accept such a change.

The proposal for a new pension plan contribution system called for teams with higher payrolls to put more into the plan. However, players would still receive the same pension benefit. This proposal, in effect, would constitute an indirect tax on high payrolls supplementing the impact of the luxury tax proposal.

Selig, then, loaded the bargaining table with what the players perceived to be harsh, unacceptable demands. None of these demands was incorporated into the final settlement, and there is no direct evidence that they yielded any incremental bargaining leverage for the owners. They did, however, encumber the bargaining process and slow down the already time-pressed negotiations.[6]

I suspect that either side would maintain that the bargaining dance with all its bluster is necessary. And each side would claim that its strategy softened the other. But how many curve balls can you throw an experienced batter before he makes adjustments? It seems more likely that the final outcome has more to do with the relative unity and conviction of each side as well as the underlying economic realities than with the smoke-and-mirrors game of the bargaining process. . . .

Notes

1. This figure possibly should be adjusted for the superstation payments that the Cubs make to Major League Baseball (MLB), which are probably on the order of $15 million annually. However, it is also likely that the *Broadcasting and Cable* figure is conservative.

2. For more on related party transactions (RPTs) and how they affect other franchises, see Zimbalist, 2003, chapter 4.

3. Goldman Sachs reportedly purchased a 40% stake in the Yankee Entertainment and Sports (YES) Network in 2001 for $340 million. Assuming no minority discount, the Goldman Sachs's acquisition implies an $850 million value for YES.

4. Doubleday's complaint was against his erstwhile Mets partner, Fred Wilpon. According to Doubleday's counterclaim, Selig also included team stadium debt in liabilities where it was not counted in the original 60/40 rule implementation guidelines.

5. When players are paid in future years, they also generate revenue. This type of long-term contract does not accord with traditional notions of debt, save for the special case of uninsured injury. Deferred compensation is a different matter and is discussed below.

6. Arguably, one of the reasons why Selig put the harsh demands on the table was that the owners really wanted the outcome of the Blue Ribbon Panel's recommendations. If they put those recommendations forth as their initial demands, the final outcome would have compromised and vitiated the magnitude of the desired changes. Thus, the owners instead decided to put extreme demands on the table with the hope of compromising to the Blue Ribbon Panel report. Of course, the natural response to such an explanation is that the bargaining *pas de deux* that ensued during 2001 to 2002 was the product of Selig establishing a *unilateral* study commission—one that did not include player representatives. Had they been included, not only could the histrionics have been avoided, but the final outcome could have been more thoughtfully, purposefully, and effectively designed.

References

Levin, R. C., Mitchell, G. J., Volcker, P. A., & Will, G. F. (2000). *The report of the Independent Members of the Commissioner's Blue Ribbon Panel on baseball economics*. New York: Major League Baseball.

Major League Baseball Staff. (2001, December). *MLB updated supplement to the report of the Independent Members of the Commissioner's Blue Ribbon Panel on baseball economics*. New York: Major League Baseball. Available at roadsidephotos.com/baseball/BRPanelupd.htm

. . . .

McAvoy, K. (2002, April 1). Yanks, others get in the game. *Broadcasting and Cable*.

. . . .

Shaikin, B. (2001, December 13). Fox reaches Dodger goals. *Los Angeles Times*, p. Sports-8.

. . . .

Sports Business Daily. (2002a, July 25). Author, p. 11.

. . . .

Sports Business Daily. (2002d, September 6). Author, p. 13.

. . . .

Vincent, F. (2002). *The last commissioner*. New York: Simon & Schuster.

. . . .

Zimbalist, A. (2003). *May the best team win: Baseball economics and public policy*. Washington DC: Brookings Institution Press.

MACROPERSPECTIVE

BEYOND THE BOX SCORE: A LOOK AT COLLECTIVE BARGAINING AGREEMENTS IN PROFESSIONAL SPORTS AND THEIR EFFECT ON COMPETITION

Ryan T. Dryer

I.   INTRODUCTION

Most sports fans have at least the limited understanding that collective bargaining agreements govern the employer–employee relationships between the owners of professional sports teams and players' associations. Indeed, sports have become a big business in the United States, and the media coverage of sports has extended beyond reporting statistics and scores to include all dealings associated with the business.[1] Every year (at various times depending on the sport), fans are bombarded with numbers detailing signing bonuses, salary cap implications, arbitration results, incentive-laden contracts, and a multitude of other terms that boggle the mind of the layperson. As most sports fans (and reporters) take a what-have-you-done-for-me-lately attitude toward the performance of their teams and the organizations that assemble them, little attention has been paid to the historical progression that has led to the current state of professional sports. A historical analysis is critical to understanding why Major League Baseball, the National Basketball Association, and the National Football League[2] each have separate agreements governing their leagues. Such an examination helps to explain why the Collective Bargaining Agreements (CBAs) exist in their current structure. The articles of the various CBAs govern the professional sports players' compensation, the procedures for settling disputes, and address a myriad of other issues relating to the employer–employee relationship in sports.[3] This comment will examine the history of the three most prominent leagues in U.S. professional sports, the CBAs that govern the employer–employee relationship in each league, the provisions of those CBAs that influence player contracts and contract disputes, the perceptions about competition that have resulted from CBA governance of the leagues, and possible solutions to problems that exist within those leagues.

II.   MLB: THEN AND NOW

Baseball has been played in America since the first half of the nineteenth century, though it was not played professionally until 1868.[4] In 1871, twenty-five professional clubs formed the National Association of Baseball Clubs, which would later become the National League.[5] The American League, lagging behind slightly, was formed in 1900.[6] Players switched teams incessantly during the baseball's infancy.[7] Contracts lasted only for a year, after which time the players were able to offer their services out on the open market.[8] This process of exclusively playing one-year contracts would soon prove to be short-lived. Shortly after organized professional play began, baseball "sought to establish a policy of self-governance in all matters," including player contracts and salary disputes.[9] This power, once established, allowed owners to be inconsiderate in compensating their players, which often led to labor disputes.[10] In 1879, these disputes led to the inception of baseball's reserve system.[11] The reserve system was first a secret "gentleman's agreement" among owners that provided a list of five players on each team to be protected and reserved for the owner of each team.[12] The other owners acknowledged this system by agreeing not to sign protected players away from their current team.[13] This "gentleman's agreement" proved very successful, and by the late 1880s the owners included a reserve clause in every player contract.[14] The clause gave the owners the option to continue renewing each player's contract indefinitely at a salary chosen at the owner's discretion.[15] If the player refused to sign the new contract, he was left with two options: (1) continue to play for the current team, or (2) permanently retire from baseball.[16] This new system was a substantial departure from the early days of professional baseball, which more closely resembled "the early forerunner to today's free agency."[17]

The reserve system, as well as the owners' practice of trading players for cash at will, led to even greater player discord.[18] Thus, by 1885, player John Montgomery Ward helped to organize the Brotherhood of Professional

Baseball Players.[19] Although the Brotherhood attracted many of the great players of its day, its attempt at self-help failed as the Brotherhood "lost money and many of its star players were lured back by the owners' promises of steady pay and steady work."[20] As a result, in December of 1890, the Brotherhood folded after just one season.[21] The players next sought relief from the courts, and in 1922, challenged the reserve clause on the grounds that the League had conspired to monopolize the baseball business.[22] The players' case went to the U.S. Supreme Court. However, the Court ruled for the league, stating that the reserve clause did not violate antitrust laws because baseball was not engaged in interstate commerce.[23] The court reasoned that "[t]he business is giving exhibitions of baseball, which are purely state affairs."[24] Therefore, the transportation of persons across state lines was considered an insignificant interference with interstate commerce.[25] In 1953, the league's reserve system was again challenged in *Toolson v. New York Yankees*,[26] with the players now using the advent of interstate baseball broadcasts to bolster their antitrust claim.[27] But, once again, the Supreme Court upheld the reserve clause, noting that invalidation of the reserve system would cause the end of competitive baseball, and thus death to the sport.[28] In 1972, the Supreme Court again heard a challenge to the reserve system in *Flood v. Kuhn*.[29] In *Flood*, "[a player] challenge[d] the reserve clause on the basis that it violated antitrust laws after he was refused the right to negotiate a new contract with another club."[30] The court again sided with the owners, upholding the antitrust exemption, stating that "the reserve clause was necessary to preserve baseball's economic stability and competitive balance."[31]

In 1966, the players, led by United Steelworkers of America economist Marvin Miller, formed the Major League Baseball Players Association (MLBPA).[32] In 1968, the MLBPA and baseball owners negotiated a collective bargaining agreement, Major League Baseball's First Basic Agreement.[33] The agreement established a minimum salary and a grievance procedure for settling disputes whereby the Commissioner, a position chosen by the owners, would be the ultimate arbitrator of any grievance.[34] Two years later, the Second Basic Agreement raised the minimum salary from ten to fifteen thousand dollars and changed the grievance procedure to one where a panel of arbitrators outside the Commissioner's office could be chosen to handle disputes.[35] This change in procedure would mark the first time in the history of the league that the owners would not have total control over player disputes.[36] The next major change occurred five years later with the 1973 Basic Agreement, which granted the players the ten and five rule.[37] This rule allowed players with ten years of major league experience and five years with his current team both the right to refuse a trade and salary arbitration.[38] In 1975, the reserve system was finally eliminated as arbitrator Peter Seitz declared that the reserve clause in a player's contract would apply only for that contract, and therefore ended clubs' use of the option clause as perpetual right to renew.[39] As a result of this ruling, the 1976 Basic Agreement allowed players with six years in the major leagues to qualify for a limited form of free agency, whereby those players would participate in a re-entry draft that would allow teams to bid for free agents in reverse order of finish to encourage competitive balance.[40] This provision was later eliminated to allow players qualifying for free agency to be available to the highest bidder.[41] Salary arbitration was available to those players ineligible for free agency who had at least two years of major league experience.[42] Free agency and salary arbitration have had a major effect on player salaries.[43] One year after salary arbitration was initiated in 1975 the average player salary was $44,676.[44] In 2005, the average player salary was $2,632,655.[45]

Despite this rapid increase in player salaries, the MLB does not have a salary cap.[46] The MLB owners' last attempt to enact a salary cap in 1994 failed miserably.[47] During this year, the CBA was scheduled to be renegotiated, but serious new issues in the professional baseball arena threatened the success of this renegotiation.[48] The most important issue confronting the owners was a glaring disparity in television revenue between larger and smaller market teams.[49] Local, unshared television revenues for large-market clubs were becoming increasingly profitable, to the point that the increased wealth allowed those clubs to sign many more high-priced (and presumably better) free-agent players than their small market counterparts.[50] The small-market teams were demanding that the large-market teams share their television revenues, and were prepared to vote down any new CBA that did not include such a provision.[51] The large-market teams would only agree to such a revenue-sharing arrangement if the new CBA included a salary cap, so that their lost television profits could be recouped in the form of reduced labor costs.[52] The players rejected the proposed salary cap offer, ultimately resulting in a players' strike that lasted over two hundred days, and the unprecedented canceling of baseball's postseason, including the World Series.[53] While the strike lasted through most of spring training of the following season, the strike ended shortly before the first games of the 1995 season, when the National Labor Relations Board (NLRB) agreed to seek an injunction against the owners, which allowed for the 1995 and 1996 seasons to be played under the old CBA.[54]

In 1996, the owners and players finally reached an agreement.[55] The approved new CBA, which came into effect in 1997, included some interesting changes. First, the agreement included a "competitive balance" or "luxury tax" that called for the teams with the five highest payrolls to pay a 35% tax on payroll spending over a set threshold amount, thus hopefully discouraging high player salaries.[56] Additionally, the owners implemented a revenue-sharing plan that would transfer revenue from the thirteen wealthiest clubs to the rest of the franchises by the year 2000.[57] Salary arbitration remained largely unchanged, with the exception that the number of arbitrators was increased from one to three in order to reduce the number of "aberrant" decisions.[58] Finally, the owners and players agreed to jointly petition Congress to eliminate MLB's anti-trust exemption as it pertained to labor matters.[59]

The current MLB CBA, which has been in effect since 2003,[60] maintains many of the provisions that were negotiated into the 1997 agreement. Major League clubs may have title to and reserve up to a maximum of forty player contracts.[61] These contract rights are maintained by the club until a player becomes a free agent or his contract is assigned. A player can achieve free agency if he has (1) fulfilled his current contract; (2) completed at least six years of major league service; and (3) not executed a contract for the next succeeding season.[62] There is a fifteen-day election period, beginning on the latter of October 15 or the day following the last game of the World Series, for a player choosing to pursue free agency to give notice of his intentions to the Players Association.[63] After free agency notice has been given to the Association, the player is available to meet with any team to discuss the possibility of signing a contract.[64] Once the free agency election period has expired, the player can then negotiate and contract with any team he chooses.[65] However, if the player has not contracted with another team prior to December 1 of that year, the former club of that player has the right to proceed to salary arbitration and retain the player for the upcoming season.[66] If the player does sign a contract with a new club following the election period, the player's former club is entitled to compensation in the form of amateur draft picks.[67]

There is no maximum player salary or salary cap, though there are established minimum player salaries as well as a unique system for arbitration. Salary arbitration, without the consent of the other party, is available to any club or any player with three to six years of service in MLB.[68] Additionally, a player with two to three years of service is eligible for arbitration if he has accumulated at least eighty-six days of service during the immediately preceding season and ranks in the top 17% in total service in that class of players that have two to three years of service with at least eighty-six days of service in the preceding season.[69] The arbitration process is as follows: After the player or club has submitted notice of the intent to pursue arbitration, the player and club exchange the figures that each side will submit for arbitration.[70] If the club submits the matter to arbitration, the player has seven days after receipt of the club's proposed figure to withdraw from arbitration (and thus continue performance at the rate contracted).[71] Submissions to arbitration are made between January 5 and January 15 of each year, and the hearings are held between February 1 and February 20.[72] The arbitration hearings are typically held before a three-person panel.[73] The arbitrators are selected annually by the MLB Players Association and the MLB Labor Relations Department ("LRD"), and these two groups designate one arbitrator to serve as the panel chair.[74] The procedure of the

actual hearings is unique. The player and club each submit a salary figure, along with a contract for the player's services that is complete except for the blank that would normally include the player's salary.[75] "The hearings [are] conducted on a private and confidential basis."[76] Each of the parties to the case is permitted just "one hour for initial presentation and one-half hour for rebuttal and summation."[77] The arbitration panel is allowed to consider as criteria for its decision "[1] the quality of the Player's contribution to his Club during the past season . . . [2] the length and consistency of his career contribution, [3] the record of the Player's past compensation, [4] comparative baseball salaries . . . [5] the existence of any physical or mental defects on the part of the Player, and [6] the recent performance record of the Club including but not limited to its League standing and attendance as an indication of public acceptance . . . ."[78] The arbitrators may not consider as criteria "(i) The financial position of the Player and the Club [including the competitive balance tax consequences]; (ii) Press comments, testimonials or similar material bearing on the performance of either the Player or the Club . . . (iii) Offers made by either the Player or the Club prior to arbitration; (iv) The cost to the parties of their representatives . . . [or] (v) Salaries of other sports or occupations."[79] After considering the allowed relevant criteria for determining the player's value, the arbitration panel renders a decision, awarding either the player's or the club's submission within twenty-four hours.[80] The arbitration award is an either/or proposition, thus the process is sometimes termed "final offer" arbitration.[81] One submission or the other must be chosen, and the decision is reached without issuance of an opinion.[82] The Players Association and the LRD are initially informed only of the award and not how the panel members voted.[83]

MLB also uses arbitration in its procedure for settling "grievances."[84] A grievance within the CBA is defined as "a complaint which involves the existence or interpretation of, or compliance with, any agreement, or any provision of any agreement, between the [Players] Association and the Clubs or any of them, or between a Player and a Club."[85] This procedure requires a player to file a written notice of a grievance to his club's designated representative no later than forty-five days after the facts of the matter became known.[86] Within ten days of the player's notice, the club's representative makes a decision on the matter and then furnishes that decision in writing to the Players Association.[87] The representative's decision is then considered final, unless the player appeals the decision within fifteen days.[88] If the player elects to appeal, the Association and a designated representative of the LRD discuss the grievance, after which the LRD representative issues an opinion to the Association.[89] Once again, if the player does not appeal this decision within fifteen days, the matter is considered settled.[90] However, if the player appeals this decision, either the player or the association may appeal to the Panel Chairman for impartial arbitration.[91] Upon receipt of notice for appeal, the Panel Chairman will set a time and date for a hearing, not to be more than twenty days from the receipt of notice.[92] The hearings are then heard by an arbitration panel and conducted in accordance with Rules of Procedure set out in the CBA.[93] The hearings are informal, and begin by first allowing the initiating party to present its case, and then allowing all interested parties the opportunity to be heard.[94] Legal rules of evidence do not apply to the proceedings, so that all evidence desired to be offered by the parties is allowed, and the Panel Chairman judges its relevancy and materiality.[95] Additionally, the Panel Chairman may request that the parties produce additional evidence that the chairman deems necessary to understanding and adjudicating the dispute.[96] Following a determination by the panel, two copies of the written decision are given to each party.[97] The panel's decision is considered the full and final disposition of the matter.[98]

III. NBA: THEN AND NOW

The National Basketball Association (NBA) was founded in 1949, when the remaining six teams in the National Basketball League (NBL) combined with the Basketball Association of America (BAA).[99] In 1954, Boston Celtics star Bob Cousy attempted to organize NBA players, becoming the first president of the National Basketball Players Association (NBPA).[100] At that time, the NBA had no minimum wage, no health benefits, no pension plan, no per diem, and the average player salary was $8,000.[101] From 1957–58, the NBA first began to enter into discussions with the NBPA.[102] But it was not until 1964, when the players threatened to strike for the first televised NBA All-Star game, that the NBA recognized the NBPA as the exclusive collective bargaining representative of the players.[103] Negotiations, and the CBA that followed, resulted in the players receiving an eight dollar per diem and a pension plan (albeit funded in part by the players themselves).[104] "In 1976, the NBA and NBPA entered into a . . . settlement agreement which [changed] a number of . . . operation[s in] the NBA, including a modification of the college draft and [the] institution of the right of first refusal."[105] This agreement was known as the Robertson Settlement Agreement (RSA) and was set to expire at the end of the 1986–87 season.[106] The RSA eliminated the "reserve" or "option" clauses that, like those clauses that were common in the old days of the MLB, would bind a player to his team after his contract had expired.[107] Concurrent with the adoption of the RSA, the NBA and NBPA entered into a multi-year CBA, which incorporated the substantive terms of the RSA and would be in effect until 1979.[108] In 1980, the parties sought to preserve the status quo, and "executed a two-year CBA expressly incorporating the terms of the RSA."[109] In 1983, many NBA teams were experiencing financial difficulty, both spending and losing a lot of money.[110] As a result, the NBPA and the Commissioner decided to implement a salary cap in order to create a salary structure capable of accommodating the interests of both sides.[111] The cap was to be the first of any kind seen in professional sports, and the decision was predictably met with huge opposition from the players.[112] Though the players challenged the cap in court,[113] they ultimately "yielded to financial pressure and agreed to institute [a] salary cap to restore the league's financial health."[114] The salary cap that was ultimately approved by the players in 1983 called for a sharing of league revenues, appropriating 53% to the players.[115] The salary cap also limited the amount of compensation that teams could offer new players, regardless of whether the new player was a free agent or a rookie.[116] Additionally, the salary cap provided for a minimum total team payroll and a predetermined cap for rookie salaries.[117] Along with the salary cap, the 1983 agreement included the "Larry Bird Exception."[118] The Larry Bird exception allows teams to exceed the salary cap when signing free agents in limited circumstances.[119] Basically, the exception provides teams resigning their veteran free agents the ability to offer up to 12.5% more of the player's salary per season, regardless of the salary cap.[120] The effect of the luxury tax is to limit team abuse of salary cap exceptions, such as the Larry Bird exception, by doubling the expense of excess spending and redistributing that penalty amount to those teams not exceeding the luxury tax threshold.[121] To deter teams from using this exception to substantially exceed the salary cap, the luxury tax penalty was set to be 100% of any overage.[122]

At the end of that season, the players sued the owners once again on antitrust grounds.[123] Though the lawsuit was ultimately settled out of court, the 1988 CBA was a landmark lawsuit for professional sports.[124] The 1988 agreement was an incorporation of the Bridgeman Settlement Agreement which brought the first unrestricted free agency to any professional sports league, among other player-favorable provisions, and was set to run through 1994.[125] At the expiration of that agreement, the players again unsuccessfully sought relief in the courts, again challenging the salary cap, the college draft, and the right of first refusal.[126] However, the parties entered into a no-lockout, no-strike agreement which effectively extended the CBA through the end of the 1994–95 season.[127] After a short lockout in 1995, the NBPA and NBA agreed to a new CBA that was in effect until 1998.[128] In 1998, the NBA exercised its option to terminate the 1995 agreement and attempted to roll back salaries and institute a hard salary cap.[129] The NBPA refused to submit to these demands, resulting in the longest lockout and work stoppage in NBA history.[130] The two sides finally reached an accord, and in 1999 a new six-year CBA was reached.[131] The latest CBA was reached in July 2005 and will remain in effect until the end of the 2010–2011 season.[132]

As previously stated, the NBA was the first professional sports league to establish a salary cap. The current NBA CBA defines the term "salary cap" as the "maximum allowable Team Salary for each Team for a Salary Cap Year," and this amount is determined each year as a percentage of projected operating revenues.[133] The current salary cap provides for a 51% share of revenues, calculated as a percentage of projected Basketball Related Income (BRI) for the current salary cap year, minus projected benefits, divided by the number of teams scheduled to play in the NBA during the salary cap year.[134] The CBA also mandates a yearly minimum team salary, which is calculated as 75% of that year's salary cap.[135] In addition to the salary cap and minimum salary limitations, there is also a luxury tax that mandates a dollar-for-dollar penalty tax for any team spending over the "Tax Level," which is also defined in the CBA.[136] This amount differs from the amount listed as the salary cap because the NBA has what is referred to as a "soft" salary cap, meaning that there are exceptions that allow a team to exceed the cap. For example, the NBA salary cap for 2006–07 was $53.135 million, while the tax level was not breached until teams passed the $65.42 million spending mark.[137] Therefore, teams could spend in excess of $12 million over the stated salary cap before they would be taxed, provided their spending fell within an approved exception, most notably the Larry Bird exception.[138]

While the free agency systems of the NBA and MLB are similar, the NBA's system differs from MLB in several respects. While it is easiest to think of unrestricted free agency as the rule and restricted free agency as the exception, the restricted form plays a major role in the NBA. Understanding restricted free agency begins with determining whether a rookie player was signed to a "Rookie Scale Contract" or a "regular contract."[139] Rookie Scale Contracts are for those players who are drafted in the first round of the NBA Amateur draft.[140] These "rookies" are slotted into predetermined contract amount scale (determined by each player's draft position) and are signed to two-year contracts that give the signing team an option to renew for a third and fourth year.[141] These rookie players become unrestricted free agents after their third season if the team does not choose to exercise the option for the fourth season.[142] If the team does choose to exercise the option for the fourth year, the team may then make what is termed a "qualifying offer" for the player's service for a new contract. By making a qualifying offer, the player becomes a restricted free agent, and his current team has the right of first refusal on competing offers.[143] This offer is a one-year proposition, and if accepted, will allow the player to become an unrestricted free agent after that year of service.[144] If another team wishes to sign that player for a higher amount than what his current team has offered as its qualifying offer, they will submit an offer sheet that provides terms for a contract lasting for at least two years. If the player wants to accept the offer from the other team, he would sign the offer sheet, and his current team then would have seven days to match the offer and keep the player.[145] If that team fails to do so, the player is deemed to have automatically entered a contract with the new team at the offered rate.[146] Likewise, if the current team chooses to exercise its right of first refusal and match the

offer, the exercise of that right binds the player and the team to a new contract at the offered terms.[147] Additionally, if the player's current team submits what is termed a "Maximum Qualifying Offer," it must be for a minimum of six years and all guaranteed compensation.[148] Maximum qualifying offers are based on the provision restricting the maximum annual salary a player may receive, which is defined as a certain percentage of the total salary cap of each team.[149] Thus, a maximum qualifying offer states the player's first year salary as the maximum annual salary for players with his years of service, with 10.5% increases per year for the rest of the contract.[150] This offer puts other teams who would consider exceeding this maximum contract offer in a difficult position, because unlike the player's current team, new teams would not qualify for a salary cap exception with respect to that player and thus all of the money offered would count against the salary cap.[151] Finally, unlike the MLB, there is no compensation for teams whose free agents sign with new teams.[152]

Like Major League Baseball, the NBA also employs an arbitration procedure for settling grievances, as well as a system arbitrator to settle any and all disputes relating to the specific articles of the CBA.[153] The NBA grants a "Grievance Arbitrator" the exclusive jurisdiction to settle "all disputes involving the interpretation or application of, or compliance with, the provisions of [the CBA] or the provisions of a Player Contract, including a dispute concerning the validity of a Player Contract."[154] The grievance arbitrator also has jurisdiction to settle disputes relating to the various trusts created by the NBA and NBPA for the benefit of the players.[155] The grievance arbitrator is appointed by joint agreement of the NBA and the NBPA, as is any successor grievance arbitrator that may be necessary due to the discharge or resignation of the original arbitrator.[156] The process used for grievance arbitration may be initiated by a player, a team, the NBA, or the players association.[157] Before the process may be initiated, the party with the grievance must first discuss the matter with the opposing party in an attempt to settle.[158] The grievance must then be initiated within thirty days of the occurrence upon which the grievance is based (or within thirty days of when the party initiating the grievance first learns of the facts of the matter, whichever is later).[159] The party initiating the grievance then files notice with the opposing party that they are initiating a grievance.[160] Upon at least thirty days of written notice to the other party, the NBA and NBPA may schedule a hearing on a date that is convenient to all the parties of the dispute.[161] The parties then submit, no later than seven days prior to the hearing, a "joint statement of the issue(s) of the dispute."[162] Then, "no later than three (3) business days prior to the hearing, the parties shall exchange witness lists, relevant documents and other evidentiary materials, [as well as] citations of legal authority that each side intends to rely on [at the hearing]."[163] The arbitrator may also allow any party wishing to file a pre- or post-hearing brief to do so at least three business days before the hearing, unless an opposing party can show that it is unreasonable under the circumstances.[164] All hearings are then "conducted in accordance with the Labor Arbitration Rules of the American Arbitration Association," as long as those rules do not conflict with the provisions of the CBA.[165] Following the hearing, the arbitrator is instructed to render a decision as soon as possible.[166] The decision is to be accompanied by a written opinion, or if both the NBA and NBPA agree, a written opinion may follow soon after the decision.[167] The arbitrator's decision is considered the full and final disposition, binding all the parties to the matter.[168]

In addition to "grievance arbitration," the NBA also has what is termed "system arbitration."[169] The NBA uses system arbitration to resolve disputes arising out of the CBA provisions relating to some of the structural provisions of the CBA such as the salary cap, minimum team salary, rookie scale contracts, the NBA draft, free agency, and league expansion.[170] A system arbitrator is selected by the NBA and NBPA jointly, and serves for continually renewable two-year terms.[171] Like grievance arbitration, the parties to a system dispute must first attempt to settle the matter prior to initiating arbitration proceedings.[172] However, unlike grievance arbitration, system arbitration may only be initiated by the NBA or NBPA, and the initiation must be started within three years of the date of the act upon which the system arbitration is based, rather than the thirty-day deadline for grievances.[173] The party initiating the arbitration then provides notice to both the system arbitrator and the opposing party, after which time a hearing may be commenced in as soon as seventy-two hours.[174] Upon notice of arbitration, the arbitrator has the authority to order the production of documents, conduct pre-hearing dispositions, and compel the attendance of witnesses to the extent necessary to make findings of fact and issue a decision.[175] As in grievance arbitration, the arbitrator then issues a decision, which may be accompanied by a full written opinion of the grounds upon which the decision is based.[176] This decision is typically the final resolution of the matter, though system arbitration does include the availability of an appeal process in most cases.[177] Appeals are heard before a three-member panel chosen jointly by the NBPA and the NBA.[178] A party seeking to appeal the decision of a system arbitrator must serve upon the other party and file with the system arbitrator notice of appeal within ten days of the decision appealed.[179] This service and filing of notice of appeal automatically stays the system arbitrator's decision pending the outcome of the appeal.[180] The appeal process begins with the parties setting a briefing schedule,[181] after which time each party has between fifteen and twenty-five days to serve the brief to the opposing party and file the brief with the appeals panel.[182] The appeals panel then schedules oral arguments on the parties' briefs between five and ten days after the filing.[183] The appeals panel then reviews the system arbitrator's findings of fact and conclusions of law and issues

a written decision on the matter within thirty days of that argument.[184] This decision constitutes the full, final, and complete resolution of the matter.[185]

IV.   NFL: THEN AND NOW

The National Football League (NFL) has been in existence since 1922,[186] although the NFL as we now know it did not exist until the 1966 merger of the American Football League (AFL) and the existing National Football League (NFL).[187] In 1956, the players of the NFL organized to back a representative body, the National Football League Players Association (NFLPA).[188] At that time, the players had virtually no bargaining power, and although several proposals, such as a minimum salary requirement, were made to the owners, those proposals were likely not even considered.[189] The NFLPA continued to be a fairly weak organization after the AFL–NFL merger until 1970, when the players first threatened to strike.[190] Though the players' threat was essentially empty,[191] the NFLPA and the owners soon reached a four-year agreement (the 1968 Agreement) providing for a minimum wage and an improved pension and insurance plan.[192] The agreement solidified the NFLPA as an established entity and formidable bargaining force, and the union then moved for larger concessions. In 1974, the NFLPA challenged the 1968 Agreement's "Rozelle Rule," which required any team signing a free agent from another team to compensate that team in the form of draft picks and players.[193] In *Mackey v. National Football League*,[194] the Eighth Circuit Court of Appeals found that the Rozelle rule violated the Sherman Act by creating an unreasonable restraint on trade.[195] The adverse court ruling prompted owners to negotiate with the NFLPA, and in 1977 a new CBA was formed.[196] The new CBA included increased benefits, arbitration of grievances, and reforms of the waiver system and the option clause.[197] In 1987, the players attempted to negotiate a new CBA that allowed for more meaningful free agency, but the inability to agree to terms led to a strike season.[198] The owners rendered the players' strike unsuccessful by employing replacement players and allowing players to cross the picket line and play under the existing terms, which many players did.[199] Recognizing the situation as futile, the players ended the strike and filed a lawsuit.[200] In 1993, after five years of litigation, the NFL reached a settlement that created a new CBA with a new system of free agency, a salary cap, and a salary floor.[201] The 2006 NFL CBA maintains these provisions and is to remain in effect through the 2010 season.[202]

Like the NBA, the NFL has a salary cap and a guaranteed minimum salary provision.[203] However, unlike the "soft" salary cap of the NBA, the NFL salary cap does not allow teams to use exceptions to exceed the cap. Thus, the NFL's salary cap is termed a "hard" cap, and attempted violations of the cap may be voided or result in stiff penalties.[204] While the current CBA has prescribed actual dollar figure amounts for the 2006 and 2007 seasons, the balance of the agreement defines the salary cap in terms of a percentage of the projected total league revenues, minus projected total league benefits, divided by the number of NFL teams.[205] The agreement, after defining the percentage upon which the cap is based, allows for future adjustments if the salary cap does not match the agreed percentage after the season is over and the actual numbers are tallied.[206] The agreement also provides an exception if the final numbers substantially deviate from the projected percentage of profit that the cap is based upon.[207] For instance, the CBA provides that an adjustment (up or down) will be made to the 2009 cap if the 2007 total league-wide cash player costs exceed or fall below a triggering percentage of the total revenues for that year.[208] This provision ensures that the cap will not begin to substantially deviate from the bargained-for percentage of profits that either the players or owners actually receive. The exception/guarantee provisions in the agreement are an extension of this adjustment formula and exist to ensure that both the minimum salary guarantees and the cap have been followed once the actual dollars are received.[209] For example, the guaranteed league-wide salary is set at 50% of total revenues.[210] If the final accounting reflects that the player compensation falls below that amount for a given year, then the teams must disburse the difference to the players.[211] A "trigger/bail-out" provision of the agreement ensures that the minimum guarantee is further complied with, in that if the percentage of total revenue paid to the players stays at least at 56.074%, then the salary cap stays in effect for the duration of the agreement.[212] However, if that amount falls below 46.868% in a given year, then there will be no salary cap for the league until the amount again breaks the 56.074% mark for a year.[213] Without these provisions, owners could constantly pay the players based on the lowest projection of league revenues, and then pay whatever difference there was up to the league-wide minimum every year.

The NFL has a relatively complex system of free agency. The system is best understood by dividing the free agents into restricted or unrestricted categories, with sub-categories of "transitional" and "franchise" players.[214] Unrestricted free agents consist of those players whose contracts have expired and have completed five or more accrued seasons,[215] or four or more accrued seasons in any capped year.[216] Such players have the right to negotiate and sign a contract with any team that the player chooses.[217] The only caveat to this unrestricted negotiation is that if the player has not signed with another team by the time NFL training camp begins or July 22, whichever is later, he may only sign a one-year contract with his current team with a pay of at least 110% of his prior year salary.[218] The player then has until the tenth week of the NFL regular season to sign this contract, or he is prohibited from playing in the NFL that year and will begin the next free agency period as an unrestricted free agent once again.[219]

Restricted free agents fall into two categories: (1) players with less than three accrued seasons; and (2) players

with at least three but less than five accrued seasons.[220] A player "with less than three Accrued Seasons whose contract has expired may . . . sign a Player Contract only with his Prior Club," if that club offers him a one-year contract on or before the March 1 deadline.[221] If the prior club makes no such offer, the player then becomes an unrestricted free agent, available to negotiate and sign with any club.[222] A player with at least three but less than five accrued seasons has the right to sign with any club just as an unrestricted free agent would, but with restrictions.[223] The main restriction includes giving the prior club a right of first refusal and/or draft choice compensation if that club tenders a qualifying offer on or before the first date of the free agency signing period.[224] The CBA establishes the minimum qualifying offer that a current club must make in order to maintain their right of first refusal, though clubs may make offers in excess of that minimum amount to increase the amount of draft choice compensation that the team would receive if the player signs with a new team.[225] For example, if a team makes the minimum qualifying offer to a player who was originally drafted in the fourth round, and a new team makes a higher offer, the current team has two options: (1) match the new team's higher offer and keep the player, or (2) allow the player to sign with the new team and receive a compensatory draft choice from that player's original draft round (in this example, a fourth round draft pick).[226] If the current team's qualifying offer is in excess of the minimum allowable qualifying offer, thus placing the offer in a category requiring additional draft compensation, the cost to the new team for signing what was originally a fourth round draft choice could be as much as a first and third round draft choice.[227] However, if the current club chooses not to make a qualifying offer to a player who would otherwise be a restricted free agent, that player will become an unrestricted free agent and able to sign with any new team he chooses.[228]

Two subsets of the NFL free agency system, "franchise" and "transition" player designations, further restrict player movement. Every year, a team is permitted to choose one player who would otherwise be a free agent to be a "franchise player."[229] A team designating a franchise player has the option of two required tenders that will make the player an "exclusive" or "nonexclusive" franchise player.[230] If the team offers the designated franchise player a one-year contract of at least the average of the top five salaries of that player's position as of the end of the restricted free agent signing period *of that year*, that player is an exclusive franchise player.[231] An exclusive franchise player may not negotiate or sign a contract with any new club.[232] To make a player a nonexclusive franchise player, a club must only offer a one-year contract of the greater of the average of the top five salaries of that player's position from *the prior year* or 120% of the player's salary from the prior year.[233] If the team makes this designation, the player may still negotiate and sign a contract with a new team, but the former team must then be compensated in the form of two first round draft choices.[234]

Finally, if a team chooses to designate the same player with the franchise label for a third time, the required tender for that player is increased to either (1) the average of the highest five salaries for the position with the highest average; (2) 120% of the average of the five highest salaries of the prior year at the player's position; or (3) 144% of the player's salary of the prior year, whichever is greater.[235] NFL clubs also have the ability to designate up to two players per year as "transition" players.[236] Once a club has designated a player as a transition player, that club is deemed to automatically have offered the player a one-year contract worth the greater of the average of the highest ten player salaries for the player's position from the previous year, or 120% of that player's prior year salary.[237] A transition player maintains the right to negotiate a contract with any team he chooses, but his prior team gains the right of first refusal.[238] And unlike the franchise player designations, if the prior team does not exercise its right of first refusal, that team is not entitled to draft choice compensation.[239]

The NFL also has an arbitration system in place for injury[240] and non injury grievances.[241] The non-injury grievance procedure is in place for disputes that relate to the interpretation of, compliance with, and application of the provisions of the CBA, player contracts, and other rules and bylaws of the league.[242] The process begins when a player, club, the NFL Management Council, or the NFLPA files a written notice of the grievance with the opposing parties within forty-five days of the occurrence upon which the grievance is based.[243] The parties to whom the notice is sent then have a week to answer the complaint by setting forth admissions to or denials of the facts alleged in the grievance.[244] "If the answer denies the grievance, the specific grounds for denial [must be stated]."[245] If the answer does not settle the grievance, any of the parties may appeal the grievance by filing a notice to the Notice Arbitrator and sending notice of appeal to the other parties involved.[246] The appeals are then scheduled based upon a series of dates available to four separate arbitrators and are typically heard upon the next available date.[247] "No later than ten (10) days prior to any hearing, each party [must send] to the other copies of all documents, reports and records relevant to the dispute."[248] Failure to do so bars the party from offering that evidence at the hearing, although the opposing party will still have the opportunity to examine those documents and use them as it so desires.[249] Following this disclosure, the parties have the opportunity to present all relevant evidence at the hearing—testimony and otherwise.[250] After the presentation of evidence, either party may request post-hearing briefs, which each party will then simultaneously submit.[251] The arbitrator must then "issue a written decision within thirty days of the submission of briefs," or sixty days of the end of the hearing, whichever is sooner.[252] The arbitrator's decision is considered the full and final disposition of the dispute, binding all of the parties.[253] One caveat to this procedure involves the "grievance settlement committee," which consists of the Executive Director of the NFLPA and the Executive Vice President for Labor Relations of the NFL.[254] This committee meets periodically to discuss pending grievances. If the committee so chooses, they may contact parties to a grievance and, with the parties' consent, attempt to settle the grievance themselves.[255] If the committee is successful, that settlement constitutes the full and final disposition of the matter.[256]

V. ACTUAL CBA EFFECTS ON ON-FIELD COMPETITION VS. PERCEPTION

Comparing the success of different professional sports leagues is a difficult task. Part of this difficulty stems from the different structures of the leagues—depending on the sport, regular season games vary from 162 to 16, league mandated roster limits range from 14 to 53, the number of playoff teams may be 16 or 8, and the playoff formats may be "sudden death" or best of seven-game series. The complexity of the comparison task is compounded by the lack of a uniform opinion on what constitutes success. Are champions more attractive in "Cinderella" or "Dynasty" form? Is the success of a league better measured by its weakest teams or strongest? The answer to such questions depends on the individual fan, though a popular opinion seems to be that parity is the goal, and that competitive balance is the best indicator of success.[257] The NFL is generally viewed as the model of parity in professional sports, while the MLB has come to represent professional sports in its most dynastic form.[258] This is due to the perception that any NFL team may become playoff eligible in any given year regardless of their market or win-loss record from the prior season, while poor performing MLB teams are deemed resigned to a perpetual state of mediocrity.[259]

The question remains whether these perceptions are justified. Considering the popular adage that only champions are remembered, a closer examination of each sport is necessary to determine whether a disparity exists in some sports as opposed to others or if that perception is unfounded. As previously stated, developing a uniform system of comparison is difficult due to the differences in the format and schedule of each league. However, one way to determine whether real competition exists within the various leagues is to examine the chance that any given team has to achieve a berth in the league's postseason playoff system. In examining five seasons of professional sports seasons from 2001–2005, the argument for the NFL system appears to be the most persuasive. In the NFL's 12-team playoff format, 25 of its current 32 teams (78.1%) became playoff eligible in the five year period.[260] Of those teams that participated in the playoffs, only one was able to accomplish the feat in all five years, while 13 of those teams only made the playoffs two or fewer times.[261] An examination of the NBA's 16-team playoff format over the same time period reveals that 25 of its 30 teams (83.3%), participated in the playoffs.[262] Of those teams, five participated in the playoffs all five years, while just eight made the playoffs two or fewer years.[263] And finally, in the MLB's eight-team playoff system, only 17 of its 30 teams (56.7%) attended the playoffs from 2001–2005.[264] Two of those teams were in the playoffs in all five years and nine of those teams played in the playoffs in two or fewer years.[265] Over the five sample years the NBA, NFL, and MLB had 80, 60, and 40 playoff positions available respectively.[266] If the playoff positions occupied by the teams that made the playoffs in every year are removed, assuming that those teams were in fact superior to the rest of the teams in their league due to consistent performance,[267] then what remains is the pool of playoff slots that the rest of the teams can realistically hope to obtain. Thus, from 2001–2005 in MLB there were 28 teams (93.3% of the league) competing for 30 (75%) of the playoffs spots.[268] The NBA had 25 teams (83.3% of the league) competing for 55 (68.8%) playoff spots, and the NFL had 31 teams (96.9% of the league) competing for 55 (91.7%) of its playoff spots.[269] These numbers suggest that the playoff races are more consistently "open" in the NFL than in the NBA or MLB.

The percentages for the NBA and MLB are actually almost equal, even taking into consideration the fact that the MLB's playoff system is half the size of the NBA. So then why is the NBA system generally accepted and the MLB system shrouded in controversy? One explanation may simply be the perception that meaningful competition is impossible with the rising salaries of professional athletes without a salary cap or significant restrictions on free agency. The concept that revenue sharing in the MLB would help level the playing field took a significant hit in 2000 when it was reported that the lower-payroll, small-market clubs were using the money that they were receiving as part of revenue sharing to turn a profit, rather than to increase payroll, as it was designed to do.[270] Also, the baseball system of arbitration is not nearly as effective at restraining player movement as the other systems of free agency. This is due in part to the fact that the financial position of each club cannot be taken into account when reaching an arbitral award, thus the salaries of the players on small-market teams are measured against the salaries of the highest paying big-market clubs.[271] Because each club's particular financial position is not considered, the placement of all players is determined by a market value that is based upon an inflated market that only exists for teams with the highest revenues and highest payrolls. The result is that owners (especially those from smaller markets) must either grant significant pay raises to the player contemplating arbitration or bid considerably more than they would otherwise be willing to pay in order to have a realistic chance of winning should a matter proceed to arbitration. For example, one study of arbitration results showed that although owners succeeded in most arbitration proceedings, the average salary of

players invoking the arbitration process increased at a rate of 95%![272] While the study takes into account a large number of players who reached a settlement prior to an arbitrator issuing a final decision,[273] it nonetheless illustrates the notion that arbitration is a win–win situation for the players. However, the result of the arbitration process for many of the smaller market teams is that these teams are either "priced-out" of retaining players or forced to reduce salary in other areas of their rosters in order to keep the arbitrating players on staff. Thus, for some teams, the arbitration system actually forces player movement instead of restraining it. The best players (or at least the most valuable based on the criteria considered during salary arbitration) are therefore shuttled to the teams that can afford to pay their salaries, a continuous cycle that effectively ruins any attempt at equality amongst all teams in the league.

Meanwhile, the NBA seems fortunate that either the number of teams in its playoff system or a relative lack of knowledge by the average fan hides the flaw in its "soft" cap. One Larry Bird exception in the NBA is the free agency equivalent of allowing an NFL team to designate five franchise players, but without salary cap consequences.[274] Considering that only five players are playing for an NBA team at any one time, this exception can swallow the salary cap-rule for teams that strike it rich in the draft. The Larry Bird exception was a major point of controversy in the 1998 lockout just as it was during settlement discussions prior to the 1995 CBA agreement, but the exception has survived negotiations again and again and so is not likely to be deleted anytime soon.[275] The problem is that the effects of the exception could subject the NBA to issues similar to those that exist in Major League Baseball. Considering that wealthier NBA clubs can afford to pay not only the extremely high salaries for star players regardless of the salary cap, but also the contracts of star rookies, the Larry Bird exception limits competition by discouraging player movement.[276] The question, then, is whether the NBA "soft cap" is actually any more effective at maintaining competitive balance than no cap at all. The playoff numbers indicate that the NBA's soft cap has little effect on maintaining competitive balance, and thus suggest the answer to the question is "no." There remains a real chance in the NBA that a team with good fortune in its choice of draft picks could conceivably lock-in a serious competitive advantage for years and years with skillful use of the salary cap exceptions.[277] This situation essentially existed for the Chicago Bulls in the 1990s when that team won six championships in eight years (using the Larry Bird exception for star Michael Jordan during that period), and they could have been even more dominant had Jordan not elected to play baseball instead of basketball for a year and a half in the mid-90s.[278] If such a circumstance comes to fruition again, critics of the soft cap demanding to be heard will have many fans listening to their howl.

. . . .

VII. CONCLUSION

The historical progression of the NBA, MLB, and NFL have created entities whose modes of operation, as defined in their respective collective bargaining agreements, make each distinct but popular among sports fans. While each league has undergone its own series of problems and renovations, the results have thus far been exciting and successful. The activities of the several sports leagues are monitored and discussed long after each season's end, and while the arguments over some aspects of the leagues sometimes drown out the cheers, it is generally agreed that business is good.[287] . . .

Despite the success of various professional sports, a balancing act is constantly performed to account for the interests of players and owners alike that can be profitable to both and enjoyed by fans. With both sides always jockeying for the best financial position, it seems that as soon as a potential disaster is avoided in one sport by way of a new collective bargaining agreement, another sport is furiously negotiating to avoid a ruinous strike or lockout. Throughout most of professional sports history, collective bargaining has done a brilliant job of calculating the interests of teams, players, and fans, and carrying the sports forward to successful, profitable ends. "Soft" cap or "hard" cap, free agency or arbitration, professional sports continue to represent one of the most popular forms of entertainment and most passionate outlets for fans across the country and around the world. Meanwhile, the struggle to maintain competitive balance continues, and the face of sports continues to evolve with each new CBA.

Notes

1. *See e.g.,* SportsBusiness Journal, http://www.sportsbusinessjournal.com/index.cfm?fuseaction=page.feature&featureId=43 (last visited Mar. 3, 2008).

2. These are the current "Big Three" of U.S. professional sports. My apologies to the NHL, which has had a substantial decline in popularity since the 2004 lockout.

3. *See generally,* 2005 NBA/NBPA CBA, *available at* http://www.nbpa.com/cba.php.

4. Frederick N. Donegan, *Examining the Role of Arbitration in Professional Baseball,* 1 SPORTS LAW J. 183 (1994).

5. *Id.*

6. *Id.* at 184.

7. Jonathan M. Conti, *The Effect of Salary Arbitration on Major League Baseball,* 5 SPORTS LAW J. 221, 223 (1998).

8. *Id.*

9. Thomas J. Hopkins, *Arbitration: A Major League Effect on Players' Salaries,* 2 SETON HALL J. SPORT L. 301, 303 (1992).

10. *Id.*

11. *Id.*

12. *Id.*

13. *Id.*

14. *Id.* at 303-04.

15. *Id.*

16. *Id.*

17. Conti, *supra* note 7, at 223.

18. Hopkins, *supra* note 9, at 304. Owner abuses included the suspension of a sick player (forcing his retirement) and the sale of players to different teams for cash. *Id.*

19. *Id.*

20. *Id.* at 305.

21. *Id.*

22. *Id.*

23. *Id.* (citing *Fed. Baseball Club v. Nat'l League of Prof'l Baseball Clubs,* 259 U.S. 200, 209 (1922)).

24. *Id.* (quoting *Fed. Baseball Club,* 259 U.S. at 208).

25. *Id.*

26. 346 U.S. 356, 361-62 (1953).

27. Hopkins, *supra* note 9, at 305-06 (citing *Toolson,* 346 U.S. at 356-57 (1953)).

28. *Id.*

29. 407 U.S. 258, 258 (1972).

30. Hopkins, *supra* note 9, at 306.

31. *Id.* (citing *Flood,* 407 U.S. at 272-73).

32. Major League Baseball Players Association: MLBPA History, http://mlbplayers.mlb.com/pa/info/history.jsp (last visited Mar. 3, 2008).

33. Hopkins, *supra* note 9, at 307

34. *Id.*

35. *Id.*

36. *Id.*

37. *Id.*

38. *Id.* at 335 n.50.

39. *Id.* at 309.

40. *Id.*

41. *Id.*

42. *Id.*

43. *Id.*

44. Major League Baseball Salaries by Baseball Almanac, http://www.baseball-almanac.com/charts/salary/major_league_salaries.shtml (last visited Mar. 3, 2008).

45. *Id.*

46. *See* 2007–2011 MLB Basic Agreement, *available at* http://mlbplayers.mlb.com/pa/pdf/cba_english.pdf (last visited Mar. 29, 2008) [hereinafter MLB CBA].

47. Daniel C. Glazer, *Can't Anybody Here Run This Game? The Past, Present, and Future of Major League Baseball,* 9 SETON HALL J. SPORT L. 339, 363 (1999).

48. *Id.* at 362-63.

49. *Id.* at 363.

50. *Id.*

51. *Id.*

52. *Id.*

53. *Id.*

54. *Id.* at 364.

55. *Id.*

56. *Id.* The money collected under the luxury tax is as follows: The first $5 million is held in reserve in the event a team should earn a tax refund during that year. The remaining balance is contributed to the Industry Growth Fund (IGF) used to help expand the baseball industry generally. Fifty percent of the proceeds over that amount go to player benefits. Twenty-five percent of those remaining proceeds go to fund high school and other projects where baseball is not played, and the last twenty-five percent goes back to the IGF. *See* 2007–2011 MLB Basic Agreement art. XXIII, § H, *available at* http://mlbplayers.mlb.com/pa/pdf/cba_english.pdf (last visited Mar. 29, 2008).

57. Glazer, *supra* note 47 at 365.

58. *Id.*

59. *Id.* Congress finally acquiesced by passing the Curt Flood Act in 1998. *Id.* at 365 n.166.

60. It is important to note here that a new MLB CBA was recently negotiated and will be in effect through 2011. While some minor changes were made from the 2003 agreement, most of that agreement incorporated into the new one. Changes of note include increasing the luxury tax by $40 million, eliminating deadlines for free agents to sign with their former teams, elimination of the ability of a player who was traded in the middle of a multi-year contract to demand a trade, and the ability of teams who are unable to sign their first-round amateur draft choices to be compensated with comparable choices in the subsequent year's draft. *See* Barry M. Bloom, *MLB, Union Announce New Labor Deal,* MLB.com, Oct. 25, 2006, http://mlb.mlb.com/news/article.jsp?ymd=20061024&content_id=1722211&vkey=ps2006news&fext=.jsp&c_id=mlb.

61. MLB CBA art. XX, § A.

62. *Id.* art. XX, § B(1).

63. *Id.* art. XX, § B(2)(a).

64. *Id.* art. XX, §§ B(2)(a) & (b).

65. *Id.* art. XX, § B(2)(c).

66. *Id.* art. XX, § B(3).

67. *Id.* art. XX, § B(4)(a).

68. *Id.* art. VI, § F(1).

69. *Id.* art. VI, § F(1).

70. *Id.* art. VI, § F(3). The clubs are bound by special exceptions from maximum salary reduction rules in the CBA that provide that the club must submit a salary figure for arbitration that is at least 80% of the player's previous year salary and earned performance bonuses (or at least 70% of his salary and earned performance bonuses for the previous two years), unless that player received an increase of at least 50% of his previous year's salary in an arbitration proceeding in the immediately preceding year. *Id.*

71. *Id.* art. VI, § F(4).

72. *Id.* art. VI, § F(5).

73. *Id.* art. VI, § F(7).

74. *Id.*

75. *Id.* art. VI, § F(6).

76. *Id.* art. VI, § F(9).

77. *Id.*

78. *Id.* art. VI, § F(12)(a).

79. *Id.* art. VI, § F(12)(b).

80. *Id.* art. VI, § F(5).

81. *Id.*

82. *Id.*

83. *Id.*

84. *Id.* art. XI.

85. *Id.* art. XI, § A(1) (a). The definition of a grievance is pretty well comprehensive of any dispute that might occur, although it does list complaints regarding the players' benefit plan and dues as exempt from this procedure, as well as actions taken with respect to a player by the commissioner involving "the integrity of the game." *Id.*

86. *Id.* art. XI, § B.

87. *Id.*

88. *Id.*

89. *Id.* Grievances involving more than one Club or a player not under contract can be filed to begin at this stage. *Id.*

90. *Id.* Note that there are also special procedures for grievances necessitating a medical expert. *Id.*

91. *Id.*

92. *Id.*

93. *Id.* (The Rules are contained in Appendix A of the Agreement).

94. *Id.* app. A, §§ 3 & 6.

95. *Id.* app. A, § 8.

96. *Id.*

97. *Id.* app. A, § 13.

98. *Id.* art. XI, § B.

99. NBA.com: Powerful Lakers Repeat, http://www.nba.com/history/season/19491950.html (last visited Mar. 3, 2008).

100. NBA Players Association: NBPA History, http://nbpa.com/history.php (last visited Mar. 3, 2008).

101. *Id.*

102. *Id.* These discussions could not be termed "negotiations," as the NBA had not yet recognized the NBPA as the voice of the players.

103. *Id.*

104. *Id.*

105. Michelle Hertz, *The National Basketball Association and the National Basketball Players Association Opt to Cap Off the 1988 Collective Bargaining Agreement with a Full Court Press:* In re Chris Dudley, 5 MARQ. SPORTS L.J. 251, 252 (1995).

106. *Id.* The agreement was named the "Robertson Settlement Agreement" after Oscar Robertson. Robertson was the president of the NBPA until 1974, and the agreement came after a class action lawsuit instituted by the players challenging some of the League's actions as violative of antitrust laws. *See id.;* National Basketball Players Association: NBPA History, *supra* note 100 (in the 1964 and 1970 sections).

107. National Basketball Players Association: NBPA History, *supra* note 100.

108. *See* Hertz, *supra* note 105, at 252-53.

109. *Id.* at 253.

110. *See* Melanie Aubut, *When Negotiations Fail: An Analysis of Salary Arbitration and Salary Cap Systems,* 10 SPORTS LAW. J. 189, 218 (2003).

111. *Id.* at 218-19.

112. *Id.* at 220-21.

113. *Id.* at 253 (citing Lanier v. NBA, 82 Civ. 4935 (S.D.N.Y.)).

114. *See* Hertz, *supra* note 105, at 253.

115. NBPA History, *supra* note 100.

116. *See* Aubut, *supra* note 110, at 219.

117. *Id. See infra* footnotes 139-142 and accompanying text for a discussion of rookie contracts.

118. Aubut, *supra* note 110, at 219.

119. *Id.*

120. *Id.* (citing Larry Coon, *NBA Salary Cap FAQ,* http://members.cox .net/lmcoon/salarycap.htm#16 (last visited Mar. 1, 2008) and 1999 NBA/NBPA CBA art. VII, §5(a)). Note that the application of the Larry Bird exception has several subtle yet complex variations that are outside the scope of this article. For a thorough explanation of this exception, see Larry Coon, *NBA Salary Cap FAQ,* http:// members.cox.net/lmcoon/salarycap.htm# 16 (last visited Mar. 1, 2008).

121. *See* Aubut, *supra* note 110, at 219-20.

122. *Id.* at 220.

123. NBPA History, *supra* note 100 (Under the 1987–88 section).

124. *Id.*

125. *Id.*

126. *Id.* (Under the 1994 section).

127. *Id.* This agreement was made to ensure the 1994–95 season would be played in its entirety. *Id.*

128. *Id.* (Under the 1995 section).

129. *Id.* (Under the 1997–98 section).

130. *Id.* The lockout extended from late summer of 1998 to January 20, of 1999. *Id.*

131. *Id.* The CBA also included an owner option to extend to a seventh season, which was exercised for 2004–05. *Id.*

132. 2005 NBA Players Association Collective Bargaining Agreement art. XXXIX, § 1, *available at* http://www.nbpa.com/cba_articles.php (last visited Mar. 1, 2008) [hereinafter 2005 NBA CBA]. Again, the owners have the option of extending the CBA by one year to include the 2011-12 season. *Id.* art. XXXIX, § 2.

133. *Id.* art. I, §§§ ggg, hhh, mmm. A salary cap year begins July 1 and ends the following June 30. *Id.* art. I, § hhh.

134. *Id.* art. VII, § 2(a)(1). "Basketball Related Income" means the aggregate operating revenues received by the NBA or any of its subsidiaries during the salary cap year. *Id.* art. VII, § 1(a).

135. *Id.* art. VII, § 2(b)(1).

136. *Id.* art. VII, §§ 12(a)(17) & (f).

137. NBA News, http://www.nba.com/news/NBA_salarycap_060711 .html (last visited Mar. 1, 2008).

138. *See* Aubut, *supra* note 110, at 219-20. The Larry Bird exception is termed the "Veteran Free Agent Exception" in the CBA. Other exceptions include the "Existing Contracts Exception," the "Disabled Player Exception," the "Bi-Annual Exception," the "Mid-level Salary Exception," the "Rookie Exception," the "Minimum Player Sal-

ary Exception," and the "Traded Player Exception." *See* 2005 NBA CBA art. VII, § 6.

139. 2005 NBA CBA art. VIII, § 1.

140. *Id.*

141. *Id.* art. VIII, § 1(a).

142. *Id.* art. XI, § 4(a)(i).

143. *Id.* art. XI, § 5(a). Other than the specific provisions for Rookie Scale Contracts, the rest of the restricted free agency rules apply to all veteran free agents with three or fewer years of NBA service. *Id.* art. XI, § 4(b).

144. Coon, *supra* note 120 (number 36). If the qualifying offer is neither accepted nor withdrawn and the time for accepting it passes, the current team's right of first refusal continues. 2005 NBA CBA art. XI, § 4(c)(ii).

145. Coon, *supra* note 120 (number 36).

146. *Id.*

147. *Id.*

148. *Id.*

149. *Id. See also* 2005 NBA CBA art. II, § 7 (defining the maximum annual salary). Note that the maximum annual salary is also dependent on how many years the player has been in the NBA.

150. 2005 NBA CBA art. XI, § 4(a)(ii)(B).

151. See *id.;* Coon, *supra* note 120 (number 19).

152. *Id.* art. XI, § 1.

153. *Id.* art. XXXI-XXXII.

154. *Id.* art XXXI, § 1(a)(i). Any dispute involving the provisions of the CBA or player contracts are defined in this section as a "grievance." *Id.*

155. *Id.* art. XXXI, § 1(a)(ii). These trusts include the National Basketball Association Supplemental Benefit Plan and the Agreement and Declaration of Trust Establishing the National Basketball Players Association/National Basketball Association Labor-Management Cooperation and Education Trust. *Id.*

156. *Id.* art. XXXI, § 6. The grievance arbitrator is set to serve for the duration of the CBA, although he may resign or be discharged by either the NBA or NBPA upon notice to the arbitrator and the other party. *Id.* In the event of a notice of discharge, the arbitrator maintains jurisdiction to settle disputes for which a date has been set or are filed in the thirty days preceding the notice of discharge. *Id.*

157. *Id.* art. XXXI, § 2(a).

158. *Id.* art. XXXI, § 2(b).

159. *Id.* art. XXXI, § 2(c).

160. *Id.* art. XXXI, § 2(d):

(i) a player or the Players Association may initiate a Grievance (A) against the NBA by filing written notice . . . with the NBA, and (B) against a Team, by filing written notice . . . with the Team and the NBA; (ii) a team may initiate a Grievance by filing written notice . . . with the Players Association and furnishing copies of [the] notice to the player(s) involved and to the NBA; and (iii) the NBA may initiate a Grievance by filing written notice . . . with the Players Association and furnishing copies of [the] notice to the player(s) and teams involved.

Id.

161. *Id.* art. XXXI, § 3(a). Once a hearing is scheduled, neither the NBA nor NBPA may postpone it more than once. *Id.* art. XXX, § 3(d).

In the event that a hearing is postponed, the party seeking the postponement pays the arbitrator's postponement fee. *Id.* art. XXX, § 3(c). However, if the opposing party objects to the postponement and the arbitrator finds the request was for good cause, the parties then share the postponement fee. *Id.*

162. *Id.* art. XXXI, § 4(a). If the parties cannot agree on a joint statement, each party may issue a separate statement that is given to the opposing party at the same time as it is given to the grievance arbitrator. *Id.*

163. *Id.* art. XXXI, § 4(c). Unless the proffering party has good cause, the parties may not rely on any material or witnesses not identified and given to the opposing party in advance of the hearing to prove its case. *Id.*

164. *Id.* art. XXXI, § 4(d).

165. *Id.* art. XXXI, § 3(g). Additionally, the arbitrator has jurisdiction and authority only to go so far in resolving disputes, including the ability to: "(i) interpret, apply, or determine compliance with the provisions of [the CBA]; (ii) interpret, apply or determine compliance with the provisions of Player Contracts; (iii) determine the validity of Player Contracts; (iv) award damages; (v) award declaratory relief . . . ." *Id.* art. XXXI, § 5(b). However, he may only decide questions of procedural arbitrability, and he may not modify terms of the CBA or any player contract. *Id.*

166. *Id.* art. XXXI, § 5(a).

167. *Id.*

168. *Id.*

169. *Id.* art. XXXII.

170. *Id.* art. XXXII, § 1.

171. *Id.* art. XXXII, §§ 6(a)-(b).

172. *Id.* art. XXXII, § 2(b).

173. *Id.* art. XXXII, §§ 2(c)-(d).

174. *Id.* art. XXXII, §§ 2(d) & 5.

175. *Id.* art. XXXII, § 3(c).

176. *Id.* art. XXXII, § 3(b).

177. *Id.* art. XXXII, § 3(d).

178. *Id.* art. XXXII, § 7.

179. *Id.* art. XXXII, § 3(d).

180. *Id.* art. XXXII, § 8(a).

181. *Id.* art. XXXII, § 8(b). The schedule may be agreed upon by the NBA and NBPA, or by the appeals panel if the parties are unable to come to an agreement. *Id.*

182. *Id.*

183. *Id.*

184. *Id.* art. XXXII, §§ 8(b)-(c).

185. *Id.* art. XXXII, § 8(c).

186. NFL—History, 1921–1930, http://www.nfl.com/history/chronology/1921-1930 (last visited Mar. 2, 2008). This was following a name change from the American Professional Football Association. *Id.*

187. NFL—History, 1961–1970, http://www.nfl.com/history/chronology/1961-1970 (last visited Mar. 2, 2008).

188. NFL Players Association: History, The Beginning–1956, http://www.nflplayers.com/user/template.aspx?fmid=182&lmid=239&pid=0&type=c (last visited Mar. 29, 2008).

189. *Id.* The representative for the NFLPA was quoted as saying that when he went to New York to present their proposals, "We never did get a chance to meet with the owners and we never got a response from any of the proposals at that time." *Id.*

190. *Id.*

191. *Id.* The players were in a weak bargaining position, and after the owners threatened to cancel the season the strike ended after only two days. *Id.*

192. *Id.*

193. Aubut, *supra* note 110, at 212.

194. 543 F.2d 606 (8th Cir. 1976).

195. *Id.* at 623.

196. NFL Players Association: History, The 1970's—AFL and NFL Players Associations Merge, http://www.nflplayers.com/user/template.aspx?fmid=182&lmid=239&pid=1036&type=c (last visited Mar. 28, 2008).

197. *Id.*

198. Aubut, *supra* note 110, at 212. The right of first refusal and the compensation system limited player movement. *Id.*

199. *Id.*

200. *Id. See also* Powell v. NFL, 678 F. Supp. 777 (D. Minn. 1978).

201. Aubut, *supra* note 110, at 213.

202. 2006 NFL CBA art. I, § 4(aw), *available at* http://www.nflplayers.com/user/template.aspx?fmid=181&lmid=231&pid=507&type=c (last visited Apr. 18, 2008) (membership required to access the full CBA).

203. *Id.* art. XXIV.

204. *Id.* art. XXV, § 6(a). *See also* Aubut, *supra* note 110, at 216 (mentions "hard" salary cap).

205. 2006 NFL CBA art. XXIV, § 4(a). The agreement does provide that the last year of the agreement will be an uncapped year, though the same provision was included in previous CBAs and the parties have renegotiated or extended the agreements without ever actually going to an uncapped year. *Id.*

206. *Id.* art. XXXII, § 4(b).

207. *Id.* art. XXIV, § 4(d).

208. *Id.* art. XXIV, § 4(b)(i).

209. *See generally id.* art. XXIV, § 4.

210. *Id.* art. XXIV, § 3.

211. *Id.*

212. *Id.* art. XXIV, § 2(a).

213. *Id.* art. XXIV, § 2(b).

214. Aubut, *supra* note 110, at 213.

215. 2006 NFL CBA, art. XIX, § 1(a). An "accrued season" is defined as each season a player was or should have been on full pay status for at least six or more regular season games. *Id.* art. XVIII, § 1(a).

216. *Id.* art. XIX, § 1(a).

217. *Id.*

218. *Id.* art. XIX, § 1(b)(i).

219. *Id.* art. XIX, §§ 1(b)(ii)-(iii).

220. *Id.* art. XVIII-XIX.

221. *Id.* art. XVIII, § 2.

222. *Id.*

223. *Id.* art. XIX, § 2(a).

224. *Id.* art. XIX, §§ 2(b)(i)-(ii). The signing period dates are determined by the league and the players association every year by September 1st, and the period lasts at least forty-five days. *Id.* art. XIX, § 2(h).

225. *Id.* art. XIX, §§ 2(b)(i)-(ii).

226. *Id.* art. XIX, §§ 2(c)(i)-(ii).

227. *See id.*

228. *Id.* art. XIX, § 2(j).

229. *Id.* art. XX, § 1.

230. Aubut, *supra* note 110, at 215 (citing 2006 NFL CBA art. XX, §§ 1-2).

231. *Id.*

232. *Id.;* 2006 NFL CBA art. XX, § 1.

233. Aubut, *supra* note 110, at 215; 2006 NFL CBA art. XX, § 2(a)(i).

234. 2006 NFL CBA art. XX, § 2(a)(i).

235. *Id.* art. XX, § 2(b).

236. *Id.* art. XX, § 3(a).

237. *Id.* art. XX, § 4(a).

238. *Id.* art. XX, § 3(b).

239. *Id. See also supra* text accompanying note 224.

240. *Id.* art. X, § 1. An "injury grievance" is defined as "a claim or complaint that, at the time a player's NFL Player Contract was terminated by a Club, the player was physically unable to perform the services required of him by that contract because of an injury incurred in the performance of his services under that contract." *Id.* While this is an important provision of the NFL CBA, especially due to the physical nature of the sport, the discussion of this process is outside the scope of this article.

241. *Id.* art. IX.

242. *Id.* art. IX, § 1.

243. *Id.* art. IX, § 2.

244. *Id.* art. IX, § 3.

245. *Id.*

246. *Id.* art. IX, § 4.

247. *Id.* art. IX, §§ 6-7.

248. *Id.* art. IX, § 5.

249. *Id.*

250. *Id.* art IX, § 7.

251. *Id.*

252. *Id.* art IX, § 8.

253. *Id.*

254. *Id.* art IX, § 13.

255. *Id.*

256. *Id.*

257. *See e.g.,* Branden Adams, *Streaks, Stats, and Minutiae,* THE HARVARD INDEPENDENT, Nov. 1, 2007, *available at* http://www.harvardindependent.com/node/20 (last visited Mar. 3, 2008).

258. For example, Major League Baseball currently has six teams who have not reached the playoffs in the last ten years, while every team in the NFL has made the playoffs at least once in that span except for the Houston Texans, who were founded in 2002. *See e.g.,* Pro Football Hall of Fame: Playoff Results, http://www.profootballhof.com/history/release.jsp?RELEASE_ID=584 (last visited Mar. 3, 2008); Major League Baseball: History: Division Series Overview, http://mlb.mlb.com/mlb/history/postseason/mlb_ds.jsp (last visited Mar. 3, 2008).

259. *See* Pro Football Hall of Fame: Playoff Results, *supra* note 258; Major League Baseball: History: Division Series Overview, *supra* note 258.

260. *See* NFL Standings: Division (years 2001-2005), www.nfl.com/standings (last visited Mar. 3, 2008).

261. *See id.*

262. *See* NBA.com: Season by Season Index, http://www.nba.com/history/season/index.html (last visited Mar. 14, 2008); NBA.com: 2001 Playoff Results, http://www.nba.com/history/playoffs/20002001.html (last visited Mar. 14, 2008) (only 2000-2001 through 2002-2003 seasons).

263. *See id.*

264. *See* The Official Site of Major League Baseball: Schedule: 2005 Postseason, http://mlb.mlb.com/mlb/schedule/ps_05.jsp (last visited Mar. 14, 2008); The Official Site of Major League Baseball: Schedule: 2004 Postseason, http://mlb.mlb.com/mlb/schedule/ps_04.jsp (last visited Mar. 14, 2008); The Official Site of Major League Baseball: Standings: Regular Season Standings, http://mlb.mlb.com/mlb/standings/index.jsp?ymd=20051002 (last visited Mar 14, 2008) (2001–2003 seasons).

265. *See id.*

266. *See, e.g.,* John Clayton, *Playoff Format is Matter of Integrity,* Dec. 30, 2005 http://proxy.espn.go.com/nfl/columns/story?columnist=clayton_john&id=2275183; NBA.com: The Playoffs, http://www.nba.com/analysis/00423850.html (last visited on Mar. 3, 2008); Baseball Post-season Playoffs by Baseball Almanac, http://www.baseball-almanac.com/ws/postseason.shtml (last visited on Mar. 3, 2008).

267. This may assume too much, but it is for argument's sake.

268. The Official Site of Major League Baseball: Standings, *supra* note 264.

269. *See* NFL History, http://www.nfl.com/history (last visited Mar. 3, 2008); NBA.com: History, http://www.nba.com/history/ (last visited Mar. 3, 2008).

270. *See* Richard C. Levin et al., *The Report of the Independent Members of the Commissioner's Blue Ribbon Panel on Baseball Economics* (2000), *available at* http://www.mlb.com/mlb/downloads/blue_ribbon.pdf (last visited Mar. 3, 2008).

271. *See* 2007–2011 MLB Basic Agreement art. VI, § F(12)(b)(i), *available at* http://mlbplayers.mlb.com/pa/pdf/cba_english.pdf (last visited Mar. 29, 2008) (MLB CBA).

272. Conti, *supra* note 7, at 235.

273. *See id.*

274. This is based on the number of players allowed in each league's active roster.

275. *See* Aubut, *supra* note 110, at 235.

276. *See id.* at 234.

277. *See id.* at 235.

278. *See* NBA.com: NBA Finals: All-Time Champions, http://www.nba.com/history/finals/champions.html (last visited Mar. 3, 2008);

NBA.com: Michael Jordan Career Perspective, http://www.nba.com /jordan/index.html (last visited Mar. 3, 2008).

287. *See* Monte Burke, *The Big Trend,* Dec. 27, 2006, http://www.forbes .com/business/2006/12/09/sports-2007-predictions-sneakpeek _sp07_22_monteburke_sports.html.

. . . .

. . . .

MICROPERSPECTIVE: THE HOCKEY STORY

THE HOCKEY LOCKOUT OF 2004–05

Paul D. Staudohar

The lockout in the National Hockey League (NHL) gave new meaning to the old sports adage "Wait till next year." The aborted schedule of games in 2004–05 set records that the fans would rather not see: the first professional sports league to lose an entire season, the most games lost (1,230) due to a work stoppage, and the longest-lasting shutdown (310 days) in sports history. Moreover, there was no guarantee that there would even be a "next year," as key issues on the bargaining table remained unresolved. But in July 2005, the NHL and its players' union finally reached a new collective bargaining agreement, allowing the 2005–06 season to start on time.

Lengthy work stoppages in professional sports are not new. In 1994–95, Major League Baseball lost 921 games over a period of 232 days from a strike, and the National Basketball Association cancelled 428 games during its 1998–99 lockout.[1] Hockey had a lengthy shutdown in 1994–95 when 468 games were wiped out during a 103-day lockout.

Team owners have increasingly relied on lockouts to put pressure on players to accede to their demands. Lockouts usually occur before or early in a season, when players have not received much, if any, of their pay. However, it is not uncommon for players to strike late in a season, when they have received most of their salaries while owners have yet to take home big payoffs from postseason television revenues.

These conflicts are costly, and perhaps it is past the time for the parties to pursue new approaches that promote a partnership between owners and players. This is especially the case with hockey, because the future of the league is threatened by the frequent wrangling over money and power. Unless a more cooperative model of negotiations is developed, the NHL could continue to recede from public view and lose its standing as a major professional sport.

BACKGROUND

The National Hockey League Players' Association (NHLPA) was formed in 1957 by players protesting a television deal between the league and CBS that gave all of the money to the owners. Detroit Red Wings star Ted Lindsay was the first president of the union, which was able to secure a minimum salary of $7000 and additional pension contributions from the owners. But a lack of player solidarity and failure to achieve recognition from the owners caused the union to falter after only about a year of operation.[2]

The union came back to life in 1967 when Toronto lawyer and players' agent Alan Eagleson took over the reconstituted NHLPA. Eagleson quickly established formal recognition of the union by the league and became the most powerful operative in the sport by gaining control of staging international hockey events and continuing to serve as an agent for several players. However, he also mishandled the financial affairs of Bobby Orr, the famous Boston Bruins defenseman, and manipulated union funds to his advantage. These missteps forced Eagleson to resign, and in 1994, following a 2-year FBI investigation, he was convicted of 32 counts of racketeering, embezzlement, and fraud. As a result, he served 6 months in prison.[3]

Eagleson was replaced as executive director by Bob Goodenow in 1992. . . .

In sharp contrast to the "company union" approach of Eagleson, Goodenow adopted an adversarial posture with the owners. To demonstrate his tenacity, he led the union in a 10-day strike at the end of the 1992 season, the first ever in hockey. The union won concessions such as the right to choose arbitrators in salary disputes, a reduction in the age for unrestricted free agency from 31 to 30, and an increase in the players' postseason revenue share.

Following the 1992 strike, the NHL hired Gary Bettman as its first commissioner, succeeding John Ziegler and then Gil Stein, who both had the title of league president. Bettman, a graduate of Cornell University and the law school at New York University, had done an excellent job as the third-ranked executive in the National Basketball Association (NBA) under Commissioner David Stern. Importantly, while at the NBA, Bettman designed and implemented basketball's salary cap, the first in modern-day sports. He was viewed as an energetic, marketing-oriented innovator and a perfect fit for the less-than-pacesetting NHL.[4] Like Goodenow, Bettman showed his mettle soon after becoming commissioner by dealing severely with a 17-day strike by hockey referees in 1993, when he hired replacement officials and then negotiated a 4-year agreement for little more than the league had initially offered.

When the players-owners' agreement expired in September 1993, the union agreed to play the 1993–94 season uninterrupted. This appeared to be an encouraging sign, but negotiations proceeded at a snail's pace and turned out fruitless. Faced with the likelihood of a strike at the end of the season, the owners took the preemptive action of a lock-out. The venture proved costly, however, because it came at a time when hockey's economic prospects never looked brighter. Although serious negotiations commenced, they soon turned rancorous, and it began to look like the season would be lost.

Similar to what would occur in 2004–05, the big issue was a so-called salary cap. The league's proposal, however, did not seek to cap payrolls generally. Instead, it was designed to limit salaries by requiring big-spending teams to contribute to revenue sharing with low-spending teams, enabling the latter to compete more effectively for signing and retaining top-quality players. In effect, the measure was akin to the luxury tax that was adopted in baseball in 1995. The union was amenable to a payroll tax, but at far lower levels than what the owners proposed. A true salary cap was proposed by the league for rookies, whose salaries had been escalating rapidly.

The lockout ended in mid-January 1995, barely saving the season, which was cut from 84 to 48 regular-season games. As a result, the owners dropped the payroll tax idea, but achieved a salary cap for rookies under the age of 25, who were limited to an $850,000 salary in 1995, with the cap rising annually to $1,075,000 in 2000. Eligibility for free agency was severely limited. Players who completed their first contract were no longer eligible for free agency. Although players aged 25–31 could still become free agents, their movement to other teams was stifled by stiff draft choice penalties that had to be paid by teams signing such players. Unrestricted free agency could be achieved only at age 32 (up from age 30 under the old contract) for the first two seasons of the agreement and at age 31 after that. It was the most restrictive free agency system in sports.[5]

The owners appeared to get much the better of the settlement, which was reported in the media as a solid victory on their part. Nick Kypreos of the New York Rangers, returning from Canada after the lockout, expressed the players' view with gallows humor. Asked by customs officials if he had anything to declare, he said, "No, the owners took it all."[6] But there was a delicious irony in store for the players. Although the owners appeared to have "taken it all," they nonetheless wasted little time in bestowing lavish salaries on players in individual negotiations with agents. This largesse would eventually lead to the league's insistence on a salary cap applicable to *all* players, a turn of events that became the major cause of the 2004–05 lockout.

Causes

Table 2 shows average salaries in the NHL since the 1993–94 season. During this period, salaries more than tripled. Because revenues did not keep pace with salaries, the league contended that it lost approximately $1.8 billion over the

Table 2   Average Salaries in the National Hockey League, 1993–94 to 2003–04

Year	Average Salary	Percent Increase Over Previous Year
1993–94	$558,000	. . .
1994–95	730,000	30.8
1995–96	890,000	21.9
1996–97	980,000	10.1
1997–98	1,170,000	19.4
1998–99	1,290,000	10.3
1999–2000	1,360,000	5.4
2000–01	1,430,000	5.1
2001–02	1,640,000	14.7
2002–03	1,790,000	9.1
2003–04	1,830,000	2.2

Source: National Hockey League. Courtesy of the Bureau of Labor Statistics.

previous decade.[7] The increase in NHL salaries over the period was significantly greater than corresponding increases in Major League Baseball, the NBA, and the National Football League (NFL).[8]

In a widely publicized study, the NHL retained Arthur Levitt, former chairman of the U.S. Securities and Exchange Commission, to examine its finances. Although Levitt's work was an "independent study," he was paid $250,000 by the league, apparently without the union's knowledge. Levitt found that the league lost $273 million in the 2002–03 season, with 19 teams losing money and 11 teams profitable.[9] In an earlier internal report, the league found that it spent 76 percent of its annual revenue on player salaries, significantly more than corresponding spending in other sports.[10] For instance, in the NBA, the players' share is about 58 percent of revenue.[11] The union was critical of the Levitt report, contending that teams understate revenues by directing them to related business entities, thereby creating a falsely bleak picture.

Nearly a year after Levitt's report, *Forbes* magazine also did a study of league revenues and expenditures for the 2002–03 season. This report found that teams lost $123 million, considerably less than the $273 million claimed by Levitt, and that salaries consumed only 66 percent, rather than 76 percent, of league revenue.[12] The *Forbes* article attributed the difference in its numbers to what the league considers to be revenue. For example, although the Chicago Blackhawks claimed no revenue from the 212 suites the team owns in the United Center, where it plays its home games, [the family of the late] Blackhawks owner William Wirtz owns half of the arena in a separate corporation.[13]

Notwithstanding creative accounting and any discrepancy in figures, it is clear that the NHL was losing money, even though the economics of owning a particular team might be quite favorable. In a sense, the owners had no one to blame but themselves: no one had forced them to pay high salaries. For instance, rookie salaries were supposedly capped under the old agreement. But a loophole developed in this cap when the owners circumvented it by paying bonuses to rookies.[14] Perhaps they took a cue from the NFL, which allows signing bonuses to be excluded from its salary cap.[15] As a result of the loophole, rookie salaries soared. For example, Marian Gaborik, a rookie with the Minnesota Wild, earned 3 times his million-dollar salary in bonuses.[16]

Another complicating factor for the league was the financial circumstances of its Canadian teams. In recent years, the Canadian dollar has varied between two-thirds and three-fourths the value of the American dollar. Teams in Canada have to compete with American-based teams for players, yet they do not usually receive as much in revenues. Also, whereas U.S. team owners have been adept at getting local governments to pay for stadiums, Canadian clubs typically have to pay for their own arenas.[17] Adding to the problem are the higher individual and corporate tax rates in Canada. Well aware of these circumstances, the NHL set up the Canadian Currency Assistance Plan in 1999, to help franchises defray some of their losses. Still, the plan is not nearly enough to overcome the inherent disparities. [*Ed. Note: The NHL ended the plan when the Canadian dollar grew stronger against the US dollar.*]

The NHL contracts with national television networks have always yielded far less revenue than those in football, baseball, and basketball. In 1999, the league began a 5-year contract with the Walt Disney Company for the rights to show games on ABC and its ESPN cable network. For the last year of the contract, the league received $120 million, which, when divided among the teams, amounted to $4 million for each team. Television ratings for NHL games were trending lower, and at the time of negotiations for a new contract, networks were wary of making a deal because of the possibility of a lockout. As a result, the new 2-year agreements reached with NBC and ESPN provided for only about half the previous annual return to the league. This reduction in revenue contributed to the owners' tougher stance with the union.

The lower television ratings and right fees are symptoms of other problems facing the league, such as the suitability of the game for television, overexpansion, and the style of play. First, hockey does not translate well to television screens because the puck is small and not easily followed. (High-definition television is expected to give a boost to viewing. . . .) Second, in a growth spurt in the 1990s, the league added nine franchises in 9 years. Because the new clubs, mostly from Sunbelt cities, paid $50–70 million entry fees to the league, expansion resulted in short-term rewards. But the novelty of the game has worn off in those cities, diminishing attendance and profits. Finally, the game featured a defensive style with a lot of pushing and grabbing that dulls fan interest. The league promotes its hard hitting and fights, which appeal to some fans, but tragedy struck in 2004 when Todd Bertuzzi of the Vancouver Canucks severely injured Steve Moore of the Colorado Avalanche by slugging him from behind and repeatedly driving his face into the ice.

ISSUES AND NEGOTIATIONS

There were numerous issues on the bargaining table in 2004–05: higher player fines for misbehavior, reducing the schedule of games, minimum salaries, playoff bonuses for players, free agency, operation of the salary arbitration process, and revenue sharing. Overshadowing all other issues, however, was the league's desire for "cost certainty," provided by a maximum team salary cap linked to league revenues. In the early stages of negotiations, for example, the league wanted a salary cap of $35 million per team, with the players guaranteed about 50 percent of league revenues. The union offered a rollback of 5 percent on player salaries, a luxury tax on payrolls of more than $50 million (with money going into a revenue-sharing pool), and a rollback on the rookie salary cap to 1995 levels.

What the negotiations boiled down to was that the league insisted that it get a salary cap while the union was equally adamant that it wanted salaries based on market conditions and would never agree to cap payrolls. At this juncture and for a long time to come, the dispute was more about each side's philosophical approach than numbers. The rigid positions of the two sides resulted in the league's announcing a lockout on September 15, 2004, the day the collective bargaining agreement expired. In anticipation of a lockout, each side established funds from which to draw, with the 730 union players eligible for payments of either $5,000 or $10,000 per month and the owners having a $300 million war chest available.

One of the problems common to sports negotiations is that the public wants to know what is happening at the bargaining table and the media are determined to supply this information. Bettman and Goodenow engaged in a battle of words in the media, as did Bill Daly, the league's vice president and chief legal officer, with Ted Saskin, the union's senior director of business affairs. Although several players—particularly union president Trevor Linden of the Vancouver Canucks—made public comments, the owners were relatively quiet because the league instituted a gag order. When Steve Belkin, an owner of the Atlanta Thrashers, stated in the *Boston Herald* that the league would use replacement players the next year if a new collective bargaining agreement was not reached, he was fined $250,000 by the league.[18] Tim Lieweke, president of the Los Angeles Kings, was fined an undisclosed amount for making a derogatory comment about Goodenow.

Twice during the lockout it appeared that the stalemate might be broken. In December 2004, the union offered to cut wages by 24 percent and dropped the amount of payroll on which the luxury tax would be levied to $45 million. Although Bettman called the union's concessions a "big-time move," he rejected the proposal and continued to insist on a salary cap and guaranteeing players a fixed percentage of revenue as wages, while raising the guarantee to 54 percent.[19] The league's counterproposal of continuing to link salaries with revenues was rebuffed by the union, because it did not trust the owners' revenue reporting methods.

The other significant shift in the parties' positions occurred in a last-ditch effort to save the season. Time was running out to hold a week or so of training camp and play a reasonable number of regular-season games prior to the postseason playoffs. In a major concession, on February 15, 2005, the league dropped its demand that salaries could not exceed 55 percent of revenue, thus abandoning the notion of cost certainty. The union's response was to accept the concept of a salary cap. These concessions brought a glimmer of hope to salvaging the season, because the focus of bargaining would now be on the numbers rather than a philosophical approach. However, even after some give-and-take with assistance from the Federal Mediation and Conciliation Service, the numbers were still far apart, with the league proposing a salary cap of $42.5 million per team and the union $49 million. Although there was a $6.5 million gap in the offers, they would apply to 30 teams and therefore caused a difference of $195 million in the positions.

IMPACT OF THE LOCKOUT

With neither side making further concessions and with time having truly run out, the league announced on February 16 that the season was cancelled, for the first time in 86 years. (The Stanley Cup was not awarded in 1919 because of the Spanish influenza epidemic.)

As a result of the work stoppage, there were layoffs of team office personnel and stadium attendants. The economic impact on league cities was not great, because fans redirected their spending from attending games to other forms of entertainment. Teams lost an estimated $2 billion in revenue from tickets, media, sponsorships, and concessions, while players gave up about $1 billion in lost salaries.[20] Revenue was lost by government agencies that owned stadiums, but some of this income was made up through booking other events into the facilities.

According to an estimate by the Canadian government, the country's gross domestic product diminished by $170 million Canadian dollars as a result of the cancelled season.[21] Because of debt servicing, the need to retain some office staff, and overhead expenses, teams spent approximately $7 million to $10 million each in American dollars during the lost season.[22] These expenditures would constitute losses, but given the likelihood that owners collectively would have lost money had the season been played, the losses are not significant, and in some cases teams actually made money.

Players, too, had offsets to lost income, such as the monthly payments from the NHLPA. About 380 NHL players were playing overseas in European leagues at the time the season was cancelled.[23] The biggest number of these players signed with Russian teams, with professional leagues in Sweden, Finland, and the Czech Republic also popular destinations. Many other players signed on with minor league clubs in North America. After the cancellation of the season was announced, still more players joined teams home and abroad. The salaries of these players were far less than what they made in the NHL, although a few lucky ones did fairly well. For instance, Vincent Lecavalier and Brad Richards each signed for $1.5 million with Ak Bars Kazan, a team from the autonomous Russian Republic of Tatarstan that plays in the 16-team Russian Superleague. Lecavalier was scheduled to make $4.4 million and Richards about $2.6 million for the Tampa Bay Lightning.[24]

At around the time the season was cancelled, cracks began appearing in the players' solidarity. Hockey's greatest-ever player, Wayne Gretzky, . . . [then] coach of the Phoenix Coyotes, said he wanted a salary cap in a new collective bargaining agreement. The league released the gag order on owners and team executives, allowing them to talk to the media and seek to influence players. About a dozen players . . . indicated that they would accept a salary cap, but not one linked to league revenues. This groundswell gained momentum after the season was cancelled, putting pressure on the union to settle.

The owners also were under mounting pressure. The aborted season left them with franchises devalued to a much lower level than before. On the one hand, further devaluation could occur if fans turned away from the game. Hall of Fame goalie Ken Dryden, a former president of the Toronto Maple Leafs and now Canada's Minister of Social Development, prophetically stated, "You never want to give a fan a chance to find out whether it was passion or habit."[25] On the other hand, the owners are well endowed financially, with nine of them among *Forbes* magazine's 400 richest Americans.

It appeared inevitable that the players would have to accept a salary cap. Payroll limits have existed in the NBA since the 1984–85 season and in the NFL since 1994. Only Major League Baseball lacks a cap, and the union there is much stronger than the one in hockey. Moreover, basketball and football have prospered despite (or perhaps because of) a salary cap.

Commissioner Bettman indicated that the league would not start the 2005–06 season on time if a collective bargaining agreement was not in place. Yet he also was committed to the idea of beginning the season on time in October. These conflicting aims raised the possibility of the league seeking a declaration of impasse from the National Labor Relations Board (NLRB). Because the league had been responsive to the union's demands and had made a sincere effort to reach an agreement, it would likely have been found to have engaged in good-faith bargaining, which is a necessary condition for declaring an impasse. Although the baseball owners' attempt to declare an impasse in 1995 was thwarted by the NLRB and a U.S. district court judge, the 2005 board could very well rule in favor of the hockey owners.

Should the league have achieved a declaration of impasse, an available option was to use replacement players. This tactic was employed successfully by the NFL during its 1987 strike, and the threat of using replacement players was instrumental in ushering in the end of the baseball strike in 1995. If necessary, the NHL probably would have used replacement players to get the 2005–06 season started on time, but as it turned out, the parties reached an agreement beforehand, avoiding what could have been an ugly confrontation.

SETTLEMENT AT LAST

On July 13, 2005, the NHL and the NHLPA reached a settlement on a 6-year collective bargaining agreement.[26] The union can reopen negotiations after the 4th year and can also extend the agreement by a year. The centerpiece of the nearly 600-page agreement is a team payroll cap of $39 million for 2005–06, with player compensation limited to 54 percent of league revenues. [*Ed. Note: The salary cap was $59.4 million in 2010–2011.*] The agreement achieves the cost certainty that Bettman and the owners wanted. The cap will be adjusted annually: if revenue goes up, the cap will rise; if revenue goes down, the cap will fall. There is a minimum payroll of $21 million. [*Ed. Note: The salary floor was $43.4 million in 2010–2011.*] Rookie salaries are capped at $850,000 per season, with a top signing bonus of 10 percent annually. Also, like NBA players, NHL players will deposit an adjustable percentage of their salaries into an escrow account. If, after the season, the leaguewide payroll exceeds 54 percent of revenues, the teams will receive funds from the escrow account. If total payrolls are less than 54 percent, the account will be paid to the players.

Players under contract had their pay cut by 24 percent. Teams had a one-time opportunity to buy out player contracts for two-thirds of their remaining value, minus the 24-percent cut. No player can account for more than 20 percent of a team's total payroll, which means that no player can earn more than $7.8 million in 2005–06. Minimum salaries were raised from $175,000 under the old agreement to $450,000 in 2005–06. Every 2 years, the minimum rises again, to $475,000 and finally to $500,000.

Free agency rules are liberalized. Players still will become unrestricted free agents at age 31 for 2005–06, but the age will gradually decrease to 29 and then to 27.[27] This seeming benefit to players is diminished somewhat by the hard cap on team payrolls.

The rules on salary arbitration were changed so that teams now can opt to take players to arbitration, whereas only players had the option before. . . . The number of rounds in the player draft was reduced from nine to seven, a feature that will make more incoming players free agents. The league will take a hiatus. . . so that players can represent their countries at the Winter Olympics . . . There will be no all-star game in years that include an Olympic break.

Prior to the 2005 agreement, the NHL did not have a formal drug-testing policy. The new arrangement calls for a minimum of two random tests per year for performance-enhancing drugs. First-time offenders get a 20-game suspension, a second offense results in a suspension for 60 games, and a player caught a third time suffers a lifetime ban. Compared with punishments in other professional team sports, these are stiff penalties, although the NHL program may be criticized for being vague in its enforcement provisions and lax on testing procedures.

CONCLUDING THOUGHTS

Although both sides typically lose in a lengthy work stoppage, the hockey lockout is notable in that the owners achieved such a dominant outcome. On nearly all issues in contention, the end result was solidly in the owners' favor. The union appears to have underestimated the need for economic restructuring, Bettman's determination to prevail, and the commitment and financial resources of the owners. The players would have been far better off if they had accepted the league's offer in February 2005, just before the season was cancelled. Probably for this reason, Goodenow resigned as head of the union with 3 years remaining on his contract and was succeeded by Ted Saskin. [*Ed. Note: Saskin was replaced by Paul Kelly, who has since left the position as well.*]

A major problem for the league was its deteriorating television situation. In late May 2005, ESPN declined to exercise its $60 million option for broadcast rights for the 2005–06 season, but in August the NHL reached an agreement with OLN (formerly called the Outdoor Life Network) for a rights fee of $65 million in 2005–06 and $70 million in 2006–07. Known chiefly for its coverage of the Tour de France and hunting shows, OLN [*now known as Versus*] is owned by Comcast, the nation's largest cable provider. However, OLN [*Versus*] is available in only about 64 million homes, compared with ESPN's 90 million homes.

There was also a need to address the high cost of attending games. Even before the agreement was reached, some teams announced that they were slashing ticket prices. Most teams eventually did this, as well as spending more money on special promotions to entice fans back to the arenas.

The games themselves should be more exciting as a result of rule changes. There will be Olympic-style shootouts at the end of a tie overtime game to determine a winner. The center red line no longer will be counted for offsides purposes, thereby allowing longer breakout passes that should result in more scoring. A third major change involves goaltenders: their equipment is reduced in size and their range of mobility behind the net is limited, making goalies less effective in stopping pucks.

Clubs agreed to share revenues, with the top 10 revenue producing teams contributing to a fund from which the bottom 10 teams can draw. The amount shared is variable, depending mainly on differences between hockey-related revenue and player salaries. Revenue sharing should stimulate competitive balance, so that all clubs have a better chance of winning the Stanley Cup, and smaller clubs should be more profitable as well. After the agreement was settled, the league moved forward with the player draft. . . .

Although in the end the union had to swallow the dreaded salary cap, it may not turn out to have such an ominous impact. Small-market teams will have a better chance of retaining talented players formerly lost to rich teams that bid salaries upward. Player mobility increases under the new free agency rules, although equalized team payroll limits will prevent salaries from escalating rapidly. Perhaps the biggest advantage to players is that they can move to teams and areas they prefer. While the payroll cap keeps costs under control, it also promotes a partnership between owners and players. Under the 54-percent guarantee to the players, the more money the owners make, the more money the players can earn, so their fates are intertwined.

In the recent past, four teams—Buffalo, Los Angeles, Ottawa, and Pittsburgh—were saved from bankruptcy by new owners or internal refinancing. Overexpansion and flagging popularity have left several other clubs, including Anaheim, Atlanta, Carolina, Florida, Nashville, and Phoenix, vulnerable to bankruptcy or purchase at fire-sale prices. The elimination of some of these teams, located in Sunbelt States where hockey is not a traditional sport, would place the league on a sounder financial footing and improve the overall quality of play. The contraction of the league, however, raises a number of legal issues. Moreover, should the league itself decide to buy out and fold franchises, the union, cities, and fans would be up in arms, as occurred when baseball proposed eliminating two teams in 2002.

Although the future is unclear, it seems certain that the NHL will be a troubled league for a while. Profitable television contracts, financial restructuring, and making the game more exciting to fans will have to occur before long-term economic stability can emerge. The surest way of achieving this objective is through cooperation between the league and its union.

Notes

1. These work stoppages are discussed in Paul D. Staudohar, "The Baseball Strike of 1994–95," *Monthly Labor Review*, April 1999, pp. 3–9.

2. David Cruise and Alison Griffiths, *Net Worth: Exploding the Myths of Hockey* (Toronto, Penguin Books Canada, 1991), pp. 110–11.

3. For an interesting case study, see Russ Conway, *Game Misconduct: Alan Eagleson and the Corruption of Hockey* (Toronto, Macfarlane Walter & Ross, 1995).

4. Paul D. Staudohar, *Playing for Dollars: Labor Relations and the Sports Business* (Ithaca, NY, Cornell University Press, 1996), p. 146.

5. The 1995 contract was extended to secure the players' agreement to participate in the 1998 Winter Olympics and again as part of a four-team expansion, causing a new expiration date of September 15, 2004.

6. Quotation from *Sports Illustrated*, "Scorecard" section, Jan. 23, 1995, p. 23.

7. Stefan Fatsis, "Hockey League Locks Out Players," *Wall Street Journal*, Sept. 16, 2004, p. D8.

8. Michael Hiestand, "Put a Lid on Pro Player Salaries," *USA Today*, Sept. 2, 2004, p. 4B. Team success does not necessarily correlate with high salaries. The New York Rangers typically have the highest team payroll in the league, but have not performed well for several seasons. The two teams that competed for the 2004 Stanley Cup—the Calgary Flames and the Tampa Bay Lightning—had the 19th- and the 20th-highest payrolls in the league.

9. Arthur Levitt, Jr., *Independent Review of the Combined Results of the National Hockey League 2002–2003 Season* (Westport, CT, Arthur Levitt, Jr., 2004); and Helene Elliott and Elliott Teaford, "A Frozen Pond of Red Ink?" *Los Angeles Times*, Feb. 13, 2004, p. D1.

10. Stefan Fatsis, "NHL Says Players' Salaries Put League in Financial Peril," *Wall Street Journal*, Sept. 19, 2003, p. B1.

11. Joel Stein, "Can the NHL Save Itself?" *Time Magazine*, Mar. 22, 2004, p. 62.

12. Michael K. Ozanian, "Ice Capades," *Forbes*, Nov. 29, 2004, p. 124.

13. *Ibid.*

14. For a discussion of how players and their agents drove up salaries, see Bruce Dowbiggin, *Money Players: How Hockey's Greatest Stars Beat the NHL at Its Own Game* (Toronto, McClelland & Stewart, 2003).

15. Paul D. Staudohar, "Salary Caps in Professional Team Sports," *Compensation and Working Conditions*, spring 1998, pp. 6–8.

16. Kevin Allen, "Lockout Threat Has Both Sides on Edge," *USA Today*, international edition, Sept. 17, 2003, p. 5B.

17. L. Jon Wertheim, "Uh-Oh, Canada," *Sports Illustrated*, June 21, 2004, p. 65.

18. "NHL Fines Thrashers' Co-Owner $250,000," *Los Angeles Times*, Oct. 13, 2004, p. D4.

19. Joe Lapointe, "N.H.L. and Union Each Reject Proposals," *New York Times*, Dec. 15, 2004, p. C13; and Alan Adams, "NHL Season Hanging by Thread," *USA Today*, Dec. 15, 2004, p. 1C.

20. Stefan Fatsis, "NHL Calls Off Its Entire Season With Labor Face-Off Cold as Ice," *Wall Street Journal*, Feb. 17, 2005, p. B2.

21. "Go Figure," *Sports Illustrated*, "Scorecard" section, Feb. 14, 2005, p. 16.

22. Darren Rovell, "Lockout Will Test Depth of Owners' Pockets," on the Internet at ESPN.com, Feb. 11, 2005, p. 2.

23. Figure from the International Ice Hockey Federation, reported in *Time Magazine*, Feb. 21, 2005, p. 19.

24. Michael Farber, "Tampa Bay to Tatarstan," *Sports Illustrated*, Jan. 10, 2005, p. 62.

25. Quotation from Helene Elliott, "Union Says NHL Players' Solidarity Intact," *Los Angeles Times*, Feb. 8, 2005, p. D3.

26. The players subsequently voted 464–68 (87 percent) in favor of the agreement, while the owners ratified it by a 30–0 vote.

27. An exception is made for 18-year-old players, who can become become eligible for free agency as early as age 25.

Discussion Questions

1. Discuss the importance of trust in management–labor relations. What do you gain when you have it? What do you lose when you don't?

2. Why did the 2002 MLB agreement lead to unforeseen ramifications?

3. What is the benefit of a salary cap to management? Does that differ from the benefit to labor?

4. What lessons should Major League Baseball management learn from past labor disputes? What about the players?

5. What are some of MLB and MLBPA's shared interests today that were not so prominent in 1994?

6. What are some of the factions that management and labor must bring to consensus on their own side before (or during) negotiations with the other side?

7. What are the practical problems with competing interests within the respective bargaining units?

8. Are draconian opening bargaining positions effective to ultimately gain concessions in the final agreement, or counter-productive as a method of eroding trust?

9. Compare and contrast the similarities and differences between the major provisions of labor agreements in the four major sports.

10. How will the recent economic recession impact upcoming labor negotiations in the major sports?

11. How could you formulate provisions in a labor agreement to create common interests between labor and management going forward?

12. Did the most recent NHL agreement create any of those forward-looking mutual interests between owners and players?

CHAPTER TEN

Labor Matters: Athlete Compensation

INTRODUCTION

It is well known that professional athletes competing in each of the four major North American sports leagues receive lucrative compensation. In 2008 and 2009, average salaries across these leagues were $5.585 million in the NBA, $3.26 million in MLB, $1.9 million in the NHL, and $1.9 million in the NFL. What is not well known is how these salaries are determined. Professional athletes are often perceived as being overpaid instead of merely well paid. This reflects a misunderstanding of the relevant marketplace for athlete compensation. A comparison of athlete salaries to those of the average person is misleading. Instead, athletes should be regarded as entertainers when it comes to compensation. When considered in this manner, athlete compensation is quite reasonable. Much like entertainers, there is a limited supply of highly skilled athletes who the average person desires to watch either live or on television. This is a significant reason why athletes (and entertainers) are able to earn such high salaries. (See **Table 1** for a list of the average salary growth in each league.)

There is, however, an area in which it is fair to compare an athlete's salary to the average worker's—the economic justification for how much one is paid. Individuals who are employed in a free and open marketplace are compensated based on their marginal revenue product (MRP); that is, how much the individual employee contributes to the employer's revenues. Conversely, individuals who are employed in a restricted, uncompetitive marketplace are not compensated based on their MRP. Instead, the employer retains most of the MRP, and the individual is compensated (and some would say *exploited*) at a more conservative rate. See **Table 2** for the top American earners in U.S. sports.

The MRP concept explains why the salaries of professional athletes typically increase with the athletes' years of experience. A truncated version of the reserve system that

set athlete salaries in each league at artificially low rates until the mid-1970s in MLB (and later in other leagues) still exists. Similar to the reserve system that perpetually bound a player to a team at the team's discretion, each league limits player access to a competitive marketplace for a period of years at the beginning of a player's career. Not surprisingly, most studies indicate that athletes tend to earn close to the minimum salary established in the league's collective bargaining agreement during this monopsonistic period. The team captures most of the athlete's MRP at this stage of his career. After this initial period, the player in each league gains increased but still restricted access to the marketplace (and the full value of the MRP) for a period of years as a result of restricted free agency, salary arbitration, or both. Upon completing this stage, the athlete gains access to the open marketplace via unrestricted free agency. This allows the player to realize close to the full value of his MRP.

In professional sports leagues, the salary of an individual athlete is determined pursuant to the athlete compensation framework established by collective bargaining between the union and management. This determination is typically accomplished through a negotiation between a team and the athlete's representative. Although the collective bargaining agreement establishes the parameters for this negotiation, the salary for any particular athlete depends on a number of factors both internal and external to that athlete. First, of course, are the factors internal to the athlete, which exist outside of the context of the collective bargaining agreement. The athlete's skill level, position, experience, injury history, drawing power, and league all impact the compensation earned. A highly skilled, experienced, and seldom-injured athlete playing a "glamour" position in a thriving league will be better compensated than one lacking any of these qualities. In addition, several external factors that are products of the collective bargaining agreement can either increase or decrease athlete salaries. Free agency and

Table 1   League Average Salary Increases From 1990–1991 to 2008–2009

Year	MLB	NFL	NBA	NHL
2008–2009	$3,260,000	$1,896,000	$5,585,000	$1,906,793
2002–2003	2,555,476	1,316,000	4,540,000	1,640,000
1999–2000	1,938,849	996,000	3,170,000	1,350,000
1997–1998	1,341,000	751,000	2,600,000	1,200,000
1993–1994	1,012,424	645,000	1,350,000	430,000
1990–1991	597,537	351,800	990,000	320,000

Sources: National Football League Players Association, National Basketball Players Association, National Hockey League Players Association, and Associated Press.

salary arbitration increase athlete salaries, whereas a salary cap, luxury tax, and the presence of a reserve system can all decrease athlete salaries. Outside of the collective bargaining agreement, the presence of a competitor league typically leads to dramatic salary increases. These external factors require further elaboration.

As previously mentioned, free agency grants athletes access to a more open marketplace for their services. There are two basic types of free agency: restricted and unrestricted. An athlete is granted restricted free agency after completion of the initial reservation period at the beginning of his career. Restricted free agency provides the athlete whose contract has expired the ability to receive employment offers from other teams in the same league. The athlete's movement to other teams is restricted, however, because the current employer typically has a right to match the outside offer and maintain the athlete's services under those exact terms. Alternatively, the team can choose to allow the player to defect and may receive compensation from the new team in exchange for this player. Thus, restricted free agency allows the athlete to obtain a salary increase through the introduction of a quasi-open marketplace. The salary effect is lower if a compensation mechanism is in place, because this places a cost on outside teams that solicit new players. Conversely, the less restrictive the compensation mechanism, the greater the effect of restricted free agency on player salaries.

Unrestricted free agency provides more experienced athletes whose contracts have expired with the opportunity to receive offers from all league teams in an open marketplace. This allows players to receive fair market value for their services. Athlete compensation increases significantly with the arrival of free agent eligibility. It should not be surprising, then, that owners are generally opposed to free agency because of the effects that it has on player salaries. Though now accepted as an essential characteristic of the athlete compensation framework, owners still attempt to impose as limited a system of free agency as possible. However, free agency itself is not necessarily bad for owners. Rather, it is the intersection of free agency with the laws of supply and demand that negatively impacts owners. Unrestricted free agency is not available to every athlete every

year. Instead, only those athletes with a particular level of experience whose playing contracts have expired are eligible for free agency. By limiting the number of athletes who are eligible for free agency each year, the supply of players entering the free agent marketplace is artificially lowered. This allows free agents to receive higher salaries than they would in a truly open marketplace where every player is a free agent every year. Doing so would flood the marketplace and depress salaries. So athletes actually have an interest in limiting their access to free agency in order to reap its maximum benefits.

Salary arbitration provides owners and athletes with a method of resolving disputes over the athlete's salary for the upcoming season while ensuring that the athlete will continue his employment with the team uninterrupted by a holdout over salary. Salary arbitration allows athletes who have completed the initial phase of their careers to compare themselves to other similarly situated athletes in the marketplace in order to obtain salary increases. Athletes have been quite successful in doing so, especially because of the intersection that has occurred between free agency and salary arbitration. The free market effects of free agency have trickled down to the salary arbitration process.

The presence of a competitor league provides athletes with an attractive employment alternative. A new league needs players, the most talented and well known of whom are employed in the established league. These leagues do not abide by their rivals' collective bargaining agreements. Thus, unencumbered by the established league's reserve system, all athletes whose contracts have expired are able to gain access to an open marketplace regardless of experience. Historically, the introduction of another bidder for their services has led to a dramatic increase in players' salaries. Similar to other industries, competition among employers in the labor marketplace benefits the employees—in this case, the athletes.

Over the years, owners have devised various tactics that attempt to depress athlete compensation below competitive levels. The reserve system accomplished this very effectively by perpetually binding a player to a team, thereby preventing him from obtaining a market-level salary. Since

Table 2   Top American Earners in U.S. Sports, 2008

Rank	ATHLETE	Salary	Endorsements	Total
1	Tiger Woods (Golf)	$7,737,626	$92,000,000	$99,737,626
2	Phil Mickelson (Golf)	6,350,356	46,600,000	52,950,356
3	LeBron James (Cavaliers)	14,410,581	28,000,000	42,410,581
4	Alex Rodriguez (Yankees)	33,000,000	6,000,000	39,000,000
5	Shaquille O'Neal (Cavaliers)	20,000,000	15,000,000	35,000,000
6	Kevin Garnett (Celtics)	24,750,000	10,000,000	34,750,000
7	Kobe Bryant (Lakers)	21,262,500	10,000,000	31,262,500
8	Allen Iverson (Free Agent)	21,937,500	7,000,000	28,937,500
9	Derek Jeter (Yankees)	20,000,000	8,500,000	28,500,000
10	Peyton Manning* (Colts)	14,500,000	13,000,000	27,000,000
11	Dale Earnhardt Jr. (NASCAR)	4,611,290	22,000,000	26,611,290
12	Dwyane Wade (Heat)	14,410,581	12,000,000	26,410,581
13	Dwight Howard (Magic)	13,758,000	12,000,000	25,758,000
14	Mark Teixeira (Yankees)	25,000,000	250,000	25,250,000
15	Tracy McGrady (Rockets)	21,126,874	4,000,000	25,126,874
16	Tim Duncan (Spurs)	20,598,705	3,500,000	24,098,705
17	Stephon Marbury (Free Agent)	21,937,500	2,000,000	23,937,500
18	CC Sabathia (Yankees)	23,000,000	250,000	23,250,000
19	Jason Kidd (Free Agent)	21,372,000	1,500,000	22,872,000
20	Jermaine O'Neal (Heat)	21,352,500	750,000	22,102,500
21	Jeff Gordon (NASCAR)	5,944,140	15,000,000	20,944,140
22	Steve Francis (Free Agent)	19,862,275	500,000	20,362,275
23	Vince Carter (Magic)	15,200,000	5,000,000	20,200,000
24	Paul Pierce (Celtics)	18,077,903	1,500,000	19,577,903
25	Carmelo Anthony (Nuggets)	14,410,581	5,000,000	19,410,581
26	Barry Zito (Giants)	18,500,000	100,000	18,600,000
27	Ray Allen (Celtics)	17,388,430	750,000	18,138,430
28t	Tom Brady (Patriots)	8,000,000	10,000,000	18,000,000
28t	Torii Hunter (Angels)	17,500,000	500,000	18,000,000
30	Rashard Lewis (Magic)	17,238,000	750,000	17,988,000
31	Shawn Marion (Free Agent)	17,180,000	600,000	17,780,000
32	Amare Stoudemire (Suns)	15,070,550	2,500,000	17,570,550
33	Matt Schaub (Texans)	17,000,000	300,000	17,300,000
34t	David Ortiz (Red Sox)	12,500,000	4,500,000	17,000,000
34t	Albert Pujols (Cardinals)	13,000,000	4,000,000	17,000,000
36	Julius Peppers (Panthers)	16,700,000	150,000	16,850,000
37t	Todd Helton (Rockies)	16,600,000	150,000	16,750,000
37t	A. J. Burnett (Yankees)	16,500,000	250,000	16,750,000
39	Ryan Howard (Phillies)	15,000,000	1,500,000	16,500,000
40	Dwight Freeney (Colts)	16,220,000	250,000	16,470,000
41	Jim Furyk (Golf)	5,263,127	11,000,000	16,263,127
42	Michael Redd (Bucks)	15,780,000	250,000	16,030,000
43	Eli Manning (Giants)	8,950,000	7,000,000	15,950,000
44	Jason Schmidt (Dodgers)	15,500,000	250,000	15,750,000
45	Antonio Smith (Texans)	15,500,000	150,000	15,650,000
46	Mike Bibby (Free Agent)	15,225,000	250,000	15,475,000
47	Ben Roethlisberger (Steelers)	12,750,000	2,500,000	15,250,000
48t	Derek Lowe (Braves)	15,000,000	150,000	15,150,000
48t	Jason Brown (Rams)	15,000,000	150,000	15,150,000
50	Lance Berkman (Astros)	14,500,000	500,000	15,000,000

Source: Reprinted courtesy of SPORTS ILLUSTRATED: "The Fortunate 50" by Jonah Freedman, August 2, 2010. Copyright © 2010. Time Inc. All rights reserved. With data from "Tiger Tops SI's List of Top Earners for Sixth Consecutive Year," *SportsBusiness Daily,* July 2, 2009.

Notes: *Manning in 2009 has distributed $500,000 in grants through his PayBack Foundation to charities in Indianapolis, near the University of Tennessee (his alma mater), and in his hometown of New Orleans.

Candidates for the U.S. 50 had to be American citizens. SI consulted players associations, tour records, agents, and news reports to compile the list. Endorsement estimates came from Burns Entertainment & Sports Marketing, other sports-marketing execs and analysts, and agents. [*Ed. Note: Covers the period from July 1, 2008–June 30, 2009.*]

the evisceration of the reserve system nearly a generation ago, the collective bargaining process has yielded the development of salary caps and luxury taxes.

The presence of a salary cap provides a team with a degree of cost certainty in addressing their single highest expenditure—athlete salaries. A salary cap is actually a revenue sharing device for owners and athletes, with the owners guaranteeing the players a significant percentage of certain revenue streams. A hard cap places an absolute limit on this percentage and allows for few exceptions to this limit. A soft cap sets a limit but allows for a number of exceptions.

Another type of cost-containment mechanism is a luxury tax. Rather than limit the amount that each team can pay its players, a luxury tax gives a team a disincentive to exceed paying its players beyond certain salary levels by penalizing them for their excessive spending. This penalty is set at a percentage of the dollar amount of the excess. The higher the percentage and the lower the tax threshold, the greater the disincentive on the team.

The excerpts chosen for this chapter describe all of the aforementioned issues and ideas in great detail. In the first article, Quirk and Fort establish the broad framework for the discussion of athlete compensation. In the next selection, Kahn explains the impact of reserve systems, rival leagues, free agency, and incentives on the labor market for professional athletes. Berri, Brook, and Schmidt analyze the statistical determinants of salary for NBA players in the next selection. Michael Lewis' bestseller *Moneyball* brought significant attention to the use of statistical information by teams attempting to gain a competitive advantage, a tactic that has since proliferated not only in baseball but in other sports as well. The reading from Hakes and Sauer examines the economics of this phenomenon in MLB, whereas Bill Gerrard's excerpt does so in the context of more complex sports that rely on a greater degree of interdependence of players, specifically looking at English professional soccer. The next three readings review provisions of the collective bargaining agreements in North American professional sports leagues that inflate and deflate player salaries. Andrew Healy reviews teams' inefficient use of the free agency system in MLB, whereas Stephen Yoost examines salary arbitration in the National Hockey League. Richard Kaplan then reviews the deflationary luxury tax system utilized in the NBA since the late 1990's. In the final article, Duffy reviews the *Bosman* decision that led to the demise of the reserve system in European soccer and introduction of unfettered free agency, analyzing its impact on the sport throughout the continent.

FRAMEWORK

PAY DIRT: THE BUSINESS OF PROFESSIONAL TEAM SPORTS

James Quirk and Rodney D. Fort

PRO ATHLETES AS ENTERTAINERS

. . . Unlike unions in most industries, players' unions do not negotiate "standard wage" policies binding on most or all members. Instead, individual player salaries are determined by direct negotiation between the player and the team owner. Unions do bargain for league-wide minimum salaries, so the changes over time in minimum salaries reflect in part changes in the bargaining power of unions. . . .

While average salary levels are much lower for football and hockey, football (and, to a lesser extent, hockey) also showed marked increases in real salary levels in the 1980s, despite the restrictions on player mobility (free agency) for NFL football relative to baseball and basketball. Thus, in rounding up the usual suspects to explain the real growth in player compensation in all sports, free agency is not the only candidate. Other factors must be at work as well, including the impressive increase in demand for pro team sports tickets, and the striking increase in value of pro sports television rights for all pro team sports. . .

But the common perception of fans is that pro athletes are wildly overpaid, and that free agency is the culprit. Every red-blooded American boy wants to grow up to be a major leaguer in some sport, and most red-blooded American adult males would toss their careers in a minute if they thought they had a chance to make it in the pros. One example of this sports idolatry can be found in the vastly overinflated assessments that high school athletes make about their chances of turning pro, and, in turn, the similar mistaken perceptions that possess college athletes. Given that many fans would pay for the privilege of playing in the majors (and some actually do pay for the major league experience at adult major league baseball fantasy camps), fans find it a little difficult to accept the fact that pro athletes demand and get salaries in the six- or seven-figure range.

One way to add some perspective to the rise in real salaries for pro athletes is to look at the compensation paid to other entertainers. Perhaps Norby Walters put it best during his 1988 trial for signing college athletes to pro contracts prior to expiration of their college eligibility: "No difference. A sports star is a rock star. They're all the same."[1]

Walters' insight is right on the mark—star pro athletes are entertainment stars every bit as much as movie and rock stars. The same factors are at work determining the sizes of the big incomes in sports as in other areas of entertainment. These factors are demand by the public for tickets to see stars, the rarity of skilled and/or charismatic individuals with star qualities (in the economist's jargon, an inelastic supply of talent), and the bargaining power of stars relative to that of the promoters who hire them (team owners in the case of pro sports). In explaining the rise in salaries for sports stars, both increases in the demand for their output and changes in their bargaining power (for example, free agency's replacing a reserve system) are relevant.

. . . .

In an interesting analogy to the elimination of the reserve clause in baseball, movie entertainers' earnings skyrocketed with the breakdown of the "contract player" mode of operation in place in the motion picture industry until the 1950s. Studio owners of that era, much as sports team owners today, argued vigorously that the runaway growth in star salaries spelled disaster for their industry. True to predictions, the earnings of movie stars did go up dramatically, but the U.S. motion picture industry remains quite healthy even up to the present time, and is one of the few American industries that has retained its competitive edge in an international setting.

It is interesting that the public perception of the importance of rising salaries for entertainers is so different between movie stars and pro athletes. That star salaries in pop music or the movies cause little public concern is borne out by where news on salaries can be found. . . . If the level of discussion about salaries in movies and in popular music is a murmur, then it is a high-pitched scream in pro sports. . . .

To fans, the answer to why pro sports are different from other entertainment endeavors is obvious. Other mass entertainment media do not bring philosophers to their defense, lead presidents of the United States to throw out first pitches, or give poets pause to reflect. Whatever the reason, pro team sports are viewed differently from the other mass entertainment industries by almost everyone—fans, sportswriters, players, and owners. But there are some fundamental economic facts of life that apply across the board to all labor markets, including the market for rock stars and pro sports players.

THE WORKINGS OF THE PLAYER MARKET

The market for any labor service, such as the market for the services of pro athletes, follows the good old law of supply and demand and operates on the basis of bids and offers by teams and players. Looking at things from the point of view of any team, we can calculate the *most* that a profit-oriented team would offer a player; it is the amount that the player would add to the team's revenue if he were signed. In the jargon of economists, as noted earlier, this is the player's *marginal revenue product*, which we will refer to as his *MRP*. The player's MRP is the most a team would pay a player because paying a player more than this would decrease team profits; on the other hand, signing a player for anything less than his MRP means that adding the player increases profits for the team.

. . . George Steinbrenner . . . was asked once how he decided how much to pay a player. He said, "It depends on how many fannies he puts in the seats." That was George's way of saying it depends on the player's MRP. . . .

From the player's point of view, the least he would be willing to accept as a salary offer to sign with a team is what he could earn in his next-best employment opportunity (taking into account locational and other nonmonetary considerations). We hesitate to push our luck, but economists refer to this next-highest employment value as the player's *reservation wage*. If a team offers a player less than his reservation wage, the player would simply reject the offer and remain employed in his next-best opportunity.

The player's MRP and reservation wage give the maximum and minimum limits on the salary that a player can be expected to earn. Just where the player's salary will end up within these limits depends on a number of considerations. Union activities have an impact, especially on players whose reservation wage would have been below the league-wide minimum salary resulting from collective bargaining. The most important consideration is the bargaining power of the player relative to that of the owner. Generally, the more close substitutes there are (that is, the easier he is to replace), the more bargaining power the team has, and the salary will be closer to the player's reservation wage than to his MRP. The more unique are the skills and drawing power of the player (that is, the tougher he is to replace), the more bargaining power the player has, and the closer the salary will be to the player's MRP.

Just how far apart the reservation wage and MRP limits on a player's salary will be depends critically on the negotiating rights for players and owners, built into the player market by the rules of the sport. At one extreme is complete free agency, where the ability of players and owners to negotiate with whomever they choose is unrestricted. At the other extreme is the reserve clause system that operated in baseball until 1976. Under the reserve clause . . . a player can negotiate only with the team owning his contract. Generally speaking, the more freedom there is for players and owners to negotiate, the closer the minimum (reservation wage) and maximum (MRP) limits on a player's salary will be. However, there can be substantial remaining bargaining room even under unrestricted free agency.

Suppose first that there is unrestricted free agency, with players and owners free to negotiate with whomever they choose. Under such circumstances, if we ignore locational and other nonmonetary considerations, each player will end up signing with the team to which he is most valuable (the team for which the player has the highest MRP). He will be paid a salary that lies between his MRP with that team, and his MRP with the team to which he is second most valuable (the team to which he has the second-highest MRP). The reason for this is that the team to which the player is most valuable can outbid any other team for the player's services, and still increase its profits by hiring him. But the team can sign the player only if it offers him at least as much as the player can earn elsewhere (the player's reservation wage), and the most the player can earn elsewhere is clearly his MRP with the team to which he is second most valuable. In a market with completely unrestricted free agency, if we ignore nonmonetary considerations, the grand conclusion is that the highest salary offered to the player will capture at least his second-highest value in the league, and can be up to (but not exceeding) his *highest* value in the league.

Under a reserve clause system, the team owning a player's contract has exclusive negotiating rights to the player. Similarly, the college draft gives the team holding a player's draft rights exclusive rights to negotiate with him (in baseball, for up to six years. . .). Instead of a competitive market for the player's services, under a reserve clause system, there is only one bidder for the player's services. The highest salary the team holding the player's contract would be willing to pay the player still is the MRP of the player for that team; but under the reserve clause, there is no competitive pressure on the owner of the contract. As a result, the player's reservation wage is not bid up to his second-highest MRP in the league. Instead, the player's reservation wage under a reserve clause system is what the player can earn *outside* of the league, or the league minimum salary, whichever is higher.

Needless to say, for most athletes, the reservation wage calculated in this way lies far below the player's value to *any* team in the league. Under the reserve clause system, a player's wage will end up some place between his reservation wage and his MRP with the team owning his contract. The reserve clause system lowers the value of the player's reservation wage by eliminating competing offers by other teams, and, unless the player happens to be under contract with the team in the league to which he is most valuable, the upper bargaining limit has been reduced as well. Predictably, the overall effect of a reserve clause system is to lower player salaries relative to what they would earn under free agency.

Put another way, a reserve clause system acts to direct more of the revenue that a player produces to the team owner than to the player. The effect of unrestricted free agency on a league that previously was under a reserve clause system, as in the case of baseball since 1976, would be a bidding up of player salaries to the point where most of the revenue that is linked to the performance of the team ends up in player salaries. Under a reserve clause system, the team can capture a significant fraction of the revenue linked to a team's performance, as well as revenue that is not so linked.

For both players and owners, the issue of free agency is critical to their economic well-being. While claims that free agency will destroy pro sports thus far are clearly exaggerated, the division of the monopoly rents created by pro sports certainly is at stake. It should come as no surprise, then, that free agency is the central issue in pro team sports collective bargaining. A secondary collective bargaining concern is the league minimum salary, which under a reserve clause system becomes the reservation wage for most players. Under free agency, the league minimum salary is no longer relevant to regulars, but it remains an important bargaining element for other players not yet eligible for free agency.

The point of all this is that the sports labor market has the same fundamental driving forces as any other labor market, that is, the value produced by an employee and his or her bargaining power, with the wage rate ending up somewhere between the reservation wage and the player's MRP, and with the player's MRP depending upon the demand by the public for the sport. Interestingly, what goes on in the player market is often portrayed in the press in exactly the opposite fashion, as though it were changes in player salaries that controlled ticket prices and TV revenues.

TICKET PRICE AND PLAYER SALARIES

Owners of sports teams understandably are concerned about escalating salaries for players. After all, they have to pay the bills. But when owners and league commissioners express their opinions about the level of player salaries in public, they like to come on in their self-appointed role of protectors of the fans. Owners are fond of pointing out that if player salaries increase, they (the owners) will be forced to raise ticket prices, or turn to pay-per-view alternatives, in order to obtain the revenues to pay those salaries. The owners' line would have it that putting a brake on salary increases really is in the interest of fans, who prefer low ticket prices to high ones. This argument seems to be very effective, because fans typically side with the owners in salary disputes with players and in labor negotiations with player unions. . . .

While the owners get effective mileage from this line, it makes very little economic sense. With some rare classic exceptions, such as Phil Wrigley and Tom Yawkey, owners of sports teams are in the business to make money, or at least not lose money. Nobody has to force an owner to raise ticket prices if he or she is fielding a successful team with lots of popular support and a sold-out stadium. Put another way, even if player costs did not rise, one would expect that ticket prices and TV contract values would rise in the face of increasing fan demand. On the other hand, if the team already is having trouble selling tickets, only sheer folly would dictate raising ticket prices.

Given a team's roster of players, the simple economic fact of life is that the ticket pricing decision by a profit-oriented owner is completely independent of the salaries paid to those players. Profit-oriented ticket-pricing decisions depend solely on the demand by fans for tickets to the team's games. The demand for the inputs used to produce the games, including players, is derived from this profit-oriented decision, not the other way around. Ticket prices rise when fan demand rises, which in turn increases player MRPs, which spills over into higher salaries for players.

Nowhere is this logic more clearly evident than in the case of baseball in the period just after the beginning of free agency. Free agency acted immediately to raise player salaries. . . . But fans would not pay more to watch the same players just because they started earning more. The initial effect of free agency was to lower team profits with little impact on ticket prices. . . . With few exceptions, ticket prices *fell* in real terms during the very first years of free agency! Indeed, only the Boston Red Sox and New York Yankees had ticket prices in excess of their 1971 levels as late as 1980, four years after free agency. Thus, salaries rose, but ticket prices did not. Ticket prices prior to free agency were already set by owners at levels representing their best guesses as to what would maximize revenue for their teams. Free agency shifted the bargaining power in the direction of players, and player salaries went up. But changes in player salaries per se had no effect on the demand for tickets and no effect on ticket prices.

. . . This has been a period of rising demand by the public for the major pro team sports. Rising demand led to increases in both ticket prices and TV contract revenues. In turn, the increased demand for pro sports tickets and TV coverage acted to increase the value of skilled players to teams, that is, their MRPs rose. Then, the bargaining process translated the increased value of player skills into higher player salaries. Salaries continued to grow . . . for all pro sports, spurred on by the growth in team revenues. Under free agency, as in baseball and basketball, more of the increased revenue goes to players than under a reserve clause system . . . but salaries go up in either case when demand for the sport increases, and, contrary to the argument of owners, they are the effect and not the cause of higher ticket prices.

It might be that the mistaken perception about the link between player salaries and ticket prices comes from a confusion of two different sources of salary escalation. If a team's salary bill rises because the team has acquired more expensive talent, then the owner can and undoubtedly will raise ticket prices, not because he or she is paying more in salaries, but because he or she is fielding a more attractive team. That was certainly the case with the Yankees in the early days of free agency. . . . But looking at the league as a whole, the same group of players was around right after free agency as before, so for an average team, the quality of players didn't change. Consequently, there was no way that the average owner could pass on to fans the increase in salaries that came with free agency; the salary cost increase came directly out of profits, instead.

THE WINNER'S CURSE

Things are not quite as simple as we have been making them, of course—general managers and scouts really do earn the money they are paid. It is no easy task to predict how a player will perform next season, what his contribution to the team will be, and the size of the crowds the team will draw. . . .

We do not pretend to any such skills. Instead, we assume that the market for players "works" in the sense that, on average, bids by skilled general managers and offers by skilled player agents lead to a situation in which players get paid pretty much according to what we have outlined, that is, what they would be worth in their second-best employment in the league.

Well, actually, they may get a little more than that, and maybe even more than their MRPs to the teams that sign them. There is a well-known phenomenon in bidding theory known as "the winner's curse," which might be operative in the player markets of the free agency period. . . .

In a sealed-bid auction, say, for league TV rights, the prospective bidders (the networks and cable systems) each evaluate the revenue potential of the TV rights and then, at a specified time, each in effect submits a dollar bid in a sealed envelope. The "lucky" winner is the individual submitting the highest bid. "Lucky" is in quotes, because, by definition, the winning bidder ends up paying more for the right to televise games, and occasionally much more, than any other bidder was willing to offer. Given that all bidders had access to pretty much the same information about the potential market for TV, this suggests that the winner might well have made a mistake in overvaluing the revenue potential of the contract. This is the "winner's curse"—winning in a sealed-bid auction means the winner might very well have bid too much, and maybe far too much, for the property. In particular, a measure of how much the winner has overbid is the difference between the winner's bid and the second-highest bid. In the jargon of the field, this difference is what is "left on the table."

The free agent market in baseball is not as formal as a sealed-bid auction, but there are problems for a general manager in determining how much a player will be worth to his team and in guessing how much other teams will be willing to offer the player. Ideally, a general manager would like to pay any player just $1 more than the player's best offer anywhere else, but this option is only available in cases where the team has "right of first refusal," that is, the right to match any outside offer.

With lots of teams out there operating in the free agent market (and assuming no collusion), there will be vigorous competitive bidding for players. Clearly, teams underestimating the MRPs of free agents will typically not be the teams signing them; instead, there is better chance that the "winners" in the free agent market will be teams overestimating player MRPs, and these are the teams stuck with the "winner's curse." And, in turn, the presence of the winner's curse means that players get paid on average even more than their value in their second-best employment opportunities in the league. This cannot be too surprising. Sportswriters, each year, are fond of rubbing owners' noses in the winner's curse by pointing out how overpaid many (some would say most) free agents are, relative to their subsequent performance.

SALARY DETERMINATION IN BASEBALL

Assuming that the baseball player market operates to generate salary offers that correlate roughly with player MRPs, we can identify factors that can be said to "determine" baseball player salaries in the sense that these factors are highly correlated with market-determined salary levels, and thus do a good job of predicting the level of baseball player salaries. . . . The equation is a "best fit" model of salary determination in the sense that (1) it explains a large portion of the total variation in player salaries, and (2) adding other factors to the equation would not significantly improve its predictive power. Models . . . are used both by players and by owners in justifying their positions on salary demands in the baseball salary arbitration process. . . .

. . . The clear conclusion is that income inequality in the rest of the U.S. economy, although high relative to other countries, pales in comparison to the inequality in recent years in baseball salaries.

It is also clear that baseball salaries have become less equally distributed over time, and skewed toward the top of the salary scale, with a noticeable jump between the reserve clause and free agency periods. . . Overall, from the baseball salary data, we can conclude that while all players benefited from free agency, a disproportionate share of the benefits went to the top players, who were the big gainers from free agency. Players at the lower end of the distribution, still held captive by united mobility for their first six years, lost ground relative to their star teammates.

. . . .

Notes

1. Quoted in Rick Telander, *The Hundred Yard Lie,* New York: Simon & Schuster 1989, at 41.

THE SPORTS BUSINESS AS A LABOR MARKET LABORATORY

Lawrence M. Kahn

Professional sports offers a unique opportunity for labor market research. There is no research setting other than sports where we know the name, face, and life history of every production worker and supervisor in the industry. Total compensation packages and performance statistics for each individual are widely available, and we have a complete data set of worker–employer matches over the career of each production worker and supervisor in the industry. These statistics are much more detailed and accurate than typical microdata samples such as the Census or the Current Population Survey. Moreover, professional sports leagues have experienced major changes in labor market rules and structure—like the advent of new leagues or rules about free agency—creating interesting natural experiments that offer opportunities for analysis.

. . . .

Of course, it is wise to be hesitant before generalizing from the results of sports research to the population as a whole. The four major team sports employ a total of 3,000 to 4,000 athletes who . . . earned . . . far above the . . . median earnings of full-time, full-year equivalent workers. . . . But at a minimum, sports labor markets can be seen as a laboratory for observing whether economic propositions at least have a chance of being true. . . .

MONOPSONY AND PLAYER SALARIES

Sports owners are a small and interconnected group, which suggests that they have some ability to band together and act as monopsonists in paying players. The result is that player pay is held below marginal revenue product. I discuss three sources of evidence on monopsony in sports: evidence from the rise and fall of rival leagues, evidence from changes in rules about player free agency, and studies comparing the marginal revenue product of players with their pay. Sports owners have often had monopsony power over players in the sense that in many instances players have the option of negotiating only with one team. Here, salaries are determined by individual team–player bargaining in which marginal revenue product, and the outside options available to teams and players, will affect the outcome. Rules changes and the rise and fall of rival leagues have their effects by changing players' and teams' outside options.

RIVAL LEAGUES

There have been two time periods in which rival leagues posed a substantial threat to existing professional sports. The first is the period from 1876 to 1920, when there was a scramble of professional baseball leagues forming, merging, and dissolving. The second is the period from the late 1960s into the early 1980s, when new leagues were born in basketball, hockey, and football.

. . . Baseball is the oldest major league sport in the United States, beginning with the birth of the National League in 1876. In this early period, there was competition for player services from other baseball leagues. To protect itself against the competition of rival leagues and improve the team owners' balance sheets, the National League introduced the "reserve clause" in 1879, which meant that players were bound to the team that originally acquired the rights to contract with them. Owners now had additional monopsony power over players, and player salaries dropped.

However, the lower salaries may have contributed to the birth of a new league in 1882, the American Association. . . . Average nominal National League salaries rose from $1,375 in 1882 to $3,500 in 1891. . .

This increase in salaries is not conclusive evidence that monopsony power of owners decreased; after all, salaries could have risen for other reasons, like the growth of baseball's popularity. However, in 1891, four of the American Association teams were absorbed into the National League, and five dissolved AA franchises were bought out by the survivors. . . . [which coincided with] an abrupt, massive decline in National League player salaries starting in the first season of the merger: player pay fell from $3,500 in 1891 (before the merger) to $2,400 in 1892 to $1,800 in 1893. This pay cut was accomplished as the outcome of the National League owners announcement in 1893 of a new salary policy: the maximum pay for a player was to be $2,400. Indeed, some teams imposed lower caps: eight top players on the Philadelphia Phillies who were all paid more than $3,000 in 1892 found that they were all paid exactly $1,800 in 1893. The sharp decline in player salaries does not appear to reflect a major decline in the demand for baseball entertainment, as attendance climbed through the 1895 season.

The success of the National League waned somewhat in the late 1890s, partly due to a lack of competitive balance, but the baseball market was growing. A new rival league, the American League, began in 1901 with eight teams. It successfully lured many star players from the older league and actually outdrew it in attendance in 1902 by 2.2 million to 1.7 million. In response, the National League attempted to have its reserve clause enforced by state courts to prevent players from jumping leagues; however, because state courts have no jurisdiction for player movements outside a given state, it was ultimately unsuccessful in this effort.

A familiar pattern then emerges. The huge success of the American League brought with it a dramatic rise in player salaries. In fact the salary increase appears to begin in 1900, perhaps reflecting anticipation of the new league. The two leagues merged during the 1903 season, at the end of which the first World Series was played. Then in 1903, salaries in Major League Baseball fell immediately by about 15 percent. . . . Again, this decline does not seem to reflect any fall in baseball's popularity that year.

Major League Baseball prospered for the rest of the first decade of the twentieth century, with player costs under control and attendance on the rise. However, attendance fell beginning in 1910, and owners kept a tight lid on salaries. Player discontent resulted in the formation of a union, the Fraternity of Professional Baseball Players of America, at the end of the 1912 season. The owners were under no legal obligation to bargain with a union and reacted to it with some hostility.

This dissatisfaction among players helped pave the way for the Federal League, which was able to recruit to long-term contracts several well-known Major League ballplayers beginning in 1913. The pay cycle began again. While the Federal League was in existence from 1913 through 1915, many players jumped leagues, and major league salaries went from about $3,000 in 1913 to $5,000 in 1915. After the 1915 season, most of the Federal League's owners were "bought out" in December 1915 by the major leagues, and nominal salaries plummeted back to $4,000 by 1917, a fall that was even larger in real terms due to the inflation of the World War I period.

The Federal League owners who were not part of the settlement pursued an antitrust suit against the settling parties for creating a monopoly; however, this suit was lost in 1922, when the U.S. Supreme Court declared that baseball was not a business.[1] This decision began baseball's antitrust exemption, which was upheld several times, most notably in an unsuccessful attempt by a player named Curt Flood to become a free agent in 1969.[2] While Flood lost his case, it may have set the stage for baseball players' ultimately successful quest for free agency. However, this goal was not achieved through the antitrust laws; in fact, baseball's exemption lasted with respect to player relations until legislation ending it was passed in 1998. Rather, collective bargaining brought free agency to baseball, as discussed below.

The early experiences of Major League Baseball provide some compelling evidence for the potential impact of monopsony in this labor market. However, the comparisons just discussed all concern baseball, and thus have no real control group. In the modern period, we can use salaries in some sports as control groups for other sports.

From the late 1960s into the 1970s, highly credible rival leagues were born in basketball and hockey. The American Basketball Association (ABA), which lasted from 1967 to 1976, was able to field some very good teams. In 1976, four of its teams were absorbed into the NBA, and these all made the NBA playoffs in several seasons after the merger. The NBA Players Association (NBPA) challenged the merger on antitrust grounds, but then withdrew its lawsuit as the result of a settlement which granted free agency rights to NBA players. The World Hockey Association (WHA), which lasted from 1971 to 1979, also had several excellent teams which were absorbed into the NHL starting in 1979.

The rise and fall of these two rival leagues offer another opportunity to test how monopsony might affect salaries since the other two major team sports—baseball and football—had no such competition in their labor markets until the advent of free agency in baseball in 1976 and the birth of the United States Football League (USFL) in 1982.

. . . In 1967, there were no rival leagues in baseball, football, or hockey, and the ABA was just getting started. Further, there was no free agency, and players unions had not yet negotiated their first agreements. Thus, the 1967 salaries can be viewed as representing common initial conditions with respect to negotiating rules, although not necessarily with respect to demand conditions.*

By 1970 and 1972, the ABA had been in existence for several years, and NBA players rapidly became the highest paid of the major team sports. The World Hockey Association started in 1971, and by 1972, NHL players outearned football and baseball players by similar margins. These upward movements in the relative salaries of basketball and hockey players, while consistent with effects of the new competition, need to be judged against the changing popularity of these two sports. For example, in the NBA, total attendance rose by 120 percent between 1966–67 and 1971–72, while television revenues went from $1.5 million to $5.5 million during the same period, rises that were much, much greater than the increases for football or baseball during this time. . . . The shock of higher salaries may also have spurred the teams to market themselves better. Moreover, NBA salaries as a percentage of gross basketball revenues rose from 30 percent in 1967 to 66 percent in 1972, which suggests a structural shift in salary determination that goes beyond a rise in revenues. In the NHL, attendance growth was actually much faster in the five years before the birth of the WHA (135 percent) than while the WHA was in business (7 percent). Thus, the acceleration of NHL salaries after 1971 is telling indeed.

There is one more important example of the impact of a rival league on player salaries, the United States Football League (USFL). Like some of the baseball experiences earlier in the century, the USFL was born out of labor strife in the established league; in this case, it was a seven-week NFL strike in 1982, in which the players had failed to gain any significant ground in their fight for free agency or a share of revenues. From 1982 to 1985, the USFL posed a challenge to the established NFL. The USFL had strong financial backing from such owners as Donald Trump; many NFL players switched leagues; and the USFL was able to sign some high-profile college players such as Anthony Carter and Herschel Walker. However, poor television ratings for the USFL ultimately signaled its demise.

The pattern of football player salaries during the USFL years follows that set by the example of other rival leagues. Real salary increases for NFL players averaged 4 percent per year from 1977–1982, before the USFL, and 5 percent per year from 1985–1989, just after the USFL. In between, real player salary increases were 20 percent per year from 1982–1985. Changes in the popularity of football do not seem sufficient to explain the explosion of salaries during the USFL years. From 1977 to 1981, NFL attendance rose 23 percent, but attendance was actually 2 percent lower in 1985 than in 1981; further, NFL television revenues rose by similar rates before and during the USFL years. Overall, NFL salaries during the USFL period were much higher than could have been predicted on the basis of revenues during that time.†

If one uses other sports as a control group for the experience of football salaries in the USFL years, the same lesson emerges. The salary growth for football players from 1982 to 1985 was 8–10 percentage points per year higher than baseball and basketball, and 17 percentage points per year higher than for hockey players. However, during the 1981–85 period, attendance grew 5 percent in baseball, 11 percent in the NBA, 11 percent in the NHL, and, as noted, fell 2 percent in the NFL; television revenues grew 211 percent in baseball and 35 percent in the NBA, compared to 29 percent in the NFL. The faster growth of NFL salaries during the 1982–85 period despite worse attendance and television revenue increases again suggests the importance of the USFL.

FREE AGENCY

Until 1976, players in each of the four major sports were bound by the reserve clause to remain with their original team, unless that team decided to trade or sell them to another team. They were not allowed to become free agents, who could sell their services to any team.

The path toward free agency started in baseball. The Major League Baseball Players Association (MLBPA) was started in 1952, but it didn't become a modern union until the former United Steelworkers negotiator, Marvin Miller, took over in 1966. The MLBPA achieved a collective bargaining

---

*The higher NFL salary level may have represented the lingering effects of the bidding war between the National Football League and the American Football League earlier in the 1960s. The two leagues agreed to merge in 1966, a merger that required Congressional approval. This episode is not discussed here because NFL salary level information is not available before 1967. However, there is strong anecdotal evidence of a bidding war between the two leagues over college stars such as Joe Namath.

†Deceleration of the growth of NFL television revenues from nearly 30 percent per year from 1981 to 1985 to just 2.6 percent annual growth from 1985 to 1988 could also have explained the deceleration of salaries after 1985. However, it is also true that attendance in the NFL picked up from 1985 to 1988, rising 1.5 percent, in contrast to the 2 percent fall from 1981 to 1985. Quirk, James and Rodney D. Fort. 1997. *Pay Dirt: The Business of Professional Team Sports.* Princeton, NJ: Princeton University Press.

agreement in 1968, and in 1970 the National Labor Relations Board ordered the parties to use outside arbitrators for resolving grievances. In a farsighted decision, Miller obtained management's agreement to incorporate the standard player contract, which included the reserve clause, into the collective bargaining agreement. This meant that grievances about the interpretation of this clause were a proper subject for arbitration. In December 1975, an arbitrator ruled that the reserve clause meant that the team could reserve a player for only one year beyond the expiration of any current contract. With the reserve clause in place, almost all teams signed players exclusively to one-year contracts, and so this ruling would have freed virtually all of the veteran players after the 1976 season. The teams, threatened with this possibility, were thus moved to negotiate a formal system of free agency with the union in 1976, calling for free agency (with some relatively minor compensation to any team losing a free agent) for players with at least six years of Major League Baseball service. This provision remains basically in place. In 1994, about 33 percent of players had at least six years' service. [*Ed. Note: In 2009, 308 of the 1,293 players on MLB teams' 40-man rosters, voluntarily retired lists and disabled lists had at least 6 years of service.*]

The rise of free agency in the 1976–77 period had a powerful impact on the salaries of baseball players. The average real increase in baseball salaries was from 0–2 percent per year from 1973–75. In 1976 the average real salary increase was almost 10 percent; in 1977, the first year under the new collective bargaining agreement, 38 percent (!); in 1978, 22 percent, before falling back into single digits growth in 1979. Moreover, baseball salaries as a percentage of team revenues rose from 17.6 percent in 1974 to 20.5 percent in 1977 to 41.1 percent in 1982, further suggesting that free agency has had a structural effect on baseball salary determination.* A final point to note about baseball salary determination is that in a series of grievance arbitration decisions in the 1980s, the owners were found guilty of colluding by not making offers to free agents. This reassertion of cartel wage-setting behavior appeared to be successful in restraining salary growth. Real annual growth in baseball salaries fell from 11 percent in the 1982–85 time period to 3 percent from 1985–87. Moreover, salaries as a percent of revenues fell from about 40 percent in 1985 to 32 percent in 1989 during the collusion period. In 1989, arbitrators levied

a $280 million back pay penalty on the owners to be paid out over the 1989–91 period as compensation for the losses imposed by collusion, and salaries as a percent of revenue bounced back to 43 percent by 1991. The collusion episode provides a further illustration of the potential impact of monopsony on salaries.

Basketball players also won free agency in 1976, but by a different route, through the settlement of the players' antitrust suit challenging the ABA–NBA merger. As a result, free agency in the NBA came on the heels of the ABA–NBA salary war period of 1967–76. Possibly as a result, average salaries grew more slowly in the NBA in the 1977–82 period than in football or baseball, a comparison which does not suggest a major impact of free agency in the NBA in addition to the impact of competition from the ABA. On the other hand, NBA salaries amounted to about 70 percent of revenue in 1977 and "nearly three quarters" in 1983, suggesting some further increase in basketball players' relative power after the coming of free agency even without the benefit of an alternative league.[3] Finally, basketball imposed a salary cap in 1983, and salaries did indeed decelerate after 1985. However, there were many exceptions to the salary cap, and it may ultimately have had little effect on salaries during this period.

EVIDENCE OF THE DEGREE OF MONOPSONISTIC EXPLOITATION

To this point, the argument has relied on presenting abrupt shifts in salaries that are difficult to explain without appealing to the theory of monopsony. An alternative mode of research on salary determination is to compare estimates of players' marginal revenue products to salaries, and in this way to approximate the degree of monopsonistic exploitation. . . .

. . . Scully found that star players in 1987 were paid 29–45 percent of marginal revenue product; even though this was the height of the collusion period, the percentage was still much higher than the 15 percent he found for the reserve clause days.[4] Zimbalist's approach compares the players eligible and not eligible for free agency.[5] In 1989, for those players with less than three years service, and thus not eligible for salary arbitration or free agency, the ratio of salary to marginal revenue product was just .38 times what it was for those eligible for salary arbitration only and .18 times that for those eligible for free agency.†

These measures of monopsonistic exploitation must be interpreted cautiously since (as noted by the authors of the studies) they do not control for a player's effects on revenue other than through his own playing statistics' effects on

---

*In the 1974 and 1975 seasons, many players were eligible for salary arbitration, but without free agency, arbitration alone seemed to have little impact on average salaries, because arbitrators are often entitled to compare players' demands and team offers to the salary levels of free agents. Using fixed effects methods on panel data for individual players for the late 1980s, I found that, other things equal, being eligible for the salary arbitration increased players' salary by about 30–45 percent. See Kahn, Lawrence M. "Free Agency, Long-Term Contracts and Compensation in Major League Baseball: Estimate from Panel Data." *The Review of Economics and Statistics.* 75:1, pp. 157–64.

---

†The low relative levels of exploitation for the free agency eligible suggest that in the free agent market, teams may have been affected by the "winner's curse." . . . .

winning.* However, taken as a whole, this line of research produces additional evidence that making the labor market more competitive leads to higher salaries than would be the case under monopsony. Nonetheless, during the 1980s there still appeared to be widespread monopsonistic exploitation in baseball, and research from this period also showed similar results for basketball.

[Ed. Note: The author's discussion of the Coase theorem and sports and racial discrimination is omitted. See Chapter 18 for a discussion of the latter topic.]

. . . .

INCENTIVES, SUPERVISION, AND PERFORMANCE

Some of the most intriguing evidence on the links from incentives to performance comes from sports that have not been much discussed to this point, like golf and marathon running. Ehrenberg and Bognanno used data from the 1984 U.S.-based Professional Golf Association (PGA) and 1987 European PGA tours to estimate the impact of incentives on player performance.[6] Because the prize structure of a given tournament is known in advance, one can compute the dollar gain to improving one's finishing position in a tournament. Ehrenberg and Bognanno found that a greater dollar gain to a better finish had a statistically significant favorable effect on a player's performance, controlling for the player's ability, his opponents' ability, and the difficulty of the course. In addition, golfers appear to perform better when it matters more, particularly in the later rounds of a tournament. Finally, golfers' labor supply, as measured by their propensity to enter a given tournament, is positively affected by the expected gain to participating, implying an upward-sloping labor supply schedule.† However, a more recent replication study, using 1992 PGA data, found that monetary incentives had small and statistically insignificant effects on player performance and that results were sensitive with respect to who rated the weather that prevailed during a tournament.[7]

The framework devised by Ehrenberg and Bognanno has been used to examine the incentive impact of prize money in two additional sports: marathon running and auto racing.[8] In auto racing, Becker and Huselid found that larger monetary rewards to better finishes lowered individual racers' finishing times and raised the incidence of accidents, presumably due to a greater effort to go fast.[9] In marathon

races, Frick found that better prize money and performance bonuses for setting records lowered racing times.[10]

In the major team sports that have been the primary focus of this paper, free agency has brought with it an increased incidence of long-term contracts, a finding Lehn argued was consistent with wealth effects, as players in essence buy long-term income insurance.[11] He noted that as the incidence of long-term contracts went from virtually zero during the days of the reserve clause to 42 percent of baseball players with at least two years pay guaranteed as of 1980, the share of baseball players who spent time on the disabled list rose from an average of 14.8 percent from 1974 to 1976 (before free agency) up to 20.8 percent from 1977 to 1980 (the early years of free agency). Lehn surmised that this increase was a moral hazard response by players on guaranteed long-term contract. In this instance, moral hazard refers to a player's impact on the decision to go or stay on injured reserve.

To perform a sharper test of this hypothesis, he compared players in 1980 who had long-term contracts of three years or more with those who had short-term contracts of two years or less. Prior to signing these contracts, those with long-term contracts were almost two years younger and had 2.2 days per season less disability than those who signed short-term contracts. Thus, those with long-term contracts do not appear to be an especially injury-prone group. Nonetheless, after signing their agreements, those with long-term contracts averaged 12.6 disabled days per season, compared to only 5.2 days for those with 0–2 years. Lehn confirms in a regression setting that this effect is highly statistically significant.[12] The finding is strongly suggestive of a moral hazard effect, although one cannot completely rule out that players who had private information that they were fragile were more likely to sign long-term contracts, in which case the results could also reflect adverse selection.

Of course, one way for a team to reduce the moral hazard response is to reward players for not being injured. Lehn notes that 38 out of 155 players with contracts of three or more years, or about 25 percent, had incentive clauses in their contracts.[13] These clauses sometimes rewarded either

---

*As an extreme example of such effects not captured by the revenues of the player's home team, Hausman and Leonard estimate Michael Jordan's value to other NBA teams during the 1991–92 season to be roughly $53 million. This consisted of effects on attendance at away games, television ratings, and merchandise sales. Hausman, Jerry A. and Gregory K. Leonard. 1997. "Superstars in the National Basketball Association: Economic Value and Policy." *Journal of Labor Economics.* 15:4, pp. 586–624.

†Labor supply effects also appear in men's professional tennis. The Association of Tennis Professionals (the governing body of the men's pro tour) decided several years ago to consider just a player's results in the most recent 14 events in which [he has] competed in computing his ranking, which affects his seeding and therefore success probability in future tournaments. For example, in 1999, one player was ranked first in the world for part of the year, despite a string of first round tournament losses. These did not count in his ranking point total, and observers surmised that he would have entered fewer tournaments (and thus conserved his energy) if the costs of losing were higher. Because of these poor incentives, the Association of Tennis Professionals (the ruling body of men's tennis) has instituted a new system which will count in a player's ranking a core set of tournaments, whether the player plays in the tournament or not, and then some other tournaments as well. See the ATP's Web site at (http://www.atptour.com).

Table 3   Salary Cap Growth in NBA and NFL

NBA	
Year	Value
1984–1985	$3.6 million
1985–1986	4.2 million
1986–1987	4.9 million
1987–1988	6.2 million
1988–1989	7.2 million
1989–1990	9.8 million
1990–1991	11.9 million
1991–1992	12.5 million
1992–1993	14.0 million
1993–1994	15.1 million
1994–1995	16.0 million
1995–1996	23.0 million
1996–1997	24.4 million
1997–1998	26.9 million
1998–1999	30.0 million
1999–2000	34.0 million
2000–2001	35.5 million
2001–2002	42.5 million
2002–2003	40.3 million
2003–2004	43.9 million
2004–2005	43.9 million
2005–2006	49.5 million
2006–2007	53.1 million
2007–2008	55.6 million
2008–2009	58.7 million
2009–2010	57.7 million

NFL	
Year	Value
1994	$34.6 million; average club salary expenditures of $36.6 million
1995	37.1 million; average club salary expenditures of 41.9 million
1996	40.7 million; average club salary expenditures of 44.9 million
1997	41.5 million; average club salary expenditures of 42.7 million
1998	52.4 million; average club salary expenditures of 61.4 million
1999	57.3 million; average club salary expenditures of 64.7 million
2000	62.2 million; average club salary expenditures of 68.3 million
2001	67.4 million; average club salary expenditures of 66.8 million
2002	71.1 million; average club salary expenditures of 64.5 million
2003	75.0 million; average club salary expenditures of 77.4 million
2004	80.6 million; average club salary expenditures of 83.8 million
2005	85.5 million; average club salary expenditures of 82.6 million
2006	102.5 million; average club salary expenditures of 104.8 million
2007	109.1 million; average club salary expenditures of 107.0 million
2008	116.7 million; average club salary expenditures of 113.8 million
2009	128.0 million; average club salary expenditures of 114.6 million

Source: ESPN.com, NFLPA documents, additional data on file from authors.

being available to play for most of the season or postseason awards won (such awards typically require being active for all or most of the year). Before signing such long-term contracts, those who ended up with incentive bonuses had virtually identical average propensities to be injured as those without such incentive bonuses. However, after signing, the injured time of players without incentive bonuses was 2.4 times that of those with bonuses. Again, a strong moral hazard response is suggested, although as before, we cannot rule out the adverse selection possibility that players who suspected that they were likely to be fragile have turned down the opportunity to sign a contract with an incentive bonus.

Hiring better quality management is an alternative route, along with contract incentives, for eliciting desired performance levels. In a study of the impact of baseball managers, I estimated the effect of better managers on team and individual player performance.[14] Managerial quality was measured by first running a 1987 regression with manager salary as the dependent variable and managerial experience, career winning percentage, and a National League dummy variable as the explanatory variables. Then, using the coefficients from the regression, I plugged in each manager's actual experience and winning percentage to get a predicted salary level. I then calculated that during the 1969–86 period, hiring a better quality manager significantly raised the team's winning percentage relative to its past level—even if one also controls for team scoring and runs allowed, suggesting that good managers win the close games. The effect of good managers was even larger when I didn't control for offense and defense. The latter effect could indicate that better managers are superior judges of talent, or motivate their players, and thus indirectly contribute to offense and defense.

I also studied individual player performance relative to established career levels when the team was taken over by a new manager. The better the quality of the new manager, the better a player's future performance relative to his past performance. In related calculations, I found an increase in managerial quality more than pays for itself based on Scully's results for the effect of winning on revenue.[15] Because of this, one might have expected the salaries of highly talented managers to be bid up. The fact that they weren't as measured in the 1987 salary data used in this study may be further indirect evidence of collusion between baseball owners during this time period.

FINAL THOUGHTS

Labor issues in sports may seem distant from the rest of the economy, since they often seem to pit millionaire players against billionaire owners. But while it would be unwise to extrapolate too strongly from the labor market experience of sports, evidence on a particular labor market should not be discounted just because the market has a high profile,

either. The strong evidence for monopsony in spo some parallels to a similar effect that has been found groups such as public school teachers, nurses, and uni professors.[16] The evidence from these areas suggests tl phenomenon of employer monopsony power could be widespread than is commonly acknowledged by econor The presence of customer discrimination in sports rer us that there are many sectors in the economy with ducer–customer contact where discrimination could pe The results on player performance suggest that athletes motivated by similar forces that affect workers in gener

While this paper has concentrated on sports in N America, many of the same economic issues arise in sports industry elsewhere. Professional soccer leagues Europe are tremendously lucrative and also must be c cerned with player movement and competitive balance. In fact, European soccer draws more TV revenue than t NBA, Major League Baseball, or the NHL. The promoti and demotion of individual teams to and from a. . . Europe superleague involving teams from several countries rai fascinating questions about the role of competitive balance

. . . .

(See **Table 3** for salary cap growth in the NBA and NFL.)

Notes

1. Federal Baseball Club of Baltimore, Inc. vs. National League of Baseball Clubs, et al., 259 U.S. 200 (1922).

2. Flood vs. Kuhn, 407 U.S. 258 (1972).

3. Staudohar, Paul D. 1996. *Playing for Dollars: Labor Relations and the Sports Business.* Ithaca, NY: Cornell University Press, at 108.

4. Scully, Gerald W. 1989. *The Business of Major League Baseball.* Chicago: University of Chicago Press.

5. Zimbalist, Andrew. 1992. *Baseball and Billions.* New York: Basic Books.

6. Ehrenberg, Ronald G. and Michael L. Bognanno. 1990. "Do Tournaments Have Incentive Effects?" *Journal of Political Economy.* 98:6, pp. 1307–1324; Ehrenberg, Ronald G. and Michael L. Bognanno. 1990. "The Incentive Effects of Tournaments Revisited: Evidence from the European PGA Tour." *Industrial & Labor Relations Review.* 43:3, pp. 74–88.

7. Orszag, Jonathan M. 1994. "A New Look at Incentive Effects and Golf Tournaments." *Economics Letters.* 46:1, pp. 77–88.

8. Ehrenberg, Ronald G. and Michael L. Bognanno. 1990. "Do Tournaments Have Incentive Effects?" *Journal of Political Economy.* 98:6, pp. 1307–1324; Ehrenberg, Ronald G. and Michael L. Bognanno. 1990. "The Incentive Effects of Tournaments Revisited: Evidence from the European PGA Tour." *Industrial & Labor Relations Review.* 43:3, pp. 74–88.

9. Becker, Brian E. and Mark A. Huselid. 1992. "The Incentive Effects of Tournament Compensation Systems." *Administrative Science Quarterly.* 37:2, pp. 336–50.

10. Frick, Bernd. 1998. "Lohn und Leistung im Professionellen Sport: Das Beispiel Stadt-Marathon." *Konjunkturpolitik.* 44:2, pp. 114–40.

11. Lehn, Kenneth, 1990. "Property Rights, Risk Sharing and Player Disability in Major League Baseball," in *Sportometrics.* B. Goff and

R. Tollison, eds. College Station, Texas: Texas A&M Press, pp. 35–58.

12. Id.

13. Id.

14. Kahn, Lawrence M. 1993. "Managerial Quality, Team Success and Individual Player Performance in Major League Baseball." *Industrial & Labor Relations Review*. 46:3, pp. 531–47.

15. Scully, Gerald W. 1989. *The Business of Major League Baseball*. Chicago: University of Chicago Press.

16. Ehrenberg, Ronald G. and Robert S. Smith, 2000. *Modern Labor Economics*, 7th ed. Reading, Mass.: Addison-Wesley.

SPORTS ANALYTICS

DOES ONE SIMPLY NEED TO SCORE TO SCORE?

David J. Berri, Stacey L. Brook, and Martin B. Schmidt

"Players must not only have objectives, but know the correct way to achieve them. But how do the players know the correct way to achieve their objectives? The instrumental rationality answer is that, even though the actors may initially have diverse and erroneous models, the informational feedback process and arbitraging actors will correct initially incorrect models, punish deviant behavior, and lead surviving players to correct models." Douglass North (1994)

INTRODUCTION

The writing of Douglass North lays forth the role instrumental rationality plays in the workings of an efficient market. Given the requirements outlined above and the prevalence of imperfectly competitive industries, one may not expect many markets to be characterized as efficient. A potential exception is the professional sports industry. Unlike most industries, professional team sports have an abundance of information on individual workers and stark consequences for failure. Failure in sports is not only met with a loss of revenues and employment, but public derision via various media outlets. Given the severity of consequences and abundance of information, it is not surprising that economists expect economic actors in professional team sports to follow the dictates of instrumental rationality.

Despite this expectation, there is some research that suggests that instrumental rationality does not always characterize decision-making in professional sports. In baseball we have the "Moneyball" story [see Lewis (2003) and Hakes & Sauer (2006)], or the argument that on-base percentage was under-valued by decision-makers in Major League Baseball. Michael Lewis (2003) told this story primarily with anecdotal evidence in his best-selling book. Hakes and Sauer (2006) confirmed that the empirical evidence was at one point consistent with the *Moneyball* story. Historically

decision-makers in baseball did undervalue on-base percentage.

Turning to the National Football League we see the work of Romer (2006). Romer investigated how often NFL head coaches choose to "go for it" on fourth down and found that coaches were far too conservative. Going for it more frequently would increase the probability that coaches would win games; hence, the actions of the head coaches actually ran counter to their stated objective.

Staying in the NFL we see the work of Massey and Thaler (2006). This work offered evidence of inefficiency in the amateur draft of the National Football League. Specifically, high draft choices were consistently over-valued, in a fashion the authors argue is inconsistent with the precepts of rational expectations.

With respect to professional basketball—the subject of this study—we have the work of Staw and Hoang (1995) and Camerer and Weber (1999). Each of these authors examined the escalation of commitment in the NBA, defined by Camerer and Weber as follows:

"when people or organizations who have committed resources to a project are inclined to 'throw good money after bad' and maintain or increase their commitment to a project, even when its marginal costs exceed marginal benefits." [Camerer and Weber: 59–60]

With respect to the NBA, Staw and Hoang (1995) and Camerer and Weber (1999) investigated the impact a player's draft position has on playing time. Both of these sets of authors offer evidence that, after controlling for the prior performance of the player, where a player was chosen in the draft still impacts the amount of playing time the player receives after the first two years of the player's career. Such a finding suggests that NBA decision-makers are slow to adopt new information, maintaining an assessment of a player when the available evidence suggests that the initial perspective is incorrect.

The purpose of this present inquiry is twofold. First we wish to re-examine several pieces of evidence previously presented in the literature. As we will demonstrate, much of this research suggests that decision makers in the National Basketball Association (NBA)—as suggested by the study of escalation of commitment—do not process information efficiently. Our review will be followed by two empirical models. The first will update Berri and Schmidt (2002), which examined the coaches' voting for the All-Rookie team in the NBA. A second model will ascertain the relationship between player salary and various measures of player productivity. Each of these models— previously described in less detail in *The Wages of Wins* [Berri, Schmidt, and Brook (2006)][1]—will shed light upon the extent information is utilized efficiently in the evaluation of players in the NBA.

THE LESSONS LEARNED

Our story begins with a review of the lessons the current body of literature teaches about the economics of professional basketball. We begin this list of lessons with the story told by a number of published works examining racial discrimination in professional basketball.

Lesson One: Points Scored Dominates the Evaluation of Player Productivity in the NBA

. . . Berri (2006) surveyed twelve studies examining racial discrimination in the NBA.[7] . . . Given that some papers offered more than one model, Berri's survey examined fourteen specific models.

Surprisingly, most aspects of player productivity were not consistently linked statistically to the decision-variable examined. In fact, the only factor consistently found to be correlated with player evaluation in the NBA is points scored. In fourteen of the fifteen models examined, points scored was found to be both the expected sign and statistically significant.[8] Of the other factors employed by researchers, only total rebounds and blocked shots were statistically significant more often than not.[9] The significance of assists was evenly split,[10] while field goal percentage was significant in only four of the nine models where it was employed. Every other factor was not significant more than once. In sum, player evaluation in the NBA appears to be driven by points scored and, perhaps, total rebounds, blocked shots, and assists.

Such results tell two important stories. The first centers on the importance of scoring in the NBA. Virtually every study employed a player's total points or points scored per game.[11] One should note, though, that a player's accumulation of points is dependent on the playing time the player receives and the number of shots taken. Simply staying on the floor and taking a large number of field goal and free throw attempts can lead to the accumulation of lofty point totals. Clearly, efficiency in utilizing shot attempts would also be an indicator of a player's worth to a basketball team. As noted, though, field goal percentage was not statistically significant in the majority of studies where this factor was considered.[12]

In other words, a player who scores points can expect to receive a higher salary. Evidence that scoring needs to be achieved via efficient shooting is not quite as clear.

The second story told is about the insignificance of many other facets of a player's performance. Players do not appear to be evaluated in terms of free throw percentage, steals, or personal fouls. Turnovers, a factor Berri (2009, in press) has identified as significant in determining wins in the NBA, has only been included once and was found to be insignificant. Given the ambiguous results uncovered with respect to everything else besides a player's points scored per game, these results suggest that a player interested in maximizing salary, draft position, employment tenure, and playing time should primarily focus upon taking as many shots as a coach allows.

Lesson Two: Player Productivity on the Court Creates Team Wins

The literature on team-wins production, though, suggests that wins are about more than points scored per game. We begin this discussion with an obvious statement. The actions of the players on the court determine the outcome of the contest observed. The key to understanding the individual contribution to team wins, though, requires a bit more investigation.

The seminal work of Gerald Scully (1974) provides a guide to those seeking to uncover the relationship between player action and team wins in professional team sports. Scully, in an effort to measure the marginal product of a baseball player, offered a model connecting team wins to player statistics.[13]

Berri (in press) recently adopted the Scully approach in developing a simple measure of marginal product in professional basketball. This model,[14] indicates that points scored, rebounds, steals, turnovers, and field goal attempts each had an equal impact on team wins. Although points scored are important in determining outcomes, factors associated with acquiring possession of the ball also significantly impact a team's on-court success.

The review of the literature on racial discrimination revealed the importance of points scored, as well as rebounds, blocked shots, and assists. This list of factors can be thought of as highlight variables, since any collection of highlights from the NBA will consists of players scoring points, collecting rebounds, blocking shots, or making creative passes. Although these highlight variables are often correlated with player compensation, wins in the NBA are about more than these highlight factors.

Lesson Three: Team Wins Drive Team Revenue

Perhaps team wins, though, are not the objective of NBA organizations. Such a possibility was considered in the work of Berri, Schmidt, and Brook (2004). These authors examined the importance of winning games as opposed to the star power of a team's roster. Specifically, a team's gate revenue was regressed upon team wins, all-star votes received, and a collection of additional explanatory variables. The results indicate that it is wins, not star power, which primarily determines a team's financial success.

Two anecdotes support this empirical finding. The team who led the league in attendance during the 2003–04 regular season was the Detroit Pistons. Although the Pistons eventually won the 2004 NBA championship, Detroit achieved its success via team defense. Only five teams scored fewer points than the Pistons. Detroit's regular season scoring leader, Richard Hamilton, ranked only 27th in the league with 17.6 points per game.[15]

The story of Allen Iverson and the Philadelphia 76ers further supports the low economic value of star power and scoring for an NBA team. In 2005–06 the 76ers sold out every game on the road.[16] At home, though, the 76ers were one of only three teams to play before crowds that were less than 80 percent of their home arena's capacity. Although the 76ers employed a major star and scorer in Allen Iverson, the team's sub-0.500 record resulted in below average home crowds.

Lesson Four: Team Payroll is not Highly Correlated with Team Wins

Given the abundance of information on player productivity and the expectation that player productivity is linked to player salary, one might expect payroll and wins to be correlated. Stefan Szymanski (2003) investigated the link between wages and team success in a variety of professional team sports, including the NBA. Although the relationship between relative payroll and wins was found to be statistically significant, only 16% of winning percentage in the NBA was explained by relative payroll.[17]

A similar result was reported by Berri and Jewell (2004). Specifically, a model was offered that looked at the importance of adding payroll, via the addition and subtraction of players, and simply giving existing players an increase in salary. Of these two factors, only adding payroll was statistically significant. Of interest, though, was that the explanatory power of the model employed was only 6%. Much of the changes in team success upon the court in the NBA are not explained by alterations to a team's level of talent, as measured by additions to team payroll.

Lesson Five: Player Performance is Relatively Consistent Across Time

The lack of a strong relationship between wins and payroll is also observed in Major League Baseball and the National Football League. Berri, Schmidt, and Brook (2006) report that relative payroll in baseball only explains 18% of team wins in MLB from 1988 to 2006. If we look at the NFL from 2000 to 2005 we find that only 1% of wins are explained by relative payroll.[18]

The inability of payroll to explain wins can at least partially be explained when we look at how difficult it is to project performance in both football and baseball. Berri (2007) and Berri, Schmidt, and Brook (2006) present evidence that performance in football is quite difficult to predict. Summary measures such as the NFL's quarterback rating, metrics like QB Score, Net Points Per Play, and Wins Per Play—introduced in Berri, Schmidt, and Brook (2006)—and various metrics reported by FootballOutsiders .com tend to be quite inconsistent across time. Less than 20% of what a quarterback does in a current season, measured via any of the above listed metrics, is explained by what a quarterback did last season. A similar result is reported for running backs by Berri (2007).

When we look at baseball we also see a problem with projecting performance. Berri, Schmidt, and Brook (2006) report that less than 40% of what a hitter does in the current season can be explained by what he did last season.[19] These results suggest that even if teams were perfectly rational, the inability to project performance is going to result in a weak link between pay and wins.

Although performance inconsistency can explain what we see in the NFL and MLB, in the NBA a different story is told. The aforementioned work of Berri (in press) and Berri, Schmidt, and Brook (2006) detailed a metric called Win Score. . .

Berri, Schmidt, and Brook (2006) reports that 67% of a player's Win Score per-minute is explained by what the player did the previous season. . . . . A virtually identical result can be seen with respect to metric reported by the NBA entitled NBA Efficiency.[20] . . . The correlation between NBA Efficiency per minute this season and last season is 0.82.[21]

These results indicate that player performance in basketball— relative to what we see in football and baseball— is quite consistent. Yet payroll and wins do not have a very strong relationship in the NBA. Hence we need to look for another story beyond inconsistent performance. Before we get to this, though, we need to spend just a moment on one last lesson.

Lesson Six: NBA Efficiency is not About Efficiency

The Win Score metric is based on the statistical relationship between wins and a team's offensive and defensive efficiency. The estimation of this relationship—reported in Berri (in press) and Berri, Schmidt, and Brook (2006)—reveals that 94% of team wins can be explained by the team's efficiency metrics. Furthermore, teams tend to average one point per possession. Consequently, factors such as points scored, rebounds, turnovers, steals, and field goal attempts have the same impact, in absolute terms, on team wins.

When we turn to NBA Efficiency we see a similar result. Points scored, rebounds, turnovers, and steals have the same valuation in absolute terms. But rather than consider shot attempts, the NBA's metric considers missed shots. As a result, an inefficient scorer can increase his value just by increasing his shot attempts.

Consider an NBA player who makes one of the three shots from two-point range. According to NBA Efficiency, his value rises by two from the made shot, and falls by two from the missed shots. So he breaks even. From three-point range he only needs to make one of four to break-even. Most NBA players, though, make at least 33% of their shots from two point range and 25% of shots from beyond the arc. Consequently most NBA players can simply increase their value, according to the NBA's metric, by simply taking more shots.[22]

Now consider the story told by Win Score, and the more complex metric introduced by Berri, Schmidt, and Brook (2006), Wins Produced. Both of these metrics note that a field goal attempt uses the team's possession. For a player to break-even he must make 50% of his two-point shots and 33% of shots from three-point range. Players who fail to shoot efficiently are wasting possessions and hurting a team's chances to win.

So we have two picture of player performance. Which of these are most consistent with player evaluation in the NBA?

EXAMINING THE ALL-ROOKIE TEAM

To answer this question, let's first consider voting for the All-Rookie team. Each year the NBA coaches vote for the members on this team. This is the only award—other than the All-Defensive team—that is determined by the NBA's coaches (as opposed to the media). The voting for this award hence gives us a quantitative measure of the coaches' evaluation of playing talent.

Berri and Schmidt (2002) examined the voting for this award across four seasons, beginning with the 1994–95 season. Berri, Schmidt, and Brook (2006) updated this analysis with additional seasons. The paperback edition of Berri, Schmidt, and Brook offered a further update, extending the analysis from 1994–95 to 2006–07. It is these empirical results we wish to review.

. . . The minimum number of voting points a rookie could receive is zero. We considered in our study all rookies who might have received consideration. The sample we chose included all rookies who played at least 12 minutes per game and appeared in 41 contests. In all, 354 rookies were examined. Of these, 21 received the maximum number of votes while 92 were not chosen by any coach.

To explain the variation in this data we considered three variables. The first is player performance (PROD), which can be measured via NBA Efficiency, Wins Produced, points scored, or a collection of player statistics. The other two variables include the initial assessment of a rookie's value, or his draft position (DFT). We also considered the number of games the rookie played . . . .

The three estimations. . . rely upon three different measures of player performance. The first is NBA Efficiency, per game.[24] . . . we see that 73% of the natural log of voting

points can be explained by our model. When we turn to Wins Produced per game, a measure highly correlated with team wins,[25] we find that only 50% of the variation in voting points can be explained.

What is interesting is that if you turn to a third measure, points scored per game[26], we find that we can explain 74% of the variation in voting points. In other words, if we only consider one facet of player performance—scoring—we can explain more of the variation in the coaches' voting than either of our metrics that summarize much of what a player does on the court. . . .

. . . . In sum, factors associated with scoring dominate the coaches' evaluation of rookie performance.

Beyond the statistics, it is interesting that draft position was statistically significant in each estimation of our model. This result suggests that independent of player performance, how a player was viewed on draft night still influences the coaches' evaluation of a player after an entire year of NBA performance. In other words, like the aforementioned work examining the escalation of commitment, we see evidence that coaches are slow to change their initial assessment of a player.

A TEST OF RECENT FREE AGENTS

One could argue that voting for the All-Rookie team is not indicative of how coaches evaluate talent. It is possible that these votes are not taken seriously and may even be filled in by assistant coaches. Although it seems unlikely that coaches would consistently endorse performances that they know are inferior, one might still wish to see if a more substantive decision suffers from the overemphasis on scoring.

The more substantive decision is the salary paid to free agents. . . .

Beyond simply re-visiting the basic approach in the literature, we also will address a criticism initially noted by Jenkins (1996). Specifically, researchers often regressed current salary upon current player statistics. The NBA, though, often signs players to multi-year contracts. As noted by Berri and Krautmann (2006), for the 2002–03 season, 70% of players labored under a contract that was at least three years in length. More than 14% of the league had a contract that was seven years or longer. Jenkins (1996) argued that to ascertain the relationship between productivity and salary, one must consider measures of productivity at the time the salary is determined.[29] In other words, one should restrict the study of salary in professional sports to recent free agents.

Following the lead of Jenkins (1996), we collected data on 255 players who had a multi-year contract begin from the 2001–02 season to 2006–07 campaign. We then constructed a model of player salary. . . Specifically, we employed as our dependent variable the log of average real salary the player was scheduled to receive over the life of the contract.[30] Our choice of independent variables begins with the same collection of performance statistics we employed in our examination of the All-Rookie team. Additionally we considered a number of non-performance factors that might impact player compensation. The first is player injury, which we attempt to capture by considering the number of games played the past two seasons (GP).[31] Additionally we consider the size of the market where the player signs (POP).[32] Theoretically increases in both games played and market size should lead to larger salaries.

In addition to injury and market size, we also consider the position the player plays. There are five positions in the game of basketball: center, power forward, small forward, shooting guard, and point guard.[33] Each of these positions is typically assigned a number, with centers typically listed as a five and the point guard position labeled with the number one. Centers and power forwards are generally taller than guards and small forwards, with many players in excess of seven feet tall. Such height is scarce in the general population, potentially driving up the price of talented front court players. In contrast, quality guards might be in greater abundance, hence driving down the price of these players.[34]

The final player characteristic we consider is experience (XP), which we incorporate with the number of years played. The guaranteed rookie contracts that first round draft choices receive causes our sample of free agents to generally consist of older players. We suspect that holding performance constant, teams will prefer younger players to older players, so experience should diminish free agent salary.

The final variable we consider is the primary focus of each salary model we have previously noted, the race of the player.

. . . .

As with our examination of the All-Rookie team. . . first estimated with three different measures of player performance: NBA Efficiency, Wins Produced, and points scored. . . .

All three estimations reveal that market size, playing power forward or small forward, and the race of the player do not impact player compensation. The results with respect to the other non-performance variables were mixed, with both insignificant and significant results reported.

How much of salary we can explain depends on which performance measure we employ. When we utilized NBA Efficiency per game, we can explain 64% of player salary. When we turn to Wins Produced our explanatory power falls to 41%. We can improve upon what we see from Wins Produced when we turn to points scored. When we consider points scored per game as our sole measure of player performance we can explain 59% of a player's average wage.

What if we turn to the entire collection of player statistics? . . . [W]hen we utilize the entire vector of player statistics we again find that race is insignificant. We also find that we can explain 64% of player salary, which is the same result we uncovered for NBA Efficiency. Interestingly, beyond points scored, we find that only rebounds and blocked shots statistically impact player compensation. Shooting

efficiency, turnovers, steals, assists, and personal fouls do not appear to change the average wage a player commands.

. . . Once again, it is points scored that have the largest economic impact on player evaluation. A 10% increase in points scored per game increases average salary by 7.7%. A similar increase in rebounds only leads to a 4.8% increase in compensation.

In sum, as we move from a vector of player statistics or the NBA Efficiency model, to a measure of productivity based upon the statistical relationship between player statistics and team wins, our ability to explain player salary declines. Such a result is quite consistent with the argument laid forth in our review of the literature. Player evaluation in the NBA seems overly focused upon scoring. Negative actions, such as inaccurate shooting or accumulating turnovers, do not seem to result in corresponding declines in player compensation.

CONCLUDING OBSERVATIONS

Our review of the literature, as well as our own analysis of the voting for the All-Rookie team and the wages paid to free agents, tell the same story. Players in the NBA need to score to score a major payday.

This was actually the same story told by Glenn Robinson, the first player chosen in the 1994 NBA Draft. Five games into his NBA career the young Glenn Robinson made the following observation: "I expect to do what I'm supposed to do. But a lot of people that don't know the game, they think it's all about scoring. I look at it from a team perspective. We have to do well as a team. I don't need to go out there and score 30 points a game and have us lose. That won't do us any good. It would help me individually." Robinson added: "But I want to see all of us get something done."[37]

A point similar to Robinson's observation was also offered by the legendary coach, Red Auerbach.[38] From 1950 to 1966, Auerbach guided the Boston Celtics to nine championships, including eight in a row from 1959 to 1966. What was the key to this team's success? In a biographical sketch posted at ESPN.com it was noted that Auerbach didn't focus on the individuals on his teams. He looked at the "whole package." While many of his players were outstanding, the Celtics were the first organization to popularize the concept of the role player. "That's a player who willingly undertakes the thankless job that has to be done in order to make the whole package fly," Auerbach said. Auerbach went on to add that the Celtics represent a philosophy that in its simplest form maintains that victory belongs to the team. "Individual honors are nice, but no Celtic has ever gone out of his way to achieve them," he said. "We have never had the league's top scorer. In fact, we won seven league championships without placing even one among the league's top 10 scorers. Our pride was never rooted in statistics."

Auerbach also bemoaned in an interview broadcast on ESPN Classic that the focus of today's players is on statistics, as opposed to winning. In Auerbach's view, Bill Russell was a great player because he didn't obsess on his own statistics, but rather sacrificed his stats so the team could win. Although Russell averaged only fifteen points per contest, he did grab 22.5 rebounds per game. In other words, although Russell was not much of a scorer, he was an amazing rebounder.

Of course rebounds are a stat. Looking over Auerbach's comments it appears that when he references statistics, he is talking about scoring. And that appears to be the wisdom of Auerbach: Wins are not just about scoring.

Both Robinson and Auerbach argued that scoring can help individual players, but not necessarily produce wins. Assuming teams and players are trying to win, why does scoring dominate the evaluation process?

In *The Wages of Wins* a possible answer to this question was provided. Player evaluation in the NBA tends to rely upon visual observation of the player, as opposed to analysis of the numbers. Visual observation would tend to be drawn to the most dramatic event on the court, scoring. Factors such as missed shots and turnovers would not tend to stand out in the mind of the observer. Consequently, these factors tend to be downplayed in the evaluation of players.

Such a story suggests that decision makers need to do more than just possess the necessary information to make the "correct" decision. This information also has to be well understood. Often, though, decision makers have not been trained in the statistical techniques necessary to uncover the statistical relationships necessary for good decision making. As a result, on-base percentage can be undervalued in baseball. NFL coaches can often fail to go for it on fourth down when the data say they should. And finally, scoring can be over-valued in the NBA.

Once again we note that sports have an abundance of information and clear consequences of failure. Yet, decision making in sports has been shown to be inconsistent with the precepts of instrumental rationality. Given this result, we have to wonder: If decision makers in sports are not fully rational, should we expect decision-makers in non-sports industries—where information is less abundant and consequences less severe—to process information efficiently?

Notes

1. This paper was originally presented at the Western Economic Association meetings in 2004 and served as the foundation of chapter 10 of *The Wages of Wins*. This book did not provide any equations or econometric tables, hence this paper will also serve the purpose of presenting these findings more formally.

. . . .

7. These 12 studies included Kahn and Sherer (1988), Koch and Vander Hill (1988), Brown, Spiro, and Keenan (1991), Dey (1997), Hamilton (1997), Guis and Johnson (1998), Bodvarsson and Brastow (1998, 1999), Hoang and Rascher (1999), Bodvarsson and Partridge (2001), McCormick and Tollison (2001), and Eschker, Perez, and Siegler (2004). With the exception of Hoang and Racher,

who considered employment discrimination, and McCormick and Tollison, who considered the allocation of playing time, each study considered the subject of wage discrimination. Kahn and Sherer, in addition to wage discrimination, also presented a model examining the role race played in determining a player's initial draft position.

8. The term statistical significance is open to interpretation. A common rule of thumb is that the t-statistic should be greater than two. Such a rule, though, could be thought of as too restrictive. Consequently, Berri (2006) argued that a coefficient was only to be considered insignificant in this discussion if its t-statistic falls below 1.5. In other words, an effort was made to increase the likelihood that a variable was significant. Even with this effort, often the non-scoring factors were found to be insignificant.

9. Ten models considered blocked shots and six found this factor to be statistically significant. Eight models considered total rebounds, while seven others broke total rebounds into offensive and defensive rebounds. Total rebounds was statistically significant in five of the eight models. Of those that considered the type of rebound, none found offensive rebounds to be statistically significant. Only one study, McCormick and Tollison (2002), found defensive rebounds to be significant.

10. The ambiguous nature of assists was highlighted in the work of Koch and Vander Hill (1988). These authors found that assists were statistically significant and positive in one regression examining player salary. In another regression, though, assists were statistically significant and negative.

11. Of the studies examining wage discrimination, only Brown, Spiro, and Keenan (1991) considered a player's per-minute performance. In examining the player draft, Kahn and Sherer (1988) also considered a player's total accumulation of the statistics employed. Both Hoang and Rascher (1999) and McCormick and Tollison (2001) employed a player's per-minute production.

12. Six models of wage discrimination considered the impact of field goal percentage. Of these, only the studies that examined the 1985-86 season found shooting efficiency to be both statistically significant and positively correlated with a player's salary. This point is highlighted in the work of Bodvarsson and Brastow (1999). These authors tested the same model with data from the 1985-86 and 1990-91 seasons. For the former campaign, field goal percentage is statistically significant. For the latter season, though, it is insignificant.

13. Scully's approach was also employed by Medoff (1976), Raimondo (1983), Scott, Long, and Sompii (1985), Zimbalist (1992a, 1992b), Blass (1992), and Berri (1999), among others.

14. This model was originally detailed in a working paper by Berri. The appendix to Berri and Krautmann (2006) sketched out the basic idea. In Berri, Schmidt, and Brook (2006) more details were provided. Finally, the original working paper was completed and is scheduled for publication as Berri (in press).

15. Data on team attendance, team scoring, and individual scoring can be found at ESPN.com. Further evidence of the lack of impact from points scored can be found in Berri, Schmidt, and Brook (2006), who report that increases in a team's points scored per game does not lead to increases in gate revenue in the NBA.

16. This result is consistent with Berri and Schmidt (2006) which reports star power is quite valuable on the road. The NBA does not split regular season gate revenue, so the money a star generates on the road goes to the star's opponent.

17. Relative payroll is a team's payroll divided by the league average. Szymanski looked at 1986 to 2000. Berri, Schmidt, and Brook (2006) updated this work via an examination of wins and payroll in

the NBA across 15 seasons, beginning with the 1990-91 season and ending with the 2006-07 campaign. For these 15 seasons, relative payroll only explains 10% of team wins.

18. The NFL regression had 190 observations. Relative payroll was also only significant at the 10% level.

19. The metrics considered included OPS (On base percentage + Slugging average), SLOB (On base percentage multiplied by slugging average), and Runs produced per plate appearance. Runs produced is calculated via the linear weights measure developed by Thorn and Palmer (1984) and utilized by Blass (1992). Across a sample that began in 1994 and concluded in 2004, only 29% of runs produced per plate appearance were explained by past performance. For OPS and SLOB the explanatory power was 33% and 37%, respectively.

20. The NBA's efficiency measure is reported at NBA.com. This metric is quite similar to Heeran's (1992) TENDEX system and Bellotti's (1993) Points Created model. TENDEX was first formulated by Heeran in 1959. Heeran begins with a model identical to the one currently employed by the NBA, but then weights each player's production by both minutes played and the average game pace his team played throughout the season being examined. Bellotti's Points Created model is also quite similar. Bellotti begins with the basic TENDEX model and then simply subtracts 50% of each player's personal fouls.

21. The result is a sample of 2,836 NBA players from the 1994-95 season through 2003–04.

22. A paperback edition of *The Wages of Wins* was prepared in 2007. The updated version noted that the critique of NBA Efficiency also applies to the Player Efficiency Rating developed by Hollinger (2002). "In devising his metric Hollinger argued that each two point field goal made is worth about 1.65 points. A three point field goal made is worth 2.65 points. A missed field goal, though, costs a team 0.72 points. Given Hollinger's values, with a bit of math we can show that a player will break even on his two point field goal attempts if he hits on 30.4% of these shots. On three pointers the break-even point is 21.4%. If a player exceeds these thresholds, and virtually every NBA played does so with respect to two-point shots, the more he shoots the higher his value in PERs. So a player can be an inefficient scorer and simply inflate his value by taking a large number of shots."

. . . .

24. The NBA Efficiency measure varies depending upon position played. On a per-minute basis, power forwards and centers average between .49 and .50, while small forwards and guards range from 0.41 to 0.43. To overcome this position bias, we calculated a position adjusted NBA Efficiency measure. Specifically we determined each rookie's per-minute NBA Efficiency value. We then subtracted the average at each position, and then added back the average value for NBA Efficiency across all positions, or 0.45. Once we took these steps, we then multiplied what we had by the number of minutes a player played and divided by games played.

25. As noted by Berri, Schmidt, and Brook (2006) the average difference between team wins and the summation of the Wins Produced by a team's players is 2.4 from 1993-94 to 2004-05.

26. Like NBA Efficiency per game, points scored per game was adjusted for position played.

27. We took the concept of points-per-shot (PPS) from an article by Neyer (1996). As Neyer explained, this is the number of points a player or team accumulates from its field goal attempts. Its calculation involves subtracting free throws made from total points, and then dividing by field goals attempted. Employing points per shot,

rather than field goal percentage, allowed for the impact of three-point shooting to be captured more efficiently.

28. Except for points-per-shot and free throw percentage, all measures were adjusted for position played in a fashion consistent with our adjustment of NBA Efficiency.

29. The work of Jenkins (1996) employed data from the 1980s and 1990s, representing perhaps the longest time period employed in studies of salary discrimination in the NBA. Unfortunately, Jenkins also differed from other works in his choice of player productivity measures. Unlike studies that employed a collection of player statistics, Jenkins followed the lead of professional baseball studies by employing an index of player performance. Hence, we cannot use Jenkins's work to ascertain the relative importance of points scored, blocked shots, assists, etc.

30. The data on player salary came from USAToday.com: *Basketball Salaries Database* (http://www.usatoday.com/sports/basketball/nba/salaries/default.aspx). The salary data was converted into constant 2004 dollars.

31. We wish to thank Justin Wolfers for suggesting this variable.

32. Data for U.S. cities was found at the website of the U.S. Census Bureau (http://www.census.gov). Data for Canadian cities was found at Statistics Canada: (http://www.statcan.ca/start.html).

33. Data on player position was taken from various web sites, including ESPN.com. In general, centers and power forwards play closer to the basket and are primarily responsible for rebounds and blocked shots. Point guards and shooting guards play further from the basket and are responsible for ball handling. Small forwards have a mixture of responsibilities.

34. The scarcity of tall people, or "the short supply of tall people" was examined in the work of Schmidt and Berri (2003), Berri et. al. (2005), and Berri, Schmidt, and Brook (2006).

. . . .

37. This was quoted in an *Associated Press* article written by Jim Litke (1994).

38. The following discussion of Auerbach was first offered at *The Wages of Wins Journal* (http://dberri.wordpress.com) and also offered in the updated version of *The Wages of Wins*.

References

. . . .

Berri, D. J. (1999). Who is most valuable? Measuring the player's production of wins in the National Basketball Association. *Managerial and Decision Economics, 20*(8), 411–427.

Berri, D. J. (2006). Economics and the National Basketball Association: Surveying the literature at the tip-off. In J. Fizel's (Ed.) *The handbook of sports economics research,* (pp. 21–48). Armonk, NY: M.E. Sharpe, Inc.

Berri, D. J. (2007) Back to back evaluation on the gridiron. In J. H. Albert & R. H. Koning's (Eds.) *Statistical thinking in sport*, (pp. 235–256). Boca Raton, FL: Chapman & Hall/CRC.

Berri, D. J. (in press). A simple measure of worker productivity in the National Basketball Association. In B. Humphreys & D. Howard's (Eds.) *The business of sport*. Westport, CT: Praeger.

. . . .

Berri, D. J., & Jewell, T. (2004). Wage inequality and firm performance: Examining a natural experiment from professional basketball. *Atlantic Economic Journal, 32*(2), 130–139.

Berri, D. J., & Krautmann, A. C. (2006). Shirking on the court: Testing for the incentive effects of guaranteed pay. *Economic Inquiry, 44*, 536–546.

Berri, D. J., & Schmidt, M. B. (2002). Instrumental vs. bounded rationality: The case of Major League Baseball and the National Basketball Association. *Journal of Socio-Economics*, *31*(3), 191–214.

. . . .

Berri, D. J., Schmidt, M. B., & Brook, S. L. (2004). Stars at the gate: The impact of star power on NBA gate revenues. *Journal of Sports Economics*, *5*(1), 33–50.

Berri, D. J., Schmidt, M. B., & Brook, S. L. (2006). *The wages of wins: Taking measure of the many myths in modern sport*. Palo Alto, CA: Stanford University Press.

. . . .

Camerer, C. F., & Weber, R. A. (1999). The econometrics and behavioral economics of escalation of commitment: A re-examination of Staw and Hoang's NBA data. *Journal of Economic Behavior and Organization*, *39*, 59–82.

. . . .

Football Outsiders. *Method to our madness*. Retrieved February 2007, from http://www.footballoutsiders.com/methods.php

. . . .

Hakes, J. K., & Sauer, R. D. (2006). An economic evaluation of the *Moneyball* hypothesis. *Journal of Economic Perspectives*, *20*(3), 173–185.

. . . .

Jenkins, J. A. (1996). A re-examination of salary discrimination in professional basketball. *Social Science Quarterly*, *77*(3), 594–608.

. . . .

Lewis, M. (2003). *Moneyball: The art of winning an unfair game*. New York, NY: W.W. Norton & Company.

. . . .

Massey, C., & Thaler, R. (2006). The loser's curse: Overconfidence vs. market inefficiencies in the National Football League draft. Unpublished paper.

. . . .

North, D. (1994). Economic performance through time. *American Economic Review*, *84*(3), 359–368.

. . . .

Romer, D. (2006). Do firms maximize? Evidence from professional football. *Journal of Political Economy*, *114*(2), 340–365.

. . . .

Scully, G. W. (1974). Pay and performance in Major League Baseball. *American Economic Review*, *64*(6), 917–930.

. . . .

Staw, B. M., & Hoang, H. (1995). Sunk costs in the NBA: Why draft order affects playing time and survival in professional basketball. *Administrative Science Quarterly*, *40*(3), 474–494.

. . . .

Szymanski, S. (2003). The economic design of sporting contests. *Journal of Economic Literature*, *XLI*(4), 1137–1187.

. . . .

AN ECONOMIC EVALUATION OF THE *MONEYBALL* HYPOTHESIS

Jahn K. Hakes and Raymond D. Sauer

In his 2003 book *Moneyball,* financial reporter Michael Lewis made a striking claim: the valuation of skills in the market for baseball players was grossly inefficient. The discrepancy was so large that when the Oakland Athletics hired an unlikely management group consisting of Billy Beane, a former player with mediocre talent, and two quantitative analysts, the team was able to exploit this inefficiency and outproduce most of the competition, while operating on a shoestring budget.

The publication of *Moneyball* triggered a firestorm of criticism from baseball insiders (Lewis, 2004), and it raised the eyebrows of many economists as well. Basic price theory implies a tight correspondence between pay and productivity when markets are competitive and rich in information, as would seem to be the case in baseball. The market for baseball players receives daily attention from the print and broadcast media, along with periodic in-depth analysis from lifelong baseball experts and academic economists. Indeed, a case can be made that more is known about pay and quantified performance in this market than in any other labor market in the American economy.

In this paper, we test the central portion of Lewis's (2003) argument with elementary econometric tools and confirm his claims. In particular, we find that hitters' salaries during this period did not accurately reflect the contribution of various batting skills to winning games. This inefficiency was sufficiently large that knowledge of its existence, and the ability to exploit it, enabled the Oakland Athletics to gain a substantial advantage over their competition. Further, we find that, even while various baseball interests denounced Beane and Lewis as charlatans in a stream of media reports, market adjustments were in motion (for discussion, see Lewis, 2004; Craggs, 2005). These adjustments took place around the time Lewis's book was published, and with sufficient force that baseball's labor market no longer exhibits the *Moneyball* anomaly.

Because sports often embody situations where choices are clear and performance and rewards are measurable, they generate useful conditions for studying the behavior of market participants. There are many examples. McCormick and Tollison (1986) use variation in fouls from basketball games to illustrate how the likelihood of punishment affects crime. Brown and Sauer (1993a, 1993b) used point spreads for professional basketball games to consider the influence of psychology and information on market prices. Studies find that the behavior of soccer players conforms well with game-theoretic predictions of equilibrium behavior in penalty kick situations (Chiappori, Levitt and Groseclose, 2002). Moreover, in laboratory experiments that are analytically similar to penalty kick situations (but not described in a soccer context) soccer players act as predicted, whereas students from the general population do not, highlighting the relevance of experience in natural settings to results in the lab (Palacios-Huerta and Volij, 2006).

The present paper depicts a particularly clear case of mispricing in the baseball labor market, accompanied by successful innovation and subsequent adjustment in market prices. Although reasons for the failure of efficient pricing are not fully understood, it seems clear that the correction in market prices was tied to the diffusion of knowledge, as competing franchises mimicked the Athletics' strategy, in part by hiring Beane's chief assistants away from the Oakland organization.

MEASURES OF OFFENSIVE PRODUCTIVITY IN BASEBALL AND THEIR CONTRIBUTION TO WINNING

Measures of Batting Skill

A Major League Baseball game consists of nine scheduled innings, in which each team has an opportunity to score runs on offense in its half of each inning. The team on offense is limited to three outs per inning, after which play and scoring cease. Play then resumes with the opponent taking its turn at bat. The limit on outs is crucial. Scoring runs is the objective of the team at bat, and this is accomplished by a combination of skills: in particular, skill at hitting the ball and the ability to avoid making an out.

The most common measure of batting skill is the *batting average*, which is the ratio of hits to total at-bats. The batting average is a crude index. By weighting singles and home runs the same, it ignores the added productivity from hits of more than a single base. Much better is the *slugging percentage*, which is total bases divided by at-bats, so that doubles count twice as much as singles, and home runs twice as much as doubles.

Nevertheless, both the batting average and slugging percentage ignore potentially relevant dimensions of batter productivity. When baseball statistics are calculated, sacrifices and walks are not counted as official at-bats, and so they do not figure into either batting average or slugging percentage. In particular, since a fundamental element

of batting skill is the ability to avoid making an out, the failure to account for walks is a serious omission. Hitting a single leads to a higher batting average, and receiving a walk doesn't show up in batting average, but in both cases the batter ends up at first base. The statistic that takes walks into account is called *on-base percentage*, which is defined as the fraction of plate appearances (including both official at-bats as well as walks) in which the player reached base successfully through either a hit or a walk.

Members of the Society for American Baseball Research (SABR) have studied a variety of combinations of on-base percentage and slugging percentage in the hope of generating a single statistic that will capture a batter's contribution. It has long been known among this group, dubbed sabermetricians, that linear combinations of these two percentages are very highly correlated with runs scored, the primary objective of an offense. The essence of the *Moneyball* hypothesis is that the ability to get on base was undervalued in the baseball labor market.

Contribution to Winning

We use linear regression analysis to confirm that on-base percentage is a powerful indicator of how much a batter contributes to winning games. In **Table 4**, the dependent variable in the regression is the team's winning percentage. The data for these calculations are performance data over five seasons from 1999 to 2003. Column 1 of Table 4 shows that looking only at a team's own on-base percentage and the on-base percentage of its opponent can explain 82.5 percent of the variation in winning percentage. Column 2 shows that looking only at a team's own slugging percentage and the opponent's slugging percentage can explain 78.7 percent of the variation in winning percentage. Column 3 incorporates both measures of batting skill, which improves the explanatory power of the regression to 88.5 percent of variance. The coefficients on skills for a team and its opponents are quite close to each other, as would be expected in a two-sided symmetric game.[1] This is to be expected given the well-documented high correlation between runs scored and linear combinations of on-base and slugging percentage.

The final column of Table 4 is used to assess *Moneyball's* claim (Lewis, 2003, p. 128) that, contrary to then-conventional wisdom, on-base percentage makes a more important contribution to winning games than slugging percentage. To facilitate the comparison, the "on-base" and "on-base against" coefficients are restricted to be the same, as are the "slugging" and "slugging against" coefficients. The coefficients in this regression for on-base percentage are more than twice as large as the coefficients for slugging, which supports Lewis's claim. A one-point change in a team's on-base percentage makes a significantly larger contribution to team winning percentage than a one-point change in team slugging percentage.

Table 4   The Impact of On-Base and Slugging Percentage on Winning

	Model			
	1	**2**	**3**	**4**
Constant	0.508 (0.114)	0.612 (0.073)	0.502 (0.099)	0.500 (0.005)
On-Base	3.294 (0.221)		2.141 (0.296)	2.032 (0.183)
On-Base against	−3.317 (0.196)		−1.892 (0.291)	−2.032^R
Slugging		1.731 (0.122)	0.802 (0.149)	0.900 (0.106)
Slugging against		−1.999 (0.112)	−1.005 (0.152)	−0.900^R
Number of observations	150	150	150	150
R^2	.825	.787	.885	.884

Source: Journal of Economic Perspectives. Used with permission.

Notes: Data are aggregate statistics for all 30 teams from 1999–2003. Coefficient estimates were obtained using ordinary least squares. Coefficients for annual 0/1 dummy variables are suppressed. Standard errors are in parentheses. Superscript "R" indicates that the coefficient was restricted to equal its counterpart in the regression. The *p*-value for the null hypothesis that restrictions are valid is 0.406 ($F = 0.52$).

THE LABOR MARKET'S VALUATION OF SKILL AND THE ATHLETICS' MANAGEMENT STRATEGY

Wages in Major League Baseball

We now turn to the question of the labor market's valuation of batting skills. . . . during the five seasons spanning 2000–2004. The average wage for position players increased over the sample period, from $2.56 million to $3.32 million, with the figure for 2004 slightly lower than the prior year. Home run hitters, defined as those with more than 25 homers in a season (roughly one standard deviation above the mean), earn $3 million to $4 million more than the average player.

Valuation of Batting Skill in Baseball

An efficient labor market for baseball players would, all other factors held constant, reward on-base percentage and slugging percentage in the same proportions that those statistics contribute to winning. We assess this proposition by estimating earnings equations for position players (which means that we exclude pitchers) for the 2000–2004 seasons.

. . . .

Relative to younger players who have limited ability to negotiate their pay, players who are eligible for arbitration earn more, with an additional increment for players eligible to become free agents. We also obtain positive and statistically significant returns to expected playing time. The returns to on-base percentage and slugging are both positive, as expected. However, the coefficient for slugging on the income of a player is considerably larger than the coefficient for on-base percentage, which is the reverse of their importance to team success. This is consistent with *Moneyball*'s claim that on-base percentage is undervalued in the labor market.

. . . .

A sense of the absolute magnitude of the premium for sluggers can be obtained for each year by evaluating the effect on salary of one-standard-deviation increases in slugging percentage and on-base percentage. . . . The incremental salary impacts for slugging percentage in the first four years range from $0.52 million to $0.70 million and are three to four times as large as the incremental impact of a standard deviation increase in on-base percentage.

This finding contrasts with the evidence. . . which indicates that swapping a small increment of slugging percentage in return for a small increment of on-base percentage would increase a team's winning percentage. The lack of a market premium for hitters with superior skill at the patient art of reaching base through walks validates the systematic approach taken by the Oakland Athletics in identifying such players, and thereby winning games at a discount relative to their competition.

The relative valuation of on-base and slugging percentage is abruptly reversed for the year 2004—and this result exists despite the inertia produced by long-term contracts. The salary returns to slugging are similar in 2004 to prior years, but 2004 is the first year in which on-base percentage becomes statistically significant. The labor market in 2004 appears to have substantially corrected the apparent inefficiency in prior years. . . and the ratio of the monetary returns to reaching base and slugging is very close to the ratio of the statistics' contributions to team win percentage.

We have thus verified a central claim in *Moneyball* by showing that on-base percentage was undervalued at the beginning of the 2000–2004 period in Major League Baseball. There are two obvious caveats which should be addressed before accepting Lewis's argument completely. First, it might be that fans prefer watching sluggers, and that the allegation of mispricing confuses the ability to "win ugly," but unprofitably, with profit maximization. Second, the analysis thus far does not link the Oakland A's success to an explicit strategy capitalizing on the alleged mispricing of skill. We turn to these questions now.

Efficiency and Management Strategy in the Oakland A's Personnel Decisions

The Oakland Athletics' management strategy, as reported by Lewis (2003, p. 124) was to minimize the payroll required to build a team which would successfully contend for a playoff spot. . . . [A] scatterplot of team salaries and winning percentage . . . demonstrates the Athletics' ability to win "on the cheap." Because Major League Baseball salaries were increasing rapidly during this period, each team payroll is indexed to the league-wide average for that season. . . .

Other teams along the "frontier" of efficiently converting payroll into wins usually either failed to have enough on-field success to make the playoffs (like the 2003 Tampa Bay Devil Rays, 2000 Florida Marlins and 2001 Minnesota Twins), or, like the 2001 Seattle Mariners, were far better on the field than their nearest competition during the regular season. As the baseball labor market corrected in 2004, the Athletics remained near the frontier of salary efficiency, but their advantage was narrowed. Despite increasing their payroll to 86 percent of league average, they finished just behind the California Angels (now called the Los Angeles Angels of Anaheim) in 2004, missing the playoffs for the first time since 1999.

In effect, the A's were able to purchase a successful team less expensively by focusing on players with a higher on-base percentage, chiefly players who excelled at receiving walks. Disciplined hitters avoid swinging at balls, forcing a pitcher to throw strikes to get an out. A team of disciplined hitters is rewarded in several ways. More walks occur, raising on-base percentage. A reputation for discipline causes pitchers on the other team to throw more pitches in the strike zone, which are easier to hit. Finally, patient hitters cause pitchers to throw a greater quantity of pitches, which raises the chance that a tiring pitcher will start to throw pitches that are easier to hit successfully.

The emphasis on taking walks is apparent in the Oakland A's aggregate batting statistics. They led the American League in walks in 1999 and 2001, were second or third in 2000, 2002 and 2004, and fifth in 2003 (as shown at http://www.baseballreference.com/leagues/AL.shtml). Coupled with the emphasis on walks in player development, this success suggests that an explicit strategy was being followed.

Although the interpretation . . . treats player skills as strictly fixed, observed skill is a combination of innate skill with team investment in player development. The A's strategy was carried out both in signing players and in coaching. In signing position players, Oakland looked for hitters who did not appear outstanding in batting average or slugging percentage, and thus who commanded only moderate salaries, but who made a substantial contribution to winning baseball games when on-base percentage and the ability to draw walks were taken into account. At the same time, the Oakland coaching staff preached the virtues of disciplined hitting and not swinging at bad pitches (or even at certain strikes that cross the plate in a way that would be hard to hit solidly). Third baseman Eric Chavez said: "The A's started showing me these numbers . . . how guys' on-base percentages are important. It was like they didn't want me to hit for average or for home runs, but walks would get me to the big leagues" (Lewis, 2003, p. 151). Miguel Tejada, who won the 2002 American League Most Valuable Player Award, was quoted as saying (presumably half-joking): "If I don't take twenty walks, Billy Beane send me to Mexico."

Personnel movements during these years illustrate that the Athletics were able to substitute new players to maintain team success when individual players became too expensive to keep. As one example, the A's had a player named Jason Giambi who won the Most Valuable Player award in the American League in 2000 for his hitting prowess. After the 2001 season, Giambi had enough major league experience to qualify for free agency. After making $4.1 million in 2001, Giambi signed a seven-year contract with the New York Yankees for $120 million dollars. Oakland made no serious effort to match this offer. However, by signing inexpensive players to replace the lost superstar with incremental improvements across several positions, the Athletics repeated as division champions in 2002, actually improving their season record by one win. The replacement of offensive production from a now expensive Jason Giambi with an array of undervalued talent—notably high on-base percentage hitters Scott Hatteberg and David Justice—neatly encapsulates Lewis's argument, and ours.

Winning the Oakland A's Way and Profit Maximization

Although a comprehensive analysis of revenues and costs for the Oakland franchise is beyond the scope of this paper, suggestive evidence is readily available that is consistent with the Athletics' strategy being both an on-field and financial success. . . . In 1995, new ownership dismantled the team roster to cut costs, and performance declined. The low-budget strategy centering on on-base percentage was put in place at this time (Lewis, p. 58), and performance began to improve in 1999. . . . [T]he A's revenues were sensitive to performance: attendance increased sharply while average ticket prices rose as on-field success improved. Thus, while the Oakland organization focused on winning games cheaply, their improved performance increased demand. The evidence. . . is fully consistent with our view that the Oakland strategy for winning games was a successful exploitation of a profit opportunity.

CONCLUDING REMARKS

Our analysis supports the hypothesis that baseball's labor market was inefficient at the turn of the twenty-first century. Arguably, this mispricing of skill had been present for a sustained period of time, perhaps decades. Dodgers General Manager Branch Rickey—perhaps best-known for breaking the color barrier in baseball with Jackie Robinson—argued in print for the importance of on-base percentage during the 1950s, but he failed to win converts (Rickey, 1954; Schwartz, 2004, p. 59). Bill James, a pioneer among sabermetricians, published a series of statistical analyses of scoring beginning in the late 1970s, and came to a similar conclusion (Lewis, 2003, pp. 76–77; James, 1982).

Consistent with the vociferous objections of baseball insiders to the possibility that quantitative analysis could help guide team management, the sabermetric insights of Rickey, James and others were apparently ignored. James in particular grew frustrated that his careful work was dismissed by the game that was his passion: "'When I started writing I thought if I proved X was a stupid thing to do that people would stop doing X,' he said. 'I was wrong'" (Lewis, 2003, p. 93).

Apparently only Oakland executive Sandy Alderson read, absorbed and incorporated Bill James's analysis into an explicit organizational strategy (Lewis, 2003, p. 63, p. 142). To execute the strategy, Oakland reached outside baseball circles and hired two young Ivy League graduates with quantitative backgrounds to evaluate personnel.

Oakland's on-field performance, combined with their radical low-budget approach, exposed a flaw in the way personnel decisions were made in baseball. Once exposed (with the help of Lewis's best-seller), competitive forces were set in motion as teams sought to replicate or improve upon the A's formula. Oakland's competitors sought success by attempting to hire the personnel management team assembled by Alderson. The two Ivy Leaguers mentioned above were hired as General Managers (that is, as executives with authority over personnel decisions) by the Toronto Blue Jays and the Los Angeles Dodgers during and after the 2003 season (Saraceno, 2004). Although the Boston Red Sox failed in their attempt to hire both the Athletics' General Manager (Billy Beane) and Assistant General Manager, they followed Beane's advice by hiring the similarly inclined Theo Epstein, making him the youngest General Manager in baseball history (Shaughnessy, 2003). In addition, the Red Sox hired the dean of sabermetrics, Bill James himself, in an advisory capacity. The Red Sox proceeded to win the World Series in 2004.

This diffusion of statistical knowledge across a handful of decision-making units in baseball was apparently sufficient to correct the mispricing of skill. The underpayment of the ability to get on base was substantially if not completely eroded within a year of *Moneyball's* publication.

Notes

1. Similar results are obtained using a team's Earned Run Average, a measure of the runs given up by a team's pitchers, as a measure of the quality of a team's pitching and its defensive ability.

References

Brown, William O. and Raymond D. Sauer. 1993a. "Fundamentals or Noise? Evidence from the Basketball Betting Market." *Journal of Finance.* September, 48:4, pp. 1193–1209.

Brown, William O. and Raymond D. Sauer. 1993b. "Does the Basketball Market Believe in the Hot Hand: Comment." *American Economic Review.* December, 83:5, pp. 1377–86.

Chiappori, Pierre-Andre´, Steven Levitt and Timothy Groseclose. 2002. "A Test of Mixed Strategy Equilibria: Penalty Kicks in Soccer." *American Economic Review.* September, 92:4, pp. 1138–51.

Craggs, Tommy. 2005. "Say-It-Ain't-So Joe." *SF Weekly.* July 6. Available at http://www.sfweekly.com/Issues/2005-07-06/news/feature.html.

James, Bill. 1982. *The Bill James Baseball Abstract 1982.* New York: Ballantine Books.

. . . .

Lewis, Michael. 2003. *Moneyball: The Art of Winning an Unfair Game.* Norton: New York.

Lewis, Michael. 2004. "Out of Their Tree." *Sports Illustrated.* March 1.

McCormick, Robert E. and Robert D. Tollison. 1984. "Crime on the Court." *Journal of Political Economy.* April, 92:2, pp. 223–35.

Palacios Huerta, Ignacio and Oscar Volij. 2006. "Experientia Docet: Professionals Play Minimax in Laboratory Experiments." NajEcon Working Paper Reviews No. 122247000000001050. Available at: http://www.najecon.org/naj/v12.htm.

. . . .

Rickey, Branch. 1954. "Goodbye to Some Old Baseball Ideas." *Life Magazine.* August 2. Reprinted at http://www.baseballthinkfactory.org/btf/pages/essays/rickey/goodby_to_old_idea.htm.

Saraceno, Joe. 2004. "Dodgers Turn to Ivy League," *USA TODAY,* March 17.

Schwartz, Alan. 2004. *The Numbers Game: Baseball's Lifelong Fascination with Statistics.* New York: Thomas Donne Books, St. Martin's Press.

Shaughnessy, Dan. 2003. "Beane Has Looked Sharp By Doing Things His Way." *Boston Globe.* September 28.

IS THE *MONEYBALL* APPROACH TRANSFERABLE TO COMPLEX INVASION TEAM SPORTS?

Bill Gerrard

INTRODUCTION

Michael Lewis' bestseller, *Moneyball: The Art of Winning an Unfair Game* (2003), tells the story of how the Oakland Athletics in Major League Baseball (MLB) have achieved a sustained competitive advantage over an eight-year period despite being one of the lowest wage spenders. At the core of the *Moneyball* story is the systematic use of player performance data to guide player recruitment, player valuation, and field tactics as championed by Oakland's general manager, Billy Beane. *Moneyball* has attracted an international audience and, inevitably, raised questions on the extent to which the approach of the Oakland A's can be replicated in other team sports. For example, the transferability of *Moneyball* to association football (i.e., soccer) featured recently as the cover article in a leading UK sports monthly (Runciman, 2007).

The objective of this paper is to explore the degree to which *Moneyball* represents transferable knowledge. Specifically, the paper poses the question: Can *Moneyball* be transferred to complex invasion team sports such as the various codes of football? It is argued that atomistic striking and fielding team sports such as baseball are most conducive to the systematic exploitation of player performance data because of the high degree of separability of individual playing contributions. However, the approach can be applied in more complex invasion team sports. This is illustrated with a benchmarking analysis of team performance in English Premiership soccer.

The structure of the paper is as follows. The following section provides a statistical analysis of the *Moneyball* effect, measuring the magnitude of Oakland's competitive success over the period of time since Billy Beane's appointment as general manager in 1998. The results of benchmarking using both structural regression models and payroll costs per win are presented. The next section analyzes Oakland's knowledge-based "David" strategy that involves utilizing the insights of the statistical analysis of baseball data (i.e., sabermetrics). The following section discusses the difficulties in moving beyond atomistic striking and fielding team sports to apply *Moneyball* to more complex invasion team sports such as soccer. The application section illustrates the application of statistical performance analysis to English Premiership soccer over a four-year period and attempts to differentiate strategically between the alternative approaches of the two most successful teams. The conclusion section offers some thoughts on the barriers to the transferability of *Moneyball* to other team sports.

OAKLAND A'S: MEASURING THE MONEYBALL EFFECT

Moneyball: The Art of Winning an Unfair Game (Lewis, 2003) provides an account of how the Oakland A's have consistently been contenders for the postseason playoffs in the MLB in recent years despite having one of the lowest payroll budgets in the league. The turnaround from a low-budget, low-achievement team to a low-budget, high-achievement team began in 1998 with the appointment of a former player, Billy Beane, as general manager. *Moneyball* is the Billy Beane story. . . . [T]he turnaround has been truly remarkable. In his first season in charge, Beane's Oakland team posted a losing regular season with a win ratio of .457, which ranked 21st out of 30 teams. But even this marked a significant achievement since Oakland ranked as the third lowest payroll spenders in 1998. Every season since 1998 has been a winning season [*Ed. Note: The A's subsequently posted losing seasons in 2007, 2008, and 2009.*] but Oakland has remained one of the lowest spending teams with 2004 as the only year in which Oakland's payroll expenditure was ranked above the lowest third.

Seasons 2001 and 2002 are the principal focus of *Moneyball*. In both seasons Oakland had the second highest regular-season win ratio winning in excess of 100 games (in a regular-season schedule of 162 games) yet were the second lowest payroll spenders in 2001 and third lowest in 2002. The scale of Oakland's achievement can only be properly appreciated if compared with the record of the MLB's goliath, the New York Yankees, over the same period. . . . Oakland has trailed the Yankees most seasons in terms of games won but the gap has been relatively small. Over the eight seasons from 1999-2006, the Yankees have averaged 3.9% more wins per season than Oakland (i.e., just over six wins). Yet over the same period the Yankees outspent Oakland by a factor of 3.22. In other words a 216.7% payroll premium has yielded only a 3.9% win advantage. And indeed in 2000 and 2002 Oakland returned a higher win ratio than the Yankees. (See **Table 5**.)

The Yankees represent an extreme case of a high-budget, high-achievement team. A fuller evaluation of the extent of the *Moneyball* approach requires a benchmarking analysis of Oakland's pay and performance record against all of the other MLB teams since 1998. There are two basic methods of quantitative performance benchmarking. The simplest method is to use ratio analysis to calculate the efficiency of an organization in terms of output per unit of input. Ratio analysis has the advantage of simplicity and transparency, allowing a direct comparison of organizations with very different scales of operation by standardizing on the basis of per unit of input. The disadvantage of ratio analysis is that it is bivariate (i.e., one input and one output) with limited value in organizations with multiple inputs and/or multiple outputs unless the individual input–output relationships are clearly separable or all of

Table 5   Pay and Performance, Oakland A's versus New York Yankees, 1998–2006

	Oakland A's		New York Yankees	
Year	Regular Season Win Ratio	Payroll	Regular Season Win Ratio	Payroll
1998	.457	$20.1m	.704	$63.5m
1999	.537	24.2m	.605	85.0m
2000	.565	32.1m	.540	92.5m
2001	.630	33.8m	.594	109.8m
2002	.636	40.0m	.640	125.9m
2003	.593	50.3m	.623	149.7m
2004	.562	59.4m	.623	182.8m
2005	.543	55.4m	.586	208.3m
2006	.574	62.2m	.599	194.7m

Source: International Journal of Sport Finance. Used with permission from Fitness Information Technology.

the inputs and all of the outputs can be converted to a standard unit of measurement (usually monetary value). A more complex method of quantitative benchmarking is to develop a structural statistical model of the relationship between the organization's output and its inputs including other relevant control variables such as differences in external environmental conditions.

Two benchmarking analyses have been developed for the relationship between win ratios and payroll costs for all of the MLB teams over the nine-year period, 1998–2006. The first benchmark analysis is a ratio analysis using average payroll costs per win. The cost-per-win ratio is the inverse of the output-input efficiency ratio with payroll costs as the input and games won as the output. There are two methodological issues involved in calculating the cost-per-win ratio for MLB teams. First, given that the data set includes nine years with substantial salary inflation, it is necessary to convert the nominal payroll costs into inflation-adjusted (i.e., real) payroll costs. In both benchmarking analyses payroll costs have been converted to 1998 MLB dollars using a conversion factor calculated as the total MLB payroll costs in the specified year divided by the total MLB payroll costs in 1998. This provides a measure of the cumulative salary inflation between 1998 and the specified year. Dividing all team payroll costs in the specified year by the conversion factors converts the team's payroll costs into 1998 MLB dollars. The second methodological problem with the cost-per-win ratio is the choice of an appropriate baseline from which to calculate the (marginal) cost-per-win ratio. Exploratory data analysis (both graphical and simple regression analysis) indicates that in terms of 1998 MLB dollars the appropriate pay-performance baseline is $8.75 million payroll costs and 50 wins.

Table 6 lists the average cost-per-win for all MLB teams over the period 1998–2006 calculated in 1998 MLB dollars using the baseline of 50 wins and $8.75 million payroll costs. It can be seen that the MLB average is $1.02 million dollars for each win over 50. Oakland ranked first as the most efficient MLB team over the period with a cost-per-win ratio of $414,647 representing an efficiency gain

of 59.3% relative to the MLB average. The second most efficient team is the Minnesota Twins with a cost-per-win ratio of $470,990 (implying an efficiency gain of 53.8%). The other highest ranking teams are the Florida Marlins ($514,884 per win), Montreal Expos ($556,674 per win), and Pittsburgh Pirates ($716,905). (It should be noted that the cost-per-win ratio for the Expos is based only on seven seasons since the franchise has been replaced by the Washington Nationals from season 2005 onwards.)

The three most inefficient teams over the period have been Baltimore ($1,680,911 per win) and the two New York teams, the Yankees ($1,535,662 per win) and the Mets ($1,432,323 per win). Baltimore's cost-per-win ratio is 64.9% above the MLB average. The Yankees show an efficiency loss of 50.7%. Hence, it is clear that the *Moneyball* effect has been considerable whether you compare Oakland with the extreme of the Yankees or the MLB average. A 59% efficiency gain over a nine-year period indicates a truly remarkable sustained competitive advantage in a highly competitive industry with competition at the core of the production process not just limited to the market process.

. . . .

The . . . differences in payroll costs between MLB teams explain just less than one quarter of the variation in win ratios between teams and between seasons. Inclusion of the persistence effects of performance in the previous season increases the explanatory power to around 37%. Although payroll costs are clearly an important explanation of why some MLB teams win more regular-season games than other teams, financial differences are not overwhelmingly dominant in determining win–loss records. The MLB is not a league that exhibits a high degree of financial determinism compared with, for example, the leading professional soccer leagues in Europe in which the static pay-performance relationship accounts for two-thirds or more of the differences in sporting performance of teams. . . .

The structural . . . analysis again highlights the exceptional achievement of Oakland as an organization. It is

Table 6   Benchmarking Analysis (I)—Average Payroll Costs Per Win, MLB, 1998–2006

Team	Average Payroll Cost Per Win	Ranking	Percentage Efficiency Gain(−)/Loss(+)
Arizona	$1,195,796	22nd	17.32%
Atlanta	1,033,084	19th	1.36%
Baltimore	1,680,911	31st	64.92%
Boston	1,312,086	24th	28.73%
Chicago Cubs	1,378,256	26th	35.23%
Chicago White Sox	737,740	6th	−27.62%
Cincinnati	779,484	7th	−23.52%
Cleveland	971,878	17th	−4.65%
Colorado	1,230,981	23rd	20.78%
Detroit	1,313,116	25th	28.83%
Florida	514,884	3rd	−49.48%
Houston	850,381	10th	−16.57%
Kansas City	871,815	11th	−14.46%
LA Angels	1,008,031	18th	−1.10%
LA Dodgers	1,381,083	27th	35.50%
Milwaukee	878,277	12th	−13.83%
Minnesota	470,990	2nd	−53.79%
Montreal (1998–2004)	556,674	4th	−45.38%
NY Mets	1,432,323	29th	40.53%
NY Yankees	1,535,662	30th	50.67%
Oakland	414,647	1st	−59.32%
Philadelphia	971,492	16th	−4.68%
Pittsburgh	716,905	5th	−29.66%
San Diego	844,471	9th	−17.15%
San Francisco	903,093	13th	−11.39%
Seattle	1,097,279	20th	7.66%
St. Louis	938,819	15th	−7.89%
Tampa Bay	1,100,790	21st	8.00%
Texas	1,383,099	28th	35.70%
Toronto	910,068	14th	−10.71%
Washington (2005–2006)	810,986	8th	−20.43%
MLB Average	**1,019,228**		

Source: International Journal of Sport Finance. Used with permission from Fitness Information Technology.
Notes:
1. All payroll costs converted to MLB dollars to remove inflation effect. Conversion factors calculated by dividing total MLB payroll costs in specified year by total MLB payroll costs in 1998.
2. Average payroll costs per win calculated relative to baseline of 50 wins and $8.75m payroll costs (1998 MLB dollars).

estimated that over a nine-year period Oakland won 144 games more than would have been predicted by a simple win-payroll benchmark model. . . . Sporting competition tends to create a reversion-to-mean process in which teams tend to gravitate towards a long-term equilibrium determined by the market fundamentals (i.e., the financial size of a team's local market). To deny the sporting equivalent of the law of gravity for nine seasons is indeed remarkable. It should be noted that the Yankees emerge as a better-than-benchmark team with 18.2 wins more than predicted by their payroll costs. The Yankees are big spenders but the benchmark analysis suggests that the team spends its money effectively so that it is a high-budget, high-achievement organization. In contrast, Baltimore is a high-budget, low-achievement team with the sixth highest average payroll

expenditure over the period but an average win ratio of .449. Baltimore is estimated to have lost 96.4 games more than would be expected by an average efficiency team with the same level of payroll costs. Only Tampa Bay has shown greater inefficiency than Baltimore with 96.6 games below benchmark.

OAKLAND A'S: EXPLAINING THE *MONEYBALL* EFFECT

Successful organizations with a sustainable competitive advantage over rival organizations can be viewed as having either resource-based or knowledge-based advantages (or a combination of both). The resource-based view (RBV) of the firm (Wernerfelt, 1984) focuses on qualitative resource-based advantages in industries characterized by resource heterogeneity. In such industries the firms with a sustainable competitive advantage are those that possess rare, unique strategic resources that are specific to the individual firm and difficult for rival firms to imitate and replicate. By contrast, in industries in which there is a high degree of resource homogeneity in the sense that the higher-quality strategic resources that yield a competitive advantage are more mobile between firms and potentially tradable on a market, the more successful firms tend to have a quantitative resource-based advantage, and are able to utilize their greater economic power to purchase the higher-quality strategic resources. In order to compete effectively with resource-rich firms, resource-poor firms need to develop a "David" strategy in which they create knowledge-based advantages. Using a distinction originally proposed by Makadok (2001), there are two types of knowledge-based advantages—resource-picking advantages and capability-building advantages. Resource-poor organizations can compete effectively if they are better at selecting resources and/or deploying resources. A successful resource-picking "David" strategy involves developing mechanisms that allow the organization to be more effective in identifying higher-quality resources at lower per unit cost in competitive situations with significant uncertainty over the future performance of individual resources. A successful capability-building David strategy requires the organization to develop mechanisms for the utilization of individual resources that yields higher levels of future performance from resources than can be achieved by rival organizations.

In professional team sports, the economic power of teams is a product of history and geography. Teams located in large metropolitan areas and a history of sporting success have the largest fan bases and are, therefore, more able to compete for the best playing talent. It is the concern with maintaining competitive balance to ensure the continuing interest of fans and financial viability of the league that has led professional sports leagues to introduce various product-market and labor-market restrictions to limit the ability of big-market teams to corner the market for the best players (Quirk & Fort, 1992). Professional sports leagues have tried to equalize team revenues through cross-subsidization mechanisms such as sharing gate receipts and collective selling of media and other image rights. Alternatively, leagues have regulated the players' labor market via salary caps, luxury taxes on excessive payrolls, reserve clauses, transfer fees, and centralized drafting of new players.

The MLB has been one of the least regulated professional sports leagues. . . . [T]here has been a three- or four-fold difference in payrolls between the big-market goliaths in the MLB such as the New York Yankees and the smaller-market teams such as the Oakland A's. The core of the knowledge-based "David" strategy developed by Billy Beane has been the systematic use of player performance data in player recruitment, player valuation, and team field tactics. Beane recognized the value of the insights provided by sabermetrics, the statistical analysis of baseball, particularly the work of Bill James. James is the guru of sabermetrics who had started to publish his statistical analysis of baseball in his *Baseball Abstract* annually in the 1980s but had remained largely ignored by MLB teams (Gray, 2006). *Moneyball* tells the story of how Beane has used the insights of sabermetrics to develop resource-picking and capability-building advantages.

Much of *Moneyball* deals on the resource-picking strategies of Oakland, particularly in the player draft. Beane shifted the team's recruitment strategy away from high school graduates towards college players with exceptional playing records. There are three advantages of focusing more on college players as draft picks. First, college players are older with more playing experience at an elite level and, as a consequence, teams can have a better appreciation of whether or not players can cope with the demands of professional baseball. Second, the playing records of college players are much better recorded in much greater detail than high school playing records. College baseball statistics are also much more informative since the quality of the opposition is more uniform. Finally, since other teams are predominantly chasing after high-school draft picks and college players are often perceived as "rejects" who have previously failed to be drafted to the MLB, the market valuations of college players tend to be significantly lower. Hence there is a potential profitable trading opportunity to sign playing talent at a lower cost. Oakland's focus on college players in the draft is one of the factors explaining their significant efficiency gains in the average cost per win. . . .

Another key factor in the Oakland's low cost per win has been the exploitation of the market inefficiency in the valuation of hitters. It is the proposition that the MLB players' labor market has systematically undervalued the productive value of hitters that Hakes and Sauer (2006) refer to as "the *Moneyball* hypothesis". Batting and slugging averages are the conventional baseball statistics for hitters but these statistics only measure hitting. Statistical analysis shows that on-base percentage (OBP), measuring the proportion of at-bats that the hitter reaches base either by hits or walks, is a better predictor of win ratios. Since MLB teams have focused on the conventional measures of hitter performance rather than OBP, this would imply that the market valuation of players would tend to undervalue players who rank much better on their OBP statistics than batting and slugging averages. This market inefficiency would, in turn, create a potential profitable trading opportunity that could allow teams using OBP to identify potential recruits and effectively buy runs more cheaply than rival teams.

Hakes and Sauer tested the *Moneyball* hypothesis. . . . Hakes and Sauer estimated a statistical model of team win-ratios in the MLB using data for seasons 1999–2003. They found that the best predictive model of MLB win-ratios included both OBP and the slugging average. These two hitter performance variables jointly explained 88.2% of the variation in regular-season win-ratios between teams over the five seasons. The estimated coefficient on OBP was found to be more than twice as large as that for the slugging average. Thus, the production (i.e., win contribution) value of OBP is significantly greater than the production value of the slugging average. Hakes and Sauer estimated a benchmark salary model for hitters for seasons 2000–2004. Their benchmark salary model included OBP, the slugging average and a set of control variables—plate appearances, arbitration eligibility, free-agent status, catcher, and in-fielder. Hakes and Sauer discovered that slugging average was a highly significant determinant of hitter salaries in each season between 2000 and 2003. In contrast, OBP was statistically insignificant every season over the same period and the magnitude of the estimated coefficient was much smaller (and, indeed, had a small negative effect in 2001). Thus, Hakes and Sauer found very strong evidence of mar-ket inefficiency with a significant discrepancy between the production value of OBP and the market (i.e., salary) value. It is this market inefficiency that Billy Beane exploited very effectively. Interestingly, Hakes and Sauer extended their benchmark salary model to 2004, the season after the pub-lication of *Moneyball*. By 2004, OBP had become a highly significant determinant of hitter salaries in the MLB with an estimated coefficient larger than that for the slugging aver-age. The market inefficiency had been corrected following the publication of *Moneyball* which, of course, begs the question as to why Oakland allowed the publication of a book that made public some of the sources of their competi-tive advantage. The lesson is clear: if you have a knowledge-based competitive advantage, keep it secret from your rivals as long as possible.

Moneyball also outlines that Oakland's "David" strategy is not purely a resource-picking knowledge-based advantage in the identification and remuneration of new recruits. It is clear that the analysis of player performance data has led to capability-developing knowledge-based advantages in the deployment of players during games. The team's field tactics are also influenced by the statistical analysis of what wins and loses games. For example, in line with the produc-tion value of OBP, Oakland stresses the importance of pitch selection for hitters. Team tactics also put much less impor-tance on stealing bases compared to other teams. Oakland believes that statistical analysis shows stealing bases to be a high-risk, low-reward tactic.

BEYOND BASEBALL: FROM ATOMISTIC TO COMPLEX TEAM SPORTS

The *Moneyball* approach requires reliable performance data for individual players in order for teams to be able to evaluate formally using, for example, statistical analysis to quantify what each player has contributed to the overall team performance. However, player performance is only highly separable in atomistic striking and fielding team sports such as baseball and cricket. It is no surprise that the academic research on the economic value of elite athletes in professional team sports has been concentrated in the MLB beginning with the estimation of the marginal revenue product (MRP) of hitters and pitchers by Scully (1974). Not only is there extensive publicly available data on individual player salaries in the MLB (e.g., the *USA Today* website) but there is also a strong statistical relationship between perfor-mance statistics for hitting and pitching, and the team's win-loss record. For example, in his 1974 study Scully found that around 88% of the team win percentage could be explained by the team slugging average and the team strikeout-to-walk ratio after controlling for league affiliation and divi-sional standing. Decomposing the aggregate team hitting and pitching statistics into individual player components allowed Scully to estimate the win-equivalent contribution of each hitter and pitcher, which he then translated into a financial valuation using the estimated relationship between team revenues and team wins.

Replicating *Moneyball* and Scully's pay-and-perfor-mance analysis in invasion team sports such as the various codes of football, field and ice hockey, and basketball is much more problematic. Invasion team sports are much more complex and hence the separability of individual player contributions is considerably more difficult. Inva-sion team sports involve a group of players co-operating to move an object (e.g., a ball or puck) to a particular loca-tion defended by opponents (e.g., across a line or between goalposts). There are several dimensions of complexity in invasion team sports. First, the range of player actions is much greater and includes tackling to regain possession, moving the ball forward via passing, receiving, running and/or dribbling, and attempting to score by shooting or crossing the line. Second, player actions are highly inde-pendent. Scoring requires the ball to be moved forward which, in turn, requires the team to have regained posses-sion. Defensive and offensive plays are interdependent. Third, many player actions are joint actions. For example, more than one player may join together to tackle an oppo-nent in possession in some codes of football. Fourth, inva-sion games vary in the degree to which there is continuity or segmentation between offensive and defensive plays. Association football (i.e., soccer) is the most complex in this respect with a continuous flow, whereas American football is highly segmented with play stopped and players interchanged after turnovers in possession. Finally, linked to the degree of continuity in play, invasion games vary in the extent to which playing roles are specialized. Again soccer is the most complex in this respect with all outfield players required to be highly competent both defensively and offensively. In contrast, American football has highly specialized defensive, offensive, and kicking units.

There are three measurement problems that must be resolved in order to undertake detailed player performance analysis in complex invasion team sports—the tracking problem, the attribution problem, and the weighting problem. The tracking problem refers to the identification, categorization, and enumeration of different types of player actions in and out of possession and including spatial coordinates of where the actions have taken place on the field of play. The attribution problem is the problem of how to allocate the individual contributions to joint and interdependent actions. The weighting problem is that concerned with determining the significance of each individual action to the overall match outcome.

The tracking problem is largely an issue of technology. Historically, performance statistics in complex team sports were limited to appearances, scoring, and discipline. Statistics on players' actions were recorded during matches by coaches and other observers using basic "paper-and-pencil" notational analysis. The advent of TV video playback at the elite level allowed coaches to develop much more sophisticated systems of notational analysis for private use by teams but the time-demands limited how much information was extracted. The tracking problem has been largely solved in recent years by two IT developments: (i) software for automated video analysis of matches and (ii) in-stadium sensors and image recognition software to allow the direct tracking of players. For example, in several leading professional soccer leagues, many of the top teams now use player tracking systems developed by the French company, Sport-Universal Process, or the UK-based company, ProZone. These systems provide data on player actions in possession and spatial movements including speed and distance covered by players. These tracking systems allow "bird's-eye" animated reconstructions of games to facilitate the analysis of individual player decisions as well as team shape and spatial coordination in and out of possession. The next stage in the development of tracking systems will be the provision of real-time feed including the use of some form of chip technology to transmit location and physiological data directly from players.

With the tracking problem solved by technology and the attribution problem amenable to agreed decision rules and conventions for the allocation of individual contributions to joint/interdependent actions, the principal measurement issue that remains is the weighting problem of how to determine the relative importance of different player actions toward overall match outcomes. There are two general types of solution to the weighting problem—a subjective, judgment-based approach or a more "objective" statistical approach. The subjective judgment-based approach involves an expert developing a weighting system based on their own experience and judgment. This is the approach adopted by, for example, the Opta Index in English soccer which provides player ratings based on a composite of player actions

using a weighting system developed by Don Howe, the former Arsenal and England coach.

The statistical approach involves the determination of an appropriate set of weightings by estimating the degree of statistical association between match outcomes and the number of different types of player actions using a sample of games. One particular statistical method is multiple regression analysis, which involves specifying and estimating a linear relationship between outcomes and the frequency of different actions. However, the problem with the statistical approach in invasion team sports is the hierarchical nature of the game with the higher-level actions, scores, and saves (i.e., the blocking of scoring attempts by opponents) dependent on lower-level actions to create scoring opportunities and limit opposition scoring opportunities. **Figure 1** provides a graphical illustration of the hierarchical structure of a complex invasion game. Higher-level actions are causally closer to final match outcomes and, as a consequence, are likely to be the best statistical predictors of outcomes with the highest weightings. Hence, players who specialize more in higher-level actions will tend to receive a disproportionately high estimated win contribution compared to players specializing in more lower-level actions if a purely statistical approach is adopted with no recognition of the dependency of higher-level actions on lower-level actions.

The statistical approach toward the weighting of player actions necessarily requires expert judgment to determine the relative weightings between different levels in the structural hierarchy, with statistical estimation used to determine the relative intra-level weightings between actions at the same level. Expert judgment may also be needed to adjust the estimated statistical weightings of those player actions that act as a good statistical predictor of opposing player actions. For example, a high observed frequency of positive

Figure 1 A Hierarchical Structural Model for Invasion Team Sports

Source: International Journal of Sport Finance. Used with permission from Fitness Information Technology.

defensive actions that prevent scoring opportunities for the opposing team can statistically be a good proxy for the amount of offensive activity by opponents leading to a negative weighting reflecting that the more opponents attack the more likely a team is to lose.

The hierarchical structural model of a complex invasion game illustrated in Figure 1 can be used to provide a framework for analyzing the drivers of match outcomes. The contributions of different types of general play to creating scoring opportunities and limiting opposition scoring opportunities can be estimated statistically. The win contribution of general play can be determined using the average league conversion of scoring opportunities. This provides a benchmark to determine the extent to which a team has deviated from the average league performance because of differences in player effectiveness with respect to identifiable individual contributions in the form of different types of general play, scoring conversion rates and save rates in games with a designated goalkeeper/goalminder. The residual component can be categorized as team effectiveness referring to deviations from the average league benchmark that cannot be predicted on the basis of individual player contributions. Offensive team effectiveness can be measured as the difference between the actual frequency of scoring opportunities created and the predicted frequency given the observed own-team general play. Similarly, defensive team effectiveness can be measured as the difference between the actual frequency of opposition scoring opportunities and the predicted frequency given the observed own-team general play. An application of this performance analysis and benchmarking in English Premiership soccer is discussed in the next section.

APPLICATION: ANALYZING TEAM PERFORMANCE IN ENGLISH PREMIERSHIP SOCCER

The complexities of analyzing player performance in a complex invasion team sport are best appreciated by examining an actual application. Detailed player performance data is often confidential and provided to teams on a commercial basis, and hence is usually either unavailable or prohibitively expensive for academic researchers. However, the Opta Index (1999, 2000, 2001, 2002) has published detailed soccer player performance data in the *Football Yearbook* covering four seasons—1998–99 through 2001–02 of the FA Premier League (FAPL) in England. The *Yearbook* contains season-total data for 25 player statistics for every outfield player including passing, crossing, dribbling, defending, and goal attempts. In addition there are 14 player statistics for goalkeepers including the save-shot ratio. With 20 teams competing in the FAPL annually, it is possible to construct a team dataset with 80 team-season observations for each variable.

A hierarchical structural model based on the framework shown in Figure 1 was estimated using multiple regression analysis.

. . . .

A bottom-up hierarchical analysis of deviations from benchmark was conducted in which the League Points value of lower-level actions is determined by assuming average-league performance at higher levels. This allows the team's deviation from average-league performance (= 51.887 points) to be decomposed. Six types of deviation from benchmark are identified:

(i) General Play: deviation due to difference between team and average-league frequency of different types of general play

(ii) Striking: deviation due to difference between team and average-league conversion rates

(iii) Goalkeeper: deviation due to difference between team and average-league save-shot ratio

(iv) Offence: deviation due to difference between actual frequency of own shots at goal and predicted number given own general play

(v) Defense: deviation due to difference between actual frequency of opposition shots on goal and predicted number given own general play

(vi) Result: deviation due to difference between actual League Points and predicted League Points given actual number of goals scored and conceded

The first three categories are defined as (individual) player effectiveness since the deviations can be clearly attributed to individual players. Categories (iv)–(vi) are defined as team effectiveness since the deviations can only be attributed to the team as a whole and not to any specific player.

An illustration of the hierarchical analysis of deviations from benchmark is provided in **Figure 2** for Arsenal in season 2001–02. Arsenal finished as Premiership champions with 87 points, which represents a benchmark deviation of 35.11 points (relative to the league average over the four sample seasons). This benchmark deviation is fairly evenly allocated between player effectiveness and team effectiveness. It is estimated that if goal conversion rates for both Arsenal and their opponents are set equal to the league average, then the greater frequency of general play actions (e.g., passing, dribbling, crossing, and defending) by Arsenal's outfield players relative to the Premiership average contributed 12.86 points (i.e., 36.63%) of the total benchmark deviation. Arsenal's better than average shot conversion rate contributed another 9.38 points above the league average. The only category in which Arsenal had a negative deviation was goalkeeping. Arsenal's save-shot ratio was lower than the league average due to their

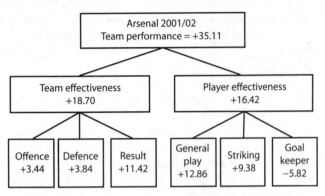

Figure 2 Benchmark Analysis, Arsenal, FA Premier League, 2001–02

Source: International Journal of Sport Finance. Used with permission from Fitness Information Technology.

first-choice goalkeeper being injured for a significant part of the season with no adequate backup replacement. Arsenal's team effectiveness shows that their outfield players jointly created more shooting opportunities and allowed fewer opposition scoring opportunities than would have been predicted by the general play of their individual players. However, most of the team effectiveness is due to results deviation with Arsenal gaining 11.42 points more than would have been predicted given the total goals scored and conceded. This fits with the general perception of Arsenal as a team that is defensively strong and maximizes its return from goals scored. (Indeed Arsenal fans have long used the chant "one-nil to the Arsenal" to intimidate the opposition with the belief that once their team had scored, the defense would ensure that the lead was protected.) . . .

The two dominant teams over the four seasons were Manchester United and Arsenal. Manchester United won the Premiership in seasons 1998–99, 1999–00, and 2000–01 and finished third in season 2001–02. Arsenal won the Premiership in season 2001–02 and finished runners-up to Manchester United in the other three seasons. . . . [T]here is a very different distribution between the two teams as regards the extent to which their deviation from the average-league benchmark is due to player effectiveness or team effectiveness. In the case of Arsenal, the team averaged 77 points (benchmark deviation = 25.11 points) over the four seasons with a relative equal balance between player effectiveness and team effectiveness. By contrast Manchester United's average-league deviation of 29.86 points is almost entirely due to player effectiveness. Indeed over the four seasons it is estimated that team effectiveness cumulatively contributed only around 0.5 league points out of total benchmark deviation of 119.5 points.

This benchmark analysis suggests that the two teams adopted very different strategies towards achieving a sustainable competitive advantage. Using the distinction proposed by Makadok (2001), Manchester United could be considered as adopting a resource-picking strategy whereas Arsenal developed more of a capability-building strategy.

Financially, Manchester United is one the biggest soccer teams in the world and over the sample period outspent Arsenal on wages by a margin of around 25%. There is a high statistical correlation of 0.801 between total wage costs and player effectiveness across all teams over the four seasons whereas the corresponding correlation between total wage costs and team effectiveness is only 0.195. In other words, player effectiveness can be acquired. Manchester United has had the necessary financial resources available and has been successful in its ability to identify and recruit highly effective players. Arsenal, on the other hand, has had more limited financial resources although still significantly more than the average Premiership team. As well as acquiring above-average player effectiveness, Arsenal has been able to develop the highest level of team effectiveness in the FAPL in the four sample seasons. Hence it could be considered that Arsenal, at least in terms of achieved results, has emulated the Oakland A's in the sense of bridging the gap with a resource-richer rival by developing more knowledge-based David strategy. Unlike Oakland, however, the details of that knowledge-based advantage have not been made public. What is known is that the Arsenal head coach, Arsene Wenger, is an economics graduate who makes extensive use of player tracking data and has a reputation for spotting and developing young players.

CONCLUSION

The *Moneyball* message from the achievements of the Oakland A's under the leadership of Billy Beane is that there is significant value to be derived from systematic (i.e., statistical) analysis of player performance. Oakland has achieved a sustained competitive advantage over an eight-year period to date by using statistical analysis to inform their decisions on recruitment, remuneration, and field tactics. Sabermetrics has become a key input into the knowledge-based "David" strategy that has allowed the low-budget A's to compete effectively with the big-market goliaths such as the New York Yankees. The strategic resource in Oakland's success has not been the player performance data which is a commodity available to all MLB teams. The strategic resource has been the ability of the Oakland management under the leadership of Billy Beane to create valuable private information through the analysis, interpretation, and application of the data.

There are three barriers to the transferability of the *Moneyball* approach to other team sports—the technological barrier, the conceptual barrier, and the cultural barrier. The technological and conceptual barriers are created by the complexity of invasion team sports. Teams need the technological capability to be available to track individual player actions and movements. Teams also need the conceptual framework to analyze player performance in the context of highly interdependent team play in which individual player actions are not separable. The technological barrier has been largely overcome through the development of video analysis and tracking systems. The conceptual barrier is more difficult but, as the analysis of Premiership soccer in this study has illustrated, it is possible to develop hierarchical structural models that can provide a conceptual framework to analyze and evaluate the contributions of individual players in complex invasion team sports.

The most enduring barrier towards the transferability of the *Moneyball* approach is the cultural barrier. *Moneyball* is a very different mindset in which statistical analysis is integrated into expert judgment-based decision-making systems. It is a different way of doing things that inevitably is dismissed as useless and inappropriate by those wedded to existing methods. Indeed much of the *Moneyball* story is about the clash of cultures between those committed to more subjective methods of analysis such as the scouts and those led by Billy Beane who relied more heavily of statistical analysis of performance data. It is a classic case of the "shirts" and the "suits". The shirts are those who are experienced in the specifics of the production process. In the case of professional team sports, the shirts are ex-players. The suits are those with more general management experience. *Moneyball* is the story of the suits invading the domain of the shirts and the tensions and conflict generated between two different mindsets. The cultural barrier is the most difficult to overcome. A successful champion of the new approach is crucial. Michael Lewis's best-selling book, *Moneyball*, has helped to establish Billy Beane as the successful champion of player performance analysis in sports around the world. But, of course, it is important to differentiate between bestseller hype and management reality. The book focuses on the science of player performance analysis but, as the subtitle of the book highlights, the application is an art. Billy Beane is a "shirt-suit," an ex-MLB player who is a talented talent-spotter and

player trader using both expert judgment and data analysis. After all, player performance analysis can only ever make a team competitive by calculating systematically the expected returns from alternative options in player recruitment and remuneration and field tactics. Winning also requires taking risks and that can never be a matter of pure calculation. Knowing which risks to take always involves judgment. Ultimately the main lesson of *Moneyball* is transferable to other sports and also to non-sporting organizations. Organizational effectiveness is both an art and a science; ignoring one in favor of the other is likely to diminish rather than enhance the organization's effectiveness. Successful performance management requires both "hard" data analysis and "soft" expert judgment.

References

. . . .

Gray, S. (2006). *The mind of Bill James: How a complete outsider changed baseball*. New York, NY: Doubleday.

Hakes, J. K., & Sauer, R. D. (2006). An economic evaluation of the *Moneyball* hypothesis. *Journal of Economic Perspectives, 20,* 173–185.

Lewis, M. (2003). *Moneyball: The art of winning an unfair game.* New York, NY: Norton.

Makadok, R. (2001). Toward a synthesis of the resource-based and dynamic-capability views of rent creation. *Strategic Management Journal, 22,* 387–401.

Opta Index (1999, 2000, 2001, 2002). *Football yearbook* (various editions). London: Carlton Books.

Quirk, J., & Fort, R. D. (1992). *Pay dirt: The business of professional team sports.* Princeton, NJ: Princeton University Press.

Runciman, D. (2007). Can this American coach and this book deliver success in English football? *The Observer Sport Monthly, 84,* 20–29.

Scully, G. W. (1974). Pay and performance in Major League Baseball. *American Economic Review, 64,* 915–930.

Wernerfelt, B. (1984). A resource-based view of the firm. *Strategic Management Journal, 5,* 171–180.

INFLATIONARY SALARY MECHANISMS

DO FIRMS HAVE SHORT MEMORIES?: EVIDENCE FROM MAJOR LEAGUE BASEBALL

Andrew Healy

A growing, and now large, body of evidence indicates that economic agents often do not conform to the classical rational model of behavior. In many cases, bounded rationality better describes behavior (Kahneman, 2003; Simon, 1957). Rather than carefully considering all available information, agents often rely on rules of thumb to solve problems, particularly when those problems are complex (Tversky & Kahneman, 1974). One rule of thumb that may cause

significant inefficiencies involves limited memory. Psychological research shows that people tend to primarily remember only salient events (Thompson, Reyes, & Bower, 1979). If economic agents forget or ignore less salient information, they will fail to act optimally when making decisions that could be improved by that information. This article shows that these limits to memory lead firms to make systematic mistakes in their salary offers.

Because performance and pay are easily measured, the market for baseball players offers an ideal laboratory for testing theories about compensation (Kahn, 1993; Sommers & Quinton, 1982), including theories relating to the effect of limited memory on salary offers. Also because salaries are so high, the costs of any mistakes are amplified. The presence of inefficient behavior in the market for baseball players would likely extend to other environments where the stakes are lower. The data show that teams are susceptible to a specific kind of inefficient behavior. Teams reward players for performing well in the immediate past, ignoring other evidence of a player's quality from his earlier performance. When choosing salary offers, teams have short memories.

This finding will likely not surprise baseball fans. Many anecdotes suggest that players often receive excessively lucrative contracts after one anomalous good season. For example, Adrian Beltre, a third baseman for the Los Angeles Dodgers, had an exceptional season in 2004. After the 2004 season, despite the absence of any similar success in the preceding years, the Seattle Mariners offered Beltre a 5-year $64 million contract. The contract paid Beltre as if he would continue to perform at his 2004 level, but he has instead reverted to his pre-2004 form.[1] Although other anecdotes also suggest that players are excessively rewarded for performing well in the final years of their contracts, testing the hypothesis that teams have short memories requires a comprehensive analysis of players' salaries.

In this article, I analyze salary and performance data for all major league baseball hitters who signed free agent contracts from 1985 to 2004. The data show that a player's performance this year is predicted about 20% more strongly by his performances from 2 and 3 years ago than by his performance from last year by itself. In contrast, a player's salary this year depends only half as much on his performances from 2 and 3 years ago as on his performance from last year. In other words, for determining future performance, there is more information in a player's earlier performance history than in his performance last year alone. Salaries, however, respond much more strongly to performance in that most recent year than to the earlier performance history.

Teams are not equally prone to underweighing earlier performance relative to recent performance. Controlling for total payroll, the teams that win the most games use past performance data most effectively. Only the unsuccessful teams put significantly too much weight on recent performance relative to earlier performance. One plausible explanation for this result is that well-managed teams are less susceptible to making memory-based mistakes in their salary offers.

What could cause memory-based biases to affect baseball salaries? Previous research in the psychology of memory offers a compelling explanation. People often access the most salient memories when making decisions. Reacting primarily to salient memories in this way corresponds to the availability heuristic (Kahneman & Tversky, 1973; Mullainathan, 2002). The most salient memory about a player who just had a remarkable season may be his recent outstanding play, whereas other relevant performance data fail to stand out as much. Availability could have caused the Seattle Mariners, for example, to believe that Adrian Beltre's lone exceptional season more accurately described the player's skills than his previous years of unexceptional play.[2] In general, this sort of behavior could explain why teams fail to take into account a player's performance in earlier years when making a salary offer.

. . . .

ESTIMATION STRATEGY

As in previous research using baseball data, I focus on a player's contribution toward winning games, through which the player affects a team's revenues (Quirk & Fort, 1992; Scully, 1974; Sommers & Quinton, 1982). The previous research indicates that, to maximize revenues, a team primarily needs to focus on winning games. To the extent that other factors influence salary offers, the estimation strategy only requires that those other factors are not related to changes in a player's performance history over time.

In this article, I will focus entirely on hitters. A variety of measures captures different aspects of a hitter's value to his team. The number of homeruns that a player hits, a player's on-base percentage, and his slugging percentage are three such measures. Previous research suggests that a measure called OPS, the sum of on-base percentage and slugging percentage, is the best single measure of a player's offensive value (Albert & Bennett, 2001). In this article, I use OPS to measure a player's worth.

. . . .

THE DATA

To test hypotheses relating to how effectively teams use past performance data to make salary offers, I use data on free agent signings in major league baseball from 1985 to 2004. The term free agent refers to a player whose contract has expired and who is free to negotiate with all teams except his original team. The competition for highly valued free agents can be fierce.[3]

For the analysis, I focus on free agent signings that occur between October and April, when regular-season games are not taking place and the vast majority of free agent signings occur. Focusing on off-season signings allows for a clear comparison between a player's performance before and after the contract is signed. Of those signings, the regressions in this study are based on all observations for which players have at least 200 at-bats in the previous two or three seasons.[4] By using this sample, I analyze the performance and salary data for all players who have played a significant amount of time in each of the 3 years preceding the signing of the free agent contract.

The data on players' salaries and past performances are obtained from The Baseball Archive.[5] The past performance data include measures of every standard statistic for each player. I construct a player's OPS by adding his on-base percentage and slugging percentage. The salary information refers to a player's base salary for the given years. To determine free agent signings, I use the data on baseball transactions compiled by Retrosheet (2006). These data contain information on all free agent signings that occur from 1985 to 2004.

The data show that the average salary has increased from $500,000 in 1985 to $2.8 million in 2004. Baseball salaries are also highly skewed and have become more skewed over time. The median baseball salaries in 1985 and 2004 were $410,000 and $870,000, respectively. . . .

RESULTS

In this section, I estimate how a player's performance history affects current performance and salary. The data show that past performance predicts current performance and salary in strikingly different ways. In addition, the data show that these differences and the inefficiencies they imply do not occur for the teams that are generally managed more effectively.

Testing for Short Memories

. . . [A] player's performance is predicted only slightly more effectively by last year's performance than by his performance from 2 years ago. . . . On the other hand, an increase in last year's performance is about twice as effective at increasing that player's salary as is an increase in performance from 2 years ago. . . .

Although teams could do somewhat better by assigning more weight to performance data from 2 years ago, they are even more ineffective at using earlier performance data. . . .

Teams' incorrect weighting of previous performance information occurs primarily for older players, as shown in **Table 7**. Comparing players who are 32 and younger to those who are 33 and older breaks the data roughly in half. Relative to last year's performance, earlier performances predict current performance about equally well for older and younger players. To some extent, all previous performances

(last year and earlier) predict current performance less well for older players. The stark difference between older and younger players, however, occurs for salary. For younger players, performance last year predicts salary about 1.5 times more strongly than performance from 2 years ago. For older players, this ratio is more than 4. Teams appear to have particularly short memories for older players. Teams pay older players almost entirely based on their performance in the previous season, and the data show that, by doing so, they make significant mistakes in their salary offers.

Testing for Optimal Use of Previous Performance Data

. . . . If teams use past performance data in an optimal way, they will use past performance data to determine salary offers in the same way that those performances affect current performance. . . . For example, for current performance, the predictive power of performance from 2 years ago is about 0.864 times as large as performance from last year. For salary, the predictive power of performance from 2 years ago relative is about 0.451 times as large as performance from last year. . . . In predicting current performance, the effect of performance from 3 years ago is about 0.448 times the effect of performance from last year. The estimated effect of performance from 3 years ago on salary is only 0.053 times the effect of last year's performance. . . .

Taken together, the effects of all three earlier years on performance and salary indicate the significant gap between how teams actually use past performance data and how they would optimally use that information. For current performance, the predictive power of performance from 2 and 3 years ago is about 1.312 times larger than performance from last year. For salary, the predictive power of performance from 2 and 3 years ago is only 0.505 times the performance from last year. The difference between these two ratios is significant ($p = .016$). If the goal is to predict how well a player will perform, there is more

Table 7   Comparing Across Age Groups

	Performance		Salary	
	Age ≤ 32 (1)	Age ≥ 33 (2)	Age ≤ 32 (3)	Age ≥ 33 (4)
Performance last year	0.399 (0.074)	0.296 (0.059)	2.593 (0.453)	4.155 (0.475)
Performance 2 years ago	0.287 (0.087)	0.201 (0.063)	1.975 (0.487)	0.775 (0.49)
Performance 3 years ago	0.136 (0.087)	0.135 (0.064)	0.545 (0.545)	0.160 (0.512)
At-bats last year	−0.002 (0.05)	−0.002 (0.026)	1.338 (0.279)	1.120 (0.209)
At-bats 2 years ago	0.000 (0.06)	0.076 (0.035)	0.867 (0.37)	1.237 (0.273)
At-bats 3 years ago	0.015 (0.056)	−0.038 (0.049)	0.522 (0.355)	0.782 (0.387)
Number of observations	232	268	232	268
R^2	.602	.541	.976	.941

Source: Journal of Sports Economics. Used with permission.

combined information in that player's performances from 2 and 3 years ago than in his performance from last year by itself. Nevertheless, teams put about twice as much weight on last year's performance as on a player's performance from 2 and 3 years ago. The data thus reject the hypothesis that teams correctly use players' past performance histories to determine their salary offers.

Successful and Unsuccessful Teams

. . . I plot average wins against a team's average payroll relative to the other major league baseball teams from 1985 to 2004. To calculate relative payroll in a season, I divide each team's total payroll in a season by the mean payroll for all teams. Then, I take the mean relative payroll for each team across seasons. . . . In the discussion below, I refer to the teams that have achieved more wins than their payrolls would predict as successful teams. I refer to the teams that have achieved fewer wins than their payrolls would predict as unsuccessful teams.

By the standard of getting the most wins out of the salaries it has paid, Oakland has been the most successful team in baseball. Oakland averaged 86 wins per season from 1985 to 2004, even though its average payroll during that time predicts only 79 wins. On the other end, Tampa Bay was the least successful team, averaging only 65 wins from 1998 to 2004, 10 fewer wins than the 75 wins that its average payroll predicts.[8] . . .

This classification makes it possible to test for differences in how successful teams use past performance information compared with how unsuccessful teams use that information. . . .

. . . [S]uccessful teams do a better job of making their salary offers match up with how past performance data predict players' present performances.[9] This result comes from two different sources. (See **Table 8**.) First, compared with unsuccessful teams, successful teams put higher relative weight on performances from 2 and 3 years ago when determining their salary offers. Second, successful teams sign players whose current performance is better predicted by last year's performance. In other words, successful teams base their salary offers more on earlier performances than unsuccessful teams and, to the extent that successful teams

sign players who performed well in the most recent year, those teams pick players for whom that recent success actually does foretell future success.

. . . One possible explanation for these differences in the types of players that successful and unsuccessful teams sign is that unsuccessful teams are more susceptible to overpaying players who have good statistics in the most recent season because of luck. To illustrate this idea, consider the example of Adrian Beltre, the player who signed a lucrative contract after one anomalous excellent season and then did not perform as well in the following season. If unsuccessful teams are particularly prone to signing players after one anomalous good season, then the players that these teams sign will have their performances better predicted by earlier years than players signed by successful teams.

. . . [O]nly the unsuccessful teams show significant memory-based biases in their salary offers. The successful teams treat past performance data similar to how they optimally would. . . .

In contrast, the unsuccessful teams use past performance data to determine salaries in a significantly different way than that information predicts future performance. . . . Relative to last year's performance, a player's earlier performances from 2 and 3 years ago predict current performance almost 4 times more effectively than it predicts that player's salary. No such difference is present for the successful teams.

CONCLUSION

To best use the dollars that they spend on salaries, organizations need to predict how well players will perform in the future. The data show that organizations make systematic mistakes in how they make these predictions. Teams infer too much from players' performances in the most recent season relative to performances from earlier years. The organizations that make these mistakes are the same ones that generally fail to spend their resources well. Organizations that are otherwise more successful also use past performance data more effectively. The sizeable mistakes that unsuccessful teams make could arise from two different hypotheses about player behavior in the final year of a contract. First,

Table 8 Last Year's Effect Compared with Earlier Years

Relative Effects of Performance in Different Years	Effect on Performance	Effect on Salary	P Value for Test of Equality
Two years ago Last year	0.864 (0.192)	0.451 (0.112)	.052
Three years ago Last year	0.448 (0.184)	0.053 (0.111)	.062
Two years ago + 3 years ago Last year	1.312 (0.291)	0.505 (0.162)	.016

Source: Journal of Sports Economics. Used with permission.

it may be the case that players are rewarded for good luck in the last season of their contract, as previous research has demonstrated that CEOs are rewarded for luck (Bertrand & Mullainathan, 2001). In support of this hypothesis, Albert and Bennett (2001) show that a player's performance in any given year reflects a great deal of luck. On the other hand, there may be certain players who exert greater effort in the final years of their contracts and certain teams repeatedly fail to recognize this behavior. The tendency shown in this article for teams to excessively reward performance at the end of a contract would amplify a player's incentive to try harder in his contract year. Future research could attempt to determine whether teams are rewarding players for luck in the final years of their contracts or for extra effort that they exerted in their contract years.

. . . .

Notes

1. Statisticians often use on-base plus slugging percentage (OPS) to measure a hitter's performance (Albert & Bennett, 2001). From 1999 to 2003, Beltre averaged a 0.756 OPS with a highest value of 0.835 in 2000. Then in 2004, his OPS jumped to 1.017. In the two seasons since, Beltre had a 0.716 and 0.793 OPS, respectively.

2. A related phenomenon, the "hot hand," can also be understood by invoking the availability heuristic as it applies to memory. Camerer (1989), for example, found that bettors incorrectly believe that a basketball team that has had recent success will also have future success. Likewise, Gray and Gray (1997) found that odds for football games are skewed toward teams that have had recent success. They find that bettors' behavior "is consistent with the idea that the market overreacts to recent form, discounting the performance of the team over the season as a whole."

3. Baseball players gained the right to free agency in 1976. Even though owners of baseball teams have been found guilty of colluding to keep players' salaries down as recently as the early 1990s, there is sufficient competition in the market for baseball players that experienced players have been receiving approximately marginal product wages going back to at least 1986 (MacDonald & Reynolds, 1994).

4. Using other at-bat thresholds, such as 150 or 300 at-bats has no effect on the general results.

5. I thank Sean Lahman of The Baseball Archive (2006) for help in accessing these data.

. . . .

8. Tampa Bay entered major league baseball as an expansion team in 1998.

9. In addition, the R^2 for the salary regressions is larger for the successful teams than for the unsuccessful teams, indicating that there is less unexplained variation in the salary offers made by successful teams.

References

Albert, J., & Bennett, J. (2001). *Curve ball: Baseball, statistics and the role of chance in the game.* New York: Springer.

Bertrand, M., & Mullainathan, S. (2001). Are CEOs rewarded for luck? The ones without principals are. *Quarterly Journal of Economics, 116,* 901–932.

Camerer, C. (1989). Does the basketball market believe in the "hot hand"? *American Economic Review, 79,* 1257–1261.

Gray, P., & Gray, S. (1997). Testing market efficiency: Evidence from the NFL sports betting market. *Journal of Finance, 52,* 1725–1737.

Kahn, L. (1993). Free agency, long-term contracts and compensation in major league baseball: Estimates from panel data. *Review of Economics and Statistics, 75,* 157–164.

Kahneman, D. (2003). Maps of bounded rationality: Psychology for behavioral economics. *American Economic Review, 93,* 1449–1475.

Kahneman, D., & Tversky, A. (1973). Availability: A heuristic for judging frequency and probability. *Cognitive Psychology, 4,* 207–232.

Lahman, S. (2006). The baseball archive. Retrieved August 20, 2006, from http://www.baseball1.com

MacDonald, D. N., & Reynolds, M. O. (1994). Are baseball players paid their marginal products? *Managerial and Decision Economics, 15,* 443–457.

Mullainathan, S. (2002). A memory-based model of bounded rationality. *Quarterly Journal of Economics, 117,* 735–774.

Quirk, J., & Fort, R. (1992). *Pay dirt: The business of professional team sports.* Princeton, NJ: Princeton University Press.

Retrosheet (2006). Transactions. Retrieved August 20, 2006, from http://www.retrosheet.org

Scully, G. (1974). Pay and performance in major league baseball. *American Economic Review, 64,* 915–930.

Simon, H. A. (1957). A behavioral model of rational choice. In *Models of man: Social and rational; mathematical essays on rational human behavior in a social setting.* New York: Wiley.

Sommers, P., & Quinton, N. (1982). Pay and performance in major league baseball: The case of the first family of free agents. *Journal of Human Resources, 17,* 426–436.

Thompson, W.C., Reyes, R. M., & Bower, G. H. (1979). Delayed effects of availability on judgment. Unpublished manuscript, Stanford University.

Tversky, A., & Kahneman, D. (1974). Judgment under uncertainty: Heuristics and biases. *Science, 185,* 1124–1131.

THE NATIONAL HOCKEY LEAGUE AND SALARY ARBITRATION: TIME FOR A LINE CHANGE

Stephen M. Yoost

I. INTRODUCTION

. . . On February 16, 2005 the National Hockey League (NHL or League) became the first professional sports league in North America to ever cancel an entire season on account of a labor dispute.[3] Three-hundred and one icy days of bitter conflict-the longest labor dispute in North American professional sports history-finally ended on July 13, 2005 with a new collective bargaining agreement (CBA) between NHL players and owners.[4] Much of the excitement surrounding the end of the lockout focused on the League's new rules of play, which the owners hope will promote scoring, speed, and excitement in the game.[5] In an effort to put the 2004–05 lockout firmly in the League's past, the NHL also unveiled a new logo.[6]

While an offense-friendly rulebook and a fresh look will help bring back some excitement to a League that has lost its luster, low-scoring games and a logo reminiscent of the 1970s did not cause the NHL's labor lockout or its financial woes.[7] Although the NHL has traditionally enjoyed its status as one of North America's four major professional sports leagues,[8] the NHL has recently been in serious danger of losing its prominence among sports fanatics throughout the United States and even in Canada.[9] With player salaries soaring[10] and big-time television contracts falling,* the NHL has turned off much of its fan base.[12] The League's operating costs have reached an all-time high,[13] and fan interest has sunk to an unprecedented low.[14] The business model of the NHL's old collective bargaining agreement led to this financial disarray and the labor lockout of 2004–05.[15] In an effort to ameliorate the League's fiscal crisis and prevent another labor dispute, the League's new CBA includes some necessary changes to its plan of business.[16]

Salary arbitration was a key element of the NHL's old collective bargaining agreement with its players, and it remains the cornerstone of the League's settlement of salary disputes under the new CBA.

. . . .

II. THE FINANCIAL DECLINE OF THE NATIONAL HOCKEY LEAGUE

The NHL hopes the new CBA will stop the League's serious financial decline that occurred over the life of the last collective bargaining agreement.[30] Following the 2002–03 season, nineteen of the NHL's thirty teams reported an operating loss.[31] Those nineteen teams lost a combined $342.4 million in that one season alone.† Four teams lost over $30 million,

only one team lost less than $5 million, and the remaining fourteen clubs lost between $5 million and $30 million.[33] The average loss of these nineteen franchises was $18 million.[34] In addition, four teams have gone bankrupt.[35]

The few profitable teams do not sufficiently counter the failing teams: of the eleven teams that reported a net profit for the 2002–03 season, only two clubs produced over $10 million.[36] The average profit of these eleven clubs was a meager $6.4 million, and their combined profit was just under $70 million.[37] As a result of these figures, the NHL as a whole lost around $273 million during the 2002–03 season.[38] The NHL's dire financial situation has prompted the League's commissioner to admit that "we lose less money by not playing."[39]

These figures beg the following question: why did the NHL lose so much money? Several factors, including an overall decreasing fan interest[40] and rapid expansion to relatively uninterested markets, contributed to the problem.[41] In the decisive Game Seven of the Stanley Cup Finals in June 2004,[42] ABC registered a 5.4 viewer rating, which was 0.4 lower than the previous season's Game Seven rating.[43] Earlier games in the 2004 Stanley Cup finals attracted the lowest ratings in twenty years.[44] The 2004 World Series of Poker attracted higher ratings on ESPN, a national cable network, than the first two games of the Stanley Cup Finals on ABC, a national network with a greater potential audience than ESPN.[45] Reflecting the reality that hardly anybody watches the NHL on television anymore, NBC paid the NHL no money upfront in the League's latest TV deal.[46] The NHL hopes that the newly unveiled rules of play for the 2005–06 season will help spark fan interest and reverse these recent trends.[47]

Between 1991 and 2001, the NHL added nine new franchises.[48] In addition, the League placed some of these teams in warm places where one would not expect to see ice hockey.[49] At the same time, traditional hockey towns like Winnipeg and Quebec, Canada lost their teams to less-interested American markets.[50] This expansion to weak markets, coupled with a decreasing fan base, helped to create the NHL's financial difficulties.

While the NHL's poor business decisions helped run the League into the ground, out-of-control player salaries have played the largest part in creating the NHL's money problems.[51] The NHL's 2002–03 audit revealed that the League spent only thirty-nine percent, or roughly $775 million, of its total operating costs on expenses other than players' salaries.[52] The NHL spent about seventy-five percent, or roughly $1.5 billion, of its revenues on players' salaries in that same season.[53] By comparison, players' costs accounted for only about fifty-seven percent of the NHL's revenues in 1994.[54]

---

*See Etan Vlessing, *A Salary Cap: The NHL "Doesn't Have a Choice,"* Amusement Bus., July 31, 2004, at Up Front.

†2002–03 URO, *supra* note 27.

Inflationary Salary Mechanisms **375**

The NHL has spent, proportionally, much more on paying its players than the other three major professional leagues.[55] To amplify this financial strain, the NHL is consistently fourth in total annual revenue as well, earning about $1.1 billion less than its next closest counterpart, the National Basketball Association (NBA).[56] The NHL has the dubious distinction of being the only league to have any of its franchises file for bankruptcy.[57]

While the NHL's popularity has been in steady decline, players' salaries have increased at a staggering rate. In 1994, the average NHL salary was $560,000.[58] In 2004, the average salary was about $1.8 million, well over three times the average salary just ten years before.[59] The League's highest-paid players, Peter Forsberg and Jaromir Jagr, earned $11 million in 2004.[60] As recently as 1996, the NHL's highest-paid player earned half that—$5.5 million.[61] These statistics readily show that, over the life of the latest collective bargaining agreement, players' salaries have exploded and destroyed the viability of the NHL.

III. PROFESSIONAL SPORTS AND SALARY ARBITRATION

A. The Business Model of the NHL and Arbitration in General[62]

Disputes over labor are common, and there is no indication that this prevalence will decrease.[63] There will always be disagreements in labor regarding compensation, because management and labor of any given company will disagree over how to distribute that company's profits.[64] Professional hockey is no exception to this phenomenon,[65] and indeed, as long as there is big money at stake and there are even larger egos involved, professional hockey's salary disputes will represent some of the most heated disputes in the entire field of labor.[66]

The National Hockey League operates like a large company with local franchises.[67] The NHL is essentially a large multi-national company consisting of many subparts.[68] Each of the thirty teams within the NHL operates as a franchise, which means that the overall system of labor is the same throughout the League, even though different entities own each team.[69] The thirty team owners collectively act as the NHL,[70] agreeing to all sorts of collective business decisions.[71] As franchise owners, however, the owners make team decisions for their individual franchises like local franchise owners of McDonald's restaurants do.[72] Owners decide, within the general rules of the NHL, what players to sign, how much to pay them, who coaches and manages their teams, and other important business decisions.[73] This is the ownership side of the NHL's labor system.

The players' side of the NHL is slightly less complicated. Players negotiate and sign contracts with the teams for whom they want to play.[74] Collectively, however, the players of the NHL act as the National Hockey League Players'

Association (NHLPA).[75] The NHLPA is the players' union.[76] As the NHLPA, the players negotiate with the League and agree upon[77] a method to govern the general labor system of professional hockey. The result of these negotiations is the collective bargaining agreement (CBA), which covers details from player eligibility to baseline compensation to training camps to salary arbitration and free agency.[78] As with agreements between large companies and their labor unions, the NHL CBA periodically runs out and must be renewed by both sides for the League to continue operating.[79]

In the NHL, players occasionally become free agents—that is, their contracts either expire or contain provisions allowing the players to renegotiate their contracts or to offer their talents to other teams.[80] Additionally, the CBA provides for salary arbitration, which gives players who meet certain criteria the opportunity to settle salary disagreements with their teams by submitting their cases to third-party arbitrators.[81]

Arbitration is traditionally defined as "a method of dispute resolution involving one or more neutral third parties who are usually agreed to by the disputing parties and whose decision is binding."[82] The NHL has utilized its own version of arbitration, defining those procedures in Article 12 of the old CBA.[83] One of the main differences between traditionally defined arbitration and the old CBA's version is the unique and limited "walk-away" provision, wherein one party can refuse to bind itself to the arbitrator's decision.[84]

B. The Emergence of Salary Arbitration in Professional Sports

. . . .

Salary arbitration's roots in professional sports traces back to 1970, when the NHL first used the process to settle compensation disputes between players and teams.[91] Not long after, the MLB followed the NHL's lead by including an arbitration procedure in its 1973 CBA.[92] Both leagues continue to employ salary arbitration in their respective collective bargaining agreements[93] and remain the only two (of the four major professional sports) leagues to use salary arbitration.[94]

C. Major League Baseball's "Final-Offer" Salary Arbitration System

Major League Baseball's salary arbitration system is known as "final-offer" arbitration.[95] When an MLB arbitration case proceeds, the player and the team's ownership each propose a salary figure.[96] Within one day of the arbitration hearing, a panel of three baseball "arbitrators must select either the player's demand or the club's offer.[97] There can be no compromise, no explanation, and no delay."[98] Furthermore, neither the players nor the team may appeal the arbitrators' decisions, and players may not hold out for better deals.[99] The final-offer system is simple enough: for example, if the ballplayer asks for $750,000 and the owner offers $500,000, the arbitrator must choose either $750,000 or $500,000, one or the other.

The final-offer feature is designed to stimulate negotiations and to discourage arbitration.[100] The final-offer system "encourages each side to put forward more realistic figures."[101] The higher chance that the arbitrator will choose the opposing side's offer leads to this anticipated effect. In other words, if the arbitrator must choose either the player's high demand or the club's low offer, the parties will compromise between the two extremes rather than risk having the arbitrator rule in favor of one or the other party.[102] "If either side gets too far out of line, the other's position will be adopted by the arbitrator."[103] The desire to win the arbitration equals an incentive to be as realistic as possible, and the less extreme demand or offer typically becomes the winning position.

1. The Advantages of MLB's Final-Offer Arbitration

There are several advantages to the MLB's final-offer system. The final-offer approach facilitates negotiation.[104] While the main advantage of settling before going to final-offer arbitration is obtaining a more favorable outcome, there are other benefits to settling salary disputes rather than going to trial or arbitration. First, arbitration hearings, like court proceedings, are adversarial and can strain the relationship between players and management.[105] Second, the parties must finance their arbitrations,[106] including paying the panel of arbitrators and funding their side's costs of discovery, which yields the evidence that they submit at the hearings.[107] Some elements of discovery, especially depositions, can be incredibly expensive.[108] Third, when parties settle, they can devise creative multi-year deals or compensation packages that involve bonuses or no-trade clauses,[109] whereas baseball's system allows arbitrators to award only single-year contracts for specified salaries.[110] Finally, settlement creates an atmosphere of cooperation, rather than of contention.[111] Settlement can "build the parties' relationship rather than rupture it"[112] by allowing the players and owners to reach a mutually acceptable common ground. On the other hand, the arbitrators' decision in an MLB salary dispute is exactly what one of the parties wanted and exactly what the other party did not want. In other words, "there is always one winner and one loser."[113] Settlement, therefore, can be superior to arbitration in many ways.

If the purpose of baseball's final-offer arbitration system is to encourage the clubs and players to resolve their disputes without resorting to arbitration, then the MLB's salary arbitration system operates properly when parties settle. Evidence shows that in the area of public employment labor disputes, the final-offer element encourages negotiations and settlement.[114] In the Major Leagues, however, players continually resort to salary arbitration rather than settle their disputes with management, leading to speculation regarding the cause of this phenomenon.[115] Disputes end up in arbitration for any of the following reasons: (1)

players have "distinctly mixed profiles," (2) one party "fails to correctly gauge the market value of a player's services," (3) a club may not have "the financial resources to pay" what the player demands, (4) the club may want to avoid the spiraling effects that increased compensation has on other players' salaries, and (5) the "personalities and egos of the participants" may preclude settlement.[116]

When baseball players have resorted to arbitration, the owners have been more successful, at least in the relative number of times that arbitrators have picked owners' offers.[117] . . .While owners have won most arbitrations, the players have benefited from the MLB's arbitration system.

2. MLB's Salary Arbitration System's Effect on Players' Salaries

The salary arbitration system has led to sky-rocketing salaries in Major League Baseball.[121] Even when players lose their arbitrations, their salaries tend to rise nonetheless.[122] Increasing salaries result from arbitration because a player always wins his arbitration hearing, even if the arbitrators pick the owner's offer.[123] There are three ways players win salary arbitrations. First, players win arbitration by filing for arbitration in the first place.[124] Simply by filing for arbitration, players consistently double their salaries.[125] "Even if they never have to go through an arbitration hearing, players receive higher salaries than they otherwise would have received if they were not eligible for arbitration."[126] The reasons for this phenomenon are elusive. At least in theory, the threat of going to arbitration "tends to move both parties to negotiate in good faith."[127] Since the final-offer system encourages players and owners to settle before arbitration, perhaps the system itself, without actually using arbitration, leads to increased salaries. Additionally, owners know that arbitrators will compare their players to high-priced talent from other teams, and rather than risk losing the arbitration, owners tend to settle for a premium.[128] Whatever the case, simply filing for arbitration tends to handsomely increase players' salaries.

Second, players win arbitration by going through arbitration and losing their case.[129] Like those who file and then settle before arbitration, players who lose their cases still have the market potential that comes with being a player who is eligible for salary arbitration. A player wins by losing his arbitration case, because his club must offer a reasonable market value in arbitration, and this number is always higher than what the player had previously earned.[130] If this were not the case, the player would not have filed for arbitration in the first place. For example, a player who earns $500,000 the previous season demands $1.5 million dollars for next season from his team. The club offers $1 million dollars instead. If the case proceeds to arbitration, the arbitrator will award the player either $1.5 or $1 million. Either way, the player will make at least twice as much as he did the previous year.[131] Studies have shown that players who "lose" their arbitrations still make an average of 150 percent their previous season's salary.[132]

Third and finally, players win arbitrations by getting arbitrators to decide in their favor.[133] In the previous hypothetical, if the player wins his arbitration, he earns three times what he earned during the previous season. This is a likely phenomenon, because players' salaries have increased at an alarming rate since the MLB started using salary arbitration.[134]

. . . .

While salary arbitration pushes baseball players' salaries up and up,[140] MLB management has blamed two aspects of the arbitration system for this phenomenon. For one, because arbitrators compare the player in dispute with the performances and salaries of other players in the same relative position, salary arbitration "makes one team pay for another team's extravagance."[141] Secondly, the system does not allow arbitrators to consider teams' market sizes, so arbitrators award players of small market teams the same salaries as their large market counterparts.[142]

In reality, both of these complaints revolve around baseball's existence in large and small markets alike. Those teams that have the capacity to pay their players "extravagantly" are the same teams that operate in a "big market."[143] In the 2004 baseball season, the teams with the three highest payrolls were the New York Yankees (with a record $180 million-plus payroll), the Boston Red Sox, and the Anaheim Angels.[144] New York and Anaheim have the two largest potential markets in baseball, with the New York and Los Angeles metropolitan areas topping out as the only two markets with more than ten million people.[145] Along with the Big Apple and Southern California, Boston ranks among the nine markets containing five million or more people.[146]

No doubt these teams can afford to pay such ridiculously high salaries because they benefit from lucrative media contracts.[147] . . . The smaller markets simply cannot match the salaries that the bigger teams lay out.[152]

Baseball's salary arbitration scheme fails to take this into account.[153] Arbitration relies on the salaries and statistics of all players regardless of where they play.[154] The big market/small market dynamic leads to increasing player salaries across the league, at least in part due to the MLB's salary arbitration system.

3. MLB's Final-Offer System: Does It Work?

The crucial question about final-offer arbitration is this: does it work? That is, does the final-offer system really encourage parties to settle and to avoid actual arbitration? . . . Between 1990 and 2004, players filed 1469 arbitration cases and only 182 went to arbitration.[157] In other words, baseball players and owners settle about ninety percent of all arbitration cases. Additionally, not all arbitration-eligible players file for arbitration,[158] suggesting that the mere possibility of going to arbitration leads clubs (and players, if in their interest) to settle.[159] These statistics reflect that baseball's final-offer system decreases the number of disputes resolved by arbitration.

While the final-offer system encourages players and owners to settle instead of arbitrate, the result—increased player salaries—is the same either way. In 1974, when the MLB first relied on arbitration to settle salary disputes, the average salary in baseball was $40,839.[160] Today, the average MLB salary is well over $2 million.[161] While the advent of free agency no doubt played a large role in this astronomical rise,[162] free agency's coexistence with arbitration pushes baseball's salaries up even more.[163] Unrestricted free agents can seek higher salaries from other teams, and restricted free agents who qualify for salary arbitration employ the arbitration system to obtain impressive pay raises.[164] As a result, Major League Baseball's use of salary arbitration has led to a profound increase in player salaries across the league. [See **Table 9** for the history of the number of cases that have proceeded to a salary arbitration hearing.]

D. The National Hockey League's Salary Arbitration System Under the Old CBA (1995–2004)

1. The Mechanics of the NHL's Salary Arbitration System

The MLB and the NHL are the only two of the major four professional sports leagues to have salary arbitration.[165] Due to baseball's tremendous popularity advantage over hockey[166] and the MLB's unique "final-offer" system of arbitration,[167] professional baseball's handling of salary arbitration is the benchmark from which practitioners and fans judge the NHL's version of arbitration.[168]

While baseball's arbitration system typically receives more attention than its NHL counterpart,[169] the NHL was the first professional sports league to use salary arbitration when the League and the players' union included the process in its collective bargaining agreement for the 1970 season.[170] NHL salary arbitration has been renewed with each new collective bargaining agreement, including the seventh and most recent CBA.[171]

Article 12 of the old NHL CBA governed hockey's use of salary arbitration until the 2004–05 season.[172] Only restricted free agents—i.e., players who still "belonged" to a particular team but who could not renegotiate their contracts with that team—qualified for salary arbitration.[173] Although the arbitrators' decisions were "final and binding on the parties," owners retained limited "walk-away rights."[174] Since the hockey season typically begins mid-October of each year,[175] all arbitration hearings occurred in the first two weeks of August and concluded before August 15.[176]

Under the last CBA, only the players were able to file for arbitration.[177] The team ownership, on the other hand, decided "whether the arbitration award shall be for a one or two year contract."[178] The default term was one year if the club failed to delineate this detail.[179] This provision favored the players because the ruling locked in the players for only one year rather than holding them to a two-year contract.[180] After just one more year, the players could then renegotiate

Table 9   Salary Arbitration Results and Data, MLB Arbitration (Year-by-Year)

Year	Players	Owners
2010	3	5
2009	2	1
2008	2	6
2007	3	4
2006	2	4
2005	1	2
2004	3	4
2003	2	5
2002	1	4
2001	6	8
2000	4	6
1999	2	9
1998	3	5
1997	1	4
1996	7	3
1995	2	6
1994	6	10
1993	6	12
1992	9	11
1991	6	11
1990	14	10
1989	7	5
1988	7	11
1987	10	16
1986	15	20
1985	6	7
1984	4	6
1983	13	7
1982	8	14
1981	11	10
1980	15	11
1979	8	5
1978	2	7
1977	No arbitration	
1976	No arbitration	
1975	6	10
1974	13	16
Total	209	281

Source: The Associated Press; additional data on file from editors.

their contracts[181] or enter into unrestricted free agency.[182] On the other hand, a default term of two years favored club owners by limiting their players' ability to match the yearly increase of salaries of other players from around the League.[183]

As with their baseball counterparts, NHL arbitrators were required to take into account various statistics and factors to guide them in making a final decision, including "the Compensation of any player(s) who is alleged to be comparable to the party Player."[184] The reliance on relative compensation created an undeniable upward spiral effect on players' salaries throughout the NHL. Arbitrators had to have some figure regarding the market value of comparable players in order to determine the market value of the player who was party to the arbitration.[185] Such a figure was necessary because NHL arbitrators were free to award any salary figure, unlike in Major League Baseball.[186] Since NHL arbitrators had unlimited options, they relied more heavily on comparable players' salaries to decide the arbitrations rather than on the players' demands or the clubs' offers.[187]

The result of this heavy reliance on comparable players' salaries was an increase in salaries across the NHL. If one player had a successful year and he negotiated a new contract with a higher salary, comparable players demanded the same higher compensation. One player's increased salary created a boon for comparable players.[188] In NHL arbitration under the old CBA, the key for the player was to prove that he was comparable to another, more highly paid player.[189] The pivotal role that comparable players' salaries played in salary arbitration led to a relative increase in overall salaries.

NHL arbitrators had to decide their cases within forty-eight hours of the end of the arbitration hearings.[190] Moreover, NHL arbitrations required only one arbitrator, while three person panels of arbitrators decide MLB hearings.[191] In addition, NHL arbitrators' decisions had to include both the "salary to be paid to the Player by the Club" and "a brief statement of the reasons for the decision, including identification of any comparable(s) relied on."[192] This differed from professional baseball's arbitration rules, which do not provide for any explanation of the arbitrators' decisions.[193] In baseball, the final-offer element begs little need for such details since MLB arbitrators simply choose between two figures.

2.   The Decisionmakers: How the NHL Chose Arbitrators Under the Old CBA

A potential distinction between the arbitration systems of hockey and baseball was the selection of arbitrators.[194] Under the old NHL CBA, the League and the NHLPA jointly appointed eight arbitrators who were members of the National Academy of Arbitrators, and only one arbitrator decided each case.[195] Likewise in the MLB, the owners and players' association "annually select the arbitrators."[196] But MLB arbitrations are "assigned to three-arbitrator panels."[197]

In a system of arbitration, a potential issue can be the procedure for selecting the arbitrators and the concern over the "repeat-player phenomenon."[198] For three reasons, the arbitrator-selection processes in both the MLB and the NHL (under the old CBA) avoided these potential problems. First, in both leagues, the opposing sides - the owners and the players - equally shared the ability to choose arbitrators.[199] Second, the two sides in each league split the costs of the arbitrations, including paying the arbitrators.[200] Finally, NHL and MLB arbitrations involved repeat-players on both sides of the hearing, so neither side had an advantage.[201] Therefore, by the terms of their respective collective bargaining agreements, both the MLB and the NHL (under the old CBA) avoided potential problems in the selection of arbitrators.

3. The NHL's Unique "Walk-Away" Provision

The last distinction of the NHL's old salary arbitration system was that NHL arbitrations were not always final; the CBA provided owners limited "walk-away rights."[202] The walk-away right meant that arbitrations could have been appealed in certain circumstances,[203] which differed from the absolute finality of the MLB's salary arbitrations.[204] The old CBA dealt with one and two-year arbitration decisions differently in regards to walk-away rights.[205] If a team's ownership chose to arbitrate a player's salary on a one-year contract, the ownership had the option of walking away from the arbitration within seventy-two hours after the arbitrator announced his or her decision.[206] Once the club did so, the player automatically became an unrestricted free agent, except in two circumstances.[207] First, if the player accepted from another team an offer that was less than eighty percent of the award from the arbitration with the original club, the original club could elect to match the offer of the other team.[208] Second, under certain circumstances and after the club had walked away from the arbitration, the player could have elected to accept the original club's "qualifying offer" for one year and become a free agent at the end of that term.[209]

If a team's ownership chose to arbitrate for a two-year contract, the ownership could again walk away from the arbitration decision within seventy-two hours of the announcement of the arbitration result.[210] The difference, however, was the result of the team's walking away. If a club walked away from a two-year arbitration decision, the player and the team had to enter into the one-year contract under the terms of the arbitration, and the player became an unrestricted free agent at the end of that one year.[211]

Thus, walking away from an arbitration decision on a two-year contract, as opposed to a one-year contract, created different results. Clubs could not fully walk away from arbitration on two-year contracts. They were stuck with the arbitration for a full year. This system yielded various incentives, including the incentive for a club unsure of losing the arbitration hearing to elect to arbitrate a one-year contract.[212] In choosing to arbitrate a one-year deal, the club preserved full walk-away rights.

The final important aspect of the NHL's walk-away right was the limit on the total number of times a club could exercise the right.[213] Teams could walk away from arbitration decisions no more than three times in any two consecutive NHL years and no more than two times in a single arbitration season.[214] The cap on walk-away rights encouraged teams to exercise the option sparingly. Since there was no limit to the number of restricted free agents on each team who could elect

arbitration, the walk-away cap could have played a significant role in clubs' arbitration strategy.[215]

4. The Latest Round of NHL Salary Arbitrations: Demonstrating How the Old CBA's Arbitration System Malfunctioned

Although the 2004 NHL season did not commence as originally scheduled, off-season salary disputes during the summer of 2004 continued as usual.[216] From August 1 to 15, 2004, arbitrators heard all of the League's arbitration cases in Toronto.[217] Arbitrators heard and decided nineteen disputes.[218] Sixty-six players filed for arbitration, and the remaining forty-seven cases settled before going to arbitration.[219]

These numbers immediately reflect that, at least in theory, the NHL's system operated as it should. The MLB's "final-offer" system, by its very structure, encourages players and owners to settle before going to arbitration. Since the NHL did not use the final-offer system, players and owners should have resorted to arbitration more frequently than their baseball counterparts. Since 1990, 1469 baseball players have filed for arbitration, and only 182 went before arbitrators.[220] Roughly ninety percent of the cases settled before arbitration.[221] Of the 108 potential MLB arbitrations in 2004, only seven actually went to hearing.[222] On the other hand, about twenty-eight percent of NHL cases typically end in arbitration.[223]

Baseball's high settle rate was the subject of much interest on the part of the NHL owners during the 2004–05 lockout.[224] Owners felt that players and agents held too much influence over the arbitration procedures of the old CBA[225] and complained that the NHLPA won the majority of arbitration cases.[226] As a result, NHL owners pushed for a final-offer system to replace the traditional arbitration procedures that the NHL used for decades.[227] The results of the latest round of arbitrations undoubtedly encouraged owners to change the system. In 2004, the nineteen arbitrations yielded an average award of $3.12 million.[228] Less than ten years ago the highest paid NHL player earned $5.5 million.[229]

While NHL owners at least recognized that there was something seriously wrong with the League's salary arbitration system, baseball's final-offer model would not slow the growth of the NHL players' salaries. Although the NHL and MLB have used somewhat different arbitration systems over the years, the result has been the same in both leagues: skyrocketing salaries.[230] The NHL need only look to the rising average and highest salaries in professional baseball to see that the MLB's arbitration works no better than the NHL's in keeping player salaries in check. Baseball players' salaries have multiplied along with those in the NHL.[231] The MLB system may encourage more settling and less arbitrating, but the product of the two leagues' systems is the same. Moving to a final-offer system is a myopic suggestion that would fail to ameliorate the NHL's systemic problem.

E.   The National Hockey League's Salary Arbitration System Under the New CBA (2005)[232]

1.   The Mechanics of the NHL's Salary Arbitration System Under the New CBA

Salary arbitration remains unchanged under the new CBA, except in two regards.[233] First, players are eligible for salary arbitration after four years in the League instead of three.[234] This provision favors the owners and signals their intent to decrease the prevalence of arbitration and its effects on players' salaries.

The other change that the new CBA makes to arbitration relates to who can elect arbitration. For the first time in the history of NHL salary arbitration, teams also have the right to elect salary arbitration.[235] For players who earn more than $1.5 million in their prior year, teams have the right to elect arbitration in lieu of making a "qualifying offer."[236] Teams also have the right to elect salary arbitration with respect to other certain restricted free agents who choose not to take the team to arbitration.[237]

The new CBA's qualifying offer system should increase players' salaries at a modest rate, while keeping players from resorting to arbitration. Players earning $660,000 or less are entitled to qualifying offers ("QOs") at one-hundred and ten percent of their prior year's salary.[238] Players earning more than $660,000 and up to $1 million are entitled to QOs at 105 percent of their prior year's salary.[239] Finally, players earning more than $1 million are entitled to QOs at 100 percent of their prior year's salary.[240]

These amendments to the old CBA's salary arbitration system should help make the process more equal between owners and players. Since teams can elect arbitration in some circumstances, they will have the potential of lowering highly-paid players' salaries when those players are not performing to their potential.[241] Besides these minimal alterations, the new CBA leaves salary arbitration untouched.[242] However, as the following analysis shows, other provisions of the new CBA render further changes to salary arbitration rules unnecessary.

2.   Other Provisions of the New CBA and How They Relate to Salary Arbitration

As with the old CBA, the NHL's new system of salary arbitration exists within the broader context of the entire collective bargaining agreement. The pertinent parts include: (1) players' League revenue share, (2) team salary caps and floors, (3) maximum and minimum individual player salaries, (4) team revenue sharing, and (5) free agency.[243]

The first major step that the NHL took with the new CBA involves guaranteeing a player's share of League revenues from each year.[244] The player's share will be fifty-four percent to the extent League revenues in any year are below $2.2 billion; fifty-five percent when League revenues are between $2.2 billion and $2.4 billion; fifty-six percent when League revenues are between $2.4 billion and $2.7 billion; and fifty-seven percent when League revenues in any year exceed $2.7 billion.[245]

These guarantees seem to favor the players at first glance. However, during the 2002–03 season, the NHL spent seventy-five percent of League revenues on players' salaries.[246] The NHL has not spent fifty-seven percent of its revenues on player costs since 1994.[247] The players' share appears to represent a significant step backwards. The NHL is attempting to use this provision to curb player costs that spiraled out of control during the life of the last CBA.

. . . .

The CBA's limitation of the players' share of League revenues relates to salary arbitration because salary arbitration has played a pivotal role in pushing players' salaries up.[250] Arbitration under the old CBA inflated players' salaries without a real limit.[251] However, under the new CBA, the limitation on the players' share of League revenues creates somewhat of a cap on the augmenting effect that arbitration can have on players' salaries.[252]

This limitation on salary growth is displayed no more prominently than in the new CBA's imposition of a team salary floor and cap.[253] Under the new CBA, the payroll range for each franchise in season one (2005–06) is $21.5 million to $39 million.[254] [*Ed. Note: The payroll range in 2010–11 was $43.4 million to $59.4 million.*] The salary range should help create more parity among the League's teams, but more importantly, the hard salary cap will effectively restrain players' salaries.[255] The pitfall of the NHL's salary arbitration scheme under the old CBA was that player-friendly arbitration artificially inflated salaries across the League without any real restraint.[256] The new CBA's hard salary cap will effectively eliminate this problem.

Similarly, the new CBA's cap on individual player salaries will curtail the inflationary effects of salary arbitration.[257] Under the old CBA, one aspect of salary arbitration that tended to increase players' salaries League-wide was the relative nature of arbitrators' decisions combined with the lack of a cap on individual salary awards.[258] The new CBA ameliorates this problem by regulating the maximum amount that any one player may make on each team.[259]

. . . .

Notes

. . . .

3. Bob Foltman, *Hockey May Rise from Grave*, CHI. TRIB., Feb. 19, 2005, § 3, at 1.

4. *Rev Up the Zamboni*, TORONTO STAR, July 14, 2005, at A20. The end of the lockout was a long-time coming, as players and owners expressed their desire to simply get the game back on the ice. *Id.* "To be totally honest, I really don't care what the deal is anymore," Philadelphia Flyers player Jeremy Roenick said. "All I care about is getting the game back on the ice." *Id.*

5. Helene Elliott, *New Game for the NHL,* L.A. TIMES, July 23, 2005, at D1. Some highlights of the new rules include: no more ties (shootouts will be played until there is a winner), a larger offensive zone (goals will be closer to the boards and the neutral zone will be reduced), a bigger shooting area in the goal (goaltenders' pads, gloves, and other equipment will be reduced in size), and fewer slowdowns (officials will show "zero tolerance" to interference, hooking, and holding obstruction by defenders). *Id.* at D9.

6. *Id.* The new logo has the same shield used in the previous NHL logo, but it is now silver and white. *Id.*

7. It is difficult to distinguish between the League's desire to update the game's rules and its fervent pleading with fans to return. *See* Tim Tucker, *Image, Scoring Require a Boost: The New NHL; League Outlines Plans to Increase Offense and Accessibility in Hopes of Coaxing Fans to Return after Costly, Unprecedented Lockout,* ATLANTA J.-CONST., July 24, 2005, at 1E. Fans' support of the NHL no doubt supplies cash to the League for it to operate and pay its players. However, disagreement over how the League divides that money between its owners and players caused the 2004–05 labor dispute.

8. Of all of the professional sports leagues in North America, the National Football League (NFL), the Major League Baseball (MLB), the National Basketball Association (NBA), and the NHL gross the highest revenue. *See* Ted Kulfan, *Comparing the Leagues' Financial Arrangements,* DETROIT NEWS, Oct. 13, 2004, at 6G. The above list is in order of estimated annual revenue, with the NFL grossing the greatest amount and the NHL hanging on at the bottom of the list. Although the NBA and the NHL include "national" in their proper names, these two leagues have franchises in both the United States and Canada. NBA.com, Teams, http://www.nba .com (place cursor on the "Teams" hyperlink at the top of the page for a drop-down menu) (last visited Dec. 17, 2005); NHL.com, Teams, http://www.nhl.com/teams/index.html (last visited Dec. 17, 2005). Although presently both leagues consist of fewer Canadian Franchises than previously, the NBA still includes the Toronto Raptors, and the NHL has six Canadian teams. *Migration of Franchises: Teams on the Move,* SPORTS ILLUSTRATED, Dec. 27, 2004, at 110, 110-12. The NBA's only other Canadian team, the Vancouver Grizzlies, moved to Memphis, Tennessee in 2001, after existing just six years in British Columbia. *Id.* at 112. The NHL started with two of its "original six" teams playing home games on Canadian ice (Montreal and Toronto). *Id.* There have been as many as eight Canadian hockey franchises in the NHL at one point, but as of 2005 there were only six (Montreal, Toronto, Ottawa, Edmonton, Calgary, and Vancouver). *Id.* The NFL has never had a Canadian franchise, due partly to the presence of the Canadian Football League. *See generally* The Official Site of the Canadian Football League, http://www .cfl.ca (last visited Dec. 17, 2005). Major League Baseball had two Canadian teams (Montreal and Toronto) from 1977 to 2004, but the Montreal Expos moved to America's capital and became the Washington Nationals in 2005. *Migration of Franchises: Teams on the Move, supra,* at 111. Before relocating the Expos to Washington, D.C., the MLB considered several other more southerly locations, including Monterrey, Mexico. Ed Waldman, *Also-ran Cities Set to Pinch Hit if D.C. Drops Out of Race,* BALT. SUN, Dec. 16, 2004, at 5C. The four major leagues have never actually had a franchise in Mexico. *Id.* For a comprehensive look at the past and future of professional sports franchises in Canada *see* Heather Manweiller & Bryan Schwartz, *Time Out: Canadian Professional Sports Team Franchise-Is the Game Really Over?,* 1 ASPER REV. INT'L BUS. & TRADE L. 199, 199-210 (2001).

9. Americans follow other sports much more intensely than hockey, as shown by the revenue differences in the four largest leagues. Kulfan, *supra* note 8, at 6G. The NHL, for instance, generates gross revenues that are less than half of what the NFL makes. *Id.* According to a December 2004 Gallup poll, over three-fourths of the people surveyed did not consider themselves fans of hockey. Gallup Poll Social Series: Lifestyles (Dec. 5, 2004—Dec. 8, 2004), http://institution.gallup.com/documents/question.aspx?question=1 51494&Advanced=0&SearchConType=1&SearchTypeAll=hockey (last visited Dec. 17, 2005). Less than twenty percent of responders considered themselves fans of hockey. *Id.* Another Gallup poll found that only twenty-three percent of Americans described themselves as hockey fans. *Go Figure,* SPORTS ILLUSTRATED, Dec. 27, 2004, at 36. In that same poll, respondents ranked hockey tenth among the eleven sports listed in the survey, with hockey coming in behind figure skating. *Id.* These numbers demonstrate that a further decline in hockey's popularity among Americans would be no shock; however, hockey is a part of the history and national pride of Canada. Soriano, *Rangers Avoid Arbitration,* ORLANDO SENTINEL (FLA.), Jan. 18, 2005, at C3. Historians believe that the first modern hockey league started in Kingston, Ontario in 1885. NHL.com Hockey History, http://nhl.com/hockeyu/history/evolution.html (last visited Dec. 17, 2005). The champion of professional hockey has won the Stanley Cup—one of the most recognizable trophies in the world— since 1893. NHL.com Stanley Cup History, http://nhl.com/hockeyu/ history/cup/cup.html (last visited Dec. 17, 2005). Over a century ago, Lord Stanley, the late Earl of Preston and Governor General of Canada, purchased the first Cup for the "champion hockey team in the Dominion (of Canada)." *Id.* Canada continues to support a strong Olympic hockey program, with the Canadian team winning the 2002 Olympic Gold Medal. Stand on Guard for Thee: Canada Captures First Hockey Gold Medal in 50 Years, CNNSI.com, Feb. 24, 2002, http://sportsillustrated.cnn.com/olympics/2002/icehockey/ news/2002/02/24/usa canada ap/ (calling hockey Canada's "national sport"). The NHL is to Canada what the NFL is to the United States. Soriano, *Rangers Avoid Arbitration,* supra, at C3. During the cancelled season of 2004–05, a bored and disappointed NHL fan from Winnipeg, Manitoba wrote to the Kansas City Star: "Now we just sit around in our basements and drink antifreeze." *Id.*

10. Pierre Lebrun, *Blame it On '97–'98,* EDMONTON SUN (ALTA., CAN.), Sept. 21, 2004, at SP2.

. . . .

12. Michael Rosenberg, *Bettman Created this Mess,* THE RECORD (Bergen County, N.J.), Oct. 24, 2004, at S6. As with any spectator sport, the NHL's fan base is integral to its success as a financially viable and socially important entity. NHL CBA, CBA FAQ: NHL Announces Cancellation of 2004–05 Season, http://www.nhl.com /nhlhq/cba/index.html (last visited Dec. 17, 2005). When NHL Commissioner Gary Bettman officially cancelled the 2004–05 season, he apologized to the fans, saying he "[was] truly sorry." *Id.* "Every professional sports league owes its very existence to its fans," he added. *Id.*

13. *See* Michael Steinberger, *Cap Row May Stop the Puck Here,* FIN. TIMES (LONDON), Sept. 14, 2004, at 18.

14. Kulfan, *supra* note 8, at 6G; Larry Brooks, *Paying for Lockout Tix off Fans,* N.Y. POST, Oct. 3, 2004, at 60; Doug Robinson, *NHL's on Strike and Nobody Even Noticed,* DESERET MORNING NEWS (SALT LAKE CITY), Nov. 1, 2004.

15. Helene Elliott, *The NHL Lockout: A "Bleak Day,"* L.A. TIMES, Sept. 16, 2004, at D1.

16. Elliott, *supra* note 5, at D1. The new CBA imposes a salary cap and floor ($39 million and $21.5 million, respectively for the 2005–06 season) on each team. *Id.* Additionally, the new CBA guarantees players will receive between 54% and 57% of League revenues each

year, depending on the level of League revenues for those years. *Id.* The new CBA also imposes restrictions on individual salaries. *Id.*

. . . .

27. NHL.com, 2002–03 League-Wide URO Results, http://www.nhl .com/nhlhq/cba/archive/bythenumbers/uro results.htm l (last visited Dec. 17, 2005) [hereinafter 2002-03 URO]. These numbers indicate that the NHL operated at a $273 million deficit for the 2002–03 season alone. *Id.*

. . . .

30. *See* Tucker, *supra* note 7, at 1E. In 2004, the Former Chairman of the Securities and Exchange Commission (SEC), Arthur Levitt, called professional hockey a "dumb investment" after heading a year-long assessment of the NHL's financial situation. Scott Van Voorhis, *On Thin Ice: Report: Most NHL Teams Lose Millions,* BOSTON HERALD, Feb. 13, 2004, at 39. Levitt's study produced the Unified Report of Operations (URO), which revealed that the NHL lost about $300 million during the 2002–03 season. *Id.* The study, however, has been a source of continued controversy, as the NHLPA and the NHL quarrel over just how bad is the NHL financial situation. *Id.* (quoting the NHLPA referring to Levitt and his associates as a "team of hired gun accountants," who the NHL paid "in the $500,000 range" to produce a "sobering" survey to convince the NHLPA and fans that drastic changes to the League's salary system must follow). The Levitt Report revealed, not surprisingly, that the greatest source of income for the NHL is the money fans pay to see games. *Id.* Gate receipts totaled $997 million of the League's combined $1.494 billion revenue in 2002–03. *Id.* Broadcasting-media brought in less than half of the total from gate receipts, or $449 million. *Id.* The NHLPA continued to challenge the accuracy of these numbers as the labor lockout of 2004–05 continued. Dave Hannigan, *Ice Hockey: Impasse in Labour Dispute Means Big Freeze for Whole NHL Season: Greed Blamed for Shut-down,* THE GUARDIAN (LONDON), Feb. 17, 2005, at 29 (noting that "[a]fter 38 meetings over two years, their [owners' and players'] evaluations of the sport's [NHL's] financial condition still differed too greatly [to reach a labor agreement]").

31. 2002–03 URO, *supra* note 27; *see also* http://www.nhl.com/nhlhq /cba/archive/bythenumbers/historical results.html (last visited Dec. 17, 2005).

. . . .

33. *Id.*

34. *Id.*

35. Chris Snow, *You Say Tomato, I say . . . ; Here are the Key Issues the League and the National Hockey League Players' Association Dispute,* STAR TRIB. (MINNEAPOLIS), Sept. 15, 2004, at 3C. The Pittsburgh Penguins filed for bankruptcy in 1974 and 1998, while the Los Angeles Kings went bankrupt in 1995. Kevin Allen, *Senators File for Bankruptcy, but Will Keep Skating,* USA TODAY, Jan. 9, 2003, available at http://www.usatoday.com/sports/hockey/nhl /senators/2003-01-09-bankruptcyx.htm. The Ottawa Senators filed for bankruptcy in January 2003. *Id.* A week later, the Buffalo Sabres followed suit. *Sports FYI: Solich Names Assistants,* TULSA WORLD (OKLA.), Jan. 14, 2003, at B2. These are the only four existing major professional sports franchises to go bankrupt. *Id.*

36. 2002–03 URO, *supra* note 27.

37. *Id.*

38. *Id.*

39. Elliott, *supra* note 15, at D9; Commish Claims Locked-out Union in Denial, ESPN.com, Nov. 2, 2004, http://sports.espn.go.com/espn /print?id=1914328&type=story.

40. A January 2005 USA Today/Gallup Poll discovered that fifty percent of sports fans would "not be disappointed at all" if the NHL/ NHLPA labor disputes cancelled the 2004–05 NHL season. Mike Brehm, *Poll: No NHL Would be No Biggie for Sports Fans,* USA TODAY, Jan. 11, 2005, at 3C. ESPN Analyst and Former NHL Goaltender Darren Pang believed that "even the casual sports fans last year, going into Game 7 of [the] Tampa Bay-Calgary (Stanley Cup Finals), were somewhat excited about our sport." *Id.* However, fan interest has considerably declined, as another recent Gallup Poll conducted in December 2004 found that only 23 percent of Americans considered themselves hockey fans. *Go Figure, supra* note 9, at 36.

41. Rosenberg, *supra* note 12, at S6.

42. The Stanley Cup Finals are the championships of the NHL. *See* NHL.com, Stanley Cup, http://nhl.com/hockeyu/history/cup/index .html (last visited Dec. 17, 2005). The Stanley Cup finals are a best-of-seven format, which means that the first team to win four games wins the NHL championship. *Id.* The seventh game of the series, then, is the "decisive" game, since the winner of Game Seven also wins the championship. Therefore, given the relative importance and decisiveness of the final game in the series, Game Seven of the 2004 Stanley Cup Finals should have attracted a large audience.

43. Vlessing, *supra* note 11, at Up Front. A TV rating is "the estimate of the size of a television audience relative to the total universe, expressed as a percentage." Top Ten Primetime Broadcast TV Programs for Week of 2/07/05–2/13/05, Nielsen Media, http://www .nielsenmedia.com/index.html (last visited Sept. 19, 2005). "As of September 20, 2004, there [were] an estimated 109.6 million television households in the U.S. A single national household ratings point represents 1%, or 1,096,000 households." *Id.* Therefore, the 5.4 rating from the final game of the 2004 Stanley Cup Playoffs translated to about 5,918,400 viewers. Comparatively, on February 6, 2005, Super Bowl XXXIX—the NFL's championship equivalent of Game Seven of the Stanley Cup Playoffs—attracted a 41.1 rating, or about 45,045,600 viewers. David Barron, *Hamilton Eagerly Eyes His Milestone Season,* HOUSTON CHRON., Feb. 11, 2005, Sports, at 2.

44. Vlessing, *supra* note 11, at Up Front.

45. Rick Reilly, *TV Poker's a Joker,* SPORTS ILLUSTRATED, Oct. 25, 2004, at 156; *see generally* Larry Brooks, *Eve of Destruction; Owners Are Out to Ruin NHL,* N.Y. POST, Sept. 12, 2004, at 62. ABC is a basic channel that has a potential of reaching 109.6 million television households in the United States alone. Top Ten Primetime Broadcast TV Programs for Week of 2/21/05-2/27/05, Nielsen Media Research, available at http://www.nielsenmedia.com/index.html (last visited Sept. 20, 2005). Fewer television households subscribe to a cable service, so cable networks, like ESPN, have fewer potential viewers. *Id.*

46. Vlessing, *supra* note 11, at Up Front. Before 2005, the NHL had a five year, $600 million contract with ABC and ESPN. Joe LaPointe, *ABC and ESPN Script Grabs More Eyeballs,* N.Y. TIMES, June 6, 2003, at D5. The NHL has traditionally had smaller television contracts than the NBA, NFL, and MLB. *Id.* Other professional sports leagues consistently sign television contracts that dwarf the NHL's largest TV deal ever: five-years, $600 million (from 1999–2004). Todd Jones, *NHL Reached for the Sky, But It Really Needed Firm Foundation,* COLUMBUS DISPATCH, Feb. 18, 2005, at B3. The 2005 network television deals of other pro sports leagues included $17.6 billion for the NFL, $4.7 billion for the

NBA, and $3.35 billion for the MLB. *Id.* Even professional racecar driving demanded a larger TV deal than professional hockey, with NASCAR holding on to a $2.8 billion deal from network TV during 2005. *Id.*

47. Elliott, *supra* note 5, at D1. Speaking on the need for these rule changes, Commissioner Gary Bettman emphasized the need to "drop the puck on a fresh start for the NHL." *Id.* The NHL unveiled its new rules in an effort to divorce fans' feelings about "the long, dark days of the lockout" and cancelled season of 2004–05 with the NHL and professional hockey in general. *Id.*

48. *Migration of Franchises, supra* note 8, at 112. Those nine expansion teams and the years the NHL introduced them are: San Jose Sharks (1991), Ottawa Senators (1992), Tampa Bay Lightning (1992), Florida Panthers (1993), Anaheim Mighty Ducks (1993), Nashville Predators (1998), Atlanta Thrashers (1999), Columbus Blue Jackets (2000), and Minnesota Wild (2000). *Id.*

49. Elliott, *supra* note 15, at D1. Examples of recently created or relocated southerly NHL franchises include the Phoenix Coyotes (formerly the Winnipeg Jets until 1996), Nashville Predators (expansion team of 1998), and Carolina Hurricanes (formerly the Hartford Whalers until 1997, when they relocated to Raleigh, North Carolina). *Migration of Franchises, supra* note 8, at 112.

50. *See* Chris Snow, *The Lost Season?: Lockout Begins Tonight; The Puck Stops Here; NHL, Players Remain Miles Apart as Lockout Appears Certain,* STAR TRIB. (MINNEAPOLIS), Sept. 15, 2004, at 1C.

51. In 2004, players' salaries ate up seventy-five percent of the NHL's revenues. Dave Joseph, *NHL Season Put on Ice: Life Goes On,* SUN-SENTINEL (FT. LAUDERDALE, FLA.), Feb. 17, 2005, at 1A.

52. 2002–03 URO, *supra* note 27.

53. *Id.*

54. Mike Loftus, *NHL Update; Little Movement in Negotiations; Owners, Players Still Heading Toward Lockout,* THE PATRIOT LEDGER (QUINCY, MASS.), Sept. 4, 2004, at 47. The NHL's losses continued to mount, as the 2004–05 non-season prevented even the possibility that the NHL could generate a profit. J.P. Giglio, *RBC, Canes Made Provisions,* THE NEWS & OBSERVER (RALEIGH, N.C.), Feb. 19, 2005, at C3. While the owners amassed a $300 million reserve fund to survive the cancelled season, the teams cannot produce revenues without conducting any games. *Id.*

55. Kulfan, *supra* note 8, at 6G. Major League Baseball (MLB) dedicates 63% of its revenue to players' salaries, while the NBA and the NFL spend 58% and 64%, respectively, of their revenues on their players. *Id.*

56. *Id.* The MLB earns about $4.1 billion per year, while the most successful league, the NFL, grosses about $5 billion. *Id.*

57. The first franchise to file for bankruptcy was the Pittsburgh Penguins. Jenny Wiggins, *US Sports Tackle TV Cash Issue: Credit Analysts are Watching for Moves off the Screen,* FINANCIAL TIMES (LONDON), Nov. 14, 2003, at 45. Three other teams—Los Angeles, Ottawa, and Buffalo—have since done the same. *See* Allen, *supra* note 35; *Sports FYI: Solich Names Assistants, supra* note 35, at B2.

58. Loftus, *supra* note 54, at 47.

59. *Id.*

60. Kulfan, *supra* note 8, at 6G.

61. *See* Tim Sassone, *Looks Like a Lockout as Deadline Looms: All Signs Pointing to Long Labor Dispute for NHL,* CHI. DAILY HERALD, Sept. 14, 2004, at Sports 1.

62. This subsection gives the reader a basic understanding of the general business structure of the NHL and of the traditional procedural ele-

ments of arbitration as one of the basic forms of alternative dispute resolution. For a more detailed look at the franchise system of professional sports *see* Kenneth L. Shropshire, THE SPORTS FRANCHISE GAME (1995).

63. The American Arbitration Association (AAA), the largest alternative dispute resolution institution in the world, has handled over two million cases, with many in the field of labor. *See* American Arbitration Association Dispute Resolution Services Worldwide, Fast Facts, http://www.adr.org/FastFacts (last visited Dec. 17, 2005). In 2002 when commercial disputes declined, the AAA handled an increased number of labor cases. American Arbitration Association Dispute Resolution Services Worldwide, 2003 President's Letter and Financial Statements 4, available at http://www.adr.org/si.asp?id=1543, at 4 (last visited Dec. 17, 2005).

64. *See* Michael Arace, *NHL's Lost Season: Nuclear Winter,* COLUMBUS DISPATCH, Feb. 17, 2005, at E1. "The reason" for the 2004–05 NHL lockout and eventual season cancellation was that "the NHL and its players' association couldn't resolve how to split revenues from the $2.1 billion industry." *Id.*

65. Thirty-four players resorted to salary arbitration in the 2003 off-season alone. SI.com, 2003 NHL Salary Arbitration List, http://sportsillustrated.cnn.com/hockey/news/2003/07/16/arbitrationlist/ (last visited Dec. 17, 2005).

66. During the labor lockout of 2004–05, the NHL and the NHLPA hurled insults at one another, while fans from across North America grew impatient with the lack of a hockey season. *See* Andrew Gross, *The Puck Stops Here,* J. NEWS (N.Y.), Feb. 17, 2005, at 1C. At the news conference during which Commissioner Bettman cancelled the 2004–05 season, Bettman jabbed at NHLPA Executive Director Bob Goodenow for not being an honest negotiating partner during the lockout. *Id.* Goodenow responded by placing the blame for the cancelled season on the shoulders of the owners. *Id.* This war of words continued throughout the entirety of the lockout. Tom Jones, *Agreement, Optimism Far Away,* ST. PETERSBURG TIMES (FLA.), Sept. 5, 2004, at 1C (noting that both the NHL and NHLPA appeared "more concerned with lobbing insults and questioning whether the other side is even interested in a settlement" than with coming to an agreement).

67. Compare NHL CBA Preamble, http://web.archive.org/web/20040428065307/http://www.nhlcbanews.com/cba/preamble.html (last visited Dec. 17, 2005), with McDonald's Corporation, Franchising Home, http://www.mcdonalds.com/content/corp/franchise/franchisinghome.html (last visited Dec. 17, 2005) (noting that McDonald's has "always been a franchising company").

68. NHL Rulebook, http://nhl.com/rules/index.html (last visited Dec. 17, 2005).

69. *Id.*

70. NHL CBA Preamble, *supra* note 67.

71. *See,* e.g., NHL Collective Bargaining Agreement expired on September 15, 2004, http://www.nhl.com/nhlhq/cba/archive/cba/index.html (last visited Dec. 17, 2005). The CBA is the most visible example of any NHL/NHLPA agreement.

72. *See* McDonald's Franchising, *supra* note 67.

73. National Hockey League, National Hockey League Players' Association Collective Bargaining Agreement, (July 22, 2005), art. 5, http://web.archive.org/web/20041012101809/www.nhlcbanews.com/cba/ index.html (last visited Dec. 17, 2005) [hereinafter NHL CBA] (noting that "[e]ach club . . . shall . . . have the right at any time and from time to time to determine when, where, how and under what circumstances it wishes to operate, suspend, discontinue, sell or move and to determine the manner and the rules by which its team shall play hockey").

74. NHL CBA, *supra* note 73, at art. 6, § 2. Under the rules of the old CBA, players relied on the Union's representation, or operated on their own. *Id.* "No Club shall enter into a Player Contract with any player and the NHL shall not register or approve any Player Contract unless such player: (i) was represented in the negotiations by a Certified Agent as designated by the NHLPA under Section 6.1; or (ii) if Player has no Certified Agent, acts on his own behalf in negotiating such Player Contract." *Id.*

75. *Id.*

76. *Id.*

77. Ideally the players' union and owners agree on a collective bargaining agreement. The events of 2004–05, however, demonstrated that such cooperation cannot be taken for granted. *See* Wes Goldstein, Players Lose It All After Union Chief Hedges Bet, CBS Sportsline.com, Feb. 16, 2005, http://www.sportsline.com/nhl/story/8201334.

78. NHL CBA, *supra* note 73, http://www.nhl.com/nhlhq/cba/index.html.

79. NHL CBA, *supra* note 73, at art. 3, § 1(a). The last CBA lasted from September 16, 1993 to September 15, 2004. *Id.* The new CBA is six years in duration (through the 2010–11 season) with the NHLPA having the option to re-open the agreement after the fourth year (the 2008–09 season). *See also* CBA FAQs, *supra* note 29. The NHLPA also has the option of extending the CBA for an additional year at the end of the 2010–11 season. *Id.*

80. Players exercise these options in an attempt to increase their salaries. NHL CBA, *supra* note 73, at art. 10.

81. NHL CBA, *supra* note 73, at art. 12.

82. BLACK'S LAW DICTIONARY 41 (2d pocket ed. 2001). Typically, an arbitrator's decision is binding. *Id.*

83. NHL CBA, *supra* note 73, at art. 12. Article 12 of the old CBA did not have an explicit definition for "salary arbitration." *Id.* Instead, the entire article defined how the NHL uses arbitration by outlining the specific guidelines for League's use of the procedure. *Id.* Mediation, another form of alternative dispute resolution, is less formal than arbitration. BLACK'S LAW DICTIONARY 444 (2d pocket ed. 2001). In addition, parties typically resolve their own disputes in mediation, while arbitrators, as agreed-upon third parties, decide cases in arbitration. *Id.* Moreover, mediation may produce a settlement agreement, whereas a settlement agreement may avoid the need for arbitration. *Id.*

84. NHL CBA, *supra* note 73, at art. 12, § 6. Thus, with a walk-away right, the arbitrator's decision may not have been binding after all. This limited right, which was retained by only the clubs and not the players, is explored in detail, *infra* Part III(D)(2).

. . . .

91. Roger I. Abrams, THE MONEY PITCH: BASEBALL FREE AGENCY AND SALARY ARBITRATION 146 (2000). In 1969, a group called the Task Force on Sports in Canada produced a report that criticized the NHL's owner-friendly labor structure. *See* Robert C. Berry et al., LABOR RELATIONS IN PROFESSIONAL SPORTS 209 (1986). Using this report as leverage, the NHLPA convinced the owners to consent to salary arbitration for the 1970 season. *Id.* At that time, however, the NHL still used the "reserve clause" in the standard player contract, meaning that free agency did not exist in professional hockey. *Id.* at 211. The owners agreed to salary arbitration while keeping the reserve system intact. *Id.* Much like the emergence of free agency in the MLB, the NHL did not allow free agency until 1972. *Id.*

92. Paul D. Staudohar, THE SPORTS INDUSTRY AND COLLECTIVE BARGAINING 41-42 (2d ed. 1989). Following the NHL's lead, the MLB finally succumbed to a free agency system in December of 1975. *Id.* at 34.

93. *Id.* at 41, 150. The NHL's new CBA also includes provisions for salary arbitration. CBA FAQs, *supra* note 29.

94. Kulfan, *supra* note 8, at 6G. The NHL and the MLB have salary arbitration, while the NFL and NBA do not. *Id.*

95. *See* Abrams, *supra* note 91, at 146-47. Berry et al., *supra* note 91, at 58.

96. *See* Andrew Zimbalist, BASEBALL AND BILLIONS: A PROBING LOOK INSIDE THE BIG BUSINESS OF OUR NATIONAL PASTIME 82 (1992).

97. Abrams, *supra* note 91, at 146-47.

98. *Id.*

99. *Id.* at 147.

100. *See* Staudohar, *supra* note 92, at 43.

101. Zimbalist, *supra* note 96, at 82.

102. *See* Staudohar, *supra* note 92, at 44.

103. *Id.*

104. Elissa M. Meth, *Final Offer Arbitration: A Model for Dispute Resolution in Domestic and International Disputes,* 10 AM. REV. INT'L ARB. 383, 384-85 (1999).

105. Abrams, *supra* note 91, at 149; *NHL: Kiprusoff Arbitration Gets Nasty,* EDMONTON SUN (ALTA. CAN.), Aug. 22, 2004, at SP14; Chris Snow, *Wild Wraps Up Two More; Brunette, Mitchell Deals will Avoid Arbitration,* STAR TRIB. (MINNEAPOLIS), Aug. 13, 2004, at 2C (noting that the salary arbitration process can be "degrading" and "potentially risky").

106. Abrams, *supra* note 91, at 149.

107. 2003–2006 Basic Agreement between the MLB and MLBPA, art. VI(F)(11), http://us.i1.yimg.com/us.yimg.com/i/spo/mlbpa/mlbpa cba.pdf (last visited Dec. 17, 2005). "The Player and Club shall divide equally the costs of the hearing, and each shall be responsible for his own expenses and those of his counsel or other representatives." *Id.* at 17.

108. *See* Stephen C. Yeazell, CIVIL PROCEDURE 419 (6th ed. 2004). "In a full-blown deposition both sides have their lawyers there; if the witness is not one of the parties he or she may also be represented by a lawyer. In addition, the deposing party must arrange for some form of recording or transcription of the deposition. . . . [E]ach hour of deposition time may amount to thousands of dollars in legal fees and costs." *Id.*

109. *See* Abrams, *supra* note 91, at 149. Settling allowed Johan Santana and the Minnesota Twins to sign a four-year, $40 million contract in 2005. Twins Agree to Four-Year, $40M Deal with Santana, CBS Sportsline.com, Feb. 14, 2005, http://www.sportsline.com/mlb/story/819457. If the two sides would have relied on arbitration, the arbitrator could have picked a one-year deal worth either $5 million (the club's expected offer) or $6.8 million (Santana's expected salary demand). *Id.*

110. *See* Abrams, *supra* note 91, at 149.

111. *Id.*

112. *Id.*

113. *Id.*

114. *See* Dale Yoder & Paul D. Staudohar, PERSONNEL MANAGEMENT AND INDUSTRIAL RELATIONS 488-89 (7th ed. 1982).

115. *See* Abrams, *supra* note 91, at 150-51.

116. *Id.*

. . . .

121. Some followers of baseball refer to the time of the year for MLB arbitrations as baseball's "get-rich season." *Who's Hot, Who's Not,* SPORTS ILLUSTRATED, Feb. 21, 2005, at 31. The first MLB arbitration of 2005 yielded a classic example of the arbitration system's effect on salaries. Kyle Lohse, a right-handed pitcher for the Minnesota Twins who went 9-13 and had a 5.34 ERA (earned run average) in 2004, won that arbitration hearing with a $2.4 million award. *Id.* In 2004, he grossed $395,000, but he will earn over six times that in 2005, thanks to this favorable arbitration. *Id.*

122. Zimbalist, *supra* note 96, at 83.

123. *See* James B. Dworkin, *Final Offer Salary Arbitration (FOSA)— a.k.a Franchise Owners' Self Annihilation,* in STEE-RIKE FOUR!: WHAT'S WRONG WITH THE BUSINESS OF BASEBALL? 73, 79 (Daniel R. Marburger ed., 1997).

124. *Id.*

125. *Id.*

126. *Id.*

127. *Id.*

128. *Id.*

129. *Id.* Dworkin, *supra* note 123, at 79.

130. A few factors lead to this phenomenon. First, only players can file for arbitration. *Id.* As a result, owners cannot utilize arbitration on a player who had a bad season. Therefore, owners cannot reverse the upward trend of players' salaries that the system tends to create. Players will not file for arbitration if they are coming off of bad seasons. *Id.* Arbitration, then, is a strategic means for players to jockey for more money after a good year. Second, the interlocking nature of free agency and arbitration, combined with arbitration's reliance on comparative players' statistics and salaries, causes an increase in players' salaries each year across the board. The arbitrators rely on these figures when deciding between the players' demands and the owners' offers. *Id.* Finally, natural market forces, such as inflation, cause salaries to rise. The American inflation rate in 2004 was 3.3%, which represents $33,000 on a $1 million salary. Jonathan Riskind, *Bush's 2006 Budget Full of Cuts,* COLUMBUS DISPATCH, Feb. 8, 2005, at A1. The first factor—the players' strategic edge—likely explains the increasing arbitration figures the most.

131. To use a real-life example, Johan Santana of the Minnesota Twins earned $335,000 in 2003. Dennis Brackin, *Signing of the Times,* STAR TRIB. (MINNEAPOLIS), January 9, 2005, at 1C. He filed for arbitration and asked for $2.45 million, while the Twins offered $1.6 million. *Id.* Since the arbitrators found for the team, technically Santana lost his arbitration. Even so, in 2004 he still made over four times more than he did the previous season. KFFL.com, Free Agents 2004: 2004 MLB Arbitration Results, http://kffl.com/article.php/4234/227 (last visited Dec. 17, 2005). Santana was arbitration-eligible in 2005 as well, and the system, once again, helped to increase his salary handsomely. Twins Agree to Four-Year, $40M Deal with Santana, *supra* note 109. Santana and the Twins were scheduled for arbitration on February 15, but the two sides settled the day before. *Id.* Even though "[b]oth sides were more than happy to avoid arbitration," the team will be paying Santana a vastly increased salary for the next four years. *Id.* Santana made $1.6 million in 2004, and his new salary—the product of arbitration—avoidance settlement—will average out to $10 million per year for the next four years. *Id.* Santana intended to ask for $6.8 million in arbitration, as opposed to the $5 million the Twins expected to offer him. *Id.* However, the Twins agreed to double their offer in exchange for a longer term commitment from the pitcher. *Id.* Since salary arbitration produces a one-year compromised deal, avoiding arbitration allowed the Twins to lock Santana in for four years. *Id.* Assuming

no settlement, Santana would have made more than three times his previous year's salary had the two sides proceeded to arbitration and had Santana "lost" that arbitration. He would have had a one-year, $5 million contract. *Id.* Instead, he will be making approximately $10 million in 2005. *Id.* His 2005 salary—$10 million—is thirty times his salary from 2003—$335,000. Compare Free Agents 2004: 2004 MLB Arbitration Results, *supra,* with Twins Agree to Four-Year, $40M Deal with Santana, *supra* note 109.

132. James B. Dworkin, *Collective Bargaining in Baseball: Key Current-Issues,* LABOR L.J. 480, 480-86 (1988).

133. Dworkin, *supra* note 123, at 80.

134. Rich Fletcher, *Show Everybody the Money,* PLAIN DEALER (CLEVELAND, OHIO), Nov. 14, 2004, at C15.

. . . .

140. Zimbalist, *supra* note 96, at 83.

141. *Id.*

142. *Id.* at 83-84.

143. According to Nielsen Media Research, the top ten American television markets of 2004–05 were (from largest to smallest): (1) New York, (2) Los Angeles, (3) Chicago, (4) Philadelphia, (5) Boston, (6) San Francisco-Oakland-San Jose, (7) Dallas-Ft. Worth, (8) Washington, D.C., (9) Atlanta, and (10) Detroit. The 56 NSI Metered Markets (U.S.), Nielsen Media Research, http://www.nielsenmedia.com/ (last visited Oct. 11, 2005). In 2004, the ten highest team salaries in the Major Leagues were (from highest to lowest): (1) New York (Yankees), (2) Boston, (3) Anaheim, (4) New York (Mets), (5) Philadelphia, (6) Chicago (Cubs), (7) Los Angeles, (8) Atlanta, (9) San Francisco, and (10) St. Louis. ESPN.com, Cleveland Indians 2004 Salaries, http://sports.espn.go.com/mlb/teams/salaries?team=cle (last visited Dec. 17, 2005). Detroit was the only metropolitan area with a baseball team that was among the top ten largest television markets but not among the top ten highest teams' salaries of 2004. Id. The Detroit Tigers team salary was twenty-first among the thirty MLB teams that year. Id.

144. John Donavan, The Year that Was: Yankees, Cardinals, Tantrums, Milestones Highlighted Regular Season, SI.com, Oct. 1, 2004, http://sportsillustrated.cnn.com/2004/writers/john donovan/09/30/season.review/.

145. Al Streit, Baseball Markets, Baseball Almanac, http://www.baseball-almanac.com/articles/baseball markets.shtml (last visited Dec. 17, 2005).

146. *Id.*

147. Richard Sandomir, *Steinbrenner Has Got It, and He Loves to Flaunt It,* N.Y. TIMES, Feb. 17, 2004, at D1.

. . . .

152. The disparity between baseball's rich and poor teams is staggering. "The combined 2005 salaries of the five projected [New York] Yankee start[ing pitchers] will total $67 million, which is more than the 2004 payrolls of 18 of the other 29 teams." Phil O'Neill, *Payroll Budgets Spiraling Out of Control,* SUNDAY TELEGRAM (WORCESTER, MASS.), Jan. 16, 2005, at D6. The payroll of the entire Cleveland Indians team was $34 million in 2004. Scott Priestle, *Indians, Shapiro Agree on 2-Year Contract Extension,* COLUMBUS DISPATCH, Dec. 23, 2004, at B5. In that same year, the New York Yankees doled out over $180 million, while the Boston Red Sox disbursed about $130 million in players' salaries. *Id.* Cleveland's paltry $34 million was the MLB's fourth-lowest team payroll. *Id.; see also* Jones, *supra* note 66, at 1C (pointing out the "haves and have nots" of the MLB,

where "only a handful of teams reasonably expect to vie for a title each season").

153. A potential counterargument is that arbitrators should not take the size of the team's market into account, because the value of the player in question is a matter of how the entire MLB values him, not just that particular team. In other words, it would be unfair for an arbitrator to "undervalue" a player from the Cleveland Indians, when the New York Yankees, with higher revenues and spending power than the Indians, would pay that player a higher salary. But the problem with that argument is that it fails to take into account the effect such a system has on the entire MLB. It would be absurd to require a law firm in Cleveland to pay its attorneys the same salary a law firm in New York City pays its similarly situated attorneys, yet both firms are part of the national legal community. In the attorney market, a lawyer from Cleveland could leave his or her job and take a new, higher paying position in New York, and the result would have very little effect on the salaries of lawyers across America. The same does not happen in Major League Baseball. The player who leaves the Indians for a higher salary with the Yankees creates a new baseline to which arbitrators look as a factor in deciding what a player with similar talents should be paid.

154. Parties in baseball arbitrations offer salary numbers for comparable players, regardless of those players' current teams. 2003–2006 Basic Agreement between the MLB and MLBPA, *supra* note 107, at art. VI(F)(12)(a). The MLB CBA requires arbitrators to use "comparative baseball salaries" from across the League as a part of the criteria for deciding arbitrations. *Id. See also* Mike Klis, *Twins Lose Koskie to Jays: Third Baseman Gets $17 Million,* DENVER POST, Dec. 13, 2004, at 9C. In the 2004 off-season, the Minnesota Twins, who are notorious for being a small market team, lost several members of their starting line-up to teams in larger markets. *Id.*

155. Dennis Brackin, *Twins, Santana are Far Apart; Lefthander is Asking for $6.8 million,* STAR TRIB. (MINNEAPOLIS), Jan. 19, 2005, at 4C. By comparison, sixty-five players filed for arbitration in 2004. Gagne, Halladay Among 65 Players to File for Arbitration, The Sports Network, Jan. 15, 2004, http://www.sportsnetwork.com/default .asp?c=sportsnetwork&page-lb/news/aan3004555.htm.

156. Brackin, *supra* note 155, at 4C.

157. Carrie Muskat, Free Agency Facts, MLB.com, Nov. 2, 2004, http://mlb.mlb.com/NASApp/mlb/mlb/news/mlb news.jsp?ymd =20041102& content id=908940&vkey=news mlb&fext=.jsp.

158. Following the 2004 baseball season, many arbitration-eligible players opted not to file for arbitration. Thirty-nine arbitration-eligible players inked new contracts without actually going to arbitration. Brackin, *supra* note 155, at 4C; *see also* Gordon Edes, *Varitek Gives a Signal: He Passes on Sox' Arbitration Offer,* BOSTON GLOBE, Dec. 20, 2004, at E2 (noting that two of the arbitration-eligible players from Boston declined arbitration and signed with other teams). Other arbitration-eligible players reached agreements with their teams before filing for arbitration. Juan C. Rodriguez, *Beckett Avoids Arbitration; Pitcher Signs; Marlins Talk to Delgado's Agent,* SUN-SENTINEL (FT. LAUDERDALE, FLA.), Jan. 19, 2005, at 9C (noting that Josh Beckett re-signed with the Marlins before going to arbitration).

159. One factor that could induce settlement is the cost of arbitrations. The cost of MLB arbitrations is typically greater than NHL arbitrations, because professional baseball requires three arbitrators per hearing, while the NHL has used a single-arbitrator system. The AAA supplies arbitrators for most MLB salary arbitrations. American Arbitration Association, Sports Arbitration including Olympic Athlete Disputes, http://www.adr.org/sp.asp?id=22022 (last visited Dec. 17, 2005). "Arbitration costs through the AAA can be astronomical." Robert J. Miletsky, How to Make Sure Your Arbitration Clauses Do Exactly What You Want Them to Do, CONTRACTOR'S

BUS. MGMT. REP., February 2005, at 10. Usually, each side pays for their own portion of the arbitration costs. Under the most recent NHL CBA, participants in salary arbitrations are responsible for their "own expense of participation in the arbitration." NHL CBA, *supra* note 73, at art. 12, § 5(n) (noting that "[t]he cost of the arbitration proceedings, including the Arbitrator's fees and expenses, shall be shared equally among the parties"). Since baseball's final-offer system creates results that are much more predictable than hockey's version, these known procedural costs of arbitration make actually proceeding to arbitration that much more illogical. For example, if a player demands a $1 million salary and his club offers $500,000, baseball arbitrators will rule for either one or the other salary figure. With the known economic costs of arbitration (i.e., paying for the arbitrators, discovery, and travel costs to and from the arbitration), both parties' incentives favor settlement. On the other hand, in an NHL arbitration without the final-offer system, the outcome of arbitration is much less predictable, so the parties may be more willing to invest greater amounts of money in obtaining a potentially favorable arbitration result. In addition, the cost of NHL arbitrations, which utilize only one arbitrator, should be lower than the expense of MLB arbitrations, which require a three-arbitrator panel. However, NHL arbitrations require full opinions and justifiable awards, so arbitrators who handle NHL cases typically demand higher remuneration per arbitration. Symposium, Sports Law and Alternative Dispute Resolution, 3 CARDOZO J. CONFLICT RESOL. 1 (2001), http://www.cardozojcr.com/vol3no1/symposia.html (relating that hockey arbitrations result in higher pay for the arbitrator/symposium participant than do baseball arbitrations). Another reason for settling before going to arbitration is a "desire to avoid a public exchange of numbers." Brackin, *supra* note 155, at 4C. Up to a certain deadline, the two sides can negotiate in private. *Id.* Once that deadline passes, the offers of the clubs and the demands of the players become public. *Id.* As with any negotiation with potentially high media and public interest, privacy can play a large role in these pre-arbitration negotiations. *Id.*

160. Lindsay, *supra* note 137, at SPORTS.

161. Tom Verducci et al., *The 20 Great Tipping Points; Many of the Most Important Events in Sports over the Past 50 Years Happened Far from any Field or Arena. Let the Countdown begin . . .,* SPORTS ILLUSTRATED, Sept. 27, 2004, at 114, 119.

162. *Id.* Sports Illustrated ranked the birth of free agency in professional sports as one of the most important events in all of sports from 1954 to 2004. *Id.* The history of free agency in baseball traces its roots back to Curt Flood, a baseball player who made $90,000 in 1970 for playing for the St. Louis Cardinals. *Id.* In 1970, baseball's reserve clause tied players to teams, and players had no power to choose for whom they played or how much money they made. *Id.* The Cardinals attempted to trade Flood to Philadelphia, and Flood challenged the trade and the reserve clause on anti-trust grounds. *Id.* The case went all the way to the Supreme Court, which ruled against Flood and preserved the reserve clause's exemption from anti-trust laws. Flood v. Kuhn, 407 U.S. 258 (1972). A few years later, in 1975, free agency was born through the Messersmith-McNally Arbitration. Nick Acocella, Flood of Free Agency, ESPN Classic, http://espn.go.com/classic/biography/s/Flood Curt.html (last visited Dec. 17, 2005). Dave McNally, a four-time twenty-game-winning pitcher from the Baltimore Orioles, earned $100,000 in 1974 before being traded to the Montreal Expos. Abu Abraham, *Deaths of Note,* CHARLESTON DAILY MAIL (W. VA.), Dec. 3, 2002, at P3C. The Expos offered him $125,000 in 1975, but McNally thought he was worth more. *Id.* He refused to sign with the Expos and instead filed a grievance with Andy Messersmith of the L.A. Dodgers and the Major League Baseball Players Association. *Id.* The arbitrator in the grievance, Peter Seitz, ruled in favor of the players, thereby killing the reserve clause and ushering in the era of free agency on

December 23, 1975. *Id.* In 1998, Congress passed the "Curt Flood Act," which partly removed baseball's exemption from federal anti-trust law. *See* J. Philip Calabrese, *Recent Legislation: Antitrust and Baseball,* 36 HARV. J. ON LEGIS. 531, 540 (1999). Unrestricted free agency began in the NHL in 1994. Damien Cox, *Top 5 Things NHL, Union Should Say (But Won't),* TORONTO STAR, Sept. 25, 2004, at E2. The NFL instituted free agency for the first time in 1993. *Cornerbacks Pick Off Biggest Pay Increases of Any Position,* BUFFALO NEWS, Feb. 15, 2004, at C8.

163. Free agency has given players the power to bargain for higher salaries by removing the reserve clause's barrier to the free market. Jones, *supra* note 66, at 1C (noting that unrestricted free agency constitutes "a free-market system . . . where owners could outbid one another for players," causing salaries to go "through the roof"). But *see* Dave Sheinin, *This Winter, Free Agents See Less Green,* WASH. POST, Jan. 31, 2004, at D1 (claiming that "the size and length of player contracts have fallen for a second straight offseason"). Due to an apparent decrease in free agency market power, the MLBPA began investigating the owners' "negotiating practices" to see whether they are illegally conspiring to "keep salaries low." *Id.* In the 1980s, MLB owners were actually found guilty of such conspiracy and ordered to pay a $280 million penalty. *Id.* When free agency started in the NFL in 1993, 132 unrestricted free agents signed fresh contracts worth an average of $1.227 million, which represented a 231% increase from the year before. Kimberly Jones & Steve Politi, *Cap I$ King: Patriots, Eagles Master NFL Salary System,* NEWHOUSE NEWS SERVICE (WASH. D.C.), Jan. 31, 2005, at SPORTS, available at LEXIS News Library, NHSNWS File. In that one season, the average NFL salary rose $104,000 to $600,000. *Id.* "The highest [team] payroll in 1992 was $31 million. Two years later, that was the minimum payroll." *Id.*

164. In 2005, Adam Dunn of the Cincinnati Reds received the MLB's highest pay raise from arbitration, as he netted a 934% increase to $4.6 million from $445,000. *Sports Shorts—Red Sox to Issue 500 Series Rings,* THE PROVIDENCE J. (R.I.), Feb. 20, 2005, at C12. The eighty-nine baseball players who went to arbitration in 2005 averaged a pay increase of 123% from those hearings. *Id.*

165. Kulfan, *supra* note 8, at 6G. On the other hand, the NBA and the NFL both have salary caps. *Id.* As of 2005, the NBA had a "soft cap," which meant that the cap is calculated "as a percentage of league income," and there are "various free-agent exemptions." *Id.* In 2003–04, the NBA cap figured out to $43.9 million, but the exemptions made the average expenditure $59 million. *Id.* This means that each NBA team could not spend more than $43.9 million on players' salaries in 2003–04, but the "softness" of the cap caused the average team to spend $59 million on salaries that year. *Id.* In 2004, the NFL had a hard cap set at 64.8% of "defined gross league revenues." *Id.* In that year, the maximum each team could spend on salaries was $80.6 million. *Id.* That year, the NFL also had a salary floor, which was $67.3 million. *Id.*

166. Both total yearly attendance and total annual revenues of the MLB and NHL reveal the disparity between the popularity of the two leagues. The MLB attracted a record-high 73,022,969 fans to see games in 2004. Collene Kane, *The Spector of Steroids,* CINCINNATI ENQUIRER, Jan. 16, 2005, at 14B. The NHL's total attendance for 2004 was about 20 million. Kevin Paul DuPont, *This Union Could Use a Few More 'Yes' Men,* BOSTON GLOBE, Feb. 20, 2005, at C11 (quoting interviews with NHL Commissioner Gary Bettman in which he "referred to the total attendance [of the 2004 NHL season]" as being "some 20 million"). Although there are 162 baseball games in a regular season compared to hockey's eighty-two, the total attendance for the two leagues is not even close. Compare MLB Team-by-Team Schedule 2005, http://mlb.mlb.com /NASApp/mlb/mlb/schedule/team by team.jsp (last visited Dec. 17,

2005) (showing that each team plays 162 games during baseball's regular season), with NHL.com, Teams, http://nhl.com /lineups/team/index.html (last visited Dec. 17, 2005) (including team schedules with eighty-two regular season matches). Baseball was also the most popular spectator sport among North Americans in 2004, with over 120 million observers attending MLB, minor league, and college baseball games. Paul Grimaldi, *Still Hot,* PROVIDENCE JOURNAL (R.I.), Jan. 1, 2005, at B1. Just under 60 million people attended NHL, minor league, and college hockey games in that same year. *Id.*

167. *See supra* Part III(C).

168. As such, the rest of this Note will build on the discussion of the MLB's final-offer system and focus almost exclusively on the NHL.

169. Even among NHL players and owners, their focus typically has been on baseball's style of arbitration. Larry Brooks, *Union, NHL Set to Talk,* N.Y. POST, Dec. 9, 2004, at 104. In the final stages of negotiations between the players' union and the owners before the cancellation of the 2004–05 season, the NHLPA offered to change the NHL's arbitration system to mirror the "final offer (either/or) system" of the MLB. *Id.*

170. Abrams, *supra* note 91, at 146.

171. Adrian Dater, *Changes Needed to Save NHL,* DENVER POST, Feb. 15, 2005, at D1 (highlighting the history of the NHL and its labor system); CBA FAQs, *supra* note 29.

172. NHL CBA, *supra* note 73, at art. 12.

173. *Id.* at art. 12, § 1(c).

174. *Id.* at art. 12, §§ 2(b), 6. After the arbitration concluded and the parties knew the arbitration award, the club could, according to the strict guidelines of CBA Article 12.6, refuse to accept the arbitration and allow the player to approach other teams as a free agent. *Id.*

175. *See* NHL Schedules, http://nhl.com/onthefly/schedules/index.html (last visited Dec. 17, 2005) (listing NHL games for the 2005–06 season from October to June).

176. NHL CBA, *supra* note 73, at art. 12, § 3.

177. *Id.* at art. 12 § 1(a) (stating that only "a player is eligible to elect salary arbitration"). This has been a major point of contention between the owners and the union. Alan Hahn, *NHL Lockout; Last Minute to Play . . .; Today is Likely Final Shot for League, Union to Save NHL Season,* NEWSDAY (N.Y.), Feb. 13, 2005, at B13. In its final CBA offer to the NHLPA before canceling the 2004-05 season, the NHL proposed a "two-way [arbitration] system in which a restricted free agent can file for arbitration or a team can take a restricted free agent to arbitration." *Id.*

178. *Id.* at art. 12, § 5(b).

179. *Id.*

180. *Id.*

181. *Id.*

182. *Id.*

183. NHL CBA, *supra* note 73, at art. 12, § 5(b).

184. *Id.* at art. 12, § 5(f), These pieces of evidence also include the following: (1) "the overall performance . . . of the Player in the previous season or seasons," (2) "the number of games played by the Player" and "his injuries or illnesses during the preceding seasons," (3) "the length of service of the Player in the League and/or with the Club," (4) "the overall contribution of the Player to the competitive success or failure of his Club," (5) "any special qualities of leadership or public appeal," (6) "the overall performance in the previous season or seasons of any player(s) who is alleged to be comparable

to the party Player," and (7) "the Compensation of any player(s) who is alleged to be comparable to the party Player." *Id.*

185. *Id.*

186. Abrams, *supra* note 91, at 146. Theoretically, NHL arbitrators were bound to the final-offer system of the MLB, the market value of comparable players could play a less important role. In reality, MLB and NHL players are motivated to initiate arbitration based on the performances and salaries of comparable players. Both MLB and NHL arbitrators rely heavily on data regarding comparable players. *See* NHL CBA, *supra* note 73, at art. 12,§ 5(m)(2)(e) (detailing that the arbitrator's decision must include "identification of any comparable(s) relied on"); *see also* 2003–2006 Basic Agreement between the MLB and MLBPA, *supra* note 107 (holding that "the criteria [for deciding an arbitration] will be . . . comparative baseball salaries").

187. In an MLB arbitration, the decision of the arbitrator is relatively easy. The arbitrator picks one or the other number, and has no obligation to explain his or her decision. Under the old NHL CBA, the arbitrator was not bound by the either/or element of the MLB's final-offer system, so he or she could have settled on any salary figure. NHL CBA, *supra* note 73, at art. 12, § 5(m). That the arbitrator had to explain his or her decision in a formal opinion was the limiting factor. *Id.* at art. 12, § 5(m)(ii)(e).

188. NHL analyst and retired coach Pierre McGuire described arbitration's affect on players' salaries in the following way: "[e]verything just became a big apples to apples thing—and I don't blame the players at all for doing it—they went to their GMs [general managers] and said, 'Hey, that guy got so and so; I'm as good as he is, I want that.'" Dater, *supra* note 171, at D1. McGuire added: "A lot of owners said to themselves, 'Hey, I've got seats to fill and games to win, I have to give him the money.' It all just became a self-fulfilling prophecy that wouldn't stop." *Id.* Once a player receives a higher salary, all comparable players then demand to be paid the same as him, and salaries across the League increase accordingly. *Id.* Then, one of those players has an outstanding year and demands a pay increase. *Id.* That player receives his raise, and the cycle starts all over again, continuously ratcheting up the League's salaries. *Id.*

189. Comparable players' salaries make up just one of many pieces of evidence submitted in an NHL arbitration under the old CBA. NHL CBA, *supra* note 73, at art. 12, § 5(f)(ii) (addressing admissible evidence). However, all of these pieces of evidence are meaningless without a reference point, and comparable players' statistics, including salaries, provided that reference point. For example, arbitrators had to have some vantage point to assess the value of "the overall performance" of a player. *Id.* Without comparable players' salaries and performances, NHL arbitrators would have had no framework with which to craft their decisions.

190. *Id.* at art. 12, § 5(m).

191. Compare *id.* at art. 12, § 5, (referring to "the Arbitrator" and "the decision of the Arbitrator"), with 2003–2006 Basic Agreement between the MLB and MLBPA, *supra* note 107, at art. 6(F)(7) (providing that "[a]ll cases shall be assigned to three-arbitrator panels").

192. NHL CBA, *supra* note 73, at art. 12, § 5(m)(i). While those comparables may come from players in smaller markets, the overwhelming incentive of the players was to present evidence of a large market player who made more money than, but who performed roughly on par with, the player whose salary was in dispute. NHL arbitrators did not pick what the evidence at the hearing would be; rather, the parties presented all of the evidence upon which the arbitrators had to rely to make their decisions. *Id.* § 5. This was another reason for the often large disparity between the clubs' offers and the players' demands.

193. Abrams, *supra* note 91, at 146-47.

194. Michael H. LeRoy & Peter Feuille, *Judicial Enforcement of Predispute Arbitration Agreements: Back to the Future,* 18 OHIO ST. J. ON DISP. RESOL. 249, 265 (2003) (noting that "the method of an arbitrator's appointment caused courts to vacate awards" and that "[e]ven if such selection did not bias the arbitrator, courts viewed it as an inherent conflict of interest").

195. NHL CBA, *supra* note 73, at art. 12, § 2(e)(ix).

196. 2003–2006 Basic Agreement between the MLB and MLBPA, *supra* note 107, at art. VI(F)(7). "In the event they are unable to agree by January 1 in any year, they jointly shall request that the American Arbitration Association furnish them lists of prominent, professional arbitrators." *Id.* Once the parties had that list, they alternated in "striking names" from the list until a mutually agreeable group remained. *Id.*

197. *Id.*

198. Sarah Rudolph Cole, *A Funny Thing Happened on the Way to the (Alternative) Forum: Reexamining Alexander v. Gardner-Denver in the Wake of Gilmer v. Interstate/Johnson Lane Corp.,* 1997 BYU L. REV. 591, 619-24 (1997) (relating repeat-players' advantages in negotiating contracts); Mark Galanter, *Why the "Haves" Come out Ahead: Speculations on the Limits of Legal Change,* 9 LAW & SOC'Y REV. 95, 110-12 (1974). *See generally* Lisa B. Bingham, On Repeat Players, Adhesion Contracts, and the Use of Statistics on *Judicial Review of Employment Arbitration Awards,* 29 MCGEORGE L. REV. 223, 258-59 (1998). The concern is, if one party always picks the arbitrator(s), the arbitrator(s) will tend to favor that party. Additionally, a repeat-player has an institutional knowledge advantage over the arbitration neophyte.

199. NHL CBA, *supra* note 73, at art. 12, § 2(e)(ix); 2003–2006 Basic Agreement between the MLB and MLBPA, *supra* note 107, at art. VI(F)(7).

200. NHL CBA, *supra* note 73, at art. 12, § 5(n). "The cost of the arbitration proceedings, including the Arbitrator's fees and expenses, shall be shared equally among the parties." *Id.*; 2003–2006 Basic Agreement between the MLB and MLBPA, *supra* note 107, at art. VI(F)(11). "The Player and Club shall divide equally the costs of the hearing." *Id.*

201. In a repeat-player problem, the advantage/bias arises when one party is constant (i.e., the "repeat-player") and the other party arbitrates once or only a few times. Although the teams are individual parties to arbitrations in both the MLB and the NHL (under the old CBA), they are "repeat-players" who deal with arbitrations on a yearly basis. The players also file for arbitration as individuals, but they receive representation from the players' union, which is also a "repeat-player." NHL CBA, *supra* note 73, at art. 12, § 5(d) (stipulating that a "[p]layer shall be represented at the hearing by the NHLPA"); 2003–2006 Basic Agreement between the MLB and MLBPA, *supra* note 107, at art. VI(F)(3).

202. NHL CBA, *supra* note 73, at art. 12, § 6.

203. NHL arbitrations are binding unless the team walks away. *Id.*

204. *See* Dworkin, *supra* note 123, at 78.

205. NHL CBA, *supra* note 73, at art. 12, § 6.

206. *Id.* at art. 12, § 6(a).

207. *Id.*

208. *Id.* at art. 12, § 6(c)(i).

209. *Id.* at art. 12, § 6(c)(ii).

210. *Id.* at art. 12, § 6(b).

211. *Id.*

212. By choosing to arbitrate for a one-year contract, the franchise could still walk away from the arbitrator's decision, if the club so chose. *Id.*

213. NHL CBA, *supra* note 73, at art. 12,§ 6(d).

214. *Id.*

215. In 2004, the Buffalo Sabres had the most players file for arbitration, eight. TSN.ca, 2004 Arbitration Cases, http://www.tsn.ca/nhl/feature .asp?fid=7545 (last visited Dec. 17, 2005). The cases of only two of those players, Martin Biron and Daniel Briere, ended in actual arbitration. *Id.* The six others settled before their hearings. *Id.* Given the low cap on a team's ability to walk away from the arbitrators' decisions, a team with eight potential arbitrations must exercise the walk-away right with the other arbitrations in mind.

216. *Id.*

217. *Id.*

218. *Id.*

219. *Id.*

220. Muskat, *supra* note 157.

221. *See id.*

222. MLB.com, 2004 Salary Arbitration Figures, http://mlb.mlb.com /NASApp/mlb/mlb/news/mlb news.jsp?ymd=20040120&content id=629358&vkey=news mlb nd&fext=.jsp (last visited Dec. 17, 2005).

223. 2004 Arbitration Cases, *supra* note 215. . .

224. Brooks, *supra* note 169, at 104 (noting that the NHL owners tried to alter the CBA to implement a MLB-like final-offer system in the NHL).

225. CBC Sports, Arbitration, http://www.cbc.ca/sports/indepth/cba /issues/arbitration.html (last visited Dec. 17, 2005).

226. *Id.*

227. *Id.*

228. 2004 Arbitration Cases, *supra* note 215. . . .

229. Sassone, *supra* note 61, at Sports 1.

230. Kulfan, *supra* note 8, at 6G. The highest paid player in baseball in 2004 was Manny Ramirez, who made $22.5 million, while his NHL counterparts were Peter Forsberg and Jaromir Jagr, who each earned $11 million. *Id.* In the 2005 baseball off-season, Roger Clemens, age forty-two, became the highest-paid pitcher in MLB history. Guy Curtright, *Clemens Gets His Payday,* ATLANTA J.-CONST., Jan. 22, 2005, at 3D. He filed for arbitration, asking for $22 million, while his team, the Houston Astros, offered a figure of $13.5. *Id.* The two sides settled, however, for a one-year, $18 million deal. *Id.* The breakdown of Clemens's salary reveals the staggering state of players' salaries in professional sports. *Id.* If Clemens matches his performance from 2004, he would make $1 million per win in 2005. Put differently, he would make $83,994 for every inning he pitches. *Id.* This story is a great example of how baseball's salary arbitration system would fail to ameliorate the NHL's woes. Clemens and the Astros settled, as the final-offer system encourages participants to do. However, the result was a record-breaking salary figure. *Id.*

231. Kulfan, *supra* note 8, at 6G.

232. As of December 18, 2005, the NHL had not released the text of the new CBA. *See* NHLPA.com, Collective Bargaining Agreement, http://www.nhlpa.com/CBA/index.asp (last visited Dec. 18, 2005) (noting that the "new collective bargaining agreement will be made available here in the near future"). Until the NHL released the full contents of the new CBA, it provided a website that highlights many of the CBA's important provisions. *See* CBA FAQs, *supra* note 29. As a result, this section will refer to the answers the NHL provided on that website, rather than referring to specific portions of the CBA. The wording of the CBA may differ from the NHL's CBA FAQs website, but the essential principles will likely be the same.

233. CBA FAQs, *supra* note 29.

234. *Id.*

235. *Id.* Since the beginning of salary arbitration, the NHL has had player-only election of salary arbitration. This right is somewhat limited; however, teams may elect to arbitrate the salaries of only two classes of players. *Id.*

236. *Id.*

237. *Id.*

238. CBA FAQs, *supra* note 29.

239. *Id.*

240. *Id.*

241. *Id.* The CBA limits teams' ability to do this only with players who earn more than $1.5 million in the previous year or those restricted free agents who qualify. *Id.*

242. *Id.* There was some speculation that the NHL would emerge from the lockout with a baseball-style final-offer system, but these predictions proved incorrect. Brooks, *supra* note 169, at 104 (noting that the NHL owners tried to alter the CBA to implement a MLB-like final-offer system in the NHL).

243. CBA FAQs, *supra* note 29. The other parts of the new CBA will likely have a minimal effect on, or be minimally affected by, salary arbitration.

244. *Id.*

245. *Id.*

246. *See* 2002–03 URO, *supra* note 27.

247. Loftus, *supra* note 54, at 47.

248. CBA FAQs, *supra* note 29.

249. 2002–03 URO, *supra* note 27.

250. *See supra* Part III.D.

251. CBA FAQs, *supra* note 29.

252. *Id.*

253. *Id.*

254. *Id.* The franchise's "payroll" includes all salaries, signing bonuses, and performance bonuses paid to players. *Id.* Except in the case of a bona fide long-term injury (injuries that sideline a player for a minimum of twenty-four days and ten games) to one or more of a team's players, team payrolls will never be permitted to be below the minimum or in excess of the maximum. *Id.* Teams at or near the upper limit that have players who incur a bona fide long-term injury are entitled to replace up to the full value of the injured player's NHL salary (even if such salary would result in the team's salary exceeding the cap). *Id.* The "replacement salary" does not count against the team's cap, but will count against the League-wide players' share. *Id.* Upon return of the injured player, the team must come into immediate compliance with the requirements of the payroll range. *Id.*

255. The lack of a salary cap was certainly the main failure of the previous CBA. Players' salaries exploded across the League from 1994–2004. Loftus, *supra* note 54, at 47. The League's average salary in 1994 was $560,000 and grew to $1.8 million by 2004. *Id.*

256. *See supra* Part III.D.

257. CBA FAQs, *supra* note 29. Under the new CBA, no player is eligible to contract for or receive in excess of twenty percent of his team's upper limit in total annual compensation (NHL salary plus signing, roster, reporting, and all performance bonuses). *Id.* Put in terms of the 2005–06 salary cap figures, the CBA prohibits players from contracting for total compensation in excess of $7.8 million in any year of his contract. *Id.* This represents a significant departure from the previous unlimited salary scheme of the old CBA. In 2004 alone, the two highest-paid NHLers, Peter Forsberg and Jaromir Jagr, earned $11 million each. Kulfan, *supra* note 8, at 6G. To bring these and other contracts in line with the new CBA, it eliminated all contracts signed for the 2004–05 season. CBA FAQs, *supra* note 29. The NHL essentially started the 2005–06 season with a clean slate.

258. *See supra* Part III.D.

259. CBA FAQs, *supra* note 29. The new CBA also sets the minimum League salary at $450,000 for the 2005–06 and 2006–07 seasons. *Id.* This provision will help to decrease the disparity between the highest-paid and lowest-paid players.

DEFLATIONARY SALARY MECHANISMS

THE NBA LUXURY TAX MODEL: A MISGUIDED REGULATORY REGIME

Richard A. Kaplan

INTRODUCTION

Professional team sports leagues have struggled for nearly half a century to develop effective economic regulatory mechanisms to govern their operations to the satisfaction of both team owners and players. Meeting that goal has proven quite difficult, as the division of league revenue raises issues between owners and players as well as among the members of each group individually.[1] In addition, league regulatory architects must contend with the call for "competitive balance," which posits that for a league to be financially successful, it must foster competitiveness among its member organizations.[2]

Revenue distribution was substantially less complicated during the early days of American professional team sports, as team owners essentially possessed unilateral power over the terms and conditions of the players' employment. One result of this dominance was the owner-imposed "reserve clause," which was used to depress players' salaries by forbidding players from negotiating with teams other than the ones that reserved them.[3] Economic regulation of this type became more contentious, however, with the advent of the players' unions in the 1960s and 1970s. After the Major League Baseball Players Association (MLBPA) and National Football League Players Association (NFLPA) both weakened their respective league's reserve clauses through arbitration and litigation in the mid-1970s,[4] leagues sought alternative ways to control costs through player movement limitations.[5] Even these models of restriction—such as requiring teams that sign a free agent to provide the player's previous team with player or draft pick compensation—were constrained further as the strength of the players'

unions grew. New and innovative regulatory systems were eventually needed to assuage the growing economic concerns of players and owners alike.

One modern solution has been to adopt a "luxury tax." Pioneered by Major League Baseball (MLB) in the mid-1990s and . . . adopted by the National Basketball Association (NBA), the luxury tax as it currently exists is a penalty imposed on teams that spend above a collectively bargained level.[6] The luxury tax is an attractive regulatory device because, in theory, it addresses the concerns of all parties. For owners, depending on the level of taxation, the luxury tax can be viewed as a quasi-salary cap; it may serve as a roadblock to continued spending. For players, the tax represents freedom from a salary cap and still offers the promise of unlimited salary growth. And finally, competitive balance may be achieved through a luxury tax regime by punishing big-spending teams and perhaps even redistributing the money collected to less affluent teams.

This Note explores the implications of the NBA luxury tax model (NBA Model), which packs the sort of regulatory punch that potentially makes it an example for other leagues to follow. This robust model, a complicated combination of escrow, tax, and distribution components, encourages teams to spend less on player salaries with the goal of increasing the profitability of the league as a whole.[7] This Note demonstrates how the NBA Model, although successful in discouraging some team player salary expenditures, creates perverse incentives that in fact lead to greater disparity in team spending and frustrate the objectives of other important aspects of the NBA's current collective bargaining agreement. These problems combine to produce a perpetual cycle where free-spending owners reap the benefits of better and cheaper talent while avoiding tax assessments. This sequence is the result of a number of imperfections in the design of the NBA Model, including a wildly inconsistent marginal tax rate.

Part I of this Note traces the various attempts to regulate the economics of professional team sports prior to the arrival of the luxury tax. Part II explores the operation of the MLB and NBA luxury taxes, including an examination of their corresponding tax distribution systems. . . .

I. THE HISTORICAL DEVELOPMENT OF ECONOMIC REGULATORY MECHANISMS WITHIN PROFESSIONAL SPORTS LEAGUES

The primary mechanisms employed to internally regulate professional team sports leagues can be parceled into three major categories of both direct and indirect salary regulation: (1) restricting free agency; (2) "capping" team and individual player salaries; and (3) taxing team and individual player salaries.[8] A brief review of these first two devices provides an understanding not only of what regulatory models have been tested, but also highlights the problems they have wrought that the third mechanism, the luxury tax, is intended to address.

Part I.A traces the development of restrictions on free agency, the original form of player market regulation. Teams have restricted players' free agency in a variety of ways over the last century and still do so in a mixture of forms in all four major professional sports.[9] Beginning in the early 1980s, some leagues embarked upon a different approach, instituting limits on the amount each team could allocate toward player salaries. This concept was taken one step further in the 1990s, when leagues began restricting the levels at which individual players could be paid. These more modern forms of economic regulation are called "salary caps," and are detailed more fully in Part I.B.

A. Restricting Free Agency

The oldest method of limiting player salary growth in American professional team sports is restricting market competition for players. In a pure market setting, players can freely offer their services to each team and create competition among those teams to achieve the highest possible compensation. By instituting restrictions on player movement in an attempt to regulate supply—e.g., permitting players to become unrestricted free agents[10] only when certain conditions are met—teams can limit the ability of players to extract their pure market value, potentially driving down the overall growth of salaries.[11] The market can also be regulated from the demand side by discouraging teams from participating in the market through mechanisms that require teams to provide some form of compensation when they sign a free agent from another team.

1. The Reserve Clause.—The first attempt to curb the market through free agency restriction was the reserve clause. The reserve clause was shaped by professional baseball in the late nineteenth century,[12] as team owners were able to protect team rights to certain players permanently so that no other team could negotiate with them.[13] Players

therefore either played for the team that reserved them or were forbidden from playing in the league at all.

Given this significant advantage for team owners, it was not long before professional basketball, football, and hockey leagues employed varying forms of the reserve clause.[14] Oddly enough, the reserve system had the support of the players, who were convinced by management that the reserving power was necessary to maintain the economic viability of the game.[15] It was not until the rise of the players' unions that the athletes' naivete faded, and they realized how such systems worked against their earning power.[16] Baseball's reserve clause, for example, was eviscerated by arbitration and subsequent collective bargaining with the MLBPA in the mid-1970s.[17]

2. The Rozelle Rule and Its Offshoots.—The NFL encountered problems with its own reserve system ten years before baseball's was dismantled.[18] As a result, NFL Commissioner Pete Rozelle developed what widely became known as the "Rozelle Rule," which was designed to restrain player salaries by empowering the Commissioner to award compensation to a team losing its own free agent by the team signing that free agent.[19] The result was striking: Between 1963 and 1974, of the 176 players to play out their option years, a paltry thirty-four signed with other teams, and only in four of those cases was compensation necessary.[20] After feeling the harsh effect of the Rozelle Rule, the NFLPA brought a series of legal actions against the NFL, weakening the Rule in one federal district court,[21] considerably circumscribing it in another,[22] and finally getting it struck down by the Eighth Circuit in 1976.[23]

The demise of the reserve system and Rozelle Rule led all four leagues to develop more limited forms of restricted free agency. These systems run the gamut in terms of the role they play within league regulatory systems overall. For example, the NFL . . . utilizes a mild form of restricted free agency that only affects a couple of players per team per season.[24] On the other end of the spectrum is the National Hockey League (NHL), which employs a sophisticated restricted free agency compensation system as its chief mechanism for limiting player salaries.[25] Not unlike the Rozelle Rule, the NHL requires compensation for many (but not all) of the free agents signed by another team—using the player's age and playing experience to determine the compensation required on the part of the signing team.[26]

3. The Entry Draft.—In addition to the reserve clause and Rozelle Rule, leagues also have experimented with less explicitly severe—yet perhaps equally effective—means of limiting player salaries through other mechanisms for restricting player movement. The entry draft is one derivative of the reserve clause that still exists in every major professional team sport. Prior to the season, each league conducts a draft whereby teams select new players to join the league.[27] The draft resembles the old reserve system by enabling teams to acquire exclusive rights to negotiate with players, thereby seriously constricting the players' ability to

seek compensation in a competitive market.[28] To temper this restriction, however, each league designates a limit to the number of years this reservation is enforceable.[29]

B.   Salary Caps

The most effective way to temper labor costs is simply to impose a cap on the amount of money teams can spend either for players individually or their roster as a whole.[30] . . . Team Cap models are based on intricate revenue-sharing schemes where a specified percentage of league revenue is codified as a ceiling on aggregate player salaries for the following season. Individual salary caps (Individual Caps), on the other hand, are currently employed by the NBA and NHL to offer a more limited avenue to team owners for curtailing spending on individual players.

1. The Team Cap.—The NBA pioneered the Team Cap in its collective bargaining agreement with the National Basketball Players Association (NBPA) in the spring of 1983.[32] In its original incarnation, the NBA Team Cap was set at the greater of either a predetermined fixed sum[33] or 53% of the league's gross revenue minus player benefits divided by the number of teams in the league.[34] To this day, the main feature of the NBA Team Cap is that it is "soft" (Soft Cap), meaning that there are a number of "exceptions" teams may employ to spend beyond the Team Cap.[35] These are potent exceptions. . .

Under the. . . NBA collective bargaining agreement (1999 NBA CBA), the NBA Team Cap is derived from a predetermined percentage of "Basketball Related Income" (BRI), which is a measure of the aggregate revenue produced by the league and its teams from sources such as ticket sales, corporate sponsorships, and broadcast revenue.[37] The Team Cap is established by taking 48.04% [*Ed. Note: The percentage is now 51% as per the most recent NBA CBA*] of "Projected BRI,"[38] deducting "Projected Benefits"[39] for the coming season, and dividing that number by the number of teams in the league.[40] . . .

In 1993, the NFL became the second league to institute a Team Cap after years of acrimonious dealings between the league and the NFLPA.[42] [*Ed. Note: The NFL salary cap expired prior to the 2010 season and future iterations depend on the results of the subsequent collective bargaining negotiation.*] Although the NFL's version of the Team Cap borrows the NBA's revenue-sharing concept, it is a "hard" or "actual" cap (Hard Cap), meaning that teams cannot exceed the designated threshold by any amount at any time. In exchange for accepting this rigid salary restriction,[43] NFL players receive a greater formal percentage of league revenue than their NBA counterparts.[44]

2. Individual Salary Caps.—For a league unable to compel its players to agree to a Hard Cap, a backdoor means of achieving some measure of salary control is to limit the amount of money that may be paid to individual players. The NBA and NHL both employ Individual Caps

for rookies' salaries (Rookie Cap),[45] . . . *[and]* a generally prescribed maximum salary applicable to veterans (Veteran Cap).[46] The Rookie Caps were instituted as a two-tiered attack on player salaries. First, such caps were specifically aimed at slowing the rate of escalating salaries for young players who had yet to prove their worth in the professional sports context. Second, when first-year players receive large payouts in a system without a Hard Cap, the overall market for player salaries is driven upward.

The Veteran Cap also has a two-prong effect. Much like the Rookie Cap, the Veteran Cap curtails spending on player salaries by limiting the amount a team spends on any one player's salary.[47] In addition, by creating a ceiling on the highest revenue-producing players, the market will readjust downward, and nonmaximum salary players will be measured against those whose salaries have been artificially limited by the collective bargaining agreement.[48]

These Individual Caps, along with the Team Caps and restrictions on player movement, have been designed to foster an acceptable economic and legal balance between owners and players. Only the NFL, however, notable for its relatively weak players' union and exceptionally profitable product, has managed a modicum of labor peace under its economic regulatory system.[49] The three other major professional sports leagues, on the other hand, are still struggling to achieve stable regulatory regimes. In searching for new ways to address these issues, MLB, [and the] the NBA . . . have turned to the idea of taxing high-spending teams in an effort to appease both owners and players.[50]

II.   THE LUXURY TAX

The luxury tax, an idea that first materialized during the labor negotiations of both MLB and the NHL in 1994,[51] was first realized in the 1997 MLB collective bargaining agreement (1997 MLB CBA).[52] Today, differing forms of luxury taxes exist in both MLB and the NBA. While these two versions of the luxury tax have varying components, their conceptual frameworks share one major feature: The entity taxed is required to pay a specified percentage of the margin by which its spending exceeds a mandated threshold.[53]

There are a number of ways in which the luxury tax concept attempts to meet the challenges facing professional team sports' economic regulatory systems. First, when owners are unable to secure a Hard Cap, the best substitute may be taxation's near-certain drag on players' salaries.[54] In essence, if teams are forced to pay back to the league—perhaps even to other teams[55]—some percentage of what they pay their players, they will be encouraged to rework traditional formulas for assessing the marginal benefits of player signings.[56] Second, players, along with the minority of owners who have the ability and willingness to outspend other owners, appreciate that the luxury tax is not an absolute ceiling on salaries. Third, leagues argue that league-wide revenue will rise under a luxury tax system because it promotes greater competitive balance.[57]

. . . .

A. The Two Incarnations of MLB's Luxury Tax

After highly contentious negotiations beginning in 1994 and lasting until 1996,[58] MLB and the MLBPA finally came to an agreement[59] over acceptable salary control mechanisms, including the first ever professional sports luxury tax.[60] The tax operated based on an adjustable threshold level that determined which teams were deemed to be overspenders.[61] The tax adjusted by permitting the minimum threshold to be raised such that a maximum of only five teams could exceed it in any given year.[62] The tax was to be assessed for only three of the agreement's five years, at a minimum total payroll of $51 million in 1997, $55 million in 1998, and $58.9 million in 1999.[63] In terms of the level of taxation, there was a flat rate of 35% charged on each dollar a team spent above the threshold in 1997 and 1998 and 34% in 1999.[64] The proceeds of the luxury tax payments were divided in several ways. The first $17 million was earmarked for the League revenue sharing plan,[65] at least $3 million to the Industry Growth Fund (IGF),[66] and up to $2.5 million to teams overcharged during previous luxury tax calculations.[67]

As one might expect, the taxes were rather "soft."[68] For example, the greatest tax imposed in 1998 was on the Baltimore Orioles, whose $79.5 million payroll earned them a meager $3.1 million tax, or 3.9% of their aggregate player salary expenditures.[69] The adjustable mechanism kicked in because the midpoint between the fifth and sixth teams was approximately $70 million,[70] and as a result, every player the Orioles signed over that mark cost the team 135% of his actual salary.

In the . . . 2002 MLB CBA, the two sides again agreed on a luxury tax, although this time it has a different name and structure. As opposed to being called a "luxury tax" as it was in the 1997 MLB CBA,[71] the updated article XXIII is now called the "Competitive Balance Tax."[72] In addition, the adjustable threshold mechanism was eliminated. The tax threshold is now simply a flat number—$117 million in 2003, $120.5 million in 2004, $128 million in 2005, and $136.5 million in 2006.[73] [*Ed. Note: The thresholds were set at $148 million in 2007, $155 million in 2008, $162 million in 2009, $170 million in 2010, and $178 million in 2011.*] In terms of the percentage that offenders are taxed, in 2003 the tax rate was a straight 17.5% for every dollar spent above the threshold.[74] Beginning in 2004, however, different rates apply, depending on whether a team is a first-time, second-time, and/or consecutive-year offender.[75] The tax distribution system also was altered, with the first $5 million of tax proceeds held in reserve for any tax refunds based on after-calculation adjustments,[76] 50% of the remaining

proceeds used to fund active player benefits,[77] 25% designated for "projects and other efforts to develop baseball players in countries where organized high school baseball is not played,"[78] and 25% once again dedicated to the IGF.[79]

The early returns on the 2002 version of the MLB tax demonstrate its utter ineffectiveness.[80] The first year of the new taxation system, 2003, produced only one taxpayer, the New York Yankees.[81] From this data it might appear that the taxation system was in fact effective because teams were forced to hold down their salary expenditures, leaving only the Yankees in violation. However, only three teams spent within 10% of the $117 million mark during the previous season,[82] suggesting that most teams' decisions to stay below the tax threshold in 2003 were based less on the impending imposition of the luxury tax than they were on preexisting economic considerations.

B. The History of the NBA Luxury Tax

The more intriguing of the two taxation systems is the NBA Model. While MLB's luxury tax model is quite limited, the one currently employed by the NBA clearly has been designed and implemented to have a major impact on the league's overall regulatory regime.

The current version of the NBA luxury tax was the product of two rounds of collective bargaining. The first round occurred in 1994–1995, after the previous collective bargaining agreement expired and the season was played under a "no strike/no lockout" agreement. These negotiations were extremely contentious, causing one union chief to resign[83] and another almost to lose his constituency altogether.[84] The main source of disagreement was over the league's desire to implement a luxury tax. Given the players' conviction on the issue, the two sides eventually reached an agreement that left the luxury tax behind.[85]

Luxury tax consideration was not dormant for long, as the NBA owners, who voted to reopen the collective bargaining agreement during the 1997–1998 season,[86] locked out the players on July 1, 1998, with intentions of garnering greater cost-control mechanisms.[87] The players' share of BRI under the Soft Cap regime had risen to 57%.[88] This led the owners to stand firm on their demands, resulting in the first work stoppage involving cancelled games in the NBA's labor history.[89] When a deal was finally reached in January 1999 (1999 NBA CBA), in addition to limiting individual player salaries[90] and gaining longer-term commitments from rookies to the teams holding their rights,[91] the NBA's biggest achievement was its coveted luxury tax system.[92]

C. How the NBA Luxury Tax System Works

The NBA luxury tax operates as part of a larger regulatory scheme called the Escrow and Team Payment (or tax) system.[93] To fully comprehend the NBA Escrow and tax system, it first is necessary to understand its conceptual foundations. Not only did the NBA set out to limit player salaries as a general matter, it chose to do so in a way that approximated its preferred regulatory mechanism: the Hard Cap. . . .

With the owners' desire to limit player salaries to a specified percentage of league revenues and the players' steadfast rejection of a Hard Cap, the two sides developed a creative mechanism aimed at further limiting the players' share of BRI while not quite using it as an absolute ceiling. From the league perspective, the Escrow and tax system is designed to serve both as a form of "insurance" against player salaries rising above a specified percentage of league revenue and as a penalty against free-spending teams. To accomplish this, the Escrow component dictates that, during each season in which there is a "Projected Overage," team owners withhold and put into escrow 10% [*Ed. Note: 9% is now held in escrow*] of all players' salaries.[94] At the conclusion of each season, if after calculating that season's BRI, final team salaries, and player benefits, it is determined that player salaries and benefits have exceeded a designated percentage of league revenues . . . (Escrow Threshold),[95] then the Escrow funds will be used to reimburse the owners to the point where the players' total salaries are reduced to that percentage. . . . The remaining escrowed money would be returned to the players relative to their individual contributions.

The Escrow has a ceiling, however, of 10% of the players' salaries and benefits.[96] Should the . . . Escrow not cover the "Overage" (i.e., the amount by which the players' share of BRI exceeds the designated percentage), the Escrow account would be exhausted and the luxury tax would be activated. . . . It is important to underscore that the tax is not assessed on teams merely exceeding the Team Cap figure . . . or even the Escrow Threshold number . . . ; rather the Penalty Threshold only becomes effective when player salaries and benefits exceed the escrowed money . . . and is only applied to teams whose expenditures exceed that same threshold.

The 1999 NBA CBA also sets forth the level at which Penalty Threshold violators are taxed. During negotiations, the NBA pushed for as much as a 200% tax[100] and settled for a 100% tax rate on any money spent by teams beyond the Penalty Threshold.[101] Therefore, if a team was $5 million over the . . . Penalty Threshold . . . , it would be assessed $5 million in taxes.

. . . .

Notes

1. For example, one major source of disagreement among team owners is whether to cap player salaries. While most teams advocate a "salary cap" system because it controls rising player salaries and helps equalize the commitment of resources to talent across a league's teams, *see infra* Part I.B, owners with greater resources generally prefer a system more closely resembling a free market so they can use their substantial wealth to outbid others for premier talent.

2. Those who believe that enhanced competitive balance positively affects revenue argue that, if a league's teams coordinate their economic behavior, they can maximize their revenue production by enabling even distribution of on-field, on-ice, or on-court success.

Without such cooperation, however, "teams in certain markets will systematically outbid others for talented players," allowing these teams to "systematically dominate league play," resulting in a "competitive imbalance [that] will reduce the quality and attractiveness of the league's product." Stephen F. Ross, *The Misunderstood Alliance Between Sports Fans, Players, and the Antitrust Laws*, 1997 U. ILL. L. REV. 519, 560; *see* Joseph P. Bauer, *Antitrust and Sports: Must Competition on the Field Displace Competition in the Marketplace?*, 60 TENN. L. REV. 263, 274-75 (1993) ("While the individual teams. . . can be competitors in a number of respects, some measure of cooperation is essential for success of the entire enterprise.").

It should be noted, however, that those who hold this view often assume that team spending regulation necessarily equalizes the level of each team's talent. One argument supporting that assumption is that big-market teams have wellsprings of revenue, thereby allowing them—in an unregulated market—to expend more revenue to attract the best players at the expense of small-market teams. *See* James Quirk & Rodney Fort, HARD BALL: THE ABUSE OF POWER IN PRO TEAM SPORTS 56-57 (1999) [hereinafter, Quirk & Fort, HARD BALL] (stating that some argue "the. . . lack of 'competitive balance' . . . leads to a fall in gate receipts at small-market teams as their won–lost records decline[], and might even lead to bankruptcy and exit from the league for some small-market teams"); Kevin E. Martens, *Fair or Foul? The Survival of Small-Market Teams in Major League Baseball*, 4 MARQ. SPORTS L.J. 323, 362-63 (1994) ("In an environment where large-market teams have the financial resources to attract the greatest number of quality free agents, small-market clubs must. . . operate at a competitive disadvantage."). At the very least, proponents of this theory argue that the ability of some teams to spend more on player salaries than others gives them "more margin for error" and therefore a better chance at success. Andrew Zimbalist, MAY THE BEST TEAM WIN 47 (2003) [hereinafter Zimbalist, MAY THE BEST TEAM WIN].

Others dispute these claims: "Empirical evidence rejects both the claim that a handful of rich teams systematically outbid their rivals for star players and the claim that dynasties result from an unrestrained labor market." Ross, *supra*, at 560-61; *see* Christopher D. Cameron & Michael J. Echevarria, *The Ploys of Summer: Antitrust, Industrial Distrust, and the Case Against a Salary Cap for Major League Baseball*, 22 FLA. ST. U. L. REV. 827, 853 (1995) ("The main problem with competitive balance theory is the lack of empirical evidence supporting it. . . . Indeed, all the evidence points in precisely the opposite direction: baseball enjoys remarkable competitive balance without a salary cap."); *see, e.g.,* Larry Brooks, *Owners' Claims Are Hot Air*, N.Y. POST, Jan. 4, 2004, at 81 (rebutting National Hockey League's (NHL) calls for increased competitive balance when "eight different teams have filled the last eight conference slots[,] . . . and only four [were] out of playoff contention [at mid-season]"). *See generally* Michael Lewis, MONEYBALL: THE ART OF WINNING AN UNFAIR GAME (2003) (chronicling success of perennially frugal Oakland Athletics).

One may be distrustful of league-based calls for greater competitive balance because they often correspond to a request for further salary regulation. *See* Robert C. Berry et al., LABOR RELATIONS IN PROFESSIONAL SPORTS 6-7 (1986) (declaring that leagues use mechanisms to regulate salaries "in the name of competitive balance" while those mechanisms not-so-coincidentally "restrict[] competitive bidding for players' services"). Regardless, this Note assumes that competitive balance is a goal of team owners in part because it is often the very aim for which they advocate. *See, e.g., Pre-Hearing Brief of Nat'l Basketball Ass'n at 6*, Nat'l Basketball Players Ass'n and Nat'l Basketball Ass'n (System Arbitrator 2002) (No. 02-01) (on file with the COLUMBIA LAW REVIEW) (calling competitive balance one of two of league's "broad objectives").

3. *See infra* notes 12-17 and accompanying text.

4. *See* Charles P. Korr, THE END OF BASEBALL AS WE KNEW IT: THE PLAYERS UNION, 1960-81, at 149-67 (2002) (detailing the "Messersmith Case," an arbitration case between Major League Baseball and its union, which resulted in dismantling of reserve clause).

5. *See infra* Part I.A.3.

6. A tax can also be placed on the revenue teams earn. *See, e.g.,* Basic Agreement Between the 30 Major League Clubs & Major League Baseball Players Association, Effective Sept. 30, 2002, art. XXIV, at 100 [hereinafter 2002 MLB CBA].

7. *See* Pre-Hearing Brief of Nat'l Basketball Ass'n at 6, Nat'l Basketball Players Ass'n (No. 02-01).

8. This list is not exhaustive—it only covers the most significant forms of regulation. For example, team revenue sharing, player-team salary arbitration, guaranteed versus non-guaranteed contracts, and limits on the number of total contract years available may influence the growth of player salaries. In the mid-1980s, MLB attempted to limit player salary growth through collusion, whereby owners jointly decided not to make bids for free agents. Quirk & Fort, HARD BALL, *supra* note 2, at 90-91; Gerald W. Scully, THE BUSINESS OF MAJOR LEAGUE BASEBALL 39-43 (1989) [hereinafter Scully, BUSINESS OF BASEBALL]; James B. Dworkin & Richard A. Posthuma, PROFESSIONAL SPORTS: COLLECTIVE BARGAINING IN THE SPOTLIGHT, IN COLLECTIVE BARGAINING IN THE PRIVATE SECTOR 217, 236-37 (Paul F. Clark et al. eds., 2002).

9. They are MLB, the NBA, the National Football League (NFL), and the NHL.

10. An "unrestricted" free agent is one for whom the original team has no matching rights and/or for whom no compensation is required. *See, e.g.,* NFL Collective Bargaining Agreement, Jan. 8, 2002 (as amended), art. I, 2(ah), at 6 [hereinafter 2002 NFL CBA] (stating that an unrestricted free agent is a player "who completes performance of his Player Contract, and who is no longer subject to any exclusive negotiating rights").

11. This is not to say that a "pure" market setting would yield net benefits for every player. For example, certain collectively bargained guarantees, such as a minimum allowable salary, enable some players to earn more than would otherwise be available if no regulation existed whatsoever.

12. The "reserve rule" was invented by Boston Braves owner Arthur Soden in 1879 but was not officially installed until 1883. Quirk & Fort, HARD BALL, *supra* note 2, at 55; Scully, BUSINESS OF BASEBALL, *supra* note 8, at 2-3. The National League, which was formed prior to the American League in 1876, instituted its reserve clause as a private agreement among the teams in which "exclusive property rights" were granted to five players for each team. *Id.* at 2. The system apparently worked, as player salaries fell in relation to revenues, and teams began to make profits for the first time. *Id.*

13. *See* Am. League Baseball Club of Chi. v. Chase, 149 N.Y.S. 6, 10 (Sup. Ct. 1914) (quoting section 3, article VI of the National Agreement [for the government of professional baseball]: "The right and title of a major league club to its players shall be absolute. . . ."). For more on the history of the reserve clause, *see* Gerald W. Scully, THE MARKET STRUCTURE OF SPORTS 11-12 (1995); Jack F. Williams & Jack A. Chambless, *Title VII and the Reserve Clause: A Statistical Analysis of Salary Discrimination in Major League Baseball,* 52 U. MIAMI L. REV. 461, 472-73 (1998).

14. Quirk & Fort, Hard Ball, *supra* note 2, at 11-12, 18, 22.

15. *Id.* at 52, 58. Some players even testified before Congress in the 1950s in an effort to keep the reserve system intact. *See* Andrew Zimbalist, *Baseball Economics and Antitrust Immunity,* 4 SETON

HALL J. SPORT L. 287, 290 (1994). Some of this thinking can be ascribed to the fact that, until the mid-1970s, most professional sports associations or unions were essentially "company unions." Quirk & Fort, HARD BALL, *supra* note 2, at 51. Another major factor was the general societal sense that athletes were fortunate to be getting paid for playing essentially a "kids" game. *Id.*; Paul D. Staudohar, PLAYING FOR DOLLARS: LABOR RELATIONS AND THE SPORTS BUSINESS 3 (1996) [hereinafter Staudohar, PLAYING FOR DOLLARS] ("In the decades before unions and collective bargaining became ingrained in the sports industry, professional athletes were treated like privileged peons.").

16. *See* Quirk & Fort, HARD BALL, *supra* note 2, at 51-52; Staudohar, PLAYING FOR DOLLARS, *supra* note 15, at 3-4. Professors James Quirk & Rodney Fort put the impact of the MLBPA on the reserve clause plainly: "Changes in the player reservation system that have taken place in baseball since the early 1970s are due almost exclusively to the action of the Major League Players Association. . . ." James Quirk & Rodney D. Fort, PAY DIRT: THE BUSINESS OF PROFESSIONAL TEAM SPORTS 192-93 (1992) [hereinafter Quirk & Fort, PAY DIRT].

17. The MLB reserve clause was dealt its first major blow in late 1975, when arbitrator Peter Seitz ruled that pitchers Andy Messersmith and Dave McNally were "free agents" after each played the season without a contract (i.e., their "option" season) as a result of refusing their clubs' offers following the previous season. Scully, BUSINESS OF BASEBALL, *supra* note 8, at 37; *see* Quirk & Fort, HARD BALL, *supra* note 2, at 61-62 ("Arbitration accomplished what one hundred years of baseball history had been unable to do, namely eliminating the reserve clause."). Professor Scully claims that "prior to the Messersmith decision players were paid just a small fraction of their actual contribution to team revenues" and with "the coming of free agency, clubs bid against each other for. . . talent, making rational decisions about the value of the player to the club relative to his market price." Scully, BUSINESS OF BASEBALL, *supra* note 8, at 153. In basketball, the reserve clause was terminated through a court-approved settlement in Robertson v. National Basketball Association, 72 F.R.D. 64, 67 (S.D.N.Y. 1976) (approving settlement that "provided for the elimination of the reserve clause, a phaseout of reserve compensation, [and] a settlement fund for the class of $4.3 million").

18. The NFL's reserve structure, like that of baseball, operated as part of an option system. *See supra* note 17. While teams technically could sign players that played out their option years, there was a "gentleman's agreement" among the owners not to do so. Quirk & Fort, PAY DIRT, *supra* note 16, at 190-91. When the Baltimore Colts' owner violated this agreement in 1963, the NFL moved quickly to formalize its previous policy. *Id.*

19. The rule stated: [A] player, even after he has played out his contract under the option rule and has thereby become a free agent, is still restrained from pursuing his business to the extent that all league members with whom he might otherwise negotiate for new employment are prohibited from employing him unless upon consent of his former employer or, absent such consent, subject to the power of the NFL Commissioner to name and award one or more players to the former employer from the active reserve or selection list of the acquiring club—as the NFL Commissioner in his sole discretion deems fair and reasonable. Kapp v. Nat'l Football League, 390 F. Supp. 73, 82 (N.D. Cal. 1974) (emphasis added).

20. Mackey v. Nat'l Football League, 543 F.2d 606, 611 (8th Cir. 1976). Compare this with the most recent data, which shows that, prior to the 2004 NFL season, a whopping 515 free agents changed teams. M. J. Duberstein, NAT'L FOOTBALL LEAGUE PLAYERS ASS'N, NFL OFF-SEASON SALARY AVERAGES & SIGNING TRENDS 145 (2004).

21. Kapp, 390 F. Supp. at 82 ("We conclude that such a rule imposing restraint virtually unlimited in time and extent, goes far beyond any

possible need for fair protection of the interests. . . or the purposes of the NFL and that it imposes upon the player-employees such undue hardship as to be an unreasonable restraint. . . .").

22. *See* Bryant v. NFL, No. CV 75-2543 HP, 1975 U.S. Dist. LEXIS 11224, at 3-6 (C.D. Cal. 1975) (granting restraining order temporarily preventing enforcement of Rozelle Rule).

23. Mackey, 543 F.2d at 615 (ruling that Rozelle Rule was mandatory subject of bargaining under National Labor Relations Act, and NFL's failure to bargain over the issue was violation of law). In 1977, however, the NFLPA agreed to a right of first refusal compensation system in a new collective bargaining agreement. Matthew S. Collins, *Note C: C as in Cash, Cough it Up, and Changes—NFL Players Score with Free Agency Following Freeman McNeil's Big Gain,* 71 WASH. U. L.Q. 1269, 1274–75 (1993).

24. The NFL's current free agent system has two major components. First, any player with five or more "accrued" seasons of NFL playing service is automatically an "unrestricted" free agent. 2002 NFL CBA, *supra* note 10, art. XIX, 1(a), at 59. A player with at least three but fewer than five accrued seasons is authorized to seek offers from other clubs after his contract expires, but if the player receives an offer, his old club must choose between matching it and retaining him, or letting him go to the new club in return for draft choice compensation. *Id.* art. XIX, 2(a)–(b), at 60-61. Also, any player who has accrued fewer than three seasons and whose contract has expired is a restricted free agent—his free agent team is only required to offer a one-year contract at the minimum salary under the CBA. *Id.* art. XVIII, 2, at 57.

Second, free agency is subject to a relatively minor constraint under the "Franchise" and "Transition" player tags. A player subject to the Transition tag must be offered the average of the top ten salaries league-wide in the player's position, and he is subject to a right of first refusal by his original club. *Id.* art. XX, 3-5, at 72–74. The Franchise tag, which can only be used once per season and not in conjunction with the Transition tag, requires teams to make an offer equal to the average of the top five salaries in the player's position. *Id.* art. XX, 2(c)(ii), at 70. Included in salaries are "roster and reporting bonuses, pro-rata portions of signing bonuses, and other payments to players in compensation for the playing of professional football." *Id.* art. XX, 2(e), at 71.

25. The system is a holdover from the 1970s and early 1980s, when the NHL originally operated based on a "modified" Rozelle Rule. McCourt v. Cal. Sports, Inc., 600 F.2d 1193, 1194 (6th Cir. 1979). The only major difference is that compensation designed to equalize the signing team and the former team would be awarded by an arbitrator instead of the commissioner. *See* Berry et al., *supra* note 2, at 211 (describing "equalization," whereby if signing team and former team of free agent cannot agree on compensation, dispute is heard by arbitrator). Unlike the NFL model, the NHL's regulatory regime withstood litigation despite having similarly stern consequences. Only three arbitration cases based on equalization were decided during that period. *Id.* at 212; Staudohar, PLAYING FOR DOLLARS, *supra* note 15, at 155.

26. *See* Collective Bargaining Agreement, NHLPA/NHL, Effective June 26, 1997 (as amended), art. 1, at 3, art. 10, at 23-37 [hereinafter 1997 NHL CBA]. At one time, NHL teams losing a free agent had the option of selecting an active player—as opposed to a draft pick—from the signing team's roster, although compensation now is restricted solely to draft choice compensation. *See id.* art. 10, at 35-36. Under the 1982 NHL collective bargaining agreement, a team that signed another team's free agent for $200,000 or more had to compensate the original team with two first-round draft choices or a first-round draft choice plus a player on the active roster. Berry et al., *supra* note 2, at 227.

27. To foster competitive balance, each league allows its teams to pick incoming players in the reverse order of the teams' winning percentages at the conclusion of the regular season. What varies among leagues is who is eligible for the draft, how many players are drafted, and whether some form of lottery system is used whereby teams are assigned a percentage chance of being among the first teams to draft according to how poorly they did in the previous season.

28. *See* Smith v. Pro-Football, 420 F. Supp. 738, 746 (D.D.C. 1976) (describing NFL Draft as one that "leaves no room whatever for competition among the teams for the services of college players, and utterly strips them of any measure of control over the marketing of their talents"). In Robertson v. National Basketball Association, the court outlined what was at stake in the collegiate draft system: Whereas the reserve clause prevents teams from competing for veteran players, the draft prevents bidding for rookies. The net effect of the two mechanisms is to force a player to deal only with the NBA club which "owns" the rights to him. If the player refuses to go along with the system, he will not play ball in the NBA. . . . 389 F. Supp. 867, 892 (S.D.N.Y. 1975).

It should be noted, however, that another key function of the draft is to spread the league's incoming talent "among the various teams . . . and help the weaker teams in the league improve." Glenn M. Wong, ESSENTIALS OF SPORTS LAW 545 (3d ed. 2002).

29. *See, e.g.,* NBA Collective Bargaining Agreement, Jan. 20, 1999, art. VIII, 1(c), at 137 [hereinafter 1999 NBA CBA] (indicating that teams have rights to players chosen in first round of draft for four years, including one "option" year); 2002 NFL CBA, *supra* note 10, art. XVI, 1-8, at 46–49.

30. While caps on salaries might appear to be anticompetitive restrictions on trade, they have been deemed permissible if imposed as part of a collective bargaining agreement. *See* Wood v. Nat'l Basketball Ass'n, 809 F.2d 954, 961-62 (2d Cir. 1987) ("Were a court to intervene and strike down the draft and salary cap, the entire agreement would unravel. This would force the NBA and [National Basketball Players Association] to search for other avenues of compromise . . . less satisfactory to them than the agreement struck down. . . . We decline to take that step.").

. . . .

32. Berry et al., *supra* note 2, at 183. While the NBA was the first league to employ the Team Cap, the concept of "free player movement with salary constraints" was first proposed by NFLPA Executive Director Ed Garvey in the NFL's 1982 collective bargaining negotiations. *See* Paul C. Weiler & Gary R. Roberts, SPORTS AND THE LAW 315 (2nd ed. 1998).

33. Berry et al., *supra* note 2, at 184. The fixed sum was $3.6 million in the first year, $3.8 million in 1985–1986, and $4 million in 1986–1987. *Id.*

34. Player benefits are costs paid by the NBA and include, but are not limited to, pensions, life insurance, disability insurance, medical and dental insurance, the employer's portion of payroll taxes, and a share of costs of the anti-drug program. 1999 NBA CBA, *supra* note 29, art. IV, 1, at 34-40. Subtracting benefits further limits the growth of the salary cap; since benefits are paid separately from salaries, this formula now incorporates—or gives credit to the owners for paying—benefits in the formula.

35. Examples of these are the $1 Million Exception, Mid-Level Salary Exception, and the "Larry Bird" Exceptions. . . .

36. *See* Nat'l Basketball Players Ass'n, 2003–2004 NBA Preliminary Projected Calculation of Escrow and Tax To Be Distributed to Teams (June 2004) (on file with the COLUMBIA LAW REVIEW) [here-

inafter 2003–2004 Escrow & Tax Payout]; Nat'l Basketball Players Ass'n, 2002–2003 NBA Preliminary Projected Calculation of Escrow and Tax To Be Distributed to Teams (June 2003) (on file with the COLUMBIA LAW REVIEW).

37. 1999 NBA CBA, *supra* note 29, art. VII, 1(a), at 52. BRI is: "The aggregate operating revenues [including the value of barter transactions] received or to be received on an accrual basis . . . by the NBA, NBA Properties, Inc., including any of its subsidiaries . . . any other entity which is controlled by, or in which the NBA, Properties . . . and/or a group of NBA Teams owns at least 50% of the issued and outstanding ownership interests . . . granted to ownership interests not owned by the NBA . . . from all sources, whether known or unknown, whether now in existence or created in the future, to the extent derived from, relating to or arising directly or indirectly out of the performance of Players in NBA basketball games or in NBA related activities."

Id. The agreement also includes income derived from things such as "regular season gate receipts," "all proceeds . . . from the broadcast or exhibition of, or the sale, license or other conveyance or exploitation of the right to broadcast or exhibit" NBA games, "all Exhibition game proceeds," "playoff gate receipts," "in-arena sales of novelties and concessions, sales of novelties in team-identified stores within a 75-mile radius of the area, NBA game parking and programs, Team sponsorships . . . Team promotions, temporary arena signage, arena club revenues, summer camps . . . mascot and dance team appearances," "proceeds from premium seat licenses," and "forty (40) percent of the gross proceeds from fixed arena signage" and "of the gross proceeds. . . from the sale, lease, or licensing of luxury suites." *Id.* art. VII, 1(a)(1)(i)-(ix), at 53-57.

38. Projected BRI is the sum of (1) BRI from the previous year plus 8% and (2) "the rights fees or other non-contingent payments stated in [the NBA's television contracts] with respect to the [upcoming season]." *Id.* art. VII, 1(c)(1)-(2), at 68-69.

39. Projected Benefits are "the projected amounts to be paid or accrued by the NBA or the Teams. . . for the upcoming Season with respect to the [players'] benefits to be provided for such Season." *Id.* art. IV, 6, at 44.

40. There were twenty-nine teams in the NBA in 2003–2004, and there will be thirty in 2004–2005 with the addition of the Charlotte Bobcats. Since the most reliable data available is based upon a twenty-nine-team league, this Note assumes in its calculations that there are twenty-nine teams in the NBA except where otherwise noted.

. . . .

42. This period included a players' strike, the use of replacement players, the voluntary decertification of the NFLPA, a precedent-setting lawsuit, and a class action lawsuit. *See* Paul C. Weiler, LEVELING THE PLAYING FIELD: HOW THE LAW CAN MAKE SPORTS BETTER FOR FANS 108-10 (2000); Dworkin & Posthuma, *supra* note 8, at 247-49.

43. Although, to be more precise, the NFLPA actually proposed the salary cap—first a loose version in 1982 and then a more definite one prior to the 1993 agreement. *See* Weiler, *supra* note 42, at 108 ("Ironically, in football [the team salary] cap had been won by the players. . . ."); Dworkin & Posthuma, *supra* note 8, at 247 ("In 1982 the players demanded a fixed percentage of NFL gross revenues (55 percent) for their salaries.").

44. The NFL salary cap percentage is 64.75%, 2002 NFL CBA, *supra* note 10, art. XXIV, 4(a), at 95, while the NBA salary cap is 48.04%, 1999 NBA CBA, *supra* note 29, art. VII, 2(a)(1), at 71. . . .

There is one additional relevant difference between the two systems. In both leagues, when a player is released from the team, the residual amount owed to the player still counts against the team's Team Cap number. Therefore, if Team P waives Player Q, and the team is still obligated to pay Player Q $1 million per year for the next three years even though Player Q is no longer with Team P, his salary still counts against the Team Cap. Most NBA contracts are guaranteed for what is termed "lack of skill." Thus, when a team releases a player whose contract contains this guarantee, his salary remains on its Team Cap. 1999 NBA CBA, *supra* note 29, art. VII, 4(a)(1), at 86. By contrast, less than five percent of active NFL players between 1995 and 2002 had guaranteed base salaries, which significantly reduces the Team Cap implications of releasing a player. *See* Nat'l Football League Players Ass'n, A New Look at Guaranteed Contracts in the NFL 3, available at http://www.nflpa .org/PDFs/Shared/Guaranteed Contracts.pdf (last visited Sept. 15, 2004) (on file with the COLUMBIA LAW REVIEW) (stating that "the average number of players with guaranteed base salary from 1995 through 2002 is 40 per season"). It must be noted, however, that a number of NFL contracts often include "signing bonuses," which are prorated for Team Cap purposes across the life of the contract and therefore would still count against the Team Cap even if a player is waived. 2002 NFL CBA, *supra* note 10, art. XXIV, 7(b)(i), at 100.

45. The "Rookie Scale" in the NBA provides for a maximum salary for each first-round draft pick based on what number selection that player is in the draft. *See* 1999 NBA CBA, *supra* note 29, Exhibit B, at B-1 to B-7. The 1997 NHL CBA provided for a maximum dollar amount that limited the compensation teams could offer draft picks. 1997 NHL CBA, *supra* note 26, 9.3(a). Unlike the NBA agreement, the NHL agreement incorporated only one dollar amount that applies to all picks—there is no "slotting" based on where a player is drafted.

46. Players who made more than the prescribed maximums at the time of the signing of the 1999 NBA CBA were granted an exception to the new individual salary limits. Paul D. Staudohar, *Labor Relations in Basketball: The Lockout of 1998-99,* MONTHLY LAB. REV., Apr. 1999, at 3, 8.

47. In the NBA, the maximum prescribed salary depends on the number of years a player has played in the league. For any player who has completed fewer than seven years of service, the maximum salary of the first year of a new contract is the greater of 25% of the team salary cap, 105% of his previous year's salary, or $9 million. 1999 NBA CBA, *supra* note 29, art. II, 7(a)(i), at 23. For any player with between seven and nine years of service, the maximum salary is the greater of 30% of the salary cap, 105% of his previous year's salary, or $11 million. *Id.* art. II, 7(a)(ii), at 23. Any player who has completed ten or more years of service can receive in the first year of his new contract the greater of 35% of the salary cap, 105% of his previous season's salary, or $14 million. *Id.* art. II, 7(a)(iii), at 23.

48. An argument can be made, however, that the maximum also becomes a number that is more "reachable" by certain players and therefore drives some salaries that would fall just below that level up to that level. For example, a ten-year veteran who may otherwise be worth $12 million annually may receive the maximum salary of $14 million as a measure of respect by the signing club.

49. *See* Daniel Kaplan & Liz Mullen, *Upshaw to Announce Early Extension Talks,* STREET & SMITH'S SPORTS BUSINESS J., Jan. 19, 2004, at 1 (stating that NFLPA and NFL will begin talks to extend their current agreement three years before its expiration, which would give NFL "the longest period of labor peace enjoyed by any of the Big Four team sports").

50. In the 1999 NBA CBA, the tax is never given a formal name other than "Team Payments." 1999 NBA CBA, *supra* note 29, art. VII, 12(g), at 135. In the 2002 MLB CBA, it is referred to as the "Competitive Balance Tax." 2002 MLB CBA, *supra* note 6, art. XXIII,

at 78. This represented an interesting change for baseball, which, under a somewhat similar taxation system in its prior agreement, termed the article XXIII tax the "Luxury Tax." Basic Agreement between The American League of Professional Baseball Clubs and The National League of Professional Baseball Clubs and Major League Baseball Players Association, Effective Jan. 1, 1997, art. XXIII [hereinafter 1997 MLB CBA], reprinted in Jeffrey S. Moorad, *Negotiating for the Professional Baseball Player* appx. 5A at 5-39, in 1 LAW OF PROFESSIONAL & AMATEUR SPORTS 5-1, 5-104 (Gary A. Uberstine ed., 2002).

51. Weiler & Roberts, *supra* note 32, at 317; Taylor Buckley, *Baseball Luxury Tax Will Land in the Lap of Spectating Public,* USA TODAY, Nov. 17, 1994, at 10C. The first serious discussions regarding the use of a tax on team payrolls occurred between the NHL and the NHLPA during their 1993–1995 labor negotiations. The NHL negotiations resulted in a three-month shutdown of the 1994–1995 NHL season, and the NHL's proposal that included a 200% tax on team salaries that exceeded the average team salary was not part of the resulting agreement. *See* Helene Elliott, *Season Now in Jeopardy,* L.A. TIMES, Oct. 6, 1994, at C1 (stating that NHL backed off its 200% tax proposal).

52. 1997 MLB CBA art. XXIII, reprinted in Moorad, *supra* note 50, at 5-104.

53. Baseball also has a process by which it taxes team revenue, under the heading of "revenue sharing."

54. *See* Lisa Dillman, *Players Submit New Plan,* L.A. TIMES, Oct. 11, 1994, at C1 (quoting NHLPA boss Bob Goodenow as saying that "any tax is a drag on salaries"); Len Hochberg, *Hockey Stays in Deep Freeze,* WASH. POST, Oct. 29, 1994, at H1 (citing league officials as wanting a substantial tax to "slow" salary growth).

55. *See infra* notes 102-107 and accompanying text.

56. Indeed, if a player expected to produce $1 million in revenue actually cost his team $1 million plus a 50% tax on that salary, the total $1.5 million signing cost would no longer be efficient for that organization.

57. *See supra* note 2 and accompanying text.

58. This included what Professor Paul Staudohar called "the mother of all sports strikes." Staudohar, PLAYING FOR DOLLARS, *supra* note 15, at 49. The strike to which he refers lasted 232 days and forced the cancellation of the 1994 World Series. *Id.* at 49-50.

59. This agreement, which was signed in December, 1996, followed the 1994–1995 strike. Dworkin & Posthuma, *supra* note 8, at 239.

60. Weiler, *supra* note 42, at 116; Dworkin & Posthuma, *supra* note 8, at 239.

61. 1997 MLB CBA art. XXIII, B(3), reprinted in Moorad, *supra* note 50, at 5-105.

62. *Id.* art. XXIII, B(3)(b), at 5-105 to 5-106. The CBA took the midpoint between the fifth and sixth teams at the threshold as long as it was above the minimum designated level.

63. *Id.* art. XXIII, B(2), at 5-105. This "minimum" was only necessary if the "arithmetic mean" of the fifth and sixth highest spending teams fell below those numbers. *Id.* art. XXIII, B(3)(a), at 5-105.

64. *Id.* art. XXIII, B(5), at 5-106.

65. *Id.* art. XXIII, H(1)-(2), at 5-119. Under this plan, only the bottom five American League clubs in net local revenue receive luxury tax distribution payments. "Each of the five (5) American League Clubs that rank[] the lowest in Net Local Revenue for 1996 shall be paid an additional $1.4 Million on February 1, 1998. Such payments shall be funded by Luxury Tax proceeds for the 1997 Contract Year pursuant to Article XXIII. . . ." *Id.* art. XXV, C(1)(b), at 5-126 to 5-127.

66. *Id.* art. XXIII, H(3), at 5-119. "The objective of IGF is to promote the growth of baseball in the United States and Canada, as well as throughout the world." *Id.* art. XXVI, A, at 5-136.

67. *Id.* art. XXIII, H(4), at 5-119 to 5-120. "Overcharging" may occur if a player does not receive an option buyout, *id.* art. XXIII, E(5)(b)(ii), at 5-112, if a club option year is not exercised, *id.* art. XXIII, E(5)(c)(ii)(C), at 5-113, or if a player nullifies an option year, *id.* art. XXIII, E(5)(d)(iii), at 5-114.

68. Weiler, *supra* note 42, at 116; *see also* Bryan Day, *Labor Pains: Why Contraction Is Not the Solution to Major League Baseball's Competitive Balance Problems,* 12 FORDHAM INTELL. PROP. MEDIA & ENT. L.J. 521, 572 (2002) ("It is worth noting that in the three seasons in which the luxury tax was in effect the tax had no discernible impact on the growth of player salaries.").

69. Mark Maske, *Orioles to Pay Most in Luxury Tax,* WASH. POST, Jan. 9, 1999, at D8.

70. *See supra* note 62 and accompanying text.

71. 1997 MLB CBA art. XXIII, reprinted in Moorad, *supra* note 50, at 5-104.

72. 2002 MLB CBA, *supra* note 6, art. XXIII, at 78.

73. *Id.* art. XXIII, B(2), at 80. According to Professor Andrew Zimbalist, the owners' initial proposal was for a threshold beginning at $98 million taxed at a rate of 50%, while the players countered with a threshold of $137.5 million taxed at 15%. Zimbalist, MAY THE BEST TEAM WIN, *supra* note 2, at 111.

74. 2002 MLB CBA, *supra* note 6, art. XXIII, B(3)(a), at 80.

75. In 2004 and 2005, a first-time tax threshold violator will be assessed a 22.5% tax on its overage. *Id.* art. XXIII, B(3)(b), at 80. For second-time offenders, the tax rate will be 30%, while the rate for a third-or fourth-time offender is 40%. *Id.* art. XXIII, B(3)(c)-(d), at 80-81. To round out the system, a first-time offender in 2006 is not assessed any tax, while a team above the threshold in 2006 but not in 2005 also avoids any penalty. *Id.* art. XXIII, B(3)(b)-(c), at 80.

76. *Id.* art. XXIII, H(1), at 99. This section also allows for an additional $5 million to be dedicated for the same purpose should the parties to the agreement agree to this adjustment. *Id.*

77. *Id.* art. XXIII, H(2), at 99.

78. *Id.* art. XXIII, H(3), at 99.

79. *Id.* art. XXIII, H(4), at 100.

80. Murray Chass, *Marlins Rebuild, but Uncertainly,* N.Y. TIMES, Jan. 10, 1999, 8, at 8 (saying that "the tax hasn't worked"); Tom Haudricourt, *Tax Provides Little Luxury: Product of Labor Dispute Fails to Curb Spending,* MILWAUKEE J. SENTINEL, Jan. 17, 1999, at Sports 15, available at 1999 WL 7652912 ("The tax. . . is a joke."). Respected baseball writer Bob Verdi referred to the baseball luxury tax as "flimsy" and "annoying" at best. Bob Verdi, *Falling in Love Again with the Old Pastime,* CHI. TRIB., Oct. 26, 2003, 3, at 13.

81. Bill Shaikin, *Rich Tradition: Yankees' Uncanny Ability to Make Money and Spend on Talent Cuts into the Attempts at Parity,* L.A. TIMES, Apr. 1, 2004, at D1.

82. Ross Newhan, *Start Spreading the Payroll Blues,* L.A. TIMES, Nov. 13, 2002, at D1.

83. *See* Richard Justice, *Finally, NBA Reaches Its Own Labor Day,* WASH. POST, Sept. 5, 1995, at C1 [hereinafter Justice, *NBA Reaches*]. Justice says sources told him that former NBPA chief Charles Grantham "was forced out because of alleged questions regarding his handling of his expense account [while o]ther sources said players didn't like the slow pace of negotiations, they didn't like the strike talk and they didn't like the fact that no new agreement was in place." *Id.*

84. Grantham was replaced by Simon Gourdine, a former NBA deputy commissioner who had joined the union in 1990. *See* John Helyar, *Pro Basketball Loses Its 'Feel Good' Image in Nasty Labor Dispute,* WALL ST. J., Aug. 7, 1995, at A1 (documenting summer of discontent between NBA and NBPA in 1995). Gourdine proceeded to negotiate a deal with the league that included a luxury tax. Richard Justice, *NBA Owners Prepare for Lockout,* WASH. POST, June 30, 1995, at B8. When the majority of players, largely left uninformed as to the specifics of Gourdine's negotiations, were let in on the terms of the deal, they were outraged. *See* Mark Asher, *Jordan, Ewing Join Class-Action Lawsuit,* WASH. POST, June 29, 1995, at B6 (describing actions of several star players trying to overturn new collective bargaining agreement agreed to in principle by union); Jackie MacMullan, *Players Suing NBA,* BOSTON GLOBE, June 29, 1995, at 39 (quoting former New York Knick and NBPA President Patrick Ewing as saying, "The deal the union accepted was not a fair deal"). The agreement allowed teams to continue exceeding the Team Cap, but, beginning in the third year of the deal, a team exceeding the cap would be assessed a "luxury tax"—a 100% tax for every dollar of a free agent contract that was raised over the final year of the previous deal by more than 10%. Justice, NBA *Reaches, supra* note 83. For example, "if a team wanted to sign a player making $1 million to a new contract at $2 million, it would have to pay the league another $900,000." *Id.*

    In response to the deal Gourdine originally negotiated, some players began a movement to decertify the NBPA under the theory that labor law would no longer apply to the bargaining relationship if there were no union representing the players, thereby opening up the NBA to potential antitrust violations. *See* Marc J. Yoskowitz, *Note, A Confluence of Labor and Antitrust Law: The Possibility of Union Decertification in the National Basketball Association to Avoid the Bounds of Labor Law and Move into the Realm of Antitrust,* 1998 COLUM. BUS. L. REV. 579, 596-99, 611 (detailing unique factors of potential decertification within realm of professional sports). The pressure applied by these players resulted in Gourdine returning to the bargaining table, which in turn, led to the failure of the decertification movement. *Id.*; Justice, NBA Reaches, *supra* note 83.

85. Murray Chass, *N.B.A. Owners Settled Rather than Risk More,* N.Y. TIMES, Aug. 10, 1995, at B11; *see* Mark Asher, *NBA, Union Beat Deadline with New Deal,* WASH. POST, Aug. 9, 1995, at C1 (describing owners' capitulation on luxury tax after players' strong opposition to provision in summer's first tentative deal); Anthony Bianco, *David Stern: This Time, It's Personal,* BUS. WK., July 13, 1998, at 114, 116 ("In the end, it was [NBA Commissioner David] Stern who blinked, recommending that the owners accept a new contract that. . . scuttled the luxury tax.").

86. The 1995 NBA collective bargaining agreement originally had a six-year term, although the NBA had the right to reopen negotiations if the players' share of BRI exceeded 51.8%. NBA Collective Bargaining Agreement, Sept. 18, 1995, art. XXXVIII, 2(a), at 185.

87. Mark Asher, *Lockout Issues Began Long Time Ago; Players Union, NBA Owners Have Not Met Face-to-Face in 23 Days,* WASH. POST, July 15, 1998, at C6.

88. Weiler, *supra* note 42, at 107.

89. *See* Dworkin & Posthuma, *supra* note 8, at 244 (stating that 437 games were missed due to lockout).

90. *See supra* Part I.B.2.

91. Frank Swoboda, *This Round May Go to Owners,* WASH. POST, Jan. 8, 1999, at C5.

92. It should be noted that the players presented their own version of the luxury tax; had it been implemented, it would have had little or no effect on team spending. The NBPA proposed to tax individual salaries above $18 million, which would only affect a handful of players. *See* Mike Wise, *N.B.A. Is Canceling Its First Two Weeks,* N.Y. TIMES, Oct. 14, 1998, at A1.

93. This is the closest thing to an official name for the system, although there is no formal equivalent to MLB's Competitive Balance Tax. The luxury tax—called "Team Payments" in the agreement—is tucked away under section 12(g) of article VII, which is entitled "Escrow Arrangement." While most of section 12 deals with the Escrow piece of the regulatory system, there is no "escrow" component to the luxury tax other than that it kicks in when the escrow account has been depleted. *See infra* notes 96-99 and accompanying text.

94. 1999 NBA CBA, *supra* note 29, art. VII, 12(d)(1), at 128-29. A Projected Overage is the forecasted amount by which players' salaries and benefits will exceed the Escrow Threshold. *Id.* art. VII, 12(b)(14), at 127.

95. The current NBA CBA calls for the designated compensation adjustment percentage to be 55% in years 2001–2002, 2002–2003, and 2003–2004, and 57% in 2004–2005. *See id.* art. VII, 12(c)(3), at 128. This Note will operate on the basis of the 2001–2004 figure.

96. *Id.* art. VII, 12(c)-(d), at 128-30. For example, after the 2001–2002 season, players' salaries and benefits were approximately 59.8% of league revenues, which did not require the full 10% Escrow. Chris Sheridan, *Arbitrator Rules in Favor of NBA,* Associated Press Online, Sept. 25, 2002, available at http://global.factiva.com (on file with the COLUMBIA LAW REVIEW) (noting that, of $154 million collected, approximately $23 million was returned to players). Therefore, not only was the luxury tax portion of the Escrow arrangement dormant, but the players were eligible to receive back some of their escrowed salary money as well. In addition, for the "transition" season into the Escrow and tax arrangement, the NBPA negotiated for a payment to the players should BRI and benefits not increase over the prior year by at least $50 million. 1999 NBA CBA, *supra* note 29, art. VII, 2(d)(7), at 75.

· · · ·

100. Mark Asher, *NBA Calls Off Meeting with the Players' Union: Cancellation of Entire Season Looms Larger,* WASH. POST, Nov. 26, 1998, at B1.

101. 1999 NBA CBA, *supra* note 29, art. VII, 12(g)(1), at 135.

102. *Id.* art. VII, 12(h)(1), at 135-36.

FOOTBALL MAY BE ILL, BUT DON'T BLAME BOSMAN

William Duffy

I. INTRODUCTION

. . . European football (soccer) has experienced a fundamental shift in the employment relationships between players and their clubs. Traditionally, the power of employment resided firmly with the national associations and private clubs, with the players having a relatively weak union and (with very few exceptions) little to say about their careers. That balance of power began to shift when Jean-Marc Bosman, a midfielder from the Belgium team RC Liege, attempted to transfer to the French team US Dunkerque in July of 1990. Although Bosman was no longer under contract, his Belgian employer demanded compensation (a so-called "transfer fee") from the French club with which he wished to sign, and refused to allow Bosman to play until payment was received.

Bosman subsequently sued RC Liege, the Belgian Football Association (URBSFA), and the Union of European Football Associations (UEFA), alleging that the rules governing the transfer of players among clubs in the Union were unfairly restrictive. . . . The specific issue was whether the rules regarding the movement of players from between clubs and the rules governing the number of foreign players allowed to play for a team during a match were in violation of the European Community Treaty.

After a protracted and complex legal battle that effectively ended Bosman's playing career, the E.C.J. [European Court of Justice] agreed with Bosman and found the transfer rules to be in violation of the European Treaty. The Court ordered the Federation Internationale de Football Associations (FIFA), UEFA, and the national football organizations of every member state to implement fundamental changes in the way they administer the movement of players between clubs within the European Union. As a result of Bosman's lawsuit and the ruling that bears his name, football players in Europe today enjoy a great deal of professional freedom.

. . . .

II. THE FACTS OF MR. BOSMAN'S CASE

A. The Structure of Football: Organization, Transfer of Players, Restrictions on Foreign Players

1. The Organization of Football

The structure of football clubs, leagues, and associations is basically the same world-wide. Organized amateur and professional football is played under a structure called an "association." In order to participate in international competition, clubs and leagues, as well as the national associations that govern them, are required to conform to certain guidelines prescribed by regional international confederations (in the case of Europe, the UEFA). Each level of the structure is afforded a certain amount of responsibility for the administration of the game. At the base, each club is responsible for its players. In order to be eligible for a match played by his club, each professional player must be registered as a professional with his national association. As a registered professional, the player is considered an employee of the club which holds his registration.

National associations are comprised of clubs playing organized competitions within the nation's borders. These associations organize league competitions and national knock-out cup competitions, and administer the national team. The associations also draft the regulations by which the game functions. . . .

The regional confederations comprise the membership of the international organizational body known as FIFA. The regulations of the regional confederations are subject to the approval of FIFA. . . .

2. The Transfer Rules: Belgium, UEFA, and FIFA

. . . The FIFA rules were important to Bosman, in that they expressly stated that the registration of players in national associations (which made the player eligible for competition) was dependent on the release and receipt of the player's professional registration certificate. While the rules stated that the out-of-contract player could not play until his certificate was received, they did not state that the former club would be required to release the player's certificate once a new contract had been reached between the player and the new club. Thus, the former club effectively retained control over the player's career. This issue led Bosman to sue RC Liege.

3. Restrictions on Foreign Players

. . . The rules regarding participation in national competitions by foreign players were, until the Bosman ruling, deliberately restrictive. As stated in Advocate General Lenz's opinion, "(f)rom the 1960s on, many—but not all—football associations introduced rules restricting the possibility of engaging players of foreign nationality."[31] . . . UEFA introduced a rule in 1991 that fixed the number of foreign players allowed to play in a UEFA sanctioned match. The rule, which became known as the "3+2 Rule," required that teams limit the number of foreign players included on the team sheet for any one match to three, plus two additional foreign players who had played professionally in the host country for a period of five uninterrupted years, including three years in junior teams.

The abolition of the 3+2 rule by the European Court of Justice in the *Bosman* decision has impacted football at least as much as the abolition of transfer fees. Its impact is seen in the increased availability of movement for all players within UEFA. It is curious that the abolition of the foreign player restriction does not receive as much attention as the transfer fees rules.

. . . .

III. THE OPINION OF THE ADVOCATE GENERAL AND THE RULING BY THE EUROPEAN COURT OF JUSTICE

A. The Opinion of the Advocate General

1. The Transfer Rules

In his advisory opinion to the European Court of Justice, Advocate General Lenz found the transfer rules to be "a *direct* restriction on access to the employment market." The Advocate General stated, "the transfer rules are in breach of Article 48, and would be lawful only if they were justified by imperative reasons in the general interest and did not go beyond what is necessary for attaining those objectives (emphasis included in original text)."[47] One such "imperative reason in the general interest" that was advanced during litigation, according to the Advocate General, was the protection of the financial and sporting equilibrium necessary to preserve the balance between competing clubs.[48] It was argued that because clubs are compensated for players moving from club to club, money remains circulating within the game, and that it is more efficient for teams to exchange cash for players, rather than players for players (i.e., a barter system, as exists in the United States professional sports leagues). This compensation was alleged to be necessary for the survival of small clubs, who reap big rewards for selling their prized assets.

For the purpose of maintaining the financial and sporting equilibrium, the Advocate General found the transfer rules to be an inadequate measure, and therefore still unlawful under Article 48. The transfer rules, he said, often force small clubs to sell their best players to generate income for their survival as entities.[51] While this certainly generates revenue for the club, it significantly weakens the club on the playing field. The movement of the best players was decidedly one way, as the small clubs were not in the financial position to lure players from the wealthiest clubs. Finally, since only the wealthiest clubs could afford the transfer fee to begin with, less wealthy clubs could seldom enjoy the benefit of the transfer fee arrangement. This further weakens the argument that it was necessary to maintain the sporting and financial equilibrium.

. . . .

Besides maintaining the sporting equilibrium among clubs, Advocate General Lenz addressed (and refuted) the argument that transfer fees were necessary to compensate clubs for the cost of training players that are eventually sold to other clubs. The Advocate General found this argument invalid based on two main points: the fee is not calculated according to the club's investment in the player, and applies to all players.[59]

The transfer fee's calculation, by its nature, does not account for the amount invested by a club in training a player, but is instead tied to the player's salary. . . .

Second, the clubs demand a transfer fee when selling established professional players as well as new players. . . .

2. The Restrictions on Foreign Players

In his opinion, the Advocate General stated,

> *No deep cogitation is required to reach the conclusion that the rules on foreign players are of a discriminatory nature. They represent an absolutely classic case of discrimination on the ground of nationality. . . . The rules on foreign players are therefore incompatible with the prohibition of discrimination under Article 48(2), in so far as they relate to nationals of other Member States.*[62]

UEFA tried to argue that the rule was not actually in violation of the Article, however, because the restriction was only against the number of foreigners who could play in a match, and not against the number that could be employed by a particular club. The Advocate General was not persuaded by this argument, because the purpose of employing a football player is to actually play him in a match. He reasoned, therefore, that because a club would be limited in the number of foreign players it could use in any one match, the club would not hire more foreign players than it needed, thus restricting the opportunities for players to move freely about the European Union.

This is a rather important part of the decision, but it receives far less attention than the transfer rules, though it arguably has a similarly prominent place in the economics of the sport following the ruling. This part of the decision effectively deepened the pool of football talent available to clubs. In effect, the shopping market for all clubs became exponentially larger than it had been before Bosman. As such, the clubs with money to spend could buy foreign players that they may have previously refrained from buying because they did not have space in their starting eleven. As a result of the Court's decision, the supply of players increased. Along with the increase in supply, should a decrease in the amount clubs are willing to pay for players be expected? Whether or not that is the expectation, it clearly has not happened. Although the supply of players increased, demand for their services also increased. From the player's point of view, the number of potential employers also increased following the Bosman decision. For the best players, that means more suitors who might view them as attractive investments. As such, the clubs who can afford to pay out large sums of cash have driven the cost of the best players higher, taking them out of the reach of more modest clubs. At the same time the clubs increased the value of merely mediocre players. The effect of this has been to concentrate the quality of players at the top of the economic pyramid. . . .

B.   The Ruling by the European Court of Justice

1.   The Transfer Rules

The ruling of the European Court of Justice, with regard to Article 48 and the transfer rules, states:

> *Article 48 EEC precludes the application of the rules laid down by sporting associations, under which a professional footballer who is a national of one Member State may not, on the expiry of his contract with a club, be employed by a club of another Member State unless the latter club has paid to the former club a transfer, training, or development fee.*[64]

In its brief discussion, the court essentially agreed with the points made by the Advocate General, namely that no justification put forward by UEFA, URBSFA, or any national association would allow the existence of the restriction on the movement of football players within the European Union.

2.   The Restrictions on Foreign Players

With regard to the restrictions on the number of foreign players allowed to play in any given match between clubs sanctioned by UEFA, the European Court of Justice ruled that those rules were also precluded by Article 48.[65] As such, the restrictions on the limitations regarding foreign players were abolished.

IV.   THE EFFECTS OF THE BOSMAN RULING

A.   The Lawsuit Within the Economics of the Game

It would be inaccurate to describe the Bosman case as the only economic turning point in football since 1996. In reality, the Bosman ruling exists within a larger context. Football's explosive growth began in the early 1990s, when some of the bigger leagues in Europe aggressively began to sell television rights as a commodity. The traditional source of revenue for clubs, gate receipts, was becoming marginalized even as early as the 1980s. Television rights, sponsorship deals, and savvy marketing were on their way to replacing gates as the main source of income. . . . The gap between rich clubs and poor clubs, part of the argument in favor of transfer fees, was demonstrated by the distribution of this income: three-quarters to the first division clubs, one-eighth to the third and fourth divisions combined. . . . Clearly, football was changing, whether Bosman brought his lawsuit or not.

B.   Arguments Against the Lawsuit

In their 1998 article, The Impact of the Bosman Ruling,[69] Gardiner and Welch addressed concerns that Bosman, fairly or unfairly, could become "a scapegoat, for all the perceived ills in the game, such as the problems that some club managers report in exerting discipline over star players who earn more than they do even when not being selected for first team football."[70] Although they acknowledge that Bosman may or may not have been the actual cause of "the big money circulating in the upper echelons of the game,"[71] . . . they argue that Bosman's lawsuit effectively attacks the codependent nature of the football leagues, and furthers the commercialization of the game. They further argue that the lawsuit broke down an invisible barrier between sport and society by needlessly introducing the societal instrument of law into what amounted to an internal disagreement between an employee and employer. In their own words:

> *There is a need for competition and although this may be keen on the field, the clubs are dependent on each other to a much greater extent than in other businesses. Therefore, until now, there have been collective interests between clubs not to allow free market principles to operate so that the top clubs buy all the best players. An issue of ongoing major concern for football clubs and supporters alike which has been facilitated, if not created, by Bosman is the way that the top clubs no longer appear to regard themselves bound by the collective interest as they look for ever greener pastures anew, such as the European Super League. . . . The attack on the transfer system in football can be seen as a classic battle concerning the legitimacy of intervention in particular sectors of industry and employment. . . . The partial removal of the transfer system that Bosman represents increases the view that football is no longer intrinsically and essentially a sport, but merely a product to be consumed. . . . As football has increasingly become subject to this process of commodification, so juridification has operated as a concomitant process. The intervention of the law into new areas of social life, and in this case, "sporting arenas" modifies what are intrinsically social relationships between humans within a "social field. . . ." The football industry has been adept in the past in insulating itself from the impact of legal regulation. However, Bosman exemplifies this process: the system of transfer of players has historically primarily been seen as determined by the football authorities; now it is one primarily determined by law.*[72]

There are two general points upon which I disagree. First, the commodification of the game, which the authors claim was exacerbated by Bosman's lawsuit, was happening regardless of the lawsuit. This was evidenced by the influx of money into the game via television rights deals. Second, in linking the commodification and juridification of the game, the authors seem to suggest that Bosman was somehow wrong to go outside of the authorities of the game for relief from his employer, as if he should have considered the deleterious effects upon football that his personal relief would have brought.

These are the primary anecdotal arguments used against the Bosman ruling in general, and against Bosman himself, by his and the ruling's detractors. The arguments suggest that Bosman is to blame for dragging football down to the same level as society and that his lawsuit helped entrench the sharp claws of capitalist and consumerist power into the game. The commodification argument is particularly ironic, since Bosman's lawsuit was arguably the classic worker's struggle against a repressive system of employment. The transfer system, after all, was designed by a cartel of employers living off the exploitation of the working class.

To place Bosman in the same category as television rights and kit sponsorships, and to call him equally responsible for the disproportionately large sums of money being traded between rich clubs and an elite mix of mercenary-like players places blame where it simply does not belong. There are serious issues of causation to consider: did Bosman start the trend, or was the trend towards commodifications well underway before he brought suit? Gardiner and Welch claim that Bosman was a reflection of the financial pressures of the game. They say that clubs were looking for legal ways to purchase the greatest number of the most highly skilled players available.[73] They assert that players were seeking to increase their bargaining power before the Bosman decision. To include Bosman in this category of players is fundamentally wrong. Bosman was not trying to increase his bargaining power; he was trying to earn a living in his chosen profession. Bosman simply argued that he was being prevented from doing so by his former employer, in direct violation of European law.

C. Ramifications of the Lawsuit on the Game

Without the restrictions of transfer fees or limitations on the number of foreign players that a team may have, players are more free to move from club to club and league to league. Clubs are now more inclined to offer longer contracts, thus making it more likely that they will be able to secure a fee of some kind when it comes time to sell a player. As a result, players are in a much stronger bargaining position when negotiating their contracts with clubs. All players are free agents once their contracts have expired. However, a select few players are effectively free agents even while under contract, because their exceptional skills are in such demand.

Since the Bosman decision took effect, players have acquired the power to demand and extract transfers in a way that would have been unthinkable before the lawsuit. Players who are unhappy with a club's management, who think that their club does not have a realistic chance of winning a title or trophy, or players who are simply bored or petulant, now have the leverage to demand to be transferred without fear of repercussion as long as they are skilled enough as players.

. . . .

Not surprisingly, the national footballing organizations of Europe have come together to solve what they view as a problem that could undermine the game. . . . The organizations agreed in December 2001, to set up two transfer "windows" per year, one each in summer and winter, to limit when clubs may buy and sell players. The hope is that the windows will add some stability to a system that is perceived to be out of control. By making it impossible for all players to move outside of the windows, clubs hope to remove the incentive for players to demand transfers in the middle of a season. An obvious flaw in that reasoning, however, is that players who demand transfers may simply . . . sit out until the next window allows them to leave.

With regard to the second half of the Bosman ruling, an interesting result of the abolition of foreign players has been what I call the "cosmopolitization" of clubs. Before Bosman, eight (sometimes six because of the "3+2 Rule") of the eleven players on the pitch were of the club's nationality. So, for example, a German team would have eight Germans. The rules defining a "foreign player," however, were set by the national associations. In England, for example, a player from any of the "Home Countries" counted as "domestic." An English team could include any British citizen, as well as those of the Republic of Ireland. Today, however, clubs can, and do, field any combination of players, from all over Europe and the world. Some complain that the importation of foreign players into the highest leagues in their respective countries inhibits the development of youth talent to the detriment of their national team. They blame this on the limitation of first team action for citizens of the home country.

Whether this is true or not should be the subject of another study. . . .

V. WHY BOSMAN IS NOT TO BLAME FOR THE POOR STATE OF THE GAME

The timing of Bosman's case was particularly important, given the fact that football began an economic boom at about the time he initiated his litigation. Despite the apparent economic rebirth of the game, however, all is not well. There is legitimate criticism that only a very few of the hundreds of clubs in Europe have actually benefited from the explosive growth in the game, and that the money now flowing freely has caused the game to lose touch with its working class roots. Bosman is frequently faced with criticism that his personal greed resulted in the explosive growth in players' salaries and that he has changed the game forever. Although Bosman makes an attractive target, especially for club owners and chairpersons, this attack on him is disingenuous in that it seeks to shift the blame for the current rot in the administration of the game.

. . . .

While one exceptionally bad deal does not necessarily represent the entirety of the business, it does illustrate the point that Jean-Marc Bosman's impact upon football in Europe must be examined in a larger context.

Bosman represents an opportunity for those in positions of authority to deflect criticism from where it really belongs—on them. Bosman never made a policy decision that had wide ranging implications for the game. Bosman never negotiated a television rights deal, a kit sponsorship deal, or even a player transfer (his own transfer was voided when RC Liege failed to release his player's certificate). Bosman never offered an inflated contract to a young player (or a highly skilled player for that matter), nor did he refuse to field a skilled player under contract without explanation. Bosman never had the opportunity to exercise complete control over an entire group of young men's careers. Bosman was not responsible for the decline in conditions at the

football stadia, nor for any other reason that the supporters left the game in droves in the 1980s.

Notes

31. 1 CMLR 645, P 37, at 662.

47. *Id.* P 212, at 728.

48. *Id.* P 218, at 730.

51. *Id.* P 226, at 733.

59. *Id.* P 237, at 737.

62. *Id.* P 135, at 693.

64. *Id.* Ruling 1, at 778.

65. *Id.* Ruling 2, at 778.

69. 3 [1998] CIL, no. 4, 289–312.

70. *Id.* at 309.

71. *Id.*

72. *Id.* at 307–08.

73. *Id.* at 303.

Discussion Questions

1. Why does the public tend to support management over labor during sports work stoppages?
2. What are the inflators and deflators of player salaries?
3. Is it more appropriate to compare athletes' compensation to popular entertainers or to CEOs and business leaders?
4. Are professional athletes overpaid? Explain.
5. Explain the relationship between ticket prices and player salaries.
6. Are there potential downsides for teams if athlete compensation shifted to an incentive-based model?
7. Does athlete performance have a direct or indirect impact on wins? Direct or indirect impact on profits? How do those answers affect decisions on incentive-based compensation, if at all?
8. What league has the most restrictive system of free agency? The least?
9. If the offers that a party makes during negotiations are an indication of its belief of the player's value, why are they inadmissible as evidence during the salary arbitration hearing?
10. How are small-market clubs disadvantaged by salary arbitration?
11. Should a party be able to discuss its financial situation in a salary arbitration hearing? Why or why not?
12. When considering incentive-based player contracts, how can management ensure that it is incentivizing the kind of performance that will actually lead to team success?

13. What does your knowledge of the reserve system, salary arbitration, and the performance of free agents in MLB tell you about the optimal method of building a club?
14. Design an athlete compensation framework that best balances the interests of both owners and athletes.
15. Should teams create negative-compensation incentives for poor play (such as missed shots, strikeouts, etc.)?
16. What offers the fullest pictures of a player's performance: statistical metrics or "eyeball" scouting?
17. If "box score statistics" are overvalued in sports, what kinds of performance are undervalued?
18. What is the next frontier of player evaluation (after scouting and statistical evaluation)?
19. Is there a way to more effectively predict injury risk in player evaluation and compensation decisions?
20. Where are the inefficiencies in player evaluation and compensation today? Apply this question to the four major sports.
21. Can statistical modeling accurately assess player performance in sports like soccer, basketball, etc. where individual performance is interdependent with the play of several teammates?
22. Do you agree with Gerrard that technology can effectively deal with the tracking, attribution and weighting problems when evaluating players in an interdependent sport?

23. Healy says, "Performance and pay are easily measured" in MLB. In light of the other readings in this chapter, do you agree?
24. How should teams properly assess a player's most recent performance that is either significantly better or worse than how he has performed in the past?
25. Is past performance an accurate predictor of future performance? What other factors should teams consider when making evaluation and compensation decisions?
26. What was the primary problem with the NHL's arbitration process—too few settlements between management and labor, or salaries escalating to unsustainable levels? Does the NHL's new CBA solve these problems?
27. Should the NHL and MLB consider offering earlier free agency to their players in exchange for eliminating the arbitration process altogether?
28. Can a luxury tax system be effective if few (if any) teams pay the tax?
29. What are the advantages and potential disadvantages to the NBA's luxury tax system, as compared to the MLB system or other leagues with different cost containment mechanisms?

CHAPTER ELEVEN

Sports Franchise Valuation

INTRODUCTION

Whether for a prospective sale, a bankruptcy, or leveraging debt, at various times it is necessary to place an accurate value on a sports franchise. As this chapter reveals, valuation of professional sports franchises is no simple task. As evidenced by the numerous sales of both established and expansion teams in the four major North American sports leagues and clubs in many European soccer leagues for seemingly ever-increasing amounts of money, the market for professional sports franchises continues to be robust. Although the study of firm and asset valuation has been a common area of research in finance, there has been little application of these principles to professional sports franchises.

Valuation of professional sports franchises is much different than valuations of most other assets. This is likely because of the idiosyncratic nature of sports franchises, which are somewhat comparable to the valuation of art in that, ultimately, beauty is in the eye of the beholder. Thus, there is significant volatility in the marketplace. The total financial return to owners of professional sports franchises is determined by calculating a team's profitability and capital appreciation. Although the franchise's ability to earn a profit and its likelihood of increasing in value in the long term play important roles in determining a team's present value, numerous other factors impact franchise value.

The nature and quality of a team's facility arrangement is one factor. Given the increase in the number of new, revenue-generating facilities in the last 15 to 20 years, it is important to gauge the impact that these stadia and arenas have on franchise values. The building boom that has occurred since the late 1980s has resulted in new or renovated stadia for most of the teams in the four major North American sports leagues. Globally, European soccer clubs are still in the early stages of the stadium construction era. The presence of a playing facility with a lease arrangement that

allows the team to generate and retain significant revenues from luxury boxes, club seats, signage, naming rights, concessions, parking, and outside events at a low cost (i.e., little rent) will drive franchise values upward. The absence of such an agreement will have the opposite effect.

In addition, a team's media contracts impact its value. The size of the league-wide television contract provides guaranteed revenues to each team and indicates the nationwide popularity of the sport. However, the size of the local television contract secured by a club varies greatly. The local television contract provides a team with revenue that is largely unshared and is an indicator of a team's popularity in its home market. Increased involvement of teams in the ownership of regional sports networks not only provides the opportunity for a team to dramatically increase revenues earned from local broadcasting, but it also provides the team owner with a valuable asset against which capital can be raised. Therefore, a team's national and local television contracts are important factors in determining the team's value. Global media contracts are a possibility for some of the biggest European soccer clubs, which provide them with a revenue stream that is unavailable to their North American counterparts due to the more restrictive league rules regarding global broadcasting found domestically.

The league in which a franchise plays impacts its value in several ways. As previously mentioned, the league's national broadcasting contract guarantees revenue to the franchise. Second, the league's revenue sharing agreement can either enhance or hinder the value of its franchises. A league with a high degree of revenue sharing can ensure the long-term viability of its franchises by guaranteeing them monies every year and protecting them against a shortfall in nonshared revenues in any particular year. However, this may harm the short-term value of franchises that generate significant amounts of revenue by redistributing their wealth to other franchises. The lack of a meaningful revenue sharing plan in European soccer leagues can either help or hinder the value of a club depending on its ability to generate revenues on its own.

A league's collective bargaining agreement with its athletes can affect the value of its franchises. A settled labor situation with a mechanism for control over player compensation benefits owners by providing them with an assurance that their revenue-generating games will continue to be played. A mechanism for controlling player compensation is vital in that, similar to most businesses, a sports franchise's ability to predict and control its costs is a very important aspect of its operations. The single greatest cost to professional sports franchises is player salaries; a salary cap provides a team with a degree of cost certainty by dictating the amount of money that it can spend on athlete compensation. Although loopholes and exceptions to these salary-containment systems have somewhat eroded their benefits, they still enhance team values. It follows then that the legal prohibition of cost containment mechanisms in European soccer leagues inhibits the value of most of the clubs.

The debt accumulated by a team also requires consideration. Team debt typically arises when an owner purchases a team and when the team must pay for part, or all, of the construction costs of a new facility; this obligation may be onerous and can ultimately cause the transfer of a team for a lower cost. It is for this reason that it is often better for a sports franchise to lease rather than own its playing facility, especially if the lease terms are advantageous. A team's debt is often guaranteed by a revenue stream accruing from its facility. This negatively affects a team's cash flow because the revenues that would otherwise be used for team operations must be utilized to service the debt. In an attempt to protect its members, each league has enacted rules that limit the amount of debt that can be accumulated by a team. However, these debt limitation rules have numerous exceptions and are rarely enforced. Again, the contrast with European soccer leagues is striking. A number of European clubs have amassed stifling amounts of debt due to the run up of franchise acquisition costs, facility-related costs, and player acquisition and salary costs.

Table 1   *Forbes* Franchise Values as of January 2010

Team	League	Owner	Current Value ($millions)
Dallas Cowboys	NFL	Jerry Jones	1,650
Washington Redskins	NFL	Daniel Snyder	1,550
New York Yankees	MLB	George Steinbrenner	1,500
New England Patriots	NFL	Robert Kraft	1,361
New York Giants	NFL	J. Mara/S. Tisch	1,183
New York Jets	NFL	Woody Johnson	1,170
Houston Texans	NFL	Robert McNair	1,150
Philadelphia Eagles	NFL	Jeffrey Lurie	1,123
Tampa Bay Buccaneers	NFL	Malcolm Glazer	1,085
Chicago Bears	NFL	Virginia McCaskey	1,082
Denver Broncos	NFL	Pat Bowlen	1,081
Baltimore Ravens	NFL	Steve Bisciotti	1,079
Carolina Panthers	NFL	Jerry Richardson	1,049
Cleveland Browns	NFL	Randy Lerner	1,032
Kansas City Chiefs	NFL	Clark Hunt	1,027
Indianapolis Colts	NFL	Jim Irsay	1,025
Pittsburgh Steelers	NFL	Dan Rooney	1,020
Green Bay Packers	NFL	Public	1,019
Miami Dolphins	NFL	Stephen M. Ross	1,015
Tennessee Titans	NFL	Bud Adams	1,000
Seattle Seahawks	NFL	Paul Allen	994
Cincinnati Bengals	NFL	Mike Brown	953
New Orleans Saints	NFL	Tom Benson	942
Arizona Cardinals	NFL	Bill Bidwill	935
San Diego Chargers	NFL	Alex Spanos	917
St Louis Rams	NFL	Chip Rosenbloom	913
New York Mets	MLB	Fred Wilpon	912
Buffalo Bills	NFL	Ralph Wilson	909
San Francisco 49ers	NFL	Denise DeBartolo York	875
Detroit Lions	NFL	William Ford	872

Table 1   *(Continued)*

Team	League	Owner	Current Value ($millions)
Jacksonville Jaguars	NFL	Wayne Weaver	866
Atlanta Falcons	NFL	Arthur Blank	856
Minnesota Vikings	NFL	Zygi Wilf	835
Boston Red Sox	MLB	John Henry	833
Oakland Raiders	NFL	Al Davis	797
Los Angeles Dodgers	MLB	Frank McCourt	722
Chicago Cubs	MLB	Tom Ricketts	700
Los Angeles Lakers	NBA	Jerry Buss and Philip Anschutz	607
New York Knicks	NBA	Cablevision Systems	586
Chicago Bulls	NBA	Jerry Reinsdorf	511
Los Angeles Angels of Anaheim	MLB	Arturo Moreno	509
Philadelphia Phillies	MLB	William Giles	496
St Louis Cardinals	MLB	William DeWitt Jr	486
Detroit Pistons	NBA	Karen Davidson	479
Cleveland Cavaliers	NBA	Daniel Gilbert	476
San Francisco Giants	MLB	William Neukom and the Burns Family	471
Houston Rockets	NBA	Leslie Alexander	470
Toronto Maple Leafs	NHL	Maple Leaf Sports & Entertainment	470
Chicago White Sox	MLB	Jerry Reinsdorf	450
Dallas Mavericks	NBA	Mark Cuban	446
Atlanta Braves	MLB	Liberty Media	446
Houston Astros	MLB	Robert McLane Jr	445
Boston Celtics	NBA	Wycliffe Grousbeck	433
Phoenix Suns	NBA	Robert Sarver	429
Seattle Mariners	MLB	Nintendo	426
New York Rangers	NHL	Cablevision Systems	416
Washington Nationals	MLB	Theodore Lerner	406
Texas Rangers	MLB	Thomas Hicks	405
San Diego Padres	MLB	John Moores	401
Baltimore Orioles	MLB	Peter Angelos	400
Toronto Raptors	NBA	Maple Leaf Sports & Entertainment	400
Cleveland Indians	MLB	Lawrence Dolan	399
San Antonio Spurs	NBA	Peter Holt	398
Arizona Diamondbacks	MLB	Ken Kendrick	390
Colorado Rockies	MLB	Charles Monfort and Richard Monfort	373
Detroit Tigers	MLB	Michael Ilitch	371
Miami Heat	NBA	Micky Arison	364
Orlando Magic	NBA	Richard DeVos	361
Minnesota Twins	MLB	James Pohlad	356
Toronto Blue Jays	MLB	Rogers Communications	353
Hendrick Motorsports	NASCAR	Rick Hendrick	350
Milwaukee Brewers	MLB	Mark Attanasio	347
Philadelphia 76ers	NBA	Comcast Spectacor	344
Utah Jazz	NBA	Greg Miller	343
Cincinnati Reds	MLB	Robert Castellini	342
Montreal Canadiens	NHL	Molson Family	339
Portland Trail Blazers	NBA	Paul Allen	338
Detroit Red Wings	NHL	Michael Ilitch	337
Denver Nuggets	NBA	Stanley Kroenke	321
Tampa Bay Rays	MLB	Stuart Sternberg	320
Oakland Athletics	MLB	Lewis Wolff	319
Golden State Warriors	NBA	Christopher Cohan	315
Kansas City Royals	MLB	David Glass	314
Washington Wizards	NBA	Theodore Leonsis	313

(continued)

Table 1   *(Continued)*

Team	League	Owner	Current Value ($millions)
Oklahoma City Thunder	NBA	Clay Bennett	310
Atlanta Hawks	NBA	Atlanta Spirit	306
Sacramento Kings	NBA	Gavin Maloof and Joseph Maloof	305
Los Angeles Clippers	NBA	Donald Sterling	295
Pittsburgh Pirates	MLB	Robert Nutting	288
Indiana Pacers	NBA	Herbert Simon	281
Charlotte Bobcats	NBA	Michael Jordan	278
Florida Marlins	MLB	Jeffrey Loria	277
Philadelphia Flyers	NHL	Comcast Spectacor	273
Boston Bruins	NHL	Jeremy Jacobs	271
Roush Fenway Racing	NASCAR	Jack Roush and John W. Henry	270
New Jersey Nets	NBA	Mikhail Prohorov	269
Minnesota Timberwolves	NBA	Glen Taylor	268
New Orleans Hornets	NBA	George Shinn and George Chouest	267
Chicago Blackhawks	NHL	Wirtz Family	258
Memphis Grizzlies	NBA	Michael Heisley	257
Milwaukee Bucks	NBA	Herbert Kohl	254
Dallas Stars	NHL	Thomas Hicks	246
Vancouver Canucks	NHL	Francesco Aquilini	239
New Jersey Devils	NHL	Jeffrey Vanderbeek	223
Pittsburgh Penguins	NHL	Mario Lemieux and Ronald Burkle	222
Minnesota Wild	NHL	Craig Leipold and Philip Falcone	210
Los Angeles Kings	NHL	Philip Anschutz	208
Anaheim Ducks	NHL	Henry Samueli and Susan Samueli	206
Colorado Avalanche	NHL	Stanley Kroenke	205
Calgary Flames	NHL	Calgary Flames LP	200
Ottawa Senators	NHL	Eugene Melnyk	197
Tampa Bay Lightning	NHL	Jeff Vinik	191
San Jose Sharks	NHL	Kevin Compton and Greg Jamison	184
Washington Capitals	NHL	Theodore Leonsis	183
Carolina Hurricanes	NHL	Peter Karmanos, Jr	177
St Louis Blues	NHL	David Checketts	176
Buffalo Sabres	NHL	Thomas Golisano	170
Richard Childress Racing	NASCAR	Richard Childress	167
Edmonton Oilers	NHL	Daryl Katz	166
Columbus Blue Jackets	NHL	John P McConnell	165
Florida Panthers	NHL	Stu Siegel and Cliff Viner	159
Nashville Predators	NHL	David Freeman	156
New York Islanders	NHL	Charles Wang	149
Joe Gibbs Racing	NASCAR	Joe Gibbs	144
Atlanta Thrashers	NHL	Atlanta Spirit	143
Phoenix Coyotes	NHL	NHL	138
Richard Petty Motorsports	NASCAR	Richard Petty	131
Penske Championship Racing	NASCAR	Roger Penske	111
Los Angeles Galaxy	MLS	Philip Anschutz	100
Michael Waltrip Racing	NASCAR	Michael Waltrip	100
Stewart-Haas Racing	NASCAR	Tony Stewart and Gene Haas	80
Earnhardt Ganassi Racing	NASCAR	Teresa Earnhardt	70
Red Bull Racing Team	NASCAR	Dietrich Mateschitz	55
Toronto FC	MLS	Maple Leaf Sports & Entertainment	44
Chicago Fire	MLS	Andrew and Ellen Hauptman	41
FC Dallas	MLS	Hunt Sports	39
New York Red Bulls	MLS	Red Bull GmbH	36
D.C. United	MLS	Victor MacFarlane and William Chang	35

Table 1   *(Continued)*

Team	League	Owner	Current Value ($millions)
Houston Dynamo	MLS	Philip Anschutz, Golden Boy Promotions and Brenner International	33
Colorado Rapids	MLS	Stanley Kroenke	31
Real Salt Lake	MLS	David Checketts	30
New England Revolution	MLS	Robert and Jonathan Kraft	27
Chivas USA	MLS	Antonio Cué and Jorge Vergara	24
Columbus Crew	MLS	Hunt Sports	23
Kansas City Wizards	MLS	OnGoal	22

Source: Forbes.

The tax benefits associated with ownership of professional sports franchises have an impact on value, as well. (See Chapter 1 for further discussion of this topic.)

The real estate value of the sports franchise must also be considered. A real estate developer may purchase a sports franchise as part of a larger development scheme upon which profits can be realized, even if the team itself may suffer operating losses. This will increase the transfer price of the franchise. The nature of the seller will affect team value as well. A corporate owner typically must sell the franchise fairly quickly in order to appease analysts or shareholders, whereas an individual owner, realizing the significant consumption value associated with team ownership, must be compensated for the loss of the psychological premium that team ownership brings. Consequently, an individual owner is less likely to sell the team with any degree of urgency and can thus afford to "hold out" until obtaining the desired price. Thus, the purchase price of a team sold by a corporation may be lower than a comparable franchise sold by an individual.

The quality or reputation of a team as measured in terms of its win–loss record also may impact value, as may the value of its brand. Although seemingly irrational due to the cyclical nature of sports, a team's recent performance

Table 2   Franchise Sales Before, During, and After Bear Market

	Years Before and After	Team	Sale Price	Sale Year	Previous Purchase Price	Previous Purchase Year
	1972	Boston Celtics	$4,000,000	1972	$6,000,000	1970
		Chicago Bulls	5,100,000	1972	1,300,000**	1966
		St. Louis Rams	19,000,000	1972	7,100,000	1962
Bear market	January1973 to December 1974	Vancouver Canucks	8,500,000	1974	6,000,000	1970
		San Diego Padres	12,000,000	1974	12,500,000	1968
	1975	Pittsburgh Penguins	3,800,000	1975	7,000,000	1971
		Chicago White Sox	10,700,000	1975	7,800,000	1961
	1980	Cleveland Cavaliers	7,000,000	1980	3,700,000	1970
		Calgary Flames	16,000,000	1980	6,000,000	1972
		Oakland Athletics	12,700,000	1980	3,800,000	1960
		New York Mets	21,000,000	1980	1,800,000**	1960
Bear market	March 1981 to August 1982	Houston Rockets	11,000,000	1982	2,000,000	1973
		New Jersey Devils	30,000,000	1982	6,000,000**	1974
		Seattle Mariners	13,000,000	1981	6,250,000**	1976
		Chicago White Sox	20,000,000	1981	10,700,000	1975
	1983	Kansas City Royals	22,000,000	1983	5,550,000**	1968
	1986	Utah Jazz	20,000,000	1986	6,150,000**	1974
		New York Mets	80,750,000	1986	21,000,000	1980

(continued)

Table 2   (Continued)

	Years Before and After	Team	Sale Price	Sale Year	Previous Purchase Price	Previous Purchase Year
Bear market	August 1987 to November 1987	Phoenix Suns	$52,000,000	1987	$2,000,000	1968
	1988	Portland Trail Blazers	70,000,000	1988	3,700,000**	1970
		Dallas Cowboys	95,000,000	1988	60,000,000	1984
		Seattle Seahawks	80,000,000	1988	16,000,000**	1974
		Los Angeles Kings	39,000,000	1988	2,000,000**	1967
		Quebec Nordiques	16,500,000	1988	6,000,000**	1979
		Baltimore Orioles	70,000,000	1988	13,100,000	1979
	1989	Denver Nuggets	54,000,000	1989	19,000,000	1985
		Toronto Maple Leafs	104,000,000	1989	2,000,000	1961
		Seattle Mariners	80,000,000	1989	13,000,000	1981
		Texas Rangers	80,000,000	1989	11,100,000	1971
Bear market	June 1990 to October 1990	Dallas Stars	31,500,000	1990	5,300,000	1977
		Montreal Expos	86,000,000	1990	12,500,000**	1968
		San Diego Padres	75,000,000	1990	12,000,000	1974
	1991	Denver Nuggets	70,000,000	1991	54,000,000	1989
		Orlando Magic	110,000,000	1991	32,500,000**	1989
		Minnesota Vikings	102,000,000	1991	54,300,000	1985
		Toronto Blue Jays	134,000,000	1991	7,000,000**	1976
	1999	Pittsburgh Penguins	70,000,000	1999	3,800,000	1975
		St. Louis Blues	96,000,000	1999	2,000,000**	1967
		Tampa Bay Lightning	115,000,000	1999	45,000,000**	1991
		Washington Capitals	85,000,000	1999	6,000,000	1975
		Montreal Expos	214,000,000	1999	86,000,000	1990
		Cleveland Indians	323,000,000	1999	4,000,000	1956
		Florida Marlins	150,000,000	1999	95,000,000**	1991
		Cincinnati Reds	186,000,000	1999	24,000,000	1984

record may factor into the valuation equation. A team's brand may come into play and enhance the franchise's value if the team is one of the handful of "trophy" teams in both the North American and European soccer leagues that resonate well beyond their home market.

The market size of the city in which a team is located may be important because of its potential effect on the size of the team's fan base, the local television contract, local sponsorship and advertising agreements, and the number of large corporations and wealthy individuals in the city with the ability to afford luxury seating. In addition, the degree to which the market is saturated by the presence of other professional sports franchises may impact a team's value.

It is for all of these reasons that valuation of professional sports franchises is considered more of an art than a science. The selections used in this chapter shed additional light on the valuation process. In the first article, Ziets and Haber of sports advisory firm MZ Sports establish the background for the discussion that ensues in the remainder of the chapter. The chapter continues with a Fitch Ratings research publication that provides an overview of the rating process for sports-related transactions. In the third and fourth excerpts, Humphreys and Mondello and then Alexander and Kern offer in-depth scholarly analyses of the determinants of the valuation of a sports franchise. Phillips and Krasner take a peek into the future of sports franchise values in the final selection.

See **Table 1** for a list of *Forbes* franchise valuations; **Table 2** for a list of franchise sales before, during, and after bear markets; and **Table 3** for a list of average league franchise valuations.

Table 2 *(Continued)*

	Years Before and After	Team	Sale Price	Sale Year	Previous Purchase Price	Previous Purchase Year
Bear market	January 2000 to 2002	Dallas Mavericks	$195,000,000	2000	$12,000,000**	1980
		Seattle SuperSonics	200,000,000	2001	21,000,000	1984
		Vancouver Grizzlies	170,000,000	2000	125,000,000**	1994
		Denver Nuggets	455,000,000	2000	755,000,000***	1997
		Atlanta Falcons	545,000,000	2001	8,500,000**	1965
		Baltimore Ravens	600,000,000	2000	4,000,000	1961
		Colorado Avalanche	202,000,000	2000	755,000,000***	1997
		New Jersey Devils	175,000,000	2000	30,000,000	1982
		New York Islanders	190,000,000	2000	6,000,000**	1972
		Phoenix Coyotes	127,000,000	2001	68,000,000	1995
		Boston Red Sox	700,000,000***	2001	22,500,000	1978
		Toronto Blue Jays	137,000,000	2000	134,000,000	1991
	2007	Oklahoma City Thunder	350,000,000	2007	200,000,000	2001
		New Orleans Hornets	248,000,000	2007	33,000,000	1987
		Nashville Predators	174,000,000	2007	80,000,000	1997
		Atlanta Braves	400,000,000	2007	12,000,000	1976
Bear market	2008–2009	Miami Dolphins	1.1 billion	2009	165,000,000	1994
		Montreal Canadiens	550,000,000***	2009	181,000,000	2000
		Minnesota Wild	225,000,000	2008	80,000,000**	1997
		Tampa Bay Lightning	204,000,000	2008	100,000,000	1999
		San Jose Sharks	147,000,000	2002	20,000,000**	1990

*Except for sales occurring in 2001, represents the percent change from last close in January in the year of the prior sale to the last close in December of the sale year.
**Expansion fee
***Sale includes other assets
Sources: Moag and Company Research; *Pay Dirt*; additional data on file from authors.

Table 3   Average League Franchise Values (in Millions)

Year	Average/High/Low	NHL	NFL	NBA	MLB
2009	Average	$223	$1000	$367	$481
	High	*470*	*1650*	*607*	*1500*
	Low	*138*	*797*	*254*	*277*
2008	Average	$220	$1040	$379	$472
	High	*448*	*1612*	*613*	*1306*
	Low	*142*	*839*	*278*	*256*
2007	Average	$200	$957	$372	$431
	High	*413*	*1500*	*608*	*1200*
	Low	*143*	*782*	*253*	*244*
2006	Average	$180	$898	$353	$376
	High	*332*	*1423*	*592*	*1026*
	Low	*127*	*720*	*230*	*209*
2005	Average	$131	$818	$326	$332
	High	*325*	*1264*	*543*	*950*
	Low	*65*	*658*	*225*	*176*

(continued)

Table 3   (Continued)

Year	Average/High/Low	NHL	NFL	NBA	MLB
2004	Average	$163	$733	$302	$295
	High	282	1104	510	832
	Low	100	552	199	145
2003	Average	$164	$628	$248	$295
	High	266	952	426	849
	Low	86	505	168	113
2002	Average	$157	$531	$223	$286
	High	277	845	403	730
	Low	79	374	135	108
2001	Average	$148	$466	$207	$263
	High	263	796	395	635
	Low	77	338	118	92
2000	Average	$135	$423	$183	$233
	High	235	741	334	548
	Low	73	305	103	89
1999	Average	$125	$385	$167	$220
	High	195	663	303	491
	Low	67	293	94	84

Source: Forbes.

OVERVIEW

THE FINANCIAL VALUATION OF SPORTS FRANCHISES

Mitchell Ziets and David Haber

INTRODUCTION

As the sports industry has grown into big business over the past twenty years, the need to drill down on the value of sports assets has grown. From estate tax planning to limited partnership sales, from change-in-control events to put features incorporated into partnership agreements, franchise valuations have become a part of the sports business landscape.

A number of texts have focused on sports franchise valuation methodology. Rather than repeat what has already been written, this . . . takes a different approach—it raises the question as to the appropriate methodology of sports franchise valuation and provides the reader with the tools to develop an informed opinion.

While the value of sports franchises has grown dramatically in recent years—according to *Forbes* and *Financial World* magazines, values in the four major U.S. sports leagues—Major League Baseball ("MLB"), National Basketball Association ("NBA"), National Football League ("NFL"), and National Hockey League ("NHL")—have grown at an average annual rate of 10.8% from 1991–2008—valuation techniques differ from those in other businesses, both in methodology and rigor. While many well-established industries are valued based on operating profits or cash flow, the sports industry derives value based on revenue multiples. This methodology frequently discounts the expense side of the ledger and pays short shrift to the unique features inherent in a sports franchise.

After providing background on trends in sports franchise values, this . . . focuses on the differentiating factors, or drivers, of franchise value. It then discusses key considerations regarding the current preferred sports franchise methodology, revenue multiple analysis. Finally, it makes a case for valuing franchises based on the discounted cash flow. It is important to note that this . . . does not conclude that revenue multiples valuation methodology should be scrapped in favor of discounted cash flow. It simply raises the question and provides sufficient ammunition for the reader.

HISTORICAL FRANCHISE VALUES

In order to analyze trends in sports franchise values, it is useful to examine franchise valuations from a historical context. In that regard, **Figure 1** shows the average franchise valuations for each of the four leagues since 1991, as reported by *Financial World Magazine* and *Forbes Magazine*:

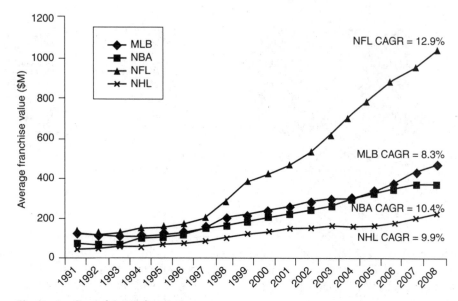

Figure 1   Franchise Valuations

Source: Rodney Fort, "Rodney Fort's Sports Economics," Sports Business Data page, 2005, http://www
.rodneyfort.com/SportsData/BizFrame.htm, accessed January 2007. Reproduced with permission of
ABC-CLIO, LLC.

Clearly, franchise values have steadily increased across all four leagues since 1991. There are a number of factors to which this can be attributed, but perhaps the most relevant is the evolution of the overarching attitude towards sports franchise ownership. In recent years, an increasing emphasis has been placed on the business operations of franchises, as opposed to the traditional focus on the competitive, game-related aspects. Historically, sports franchises were generally considered to be expensive toys or hobbies for wealthy individuals. However, as the dollars associated with franchise operations increased exponentially in recent years, owners began to recognize and take advantage of opportunities to turn their franchises into real moneymaking ventures, rather than mere outlets for their competitive instincts. Accordingly, demand and sales prices for franchises have increased across all four leagues, as seen in Figure 1.

It should be noted that these valuations, while providing public benchmarks, are a source of debate within the sports finance community. *Forbes* began attempting to value franchises in the four primary leagues in 1998, picking up where *Financial World Magazine* left off in 1997. *Forbes'* valuation methodology is kept confidential, but does ultimately result in valuations for each franchise based on four primary components: 1) value attributable to revenues shared by all franchises within a given league; 2) value attributable to a franchise's city and market size; 3) value attributable to a franchise's stadium/arena; and 4) value attributable to a franchise's brand management.[1] With respect to those four value components, all but the first are primarily intangible and difficult to approximate without a rigorous methodology. Accordingly, one frequent assessment is that, while the analysis serves as a useful tool in valuing franchises, the accuracy of

the underlying individual team data limits the veracity of the analysis on a team-by-team basis.

At the same time, there is certainly something to be said for a valuation approach that is consistently applied over time. Regardless of the accuracy of any particular franchise valuation, a review of a set of the *Forbes* valuations over time can reveal trends for specific leagues, as well as across leagues. For example, the chart in Figure 1 shows that as of 1997, average franchise values for all four leagues were still relatively tightly grouped, whereas NFL valuations have spiked significantly since then, outstripping the growth in values of the other leagues fairly significantly. With respect to the growth rates of franchise values, all four leagues have demonstrated impressive results in the *Forbes* data. Since 1991, the average value of an NFL franchise has grown by 12.9% per year, which is closely trailed by the growth rate of the average franchise in the NBA at 10.4%. The other two leagues' average franchise values have also grown steadily since 1991, with the NHL at 9.9% and MLB at 8.3% per year.

DRIVERS OF FRANCHISE VALUES

From the *Forbes* data in Figure 1, the overall trends in franchise values can be understood. However, when valuing a particular franchise, factors that are specific to the league, city, and team in question must be taken into consideration.

League Issues

As seen in Figure 1, there is a clear disparity (which has become increasingly pronounced in recent years) in valuations of franchises in different leagues. It stands to reason that the league in which a franchise is a member is a highly

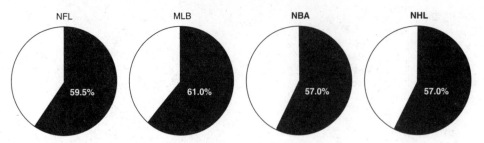

Figure 2   Average Percent of Revenues Spent on Player Salaries by League
Source: MZ Sports LLC proprietary research. Reproduced with permission of ABC-CLIO, LLC.

significant driver of franchise value. Leagues can affect franchise value in three primary ways: (i) labor situation, (ii) league-developed revenue streams, and (iii) league rules regarding ownership and debt. Among the most publicized areas of league rules are player salary constraints, which vary widely across leagues. It stands to reason that a league with tight controls on player salaries creates a greater degree of cost certainty for its franchises, which in turn, should have a positive effect on franchise value. In practice, the NFL has a tight salary cap that is tied to a fixed portion of leaguewide revenues, and the NHL has gone to a similar system as of its latest Collective Bargaining Agreement ("CBA"). Meanwhile, the NBA does have a salary cap, but there are exceptions which lead to a slightly higher degree of variance in player salaries. And lastly, MLB does not have a salary cap—its main salary constraint is a 'luxury tax'—a tax on salaries over a certain level—which to date has directly impacted only a few franchises. **Figure 2** shows that the average percent of revenues dedicated to covering player salary expenditures (including player development costs) is higher for MLB than for the other three leagues.

Labor stability, or lack thereof, is another important driver of franchise value. A league with no labor problems on the horizon is not likely to experience any value-depleting work stoppages. Noting the fact that the aforementioned

issues with salary constraints are usually the primary cause of labor strife, an ideal situation from a franchise value perspective would be a CBA which is lucrative for franchise owners, yet still provides players with an acceptable level of compensation to ensure labor peace. Any deviation in either direction from this equilibrium can lead to potential work stoppages which can be extremely damaging to franchise values in the short term. **Figure 3** shows the current term of the active CBA for each league.

Revenue sharing can also significantly drive value. Leagues with a relatively high degree of local revenue sharing are likely to have smaller disparities in valuations between higher revenue franchises and lower revenue ones. The NFL has the highest degree of revenue sharing; a policy that has helped drive franchise value. MLB, in recent years, has increased revenue sharing in response to a growing gap in revenues between large market and small market teams. The same can be said for the NHL, which determined that a higher degree of revenue-sharing was vital to the survival of many of its franchises during its CBA negotiations of 2004–05. The NBA also can have a significant degree of revenue-sharing, though it is not as clear-cut as the systems employed by the NFL and NHL. In the NBA, revenue-sharing is derived from a luxury tax on player salaries over a specific threshold. Depending on player compensation as

League	CBA Starts	CBA Terminates	Extension/Early Termination Options
MLB	2007 Season	After 2011 Season	None
NBA	2005–06 Season	After 2010–11 Season	The League has the option to extend the agreement through the 2011–12 season
NFL	2005 Season	After 2010 Season	The League exercised its option to end the agreement after an uncapped year in 2010
NHL	2005–06 Season	After 2010–11 Season	The Players Association has the option to extend the agreement through the 2011–12 season

Figure 3   CBA Term for Each League
Source: MZ Sports LLC proprietary research. Reproduced with permission of ABC-CLIO, LLC.

a percentage of overall league revenues as well as individual team spending, the luxury tax trigger may or may not be tripped in a given year.

It should also be noted that local revenue sharing is one value driver that should be examined in conjunction with national revenues, as leagues which have a large amount of the latter will be able to lessen the relative importance of local revenues. The primary sources of national revenues, which are shared equally among all franchises within a given league, are national TV rights contracts. **Figure 4** shows the average per-team national media revenue for each league from 1991–2010.

Figure 4 shows that per-team national media revenues in the NFL exceed those of the other three leagues. These figures depict why national TV revenues are a highly significant value driver. An NFL franchise starts out with nearly $100M of guaranteed revenue without ever having to sell a ticket, or a sponsorship package, whereas an NHL franchise would only have roughly $3M guaranteed from national TV rights.

It is not surprising that the relative size of the rights fees received by each league are generally correlated to the average Nielsen ratings of their respective game broadcasts, as seen in **Figure 5** for 1999–2007.

At the same time, these national TV revenues only tell part of the national media story for each league, and the remaining parts of that story are constantly evolving. The concept of "new media", a term intended to encompass Internet, wireless, and cellular-based revenue streams, has become more and more of a focal point for sports leagues. As the U.S. population becomes more attuned to new media entertainment opportunities, the leagues are positioning themselves to create heretofore untapped revenue sources. MLB appears to be at the forefront of this initiative, with its creation and ownership of MLB Advanced Media ("MLBAM"), a venture focused on the delivery of MLB-related content over new forms of media. Thus far, MLBAM has proven itself to be extremely successful, maintaining a position on the forefront of this type of technology while simultaneously managing to generate positive cash flows. While the other leagues are trailing behind MLB in these endeavors, they too are placing an increasing emphasis on the development of business models that capitalize on these newfound opportunities. All four leagues have formed partnerships with cutting-edge companies like YouTube and Google, along with cell phone service providers, for the delivery of for-sale content to consumers through all means

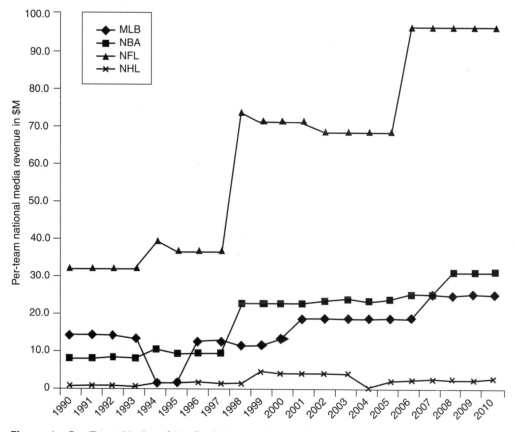

Figure 4   Per-Team National Media Revenues by League

Source: Street & Smith's Sports Business Journal Research, "Sports Rights Fees," *Street and Smith's Sports Business Daily,* 2006, http://www.sportsbusinessdaily.com/index.cfm?fuseaction=tdi.main&departmentId=24#sportsrightsfees, accessed January 2007. Reproduced with permission of ABC-CLIO, LLC.

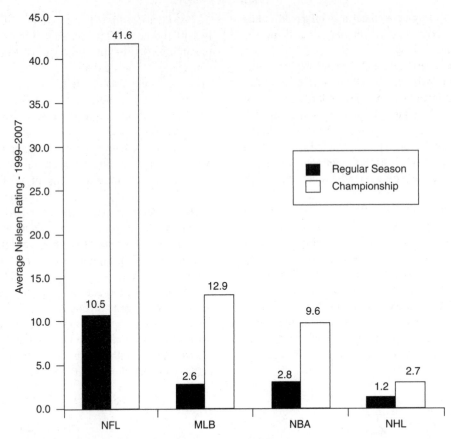

Figure 5   Average Nielsen Ratings (1999–2007) by League

Source: Street & Smith's Sports Business Journal Research, "Final Nielsen TV Ratings," *Street and Smith's Sports Business Daily*, 2006, http://www.sportsbusinessdaily.com/index.cfm?fuseaction=tdi .main&departmentId=24#finaltvratings, accessed January 2007. Reproduced with permission of ABC-CLIO, LLC.

other than the television set. While these business models are nowhere near being fully fleshed out, a key driver of franchise value into the future will be how prepared each league (and thus, each franchise) is for the next wave of media opportunities.

Even as new media revenue streams are still evolving, each league has become increasingly adept in recent years at generating significant non-television revenues on a national basis to be distributed to all of the member franchises. Specifically, each league has established marketing arms that generate a great deal of sponsorship and licensing revenues at the league level. With all of the diversified entertainment options available in today's society, association with powerful, established, highly relevant entities like the four major leagues has become extremely attractive to corporations. Accordingly, the leagues have not hesitated to financially capitalize on the attention they receive from the corporate world. With that in mind, it is clear that a significant portion of any franchise's revenues are being generated from a highly advantageous position by the leagues themselves, and the subsequent value-enhancing benefits are passed along to the franchises.

In addition to leaguewide revenues, each league has policies regarding debt and ownership which impact value. The limits on the amount of debt a franchise can carry is as follows: NFL ($150M); NBA ($100M); NHL (50% of franchise value); and MLB (10x EBITDA or 15x EBITDA in the case of a new ballpark). These rules are intended to ensure that each franchise has a limited amount of debt in the event of an economic downturn. The nature of the debt rules has caused debate within each league as to which method best drives value—a fixed debt amount (NFL and NBA), a value based test (NHL), or a profitability based test (MLB).

Furthermore, the debt rules also ensure that each franchise's owners have some "skin in the game", which incentivizes the owners to make decisions that should be at least partially driven by the franchise's best financial interests. Along these lines, the NFL and NBA each impose fixed minimum equity requirements on the franchise's controlling general partner ("GP"), or controlling owner of the franchise. One could surmise that debt limits, especially fixed debt limits, serve to limit growth in franchise value by reducing the universe of potential owners/acquirers. On the other hand, the tradeoff for this reduced franchise demand is increased franchise stability as poorly capitalized owners are less likely to be involved.

Another important league related value driver is the potential availability of financial capital. Each league works to increase the values of each of its franchises, and one example of this is in the leagues' willingness to establish leaguewide credit facilities to allow its franchises to access debt at below-market prices and terms. Due to each league's aggregate financial strength, the financial markets are often willing to provide extremely favorable lending terms, which the leagues can pass on to their respective franchises. This has been an important factor in franchises' ability to finance the construction of new/renovated facilities, which in turn allows them to potentially increase their revenues significantly, benefiting the league as a whole. Leaguewide credit facilities exist in the NFL, MLB, and the NBA. In addition to its leaguewide credit facility, the NFL established a well-received program entitled "G-3" in order to provide an additional source of favorably priced debt to be used specifically for new facility construction. Access to inexpensive debt is highly attractive for a team owner and thus drives franchise value.

Specific Team Issues

On a franchise specific level, there are also numerous drivers of value. Within a given league, market size is the most important driver. A larger market translates to a larger potential fan base to purchase tickets and to watch or listen to games. Increased demand for tickets helps drive ticket prices as well. In addition, a larger market usually means a stronger corporate presence, resulting in increased demand for premium seating and sponsorships. While it would appear obvious that there would be a direct correlation between franchise size and franchise value, this is not always the case. **Figure 6** shows the sale prices of franchises recently sold in each of the four major leagues in comparison to the market size of each of those franchises.

Figure 6 demonstrates that the correlation between franchise sale price and market size varies by league. For MLB franchises, there appears to be a clear relationship between market size and sale price—this also appears to ring true for NHL franchises. Meanwhile, for NBA and NFL franchises, it appears as though market size is significantly less of a determining factor. This dichotomy is explained, at least in part, by the aforementioned discussion of the disparities between leagues. As mentioned earlier, leagues with a relatively high degree of local-revenue sharing and a large amount of national revenues inherently deemphasize, at least partially, local revenues as a driver of franchise value. Of course, it is probably dangerous to attempt to draw a meaningful conclusion with any degree of confidence from the sample set detailed in Figure 6, as market size is only the starting point of the examination of the potential drivers of franchise value.

In addition to market size, a team's arena situation is a large driver of value. The most important question is

League	Franchise	Sale Price	Market Size Ranking
MLB	Atlanta Braves	$450M	#8
MLB	Washington Nationals	$450M	#9
MLB	Los Angeles Dodgers	$421M	#2
MLB	Cincinnati Reds	$260M	#34
MLB	Milwaukee Brewers	$220M	#35
NBA	Cleveland Cavaliers	$375M	#17
NBA	Boston Celtics	$360M	#7
NBA	Seattle Supersonics	$350M	#14
NBA	New Jersey Nets	$300M	#1
NBA	Charlotte Bobcats	$300M	#24
NFL	Miami Dolphins	$1,100M	#16
NFL	New York Jets	$635M	#1
NFL	Minnesota Vikings	$600M	#15
NFL	Baltimore Ravens	$600M	#26
NFL	Atlanta Falcons	$545M	#8
NHL	Minnesota Wild (2)	$250M	#15
NHL	Tampa Bay Lightning (2)	$200M	#13
NHL	Nashville Predators (2)	$193M	#29
NHL	St. Louis Blues (2)	$135M	#21
NHL	New Jersey Devils (1)	$125M	#1

Figure 6   Franchise Sale Prices vs. Market Size

Sources: MZ Sports LLC proprietary research; and AR&D Television Branding, "Nielsen Media Research Local Universe Estimates," AR&D Television Branding website, www.ar-d.com/pdf/DMAListing_2005-2006.pdf, accessed January 2007. Reproduced with permission of ABC-CLIO, LLC.

Note: (1) Franchise was sold during the term of the 1994–2004 Collective Bargaining Agreement

(2) Franchise was sold during the term of the Collective Bargaining Agreement signed in 2008

the ability of the building to maximize revenues. A newer facility will generally be fully equipped with amenities that have been proven, in recent years, to be better revenue drivers than those of venues of the past. This is generally reflected in the quality and availability of premium seating and sponsorship opportunities, but also carries over into the quality and accessibility of concessions and merchandise sales points, on-site tertiary businesses (restaurants, lounges, etc.), and general fan-friendliness. A new facility is very likely to have been constructed with all of the aforementioned concepts near the top of the priority list, whereas franchises in outdated venues may be facing an uphill battle in one or more of those areas. Of course, merely examining the quality of the venue would be missing another huge component of this particular revenue driver—the franchise's lease arrangement.

While the facility quality may determine revenue potential, the lease will ultimately define how much of that revenue the team gets to keep. Most facilities are funded in part by the public sector and franchises and their public partner negotiate the financial and operating arrangements. Some leases are fairly straightforward rental arrangements—the team pays a designated amount of rent to the public sector in exchange for the right to play at the facility, and in return, keeps all of the revenues and is responsible for all of the expenses associated with the facility. However, there is an entire continuum of lease arrangements which result in revenue and/or expense sharing between the franchise and the public sector. In these cases, the proportion of revenues and expenses that are directed to the franchise is just as important in terms of franchise value as the overall size of the revenue pool.

Furthermore, the notion of potential ancillary real estate opportunities on or near the facility's site and the division of any potential revenues from those possible ventures is another factor in the ultimate determination of how a franchise's facility can drive value. Numerous examples of development surrounding sports facilities exist, as team owners look for additional sources of income. For example, in Dallas, Texas, the Victory development is a $3 billion development project surrounding the arena that hosts the Dallas Mavericks and Dallas Stars.[2] Meanwhile, in Glendale, Arizona, the Westgate development, adjacent to the arena for the Phoenix Coyotes, features 6.5 million square feet of mixed-use property.[3] In Columbus, Ohio, the Arena District, anchored by Nationwide Arena, is a 75-acre, $540 million mixed-use development.[4] In these instances, the franchise owners have played and/or will play a large role in the development of this valuable real estate, as their respective franchises have served as the anchors for the surrounding areas.

Local media opportunities also drive value. A franchise's territory determines the size of the viewer base in its local media market, which in turn dictates the potential revenues that teams can generate through local broadcast rights. An additional factor to be considered in the valuation of a franchise is the duration of its existing local media contracts. If a franchise is locked into a long-term local media deal at rates which are or will be below market, franchise value would be impacted. On the other hand, a franchise that is at or near the end of an existing broadcast agreement has a great deal of flexibility. The franchise will be able to negotiate a new set of agreements, most likely under favorable terms, given the inevitable fight for local media rights among the various outlets. A strategy that has become increasingly desirable in recent years has been the formation of Regional Sports Networks ("RSNs"). Under the traditional model, franchises would sell the broadcast rights to their games to local television networks in exchange for a rights fee. However, franchises have become more attuned to the idea of filling the role of their traditional broadcast partners themselves in order to directly access the consumers. **Figure 7** shows a list of franchise-owned RSNs.

As demonstrated in Figure 7, RSNs are most prevalent in the largest markets—these are the locations in which the television rights are most valuable, and accordingly, the franchises have the most incentive to retain those rights themselves. Clearly, the existence or potential existence of an RSN has the potential to have a big impact on franchise value. At the same time, it is very important to note that the vast majority of franchises are not involved with RSNs, which adds complexity to any attempts to compare values between two or more franchises with different approaches to local media opportunities.

Another key driver is how a franchise has been operated in the past, as well as how it might be operated on a going-forward basis. If a franchise has been governed in

Franchise(s)	Regional Sports Network	Market Size Ranking
New York Mets	Sportsnet New York (SNY)	#1
New York Yankees	Yankees Entertainment and Sports Network (YES)	#1
Chicago Blackhawks, Bulls, Cubs, and White Sox	Comcast SportsNet Chicago (CSN-Chicago)	#3
Philadelphia Flyers and 76ers	Comcast SportsNet Philadelphia (CSN-Philadelphia)	#4
San Francisco Giants, Golden State Warriors, and San Jose Sharks	Comcast SportsNet Bay Area (CSN-Bay Area)	#6
Boston Bruins and Red Sox	New England Sports Network (NESN)	#7
Baltimore Orioles and Washington Nationals	Mid-Atlantic Sports Network (MASN)	#9/#26
Cleveland Indians	SportsTime Ohio (STO)	#17
Colorado Avalanche and Denver Nuggets	Altitude Sports and Entertainment Network (ASE)	#18

Figure 7   Franchise-Owned Regional Sports Networks

Source: AR&D Television Branding, "Nielsen Media Research Local Universe Estimates." Reproduced with permission of ABC-CLIO, LLC.

such a way as to have created significant and unavoidable operating losses in the near future, then those losses need to be considered as a detractor from franchise value. For example, a franchise may have signed up to long-term below-market sponsorship and local media deals, or taken on significant long-term player salary commitments. These dynamics could lead to future operating losses that will need to be funded by the owner, and should be factored into any valuation accordingly.

At the same time, a given franchise may have potential synergies that could create added value to a specific owner. For example, the owner of a local television network might need entertainment content for the network. In this case, franchise ownership would also increase the value of a related property, the network, as well. A similar example would be an individual who already owns one sports franchise in a specific market, and is considering the acquisition of a second franchise in a different league in that market. In this scenario, that owner may be able to combine back-office and sales/marketing staffs, which would enable them to reduce consolidated operating expenses, creating added value.

In addition, the potential for unrealized upside in revenues and profit drives value. Often, team owners sell franchises that are under-performing in their market for any number of reasons and a new owner can greatly enhance revenue performance. For example, a franchise may be located in a large market with a great deal of disposable income, but may also have a sales staff that is inefficiently incentivized and/or managed or have a ticket pricing policy that leaves substantial dollars on the table.

VALUATION METHODOLOGY— REVENUE MULTIPLES

It is clear that there are a wide variety of factors that drive franchise valuation, factors that impact both revenues and expenses. Thus, like any other business, valuing a sports franchise must be undertaken with the requisite amount of rigor, focusing not only on a team's current state of affairs, but its potential future financial profile.

Taking into account profitability and future growth are staples in valuing assets in most industries. Whether one is looking to acquire assets in the real estate business, which often trade as a multiple of FFO (Funds From Operations— a cash flow measure) or media, which trade as a multiple of EBITDA or on price/earnings ratios, the basis for the analysis is profitability.

However, sports franchises are typically valued based on revenue multiples. This approach requires minimal information—franchise revenues along with historical revenue multiples for the league. For example, if a buyer and seller agreed on a set of comparable franchise sale transactions that ended up reflecting an average revenue multiple of 2.5x, and the franchise under consideration had annual revenues

of $100M, then the valuation dictated by this approach would be $250M.

This approach is preferred due to several factors. First, this approach intentionally disregards cash flow variability. If a franchise is hypothetically on track to generate $10M of net cash flow, when suddenly the owner decides to pour an additional $30M into player salaries that year, then the projected $10M profit instantly become $20M of losses. It can be reasonably argued that the $30M player salary expenditure was merely a one-off decision made unilaterally by the previous owner on a non-repeating basis and, as a result, should not have any effect on the true value of the franchise. Because sports franchises' profitability are so heavily dependent on discretionary owner-specific operational decisions, one might argue that it would not be fair to base a valuation on any metric that takes these decisions into account, as they will not reoccur in the future. In addition, a revenue-based multiple approach makes the assumption that all franchises could theoretically be operated with an identical expense structure, which would imply that the only differentiating factor between franchises would be their respective revenues.

Sellers of teams favor use of the revenue multiple approach for the very reasons described in the previous paragraph. By focusing the valuation on the revenue-side of a franchise's financial statements, they are able to short-circuit any potential value-depressing issues with the franchise's actual operations. Furthermore, this approach also is fairly easy to grasp, which makes it easier for the seller to try and keep the revenue multiple as the focal point of discussions and negotiations, which can further distract a potential buyer from a deeper investigation of the franchise's current state of operations. If the seller is successful in this endeavor, then the buyer will not spend time thinking about potential upside opportunities or ongoing operating losses, but rather, will be focused on debating the fairness of the applicable multiple itself.

In order to derive the appropriate revenue multiple, the universe of comparable transactions should be as large as possible to minimize the impact of any particular off-market deal. **Figure 8** shows historical revenue multiples for the eight most recent franchise sales in each league.

Figure 8 shows clear disparities in the average revenue multiple for each of the four major leagues. However, of equal importance is the wide variation of multiples within a given league. This variation hints at the fact that a revenue multiple-based valuation should be based on a carefully culled set of comparables. Numerous factors are used to narrow the pool of potential comparable transactions. CBA changes, market size, type of seller all can impact whether or not a prior transaction is included.

Once an agreed upon set of comparable transactions is established, the revenue multiple will be adjusted based on team and league specific value drivers as described earlier. This could include potential upside at the team or league

League	Year	Franchise	Revenue Multiple at Acquisition (1)	Acquirer
MLB	2002	New York Mets	2.4x	Fred Wilpon
MLB	2003	Los Angeles Angels of Anaheim	1.5x	Arturo Moreno
MLB	2004	Los Angeles Dodgers	2.4x	Frank and Jamie McCourt
MLB	2004	Milwaukee Brewers	1.8x	Mark Attanasio
MLB	2005	Oakland Athletics	1.4x	Lew Wolff
MLB	2005	Cincinnati Reds	2.0x	Robert Castellini
MLB	2006	Washington Nationals	3.7x	Lerner Family
MLB	2007	Atlanta Braves	2.8x	Liberty Media
		Average MLB Multiple	**2.2x**	
NBA	2000	Vancouver Grizzlies	3.2x	Michael Heisley
NBA	2001	Seattle Supersonics	2.7x	Howard Schultz
NBA	2002	Boston Celtics	3.8x	Wyc Grousbeck and Stephen Pagliuca
NBA	2003	Charlotte Bobcats	3.3x	Robert Johnson
NBA	2004	Phoenix Suns	4.0x	Robert Sarver
NBA	2004	New Jersey Nets	3.0x	Bruce Ratner
NBA	2005	Cleveland Cavaliers	4.7x	Dan Gilbert
NBA	2006	Seattle Supersonics	3.9x	Clay Bennett
		Average NBA Multiple	**3.6x**	
NFL	1999	Houston Texans	3.7x	Robert McNair
NFL	1999	Washington Redskins	5.3x	Daniel Snyder
NFL	2000	Baltimore Ravens	5.0x	Art Modell
NFL	2000	New York Jets	6.1x	Woody Johnson
NFL	2002	Atlanta Falcons	4.9x	Arthur Blank
NFL	2004	Baltimore Ravens	3.5x	Steve Bisciotti
NFL	2005	Minnesota Vikings	4.2x	Zygmunt Wilf
NFL	2007	Miami Dolphins	5.1x	Stephen Ross
		Average NFL Multiple	**4.7x**	
NHL	2004	New Jersey Devils	1.7x	Jeffrey Vanderbeek
NHL	2005	Anaheim Mighty Ducks	1.0x	Henry Samueli
NHL	2006	St. Louis Blues	1.9x	Dave Checketts
NHL	2006	Vancouver Canucks	2.7x	Francesco Aquilini
NHL	2007	Nashville Predators	2.5x	David Freeman
NHL	2007	Tampa Bay Lightning	2.2x	Oren Koules, Jeff Sherrin, and Doug MacLean
NHL	2008	Edmonton Oilers	2.6x	Daryl Katz
NHL	2008	Minnesota Wild	3.2x	Craig Leipold
		Average NHL Multiple	**2.2x**	

(1) Revenue Multiple at Acquisition is equal to the price paid for the franchise divided by the franchise's revenues. For example, a team with $100M of revenues and a sale prive of $300M will have a venue multiple of 3.0x.

Figure 8   Historical Revenue Multiples

Source: MZ Sports LLC proprietary research. Reproduced with permission of ABC-CLIO, LLC.

level, inclusion of new media opportunities, local media opportunities or long-term obligations to players or front-office staff. For example, assume that, based on comparable transactions (large market for example), both parties agree as a starting point on a revenue multiple of 2.5x. Then the negotiations regarding value will be based on adjustment factors to the 2.5x multiple. A buyer may argue, for example, that long-term player commitments should work to adjust the multiple to 2.3x revenues or that a long-term

media deal that does not let the buyer take advantage of a potential RSN reduces the multiple to 2.0x.

The most notable shortcoming to this type of approach is that the adjustments are done at a very high level and are not based on a rigorous financial analysis, especially on the expense side. Existing team losses, high payroll, large front office costs, and inflexibility regarding local media are but a few examples that can dramatically impact value. Simple adjustments in revenue multiples cannot adequately replace rigorous financial analysis in determining the bottom line impact.

VALUATION METHODOLOGY— DISCOUNTED CASH FLOW

A valuation approach that should be more effective in incorporating the franchise specific drivers described above is the Discounted Cash Flow ("DCF") approach. The DCF approach bases valuation on projected annual operating cash flows discounted at the buyer's hurdle rate. While comparable transactions provide a handy benchmark, DCF allows a franchise to be examined based on its own merits and unique attributes.

The DCF approach historically has been considered difficult to implement for the reasons listed above including lack of profitability and dramatic swings in income due to player payroll. However, buyers that are spending multiple hundreds of millions of dollars on a franchise are taking the position that they will run the franchise as a business, in some cases targeting a specific cash flow profit (net of debt service) and in the worst-case, as a break-even proposition. This line of reasoning eliminates the concerns, on a DCF basis, of on-going losses. Clearly, the notion of a break-even or better bottom line must be grounded in reality. However, with the leagues reining in player costs, for the most part tying player payroll to a percentage of league revenues, owners are now better positioned to argue that future profits are achievable. In addition, numerous recent buyers have been able to dramatically increase revenues and profitability, again creating the argument for DCF. Finally, with increased information sharing among teams, franchise buyers can more effectively create business plans that tie expenses to revenues.

In addition to annual operating cash flow projections, a DCF analysis will include a projected exit value or terminal value, which can be calculated using either multiples or growth rates in conjunction with discount rates. Typically, if a multiple is used for the exit value, the multiple will be based on an implied revenue multiple at the time of purchase, with sensitivity analysis to test various exit values.

DCF relies on numerous assumptions, both in terms of operating projection and exit value. Clearly, then, one has to have a high degree of confidence in the assumptions and significant knowledge and understanding of a franchise's operations. Testing for various operating and exit value scenarios helps greatly in this regard. While the assumptions in question are just that, assumptions, this approach, if undertaken with the appropriate level of rigor, should produce more appropriate results compared to a revenue multiple approach, which often fails to properly account for or measure certain operating factors and future profitability.

Notes

1. Michael K. Ozanian and Kurt Badenhausen, "The Business of Baseball," *Forbes*, April 20, 2006, http://www.forbes.com/2006/04/17/06mlb_baseball_valuations_land.html, accessed January 2007.

2. Christine Perez, "Woods Takes Victory Park to New Level," *Dallas Business Journal*, December 29, 2006, http://www.bizjournals.com/dallas/stories/2007/01/01/story1.html?t=printable, accessed January 2007.

3. Scott Wong, "Westgate Gears Up for Parties," *The Arizona Republic*, December 27, 2006, http://www.azcentral.com/community/glendale/articles/1227gl-lockparty27Z18.htmll, accessed January 2007.

4. Mark Belko, "Penguins Taking Delegation to See Columbus' Arena District Development," *Pittsburgh Post-Gazette*, January 11, 2006, http://www.post-gazette.com/pg/06011/635718-61.stm, accessed January 2007.

CREDIT RATINGS

FITCH RATINGS—CRITERIA REPORT GLOBAL SPORTS RATING GUIDELINES, MAY 9, 2007

Chad Lewis, Jessica Soltz Rudd, Laurence Monnier, and Cherian George

SUMMARY

The continued evolution of professional sports from entertainment to big business has spurred billions of dollars of capital-market transactions in the past two decades at the league, franchise and facility level. Fitch's core credit view of the underlying factors associated with sports-related transactions has not changed. Primary factors that Fitch analyzes to determine all sports ratings include the following:

- League economic model.
- National television contracts.
- Player salary structure.
- Revenue sharing among member clubs.
- Role of league in team financial matters.
- League debt limits and other financial policies on franchises.
- Relationship between league and players' union.
- Locally generated revenues.

This report lays out Fitch's view in more detail and guides readers through the analytical framework used in assessing the credit quality of a professional sports league, a professional sports franchise and various types of sports facilities based on the underlying financial viability and fundamentals, economic factors and legal analysis. The underlying economics of a professional sports league play the most critical role in assigning sports ratings. Professional sports' economic models (consisting of players' salary structures, media contracts and revenue-sharing policies, among other factors) have become more evident and highlight the leagues' structural credit differences.

Fitch's universe of sports ratings includes leaguewide credit facility ratings, franchise ratings, and stadium and arena ratings. Specifically, within the franchise ratings, Fitch has analyzed both corporate and asset-backed transactions. Fitch's stadium and arena ratings universe includes transactions involving the four major U.S. sports leagues—the National Football League (NFL), Major League Baseball (MLB), the National Basketball Association (NBA) and the National Hockey League (NHL)—as well as European soccer leagues. The primary security structures in the stadium and arena ratings universe include a pledge of all facility-generated revenue, a pledge of selected facility-generated revenues, a pledge of various tax-generated revenues and asset-backed structures.

Fitch views sports ratings from a top-down perspective for team-related ratings, as well as project finance stadium and arena financings. From this perspective, team and sports facility ratings are analyzed within the operating and regulatory environment of their parent league, which provides analysis of that league's economic model, financial policies and legal structure. Consequently, determining these ratings is in some ways analogous to the "sovereign ceiling" concept of the international bond markets when rating the debt instruments of nations and their subsovereigns or applicable corporate entities, such as provinces, states or corporates that are part of and operate within that respective nation's laws and financial regulations. For example, Fitch maintains an 'A+' rating for the NFL's senior unsecured notes, and it is unlikely that an individual franchise in the NFL would be rated on par or above the league. For sports facilities, the rating ceiling could be somewhat different, though this is generally unlikely, as stadiums and arenas may have strong economic characteristics stemming from multiple anchor tenants and the ability to host many other revenue-producing events.

The first two sections of this report specifically detail Fitch's underlying analytical approach and the credit factors incorporated in rating the four U.S. professional sports and the franchises within those leagues. An appendix has been provided that specifically discusses credit fundamentals associated with European soccer transactions. Many of the facility-based credit factors are amendable to European soccer transactions, provided a thorough understanding of the league and franchise exist.

Construction and environmental risk factors and analyses are largely similar and applicable across countries. The legal framework in which a facility is developed is also generally similar across countries, with the stipulation that more or less stringent applicable laws may have a positive or negative rating effect, depending on legal impediments specific to an area that are more favorable or detrimental to a transaction.

PROFESSIONAL SPORTS LEAGUES

A professional sports league analysis is the backbone for all sports-related transactions. The fundamental makeup and economic model of a league is the most significant rating factor in assessing the credit quality for the league, as well as franchise and facility transactions. The primary source of revenues, national television contracts, provides a strong, stable revenue source. Additional shared revenues, such as pooled suite, club seat and ticket revenues, are viewed favorably as they provide revenue diversity. The framework set in place for the largest expense item, player salaries, is the second most important factor in assessing league credit. In addition to the financial and economic profile of a league and potential changes to the general economic framework, Fitch carefully monitors fan attendance levels, television ratings, average ticket prices, changes and trends in ownership, player and union relations and other factors that may have a material effect on the quality of the sports product.

A league structure incorporating strong national television contracts, appropriate salary structure, a strong diverse corporate sponsorship and advertising base, established strong debt policy, league-level support to assist distressed franchises, a solid history of limited work stoppages, and strong covenants and legal provisions is viewed most favorably by Fitch and would be a strong candidate for an investment-grade rating. Leagues that incorporate some of the key rating factors may also achieve investment-grade ratings.

League Revenues

Fitch views positively league policies that share national television revenues equally, as compared with a league that distributes national television revenues based on a team's performance. From a ratings perspective, equal distribution provides, to some extent, additional parity among franchises by providing some level of revenue certainty per franchise, resulting in a more level playing field for franchises. While locally generated revenues may be dramatically different between small and large market teams, significant revenue sharing from a league level helps to mitigate significant disparities among franchises. Leagues that equally distribute revenues, rather than distribution based on a franchise's on-field performance and winning record, provide greater revenue certainty and less potential for revenue disparity among franchises. The concept of distribution of revenues based on performance-based measures may be exacerbated if a franchise is unable to generate significant local revenues from ticket sales and other stadium-derived revenues. From Fitch's standpoint, a league structure that bolsters financial parity among franchises has the potential to drive competition between franchises and grow and maintain spectator interest.

Salary Structure

The various salary structures across existing professional leagues around the world can have a substantial effect on the credit ratings of those leagues. Salary structures ranging from a "hard salary" cap to a "soft salary" cap to no salary cap exist in professional sports today. A hard salary cap establishes a maximum for player payroll. The player payroll may be adjusted upward or downward based on the index to which it is linked. For example, a hard salary cap may be linked to a percentage of the national television broadcast rights fees or a percentage of total league-generated revenues, including national television broadcast rights fees, shared suite and club seat and other nationally shared advertising and sponsorship agreements. Essentially, the player payroll and a team's share of the national media contracts and other revenue agreements are adjusted in tandem. This is viewed as a credit strength because a franchise's largest expense item, player salaries, are not able to exceed a certain percentage of defined revenues; thus, it is highly unlikely that expense growth would largely increase at a rate greatly exceeding total revenue growth. Additionally, given that franchises spend the same amount of money on player salaries, teams should have a similar talent level, which drives competition. In Fitch's opinion, competition between franchises is a key underlying factor for the ability of a league to sustain strong spectator interest over the long term.

A soft salary cap may generally have the same structure as a hard salary, with exceptions for veteran or key franchise players. Exceeding the soft salary cap requires a franchise to pay a fixed amount of money, often equal to the amount above the threshold, into a league's central fund for equal distribution to the other franchises in the league. The absence of a salary cap (i.e., an owner may choose to spend as much or as little on a franchise payroll) is viewed as a weakness to a league, because there is less expense certainty. Additionally, a significant disparity between franchise payrolls and the subsequent higher talent levels lured by larger payrolls has the ability to risk the long-term competitive nature of the league.

Fitch views the combination of equal distribution of revenues, coupled with a hard salary cap, as a strong foundation for a professional sports league. The current U.S. (NFL) economic model is an example of this. The NFL has a hard salary cap and adjusts player payroll according to the annual amount of national broadcast rights fees and other shared pooled revenues, which are distributed among all the franchises equally.

League Debt Policies

An established debt policy at the league level for franchise-level debt is viewed positively by Fitch. A debt policy that caps a franchise's maximum debt to an established fixed asset value based on recent historical franchise sales is viewed more favorably than a debt policy that links maximum debt levels to a financial indicator, such as EBITDA. While an EBITDA debt test provides a solid financial indicator, Fitch generally views possible short- to medium-term fluctuations in EBITDA as more volatile than possible declines in franchise values. A franchise may decide to sign a "high profile" player in a year and cause financial margins to decline for that year or the next. Conversely, Fitch's proactive monitoring of franchise sales across the leagues for the past 10 years supports this premise of greater stability in franchise values. Fitch would expect that, and views favorably, a debt policy linked to the franchise value would yield no more than a debt-to-franchise value of 25% and a debt policy linked to EBITDA would link maximum debt to no less than 10 times ($\times$) EBITDA, which Fitch notes as being on the high end of the spectrum for EBITDA tests.

League Work Stoppage History

The relationship between the players' associations and league and history of work stoppages is a key factor in rating leagues. Fitch assesses the historical labor environment and any material changes that have occurred to the current environment. A strong history with limited disputes from both sides is viewed positively. Historical disputes over key elements of labor agreements that have been changed and agreed upon, as well as an overall current peaceful labor environment, are viewed favorably.

SPORTS FRANCHISES

An understanding of league policy and procedures, as well as its underlying economic model, is a prerequisite for considering franchise fundamentals. It is the competitive nature and long-term stability of these associations that foster and preserve fan interest, which, in turn, attracts advertisers and broadcasters. Macro- and microinfluences, such as demographics, stadium and arena issues, as well as management ultimately differentiate the financial profiles at the team level. These influences help serve as key credit support measurements.

Fitch also notes, with the advent of various leaguewide borrowing programs in the United States, the majority of franchises seeking capital markets debt have elected to borrow from leaguewide programs as opposed to entering the capital markets. Arguably, the leaguewide programs in the United States give franchises a lower cost of borrowing, because the debt is secured by league revenues and debt service is paid prior to franchises receiving the revenues, which Fitch views more favorably.

Although general rules can be applied, rating debt at the franchise level remains a case-by-case analysis. In reviewing an individual team transaction, several key questions need to be asked, including the following:

- Can a team support both its operating cost and its debt obligations?

- Are there appropriate credit-protection measures in place to support debt service and asset valuations in a downside scenario?

- Does the league take an active role in ensuring the financial viability of its member teams, as well as the financial claims of creditors?

- What has been the track record of ownership in generating consistent financial results?

- Has the team forged a special relationship within a community that makes it an invaluable asset and source of pride?

A thorough understanding of the answers to these questions serves as the basis for Fitch's sports ratings at the team level.

Because most debt at the team level is secured by a direct lien on the franchise, team debt can be considered a hybrid transaction, incorporating elements of both a traditional cash flow obligation, as well as elements of an asset-based transaction. As a result, Fitch's approach gives appropriate consideration to both of these measures in establishing a senior secured rating. A more favorable rating will be considered where the team is the legal obligor (team-level debt), as opposed to holding company or partnership (holdco. or partnership) debt. The position of the borrower addresses such issues as structural subordination. Debt at the holdco. level is structurally subordinate to debt at the team level, similar to the concept of a holdco. in traditional corporate finance.

Establishing a senior secured rating is a two-step process. The first step involves establishing a timeliness of repayment rating or implied senior unsecured rating. The second step involves notching from the implied senior unsecured rating based on the collateral coverage provided by the value of the franchise.

IMPLIED SENIOR UNSECURED RATING IN SENIOR SECURED RATINGS

The implied senior unsecured rating effectively serves as the starting point for the secured rating. Key considerations for establishing an implied senior unsecured rating consider the overall quality of the team's key revenue components. More specifically, Fitch differentiates contractual revenue streams from noncontractual revenue streams. Contractually

obligated revenues (COR) primarily include national and local media contracts, local sponsorship agreements and luxury suite rentals. Sometimes revenues are referred to as "highly probable." These revenues are not explicitly contractual but have a contractual component that may be represented as highly probable. Highly probable revenues are analyzed and reviewed to determine the likelihood that they will be realized. Fitch will only consider such sources if historical evidence suggests a high probability of realization. Season ticket sales, which have demonstrated consistent renewals over a long period of time, may be considered highly probable. The greater portion of revenues deemed contractual and/or highly probable, the higher the "quality" assigned to these revenue streams.

Another key analytical factor is a team's COR as a percentage of player payroll. Because player payroll constitutes the largest cost component for a team, the extent to which player cost can be matched against contractual revenue streams helps to assess a team's reliance on less certain revenue streams to support player payroll, operating expenses and debt service. COR representing more than 70% of total player expenditures will, on average, result in a higher implied senior unsecured rating. Conversely, teams with COR substantially less than 70% of player cost will likely receive lower implied senior unsecured ratings. Teams operating in leagues with weak restraints on player costs and loose debt limitations, as well as those in which the COR is less than 70%, would most likely have the lowest implied senior unsecured rating.

EBITDA may not be the most accurate proxy for a team's cash flow, given that GAAP EBITDA does not take into account items such as cash bonuses, deferred compensation and other cash items that are not reflected in the income statement. Therefore, traditional cash flow based credit metrics, such as total debt/EBITDA and EBITDA/interest expense, have limitations when valuating team-level debt obligations. With this in mind, Fitch uses slightly altered credit measures in rating team debt.

Leverage

The ratio of debt (at the team level) to a team's annual COR should not exceed 2.0x for investment-grade consideration.

Debt-Service Coverage

Depending on the league, as a general guideline, the Fitch base case and Fitch stress case have targeted minimum ratios of operating income (total revenues less total operating expenses and cash bonuses) to annual debt service to range between 2.25x and 1.75x and 1.75x and 1.40x, respectively, for investment-grade consideration.

As mentioned previously, the relative strength of a league's economic model is also considered in establishing an implied senior unsecured rating. For example, the NFL's economic model is extremely strong and helps to create a favorable credit environment for the league's individual franchises. This is in part due to the NFL's robust television contracts that roughly match a team's largest expenditure: player payroll. For leagues in which revenues are not as equitably distributed, the effect is illustrated via a performance gap. Small-market franchises find it increasingly more difficult to compete with large-market teams, as they do not have comparable economic resources to procure top player talent. From a ratings perspective, a lower shared percentage requires greater scrutiny on a franchise's local revenues. These include gate receipts, local broadcasting rights and stadium-related revenue. These revenues are more closely tied to market demographics and team performance.

Collateral Coverage in Senior Secured Ratings

The second step in rating franchise debt assesses the overall collateral coverage provided by a pledge of the franchise. Recent transaction prices serve as the most relevant valuation measure. From an asset coverage standpoint, most teams exhibit significant asset coverage over committed secured debt amounts. Additionally, leagues with actively enforced debt policies that limit an owner's ability to leverage a team help to ensure sufficient overcollateralization. Fitch will notch above the implied senior unsecured rating by as many as three notches where ultimate recovery of principal is certain. In general, to receive a three-notch enhancement, loan to value (LTV) should be 50% or less. The 50% LTV guideline is a general rule and should be matched against the overall credit quality of the team.

ANATOMY OF A SPORTS FRANCHISE TRANSACTION

The primary credit risks in a sports franchise transaction involve renewal of the national media contracts (as well as local media contracts and other COR, where appropriate), the possibility of a work stoppage and a deterioration in franchise values. Fitch views favorably debt obligations that contain structural features that help to offset these risks.

National Media Contracts

Fitch considers renewal risk of national media contracts to be among the most important factors in assessing the creditworthiness of sports franchises. Because broadcasting rights fees provide a substantial portion of a team's revenues, any adverse change in these contracts would likely have a material effect on a team's overall credit profile. Ideally, the tenor of the debt obligation should expire prior to the expiration of the national media contracts so as to avoid renewal risk. When the maturity of the rated debt obligation goes beyond the expiration of the national media contracts, Fitch considers the historical trends in renewals for sports programming and for the respective league. In cases where creditors are exposed to broadcast contract renewal risks, covenants that set minimum thresholds for national broadcasting renewals are helpful in providing remedies in the event leaguewide broadcasting contracts are lower than anticipated. Possible remedies may include mandatory ownership capital calls and cash lockups prior to the renewal of national broadcast contracts. Fitch views positively structural features, including covenants, that allow creditors to readjust credit risk in light of lower than anticipated league wide broadcasting renewals.

Labor Environment

Fitch views positively structural provisions that address potential work stoppages. This applies to instances where the collective bargaining agreement (CBA) expires prior to the maturity of the rated debt obligation. While the contractual terms of the national media contracts may provide for the continued receipt of broadcasting fees during a work stoppage, teams will not receive any game-related income (ticket sales) and may have to remit refunds to ticketholders and sponsors. A labor contingency reserve helps to offset this risk by protecting debt service in the event of a work stoppage. Typically, labor contingency reserves will fund one year of debt service. Similar structural protections are required for investment-grade sports facility ratings.

Collateral Coverage

Similar to an asset-based transaction, collateral valuations are a key measure of credit support. Fitch views favorably covenant triggers that set minimum team valuations. Periodic appraisals and/or recent purchase transactions may serve as the mechanisms for collateral monitoring. Fitch examines the rights of creditors to readjust credit risk if asset valuations decline. A mandatory debt repayment to reduce LTVs and asset coverage to prevailing rates is viewed most favorably as an offset to potentially declining franchise values.

Support Agreements/Guarantees

In some cases, a team's underlying credit profile may be extremely weak and rated low on a stand-alone basis. In these instances, a credit may require some type of third-party support. This support usually takes the form of an operating support arrangement in which the owner or supporting entity agrees to fund operating losses unconditionally or up to a specified, agreed-upon amount. Fitch's implied senior unsecured rating starts with the team's creditworthiness on a stand-alone basis and is adjusted to reflect the level of support provided by the outside party. In considering the level of support, a review of the outside party's financial ability to cover operating losses and debt repayment is considered. The financial strength of the support provider, as well as the level of support required by creditors, helps determine the level of enhancement given to the implied senior unsecured rating.

Lockbox Mechanisms/Accounts

Certain lockbox or debt-service account (DSA) structures may be established to provide debt service through contractual revenue streams. Franchise debt transactions may attempt to somewhat mitigate team financial risk by creating a lockbox structure that directs national broadcasting rights fees into a lockbox account. The lockbox account deducts amounts required for debt service and remits the remaining portion to the team. Furthermore, the transaction may require additional funds be held in the DSA as added debt-service protection. The DSA and lockbox arrangement somewhat insulate creditors from team-related risk. It should be noted that these structures only serve as a method of payment and do not necessarily protect creditors' claims should the team file for bankruptcy. The automatic-stay provision within the bankruptcy code could freeze interest and principal payments owed to creditors.

FRANCHISE VALUES

One of the biggest unknowns in sports financing is the future of team valuations, which is a key component in a sports franchise rating analysis. Rather than trying to predict the future of team valuations, it may be more useful to understand the underlying fundamentals that support franchise values. Some of these fundamentals include the relative scarcity of sports assets, the exclusive right to operate, the economics of the respective league and the prestige associated with owning a sports team.

Relative Scarcity of Sports Assets

The consensus from officials across all leagues seems to suggest that demand far exceeds supply for ownership of a professional sports team, although Fitch notes that current demand may change in the future. However, given franchise sales over the past 10 years, Fitch believes the likelihood that franchise values would decline in the near term is highly unlikely; thus, demand will remain strong. With waiting lists of buyers and a limited amount of teams available for purchase, competition for ownership can be intense and drive up the price paid for a team, in many cases. However, demand for clubs can differ significantly based on the team's local market, history of support and the league in which it plays, among other factors.

The Exclusive Right to Operate

The right to operate a team is solely and exclusively granted by the governing league. The right granted by the respective league effectively serves as a key barrier to entry. This right to operate allows an acquiring owner exclusive access to national media revenues and other team-generated revenue streams. Moreover, each major sports league has explicit rules prohibiting competing ownership within the same market. This effectively provides an owner with the ability to operate in noncompetitive geographical markets (for the respective sport).

The Economics of the League

As discussed in the league analysis section, the underlying economics of a league help determine the overall attractiveness of a franchise. One of the major differentiating factors between sports leagues is the allocation of revenues among member teams. For example, the NFL equitably distributes a high percentage of total leaguewide revenues and places a hard cap on players' salaries. This policy puts franchises on generally level fiscal terms, translating into greater on-field competition and fan interest. As a result of these policies, the overall attractiveness, from a financial standpoint, of NFL member teams is increased.

Trophy Assets

The prestige associated with owning a professional sports team is an intangible benefit that is not easily measured. Instant visibility is gained upon owning a sports team, as fans and local media perceive the owner as a key community figure. Like a valuable piece of art, some of the benefits of owning a professional sports team are less scientific. The emotional aspects of ownership may play a big role in the overall purchase decision.

To the extent that debt is used to finance a significant portion of a purchase price, prudent credit decisions must still be made. Depending on the operating history of the respective franchise and prevailing macroeconomic trends in the industry, credit-protection measures, such as material debt amortization and/or mandatory debt reductions, may help offset credit concerns relating to future franchise values and refinancing risks.

Cash Flow Analysis

In addition to the aforementioned factors analyzed in determining franchise values, the ability and amount of positive cash flow a franchise generates is also analyzed. It is important to note that a thorough understanding of the league framework in which a franchise operates in is a pivotal factor when analyzing cash flows of a franchise in the value of a franchise. A franchise that plays in a league where there is substantial leaguewide revenue sharing and a salary cap has a stronger foundation to produce positive cash flow, because a significant amount of overall revenues flow from national television contracts and the largest expense item, player salaries, is fixed. While franchise performance may affect other revenues, a franchise in a league that does not have significant revenue sharing from a national broadcast agreement and a salary cap may be more susceptible to revenue fluctuations based on on-field performance, which would ultimately have a greater effect on cash flow. Management's ability to grow revenues in addition to leaguewide revenues from local media contracts, average ticket prices, advertising and sponsorships, and concessions and novelties is an important rating factor.

Management's historical track record and ability to manage and adjust expenses in a period of declining revenues is also a key credit consideration. Fitch recognizes that while other team-level expenses, such as player development, general administrative costs and benefits are a small portion of total expenses, they are important to a franchise. Historical demonstration and understanding management's ability, plan and implementation to manage expenses is crucial. Fitch will carefully monitor any changes in league revenues and locally generated franchise revenues and any potential short-term and long-term effects on cash flows.

SPORTS FACILITIES

The increasing importance of sports facility generated revenue to teams' financial health spurred a significant surge of new construction, as the changing model of professional sports has proven that new facilities are vital to a franchise's financial success. New facilities have the ability to generate new revenue streams, such as naming rights, club seats and suite revenues and, generally, strong corporate advertising and sponsorship revenues. Older stadiums that have not benefited from the aforementioned new revenue streams and, in many cases, lease agreements that limited financial growth often impede the financial potential of a franchise.

Historically, most stadiums and arenas were financed under the same city-building infrastructure theory as municipal properties; that is, the buildings were intended to be used by all and constructed solely with public dollars for the benefit of the town and people. However, as professional sports leagues expanded into big business, the pressure for modern stadiums with new and increased revenue drivers pushed the trend of facility construction into a new era, much of which with private dollars. Several methods of financing construction have been used, including public financing via tax-generated sources, stand alone nonrecourse project financing and asset-backed securitization of stadium revenues. It is important to note that almost every sports facility financing package is different and has consisted of elements of either tax-backed or project financing, or both, as well as private loans or private cash. However, certain underlying factors are similar and necessary in all sports facility transactions, such as the franchise's lease agreement with a nonrelocation agreement or a "promise to play" for the term of the debt.

From a project finance perspective, public dollars are considered pseudo equity, helping to bolster the economics of the project finance bond transaction. Fitch observes that there is not a consistent debt-equity structure utilized, as there are many different ways to finance a large-scale project, and that each transaction is structurally different. From a bondholder's perspective, the lower the leverage and the higher the debt-service coverage the better, but both factors are different in every transaction. While there is almost always a mixture of public debt, private debt and private equity contributed to sports facilities, Fitch notes that, in many cases, the public sector retains the title and ownership to the stadium or arena.

Projected cash flows, debt-service coverage and liquidity levels for these types of project financing transactions must undergo various base and stress test case scenarios. Pro forma projections must be able to withstand several sensitivity analyses. Generally, assumptions in the stress test include reductions in base attendance levels, decreased percentages of premium seating renewals, the exclusion of certain revenue from other events and a significant reduction of other revenue, such as naming rights, concessions, advertising and parking. Structural protections, such as debt-service reserve funds, must also be included in the transaction to mitigate the risk of a work stoppage. The appendix attached to this report, and further discussed below, provides an indication of various assumptions Fitch will build into a base-case and stress-case scenario.

Furthermore, Fitch assesses the viability of each sports project finance transaction through a detailed analysis of the facility's service and market area, franchise and venue competition, project construction risk, the respective league of the tenant franchise, the quality of the franchise and the strength of facility management and operations.

PROJECT FINANCE—FINANCIAL PROFILE

In general, for project finance sports facility ratings, it is important to note that Fitch uses fan attendance averages from historical trends, rather than from pro forma attendance estimates. Additionally, the rating is based largely on COR, which is not directly dependent on the on-field success of the home team but rather on presigned long-term leases the sports facility enters into with the various counterparties, such as naming rights partners, advertising partners, long-term suites and club seat agreements, guaranteed concession agreements and team rent payments.

Although revenues in entertainment-dependent facilities are often considered volatile because of their nonessential nature, a high percentage of COR provides a degree of stability and predictability to the revenue stream. Key elements of COR include solid lease agreements with the anchor tenants, premium seat license agreements, long-term contracts with concessionaires and advertisers and, possibly, some type of guaranteed public support (such as a sales tax rebate). It is important, for investment-grade consideration, that transactions have at least 60% of projected pledged revenues contractually obligated.

Luxury Suites and Club Seats

Premium seating has become a major source of security for project finance transactions. Premium seating generally consists of luxury suites and club seats that range in price from $50,000–$350,000 and $500–$5,000 per annum, respectively.

The pricing structure is driven by demand, actual suite location and associated amenities, the strength of the tenant franchises and the number of included events. Due to their high cost, suites are normally leased by corporations, and Fitch analyzes the service area's corporate base compared with the overall supply of suites in the area. The length of premium seat leases varies, with average terms ranging between three and 10 years. From a debtholder's perspective, a transaction with staggered lease expiration dates mitigates the risk of a significant percentage of leases expiring in any given year, which poses renewal risk. Demand factors for luxury seats are based on economic conditions in the local area, historical franchise performance and fan support. For luxury suite agreements, Fitch generally assumes the payment schedule according to the initial terms of the agreement and stresses the renewal of those agreements. Club seat revenue can also represent a significant amount of pledged revenue. Club seat holders are typically small businesses and wealthy individuals, and Fitch believes club seat demand is more dependent on the franchise record than luxury suites.

Naming Rights and Sponsorship Agreements

Naming rights agreements are another revenue source that can be part of a basket of revenue streams that can secure project bonds. Naming rights enable a corporation to name the facility after itself or one of its products. Naming rights agreements may include a substantial upfront payment, in addition to annual payments, typically well in excess of $1 million. A naming rights counterparty analysis is important to the rating of the project debt, and the underlying rating of the corporation is considered. Projected income may be discounted for low-rated counterparties. Additional corporate-related income may be derived through sponsorship and advertising agreements.

Personal Seat Licenses

Personal seat licenses (PSLs) are another source of revenue earned by facilities. A PSL is purchased by individuals, giving them the right to buy season tickets for a certain period of time or for the life of the facility. PSL revenue is typically collected in the initial stages of the construction process, so it is often used as equity to partially fund facility construction, as opposed to being utilized to retire debt.

Season Ticket Sales and Concessions Revenue

Season tickets, and to a greater extent gate receipts, comprise relatively volatile revenue streams in certain sports and markets, since the demand is highly correlated to the franchise's current performance and economic conditions. Stress levels for these revenue streams are significant and depend on market location, the inclusion of an upfront payment or PSL, franchise support and demonstrated continued demand, such as historical revenues and the existence of a ticketholder waiting list. The guaranteed revenue under a concession agreement is based on calculations that incorporate fan attendance levels and varying percentages of gross annual receipts net of sales taxes. To determine the likelihood of payment of the guaranteed portion of the concession revenue stream, Fitch analyzes the historical concession revenue performance. The strength of the guaranteed revenue stream is also based on the counterparty's credit rating and its position in the industry. The agreement may include a substantial upfront fee to the facility and a guaranteed portion that is significantly lower than the historical concession revenue generated. Inclusion of these provisions partially mitigates the risk that an obligor may default on its obligation and increases the ability to attract a replacement concessionaire in the event of unacceptable performance.

PUBLIC FINANCING

Traditionally, there has been substantial public support in sports financing, as state governments, local governments and special tax districts pledge support to the projects in various ways. Tax-supported sports transactions have been structured as general obligation bonds, lease-backed bonds and dedicated tax bonds, among others. Specific taxes earmarked to support facilities, including taxes on tobacco and alcohol, general sales taxes, accommodations taxes for hotels and motels, and ticket surcharges, among others, have been used to secure the debt issued for sports facilities. The use of accommodations taxes is a popular method of financing the debt, because it is perceived that the project will attract visitors who, in turn, will occupy the hotels and motels. This method of financing, along with similar tourist development taxes, such as those on rental cars, are politically more palatable and, consequently, may be more successful in gaining local support, because they primarily affect visitors, as opposed to local residents.

LEGAL STRUCTURE

Various legal agreements establish a project framework and each party's obligations. Fitch analyzes project documents and their legal implications to ensure full and timely principal and interest payments and to evaluate bondholder security. Although there are several primary legal considerations inherent in all sports facility financings, all legal analyses focus on the bondholders' legal right to receive project revenues on time and in full. Fitch first focuses on collateral pledged to the bondholders. In all sports facility financing structures, a team nonrelocation covenant is required. These agreements protect the economic value of the project by legally requiring the teams to play their games at the facility, thereby mitigating the risk that there will be insufficient revenues due to a team's departure.

Project Finance and Securitization

In traditional project finance and those structures incorporating elements of securitization, security is derived from pledged revenues and, in some cases, a mortgage on the building, as well as a ground lease. The pledged revenues usually include several revenue streams, the right to future revenues, the right to enter into future contracts and the right to renew contracts. Fitch then evaluates the potential bankruptcy of all parties to the transaction, with a particular focus on the issuer and/or its parent, analyzing the possible delay and the potential of total disruption in bondholder payments.

Bankruptcy analysis is paramount to these transactions. The legal structure and/or supporting credit solutions are evaluated when analyzing the potential bankruptcy of all parties where their bankruptcy could affect full and timely payment to the noteholders. The primary focus is usually on the issuer, parent(s) and affiliates. Fitch's bankruptcy analysis evaluates the ability of the entity to make timely payments to the bondholders without any interruption in the cash flows and the potential for the complete termination of those cash flows.

In project finance sports facility transactions, the debt-issuing entity is either a newly formed special-purpose vehicle (SPV) or operating subsidiary. Traditionally, the issuer has a first perfected security interest in the collateral, which is then pledged to the indenture trustee for the benefit of the bondholders. If the issuer is not an SPV, Fitch performs a financial analysis of the issuer to ensure that its bankruptcy risk is commensurate with the rating level assigned to the transaction. Transactions incorporating elements of securitization generally involve the sale of the collateral from the operating subsidiary to a bankruptcy-remote SPV created to serve as the issuer of the financing. The issuer SPV then issues bonds supported by the assets acquired by the issuer SPV. Fitch expects the counsel to the transaction would confirm that a true sale of the assets has occurred, such that the assets would not form part of the transferor's estate if such transferor filed a petition in bankruptcy. Fitch further expects, with respect to the SPV's issuance of the bonds, that the counsel validate that the issuer SPV has granted the indenture trustee a first-priority perfected security interest in all of the issuer SPV's assets. Also, Fitch expects that all relevant enforceability opinions required for the transaction will be provided. Generally, both of these transaction structures include the use of a lockbox for bondholder protection.

Fitch expects that the transaction's counsel would furnish a nonconsolidation opinion with respect to any owner holding more than 50% interest in an SPV. If an SPV has been created, Fitch evaluates the credit strength and financial viability of the SPV's parent and affiliates. This analysis sometimes provides adequate assurance that voluntary and involuntary bankruptcy of the parent and affiliates is unlikely. In those cases in which parents and affiliates hold real estate interests or are the operator, Fitch, in addition to analyzing the parent's and affiliates' credit quality, assumes they become insolvent and declare bankruptcy. Since the operation of the sports facility is usually necessary to generate revenues for the parent or affiliates, Fitch, on a case-by-case basis, will analyze the business incentives for a parent or affiliate to cause consolidation. Fitch has consistently reached the conclusion that bondholders will be ultimately paid. However, a lapse in the timely payment of principal and/or interest is likely while the entity restructures. Certain reserve requirements are traditionally provided to ensure timely payment to the bondholders.

Real Estate Structures

In many tax-supported and project finance structures, as well as structures incorporating elements of securitization, the land is owned by the municipality or other parties and leased via a triple-net ground lease to the issuer through the term of the debt. Traditionally, the improvements are either transferred to the issuing entity through the sale of a fee—simple interest in the building after construction is complete or leased in the form of a triple-net lease through the term of the debt. In either instance, the interest in the building and its fixtures provide lenders with additional repayment security.

Under a triple-net lease, the lessee bears all responsibility on real estate issues, costs of operation, insurance, abatement, assignments and sublets. The leasehold and/or fee interest is sometimes pledged to the bondholders, providing additional security and often the right to replace the operator if the facility is not managed as a first-class facility or up to certain identified industry standards. However, Fitch will evaluate a structure that does not include a mortgage interest granted to the bondholders. For example, instead of a mortgage interest, the issuer and other appropriate parties may incorporate either a pledge not to encumber the fee simple while bonds are outstanding, which is offset by additional overcollateralization or a springing mortgage. Both of these structures are inherently weaker from a credit perspective but can be evaluated and included in investment-grade credits if they have appropriate offsetting strengths.

Construction Risk

As with other types of projects, construction risk often constitutes the greatest risk in the credit quality chain of a stand-alone sports facility project. In certain circumstances, it can constrain the rating to a level below what it would be after completion. Completion risk refers to the risk that the facility will not be completed on time, on budget or up to the required performance standards. For strong, economically viable projects, construction completion risk can be mitigated and investment-grade ratings can be achieved. Fitch will carefully consider the project's complexity and technology, projected costs, delay risk and quality of contractors, as well as the terms of the construction contract.

Sports facilities vary widely in complexity, ranging from less complex open-air, single-level stadiums on undeveloped land to multilevel, retractable roof stadiums in densely populated areas and arenas in earthquake-prone areas. Fitch relies on the expertise and opinion of independent and reputable engineers (I/Es) to evaluate the design specifications of the project and the reasonableness of the development cost estimates and ongoing maintenance expenditures. The role of the I/E is crucial during the development phase, as one of the critical tasks is to monitor the works process, milestone compliance, and critical path or schedule. Typically, the I/E also approves the release of escrowed funds to compensate the contractors from proceeds of rated debt.

Construction quality and proper maintenance are fundamental for sports facilities, as they are generally considered assets with a useful life of 30–40 years that can support long-term, nonrecourse financing. The I/E's assurances regarding construction quality and maintenance represent a vital link between the sports facility (the asset) and the financing's structure.

Project complexity will affect the likelihood that the facility will be completed on time (delay risk). Delays can also occur due to permitting, stop-work orders, availability of critical equipment or labor, weather or seasonal conditions, and other factors. Delays that cannot be controlled by the contractor, such as force majeure and permitting, must be addressed by other means, such as compensation from insurance. Of note, potential delays and construction cost overruns caused by incomplete, ambiguous or evolving specifications, beyond the customary and often inevitable work changes requested by either the sponsors or contractor, are of great concern. Fitch expects projects financed by the capital markets will be undertaken on the basis of minimal design risk. Neither Fitch nor the I/E has the capacity to estimate the ultimate effect on project costs and cash flows from material changes in design once a project has initiated construction, especially if appropriate mechanisms, such as completion and performance guarantees from sponsors, governments or solid third parties, are insufficient or not provided.

Environmental Risk

Another major consideration is environmental risk, including remediation efforts, cost overruns, timing and insurance. Environmental issues are of greatest concern during the construction phase of a project, because unexpected expenses during this period can seriously deteriorate the credit quality of the project. Traditionally, the environmental concerns are identified, and mitigation procedures have been established prior to the project being brought to the capital markets. Also, most project finance and structures incorporating elements of securitization involve guaranteed maximum price contracts, thereby transferring responsibility for unexpected costs. Fitch will review the guaranteed maximum price contract to ensure that such risks are shared by the public and private entity. If the contractor bears the burden for pre-existing conditions, the risk could limit the rating. In some instances, the municipality bears all responsibility for environmental risks and will cover the costs associated at the various stages of buildout. Fitch's concern is for the overall viability of the project: how unexpected environmental costs will be paid for, are there adequate reserves and insurance, or are the risks assumed by the party best able to handle such issues.

FITCH BASE-CASE AND STRESS-CASE SCENARIOS

To assess the ability to repay debt in a full and timely manner, Fitch will first evaluate the economic profile of the project and then layer onto it any legal, financial and policy constraints. To accomplish this, Fitch will initially design base and stress cases solely based on economic factors that incorporate reasonable scenarios that can occur based on Fitch's experience with the sports industry as a whole and with similar projects. As an illustration, Fitch provides some guidance on how we might design these cases in the matrix . . . [that follows]. While the appendix is largely a general guide, tailored assumptions may be necessary based on local experience and broader legal, political, economic and financial considerations. The application of each of the factors identified will be a function of the type of the sports facility (new construction or facility with an operating history), the level of conservatism in key finance plan assumptions and the level of financial flexibility maintained.

For each factor, Fitch identifies an analytical approach and a range of possible adjustments. The level of adjustment within the identified ranges will be a function of the nature of the project and its risk profile, which incorporates service area analysis, historical franchise operations and the league framework, as well as Fitch's assessment of the conservatism or aggressiveness built into the plan of finance provided. Fitch will then layer noneconomic factors to finalize our base and stress cases. Generally, Fitch's base case will be more conservative than the base case provided by the entity, as Fitch's base case seeks to establish a scenario that is highly probable under normal conditions. For example, Fitch's scenarios eliminate any built-in optimism in assumptions with future attendance levels and any additional revenue assumptions, including higher concession, novelty, parking and ticket revenues. Fitch's stress case then seeks to assess the ability of the structure to withstand a combination of severe, but reasonably probable, stress situations while still paying debt service on a full and timely basis.

The level of financial flexibility that remains after the application of the stress test to absorb further downside events will be an important driver of the facility's debt rating. Facilities with minimal remaining flexibility will at best achieve low investment-grade ratings. Facilities with higher levels of remaining flexibility and strong structural enhancements may be able to achieve higher ratings, although they will be generally capped in the 'A' category.

APPENDIX TO SPORTS RATING GUIDELINES

Sports Financing in Europe

A small number of European football-related (often referred to as soccer in the United States) financings have been completed, mostly via private placements with banks or with institutional investors (frequently in the U.S. market), with the most notable public financing being that for Arsenal Football Club (a soccer club in the English Premiership League) in 2006. In order to understand the importance of relegation risks and other credit factors in European football, as compared to U.S.-based sports, it is necessary to understand how the English Premiership League system and other European counterparts operates. Although all of the specific features of the English Premier League are not necessarily common across the other European leagues, Fitch's approach to analyzing key credit factors serves to illustrate the differences and specific risks addressed to transactions in Europe.

Because the role of European sport leagues differs significantly from the role of those in the United States, Fitch does not need to rate the league in order to rate a sports transaction. While the rules of the leagues in terms of broadcasting revenue distribution, financial control and sporting sanctions in case of financial difficulties will be reviewed, there is no concept of a league-related rating cap for European football transactions. However, given that Fitch compares sports-related credit ratings across various countries and the risks of relegation in Europe, Fitch notes that European soccer ratings may be limited to rating ceilings based on the league fundamentals analyzed in U.S. sports transactions.

Leagues

Arguably, European football is the most highly developed and popular sport in Europe. The Barclays English Premier League (the top league in England), Serie A (the top Italian Soccer League), Liga de Futbol Profesional (commonly known as La Liga, the top league in Spain), the Bundesliga (the top league in Germany) and Ligue de Football Professionnel (the top league in France) are widely regarded as the top five leagues in Europe. Each league operates and competes within their respective country, as well as in competitions across Europe.

Qualification for the two major European competitions, the Union of European Football Association (UEFA) Champions League and UEFA Cup, is available to clubs finishing in the top 4–8 spots in the league (the exact number depending on the size of the league and past performance of its clubs in the European competitions). At the opposite end of the scale, clubs can be relegated to a lower league if they finish the season in the bottom two or three spots in the league.

This structure has the effect of making virtually all games have some importance, whether for the top clubs seeking to win the league, the middle-ranking clubs seeking to qualify for European competition and the extra income that brings or the bottom clubs seeking to avoid relegation. This apparent lack of a widely competitive league structure has not detracted from the popularity of the game, which continues to improve annually, given Fitch's observation of attendance levels across Europe. This is undoubtedly partly a result of increased interest in the pan-European competitions, where there are no dominant teams or countries.

Relegation

The major European soccer leagues practice a system of promotion/relegation. This is the key difference in league structures between the U.S. and European soccer leagues and raises unique credit risk concerns. Relegation is the process by which poorly performing teams at the bottom of league standings are demoted to a lower division and replaced by top teams in the next lowest division. This performance-related risk can have significant implications on two fronts. First, broadcast rights fees can be dramatically different from one division to the next, creating a greater degree of uncertainty with regard to revenue flows. Second, attendance figures will be affected, as fan interest is a function of the level and quality of competition. Some leagues provide an element of compensation for relegated teams in the form of a "parachute payment," payable for two years in the case of the English league, to offset the effect of lower revenues (mostly media), which may not be immediately fully reflected in lower player salaries. Despite the parachute payments (which are not common to all European leagues), relegation is a considerable rating stress scenario for which Fitch seeks reassurance that the relevant club would have adequate financial resources to meet its debt payments.

Locally Generated Revenues

Ticket sales are widely viewed as the most stable revenue source, but they can vary significantly between the largest clubs with stadium capacity of more than 70,000 to the smallest clubs with stadium capacity of 20,000. Historically a club's revenues would have been principally generated by ticket sales to the local community, in addition to a small proportion of sales to traveling fans. The increased influence of television broadcasting rights, sponsorship, advertising and retail sales via club Web sites has changed the revenue mix significantly, but the importance of local support is a key rating factor and has historically contributed to a significant proportion of total club revenues.

Given the large dependence on ticket revenues, Fitch will review the history of a football club over the past 10–30 years, with particular focus on its league position and the effect on ticket prices and the stadium occupancy rate. The history of the club in terms of ticket sales and prices in different league positions will be taken into account in applying stresses, but recent evidence of the effect of relegation may be unlikely for one of the leading clubs. In this case, stresses will be based on the experiences of other clubs relegated in more recent years. Some clubs, which are notable for having a very loyal local following, may be stressed less in terms of match attendance.

Similar to U.S. transactions, Fitch will generally use a historical occupancy/attendance average of the stadium as a floor for attendance and create a stress scenario that will apply a steady fall in the premier league position from its most recent performance and, given the long term of these transactions, a relegation scenario one or more times during the life of the transaction for one or more years on each occasion. Fitch will then assess the effect of declining ticket revenues on the transaction's ability to service the debt. A club that has occupied a high league position over a long period of time or has never been relegated into a lower league will provide guidance in assessing the future financial performance of the club.

Television Contracts

Although generally a less important source of revenue than ticket sales, certainly as compared with U.S. sports, television/media contracts are still crucial to the financial success of a club. Contracts have historically been renewed every 3–4 years, and recent experience has been that significant increases have been achieved with new contracts. This provides Fitch some comfort that future negotiations would be positive, although, there is no certainty the value of future broadcasting contracts will be of equal or greater value. Consequently, Fitch generally will assume minimal, if any, increases in renewal amounts.

The split of media revenues varies from country to country. In England, approximately 50% of the revenues is shared equally across the top 20 premier league teams, 25% is shared by reference to the number of games of a particular club that are televised (inevitably a larger share for the more successful and more widely supported clubs) and the remaining 25% is split by league position on a sum of the digits basis (i.e., the top club receives 20/210th, the bottom team 1/210th). Similar to ticket receipts, there is a built-in bias toward the larger and more successful clubs, thus consolidating their ability to remain larger and more successful.

The broadcasting rights in English football are contracted on a pool basis (i.e., the contracts are negotiated by Football Association [FA], the governing body, on behalf of all the clubs). The revenue is then shared among Premiership League teams according to the above formula. However, as noted, there is a built-in bias toward the larger clubs. This is regarded as a necessary in order to prevent each club from negotiating its own contracts and creating a more size-biased distribution.

Fitch notes the key difference in the distribution of national broadcast revenues in Europe, as compared with the United States, is that the four major sports receive an equal distribution of national broadcast revenues. While this provides some revenue certainty, locally generated media outlets can vary between large and small market teams. Given this key difference, Fitch typically assumes that a club's share of broadcasting revenue decreases in line with the formula set out above as it moves down the league table. Fitch will create a stress scenario by applying a steady fall in the premier league position from its most recent performance and, given the long term of these transactions, a relegation scenario one or more times during the life of the transaction and for one or more years on each occasion. Again, the extent of the decrease will be based on the experience of relegated clubs in the past. Fitch will then assess the effect of media and other revenues on the transaction's ability to service the debt.

Sponsorship and Advertising Agreements

The wide appeal of football has seen a huge growth over the past decade in terms of advertising and sponsorship revenue. Similar to the growth in broadcast contracts, sponsorship and advertising agreements, for clubs in comparable league positions, have experienced similar growth. While sponsorship and advertising agreements are usually negotiated on a club-by-club basis with clubs with the biggest fan bases and stadiums commanding the best deals, sponsorship and advertising agreements are key to each club's financial existence.

Other revenues, such as merchandising, have historically followed similar patterns, but many clubs have developed more sophisticated approaches to exploiting the potential for increasing match day revenues and sales via the Internet to, in many cases, a worldwide audience. The clubs with the bigger grounds also have the ability to use their corporate hospitality facilities on nonmatch days for conferences, weddings, etc. Only this latter source is likely to be delinked from on-the-field performance.

Fitch generally takes a similar approach to creating stress scenarios for sponsorship and advertising, as compared with ticket sales and broadcast revenues, whereby a team performance and league standings are analyzed. Stressed sponsorship revenues will typically follow the terms of the contracts, which often contain reductions for poor performance. In the event that a sponsorship contract expires during a period of relegation, Fitch would assume renewal at a stressed rate. Other commercial revenues that are likely to be directly linked to team performance will be stressed accordingly.

Player Salary Structure

As noted earlier, there are no salary restrictions in European football. However, salary costs as a percentage of overall turnover are a standard measure of financial prudence, with 55% being the average for an English club. There are, of course, anomalies, particularly where the club has been purchased by a wealthy individual who is prepared to buy success. The notable example is Chelsea in the English League, which was purchased by Roman Abramovich, the Russian oil magnate, in 2003. Since then, the club has purchased several players at huge transfer fees and has the highest wage bill in the country.

In terms of costs, Fitch will review player contracts to see whether a club has some flexibility in managing the overall cost (e.g., by staggering contract maturities so as to be able to take the opportunity not to renew a contact for a particularly expensive player). In reality, the better players will seek a transfer to a more successful club, especially in the event of relegation. So, the decline in costs is, to a degree, inevitable even with careful management. However, Fitch will always assume some lag relative to the decline in revenues. Most other costs are seen as independent of league position, so they will not typically be adjusted.

In addition to adjustment to player salaries when a club is relegated, Fitch will also look for features that restrict the net transfer spend (i.e., cost of new players less proceeds from players sold) and, even in a period of strong performance, restrict the use of transfer fees received for football-related assets, usually new players. In the absence of these features, further stresses will be applied.

Relationship Between League and Players' Unions

Players' unions exist within European sports leagues, but their role has little overall financial effect because it tends to be focused on protecting players against harsh disciplinary measures (usually by the league rather than an individual club) and securing appropriate compensation in the event of career-threatening injury. There have been no incidents of strike action in recent years, and Fitch generally views this as a strength of European soccer transactions. Furthermore, given the minimal risks associated with work stoppages, stress scenarios for a club or stadium transaction generally do not incorporate a work stoppage, where, given the history of work stoppages in U.S.-based sports, are applied.

Role of League in Team Financial Matters/Debt Limits

The governing body of the league typically has very limited powers over a club's financial matters, with the exception of some quite draconian sanctions in the event of a club becoming insolvent. An example is the English Premier League, where a club has 10 points deducted from its total for the season—38 games, three points for a win and one for a draw—which could have the effect of taking the club from midtable to relegation, thus potentially compounding its financial problems yet further.

Another example is the Dutch League, which has similar sanctions for insolvency. The Dutch League does, however, have something of an early warning system in the form of a ranking scale for clubs relating to their financial stability. Those clubs falling below a certain score measured across 12 separate criteria (including liquidity and player costs as a percentage of turnover) are subject to a degree of supervision (e.g., player purchases are subject to approval).

Clubs entering European competitions are required by the European governing body, UEFA, to obtain a license confirming their ability to meet their financial obligations for a period of 18 months.

Although all of these methods of the supervision are somewhat passive, Fitch views them as credit positive for the football industry. The management of a club will have a strong incentive to manage a club cautiously to avoid being ejected from any competitions.

[*Ed. Note: See **Table 4** for characteristics of a typical Fitch analysis for sports facilities.*]

DETERMINANTS OF FRANCHISE VALUES

DETERMINANTS OF FRANCHISE VALUES IN NORTH AMERICAN PROFESSIONAL SPORTS LEAGUES: EVIDENCE FROM A HEDONIC PRICE MODEL

Brad Humphreys and Michael Mondello

INTRODUCTION

There has been a recent increase in scholarly research on the determinants of professional sports franchise values. This research is limited by the fact that the fundamentals used to value typical businesses are not readily available for North American professional sports teams, which are privately held corporations and do not release audited financial data to the general public. In addition, a distinguishing characteristic differentiating sport franchises from traditional businesses is their dependence on intangible assets. These intangible assets, including player contracts, television rights, stadium agreements, and relationships with fans, are important factors contributing to the overall financial status of professional sports teams. Although intangible assets are present within traditional businesses, tangible assets such as plant, property, and equipment are generally considered the drivers of valuation.

Despite anecdotal evidence primarily filtered through the mass media reporting imminent bankruptcies and claims of individual team owners losing significant dollars, few

Table 4   Characteristics of a Typical Fitch Analysis for Sports Facilities to Achieve Investment-Grade Ratings

	Fitch Base Case	Fitch Stress Case
Construction **Simple Project**		
Cost	0%–5% overrun	5%–10% overrun
Schedule	0–3 month delay	3–6 month delay
Complex Project		
Cost	0%–10% overrun	10%–20% overrun
Schedule	3–12 month delay	6–24 month delay
Attendance		
Established	5–15 year historical average	(Base case) — (10%–15%)
New Facility	10–15 year historical average	(Base case) — (10%–15%)
Suite and Premium Seat Renewal Rates **Established**		
Staggered Lease Agreements	CPI + (50 bps–100 bps)	CPI – (50 bps–100 bps)
Nonstaggered Lease Agreements	CPI – (0 bps–50 bps)	CPI – (50 bps–150 bps)
New Facility		
Staggered Lease Agreements	CPI + (50 bps–100 bps)	CPI + (50 bps–100 bps)
Nonstaggered Lease Agreements	CPI + (50 bps–100 bps)	CPI + (50 bps–100 bps)
Sponsorship and Advertising Revenues		
Established	5–15 year historical average	(Base case) — (50 bps–100 bps)
New Facility	10–15 year historical average	(Base case) — (50 bps–100 bps)
Other Revenues		
Established	5–15 year historical average	(Base case) — (50 bps–100 bps)
New Facility	10–15 year historical average	(Base case) — (50 bps–100 bps)
O&M Growth		
Established	5–10 year historical average	(Base case) — (50 bps–100 bps)
New Construction	10–15 year historical average	(Base case) — (50 bps–100 bps)
Financial Ratios (×) **Established—Minimum DSCR**		
Contractually Obligated Revenue	1.50–1.75	1.20–1.45
Total Pledged Revenue	2.00–2.25	1.50–1.75
New Facility—Minimum DSCR		
Contractually Obligated Revenue	1.75–2.00	1.45–1.70
Total Pledged Revenue	2.25–2.40	1.75–2.00
Reserve Levels		
Debt-Service Reserve	Six-month minimum	Six-month minimum
Operations and Maintenance	3–6 month minimum	3–6 month minimum
Strike Reserve	Single anchor tenant facility. In addition to debt-service reserve, additional six-month reserve prior to the signing of a CBA	Single anchor tenant facility. In addition to debt-service reserve, additional six-month reserve prior to the signing of a CBA
Capital Expenditure Reserve	Buildup over initial 10 years	Buildup over initial 10 years
Other		
Lease Agreement	At a minimum for a term equal to the term of bonds	At a minimum for a term equal to the term of bonds
Term	20–25 year maximum debt term	20–25 year maximum debt term

CPI—Consumer Price Index. bps—Basis points. DSCR—Debt-service coverage ratio. CBA—Collective bargaining agreement. 1. Suite and premium seat renewal rates are for existing and new facilities with a waiting list; base- and stress-case scenarios may not include reduction amounts. 2. Other revenues are noncontractually obligated and dependant on attendance levels, which include parking revenues, concessions revenue that is not guaranteed by the concession provider, novelty revenues and ticket revenues. 3. A peer analysis is also incorporated into Fitch's assumptions and may affect ranges.
Source: Fitch Ratings. Reprinted by permission of Fitch, Inc.

professional sports teams in North America have been forced into bankruptcy, and only a few empirical studies examining the determinants of franchise valuation exist. This study adds to the existing research by identifying factors associated with franchise valuation.

In one of the first empirical studies of professional sport team values, Alexander and Kern (2004) examined the effects of team classification, relocation, and the impact of a new stadium on franchise values in the National Football League (NFL), National Basketball Association (NBA), National Hockey League (NHL), and Major League Baseball (MLB). Variables including market size, team performance, and the presence of new stadiums were all found to increase a team's franchise value. Furthermore, playing in a new stadium increased MLB team values an average of $17 million; however, NBA team values increased only by $6.6 million. In addition to the impact of a new stadium, teams using a regional identifier, for example the Tampa Bay Devil Rays (a team identified with a single city) as compared to the Florida Marlins (a team identified with a larger region, the entire state of Florida) had increased franchise values in MLB but not in the other three leagues. Alexander and Kern (2004) posited that this finding may be attributed to the fact that other leagues have institutional policies, like revenue sharing, in place, minimizing any differences among the teams.

. . . .

Finally, Miller (2007) analyzed MLB panel data from 1990 to 2002 and found teams playing in new stadiums demonstrated an increase in franchise value after controlling for team quality and city demographic differences. Furthermore, Miller (2007) found that teams playing in private stadiums had higher franchise values compared to teams playing in public stadiums, although this difference was insufficient to cover the average construction cost of the stadium.

. . . In this paper, we examine the fundamental determinants of franchise sale prices. Although a large number of anecdotal sources have addressed this phenomenon, only a few empirical papers have examined franchise valuation thus far. Fort (2006) found relatively high variation in the appreciation of franchise values over time but did not examine the relationship between fundamentals and sale prices. Similarly, Alexander and Kern (2004) reported that market size, on-field performance, and new facilities were associated with higher franchise values over the period 1991–1997.

METHOD

Several empirical approaches for analyzing changes in the prices of fixed assets like houses and real estate exist. These methods have been used to analyze changes in the prices of assets like art (Beggs & Graddy, 2006; Goetzmann, 1993), wine (Burton & Jacobsen, 2001), and antique furniture

(Graesner, 1993). We apply one of these techniques, hedonic price index method (HPI), to the analysis of the prices paid for professional sports franchises.

The hedonic price framework was first proposed by Rosen (1974). The hedonic method uses variation in observable characteristics of an asset, in this case a professional sports franchise, to explain observed variation in the sale price of that asset. The parameters on the variables capturing the characteristics can be interpreted as hedonic prices of those characteristics.

. . . .

DATA

. . . .

We analyze franchise sale prices over the period 1969–2006. Note that we are not using the estimated franchise values reported annually in *Forbes* magazine; we restrict our analysis to only reported franchise sales prices. We restrict our sample to the post-1969 period because no annual metropolitan area economic data exist before this year, and market characteristics may affect franchise sales prices. Many franchise sales are fractional—an individual or group of investors buys a portion of a professional sports franchise. Following the method used by Fort (2006), we converted all fractional sales to full value. So if 50% of a franchise was sold for $10 million dollars, we count the estimated franchise value as $20 million dollars.

. . . Collectively, there were 184 sales of existing franchises during the sample period across the four leagues. Specific to these 184 sales, 63 occurred in MLB, 51 in the NBA, 35 in the NFL, and 35 in the NHL.

Table 5 contains summary statistics on the franchise sales over the sample period, in current dollar or nominal terms. Research on the sale price of houses, art, and other assets typically works with nominal prices rather than real prices to avoid bias introduced by the deflation process and to make the results comparable to the nominal rate of return on other traded assets like stocks and bonds. We follow this convention in this paper.

The NFL franchises possessed the largest mean sale price, and NHL franchises the smallest. Moreover, NBA

Table 5 Nominal Sale Prices 1969–2006

Sport	# Sales	Avg. Franchise Sale Price in $ Millions	Std. Dev.	Min.	Max.
MLB	63	132.4	154.6	7.1	700
NBA	51	176.2	336.1	2.0	2125
NFL	35	186.6	336.1	10.0	1000
NHL	35	85.9	76.8	3.8	250

Source: International Journal of Sport Finance. Used with permission from Fitness Information Technology.

franchise sale prices were more volatile than other leagues; NHL franchise sale prices the least variable. The largest price paid for a sports franchise in the sample was $2.125 billion, paid for the New York Knicks in 1997. Although this transaction would appear to be an outlier, additional examination revealed this transaction also included their home facility Madison Square Garden, a 19,763-seat arena in midtown Manhattan that is the largest revenue-generating sports venue in the world. Likewise, the largest price paid for an NFL franchise was $1.0 billion, paid for the Washington Redskins in 2003, and that transaction included the 80,000-seat stadium in which the Redskins played, named FedEx Field. The largest price paid for a MLB franchise was $700 million, paid for the Boston Red Sox in 2002, including Fenway Park and an 80% ownership interest in a regional sports television network, the New England Sports Network. Lastly, the largest price paid for an NHL franchise was $250 million, paid for the Philadelphia Flyers in 1996. Undoubtedly, ownership of a stadium or arena had a significant effect on the sale price.

The franchise sales were evenly distributed over the sample period. For example, 44 transactions occurred between 1969 and 1979, 49 took place in the 1980s, 54 in the 1990s, and 37 since 2000. Only 3.3% of the sales involved a move of the franchise from one city to another, and 18.5% of the transactions involved both a team and a sports facility. Seven percent of the transactions (15 in total) involved franchises located in Canada. These transaction prices were converted to U.S. dollars at the exchange rate at the time of the transaction.

Our final data set consisted of 184 franchise sale prices from the four major professional sports leagues in North America over the period 1969–2006. We augmented these data with additional variables capturing the ownership of the facility the team played in, the success of the team on the field, the age of the franchise and facility, and market characteristics like metropolitan area population and the number of other professional sports franchises in the metropolitan area. Note that NHL standings are based on points, not wins, so NHL team performance, unlike NFL, NBA, and MLB performance, is not based on winning percentage. For the NHL, we estimated winning percentage by dividing the number of points earned in each season by 162, the maximum number of points possible in an 81-game season. This transformation makes NHL on-ice success comparable to the other three leagues while still preserving the relative within-season and across-season relative standings of NHL teams.

RESULTS

. . . .

[T]he average price of NBA franchises is equal to the average price of an MLB franchise, and the average price of an NHL franchise is lower than a MLB franchise. NFL franchises are the most expensive, and NHL franchises are the least expensive.

Franchises in larger markets command a premium, probably because of the larger revenue potential. The parameter on the log of the metropolitan area population can be interpreted as elasticity in this setting, and the parameter estimate suggests that for each additional 1% increase in the metropolitan area population the franchise sale price increases by 0.67%. Both Alexander and Kern (2004) and Miller (2007) found metropolitan population to have a positive effect on franchise values. Teams owning their facility also command a premium, and the franchise age also carries a positive hedonic price. Team buyers are effectively buying the history of the team, and the longer the team has been in existence, the more team history there is to buy. The age of the facility the team plays in has no effect on franchise sale prices. Recent on-field success, as measured by the average winning percentage in the five seasons before the sale, also had no effect on sale prices. These three results differ from Miller (2007), who found that: (a) franchise age had no effect on franchise value, (b) facility age had a negative effect on franchise value, and (c) current and lagged winning percentage had a positive effect on franchise value. Miller (2007) analyzed annual franchise value estimates from MLB; we analyze transaction prices across all four major leagues. Both Fort (2006) and Miller (2007) remarked that the franchise value estimates typically differ from actual sale prices. Since 1990, when the *Forbes/Financial World* franchise value estimates were first published, there have been 91 franchise sales in the four North American professional sports leagues studied here. On average, the estimated franchise value was $31.6 million less than the actual sale price for these franchises. This average difference obscures some asymmetry in the difference; for 57 of the sales, the estimated franchise value was less than the sale price, with an average difference of $75 million; for 30 of the sales, the estimated franchise value was greater than the sale price, with an average difference of $49 million; in two instances, the 1991 sale of the New York Giants and the 2001 sale of the Seattle SuperSonics, the sale price and the estimated franchise value were identical.

These differences in parameter estimates help identify why the *Forbes* franchise estimates differ from actual sale prices. Based on Miller's (2007) results, the annual franchise value estimates depend more on facility and on-field success, and the sale prices depend more on franchise and market characteristics. Our results suggest that facility age and on-field success have no effect on sale price. Miller's (2007) analysis of estimated franchise values suggests that on-field success and facility age systematically affect estimated franchise values. Thus, one reason for the systematic difference between the estimated franchise values and actual franchise sales price is that the estimated franchise values take into account on-field success and facility age while franchise buyers do not.

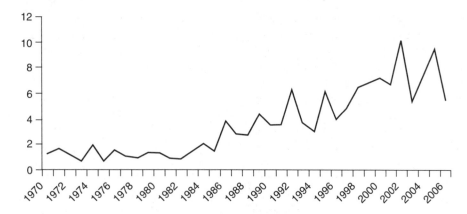

Figure 9   Quality-Adjusted Franchise Price Index 1970–2006

Source: International Journal of Sport Finance. Used with permission from Fitness Information Technology.

. . . It appears team success does not have an important hedonic price in this setting.

The higher the number of competing professional sports teams in the metropolitan area, the lower the franchise sale price, other things being equal. This result is consistent with the idea that other professional teams in the metropolitan area are competitors, and the presence of more competitors reduces the franchise sale price, holding other market characteristics like metropolitan population constant.

. . . .

First, the quality-adjusted price index has increased steadily over the sample period. Despite some short-term downturns in franchise prices, the quality-adjusted price of an average sports franchise has increased steadily over the past 38 years. It is difficult to reconcile this increase with the periodic claims of large and persistent losses incurred by team owners. If professional sports teams consistently lose money, why does the quality-adjusted price index continue to increase?

Second, based on **Figure 9**, it is difficult to incur a capital loss on the purchase of a professional sports franchise. The average annual increase in the quality-adjusted franchise price was 16% over the sample period, a nominal rate of return far exceeding the annual 3% per year rate of return used by Fort (2006) as a comparison. Based on this price index, a generic sports franchise bought for $5 million in 1970 and held for 35 years would have been worth $48 million in 2005, holding quality constant over the period. However, the quality-adjusted price index on Figure 9 does exhibit quite a bit of variation, and there are several years with a negative rate of return on the average franchise value.

The average rate of increase also varies considerably by decade. The average annual increase was 21% from 1969 to 1979, 23% in the 1980s, 13% in the 1990s, and just 4% after 2000. It is useful to compare these numbers with the decade-by-decade unconditional results in Fort (2006) for MLB. Fort reports a 5.3% increase for the 1970s, 9.5% for the 1980s, and 3% for the 1990s, based on unconditional

repeat sales for specific MLB franchises. Fort's decade-by-decade annual growth rates are lower because he focused on a single sport and his increases do not hold franchise quality constant over the period. These results suggest that a buy-and-hold team owner could expect a much larger annual rate of return in an investment in a sports franchise than Fort's (2006) results.

The lower annual increase in the quality-adjusted price index after 1990 suggests that there may have been an important change in the market for sports franchises in the latter part of the sample period. Fort (2006) also noted the decline in the value of ownership of professional sports teams in the past 10 years, asking of MLB, "Why did the fall off to essentially zero growth rates in the 1990s occur?" Although we have no evidence to point to in this paper, we can rule out a decline in the quality of sports franchises in the past 20 years as the culprit because the decline is also present in our quality-adjusted price index.

SUMMARY AND CONCLUSIONS

In this paper we analyze the evolution of the sales price for professional sports franchises in North America using a hedonic price model. This approach has been used to investigate changes in the price of other assets like residential real estate, art, and wine. The hedonic price method allows us to identify certain characteristics of sports franchises affecting their sale price and to estimate a hedonic price for each of these characteristics. Our results suggest that the nature of the league, local market size, franchise age, the number of competing professional teams in the market, and the ownership of the facility in which the team plays all have significant hedonic prices, but the team's on-field success and facility age do not. We construct a quality-adjusted price index for an average professional sports franchise. The average annual rate of increase of this index is over 20% over the period 1969–2006, signifying owners of professional sports teams earned significant capital gains over the period. This estimated increase in franchise prices is also significantly larger than previously reported in the literature, suggesting sports team owners have financially benefited, even better than previously thought, over the past 38 years.

The results in this paper have several important limitations. First and foremost, the results of the hedonic model estimation depend critically on a properly specified model. If we have failed to include important indicators of franchise quality in the empirical model, then the quality-adjusted price index will be biased and may not reflect the actual benefit from owning a professional sports team. Also, we have pooled team sales prices across leagues in order to increase the efficiency of our estimates of the parameters of the hedonic model. If there are important differences in the changes in franchise values across leagues that are not captured by our league-varying intercepts, then our results will be affected. Unfortunately, our sample contains only about 25 observations for some individual sports, making specification tests by sport difficult.

Our results also suggest potential areas for further research. The franchise sales data analyzed here can also be analyzed using other techniques. Foremost among these is the repeat sales method developed by Case and Schiller (1989). This method has the advantage of placing much less emphasis on model specification. Also, the decline in the annual increase in the quality-adjusted franchise price index beginning in the 1990s deserves more attention. Researchers with access to additional franchise sale data from the 2000s should further investigate the nature and causes of this change. Specifically, additional research could accurately determine if this reduction in franchise appreciation represents a permanent trend or if this was just a transitory period in team ownership values.

References

Alexander, D. L., & Kern W. (2004). The economic determinants of professional sports franchise values. *Journal of Sports Economics, 5*(1), 51–66.

Beggs, A., & Graddy, K. (2006). Failure to meet the reserve price: The impact on returns to art. University of Oxford Department of Economics Discussion Paper number 272.

. . . .

Burton, B. J., & Jacobsen, J. P. (2001). The rate of return on investment in wine. *Economic Inquiry, 39*(3), 337–350.

Case, K. E., & Shiller, R. J. (1989). The efficiency of the market for single family homes. *American Economic Review, 79*(1), 125–137.

Fort, R. (2006). The value of Major League Baseball ownership. *International Journal of Sport Finance, 1*(1), 9–20.

Goetzmann, W. N. (1993). Accounting for taste: Art and the financial markets over three centuries. *American Economic Review, 83*(5), 1370–1376.

Graeser, P. (1993). Rate of return to investment in American antique furniture. *Southern Economic Journal, 59*(2), 817–821.

Miller, P. A. (2007). Private financing and sports franchise values: The case of Major League Baseball. *Journal of Sports Economics, 8*(5), 449–467.

Rosen, S. (1974). Hedonic prices and implicit markets: Product differentiation in pure competition. *Journal of Political Economy, 82*(1), 34–55.

. . . .

THE ECONOMIC DETERMINANTS OF PROFESSIONAL SPORTS FRANCHISE VALUES

Donald L. Alexander and William Kern

During the past several decades, professional sports have undergone tremendous changes relative to earlier eras. We have seen changes in the location of teams, ownership, the structure of labor/management relations, the names of teams, the emergence of corporate ownership, a stadium building boom, and the sale of stadium naming rights, just to name a few examples. The economic impact and rationale for these changes have been the fodder for recent research by sports economists. Analysis of the economic incentives motivating team relocation and new stadium construction has generated considerable attention. Economists have explored the underlying rationale for the movement of franchises and the building of new stadiums, and have attempted to measure the effects of these changes on outcomes such as the amount of employment and economic growth generated in local and regional economies.[1]

In this article, we take a different perspective on several of these changes noted above. We examine them from the standpoint of their managerial efficiency—the payoff derived from these strategies for the firm/team rather than the economy as a whole. That is, we attempt to assess the value or payoffs derived from several management strategies commonly employed by team owners during the past several decades. The values of some of these strategies are readily ascertained. For instance, it is easy to determine the value of the decision of any franchise to sell the naming rights to their stadium. There is a market for such rights and they go to the highest bidder. The price those rights command (which are commonly public knowledge) are additions to the franchise's revenue stream, and their effect on the value of franchises is a clear indication of the payoff to this strategy.

Although the payoff to some of these strategies is less obvious, they presumably (certainly the owners expected them to) have a positive effect on franchise value. For instance, when Bud Adams relocated the Houston Oilers to become the Tennessee Titans, and when Bill Bidwell renamed the Phoenix Cardinals the Arizona Cardinals, and when the Baltimore Orioles built Camden Yards, we can presume that they did so because they felt these decisions would enhance the value of their franchises. The questions that arise and that we seek to answer in this article are whether in fact franchise value is positively enhanced by such strategies and, if so, to what magnitude? What is the incremental value of choosing a regional as opposed to a city-specific identity for your team? What are the effects of team relocation and new stadium construction on franchise values?

AN OVERVIEW OF PROFESSIONAL SPORTS NOMENCLATURE

In the four American professional sports leagues (baseball, basketball, football, and hockey), teams are named either for the city in which they are located (e.g., Miami Dolphins, Los Angeles Dodgers) or in reference to a much broader geographic area (e.g., Florida Marlins, California Angels).

To our knowledge, there has been no formal analysis examining whether having a regional identity rather than a city identity has any effect on a franchise's economic value. One might argue that if it did matter, then we would expect to see more team owners adopting regional names if it was perceived to be profitable or changing their identities from regional ones if it were perceived to be less profitable than having a city name. We agree in part. We recognize, however, that this is not a simple decision but a more complex calculation that is likely to be affected by considerations such as tradition and the source of funding for stadium construction, as well as the size of the prospective marketing area (i.e., fan base) and cable television market targeted by the team owners.

In this article, we compiled franchise value data for teams in Major League Baseball (MLB), the National Basketball Association (NBA), the National Football League (NFL), and the National Hockey League (NHL). In the empirical analysis described below, we treated each league separately because each has different rules and traditions that affect each franchise's economic value. For example, MLB is exempt from antitrust laws, whereas the other leagues are not. In addition, the extent of revenue sharing varies across leagues as well. For instance, ticket revenues are shared between the home and visiting teams on a 100-0 basis in the NBA and NHL, on an 85-15 basis [formerly] in MLB, and on a 60-40 basis in the NFL.[2] Thus, we believe that it is plausible to consider the leagues as different samples. We can also gain additional insight when we compare some of the trends that have emerged in each of the four professional sports.

Table 6 presents an overview of the situation in each of the four major professional sports leagues. The data summarized in this table span the period from 1991 to 1997. These data show that the number of teams with regional identities is evenly distributed across MLB, the NBA, the

Table 6   Descriptive Analysis

	League			
	MLB	**NBA**	**NFL**	**NHL**
Regional identity	5	5	5	4
New stadium	4	12	5	9
New location	0	0	3	2
New team	2	0	2	4
Changed identity	0	0	2	1

Source: Authors' calculations and Keating (1999). Reproduced from *Journal of Sports Economics.* Used with permission.

Note: MLB = Major League Baseball; NBA = the National Basketball Association; NFL = the National Football League; NHL = the National Hockey League. The following lists the teams with regional identities: MLB (California, Colorado, Florida, Minnesota, and Texas); NBA (Golden State, Indiana, Minnesota, New Jersey, and Utah); NFL (Carolina, Minnesota, New England, Arizona, and Tampa Bay); and NHL (Colorado, Florida, New Jersey, and Tampa Bay). We recognize that several of these regional identities have changed since the end of our sample period in 1997.

NFL, and the NHL. The interesting feature is that different teams in the same location have adopted regional identities, as indicated by the following clustering in certain cities: the Minnesota Twins (MLB), Minnesota Timberwolves (NBA), and Minnesota Vikings (NFL) in Minneapolis;[3] the Colorado Rockies (MLB) and Colorado Avalanche (NHL) in Denver; the Tampa Bay Buccaneers (NFL), Tampa Bay Lightning (NHL), and Tampa Bay Devil Rays (MLB) in Tampa;[4] the New Jersey Nets (NBA) and New Jersey Devils (NHL); and the Florida Marlins (MLB) and Florida Panthers (NHL) in South Florida. This commonality can be explained in a number of different ways. For example, the Minnesota situation may reflect an implicit compromise between the Minneapolis and St. Paul fans, or it could be an attempt to attract a larger fan base beyond the twin cities. Similarly, the Tampa Bay example may reflect an attempt to draw fans from the greater Tampa, St. Petersburg, and Clearwater communities. The Florida situation is quite similar. In contrast, the New Jersey situation appears to be an attempt to separate itself from New York, but with greater appeal than might be generated by naming the team for Newark or East Rutherford. Indeed, the New Jersey situation may simply reflect a Hotelling-like equilibrium in which competitors achieve some minimal level of product differentiation at the margin while at the same time attempting to maintain a monopoly on the inframarginal consumers.

Another interesting feature of these data is the relatively few situations (at least during our sample period) in which teams have changed their identities. Two are particularly noteworthy and merit some discussion. The first involves the Phoenix Cardinals (NFL) changing their identity to the Arizona Cardinals. This is an example in which team owners have adopted a regional identity, perhaps trying to establish a broader fan base beyond the Phoenix area. The second involves the change that occurred when the Minnesota North

Stars (NHL) moved to Dallas. Instead of changing the name to the Texas North Stars, the owners adopted Dallas Stars as the new team name. This contrasts with the Phoenix situation in which the owners chose to use a regional identity, whereas the owners of the Stars chose to use a city-specific identity. [*Ed. Note: Subsequently, the Anaheim Angels changed their name to the Los Angeles Angels of Anaheim after withstanding a legal challenge to the change brought by the City of Anaheim.*]

These data also illustrate several other features of professional sports. First, there was expansion in three of the four leagues as several new teams were formed. In our sample, the new teams were formed mainly in California and Florida. Second, several existing teams changed locations. In the NFL, the Cleveland Browns moved to Baltimore, the Los Angeles Rams moved to St. Louis, and the Los Angeles Raiders moved back to Oakland. Third, there were a considerable number of new stadiums or arenas built during our sample period, which represents a trend that has continued into the new century. With the exception of new stadium construction, these changes were confined to MLB, the NFL, and the NHL.

THE EMPIRICAL MODEL

The sample consists of a pooled, cross-sectional, time-series panel of team specific data for each of the four major professional sports leagues. Each sample spans the period from 1991 to 1997 and includes data for only U.S.-based franchises. . . . We used the franchise value for each team as the dependent variable. *Financial World* (*FW*) magazine reported these data annually for MLB, NBA, NFL, and NHL.[5] In general, these data represent *FW*'s estimate of the present discounted value of the team's net revenue stream at a point in time. We acknowledge that these are only crude estimates and are not determined in organized financial markets through the interaction of supply and demand. Nevertheless, there has been a reasonable attempt to estimate the net revenue flow for each team. For example, revenue estimates are based on gate receipts, television contracts (national and local including cable), concessions, parking, venue advertising, naming rights, licensing, and merchandising. Cost estimates are based on player costs, pensions, travel, marketing, administrative, and media expenses. Moreover, we compared the estimates reported in *FW* to the prices paid for various franchises sold during the sample period, and several conclusions emerge from this informal comparison.[6] First, the *FW* estimates were typically lower than the reported transaction prices but always within an order of magnitude of the sales price. Scully (1995), however, argues that the premium paid for various franchises may simply reflect the "winner's curse" in the bidding competition for that franchise, especially for teams with good reputations. Second, in many instances it appeared that *FW* adjusted the franchise value estimate in the following year, and this may

simply reflect the fact that the *FW* estimates were published before the franchise sales were consummated. Third, this pattern did not appear to vary across the four professional sports, which leads us to believe that if there are any biases in the *FW* procedure used to compute those estimates, those biases will affect all the estimates within the sample. . . .

[The following anticipates] the various factors that are likely to influence the determination of a team's franchise value.[8] On the demand side, we use real, per-capita income (*INCOME*) to control for differences in ticket demand that will affect a team's revenue and, hence, franchise profitability. We anticipate a positive sign for this variable. We also include a city's population (*POP*) to control for market-size effects on franchise profitability. Generally, we expect that teams located in larger markets will be more profitable than teams located in smaller markets, ceteris paribus.[9] The major reason is that large market teams have a larger potential fan base to support their franchises. In addition, large market teams are in a better position to negotiate lucrative cable television contracts if for no other reason than the advertisers, who pay premium rates to the local cable service provider, would gain exposure to a large number of potential customers.[10]

Team performance during the season is another factor that will likely affect demand and, hence, franchise value.[11] In this case, we used team's final standings from the previous season (*PLACE*) to control for this influence. We expect a negative sign for this variable because as team performance worsens (e.g., first to fourth), revenue will likely decrease. The reason may be that the team's reputation is diminishing (Scully, 1995), which is diminishing the franchise value, or it simply may be that some season ticket holders are less likely to renew their season tickets (Salant, 1992), which is also likely to reduce profitability.

. . . .

We also included several indicator variables to account for other factors that will likely affect a team's profitability. The first is. . . if a team has what we characterize as a regional identity . . . . We anticipate a positive sign for this variable. For example, a regional identity (e.g., Tennessee Titans instead of the Nashville Titans) may represent an appeal to a larger geographic fan base, which will enhance a team's profitability, ceteris paribus. If this is the case, then we should see more teams adopting regional type identities whenever possible. We recognize, however, that tradition may well interfere here and significantly restrict an owner's abilities to carry out such a strategy. For instance, it is hard to imagine the Cleveland Indians becoming the Northern Ohio Indians or the Green Bay Packers becoming the Wisconsin Packers. The creation of a regional identity is more easily accomplished and, therefore, more likely when a team changes location or when a new franchise is created through league expansion.

A regional identity could also possibly arise as a consequence of the nature of the financing that has been employed as part of the package used to lure a team to an area. When taxpayers from across the state are compelled to pay taxes to build arenas and stadiums, there may arise a sort of stakeholder effect whereby citizens of that state feel as though they have some claim on that team. The team may therefore feel obligated to adopt a state or regional identity to appease potential fans. Leeds and von Allmen (2002, p.172) argue that the common practice during the 1962 to 1991 period of naming stadiums after the municipalities in which they are located could be traced to the fact that the cities were paying for the new stadiums.

In our opinion, the creation of a regional identity appears much more likely to be undertaken as a marketing strategy rather than a quid pro quo for a new stadium or team. An examination of the recent history of new stadiums, team relocation, and league expansion indicates that franchise owners certainly do not need to adopt a regional identity to get a new stadium deal or attract a team. Of the total of 62 new stadiums constructed, renovated, or in the planning phase during the period from 1994 to 2004, only 21 were even partially funded by state governments. Sixteen of those 21 funded by state governments were built or are being built for franchises with city identities. Of the remaining 5, 1 is the New England Patriots, who adopted a regional identity in 1971 (and also built their old stadium at their own expense), and 2 carry the regional identity of Tampa Bay.[12]

The second indicator variable is . . . if the team is playing in a new stadium or arena. . . . The construction of new stadiums or arenas marked the 1990s as team owners sought new financial arrangements and revenue sources and local governments sought to keep the home team from moving to a new location.[13] We anticipate that this variable will have a positive and permanent effect on franchise value during the stadium's economic life because it affords owners additional revenue generating means such as luxury suites and enhanced concession revenues.

The third variable . . . is a measure that attempts to account for the effect of a change in a franchise's location. . . . [T]he effect of a new location will have a positive but diminishing effect on franchise value. Hamilton and Kahn (1997, p. 253) note that several authors have hypothesized the existence of a "honeymoon effect" on attendance following a team's movement to a new location or construction of a new stadium. They report that the accepted wisdom is that this effect begins to fade after about 3 years and is zero after 8 years.

Closely related to this third variable is the case in which a team changes location and changes its identity as well. For example, when Art Modell moved the Cleveland Browns to Baltimore, he changed the team's nickname from the Browns to the Ravens. . . . Again, we anticipate that this factor will have a positive but diminishing effect on a team's value. The fifth . . . is the year the team enters the league. . .

Here we seek to account for the effect of the "newness" of the team. We hypothesize that a new team has a sort of novelty that exerts a significant effect on fan interest in the first few years of its existence.[14]

THE EMPIRICAL RESULTS

. . . For all four leagues, the empirical model performed well and as we anticipated. [See **Table 7**.] For example, the results indicate that population differences (*POP*) have a positive effect on franchise values in three of the four leagues. Not unexpectedly, it is insignificant in the NFL model and this may reflect the fact that the NFL's extensive system of revenue sharing among its teams minimizes any market-size effects arising from population differences across cities. The results also show that team performance (*PLACE*) matters, as this variable has the expected negative sign and is significant at conventional levels in all four models.

In the MLB sample, there were no teams that changed locations or their identities and, consequently, we did not include *NEWLOC* and *CHGID* in the MLB model. However, there were several new teams that joined the league and several that moved into a new stadium. The results show that there was no significant difference between new teams (*NEWTEAM*) and established teams in terms of average franchise values. One explanation for this result may be that new teams have yet to establish a strong fan base and lucrative revenue sources to enhance their profitability as compared to the older teams that have been in the league for some time. This may be explained by the fact that in all leagues, previous growth and expansion have already taken the best locations. Expansion during the sample period was generally toward more marginal market areas such as the formation of the Florida Marlins and Tampa Bay Devil Rays. These areas may be classified as marginal because they are smaller in terms of population, income, and, perhaps more important, fan interest relative to some of the older, more established franchises.

By contrast, we did find that teams playing in new stadiums (*NEWFACILITY*) have, on average, higher franchise values. The plausible explanation for this result is that the new stadium provides the owners with new revenue sources such as the sale or rental of additional corporate boxes and the opportunity to sell the naming rights which, all taken together, increase a team's franchise value. Indeed, the results suggest that a new facility increases franchise value (in real terms) in MLB by approximately $17 million. One explanation for why *NEWTEAM* is insignificant while *NEWFACILITY* is significant is that the teams that are new also are playing in a new stadium as well. Given the construction of the empirical model, it is quite possible that we are unable to separate the effects for those teams that are new and playing in a new stadium.[17]

Table 7   Ordinary Least Squares (OLS) Regression Analysis of Professional Sports Franchise Values (Dependent Variable = Franchise Value)

Variable	League			
	MLB	NBA	NFL	NHL
Constant	52.88 (4.00)	68.60 (5.09)	98.27 (10.17)	44.16 (3.87)
INCOME	0.001 (1.76)*	−0.0008 (−1.01)	0.0003 (0.70)	−0.0006 (−0.98)
POP	3.03 (10.21)**	1.84 (3.68)**	0.19 (1.29)	0.68 (3.93)**
PLACE	−7.83 (−2.43)**	−2.45 (−3.02)**	−2.71 (−3.90)**	−2.20 (−3.49)**
NEWTEAM	5.05 (0.77)		6.68 (0.75)	−7.14 (−1.67)
NEWFACILITY	17.07 (4.74)**	6.64 (2.09)*	−2.96 (−0.90)	10.84 (3.40)**
NEWLOC			−0.88 (−0.12)	−3.73 (−0.52)
CHGID			1.67 (0.27)	−9.73 (−1.26)
REGID	11.98 (1.72)*	−5.71 (−1.61)	−2.69 (−0.64)	−11.62 (−2.17)
REFPOP	−2.90 (−4.55)***	−1.39 (−2.86)***	−1.56 (−1.66)	−0.20 (−0.55)
Adjusted R^2	0.57	0.51	0.47	0.56
B-P-G	46.11	76.62	73.63	36.96
LM	2.69	1.04	0.59	1.70

Source: Journal of Sports Economics. Used with permission.

Note: MLB = Major League Baseball; NBA = the National Basketball Association; NFL = the National Football League; NHL = the National Hockey League. The *t* values are in parentheses. The regression estimates were obtained using the HECTOV (and AUTCOV in MMLB regression) procedure in *SHAZAM*. The Breusch-Pagan-Godfrey (*B-P-G*) test statistic and the Lagrange multiplier (*LM*) test statistic were computed before correcting for heteroscedasticity. The results for the year fixed effects are available on request.

*Five percent significance level (one-tailed) = 1.65 **One percent significance level (one-tailed) = 2.33. ***One percent significance level (two-tailed) = 2.58.

The results also show that teams with regional identities (*REGID*) have, on average, higher franchise values than teams that do not.[18] The coefficient indicates that a regional identity increases franchise value by almost $12 million in MLB. We interacted *REGID* with population (*POP*) to test whether the effect of a regional identity varies with market size. We expect that a regional identity would have a larger effect on franchise value for teams located in small market areas. Thus, we anticipate a negative sign for *REGPOP* and the results support this hypothesis.

In the NBA sample, there were no new teams (*NEWTEAM*) and no teams that moved (*NEWLOC*) or changed their identity (*CHGID*). Thus, we did not include these variables in the NBA model. Nonetheless, the results show that the teams moving into new arenas (*NEWFACILITY*) did improve their franchise values, ceteris paribus, because this variable is significant at conventional levels. It is interesting that the results indicate that a new facility only increases franchise value (in real terms) by $6.64 million. This is much less than the increase reported for MLB, perhaps because MLB plays approximately twice as many home games as the NBA.

The results indicate that the regional identity variable (*REGID*) does not help to explain variations in franchise values in the NBA as it did in MLB, except that when it is interacted with population, the coefficient for *REGPOP* is negative and significant at conventional levels. We interpret this to mean that the effect of having a regional identity does vary inversely with market size. Teams with regional

identities that are located in larger markets will, on average, have lower franchise values as compared to teams with regional identities that are located in smaller markets.

The NFL sample is much more mixed than the MLB and NBA samples in terms of teams moving, new teams joining the league, and so forth. The results for the NFL model provide a mixed message as well. The variables *NEWTEAM*, *NEWFACILITY*, *NEWLOC*, and *CHGID* are all insignificant at conventional levels. We believe there are two primary reasons for why this pattern emerges in the NFL regression results. The first is that the NFL's system of revenue sharing minimizes any differences in franchise values and, consequently, we are unable to estimate the separate effects of team-specific differences (e.g., teams playing in a new stadium compared to teams playing in an older stadium) given the limited nature of our sample (7 years of data). The second reason is that there may be some correlation among the explanatory variables. For example, teams that have moved to new stadiums may also be new teams or teams that have changed location.

Again, the results indicate that the regional identity variable (*REGID*) does not help to explain variations in franchise values in the NFL as it did in MLB, except that when it is interacted with population, the coefficient is negative and significant at conventional levels. We interpret this to mean that the effect of having a regional identity does vary inversely with market size. Teams with regional identities that are located in larger markets will on average have lower franchise values as compared to teams with regional identities that are located in smaller markets. We find this result somewhat surprising, given that revenue sharing is intended to minimize differences between small and large market teams.

The NHL sample is also mixed in terms of teams moving, new teams joining the league, and so forth, but the results are similar to the pattern reported for MLB and the NBA. For example, the *NEWFACILITY* variable indicates that teams playing in new venues have higher franchise values, on average. The results suggest that a new venue increases franchise value by approximately $10.8 million, which is greater than the increase for the NBA but less than the increase for MLB. It is reasonable to expect that the increase is less than the increase reported for MLB, but at the same time it seems puzzling that it would be greater than the increase for the NBA because in many instances the NBA and NHL share the same arenas.

In contrast to the results for the other three leagues, the results for the NHL show that teams with a regional identity (*REGID*) do not have, on average, a higher franchise value and that the effect does not vary with market size. In the case of the NHL, we believe this reflects the fact the teams with regional identities in our sample are located in what we characterize as marginal or unproven markets. For example, the NHL teams are: Colorado, Florida, New Jersey, and Tampa Bay. Florida is relatively new to the NHL and is located in what many believe is an unproven hockey market. Despite the success on the ice, New Jersey has struggled at the gate and probably because it is competing against the older, more established New York teams. Consequently, it is probably difficult to appeal to loyal Ranger and Islander fans. Tampa Bay is in a situation that is similar to Florida's situation. It is a relatively new team located in a marginal hockey market at best. Thus, the appeal to draw fans from the greater Tampa area is not likely to have any positive impact, as the evidence confirms. Colorado would appear to be the exception. However, the reader may recall that Colorado previously had an NHL franchise known as the Rockies that moved from Colorado to become the New Jersey Devils in 1982.

. . . .

As we anticipated, income differences will lead to different levels of demand that will affect franchise profitability. Second, population (*POP*) and team performance (*PLACE*) also had the expected signs and were significant at conventional levels in all four models. Third, the new facility measure (*NEWFACILITY*) had a positive and statistically significant impact in all models except the NFL. Again, we believe this may reflect in part the effect of the NFL's system of revenue sharing, but also the fact that television revenues, which are shared, are relatively more important than stadium revenues.

. . . .

SUMMARY AND CONCLUSIONS

In this article, we examine the economic determinants of professional sports franchise values. The empirical results that we present indicate that market size, team performance, and the presence of a new facility increase a team's franchise value, as many would expect. Moreover, we find that the use of a regional identity increases franchise value in MLB but not in the other professional sports. We believe this may reflect the fact that the other sports have institutional arrangements that minimize any differences among the various teams unlike MLB. Consequently, this offsets the positive impact of having a regional identity.

The reader may be surprised at the small magnitude of the effects of team relocation, new stadiums, and regional identities on franchise values, given the size of the public subsidies teams often receive and new revenues these changes have generated. But our results are consistent with the claims and observations of Noll and Zimbalist (1997) and Hamilton and Kahn (1997). Noll and Zimbalist argue that although the new stadiums do enhance net franchise revenues, they also raise costs, particularly players' salaries, which they claim "are roughly proportional to the revenues that they generate," so that much of the revenue enhancement from a new stadium inevitably goes to players (p. 28). What appears to have happened is that the owners have used the additional revenues derived from the new facilities to bid players away from other teams and, thus, raising the overall pay levels in professional sports. For example, Hamilton and Kahn demonstrate that as a consequence of the Baltimore Orioles' move to Camden Yards, net revenues increased by $23 million per year, but that allowed them to spend more on players, causing salaries to rise by almost $22 million per year (p. 259). Our results are thus consistent with Noll and Zimbalist's claim that the players capture a large percentage of the economic rents generated by these changes.

This outcome in which the players capture the additional rents may not necessarily be the only possible outcome. For example, the recent sale of the Washington Redskins and the Cleveland Indians suggests that the former owners may capture some economic rents as well. On the basis of our analysis, it would be difficult to determine how much of the change in franchise value is captured by the players and how much is captured by the owners.

Notes

1. See, for example, Noll and Zimbalist (1997) for a collection of articles investigating these issues.

2. Scully (1995, p. 183, note 22). Television contracts and revenue sharing also vary widely across the four leagues. Whereas the National Football League (NFL) has a lucrative national television contract, Major League Baseball (MLB) and the National Hockey League (NHL) do not.

3. The NHL recently added the Minnesota Wild, although it is not included in our sample.

4. The Devil Rays are also not included in our sample.

5. These data are reported from 1991 to 1997. After 1997, the data were not published until 2000.

6. The franchise sales data were reported in "Most Recent Franchise Sales," Appendix 2, *Sports Facility Reports* (Spring 2001), which is published by the National Sports Law Institute of Marquette University Law School (http://www.marquette.edu/law/sports/sfr/sfr21 .html).

. . . .

8. Scully (1995, pp. 100-7) argues that teams build reputations that affect their franchise values, and one of the determinants is the team's winning percentage. The demand for wins is a function of market size, usually measured by the standard metropolitan statistical area (SMSA) and per-capita income.

9. Scully (1995, p. 116) argues that this is the conventional wisdom, except for the NFL, which has an extensive system of revenue sharing that minimizes any market-size differences on profitability.

10. For example, according to the National Center for Policy Analysis, Idea House (http://www.ncpa.org/pd/state/slaugh98c.html), the New York Yankees signed a 12-year, $500 million cable television contract in 1996 and that same year earned $69.8 million from their radio and television contracts.

11. We recognize, however, that high-valued franchises have the financial means to acquire better talent that enhances team performance. This would mean, for example, that franchise value in the year 2000 may affect team performance in 2001, which will then affect franchise value in 2002. But given that we have a relatively short time series, we are unable to construct an econometric model to account for this potential dynamic relationship.

12. These data are derived from Rappaport and Wilkerson (2001), Appendix 2.

13. See Keating (1999) for more details.

14. Alexander (2001) found that expansion teams in MLB experienced a higher demand relative to established teams, but he used a simple dummy variable classification.

. . . .

17. There is some correlation between *NEWLOC* and *NEWTEAM*, but it is not perfect.

18. An anonymous referee has pointed out that the *REGID* variable may be endogenous. Team owners that maximize profit select regional identities because they are perceived to be more profitable. We used the procedure discussed in Greene (2000, pp. 933-934) to determine whether *REGID* is endogenous, and the results indicate that it is exogenous.

References

. . . .

Hamilton, B., & Kahn, P. (1997). Baltimore's Camden Yards ballparks. In R. G. Noll & A. Zimbalist (Eds.), *Sports, jobs, & taxes: The economic impact of sports teams and stadiums*. Washington, DC: Brookings Institution.

Keating, R. J. (1999, April 5). Sports Pork: The costly relationship between major league sports and government. *Policy Analysis, 339*, 1–33.

. . . .

Leeds, M., & von Allmen, P. (2002). *The economics of sports*. Boston: Addison-Wesley.

Noll, R., & Zimbalist, A. (1997). *Sports, jobs and taxes*. Washington, DC: Brookings Institution.

Salant, D. J. (1992). Price setting in professional sports. In P. M. Sommers (Ed.), *Diamonds are forever: The business of baseball*. Washington, DC: Brookings Institution.

Scully, G. W. (1995). *The market structure of sports*. Chicago: The University of Chicago Press.

. . . .

THE FUTURE

PROFESSIONAL SPORTS: THE NEXT EVOLUTION IN VALUE CREATION

Jeff Phillips and Jeremy Krasner

The Chicago Cubs and Wrigley Field were acquired by the Tribune Company in 1981 for $20.5 million. [*Ed. Note: The team, stadium, and the Cubs 25% stake in Comcast Sportsnet Chicago were sold to the Ricketts family for $845 million in 2009.*] . . . Driving this appreciation was an increase in league-wide revenues, the participation in league-wide ventures like Major League Baseball Advanced Media and a demand for their product that has allowed the team to steadily increase prices. As noted in the chart below [**Table 8**], this type of historical appreciation is not unusual, but is it reasonable to expect similar appreciation in the future?

To understand how these assets appreciated, one must understand what drives the valuation of a sports franchise. Each year, only a few teams become available, and every sports fan would love to own a team if they had the financial wherewithal. Conceptually, the value of a sports team is more similar to a rare Picasso painting than a typical business. A Picasso has significant value, despite not generating substantial cash flow on an annual basis, because it is rare (in short supply) and many people would like to own one if they could (in high demand).

If supply is low and demand high, one might expect that teams would command similar prices in sale transactions if only the unique nature of the asset determined its value. However, as illustrated in the table below, there has been significant disparity in the valuation of franchises, both within and across the various major leagues.

Table 8   Capital Appreciation of Select Franchises

Franchise	Prior Transaction	Latest Transaction	Holding Period (Yrs)	CAGR
Cleveland Cavaliers	$20.0	$375.0	22	14.3%
Phoenix Suns	55.0	401.0	17	12.4%
Seattle Supersonics	200.0	350.0	5	10.7%
Minnesota Vikings	250.0	600.0	7	13.3%
Atlanta Falcons	8.5	545.0	37	11.9%
New York Jets	1.0	635.0	37	19.1%
Baltimore Ravens	4.0	600.0	38	14.1%
Nashville Predators	80.0	193.0	11	8.7%
Tampa Bay Lightning	115.0	206.0	9	6.9%

Source: Stout Risius Ross, Inc. Used with permission.

WHAT DRIVES THE DISPARITY IN FRANCHISE VALUES?

At some level, there is the price that is paid to join the "owners club," with anything above that generally supported by underlying economics. If all revenues within a league were shared equally, valuation ranges of a league's members would be within a fairly tight band. However, as noted previously, this is not the case. These valuation disparities are driven by significant variations in non-shared revenues.

Sports franchises have experienced significant appreciation during the last several decades. The considerable jumps in franchise values, either collectively within a league or individually, can be tied to certain fundamental changes in economics.

These fundamental changes can impact the valuation of an individual team or an entire league. Leagues with large unexpected increases in broadcast revenues or changes to their fundamental economic structure, such as the NHL's recent shift to a salary cap, have had changes that impacted the values of all teams within a given league.

On an individual franchise basis, the valuation impact was apparent as teams built new, modern stadiums with the necessary amenities, such as suites and club seats, to generate revenues from premium sources necessary to remain competitive. Teams that built stadiums had a fundamental advantage over those teams that did not have new stadiums. In leagues with salary caps, a new stadium also creates an advantage for the owner (and creates value), as the resulting higher revenue levels do not result in higher player salaries. However, the additional cash flow can be used to service debt, invest in the franchise in other ways (e.g. practice facilities) or pay distributions to the owners.

The majority of teams across the major sports have secured new facility deals that allow them to maximize revenues in their local market. In fact, over the past decade or so, over 50 new stadiums or arenas have been built. Performance can impact these revenue streams as it impacts attendance, but the amenities to generate the incremental revenue streams are in place. The franchises that successfully navigated these trends have reached the point where their ability to materially increase revenues (outside of normal price increases and league-wide ventures) has slowed.

IS THE FUTURE APPRECIATION IN VALUE OF SPORTS FRANCHISES LIMITED?

A quick look at a sports team's primary revenue categories sheds some light on future growth opportunities:

League Economics—

- National Broadcast Contracts—popularity of league drives rights fees
- Revenue Sharing Policy—shifts dollars to small market clubs
- Salary Cap—provides level of cost certainty

Stadium Economics—

- Luxury Suites
- Club Seats
  - Newer stadiums often increase number of suites and club seats
- Other Stadium Amenities—concessions, parking, sponsors and advertising

Market Demographics—

- Market Size
- Corporate Environment
  - Increases demand for premium seating, naming rights, sponsorships, etc.

A number of the revenue streams identified above have limited upside potential. A team's facility revenues are to a large degree constrained by the capacity of their facility and impacted by their ability to increase prices. Increasing prices is easier when the team is winning and the economy is strong. Some of the ancillary revenues (premium seating, advertising and naming rights) can increase based on the overall demand for the product and the health of the corporate environment.

Franchise owners that have maximized their facility revenues must look outside the confines of their stadium or arena to generate significant future appreciation in their franchise.

THE NEXT EVOLUTION IN VALUE CREATION

The major sports leagues and many of their members have effectively evolved, identifying the next opportunity to gain a competitive advantage and capitalizing on it (as illustrated in the chart below). Without identifying the next growth prospect, team valuations may be subject to fluctuations of the market that do not deviate much more than changes in GDP, or best case, increase at rates commensurate with increases in the wealth of likely buyers. Certain leagues still have the ability to positively impact traditional valuation drivers (e.g. broadcast deals and new facilities), but more mature leagues must capitalize on other opportunities to drive future appreciation in franchise value.

WHAT'S NEXT FOR PROFESSIONAL SPORTS?

The creation of value in the next decade or so will be driven by two very different opportunities: (i) the proliferation of

large, mixed-use developments in and around facilities that will allow franchises to further maximize their brands and generate incremental revenues; and (ii) the continued expansion of major sports leagues into new markets to drive league-wide revenues to new heights. How successful teams and leagues are in executing these opportunities will determine the valuation landscape in 2020.

The Real Estate Play

More recent facilities focus on providing an entertainment experience and aim to keep "traffic" at the facility before and after the game. While the real estate market has been challenging recently, it continues to pose an interesting growth opportunity for the sports team owner. Leveraging the asset that they possess and extracting value from year-round facility features or the development of the real estate within close proximity to the stadium appears to be the next big domestic opportunity. There are a number of examples that illustrate this point [**Table 9**].

Real estate development represents an ideal opportunity to expand the reach of the brand into the immediate and surrounding areas and capture incremental revenues that potentially fall outside the definitions of shared revenues. These incremental revenues can provide the owner with the economic advantages to drive investment returns, while funding

Table 9   Examples of Facilities Involving Related Real Estate Opportunities

Team	Amenities

St. Louis Cardinals	• Development of a "Ballpark Village"
	• Approximately $650 million cost
	• Phase 1: Entertainment, retail and office space
	   • 360,000 square feet of restaurant and retail space
	   • 300,000 square feet of office space
	• Phase 2: Up to 250 residential units

Dallas Cowboys	New Stadium in 2009 • Creates one of the largest entertainment venues • Legends Square provides restaurants, shops and other gathering places • Cowboys Experience includes a multi-faceted venue for community activities, fan experiences and tourism

New York Giants & Jets	New Stadium in 2010
	• Atrium consists of a hall-of-fame, team stores, dining and conference space
	• Future link with $1.3 billion Xanadu retail entertainment complex with over 4.8 million square feet of space, including:
	   • America's first snow dome for indoor skiing
	   • Luxury hotel and Class A office buildings

Toronto Maple Leafs & Raptors	Development of Maple Leaf Square with 1.8 million square feet of space • 872 condominiums • A 169 room hotel • 230,000 square feet of office space • 110,000 square feet of retail space with a grocery store, sports bar, and a fine dining establishment • A 1,700 square foot hi-definition theatre broadcasting LeafsTV and Raptors NBA TV around the clock.

Source: Stout Risius Ross, Inc. Used with permission.

stadium costs and player salaries. These new revenue streams will also lead to an escalation of franchise values.

The Impact of Globalization

Globalization is not new to the business world or professional sports. However, globalization still presents itself as an opportunity that leagues and teams should continue pursuing to elevate and accelerate revenue growth opportunities. In fact, NFL Commissioner Roger Goodell is quoted as saying "Our goal is to translate America's obsession into the world's passion." The leagues and/or teams that have the highest valuation growth in the next decade will be those that have successfully executed their globalization plans by increasing the number of eyeballs that view or develop

a passion for their product. The following chart [**Table 10**] illustrates the leagues' current global endeavors. [*Ed. Note: For more on globalization issues, see Chapter 3, "Global Leagues."*]

Clearly, the leagues recognize the opportunity. The increased exposure promotes and expands the appeal throughout the world and in turn will drive broadcasting, sponsorship and merchandise revenues, among others. Each league has a current plan and to differing degrees has been successful in the early stage of expanding their reach. For example, MLB's broadcast agreement with Dentsu has helped drive league-wide revenues, which now approach that of the NFL. NBA.com/China has become the most popular single sports site in China and the NBA is consistently the most searched sports

Table 10   Globalization Efforts of Professional Sports Leagues

League	International Movement

MLB	• International games—Season opening series
	  • Mexico (1999)
	  • Japan (2000, 2004 and 2008)
	• Exhibition series in China (2008)
	• World Baseball Classic—Inaugural competition in 2006 with follow-on in 2009 and every four years thereafter
	• Yankees plan to open an office in China to pursue media and corporate sponsorships
	• Broadcasting deal with Japanese network ($275 million)

NFL	• American Bowl Series began in 2005 with preseason games • Regular season games in Mexico and London • Commitment to play 2 regular season international games during the next four years • Buffalo plans to play 1 regular season game in Toronto each of the next five years . . . .
NBA	• One of the first leagues to recognize global opportunity • Hong Kong office opened in 1992 • Approximately 20% of all players are of international descent • Yao Ming was the first foreign born player chosen as the overall #1 in the 2002 NBA draft • Formation of NBA China in 2008—will conduct all of the league's business in Greater China • International revenue growing at double digit rates and approaching 10% of the league's total revenue • NBA will be seen in over 200 countries and broadcast in over 40 languages • International leagues competing for players
NHL	• Over 30% of all players are from non-North American countries • This high percentage underscores the potential market that exists for globalization within the NHL • NHL Premiere 2007—Game played in London • NHL Premiere 2008—Will feature games in Prague, Czech Republic and Stockholm, Sweden • International leagues competing for players

Professional Soccer	• Internationally successful with the greatest global appeal but expanding opportunity to new markets such as North America
	• Recent large broadcast deals illustrate broad appeal
	  • English Premier League recently negotiated a £2.7 billion contract over 3 years
	  • Scottish Premier League more than doubled its contract to £125 million over 4 years
	  • Introduction of David Beckham to MLS
	  • English Premier League attracting foreign investors
	    • Tom Hicks and George Gillett Jr. purchase of Liverpool Football Club
	    • Malcolm Glazer purchase of Manchester United
	    • Roman Abramovich purchase of Chelsea Football Club

Source: Stout Risius Ross, Inc. Used with permission.

term on Baidu.com, the top search engine in China. The NFL has the longest way to go given its lower international player participation, but at the same time may have the largest opportunity.

HOW DOES THIS TRANSLATE INTO VALUE CREATION?

As previously noted, many of the typical franchise's revenue streams have been maximized. While capacity at a facility may be limited, the opportunity to increase revenues through international growth and real estate development initiatives are immense. Real estate development presents opportunities for owners to differentiate their team by growing non-shared revenue streams.

As leagues pursue globalization strategies, they will elevate league-wide revenues. Since these revenue streams are typically shared by all teams equally, successful globalization strategies should increase the value of all franchises within a given league. Further, as talent from around the world continues to represent an increasing percentage of players and overall interest in sports occurs, the demand for product and content abroad will increase. This increased demand will translate into increasing revenue streams, especially for those that embrace and capture the opportunity that exists. In addition to the impact of globalization on revenue streams, globalization can impact the valuation of franchises through the incremental demand that can be created by expanding the buyer pool to include more international buyers. The tapping of the significant wealth that exists outside of the U.S. is an opportunity that cannot be overlooked.

Given the opportunities that exist within each league, it will not be surprising in the long-run, to see a convergence of franchise values between the various leagues. In the short-term, MLB and the NBA should realize greater increases in value as they benefit from an effort that is more fully developed. The NFL, on the other hand, will face a higher level of challenges due to limited participation in many international markets, and thus the opportunity may be slower to develop. The higher level of international players comprising professional soccer and the NHL provide a framework that these organizations can leverage to enhance overall league and franchise value.

Can professional sports teams achieve comparable value appreciation as the recent past? Only time will tell, but executing on both the real estate and global opportunities will certainly go a long way in helping owners maximize returns.

Discussion Questions

1. From a valuation perspective, what are the advantages and disadvantages of revenue sharing in professional sports leagues?
2. What valuation method would be better for buyers and why? Compare this method with other valuation methods used today. What valuation method would be best for sellers? Why?
3. What are the differences in the effects of team naming discussed in these articles?
4. What are the different barriers to globalization, as described by Phillips and Krasner?
5. What are the most important factors driving valuation?
6. Assuming that regional identities are more profitable to the value of a team, what barriers may prevent a team from successfully changing its name to a more regional one?
7. Provide an example of why a losing team might be purchased for a large sum of money, consistent with the material discussed in this chapter.
8. How does the impact of asymmetric information between buyers and sellers of sports franchises on the sales price of professional sports franchises differ from the impact it has on sales of nonsports businesses?
9. What is a team's "reputation," and how does it impact the value of the team? Why is this relationship irrational?
10. What are the most important factors in the credit rating process?

Part II

Olympic Sports

CHAPTER TWELVE

Olympics

INTRODUCTION

Whereas the professional sports discussed in previous chapters are all about business and the bottom line, at least in a relative sense, a greater sense of pageantry, politics, and global goodwill are associated with global events such as the Olympic Games and the FIFA World Cup. These added elements do not necessarily mesh with the goals of an enterprise striving for black ink.

The Olympic Games serve as a vivid model for the concerns that businesspeople have in bidding for global events, whether it be soccer, rugby, gymnastics or any other event with participants from around the globe. The entity in the Olympic alphabet stew that has the clearest charge to reach for financial success is the organizations for a given Olympiad. An equivalent body exists for any major global sporting event. These entities are the on-the-ground enterprises that must actually make the event happen and have financial success.

The Organizing Committee for the Olympic Games (OCOG) will be the primary focus of this chapter. However, before that focus, this introduction will describe the positioning of the various organizations in the overall Olympic world. The business of the Olympics is a combination of organizations, referred to in the industry by their abbreviations. This is the same with regard to global events for individual sports as well; for example, FIFA holds the power regarding global football. The various bodies wield a certain degree of power, and all must, sometimes with difficulty, work together to stage the Olympics in both their winter and summer forms. **Figures 1** and **2** depict the organizational structure of the Olympics.

The rights to the Olympic Games and all of the intellectual property associated with them—including the five rings, their colors, the flag, and the words Olympics, Olympiad, and Olympic Games—are held by the International Olympic Committee (IOC), which is based in Lausanne, Switzerland. The primary sources of revenue for the IOC are broadcast rights, sponsorships, ticket sales, and licensing-related revenues. The financial driver for the Olympics, just as with professional sports, is television (see **Table 1**). The numbers are truly staggering in this arena. The sale of worldwide broadcast rights from 2005 to 2008 provided the IOC with $2.568 billion—over half of its total revenues. The IOC relies heavily on the United States broadcast networks, with nearly 60% of these revenues coming from NBC, 23% from Europe, and the remainder from the rest of the world. This situation is unlikely to change in the near future, with NBC paying $2.201 billion for U.S. broadcast rights for the Olympic Games of 2010 in Vancouver and 2012 in London. The IOC distributes 51% of the broadcast rights fees of each Olympics to the OCOG responsible for the respective Olympic Games and 49% to the Olympic Movement. A broader discussion of television and the business of sports appears in Chapter 8.

Sponsorships established by the IOC sponsorship program, formally called The Olympic Program (TOP), are a vital source of revenue for the IOC, accounting for 34% of its revenues from 2005 to 2008. Composed of 12 global companies that receive broad category exclusivity, the TOP program generated $1.866 billion during the past quadrennial, from 2005 to 2008. Although less so than in the past, the IOC is heavily dependent on the United States for its sponsorships, with six TOP sponsors based in this country. (From 2009 to 2012, the TOP program will be composed of nine global sponsors, four of which are from the United States.) Ticket sales to Olympic opening and closing ceremonies and events provided $238.5 million for the IOC, or 11% of its revenues. The sale of Olympic-related licensed products, coins, and stamps completes the IOC financial picture, generating $122 million (or 2%) of the organization's revenues.

The IOC distributes over 90% of its revenues to OCOGs, National Olympic Committees (NOCs) and International

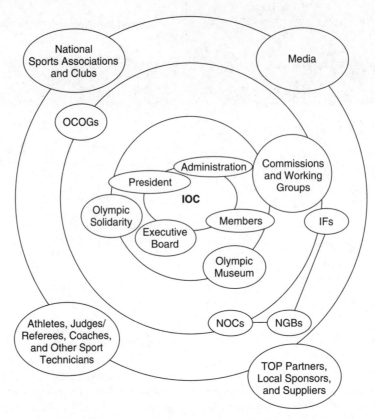

Figure 1   Structure of the Olympic Movement

Source: International Olympic Committee. Used with permission.

Federations (IFs). For example, the Turin Organizing Committee (TOROC) received $406 million in broadcast rights and $139 million from the TOP program. This $545 million represented 35% of TOROC's operating budget. The IOC provided the Athens Organizing Committee (ATHOC) with $960 million, or 60% of its operating budget, for the 2004 Games. In addition, the IOC distributed a combined $4.41 billion to the Turin Organizing Committee, the Beijing Organizing Committee, the NOCs that sent teams to the 2006 and 2008 Olympic Games, the 28 summer sport IFs for the 2008 Olympics, and the 7 winter sports IFs for the 2006 Olympic Games. The IOC retains 8% of its revenues to pay its administrative and operating expenses.

Each of the 205 countries that are a part of the Olympic family has its own NOC. A country's NOC is responsible for fielding its Olympic team. The United States Olympic

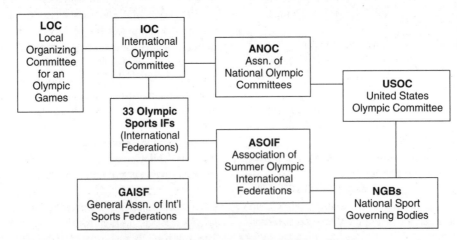

Figure 2   International Sports Organizational Relationships*

Source: United States Olympic Committee. Used with permission.

*This illustration may not accurately reflect the current organization of the USOC and is intended to provide the reader with an understanding of the USOC's complex reporting structure.

Table 1 The Games on TV: Network Ratings, Rights Fees, and Related Information Since the Olympics Were First Televised

Year	Games	Location	Network	Average Prime Time Rating	Total Network Hours	Number of Nations	Number of Events	U.S. Rights Fee (Adjusted**)
1960	Winter	Squaw Valley, Calif.	CBS	N/A	N/A	30	27	$50,000 ($299,160)
1960	Summer	Rome	CBS	N/A	20	84	150	390,000 ($2.3 million)
1964	Winter	Innsbruck, Austria	ABC	N/A	17.5	36	34	600,000 ($3.4 million)
1964	Summer	Tokyo	NBC	N/A	14	94	163	1.5 million ($8.6 million)
1968	Winter	Grenoble, France	ABC	13.5	20	37	35	2.5 million ($12.7 million)
1968	Summer	Mexico City	ABC	N/A	43.75	113	172	4.5 million ($22.9 million)
1972	Winter	Sapporo, Japan	ABC	17.2	26	36	35	6.4 million ($27.1 million)
1972	Summer	Munich, Germany	ABC	24.4	62.75	122	195	7.5 million ($31.8 million)
1976	Winter	Innsbruck, Austria	ABC	21.5	27.5	37	37	10 million ($31.1 million)
1976	Summer	Montreal	ABC	23.9	76.5	93	198	25 million ($77.8 million)
1980	Winter	Lake Placid, New York	ABC	23.6	35	37	39	15.5 million ($33.3 million)
1980	Summer	Moscow	NBC	None***	None***	81	203	87 million ($187.0 million)
1984	Winter	Sarajevo, Yugoslavia	ABC	18.4	41.5	49	40	91.6 million ($156.1 million)
1984	Summer	Los Angeles	ABC	23.2	180	140	221	225 million ($383.5 million)
1988	Winter	Calgary	ABC	19.3	95	57	46	309 million ($462.6 million)
1988	Summer	Seoul, Korea	NBC	17.9	176	160	237	309 million ($462.6 million)
1992	Winter	Albertville, France	CBS	18.7	107	64	57	243 million ($306.7 million)
1992	Summer	Barcelona, Spain	NBC	17.5	148	171	257	409 million ($516.3 million)
1994	Winter	Lillehammer, Norway	CBS	27.8	110	67	61	295 million ($352.5 million)
1996	Summer	Atlanta	NBC	21.6	164	196	271	456 million ($514.7 million)
1998	Winter	Nagano, Japan	CBS	16.3	124	80	68	375 million ($407.4 million)
2000	Summer	Sydney, Australia	NBC	13.8	162.5	199	300	705 million ($725.1 million)
2002	Winter	Salt Lake City	NBC	19.2	168.5	80	78	545 million
2004	Summer	Athens, Greece	NBC	15.0	1,210	201	301	793 million
2006	Winter	Turin, Italy	NBC	12.2	416	80	84	613 million
2008	Summer	Beijing	NBC	16.2	3,600	204	302	820 million
2010	Winter	Vancouver, Canada	NBC	13.8	835	82	86	820 million
2012	Summer	London	NBC	TBD	TBD	TBD	TBD	1.18 billion

*Total hours listed for the Winter Olympics from 1960 to 1984 are for prime time only.

**Fee converted to 2001 value using U.S. Department of Labor Bureau of Labor Statistics formula. Figure represents 2001 buying power.

***The United States boycotted the 1980 Summer Games; NBC's coverage was limited to highlights and two anthology-style specials after the Games were completed, though the network still paid the full rights fee.

Sources: Guardian, NBC, Nielsen Media Research, Street & Smith's Sports Business Journal research.

Note: For the 2008 Summer Games in Beijing, an additional 2,200 hours of live coverage were aired on NBCOlympics.com.

NA: Not available; no television ratings system was in place at the time.

TBD: To be determined.

Committee (USOC) shoulders this responsibility in the United States. **Figure 3** depicts the organization of the U.S. Olympic Movement. Empowered by the Amateur Sports Act, the USOC derives much of its revenue from the IOC. The USOC receives royalty payments from the IOC and broadcast networks for the U.S. Olympic broadcast rights; 12.75% of the IOC's American broadcast revenues ultimately are delivered to the USOC as part of a 21-year-old deal with NBC, providing the USOC with $673 million for the Olympic Games from 2000 to 2012. This bounty is not limited to television. The USOC also receives 20% of the IOC's global marketing revenues—more than all of the other 204 NOCs combined. The USOC also generates significant revenues from its own domestic sponsorships, joint ventures, and fundraising and licensing efforts. In 2008, the USOC generated $280.6 million in total revenue.

Despite its nonprofit status, the USOC has struggled to avoid red ink in recent years. The USOC has a staggering amount of overhead expenses and also provides American athletes and various National Governing Bodies (NGBs) with over $70 million of financial support each year. However, it should be noted that, unlike almost every other country's

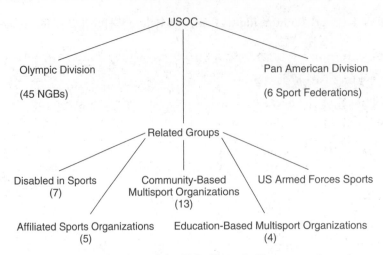

Figure 3   Organization of the U.S. Olympic Movement*

Source: United States Olympic Committee. Used with permission.

NOC, the USOC does not receive any direct government support. The fact that the IOC and USOC are so mutually dependent is thought to have generated significant resentment of the United States in the European-controlled IOC.

The next layer of governance is among the individual sports. This is where entities like FIFA come into play. Each sport is governed at its highest level by an international sports federation. Many host championships or tournaments, such as the FIFA World Cup, that are independent of the Olympic Games. There are 26 IFs involved in the 2012 Summer Olympics and 7 in the Winter Olympics. For example, the International Amateur Athletics Federation governs "athletics," popularly referred to as track and field. This organization sets the rules and holds the rights to various championships and other competitions around the globe. Each country that has athletes involved in that sport at the international level has a domestic national governing body. In the United States, the NGB for athletics is USA Track & Field (USATF). Overall, there are 45 recognized Olympic NGBs in the United States.

All of these various enterprises are permanent and often extremely political. The perks for leadership within these organizations include global travel, gifts, and important political and business relationships.

The OCOGs are the most unique of the Olympic-related organizations. In the United States, the OCOGs that people are most familiar with are the Los Angeles Olympic Organizing Committee (LAOOC), which planned and operated the 1984 Olympics, and the more recent OCOGs for Atlanta in 1996 (ACOG) and Salt Lake City in 2002 (SLOC). The uniqueness of the OCOGs comes primarily from the fact that they are disbanded once the games are completed. The

OCOGs are heavily dependent on the IOC, which provides the OCOG with revenues from its broadcasting and sponsorship rights. An OCOG generates its own revenues through the sale of local sponsorships, tickets, and licensed products. For example, SLOC earned $575 million in sponsorship revenues, $180 million in ticket sales, and an additional $25 million in sales of licensed products. The OCOG retains 95% of its local sponsorship, ticketing, and licensing revenues and gives 5% to the IOC.

A number of other chapters are of interest in conjunction with the readings on the Olympics and other global sporting events. Certainly the chapter on ethics (Chapter 20) has relevance, given the number of scandals associated with global sporting events. With regards to the Olympics, those issues range from the votes of judges to the influencing of IOC members in their site selections for the Olympic Games. The chapter on amateurism (Chapter 18) highlights the thinking behind the creation of a class of athletes characterized as "amateur." Ironically, although the concept is most often associated with the Olympic Games, there are essentially no longer any "pure" amateurs participating. Many, including members of the U.S. Olympic basketball squads, are professionals in their sports. Many others receive payment from their countries, with the highest rewards given for gold medals or the breaking of world records.

In the first reading, "Management of the Olympic Games: The Lessons of Sydney," Chappelet focuses on the key management elements of running an Olympics: time, money, human resources, and information. In the second selection, "The Financing and Economic Impact of the Olympic Games," Brad Humphreys and Andrew Zimbalist focus on the economic aspects of the Games. The final article, Giannoulakis and Stotlar's "Olympic Sponsorship: Evolution, Challenges and Impact on the Olympic Movement," offers more depth on the financing issue, addressing Olympic sponsorships.

---

*This illustration may not accurately reflect the current organization of the USOC and is intended to provide the reader with an understanding of the USOC's complex reporting structure.

ORGANIZING COMMITTEE MANAGEMENT

MANAGEMENT OF THE OLYMPIC GAMES: THE LESSONS OF SYDNEY

Jean-Loup Chappelet

. . . We shall define management as the optimization of the resources available to managers. These resources can be divided into four main categories: time, money, human resources, and information. The main features of the management of each of these resources for the Sydney Games will be examined below. Comments will then be made on the organizational structures put in place to manage these resources.

TIME

Time is the rarest resource of any major event-type project as, by definition, such an event cannot be postponed, even by a single day. The Games of the new millennium were scheduled to open on 15 September 2000, and this date had been virtually carved in stone over six years earlier. For an OCOG, every additional day is a day less. . . In this respect it is important to note that SOCOG [Sydney Organizing Committee for the Olympic Games] was very quickly set up by virtue of a law enacted by the Parliament of New South Wales on 12 November 1993, less than two months after the IOC's decision to award the Games to Australia's biggest city. A new record for diligence had been set!

One and a half years later the OCA (Olympic Coordination Authority) was created, with the principal task of building most of the sports facilities that were required, including the Olympic Park in Homebush, which would host fifteen of the twenty-eight sports on the program. All of the sports venues for the Sydney Games were thus ready around one year before the Games, except for the temporary beach volleyball stadium on Bondi Beach. This meant that test events could be organized well in advance, and provided the opportunity to correct *in situ* all manner of unanticipated organizational problems.

These dress rehearsals undoubtedly contributed to the success of the sports management of the Games. They did away with the need for last-minute fixes, which are a source of stress and additional expense. In Atlanta, the Olympic stadium was opened just three months before the Games, and work began on fitting out the Main Press Centre just three days before the Games opened. The contrast is striking: The time spent on preparation in Sydney in a sense resulted in time saved during the Games. The daily coordination meetings with the IOC each morning became progressively shorter. One was even canceled.

MONEY

Although it is still too early to draw any definitive conclusions, initial figures suggest that SOCOG's budget will balance at around A$ 2.5 billion. (In September 2000, the exchange rates were approximately A$ 1 = CHF 0.97, US$ 0.56.) This certainly owes something to the limitations placed on operating expenditure, but also and above all to the optimization of the Games revenues themselves.

After the disappointment—an understatement—that greeted the announcement of the total figure negotiated by the IOC for television rights to the Games in the United States (which were sold to NBC rather than Fox Network), SOCOG turned to other possible sources of revenue, mainly sponsoring and the sale of tickets for the competitions.

Nearly A$ 700 million were obtained from the 24 *Team Millennium* sponsors (including the 11 partners of the IOC's TOP program), the 19 Sydney 2000 Supporters, and the 60 official providers (including 23 sports equipment companies).

To this sum was added some A$ 70 million in royalties from the three thousand or so products manufactured with SOCOG's emblems by around a hundred licensed businesses. This licensing program remained within the bounds of good taste and was a considerable success. Even during the Games, long queues formed outside various "Olympic Stores" set up specially to sell these products.

A total of A$ 770 million in revenue was therefore attributable to commercialization in the strict sense of the word, compared with the A$ 1,039 million SOCOG received for the television rights. This represents approximately A$ 40 for each inhabitant of Australia, or thirteen times more than the commercial revenue from Atlanta, in terms of population. As far as tickets were concerned, SOCOG beat the sales records set by previous OCOGs despite the major difficulties caused by a multi-tiered distribution program that proved to be needlessly complicated. While over two million tickets remained unsold three months out from the Games, an average of 50,000 tickets were sold each day during the Games. For the first time in Olympic history, SOCOG's Internet site was also made to pay its way, through sales of tickets as well as licensed merchandise. The sight of the 110,000-seat Olympic stadium being filled almost to capacity during the athletics heats was particularly impressive. Approximately 87% of the Olympic tickets were finally sold, almost meeting the budgetary objective of A$ 566 million. The tickets for the cultural program also sold well.

The success of the commercial program, built up over the years of preparation and boosted towards the end by the ticketing program, enabled SOCOG to avoid digging too deeply into the A$ 140 million reserve allocated in June 2000 by the government of New South Wales to enable

SOCOG to balance its budget. This reserve also undoubtedly had a psychological effect. It helped to avoid a situation in the final months where SOCOG had to base its operational decisions solely on financial criteria, as was the case in Atlanta in 1996. We now know that, in order to avoid the slightest hint of a deficit, the organizers of the Centennial Games economized as much as possible during the final year leading up to the Games, to the point of jeopardizing the transport and information systems.

The icing on the cake in terms of optimizing financial resources came when SOCOG had the good fortune of seeing the Australian dollar decline sharply against the U.S. dollar as the Games approached, contrary to the historical tendency of host country currencies to appreciate during the Olympic year. Although the television rights negotiated in U.S. dollars had been prudently hedged against exchange rate fluctuations, this stroke of luck nevertheless provided additional revenues of the order of A$ 50 million. [*Ed. Note: Table 2* shows the cost of the Sydney Olympic Games and others.]

HUMAN RESOURCES

Preparations for the Games require putting in place an organization that in six years grows from a handful of personnel to several thousand (2,500 in Sydney), only to drop one month after the Closing Ceremony to a few hundred staff, who virtually all disappear in the year following the Games. During the Olympic period, the core staff is augmented by an army of volunteers (47,000 in Sydney). It is not difficult to imagine the enormous challenge of managing the human resources of such a business, which has virtually no past, and no future at all as soon as the Games are over.

SOCOG encountered major difficulties in this area. It went through two presidents before the appointment, after the Atlanta Games, of Michael Knight, who was already the Olympics Minister for New South Wales. The controversial management style of the last president led over the years to the voluntary and involuntary departure of several staff members, including one chief executive. Evidently, however, SOCOG's second chief executive, Sandy Hollway, was able to maintain the motivation of the majority of his troops right up to the end. This was to the detriment of his relationship with the president, who withdrew a large part of his prerogatives one month before the Games and sought to limit public recognition of the man he had appointed as his "number two."

In contrast, the volunteer program was perfectly conducted, and most certainly contributed to the success of the Games. Word quickly spread among the Olympic family, the media, and the spectators about the spontaneous friendliness of the thousands of young and less young Australians (and foreign nationals) who had volunteered their services. The volunteers were the shop window of the Games, and the main point of contact between the organization and its "clients."

Planning began almost three years before the Opening Ceremony (compared with 18 months before in Atlanta), and volunteers were recruited through a national campaign in October 1998. A complete training program was set up by the public training agency TAFE NSW, based on manuals, videos, and an Internet site. The program began in June 2000 and enabled Sydney's volunteers to fill the majority of posts during the Games, unlike in Atlanta, where the volunteers had often not been trained for the tasks they were performing. Some of the drivers even used their own leisure

Table 2   Olympic Costs

City (Year)	Bid Cost	Games Cost	Results
Beijing (2008)	$24.7 million	$43 billion	$146 million profit
Turin (2006)	$9.4 million	$1.58 billion	$32.4 million loss
Athens (2004)	$460 million*	$9 billion	$155 million profit
Salt Lake City (2002)	$7 million	$1.3 billion	$100 million profit
Sydney (2000)	$12.6 million	$3.24 billion	Broke even
Nagano (1998)	$11 million	$14 billion	$28 million profit for organizing committee, $11 billion debt to various government groups
Atlanta (1996)	$7 million	$1.7 billion	Broke even
Lillehammer (1994)	$3 million	$1.6 billion	$40 million–$50 million profit
Albertville (1992)	$2 million–$3 million	$2 billion	$57 million loss
Barcelona (1992)	$10 million	$10.7 billion	$3 million profit for the Olympic organizing committee, $6.1 billion in debt for the government and public entities

Sources: Street & Smith's Sports Business Journal research, International Olympic Committee, *USA Today,* Associated Press, *Snow Country Magazine, China Daily, Los Angeles Times,* Turin Olympic Committee, Sports Business News, BBC, CNN.

*Note: $460 million represents the alleged amount misappropriated for the Athens Olympic bid.

time to familiarize themselves with the Olympic routes. The volunteer leaders, often volunteers themselves, were also given leadership courses.

The low drop-out rate for volunteers during the Games, far lower than in Atlanta, is an indication that this fundamental human resource was well managed. Although it was not announced in advance, most of the volunteers were compensated with tickets for sports competitions or rehearsals for the Opening Ceremony. Five thousand of them were also able to attend the Closing Ceremony free of charge. They also had free use of public transport. One of Sydney's daily newspapers even published all of their names, from Naseem Aadil to Warren Zylstra, in a special section entitled: *"47,000 heroes."*

INFORMATION

Information is still all too seldom identified as a managerial resource on a par with human and financial resources. And yet it is a vital resource in today's post-industrial society, which is a service society whose main raw material is information. It is such information, in the broad sense, which the media broadcast during the Games in the form of text, images, and sound, and, which, after the Games, constitutes the only tangible trace of the Games apart from the Olympic facilities.

Information management proved particularly disastrous at the beginning of the Centennial Games: the results sent out to the Olympic Family and the media by the information system were full of errors, which meant that the press agencies were obliged to re-enter them manually for transmission around the world. Unsatisfactory transport and accommodation conditions for the journalists only increased their recriminations which, in a few short days, irretrievably damaged the reputation of Atlanta and its Games. Rightly or wrongly, IBM was held responsible. Not wishing to see a repeat of the fiasco, IBM proposed to SOCOG that it would take charge of systems integration, a role that had been filled in Atlanta by the OCOG itself.

The information system for the Sydney Games comprised four sub-systems: 1) for generating the competition results; 2) for broadcasting information on the Games to the Internet; 3) for communication within the Olympic Family through two thousand "INFO" terminals; 4) for management of SOCOG services (accreditation, accommodation, ticketing, transport, recruitment, etc.). These systems included some systems provided by other technology partners, such as Xerox for data printouts, Swatch Timing for competition timekeeping, Kodak for 200,000 accreditation photographs, and Panasonic for broadcasting text and images on giant screens. Overall, the information system for SOCOG and the Games was implemented through the efforts of 850 experts, and was accessed by nearly seven thousand networked personal computers.

We should not omit to mention the great success of the official Sydney 2000 website, managed for SOCOG by IBM (www.olympics.com). The site welcomed some 8.7 million visitors from the day before the opening until the Closing Ceremony of the Games, most of them from the United States (38%), Australia (17%), Canada (7%), Great Britain (5%), Japan (3%), and 136 further countries. These visitors—the great majority of them women—spent an average of 17 minutes on the site, and downloaded a total of 230 million pageviews. Fans from 199 countries sent 371,654 emails to the participating athletes, over four thousand of whom created a personal page on the computers available in the Olympic Village.

The site of the TV network NBC (www.nbcolympics .com), the only site, along with Australia's Channel 7, authorized to webcast short video sequences of the Games, attracted 2.2 million Americans during the Olympic fortnight. In comparison, 59 million people saw NBC's recorded coverage of the competitions. (Television viewing figures were lower than usual because of the time difference.) These statistics are particularly impressive considering that the first Internet browser became available the same year that the Games were awarded to Sydney. Thanks to the Internet, results, sound, still and moving images of the Olympic festival undoubtedly constitute a mine of new rights to be exploited by the IOC and the OCOGs, while respecting the public's right to information.

This very brief overview of information management by SOCOG would not be complete without a mention of the TOK program (Transfer of Olympic Knowledge), which was launched one year before the Games to synthesize the bulk of information essential to their organization. This work, in the form of around 100 manuals drafted during the year 2000 by SOCOG's managers, was financed by the IOC, and will be used by the OCOGs of Athens and Turin before being updated and passed on to future OCOGs. These TOK manuals will provide a useful supplement to the official report of the Sydney Games, work on which was begun very intelligently well in advance. For the first time, all of the organizational information, all of the tacit knowledge of a complete edition of the Games, will be turned into formalized knowledge for the following Games, in line with the new theories of knowledge management.

ORGANIZATION

This overview of the management of the Sydney Games would not be complete without a brief comment on their structural organization, that is, the political and administrative arrangement of the various bodies involved in organizing the Games. In addition to SOCOG, these were mainly: the OCA (Olympic Coordination Authority), responsible for building most of the sports facilities since 1995; SOBO (Sydney Olympic Broadcast Organization), founded in 1996 and responsible for producing the sound and image signal for the Games (host broadcaster); ORTA (Olympic Roads & Transport Authority), created in 1997; and the OSCC (Olympic Security Command Center), set up in 1998.

Like SOCOG, the OCA, ORTA, and OSCC were agencies belonging to the state of New South Wales. SOBO was officially a commission of SOCOG's board of directors. Apart from the OSCC, which was chaired by the state police commissioner, all of these bodies were chaired by Michael Knight, who was also New South Wales Minister for the Olympics and president of the DHA (Darling Harbour Authority), which manages the area where six of the Olympic sports were held.

The Sydney Games thus benefited from a highly decentralized structure, unlike that of Atlanta. Every organization mentioned above was responsible for one of the essential organizational tasks: general operations (SOCOG), construction and management of the facilities (OCA), production of televised images of the Games (SOBO), road and rail transport (ORTA), and public security (OSCC). It is perhaps surprising to see how, over the years of preparation, SOCOG was little by little divested of major responsibilities. Although for operational reasons the minister/president felt the need, a few months before the Games, to bring together the various bodies he chaired under a single central decision-making structure called "Sydney 2000," it is highly likely that their original autonomy—which guaranteed that they were completely focused on their mission—contributed greatly to the ultimate success of the Games.

Moreover, one can see to what extent the organizing of the Games in Sydney was state-controlled, from both a legal point of view and a personnel point of view, since the main leaders were senior government officials and civil servants. This is particularly striking as the Atlanta OCOG was entirely private (though a non-profit organization). The lack of coordination with the authorities of the state capital and the state of Georgia contributed to the various problems, particularly in terms of sponsorship, traffic, and security. These problems were naturally resolved in Sydney thanks to the active participation of elected government officials and the local and regional administrations concerned, which ended up spending over A$ 2 billion on the Games, over and above SOCOG's budget. Added to this was the coordinated contribution of some thirty agencies of the Australian Federal Government, estimated at A$ 484 million, including, for the record, the first "official poet" of the Games since Pindar.

Is Sydney's managerial model preferable to that of Atlanta? Yes, probably, because the Games have become an event that affects an entire country. Whatever their legal status, the OCOGs have to work very closely with the public authorities, with whom they have to share their goals of public service, and the harmonious development of the managerial objective should no longer be to stage bigger Games, because "gigantism" is an ever-present threat, but to stage Games that are unique and special, that leave a lasting mark in the collective history of the nation and the human race.

ORGANIZING COMMITTEE REVENUE SOURCES

THE FINANCING AND ECONOMIC IMPACT OF THE OLYMPIC GAMES

Brad R. Humphreys and Andrew Zimbalist

. . . .

FINANCING THE OLYMPICS

The modern Olympic Games began in 1896, but it was not until 1976 that a watershed event shook up the financing model for the Games and set the Olympics on its current economic course. In that year the city of Montreal hosted the summer Games. Montreal incurred a debt of $2.8 billion that was finally paid off in 2005.[1] Annual debt service created a large budgetary hole for the city for three decades.

By the end of the Montreal Games, the 1980 Games had already been set for Moscow, but no city wanted to bid for the right to host the 1984 Games.[2] After some scrambling, Los Angeles agreed to host the Games, but only on the condition that it took on no financial obligation. With

no alternative, the International Olympic Committee (IOC) accepted this condition and Los Angeles was awarded the 1984 summer Games on July 1, 1978.

1978 also marked the first significant relaxation of Olympic amateur rules under then IOC president Lord Killanin. In that year, Rule 26 of the Olympic Charter was modified so that athletes were allowed openly to earn money from endorsements, if the money went to their national sports federation or their country's National Olympic Committee (NOC). The receiving organization was then permitted to pay the athlete's expenses, including "pocket money." "Broken-time" payments for time away from the athlete's regular job were also authorized if the athlete had a regular job. But the rule continued to declare that professional athletes were ineligible.

During the 1980–2001 reign of IOC president Juan Antonio Samaranch the complete professionalization and commercialization of the Olympics were promoted by further liberalizing the amateur regulations. In 1982, the amateur rules were revised to permit payments into a trust fund that provided expenses during the athlete's active career—and substantial sums thereafter. Eventually, decisions about accepting professionals were left to the International Federation (IF) of each sport. The new professional era was heralded during the 1992 Games in Barcelona, when the United States sent its dream team of NBA stars which, unlike their more recent incarnations, went on to win the gold medal. Nominally, for the 2004 Games in Athens, boxing was the only sport that did not accept professionals, but even this distinction is dubious, because the NOCs of many countries gave their boxing medalists cash prizes.

These changes also led to increased commercialization, increased TV and sponsorship money, which, in turn, led to corruption and scandal within the IOC. Samaranch set a new tone for the IOC when he began his reign in 1980. He insisted on being referred to as "His Excellency" and to be treated as a head of state. Before he took over in 1980, the 112 IOC representatives had to pay their own way to cities bidding for the Games. Within a year they were getting not one but two first-class tickets, plus all expenses paid for as well as lavish entertainment. Samaranch himself always insisted on limousine service and the best suite in the best hotel in any city. In Lausanne, Switzerland, IOC headquarters, he had the IOC rent him a massive penthouse suite at the Palace Hotel for $500,000 a year.

IOC representatives who voted on the host city followed Samaranch's lead and payoffs grew by leaps and bounds. Outrageous tales of the excesses abounded. One surrounds the selection of Nagano, Japan to host the 1998 winter Games. The son of Samaranch's close adviser Artur Takacs was a lobbyist for Nagano's organizing committee, for which he was paid a salary of $363,000, plus a bonus if Nagano won the Games. A consortium of Japanese businessmen promised $20 million for the construction of an Olympic Museum in Lausanne, if Nagano got the Games, which, not surprisingly, it did. Salt Lake City lost out, but the city learned a lesson.

The previous winter Games were in Albertville, France. Most observers believed that Falun, Sweden had a better bid. Samaranch, however, prevailed upon the IOC members, the large majority of whom he appointed, to select Albertville for 1992; that way Paris would be effectively eliminated from competition for the 1992 summer Games, which instead went to his hometown Barcelona.

Gifts to IOC members ranged from free first-class trips, to college entrance and tuition, room and board for children, rent-free apartments, free shopping expeditions, sexual favors and tens of thousands of dollars in cash. All this fun came to a head with revelations around the Salt Lake bid for the 2002 Games. Since then, the IOC has supposedly reformed itself, inter alia, by reducing the number of voters and by officially declaring an outright ban on gifts.

Meanwhile, the modest financial success of the 1984 Games in Los Angeles led to a new era of international competition among cities to host the Games. The relative success of Los Angeles, however, was sui generis. Los Angeles had very little construction expense and the chair of the Los Angeles OCOG (Organizing Committee for the Olympic Games), Peter Ueberroth, was able to raise substantial sums by selling sponsorships to corporations. LAOCOG generated a small surplus (just over $300 million) and reset the Olympic financial model for less public and more private financing.

Nonetheless, other host cities found it impossible to procure the same proportion of private support and, instead, relied upon large public expenditures. Several billion dollars of public monies were committed in Seoul (1988), Barcelona (1992), Sydney (2000) and Athens (2004). In some cases, the local OCOG ran a modest surplus (20 percent of any surplus must be shared with the IOC),[3] but the local government laid out billions of dollars to help finance the activities of the OCOG. In the case of Athens, for instance, the public investment exceeded $10 billion—some of this public investment resulted in improved, more modern infrastructure for the city, but some of it resulted in white elephants. Many facilities built especially for the Games go un- or underutilized after the 16- or 17-day period of the Olympic competition itself, while requiring tens of millions of dollars annually to maintain and occupying increasingly scarce real estate. Public investment for Beijing (2008) is expected to well exceed $30 billion.

Salt Lake Olympiad chief and former governor of Massachusetts Mitt Romney questioned whether U.S. cities should enter bids to host the Olympic Games, stating that they were increasingly driven by "giganticism" with the addition of new sports and more frills. Romney said: "It's a fair question to ask, 'Is it worth it or not?' My own position is that the Games make sense, not as a money-making enterprise, but as a statement for peace."[4]

PRESENT DAY FINANCIAL ARRANGEMENTS

The IOC presents the financing of the Olympic Games in terms of its own organizations: the local organizing committee (OCOG), the NOC, the IFs, and itself. The OCOG budget is not the same as the budgetary impact on the local city that hosts the games. The local city, its state government and its national government may provide billions of dollars of subsidies to the OCOG, and the OCOG may report a surplus.[5] This surplus has little meaning regarding the budgetary impact on public bodies from hosting the Games. Moreover, it is common practice for the OCOG budget to consist entirely (or almost entirely) of operating, as opposed to capital, expenditures.[6] Nonetheless, to the extent that the OCOG receives funding from the IOC or from private sources, the lower will be the financing burden that falls on the local, state and national government that hosts the Games. What follows, then, is a discussion of how the IOC distributes the revenue that is collected from the staging of each Olympic Games.

Table 3 presents the total revenue that accrues to the IOC or any of its constituent organizations during each

Table 3   Olympic Movement Revenue (in Millions)

Source	1993–96	1997–00	2001–04
Broadcasting	$1251	$1845	$2230
Worldwide Sponsorship	279	579	663
Domestic Sponsorship	534	655	796
Ticketing	451	625	411
Licensing	115	66	87
TOTAL	**$2630**	**$3770**	**$4187**

Source: Adapted from IOC, 2006 Olympic Marketing Fact File, http://www.olympic.org, p. 16. Reproduced with permission of ABC-CLIO, LLC.

quadrennial Olympic cycle, consisting of one Winter and one Summer Games. It shows a healthy revenue growth in each of the major categories, with television revenues the largest single source of revenue by a factor of 3. The TOP program consists of eleven companies that hold exclusive category sponsorships as the official Olympic company.

TOP Program revenues go 50 percent to the local OCOGs, 40 percent to the NOCs and 10 percent to the IOC.[7] Broadcast revenue goes 49 percent to the OCOG and 51 percent to the IOC, which, in turn, distributes the lion's share of this revenue to the NOCs and IFs. Prior to 2004, the OCOGs received 60 percent of broadcast revenue. Beginning in 2012, it has been determined that OCOGs will receive a fixed number, rather than a fixed percentage, as broadcast revenues continue to rise.[8] Overall, the IOC retains 8 percent of Olympic revenue, the remaining 92 percent is shared by the OCOGs, NOCs and IFs.

Table 4 depicts the astronomical growth in television broadcasting revenue for the Summer and Winter Games since 1960. Not surprisingly, the largest share of broadcast revenue comes from the United States. For instance, for the

2004 Athens Games, the IOC contract with NBC yielded $793.5 million, or 53.1 percent of the total. Following the U.S. rights fee were Europe ($394 million), Japan ($155 million), Australia ($50.5 million), Canada ($37 million), and South Korea ($15.5 million). All told, there were 80 rights holders televising the Athens Games to 220 countries and 2 billion potential viewers worldwide. Ten thousand media personnel were on hand to cover the Games.[9]

OCOGs do not cover all their expenses from the above sources. For instance, the Nagano OCOG in 1998 had revenues of $990 million, of which approximately $435 million came from the IOC. Similarly, the Salt Lake OCOG had revenues of $1.348 billion, of which approximately $570 million came from the IOC.[10]

RESULTS

Economic theory would suggest that any expected local economic benefit would be bid away as cities compete with each other to host the Games. More precisely, with perfect information the city with the highest expected gain could win the Games by bidding $1 more than the expected gain to the second highest city. Such an outcome could yield a small benefit to the winning city, but this would require perfect information and an open market bidding process. In fact, the bidding process is not done in dollar amounts, but comes rather in the form of providing facilities and guaranteeing financing and security.[11] In the post-9/11 world, security costs are far from trivial. Total security costs in Athens in 2004 came to $1.4 billion, with 40,000 security people; Beijing in 2008 is projected to have over 80,000 security personnel working the Games.

It is also widely acknowledged that the bidding process is laden with political considerations. Moreover, the bidding cities are more likely to be motivated by gains to particular private interests within the city (developers, construction

Table 4   Past Broadcast Revenue (in Millions)

Summer Olympic Games	Broadcast Revenue	Winter Olympic Games	Broadcast Revenue
1960 Rome	$1.178	1960 Squaw Valley	$.050
1964 Tokyo	1.578	1964 Innsbruck	.937
1968 Mexico City	9.750	1968 Grenoble	2.613
1972 Munich	17.792	1972 Sapporo	8.475
1976 Montreal	34.862	1976 Innsbruck	11.627
1980 Moscow	87.984	1980 Lake Placid	20.726
1984 Los Angeles	286.914	1984 Sarajevo	102.682
1988 Seoul	402.595	1988 Calgary	324.897
1992 Barcelona	636.060	1992 Albertville	291.928
1996 Atlanta	898.267	1994 Lillehammer	352.911
2000 Sydney	1,331.550	1998 Nagano	513.485
2004 Athens	$1,494.028	2002 Salt Lake	$736.135

Source: Adapted from IOC, 2006 Marketing Fact File, p. 46. Reproduced with permission of ABC-CLIO, LLC.

companies, hotels, investment bankers, architects, real estate companies, etc.) than by a clear sense that the city as a whole will benefit economically.

In contrast, the IOC views its principal role as promoting sport, not economic development. It requires buildings and infrastructure to be financed with non-Olympic money.[12]

Accordingly, even though a local OCOG may break even or have a small surplus[13] the greatest likelihood is that the city itself (and state and national governments) experiences a fiscal deficit from the Games. On the one hand, the only tax revenue that would accrue to host governmental bodies would be from incremental sales and income resulting from hosting the Olympic Games. The evidence on this score is not encouraging. On the other hand, hosting governmental bodies, together with any private support, must pay for facility construction, upgrade and infrastructural improvements necessitated by the Games. It must also pay for the opening and award ceremonies, transportation of the athletes to the various venues, entertainment, a telecommunications/broadcasting center, and security, among other things.

The initial publicized budgets of the OCOGs invariably understate both the ultimate cost to the OCOG and, to a much greater degree, the total cost of staging the Games. The former escalates for several reasons. First, construction costs inflate significantly. Land values increase with growing scarcity during the ten-year cycle of Olympic host selection and preparation. Second, the early proponents of hosting the Games in a particular city find it in their interest to under-represent the true costs, as they seek public endorsement. Third, as the would-be host city enters into competition with other bidders, there is a natural tendency to match their competitors' proposals and to add bells and whistles to their plan. The latter escalates because it includes infrastructure and facility costs while the publicized OCOG budget includes only operating costs. The infrastructure and facility costs usually form the largest component of total expenses, and often do so by a substantial margin.

Thus, Athens initially projected that its Games would cost $1.6 billion, but they ended up costing closer to $16 billion (including facility and infrastructure costs). Beijing projected costs of $1.6 billion, but current estimates are that they will cost between $30 billion and $40 billion.[14] London expected its 2012 Games to cost under $5 billion, but they are now projected to cost $19 billion.[15] In a world where total revenue from the Games is in the neighborhood of $4 to $5 billion for the Summer Olympics and roughly half that for the Winter Games, costs above these levels mean that someone has to pay.[16] While private companies often contribute a share of the capital costs (beyond the purchase of sponsorships), host governmental bodies usually pick up a substantial part of the tag. Moreover, as we have seen, not all the money generated at the Games stays in the host city to pay for the Games; rather, close to half the money goes to support the activities of the IFs, the NOCs and the IOC itself.[17]

Thus, while the Sydney OCOG in 2000 reported that it broke even, the Australian state auditor estimated that the Games true long-term cost was $2.2 billion.[18] In part, this was because it is now costing $30 million a year to operate the 90,000-seat Olympic Stadium.[19] Similarly, the 1992 Olympics in Barcelona generated a reported surplus of $3 million for the local organizing committee, but it created a debt of $4 billion for the central Spanish government and of $2.1 billion for the city and provincial governments.[20]

For all of the foregoing reasons, if there is to be an economic benefit from hosting the Olympic Games, it is unlikely in the extreme to come in the form of improving the budgets of local governments. This raises the question of whether there are broader, longer-term or less tangible economic gains that accrue from hosting the Olympic Games, and it is to this question that we now turn.

HOW DO THE OLYMPIC GAMES AFFECT THE ECONOMY?

In general, sporting events produce two types of economic benefits: direct economic benefits and indirect economic benefits. Direct economic benefits include net spending by tourists who travel from out of town to attend the event, spending on capital and infrastructure construction related to the event, long-run benefits—for example lower transportation costs attributable to an improved road or rail network—generated by this infrastructure, and the effect of hosting a sporting event on local security markets, primarily stock markets. Indirect benefits include possible advertising effects that make the host city or country more visible as a potential tourist destination or business location in the future and increases in civic pride, local sense of community, and the perceived stature of the host city or country relative to other cities or countries. The Olympic Games are much like other sporting events, except that the Games involve many more participants, officials, and fans, involve more infrastructure construction, induce many more visitors from out of town, and have a much higher profile than most other sporting events.

Because of the larger size and profile of the Olympic Games, they have a greater potential to generate economic benefits than smaller sports events. However, the criticisms about overstatement of economic benefits made about smaller sporting events also apply to the Olympic Games, as we will soon see.

Among the direct economic benefits generated by the Olympic Games, tourist spending is probably the most prominent. From **Table 5,** an average of 5.1 million tickets was sold for the past six Summer Olympic Games, including almost six million tickets to the 1984 Games in Los Angeles. The Winter Games are considerably smaller, averaging 1.3 million tickets over the past five Winter Olympics. Even though selling five million tickets does not mean that there are five million spectators, and many of the tickets are sold

Table 5   Ticket Sales and Revenues (1,000,000s of Tickets and Current US$)

Games	Tickets Sold	% Capacity	Revenue to OCOG (95% total)
1984 Los Angeles	5.700	83%	$156,000,000
1988 Calgary	1.600	78%	32,000,000
1988 Seoul	3.300	75%	36,000,000
1992 Albertville	0.900	75%	32,000,000
1992 Barcelona	3.000	80%	79,000,000
1994 Lillehammer	1.200	87%	26,000,000
1996 Atlanta	8.300	82%	425,000,000
1998 Nagano	1.300	89%	74,000,000
2000 Sydney	6.700	88%	551,000,000
2002 Salt Lake	1.500	95%	183,000,000
2004 Athens	3.800	72%	228,000,000

Source: Adapted from IOC, 2006 Marketing Fact File, p. 59. Reproduced with permission of ABC-CLIO, LLC.

NB: Ninety-five percent of ticketing revenue stays with the local OCOG; 5 percent goes to the IOC.

to local residents, especially for the Summer Games which typically take place in large metropolitan areas, a sporting event of this size and scope has the potential to attract a significant number of visitors from outside the host city. Also, since the Games are often spread over more than two weeks, these visitors may spend a significant amount of time in the host area, generating substantial spending in the lodging, and food and beverage sectors.

The Olympic Games require large spending on constructing and updating venues. These include facilities for the actual competition, accommodations for the participants, and visitors, and facilities for the army of media covering the Games. Many of these venues are specific structures like a velodrome for bicycle racing, a bobsled/skeleton/luge run, etc., that involve costly construction due to their specialized nature. In addition, Olympic venues typically have huge seating capacities. The stadiums that have hosted the opening and closing ceremonies for the Summer Olympic Games often seat 100,000 spectators.

In addition to venue construction, hosting the Olympic Games often requires expansive infrastructure to move the participants, officials, and fans to and from the venues. A majority of past transportation infrastructure construction has been on roads. But host cities and regions have also spent considerable sums on airport construction as well as on the renovation and construction of public transportation systems.[21] In less developed cities, the building of a modern telecommunications capacity also represents a substantial investment.

The construction of this infrastructure generates appreciable economic activity in the host community. Large numbers of construction workers must be hired and large quantities of construction materials must be purchased and transported.

Beyond the construction period, Olympics-generated infrastructure can provide the host metropolitan area or region with a continuing stream of economic benefits. The venues built for Olympic events can be used for years or decades after the Games are over. The existence of these venues can generate some ongoing economic benefits. But more importantly, upgrades to the transportation infrastructure can provide significant benefits to the local and regional economy, if local businesses are able to make use of the improved transportation infrastructure. These benefits take the form of reduced production costs and prices charged by local businesses.[22]

The economic benefits to local securities markets are typically associated with the announcement of the awarding of the Olympic Games, and not with the hosting itself of the Games. If the awarding of the Games generates significant expected future profits in the host economy, then this could lead to a current increase in stock returns in the host country. A permanent increase in wealth, generated by increases in returns to stock shares, could lead to increases in current consumption and investment. However, the magnitude of these wealth effects are likely to be small, and a temporary increase in stock returns associated with the Olympic selection decision may indicate, at best, a small increase in future profits by firms in specific industries or, alternatively, spurious correlation.

The indirect economic benefits generated by the Olympic Games are potentially more important than the direct benefits, and also more difficult to quantify. One possible indirect benefit is the advertising effect of the Olympic Games. Many Olympic host metropolitan areas and regions view the Olympics as a way to raise their profile on the world stage. Cities and regions compete intensely for a share of international tourism spending, and the Olympic Games are possibly one way to make the host stand out in this crowded marketplace. In this sense, the intense media coverage before and during the Olympic Games is a form of advertising. If hosting the Olympic Games is an effective form of advertising in that it leads tourists who would not have otherwise considered this to be a destination to visit the host city or region, then this advertising effect can generate significant economic benefits over a long period of time. These potential economic benefits take the form of increased tourist spending, just like the direct benefits discussed above. The difference is that these potential benefits may be long lasting, and may be spread more diffusely over the host city or region, and not concentrated in and around the Olympic venues like the direct benefits associated with hosting the Games. . . .

THE PROBLEM WITH MULTIPLIERS

Multiplier-based estimates of the economic impact are subject to a number of potentially damaging criticisms.[23] Although these criticisms are widely known in academic circles, the continued use of multiplier-based estimates of the economic impact of sporting events suggests that these limitations are not understood in other settings.

One important problem with multiplier-based estimates stems from the estimate of the number of attendees. New economic impact can only be generated by the spending of spectators, participants, and officials from outside the host area. Spending by local residents does not represent new economic impact, it represents spending that would have taken place in the host area even if the Olympic Games were held elsewhere; this spending needs to be removed from the estimate.[24] However, estimating the total number of attendees is much easier than estimating the number of attendees from outside the host area. From Table 5, 8.3 million tickets were sold to events at the 1996 Atlanta Summer Olympic Games. Some of these tickets were clearly sold to residents of Atlanta. But how many of these 8.3 million tickets were purchased by Atlantans? This number is difficult to estimate accurately.

Further complicating the process are "time switchers" and "casuals." "Time switchers" are attendees who would have visited the host area at some other time, for some other reason, but instead choose to visit the host area during the sporting event. "Casuals" are attendees who visit the host area at the same time as the sporting event for some other reason and decide to attend the event out of convenience. The spending by both types of attendees needs to be removed from the economic impact estimate, as it cannot be directly attributable to the sporting event. This spending would have taken place whether or not the sporting event was in the area. Failure to remove this spending leads to over estimates of the economic impact generated by the event.

A second important problem with multiplier-based economic impact estimates is their failure to account for crowding out. In many cases, the host area for the Olympic Games is a tourist destination in its own right; tourists would visit this area even if the Olympic Games were held elsewhere; London, for example, is a major tourist destination. Crowding out takes place when outside visitors attending the Olympic Games buy hotel rooms, meals, and other travel related goods and services that would have been purchased by other visitors absent the Olympic Games. Crowding out implies that each dollar of new economic impact estimated by multiplier-based methods needs to be offset by some corresponding lost economic impact that was crowded out, or else the net economic impact will be overstated.

It is extremely difficult to determine how much crowding out actually takes place when an area hosts the Olympic Games. However, one study found that gate arrivals at the Atlanta airport during the 1996 Summer Games was identical to gate arrivals in the same months in 1995 and 1997, implying that quite a few tourists to Atlanta were crowded out by the 1996 Games.[25] In late 2004, Athens tourism officials were estimating about a 10 percent drop in summer tourism in 2004 due to the Olympics. The Utah Skier Survey found that nearly 50 percent of non-residents would stay away from Utah in 2002 due to the expectation of more crowds and higher prices.

Even though the size of crowding out is difficult to determine, it exists, and multiplier-based estimates of economic impact typically ignore it, and, consequently, over estimate the actual economic impact.

A third problem with multiplier-based estimates is the displacement phenomenon. Some local residents may choose to leave town to avoid the congestion during the Games. The displaced people spend money outside the local area that they would have spent locally absent the Games. For instance, a survey in Barcelona indicated that fully one-sixth of the city's residents planned to travel outside the city during the 1996 Olympics.

A fourth important problem with multiplier-based estimates of the economic impact of sporting events is the selection of the multiplier. Economic theory does not provide exact guidance on the size of the multiplier to use in any particular application. The size of the multiplier used is at the discretion of the analyst. More importantly, the larger the multiplier used, the larger the estimate of the economic impact. This creates an incentive for researchers to systematically choose large multipliers in order to generate large estimates of the economic impact of sporting events.

Despite all these problems, the majority of published estimates of the economic impact of the Olympic Games come from multiplier-based estimates. Multiplier-based estimates are widely used because, relative to the other approaches discussed above, this approach requires little data, little technical expertise, and very little in the way of computing power. Multiplier-based estimates are relatively cheap to produce and easy to manipulate.

EVIDENCE ON THE ECONOMIC IMPACT OF THE OLYMPICS

Considering the size and prominence of the event, relatively little objective evidence on the economic impact of the Olympic Games exists. Much of the existing evidence has been developed by the host cities or regions, which have a vested interest in justifying the large expenditures on the games that were documented above. These "promotional" studies suffer from a number of the flaws discussed in the previous section, and must be taken with a very large grain of salt. Given these caveats, **Table 6** shows some estimates of the economic impact of past Olympic Games, as well as some published estimates of the number of outside visitors

Table 6   Estimated Economic Impacts and Visitors from Promotional Studies

Host	Year	Period	Total Estimated Impact Real 2006 US Dollars	Visitors	Notes
Tokyo	1964	1964		70,000	Actual
Munich	1972	1972		1,800,000	Estimated
Montreal	1976	1976		1,500,000	Estimated
Moscow	1980	1980		30,000	Actual
Los Angeles	1984	1984	$4,488,522,780	600,000	Multiplier
Calgary	1988	1988		1,339,000	Unknown
Seoul	1988	1982–1988	$4,598,146,717	279,332	Multiplier
Albertville	1992	1992		942,000	Estimated
Barcelona	1992	1987–1992	$42,834,973	400,000	Multiplier
Lillehammer	1994	1994		1,208,000	Estimated
Atlanta	1996	1991–1997	$6,526,821,761	1,100,000	Multiplier
Sydney	2000	1994–2006	$1,565,371,660	700,000	Multiplier
Salt Lake	2002	1996–2003	$1,696,475,533	850,000	Multiplier
Athens	2004	1998–2011	$16,983,139,800	5,900,000	Multiplier
Turin	2006	2006	$2,000,000,000	1,500,000	Multiplier

Source: Compiled from various media sources, authors' calculations. Reproduced with permission of ABC-CLIO, LLC.
[*Ed. Note: Total Estimated Impact was not calculated for Tokyo, Munich, Montreal, Moscow, Calgary, Albertville, or Lillehammer.*]

who attended the Games. In all cases, the estimated dollar values of the economic impacts have been converted to 2006 US dollars using contemporaneous exchange rates.

Column four on Table 6 contains the published estimated economic impact generated in eight past Olympic Games. In all cases, these impacts were generated using multiplier-based economic impact estimates. In all but one of these Games, the estimated economic impact was significant, ranging from $1.5 billion to nearly $17 billion U.S. dollars. The time frame for these economic impacts varies significantly, from a single year to a thirteen-year period. Because the actual underlying economic impact is not constant across time, it does not make sense to express these figures on an annual basis. The extremely large estimated impact from the Athens Games, for instance, is in part due to the exceptionally long period of analysis used.

Because these estimates of economic impact are all based in part on spending by tourists who attend the Games, the information on estimated tourist attendance shown in column 5 of Table 6 is also interesting. Like the economic impact estimates, the visitor estimates show a wide amount of variation, ranging from a low of 30,000 for the 1980 Moscow Olympic Games to a high of nearly 6 million, over a thirteen-year period, for the 2004 Athens Games. Again, the host cities or regions have an incentive to overstate these estimates to justify their large expenditures on the Games.

The figures for both the 1964 Tokyo Games and the 1980 Moscow Games are interesting, in that these are actual visitor totals based on the number of tourist visas issued by these two countries. The Moscow Games are clearly an outlier, both because of the boycott of those games by the US and some other countries over the ongoing war in Afghanistan, and the difficulties of travel behind the Iron Curtain at that time. The Tokyo Games took place far from both Europe and North America, which meant considerable travel costs in the early 1960s.[26] But still, the modest size of these two actual visitor counts, even given these caveats, makes some of the larger estimates in the table questionable.

Estimates of the economic impact of the Olympic Games derived from academic research published in peer-reviewed journals is a more reliable type of evidence than the figures from promotional studies shown in Table 6, because the researchers who develop these estimates have no vested interest in the economic success of the Games and also because the peer review process provides an important check on the methods and assumptions used to generate these estimates.

Only a few such studies exist. One study focused on the effect of the 1996 Atlanta Olympic Games on the economy in Georgia.[27] The paper concludes that hosting the games increased employment in Georgia by 17%, or approximately 293,000 new jobs in the counties that contained Olympic venues or were contiguous to counties with Olympic venues in the four-year period 1996–2000, but had no effect on real wages. This result implies new employment, but no benefit for the existing workers in these counties in Georgia.

This paper used a novel, high frequency panel data set for counties in Georgia over the period 1985–2000. The results, based on estimates of reduced form econometric models of the determination of county-level employment and real wages, are strong because of the length and breadth of this panel data set and the careful econometric analysis. This paper contains the strongest evidence of economic benefits flowing from the Olympic Games. However, the reduced form nature of the analysis does not identify a particular mechanism through which hosting the Olympic

Games raises employment in the counties in and near the Olympic venues.

A second paper examined the effects of hosting the Olympic Games on migration into North American regions.[28] This paper examined population and employment in the regions surrounding Lake Placid, New York (1980), Los Angeles, California (1984), Calgary, Alberta (1988) and Atlanta, Georgia (1996). The results indicate a 1% increase in employment in these regions in a variable period following the Olympic Games, along with a decline in per capita income in this period, after controlling for other factors that affect employment and income.

The evidence in this paper is based on estimated reduced form econometric models of migration into these four regions using pooled data. While the econometric approach is appropriate, the study uses relatively little data from before the Lake Placid and Los Angeles Games and after the Atlanta Games. This data limitation reduces the strength of the results.

These two papers find evidence that hosting the Olympic Games increases employment in the host region, but do not contain any evidence that hosting the Olympics increases compensation in the host region. The lack of an effect on compensation implies that the distributional effects of the overall impact of hosting the Olympic Games may be different than the employment effects, if local prices and the local cost of living rose as a result of hosting the games. This could be the case even in Atlanta, where local wages were deflated by a national price measure, the Consumer Price Index for all Urban Employees (CPI-U). If prices and the cost of living in Atlanta increased more than national average prices reflected in the CPI-U, then real wages in the Atlanta region could have declined as a result of hosting the 1996 Games.

[*Ed. Note: The authors' discussion of two other studies is omitted.*]

. . . .

The results in these studies present a consistent picture of the economic impact of hosting the Olympic Games on regions. Some jobs will be created as a result of hosting the Games. However, there appears to be no detectable effect on income, suggesting that existing workers do not benefit from the Games. Moreover . . . the overall economic impact of hosting the Games depends on the overall labor market response to the new jobs created by the Games. When taking into account the overall labor market situation, the net impact of the Games on a region may not be positive. The negative impact on regional income found by the study that examined four North American regions is consistent with a negative overall labor market response to hosting the Games. Furthermore, the long-run impacts on tourism in the host region may be overstated, based on evidence from Lillehammer.

Clearly, the results from academic research on the economic impact of hosting the Olympic Games call into question the reported economic impact from the promotional studies shown in Table 6. Economic impacts on the order of $5 to $10 billion dollars should be easily detectable in retrospective economic data from a geographic region. The fact that no peer-reviewed research published in a scholarly journal has found any evidence of billions of dollars of new income in any Olympic host regions suggests that the promotional studies vastly overstate the economic impact of hosting the Olympic Games.

. . . .

The announcement that Sydney would host the 2000 Summer Olympic Games produced modest increases in stock returns in a limited number of industries: building materials, developers and contracts, and engineering. The announcement that Athens would host the 2004 Summer Olympic Games produced a short-term, significant increase in overall stock returns on the Athens Stock Exchange, but had no impact on the Milan Stock Exchange. Milan was one of the cities in the running for the 2004 Summer Games. Stock returns in construction related industries on the Athens Stock Exchange increased more than other sectors following the announcement, suggesting that much of the economic benefit accrues to this sector.

This evidence is limited to only two Olympic Games, and the increases in stock returns reported in the studies are modest, short term, and primarily limited to the construction industry, and related sectors of the economy. The empirical model used to analyze stock returns on the Athens Stock Exchange explains only 6% of the observed variation in returns. Overall, the evidence from this literature suggests that stock markets do not forecast large positive economic impacts flowing from the Olympic Games. While the idea that hosting the Olympic Games affects stock returns may appear important to the general public, a careful reading of this literature reveals that the underlying effects are small, transitory and limited to a few sectors of the economy. This evidence does not support net economic impact on the order of those reported on Table 6 accruing to the host city or region.

CAN THE OLYMPIC GAMES BE AN ECONOMIC SUCCESS?

Our review of the existing peer-reviewed evidence on the economic impact of the Olympic Games reveals relatively little evidence that hosting the Games produces significant economic benefits for the host city or region. If the economic gains are modest, or perhaps non-existent, what can host cities and regions do to leverage hosting the Olympic Games? A careful examination of past experiences suggests two important avenues for leveraging the Olympic Games:

host cities or regions need to make careful land use decisions and maximize the post-Olympic Games use of new and renovated facilities and infrastructure.

Land is an increasingly scarce resource in both large urban areas that typically host the Summer Games and in the mountainous areas that host the Winter Games. Hosting the Olympic Games requires a significant amount of land for facilities, the Olympic Village, housing for the media and staff, accommodations for spectators, and parking. Unsuccessful Games leave behind legacies of seldom or never used structures taking up valuable land. For example, one recent study concluded that the primary legacy of the Nagano Games are a rarely used bobsled track and a huge speed skating venue that has generated significant operating losses since the games. Likewise, the long-term impact of the Calgary Games is viewed as less important than the annual rodeo, the Calgary Stampede, and the signature venue in Calgary, the SaddleDome, is viewed as obsolete and in need of replacing less than twenty years after the end of the Games.[33] Although it was used for years following the 1976 Montreal Games, the Olympic Stadium was widely viewed as one of the worst facilities in Major League Baseball, and many "features" like the retractable roof never worked. Many of the venues used in the 2004 Athens Games are either vacant or seldom used, and occupy valuable land in a crowded urban center.

Successful Games, like the 1984 Los Angeles Summer Games, utilize existing facilities as much as possible, consuming as little scarce urban land as possible. The stadium used for the opening and closing ceremonies in the 1996 Atlanta Games was reconfigured to a baseball stadium immediately following the conclusion of the Games. The bullet train built for the Nagano Games greatly reduced the travel time between that city and Tokyo.

Tying up scarce land for seldom-used Olympic venues in both urban areas and alpine recreation areas cannot be an optimal use of this valuable resource. Olympic planners need to design facilities that will be useful for a long time after the Games are over, and are constructively integrated into the host city or region.

Clearly, the impact of the Olympic Games will vary according to the differing levels of development in the host city and country. Properly planned, hosting the Games can catalyze the construction of a modern transportation, communications and sport infrastructure. Such a potential benefit is bound to be greater for less developed areas. But even in such areas, hosting the Games will require a significant outlay of public funds to finance the infrastructural improvements. These improvements can also be made without hosting the Games. Thus, it is relevant to ask whether the planning for the Olympics produces an optimal use of scarce public monies. It is also relevant to consider that in many circumstances the public policy process is so gridlocked that needed infrastructural investments may be delayed for years, if not decades, without the Olympic catalyst and that

the Games do provide at least some capital to facilitate the completion of desirable projects.

Conversely, in more developed regions, where land is even more scarce during the initial bid planning (and destined to become scarcer still over the ten-year period of Olympic selection and preparation) and labor and resource markets are tight, hosting the Games can occasion a gross misuse of land as well as provoke wage and resource price pressure leading to higher inflation.

Finally, it is important to recognize that hosting the Olympic Games generates significant non-pecuniary benefits to the host city or region. The residents of the host city or region are likely to derive significant pride and sense of community from hosting the Games. Their homes are the focus of the world's attention for a brief, but intense period. The planning and work required to host the Games takes considerable time and effort, and much of the hard work is done by volunteers. Pulling off such a huge endeavor is a source of considerable local and national pride. These factors are both important and valuable, even though researchers find it difficult to place a dollar value on them.

. . . Economists have used the Contingent Valuation Method (CVM) to place a dollar value on such diverse intangible benefits as cleaning up oil spills in pristine wilderness areas and preserving green space in urban areas. The basic approach in CVM is to elicit people's willingness to pay for some intangible through hypothetical questions involving referendum voting or changes in taxes. A recent estimate of the total willingness to pay for the intangible benefits generated in the United Kingdom from hosting the 2012 Summer Games was in excess of two billion pounds sterling.

In the end, the economic and non-economic value to hosting the Olympic Games is a complex matter, likely to vary from one situation to another. Simple conclusions are impossible to draw. Prospective hosts of future Games would do well to steer clear of the inevitable Olympic hype and to take a long, hard and sober look at the long-run development goals of their region.

Notes

1. Montreal city officials initially projected that the Games would only cost $124 million. Rick Burton, "Olympic Games Host City Marketing: An Exploration of Expectations and Outcomes," Sport Marketing Quarterly, 12 (2003), 38.

2. According to one report, the Soviet government spent $9 billion on facilities for the 1981 games. Burton, 38.

3. Holger Preuss, The Economics of Staging the Olympic Games. Northampton, MA: Edward Elgar Publishing, 2003, 194.

4. Quoted in Burton, 35.

5. For instance, in the recent Games hosted in the United States, the federal government provided $1.3 billion in Salt Lake City in 2002; $609 million in Atlanta in 1996 and $75 million in Los Angeles in 1984 (all reckoned in 1999 prices.) Bernard L Ungar, Olympic Games: Federal Government Provides Significant Funding and Support, Collingwood, PA: Diane Publishing Co., 2000, p. 5. For the 2010 Winter Games in Vancouver, in addition to the provincial gov-

ernment of British Columbia and the federal government of Canada putting up $9.1 million each to help finance the bidding process, the provincial government is putting up an additional $1.25 billion to finance the Games (and providing a guarantee to cover cost overruns) and the federal government is contributing another $330 million. The city of Vancouver is putting $170.3 million. www.mapleleafweb.com, accessed August 22, 2007.

6. Preuss, 195.

7. International Olympic Committee, "2006 Olympic Marketing Fact File," http://www.olympic.org/uk/organisation/facts/revenue/index _uk.asp. 23. (Accessed October 28, 2007).

8. Preuss, 110.

9. IOC, 2006 Marketing Fact File, pp. 51–54.

10. IOC, 2006 Marketing Fact File, p. 82-83. From the Salt Lake Games revenues, the IOC also provided $305 million to the NOCs.

11. In addition to providing for facilities, infrastructure and security, and devoting large tracts of land on which to build the facilities, the eventual host city, along with its bidding competitors, typically spend $30 to $50 million to conduct their bid. The bidding process involves a roughly ten-year commitment for the eventual host city. Further, and as discussed elsewhere in this paper, host cities must maintain most Olympic facilities for decades into the foreseeable future.

12. Preuss, 195.

13. Of course, not all OCOGs manage to break even, the Albertville OCOG lost $57 million. Burton, 39.

14. Herein lies another conundrum. The lower figure appears to include only operating costs or the budget of the Beijing OCOG. This is the figure that is generally publicized. The higher range also includes facility and infrastructure costs. The latter includes the expansion of the Beijing subway system and, hence, will likely serve the city productively well after the Games are over. Before and after comparisons are often plagued by this apples and oranges confusion.

15. Brendan Carlin, "Olympic budget trebles to £9.3bn," London Telegraph, March 15, 2007. Also see, Bernard Simon, "Cost of Canadian 2010 Winter Olympics Escalates," Financial Times, February 6, 2006.

16. To be sure, the Winter Games involve fewer participants, fewer venues and less construction; hence, the cost of these Games is lower than for the summer Games.

17. Not surprisingly, the PR hype does not always match this reality. For instance, the director of planning and budgeting of the Atlanta Games told Holger Preuss (author of the book The Economics of Staging the Olympics): "We can only give you the analyses which carry a positive image. Other analyses remain unpublished so as not to make the population insecure."

18. The Sydney bid cost $46.2 million and its Games cost $3.24 billion. Preuss, 233. The Sydney Games were originally projected to earn the Australian Treasury a surplus of $100 million. Burton, 39. One of the goals of the Sydney Games was to generate increased tourism, yet Graham Mathews, a former forecaster for the Australian Federal Treasury stated: "While having the Olympics may have made us feel warm and fuzzy and wonderful, in cold hard terms it's actually hard in international experience to determine if there has been a positive, lasting impact on tourism from having that brief burst of exposure." Burton, 40.

19. Similarly, maintenance costs on the Athens Olympics facilities in 2005 reportedly will come in around $124 million and there appears to be little to no local interest being expressed for the two Olympic soccer stadiums. "Cost of 2004 Athens Games Continues to Esca-late," Washington Post, August 10, 2005, http://www .washingtonpost.com. Torino had several white elephants, including its bobsled-run venue which cost $108 million to construct. Deputy President of Torino Games, Evelina Christillin commented to a Wall Street Journal reporter: "I can't tell you a lie. Obviously, the bobsled run is not going to be used for anything else. That's pure cost." The speed skating arena in Nagano (1998) is sometimes used for flea markets. Gabriel Kahn & Roger Thurow, "Quest for Gold—Torino 2006," The Wall Street Journal, February 10 2006, page A1.

20. The total reported cost of the Barcelona Games was $9.3 billion, of which private sources covered $3.2 billion and public sources covered $6.1 billion. See Burton, op. cit., p. 39. For a related account of large public expenditures on infrastructure for the Salt Lake City Olympics, see D.L. Bartlett & J.B. Steele, "Snow Job," Sports Illustrated, December 21, 2001, pp. 79-98. Bartlett and Steele report that the U.S. government spent $1.5 billion of taxpayer money on the purchase of land, road construction, sewers, parking lots, housing, buses, fencing, a light rail system, airport improvements, and security equipment, inter alia. Some have argued that a part of these expenditures would have occurred even if Salt Lake City did not host the Olympics.

21. Stephen Essex and Brian Chalkley, "Mega-sporting Events in Urban and Regional Policy: A History of the Winter Olympics." Planning Perspectives 19, no. 1 (2004): 205.

22. Terance Rephann and Andrew Isserman, "New Highways as Economic Development Tools: An Evaluation Using Quasi-Experimental Matching Methods." Regional Science and Urban Economics 24, no. 6 (1994): 728.

23. John Crompton, "Economic Impact Analysis of Sports Facilities and Events: Eleven Sources of Misapplication," Journal of Sport Management 9 (1995): 15

24. This statement assumes that residents have a fixed budget for leisure spending. To the extent that they may expand their leisure spending or that they substitute local leisure spending for leisure spending outside the local area, then this claim must be modified.

25. Philip Porter, "Mega-Sports Events as Municipal Investments: A Critique of Impact Analysis." In Sports economics: Current Research, ed. J. Fizel, E. Gustafson, and L. Hadley (Westport, CT: Prager, 1999)

26. Of course, the city of Tokyo may have benefited from Japanese tourists coming from other parts of the country. Any such benefit would have been at the expense of other places in Japan and would not have constituted a benefit to the whole country.

27. Julie L. Hotchkiss, Robert E. Moore, and Stephanie M. Zobay, "Impact of the 1996 Summer Olympic Games on Employment and Wages in Georgia," Southern Economic Journal 69 (2003): 691–704.

28. Travis J. Lybbert and Dawn D. Hilmany, "Migration Effects of Olympic Siting: A Pooled Time Series Cross-Sectional Analysis of Host Regions," The Annals of Regional Science 34 (2000): 405–420.

. . . .

33. David Whitson and John Horne, Understated costs and overstated benefits? Comparing the outcomes of sports mega-events in Canada and Japan. The Sociological Review 54 (2006): 75.

. . . .

References

Atkinson, G., S. Mourato, and S. Szymanski, "Quantifying the 'Un-quantifiable': Valuing the Intangible Benefits of Hosting the Summer Olympic Games," Urban Studies (2008), in press.

Bartlett, D. L., and J. B. Steele, "Snow Job," *Sports Illustrated,* December 21, 2001, pp. 79–98.

Berman, G., R. Brooks, and S. Davidson, "The Sydney Olympic Games Announcement and Australian Stock Market Reaction," *Applied Economics Letters 7* (2000): 781–784.

Burton, Rick, "Olympic Games Host City Marketing: An Exploration of Expectations and Outcomes," *Sport Marketing Quarterly, 12* (2003): 35–45.

Carlin, Brendan, "Olympic Budget Trebles to £9.3bn," *London Telegraph,* March 15, 2007.

Crompton, John, "Economic Impact Analysis of Sports Facilities and Events: Eleven Sources of Misapplication," *Journal of Sport Management 9* (1995): 14–35.

Essex, S., and B. Chalkley, "Mega-sporting Events in Urban and Regional Policy: A History of the Winter Olympics," *Planning Perspectives 19,* no. 1 (2004): 201–232.

Hotchkiss, J. L., R. E. Moore, and S. M. Zobay, "Impact of the 1996 Summer Olympic Games on Employment and Wages in Georgia," *Southern Economic Journal 69* (2003): 691–704.

International Olympic Committee, "2006 Olympic Marketing Fact File," http://www.olympic.org/uk/organisation/facts/revenue/index_uk.asp., 23.

Kahn, Gabriel, and Roger Thurow, "Quest for Gold—Torino 2006," *Wall Street Journal,* February 10, 2006, page A1. http://www.wallstreetjournal.com.

Lybbert, T. J., and D. D. Hilmany, "Migration Effects of Olympic Siting: A Pooled Time Series Cross-sectional Analysis of Host Regions," *The Annals of Regional Science 34* (2000): 405–420.

Porter, Philip, "Mega-Sports Events as Municipal Investments: A Critique of Impact Analysis." In *Sports Economics: Current Research,* edited by J. Fizel, E. Gustafson, and L. Hadley, 61–74. Westport, CT: Prager, 1999.

Preuss, H. *The Economics of Staging the Olympic Games.* Northampton, MA: Edward Elgar Publishing, 2004.

Rephann, T. and A. Isserman. "New Highways as Economic Development Tools: An Evaluation Using Quasi-Experimental Matching Methods," *Regional Science and Urban Economics 24,* no. 6 (1994): 723–751.

Ritchie, J. R. B., and B. H. Smith, "The Impact of a Mega-Event on Host Region Awareness: A Longitudinal Study," *Journal of Travel Research 30* (1991): 3–10.

Simon, Bernard, "Cost of Canadian 2010 Winter Olympics Escalates," *Financial Times,* February 6, 2006.

Tiegland, Jon, "Mega-events and Impacts on Tourism; the Predictions and Realities of the Lillehammer Olympics," *Impact Assessment and Project Appraisal 17* (1999): 305–317.

Ungar, Bernard L., *Olympic Games: Federal Government Provides Significant Funding and Support,* Collingdale, PA: Diane Publishing Company, 2000.

Veraros, N., E. Kasimati, and P. Dawson. "The 2004 Olympic Games Announcement and its Effect on the Athens and Milan Stock Exchanges," *Applied Economics Letters 11,* no. 3 (2004): 749–753.

Washington Post, "Cost of 2004 Athens Games Continues to Escalate," August 10, 2005, http://www.washingtonpost.com.

Whitson, D., and J. Horne, "Understated Costs and Overstated Benefits? Comparing the Outcomes of Sports Mega-events in Canada and Japan," *The Sociological Review 54* (2006): 71–89.

EVOLUTION OF OLYMPIC SPONSORSHIP AND ITS IMPACT ON THE OLYMPIC MOVEMENT

Chrysostomos Giannoulakis and David Stotlar

Over the past Olympiads, the International Olympic Committee (IOC), Olympic Organizing Committees (OCOGs), National Olympic Committees (NOCs), and in general the Olympic Movement have become increasingly dependent upon the significant financial support provided by corporate sponsors. The increased dependency of the Olympic Movement on corporate sponsorship is seen in the fact that 30% of the IOC's budget and 40% of the United States Olympic Committee's (USOC) funds are derived from sponsorship and licensing income.[1] Olympic sponsorship involves not only financial support of the revenue, but provides products and services, technologies, expertise, and personnel to help in the organization of the Games.[2] Sponsorship revenue for the 2002 Salt Lake Winter Olympic Games accounted for 54% of all income.[3] In addition, the Athens 2004 sponsorship program, with the combined support from domestic sponsors and The Olympic Partners (TOP), was the second largest source of revenue for the staging of the Olympic Games, providing approximately 23% of the Organizing Committee's budget. As a result, in Greece, a nation of fewer than 11 million people, Athens 2004 sponsorship

provided the highest-ever capital support of any domestic program in the history of the Olympic Games.[4] The above-mentioned figures illustrate clearly the significant financial contribution of corporate sponsorship to the viability of the Olympic Movement and the continuation of the Olympic Games. The aim of this paper is to present financial data on the mutual beneficial relationship between the Olympic Movement and corporate sponsorship, as well as to discuss factors that may influence the nature of the Olympic Games due to their increased dependency on corporate sponsors. This discussion is conducted within the context of the IOC's marketing framework and the growing literature devoted to Olympic sponsorship. Marketing strategies of Olympic sponsors at the 2006 Torino and 2008 Beijing Olympic Games will be also discussed. Of particular concern is the way sponsors have attempted to capitalize on the elements of the Olympic Movement and what precautionary measures the IOC has implemented to maintain the spirit and true value of the Olympic Games intact.

HISTORY OF OLYMPIC SPONSORSHIP

The Olympic Games and sponsorship have had a long relationship, which was initiated with the ancient Olympic Games. Starting as an ancient Greek religious festival, where athletes competed in honor of Zeus, the Olympics have become one of the most celebrated and profitable media events in the world. In ancient Greece, cities would sponsor participant athletes by providing athletic facilities, equipment, and trainers. Although winners were only awarded a crown of wild olive leaves, they and their sponsor towns won huge renown.[5] At the first modern Olympic Games, which were revived in Athens in 1896 as athletic Games, two thirds of the funds came from private donations. Interestingly, the largest expense of the Games, the refurbishment of the Panathinaiko Stadium, was fulfilled due to the financial contribution of a single benefactor. However, "revenue was also received from private companies, including Kodak, which bought advertising in a souvenir program."[6] It was not until the Stockholm Olympic Games in 1912 that companies would purchase official rights from the International Olympic Committee, such as rights to secure pictures and sell memorabilia. At the Amsterdam Games in 1928 the Organizing Committee granted the right for concessions to operate restaurants within the Olympic stadium, and precautionary measures were implemented to restrict program advertising and to ban advertising in and around the stadium.[7]

The first financial surplus for an Olympic Organizing Committee was achieved at the 1932 Los Angeles Olympic Games. . . . Interestingly, the number of sponsors continued to grow in the following Olympiads, with 46 companies participating at the 1960 Rome Games and 250 companies at the 1964 Olympic Games in Tokyo. The participating number of corporate sponsors reached its highest peak at the 1976 Montreal Olympic Games with 628 sponsors and suppliers. Despite the extended number of corporate sponsors, the Games were a financial disaster for the Organizing Committee and the city of Montréal. The 1984 Los Angeles Olympic Games were the signature Games in regards to a financial surplus and commercialization of the Games, as they marked a turning point in Olympic sponsorship. The first privately financed Games produced a surplus of $232.5 million in Los Angeles and introduced the concept of protecting the local population from cost overruns associated with a sporting event.[9] The marketing program included 34 sponsors, 64 suppliers, and 65 licensees and sponsor hospitality centers were introduced for the first time.[10] Through its marketing program the Organizing Committee provided the opportunity for corporate sponsors to strongly affiliate themselves with the Olympic Movement in a number of different ways. . . .

THE OLYMPIC PARTNERS (TOP)

Since the unexpected financial success of the 1984 Los Angeles Olympic Games, the International Olympic Committee (IOC) realized that corporate sponsors provided the Olympic Movement with substantial profits and sponsorship became an integral part of the Movement. Simultaneously, the interconnection and interdependence between Olympic Games and sponsorship was strongly enhanced.[12]

The financial success of the Los Angeles Games was accompanied by major issues concerning over-commercialization and ambush marketing. One of the most important ambush marketing matters arose when Kodak ambushed Fuji film. Although Fuji was the official sponsor of the 1984 Games, many people were convinced that it was Kodak that was the official sponsor. Kodak was able to secure maximum media and on-site exposure by obtaining sponsorships with the United States Olympic Committee and buying numerous television advertisements during the Olympic Games. By utilizing this effective promotional strategy Kodak successfully created the perception that the company was the official sponsor of the Games.[13]

Due to the over-commercialization and the extended ambush or "parasite" marketing at the 1984 Los Angeles Games, the IOC introduced The Olympic Program (TOP) in 1985. Namely, the IOC established a marketing initiative "whereby a limited number of sponsors would receive special treatment and benefits on a worldwide basis while achieving product category exclusivity and protection for their Olympic sponsorship activities."[14] The original name of the program was changed to The Olympic Partners (TOP) in 1995. . . . [T]he change of the name reflected the nature of the relationship desired by the IOC between itself and the small number of multinational companies who are partners.[15] Sponsorship has been defined as a business relationship between a provider of funds, resources or services, and an event or organization that offers in return some rights and an association that may be used for commercial advantage.[16] Therefore, the IOC attempted through the TOP program to secure a stable and controlled revenue base, in order to maintain a successful and healthy relationship with its major corporate sponsors. In addition, the TOP program was one of the steps towards the implementation of a modernized funding process of the Olympic Movement. With the initiation of the TOP program, there was a dramatic increase in revenue throughout the five quadrenniums (**Table 7**).

The TOP program is the only sport-related marketing program in the world that provides complete category exclusivity worldwide while encompassing sponsorship of the event, the organizing body, and all participating teams.[17] By initiating the product exclusivity for its partners the IOC was able to significantly reduce the overall number of sponsors by implementing quality over quantity of sponsors while increasing the revenues for the Olympic Movement (**Table 8**). A reduction in the number of corporate sponsors was considered as the one of the most important mechanisms for the IOC to restrict ambush marketing and to control the commercial aspects of the Olympic Games. The current TOP VI partners contributed an average of $80 million each in order to secure their four year exclusive rights to two Olympic Games, both winter and summer, as well as rights to sponsor Organizing Committees and all participating National Olympic Committees.

Table 7   Evolution of TOP Olympic Sponsors

	TOP I Calgary/ Seoul	TOP II Albertville/ Barcelona	TOP III Lillehammer/ Atlanta	TOP IV Nagano/ Sydney	TOP V Salt Lake/ Athens	TOP VI Torino/ Beijing	Top VII Vancouver/ London
Number of Clients	9	12	10	11	11	12	9
Total Revenue (US $ million)	95	175	350	500	650	866	980

Source: IOC, 2006 Marketing Fact File (Lausanne: IOC, 2006). Reproduced from *Eighth International Symposium for Olympic Research*. Used with permission.

. . . the IOC stated in the 2002 Marketing Report:

The Olympic Family strives to ensure and enhance the value of Olympic sponsorship by diligently managing the partnership program, protecting the Olympic image and the rights of Olympic partners, and recognizing and communicating to a global audience the vital support that Olympic sponsors provide to the Movement, the Games, the athletes. Olympic partners have become fully integrated into the Olympic Movement, creating innovative programs that help to achieve corporate business objectives while supporting the Olympic Games and the Olympic athletes.[18]

[*Ed. Note: Discussion of corporate sponsor contributions at 2002 Salt Lake City and 2004 Athens Olympic Games omitted.*]

. . . .

OLYMPIC SPONSORSHIP AT THE 2006 TORINO AND 2008 BEIJING OLYMPIC GAMES

Current estimates of spending by TOP VI sponsors (Torino & Beijing) are $866 million with approximately 33% going to the Beijing Organizing Committee for the Olympic Games (BOCOG) and 17% to the Torino Organizing Committee (TOROC).[26] The sponsorship approach of major corporations at the Winter Olympic Games in Italy seemed to vary based on the formidable challenges the 2006 Games presented. The first challenge was the time zones and delayed TV coverage to the United States market. Consequently, the United States TV ratings for the 2006 Torino Winter Olympic Games were the lowest in 20 years. With the continuing dynamics in media preference many Olympic faithful chose to access the Olympic coverage through alternative media. The 2006 Torino Opening Ceremonies attracted 244,575 visitors to the web site. This figure represented a 95% increase over the 2004 Summer Games in Athens. A record number of daily hits to the 2006 Olympic web site occurred on February 16th with over 50 million page views.[27] While this falls short of the projected TV audience of 2 billion, the trend may signal a change for Olympic sponsors to extend their placement to additional sites.

Table 8   Sponsorship Presence at US Olympic Games

	1980 Lake Placid	1996 Atlanta	2002 Salt Lake
Local Partners	231	111	53
Licensees	165	125	69
Total Local Partners	396	236	122
Sponsorship Revenue (US $)	30,000,000	630,000,000	840,000,000
Licensing Revenue (US $)	2	91	25
Total Partner Revenue (US $)	32	724	865

Source: IOC, Marketing Matters, 2/1 (June 2002). Reproduced from *Eighth International Symposium for Olympic Research*. Used with permission.

During previous Olympic Games TV coverage produced superstars for a lifetime, yet with the fragmented media access points the Olympians of today may well prove to be very short-term stars. The Games have also encountered increasingly negative publicity as evidenced by various doping scandals among Olympic athletes. Specifically, during the 2006 Winter Games, the Austrian cross-country coach was suspended and an out-of-competition testing done on the Austrian team where blood-doping paraphernalia was found in the team residence at the Games. The much-touted US skier Bode Miller, who commented at a press conference that he skied better when he was intoxicated, subsequently failed to win a single Olympic medal. As a result, many Olympic sponsors prefer to focus their marketing dollars on the platforms created by the IOC and Games Organizing Committees instead of forming alliances with individual Olympic athletes.

As fees for Olympic sponsors continue to rise dramatically, namely $80 to $100 million for a four-year sponsorship agreement with the IOC, corporations are becoming even more strategic in how they market their brands through the Olympics in first place. By integrating Olympic sponsorships into their global marketing strategy, corporations are able to ensure greater benefit from their investment.

. . . .

IMPACT OF OLYMPIC SPONSORSHIP

It is evident that protecting the Olympic image and the value of sponsorship for the Olympic partners are major concerns for the International Olympic Committee. As a result, the IOC's marketing department has introduced a series of public relations campaigns with the main focus on raising awareness regarding the significant contribution of corporate sponsorship to the Olympic Movement. In addition to the public relations campaigns, the IOC has undertaken several market research studies in order to strengthen and promote the Olympic image and to understand attitudes and opinions towards the relationship between Olympic Games and corporate sponsorship. In the Barcelona 1992 Olympic Games, 79% of people in the United States, England, and Spain stated that the Olympic Games would not be viable without sponsorship. Furthermore, 86% stated that they were in favor of the Games being sponsored. Similar studies in 1996 found that one third of the respondents in a nine-country study suggested that their opinion of the sponsoring company was raised as a result of their Olympic sponsorship.[39] In Sydney 2000, 34% of the spectators stated "sponsorship makes a valuable contribution to the Olympics and makes me feel proud about sponsors."[40] In the recent Winter Olympic Games in 2002, the IOC commissioned Sport Marketing Surveys (SMS) to conduct market research on-site with spectators, corporate guest, and media. According to the results of the study, "research results clearly illustrate that unprompted awareness of the Olympic sponsors was very high among Olympic spectators and media, and that all possessed a strong understanding of the importance of sponsorship to the Olympic Movement and the staging of the Games."[41] The results showed that 92% of the spectators agreed that "sponsors contribute greatly to the success of the Games," 76% of the media agreed that they "welcome sponsorship support if the Games continue to be staged," and 45% of spectators stated that they would be more likely to buy a company's product or service as a result of them being an Olympic sponsor. Similar research studies in Athens 2004 Olympic Games depicted the positive attitude of spectators and media towards the support of corporate sponsorship to the Olympic Movement. In Sydney 2000, 34% of the spectators indicated "Sponsorship makes a valuable contribution to the Olympics and makes me feel proud about sponsors."[42]

In 2000, the International Olympic Committee conducted a research study in collaboration with a major Olympic sponsor and the Australian Tourist Commission (ATC). The IOC evaluated the attitudes of guests towards the Olympic brand. The sponsor evaluated the level of satisfaction expressed by its guests. Finally, the ATC examined pre- and post-Games travel patterns and the possibility for international visitors to return to Australia. Inevitably, the majority of the guests surveyed expressed a very high level of satisfaction in regards to hospitality issues and the organization of the Games. Most of the participants stated that sponsorship activities significantly affected their perception towards their Olympic experience in Sydney.

OLYMPIC SPONSORSHIP BEYOND BEIJING

The IOC has awarded the Olympic Games through 2012. The Vancouver Organizing Committee (VANOC) secured the rights to the 2010 Winter Games while London will host the 2012 Summer Olympic Games. Sponsors, both domestic and TOP VII partners, are beginning to line up. Five of the current TOP sponsors have extended through 2012 and Coca-Cola has renewed its sponsorship status through 2020. Bell-Canada bid $200 million to become the official telecommunications sponsor and RBC Financial paid $110 for the banking services rights. At this early stage it is interesting to note that VANOC's 2003 bid documents only projected a total of $200 million from all sources.[43] The 2012 London Organizing Committee is projecting revenues of $750 million from TOP sponsors and $600 million from domestic partners. While the allure of 1.3 billion Chinese fades into Olympic history, Vancouver and London are positioned to attract tourists and their economic impact to comfortable and secure destinations. In Olympic tradition, leaders of these economies will attempt to lure business development through their day on the Olympic stage.

CONCLUSION

It is evident that the complicated marketing policies and management structures of the International Olympic Committee have evolved into one of the best-managed global brand marketing association programs in the world, characterized by sophisticated and effective marketing structures. Olympic Games have become one of the most large-scale and profitable global media events. Events associated with the Olympic Games have not only become great entertainment, occupation, and lifestyle, but solid business as well.[44] The history of Olympic sponsorship has demonstrated the increased financial dependency of the Olympic Movement on corporate sponsors. Arguments have been raised about the escalating price for the TOP level sponsorships. An online 2005 poll with Marketing Magazine found that 67% of respondents thought that Olympic sponsorship was out of proportion to its marketing value. However, the authors believe that the best indicator is to watch where marketers put their money. Clearly, the pace of Olympic marketing and sponsorship has not slowed. However, a lingering question is whether the nature of the Games will be influenced and altered in the near future due to commercialization and the increased financial dependency of the Olympic Movement on sponsors. IOC President Jacques Rogge appears steadfast in his commitment to keep sponsor images off the field of play. Yet as the price increases so may the demands of the corporate sponsors.

Research studies conducted by the IOC have illustrated the significant impact of Olympic sponsorship on the spectators' perceptions of the Games. However, most of the studies were conducted with Olympic sponsors' guests as the primary participants of the studies. It is inevitable that these studies would project a highly positive perception of participants in regards to the value of Olympic sponsors to the viability of the Olympic Movement, since the results are published in the IOC's official marketing reports.

Are the Olympic Games transforming into the biggest financial opportunity for sponsors to showcase their products and services through global media exposure instead of being the biggest celebration of humanity and sportsmanship? Critics have always charged that the Olympic Games are more about marketing and less about sport. Previous Summer Olympics, such as the 1996 Atlanta Games, have been criticized for over-the-top marketing and a carnival-like atmosphere as well as for being another advertising medium deluging Olympic fans. The reality is that sponsorship has become an integral part of the Olympic Movement, which involves an ongoing commitment by Olympic partners who need to find new ways to gain the maximum returns for their investment. Olympic sponsorship has indeed a dynamic nature, since sponsors significantly support the viability of the Olympic Movement and the continuation of the Olympic Games. The question is whether the organization and staging of a mega event as the Olympic Games would be feasible without the financial contribution of corporate sponsors. The answer is that the Games would not be feasible, since the cost of staging the Games has increased dramatically over the past decade. It is clear that the current situation favors a long-term relationship between the IOC and a small number of sponsors. As Brown noted, "The IOC is placing more emphasis on promotion of the roles played by sponsors and on initiatives to ensure that sponsor exclusivity is preserved."[45] Unarguably, the IOC has achieved over the past decade, especially after the 1996 Atlanta Olympic Games, control of the commercial aspect of the Games by incorporating quality over quantity of corporate clients to the Olympic sponsorship program. However, the threat of ambush marketing and corruption scandals is always present. It would be interesting to see whether the IOC will continue to maintain its marketing and commercial control over Olympic partners based on the increased financial dependency of the Olympic Movement on corporate sponsorship. It is indeed a formidable challenge for the IOC to preserve the true essence of the Olympic Games by balancing terms such as sponsorship, return on investment, brand awareness,

and benefits with Olympic ideals such as sportsmanship, human scale, noble competition, and solidarity. In a recent interview conducted by Sports Business Journal, Jacques Rogge was asked how he balances the Olympic ideals with commercialization.[46] Rogge replied:

First, let me remind you that the games are the sole organization where there is no billboarding in the venues. There is no advertising on the bib or equipment or clothing of the athletes. That gives a kind of commercial-free environment. The second issue is that we say and we think that the support of the corporate world has led to the democratization of sport.

Olympic sponsors will continue to seek new ways to leverage benefits for their investment in the Olympics. It is the IOC's critical role to continue affiliating with sponsors that do not simply create "noise," but with those sponsors who create "meaning" and add true value to the overall Olympic experience. According to Kronick and Dome "Olympic sponsorship is a marathon, not a sprint."[47] Building relationships, whether with the 1.3 billion people in China or with corporations and consumers in the developed economies of North America or Europe, epitomizes the objectives of Olympic Movement sponsors. The impact of Olympic sponsorship extends far beyond the IOC and a relative limited number of corporate sponsors and Olympic partners.

Considerable discussion has occurred within the IOC about changing the process by which the Games are awarded. Pundits at the IOC proclaim that awarding the Games (without a bidding process) to countries that are less economically developed will expand the Olympic ideals to a more global audience. However, one would be naïve to think that the corporations that grease the wheels of the Olympic machine would not have significant influence in those decisions. Previously noted statements from Coca-Cola about the Chinese market and the implied efforts of Volkswagen to secure automobile production and sales in China indicate that Olympic sponsorship appears to be more about the market than the Olympic Games. This could lead to a situation where the IOC would become a prisoner of its own success due to the increased dependency on the revenues from corporate partners. At what point do the Olympic Games become a traveling trade show to the world's most lucrative markets where the entertainers are paid in medallions of gold, silver, and bronze?

The trend can already be seen in ticketing for the Games. For Torino, tickets to the Opening ceremony ranged from $250–850 US making it increasingly difficult for the average citizen to obtain Olympic Tickets. True there is an array of lower priced tickets, which have historically been available for less attractive sports. Unfortunately, tickets to more attractive sports are often secured by Olympic sponsors for use in corporate hospitality. Furthermore, the tickets frequently go unused as evidenced by the empty seats in lower tiers seen on the TV broadcasts of figure skating in the 2006 Games. Many true Olympic fans were left literally out in the cold. The Olympic Games are apparently following other marketing trends moving from Business-to-Consumer (B-2-C) marketing strategies to Business-to-Business (B-2-B). However the IOC needs to carefully balance the needs of corporate sponsors with the passion for the Games residing in Olympic fans around the globe. A stated goal of the IOC is "To ensure the independent financial stability of the Olympic Movement and thereby to assist in the worldwide promotion of Olympism."[48] If the IOC does not attend to this balance, Citius, Altius, Fortius may well become the motto of the Olympic sponsors rather than that of the Olympic athletes.

Notes

1. D. K. Stotlar, *Developing Successful Sport Sponsorship Plans*, 2nd ed. (Morgantown, WV: Fitness Information Technology, 2005).

2. J. Lee, "Marketing and Promotion of the Olympic Games," *Sport Marketing Quarterly*, Vol. 8, No. 3, 2005.

3. Stotlar, *Developing Successful Sport Sponsorship Plans*, 2005.

4. IOC, *Athens 2004 Marketing Report* (Lausanne: IOC, 2004).

5. P. Badinou, "Sports ethics in the ancient Games. *Olympic Review*, August September, 2001, pp. 59–61.

6. G. Brown, "Emerging issues in Olympic sponsorship; Implications for Host Cities," *Sport Management Review*, 2000, Vol. 3, No 1, pp. 71–92.

7. Ibid.

. . . .

9. R. Burton, "Olympic Games Host City Marketing: An Exploration of Expectations and Outcomes," *Sport Marketing Quarterly*, 2003, Vol. 12, No.1, pp. 37–47.

10. Brown, "Emerging issues in Olympic sponsorship; Implications for host cities," 2000.

. . . .

12. For the whole question of Olympic sponsorship and the TOP program, see R.K. Barney, S.R. Wenn, S.G. Martyn, *Selling the Five Rings: The IOC and the Rise of Olympic Commercialism* (The University of Utah Press: Salt Lake City 2004).

13. Stotlar, *Developing Successful Sport Sponsorship Plans*, 2005.

14. Ibid.

15. Brown, "Emerging Issues in Olympic Sponsorship; Implications for Host Cities," 2000.

16. S. Sleight, *Sponsorship: What It Is and How To Use It*, (London: McGraw-Hill, 1989).

17. *Salt Lake City 2002 Marketing* Report (Lausanne: IOC, 2002).

18. Ibid.

. . . .

26. IOC, *2006 Marketing Fact File* (Lausanne: IOC, 2006).

27. Ibid.

. . . .

39. Brown, "Emerging Issues in Olympic Sponsorship: Implications for Host Cities," 2000.

40. "At the Olympics, Less May Be More," http://www .performanceresearch.com/index.htm, Accessed 17 February 2006.

41. IOC, "Salt Lake 2002 Overview," *Olympic Marketing Matters*, Vol. 21, pp. 1–8.

42. "At the Olympics, Less May Be More," http://www .performanceresearch.com/index.htm, accessed 17 February 2006.

43. E. Lazarus, "Creative Games Management," *Marketing Magazine*, 110/17 (2005).

44. J. Lee, "Marketing and Promotion of the Olympic Games," *Sport Marketing Quarterly*, 8/3 (2005.)

45. Brown, "Emerging Issues in Olympic Sponsorship: Implications for Host Cities," 2000.

46. J. Genzale, "Keeper of the flame," *Sports Business Journal*, 8/99, pp. 21–23.

47. S. Kronick, & D. Dome, "Going for an Olympic Marketing Gold Beijing 2008," 2006.

48. IOC, *2006 Marketing Fact File*.

Discussion Questions

1. What is the major revenue source for the Olympics?
2. What entity is charged with running the Olympic Games?
3. What strategies might an OCOG use to make a given Olympiad more profitable?
4. What role do volunteers play in putting on the Olympic Games?
5. How are the different expenditures related to an Olympiad categorized for the determination of profit?
6. Why do corporations, such as Coca-Cola, pay such large sums for sponsorship rights?
7. What problems do people perceive with the commercialization of the Olympic Games?
8. What are the positive aspects of Olympic commercialization?
9. What is the most equitable division of IOC revenues between the various stakeholders (IOC, OCOG, IF, NOC)?

10. How has the IOC's reliance on the television networks and those contracts that are formed with these networks changed over time?

11. What city had the most substantial Olympic surplus? What is that surplus attributable to?

12. What is the true economic impact of hosting an Olympic Games?

13. How are the facilities that are built with the purpose of follow-up usage different than those that are built without any purpose of follow-up usage?

14. Whose leadership brought the Games into this era of relative financial stability? How was this done?

Part III

College Sports

History and Structure

INTRODUCTION

The National Collegiate Athletic Association (NCAA) is the dominant organization governing college sports in the United States today. Other organizations, including the National Association of Intercollegiate Athletics (NAIA), have played various roles over the years, but the NCAA has been the most prominent. Thus, this chapter and the ones that follow focus on the most important business issues related to the NCAA.

The key distinction between collegiate sports and the professional sports discussed in earlier chapters is the role of profit. College sports are focused on more than just the bottom line, in theory and in practice in most cases. Collegiate athletics are tied to interests as diverse as student morale, campus public relations, institutional profile, fundraising, and student physical fitness. As a result of this mix, athletic directors and college presidents arguably have a much more complicated juggling act than the professional sports team general manager or team owner, whose focus is much more on the bottom line.

The articles presented in this chapter provide a great deal of information on the NCAA. It is important to note that when the NCAA was originally formed at the turn of the last century it was focused on promoting safety, specifically seeking to end the deaths that had been occurring in collegiate football. The excerpted article by Smith, "A Brief History of the National Collegiate Athletic Association's Role in Regulating Intercollegiate Athletics," provides information on the organization's background, as does the material from Masteralexis, Barr, and Hums, excerpted from *Principles and Practice of Sport Management* (3rd edition).

What most informal critics miss when contemplating collegiate sports is the actual governing structure of the NCAA. Those who understand college athletics point out that the NCAA is not a monolithic organization that dictates what occurs in the governance of collegiate sports. The NCAA is, in fact, governed by its over 1000 member institutions. The NCAA is divided into three divisions. In 2008–2009, 330 institutions were competing in the three Division I subdivisions: 119 in the Football Bowl Subdivision (formerly Division I-A), 118 in the Football Championship Subdivision (formerly Division I-AA), and 93 in the Division I Without Football Subdivision (formerly Division I-AAA). The Division II level had 282 institutions, and Division III had 422 institutions. It is these member organizations that determine how collegiate sports will operate via the numerous representative paths in the NCAA. Governing rules address issues ranging from eligibility to the operation of championships. The selection from Yasser, McCurdy, Goplerud, and Weston provides a textbook overview of the organization.

The rules of the NCAA are set forth in the organization's constitution and bylaws, which are available in the NCAA Manual. Governing information may be found at http://www.ncaa.org.

A BRIEF HISTORY OF THE NATIONAL COLLEGIATE ATHLETIC ASSOCIATION'S ROLE IN REGULATING INTERCOLLEGIATE ATHLETICS

Rodney K. Smith

. . . .

II.   A BRIEF HISTORY OF THE NATIONAL COLLEGIATE ATHLETIC ASSOCIATION

A.   1840–1910

The need for regulation of intercollegiate athletics in the United States has existed for at least a century and a half. One of the earliest interschool athletic events was a highbrow regatta between Harvard and Yale Universities, which was commercially sponsored by the then powerful Elkins Railroad Line.[5] Harvard University sought to gain an undue advantage over its academic rival Yale by obtaining the services of a coxswain who was not a student.[6] Thus, the commercialization and propensity to seek unfair advantages existed virtually from the beginning of organized intercollegiate athletics in the United States. The problem of cheating, which was no doubt compounded by the increasing commercialization of sport, was a matter of concern.[7] Initially, these concerns led institutions to move the athletic teams from student control to faculty oversight.[8] Nevertheless, by the latter part of the nineteenth century, two leading university presidents were voicing their fears that intercollegiate athletics were out of control.[9] President Eliot at Harvard was very concerned about the impact that commercialization of intercollegiate athletics was having, and charged that "lofty gate receipts from college athletics had turned amateur contests into major commercial spectacles."[10] In the same year, President Walker of the Massachusetts Institute of Technology bemoaned the fact that intercollegiate athletics had lost its academic moorings and opined that "[i]f the movement shall continue at the same rate, it will soon be fairly a question whether the letters B.A. stand more for Bachelor of Arts or Bachelor of Athletics."[11] In turn, recognizing the difficulty of overseeing intercollegiate athletics at the institutional level, whether through the faculty or the student governance, conferences were being created both to facilitate the playing of a schedule of games and to provide a modicum of regulation at a broader level.[12]

Despite the shift from student control to faculty oversight and some conference regulation, intercollegiate athletics remained under-regulated and a source of substantial concern.[13]

Rising concerns regarding the need to control the excesses of intercollegiate athletics were compounded by the fact that in 1905 alone, there were over eighteen deaths and one hundred major injuries in intercollegiate football.[14] National attention was turned to intercollegiate athletics when President [Theodore] Roosevelt called for a White House conference to review football rules.[15] President Roosevelt invited officials from the major football programs to participate.[16] Deaths and injuries in football persisted, however, and Chancellor Henry MacCracken of New York University called for a national meeting of representatives of the nation's major intercollegiate football programs to determine whether football could be regulated or had to be abolished at the intercollegiate level.[17] Representatives of many major intercollegiate football programs accepted Chancellor MacCracken's invitation and ultimately formed a Rules Committee.[18] President Roosevelt then sought to have participants in the White House conference meet with the new Rules Committee.[19] This combined effort on the part of educators and the White House eventually led to a concerted effort to reform intercollegiate football rules, resulting in the formation of the Intercollegiate Athletic Association (hereinafter IAA), with sixty-two original members.[20] In 1910, the IAA was renamed the NCAA.[21] Initially, the NCAA was formed to formulate rules that could be applied to the various intercollegiate sports.[22] [*Ed. Note: The NCAA's current stated purposes are shown in* **Figure 1**.]

In the years prior to the formation of the NCAA, schools wrestled with the same issues that we face today: the extreme pressure to win, which is compounded by the commercialization of sport, and the need for regulations and a regulatory body to ensure fairness and safety.[23] In terms of regulation, between 1840 and 1910, there was a movement from loose student control of athletics to faculty oversight, from faculty oversight to the creation of conferences, and, ultimately, to the development of a national entity for governance purposes.[24]

B.   1910–1970

In its early years, the NCAA did not play a major role in governing intercollegiate athletics.[25] It did begin to stretch beyond merely making rules for football and other games played, to the creation of a national championship event in various sports.[26] Indeed, students, with some faculty oversight, continued to be the major force in running intercollegiate athletics.[27] By the 1920s, however, intercollegiate athletics were quickly becoming an integral part of higher education in the United States.[28] Public interest in sport at the intercollegiate level, which had always been high, continued to increase in intensity, particularly as successful and entertaining programs developed, and also with increasing access to higher education on the part of students from all segments of society.[29]

The purposes of this Association are:

(a) To initiate, stimulate and improve intercollegiate athletics programs for student-athletes and to promote and develop educational leadership, physical fitness, athletics excellence and athletics participation as a recreational pursuit;

(b) To uphold the principle of institutional control of, and responsibility for, all intercollegiate sports in conformity with the constitution and bylaws of this Association;

(c) To encourage its members to adopt eligibility rules to comply with satisfactory standards of scholarship, sportsmanship and amateurism;

(d To formulate, copyright and publish rules of play governing intercollegiate athletics;

(e) To preserve intercollegiate athletics records;

(f) To supervise the conduct of, and to establish eligibility standards for, regional and national athletics events under the auspices of this Association;

(g) To cooperate with other amateur athletics organizations in promoting and conducting national and international athletics events;

(h) To legislate, through bylaws or by resolutions of a Convention, upon any subject of general concern to the members related to the administration of intercollegiate athletics; and

(i) To study in general all phases of competitive intercollegiate athletics and establish standards whereby the colleges and universities of the United States can maintain their athletics programs on a high level.

Figure 1   NCAA Constitution, Article 1.2: Purposes

Source: 2009–2010 *NCAA Division I Manual,* p. 1. © National Collegiate Athletic Association. 2008–2010. All rights reserved.

With this growing interest in intercollegiate sports and attendant increases in commercialization, outside attention again focused on governance and related issues.[30] In 1929, the highly respected Carnegie Foundation for the Advancement of Education issued a significant report regarding intercollegiate athletics and made the following finding:

[A] change of values is needed in a field that is sodden with the commercial and the material and the vested interests that these forces have created. Commercialism in college athletics must be diminished and college sport must rise to a point where it is esteemed primarily and sincerely for the opportunities it affords to mature youth.[31]

The Carnegie Report, echoing themes that appear ever so relevant in the year 2000, concluded that college presidents could reclaim the integrity of sport.[32] College administrators "could change the policies permitting commercialized and professionalized athletics that boards of trustees had previously sanctioned."[33]

While the NCAA made some minor attempts to restructure rules to increase integrity in the governance of intercollegiate athletics, those efforts were insufficient to keep pace with the growing commercialization of, and interest in, intercollegiate athletics.[34] Recruitment of athletes was not new, but the rising desire to win, with all its commercial ramifications, contributed to recruitment being raised to new heights.[35] Red Grange, for example, is often given credit for "starting the competition for football talent through . . . recruiting."[36] Public interest in intercollegiate athletics continued to increase

with support from the federal government during the 1930s. The capacity of the NCAA to regulate excesses was not equal to the daunting task presented by the growth of, interest in, and commercialization of sport.[37]

After World War II, with a dramatic increase in access to higher education on the part of all segments of society, largely through government support for returning military personnel to attend college, public interest expanded even more dramatically than it had in the past.[38] Increased interest, not surprisingly, led to even greater commercialization of intercollegiate athletics. With the advent of television, the presence of radios in the vast majority of homes in the United States, and the broadcasting of major sporting events, these pressures further intensified.[39] More colleges and universities started athletic programs, while others expanded existing programs, in an effort to respond to increasing interest in intercollegiate athletics. These factors, coupled with a series of gambling scandals and recruiting excesses, caused the NCAA to promulgate additional rules, resulting in an expansion of its governance authority.[40]

In 1948, the NCAA enacted the so-called "Sanity Code," which was designed to "alleviate the proliferation of exploitive practices in the recruitment of student-athletes."[41] To enforce the rules in the Sanity Code, the NCAA created the Constitutional Compliance Committee to interpret rules and investigate possible violations.[42] Neither the Sanity Code with its rules, nor the Constitutional Compliance Committee with its enforcement responsibility, were successful because their only sanction was expulsion, which was so severe that it rendered the committee impotent and the rules ineffectual.[43] Recognizing this, the NCAA repealed the Sanity Code in 1951, replacing the Constitutional Compliance Committee with the Committee on Infractions, which was given broader sanctioning authority.[44] Thus, in 1951, the NCAA began to exercise more earnestly the authority which it had been given by its members.[45]

Two other factors are worth noting in the 1950s: (1) Walter Byers became Executive Director of the NCAA, and contributed to strengthening the NCAA, and its enforcement division, over the coming years to televise intercollegiate football; and (2) the NCAA negotiated its first contract valued in excess of one million dollars, opening the door to increasingly lucrative television contracts in the future.[46] The NCAA was entering a new era, in which its enforcement authority had been increased, a strong individual had been hired as executive director, and revenues from television were beginning to provide it with the wherewithal to strengthen its capacity in enforcing the rules that were being promulgated.[47] Through the 1950s and 1960s, the NCAA's enforcement capacity increased annually.[48]

C.   1971–1983

By 1971, as its enforcement capacity had grown yearly in response to new excesses arising from increased interest and commercialization, the NCAA was beginning to be criticized for alleged unfairness in the exercise of its enhanced enforcement authority.[49] Responding to these criticisms, the NCAA formed a committee to study the enforcement process, and ultimately, in 1973, adopted recommendations developed by that committee designed to divide the prosecutorial and investigative roles of the Committee on Infractions.[50] In the early 1970s, as well, the membership of the NCAA decided to create divisions, whereby schools would be placed in divisions that would better reflect their competitive capacity.[51] Despite these efforts, however, by 1976, when the NCAA was given additional authority to enforce the rules by penalizing schools directly and, as a result, athletes, coaches, and administrators indirectly, criticism of the NCAA's enforcement authority grew even more widespread.[52] Indeed, in 1978, the United States House of Representatives Subcommittee on Oversight and Investigation held hearings to investigate the alleged unfairness of the NCAA's enforcement processes.[53] Once again, the NCAA responded by adopting changes in its rules designed to address many of the criticisms made during the course of the hearings.[54] While concerns were somewhat abated, the NCAA's enforcement processes continued to be the source of substantial criticism through the 1970s and 1980s.[55]

The NCAA found itself caught between two critiques. On the one hand, it was criticized for responding inadequately to the increased commercialization of intercollegiate athletics, with all its attendant excesses; while on the other hand, it was criticized for unfairly exercising its regulatory authority.[56] Another factor began to have a major impact as well. University and college presidents were becoming more

directly concerned with the operation of the NCAA for two major reasons: (1) as enrollments were beginning to drop, and expenses were increasing in athletics and elsewhere, presidents began, with some ambivalence, to see athletics as an expense, and as a potential revenue and public relations source; and (2) they personally came to understand that their reputations as presidents were often tied to the success of the athletic program and they were, therefore, becoming even more fearful of the NCAA's enforcement authority.[57]

D.   1984–1999

In difficult economic times for higher education in the 1980s, university presidents increasingly found themselves caught between the pressures applied by influential members of boards of trustees and alumni, who often demanded winning athletic programs, and faculty and educators, who feared the rising commercialization of athletics and its impact on academic values.[58] Many presidents were determined to take an active, collective role in the governance of the NCAA, so they formed the influential Presidents Commission in response to these pressures.[59] In 1984, the Presidents Commission began to assert its authority, and by 1985, it took dramatic action by exercising their authority to call a special convention to be held in June of 1985.[60] This quick assertion of power led one sports writer to conclude that "There is no doubt who is running college sports. It's the college presidents."[61]

The presidents initially were involved in a number of efforts to change the rules, particularly in the interest of cost containment.[62] These efforts were not all successful.[63] Over time, however, the presidents were gaining a better understanding of the workings of the NCAA, and they were beginning to take far more interest in the actual governance of intercollegiate athletics.[64] A little over a decade later, the presidents' involvement grew to the extent that they had changed the very governance structure of the NCAA, with the addition of an Executive Committee and a Board of Directors for the various divisions, both of which are made up of presidents or chief executive officers.[65]

. . . .

During this time period, there were a number of additional developments that had an impact on the role of the NCAA in fulfilling its enforcement and governance of responsibilities. Even in a short history, like this one, a few of those developments are noteworthy.

As the role of television and the revenue it brings to intercollegiate athletics [have] grown in magnitude, the desire for an increasing share of those dollars has become intense. The first television event in the 1950s was a college football game, and the televising of college football games remained under the NCAA's control for a number of years.[83] In time, however, a group of powerful intercollegiate football programs were determined to challenge the NCAA's handling of the televising of games involving their schools.[84] In *NCAA v. Board of Regents,*[85] the United States Supreme Court held that the NCAA had violated antitrust laws.[86] This provided an opening for those schools, and the bowls that would ultimately court them, to directly reap the revenues from the televising of their football games.[87] . . . Because these schools have been able to funnel more television revenues in their direction, which has led to increases in other forms of revenue, they have gained access to resources that have unbalanced the playing field in football and other sports.[89]

Another matter that has dramatically impacted intercollegiate athletics during the past two decades is Title IX, with its call for gender equity in intercollegiate athletics.[90] With some emphasis on proportionality in opportunities and equity in expenditures for coaches and other purposes in women's sports, new opportunities have been made available for women in intercollegiate athletics.[91] The cost of these expanded opportunities has been high, however, particularly given that few institutions have women's teams that generate sufficient revenue to cover the cost of these added programs.[92] This increase in net expenses has placed significant pressure on intercollegiate athletic programs, particularly given that the presidents are cost-containment conscious, desiring that athletic programs be self-sufficient.[93] Revenue producing male sports, therefore, have to bear the weight of funding women's sports.[94] This, in turn, raises racial equity concerns because most of the revenue producing male sports are made up predominantly of male student-athletes of color,[95] who are expected to deliver a product that will not only produce sufficient revenue to cover its own expenses, but also a substantial portion of the costs of gender equity and male sports that are not revenue producing.[96]

The gender equity and television issues have been largely economic in their impact, but they do indirectly impact the role of the NCAA in governance. Since football funding has been diverted from the NCAA to the football powerhouses, the NCAA for the most part has had to rely even more heavily on its revenue from the lucrative television contract for the Division I basketball championship.[97] Heavy reliance on this funding source raises racial equity issues, since student-athletes of color, particularly African-American athletes, are the source of those revenues.[98] Thus, the very governance costs of the NCAA are covered predominantly by the efforts of these student-athletes of color.[99] This inequity is exacerbated by the fact that schools and conferences rely heavily on revenues from the basketball tournament to fund their own institutional and conference needs.[100]

Generally, developments during the past two decades have focused on governance and economic issues.[101] There have been some efforts, however, to enhance academic integrity and revitalize the role of faculty and students in overseeing intercollegiate athletics.[102] Of particular note in this regard has been the implementation of the certification process for intercollegiate athletic programs.[103] The certification process involves faculty, students (particularly student-athletes), and staff from an institution in preparing an in-depth self-study, including substantial institutional data in the form of required appendices.[104] The study covers the following areas: Governance and Rules Compliance, Academic Integrity, Fiscal Integrity, and Commitment to Equity.[105] This process helps institutions focus on academic values and related issues.[106] These efforts also provide the chief executive officers with additional information and a potentially enhanced role in intercollegiate athletics at the campus level.[107]

The past two decades have been active ones for the NCAA. With meteoric rises in television and related revenues, the commercialization of intercollegiate athletics has continued to grow at a pace that places significant strain on institutions and the NCAA. These commercial pressures, together with increasing costs related to non-revenue producing sports, costly gender equity requirements, and other resource demands (e.g., new facilities), make it challenging to maintain a viable enforcement process and a balanced playing field.

III. THE FUTURE

Over the past 150 years, the desire to win at virtually any cost, combined with the increases in public interest in intercollegiate athletics, in a consumer sense, have led inexorably to a highly commercialized world of intercollegiate athletics.[108] These factors have created new incentives for universities and conferences to find new ways to obtain an advantage over their competitors. This desire to gain an unfair competitive advantage has necessarily led to an expansion in rules and regulations. This proliferation of rules and the development of increasingly sophisticated regulatory systems necessary to enforce those rules, together with the importance that attaches to enforcement decisions, both economically and in terms of an institution's reputation (and derivatively its chief executive officer's career), places great strain on the capacity of the NCAA to govern intercollegiate athletics. This strain is unlikely to dissipate in the future because the pressures that have created the strain do not appear to be susceptible, in a practical sense, to amelioration. Indeed, the one certainty in the future of the NCAA is the likelihood that big-time intercollegiate athletics will be engaged in the same point–counterpoint that has characterized its history; increased commercialization and public pressure leading to more sophisticated rules and regulatory systems.

As rules and regulatory systems continue along the road of increased sophistication, the NCAA will more closely resemble its industry counterparts. It will develop an enforcement system that is more legalistic in its nature, as regulatory proliferation leads to increasing demands for fairness. In such a milieu, chief executive officers will have to take their responsibilities for intercollegiate athletics even more seriously.[109] It can be hoped, as well, that their involvement, and the increased involvement on the part of faculty and staff, through the certification process and otherwise, will lead to a more responsible system in terms of the maintenance of academic values. If the NCAA and those who lead at the institutional and conference levels are unable to maintain academic values in the face of economics and related pressures, the government may be less than a proverbial step away.[110]

Notes

. . . .

5. These regatta, which were student run for the most part, were among the first intercollegiate athletic events.

6. Rodney K. Smith, The National Collegiate Athletic Association's Death Penalty: How Educators Punish Themselves and Others, 62 Ind. L.J. 985, 988-89 (1987) [hereinafter Smith, Death Penalty]; Rodney K. Smith, Little Ado About Something: Playing Games With the Reform of Big-Time Athletics, 20 Cap. U. L. Rev. 567, 569–70 (1991) [hereinafter Smith, Little Ado].

7. The commercialization of intercollegiate athletics, with the payment of star athletes, was rather firmly entrenched by the latter part of the 19th Century. For example, it is reported that Hogan, a successful student-athlete at Yale at that time, was compensated with: (1) a suite of rooms in the dorm; (2) free meals at the University club; (3) a one-hundred dollar scholarship; (4) the profits from the sale of programs; (5) an agency arrangement with the American Tobacco Company, under which he received a commission on cigarettes sold in New Haven; and (6) a ten-day paid vacation to Cuba. See Smith, Death Penalty, supra note 6, at 989.

8. Id. at 989–90.

9. Smith, Little Ado, supra note 6, at 570.

10. Id.

11. Id.

12. Smith, Death Penalty, supra note 6, at 990.

13. Id.

14. Id.

15. George W. Schubert et al., Sports Law 1 (1986); Smith, Death Penalty, supra note 6, at 990.

16. Smith, Death Penalty, supra note 6, at 990.

17. Id.

18. Id.

19. Id.

20. Id. at 991; Schubert, supra note 15, at 2.

21. Id.

22. Id.

23. Smith, Little Ado, supra note 6, at 571.

24. Smith, Death Penalty, supra note 6, at 989–91.

25. Id. at 991.

26. Id.

27. Id.

28. Id.

29. Id.

30. Id.

31. Id.

32. Id.

33. Id.

34. Id. at 991–92.

35. Id. at 992.

36. Id. at 992.

37. Id.

38. Id.

39. Id. at 992.

40. Id.

41. Id.

42. Id.

43. Id. at 992–93.

44. Id. at 993.

45. Id.

46. Id.

47. Id.

48. Id.

49. Id. at 992.

50. Id. at 994.

51. Id. at 993.

52. Id. at 994.

53. Id.

54. Id.

55. Id. at 995.

56. Id.

57. Id. at 995–96.

58. Id. at 995; Rodney K. Smith, Reforming Intercollegiate Athletics: A Critique of the Presidents Commission's Role in the N.C.A.A.'s Sixth Special Convention, 64 N.D. L. Rev. 423, 427 (1988).

59. Smith, Death Penalty, supra note 6, at 996-97.

60. Smith, supra note 58, at 428-30.

61. Smith, Death Penalty, supra note 6, at 997.

62. Smith, supra note 58, at 428.

63. Id.

64. Id.

65. Manual, supra note 4, at 22–23.

. . . .

83. Schubert, supra note 15, at 2.

84. Id.

85. 468 U.S. 85 (1984).

86. Id. at 113, 120.

87. Schubert, supra note 15, at 57–58.

. . . .

89. It is clear that the membership of the College Football Association has been able to use those additional revenues to enhance their entire athletics program, giving them a competitive edge.

90. Rodney K. Smith, When Ignorance is Not Bliss: In Search of Racial and Gender Equity in Intercollegiate Athletics, 61 Mo. L. Rev. 329, 367 (1996).

91. Id. at 355.

92. Id. at 368.

93. Id. at 359-60.

94. Id. at 368.

95. Id. at 369–70.

96. Id. at 370.

97. Id. at 348.

98. Id. at 349.

99. Id.

100. Id. at 369-70.

101. Smith, Little Ado, supra note 6, at 573.

102. Smith, Death Penalty, supra note 6, at 1058.

103. This certification process has been in place for a number of years and is becoming institutionalized. Smith, Little Ado, supra note 6, at 573.

104. Id. at 573-74.

105. Id.

106. Id. at 576.

107. Id.

108. Smith, Death Penalty, supra note 6, at 991.

109. It can be anticipated, as well, that chief executive officers will be held increasingly accountable for rules violations at their institutions.

110. Just as the government (the legislative and judicial branches) became involved at the turn of the century and again in the 1970s, it is likely that similar oversight will occur in the future. With increased formalization of regulatory processes, the judiciary may well become more involved.

STRUCTURE

PRINCIPLES AND PRACTICE OF SPORT MANAGEMENT

Lisa Pike Masteralexis, Carol A. Barr, and Mary A. Hums

INTRODUCTION

Intercollegiate athletics is a major segment of the sport industry. It garners increasingly more television airtime as network and cable companies increase coverage of sporting events, it receives substantial coverage within the sports sections of local and national newspapers, and it attracts attention from corporations seeking potential sponsorship opportunities. Television rights fees have increased dramatically. Sport sponsorship opportunities and coaches' compensation figures have escalated as well. The business aspect of collegiate athletics has grown immensely as administrators and coaches at all levels have become more involved in budgeting, finding revenue sources, controlling expense items, and participating in fund development activities. The administrative aspects of collegiate athletics have also changed. With more rules and regulations to be followed, there is more paperwork in such areas as recruiting and academics. These changes have led to an increase in the number of personnel and the specialization of positions in collegiate athletic departments. Although the number of athletic administrative jobs has increased across all divisions, jobs can still be hard to come by because the popularity of working in this segment of the sport industry continues to rise.

The international aspect of this sport industry segment has grown tremendously through the participation of student-athletes who are nonresident aliens (a term used by the National Collegiate Athletic Association). Coaches are more aware of international talent when recruiting. The number of nonresident alien student-athletes competing on U.S. college sports teams has grown from an average of 1.7% of the male student-athletes in all divisions in 1999–2000 to 2.6% in 2004–2005. The male sports with the most nonresident alien representation are soccer (4.9% of all male soccer student-athletes), ice hockey (13.8%), and tennis (16.6%) (National Collegiate Athletic Association [NCAA], 2006b). On female sport teams, a similar increase in the number of nonresident alien participation has occurred. In 1999–2000, 1.5% of all female student-athletes were nonresident aliens, a percentage that increased to 2.8% in 2004–2005. The sports showing the largest representation are tennis (11.5%), ice hockey (14.5%), and badminton (17.4%) (NCAA, 2006b). Athletic teams are taking overseas trips for practice and competitions at increasing rates. College athletic games are being shown internationally, and licensed merchandise can be found around the world. It is not unusual to stroll down a street in Munich, Germany, or Montpellier, France, and see a Michigan basketball jersey or a Notre Dame football jersey.

History

On August 3, 1852, on Lake Winnepesaukee in New Hampshire, a crew race between Harvard and Yale was the very first intercollegiate athletic event in the United States (Dealy, 1990). What was unusual about this contest was that Harvard University is located in Cambridge, Massachusetts, and Yale University is located in New Haven, Connecticut, yet the crew race took place on a lake north of these two cities, in New Hampshire. Why? Because the first intercollegiate athletic contest was sponsored by the Boston, Concord & Montreal Railroad Company, which wanted to host the race in New Hampshire so that both teams, their fans, and other spectators would have to ride the railroad to get to the event (Dealy, 1990). Thus, the first intercollegiate athletic contest involved sponsorship by a company external to sports that used the competition to enhance the company's business.

The next sport to hold intercollegiate competitions was baseball. The first collegiate baseball contest was held in 1859 between Amherst and Williams (Davenport, 1985), two of today's more athletically successful Division III institutions. In this game, Amherst defeated Williams by the lopsided score of 73–32 (Rader, 1990). On November 6, 1869, the first intercollegiate football game was held between Rutgers and Princeton (Davenport, 1985). This "football" contest was far from the game of football known today. The competitors were allowed to kick and dribble the ball, similar to soccer, with Rutgers "outdribbling" its opponents and winning the game six goals to four (Rader, 1990).

The initial collegiate athletic contests taking place during the 1800s were student-run events. Students organized the practices and corresponded with their peers at other institutions to arrange competitions. There were no coaches or athletic administrators assisting them. The Ivy League schools became the "power" schools in athletic competition, and football became the premier sport. Fierce rivalries developed, attracting numerous spectators. Thus, collegiate athletics evolved from games being played for student enjoyment and participation to fierce competitions involving bragging rights for individual institutions.

Colleges and universities soon realized that these intercollegiate competitions had grown in popularity and prestige and thus could bring increased publicity, student applications, and alumni donations. As the pressure to win increased, the students began to realize they needed external help. Thus, the first "coach" was hired in 1864 by the Yale crew team to help it win, especially against its rival, Harvard University. This coach, William Wood, a physical therapist by trade, introduced a rigorous training program as well as a training table (Dealy, 1990). College and university administrators also began to take a closer look at intercollegiate athletics competitions. The predominant theme at the time was still nonacceptance of these activities within the educational sphere of the institution. With no governing organization and virtually nonexistent playing and eligibility rules, mayhem often resulted. Once again the students took charge, especially in football, forming the Intercollegiate Football Association in 1876. This association was made up of students from Harvard, Yale, Princeton, and Columbia who agreed on consistent playing and eligibility rules (Dealy, 1990).

The dangerous nature of football pushed faculty and administrators to get involved in governing intercollegiate

athletics. In 1881, Princeton University became the first college to form a faculty athletics committee to review football (Dealy, 1990). The committee's choices were to either make football safer to play or ban the sport altogether. In 1887, Harvard's Board of Overseers instructed the Harvard Faculty Athletics Committee to ban football. However, aided by many influential alumni, the Faculty Athletics Committee chose to keep the game intact (Dealy, 1990). In 1895, the Intercollegiate Conference of Faculty Representatives, better known as the Big Ten Conference, was formed to create student eligibility rules (Davenport, 1985). By the early 1900s, football on college campuses had become immensely popular, receiving a tremendous amount of attention from the students, alumni, and collegiate administrators. Nevertheless, the number of injuries and deaths occurring in football continued to increase, and it was evident that more legislative action was needed.

In 1905 during a football game involving Union College and New York University, Harold Moore, a halfback for Union College, was crushed to death. Moore was just one of 18 football players who died that year. An additional 149 serious injuries occurred (Yaeger, 1991). The chancellor of New York University, Henry Mitchell MacCracken, witnessed this incident and took it upon himself to do something about it. MacCracken sent a letter of invitation to presidents of other schools to join him for a meeting to discuss the reform or abolition of football. In December 1905, 13 presidents met and declared their intent to reform the game of football. When this group met three weeks later, 62 colleges and universities sent representatives. This group formed the Intercollegiate Athletic Association of the United States (IAAUS) to formulate rules making football safer and more exciting to play. Seven years later, in 1912, this group took the name National Collegiate Athletic Association (NCAA) (Yaeger, 1991).

In the 1920s, college and university administrators began recognizing intercollegiate athletics as a part of higher education and placed athletics under the purview of the physical education department (Davenport, 1985). Coaches were given academic appointments within the physical education department, and schools began to provide institutional funding for athletics.

The Carnegie Reports of 1929 painted a bleak picture of intercollegiate athletics, identifying many academic abuses, recruiting abuses, payments to student-athletes, and commercialization of athletics. The Carnegie Foundation visited 112 colleges and universities. One of the disturbing findings from this study was that although the NCAA "recommended against" both recruiting and subsidization of student-athletes, these practices were widespread among colleges and universities (Lawrence, 1987). The Carnegie Reports stated that the responsibility for control over collegiate athletics rested with the president of the college or university and with the faculty (Savage, 1929). The NCAA was pressured to change from an organization responsible for developing playing rules used in competitions to an organization that would oversee academic standards for student-athletes, monitor recruiting activities of coaches and administrators, and establish principles governing amateurism, thus alleviating the paying of student-athletes by alumni and booster groups (Lawrence, 1987).

Intercollegiate athletics experienced a number of peaks and valleys over the next 60 or so years as budgetary constraints during certain periods, such as the Great Depression and World War II, limited expenditures and growth among athletic departments and sport programs. In looking at the history of intercollegiate athletics, though, the major trends during these years were increased spectator appeal, commercialism, media coverage, alumni involvement, and funding. As these changes occurred, the majority of intercollegiate athletic departments moved from a unit within the physical education department to a recognized, funded department on campus.

Increased commercialism and the potential for monetary gain in collegiate athletics led to increased pressure on coaches to win. As a result, collegiate athletics experienced various problems with rule violations and academic abuses involving student-athletes. As these abuses increased, the public began to perceive that the integrity of higher education was being threatened. In 1989, pollster Louis Harris found that 78% of Americans thought collegiate athletics were out of hand. This same poll found that nearly two-thirds of Americans believed that state or federal legislation was needed to control college sports (Knight Foundation, 1993). In response, on October 19, 1989, the Trustees of the Knight Foundation created the Knight Commission, directing it to propose a reform agenda for intercollegiate athletics (Knight Foundation, 1991). The Knight Commission was composed of university presidents, CEOs and presidents of corporations, and a congressional representative. The reform agenda recommended by the Knight Commission played a major role in supporting legislation to alleviate improper activities and emphasized institutional control in an attempt to restore the integrity of collegiate sports. The Knight Commission's work and recommendations prompted the NCAA membership to pass numerous rules and regulations regarding recruiting activities, academic standards, and financial practices.

Whether improvements have occurred within college athletics as a result of the Knight Commission reform movement and increased presidential involvement has been debated among various constituencies over the years. Proponents of the NCAA and college athletics cite the skill development, increased health benefits, and positive social elements that participation in college athletics brings. In addition, the entertainment value of games and the improved graduation rates of college athletes (although men's basketball and football rates are still a focus of concern) in comparison with the student body overall are referenced. Those critical of college athletics, though, cite the continual recruiting violations, academic abuses, and behavioral problems of athletes and coaches. These critics are concerned with the commercialization and exploitation of student-athletes as well. . . .

. . . .

ORGANIZATIONAL STRUCTURE AND GOVERNANCE

The NCAA

The primary rule-making body for college athletics in the United States is the NCAA. Other college athletic organizations include the National Association of Intercollegiate Athletics (NAIA), founded in 1940 for small colleges and universities and having approximately 277 member institutions (National Association of Intercollegiate Athletics, 2006), and the National Junior College Athletic Association (NJCAA), founded in 1937 to promote and supervise a national program of junior college sports and activities and currently having approximately 550 member institutions (National Junior College Athletic Association, 2003).

The NCAA is a voluntary association with more than 1,200 institutions, conferences, organizations, and individual members. . . . All collegiate athletics teams, conferences, coaches, administrators, and athletes participating in NCAA-sponsored sports must abide by the association's rules.

The basic purpose of the NCAA as dictated in its constitution is to "maintain intercollegiate athletics as an integral part of the educational program and the athlete as an integral part of the student body and, by so doing, retain a clear line of demarcation between intercollegiate athletics and professional sports" (NCAA, 2005b, p. 1). Important to this basic purpose are the cornerstones of the NCAA's philosophy—namely, that college athletics are amateur competitions and that athletics are an important component of the institution's educational mission. [*Ed. Note: The fully stated basic purpose is shown in* **Figure 2.**]

The competitive athletics programs of member institutions are designed to be a vital part of the educational system. A basic purpose of this Association is to maintain intercollegiate athletics as an integral part of the educational program and the athlete as an integral part of the student body and, by so doing, retain a clear line of demarcation between intercollegiate athletics and professional sports.

Figure 2   NCAA Constitution, Article 1.3.1: Basic Purpose

Source: 2009–2010 NCAA Division I Manual, p. 1. © National Collegiate Athletic Association. 2008–2010. All rights reserved.

The NCAA has undergone organizational changes throughout its history in an attempt to improve the efficiency of its service to member institutions. In 1956, the NCAA split its membership into a University Division, for larger schools, and a College Division, for smaller schools, in an effort to address competitive inequities. In 1973, the current three-division system, made up of Division I, Division II, and Division III, was created to increase the flexibility of the NCAA in addressing the needs and interests of schools of varying size ("Study: Typical I-A Program," 1996). This NCAA organizational structure involved all member schools and conferences voting on legislation once every year at the NCAA annual convention. Every member school and conference had one vote, assigned to the institution's president or CEO, a structure called one-school/one-vote.

In 1995, the NCAA recognized that Divisions I, II, and III still faced "issues and needs unique to its member institutions," leading the NCAA to pass Proposal 7, "Restructuring," at the 1996 NCAA convention (Crowley, 1995). The restructuring plan, which took effect in August 1997, gave the NCAA divisions more responsibility for conduct within their division, gave more control to the presidents of member colleges and universities, and eliminated the one-school/one-vote structure. The NCAA annual convention of all member schools still takes place, but the divisions also hold division-specific mini-conventions or meetings. In addition, each division has a governing body called either the Board of Directors or Presidents Council, as well as a Management Council made up of presidents, CEOs, and athletic directors from member schools who meet and dictate policy and legislation within that division. The NCAA Executive Committee, consisting of representatives from each division as well as the NCAA Executive Director and chairs of each divisional Management Council, oversees the Presidential boards and Management Councils for each division.

Under the unique governance structure of the NCAA, the member schools oversee legislation regarding the conduct of intercollegiate athletics. Member institutions and conferences vote on proposed legislation, thus dictating the rules they need to follow. The NCAA National Office, located in Indianapolis, Indiana, enforces the rules the membership passes. Approximately 350 employees work at the NCAA National Office administering the policies, decisions, and legislation passed by the membership, as well as providing administrative services to all NCAA committees, member institutions, and conferences (NCAA, 2004c). The NCAA National Office is organized into departments, including administration, business, championships, communications, compliance, enforcement, educational resources, publishing, legislative services, and visitors center/special projects.

Two of the more prominent areas within the NCAA administrative structure are legislative services and enforcement. These two areas are pivotal because they deal with interpreting new NCAA legislation and enforcing these rules and regulations. . . .

The enforcement area was created in 1952 when the membership decided that such a mechanism was needed to enforce the association's legislation. The process consists of allegations of rules violations being referred to the association's investigative staff. The NCAA enforcement staff determines if a potential violation has occurred, with the institution being notified of such finding and the enforcement staff submitting its findings to the Committee on Infractions (NCAA, 2005g). The institution may also conduct its own investigation, reporting its findings to the Committee on Infractions.

If a violation is found, it may be classified as a secondary or a major violation. A secondary violation is defined as "a violation that is isolated or inadvertent in nature, provides or is intended to provide only a minimal recruiting, competitive or other advantage and does not include any significant recruiting inducement or extra benefit" (NCAA, 2005g, p. 343). A major violation is defined as "[A]ll violations other than secondary violations . . . , specifically those that provide an extensive recruiting or competitive advantage" (NCAA, 2005g, p. 344).

It is important to note that although the NCAA National Office staff members collect information and conduct investigations on possible rule violations, the matter still goes before the Committee on Infractions, a committee of peers (representatives of member institutions), which determines responsibility and assesses penalties. Penalties for secondary violations may include, among others, an athlete sitting out for a period of time, forfeiture of games, an institutional fine, or suspension of a coach for one or more competitions. Major violations carry more severe penalties to an institution, including, among others, bans from postseason play, an institutional fine, scholarship reductions, and recruiting restrictions.

Divisions I, II, and III

The latest NCAA organizational restructuring, which became effective in 1997, called for divisions to take more responsibility and control over their activities. This was due to the recognition of substantial differences among the divisions, both in terms of their philosophies as well as the way they do business. A few of the more prominent differences among divisions are highlighted in this section. . . . Each institution has its own philosophy regarding the structure and governance of its athletic department. In addition, generalizations regarding divisions are not applicable to all institutions within that division. For example, some Division III institutions, although not offering any athletic scholarships, can be described as following a nationally competitive, revenue-producing philosophy that is more in line with a Division I philosophy. . . . [*Ed. Note: See **Figure 3**.*]

Division I member institutions, in general, support the philosophy of competitiveness, generating revenue through

DIVISION I PHILOSOPHY

In addition to the purposes and fundamental policy of the National Collegiate Athletic Association, as set forth in Constitution 1, members of Division I support the following principles in the belief that these statements assist in defining the nature and purposes of the division. These statements are not binding on member institutions but serve as a guide for the preparation of legislation by the division and for planning and implementation of programs by institutions and conferences. A member of Division I:

(a) Subscribes to high standards of academic quality, as well as breadth of academic opportunity;

(b) Strives in its athletics program for regional and national excellence and prominence. Accordingly, its recruitment of student-athletes and its emphasis on and support of its athletics program are, in most cases, regional and national in scope;

(c) Recognizes the dual objective in its athletics program of serving both the university or college community (participants, student body, faculty-staff, alumni) and the general public (community, area, state, nation);

(d) Believes in offering extensive opportunities for participation in varsity intercollegiate athletics for both men and women;

(e) Sponsors at the highest feasible level of intercollegiate competition one or both of the traditional spectator-oriented, income-producing sports of football and basketball. In doing so, members of Division I recognize the differences in institutional objectives in support of football; therefore, the division provides competition in that sport in the Bowl Subdivision and the Championship Subdivision; (Revised: 12/15/06)

(f) Believes in scheduling its athletics contests primarily with other members of Division I, especially in the emphasized, spectator-oriented sports, as a reflection of its goal of maintaining an appropriate competitive level in its sports program;

(g) Maintains institutional control over all funds supporting athletics; and (Revised: 1/14/08 effective 8/1/08)

(h) Understands, respects and supports the programs and philosophies of other divisions. Occasionally, institutions from other divisions or athletics associations will seek membership in Division I. In such cases, the applicants should be required to meet, over a period of time, prescribed criteria for Division I membership in order to assure that such institutions agree and comply with the principles and program objectives embodied in this statement.

Figure 3   NCAA Division I Philosophy Statement

Source: 2009–2010 *NCAA Division I Manual*, p. 308. © National Collegiate Athletic Association. 2008–2010. All rights reserved.

athletics, and national success. This philosophy is reflected in the following principles taken from the Division I Philosophy Statement (NCAA, 2005h):

• Strives in its athletics program for regional and national excellence and prominence

• Recognizes the dual objective in its athletics program of serving both the university or college community (participants, student body, faculty-staff, alumni) and the general public (community, area, state, nation)

. . . .

• Strives to finance its athletics program insofar as possible from revenues generated by the program itself

Division I schools that have football are further divided into two subdivisions: Division I-A, Football Bowl Division, is the category for the somewhat larger football-playing schools in Division I, and Division I-AA, Football Championship Division, is the category for institutions playing football at the next level. Division I-A institutions must meet minimum attendance requirements for football, whereas Division I-AA institutions are not held to any attendance requirements. Division I institutions that do not sponsor a football team are often referred to as Division I-AAA.

Division II institutions usually attract student-athletes from the local or in-state area who may receive some athletic scholarship money but usually not a full ride. Division II athletics programs are financed in the institution's budget like other academic departments on campus. Traditional rivalries with regional institutions dominate schedules (NCAA, 2004d).

Division III institutions do not allow athletic scholarships and encourage participation by maximizing the number and variety of athletics opportunities available to students. [*Ed. Note: See **Figure 4**.*] Division III institutions also emphasize the participant's experience, rather than the experience of the spectator, and place primary emphasis on regional in-season and conference competition (NCAA, 2004d).

Beyond the different philosophies just discussed, it is important to note some of the other differences that exist among the divisions. Division I athletic departments are usually larger in terms of the number of sport programs sponsored, the number of coaches, and the number of administrators. Division I member institutions have to sponsor at least seven

DIVISION III PHILOSOPHY

Colleges and universities in Division III place highest priority on the overall quality of the educational experience and on the successful completion of all students' academic programs. They seek to establish and maintain an environment in which a student-athlete's athletics activities are conducted as an integral part of the student-athlete's educational experience, and in which coaches play a significant role as educators. They also seek to establish and maintain an environment that values cultural diversity and gender equity among their student-athletes and athletics staff. (Revised: 1/10/95, 1/9/06 effective 8/1/06) To achieve this end, Division III institutions:

(a) Place special importance on the impact of athletics on the participants rather than on the spectators and place greater emphasis on the internal constituency (e.g., students, alumni, institutional personnel) than on the general public and its entertainment needs;

(b) Shall not award financial aid to any student on the basis of athletics leadership, ability, participation or performance; (Revised: 7/24/07)

(c) Encourage the development of sportsmanship and positive societal attitudes in all constituents, including student-athletes, coaches, administrative personnel and spectators;

(d) Encourage participation by maximizing the number and variety of athletics opportunities for their students;

(e) Assure that the actions of coaches and administrators exhibit fairness, openness and honesty in their relationships with student-athletes;

(f) Assure that athletics participants are not treated differently from other members of the student body;

(g) Assure that athletics programs support the institution's educational mission by financing, staffing and controlling the programs through the same general procedures as other departments of the institution. Further, the administration of an institution's athletics program (e.g., hiring, compensation, professional development, certification of coaches) should be integrated into the campus culture and educational mission; (Revised: 1/9/06 effective 8/1/06)

(h) Assure that athletics recruitment complies with established institutional policies and procedures applicable to the admission process; (Adopted: 1/12/04 effective 8/1/04)

(i) Assure that academic performance of student-athletes is, at a minimum, consistent with that of the general student body; (Adopted: 1/9/06 effective 8/1/06)

(j) Assure that admission policies for student-athletes comply with policies and procedures applicable to the general student body; (Adopted: 1/9/06 effective 8/1/06)

(k) Provide equitable athletics opportunities for males and females and give equal emphasis to men's and women's sports;

(l) Support ethnic and gender diversity for all constituents; (Adopted: 1/12/99)

(m) Give primary emphasis to regional in-season competition and conference championships; and

(n) Support student-athletes in their efforts to reach high levels of athletics performance, which may include opportunities for participation in national championships, by providing all teams with adequate facilities, competent coaching and appropriate competitive opportunities.

The purpose of the NCAA is to assist its members in developing the basis for consistent, equitable competition while minimizing infringement on the freedom of individual institutions to determine their own special objectives and programs. The above statement articulates principles that represent a commitment to Division III membership and shall serve as a guide for the preparation of legislation by the division and for planning and implementation of programs by institutions and conferences.

Figure 4   NCAA Division III Philosophy Statement

Source: 2009–2010 *NCAA Division III Manual*, p. vii. © National Collegiate Athletic Association. 2008–2010. All rights reserved.

sports of all-male or mixed-gender teams and seven all-female teams, or six sports of all-male or mixed-gender teams and eight all-female teams. Division I-A football-playing institutions must sponsor a minimum of 16 sports, including a minimum of six sports involving all-male or mixed-gender teams and a minimum of eight all-female teams (NCAA, 2005i). Division I athletic departments also have larger budgets due to the number of athletic scholarships allowed, the operational budgets needed for the larger number of sport programs sponsored, and the salary costs associated with the larger number of coaches and administrators. Division II

institutions have to sponsor at least four men's sports and four women's sports, and allow athletic scholarships but on a more modest basis than Division I. Division III institutions have to sponsor five sports for men and five sports for women and do not allow athletic scholarships.

Conferences

The organizational structure of intercollegiate athletics also involves member conferences of the NCAA. Member conferences must have a minimum of six member institutions within a single division to be recognized as a voting member conference of the NCAA (NCAA, 2005c). Conferences provide many benefits and services to their member institutions. For example, conferences have their own compliance director and run seminars regarding NCAA rules and regulations in an effort to better educate member schools' coaches and administrators. Conferences also have legislative power over their member institutions in the running of championship events and the formulation of conference rules and regulations. Conferences sponsor championships in sports sponsored by the member institutions within the conference. The conference member institutions vote on the conference guidelines to determine the organization of these conference championships. Conferences may also provide a revenue-sharing program to their member institutions in which revenue realized by the conference through NCAA distributions, TV contracts, or participation in football bowl games is shared among all member institutions. . . .

Conferences have their own conference rules. Member institutions of a particular conference must adhere to conference rules in addition to NCAA rules. It is important to note, though, that although a conference rule can never be less restrictive than an NCAA rule, many conferences maintain additional rules that hold member institutions to stricter standards. For example, the Ivy League is a Division I NCAA member conference, but it prohibits its member institutions from providing athletic scholarships to student-athletes. Therefore, the Ivy League schools, although competing against other Division I schools that allow athletic scholarships, do not allow their athletic departments to award athletic scholarships.

Conference realignment is one of the . . . issues affecting collegiate athletic departments. Over a six-month period from June 2003 through December 2003, about 20 Division I-A schools alone changed conferences (Rosenberg, 2003). Some of the reasons for a school's wanting to join a conference or change conference affiliation are (1) exposure from television contracts with existing conferences, (2) potential for more revenue from television and corporate sponsorships through conference revenue sharing, (3) the difficulty independent schools experience in scheduling games and generating revenue, and (4) the ability of a conference to hold a championship game in football, which can generate millions of dollars in revenue for the conference schools if the conference possesses at least 12 member institutions.

One of the biggest conference realignments involved the demise of the 80-year-old Southwest Conference. In 1990, the Southwest Conference (SWC) comprised nine member schools (Mott, 1994). In August 1990, the University of Arkansas accepted a bid to leave the Southwest Conference and join the Southeast Conference (SEC). The university stated that the SEC gave it bigger crowds in revenue-producing sports and more national exposure ("Broyles Hopes," 1990). In 1994, four Southwest Conference schools—Texas, Texas A&M, Baylor, and Texas Tech—announced they were leaving to join the Big Eight Conference (Mott, 1994). In April

1994, three other SWC schools—Rice, Texas Christian University, and Southern Methodist University—joined the Western Athletic Conference (WAC) ("Western Athletic," 1994). Thus, the Southwest Conference had lost all of its member schools except Houston. This led to the demise of the Southwest Conference because it dropped below the six-member school minimum required by the NCAA for recognition as a member conference. Houston, the sole remaining SWC school, joined Conference USA in 1995.

The demise of the Southwest Conference due to conference realignment has been rivaled recently with the 2003–2004 realignment that has affected six Division I-A conferences. This realignment was initiated by the movement of the University of Miami, Virginia Tech, and Boston College from the Big East Conference to the Atlantic Coast Conference. With three of its eight football-playing schools leaving for the ACC, the Big East invited five schools from Conference USA (Cincinnati, Louisville, South Florida, Marquette, and DePaul) to join it (Lee, 2003). Conference USA also lost two schools, St. Louis and University of North Carolina–Charlotte, to the Atlantic 10 Conference. Conference USA subsequently went looking for schools for its conference, with Marshall and Central Florida from the Mid-American Conference, and Southern Methodist University, Tulsa, Texas–El Paso, and Rice from the Western Athletic Conference accepting the invitation (Watkins, 2004). The Western Athletic Conference added New Mexico State and Utah State from the Sun Belt Conference (Lee, 2003). There is sure to be more conference shuffling among NCAA member institutions as the conferences seek stability.

. . . .

Title IX/Gender Equity

Perhaps no greater issue has affected collegiate athletic departments over the past couple of decades than Title IX or gender equity. . . . Title IX is a federal law passed in 1972 that prohibits sex discrimination in any educational activity or program receiving federal financial assistance. Early in its history, there was much confusion as to whether Title IX applied to college athletic departments. Title IX gained its enforcement power among college athletic departments with the passage of the 1988 Civil Rights Restoration Act. In 1991, the NCAA released the results of a gender-equity study that found that although the undergraduate enrollment on college campuses was roughly 50% male and 50% female, collegiate athletic departments on average were made up of 70% male and 30% female student-athletes. In addition, this NCAA study found that the male student-athletes were receiving 70% of the athletic scholarship money, 77% of the operational budget, and 83% of the recruiting dollars available (NCAA Gender Equity Task Force, 1991). In response to such statistics, an increase in the number of sex discrimination lawsuits took place, with the courts often ruling in favor of the female student-athletes.

Collegiate athletic administrators started to realize that Title IX would be enforced by the Office for Civil Rights (OCR) and the courts, and as athletic administrators they would be required to provide equity within their athletic departments. The struggle athletic administrators are faced with is how to comply with Title IX given institutional financial limitations, knowing that lack of funding is not an excuse for not complying with Title IX. To bring male and female participation numbers closer to the percentage of undergraduate students by sex at the institution, numerous institutions are choosing to eliminate sport programs for men, thereby reducing the participation and funding on the men's side. Another method selected by some institutions is capping roster sizes for men's teams, known as roster management, thus keeping the men's numbers in check while trying to increase women's participation. A third, and most appropriate, option under Title IX is increasing participation and funding opportunities for female student-athletes. Of course, in selecting this option, the athletic administrator must be able to raise the funds necessary to add sport programs, hire new coaches, and provide uniforms for the new sport programs.

The debate surrounding Title IX continues, with numerous organizations (e.g., the National Women's Law Center, Women's Sports Foundation, and National Organization for Women), as well as advocates within the college athletic setting, arguing the merits of Title IX and that the appropriate enforcement methods are being used. In contrast, though, organizations such as USA Gymnastics and the National Wrestling Coaches Association are concerned about the effects Title IX has had on their sport (men's teams) and in particular are questioning the appropriateness of certain Title IX compliance standards. About 400 men's college teams were eliminated during the 1990s, with the sport of men's wrestling being hit particularly hard. The National Wrestling Coaches Association filed a lawsuit against the Department of Education arguing that the male student-athletes were being discriminated against as a result of the Title IX enforcement standards directly causing a reduction in men's sports. This lawsuit was dismissed in May 2004, with an appeals court panel ruling that the parties lacked standing to file the lawsuit, which instead should be litigated against individual colleges that eliminated men's sports ("Appeals Court," 2004). To date, these types of lawsuits have not been effective for male student-athletes. In May 2004, Myles Brand, [then] president of the NCAA, endorsed Title IX while speaking at a meeting of the National Wrestling Coaches Association, stating that it should not be used as an excuse or a cause for elimination of sport programs. Instead, these are institutional decisions reflected in the statistic that although the number of men's wrestling and gymnastics teams, among others, has declined over the past two decades (from 363 to 222), the number of football teams over the same time period has increased (from 497 to 619) ("Brand Defends Title IX," 2004).

A study by *The Chronicle of Higher Education* in 1995–1996 found that undergraduate enrollment on college campuses was 53% women, yet athletic departments were made up of 63% male student-athletes and 37% female student-athletes, with the women student-athletes receiving 38% of athletic scholarship funding (Naughton, 1997). More recently, the 2003–2004 NCAA Gender Equity Report found undergraduate enrollments at Division I schools to be 53.4% female, while student-athletes were 44% female. In addition, female student-athletes in 2003–2004 were receiving 45% of the athletic scholarship funding (NCAA, 2006c). Although these recent statistics do indicate improvements in gender equity, there is still much work to be done. Collegiate athletic administrators must continue to address this issue and develop strategies within their athletic departments to comply with Title IX and achieve gender equity.

Hiring Practices for Minorities and Women

In December 2003, Sylvester Croom became the first African American head football coach in the 71-year history of the Southeastern Conference (Longman & Glier, 2003). The hiring of Croom was a much needed milestone for the SEC, the last major conference to hire a black football coach. But it signified only a small step in the progress toward improvement that still needs to take place. The hiring of Mario Cristobal at Florida International and Randy Shannon at the University of Miami in December 2006 brought the total number of minority Division I-A head football coaches to 7 out of 119 positions (O'Toole, 2006).

Minority hiring has long been an issue of concern and debate within collegiate athletics. In 1993–1994, the NCAA's Minority Opportunity and Interests Committee found that African Americans accounted for fewer than 10% of athletic directors and 8% of head coaches, and when predominantly African American institutions were eliminated from the study, the results dropped to 4% representation in both categories (Wieberg, 1994). Not much improvement, if any, has taken place. . . .

The Black Coaches' Association (BCA) announced in October 2003 the establishment of a "hiring report card" to monitor football hiring practices at major institutions. Grades are based on contact with the BCA during the hiring process, efforts to interview candidates of color, the number of minorities involved in the hiring process, the time frame for each search, and adherence to institutional affirmative action hiring policies (Dufresne, 2003).

Women have also lacked appropriate representation among administrators at the collegiate level. . . . This issue continues to demand—appropriately so—the attention of college athletic directors, in the hiring of coaches, and of institutional presidents, in the hiring of athletic directors.

Academic Reform

Since the early 1990s and the publication of the Knight Commission reports that criticized the NCAA's academic legislation and academic preparation of student-athletes, the NCAA has been involved in numerous academic reform measures. The Knight Commission noted that although Proposition 48 was in place (to be eligible to play his or her first year in college, the student-athlete was required to possess a 2.0 minimum grade-point average [GPA] in 11 high school core curriculum courses while also meeting a minimum 700 SAT standard [equates to an 820 score under the "revised" SAT]), student-athlete graduation rates were low. Student-athletes could maintain eligibility to compete in athletics while not adequately progressing toward a degree (Knight Foundation, 1991). Satisfactory progress requirements were added, requiring student-athletes to possess a minimum GPA while taking an appropriate percentage of degree-required courses each year.

In response to concern that the SAT may be biased and in an attempt to increase the graduation rates of student-athletes, Proposition 16 went into effect in 1996–1997. This initial eligibility academic legislation required student-athletes to possess a minimum GPA in 13 core courses, with a corresponding SAT score along a sliding scale. If the student-athlete had a minimum GPA of 2.0, he or she needed a minimum SAT score of 1010. The student-athlete would then need to possess a corresponding GPA and SAT score along a scale to the minimum SAT of 820, which corresponded with a 2.5 GPA requirement. This legislation was changed through Bylaw 14.3, which became effective for all student-athletes entering a collegiate institution on or after August 1, 2005. Bylaw 14.3 requires student-athletes to meet a minimum GPA standard in 14 core courses, with a corresponding SAT score, but the sliding scale was changed to range from a 2.0 GPA with a 1010 SAT minimum to a 3.55 GPA with a minimum 400 SAT (NCAA, 2005f). In addition, satisfactory progress requirements were made more stringent to push student-athletes toward graduating within six years.

The NCAA initiated the latest academic reform proposal, the Academic Progress Rate (APR) or incentive/disincentive plan, in the fall of 2004. The new system collects data on a team's academic results based on eligibility and retention of student-athletes from the previous academic year. Results are then tied to recruiting opportunities, number of athletic scholarships, postseason eligibility, and NCAA revenue distribution (Alesia, 2004). The academic progress rate is calculated by awarding up to two points per student-athlete per semester or quarter (one point for being enrolled and one point for being on track to graduate). The total points earned are divided by the total possible points. A team can be subject to penalties if its score falls below 925, a figure the NCAA calculates as a predictor of a 60% graduation rate (Timanus, 2006). Penalties, such as a reduction in the maximum number of financial aid counters a sport is permitted to award, began in 2006–2007 and were based on three years of data.

In October 2005, the NCAA Division I Board of Directors approved a plan to spend up to $10 million annually on a program intended to help more college athletes graduate. The NCAA plans to give half of the money ($5 million annually) to institutions whose athletics programs make big improvements in their academic performance over the previous year. An additional $3 million would go to colleges that can demonstrate that they need money for tutors or programs that help athletes do well in the classroom. The rest of the money would reward athletics programs that are already doing well, with individual institutions receiving a maximum of $100,000 each (Wolverton, 2005).

Academic progress, academic preparations, and the graduation rate of student-athletes will continue to be issues of importance as college athletics and the educational mission of colleges and universities continue to coexist.

. . . .

References

. . . .

Alesia, M. (2004, January 10). NCAA thinks new system can aid academics. *The Indianapolis Star*. Retrieved on January 12, 2004, from http://www.indystar.com/articles/1/110210-4641-P.html

Appeals court: Individual colleges to blame for cuts. (2004, May 14). ESPN.com. Retrieved on May 17, 2004, from http://sports.espn.go.com/epsn/ news/story?id;eq1801717

. . . .

Brand defends Title IX. (2004, May 21). LubbockOnline.com. Retrieved on May 21, 2004, from http://www.lubbockonline.com

Broyles hopes a move won't end Arkansas' SWC rivalries. (1990, August 1). *The NCAA News*, p. 20.

Crowley, J. N. (1995, December 18). History demonstrates that change is good. *The NCAA News*, p. 4.

. . . .

Davenport, J. (1985). From crew to commercialism— the paradox of sport in higher education. In D. Chu, J. O. Segrave, & B. J. Becker (Eds.), *Sport and higher education* (pp. 5–16). Champaign, IL: Human Kinetics.

Dealy, F. X. (1990). *Win at any cost.* New York: Carol Publishing Group.

Dufresne, C. (2003, October 22). BCA to grade hiring efforts. *Los Angeles Times*. Retrieved on October 22, 2003, from http://www.latimes.com/sports/la-sp-bca22oct22,1,1607383

. . . .

Knight Foundation Commission on Intercollegiate Athletics. (1991, March). *Keeping faith with the student-athlete.* Charlotte, NC: Knight Foundation.

Knight Foundation Commission on Intercollegiate Athletics. (1993, March). *A new beginning for a new century.* Charlotte, NC: Knight Foundation.

. . . .

Lawrence, P. R. (1987). *Unsportsmanlike conduct.* New York: Praeger Publishers.

Lee, J. (2003, December 8–14). Who pays, who profits in realignment? *SportsBusiness Journal*, 25–33.

Longman, J., & Glier, R. (2003, December 2). The S.E.C. has its first black football coach. *The New York Times*. Retrieved on December 2, 2003, from http://www.nytimes.com/2003/12/02/sports/ncaafootball/02CROO.html

. . . .

Mott, R. D. (1994, March 2). Big Eight growth brings a new look to Division I-A. *The NCAA News*, p. 1.

National Association of Intercollegiate Athletics. (2006). About the NAIA. Retrieved on September 23, 2006, from http://naia.cstv.com/member-services/about/members.htm

. . . .

National Collegiate Athletic Association. (2004c). The history of the NCAA. Retrieved on June 14, 2004, from http://www.ncaa.org/about/history.html

National Collegiate Athletic Association. (2004d). What's the difference between Division I, II, and III? Retrieved on June 14, 2004, from http://www.ncaa.org/about/div_criteria.html

. . . .

National Collegiate Athletic Association. (2005b). Article 1.3.1: Basic purpose. In *2005–06 NCAA Division I manual*. Indianapolis, IN: Author.

National Collegiate Athletic Association. (2005c). Article 3.3.2.2.2.1: Full voting privileges. In *2005–06 NCAA Division I manual*. Indianapolis, IN: Author.

. . . .

National Collegiate Athletic Association. (2005f). Article 14.3: Freshman academic requirements. In *2005–06 NCAA Division I manual*. Indianapolis, IN: Author.

National Collegiate Athletic Association. (2005g). Article 19.02.2: Types of violations. In *2005–06 NCAA Division I manual*. Indianapolis, IN: Author.

National Collegiate Athletic Association. (2005h). Article 20.9: Division I philosophy statement. In *2005–06 NCAA Division I manual*. Indianapolis, IN: Author.

National Collegiate Athletic Association. (2005i). Article 20.9.6: Division I-A football requirements. In *2005–06 NCAA Division I manual*. Indianapolis, IN: Author.

. . . .

National Collegiate Athletic Association. (2006b). 1999–00-2004–05 NCAA race and ethnicity report. Retrieved on November 1, 2006, from http://www.ncaa.org/library/research/ethnicity_report/index.html

National Collegiate Athletic Association. (2006c). 2003–04 NCAA gender-equity report. Retrieved on February 9, 2007, from http://www.ncaa.org/library/research/gender_equity_study/2003-04/2003-04_gender_equity_report.pdf

. . . .

National Collegiate Athletic Association. (2006g). NCAA enforcement/infractions. Retrieved on October 1, 2006, from http://www.ncaa.org/enforcement

. . . .

National Junior College Athletic Association. (2003). NJCAA history. Retrieved on August 1, 2003, from http://www.njcaa.org/history.cfm

NCAA Gender Equity Task Force. (1991). *NCAA gender equity report*. Overland Park, KS: National Collegiate Athletic Association.

Naughton, J. (1997, April 11). Women in Division I sport programs: "The glass is half empty and half full." *The Chronicle of Higher Education*, pp. A39–A40.

O'Toole, T. (2006, December 20). Division I-A minority coaches grows to seven. *USA Today*, p. C1.

. . . .

Rader, B. G. (1990). *American sports* (2nd ed.). Englewood Cliffs, NJ: Prentice Hall.

Rosenberg, B. (2003, December 8). Domino effect: Division I-A conference realignment has had emotional, structural impact. *The NCAA News*. Retrieved on June 14, 2004, from http://www.ncaa.org/news/2003/20031208/active/4025n03.html

. . . .

Savage, H. J. (1929). *American college athletics*. New York: The Carnegie Foundation.

. . . .

Study: Typical I-A program is $1.2 million in the black. (1996, November 18). *The NCAA News*, p. 1.

Timanus, E. (2006, March 2). Academic sanctions to hit 65 schools. *USA Today*, p. 1C.

. . . .

Watkins, C. (2004, May 1). UTEP accepts invitation to join C-USA. *The Dallas Morning News*. Retrieved on May 4, 2004, from http://www.dallasnews.com/cgi-bin/bi/gold_print.cgi

Western Athletic Conference to become biggest in I-A. (1994, April 27). *The NCAA News*, p. 3.

Wieberg, S. (1994, August 18). Study faults colleges on minority hiring. *USA Today*, p. 1C.

Wolverton, B. (2005, November 11). NCAA will pay colleges that raise athletes' academic performance. *The Chronicle of Higher Education*, p. A39.

Yaeger, D. (1991). *Undue process: The NCAA's injustice for all.* Champaign, IL: Sagamore Publishing.

SPORTS LAW: CASES AND MATERIALS

Ray Yasser, James R. McCurdy, C. Peter Goplerud, and Maureen A. Weston

B. NATIONAL COLLEGIATE ATHLETIC ASSOCIATION—AUTHORITY AND RULES

1. Overview of the Association and Its Structure

The NCAA is an unincorporated, voluntary, private association, consisting of nearly one thousand members. Members are predominantly colleges and universities, both public and private. Athletic conferences are also members of the NCAA. Public universities constitute approximately 55 percent of the membership. All member schools and conferences are required to pay dues, the amounts varying depending upon the division in which membership is held. The association is divided into three divisions: Division I, Division II, and Division III. Division I is itself divided into Division I-A, I-AA, and I-AAA. The organization has a large permanent professional staff, with discrete departments for administration, business, championships, communications, compliance services, enforcement, legislative services, and publishing. The association is headquartered in Indianapolis.

The membership governs the organization, and since 1997, it is essentially a federation system, with each division governing itself on nearly all issues. [*Ed. Note: The NCAA governance structure is shown in **Figure 5**.*] There is, however, an Executive Committee which presides over the entire organization. It consists of 20 members. The Executive Director and the chairs of the three divisional Management Councils serve as ex officio nonvoting members. The other sixteen members include 8 Division I-A CEO's from the Division I Board of Directors, 2 Division I-AA CEO's from the Board, 2 Division I-AAA CEO's from the Board, 2 Division II CEO's from the Division II Presidents Council, and 2 Division III CEO's from the Division III Presidents Council.

The Executive Committee is to:

(a) Provide final approval and oversight of the Association's budget;

(b) Employ the Association's chief executive officer (e.g. executive director), who shall be administratively responsible to the Executive Committee and who shall be authorized to employ such other persons as may be necessary to conduct efficiently the business of the Association;

(c) Provide strategic planning for the Association as a whole;

(d) Identify core issues that affect the Association as a whole;

(e) Act on behalf of the Association to resolve core issues and other Association-wide matters;

(f) Initiate and settle litigation;

(g) Convene at least one combined meeting per year of the divisional presidential governing bodies;

(h) Convene at least one same-site meeting per year of the three divisional Management Councils;

(i) Forward proposed amendments to Constitutions 1 and 2 and other dominant legislation to the entire membership for a vote;

(j) Call for a vote of the entire membership on the action of any division that it determines to be contrary to the basic purposes, fundamental policies, and general principles set forth in the Association's Constitution. This action may be overridden by the Association's entire membership by a two-thirds majority vote of those institutions voting; and

(k) Call for an annual or special Convention of the Association.[1]

Division I is composed of the schools which are the most visible athletic competitors, the so-called "big time programs." For Division I, the primary rule making body in the new NCAA structure is a Board of Directors, made up of eighteen CEO's from Division I member institutions. [*Ed. Note: The Division I governance structure is shown in **Figure 6**.*] The following eight conferences have one representative each on the Board: Atlantic Coast Conference, Big East, Big 12, Big 10, Pac-10, Southeastern, Western Athletic Conference, and Conference USA. One member must come from either the Big West or Mid-American Conferences. The remaining six members come from Division I-AA and I-AAA (Division I schools which do not play Division I football). Each conference in the latter divisions must be represented on either the Board or the Management Council.

The primary duties of the Board are: 1) to establish and direct general policy; 2) to adopt bylaws and other operating provisions; 3) approve an annual budget for Division I; and 4) to ensure gender and ethnic diversity among the members of the governance structure. Members of the Board are elected by the constituencies they represent and serve four-year terms, with no immediate re-election. The terms are staggered to provide continuity and stability.

The NCAA openly states that one of its primary purposes is to promote the concept of amateurism. Related to this is the idea that athletics are an integral part of the educational experience at the intercollegiate level. The NCAA, of course, is big business, with a 2008–09 operating budget of $661 million. It includes a huge television contract for collegiate basketball, smaller contracts for other sports, and an extensive scholarship program. In short, the Association is the governing body, and to a great extent, business agent and primary entity for intercollegiate sports.

In order to understand the more difficult issues faced by the NCAA and its individual member schools, it is necessary to have an understanding of the critical portions of the NCAA Constitution and Bylaws. These are contained in the NCAA Manual, for the appropriate division, which is updated annually. The following is a summary of the key provisions of the Division I Manual.

A basic purpose of the Association is to ensure that intercollegiate athletics are maintained as "an integral part of the educational program and that the athlete [is] an integral part of the student body."[6] Theoretically, this should promote a clear-cut delineation between amateur sports and professional sports. The athletes who make up the program at a school are to be amateurs. Amateur is defined as one whose participation is "motivated primarily by education and by the physical, mental, and social benefits to be derived."[7] Ironically, the Association also urges that its *student-athletes,* and that is the operative term, "should be protected from exploitation by professional and commercial enterprises."[8]

The rules on amateurism are a major focal point of the Association. As noted, only an amateur student-athlete is eligible for participation in a particular sport.[9] An athlete

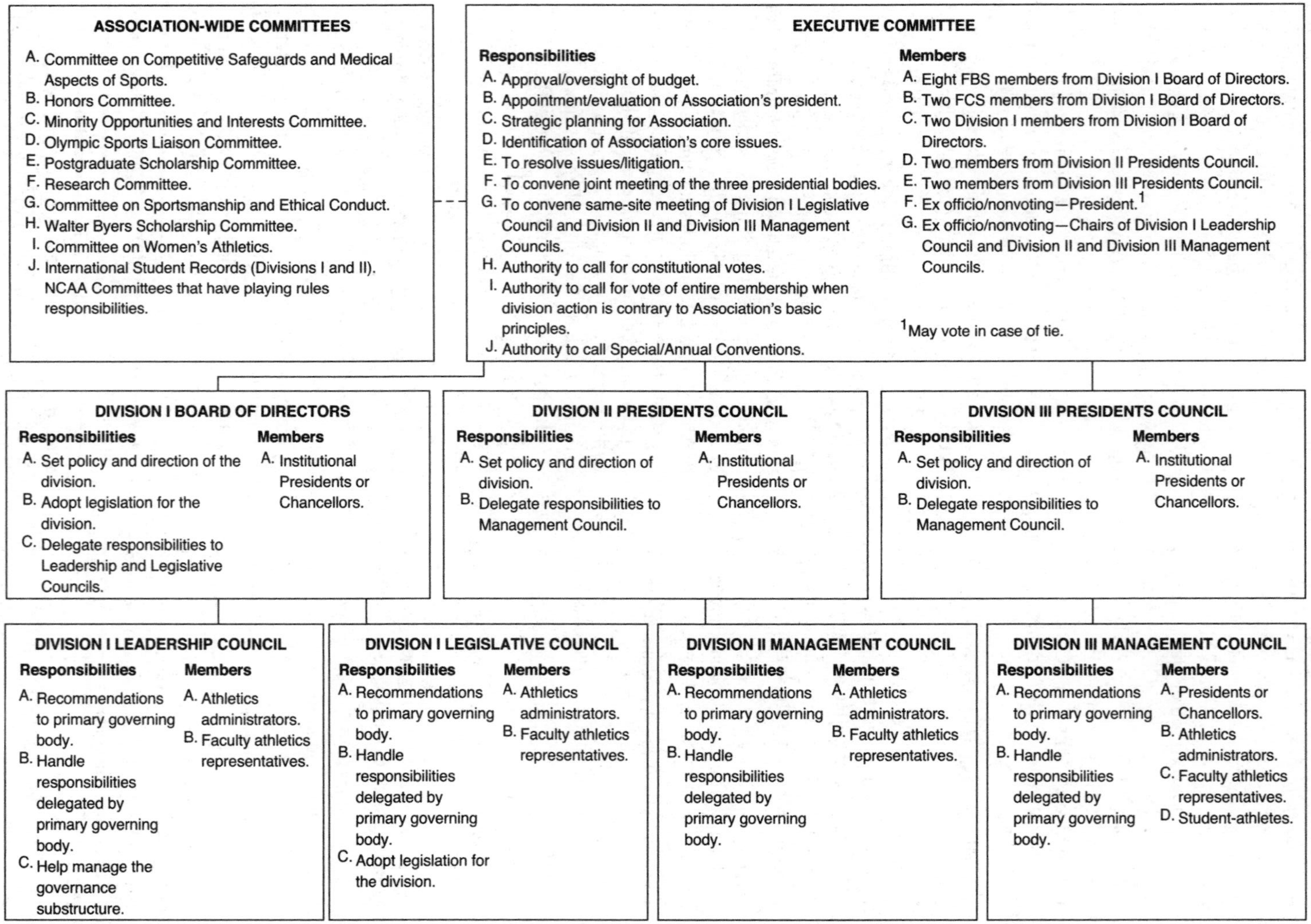

ASSOCIATION-WIDE COMMITTEES

A. Committee on Competitive Safeguards and Medical Aspects of Sports.
B. Honors Committee.
C. Minority Opportunities and Interests Committee.
D. Olympic Sports Liaison Committee.
E. Postgraduate Scholarship Committee.
F. Research Committee.
G. Committee on Sportsmanship and Ethical Conduct.
H. Walter Byers Scholarship Committee.
I. Committee on Women's Athletics.
J. International Student Records (Divisions I and II). NCAA Committees that have playing rules responsibilities.

EXECUTIVE COMMITTEE

Responsibilities

A. Approval/oversight of budget.
B. Appointment/evaluation of Association's president.
C. Strategic planning for Association.
D. Identification of Association's core issues.
E. To resolve issues/litigation.
F. To convene joint meeting of the three presidential bodies.
G. To convene same-site meeting of Division I Legislative Council and Division II and Division III Management Councils.
H. Authority to call for constitutional votes.
I. Authority to call for vote of entire membership when division action is contrary to Association's basic principles.
J. Authority to call Special/Annual Conventions.

Members

A. Eight FBS members from Division I Board of Directors.
B. Two FCS members from Division I Board of Directors.
C. Two Division I members from Division I Board of Directors.
D. Two members from Division II Presidents Council.
E. Two members from Division III Presidents Council.
F. Ex officio/nonvoting—President.[1]
G. Ex officio/nonvoting—Chairs of Division I Leadership Council and Division II and Division III Management Councils.

[1]May vote in case of tie.

DIVISION I BOARD OF DIRECTORS

Responsibilities
A. Set policy and direction of the division.
B. Adopt legislation for the division.
C. Delegate responsibilities to Leadership and Legislative Councils.

Members
A. Institutional Presidents or Chancellors.

DIVISION I LEADERSHIP COUNCIL

Responsibilities
A. Recommendations to primary governing body.
B. Handle responsibilities delegated by primary governing body.
C. Help manage the governance substructure.

Members
A. Athletics administrators.
B. Faculty athletics representatives.

DIVISION I LEGISLATIVE COUNCIL

Responsibilities
A. Recommendations to primary governing body.
B. Handle responsibilities delegated by primary governing body.
C. Adopt legislation for the division.

Members
A. Athletics administrators.
B. Faculty athletics representatives.

DIVISION II PRESIDENTS COUNCIL

Responsibilities
A. Set policy and direction of division.
B. Delegate responsibilities to Management Council.

Members
A. Institutional Presidents or Chancellors.

DIVISION II MANAGEMENT COUNCIL

Responsibilities
A. Recommendations to primary governing body.
B. Handle responsibilities delegated by primary governing body.

Members
A. Athletics administrators.
B. Faculty athletics representatives.

DIVISION III PRESIDENTS COUNCIL

Responsibilities
A. Set policy and direction of division.
B. Delegate responsibilities to Management Council.

Members
A. Institutional Presidents or Chancellors.

DIVISION III MANAGEMENT COUNCIL

Responsibilities
A. Recommendations to primary governing body.
B. Handle responsibilities delegated by primary governing body.

Members
A. Presidents or Chancellors.
B. Athletics administrators.
C. Faculty athletics representatives.
D. Student-athletes.

Figure 5   NCAA Governance Structure

Source: 2009–2010 *NCAA Division I Manual,* Figure 4-2, p. 27. © National Collegiate Athletic Association. 2008–2010. All rights reserved.

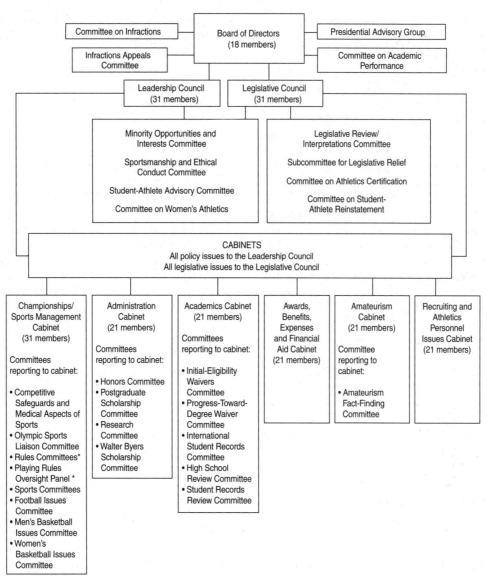

Figure 6   NCAA Division I Governance Structure

Source: 2009–2010 *NCAA Division I Manual,* Figure 4-1, p. 26. © National Collegiate Athletic Association. 2008–2010. All rights reserved.

may be a professional in one sport and still retain eligibility in other sports, however. An athlete will be deemed a professional, and thus lose his or her eligibility if the individual:

(a) Uses his or her athletics skill (directly or indirectly) for pay in any form in that sport;

(b) Accepts a promise of pay even if such pay is to be received following completion of intercollegiate athletics participation;

(c) Signs a contract or commitment of any kind to play professional athletics, regardless of its legal enforceability or any consideration received;

(d) Receives, directly or indirectly, a salary, reimbursement of expenses, or any other form of financial as-

sistance from a professional sports organization based upon athletic skill or participation, except as permitted by NCAA rules and regulations;

(e) Competes on any professional athletics team and knows (or had reason to know) that the team is a professional athletics team . . . , even if no pay or remuneration for expenses was received; or

(f) Enters into a professional draft or an agreement with an agent or other entity to negotiate a professional contract.[10]

The NCAA defines "pay" to include the following items and concepts: salaries, extra educational expenses beyond that allowed by the NCAA, expenses for parents, payment based upon performance, prizes, and preferential treatment or benefits.[11] An individual also becomes a professional in a sport if he or she signs a professional contract, regardless of its enforceability or a delayed start date. Participation on a professional sports team makes one a professional. As noted, an athlete may be a professional in one sport and retain eligibility in other NCAA sports. That individual, however, may not accept institutional financial aid while involved in professional sports or receiving remuneration from a professional sports organization.[12] An athlete's eligibility may be impacted by activity associated with a professional sports draft. A football player who declares himself available for the draft immediately loses his eligibility, regardless of whether he is actually drafted or eventually signs a contract.[13] That player may, however, make inquiry about his market value prior to declaring without jeopardizing his eligibility. A basketball player may enter a draft and, if not drafted, she has thirty days following the draft to make a decision to play professionally. The athlete may return to collegiate competition if she indicates that intention in writing to the athletic director within thirty days of the draft.[14] A college baseball player is in a different situation in that the baseball draft is conducted without the players having to declare themselves eligible. Thus, if a player meets age or collegiate progress requirements he is eligible to be drafted. A player who is drafted does not have his eligibility affected until he signs a contract. However, in all of the situations noted, the player immediately loses his or her eligibility if [he or she retains] an agent. The eligibility is lost even if the contract is for services to be rendered subsequent to completion of eligibility. In addition, an athlete may not receive benefits of any kind from an agent.[15] The only exception is for the athlete who is a professional in one sport, but continues to compete at the collegiate level in other sports. He may have an agent for the sport in which he is a professional, but the agreement with that agent must be limited, *in writing*, to that particular sport. If it is not so limited it will be deemed applicable to all sports, thus rendering the athlete ineligible. Finally, an athlete may secure advice from an attorney concerning a proposed contract, so long as the attorney does not become involved in negotiating the contract.

The NCAA has also historically been concerned about athletes becoming involved in promotional activities which benefit them solely because of their athletic abilities. The most absurd example of previously stringent policies occurred when a University of Indiana basketball player was suspended for one game because he appeared on a sorority calendar, the proceeds from which went to charity. This rule has been relaxed somewhat. Athletes may now appear or have their picture used for charitable or educational purposes if written permission is secured, no class time is missed, and there is no co-sponsorship by a commercial entity.[16]

The NCAA also has restrictions on employment for student athletes. The Association limits the scholarship of an athlete on full scholarship to tuition, fees, room, board, and books. Within limits, an athlete on full scholarship may also receive Pell Grant funds. . . . Any work obtained must be for a fair, prevailing wage, and must not be based on the athlete's athletic reputation.

The Association regulations also govern the educational status and progress of the student athlete. This area has been extremely controversial in recent years, particularly as it relates to the initial eligibility of entering student athletes. The student athlete has four years of eligibility for athletic competition for any one sport. [These] four years must be completed within five years of the time the athlete first registers for a minimum full time program of studies in a collegiate institution.[18] "To be eligible to represent an institution in intercollegiate athletics competition, a student-athlete shall be enrolled in at least a minimum full time program of studies, be in good academic standing and maintain satisfactory progress toward a baccalaureate degree."[19]

The initial eligibility rules have been the target of much criticism, tinkering and litigation. In 1983 the NCAA enacted the so-called Proposition 48 which became effective in 1986. It was intended to regulate the eligibility of incoming freshman athletes in an era when questions had arisen as to admissions practices at some institutions. This rule initially set up minimum grade point averages and college entrance examination scores which had to be attained. Failure to attain these minimal standards cost the athlete eligibility or scholarship funds or both. These rules have been amended several times since 1986 and are now even more stringent. To be eligible as a freshman for competition and scholarship funds, an incoming athlete must have a minimum grade point average in thirteen [*now 14*] core courses in high school and a corresponding minimum test score on either the ACT or SAT test. The scale slides depending upon the level of grade point average or test score. If the athlete does not satisfy the standards, he will either be labeled a nonqualifier or a partial qualifier. The specific categorization will again depend on where the test scores and grades fall. If the athlete is a nonqualifier, she will not be able to receive athletic based financial aid, cannot practice or compete as a freshman, and retains only three years of eligibility. A partial qualifier may practice, can receive an athletic scholarship, but cannot compete as a freshman and will have only three years of eligibility left.[20] [*Ed. Note: A nonqualifier may now receive non-athletics–based financial aid as a freshman. Both nonqualifiers and partial qualifiers may now regain a fourth year of eligibility if they graduate in four years.*]

. . . .

The NCAA also has extensive and complex rules governing the recruitment of prospective student-athletes by schools. These include a prohibition on involvement in the process by supporters of the institution. They also include the number of visits a recruit may make to member schools, the number of recruits a particular school may bring to its campus, and elaborate restrictions on when coaches may talk to recruits, see them play, and bring them to campus.[21] There are also detailed restrictions and requirements concerning competition and practice, including length and time of season, limitations on numbers of contests, and number of hours of practice per week during the season. Finally, the

Association conducts and regulates postseason championship events in more than two dozen sports.[22]

Another linchpin of the Association is the concept of institutional control of intercollegiate athletics.[23] Each member institution is to control its program in a manner consistent with the rules and regulations of the Association. [*Ed. Note: Figure 7 outlines the enforcement process.*] The CEO

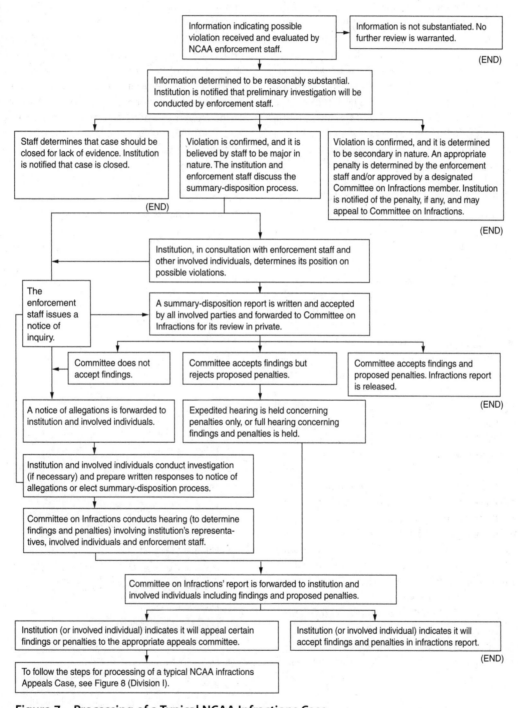

Figure 7   Processing of a Typical NCAA Infractions Case

Source: 2009–2010 *NCAA Division I Manual,* Figure 32-1, p. 399. © National Collegiate Athletic Association. 2008–2010. All rights reserved.

of the institution is ultimately responsible for the program at a given school. This responsibility extends to the conduct of administrators, coaches, athletes, and supporters of the program. When the conduct of the program transgresses the rules, the enforcement arm of the NCAA goes to work, as do the administrators and coaches of the program under investigation.

The Association has a large full time enforcement staff which handles investigations. An investigation may begin either as a result of information being given to the enforcement staff by some outside source, on the initiation of the enforcement staff itself, or as a result of a self-reported violation of the rules by the school itself. All investigations are treated as confidential until announcements are made according to the prescribed procedures.[24] The initial step in the investigative process is the evaluation of the information received concerning possible violations by the enforcement staff. If the information is not substantiated, the case will be closed. If it is determined to be reasonably substantial, the institution will be notified that a preliminary investigation is under way. This notice will provide the school with information regarding the charges, the persons allegedly involved, the time frame of the violations, and will notify the school and involved individuals that they may be represented by counsel throughout the process. Following the preliminary investigation, the process can go in one of three directions: the case may be closed for lack of evidence; a major violation may be found and summary disposal discussions begin with the school; or a lesser or secondary violation may be found and appropriate penalties are then discussed and imposed.

If the alleged violations are determined to be major and summary disposition is not possible, the NCAA then serves an Official Inquiry on the CEO of the institution. This OI will detail the allegations with perhaps even more specificity than the notice of preliminary investigation. The institution will then conduct its own investigation, often utilizing outside counsel and investigators. Individual coaches and athletes may also have their own legal representation. The rules of the Association require the institution to cooperate fully with the NCAA enforcement staff, the Committee on Infractions, Infractions Appeals Committee, and the Council. Failure to cooperate is itself a violation of the rules. (Another significant violation, frequently found in these matters, is lack of institutional control of the program.) Theoretically, then, it is not an adversarial process.

Following the investigation the Committee on Infractions will conduct a hearing to determine findings and any penalties deemed appropriate. This hearing will involve the institution's representatives, involved parties, the enforcement staff, and, where appropriate, the report of an independent hearing officer. Following the hearing the Committee on Infractions will issue its report, which will include penalties. Potential penalties range from public censure and reprimand to the "death penalty," the total shut down of a program or particular sport for a set period of time. In between are such sanctions as reduction in scholarships allowed, forfeiture of tournament money, ineligibility for championship events, limitations on recruitment activities by certain personnel, and ineligibility for appearance on television. The school has the opportunity to appeal the ruling to the Infractions Appeals Committee. [*Ed. Note: The appeals process is outlined in* **Figure 8**.] This appellate body will receive written "briefs" from the institution and from the Committee on Infractions. It will also hold a hearing involving all interested parties. Unlike earlier appeals to the NCAA Council, the Infractions Appeals Committee has actually modified or partially reversed findings of the Committee on Infractions.

The enforcement process, as set out above, has been substantially modified in the last several years. Prior to 1993 there were major concerns regarding fairness and due process raised by schools and individuals within the membership.

. . . .

Notes

. . . .

6. Division I Manual, 1.3.1.

7. Division I Manual, 2.9.

8. Id.

9. Division I Manual, 12.01.1.

10. Division I Manual, 12.1.1.

11. Division I Manual, 12.1.1.

12. Division I Manual, 12.1.2.

13. Division I Manual, 12.2.4.

14. Division I Manual, 12.2.4.2.1.

15. Division I Manual, 12.3.

16. Division I Manual, 12.5.1.

. . . .

18. Division I Manual, 14.2.1.

19. Division I Manual, 14.01.2 (1996).

20. *See generally* Division I Manual, 14.

21. Division I Manual, 13.

22. Division I Manual, 17, 18.

23. Division I Manual, 2.1.

24. Division I Manual, 32.1.1 (1996).

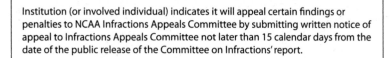

Institution (or involved individual) indicates it will appeal certain findings or penalties to NCAA Infractions Appeals Committee by submitting written notice of appeal to Infractions Appeals Committee not later than 15 calendar days from the date of the public release of the Committee on Infractions' report.

Infractions Appeals Committee acknowledges receipt of timely appeal. Institution (or involved individual) is provided a 30-day period to submit response in support of appeal.

After receiving institution's (and/or involved individual's) response, the Committee on Infractions is provided a 30-day period to submit response to the institution's (or involved individual's) written appeal.

Institution (and/or involved individual) is provided 14 days to provide a rebuttal to Committee on Infractions' response. Enforcement staff may provide written information not later than 10 days from the rebuttal deadline.

Infractions Appeals Committee reviews the institution's (and/or involved individual's) appeal and the Committee on Infractions' response. This review is completed either through a hearing or on the written record. Hearings include representatives on behalf of the institution, involved individual(s), the Committee on Infractions and enforcement staff.

Infractions Appeals Committee decision is announced.

Figure 8   Processing of a Typical NCAA Infractions Appeals Case

Source: 2009–2010 *NCAA Division I Manual,* Figure 32-2, p. 400. © National Collegiate Athletic Association. 2008–2010. All rights reserved.

Discussion Questions

1. What were some of the early complaints voiced about the growing commercialism of intercollegiate athletics? Have these complaints endured?
2. Why was the NCAA formed?
3. Describe the structural evolution of the NCAA.
4. How did the NCAA react to the critics who stated that it exercised its enforcement authority unfairly?
5. Describe the present management structure of the NCAA.
6. Is the current structure the ideal governing structure for collegiate sports?
7. Describe an alternative governing structure that might operate more effectively.
8. Give some examples of the rule violations that predominantly occur in both women's and men's sports.
9. What was the Sanity Code?
10. Why was the Sanity Code repealed?

CHAPTER FOURTEEN

The NCAA and Conference Affiliation

INTRODUCTION

Intercollegiate athletics have been infused with a degree of commercialization since the earliest days of student competition. What is not as readily apparent, however, is the size of the college sports industry. This chapter and the one that follows explain the business of intercollegiate athletics from the perspective of the NCAA as a collective, its member conferences, and its individual member institutions.

This business of college sports, other than some international student participants, is an American phenomenon. The initial selection in this chapter by Noll provides a comprehensive overview of the financial aspects of intercollegiate athletics. A subsequent excerpt by the late Myles Brand, a university president turned NCAA president, highlights the concerns and challenges brought on by commercialization of intercollegiate athletics. As shown in **Table 1**, the primary asset of the NCAA is the Division I men's basketball tournament. The NCAA budget was $661 million in the 2008–2009 season. Nearly 90%, or $590 million, of this amount was generated by the NCAA's previous 11-year, $6.2 billion contract with CBS to broadcast what has become widely known as "March Madness," as well as the NCAA's marketing rights. The NCAA replaced the last 3 years of this deal with a 14-year, $10.8 billion contract with CBS and Turner (via its TBS, TNT, and truTV networks) through 2024, which will provide the NCAA with an average of $771 million per year. The NCAA cedes it marketing rights to CBS, which sells the sponsorships. Top-level NCAA sponsors (known as 'corporate champions') pay a reported $35 million annually, with second-tier sponsors paying a reported $10 to $12 million annually. Another 6%, or $41.8 million, was earned in ticket sales for this tournament. The organization's remaining revenues (5%) were the result of gate receipts from all of its other tournaments across all three divisions ($18.6 million combined), as well as licensing efforts and other investments, sales, fees, and services ($9.8 million).

It is important to note that the NCAA does not control the revenues associated with the Division I-A football postseason, despite the fact that its revenue potential is seemingly much greater than that of basketball. Thus, individual conferences and schools (namely, Notre Dame) negotiate separate broadcast agreements for regular-season football; a separate coalition of top conferences and Notre Dame control the postseason through the Bowl Championship Series (BCS). All other postseason games are controlled by the promoters of the various independent bowl games that have entered into individual agreements with broadcast networks and cable channels to televise their contests. These bowls typically have arrangements with conferences to send predetermined place teams to play in the games. The article by Copeland explains the history of the NCAA's hands-off approach to college football, which is a result of the Supreme Court's 1984 decision in *Board of Regents v. NCAA*. The NCAA distributes the majority of its revenues to the members of Division I through various mechanisms. These distributions totaled $387.2 million, or 59% of the NCAA's expenses in 2008–2009. (The details of these distributions are provided in the NCAA's *2008–09 Revenue Distribution Plan* later in this chapter.) Another $49.9 million, or 7.5%, of the NCAA's revenues was distributed to the members of Divisions II and III, as is mandated by the NCAA constitution. The NCAA pays for all of the game and travel expenses for the schools participating in its 88 postseason tournaments in 23 sports, totaling nearly $64 million in 2008–2009, or 10% of its budgeted expenses. The NCAA also provides a number of programs and services for its members and athletes and spent $107.5 million in a wide range of areas in 2008–2009, or 16% of its budget. Finally, the NCAA's expenditures on attorney's fees, lobbyists, its internal governance and committees, staff salaries,

Table 1   The National Collegiate Athletic Association Revised Budget for Fiscal Year Ended August 31, 2009

	2008–09 Budget	Perecentage of Total Operating Revenue and Expenses
REVENUE		
Television and Marketing Rights Fees	590,730,000	89.37%
Championships Revenue	60,430,000	9.14%
TOTAL CHAMPIONSHIPS REVENUE	651,160,000	98.51%
Investments, Fees, and Services	8,830,000	1.34%
Membership Dues	1,010,000	0.15%
TOTAL NCAA OPERATING REVENUE	661,000,000	100.00%
DIVISION SPECIFIC EXPENSES		
Total Distribution to Division I members	387,227,000	58.58%
Total Division I championships and programs	64,046,775	9.69%
TOTAL DIVISION I EXPENSE AND ALLOCATION	451,273,775	68.27%
TOTAL DIVISION II EXPENSE AND ALLOCATION	28,886,000	4.37%
TOTAL DIVISION III EXPENSE AND ALLOCATION	21,020,000	3.18%
TOTAL DIVISION SPECIFIC EXPENSES AND ALLOCATIONS	501,179,775	75.82%
ASSOCIATION-WIDE EXPENSE- PROGRAMS AND SERVICES		
Total Student-Athlete Welfare and Youth Programs and Services	22,785,800	3.45%
Total Membership Programs and Services	84,682,801	12.81%
TOTAL PROGRAM AND SERVICES	107,468,601	16.26%
TOTAL ADMINISTRATIVE SERVICES	27,899,525	4.22%
Division II and III Championships and Program Support	(2,014,571)	−0.30%
TOTAL ASSOCIATION-WIDE EXPENSES	133,353,555	20.17%
TOTAL NCAA OPERATING EXPENSES	634,533,330	96.00%
Contingencies and Reserves	24,400,170	3.69%
Collegiate Sports, LLC	2,066,500	0.31%
TOTAL CONTINGENCIES AND RESERVES	26,466,670	4.00%
TOTAL	661,000,000	100%

Source: National Collegiate Athletic Association. © National Collegiate Athletic Association. 2008–2010. All rights reserved.

and general and administrative services totaled over $27.9 million, or 4% of its budget, in 2008–2009.

Although there are 31 conferences in Division I, it is not surprising that the NCAA's revenue-sharing system favors the members of the so-called BCS conferences—the "Big Six" athletic conferences that dominate Division I— the ACC, Big East, Big Ten, Big 12, Pac-10, and SEC. The NCAA's distribution to athletic programs is based on three factors. First, the number of NCAA sports that the institution offers affects the amount of money that it receives from the association. With the distributed funds being directly proportionate to the number of teams fielded, the more comprehensive athletic programs receive larger amounts of NCAA monies. Only the Ivy League received more money than the Big Ten, ACC, and Big East in 2008–2009. Second, the number of athletic scholarships that a school offers to its students impacts its receipt of NCAA funds; the more athletic scholarships offered, the greater the amount of money received. The BCS conferences occupied the top six spots

on this distribution list in 2008–2009. The third distribution is based on each conference's performance in the men's basketball tournament over the previous 6 years. Each of the BCS conferences received more from this distribution than any other conference. This should be expected given the depth and strength of these conferences and their dominance of college basketball. No school from outside of this power base has won a national championship in the sport since 1990. The dominance of these conferences is not limited to basketball. Overall, institutions from BCS conferences won 32 of the 35 Division I NCAA championships in which they competed in 2008–2009.

Though the other distributions to Division I institutions are divided far more equitably via the academic-enhancement fund, the special assistance fund for student-athletes, the student-athlete opportunity fund, and conference grants, they represent a much smaller amount of money—approximately one-quarter of the amount that is dispersed through the aforementioned athletic scholarships, sports sponsorship, and basketball funds. The chapter concludes with the NCAA's 2008–2009 revenue distribution plan, which provides the exact details of its methodology, while the accompanying NCAA budgets and audited financial statements add color.

Although the ACC, Big East, Big Ten, Big 12, Pac-10, and SEC receive favorable NCAA distributions, a far greater advantage is gained from the revenue sources that the NCAA does not control: the negotiation of television agreements by these elite conferences for regular season and postseason conference basketball and football contests, ticket sales to the postseason conference basketball tournaments and conference football championship games, and the participation in postseason BCS bowl games by members of these conferences. The pursuit of increased revenues has led to periodic, dramatic shifts in the conference landscape, with some conferences strategically adding institutions in an effort to increase their long-term media revenues by adding geographic reach, to gain the ability to play a conference championship game in football by reaching the 12 schools required by NCAA rules, and to increase their dominance within their regional footprint. Other conferences then re-align in an effort to preserve their existence. Indeed, yet another round of realignment was occurring in mid-2010 as this book was going to press, with several institutions switching membership among BCS and non-BCS conferences.

College conferences operate quite similarly to professional sports leagues in the negotiation of television agreements for football and basketball. Each conference pools certain rights of its member schools and enters into its own conference-wide broadcasting agreement, with the revenues typically divided equally among the member institutions. These contracts are lucrative. In addition, the ability of conferences either to launch or to contemplate launching their own networks to complement their existing national media contracts (a topic discussed in the context of professional sports in Chapter 8), has enabled them to dramatically increase their media-related revenues in their most recent agreements.

The Mountain West launched its own network (The Mtn.) in partnership with Comcast in 2006, which set the groundwork for the Big Ten to launch its own network (the Big Ten Network) the following year. The Big Ten Network is a 25-year deal with Fox Sports Network (a subsidiary of News Corp.) in which the conference owns 51% and Fox owns 49%. News Corp. has indicated in filings that the conference could receive $2.8 billion over those 25 years, an average annual value of $112 million. In addition, the Big Ten has a 10-year football and basketball agreement with ABC/ESPN, worth a projected $1 billion, that runs from 2008–2017 and a 10-year, $20 million football and basketball deal with CBS that runs from 2009–2018. The Big Ten's media deals compare to those of the SEC. The SEC eschewed the possibility of launching its own network in favor of signing a pair of 15-year contracts with ESPN and CBS that run from 2009–2023 that provide the conference with a total of $2.25 billion from ESPN and $825 million from CBS, an average annual value of $205 million. This is a testament to the popularity of the conference both in its own regional footprint and on a national basis, as well as its dominance in college football.

The Big 12 conference signed a more traditional rights fee agreement with ABC/ESPN—an 8-year, $480 million deal (an average annual value of $60 million) through 2015–2016 for football, basketball, and Olympic sports. It complements this deal with a 4-year, $78 million contract with Fox Sports Net running through 2011 to air football games.

The Pac-10 conference has a 5-year, $125 million deal with ABC/ESPN through 2011; a 5-year, $97 million deal with Fox Sports Net through 2011 for football; and a 6-year, $52.5 million deal with Fox Sports Net through 2011–2012 for basketball. This last agreement is a multifaceted outsourcing deal that gives the cable outlet the exclusive right to sell, among other things, all Pac-10 basketball tournament sponsorship packages.

The ACC has a 12-year, $1.86 billion contract with ABC/ESPN through 2022–23, a deal that replaced a 7-year, $258 million deal with ABC/ESPN through 2010 for football and its 10-year, $300 million deal with Raycom Sports through 2010–2011 for basketball. The 130% increase in the annual average value of the deal (from an average of $66.9 million per year to an average of $155 million annually) was a product of a bidding war for the rights between Fox and ABC/ESPN. The Big East conference has proven to be quite strong at basketball and much weaker at football. This is reflected in its relatively small football/basketball media deal among the BCS conferences—a 6-year, $200 million deal with ESPN through 2012–2013 for basketball and through 2013 for football.

In 2009–2010, the BCS conferences of the Big Ten, SEC, ACC, Big 12, Pac-10, and Big East received television revenues of $242 million, $205 million, $78 million, $67 million, $58 million, and $33 million, respectively. The non-BCS conferences in Division I-A—the Mountain West, Conference USA, Western Athletic, Mid-American, and Sun Belt—earned $12 million, $11.3 million (including media/marketing revenues), $4 million, $1.4 million, and $1 million, respectively. These contracts indicate the popularity of big-time college football and basketball. **Table 2** shows the various revenues and expenses of the SEC, ACC and Big Ten in recent years.

In addition, each of these conferences stages a profit-generating postseason basketball tournament, with revenues ranging from $2.8 million (SEC) to $7.3 million (ACC) in 2007–2008. Further, the Big 10, SEC, and ACC each have 12 schools, which allow these conferences to hold a postseason championship football game, as per current NCAA rules. These games generated $13.7 million for the SEC and approximately $5 million for the ACC in 2007–2008.

Table 2   Select Recent BCS Conference Financial Snapshots

SEC Conference Revenues, 2009–2010	
Source	**Amount**
Football television	$109.5 million
Bowl games	26.5 million
NCAA championships (all sports)	23.5 million
SEC football championship game	14.5 million
Basketball television	30.0 million
SEC men's basketball tournament	5.0 million
Total revenues	**$209.0 million***

*Each school received $17.3 million. This total does not include $14.3 million retained by institutions participating in bowls or $780,000 from the NCAA Academic Enhancement Fund.
Source: SEC.

ACC Conference, 2007–2008	
Source	**Amount**
Revenues	
Football television	$40.58 million
Basketball television	34.70 million
Bowl games	29.21 million
NCAA basketball tournament	15.07 million
Other football revenue	10.15 million
ACC men's basketball tournament	6.50 million
ACC football championship	4.14 million
Other basketball revenue	3.73 million
XM Satellite Radio fees	1.50 million
New member entry fee	500,000
ACC women's basketball tournament	330,216
Total revenues	**$162.76 million**
Expenses	
Compensation/salary/wages/benefits	4.16 million
ACC basketball tournament	1.88 million
ACC football championship	981,848
Bowl expenses	659,204
Media relations	394,580
Total expenses	**$152.09 million***

*Includes distribution of approximately $141.45 million to members.
Source: IRS Form 990.

Big 10 Conference, 2007–2008	
Source	**Amount**
Revenues	
Sports Revenue	$206.77 million
Operating revenue	7.91 million
Licensing program royalties	1.33 million
Championship events	754,566
Membership Dues and Assessments	935,000
Total revenues	**$217.7 million**
Expenses	
Officiating Expenses	551,599
Conference Office Programs	1.44 million
Distributions to member schools	206.77 million
Allen & Co.	3.5 million
Compensation of current officers, directors, key employees	2.13 million
Mayer Brown LLP	690,148
Championship events	822,890
Total expenses	**$219.4 million**

Source: IRS Form 990.

BCS is a coalition of the Fiesta, Orange, Rose, and Sugar Bowls and the BCS National Championship Game, which doled out over $125.5 million to the BCS conferences in 2008–2009. The five other Division I-A conferences, combined, shared approximately $19.3 million. There were 29 other, non-BCS bowl games in 2008–2009 that played host to a collection of lesser teams, most of which still came from the BCS conferences. The non-BCS bowl games distributed $79.9 million in 2008–2009, approximately three-quarters of which went to the elite conferences. Thus, while none of the BCS conferences earned total bowl revenues of less than the Big East's $23.3 million, no other Division I-A conference earned bowl revenues greater than $12.2 million (Mountain West). Overall, the BCS conferences collected $189.8 million from bowl games played in 2008–2009, and the other five conferences reaped $36.5 million.

In addition to the substantial amount of revenue that is generated by participation in bowl games, there is also a significant expense associated with playing in these contests. Each institution must pay for the transportation, meals, housing, entertainment, awards, and per diem allowances for its team and coaching staff, marching band, cheerleaders, and official traveling party, many of whom arrive in the host city several days prior to the game. The participating schools also must sell an allotment of tickets to the game and are responsible for the cost of any unsold tickets. These expenses are much higher for the BCS bowls than the non-BCS ones. However, the expenses are more than offset by the revenues

Football is the most important source of revenue for the elite conferences. Beyond the aforementioned television contracts and championship games, membership in a BCS conference (aside from Notre Dame) is nearly a prerequisite for participation in the Bowl Championship Series. The generated in the BCS games. The net distribution to conferences and institutions in the five BCS bowls was $125.4 million in 2008–2009. The 29 non-BCS bowls are quite different; their lower revenues resulted in a net distribution of $22.6 million in 2008–2009. Thus, the profit margin for BCS bowls was 85%, while it was only 28% for the non-BCS bowls in 2008–2009.

Each conference has a different formula for sharing the revenues that its institutions receive from bowl games and NCAA tournaments. Similar to professional sports leagues, a revenue sharing system that gives participating teams a disproportionate amount of the monies creates profit-maximizing behavior, including cheating, whereas one that is too generous to nonparticipating schools encourages free-riding among lesser teams and creates a disincentive for self-improvement. The key for each conference is to find the appropriate level of revenue sharing.

Although the BCS conferences generate substantial revenues, an existence in Division I outside of these conferences is much more difficult. At present, 25 other conferences play Division I basketball; 5 of these conferences play Division I-A football and 11 additional conferences play Division I-AA football; the remaining 9 conferences are in Division I-AAA and do not offer football. These "have-not" conferences generally struggle both competitively on the field and financially off of it. The 25 other Division I basketball conferences lag in total NCAA distributed revenues, with only two conferences (Conference USA and the Mid-American) receiving even half of what was received by any of the Big Six conferences in 2007–2008 and 16 receiving less than one-quarter. For the five other conferences participating in Division I-A football (Conference USA, Mid-American, Mountain West, Sun Belt, and Western Athletic), the situation is even more daunting. The problem facing these football programs is that they have a cost structure that is similar to the BCS conference programs (athletic scholarships, coaching staff, facility costs, etc.), but lack the popularity—the fan demand for tickets and television—to generate comparable revenues during the regular season. In addition, these schools receive a fraction of the revenues from bowl games that are earned by the BCS conferences, as previously noted. Finally, the eight conferences that participate in Division I-AA football are financially troubled. Though the cost structure is lower than it is in Division I-A because of the lower scholarship total (63) and smaller coaching staffs and infrastructure, it remains quite high in comparison to the paltry revenues generated. With its small attendance, little television coverage, and a largely ignored NCAA playoff in lieu of bowl games, Division I-AA football conferences have little hope for profitability.

FINANCIAL OVERVIEW

THE BUSINESS OF COLLEGE SPORTS AND THE HIGH COST OF WINNING

Roger C. Noll

Intercollegiate athletics is a strange business—one whose profits end up in the most unlikely pockets. But I'm getting ahead of the story.

For some 50 colleges and universities, football and men's basketball are modest enterprises that generate enough revenues to cover full scholarships for about 100 athletes—and, in a good year, to yield a profit of a few million dollars. At a few universities, women's basketball is also profitable, and baseball is more or less a break-even operation. For all other sports, and for major sports outside the top group of colleges, intercollegiate athletics is a financial drain. Yet almost all American colleges and universities field an impressive array of men's and women's teams across a variety of sports that have few players and virtually no spectators.

What's more, intercollegiate sports chronically generate serious controversy that leaves college administrators cringing behind their desks. The media regularly report scandals about drug use, criminal activity, excessive financial aid, and poor academic performance punctuated by low graduation rates. No less important, big-time sports cause friction among faculty and university administrators. Some see sports as diverting resources and attention to an unimportant—even frivolous—non-academic activity. Explicit favoritism to athletics also is controversial. If coaches are paid more than Nobel Prize winners, if athletes have larger scholarships and better dorms than academic superstars, are colleges transmitting the wrong lessons to students and society at large? And if college sports cast so dark a shadow, why do they endure?

WHY AMERICAN UNIVERSITIES SUPPORT SPORTS

To the rest of the world, American intercollegiate athletics seem like pagan rituals. Universities rarely sponsor athletics teams—let alone encourage them to play before thousands or to appear on television.

The popularity of intercollegiate sports in the United States is not driven by Americans' greater interest in sports. . . .

Nor are intercollegiate sports popular because more Americans follow sports that first interested them as students. Intercollegiate athletics in the United States has been a popular entertainment since the beginning of the century, when the fraction of Americans who had gone to college was far lower than the proportion of college-educated Europeans and Japanese today.

Finally, the special prominence of American intercollegiate athletics is not explained by television exposure. College sports were popular before radio and long before television. Moreover, since Europe has liberalized broadcasting by allowing cable television, sports on cable has proliferated—but not intercollegiate sports.

So why do American colleges devote so much effort to sports? Primarily, because their students demand it as athletes, not as spectators. Public enthusiasm focuses on the so-called revenue sports—basketball and football. But the vast majority of college athletes play other, minor sports, for which no significant demand exists other than from the athletes themselves. The inescapable conclusion: universities have comprehensive varsity athletics programs largely because students want to be athletes. And they compete to enable students to follow their interests, whether in physics or field hockey, linguistics or lacrosse.

THE FINANCIAL STAKES IN SPORTS

Colleges and universities follow diverse policies regarding intercollegiate athletics. The vast majority sponsor teams with no expectation of generating revenues. Indeed, the typical intercollegiate sports program is based on the traditional amateur model.

But focusing on the typical ignores the big-time sports schools with multimilliondollar profit centers in basketball and football, and the many other schools that dabble in the so-called revenue sports. The NCAA divides colleges and universities into three divisions according to the depth of their financial commitment. The top group, Division I, is further subdivided into I-A and I-AA for football. And even this categorization understates the extent of diversity.

In Divisions II and III, sports are relatively low-cost activities. Most schools use part-time coaches, play only nearby competitors and give few athletic scholarships. . . . This sum is not large compared to a university budget. But a small liberal arts college with 1000 students may end up spending 5 to 10 percent of tuition on a comprehensive sports program.

At the top of the heap are about three dozen Division I-A schools that compete for national championships in several sports including football and both men's and women's basketball. Just below are another dozen mostly small, Catholic colleges that have the same ambitions in all but football. At these schools, game attendance for the trophy sports approaches the numbers for professional sports. They expect to be in the NCAA championship basketball tournament and, if they play Division I football, in a postseason bowl.

PUNTING ON FOOTBALL

The financial returns from football can be very large for top teams. Typically, they play six or seven games at home, bribing weaker schools to be cannon fodder against far superior opponents in front of large crowds. . . .

The top teams also expect to appear on television almost every week . . . although in most conferences the money must be shared with other conference members. Notre Dame does even better since it sells national television rights to all its home games and does not belong to a conference.

In addition, bowl games guarantee a payoff . . . per team. For teams picked for a top bowl game . . . the payoff is several million dollars—although, for most schools, bowl income, too, must be shared with conference members. . . . [*Ed. Note: **Tables 3, 4, 5,** and **6** show revenues generated by bowl games.*]

For the rest of the Division I-A football teams and all of the ones in Division I-AA, television exposure is unusual . . . Thus, these teams must get by on revenues about one-tenth that of their superpower brethren—a reality that explains why most jump at the chance to earn a few hundred thousand dollars to be drubbed by Penn State or Michigan.

Football team operating costs are driven by the school's business strategy. Does it try to field a ranked team that will go to a major bowl? If so, the team must play interregional foes, running up travel costs of hundreds of thousands per trip. . . .

Management costs typically are attributed to something other than salary—endorsements, in-kind payments (e.g., a mansion, a Cadillac)—in order to keep compensation in line with that of top faculty. But this practice is mainly a public-relations device: competition for top coaches insures that, one way or another, they are paid according to their ability to generate revenue. By contrast, a team that does not aspire to national ranking can minimize travel costs and rely on mediocre veterans for coaching. Stadium operation costs are roughly proportional to attendance. . . .

The major source of differences among teams' financial aid budgets is tuition. Tuition depends on the quality, reputation, and scope of activities of the school as well as whether it is public or private. All athletic scholarships include about $12,000 for room and board so that 85 scholarships (the Division I-A ceiling for football) cost about $1 million plus tuition. . . .

Scholarship costs explain why two-thirds of Division I basketball schools do not play in Division I-A football. Athletics departments at private schools need to dish out two or three times more in aid to play Division I-A football as do most public schools. Thus for nearly all private schools in Division I, football revenues can't come close to covering the costs of scholarships, coaches, travel, equipment, and stadium operations. So very few opt in.

Table 3 Financial Review of 2008–2009 Postseason Bowls: 5-Year Summary of Institutional Expenses

	2008–2009 BCS	2008–2009 Non-BCS	2008–2009 Total	2007–2008 Total	2006–2007 Total	2005–2006 Total	2004–2005 Total
Bowl payout[1,2]	$148,164,228	$79,900,079	$228,064,307	$221,890,357	$217,600,717	$190,251,549	$186,373,416
Transportation							
Team and staff	2,690,132	10,041,891	12,732,023	11,300,594	10,746,540	10,294,906	8,529,472
Band and cheerleaders	1,383,979	4,165,980	5,549,959	6,602,187	5,506,093	3,826,834	4,457,282
Official party	678,714	1,194,318	1,873,032	2,888,282	2,541,241	1,454,701	1,706,343
Total transportation expense	*4,752,825*	*15,402,189*	*20,155,014*	*20,791,063*	*18,793,874*	*15,576,441*	*14,693,097*
Meals/Lodging/Per Diem							
Team and staff	5,226,258	12,119,753	17,346,011	16,285,556	15,333,584	13,068,423	12,246,030
Band and cheerleaders	1,314,920	2,802,355	4,117,275	4,437,016	3,790,209	3,315,802	3,339,261
Official party	436,069	1,182,402	1,618,471	2,289,026	2,343,383	1,566,158	1,680,240
Total meals, lodging and per diem expense	*6,977,247*	*16,104,510*	*23,081,757*	*23,011,598*	*21,467,176*	*17,950,383*	*17,265,531*
Total travel expense	**11,730,072**	**31,506,699**	**43,236,771**	**43,802,662**	**40,261,050**	**33,526,824**	**31,958,628**
Game Expense							
Entertainment	400,001	856,130	1,256,131	978,140	1,297,827	1,322,759	931,240
Promotion	196,799	629,025	825,824	787,606	1,010,303	772,062	575,305
Awards	635,985	3,245,195	3,881,180	3,866,610	3,994,163	3,644,826	3,569,593
Equipment and supplies	295,404	1,613,774	1,909,178	2,142,943	1,982,629	1,673,206	1,675,274
Tickets absorbed by participating team	2,571,315	5,099,170	7,670,485	6,865,285	9,106,185	10,799,049	9,349,515
Administrative	1,919,074	3,713,141	5,632,215	5,949,361	4,948,051	3,634,714	4,939,771
Other	2,809,707	4,918,575	7,728,282	6,603,443	7,084,487	6,227,464	5,280,656
Total game expense	**8,828,285**	**20,075,010**	**28,903,295**	**27,193,388**	**29,423,645**	**28,074,080**	**26,321,354**
Tickets absorbed by conference	2,182,910	5,677,305	7,860,215	8,023,975	—	—	—
Total expenses	**22,741,267**	**57,259,014**	**80,000,281**	**79,020,025**	**69,684,695**	**61,600,904**	**58,279,982**
Excess revenues over expenses	**125,422,961**	**22,641,065**	**148,064,026**	**142,870,332**	**147,916,022**	**128,650,645**	**128,093,434**

[1] Average expense allowance for BCS participating institutions is $1,713,406, and average expenses are $2,108,645.

[2] Average expense allowance for non-BCS participating institutions is $876,198, and average expenses are $987,224.

Source: National Collegiate Athletic Association, April 10, 2009. © National Collegiate Athletic Association. 2008–2010. All rights reserved.

Table 4   Distribution of BCS Revenue, 2008–2009

Conference	Distribution of Revenue
Big Ten	$23,172,725
Southeastern	23,172,725
Big 12	23,172,725
Pacific 10	18,672,743
Atlantic Coast	18,672,725
Big East	18,672,725
Mountain West	9,788,800
Western Athletic	3,224,000
Conference USA	2,659,200
Mid-American	2,094,400
Sun Belt	1,529,600
Notre Dame	1,331,860
Big Sky	225,000
Atlantic 10	225,000
Mid-Eastern	225,000
Gateway	225,000
Ohio Valley	225,000
Southwestern Athletic	225,000
Southland	225,000
Southern	225,000
U.S. Military Academy	100,000
U.S. Naval Academy	100,000
Total BCS Distribution	**$148,164,228**

Source: National Collegiate Athletic Association, April 10, 2009. © National Collegiate Athletic Association. 2008–2010. All rights reserved.

Table 5   Postseason Bowl Average Information, 2008–2009

	Non-BCS Bowl	BCS Bowl
Average bowl payout	$2,755,175	$29,632,858
Average expenses	1,974,449	4,546,253
Average net to conferences and institutions	780,726	25,086,605

Source: National Collegiate Athletic Association, April 10, 2009. © National Collegiate Athletic Association. 2008–2010. All rights reserved.

Tuition does not necessarily reflect actual costs to the university. A key consideration is whether the school is at its enrollment ceiling. At highly rated academic schools—California, Duke, Michigan, Northwestern, Stanford, U.C.L.A., Wisconsin—many applicants are rejected who would be willing to pay all of the university's charges. So the decision to subsidize another athlete is a decision not to admit someone who might pay full tuition.

But where an extra athlete does not displace a tuition-payer, the cost of admitting 85 football players is very small compared to the average cost of providing the education. Thus, if an under-enrolled private school can generate enough revenue from football to pay the tuition of its players, the tuition payments are gravy for the university.

Capital facilities are a very important cost of football. In theory, a university could go into debt to build a stadium, and then cover the debt from its operating budget. But, in practice, capital investments are covered by special fundraising drives or, for public universities, by separate appropriations. The reason is simple: no university generates a large enough surplus to justify the capital expenditures necessary to field a football team.

. . . .

March Madness

Basketball operates on a smaller gross, but with disproportionately lower costs. Like football, the best basketball schools play more home games than the worst, with cash changing hands to arrange unbalanced schedules. A dozen Division I men's teams have a home attendance of around 300,000 per season, while some 50 draw more than 100,000.

Colleges ration student attendance to sell more tickets at higher prices. The best men's basketball teams have game revenues . . . plus television revenues. . . . A few top women's teams take in over $1 million. But most of the 50 or so schools that try to field a ranked team and usually make the NCAA championship tournament have revenues below this.

The NCAA has a complex formula, based on past success, for dividing the profits from the NCAA tournament. Nearly all payments go to conferences that share revenues, so a school's tournament revenue depends more on the success of its conference than its own record. [*Ed. Note:* ***Tables 7 and 8 show distribution amounts to Division I conferences.***]

. . . .

Over 300 schools play Division I basketball, compared to over 100 in Division I-A football and about 80 more in Division I-AA. . . .

Basketball is far less expensive than football because teams need pay only 15 scholarships and travel with fewer than 15 players. Coaches are paid about the same as in football, but staffs are smaller. . . .

As in football, the cost of a scholarship to the athletics department can run from $12,000 to over $30,000. But even in the latter case, the total team cost is under $500,000. Thus revenue . . . is more than sufficient to pay the out-of-pocket costs of a team at a private school, and half that can do the job at an inexpensive public school. . . .

WHAT'S IN IT FOR SPORTS U?

Schools not well known outside their home region can benefit indirectly from a successful Division I team by increasing applications for admission. Whether this actually helps the school, though, depends upon its circumstances. A school at its enrollment ceiling will gain only to the extent that it can be more selective in admissions. But a private

Table 6   Summary of Bowl Excess Revenue Expenses by Conference, 2008–2009

Conference	Institution's Bowl Revenue	Participating Institution's Expense	Excess of Revenue over Expenses	Excess Revenue/Expenses per Conference
ACC	$30,913,725	$12,148,350	$18,765,375	12.70%
Big East	23,322,725	7,796,069	15,526,656	10.50%
Big Ten	36,571,930	12,725,600	23,846,330	16.10%
Big 12	34,017,340	11,496,279	22,521,061	15.20%
Conference USA	6,734,200	4,325,469	2,408,731	1.60%
Independents	3,131,860	2,157,964	973,896	0.70%
Mid-American	5,844,400	3,970,037	1,874,363	1.30%
Mountain West	12,173,629	4,623,899	7,549,730	5.10%
Pac-10	24,817,358	6,050,572	18,766,786	12.70%
SEC	40,123,711	11,761,044	28,362,667	19.20%
Sun Belt	2,604,600	856,590	1,748,010	1.20%
WAC	6,008,829	2,088,407	3,920,422	2.60%
Other distribution	1,800,000	—	1,800,000	1.30%
2008–2009 Totals	**$228,064,307**	**$80,000,281**	**$148,064,026**	**100.00%**

Source: National Collegiate Athletic Association, April 10, 2009. © National Collegiate Athletic Association. 2008–2010. All rights reserved.

Table 7   2007–2008 NCAA Total Distribution to Members

Conference	Amount
America East	$6,686,913
Atlantic 10	11,416,499
Atlantic Coast	29,422,225
Atlantic Sun	3,584,429
Big 12	28,381,052
Big East	29,949,918
Big Sky	4,961,818
Big South	4,629,776
Big Ten	31,215,888
Big West	5,191,129
Colonial Athletic	9,884,737
Conference USA	18,272,537
Horizon League	6,219,609
Independents	381,402
Ivy Group	6,784,213
Metro Atlantic	4,504,154
Mid-American	12,894,716
Mid Eastern	5,615,508
Missouri Valley	9,531,408
Mountain West	12,448,714
Northeast	6,156,454
Ohio Valley	6,180,611
Pacific-10	25,390,458
Southeastern	27,662,076
Southern	5,671,294
Southland	5,792,809
Southwestern	5,142,029
Sun Belt	9,397,222
The Patriot League	6,226,305
The Summit League	3,648,105
West Coast	4,623,771
Western	10,434,348
Total	**$358,302,127**

Source: National Collegiate Athletic Association. © National Collegiate Athletic Association. 2008–2010. All rights reserved.

Table 8   2007–2008 Division I Basketball Fund Distribution

Conference	Amount
America East	$1,337,093
Atlantic 10	4,393,307
Atlantic Coast	15,090,053
Atlantic Sun	1,146,080
Big 12	15,663,093
Big East	16,618,160
Big Sky	1,337,093
Big South	1,337,093
Big Ten	13,561,946
Big West	1,719,120
Colonial Athletic	2,674,187
Conference USA	8,213,573
Horizon League	2,865,200
Independents	0
Ivy Group	1,146,080
Metro Atlantic	1,337,093
Mid-American	1,910,133
Mid Eastern	1,146,080
Missouri Valley	4,775,333
Mountain West	4,011,280
Northeast	1,146,080
Ohio Valley	1,146,080
Pacific-10	12,606,880
Patriot League	1,528,107
Southeastern	14,708,026
Southern	1,146,080
Southland	1,337,093
Southwestern	1,146,080
The Summit League	1,146,080
Sun Belt	1,146,080
West Coast	2,674,187
Western	3,247,227
Total	**$143,259,997**

Source: National Collegiate Athletic Association. © National Collegiate Athletic Association. 2008–2010. All rights reserved.

school that has trouble filling its dorms can admit more students and collect more tuition. Even an extra 100 students at $20,000 each represents a serious piece of change for the average university.

Some claim that big-time sports can increase donations to academic programs. But several studies have concluded that athletics has essentially no effect on contributions to the school outside the athletics programs. The only plausible source of an indirect financial benefit is through the enrollment effect: if more and better students attend, the university might receive more alumni gifts a few decades later.

The vast majority of departments of athletics do not make a profit, even from the two revenue sports. Indeed, a majority of Division I schools lose substantial amounts on football and, at best, break even on basketball. Thus, for all schools outside (and most in) Division I, intercollegiate athletics is a financial drain—commonly hundreds of dollars annually per student enrolled.

For the top schools that do profit from their revenue sports, the profits are significant. But the money rarely accrues to the academic side of the university. Competition is fierce for high-end coaches—as well as for people who can run big-time athletics departments efficiently. Thus, much of the surplus from revenue sports is spent on salaries.

What's more, universities are inclined to spend anything left on unremunerative sports. This phenomenon has been boosted by the requirement for gender equality in varsity athletics. Women have no counterpart to football with its 85 scholarships. So in the wake of legal requirements to balance gender participation in varsity sports, football schools have been forced either to drop some men's sports or to add women's. Schools that make a lot of money on football pursue the second strategy. After all—returning to the earlier theme—men and women students alike want more women's sports, not fewer men's sports.

"CHEATING" AND THE ROLE OF THE NCAA

Athletics scandals typically arise from violations of the NCAA's rules, and thus are commonly labeled as "cheating" to emphasize the idea that the offending institutions are attempting to gain advantages unfairly. These scandals fall into three categories. The first is excessive financial assistance to student-athletes—under-the-table payments or no-show jobs. The second is toleration of antisocial behavior that does not directly affect athletic performance—drug use, theft, violence, or simply low academic performance that would not be tolerated for nonathletes. The third is toleration of performance-enhancing drugs or training regimes that consume most of a student's time. All of these rules violations follow from the financial incentives facing universities and, especially, coaches.

. . . To obtain a job at one of the 30 or so universities that aspire to the first tier in revenue sports, a coach must first win consistently at a lower level. Then, to keep a plum job or move on to the pros, a coach must win consistently against quality opponents. At the very top schools, winning seasons without major bowl victories in football or a shot at the quarterfinals in [the] NCAA basketball tournament will lead to dismissal.

The basic principle behind the NCAA's rules regarding competition for athletes is that it must be limited to two dimensions: the overall college environment and the skills of the coach. Many highly skilled athletes are in college to prepare for professional sports careers. They seek scholarships for one purpose: to obtain experience and training needed to advance to the pros with the least possible disruption to what they do off the playing field. And like other adolescents, some athletes cut class, take drugs, beat up other students and, on occasion, knock off a liquor store if they think they can get away with it.

For a coach, success assures a decades-long career with a salary of hundreds of thousands of dollars. And with few exceptions, coaches have no alternative employment opportunities anywhere near as lucrative. Consequently, a coach facing an athlete who wants extra money (or a free pass on school rules) has compelling reasons to succumb.

Persistent rule breaking by coaches is not likely to go unnoticed by vigilant university administrators. But the incentive to cheat spills over if they regard athletic performance as a way of attracting students or encouraging the generosity of alumni and state legislators. All that is needed to let cheating persist is inattention.

The cheating label is a device for generating adverse publicity that might pressure universities to adhere to the NCAA's rules. But looking behind the public relations, much of what the NCAA and the press call cheating is not ethically questionable.

The NCAA's financial rules are incredibly detailed, frequently picayune, and vigorously enforced. Isolated minor infractions usually lead to minor penalties: While at Stanford, Tiger Woods regained eligibility when he reimbursed Arnold Palmer for dinner. But repeated minor violations are interpreted as a sign of laxity in a university's enforcement efforts. When U.C.L.A. was placed on probation in basketball, the documented crimes were repeated gifts of T-shirts and Thanksgiving dinners.

THE NCAA CARTEL

Economists who have studied intercollegiate sports unanimously agree that the NCAA is the harshest price-fixing cartel in all athletics, amateur or professional. Recall that an athletic scholarship actually covers only about $10,000 in basic living costs. The rest goes for tuition, books, and other fees. For an athlete who has no interest in the educational aspects of being a college athlete, the part of a scholarship that covers academics has no value. If attending college were regarded as more or less a full-time job, the student-athlete could do better working an equivalent number of hours at a fast-food restaurant. The problem from the athlete's perspective is that McDonalds does not field a football team. [*Ed. Note: See* **Figure 1** *for the stated economic policy of the NCAA.*]

Financial cheating arises because an athlete is worth more to a university and its fans than the NCAA scholarship limit. If five good players can increase the revenue of a men's basketball team from $1 million to $3 million—still a modest amount—these players are worth $400,000 each. Thus if schools were to bid competitively for these athletes, the winning bids would be ten times more than the list price of a year at Stanford.

Where would this money come from? Some, presumably, from subsidies now going to minor sports. Some would

---

Intercollegiate athletics programs shall be administered in keeping with prudent management and fiscal practices to assure the financial stability necessary for providing student-athletes with adequate opportunities for athletics competition as an integral part of a quality educational experience.

Figure 1   NCAA Constitution Article 2.16

Source: 2008–2009 *NCAA Division I Manual*, p. 5. © National Collegiate Athletic Association. 2008–2010. All rights reserved.

come from coaches' salaries, because recruiting superstar athletes would no longer be as profitable. And for a handful of top sports schools, some would come out of profits now used to cover academic expenditures.

The beneficiaries of the NCAA scholarship rules are thus athletes in other sports, the very best coaches, and, in rare cases, academic programs. For the most part, these beneficiaries are either highly paid or from families with above-average incomes. By contrast, NCAA financial rules harm the star athletes in football, men's basketball, and, to a lesser degree, women's basketball—athletes who disproportionately come from lower-income families. Thus, the NCAA financial rules are primarily a means of redistributing income regressively.

The overall impact of the financial rules varies enormously among schools and students. For a minority of college athletes, including some in minor sports, the main benefit of intercollegiate athletics is preparation for a professional sports career. For those who do become pros, the payoffs are very large and college life is a far more pleasant way to gain experience and acquire training than playing in minor leagues. In this sense, college athletes are not exploited because their alternatives are less attractive.

Nevertheless, the prospects for a pro career are poor in every sport. Each year, about 1500 men receive Division I basketball scholarships, while 2000 receive Division I-A football scholarships. Of these, about 150 will ever play an N.B.A. game, and about 250 will ever play in the N.F.L. Moreover, most of the athletes who succeed as pros will come from the elite athletics programs. . . .

For scholarship athletes who never become pros, intercollegiate sports can provide two other benefits. One benefit—competition itself—is frequently overlooked because of the focus on preparing athletes for pro careers. Nevertheless, this benefit is not trivial.

Then, too, a college degree has a big effect on lifetime income. The return to the investment in college is very high and has increased sharply in the last two decades. Thus for a serious student, a free education at a private university is worth not just the $100,000-plus scholarship, but another $200,000 in the "present value" of the extra income the student will earn over a lifetime.

At the other end of the spectrum, if a school has no academic standards or graduates few athletes, restrictions on scholarships are just an instrument for taking advantage of the NCAA price-fixing cartel. In the trophy sports, many scholarship athletes do not take academics seriously and very few graduate, so that they do not enjoy the postgraduation benefits of higher education.

For these, the majority of Division I scholarship athletes, college is nothing more than an opportunity to play organized sports for a few more years before facing the reality of adulthood. The nub of the issue about the place of sports on campus is whether these athletes, numbering a few thousand in all sports combined, are better off in college than out. For the most part, they enjoy their college experiences—but not for anything having to do with academics.

PLAYING BY THE RULES

On paper, the NCAA's rules seem to say that college is for athletes ready to benefit from the academic side of school. For the most part, however, the NCAA's rules [that are] unrelated to money or the games themselves are minimal and rarely enforced. The NCAA does maintain eligibility rules for both admissions and grades. But these requirements are actually very low—well below the formal admissions requirements for universities and colleges with well-regarded academic programs, including many schools that compete in Division I athletics. Indeed, in the trophy sports only a small fraction of athletes who could play regularly for a top team satisfy the normal admissions requirements of the academically oriented colleges.

To maintain eligibility, the NCAA insists that athletes be registered as full-time students, remain in good academic standing, and make normal progress toward a degree. But since schools are extremely heterogeneous in their academic standards, these requirements boil down to very little. Good standing means whatever the university decides. Normal progress toward a degree means almost nothing, since progress is not judged retrospectively by actual graduation results. Most schools graduate a third or fewer of scholarship athletes in the trophy sports and some graduate none.

With respect to antisocial behavior, the NCAA's basic rule is that athletes should be treated like other students. As a result, if a school does not expel other students for felonies, they need not expel athletes. In most cases, universities' disciplinary actions are taken on a case-by-case basis. And some schools are perfectly happy to field a team of alleged perpetrators who, when they behave the same way in the pros, are suspended.

In theory, the NCAA also limits the time athletes can spend on sports. But these rules have no bite. If coaches and universities want a longer season, the NCAA accepts extended time limits. And for some sports, the "season" is the academic year.

The hours-per-week limit is more an accounting formality than a strict constraint. The norm is to practice far more than the limits allow, so that each athlete "voluntarily" decides to commit extra time to training in order to compete effectively against others who devote extra time to training.

By contrast, the prohibition against performance-enhancing drugs is rigidly enforced. Student-athletes sometimes are declared ineligible to compete in NCAA events after taking prescription drugs for an illness. While athletes often protest the NCAA's testing protocols, the strict rules against steroids, painkillers, and stimulants definitely serve their long-term interests.

THE TRUE IMPACT OF THE NCAA CARTEL

Step back, and the picture is clear: the NCAA is mostly a device for "cartelizing" universities while doing little to enforce standards of academic performance and social behavior among student-athletes. With the exception of the prohibition against performance enhancing drugs, the only rules that are both strict and vigorously enforced pertain to limiting financial aid. Thus, to judge solely by cause and effect, the NCAA is mostly interested in suppressing payments to athletes in a way that benefits coaches and the athletes who play minor sports.

The NCAA's inclinations are also revealed by its other business activities. Until the mid-1980s, the organization required all colleges and universities to give the NCAA a monopoly in television rights for daytime Saturday football games. The practice ended only after the rule was declared a violation of antitrust law. This court decision led to the proliferation of football telecasts on cable channels, which reduced the total fees collected by colleges, increased the disparity in television revenues among colleges (favoring the strongest football programs) and substantially increased the total number of Saturday games available to viewers.

. . . .

The NCAA's rules on the number of games go far beyond what is necessary to limit the demands on athletes. That objective could be achieved by a much simpler rule . . . . This cynical conclusion is not intuitively obvious, and to some seems to deny the organization's history. Early in the [last] century, football came very close to being banned because it had become so violent and dangerous. The NCAA rewrote the rules of play to solve this problem, and hardly anyone would dispute the legitimacy of this role.

A few decades later, as intercollegiate football became more important many schools abandoned the principle of a student-athlete, and became professional operations. The NCAA's present limits on the number and value of scholarships and its academic requirements arose to combat this professionalization.

But the NCAA's rules do not prevent professionalization among universities that seek to pursue it. Indeed, by making certain that coaches and schools—not athletes—are the main beneficiaries, the NCAA makes the problem worse by giving them a reason to abandon academic values in pursuit of athletic glory.

ARE INTERCOLLEGIATE SPORTS A DESTRUCTIVE INFLUENCE?

Perhaps 50 colleges and universities participate in trophy sports to generate revenues, with the benefits going in part to coaches and athletic administrators, in part to other sports, and, in a few cases, to academic programs. For all other sports, and even for trophy sports at all but the top programs, intercollegiate sports exist not to make money but to please important constituencies—primarily students. If all universities collectively banned intercollegiate sports or athletic scholarships, higher education as a whole probably would be stronger financially than it is.

But this is far from the complete story. Most colleges and universities also would be better off financially if they agreed to eliminate comparative literature and advanced mathematics. The difficult question is whether varsity sports bring enough value to universities to offset their costs. And part of the answer revolves around the scandals that surround athletics.

Scandals embarrass universities and undermine their moral authority as transmitters of social values. But scandals are not intrinsic to intercollegiate sports. Intercollegiate athletics create scandals only in schools that are powers in trophy sports—or seek to become powers.

The incentive of coaches to win is a necessary component of the incentive to break the rules. And much of this is created by the cartel aspects of the NCAA's rules, which limit the cost of all programs and substantially increases the profitability of trophy sports at top schools.

If the NCAA behaved less like a cartel, the financial benefit of on-field success would be smaller. In turn, salaries for top coaches would fall, and schools would have less reason to recruit athletes who seek only a pro career and not an education. Moreover, relaxed rules would lead to fewer violations and fewer scandals. Cutting to the chase, if colleges had to pay something closer to market value for top athletes, they would admit fewer of them and be less interested in athletes who are likely to be behavioral problems.

The economics of intercollegiate athletics is not a story of administrators willfully perverting academic values for the fast buck. Such things do happen, but this is not an accurate characterization of the vast majority of intercollegiate sports programs. The more fundamental force driving college sports is the intense interest that so many students and alums have in sports. And the idea that colleges would abandon something as universally popular as intercollegiate athletics is a fantasy.

But things could be far better. Higher education and society at large would be better served if the NCAA did not limit scholarships or set the price for postseason events in trophy sports.

OPTIONS

Breaking up the NCAA cartel is probably as unrealistic a goal as banning intercollegiate athletics. Any effort to eliminate the cartel aspect of the NCAA would probably lead many Division I schools to set up a rival organization that adopted the practices the NCAA now follows. If the schools that value athletics most highly all joined the new cartel, reforming the NCAA would have little effect.

So what, if anything, can be done? Perhaps, not much.

Too many people currently involved in sports, from coaches to athletes in non-trophy sports to the commercial interests that cohabit with [the] best college sports programs, would fight hard to preserve the business as usual. Moreover, as the demand for revenue sports rises along with affluence and leisure time in America, the financial incentives to do well in trophy sports will only grow. The future is likely to be a larger version of the past.

But for optimists in the crowd, there are a couple of plausible routes to reform. The first is to attack the NCAA through antitrust laws. The NCAA has already lost its television monopoly this way. And an unrelated antitrust suit forced a consortium of elite universities to abandon collusion on need-based financial aid. But an antitrust suit would be slow and expensive. And it would probably require the active involvement of the Antitrust Division of the Department of Justice, which is notably uninterested.

The Justice Department's reluctance is understandable: The Federal Trade Commission was barred from attacking the NCAA on the ground that it is only allowed to enforce competition in for-profit markets. Moreover, unlike the television case in which some universities had financial incentives to break the NCAA's control, private parties are unlikely to pursue the antitrust route on scholarships or postseason play.

Another way to castrate the cartel would be to alter the existing rules in ways that change the universities' incentives.

. . . .

The key to change in all these proposals parallels the general drift of economic policy reform in the past three decades: rely more on incentives and less on rules. The practical way to make the values of intercollegiate sports more closely parallel the academic values of universities is to give universities less incentive to abandon academic values.

UNBOUND: HOW A SUPREME COURT DECISION TORE APART FOOTBALL TELEVISION AND RIPPLED THROUGH 25 YEARS OF COLLEGE SPORTS

Jack Copeland

Twenty-five years ago this summer, the thread that leads to today's NCAA began unspooling from the chambers of the U.S. Supreme Court. That was when Justice John Paul Stevens wrote that the Association's control of football games on television violated antitrust law. Six of his colleagues signed on in agreement.

The 7–2 decision on June 27, 1984, resulted from a legal challenge filed nearly three years earlier by the Universities of Georgia and Oklahoma. The schools argued the NCAA's Football Television Plan, through which the Association controlled broadcasts of weekly national and regional games on TV and cable networks, illegally blocked them from striking their own deals.

Just two weeks later, the Association grappled during a special meeting in Chicago with a future in which members no longer would share in football-television revenues that had topped $260 million under the voided plan. There, representatives of 111 schools argued over whether the NCAA should attempt to salvage the plan with a new agreement that would address antitrust concerns, then essentially voted to leave members free to pursue their own contracts.

The Division I Men's Basketball Committee also gathered about that same time in Colorado, and Richard Schultz, then director of athletics at Virginia, was attending his first meeting as a new member. He remembers the group taking a break so that he and others could fly to Chicago for the football discussion.

"There were a lot of tensions out there as the lawsuit was coming together . . . and there was some tension once (the decision) came down," Schultz recalled. "Where I was, the tension was mainly, what's going to happen, how's this going to impact financially, and so forth."

Schultz returned to Colorado, and the basketball committee resumed planning to implement an expansion to 64 teams in 1986—a move that just seemed like a natural step at the time but that soon sparked an explosion in the tournament's popularity and value.

Then, everyone—the administrators who struggled through that postmortem in Chicago, and Schultz and the other stewards of the basketball tournament that now was the NCAA's most prized possession—went home. So did members of the newly formed NCAA Presidents Commission, which had gathered in Chicago for a scheduled organizational meeting just three days after the court ruling and whose agenda included a request from the NCAA Council for presidents to consider the idea of a major-college football playoff.

All returned home from those meetings and began picking up that thread unspooling from the Supreme Court.

That thread soon would lead Schultz into leadership of the NCAA, ultimately put presidents in charge of decision-making for the organization and lead to an array of once-unimagined challenges as it pulled the Association into the future.

Five years ago, journalist Keith Dunnavant wrote about the 1984 decision in his book titled "The 50-Year Seduction," calling *NCAA vs. University of Oklahoma Board of Regents* an "earthquake." The book detailed "how television manipulated college football, from the birth of the modern NCAA to the creation of the BCS," as the subtitle put it.

If what happened in 1984 was an earthquake, there now have been 25 years of aftershocks.

"The Board of Regents decision fundamentally shaped the future of college athletics, and college football in particular, because it created a future denominated by the chase for TV sets," Dunnavant explained. . . .

"You can draw a line from the Board of Regents decision to the expansion of the SEC to the death of the Southwest Conference to the birth of the Big 12 to the emergence of the Atlantic Coast Conference. Also, without the decision—and how it affected what I call a civil war political climate within big-time college football—you would not have the Bowl Championship Series today," he said.

"It is the absolute common denominator to the modern era of the sport that we see today."

The decision's impact on college football, that "civil war political climate" and a lengthy struggle to capitalize on the newly opened TV marketplace is well-documented in books written by Dunnavant and others, including one by the NCAA's executive director at the time of the ruling, Walter Byers.

By the time he published "Unsportsmanlike Conduct" in 1995, Byers had come to believe the organization—which he had nurtured from the establishment of a national headquarters in the 1950s through the achievement of rules-enforcement authority, financial security and new championship opportunities for both men and women—had lost its way in serving the students playing the sports.

He argued the NCAA should not limit the term or value of athletics scholarships, should not prevent athletes from holding a job or otherwise restrict outside income, should repeal restrictions on transfers and should permit consultation with agents in making decisions about sport careers. He also said if the NCAA does not take these steps unilaterally, it should be forced to do so by legislative action.

Byers looked at those contentious days around the Board of Regents case from that perspective and judged the focus on football as too narrow. He suggested that Oklahoma, Georgia and other schools that joined forces through the College Football Association could have dismantled the NCAA for the sake of reform but instead "missed a politically propitious moment to restructure control of college athletics, dazzled instead by TV glamour and the prospect of network dollars." As a result, rather than destroying the Association, the Board of Regents case prompted the NCAA

to regroup and reassess—whether through day-to-day business like that basketball committee meeting in Colorado or decisions by the NCAA Executive Committee and Council and at annual Conventions.

"Organizations, like the people who inhabit them, generally need time to absorb and operationalize major changes," wrote Joseph Crowley, a former NCAA membership president, in his history of the Association in 2006, "In the Arena: The NCAA's First Century."

"Refinements are often necessary. Midcourse corrections often occur. Leaders have the responsibility of monitoring the pace of change and maintaining a protective balance between reform and organizational stability. Hard choices have to be made in the process. Tall orders may take a while."

Perhaps those words best describe the thread that the NCAA followed through the quarter century after Justice Stevens' opinion.

During the NCAA's 2006 Convention, three of the Association's four chief executives (Schultz, Cedric Dempsey and Myles Brand) and a stand-in for Byers (retired Big Ten Conference Commissioner Wayne Duke, who had worked beside Byers after establishment of the national office in Kansas City) participated in a panel discussion celebrating the 100th anniversary of the Association's founding.

Schultz, Dempsey and Brand each stressed the importance of the Board of Regents decision, as did Duke, who recalled Justice Byron White's dissenting opinion in the case, which argued that the NCAA television plan should be preserved because it "fosters the goal of amateurism by spreading revenues among various schools and reducing the financial incentives toward professionalism."

Yet, even as the foursome agreed that the decision was a key milestone in the NCAA's history, Brand provocatively suggested that it merely altered the course that history followed—not the outcome.

"I'm of the opinion that if that case had gone the other way, we still might be exactly where we are now," he said then. "The names might have changed and some of the contractual arrangements would be different, but I'm not sure there would be anything different in the end."

It's an interesting question: Would the NCAA be different today if it had won, rather than lost, that 1984 antitrust case?

Brand's predecessor, Dempsey, largely agrees today with Brand, though he thinks some of the most difficult issues he faced during his tenure leading the NCAA from 1994 to 2003 stemmed directly from the 1984 ruling.

"It created a vulnerability that the NCAA had never had before to legal actions, an area in which it had tremendous success before that time," he said. . . . "It unfortunately, I think, began to separate out the major programs in the country, by giving them a feeling of—and in actuality—greater control. Had it not been for '84, we might not have had the same kind of restructuring approach in Division I that occurred 12 years later.

"It had a tremendous impact upon the current structure and certainly the philosophy of intercollegiate sports."

Schultz agrees that a fundamental frustration expressed via the Board of Regents case—that a relatively small number of schools were producing revenue for the Association but had limited say in how it was distributed—lingered as the newly expanded 64-team basketball tournament exploded in popularity. Eventually, it won a $1 billion television contract for the NCAA with CBS in 1989.

"I had one or two athletics directors at various times say, 'Well, we might just pull out of basketball and go out on our own.' And I said, well, fine, go ahead and do that," Schultz recalled. "I said, 'You've got a great model in front of you in football. You saw what happened to football television when you went out.'"

What happened is that football television revenue plummeted as conferences and schools began competing for the best deals from the relatively small number of media outlets available at the time to carry games. What had been a seller's market suddenly was a buyer's market, as The NCAA News reported three weeks after the Supreme Court decision, and just a week after that Chicago meeting.

"It was many, many, many years before the (football) rights fees on a per-game basis began to approach what they were at the end of the NCAA program," said Tom Hansen, the recently retired commissioner of the Pacific-10 Conference. . . .

Dempsey observed the same dissatisfaction among the membership tier that contributed most to the Association's wealth, and perhaps felt it even more acutely than Schultz.

"From '84 to '96, there were always different things that would come up, and there would always be that veiled threat, well, if you don't do this, we're going to get out," he recalled.

That dissatisfaction flowered as Schultz was leaving office in 1993 and Dempsey assumed the post at the 1994 NCAA Convention. A group of Division I-A commissioners circulated a restructuring proposal at that Convention calling for creation of a 15-member "board of trustees" consisting of institutional presidents and dominated by what it termed "equity" conferences to replace the Council and Presidents Commission, as well as an end to one-institution, one-vote rulemaking at the Convention.

"Most of it had to do with revenue-sharing and determining their own destiny, and not having it be determined by people who didn't have the same kind of challenges that they had with their programs," Schultz said.

Three years later, the NCAA membership essentially adopted the plan proposed by the commissioners, after hammering out provisions designed to maintain links between the three membership divisions even as it reorganized into a "federated" structure meant to give each division authority over its own affairs. (Divisions II and III retained the one-institution, one-vote approach to deciding issues.)

"I think that had to take place, and it would have taken place with or without the Board of Regents decision," Schultz said. "In fact, the decision to do that may have come sooner (if the NCAA had won the case)."

Dempsey agrees federation was inevitable, but worries about whether the Association got it right in the details of governance.

"Out of that, we lost a lot," he suggested. "Those institutions still could have maintained control in the way they wanted without throwing out the baby with the bath water, if you will.

"As I go to campuses, people just don't feel part of the Association any longer. And all of the benefits that used to accrue from going to the Convention—and I know there were a lot of negatives, having to sit and listen to the other two (divisions), though I think those were handled by federation—it could have been handled much differently."

Even so, restructuring brought peace organizationally that the Association had not experienced since before the College Football Association formed in the late 1970s.

For several years after the Board of Regents decision, NCAA members struggled within the Association's structure to determine who would call the shots for the organization, while vying outside that structure—sometimes in something resembling hand-to-hand combat—to capitalize on the freedom provided by the Supreme Court to sell the appeal of college sports for media consumption.

The "civil war" Dunnavant referred to essentially was a rivalry pitting the College Football Association against the Big Ten and Pacific-10 Conferences. The conflict often did resemble a series of battles, as the sides skirmished in courtrooms and schools deserted longtime conference affiliations to boost the television appeal of a rival league. One key player, Notre Dame, struck a separate peace of sorts by breaking ranks with the CFA and negotiating its own network television contract.

But just as those "equity" conferences found a way to co-exist in a shared authority over the Division I governance structure within the NCAA, they also found a way through what has come to be known as the Bowl Championship Series to work together on the problem of football television.

The Board of Regents decision led directly to a dramatic increase in the number of games aired not only by the old-line networks such as CBS, NBC and ABC, but also by then fledgling cable outlets such as ESPN and the Turner Broadcasting System. It may have driven down the amount that schools earned per game for a television appearance, but over time it opened up many more opportunities for teams to appear on TV—though leagues with less negotiating clout ended up playing on Tuesday or Wednesday or Thursday night.

"I find it ironic that today, each of the (Division I Football Bowl Subdivision, formerly Division I-A) conferences has just about the same resources committed to football television that the NCAA did to run the entire country back in those days," the Pacific-10's Hansen said. "We all have multiple staff members involved in telecasting football, and in most cases, basketball also."

Those institutions may have wrestled authority over football television away from the NCAA on antitrust grounds, but that didn't exempt those institutions from antitrust scrutiny themselves—a problem that frustrated efforts to group the most attractive games into one television package. But a breakthrough of sorts came as the conferences dealt with complaints from many quarters—ranging from broadcast partners to fans—over the traditional football bowl system's inability to satisfy the American desire to determine a national champion.

"The creation of the BCS was the symbolic reunification of big-time college football, because it effectively was what amounted to the old CFA schools coming together to create a better postseason structure, but that would not have been possible but for the inclusion of the Big Ten and the Pac-10 coalition," Dunnavant said.

"The breakdown of that resistance really placed a period at the end of a very divisive era."

The collaboration may or may not ultimately produce a football playoff (Dunnavant suspects it will), but regardless of the outcome, it's interesting to ask that question again: Would things have turned out differently if the NCAA had prevailed in the Supreme Court in 1984?

"I think there's a good possibility that we might have a limited football playoff in (the former) Division I-A if the NCAA still had control," Schultz said. "We came very close to it when I was there."

Schultz said that at one point in his administration, Division I-A presidents in the governance structure were ready to support a playoff but backed off in the face of criticism from colleagues in another division. Then, not long before his departure, Schultz unsuccessfully proposed a two-week playoff to Division I-A conference commissioners that he argued would bring schools three to four times more revenue than they were collecting from existing bowl games, while retaining those games.

Attractive as those revenues might be, it would have required the conferences to give up at least a measure of control over the playoff—and perhaps in those pre-federation days, control over who would receive the proceeds.

So, is the NCAA different today than it would have been if the Supreme Court had been persuaded to follow Justice White's lead, rather than Justice Stevens?

It lost revenue from football television, but quickly replaced it with revenue from the basketball tournament, which Schultz believes exploded in popularity and value after expansion to 64 teams because "every community, every state, that had a team with 17 or 18 wins or close to 20 wins by the time the selection process came around thought their team was going to be in the tournament for the very first time."

It afforded Schultz and the membership an opportunity to share revenues without requiring recipients to make what he has called "the $350,000 free throw" to advance deeper into the tournament, while supporting programs ranging from catastrophic-injury coverage to various initiatives directly serving student-athlete development and well-being.

"It probably satisfied some of those schools that were getting football revenue when it was controlled and then lost that football revenue afterwards, and were able to pick up the additional revenue in basketball," Schultz said. "From a financial standpoint, that eased a lot of fears."

The NCAA has changed structurally, but perhaps the Supreme Court's decision better equipped the Association to work collaboratively to address issues.

"It's still alive and, overall, well," Dempsey says. "The NCAA has adjusted to the will of the membership pretty well, and will continue to do so. It will make the changes that are necessary, from time to time, as issues come up."

Those issues are many. Can the expense of operating large athletics programs be controlled? Will the Association achieve its ambitious efforts to improve the academic performance of athletes? Should it take greater advantage of commercial opportunities to generate more revenue if doing so directly benefits students at member schools?

It likely will require another spool of thread to find those answers.

THE 2009 NCAA STATE OF THE ASSOCIATION SPEECH, AS DELIVERED BY WALLACE I. RENFRO, NCAA VICE PRESIDENT AND SENIOR ADVISOR TO PRESIDENT MYLES BRAND, JANUARY 15, 2009

Myles Brand

. . . .

This paper and speech is the result of significant thought, discussion and writing that Dr. Brand has given to the relationship of commercialism to sports, a relationship that exists because sports is a significant part of the human experience.

It is present in our lives from children's play to the most elite professional contests.

Our language is filled with sports metaphors, and we ease into deeper conversations by finding neutral ground in sports talk.

The relevance of sports to our global culture was made evident when China used the attention of the Olympics for two weeks in August to announce that it is moving back onto the world stage. In America, we have developed a rich tradition for both participation and consumption.

There are a variety of professional sports leagues in America from lacrosse to ice hockey, from soccer to football, from golf to basketball.

Indeed, there are more than two dozen professional leagues.

But, as pervasive as professional sports has become in this country, college sports occupies a central place in the American culture.

It has become integral to many of our universities and colleges, institutions which are the guardians of our traditions and histories and the harbingers of our futures. College sports generates a significant economic impact in communities all across the country.

The estimated annual budget for all of intercollegiate athletics is $6 billion.

A large number.

But to help put that number in perspective, it should be noted that the total spent by athletics departments in America each year would not fully fund even two of this nation's largest public universities for a year, where annual budgets for a single comprehensive public research university range from $3 to $4 billion.

Unlike professional sports, however, the bottom line in the collegiate model is not the bottom line.

It is not creating profits for owners and shareholders.

The reason America's colleges and universities sponsor athletics—for more than a century and a half now—is the positive effect participation has on the lives of young men and women.

We should feel good in knowing college sports empowers these young people to become contributing members of their communities and country.

College sports rely on the hard and good work of many, and we should praise those who coach and administer intercollegiate athletics.

Indeed, we could easily spend our time today citing the successes of intercollegiate athletics.

There are innumerable and wonderful stories that need to be told.

Make no mistake: sports in college are very, very good.

We should all be unabashed advocates. Nonetheless, intercollegiate athletics is faced with issues it must resolve.

There are a number of ongoing challenges—academic reform in Division I, future strategic directions for Division III, and a dearth of diversity in hiring for coaches and administrators in all three divisions.

The key overarching issue for each of the divisions, in its own way, is the integration of athletics into the life of an academic institution.

There is both good news and ongoing frustration in all these areas.

And there are serious efforts that must yet be made.

These issues are rarely subtle in their ability to grab our attention; but with persistence, they can and are being brought to manageable size.

But today, the focus will be on an even more exasperating challenge for intercollegiate athletics: the proper role for commercial activity.

Indeed, there may be no more pressing issue for us over the next decade, especially as the economy constrains university and college budgets.

Our ability to understand both the necessity of monetizing the assets of college sports and the potential dangers of commercialism gone wild . . . and to find a proper balance that helps financially support as many participation opportunities as possible without swamping the principle of amateurism . . . may either ensure the place of intercollegiate athletics in higher education and the American culture or relegate it in many instances to third-rate professional sports.

If this issue has not already reached crisis, it is certainly approaching it.

There are several reasons for that.

First, universities are accelerating their spending on college sports. For more than a decade, the rate of increase in athletics' expenditures in Division I has exceeded the rate of increase in the general university budgets by a factor of three to four.

Revenues for athletics tend to increase faster than the general university budget.

Yet, in recent years, they have not, on average, kept pace with expenditures.

As a result, just six athletics programs in Division I have been in the black for each of the past five years.

In any given year, only five percent of the FBS programs operate in the black.

Gate receipts—not an insignificant revenue source for some institutions—generally hold static.

Athletics cannot depend on increased gates to cover the increased costs.

Where do new funds come from in order to meet the increased expenditures? There are basically three potential categories: increased donor contributions; increased subsidy from the university general fund; and increased commercial activity.

There is no question that Division I athletics directors have had to increase their efforts in fundraising.

True, they have had some success.

But there are natural limits, especially in times of economic downturn.

Moreover, the successes of athletics departments in fundraising is beginning to have consequences for the rest of the university; while philanthropy is not a zero-sum game, funds raised for athletics in some instances appear to be coming from those that in the past went to other parts of the university.

Increased fundraising, while important, may not be the best solution.

Almost every campus subsidizes athletics, and there is nothing wrong with subsidization.

The issue is, rather, whether the subsidy so burdens the rest of the university that there are adverse academic consequences.

Given the budgetary difficulties for many institutions, most especially those highly dependent on state allocations or tuition, continued large increases in subsidy for athletics is proving problematic.

That, then, leaves increases in commercial activity to fund increased expenses in athletics.

The second reason why commercialism can be problematic is that there have been dramatic changes in the media, including especially the sports media, that have generated new and greater opportunities for commercial activity associated with athletics.

Nearly three decades ago, ESPN began solely featuring sports on TV.

There is no doubt that ESPN has been highly successful, its initial platform has not only turned into an entire network, but it now includes print media, radio and importantly new media configurations.

It is not an exaggeration to say that ESPN has shaped an entire generation in how sports are consumed.

Media presentation of sports—including college sports —is big—very big—business.

The desire of media outlets to obtain college sports content and to use it as programming to sell advertising sometimes seems limitless.

Media companies are quite willing to pay universities, conferences and the NCAA to present this content in ways that are attractive to audiences.

The more attractive the sports are, the more media are willing to pay.

For colleges and universities, the issue goes beyond increased revenue.

The broadcast presentation and distribution of a school's athletics events can increase its visibility and name recognition.

Athletics is one good way to market the university.

Such successful marketing can result in higher application rates for the general student body, as well as campus morale and community building.

The third reason for increased commercialism is related to the expansion of the sports media.

We are in the midst of a media revolution in which there are rapid changes in the modes of presentation and in how audiences consume media.

It was not that long ago when sports were featured only in the print media and three TV networks.

Now, the options are almost limitless.

Where television once opened us to the pictures and sounds of sports on one screen, there are now three types of screens to watch: traditional TV, including network and cable, local and national; computer screens, which not only include live Internet presentations, but also animated sporting events through video games; and hand-held devices that permit mobile viewing tailored to the audience's taste and convenience.

Indeed, video screens are becoming ubiquitous, in airports, elevators, taxis—wherever you look.

There are expanding opportunities for universities to generate revenue by selling the rights to present and distribute their sporting events to these new media outlets.

But the new media environment is highly competitive, and so expanded access becomes a condition for the sale of these rights.

Examples of expanded access include moving the games to nontraditional days of the week and adjusting the starting times to accommodate broadcast schedules.

Access includes live interactions with coaches and student-athletes in order to bring the viewer "into" the game.

The confluence of the Internet and reality animation makes difficult control by content providers—namely us.

These three primary reasons explain why there is increased commercialism and why, at this time, the challenge to finding the right balance is critical.

How do we ensure continued revenue from commercial activity, especially when these monies are needed more than ever, without abridging the values and mission of higher education?

The central questions then become: What is the balance point between too much and too little commercial activity and how do we adhere to it?

Aristotle argued for the doctrine of the Golden Mean.

The virtuous path is one that avoids the excesses of the extremes.

An example of such a virtue is courage.

Courage strikes a balance between debilitating fear and foolhardy disregard of danger.

Aristotle did not claim that the right path is always the middle one.

But warns us to avoid the ends of the spectrum.

In the case of commercialism, the extremes of unrealistic idealism and crass commercialism are not the right courses of action, but between them—somewhere—there is an acceptable balance point.

Finding this balance point, it can be argued, is the next greatest challenge we must address.

Some believe that college sports should be totally devoid of commercial interests.

They believe the enterprise should be "pure," that only the competition between student-athletes is relevant.

Advertising and other commercial activities sully the contests and the contestants.

This idealistic approach may work in the cases of recreational and club sports, but not for competitive, organized sports, including intercollegiate athletics.

Training, coaching and competition are not free in the collegiate environment.

Coaches work for salaries, equipment must be purchased, and travel to the competition and conducting the events can be costly.

Championship competitions, in which the best compete against their peers, are a key part of the collegiate athletics experience, and championships certainly are not free to conduct.

Some level of commercial activity—from nominal levels of local sponsorships to huge media and corporate contracts—touches every NCAA athletics program in the country regardless of division.

Without commercial activity, intercollegiate athletics as we know it could not exist.

This is true even on the Divisions II and III levels.

A critical part of the Divisions II and III experiences is championship competition.

Championships in these divisions are almost entirely supported by revenues generated from the Division I men's basketball tournament.

Thus, the ability of Divisions II and III to conduct championships are based—indirectly at least—in commercial activity.

Every member of the NCAA has a stake in how commercialism is conducted in college sports.

The only way to operate athletics on campuses without the revenues from commercial activity is to reduce it to recreational or club sports, without paid coaches or good equipment and facilities.

While that, of course, is always an option, the benefits of student participation in high-level, organized athletics; the branding and marketing of the institution through athletics; and the value to the community, including economic development, would all be lost.

The loss of these benefits to gain pure idealism is unwarranted.

The higher education community has understood this equation for over one hundred years. On the other hand, commercial activity can go too far and can subvert the values and mission of higher education.

Some critics of contemporary intercollegiate athletics argue that the problem is not commercialism itself, but rather the artificial limits placed on that activity by the higher education community.

Competitive success, they argue, is the goal of athletics programs.

The reason we play the games is to win.

Such success is costly, and becoming more so over time.

Since there are limitations to institutional subsidy, athletics programs should pursue commercialism, no matter its form, to pay the bills.

Intercollegiate athletics, so goes this argument, should do all that it can to generate revenues—a no-holds-barred approach.

Surely, this extreme position is mistaken.

Crass commercialism is no better than unrealistic idealism.

Both are unacceptable extremes.

There are commercial activities in which universities should not engage even if it generates substantial revenues for athletics. A crystal clear example is that student-athletes should not be commercially exploited.

They are students, not professionals.

Exploiting student-athletes for commercial purposes is as contrary to the collegiate model as paying them.

There are several orthogonal parameters that must be understood in order to find the balance point for commercial activity.

These parameters include the locus of responsibility for controlling commercial activity, the underlying types of activity relevant to college sports, and the potential for diminishing or eliminating cases of run-away commercialism.

There must be shared responsibility in the oversight of commercial activity. In particular, there are critical roles for the NCAA national office and there are critical roles for the individual campuses.

Without this complementary exercise of control, there is little opportunity to contain over-commercialism.

The role of the NCAA national office is to work with the membership to articulate the core principles that apply to commercial activity, and to disseminate these principles widely so that they are well understood within the college sports community and among the media and corporate sponsors.

The NCAA national office also has responsibility for conducting and managing the media rights for championship events (except BCS football).

It likewise has the responsibility for implementing the principles governing commercialism in these championship events.

The role of the NCAA members is to oversee their athletics programs and the events in which their teams participate, so that the core principles are followed.

That includes educating their athletics communities, including those off campus, about the nature and limits of commercial activity.

Conferences, also, have a role to play.

They oversee conference championships, and they negotiate media and corporate contracts on behalf of and at the direction of their conference members.

In some cases, conferences combine their efforts to create multi-conference events, including football bowl games in Division I.

Generally speaking, then, the national office is operationally responsible for post-season national contests, with the exception of FBS football, and the individual campuses have responsibility for all the other intercollegiate contests, including those conducted by their conferences.

This is the system of shared responsibility.

There are some who believe the NCAA national office should have oversight for commercial activity for all of college sports.

It would not be a good idea, however, for the national office to exercise campus-based control of commercialism.

Local control permits each campus to take best advantage of its unique opportunities and to market and depict itself in the manner it judges most appropriate.

The development, advancement and protection of an individual institution's brand ought to be within its purview.

If the NCAA national office were to assume this responsibility, it would become overly intrusive into the affairs of its member institutions.

That is not a recommended course of action.

So, we understand that some level of commercial activity is necessary, even appropriate.

But, we also understand that there must be a balance reached so that such activity does not overwhelm the values of higher education.

And, we understand that there is shared responsibility for finding and maintaining the balance point.

What, then, are the limits of commercial activity?

What is off the table?

What is not acceptable under any circumstances?

We need first to distinguish between two types of commercial activity.

Namely, there is commercialism that directly involves student-athletes and commercialism that does not.

The central stricture on commercial activity concerns the exploitation of student-athletes.

There must be a clear distinction between those activities that directly involve student-athletes and those that do not.

The NCAA Manuals for each division are filled with rules and bylaws that address the status and standing of student-athletes.

Fundamental to that standing is that these are young women and men who are students and not professional athletes.

The justification for this premise, we must continue to emphasize, is straightforward: The underlying reason why universities support intercollegiate athletics at all is that it provides educational value for those students who participate.

Thus, any adequate policy of commercial activity must ensure that student-athletes are not commercially exploited.

Call this the condition of nonexploitation.

. . . .

When we say "student-athlete exploitation in commercial activity," we should have a specific definition in mind.

Since student-athletes are amateurs, not paid professionals, they cannot accept payment for endorsing or advertising any commercial product or service.

It also means they should not be put in a position in which the natural interpretation by a reasonable person is that they are endorsing or advertising a commercial product or service.

But most cases of exploitation are subtle and indirect.

Instead of obvious product endorsement, the marketing can include game pictures, films, audio or video of student-athletes that make it appear to a reasonable person that a student-athlete is endorsing a specific commercial product.

The student-athlete may well have no knowledge or awareness that his or her reputation, image or name is being used for these commercial purposes.

But exploitation may be the result, nonetheless.

Generation of much needed revenue does not justify the exploitation of student-athletes.

We can—and we should—debate the nature of proper commercial conduct.

However, one principle is not subject to debate: commercial exploitation of student-athletes is not permissible.

Period.

This is the clearest and most important line of demarcation between college and professional sports.

In many ways, the two models are similar.

But the key differences are that, first, the function of college sports is based on education while the function of professional sports is based on entertainment.

And second, those who participate in college sports are students while those who participate in professional sports are paid employees.

It is critical to note that a sound definition of student-athlete exploitation does not include the promotion of most college athletics by institutions or charitable events.

Using pictures of student-athletes by athletics programs to promote the upcoming big game or to promote literacy by showing the athlete reading to young children is acceptable.

The reason that these cases are acceptable is that these are not commercial, for-profit based activities.

There is a difference between charitable and university activities, on the one hand, and commercial, for-profit activities on the other hand.

The other type of commercial activity in college sports pertains to instances not directly involving student-athletes.

There are numerous examples of this type.

For example, there can be the sale of merchandise, such as clothing, that use the athletics department logo; or a coach might endorse a commercial product or service; the institution might sell signage within its athletics facilities, including scoreboard space, in order to advertise a commercial product or service; or an institution or athletics department might adopt a certain commercial product for a fee, say a brand of athletics shoes or soft drink.

This type of commercial activity, when properly conducted, does not exploit student-athletes.

The NCAA does not regulate this type of activity.

It does not do so because that would intrude on institutional autonomy.

Some who are uncomfortable with the growth of commercialism focus on the tastelessness of some of these activities.

They may find the quantity of institutional commercial activity within athletics venues overwhelming, noisy or inappropriate; or they may find that the products or services advertised are unbecoming for higher education.

In the latter case, the NCAA does have rules prohibiting advertising that is degrading of race or gender.

But not all advertising that some find unacceptable is degrading.

For the two types of commercial activity, that which directly involves student-athletes and that which does not, should there be consistency among those who have responsibility for oversight?

The answer is: yes and no.

Without question, there should be universal rules that apply to all who have oversight responsibility prohibiting student-athlete exploitation.

These rules are not easy to formulate correctly, however.

Indeed, over the past several years the NCAA governance structure has tried and failed to do so.

A recent attempt by a committee of presidents, it is hoped, will be more successful.

Rules only make sense in this context if they are enforceable and if there are sanctions for noncompliance.

If we are serious about protecting student-athletes from commercial exploitation, and it is not merely rhetoric, then we must have enforceable rules and meaningful sanctions.

Be assured that we must be serious about this.

By contrast, the question of consistency in oversight for commercial activity not directly involving student-athletes has a different answer.

Namely, there need not be consistency at the national, conference and institutional levels in commercial activity.

As a matter of fact, to require such consistency is to try to legislate taste, and trying to do that is at best foolish.

True, not every ad or marketing ploy is appropriate, and we want institutions of higher education to use good judgment and not succumb to temptations for the outrageous or the overly provocative.

But within these boundaries, there is a great deal of room for disagreement, and trying to set national policy will only frustrate the goal of shared responsibility.

The NCAA national office takes a conservative approach to its oversight responsibilities for the championships.

The national office has, and will continue to eschew advertising and other commercial activity that can be reasonably interpreted as offensive.

Championships are conducted in "clean" venues, in that advertising and signage are kept at a minimum and the highest standards of propriety are practiced.

In the case of venues and media presentation under the control of individual institutions and conferences, it is their taste that is controlling.

There may well be differences of opinion about what is appropriate and what is too much, but these often are differences of taste rather than differences in principle.

So be it.

Rules governing commercialism not directly involving student-athletes, therefore, are to be kept at a minimum.

We already have rules about treating all people with respect, and against racism and sexism.

Nothing more may be needed. Nonetheless, there are better and worse ways to conduct commercial activity on campuses, and on conference and national platforms.

Some ways better represent higher education than others.

It is understood that commercial activity is undertaken to generate revenue.

But it does not follow that the greater the flurry, the greater the revenue stream.

Good judgment and sound contract negotiations with the media and corporate sponsors is the key to revenue generation.

Focusing on the special higher education features of college sports is more effective than emulating professional sports, with its strong entertainment focus.

While rules are not the answer, guidelines based on best practices make good sense in bringing order and propriety to commercial activity.

These guidelines should be in the form of recommendations to institutions and conferences, not enforceable requirements.

This solution is likely to be unsatisfying to some.

They would like to have rules and accompanying sanctions for all commercial activity, whether or not it directly involves student-athletes.

However, a balanced approach to commercialism recognizes the differences in regulatory conditions when student-athletes are and when they are not directly involved, and it takes into account differences in matter of taste.

The framework for commercial activity just described is based on a key premise: Namely, issues surrounding student-athletes are central to any adequate policy for commercial activity in intercollegiate athletics.

Leaving aside radical critics of one orientation or another, there likely is widespread agreement with the condition of nonexploitation of student-athletes.

But we also know that there is lack of agreement on how to apply this condition in particular cases.

Can we solve the problem of determining when student-athletes are exploited?

Not easily, we suspect.

The first inclination is to try to develop an algorithm or mechanical rule that automatically gives the right answer.

That approach seems doomed to failure.

Obviously, a student-athlete cannot be depicted holding a product and saying "Buy this."

But there is a great deal of gray area.

One recent attempt to provide a mechanical rule was to specify the percentage of space that can be devoted to advertising when a student-athlete is in the frame.

But there are multiple factors that make it appear that the student-athlete is endorsing a product beyond the percentage of space devoted to it.

No matter how carefully such mechanical rules are crafted, wily advertisers would likely find a way within the rules to give the appearance of product endorsement.

That would lead to revising the rules, and then new attempts to push the boundaries.

You can already see the NCAA rule book getting fatter.

The point is that this type of regulation cannot be mechanical.

Rather, what is required is the exercise of good judgment by sensible people who understand the rationale and purpose of the condition of nonexploitation.

This is the only reasonable way to proceed.

Even so, we will not likely achieve agreement on every case.

There will be borderline instances in which persons of good will, knowledge and experience will disagree.

We need, in particular, a systematic approach to adjudicate cases in which it is alleged that there is student-athlete commercial exploitation.

In similar cases, when good judgment is required to apply NCAA rules, such as student-athlete eligibility, we depend on trained, national office staff.

We should do so here, as well.

Moreover, as we do in other cases, there should be an appeals process involving NCAA members that would review staff decisions.

In addition, there may also be the need for an oversight committee of membership peers that will review the landscape of commercial activity in intercollegiate athletics, make binding determinations of instances in which there is student-athlete exploitation even if NCAA amateurism rules are not violated, and evaluate trends in commercial activity to ensure that the values of higher education and the best interests of the "collegiate model" of athletics are not abridged.

Actions of such an oversight committee would both guide decisions of the staff and appeals body directly with regard to student-athlete exploitation and inform the membership when trends appear to be compromising the values of higher education and the collegiate model.

Marketing expertise and new media technologies have changed the landscape in which student-athlete images and names are used.

We can expect those factors to continue to reshape the landscape.

Thus, our process of adjudicating the claim of student-athletic exploitation must be sufficiently forward-looking and flexible to take into account these factors.

It is incumbent on all to ensure that the national office staff and any oversight committee charged with undertaking decisions about student-athlete exploitation in commercial activity are knowledgeable and objective.

To sum up, then, at the highest level, there are two key principles that govern commercial activity in intercollegiate athletics.

First, student-athletes are not to be exploited in commercial activity.

Second, all such activity in college sports undertaken by universities and colleges, conferences and the NCAA national office must be consistent with the values and mission of higher education.

These two high-level principles must be translated into more specific NCAA legislative rules, as well as guides for best practices.

That detailed, careful work is necessary to assist athletics and university administrators in conducting commercial activity properly.

There is no question that commercial activity is necessary for mounting intercollegiate athletics programs, certainly in Division I, but also in Divisions II and III.

But that activity must be undertaken within the context of higher education.

It must be done the right way.

Contemporary marketing practices of college sports by the media and by corporations can unintentionally, and sometimes intentionally, abridge these two principles.

It is not easy, at times, for the college community to protect intercollegiate athletics.

The answer is to use regulation where clear prohibitions are evident—exploitation of student-athletes, for example—and apply values-driven judgment where flexibility is required.

We must not be lured into forced algorithmic solutions, which merely present a puzzle to be solved by those who want to take unfair advantage of student-athletes.

Rather, there needs to be a process by which experienced, objective, and careful judgment resolves the issues.

The NCAA staff should play that role in interpreting rules pertaining to student-athlete exploitation.

But, as we also do in other cases, there also needs to be an appropriate appeals process and oversight of staff decisions.

College sports are incredibly popular among fans and within the higher education community.

And for good reasons.

It consists of athletics contests among earnest young men and young women, who are students representing their colleges and universities.

There is a sense of exuberance, as well as high-quality performance, which is characteristic of intercollegiate athletics.

We should do everything we can to protect this significant enterprise.

But reality imposes itself.

Almost every university and college must provide financial subsidy to conduct intercollegiate athletics.

To help meet these costs, revenues from commercial activity are required.

The objective, then, is to determine the balance point, all factors considered, between crass commercialism and unrealistic idealism.

Once that occurs, we will be able to move forward in the conduct of intercollegiate athletics with a clear conscience.

Intercollegiate athletics has become an integral part of college life and culture.

Given the educational value of participation in athletics, it is important to not sell this great enterprise short. But it is immoral to sell it out.

We must do it right.

NCAA 2008–2009 REVENUE DISTRIBUTION PLAN

ACADEMIC ENHANCEMENT: DESCRIPTION

Approximately $20,667,000 is allocated for enhancement of academic-support programs for student-athletes at Division I institutions. A payment of approximately $62,438 is sent in late June to each Division I institution. In addition to funding direct benefits to student-athletes, the Academic Enhancement fund will continue to allow spending on academic support salaries and benefits and capital improvements that enhance the academic services. The Academic Enhancement checks will continue to be mailed to each institution. The institution is also encouraged to consider using this fund for the provision of other direct benefits to student-athletes that enhance student-athlete welfare. The additional benefits may be provided in accordance with the Student-Athlete Opportunity Fund guidelines. For research purposes only, institutions report on how the funds were used to enhance their academic programs and services for student-athletes. Among the common uses are tutorial services, equipment (e.g., computer), supplies and additional personnel.

Starting with the 2007–08 budget year, a portion of the increases to the Academic Enhancement Fund will be allocated to the Division I Academic Performance Program (APP) Supplemental Support Fund which was established to support campus-based initiatives designed to foster student-athlete academic success at eligible limited resource institutions. The Fund has been created to support efforts to improve team Academic Progress Rates (APR) and Graduation Success Rates (GSR). Eligibility for the fund is determined by the NCAA based on APR and GSR rankings. Grants from the Fund are awarded in response to proposals for innovative solutions and efforts to increase student-athlete retention and progress-toward degree success. Funds not utilized within the Supplemental Support Fund will be distributed among all Division I institutions with the Academic Enhancement Fund dollars in late June.

. . . .

BASKETBALL FUND: DESCRIPTION

The basketball fund provides for moneys to be distributed to Division I conferences based on their performance in the Division I Men's Basketball Championship over a six-year rolling period (for the period 2003–2008 for the 2008–09 distribution). Independent institutions receive a full unit share based on its tournament participation over the same rolling six-year period. The basketball fund payments are sent to conferences and independent institutions in mid-April each year.

If a new member participates in the Division I men's basketball championship in March-April 2009, the units for participating will be included in the Basketball Distribution sent April 2010.

One unit is awarded to each institution participating in each game, except the championship game. In 2007–08, each basketball unit was approximately $191,000 for a total $143.3 million distribution.

In 2008–09, each basketball unit will be approximately $206,020 for a total $154.7 million distribution.

. . . .

Conferences are urged, but not required, to distribute money from the basketball fund equally among all their member institutions.

. . . .

CONFERENCE GRANTS: DESCRIPTION

A total of $7,467,000 is allocated for grants to Division I men's and women's basketball-playing conferences. Grants of approximately $240,871 will be made to each Division I conference that employs a full-time administrator and that are eligible for automatic qualification into the Division I men's and women's basketball championships, regardless of whether the conference is granted automatic qualification.

These grant funds must be used to maintain, enhance or implement programs and services in each of the following areas:

a. Men's and women's officiating programs: permissible uses include the improvement of officiating programs in all sports, as opposed to just in men's and women's basketball.

b. Enhancement of conference compliance and enforcement programs.

c. Heightening the awareness of athletics staffs and student-athletes to programs associated with drug use, and assisting coaches, athletics administrators and student-athletes in this regard.

d. Enhancement of opportunities: employment, professional development, career advancement and leadership/management training in intercollegiate athletics for ethnic minorities.

e. Development of conference gambling education programs.

A conference may determine the specific amount it wishes to allocate to these five areas, but it must spend at least some portion of its grant in all five.

. . . .

GRANTS-IN-AID: DESCRIPTION

The broad-based distribution is made to all Division I institutions on the basis of the number of varsity sports sponsored (weighted one-third, totaling $51.6 million) and the number of athletics grants-in-aid awarded (weighted two-thirds, totaling $103.1 million).

. . . .

The annual distribution is based on sports-sponsorship and grants-in-aid data from the preceding academic year (e.g., the 2008–09 distribution is based on 2007–08 data). The grants-in-aid distribution is based on previously submitted squad lists, and the number of athletics grants-in-aid is calculated from those lists. . . .

The grants-in-aid component is based on the number of athletic grants awarded by each institution (based on full-time equivalencies), beginning with one grant and progressing in value in increments of 50. Grants awarded above 150 are valued at the same amount. The value of each basis point in the 2007-08 distribution was $242.67.

As examples, an institution that awarded 80.48 grants-in-aid received a check for $26,927; an institution awarding 164.89 grants-in-aids received $230,003 and an institution awarding 242.44 grants-in-aid received $606,384.

As with sports sponsorship, athletics grants are counted only in sports in which the NCAA conducts championships competition, emerging sports for women and Division I-A football. However, sports that do not meet the minimum contests and participants requirements of Bylaw 20.9.4.3 are included in the grants-in-aid component. Institutions also receive credit in the grants-in-aid component for grants awarded to fifth-year student-athletes who have exhausted eligibility and for students who, for medical reasons, do not count on the squad list but are receiving aid. Credit is not given for Proposition 48 student-athletes.

. . . .

SPORTS SPONSORSHIP: DESCRIPTION

The NCAA Committee on Infractions may consider withholding all or a portion of an institution's share of the broad-based distribution moneys as a penalty in infractions cases.

An institution receives a unit for each sport sponsored beginning with the 14th sport (the minimum requirement for Division I membership).

Only sports in which the NCAA conducts championships competition (which meet the minimum contests and participants requirements of Bylaw 20.9.4.3) and emerging sports for women are counted. In the 2007–08 distribution, for sports sponsored beginning with the 14th, an institution received approximately $26,123 per sport (i.e., an institution sponsoring 16 total sports received $78,369; an institution sponsoring 24 sports received $287,353).

[*Ed. Note: Even though the NCAA does not conduct a Division I-A football championship, that sport and athletics grants awarded in it are counted in the broad-based distribution.*]

STUDENT-ATHLETE OPPORTUNITY FUND AND SPECIAL ASSISTANCE FUND: DESCRIPTION

Special Assistance Fund

A total of $13,383,000 is sent to conference offices in early August to assist student-athletes in Division I with special financial needs. The guiding principles of the fund are to meet the student-athletes' needs of an emergency or essential nature for which financial assistance otherwise is not available. Conference interpretations not addressed by the Executive Committee should stay within this intended purpose. The responsibility for oversight and administration of the fund, including interpretations, rests solely with the conferences. The allocations are based on grants-in-aid and sports sponsorship information from two years prior (e.g. 2008–09 distribution is based on 2006–07 grants-in-aid and sports sponsorship data.)

Student-Athlete Opportunity Fund

A total of $35,393,000 will be sent to Division I conference offices in late August 2008 that will be allocated based on the 'broad-based' (sports sponsorship and grants-in-aid) distribution formula. The funds will increase in value at 13 percent annually, subject to approval by the Division I Board of Directors.

The following information demonstrates the intent of the funds:

The Student-Athlete Opportunity Fund is intended to provide direct benefits to student-athletes or their families as determined by conference offices. As a guiding principle, the fund shall be used to assist student-athletes in meeting financial needs that arise in conjunction with participation in intercollegiate athletics, enrollment in an academic curriculum or that recognize academic achievement. Accordingly, receipt of Student-Athlete Opportunity Fund monies shall not be included in determining the permissible amount of financial aid that a member institution may award to a student-athlete. Further, in as much as the fund is designed to provide direct benefits to student-athletes, the fund is not intended to be used to replace existing budget items.

The following student-athletes are eligible for funds:

All student-athletes, including international, are eligible to receive SAOF benefits, regardless of whether they are grant-in-aid recipients, have demonstrated need or have either exhausted eligibility or no longer participate due to medical reasons. Additionally, student-athletes receiving monies from the Special Assistance Fund may also receive SAOF benefits.

. . . .

The following are restrictions on the use of the funds:

Pursuant to NCAA Bylaw 15.01.6.2, member institutions and conferences shall not use monies received from the fund for the following:

A. *Salaries and benefits.*

B. *Grants-in-aid (other than summer school) for student-athletes with remaining eligibility.*

C. *Capital improvements.*

D. *Stipends.*

E. *Athletic development opportunities:*

  1. *Fees and other expenses associated with a student-athlete's participation in a sports camp or clinic;*

  2. *Fees and other expenses associated with private sports-related instruction provided to a student-athlete;*

  3. *Fees for other athletic development experiences (e.g., greens fees, batting cage rental); and*

  4. *Expenses associated with a student-athlete's participation in a foreign tour.*

. . . .

The Special Assistance Fund has three components to the calculation. It is based on current year information for Pell Grants and, starting with the 2009 distribution, one-year's subsequent information for Grants-in-Aid and Sports Sponsorship data. As an example, the August 2009 Special Assistance Fund distribution will be based on 2008–09 Pell Grant information and 2007–08 Grants-in-Aid and Sports Sponsorship information. . . . [*Ed. Note: See **Table 9** for grants-in-aid fund values and **Figure 2** for information on the special assistance fund for students.*]

. . . .

Table 9   Grants-in-Aid Fund Values

Number of Grants	Valuation Points	Grant Value
1–50	(1) point each × $242.67	$242.67
51–100	(2) points each × $242.67	$485.34
101–150	(10) points each × $242.67	$2,426.70
151 and above	(20) points each × $242.67	$4,853.40

Source: NCAA 2008–2009 Revenue Distribution Plan. © National Collegiate Athletic Association. 2008–2010. All rights reserved.

. . . .

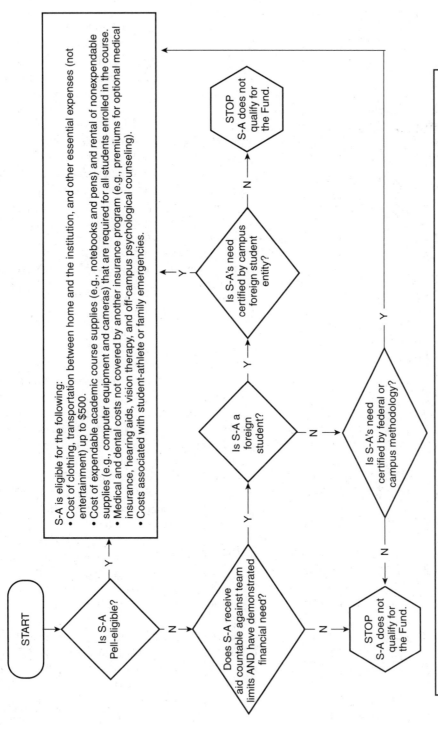

Figure 2   Eligibility for Special Assistance Fund for Student-Athletes

Source: PAC-10 Conference. Used with permission.

NATIONAL COLLEGIATE ATHLETIC ASSOCIATION AND SUBSIDIARIES

[Excerpts from] Consolidated Financial Statements [*see Table 10*]

> August 31, 2008
> (with summarized financial information for 2007)
> (With Independent Auditors' Report Thereon)

. . . .

NATIONAL COLLEGIATE ATHLETIC ASSOCIATION AND SUBSIDIARIES

Notes to Consolidated Financial Statements
> August 31, 2008
> (with summarized financial information for 2007)

Table 10   Consolidated Statement of Activities

Year ended August 31, 2008 (with comparative financial information for the year ended August 31, 2007)

	2008 Total	2007 Total
Revenues		
Television and marketing rights fees	$552,287,787	$512,026,034
Championships and NIT tournaments	70,640,409	66,198,275
Investment income, net	−3,998,529	32,981,412
Sales and services	14,519,175	7,612,372
Contributions—facilities, net	2,654,775	2,654,775
Contributions—other	191,811	318,939
Total revenues	$636,295,428	$621,791,807
Expenses		
Distribution to Division I members	$359,349,169	$331,925,602
Division I championships, programs and NIT tournaments	69,900,383	58,305,606
Division II championships, distribution and programs	29,846,478	26,639,186
Division III championships and programs	18,907,533	17,478,629
Association-wide programs	108,882,864	114,002,042
Management and general	26,060,135	26,431,656
Total expenses	$612,946,562	$574,782,721
Change in net assets	23,348,866	47,009,086
Net assets—beginning of year	$327,014,383	$280,005,297
Net assets—end of year	$350,363,249	$327,014,383

Source: National Collegiate Athletic Association. © National Collegiate Athletic Association. 2008–2010. All rights reserved.

(1) The Association

The National Collegiate Athletic Association (the NCAA or the Association) is an unincorporated not-for-profit educational organization founded in 1906. The NCAA is the organization through which the colleges and universities of the nation speak and act on athletics matters at the national level. It is a voluntary association of more than 1000 institutions, conferences and organizations devoted to the sound administration of intercollegiate athletics in all its phases. Through the NCAA, its members consider any athletics issue that has crossed regional or conference lines and is national in character. The NCAA strives for integrity in intercollegiate athletics and serves as the colleges' national athletics accrediting agency. A basic purpose of the NCAA is to maintain intercollegiate athletics as an integral part of the educational program and the athlete as an integral part of the student body.

The NCAA operates through a governance structure which empowers each division to guide and enhance their ongoing division-specific activities. In Division I, the legislative system is based on conference representation and an eighteen member Board of Directors that approves legislation. The Division II and III presidential boards are known as the Presidents Council; however, legislation in Division II and III is considered through a one-school, one-vote process at the NCAA Annual Convention. The governance structure also includes an Executive Committee composed of sixteen chief executive officers (member institution chief executive officers) that oversee association-wide issues which is charged with ensuring that each division operates consistently with the basic purposes, fundamental policies and general principles of the NCAA. The Executive Committee has representation from all three divisions and oversees the Association's finances and legal affairs.

In September, 2005, the NCAA organized the NIT, LLC, a limited liability company. The NCAA is the sole member of the company. The NIT, LLC was organized as the entity that will administer the NIT Season Tip-Off and the Postseason NIT collegiate basketball events. The financial results of the NIT, LLC are consolidated in the financial statements of the NCAA. All significant intercompany balances and transactions have been eliminated in consolidation.

In January, 2007, the NCAA organized the Eligibility Center, LLC, a limited liability company. The NCAA is the sole member of the company. The Eligibility Center, LLC was organized for the primary purpose of performing academic and amateurism eligibility certification decisions for prospective student-athletes desiring to compete for NCAA Division I and II member institutions. In October, 2007, the Eligibility Center assumed the administrative responsibility for the National Letter of Intent program. The financial results of the Eligibility Center, LLC are consolidated in the financial statements of the NCAA. All significant intercompany balances and transactions have been eliminated in consolidation.

In May, 2007, the NCAA organized the Collegiate Sports, LLC, a limited liability company. The NCAA is the sole member of the company. The Collegiate Sports, LLC was organized for the primary purpose of being the sole member of the limited liability companies organized by the NCAA. The ownership of the NIT, LLC and Eligibility Center, LLC were transferred from the NCAA to the Collegiate Sports, LLC in May, 2007.

In August, 2007, the NCAA organized the College Football Officiating, LLC, a limited liability company. Collegiate Sports, LLC is the sole member of the company. The College Football Officiating, LLC was organized to pursue the development and maintenance of a national Division I college football officiating program. The College Football Officiating, LLC did not have any transactions in the year ended August 31, 2008.

. . . .

(7) National Invitation Tournament

In August, 2005, the NCAA and the Metropolitan Intercollegiate Basketball Association (MIBA) agreed to terms under which the NCAA purchased the rights and assets identified in organizing, promoting and administering the preseason and postseason National Invitation Tournaments (NIT). The NCAA agreed to pay MIBA $56,250,000 over a nine year period pursuant to the terms and conditions of a lawsuit settlement and an asset purchase agreement (the Agreements), including guaranteed minimum profit sharing payments of $250,000 in each of those nine years. The terms of the Agreements transfer the ownership of the tournaments and settle all litigation matters between the NCAA and MIBA.

Pursuant to a third party valuation, as of August 31, 2005, the value of the intangible assets acquired by the NCAA were $34,000,000 (before imputed interest of $8,304,717) resulting in $22,250,000 (before present value discount of $3,236,399) of settlement expense in the statement of activities for the year ended August 31, 2005. Imputed interest and present value discount rates were at 6%.

. . . .

(9) Commitments and Contingencies

The NCAA acts as the governing body for college athletics. In the course of carrying out its responsibilities, the NCAA is the target of litigation from student-athletes, coaches, universities and the general public. In addition, decisions made by the NCAA to enforce legislation and rules, as well as eligibility determination for student-athletes, are often challenged by the affected parties through lawsuits. These lawsuits range from seeking to overturn NCAA committee and legislative decisions to seeking monetary damages and reimbursement of legal fees.

The NCAA and its legal counsel are defending against lawsuits and claims arising in the normal course of its day-to-day activities. The NCAA does not believe the ultimate resolution of these matters will result in material losses or have a material adverse effect on the financial position, change in net assets or cash flows of the NCAA. The NCAA has incurred attorney's fees in the process of defending against such matters, which are recorded in the accompanying consolidated financial statements.

. . . .

(12) Distribution of Revenues

In August 1990, the NCAA Executive Committee approved a plan to distribute revenues to member institutions for the year ended August 31, 1991, and each year thereafter. For Division I members, the plan consists of a basketball fund distribution based on historical performance in the Division I Men's Basketball Championship, a broad-based distribution based on Division I sports sponsored and athletics grants-in-aid, an academic enhancement fund for academic programs for student-athletes, a student-athlete opportunity fund, a conference grant program and a special assistance fund for student-athletes to be used for emergency situations. For Division II members, the plan consists of a basketball fund distribution based on historical performance in the Division II Men's and Women's Basketball Championship, sports sponsorship, and an equal distribution among all active members.

. . . .

(14) Television and Marketing Rights Fees

On November 18, 1999, the NCAA entered into an agreement with CBS (the CBS agreement) that provides CBS exclusive television broadcast rights for the Division I Men's Basketball Championship along with other championship and marketing rights effective from fiscal 2003 and continuing through fiscal 2013. The agreement is for 11 years, with the NCAA having an option to renegotiate after eight years. [*Ed. Note: The NCAA subsequently exercised their option and reached a 14 year agreement with CBS and Turner, the payments for which remain the same in the first three years of the contract as they were in the final three years of the previous contract.*] The rights fees include: telecast rights, including over-the-air cable, satellite, digital and home video, marketing rights, championships publication program rights, radio rights, internet rights, fan festival rights, and selected licensing rights. The contract also includes year-round promotion of the NCAA and its championships.

The rights fee for this package is a guaranteed minimum of $6.0 billion over the 11-year contract. Pursuant to the agreement, for the year ended August 31, 2008, the NCAA received $529,000,000 ($490,000,000 for the year

Table 11   Annual Payments from NCAA's Division I Men's Basketball Broadcasting Contract, 2009–2013

Fiscal year ending August 31	
2009	$571,000,000
2010	617,000,000
2011	657,000,000
2012	710,000,000
2013	764,000,000
	$3,319,000,000

Source: National Collegiate Athletic Association. © National Collegiate Athletic Association. 2008–2010. All rights reserved.

ended August 31, 2007). The NCAA will receive future television broadcast payments as follows [*see Table 11*]:

On June 29, 2001, the NCAA entered into an agreement with ESPN (the ESPN agreement) that provides ESPN exclusive television broadcast rights for the Division I Women's Basketball championship along with broadcast rights to other NCAA championships, excluding those to which rights have been granted to CBS. The contract is effective from fiscal year 2003 and continues through fiscal year 2013. The ESPN agreement is for 11 years, with the NCAA having an option to renegotiate after eight years.

The rights fee for this package is on a fixed, nonrefundable basis for the sum of $163 million over the 11-year contract. Pursuant to the ESPN agreement, for the years ended August 31, 2008 and 2007, the NCAA received $14,800,000 and $13,800,000, respectively.

The NCAA will receive future television broadcast payments as follows [*see Table 12*]:

. . . .

[*Ed. Note: See Table 13 for schedule of consolidating statement of activities.*]

Table 12   Annual Payments from NCAA's Division I Women's Basketball Broadcasting Contract, 2009–2013

Fiscal year ending August 31	
2009	$15,800,000
2010	16,800,000
2011	17,900,000
2012	18,800,000
2013	19,100,000
	$88,400,000

Source: National Collegiate Athletic Association. © National Collegiate Athletic Association. 2008–2010. All rights reserved.

Table 13   Schedule of Consolidating Statement of Activities, Year Ended August 31, 2008

	NCAA	NIT, LLC	Eligibility Center, LLC	Total
Revenues				
Television and marketing rights fees	549,517,787	2,770,000	—	552,287,787
Championships and NIT tournaments	67,700,370	2,940,039	—	70,640,409
Investment income, net	−4,117,052	65,404	53,119	−3,998,529
Sales and services	5,672,773	109,849	8,736,553	14,519,175
Contributions—facilities, net	2,654,775	—	—	2,654,775
Contributions—other	191,811	—	—	191,811
Total revenues	621,620,464	5,885,292	8,789,672	636,295,428
Expenses				
Distribution to Division I members	359,349,169	—	—	359,349,169
Division I championships, programs and NIT tournaments	64,231,221	5,669,162	—	69,900,383
Division II championships, distribution and programs	29,846,478	—	—	29,846,478
Division III championships and programs	18,907,533	—	—	18,907,533
Association-wide programs	100,444,796	—	8,438,068	108,882,864
Management and general	25,838,748	221,387	—	26,060,135
Total expenses	598,617,945	5,890,549	8,438,068	612,946,562
Change in net assets	23,002,519	−5,257	351,604	23,348,866
Net assets—beginning of year	327,277,446	91,521	−354,584	327,014,383
Net assets—end of year	350,279,965	86,264	−2,980	350,363,249

Source: National Collegiate Athletic Association. © National Collegiate Athletic Association. 2008–2010. All rights reserved.

Discussion Questions

1. What is the expected path that the NCAA institution will follow to limit athletic program financial losses? What are the pros and cons of this path?
2. How could the NCAA redistribute its revenues in a more effective manner?
3. Describe each facet of a successful cartel and how it applies to the NCAA.
4. Compare and contrast the motivations driving the NCAA versus those driving universities.
5. Compare and contrast those NCAA institutions that are typical versus those that profit from their athletic programs.
6. Describe how the profits are divided among teams that compete in the NCAA Men's Basketball Tournament.
7. According to Noll, how do schools benefit, or not benefit, from having large athletic programs (namely large football and men's basketball programs)? Do you agree?
8. According to Noll, what are some plausible reforms the NCAA might consider implementing? Do you have any other suggestions that might help reform the NCAA?
9. What is the rationale for casting college football programs as profit maximizers? Do you agree with this characterization?
10. What reason did the NCAA give to justify its continued control over the rights to football telecasts? Was this argument logical?
11. What would have most likely occurred if the Supreme Court had reached the opposite outcome in *NCAA vs. Board of Regents*? Would this resemble any modern organizations?
12. How did the NCAA modify its revenue distribution practices in order to place less emphasis on winning in men's basketball? Did it accomplish its goal?
13. Although the NCAA does not publicize a detailed breakdown of revenue distribution among athletic programs, how can one identify the inequality in the way the revenues are distributed?
14. Why do conferences distribute revenues in a relatively equal fashion? Do you agree with this type of distribution?

CHAPTER FIFTEEN

Member Institutions

INTRODUCTION

The vast majority of the 1000-plus NCAA member institutions find sports to be a money-losing endeavor. These losses are expected at each of the nearly 300 Division II and over 400 Division III member institutions, where the athletic department is viewed as an integral part of the university, as indicated by the Division II and Division III philosophy statements. The financial expectations for the members of Division I are typically quite different, with intercollegiate athletics viewed as a potential money-maker. However, as indicated by the NCAA's most recent financial survey covering the period from 2004–2006, published in 2008, the potential is rarely realized, and the results are usually the same as in Divisions II and III. If institutional support is excluded, none of the 118 members of Division I-AA or the 93 members of Division I-AAA operated profitable athletic departments in 2006. The median I-AA institution lost $7.1 million and the median I-AAA member lost $6.6 million that year.

The financial expectations are much greater for the 120 members of the big-time world of college sports that is NCAA Division I-A. Nineteen universities—most of whom were members of the BCS conferences—had profitable athletic programs, and the median net revenues over expenses were $4.29 million in 2006, excluding institutional support. The remaining 100 schools in Division I-A lost money, with a median negative net revenue of $8.92 million, excluding institutional support. Overall, then, the gap between the median positive net revenues and the median negative net revenues was $13.2 million in 2006, approximately $2 million more than the gap in 2004. The median member of NCAA Division I-A lost $7.27 million in 2006. A closer look behind these numbers is warranted.

In 2006, the median institution in Division I-A fielded 19 teams, the median institution in Division I-AA fielded 18 teams, and the median institution in Division I-AAA, which does not have football teams, fielded 16 teams. However, the only sports that generate net revenues over expenses at almost all of these schools are football and men's basketball, with a handful of schools also able to run profitable programs in regionally popular sports such as ice hockey, women's basketball, and wrestling. All of the other sports lose money. Thus, the football and men's basketball programs must generate significant net revenues in order for the entire athletic program to operate profitably. Despite generating far less revenues than football programs, men's basketball programs have a greater likelihood of profitability than football programs in both Division I-A and I-AA. Sixty-eight Division I-A men's basketball programs made money in 2006, with a median profit of $2.72 million. Fifty-one teams lost money, with a median loss of $812,000. Overall, the 119 Division I-A men's basketball programs had median generated revenues of $3.98 million, with median expenses of $3.06 million in 2006. The median program profited $1.58 million.

The vast majority of the Division I-AA men's basketball programs lost money in 2006, with a median loss of $529,000 at these 108 institutions. Only 10 Division I-AA men's basketball programs made money, with a median profit of $187,000. Overall, the median Division I-AA men's basketball team lost $474,600. In Division I-AAA, 84 schools had a median loss of $774,000 in 2006, while 9 teams made a median profit of nearly $1 million. In total, the median I-AAA basketball program lost $639,600 in 2006.

As noted in the previous chapter, big-time college football is a potentially lucrative business. In 2006, 56% of Division I-A institutions realized this potential, earning a median profit of $8.8 million. It is safe to say that many of these 67 institutions were members of the BCS conferences. Conversely, 52 Division I-A football programs lost money, with a median deficit of $2.5 million. Overall, the median Division I-A football team profited by $5.35 million in 2006.

The financial story is much different in the off-Broadway world of Division I-AA football, where only five football programs generated even minimal profits in 2006. However, 113 Division I-AA football programs lost money, with a median deficit of $1.28 million. Overall, the median football program in Division I-AA lost $1.30 million in 2006.

Across all three levels of Division I athletics, several items are worth noting. First, average revenues and average expenses are both increasing, with expenses growing faster than revenues. Second, there is a continually increasing separation between the "haves" and "have-nots" of college sports. The schools that are making money are making more of it, and those that are losing money are losing more of it. Finally, between 16 and 19 of the 330 Division I institutions were profitable in any given year from 2004–2006. The remainder lost money.

Although Division I-A, I-AA, and I-AAA institutions compete against each other for NCAA championships in all sports other than football, it is this one-sport distinction that marks the difference between these levels of competition. In reality, Division I-A occupies an entirely different financial stratum than the others, with the median institution having approximately four times the amount of both total revenues and expenses. A brief discussion of the sources of revenues and operating expenses in college sports sheds additional light on these differences.

Ticket sales are the single largest source of revenue for Division I-A institutions, with the median school collecting $7.4 million in 2006. This is approximately 26 times the median amount earned in I-AA and 42 times the amount in I-AAA. Fundraising is the second most important revenue source, with the median I-A member bringing in $5.8 million in 2006, or approximately 9 times the amount in I-AA and 12 times the amount in I-AAA. The median athletic department in Division I-A receives 20% of its funding—$7.2 million per year—from the institution despite the fact that most are supposed to be auxiliary enterprises that are financially self-supporting. While the athletic departments in Divisions I-AA and I-AAA receive slightly less institutional support (a median amount of approximately $7.1 million in I-AA and $6.6 million in I-AAA in 2006), it constitutes over 70% of the total revenues at these schools. When looking at the overall profits or losses at any one NCAA member, it is appropriate to exclude institutional support from the revenue equation. Although it does represent the transfer of administrative funds to the athletic department from the institution, it does not represent monies that are otherwise earned by the institution because of the athletic department. Similarly, student activity fees provide Division I-A athletic departments with slightly more revenue than in I-AA or I-AAA ($1.4 million versus $872,000 in I-AA and $511,000 in I-AAA) but constitute approximately 15% to 20% of the total revenues of the latter groups. Thus, the median Division I-AA and I-AAA schools receive over 70% of their revenue from their institutions and students, and are hardly self-sufficient. **Table 1** shows net operating results excluding institutional support.

The various NCAA and conference distributions discussed in the previous chapter bring in much more revenue to the median institution in Division I-A ($4.87 million in 2006) than in Divisions I-AA and I-AAA ($395,000 and $232,000, respectively). Again, this is largely due to the dominance of the six power conferences. Finally, the median Division I-A school earns much more from broadcast rights ($168,000 in 2006), concessions, programs and novelties ($604,000), licensing royalties, advertising and sponsorships ($1.33 million), and miscellaneous items ($592,000) than does the median school in I-AA and I-AAA (approximately $257,000 and $252,000, respectively, for all of these items combined). Overall, the median Division I-A school had revenues of $35.4 million in 2006 (or $26.4 million when excluding institutional support), whereas the median Division I-AA and I-AAA institution had revenues of $9.64 million and $8.77 million, respectively (or $2.35 million and $1.83 million when excluding institutional support).

On the expense side of the ledger, the single greatest cost at all three levels of Division I is university paid staff salaries and benefits ($12.18 million in I-A, $3.61 million in I-AA, and $3.00 million in I-AAA). The second largest expense at all three levels is funding for athletic scholarships, on which the average Division I-A school spent $6.02 million, the average I-AA institution spent $2.88 million, and the average I-AAA school spent $2.76 million. Other average operating expenses which differed significantly between Division I-A and Divisions I-AA and I-AAA include team travel ($2.67 million versus $911,000 and $762,000); guarantees and options to visiting teams

Table 1   Net Operating Results (Medians)—Division I

	2006 Median Values
Football Bowl Subdivision	
Total generated revenues	$26,432,000
Total expenses	$35,756,000
Median net generated revenue	($7,265,000)
Football Championship Subdivision	
Total generated revenues	$2,345,000
Total expenses	$9,485,000
Median net generated revenue	($7,121,000)
Division I Without Football	
Total generated revenues	$1,828,000
Total expenses	$8,918,000
Median net generated revenue	($6,607,000)

Source: Daniel Fulks, 2004–2006 NCAA Revenues and Expenses of Division I Intercollegiate Athletic Programs Report (2008). © National Collegiate Athletic Association. 2008–2010. All rights reserved.

($1.2 million versus $61,000 and $54,000); equipment, uniforms, and supplies ($1.2 million versus $381,000 and $285,000); fundraising ($1.2 million versus $215,000 and $305,000); severance pay ($189,000 versus $36,000 and $37,000); game expenses ($1.55 million versus $239,000 and $234,000); and recruiting ($677,000 versus $220,000 and $163,000).

In addition to these differences in operating expenses, Division I-A institutions spend more on facilities maintenance and rentals ($5.2 million) than Division I-AA or I-AAA institutions ($594,000 and $365,000). Capital costs constitute a major aspect of total athletic expenditures and are not included in the aforementioned discussion. The NCAA funded study "The Physical Capital Stock Used in Collegiate Athletics" and a companion study "The Empirical Effects of Collegiate Athletics," both excerpted in this chapter, detail the exorbitant spending on athletics-related facilities by Division I-A institutions and conclude that an "arms race" related to these facilities is occurring. This reflects the recent and still ongoing multibillion dollar spending spree on athletic facilities.

Overall, Division I-A athletic departments had median expenses of $35.8 million in 2006. The median expenses were $9.5 million in Division I-AA and $8.9 million in I-AAA.

See **Table 2** for a summary of revenues and expenses for 2006 for the Football Bowl Subdivision. **Table 3** details sources of revenues for 2006 for the Division I Football Bowl Subdivision, the Football Championship Subdivision, and Division I (without football). **Table 4** breaks down operating expenses for 2006 for the Division I Football Bowl Subdivision, the Football Championship Subdivision, and Division I (without football). **Table 5** offers information on the naming-rights deals at various NCAA facilities.

Although the above analysis is certainly important, it must nonetheless be taken with a requisite grain of salt. Standard accounting techniques across NCAA institutions are lacking. In addition, related-party transactions involving other departments within the university are commonly used and some revenues and costs are improperly allocated across sports within the athletic department.

Former University of Michigan President James Duderstadt addresses these topics from both a macro and micro perspective, with a focus on Michigan's athletic department in "Intercollegiate Athletics and the American University: A University President's Perspective." The review of the business of sports at the University of Michigan, one of the powerhouses of the industry and a member of the Big Ten conference, continues with a look at the athletic department's internal budget documents for 2009–2010. Michigan's profitability in intercollegiate athletics is the exception rather than the rule. In addition to gaining a university president's thoughts, the findings of a Knight Commission on Intercollegiate Athletics survey highlight another important campus constituency's perceptions of college sports—those of the faculty.

The fairly bleak financial outlook for most intercollegiate athletics programs has led to an investigation of the indirect impacts of athletics on the institution. The athletic department is often the most visible aspect of the institution. As the front porch to the institutional house, it is important to attempt to know the impact of athletics on institutional fundraising, the size and quality of the student body, and the advertising and public relations of the institution. Anecdotal evidence suggests that these impacts can be substantial, as it has been at Butler University, Gonzaga University, St. Joseph's University, George Mason University, and the University of Florida in recent years. However, Robert Frank finds that these impacts are very small, if existent at all, in his article "Challenging the Myth: A Review of the Links Among College Athletic Success, Student Quality and Donations" excerpted in this chapter. Pope and Pope examine the impact of success in major college football and men's basketball on the number and quality of applications for admission to the institution. Stinson and Howard then review the impact of athletic success on fundraising at both the institution generally and in the athletic department more specifically.

The economics of college sports—both direct and indirect, actual and theoretical—often results in institutions making strategic decisions to change either their goals or the breadth and depth of their athletic programs. These decisions have broad consequences. The addition or subtraction of a team from an institution's athletic offerings is usually spurred by programmatic, gender equity, and/or financial considerations. In the past decade, a number of institutions in pursuit of increased media attention and the big-money potential of college sports have upgraded their athletic departments to a higher NCAA division. Membership in NCAA Division I grew from 261 in 1980 to 330 in 2008–2009. The NCAA put a four-year moratorium in effect in 2007 on permitting institutions to join Division I or upgrade within Division I until 2011, though it did allow the 20 schools that were already in the process of upgrading their programs to proceed. Although there are some success stories, upgrading is typically a foolish endeavor; most schools are unprepared for the move and fail to be rewarded for it either financially or indirectly. The NCAA's longitudinal study on the impact of upgrading the athletic program on the institution provides the details.

Many athletic departments have found that it is more efficient for them to outsource their marketing and other business operations to one of a handful of third-party providers that specialize in handling these affairs. The excerpt from Burden and Li examines the outsourcing of intercollegiate athletics programs.

As per the Internal Revenue Code, universities are nonprofit entities that are generally tax-exempt. As a consequence, the revenues that university athletic departments receive are not taxed either, despite the profit-motive of Division I members. An important consequence of this

Table 2   Summary of Revenues and Expenses (By Gender), Football Bowl Subdivision, 2006

	Generated Revenues		Total Revenues		Total Expenses		Median Net Revenue	
	Median	Largest	Median	Largest	Median	Largest	Generated	Total
Men's	$17,003,000	$81,699,000	$18,824,000	$81,706,000	$15,196,000	$62,329,000	$731,000	$1,209,000
Women's	641,000	6,585,000	1,702,000	8,840,000	6,143,000	27,431,000	(4,981,000)	(4,033,000)
Coed	6,917,000	198,974,000	13,590,000	203,504,000	11,867,000	52,448,000	(3,315,000)	1,912,000
Total	26,432,000	236,835,000	35,400,000	241,365,000	35,756,000	101,804,000	(7,265,000)	163,000

Source: Daniel Fulks, 2004–2006 NCAA Revenues and Expenses of Division I Intercollegiate Athletic Programs Report (2008). © National Collegiate Athletic Association. 2008–2010. All rights reserved.
Notes: Generated revenues are produced by the athletics department and include ticket sales, radio and television receipts, alumni contributions, guarantees, and other revenue sources that are not dependent on entities outside the athletics department.
Total revenues, or allocated revenues, are composed of:
- Student fees directly allocated to athletics;
- Direct institutional support, which are financial transfers directly from the general fund to athletics;
- Indirect institutional support, such as the payment of utilities, maintenance, support salaries, etc. by the institution on behalf of athletics; and
- Direct governmental support—the receipt of funds from state and local governmental agencies that are designated for athletics.

Table 3   Sources of Revenues, Division I Football Bowl Subdivision, Football Championship Subdivision, Division I (Without Football), 2006

	Football Bowl Subdivision		Football Championship Subdivision		Division I (without Football)	
	Total Division ($ Median)	Percentage of Total	Total Division ($ Median)	Percentage of Total	Total Division ($ Median)	Percentage of Total
Total ticket sales	7,442,000	23	278,000	5	177,000	5
NCAA and conference distributions	4,863,000	14	395,000	4	232,000	4
Guarantees and options	738,000	2	234,000	2	90,000	1
Cash contributions from alumni and others	5,826,000	24	635,000	8	483,000	8
Third-party support	0	0	0	0	0	0
Other:						
Concessions/Programs/Novelties	604,000	3	4,277,000	1	14,000	0
Broadcast rights	168,000	3	611,000	0	0	0
Royalties/Advertising/Sponsorship	1,334,000	5	150,000	2	172,000	3
Sports camps	77,000	1	23,000	1	30,000	1
Endowment/Investment income	387,000	3	19,000	2	15,000	1
Miscellaneous	592,000	2	77,000	2	66,000	1
Total generated revenues	26,432,000	80	2,345,000	28	1,828,000	26
Allocated revenues:						
Direct institutional support	1,883,000	9	4,277,000	45	4,602,000	47
Indirect institutional support	0	3	611,000	10	443,000	8
Student fees	1,743,000	6	872,000	15	511,000	18
Direct government support	0	1	0	1	0	0
Total allocated revenues	6,538,000	20	7,130,000	72	6,592,000	74
Total All Revenues	32,004,000	100	9,642,000	100	8,771,000	100

Source: Daniel Fulks, 2004–2006 NCAA Revenues and Expenses of Division I Intercollegiate Athletic Programs Report (2008).
Notes: Generated revenues represent revenues earned by the athletics department and do not include allocated revenues. Allocated revenues include direct institutional support, indirect support, student fees, and governmental support.
Percentages are based on averages for entire subdivision.
Because of zero values reported by respondents, median values can be misleading.

Table 4 Operating Expenses by Object of Expenditure, Division I Football Bowl Subdivision, Football Championship Subdivision, Division I (without Football), 2006 Mean Values*

	Football Bowl Subdivision		Football Championship Subdivision		Division I (without Football)	
	Total Division ($)	% of Total	Total Division ($)	% of Total	Total Division ($)	% of Total
Grants-in-aid						
Men	3,359,000	9	1,587,000	14	1,210,000	13
Women	2,441,000	6	1,242,000	11	1,508,000	16
Administrative and Non-gender	218,000	1	48,000	0	40,000	0
Total	6,017,000	16	2,676,000	25	2,758,000	29
Guarantees and Options						
Men	1,142,000	3	55,000	0	46,000	0
Women	35,000	0	4,000	0	7,000	0
Administrative and Non-gender	27,000	0	2,000	0	1,000	0
Total	1,204,000	3	61,000	1	54,000	1
Salaries and Benefits-University Paid						
Men	5,328,000	14	1,393,000	12	984,000	10
Women	2,116,000	5	819,000	7	790,000	8
Administrative and Non-gender	4,739,000	12	1,397,000	12	1,222,000	13
Total	12,182,000	32	3,609,000	32	2,996,000	31
Salaries and Benefits-Third Party paid						
Men	153,000	0	10,000	0	10,000	0
Women	20,000	0	3,000	0	5,000	0
Administrative and Non-gender	18,000	0	3,000	0	3,000	0
Total	191,000	0	16,000	0	18,000	0
Severance Pay						
Men	157,000	0	19,000	0	30,000	0
Women	12,000	0	7,000	0	4,000	0
Administrative and Non-gender	19,000	0	10,000	0	3,000	0
Total	189,000	0	36,000	0	37,000	0
Team Travel						
Men	1,720,000	4	513,000	5	397,000	4
Women	905,000	2	351,000	3	342,000	4
Administrative and Non-gender	47,000	0	47,000	0	23,000	0
Total	2,672,000	7	911,000	8	762,000	8
Recruiting						
Men	471,000	1	144,000	1	91,000	1
Women	196,000	1	73,000	1	68,000	1
Administrative and Non-gender	10,000	0	3,000	0	4,000	0
Total	677,000	2	220,000	3	163,000	2
Equipment/uniforms/supplies						
Men	669,000	2	201,000	2	125,000	1
Women	262,000	1	105,000	1	103,000	1
Administrative and Non-gender	274,000	1	76,000	1	57,000	1
Total	1,205,000	3	381,000	3	285,000	3
Fundraising						
Men	210,000	1	49,000	0	51,000	1
Women	56,000	0	15,000	0	17,000	0
Administrative and Non-gender	921,000	2	150,000	1	237,000	2
Total	1,187,00	3	215,000	2	305,000	3

	$	%	$	%	$	%
Game Expenses						
Men	1,022,000	3	142,000	1	113,000	1
Women	239,000	1	63,000	1	75,000	1
Administrative and Non-gender	286,000	1	33,000	0	45,000	0
Total	1,547,000	4	239,000	2	234,000	2
Medical						
Men	108,000	0	15,000	0	7,000	0
Women	65,000	0	6,000	0	7,000	0
Administrative and Non-gender	371,000	1	125,000	1	81,000	1
Total	545,000	1	145,000	1	95,000	1
Membership Dues						
Men	32,000	0	8,000	0	6,000	0
Women	10,000	0	4,000	0	5,000	0
Administrative and Non-gender	196,000	1	29,000	0	33,000	0
Total	238,000	1	41,000	0	44,000	0
Sports Camps						
Men	156,000	0	28,000	0	48,000	1
Women	93,000	0	24,000	0	28,000	0
Administrative and Non-gender	43,000	0	48,000	1	19,000	0
Total	293,000	1	100,000	1	95,000	1
Spirit Groups						
Men	59,000	0	7,000	0	1,000	0
Women	9,000	0	1,000	0	1,000	0
Administrative and Non-gender	117,000	0	35,000	0	27,000	0
Total	185,000	0	43,000	0	29,000	0
Facilities Maintenance and Rental						
Men	1,130,000	3	80,000	1	83,000	1
Women	266,000	1	21,000	0	29,000	0
Administrative and Non-gender	3,846,000	10	492,000	4	253,000	3
Total	5,243,000	14	594,000	5	365,000	4
Indirect Institutional Support						
Men	216,000	1	101,000	1	66,000	1
Women	81,000	0	62,000	1	54,000	1
Administrative and Non-gender	1,087,000	3	1,001,000	9	650,000	7
Total	1,384,000	4	1,165,000	10	770,000	8
Other						
Men	924,000	2	189,000	2	107,000	1
Women	248,000	1	75,000	1	65,000	1
Administrative and Non-gender	2,475,000	6	465,000	4	346,000	4
Total	3,648,000	9	730,000	6	518,000	6
Total Operating Expenses						
Men	16,856,000	44	4,541,000	40	3,375,000	35
Women	7,056,000	18	2,874,000	25	3,108,000	33
Administrative and Non-gender	14,695,000	38	3,965,000	35	3,045,000	32
Total	38,607,000	100	11,381,000	100	9,528,000	100

*Because of zero values reported by respondents, median values can be misleading. Consequently, mean values are provided in this table.

Source: Daniel Fulks, 2004–2006 NCAA Revenues and Expenses of Division I Intercollegiate Athletic Programs Report (2008).

Table 5   Naming-Rights Deals at NCAA Facilities (Listed by Total Value)

Facility	School	Sponsor	Price	Years	Avg. Annual Value	Expires
Save Mart Center (a)	Fresno State University	Save Mart Supermarkets	$40 million	20	$2 million	2023
TCF Bank Stadium*	University of Minnesota	TCF Bank	$35 million	25	$1.4 million	2034
Comcast Center	University of Maryland	Comcast Corp.	$25 million (b)	25	$1 million	2026
Chevy Chase Bank Field at Byrd Stadium	University of Maryland	Chevy Chase Bank	$20 million	25	$800,000	2030
AT&T Stadium	Texas Tech University	AT&T	$20 million	25	$800,000	2019
Bright House Networks Stadium	University of Central Florida	Bright House Networks	$15 million	15	$1 million	NA
Papa John's Cardinal Stadium (c)	University of Louisville	Papa John's	$15 million	Indefinite	NA	2040
Summa Field at InfoCision Stadium (d)	University of Akron	InfoCision Management Corp.	$15 million	20	$750,000	NA
UFCU Disch Falk Field	University of Texas	University Federal Credit Union	$13.1 million	15	$873,333	NA
Value City Arena	Ohio State University	Value City Department Stores	$12.5 million (e)	75	$166,667	2072
Cox Arena at Aztec Bowl	San Diego State University	Cox Communications Inc.	$12 million	Indefinite	NA	NA
Cintas Center	Xavier University	Cintas Corp.	$10 million	NA	NA	NA
Fifth Third Arena	University of Cincinnati	Fifth Third Bancorp	$10 million (f)	NA	NA	NA
United Spirit Center	Texas Tech University	United Supermarkets Co.	$10 million	20	$500,000	2015
Jenny Craig Pavilion	University of San Diego	Jenny Craig Inc.	$7.0 million (g)	NA	NA	NA
Bank of Kentucky Arena	Northern Kentucky University	Bank of Kentucky	$6 million	20	$300,000	NA
The Colonial Center	University of South Carolina	Colonial Life & Accident	$5.5 million	12	$458,333	2015
Bank of America Arena	University of Washington	Bank of America Corp.	$5.1 million	10	$510,000	2009
Coors Events Center	University of Colorado	Adolph Coors Co.	$5 million	Indefinite	NA	NA
Cox Pavilion	University of Nevada	Cox Communications Inc.	$5 million	10	$500,000	2009
Houchen Industries L.T. Smith Stadium	Western Kentucky University	Houchen Industries	$5 million	Indefinite	NA	NA
Movie Gallery Veterans Stadium	Troy State University	Movie Gallery Inc.	$5 million	20	$250,000	2022
Wells Fargo Arena	Arizona State University	Wells Fargo & Co.	$5 million	Indefinite	NA	NA
Yum! Center (h)	University of Louisville	Yum! Brands	$5 million	20	$250,000	NA
Taco Bell Arena	Boise State University	Taco Bell	$4 million	15	$266,667	2019
Sioux Valley Hospital Field	Sioux Falls University	Sioux Valley Hospital	$3.2 million	20	$160,000	NA
Carrier Dome	Syracuse University	Carrier Corp.	$2.75 million	Indefinite	NA	NA
Alltel Pavilion	Virginia Commonwealth University	Alltel Corp.	$2 million	10	$200,000	2008

Facility	Institution	Company				
Franklin Covey Field	University of Utah	Franklin Covey Co.	15	$1.4 million	$93,333	2008
First United Bank Center	West Texas A&M University	First United Bank	15	$1 million	$66,667	NA
Pharmed Arena	Florida International University	Pharmed Group	NA	$1 million	NA	NA
Pomoco Stadium	Christopher Newport University	The Pomoco Group	10	$1 million	$100,000	2016
Shentel Stadium	Shenandoah University	Shenandoah Telecommunications	10	$750,000	$75,000	2010
Hanover Insurance Park at Fitton Field (i)	College of the Holy Cross	Hanover Insurance	3	$300,000	$100,000	2007
Maxwell Field at Alltel Stadium	Winona State (Minn.) University	Alltel Corp.	10	$250,000	$25,000	NA
BankUnited Center	University of Miami	BankUnited Financial Corp.	NA	NA	NA	2015
BB&T Field	Wake Forest University	BB&T Corp.	NA	NA	NA	2017
Toyota Stadium	Georgetown (Ky.) College	Toyota Motor Sales USA	NA	NA	NA	NA

NA: Not applicable or not available

*Under construction or in late stages of development.

(a) PepsiCo acquired naming rights to the venue as part of a 23-year, $40 million sponsorship - the first three years of which came while the arena was under construction – but passed the rights to Modesto, California-based Save Mart Supermarkets while retaining campuswide pouring rights. Save Mart declined to disclose its contribution for the naming-rights portion of the deal.

(b) To be paid over 10 years; additional cost of $5 million included for logo rights to the basketball floor by Comcast.

(c) In August 2007, a $10 million pledge toward Papa John's Cardinal Stadium expansion from Papa John's International and its founder, John Schnatter, extended the previous deal worth $5 million.

(d) Field title sponsorship by Summa Health System worth $5 million over 20 years.

(e) Value City Arena was part of the naming-rights deal for the Jerome Schottenstein Center.

(f) Fifth Third's naming rights to the university was part of a $10 million gift to the university that includes areas other than sports.

(g) Part of an overall $10 million gift to the university.

(h) The Yum! Center is the training facility for the University of Louisville.

(i) The stadium is owned by College of the Holy Cross and serves as home to that school's baseball team. However, the Worcester Tornadoes brokered and receive all revenue from the naming-rights deal, and Holy Cross refers to the facility as Fitton Field.

Source: Research by David Broughton, *Street & Smith's SportsBusiness Journal.* Used with permission.

favorable tax treatment is that institutions that build or renovate athletic facilities are usually eligible for tax-exempt bonds to help fund these projects, and the lower interest rate allows them to maintain substantially lower debt service than if they were otherwise ineligible for this treatment.

This not-for-profit status is quite favorable for alumni and boosters making contributions to the athletic department because their donations are fully tax-deductible. When the donation is a prerequisite to the purchase of season tickets or luxury seating, it is still 80% tax-deductible. This makes donating to colleges and universities an even more attractive option for alumni and boosters, and allows athletic departments to generate substantial amounts of revenues from fundraising. The median member of Division I-A brought in $5.8 million in cash donations in 2006, while the median Division I-AA and I-AAA institutions collected $635,000 and $483,000, respectively. Collectively, the members of

Division I-A received nearly $845 million in tax-free donations in 2005, most of which was tax-deductible for the donors.[1] As this represents forsaken taxable income, it is fair to conclude that the federal government lost hundreds of millions in uncollected taxes—and thus implicitly subsidizes the college sports industry. The tax issues surrounding college athletics are further discussed in the Congressional Budget Office's report on the topic.

Note

1. Myles Brand, Letter to William Thomas, Chairman, U.S. House of Representatives Committee on Ways and Means, Nov. 13, 2006, available at http://www.ncaa.org/wps/wcm/connect/2fa84c004e0d90 aea0caf01ad6fc8b25/20061115_response_to_housecommittee onwaysandmeans.pdf?MOD=AJPERES&CACHEID=2fa84c004e0d 90aea0caf01ad6fc8b25.

OVERVIEW OF INSTITUTIONAL IMPACT

INTERCOLLEGIATE ATHLETICS AND THE AMERICAN UNIVERSITY: A UNIVERSITY PRESIDENT'S PERSPECTIVE

James J. Duderstadt

The sports media fuel the belief that money is the root of all evil in college athletics. And, indeed, the size of the broadcasting contracts for college football and basketball events, the compensation of celebrity coaches, and the professional contracts dangled in front of star athletes make it clear that money does govern many aspects of intercollegiate athletics.

For example, Michigan, along with many other universities with big-time athletics, claims that football is a major money-maker. In fact, Michigan boasted that it made a profit of $14 million from its football program in 1997, the year it won the national championship. . . . Yet at the same time, most athletic departments plead poverty when confronted with demands that they increase varsity opportunities for women or financial aid for student-athletes. In fact, many athletic departments in Division I-A will actually admit that when all the revenues and expenses are totaled up, they actually lose money.

What is going on here? Could it be that those reporting about the economics of college sports have difficulty understanding the Byzantine financial statements of athletic departments? Are accounting tricks used to hide the true costs of intercollegiate athletics? Or perhaps those who lead and manage college sports have limited understanding of

how financial management and business accounting works in the first place?

It is probably all of the above, combined with the many other myths about the financing of college sports, which confuse not only outsiders such as the press and the public, but even those insiders such as the university administration, athletic directors, and coaches. Before we dive into a discussion of how college athletics are financed these days, I want to straighten out several of the more common misperceptions.

STRIPPING AWAY THE MYTHS

First, most members of the public, the sports press, and even many faculty members believe that colleges make lots of money from sports. In reality, essentially all of the revenue generated by sports is used by athletic departments to finance their own operations. Indeed, very few intercollegiate athletics programs manage to balance their operating budgets. The revenue from gate receipts, broadcasting rights, postseason play, licensing, and other commercial ventures is rarely sufficient to cover the full costs of the programs. Most universities rely on additional subsidies from student fees, booster donations, or even state appropriations. Beyond that, college sports benefit from a tax-exempt status on operations and donations that represents a very considerable public subsidy.

The University of Michigan provides an interesting case study of the financing of intercollegiate athletics, since it is one of only a handful of institutions that usually manages to generate sufficient revenue to support the cost of operations (although not the full capital costs) for its intercollegiate athletics programs. Even for Michigan, financing intercollegiate athletics remains an ongoing challenge. For example, during the 1988–89 fiscal year, my first year as president, the University of Michigan won the Big Ten football championship, the Rose Bowl, and the NCAA basketball championship. The university also appeared in seven national football telecasts and dozens of basketball telecasts, played in a football stadium averaging 105,000 spectators a game, and sold out most of its basketball and hockey events. Yet it barely managed to break even that year, with a net profit on operations of about $1 million on $35 million of revenue. . . .

When I was provost, football coach Bo Schembechler once complained to me about the enormous pressures to keep Michigan Stadium filled. He pointed to the losses that we would face if stadium attendance dropped 10 percent. I responded that, while this loss would be significant, it paled in comparison to the loss we would experience with a 10 percent drop in bed occupancy in the University of Michigan hospitals, which have an income more than twenty times larger than that of Michigan football. . . . Even football revenue has to be placed in perspective.

The University of Michigan, as one of the nation's most successful athletics programs, generates one of the highest levels of gross revenue in intercollegiate athletics. Despite this fact, in some years, the expenditures of our athletic department actually exceed revenues. . . . This paradox is due, in part, to the unique "business culture" of intercollegiate athletics. The competitive nature of intercollegiate athletics leads most athletic departments to focus far more attention on generating revenue than on managing costs. There is a widespread belief in college sports that the team that spends the most wins the most, and that no expenses are unreasonable if they might enhance the success of a program. A fancy press box in the stadium? First-class travel and accommodations for the team? A million-dollar contract for the coach? Sure, if it will help us win! Furthermore, the financing of intercollegiate athletics is also complicated by the fact that while costs such as staff salaries, student-athlete financial aid, and facilities maintenance are usually fixed, revenues are highly variable. In fact, in a given year, only television revenue for regular events is predictable. All other revenue streams, such as gate receipts, bowl or NCAA tournament income, licensing revenue, and private gifts, are highly variable. While some revenues such as gate receipts can be accurately predicted, particularly when season tickets sales are significant, others such as licensing and private giving are quite volatile. Yet many athletic departments (including Michigan, of late) build these speculative revenues into annual budgets that sometimes crash and burn in serious deficits when these revenues fail to materialize.

Needless to say, this business philosophy would rapidly lead to bankruptcy in the corporate world. It has become increasingly clear that until athletic departments begin to operate with as much of an eye on expenditures as revenues, universities will continue to lose increasing amounts of money in their athletic activities, no matter how lucrative the television or licensing contracts they may negotiate.

Well, even if athletic departments essentially spend every dollar they generate, don't winning programs motivate alumni to make contributions to the university? To be sure, some alumni are certainly motivated to give money to the university while (and, perhaps, only when) basking in the glow of winning athletic programs. But, many of these loyal alumni and friends give only to athletic programs and not to the university more generally. And the amounts they give are relatively modest. . . .

University fundraising staff have known for many years that the most valuable support of a university generally comes from alumni and friends who identify with the *academic* programs of the university, not its athletic prowess. In fact, many of the university's most generous donors care little about its athletic success and are sometimes alienated by the attention given to winning athletics programs.

The staggering sums involved in television contracts, such as the $6 billion contract with CBS for televising the NCAA tournament, suggest that television revenue is the goose that lays the golden eggs for intercollegiate athletics. But for most institutions, ticket sales are still the primary source of revenue. Indeed, there is some evidence that television can have a negative impact on the overall revenues of many athletic programs by overexposing athletic events and eroding gate receipts. Lower game attendance brought on by television has been particularly harmful to those institutions and conferences whose sports programs are not broadcast as primetime or national events, since many of their fans stay home from university events in order to watch televised events involving major athletic powers.

The additional costs required to mount "TV quality" events tend to track increasing revenue in such a way that the more one is televised, the more one must spend. More and more institutions are beginning to realize that there is little financial incentive for excessive television coverage. While exposure can convey the good news of successful athletic programs and promote the university's visibility, it can also convey "bad news," particularly if there is a major scandal or a mishap with an event.

If the financial and publicity impact of television is not necessarily positive, why is there then such a mad rush on the part of athletics programs for more and more television exposure? Speaking from the perspective of one of the most heavily televised universities in the country, my suspicion is that the pressure for such excessive television coverage is not coming from the most successful and most heavily televised institutions—the Michigans, Ohio States, and UCLAs. It is, instead, coming from the "have-not" institutions, those who have chosen not to mount competitive programs but who have become heavily dependent on sharing the television revenue generated by the big box office events through conference or NCAA agreements.

Stated more bluntly, the television revenue-sharing policies of many conferences or broader associations, such as the NCAA, while implemented with the aim of achieving equity, are failing. They are, in reality, having the perverse effect of providing strong incentives for those institutions that are not attractive television draws to drive the system toward excessive commercialization or exposure of popular events. While the have-not universities share in the revenues, these institutions do not bear the financial burden or disruption of providing television-quality events. In a sense, the revenue-sharing system does not allow for negative feedback that might lead to more moderate approaches to television broadcasting.

What about the suggestion that student-athletes deserve some share of the spoils? The argument usually runs as follows: College sports is golden—witness, for example, the $550 million paid each year by CBS for the NCAA tournament or the . . . payout per team for the football Bowl Championship Series games. And yet the athletes do not even get pocket money. . . . And what about college coaches, some of whom make over a million dollars a year? Shouldn't we pay the athletes who generate all this money? Late in his long tenure as executive director of the NCAA, Walter Byers argued that since colleges were exploiting the talents of their student-athletes, they deserved the same access to the free market as coaches. He suggested letting them endorse products, with the resulting income going into a trust fund that would become available only after they graduated or completed their eligibility.[2]

These myths are firmly entrenched not only in the public's mind but in the culture of the university. We need now to separate out the reality from the myth, to better understand the real nature of the financial issues facing college sports.

Reality 1: What Do Universities Really Make from Athletics?

As we noted earlier, in 1997, the University of Michigan generated $45 million from its athletics activities, of which only about $3 million came from television. Although the university actually generated far more than this from the broadcasting of events such as football and basketball games, the Rose Bowl, and the Big Ten and NCAA basketball tournaments, most of this revenue was shared with the other Big Ten and NCAA schools. How much of this revenue can we attribute to the efforts of students? This is hard to estimate. On the one hand, we might simply divide the entire revenue base by the number of varsity athletes (seven hundred) to arrive at about $45,000 per athlete. But, of course, coaches and staff also are responsible for generating revenue, by building winning sports programs or marketing or licensing sports apparel. Certain unusual assets, like Michigan Stadium, attract sizable crowds and generate significant revenue regardless of how successful the team

is. Finally, we have not said anything yet about expenses. Operating expenditures at Michigan, as at every other university in the nation, are sometimes larger than revenues. As a result, the net revenues, the profit, is zero! While it is admittedly very difficult to estimate just how much income student-athletes bring to the university, it is clear that it is far less than most sportswriters believe.

Reality 2: What Do the Players Receive from the University?

At Michigan the typical instructional cost (not "price" or tuition) of our undergraduate programs is about $20,000 per student per year. When we add to this support for room and board and incidentals, it amounts to an investment of about $30,000 per year per fully tendered student-athlete, or between $120,000 to $150,000 per athlete over four or five years of studies. The actual value of this education is far higher, since it provides the student-athlete with an earning capacity far beyond that of a high school education (and even far beyond that of most professional sports careers, with the exception of only the greatest superstars). Of course, only a few student-athletes will ever achieve high-paying careers in professional sports. Most do not make the pros, and most of those who do are only modestly compensated for a few short years.

The real reward for student-athletes is, of course, a college education. Despite having somewhat poorer high school records, test scores, and preparation for college, athletes tended to graduate at rates quite comparable to those of other students. The reasons for their academic success involved both their strong financial support through scholarships and their academic support and encouragement through programs not available to students at large. Yet it is also the case that recruiting college athletes based entirely on physical skills rather than academic promise undermines this premise. As William Dowling, professor at Rutgers, has noted, "Problems will remain as long as players in the so-called revenue sports represent a bogus category of students, recruited on the basis of physical skills rather than for academic or intellectual ability."[4]

Those who call for professionalizing college athletics by paying student-athletes—and they are generally members of the sports media—are approaching college sports as show business, not as part of an academic enterprise. Only in show business do the stars make such grossly distorted amounts. In academics, the Nobel Prize winner does not make much more than any other faculty member. In the corporate world, the inventor of a device that earns a corporation millions of dollars will receive only a small incentive payment for her or his discovery. The moral of the story is that one simply cannot apply the perverse reward system of the entertainment industry to college sports—unless, of course, you believe college sports is, in reality, simply another form of show business.

A PRIMER ON COLLEGE SPORTS FINANCING

Most business executives would find the financial culture of intercollegiate athletics bizarre indeed. To be sure, there are considerable opportunities for revenue from college sports. . . . In terms of their revenue-generating capacity, three college football teams, Michigan, Notre Dame, and Florida, are more valuable than most professional football franchises.[5] Such statistics have lured college after college into big-time athletics, motivating them to make the investment in stadiums, coaching staffs, [and] scholarships, to join the big boys in NCAA's Division I-A.

Yet most intercollegiate athletics programs at most colleges and universities require some subsidy from general university resources such as tuition or state appropriation. Put another way, most college athletics programs actually lose money. . . . And, while football coaches might like to suggest that the costs of "nonrevenue" sports are the problem, particularly those women's sports programs mandated by Title IX, before blaming others, they should first look in a mirror. While football generates most of the revenue for intercollegiate athletics, it also is responsible for most of the growth in costs. More precisely, when college sports is transformed into an entertainment industry, and when its already intensely competitive ethos begins to equate expenditure with winning, one inevitably winds up with a culture that attempts to spend every dollar that it is generated, and then some.

Stated another way, the costs of intercollegiate athletics within a given institution are driven by decisions concerning the level of competition (e.g., NCAA Division, regional, or nationally competitive), the desire for competitive success, and the breadth of programs. Although football generates most of the revenue for big time athletic programs through gate receipts and broadcasting, it is also an extremely expensive sport. Not only does it involve an unusually large number of participants and attendant coaching and support staff, but the capital facilities costs of football stadiums, practice facilities, and training facilities are very high. Furthermore, many of the remaining costs of the athletic department, such as marketing staff, media relations, and business are driven, in reality, primarily by the needs of the football program rather than the other varsity sports. In this sense, football coaches to the contrary, big-time football programs are, in reality, cost drivers rather than revenue centers.

It is instructive to take a more detailed look at the various revenue streams and costs associated with intercollegiate athletics in order to get a sense of scale. The following are the principal sources of revenues and expenditures:

Revenues

- Ticket sales
- Guarantees
- Payouts from bowl games and tournaments
- Television
- Corporate sponsorships, advertising, licensing
- Unearned revenues
- Booster club donations
- Student fees and assessments
- State or other government support
- Hidden university subsidies

Expenditures

- Salaries
- Athletic scholarships
- Travel and recruiting
- Equipment, supplies, medicine
- Insurance
- Legal, public relations, administrative
- Capital expenditures (debt service and maintenance)

Furthermore, intercollegiate athletics is highly capital intensive, particularly at a big-time program such as Michigan. Few athletics programs amortize these capital costs in a realistic fashion. Including these imbedded capital costs on the balance sheet would quickly push even the most successful programs far into the red.

To illustrate, let us walk through the budget of the University of Michigan Department of Intercollegiate Athletics. First let me note that it is the practice of the university that intercollegiate athletics be a self-supporting enterprise, not consuming university resources. It receives neither state appropriation nor student tuition. Furthermore, this financial firewall works in both directions: any revenue balance earned by the athletic department cannot, under normal circumstances, be transferred to the academic side of the university. They must pay for what they cost the university, and they keep what they make. . . .

Not included in these figures were onetime expenditures of roughly $18 million to expand Michigan Stadium, to decorate it with a gaudy maize-and-blue halo designed by the noted architect Robert Venturi, complete with the ten-foot-high words to the Michigan fight song, "Hail to the Conquering Heroes"; to install $8 million worth of "Jumbo-tron" television scoreboards; and to build a sophisticated control room for Internet broadcasts. These onetime expenses were charged against (and largely decimated) the flexible reserve funds of the department. Lest you think these latter expenses were unusually extravagant, Ohio State is in the midst of several construction projects that will leave their athletic department saddled with a $277 million debt, to be paid over the next thirty years. (And you wonder why people believe that the financial culture of intercollegiate athletics is wacko?)

As I noted earlier, the financial strategy in intercollegiate athletics is strongly driven by competitive pressures. The belief that those who spend the most win the most drives institutions to generate and spend more and more dollars. The prosperous programs at institutions such as Michigan, Penn State, and Notre Dame set the pace for the entire intercollegiate athletics enterprise, no matter what the size of the school. As expenditures on athletics programs continue to spiral out of control, there have been increasing calls for action at both the national and conference level. Yet part of the problem is that many athletic departments hide the true nature of the financial operations not only from the prying eyes of the press and the public, but even from their own universities. Several years ago, the Big Ten Conference launched an effort to contain costs by restricting the growth of institutional expenditures on athletics to the rate of inflation. At that time, many universities were suffering as their athletics revenues were insufficient to cover costs. There were also concerns about competitiveness, since the wealthier schools tended to dominate most Big Ten sports, particularly football.

More specifically, Michigan and Ohio State, because of their very large stadiums, had considerably more gate receipt revenue than the other Big Ten members. Onetime football powers such as Wisconsin and Minnesota had fallen on hard times, with mediocre teams and low stadium attendance. Minnesota was in a particularly difficult bind since it had shifted its football games to the downtown Minneapolis Metrodome and torn down its on-campus stadium. Earlier attempts to address this discrepancy among institutions through revenue-sharing formulas had finally become burdensome enough to the larger stadium schools, particularly with the entry of Penn State that the conference agreed to accept a more equitable formula.

Therefore, attempts to control expenditures rather than to redistribute revenues became the focus. But there was a big problem here. Nobody really knew how much the athletic departments in each university were spending. On top of that, no one seemed to know how much or where the revenue came from. And because most athletics programs were independent of the usual financial management and controls of their institutions, it was clear that this comparative information would be difficult if not impossible to obtain through the departments themselves.

Member institutions decided to form a special subcommittee to the Big Ten Council of Presidents comprised of the universities' chief financial officers. This CFO committee was charged with developing a system to obtain and compare annual athletics revenues and expenditures within the Big Ten. Needless to say, this decision to go outside of the athletic enterprise for supervision did not go down well in some schools where the athletic department had unusual autonomy. And while opening their books for examination was not particularly troublesome to most Big Ten universities, since as public institutions they frequently had to endure audits from state government, this was a very sensitive matter to the one private university in the Big Ten, Northwestern.

The first set of comparisons across all universities was eye opening.[8] Among the factors of particular note was the distribution of revenues.

Ticket sales	38 percent
Television and radio	13
Gift income	13
Subsidies	11
Licensing, concessions, etc.	9
Game settlements, guarantees	8
Bowls and NCAA revenue	4
Miscellaneous	4

Although broadcasting and bowl revenues were important—and are becoming more so—the largest single revenue source (38 percent) remained gate receipts. This explains why the three universities with very large stadiums (Michigan at 105,000, Ohio State at 98,000, and Penn State at 96,000) stand out in revenues. Among the public universities, there was great disparity in the capacity to generate private support for athletics (with Michigan ranking, surprisingly enough, toward the bottom of the range) and in their subsidies from state support.

The financial studies revealed that 72 percent of total athletic department revenue is attributable to football. Another 23 percent comes from men's basketball. In other words, 95 percent is generated by football and basketball combined. (Ice hockey contributes 4 percent and women's basketball 1 percent.) A further breakdown of revenue sources shows the difference between men's and women's sports.

Men's sports	71.1 percent
Women's sports	4.3
Administrative operations	24.6

In terms of expenditures, 57 percent was spent on football and men's basketball, while 24 percent was spent on women's sports, and 14 percent on all other men's sports. Despite the Big Ten Conference's efforts to achieve gender equity, women's programs amounted to only one-quarter of expenditures in the 1990s. Financial aid was distributed 67 percent to men, 33 percent to women, roughly in proportion to their representation among varsity athletes.

Two universities stood out in terms of the breadth and comprehensiveness of their programs: Ohio State, with thirty-five programs, and Penn State with thirty. Michigan's twenty-three programs were only in the middle of the pack, despite the fact that Michigan ranked number one in revenues. . . .

There was a factor-of-two difference in athletic department revenues and expenditures, ranging from Michigan and Ohio State . . . to Northwestern and Purdue. . . . The analysis also quickly made apparent why Northwestern had been so reluctant to share its financial data. In sharp contrast to the public universities, Northwestern was subsidizing its athletics programs from general academic resources to the tune of about $8 million per year (almost half their revenues). Although today, after two Big Ten football championships, faculty and students might believe it was worth the roughly eight hundred dollars per student of tuition (or other academic income) it cost to remain in the Big Ten, at the time of the first CFO surveys, this was highly sensitive information. While Northwestern's hidden subsidy was the largest among Big Ten universities, it was certainly not unique. Some institutions provided hidden subsidies by waiving tuition or granting instate tuition rates for student athletes. Others received direct subsidies for their athletics programs through state appropriations (e.g., Wisconsin received $634,000 per year).

There were a number of other significant differences among the expenditure patterns of the various universities. For example, several of the public universities charged only in-state tuition to athletes, even if they were out-of-state residents, thereby reducing very significantly their costs for athletic scholarships. In contrast, Michigan charged full out-of-state tuition levels, which were comparable to those of private institutions, thereby driving up the costs of athletic grants-in-aid programs considerably. Labor costs also varied widely among institutions, ranging from urban and unionized wage scales to rural and non-unionized wage scales.

It was finally concluded, after several years of effort, that the great diversity among institutions in terms of the manner in which revenue was generated, expenditures were managed, and accounting was performed made it almost impossible to attempt conference-wide cost containment. Hence, the Big Ten presidents adopted a policy encouraging rather than requiring cost containment. However, they also decided to continue the annual CFO comparative analysis of revenues and expenditures, if only to provide visibility for unusual practices.

SHOW ME THE MONEY!

Revenue flows into athletics departments from a number of sources and out again through a complex array of expenditures. . . . In this brief discussion, I will focus only on a few items of particular interest.

One of the most expensive elements of sports is the current grants-in-aid system for the financial support of student-athletes. In contrast to the need-based financial aid programs for regular students, colleges are allowed to provide student-athletes with sufficient support to meet "all commonly accepted educational expenses"—a full ride, regardless of financial need or academic ability. This policy, first implemented in football in the 1950s, has spread rapidly to all varsity sports. As the costs of a college education have rapidly increased over the past two decades, the costs

of grants-in-aid have risen dramatically. . . . But there is considerable variation among institutions . . . .

In some cases, this discrepancy is due to institutions that choose to subsidize financial aid by granting all athletes in-state tuition levels, in effect hiding the subsidy of the difference between in-state and out-of-state levels. Although some universities restrict the number or types of grants-in-aid they provide in various sports, the University of Michigan has long had a policy of fully funding all allowable grants-in-aid in all sports in which it competes. Since most student-athletes are subject to out-of-state tuition levels, the resulting cost of athletically related student aid is unusually high . . . .

A second factor in the inflating costs was the rapid growth in size of football programs as coaches pushed through the unlimited-substitution rules in the 1960s. This system allowed college football to develop specialists for essentially every position and every situation in the game—offense and defense, blocking and tackling, kicking and passing. Although it was promoted as a way to make the game more exciting, it was not just a coincidence that it also made football far easier to play and to coach. More significantly, it transformed college football into a corporate and bureaucratic enterprise, with teams of over one hundred players, dozens of coaches, trainers, and equipment managers, and even technology experts in areas such as video production and computer analysis. Furthermore, unlimited substitution not only transformed college football into the professional football paradigm, but it also demanded that high school football follow the colleges and the pros down the same expensive path.

The third factor driving the rapid expansion of the program's cost and complexity has been the insatiable desire of football coaches for any additional gimmicks that might provide a competitive edge, either in play or competition. Special residences for football players became common, some resembling country clubs more than campus dormitories. Many football programs have built not only special training facilities but also even museums to display their winning traditions to prospective recruits. . . . Teams usually travel in high style, with charter jet service, four-star hotels, and even special travel clothing such as team blazers. And, of course, each time a coach at one university dreams up a new wrinkle, all of the other coaches at competing universities have to have it, no matter how extravagant or expensive.

This competitive pressure from coaches and fans—and even the media—has made it very difficult for athletic departments to control costs. Each time actions are proposed to slow the escalation of costs in the two main revenue sports, football and basketball, they are countered with the argument that the more one spends, the more one will win and hence the more one will make. The relative financial inexperience of those who manage athletic departments makes it even more difficult to resist these competitive forces. They tend to develop a one-dimensional financial culture, in which all attention is focused on revenue generation, and cost controls are essentially ignored.

A conversation with any athletic director soon reveals just how much of their attention is devoted to generating revenue to cover ever-increasing costs. This preoccupation with revenue generation propagates up through the hierarchy, to university presidents and governing boards, athletic conferences, and even the NCAA. Far more time is spent on negotiating broadcasting contracts or licensing agreements than on cost containment, much less concern about the welfare of student-athletes or the proper role of college sports in a university.

Though most of the revenue for college sports has traditionally come from revenue associated with football and basketball events, several of the most popular programs have generated very extensive licensing income from the use of institutional logos and insignia. A number of major athletics programs, Michigan among them, have signed lucrative contracts with sports apparel companies. Many athletic departments have also launched extensive fundraising efforts involving alumni and fans, both for ongoing support and endowment. In fact, both athletic scholarship programs and key athletic department staff such as athletic directors and football coaches are supported by endowments in some universities.

Athletic departments go to great lengths and considerable creativity to find new sources of revenues. For example, when Michigan decided to replace its artificial turf in Michigan Stadium with natural turf in 1992, the athletic department got the bright idea that people might want to purchase a piece of the old carpet for nostalgic reasons. They chopped up the old artificial turf into an array of souvenirs, ranging from coasters to doormats to large rugs containing some of the lettering on the field. To their delight, these sold like hotcakes, and the department made over two hundred thousand dollars. . . .

Another example is the construction of an elegant new plaza and fence surrounding Michigan Stadium in 1995. The athletic department decided to sell paving bricks at a premium (one hundred to one thousand dollars apiece) and allow people to inscribe their names and perhaps even a brief message. Again, demand soared for the opportunity to become "a part of Michigan Stadium," and the department rapidly raised the several hundred thousand dollars required for the project.

Licensing provides a more standard means for generating revenue for the athletic department. Michigan moved early into a more direct merchandising effort, placing retail shops (the M-Go Blue Shops) in various athletics venues, so that it could participate directly in the profits from athletic or signature apparel. It was always a fascinating experience to browse through these shops to see what the fertile creativity of the marketing side of the athletic department had devised or approved for licensing: maize-and-blue toilet seats that play "The Victors" when raised, the Michigan football helmet chip-and-dip bowl, and hundreds upon hundreds of different sweatshirt designs. The catalog mail-order business became particularly lucrative.

. . . .

We have noted earlier the extreme volatility of most revenue sources for intercollegiate athletics. While a New Year's Day bowl appearance or success in the NCAA Basketball Tournament can provide a windfall, a poor season can trigger rapid declines in gate receipts, licensing income, and private gifts. Catastrophe awaits the naive athletic director who builds an expenditure budget based on such speculative income, since disaster awaits when the books are finally closed at year end. During my tenure as president, we not only required the athletic department to budget very conservatively, but it also was encouraged to build a reserve fund with sufficient investment income to compensate for any uncertainty in the operating budget. In fact, our athletic director generally measured financial performance in terms of the growth of the reserve fund from year to year.

FINANCIAL ACCOUNTABILITY

The athletic department at most NCAA Division I-A universities is treated as an auxiliary activity, separated by a financial firewall from the budgets of academic programs. This strategy allows athletic directors to offer up the excuse that the sometimes flamboyant expenditures of the department are not being made at the expense of the university. But it also creates major problems. It tends to focus most of the athletic department's energy (not to mention the conference's and NCAA's) on revenue generation rather than cost management. It subjects coaches and staff to extreme pressures to generate additional revenue in the mistaken belief that it will enhance the competitiveness of their programs. And, perhaps most significantly, it further widens the gap between the athletic department and the rest of the university.

Despite the boasts of athletic directors and football coaches to the contrary, intercollegiate athletics at most institutions—perhaps all institutions, if rigorous accounting principles were applied—is a net financial loser. All revenues go simply to support and in some cases expand the athletic empire, while many expenditures that amount to university subsidy are hidden by sloppy management or intricate accounting. Put more pointedly, college sports, including the celebrity compensation of coaches, the extravagant facilities, first-class travel and accommodations, VIP entertainment of the sports media, shoddy and wasteful management practices, all require subsidy by the university through devices such as student fees, hidden administrative overhead support, and student tuition waivers.

Yet our athletic departments not only tout their self-supporting status, but they vigorously seek and defend their administrative and financial independence. And well they should, since their primary activity is, increasingly, operating a commercial entertainment business. As college football and basketball become ever more commercial and professional, their claim on any subsidy from the university is diminished.

Of course, few of our sports problems are self-supporting. If we illuminate hidden costs and subsidies, we find that all intercollegiate athletics burden the university with considerable costs, some financial, some in terms of the attention required of university leadership, some in terms of the impact to the reputation and integrity of the university, and some measured only in the impact on students and staff. Experience has also shown that expenses always increase somewhat more rapidly than the revenues generated by college sports.

In conclusion, the mad race for fame and profits through intercollegiate athletics is clearly a fool's quest. Recognition on the athletic field or court has little relevance to academic reputation. Nebraska can win all the national championships it wishes, and it will never catch fair Harvard's eye. Indeed, fame in athletics is often paradoxical, since it can attract public scrutiny, which can then uncover violations and scandal. As the intensity and visibility of big-time athletics build,

the university finds itself buffeted by the passion and energy of the media and the public, who identify with their athletics programs rather than their educational mission.

Yet every year, several more universities proudly proclaim they have decided to invest the resources to build sports programs that will earn them membership in NCAA's Division I-A. Sometimes lessons are never learned.

Notes

. . . .

2. Walter Byers with Charles Hammer, *Unsportsmanlike Conduct: Exploiting College Athletes.* Ann Arbor: University of Michigan Press, 1995.

. . . .

4. William Dowling, "To Cleanse Colleges of Sports Corruption, End Recruiting Based on Physical Skills," *Chronicle of Higher Education,* July 9, 1999, B9.

5. Richard Sheehan, *Keeping Score: The Economics of Big-Time Sports,* New York: Diamond Communications, 1996, chaps. 11, 12.

. . . .

8. Athletic Operations Survey, 1993–94, Big Ten Conference, Chicago, 1994.

UNIVERSITY OF MICHIGAN DEPARTMENT OF ATHLETICS OPERATING BUDGETS, 2009–2010

For the proposed FY 2010 Operating Budget (described in detail on the following pages), we project an operating surplus of $8.8 million based on operating revenues of $94.4 million and operating expenses of $85.6 million. The budgeted surplus will be added to our operating reserves. [*Ed. Note: See Table 6*.] Highlights are as follows:

- The budget reflects an eight-game home schedule for football (seven home games were played last year).

- Budgeted sponsorship revenue (including radio rights) has increased to $13.7 million from $8 million in FY 08. Sponsorship revenue includes the IMG and Adidas agreements, both of which became effective in FY 2009.

- Included in operating expenses is a $4.5 million transfer to a deferred maintenance fund established in FY 2003. The deferred maintenance fund is used as a means to provide for major repair and rehabilitation projects for our athletic facilities. We expect to continue to set aside additional funds in future years for this purpose.

- The budget reflects operating expenditure increases of 4.8% over projected operating expenses in FY 2009, principally due to compensation, financial aid, team travel, and home game expense increases.

We are also pleased to report that based on preliminary results, we project that the operating surplus for FY 09 will be $10.2 million, approximately the same as budgeted. The accumulation of operating surpluses will be used to fund our ongoing capital needs and facility renewal projects in FY 2010 and beyond.

. . . .

UNIVERSITY OF MICHIGAN ATHLETIC DEPARTMENT 2009–2010 BUDGET NOTES AND ASSUMPTIONS (ALL DOLLAR AMOUNTS IN 000'S)

Basis for Accounting

The University of Michigan Athletic Department manages its financial activity through the use of three different funds, the Operating Fund, the Endowment Fund, and the Plant Fund.

The Operating Fund budget is presented herein. (A consolidated financial statement is prepared annually and audited by PricewaterhouseCoopers). The Operating Fund budget includes most of the revenues and expenditures of the Athletic Department, with the exception of Endowment Fund gifts and associated market value adjustments (which are recorded in the Endowment Fund), and investments in the physical plant (with the associated debt, which are recorded in the Plant Fund).

Table 6   Michigan Athletic Department FY 2010 Operating Budget (in thousands)

	FY 07/08 Actual	FY 08/09 Budget	FY 08/09 Projected	FY 09/10 Budget	% Change Budget	% Change Projected	$ Change Budget	$ Change Projected
Revenues								
Spectator admissions	$38,642	$35,551	$35,609	$37,714	6.1%	5.9%	$2,163	$2,105
Conference distributions	17,267	17,419	17,566	18,306	5.1%	4.2%	887	740
Corporate sponsorship	8,065	11,980	13,395	13,760	14.9%	−21.7%	1,780	365
Priority seating and other annual gifts	15,138	13,600	13,600	13,700	0.7%	0.7%	100	100
Licensing and royalties	5,047	3,800	3,800	4,100	7.9%	7.9%	300	300
Concessions and parking	2,221	1,860	1,860	1,887	1.5%	1.5%	27	27
Facilities	1,934	1,870	1,870	1,774	−5.1%	−5.1%	(96)	(96)
Other income	1,237	937	937	863	−7.9%	−7.9%	(74)	(74)
Investment income	4,207	3,444	3,244	2,345	−31.9%	−27.7%	(1,099)	(899)
CURRENT FUND REVENUES	$93,758	$90,461	$91,881	$94,449	4.4%	2.8%	$3,988	$2,568
Expenses								
Salaries, wages & benefits	$29,728	$30,860	$31,660	$33,958	10.0%	7.3%	$3,098	$2,298
Financial aid to students	13,584	15,129	15,029	15,734	4.0%	4.7%	605	705
Team and game expense	14,827	15,005	15,482	15,791	5.2%	2.0%	786	309
Facilities expense	8,026	7,093	7,893	7,580	6.9%	−4.0%	487	(313)
Deferred maintenance fund transfer	4,500	4,500	4,500	4,500	0.0%	0.0%	—	—
Other operating and administrative expenses	7,151	6,575	6,660	5,923	−9.9%	−11.1%	(652)	(737)
Debt service transfer to plant fund	2,411	1,029	446	2,139	107.9%	379.6%	1,110	1,693
CURRENT FUND EXPENSES	$80,227	$80,191	$81,670	$85,625	6.8%	4.8%	$5,434	$3,955
NET OPERATING SURPLUS	13,531	10,270	10,211	8,824				
Transfers and capital expenditures								
Capital expenditures from current funds and transfers to plant and other funds	(12,259)	(7,700)	(7,700)	(2,275)				
Transfer from quasi-endowment and other funds	(1,383)							
Net transfers and capital expenditures	(13,642)	(7,700)	(7,700)	(2,275)				
INCREASE (DECREASE) IN CURRENT FUND BALANCES	(111)	2,570	2,511	6,549				

Source: University of Michigan. Athletic Department. Used with permission.

Governmental Accounting Standards Board Statement No. 33 ("GASB 33") requires that the promises of private donations be recognized as receivables and revenues in the year the pledge was given, provided they are verifiable, measurable, and probable of collection. The Athletic Department Operating Fund budget presented herein records gifts when received (i.e., on a cash basis). The Operating Fund budget presented also reflects 100% of the gifts related to preferred seat donations ("PSD") as gift income. For financial reporting purposes, 20% of PSD gifts are reflected in spectator admissions.

1. Spectator admissions

Spectator admissions are net of associated guarantee payments to visiting schools and consist of the following:

	Actual FY 06	Actual FY 07	Actual FY 08	Projected FY 09	Budget FY 10
Football	$30,570	$29,819	$34,555	$31,670	$33,753
Basketball	2,354	2,104	1,908	1,921	1,975
Hockey	2,141	1,985	1,799	1,789	1,800
Other	205	163	380	229	186
Total	$35,609	$34,071	$38,642	$35,270	$37,714
Memo:					
Home football games	7	7	8	7	8
Regular season football games	11	12	12	12	12

2. Conference distributions

Expected Big 10 conference distributions consist of the following:

	Actual FY 06	Actual FY 07	Actual FY 08	Projected FY 09	Budget FY 10
Television (football and basketball)	$6,143	$9,371	$13,932	$14,393	$15,034
NCAA basketball based distributions	2,275	2,319	2,436	2,551	2,712
Football bowl games	1,917	1,947	2,038	1,841	1,775
Other miscellaneous	340	400	384	349	400
	$10,675	$14,037	$18,790	$19,134	$19,921
Less amount contributed to University		570	1,523	1,568	1,615
Net conference distributions		$13,467	$17,267	$17,566	$18,306

3. Facilities

Facility income includes the fee and rental revenue from the University of Michigan Golf Course, the Varsity Tennis Center, Yost Ice Arena, and the various other athletic department facilities.

4. Investment Income

Investment income includes the return from the University Investment Pool (UIP) program as well as the quarterly distribution from Endowment and Quasi-Endowment Funds.

5. Other Income

Other income consists of guarantees received for hockey and basketball away games, ticket handling fees, and other miscellaneous income.

6. Compensation Expense

The athletic department has approximately 245 full time employees including those that have joint appointments with other University units, and various part time employees, interns, and graduate assistants. Compensation expense by area is as follows:

	Actual FY 06	Actual FY 07	Actual FY 08	Projected FY 09	Budget FY 10
Coaches and team staff	$8,980	$11,234	$13,239	$14,670	$15,478
Compliance, sports information, and other administration	2,575	2,808	3,400	3,568	3,731
Athletic medicine, conditioning, academic support	2,316	2,498	2,841	2,809	3,277
Facilities	2,404	2,537	2,745	2,697	2,788
Sports marketing, development and studio operations	853	784	869	960	1,031
Ticket and business office	733	773	801	801	860
Fringe benefits	4,939	4,664	5,833	6,155	6,793
Total	$22,800	$25,298	$29,728	$31,660	$33,958

7. Financial aid to students

The athletic department grants the maximum allowable scholarships to all varsity sports. Total grant-in-aid equivalencies are approximately 335 with an estimated in-state to out-of-state ratio of 30%/70%.

8. Sports programs

Sports program expense is comprised of the following:

	Actual FY 06	Actual FY 07	Actual FY 08	Projected FY 09	Budget FY 10
Team travel expenses	$3,329	$4,015	$4,458	$4,655	$4,769
Equipment	1,814	1,822	2,507	2,917	2,786
Home game, hosted events, and officials	1,722	1,996	2,524	2,687	3,074
Training and medical expenses	828	810	836	818	1,044
Recruiting	993	949	1,269	1,281	1,297
Vacation board	521	560	591	766	668
Post season expenses, net	520	463	722	600	600
Booster and "special account" expenses	503	554	705	601	537
Other sport program expenses	823	863	1,215	1,157	1,015
Total	$11,053	$12,032	$14,827	$15,482	$15,790

Post season expenses are estimated based on the likelihood of participation in post season events for the majority of varsity sports. The post-season budget assumes that the football bowl expenditures will not exceed the bowl expense allowance received.

9. Facility Expenses

Facility expenses consist of the following:

	Actual FY 06	Actual FY 07	Actual FY 08	Projected FY 09	Budget FY 10
Repairs and maintenance	$2,237	$2,655	$3,714	$2,913	$2,554
Utilities	2,340	2,577	2,456	3,064	3,200
Supplies and equipment	804	702	1,020	979	1,073
Other facility expenses	749	743	836	937	753
Total	$6,130	$6,677	$8,026	$7,893	$7,580

10. Deferred Maintenance Fund Transfer

In 2002 the department established a Deferred Maintenance Fund as a means to provide for repair and rehabilitation projects for the athletic physical plant. Transfers from the Operating Fund to the Deferred Maintenance Fund are reflected as operating expenses in this presentation.

11. Other Operating and Administrative Expenses

Other operating and administrative expenses consist of the following:

	Actual FY 06	Actual FY 07	Actual FY 08	Projected FY 09	Budget FY 10
Corporate sponsor and development expenses, including television production costs	$1,806	$1,917	$2,191	$1,862	$1,262
Postage, equipment and ticket expenses	1,131	1,104	1,191	1,013	994
University re-charges	802	736	751	736	755
Insurance	462	292	326	395	455
Telephone	290	340	397	378	387
Publications and printing	366	335	385	475	364
Professional travel	298	297	349	402	402
Band expenses, excluding post-season expenses	164	219	223	236	238
Big 10 conference and other dues	98	98	102	105	105
Other expenses	739	952	1,236	1,046	961
Total	$6,156	$6,290	$7,151	$6,648	$5,923

12. Debt Service

Debt service and associated debt is summarized as follows:

	FY 2010 Budget			Scheduled Balance	
	Interest	Principal	Total Debt Service	June, 2010	June, 2009
Ross Academic Center	—	—	—	—	2,100
Stadium project	340	—	340	148,300	108,250
Fieldhouse	567	200	767	11,700	11,900
Stadium concrete	328	160	488	7,445	7,605
Hartwig renovation	134	60	194	3,005	3,065
Softball renovation	172	80	252	3,990	4,070
Rowing facility	38	60	98	805	805
Total	$1,579	$560	$2,139	$175,245	$137,795
Less amounts collected on pledges in Plant Fund			—		
Net debt service—Operating Fund			$2,139		

13. Transfers to Plant Fund for Capital Expenditures

Capital expenditures and estimated plant fund transfers are budgeted at $2.3 million for fiscal year 2010 and consist of various renovation projects.

FACULTY PERCEPTIONS OF INTERCOLLEGIATE ATHLETICS SURVEY, EXECUTIVE SUMMARY, PREPARED FOR THE KNIGHT COMMISSION'S FACULTY SUMMIT ON INTERCOLLEGIATE ATHLETICS, OCT. 15, 2007

INTRODUCTION

In a national survey of more than 2,000 faculty members at universities with the country's most visible athletic programs, a striking number of professors say they don't know about and are disconnected from issues facing college sports. More than a third say they don't know about many athletics program policies and practices, including the financial underpinnings of their campuses' athletics programs. Furthermore, more than a third have no opinion about concerns raised by national faculty athletics reform groups. The largest portion of faculty (41 percent) believe faculty governance roles on campus associated with the oversight of intercollegiate athletics are ill defined, and most believe those roles are not particularly meaningful. On other issues, faculty are often equally divided between those who are satisfied with the conduct of their institution's intercollegiate athletics programs and those who are not.

Faculty members do tend to agree on several key points:

- Athletics decisions on campus are being driven by the demands of the entertainment industry.

- Faculty members are dissatisfied with their roles in athletics governance on campus, although more of them are satisfied with presidential oversight of athletics on their own campuses.

- Salaries paid to head football and basketball coaches are excessive, and the financial needs of athletics get higher priority than academic needs. Still, half of the respondents also think athletics success results in financial gains to campus initiatives unrelated to sports.

- Professors have similar levels of satisfaction with the academic performance of students in general and athletes in sports other than football and basketball. However, they are significantly less satisfied with the academic performance of football and basketball players. They believe athletes are more burdened than other students by demands on their out-of-class time.

- Faculty members are satisfied with the practice of awarding scholarships based on athletics ability, and believe that scholarships for basketball and football athletes may not compensate them fairly for their services.

BACKGROUND

In 1989, the trustees of the John S. and James L. Knight Foundation were concerned that highly visible athletics scandals threatened the integrity of higher education. They formed the Knight Commission on Intercollegiate Athletics to develop and win acceptance of realistic reforms that would close the widening chasm between higher education's ideals and big-time college sports.

In its 1991 and 2001 reports, the Knight Commission called on university faculties to join other members of the academic community to act together to restore the balance of athletics and academics on campus. In meetings since that time, the Knight Commission has heard testimony from professors involved in campus leadership, athletics governance, and athletics reform groups such as the Coalition on Intercollegiate Athletics and the Drake Group.

Following the Knight Commission's Summit on the Collegiate Athlete Experience in 2006, members of campus reform groups approached the Knight Commission to propose a summit on the role of the faculty in maintaining a healthy relationship between academics and athletics on campus. The commission agreed to host such a summit.

In preparation for the Faculty Summit, the Knight Commission asked Dr. Janet H. Lawrence, an associate professor at the University of Michigan's Center for Postsecondary and Higher Education, to conduct a national survey of faculty members at NCAA Division I Football Bowl Subdivision (formerly Division I-A) universities. The purpose was to learn how faculty members who are most likely to have knowledge about athletics issues through university governance involvement, or faculty who are most likely to interact with athletes in the classroom, perceive a range of athletics issues. The findings are to be used as background for discussions at the summit as well as for further conversation that may follow within athletic conferences and on individual campuses. The survey was designed to answer the following questions:

- How do faculty perceive intercollegiate athletics on their campuses?

- How satisfied are they with the governance, academics and financial aspects of intercollegiate athletics?

- What most concerns them about intercollegiate athletics?

- What priority do they think campus faculty governance groups should give to intercollegiate athletics?

The survey took into account how perceptions might be affected by differences in faculty members' career experiences, campus climate, athletics success, and athletes' academic success. Finally, the study looked at the likelihood of individual professors agreeing to get involved in solving problems in intercollegiate athletics on their own campuses and whether they believed such activity would be effective.

SURVEY METHODOLOGY

The survey was sent to 13,604 faculty members at 23 institutions in the NCAA's Football Bowl Subdivision (formerly known as Division I-A). Two institutions were randomly selected from each of the eleven Football Bowl Subdivision conferences and one was chosen from the institutions not affiliated with any conference. Among those surveyed were 1) faculty currently involved in university governance (e.g., faculty senates); 2) faculty in roles associated with intercollegiate athletics oversight (e.g., faculty athletics representatives, members of campus athletics advisory boards); and, 3) tenured or tenure track faculty who teach undergraduates and, as a result, have a high probability of interacting with athletes in the classroom. Researchers received 3,005 responses from professors at all 23 institutions surveyed. However, the final sample used in the analysis consisted of 2,071 responses after adjusting for those who did not fully complete the survey, faculty currently on sabbatical, emeritus faculty, non-tenure track faculty, and administrators inadvertently included.

The sample design did not attempt to approximate a random sample of faculty that could be generalized with a margin of error since it was important to focus on faculty with governance involvement. Of this purposive sample, more than three-quarters (78 percent) are involved in faculty governance at some level and 14 percent of this group has experience with athletics governance. Only 22 percent of the respondents report no current involvement in either athletics or campus-wide governance.

SURVEY RESULTS

The overarching finding is: A striking number of professors say they don't know about and are disconnected from issues facing college sports. It's all the more striking because the survey sample included faculty involved in governance or undergraduate teaching—those more likely to be informed about these issues.

More than a third of faculty members are unfamiliar with select policies and practices pertaining to athletics, the financial underpinnings of athletics on campus, or concerns raised by national faculty athletics reform groups. Perhaps as a result, this lack of information results in large segments of faculty members responding that they have no opinion about a number of academic, governance and financial issues. Those who say they are informed about such operations are divided among those who are satisfied with the conduct of intercollegiate athletics on their campus and those who are not. The large segment of uninformed faculty is particularly noteworthy because the sample was designed to include faculty involved in governance or undergraduate teaching and, as a result, would seem more likely than a randomly drawn sample of university faculty to be informed about these issues.

Concerning academic issues, more than half (53 percent) have no opinion about their satisfaction with coaches' roles in the admissions process; nearly half (49 percent) do not know if a faculty committee on campus regularly monitors the educational soundness of athletes' programs of study; 40 percent have no opinion about the academic standards on their campus that guide admissions decisions for athletes in football and basketball, and a similar portion (38 percent) have no opinion about the attention given by campus faculty governance groups to the quality of athletes' educational experiences.

Regarding finances, 39 percent of faculty do not know if athletics programs on their own campuses are subsidized by institutional general funds. Also, nearly a third (31 percent) offer no opinion on whether they are satisfied or dissatisfied with the use of general funds to subsidize athletics on their campus—likely the result of a lack of information on which to base an opinion.

More than a third have no opinion about the types of roles faculty members play in the governance of intercollegiate athletics (35 percent) and the range of faculty perspectives considered by central administrators when institutional positions on athletics are formulated (34 percent).

While perceptions about and satisfaction with the conduct of intercollegiate athletics are mixed among faculty who do have knowledge of athletics operations, professors generally share the same beliefs about several key issues involving governance, academics, athlete welfare and finances. These shared beliefs include the following:

GOVERNANCE

1. *Faculty members say they believe intercollegiate athletics is an auxiliary service and decisions are driven by the demands of the entertainment industry.*

   More than six in 10 (62 percent) say that intercollegiate athletics is structurally separate from the academic part of their university, and half say that decisions about the athletics program are driven by the entertainment industry with minimal regard for their university's academic mission.

2. *Although faculty are more satisfied than not with their respective president's oversight of athletics, they are generally dissatisfied with their roles in faculty athletics governance and the consideration of faculty input on athletics decisions. However, when asked to prioritize issues for campus faculty governance groups, intercollegiate athletics ranks very low.*

   Faculty members are more satisfied (46 percent) than not (28 percent) with their respective president's oversight of intercollegiate athletics. But more faculty (36 percent) than not (28 percent) are dissatisfied with faculty athletics governance roles. More specifically, the largest portion of the faculty (41 percent) believe faculty governance roles associated with the oversight of athletics on campus are ill defined; 32 percent disagree with that statement and 26 percent do not know. Even a third of those with athletics governance experience (35 percent) believe these roles are ill defined. Further, professors are generally dissatisfied with the extent to which faculty input is considered when athletics decisions are made, and are more dissatisfied (44 percent) than not (25 percent) with the range of faculty perspectives considered by administrators when athletics positions are formulated. Further, more respondents (47 percent) than not (28 percent) believe faculty members are interested in intercollegiate governance issues on their campus. However, they rank intercollegiate athletics second to last, just above Greek life, in a list of 13 priorities for campus faculty governance groups.

3. *Faculty members involved in athletics governance are more positive about all aspects of intercollegiate athletics than those who are not involved.*

ACADEMICS AND ATHLETE WELFARE

1. *Faculty believe athletes are motivated to earn their degrees and are academically prepared to keep pace with other students. Faculty have similar levels of satisfaction with the academic performance of students in general and athletes participating in sports other than football and basketball. However, they are significantly less satisfied with the academic performance of football and basketball players. At the same time, they recognize that athletes have less discretionary time than non-athletes.*

A majority of faculty members (61 percent) believe that athletes are motivated to earn their degrees and are academically prepared to keep pace with the other students in their classes. Respondents rate their satisfaction with the academic integrity and performance of athletes and other students at similar levels, although they are significantly less satisfied with the academic performance of football and basketball athletes. Three-quarters of those surveyed believe athletes are more burdened than other students because of the demands on their out-of-class time, and the majority believe that athletes are not engaged in other campus activities.

2. *While most faculty members believe that academic standards do not need to be compromised to achieve athletics success, nearly a third disagree.*

While faculty acknowledge that athletes are more burdened than other students, half say they believe that academic standards do not need to be lowered to achieve athletics success. However, nearly a third (32 percent) of those surveyed believe that some com-

promises with academic standards must be made to achieve athletics success in football and basketball.

3. *Academic concerns appear to motivate faculty to join campus efforts aimed at addressing those issues.*

Faculty who are personally most concerned about the academic aspects of intercollegiate athletics are likely to join campus activities designed to ameliorate problems. Among those who think that the chances their efforts will result in meaningful campus change are greater than 50/50, the largest number said academic issues are of most concern to them. In particular, professors who are concerned about the quality of athletes' educational experiences and their academic outcomes are the most optimistic about their chances for success.

FINANCES

1. *Three in four faculty members say salaries paid to their schools' head football and basketball coaches are excessive. The majority believe athletics financial needs get higher priority than academic needs; however, half of those surveyed also think athletics success results in financial gains to campus initiatives unrelated to sports.*

Nearly three-quarters (72 percent) of faculty believe salaries paid to head football and basketball coaches on their campuses are excessive. However, with regard to finances overall, faculty members see intercollegiate athletics as a mixed blessing. On the one hand, they note the high costs associated with intercollegiate athletics, and the majority of them believe their institutions prioritize construction of state-of-the-art athletic facilities over capital projects for academic departments. On the other hand, half think the success of intercollegiate athletics fosters alumni and corporate giving to campus initiatives outside of athletics.

2. *More than half of faculty members are satisfied with the practice of awarding scholarships based on athletic ability, and more faculty than not believe scholarships for basketball and football athletes may not fairly compensate them for their services.*

More than half of faculty (53 percent) are satisfied with the practice of awarding scholarships based on athletics ability, nearly a third (31 percent) are not, and 15 percent have no opinion.

Also, 45 percent of respondents do not believe or only slightly believe that athletics scholarships adequately compensate athletes in football and basketball; 39 percent moderately or strongly believe that athletics scholarships constitute fair compensation; and 15 percent do not know. The survey did not ask additional questions that may further explain this perception, such as whether faculty who appear to support additional aid to football and basketball athletes believe additional aid should cover the full cost of attendance, be given only to those athletes with financial need, or be provided as an additional flat stipend.

3. *Faculty who believe general university funds are used to subsidize intercollegiate athletics on their campus tend to be dissatisfied with this practice.*

Of the 791 faculty members who believe that the use of general funds to subsidize intercollegiate athletics is "Slightly to Very Much" characteristic of their campus, more faculty members (64 percent) than not (24 percent) are generally dissatisfied with the use of those funds for athletics. The level of dissatisfaction dramatically decreases when the perception of the subsidization level decreases. Eighty percent of faculty who believe general fund subsidization of athletics is "Very Much" characteristic of their campus are dissatisfied with this practice, as opposed to 14 percent who are satisfied. A smaller portion (62 percent) of faculty members who believe general fund subsidization is "Moderately" characteristic of their campus are dissatisfied with the subsidization practice, while 25 percent are satisfied. Once the faculty perception reaches the level of subsidization being "Slightly" characteristic of their campus, faculty satisfaction of the practice is nearly split—41 percent are satisfied and 38 percent are dissatisfied.

4. *Faculty members cite financial issues most frequently among their own personal concerns about intercollegiate athletics.*

When asked what most concerns them about intercollegiate athletics on their respective campus, the largest number of faculty members (342) cite financial issues. In particular, faculty highlight the high costs of athletics and its subsidization with general funds. The next largest groups of faculty concerns about college sports are the treatment of athletes (209) and campus climates that prioritize athletics over academics (193).

IMPACT OF CAMPUS CONTEXT

Although it may seem obvious, it is useful to state that the survey results clearly demonstrate that faculty perceptions of their general campus context predict their perception of and satisfaction with their intercollegiate athletics program.

An experimental taxonomy was created to search for variations in the perceptions of faculty who work in universities that differ in academic and athletics success. Institutions from the sample were placed in one of four categories: Higher Athletic/Higher Academic; Higher Athletic/Lower Academic; Lower Athletic/Higher Academic; Lower

Athletic/Lower Academic. Institutions were divided among the higher/lower academic categories based on graduation rates in football and men's basketball and average test scores for all entering students. The higher/lower athletic categories are based on institutions' appearances in the men's basketball tournament and football bowl games over the most recent six-year period.

More faculty at institutions in the Higher Athletic categories believe that athletics is not subsidized by university general funds, perceive that athletics success leads to donations in other areas, and believe that their intercollegiate teams fulfill part of their university's service mission to the state.

Faculty at institutions in the Higher Athletic/Higher Academic category more often perceive that the faculty and president agree on matters related to athletics; faculty governance roles are better defined; and the athletics department runs a clean program. However, they express more concern about the demands on athletes and are most distressed by the professionalization of intercollegiate athletics on their campus.

Faculty at institutions in the Higher Athletic/Lower Academic group are more concerned about the influence of external groups on intercollegiate athletics decisions and, compared to the other groups, assign the highest priority to intercollegiate athletics for campus governance groups. Another distinguishing characteristic of this group is that they tend to be more concerned about the structural separation of athletics from the university and a campus culture that places a greater emphasis on athletics than academics. Comparatively, faculty at campuses in the Lower Athletic/Lower Academic group are most concerned with the escalating costs of athletics and are least satisfied with the subsidization of athletics with university general funds. Although this group shares similar dissatisfaction with governance aspects, it more strongly perceives that athletics administrators use their power and influence to control decisions. Faculty members at institutions in the Lower Athletic/Higher Academic group share financial concerns with their colleagues in the other lower athletic performance group; however, they do not share the same level of dissatisfaction with governance. Faculty in this group have the highest satisfaction with the academic performance of football and basketball athletes. In contrast, they have the lowest level of satisfaction with athletes in sports other than football and basketball.

CONCLUSION AND DISCUSSION

Survey findings reveal a steep challenge ahead for those seeking greater faculty involvement in intercollegiate athletics. Although faculty members are dissatisfied with many facets of college sports, their dissatisfaction may not be strong enough to motivate action given the low priority they give intercollegiate athletics when compared to other campus issues for faculty governance to consider. Perhaps the greatest challenge to increasing faculty engagement with athletics is the lack of knowledge faculty appear to have about many key policies, practices and issues. Survey results highlight the need for administrators and faculty in campus leadership positions, and particularly those involved in athletics governance, to consider opportunities and mechanisms to better inform faculty members.

The experimental taxonomy also suggests that the level of team academic and athletics success may mediate faculty perceptions, satisfaction and concerns in significant ways. It appears useful for faculty and administrators to consider the impact these institutional characteristics have as dialogue continues about the faculty's role in maintaining healthy relationships between academics and athletics on campus.

[*Ed. Note: The complete research report and data tables are accessible at www.knightcommission.org.*]

DIRECT IMPACTS OF INTERCOLLEGIATE ATHLETICS

THE PHYSICAL CAPITAL STOCK USED IN COLLEGIATE ATHLETICS

Jonathan M. Orszag and Peter R. Orszag

INTRODUCTION

In a previous interim report ("The Effects of Collegiate Athletics: An Interim Report"), we explored the financial effects of operating expenditures associated with collegiate athletics.[1] That report drew upon a comprehensive database linking information collected by the National Collegiate Athletic Association (NCAA) in conjunction with the Equity in Athletics Disclosure Act (EADA) to a variety of other data sources. The report, however, underscored a substantial concern with the existing data: poor measurement of capital expenditures and the capital stock used in collegiate athletics.

The previous report highlighted two significant problems with data on the capital stock used to support intercollegiate athletics. First, the value of the outstanding athletic capital stock is not recorded anywhere on the NCAA/EADA forms. Second, new capital expenditures are not adequately reflected in the NCAA/EADA data. For example, in a survey of chief financial officers from 17 Division I schools, roughly half the respondents indicated that all athletic capital expenditures were captured by the NCAA/EADA data, and the other half indicated that at least part of athletic capital spending was not. It is thus impossible to estimate in any rigorous fashion the value of the capital services used in the "production" of intercollegiate athletics with the NCAA/EADA data.

As a result of these shortcomings in athletic-related capital data, the previous interim report was forced to focus mostly on operating expenses. Although this approach was reasonable for the purposes of the interim report, the exclusion of capital costs nonetheless represented a gap in the analysis. For example, more than half of all Division I-A schools have either opened a new football stadium or undertaken a major renovation of their old stadium since 1990. The exclusion of capital costs may be particularly important in areas such as analyzing the potential "arms race" in college athletics.

To remedy the shortcomings in the data on intercollegiate physical capital, the NCAA has taken two major steps. First, in conjunction with National Association of College and University Business Officers (NACUBO), the NCAA has devised a new annual financial survey that will better capture ongoing capital expenditures.[2] Second, with funding from the Mellon Foundation, the NCAA commissioned this study to examine the existing physical capital stock used in intercollegiate athletics. Our analyses suggest that the survey data, combined with other readily available information (e.g., on stadium capacity), could be used on an ongoing basis as a rough historical measure of annual capital costs in Division I-A, even though such estimates will need to be viewed with some caution given the inherent difficulties in such extrapolation.

II.   ESTIMATING THE CAPITAL STOCK USED IN INTERCOLLEGIATE ATHLETICS

The analytically correct measure of the value of capital services used in intercollegiate athletics . . . is equal to the replacement value of the capital stock, K, used in intercollegiate athletics multiplied by the depreciation rate . . . plus the opportunity cost of capital. . . . Obtaining a value for K by school, however, requires a current estimate of the replacement value of the capital stock—including stadiums, training facilities, fields, and other capital—used in intercollegiate athletics.[3] In this section, we focus on estimating the current value of K.

A.   Capital Survey

To collect information on K, we constructed a survey and, working with the NCAA, sent it to selected university officials. . . . It collected information on the replacement value of facilities if the institution owned the facility; the lease cost if the institution did not own the facility; the share of time the facility was used for different purposes; and the land for the facilities, practice fields, and parking lots.

The survey was completed by 56 schools, including 28 Division I (with 8 in Division I-A), and 28 schools in Divisions II and III. **Table 7** provides the number of responses and representation rate (responses as a percentage of schools) in each Division.

The 56 respondent schools provided information on a total of 362 athletic facilities. **Table 8** shows the distribution of facilities by sport. Roughly 7.5 percent of the facilities were used for football, roughly 14 percent were used for men's basketball, and more than 15 percent were used for women's basketball. One potential explanation for the greater prevalence of women's basketball facilities than men's basketball facilities is that men's teams may be more likely to practice and play in the same facility.

B. Survey Data on Capital Stock Used in Intercollegiate Athletics

The capital stock used in intercollegiate athletics can be owned or leased by the university. In practice, however, the vast bulk of the relevant capital stock used by intercollegiate athletics is owned, not leased. **Table 9** shows the mean survey responses by division for total replacement values, and total annual lease costs (for leased facilities). These two figures are not immediately comparable, just as the value of a house is not immediately comparable to annual rent payments. To make them comparable, we transform the annual lease payments into an estimated replacement value for the underlying facility. If the annual lease payment equals five percent of the replacement value, the mean replacement value of owned facilities represents more than 99 percent of the owned and leased "facility capital stock" used in intercollegiate athletics for the schools completing the survey. (If the lease payments are more than five percent of the replacement value, the share of total facility capital stock that is owned is even higher than 99 percent.) We therefore focus our attention on athletic facilities owned by the universities.

In addition to facilities, another element of K is the land, such as practice fields and parking lots, devoted to intercollegiate athletics. **Table 10** shows the land used in

Table 7   Survey Response Rate

Division	Number of Responses	Division (%)
I	28	8.6%
I-A	*8*	*6.8*
II	11	4.0
III	17	4.0
Total	**56**	**5.5%**

Source: The Physical Capital Stock Used in Collegiate Athletics. Used with permission.

Table 8   Facilities by Sport

Sport	Number
Football	27
Men's basketball	51
Women's basketball	56
Total	**362**

Source: The Physical Capital Stock Used in Collegiate Athletics. Used with permission.

intercollegiate athletic activities, as estimated by the size of practice fields and number of parking spots (both weighted by the share of the time they are estimated to be used for intercollegiate athletics). We assume that parking spaces average 350 square feet each, including aisle space.[4] The final column in Table 10 therefore adds 350 times the weighted-average number of parking spots to obtain the total land used for practice fields and parking spots combined.

To assess the impact of including land use in evaluating the capital employed for intercollegiate athletic activities, we must assume an opportunity value of such land for each university. We estimate the opportunity value per square acre in two different ways. In our first approach, we use data from the Integrated Post-Secondary Education Data System (IPEDS) on land values, combined with campus acreages from *U.S. News and World Report*. In our other approach, we assume an average land value of $15,000 per acre based on an estimate of the value of all land in the United States.[5] We then scale this land value by the ratio of average housing values within five miles of the university's zip code to the national average housing value. The results are shown in **Table 11**. Using either approach, land values are substantially smaller than facilities values; indeed, land values are such a small share of the total that they can be ignored for practical purposes. Reasonable variation in the assumed value of land per acre will not affect this basic finding.

Our conclusion from Tables 9 and 11 is that the replacement value of facilities used in intercollegiate athletics represents the overwhelming majority of overall capital used in

Table 9   Average Replacement Values and Lease Payments by Division

Division	Avg. Replacement Values per Institution ($ thousands)	Avg. Annual Lease Payments per Institution ($ thousands)
I	$94,301	$42.4
I-A	*240,627*	*68.8*
II	10,944	1.4
III	23,482	0.2
All Divisions	**$56,429**	**$21.5**

Source: The Physical Capital Stock Used in Collegiate Athletics. Used with permission.

Note: Three schools did not provide replacement values for facilities they own. Other schools did not provide replacement costs for all their owned facilities. Such facilities are, therefore, excluded from the table.

Table 10   Average Land Use by Division

Division	Practice Fields Used for Intercollegiate Athletics, Weighted by Estimated Time Use, in Square Feet	Parking Spots Used for Intercollegiate Athletics, Weighted by Estimated Time Use	Square Footage of Practice Fields and Parking Spots, Weighted by Estimated Time Use
I	368,193	1,598	927,510
I-A	411,036	4,351	1,933,894
II	204,407	115	244,795
III	266,703	196	335,328
All Divisions	305,211	881	613,636

Source: The Physical Capital Stock Used in Collegiate Athletics. Used with permission.

those sports. Since the other components appear to represent a very small share of total athletically related capital, we focus our attention in the rest of this paper on the replacement value of facilities.

III. ESTIMATING THE COST OF CAPITAL USED IN INTERCOLLEGIATE ATHLETICS

To obtain an annual capital cost for intercollegiate athletics, we combine the estimated replacement value of facilities with different estimates of depreciation and financing costs. Winsten (1998) assumes a depreciation rate for college facilities (not just athletic ones) of 2.5 percent per year; we adopt that depreciation rate here.[6] The value of financing costs should depend on the institution's alternative investment opportunities; we assume that the alternative investment opportunities would earn 7.5 percent per year.[7] Our central estimate of depreciation and financing costs combined is therefore 10 percent; we also show the results for 7.5 percent and 12.5 percent.

. . . [U]nder our central estimate, the annual capital costs associated with intercollegiate athletics averages $9 million at Division I schools and $24 million at Division I-A schools. The average annual capital cost at Division II and Division III schools is significantly lower; an average of about $1 million at Division II schools, and an average of about $2 million at Division III schools.

To provide some points of comparison for these figures, we initially consider the Division I-A results. The

$24 million average annual capital cost for intercollegiate athletic facilities is roughly equal to the average operating cost for intercollegiate athletics in Division I-A of more than $27 million. In other words, the largely unrecorded annual cost associated with intercollegiate capital facilities is roughly equal to the reported annual operating expenditures on intercollegiate athletics.

. . . The data from the capital survey, combined with data from the Department of Education, can be used to compute the athletic share of overall institutional spending, including capital costs both in the athletic and overall figures.[8] Of the Division I respondents to the capital survey, we were able to obtain data on total institutional capital values for eight public universities.[9] For these eight schools, operating athletic spending represented 2.6 percent of total operating spending for the institutions. Including athletic and overall institutional capital costs, athletic spending represented 3.7 percent of total institutional spending. In other words, including capital costs does not alter the qualitative result that athletic spending represents a relatively small share of total institutional spending in Division I, at least for the schools for which data were available.

Other comparisons may provide further insight into the magnitude of annual athletic capital costs. (Data on annual non-athletic expenditures for these comparisons were obtained directly from financial reports posted on institutional websites.) The estimated $5 million average annual capital cost for intercollegiate athletic facilities at one Division I school is roughly equal to half of its academic support and

Table 11   Average Facility Value and Land Value

Division	Average Replacement Values for Facilities ($ thousands)	Average Land Values Using Approach #1 ($ thousands)	Land Value as Percent of Total Capital Using Approach #1 (%)	Average Land Value Using Approach #2 ($ thousands)	Land Value as Percent of Total Capital Using Approach #2 (%)
I	$94,301	$2,514	2.6%	$448	0.5%
I-A	240,627	2,852	1.2	937	0.4
II	10,944	232	2.1	62	0.6
III	23,482	254	1.1	128	0.5
All Divisions	$56,429	$1,392	2.4%	$276	0.5%

Source: The Physical Capital Stock Used in Collegiate Athletics. Used with permission.

Table 12   Annual Capital Costs of Football and Men's Basketball Facilities as a Percent of Total Annual Capital Costs for All Athletic Facilities

Division	Annual Capital Costs of Football as a Percent of Total (%)	Annual Capital Costs of Football and Men's Basketball as a Percent of Total (%)
I	34.7%	46.9%
I-A	*44.2*	*54.5*
II	6.3	26.8
III	2.1	9.6
All Divisions	**29.5%**	**41.4%**

Source: The Physical Capital Stock Used in Collegiate Athletics. Used with permission.

student aid expenses. At another Division I school, the average annual capital cost is about one-third the cost of annual library collection purchases. At one Division I-A school, the $23 million average capital cost for intercollegiate athletic facilities is roughly equal to the annual expenses associated with its libraries. At one Division III school, the $5 million average capital cost for intercollegiate athletic facilities is roughly equal to one-third the cost of research.

. . . [A]verage annual capital costs for football facilities are roughly $10.6 million for Division I-A, $69,000 for Division II, and $49,000 for Division III. By comparison, in 2003, average operating expenditures on football were roughly $7 million, $0.5 million, and $0.2 million in Divisions I-A, II, and III, respectively. . . . [A]verage annual capital costs for basketball facilities are roughly $1.1 to $1.2 million for Division I, $224,000 for Division II, and $177,000 for Division III.

. . . .

Table 12 shows that these two sports represent a significant share of athletically related capital costs: For all schools combined, they represent more than 40 percent of the total. These two sports represent an even higher share of total capital costs among Division I-A schools: 55 percent of capital costs in Division I-A are associated with football and men's basketball.

Football and basketball facilities play an even larger role in explaining the *variation* of replacement costs across schools than may be suggested. . . . To understand how this could occur, assume that every school has similar facilities for sports such as baseball, soccer, and field hockey, but have substantially different facilities for football and men's basketball. In this situation, football and basketball may, on average, represent a significant share of total costs, but explain even more of the differences in total replacement costs across schools. This is indeed what the data show: football and men's basketball facilities explain between 80 and 90 percent of the variation in total capital costs across schools; nearly all of this explanatory power comes from football facilities. These findings highlight the benefits of focusing on these two sports, especially football, in explaining the variation in capital costs across athletic programs either for all divisions or within Division I.

Outside of Division I, however, the replacement costs for football and basketball stadiums account for a much smaller share of total costs and explain a much smaller share of the *variation* of such costs across schools. In Divisions II and III, it is harder to find a single variable that explains a majority of the variation in replacement costs across schools. In those divisions, the total number of varsity teams appears to be the strongest single explanatory variable of total replacement costs.

IV. POTENTIAL APPLICATIONS OF CAPITAL SURVEY DATA

The key role of football in the overall cost of athletic capital (at least when Division I schools are included in the analysis) warrants further examination of the underlying factors affecting capital costs for that sport. In this section, we show that the annual football capital costs are largely driven by the capacity of the stadiums. Since stadium capacity is available for all schools, not just those schools in our sample, this finding may provide a mechanism for assessing changes in annual capital costs over time.

Under the assumption that the relationship between the key observed characteristics of football stadiums and the replacement costs of such stadiums is the same for those schools that completed the survey and those schools that did not complete the survey, and that the relationship holds over time, a statistical relationship can be used to estimate the value of other football stadiums.[10] That, in turn, can be used in two key settings.

First, analysts can monitor the most significant component of athletic capital costs simply by observing changes in stadium capacity. The data show that replacement costs are the key driver of total capital costs for Division I schools, that the replacement costs of football stadiums are the key driver of total replacement costs, and that football stadium capacity is the key driver of the replacement costs of football stadiums. Indeed, variation in the level . . . of football stadium capacity alone explains between 60 and 75 percent of the variation in total replacement costs (in either levels or natural logs) for all athletic facilities. This key finding may provide a simple and cost-effective means of tracking historical athletic capital costs.

Second, for Division I-A schools, football capacity can be used to examine whether an "arms race" has taken place in capital expenditures. An arms race appears to mean different things to different observers. For example, some observers define an arms race as an increase in inequality in athletic capital spending or merely an absolute increase in aggregate capital spending. A somewhat more precise definition of an "arms race" is that increased spending at School A triggers increased capital spending at School B, which then feeds back into pressure on School A to further raise its own capital spending. To examine this definition of an arms race, we examined whether an increase in football stadium capacity by other members of a school's conference statistically increased the likelihood that the school itself expanded stadium capacity. We use data on football stadium capacity for all Division I-A schools from 1991 to 2004, not just for those schools completing our survey. The analysis suggests the possible, albeit weak, presence of an arms race in football capital spending within Division I-A: The expansion of a stadium at one school within a conference appears to make it more likely that other schools within that same conference will expand the capacity of their stadiums, although this finding is sensitive to specific assumptions employed in the statistical analysis.[11] The evidence that does exist to suggest an arms race in football stadium capacity appears to be present in particular within the six major football conferences.[12] The magnitude of the effect even within the major conferences appears to be relatively weak. In other words, even in the regression specifications where the effect is statistically significant, the practical implications appear to be limited because the magnitude of the effect is small.[13]

V.   CONCLUSION

The absence of reliable data on the capital costs associated with intercollegiate athletics has significantly limited a full understanding of the finances of college sports. This study represents a useful step toward better understanding athletically related costs. In the future, analysts and university officials will have even more insight into athletically related capital spending because of the improved accounting and data collection devised by the NCAA and NACUBO.

Notes

1. Robert E. Litan, Jonathan M. Orszag, and Peter R. Orszag, "The Empirical Effects of Collegiate Athletics: An Interim Report," August 2003, available at http://www.ncaa.org/databases/baselineStudy/baseline.pdf.

2. See, for example, http://www1.ncaa.org/membership/ed_outreach/eada/forms/procedures.pdf.

3. See, for example, Gordon C. Winston, "A Guide to Measuring College Costs," Williams College, DP-46, January 1998.

4. A variety of estimates suggest an average size between 300 and 350 square feet (including aisle space) per parking spot. We choose the high end of this range to produce an upper-bound estimate.

See, for example, http://www.nuggetnews.com/archives/20040317/front13.shtml, http://www.ci.bloomington.mn.us/meetings/pc/synopsis/1996/092696pcs.htm, http://64.233.161.104/search?q=cache:l0vj7QSePacJ:gulliver.trb.org/publications/tcrp/tcrp_rpt_35.pdf+%2 2AVERAGE+PARKING+SPACE+%22&hl=en, or http://pen.ci.santamonica.ca.us/cityclerk/council/agendas/1989/s89121211-E.html.

5. J. Ted Gwartney and Nicolaus Tideman. "The Jerome Levy Economic Institute Conference: land, wealth and poverty." *The American Journal of Economics and Sociology*, July, 1996. The paper states that there is no consistent estimate of land value for the U.S., but cites an estimate that results in a total US land value of $30 trillion. We divide this by the 2,271,343,360 acres in the United States to get an estimate of $13,208 per acre, and round up to produce an overestimate and account for inflation.

6. Gordon C. Winston, "A Guide to Measuring College Costs," Williams College, DP-46, January 1998.

7. If anything, this estimate may be slightly too high, but it is possible that the depreciation estimate is slightly too low. A central estimate of 10 percent for the combined capital costs provides insight into the order of magnitude; as shown below, small variations above and below that central estimate do not change our fundamental conclusions.

8. The most recent available total institutional capital values were for 2001. We converted those figures into 2003 dollars using the Consumer Price Index. To compute the annual capital costs, we adopt the same assumptions as athletic capital costs (i.e., depreciation plus financing costs equal 10 percent of the capital stock).

9. The Department of Education does not publish data on total institutional capital values for private universities.

10. In particular, to predict the replacement cost of facilities used for football, we first attempted to explain the variation in the replacement costs for football stadiums across the schools completing our survey based on a number of key observable characteristics of the football stadiums. We estimated regressions that included characteristics of the schools (e.g., enrollment) and additional characteristics of the facilities (e.g., number of luxury boxes). We concluded that a parsimonious specification that explains a substantial degree of the variation in football stadium replacement costs (in thousands) is:

$$\ln(replacement\ \text{cost}) = 6.61 + 1.25*\ln(capacity) - 0.33*\ln(age)$$

where ln is the natural log of each variable, capacity is the stadium's seating capacity, and age is its age. The coefficients sensibly imply that larger stadiums have higher replacement costs; older stadiums have smaller replacement costs. The coefficient on ln(capacity) is statistically significantly different from zero at the one percent level and the coefficient on ln(age) statistically significantly different from zero at the 10 percent level. (The impact of age is relatively modest and reflects differences in stadium characteristics (e.g., luxury boxes, number of bathrooms, etc.) based on date of construction.) These variables explain 76 percent of the variation in the natural log of the reported replacement costs; the key variable is stadium capacity, which alone explains 72 percent of the variation in the natural log of the reported replacement costs. Age and capacity also play a key role in explaining men's basketball replacement costs, but are less effective in explaining the variation of men's basketball replacement costs than football replacement costs.

11. For example, some schools reported relatively small changes in stadium capacity from year to year that may not reflect true underlying changes in the stadium. If the analysis ignores these small and

potentially erroneous changes, the evidence for an arms race, which is not overwhelming in the first instance, is attenuated.

12. We classified as "major" conferences the SEC, Big Ten, Big 12, ACC, Big East, and Pac-10 (and their predecessors).

13. For example, under one specification, the data suggest that if the maximum capacity within one of the major conferences increases by 10,000 seats, the average predicted increase at other schools within that same conference is roughly 500 seats.

THE EMPIRICAL EFFECTS OF COLLEGIATE ATHLETICS: AN UPDATE TO THE INTERIM REPORT

Jonathan M. Orszag and Peter R. Orszag

In a previous interim report ("The Effects of Collegiate Athletics: An Interim Report"), we explored the financial effects of operating expenditures associated with collegiate athletics.[1] That report drew upon a comprehensive database linking information collected by the National Collegiate Athletic Association (NCAA) in conjunction with the Equity in Athletics Disclosure Act (EADA) to a variety of other data sources.

The interim report underscored two concerns with the existing data at that time: First, the data suffered from poor measurement of capital expenditures and the capital stock used in collegiate athletics. A companion analysis addresses this concern.[2] Second, the available data covered only an eight-year period. Using more recently available data, this update extends the analysis so that it covers a 10-year period.

The interim report specifically examined ten hypotheses about college athletics, focusing primarily on Division I-A schools. Using updated data and other recently released information, we re-examine each of the hypotheses. Our analysis confirms five of the hypotheses; the other five are not proven and require further empirical analysis:[3]

Hypothesis #1: Operating Athletic Expenditures are a Relatively Small Share of Overall Institutional Spending

- According to Department of Education data, reported athletic spending represented roughly four percent of total higher education spending for Division I-A schools in 2001 (the most recent comprehensive Department of Education data publicly available). In 1997, this share was roughly three percent.

- In 2003, NCAA/EADA data suggest that operating athletic spending represented roughly 3.8 percent of total higher education spending for Division I-A schools. By comparison, the share was roughly 3.3 percent in 2001.

- The share of operating athletic spending in a university's total budget is higher for smaller Division I-A schools than for larger Division I-A schools because of the fixed costs associated with an athletic department.

- The share of operating athletic spending in overall higher education spending has increased over time as indicated by the comparisons above. In recent years, athletic spending has been growing more rapidly than total spending, so the athletics' share of the total has been increasing. In particular, total athletic spending increased by roughly 20 percent in nominal terms between 2001 and 2003; total institutional spending rose by less than five percent during the same period, according to NCAA/EADA data.

- Despite the recent increase in relative athletic spending, we continue to conclude that operating athletic expenditures in the aggregate are a relatively small share of total higher education spending for Division I-A schools.

- These spending shares exclude capital spending. Our companion piece finds that including capital spending for both athletics and the overall university budget modestly raises the share of total spending attributed to athletics, but does not alter the fundamental conclusion that athletic spending represents a small share of total institutional spending.

Hypothesis #2: Football and Basketball Exhibited Increased Levels of Inequality in the 1990s

- A common measure of inequality is the Gini coefficient, which would equal one if one school accounted for all spending and zero if spending were the same across schools. Increases in the Gini coefficient represent increased levels of inequality and vice versa.

- Between 1993 and 2003, the Gini coefficient for Division I-A football spending rose from 0.23 to 0.30. . . . The Gini coefficient for Division I-A basketball spending also rose sharply, from 0.24 to 0.30.

- We continue to conclude that football and basketball exhibited increased levels of inequality between 1993 and 2003.

Hypothesis #3: Football and Basketball Exhibit Mobility in Expenditure, Revenue, and Winning Percentages

- More than 30 percent of the schools that were in the top quintile of Division I-A football spending in 1993 were no longer in the top quintile by 2003. More than three-fifths of the schools in the middle quintile in 1993 were no longer there in 2003; less than two-fifths had moved up and one-fourth had moved down.

- Net revenue also exhibited some degree of mobility: Among the schools in the middle quintile of football net revenue in 1993, roughly three-quarters were no longer in the middle quintile in 2003.

- A school's winning percentage exhibits only modest levels of persistence. For example, the correlation of winning percentages from one year to the next is only about 50 percent. The correlation dissipates over time: The correlation between winning percentages ten years apart is 20 to 30 percent.

- We continue to conclude that football and basketball exhibit some degree of mobility in expenditure, revenue, and winning percentages.

Hypothesis #4: Increased Operating Expenditures on Football or Basketball, on Average, are not Associated with Any Medium-Term Increase or Decrease in Operating Net Revenue

- Our statistical analyses suggest that between 1993 and 2003, an increase in operating expenditures of $1 on football or men's basketball in Division I-A was associated with approximately $1 in additional operating revenue, on average. The implication is that spending an extra $1 was not associated with any increase or decrease in *net* revenue, on average, from these sports.

- These results continue to have limitations. For example, our database covers a 10-year time period, but any effects may have longer lags. If this were the case, our database may be too short to capture the "true" effects of increased spending. In addition, as noted above, the NCAA/EADA data do not adequately record capital expenditures; our analysis therefore focuses on operating spending. It is possible that the effects of operating spending differ from the effects of capital spending.

- We continue to conclude that over the medium term (ten years), increases in operating expenditures on football or men's basketball are not associated with any change, on average, in operating net revenue.

Hypothesis #5: Increased Operating Expenditures on Football or Basketball are not Associated with Medium-Term Increases in Winning Percentages, and Higher Winning Percentages are not Associated with Medium-Term Increases in Operating Revenue or Operating Net Revenue

- A variety of econometric exercises suggests no robust statistical relationship between changes in operating ex-

penditures on football and changes in football winning percentages between 1993 and 2003.

- A variety of econometric exercises also suggests no robust statistical relationship between changes in winning percentages and changes in football operating revenue or net revenue between 1993 and 2003.

- We continue to conclude that increased operating expenditures on football or basketball are not associated with medium-term increases in winning percentages, and higher winning percentages are not associated with medium-term increases in operating revenue or operating net revenue.

Hypothesis #6: The Relationship Between Spending and Revenue Varies Significantly By Sub-Groups of Schools (e.g., Conferences, Schools with High SAT Scores, Etc.)

- With the updated database, we examined the relationship between spending and revenue across various subsets of schools. We were still not able to detect evidence of systematic differences when separating the schools by characteristics such as: public vs. private schools; schools with high SAT scores vs. schools with low SAT scores; large student populations vs. small student populations; schools that were ever in the Associated Press (AP) rankings; and schools that were ranked in the top 25 in the AP poll in 1993.

- In many cases, the sample sizes for the subsets of schools were quite small; given the paucity of data in some cases, it is difficult to reject the hypothesis outright. Instead, we continue to conclude that the hypothesis that the relationships vary significantly by subgroups of schools is not proven.

Hypothesis #7: Increased Operating Expenditures on Big-Time Sports Affect Operating Expenditures on Other Sports

- Our statistical analysis of the updated data suggests that each dollar increase in operating expenditures on football among Division I-A schools may be associated with a $0.27 increase in spending on women's sports excluding basketball and $0.37 including basketball, but the results are not robust to changes in the econometric specification. Such a potential spillover effect may be expected given Title IX and other pressures to ensure equity between men's and women's sports.

- Previous studies have found that increases in football spending are associated with increased spending on women's sports.

- Given the lack of robustness of the results, we continue to conclude that the hypothesis that increased operating expenditures on big-time sports affect operating expenditures on other sports is not proven.

Hypothesis #8: Increased Operating Expenditures on Sports Affect Measurable Academic Quality in the Medium Term

- Our statistical analysis of the updated data suggests no relationship—either positive or negative—between changes in operating expenditures on football or basketball among Division I-A schools and incoming SAT scores or the percentage of applicants accepted.

- The academic literature is divided on whether athletic programs affect academic quality. While our results suggest no statistical relationship one way or the other, our data are limited to ten years and such a relationship may exist over longer periods of time. In addition, the relationship between athletics and academic quality may manifest itself in ways other than the effect on SAT scores or other directly measurable indicators.

- We continue to conclude that the hypothesis that changes in operating expenditures on big-time sports affect measurable academic quality in the medium term is not proven.

Hypothesis #9: Increased Operating Expenditures on Sports Affect Other Measurable Indicators, Including Alumni Giving

- Econometric analysis using our updated database shows little or no robust relationship between changes in operating expenditures on football or basketball among Division I-A schools and alumni giving (either to the sports program or the university itself).

- The academic literature is again inconclusive on this issue. As with the previous hypothesis, our results suggest little or no statistical relationship—but our data are limited to ten years and such a relationship may exist over longer periods of time.

- We continue to conclude that the hypothesis that increased operating expenditures on sports affect other measurable indicators, including alumni giving, is not proven.

Hypothesis #10: Football and Basketball Exhibit An "Arms Race" in which Increased Operating Expenditures At One School Are Associated With Increases At Other Schools

- Analysts have used the term "arms race" to describe a variety of phenomena. We use the term to refer to a situation in which increased spending at one school is associated with increases at other schools.[4]

- In our updated analysis, some econometric analyses suggest that increased operating expenditures on football at one school may be associated with increases in operating expenditures at other schools within the same conference, but most specifications suggest no relationship.

- We continue to conclude that the hypothesis that football and basketball exhibit an "arms race" in which increased operating expenditures at one school are associated with increases at other schools is not proven.

- It is important to emphasize that the existence of an "arms race" may be concentrated in capital expenditures, which are not adequately recorded in the NCAA/EADA data, rather than in operating expenditures.

- In our companion paper on capital expenditures, we explore this issue in more detail. We examined whether an increase in football stadium capacity by other members of a school's conference statistically increased the likelihood that the school itself expanded stadium capacity.

- The analysis suggests the possible, albeit weak, presence of an arms race in football capital spending within Division I-A: The expansion of a stadium at one school within a conference appears to make it more likely that others schools within that same conference will expand the capacity of their stadiums, although this finding is sensitive to specific assumptions employed in the statistical analysis. Even in the regression specifications where the effect is statistically significant, the practical implications appear to be limited because the magnitude of the effect is small.

CONCLUSION

This update reflects an effort to continue exploring the empirical effects of collegiate athletics. It updates the analysis contained in the interim report with new data and information. As in the interim report, we continue to find that many widely held perspectives about spending on big-time sports by colleges—by both proponents and opponents of such spending—are not supported by the statistical evidence.

Our results must continue to be qualified, however. Although the data in this paper are more comprehensive than other datasets that have been used in the past, they remain imperfect: They are available only between 1993 and 2003, and they fail to capture fully various components of athletic activities (especially total capital expenditures and staff compensation from all sources). Further efforts are underway to improve the data; in conjunction with National Association of College and University Business Officers (NACUBO), the NCAA has devised a new annual financial survey that will better capture ongoing capital expenditures. As these new data become available, they should provide additional insights into the effects of college athletics on institutions of higher education.

Notes

1. Robert E. Litan, Jonathan M. Orszag, and Peter R. Orszag, "The Empirical Effects of Collegiate Athletics: An Interim Report," August 2003, available at http://www.ncaa.org/databases/baselineStudy/baseline.pdf ("Interim Report").

2. Jonathan M. Orszag and Peter R. Orszag, "The Physical Capital Stock Used in Collegiate Athletics," April 2005.

3. We note that since our interim report was released in August 2003, an analysis prepared for the Knight Foundation Commission on Intercollegiate Athletics reached many of the same conclusions. Robert H. Frank, "Challenging the Myth: A Review of the Links Among College Athletic Success, Student Quality, and Donations," May 2004, available at http://www.knightfdn.org/athletics/reports/2004_frankreport/KCIA_Frank_report_2004.pdf.

4. In particular, we define an "arms race" as occurring when an increase in spending at School A triggers an increase in spending at School B, which then feeds back into pressure on School A to further raise its own spending. To examine this definition of an arms race, we examined whether increased spending by other members of a school's conference was statistically associated with increased spending by the school itself.

INDIRECT IMPACTS OF INTERCOLLEGIATE ATHLETICS

CHALLENGING THE MYTH: A REVIEW OF THE LINKS AMONG COLLEGE ATHLETIC SUCCESS, STUDENT QUALITY, AND DONATIONS

Robert H. Frank

INTRODUCTION

Big-time college athletic programs are expensive. At the University of Michigan, for example, total spending on athletics approached $50 million in the 2003–2004 academic year.[1] Athletic budgets are also rising quickly. Between 1995 and 2001, they rose more than twice as fast as university budgets overall in Division I schools, the most competitive NCAA classification. In real terms, athletic program spending rose about 25 percent during that period, while overall spending rose only about 10 percent.[2]

In view of the enormous revenues that can accrue to the most successful programs, the incentives to compete for the limited number of positions at the top of the college athletics hierarchy are strong. In 2003, the NCAA's postseason football Bowl Championship Series alone distributed $104 million among 64 Division I college programs.[3] Yet the overall distribution of financial rewards is highly skewed, and at all but a small proportion of institutions, revenues are now outweighed by expenditures on athletic programs. Athletic budgets are increasingly funded by student fees, which range from $50 to $1,000 per student each year. Such fees now account for an average of 20 percent of the athletic budgets at Division I Schools.[4]

If expenditures exceed revenues in most college athletic programs, why are universities investing so much more each year in these programs? I will consider two possible explanations. The first is a structural one common to many other markets in which reward is determined by relative performance. In such markets, we will see, it is not uncommon for contestants to invest more in performance enhancement than can reasonably be justified by the expected gains. The second possibility is that although a successful athletic program may fail to cover its direct costs, it may generate indirect benefits in other domains that are of sufficient value to make up the shortfall. Two such indirect benefits have been widely claimed to exist—namely, that successful college athletic programs stimulate both additional alumni donations and additional applications from prospective students. Since tuition payments typically fall well short of the cost of educating each student, additional applications do not improve a university's financial position directly, and may even hinder it if they result in larger numbers of students admitted. Yet by enabling an institution to become more selective, additional applications could help a university move up in the race for academic prestige, a valuable benefit in its own right.

COLLEGE ATHLETICS AS A WINNER-TAKE-ALL MARKET

It might seem that a university's decision about whether to mount a big-time college athletic program is like any other ordinary business decision about whether to enter a particular market. The general rule is that if a business expects that it can enter a market profitably, it will do so; otherwise, it will not. But attempts to apply this rule often play out with unanticipated consequences when the reward from entering a market depends less on the absolute quality of the business's product than on its relative quality. Philip Cook and I use the term *winner-take-all markets* to describe arenas with this form of reward structure. In winner-take-all markets, the expectation is often that participants as a whole will not make any money, and that indeed a substantial majority will suffer losses.

A feel for how winner-take-all markets differ from ordinary markets is afforded by experiments involving a simple auction called the entrapment game. First described by the economist Martin Shubik, this game is just like a standard auction except for one feature. The auctioneer announces to an assembled group of subjects that he is going to auction off some money—say, a $20 bill—to the highest bidder. Once the bidding opens, each successive bid must exceed the previous one by some specified amount—say, 50 cents. The special feature of the entrapment game is that once the bidding stops, not only must the highest bidder remit the amount of his bid to the auctioneer, but so must the second-highest bidder. The highest bidder then gets the $20 bill and the second-highest bidder gets nothing. For example, if the highest bid were $8 and the second-highest bid were $7.50, the auctioneer would collect a total of $15.50. The highest bidder would get the $20, for a net gain of $12; and the second-highest bidder would experience a loss of $7.50.

Players in this game face incentives much like the ones that confront participants in winner-take-all markets as they consider whether to undertake investments in performance enhancement. In both cases, by investing a little more than one's rivals, one can tip the outcome decisively in one's favor.

Although the subjects in these experiments have ranged from business executives to college undergraduates, the pattern of bidding is almost always the same. Following the opening bid, offers proceed quickly to $10, or half the amount being auctioned. There is then a pause as the subjects appear to digest the fact that, with the next bid, the two highest bids will sum to more than $20, thus taking the auctioneer off the hook. At this point, the second-highest bidder, whose bid stands at $9.50, invariably offers $10.50, apparently thinking that it would be better to have a shot at winning $9.50 than to take a sure loss of $9.50.

In most cases, all but the top two bidders drop out at this point, and the top two quickly escalate their bids. As the bidding approaches $20, there is a second pause, this time as the top bidders appear to be pondering the fact that even the top bidder is likely to come out behind. The second bidder, at $19.50, is understandably reluctant to offer $20.50. But consider his alternative. If he drops out, he will lose $19.50 for sure. But if he offers $20.50 and wins, he will lose only 50 cents. So as long as he thinks there is even a small chance that the other bidder will drop out, it makes sense to continue. Once the $20 threshold has been crossed, the pace of the bidding quickens again, and from then on it is a war of nerves between the two remaining bidders. It is quite common for the bidding to reach $50 before someone finally yields in frustration.

One might be tempted to think that any intelligent, well-informed person would know better than to become involved in an auction whose incentives so strongly favor costly escalation. But many of the subjects in these auctions have been experienced business professionals; many others have had formal training in the theory of games and strategic interaction. . . .

Shubik's entrapment game obviously doesn't capture the rich details that characterize the current market for big-time college athletics. So I now consider an example that, while still highly simplified, resembles this market more closely. Suppose 1,000 universities must decide whether to launch an athletic program, the initial cost of which would be $1 million a year. Those who launch a program then compete in an annual tournament in which finishers among the top 10 earn a prize of $10 million each. To further simplify matters, suppose that those deciding to launch an athletic program all have equal access to the limited pool of talented players, skilled coaches, and other inputs required for these programs (making each participant as likely as any other to finish in the top 10). If schools make their decisions about whether to launch a program in sequence, and each school can observe how many other schools have already entered the arena, how many schools will decide to compete?

If every institution's decision were driven solely by whether it could expect to make a profit (or at least avoid a loss) by launching a program, we would expect only 100 of the 1,000 institutions to launch athletic programs and the remaining 900 to sit out. That way, the competing institutions would each have a one-tenth chance at winning a prize of $10 million, or an expected revenue of $1 million, just enough to cover the cost of entry. In any given year, the top 10 finishers will thus post net gains of $9 million each, while the 90 remaining institutions will post a net loss of $1 million each. Under the assumption that all contestants have equal access to the inputs for athletic programs, each program will end up winning once every 10 years, on average. Under these simplifying assumptions, maintaining a big-time athletic program would be, in effect, a break-even proposition over the long run. Participants wouldn't make any money, on the average. But they wouldn't lose any money, either.

This example abstracts from reality in at least two ways that make launching a big-time athletic program seem more economically attractive than in fact it is. For one, it assumes that when a university assesses its prospects, it is accurate in its estimate of the probability that its own program will be among the winners. Yet there is abundant evidence that potential contestants are notoriously optimistic in their estimates of how well they are likely to perform relative to others.

This tendency has been recognized for centuries. As Adam Smith described it,

The overweening conceit which the greater part of men have of their own abilities, is an ancient evil remarked by the philosophers and moralists of all ages. Their absurd presumption in their own good fortune, has been less taken notice of. It is, however, if possible, still more universal. There is no man living who when in tolerable health and spirits, has not some share of it. The chance of gain is by every man more or less over-valued, and the chance of loss is by most men under-valued, and by scarce any man, who is in tolerable health and spirits, valued more than it is worth.[6]

Smith's characterization of human nature is no less accurate today than when he offered it more than 200 years ago. . . .

Psychologists call this pattern the "Lake Wobegon Effect," after Garrison Keillor's mythical Minnesota town "where the women are strong, the men are good-looking, and all the children are above average."[14] The phenomenon has most often been explained in motivational terms by authors who note that the observed biases are psychologically gratifying.[15] . . .

But the Lake Wobegon bias clearly has cognitive dimensions as well. Thus psychologists Amos Tversky and Daniel Kahneman have shown that when people try to estimate the likelihood of an event, they often rely on how easily they can summon examples of similar events from memory.[17] Yet, although ease of recall does, in fact, rise with the frequency of similar events, it also depends on other factors. For example, events that are especially salient or vivid are easily recalled even if they happen only infrequently. Since teams from the most successful college athletic programs appear in a disproportionate share of the televised games and capture a disproportionate share of national media coverage, the good fortunes of these programs are nothing if not salient. In contrast, the fates of unsuccessful programs, which receive little or no media attention, are much less likely to spring to mind.

If the university administrators who decide whether to launch big-time athletic programs are like normal human beings in other domains, they are likely to overestimate the odds that their programs will be successful. The upshot is that many more institutions are likely to launch big-time athletic programs than would be warranted by unbiased profit-and-loss estimates.

A second misleading simplification in my illustrative example is the assumption that the level of expenditure required to launch and maintain a big-time athletic program is fixed. Expenditures on these programs are in fact constantly subject to reassessment and adjustment. As in Shubik's entrapment auction, any given athletic director knows that his school's odds of having a winning program will go up if it spends a little more than its rivals on coaches and recruiting. But the same calculus is plainly visible to all other schools. And again as in Shubik's auction, the gains from bidding higher turn out to be self-canceling when everyone does it. The result is often an expenditure arms race with no apparent limit.

Evidence suggests that big-time college athletic programs find themselves embroiled in just such an arms race. NCAA Division I-A head football coaches, for example, earned an average annual base salary of more than $388,000 last year, an increase of more than 80 percent in real terms over the 1998 average.[18] But base salary is often only a small component of coaches' total annual compensation. . . .

In sum, the logic of competition in winner-take-all markets suggests that participants in these markets are likely to experience much less favorable economic results than they had expected at the outset. Upward biased estimates of success will tempt more institutions to enter than would be warranted by the logic of profit and loss. And each institution, once entered, will face powerful incentives to increase its expenditures in search of a competitive edge. This logic is in harmony with the observation that the revenues generated directly by college athletic programs fall far short of covering their costs in the overwhelming majority of cases.

INDIRECT BENEFITS OF COLLEGE ATHLETIC PROGRAMS

Even if a college athletic program fails to generate sufficient direct revenue to cover its costs, it might generate indirect benefits of sufficient magnitude to bridge the shortfall. Two such indirect benefits have been widely discussed: 1) that a winning athletic program leads to additional contributions from alumni and others; and 2) that a winning program generates additional applications from prospective students (resulting, presumably, in a higher quality freshman class). How do these indirect benefits affect the theoretical presumption that an institution that launches a big-time athletic program should expect to lose money?

Consider first the issue of alumni donations. Given that many alumni donations are earmarked specifically for college athletic programs, there is no doubt that many alumni feel strongly about these programs. Whether such donations simply displace donations that would have been made for academic programs is an empirical question, one that I will address presently. But suppose, for the sake of discussion that having a winning athletic program leads to a net increase in the flow of alumni donations. How do these additional revenues alter an institution's expectation about the financial consequences of launching a big-time athletic program?

From an economic perspective, indirect revenues from donations are functionally equivalent to revenues generated directly by athletic programs, such as those from ticket sales and television contracts. Growth in direct sources of revenue has two effects: It induces more institutions to launch athletic programs, and it induces those having such programs to invest more heavily in them. Following a once-for-all increase in the revenue distributed from the NCAA's annual March Madness basketball tournament, for example, the expectation is that a new equilibrium will eventually be reached in which there are more institutions that have serious basketball programs, and in which average expenditures on such programs are higher than before. But just as each competing institution faced the expectation of an economic loss in the original equilibrium, the same will be true in the new equilibrium. From the perspective of each competing institution, the gains from the additional revenues are offset by the presence of additional competitors (which reduces each institution's odds of having a winning program) and by increased spending on coaches, recruiting, and other inputs.

Adding alumni donations into the revenue mix has precisely the same effect as increasing the payout from television contracts. In the presence of such donations, a new equilibrium results in which both the expected number of athletic programs and the expected level of total expenditures in each become larger than before.

What about the possibility that a successful athletic program might boost the number of prospective students who apply, thus enabling an institution to become more selective, in turn boosting its position in rankings such as those published by the *US News and World Report*? As in the case of alumni donations, there can be little doubt that a successful athletic program will encourage at least some additional applications. But since all institutions are likely to operate under the same expectation, the existence of this benefit is analogous in its effects to higher TV revenues and increased alumni donations. That is to say, it will cause additional institutions to enter the big-time athletic arena and those already in that arena to spend more than before on their athletic programs. So to the extent that having a successful big-time athletic program stimulates additional applications, that fact implies that institutions will have to spend more money than before to achieve a winning program.

Viewed from the perspective of institutions of higher learning as a whole, it is impossible for additional investment in athletic programs to cause schools to become more selective on the average. Selectivity, after all, is a purely relative concept: It is mathematically impossible for more than ten percent of all schools to be among the ten percent most selective. Still, if applications track athletic success closely, any single school's failure to invest in a big-time athletic program might mean that its selectivity would fall relative to that of other schools. But even that would not imply that investment in a big-time athletic program is an efficient strategy for becoming more selective. The same funds used to boost athletic performance could be used in other ways that make schools more attractive to potential applicants—financial aid, for example, or increased direct marketing, or improved academic programs. So here again, it becomes an empirical question as to whether greater investment in big-time athletic programs is likely to improve the quality of a school's entering freshman class relative to what it would have been had the same money been spent in other ways.

EMPIRICAL EVIDENCE: A SURVEY

What does the empirical evidence say about whether success in big-time college athletics stimulates additional applications and alumni giving? Different authors have attempted to answer these questions in a variety of ways. I discuss first the studies that examine the how a school's athletic success affects the size of its applicant pool.

Does Athletic Success Increase Applications?

Success in big-time college athletics may influence applications for admission in at least two ways. One is that many prospective students are sports fans, some of whom may decide where to apply in part on the basis of their assessments of which institutions are most likely to play host to exciting athletic contests. A second influence is the broader effect of university name recognition. The names of institutions with successful big-time athletic programs appear frequently in the media, making them generally more familiar to prospective students. On this view, a big-time athletic program serves much like a national advertising campaign.

Other factors held constant, if students are indeed more likely to apply to an institution with a successful athletic program, one observable consequence should be that such schools will be more selective than others on such measures as the average SAT scores of entering freshmen. How does this hypothesis fare empirically?

In a widely-cited 1987 study, Robert McCormick and Maurice Tinsley collected data on approximately 150 schools for 1971, 63 of which they identified as having big-time athletic programs. They estimated a multiple regression model in which the average SAT score of an institution's entering freshmen in any given year depended on a variety of academic control variables and on whether it was a participant in big-time college athletics. The control variables included the number of volumes in the school's library, the average salary of its faculty, as well as its student-faculty ratio, endowment per student, tuition, enrollment, age, and whether it was public or private. On the basis of various permutations of this basic model, McCormick and Tinsley estimated that a school with a big-time athletic program could expect an entering freshman class with an average SAT score roughly 33 points—or 3 percent—higher than if it did not have a big-time athletic program.

A difficulty with this type of analysis is that it is impossible to gather data on all the various causal factors that might shape an outcome like an institution's average SAT scores. If schools with big-time athletic programs are different in other ways that prospective applicants find appealing, the regression model will wrongfully attribute the influence of the omitted factors to athletic programs.

In an attempt to control for this difficulty, McCormick and Tinsley employ a second strategy in which they examine the link between changes in average SAT scores and changes in athletic success. Focusing exclusively on schools with big-time athletic programs, their measure of an institution's athletic success is the trend in its won-lost percentage between 1971 and 1984. Their dependent variable was the change in entering freshmen SAT scores between 1981 and 1984. In various permutations of their model, they found positive estimates of the effect of athletic success trends on change in SAT scores. But in each case the effects were extremely small, and none of their estimates was statistically significantly different from zero at conventional confidence levels.

In a 1993 paper, Irvin Tucker and Louis Amato examine the relationship between a school's athletic success and the size of its applicant pool by utilizing a different performance measure from one used by McCormick and Tinsley. They measure football success, for example, by assigning points based on the Associated Press's end-of-season top-20 rankings, and they construct a similar measure for basketball success. Using these measures, football success, but not basketball success, was positively and statistically significantly associated with increases in SAT scores between 1980 and 1989. But here, too, the effect was small. A school whose football program finished in the top twenty for each of the 10 years in the sample would expect to attract a freshman class with 3 percent higher SAT scores than a school whose program never finished in the top 20.

Working with data for the same set of institutions belonging to major college football conferences, Robert Murphy and Gregory Trandel (1994) utilize still another measure of football success—namely, the within-conference won-lost percentage (as opposed to the overall won-lost percentage utilized by McCormick and Tinsley). By constructing a 10-year panel from 1978-1987, they were also able to estimate separate intercept coefficients for each institution, a more reliable way of controlling for unobserved differences among institutions. Murphy and Trandel find that improvements in within-conference won–lost percentages are positively associated with the number of applications received, although the size of the effect is again small. For example, a school that posts a 50 percent increase in its percentage of games won (by moving from, say, winning half of its games to winning 75 percent of them) would on average see its number of applicants rise by only 1.3 percent. The effect they estimate is thus even smaller than the ones estimated by McCormick and Tinsley and by Tucker and Amato.

Although Tucker and Amato found that an institution's basketball success had no effect on its students' SAT scores, Franklin Mixon (1995) argues to the contrary on the basis of study in which he employs a different measure of success—the number of rounds through which the school's team advanced in the NCAA tournament in the spring before applications are filed the next fall. This measure is positively and statistically significantly associated with average SAT scores of the relevant entering class.[20] The effect, however, is extremely small. By the largest of Mixon's three published estimates, advancing an additional round in the NCAA tournament results in a 1.7 point increase in the entering class's average SAT score.

An alternative to the statistical regression approach to studying causal relationships is the event study, which focus on the experiences surrounding conspicuous examples of changes in a causal factor. For present purposes, the most spectacular such change is winning a national championship trophy in one of the two biggest sports, football and basketball. If athletic success matters, then a school should receive significantly more applications in the wake of a championship season than in the years preceding it.

In a 1996 paper, Douglas Toma and Michael Cross examined records for the 13 different institutions that won the NCAA Division I-A national football championship between 1979 and 1992[21] and the 11 different institutions that won the NCAA men's basketball tournament during those same years. For each institution with a championship, they tracked the quantity and quality of undergraduate applications for the five years before and after the championship season.

Toma and Cross report that two football championship seasons in particular were followed by large increases in applications. Applications to the University of Miami increased by 33 percent for the three years following the school's national title in 1987; and when Georgia Tech shared the national title in 1990, its applications rose by 21 percent over the following three years. Five other football championship seasons were followed by applications increases of between 10 and 20 percent, and the remaining championship seasons were followed by "only modest gains." Two schools—Alabama in 1979 and Miami in 1993—actually saw applications drop by roughly 5 percent in the three years following a championship season. Toma and Cross report a similar pattern of findings in the wake of championship seasons in basketball. Ten of the 13 schools that won the NCAA Basketball Tournament between 1979 and 1993 experienced increases in applications.

In an attempt to control for other factors that might have influenced changes in applications, Toma and Cross matched each of the championship institutions in both sports with a small number of similar peer institutions. The results of this adjustment varied considerably across institutions, but in general tended to attenuate their estimates of the gains in applications attributable to winning a championship.

Given the enormous visibility of winning a national title in football and basketball, it is perhaps not surprising that significant increases in applications followed in the wake of championship seasons in at least some schools. Much less expected, however, is that Toma and Cross were unable to find any measurable impact of these increases on the quality of admitted or entering students. Perhaps the institutions experiencing increased applications found opportunities to increase their selectivity in ways not reflected in SAT scores, grades, and other student quality measures. Or perhaps, as Toma and Cross speculate, a school's national championship visibility may have "more impact on the search phase, and less on the choice phase, of student college choice."[22] If their conjecture is accurate, it suggests the intriguing possibility that an institution's athletic success might actually reduce its admissions yield, thereby reducing its position in the US News rankings.

Perhaps the most careful study to date of the relationship between athletic success and various other outcomes was published as a 2003 interim report by the consulting firm Sebago Associates under a commission from the National Collegiate Athletics Association. In this report, authors Robert Litan, Jonathan Orszag, and Peter Orszag present statistical analyses based on a new database they compiled from information collected as part of the Equity in Athletics Disclosure Act, which was then merged with data from other sources, including proprietary NCAA data and the authors' own survey of chief financial officers from 17 Division I schools. Because of gaps in data from the various sources, the resulting data set spans only the years from 1993 to 2001. Even so, this study rests on by far the most comprehensive data set used in any of the studies on college athletics published to date. Using fixed-effects models to control for unobserved institutional characteristics, Litan et al. estimate that football winning percentage is positively associated with average incoming SAT scores, but that the effect is small and not significantly different from zero at conventional confidence levels.

How are we to interpret the disparate findings in the empirical literature on athletic success and applications? Before turning to this question, I discuss the studies that focus on athletic success and alumni giving, for these studies are also difficult to interpret, and for essentially similar reasons.

ATHLETIC SUCCESS AND ALUMNI GIVING

With the publication of their 1979 paper, Lee Siegelman and Robert Carter launched an intense debate, much of it carried out in *Social Science Quarterly*, about whether success in big-time college athletics stimulates alumni to donate more to their alma maters than they otherwise would have. The same technical issues that arose in the debate about athletic success and SAT scores surface in this debate as well. Focusing on Division I schools, Siegelman and Carter performed separate regressions to estimate how an institution's football winning percentage affected alumni donations to its annual fund for each year in a multiyear sample. Their conclusion was that such donations are essentially independent of football success.

In a follow-up study, George Brooker and T.D. Klastorin (1981) raise the familiar objection that the Siegelman and Carter study is compromised by its implicit assumption that, apart from athletic success, institutions in Division I are alike in all other important respects that influence alumni giving. In an attempt to control for institutional heterogeneity, Brooker and Klastorin estimate separate coefficients for universities in different university groupings over a multiyear sample. They find positive links between alumni giving and some measures of athletic success for some university groups and negative links for others. Unfortunately, they report only the signs of their estimated coefficients, not their numerical magnitudes, making it impossible to assess whether the links they find are economically significant.

In a 1983 paper, Siegelman and Samuel Brookheimer take even further steps to control for institutional heterogeneity by conducting a full panel study with separate fixed effects for each school. They also break alumni donations down into two components, restricted gifts made directly to the athletic department and unrestricted gifts to the annual fund. They report that the two types of giving are essentially uncorrelated with each other, and that only direct gifts to the athletic department depend in any way on athletic success, and those only on football success, not basketball success. By their estimates, a ten-percent increase in football winning percentage sustained over a four-year period would increase donations to the athletic program by more than $125,000 in 1983 dollars.

Unlike most other authors, who focus on a large sample of different institutions, Paul Grimes and George Chressanthis (1994) attempt to estimate the link between athletic success and alumni giving by confining their attention to a single school, Mississippi State University, during the 30-year period between 1962 and 1991. Grimes and Chressanthis also depart from tradition by studying the effects of athletic success not just in football and basketball, but also in baseball. They find that winning percentage in football is actually negatively associated with alumni giving, although not statistically significantly so. Basketball winning percentage has a positive estimated coefficient, but again one that is not statistically significant at conventional levels. Only baseball winning percentage is statistically significantly linked to alumni giving. But the estimated effect is extremely small. Their estimates of the effect of postseason appearances are statistically insignificant for all three sports, and actually negative for basketball.

Grimes and Chressanthis also examine one other factor ignored by the other studies just described—namely, the effect on giving of being sanctioned by the NCAA for rules violations. Being placed on NCAA probation is a nonnegligible risk for institutions seriously attempting to field winning programs, since these institutions are often forced by competition to operate close to the margins of allowable conduct. The authors estimate, for example, that a year's sanction for a rules violation in football would cost MSU more than $1.6 million in lost donations in 1982 dollars.

In a 1996 paper, Robert Baade and Jeffrey Sundberg constructed separate data sets for public universities, private universities, and liberal arts colleges to examine the factors that governed alumni giving during the period from 1973 to 1979. They also refined previous measures of athletic success by looking not only at won-lost percentages but also bowl game appearances. They concluded that although winning records do not translate into higher gifts at public and private universities, bowl game appearances do result in significantly higher gifts (an estimated average gift increment of $40 per year per alumnus at private universities, $6.50 per year per alumnus at public universities). They also found that NCAA basketball tournament appearances result in higher gifts at public universities (an annual increment of $5.60 per alumnus). At liberal arts colleges, which do not normally appear in postseason bowls, they found a "statistically significant, but very small, correlation between winning percentage and alumni giving."

In a 2000 paper, Thomas Rhoads and Shelby Gerking provide a useful illustration of the extent to which unobserved institutional heterogeneity can bias estimates in studies that fail to control for it. Focusing on much the same sample of Division I schools studied by Baade and Sundberg, Rhoads and Gerking examine the relationship between athletic success and giving for the period from 1986–87 to 1995–96. Using a standard OLS regression model without fixed effects as a baseline, they estimate that football bowl wins and NCAA basketball tournament wins have positive and statistically significant effects on both total giving and giving by alumni. These effects are about the same magnitude as those estimated by Baade and Sundberg. But when Rhoads and Gerking then run essentially the same model with fixed effects for each institution, they find that none of the athletic success variables has a coefficient that is statistically different from zero. Rhoads and Gerking also estimate that being placed on NCAA probation for a basketball violation reduces total giving by $1.6 million in 1987 dollars.

The 2003 NCAA-commissioned study by Litan et al. also examines the relationship between football success and both total alumni giving and alumni giving to football programs. As noted earlier, Litan and his co-authors have assembled perhaps the most comprehensive database employed in any of the studies described in this review. Using carefully specified fixed-effects models to control for institutional heterogeneity, they report that both football winning percentage and lagged football winning percentage are negatively linked with both total alumni giving and alumni donations to football programs. None of these estimates, however, is statistically significant at conventional levels. Litan et al. also fail to find statistically significant links between football spending or lagged football spending on either form of alumni giving.

Several other studies I will not describe in detail here also look for possible links between athletic success and alumni giving. Some (for example, Coughlin and Erekson, 1984, and Goff, 2000) report positive links. Others (for example, Frey, 1985, and Grace, 1988) do not. Still others (for example, Turner, Meserve, and Bowen, 2001) even suggest that athletic success may diminish the amount that donors contribute for general purposes.

WHAT ARE THE POLICY IMPLICATIONS OF THE EMPIRICAL LITERATURE?

As many of the authors of the studies discussed above would be quick to concede, the limitations of existing data and methods of statistical inference make it exceedingly difficult to reach definitive general conclusions about the strength, or indeed even the existence, of the causal relationships in question. Perhaps the only firm conclusion that can be drawn from a review of the empirical literature on the indirect effects of athletic success is that each of the competing claims regarding these relationships is likely to be true under at least some circumstances.

Certainly there are instances in which the presence of a specific causal link appears compelling, as when Boston College experienced a 12-percent increase in applications during the year following its football team's dramatic come-from-behind victory over Miami in 1984. [See note below.] Replays of Doug Flutie's 48-yard touchdown pass to Gerard Phelan as time expired were broadcast so frequently over the ensuing months that the drama of this story could hardly have escaped the attention of even a single American high-school sports fan. Such vivid episodes notwithstanding, the existing empirical literature suggests that success in big-time athletics has little, if any, systematic effect on the quality of incoming freshmen an institution is able to attract (as measured by average SAT scores).

By the same token, precious little can be said with confidence about the relationship between alumni giving and successful performance in big-time college athletics. That there are many wealthy donors who care deeply about the athletic success of their alma maters cannot be questioned. Nor is there any doubt that the good will generated by a successful athletic program prompts many of these people to donate more generously. Yet all major college athletics programs go through cycles of relative success and relative failure. And if success stimulates alumni giving, then failure must inhibit it. The empirical literature seems to say that if the overall net effect of athletic success on alumni giving is positive, it is likely to be small.

As the psychologist Tom Gilovich has suggested, someone who wants to believe a proposition tends to ask, "Can I believe it?" In contrast, someone who wants to deny its truth tends to ask, "Must I believe it?"[23] With such a variety of claims and findings in the empirical literature, we must expect individual differences in motivation to explain a substantial share of the variance in beliefs about the links between athletic success and other outcomes. Important players in the debate about college athletic spending are thus likely to cling to conflicting beliefs about the facts.

Under the circumstances, it is all the more important that our thinking about the effects of spending on athletic programs be informed by a clear understanding of the economic forces that govern behavior in big-time college athletic markets. Fortunately, what we know about how such markets function suggests that the answers to many important policy questions may not hinge strongly on the strength of the empirical relationships just examined.

Policy questions arise at two distinct levels in the athletic arena. First, individual institutions must decide whether, and, if so, how much, to invest in pursuit of big-time athletic success. And second, governing bodies, both public and private, must decide whether, and if so, how, to regulate the behavior of individual athletic programs.

Consider first the individual institution's investment decision. How would this decision be affected by its beliefs about whether successful athletic programs stimulate additional applications or greater alumni giving? What we know from the structure of competition in winner-take-all markets with free entry is that if the reward from successful performance increases, more contestants will compete and each will invest more heavily in performance enhancement. If prospective contestants tend toward optimism in assessing their odds of success (as we saw earlier, a near universal tendency in other domains), or if contestants become involved in expenditure arms races (as we saw in the bidding war among contestants in Shubik's entrapment game), the clear expectation is that participation in big-time college athletics will be a losing proposition for all but a handful of institutions. That is, once participants respond to an increase in the reward for successful performance, market forces all but assure that participation in big-time college athletics will again be financially unremunerative for most institutions. Indeed, with higher stakes, the expected financial losses are likely to be even larger than before. In Shubik's entrapment game, for example, bidders' losses are roughly proportional to the denomination of the bill being auctioned.

The same logic holds, irrespective of the size of the indirect effects of athletic success. So from the individual institution's perspective, even if an academic study were to establish with certainty that athletic success stimulates large increases in, say, alumni giving, this would not constitute an argument for increased investment. Competition among institutions to capture those gains would have already eliminated any unexploited opportunities for gain that might initially have been available. Conversely, discovering the link between success and alumni giving to be weak would provide no additional reason to curtail investment, since the weakness of that link would already be reflected in the current market equilibrium. Rational investment decisions are forward looking, and in either case, once the market has reached equilibrium, the expected return to additional investment is likely to be negative.

Similar conclusions apply to the relationship between an institution's athletic success and the size of its applicant pool. Here, too, if the link were known to be strong and positive, more contestants would enter the arena and each would invest more intensely in performance enhancement. A big-time athletic program might be a cost-effective means of expanding the applicant pool if a highly visible winning program could be launched at moderate expense. But as we have seen, even the cost of fielding a losing program is extremely high and growing rapidly. If expanding its applicant pool is an institution's goal, it faces many more attractive investment opportunities than those it confronts in the domain of big-time college athletics.

If investment in big-time college athletics is unlikely to yield high returns from the perspective of any given institution, it is an even less attractive proposition from the perspective of institutions as a whole. The distinction between the two perspectives is precisely analogous to the distinction we see in the entrapment game. From the perspective of any individual bidding to win the $20 bill, boosting one's bid beyond that of the current high bidder entails at least the possibility of a favorable outcome. From the perspective of bidders as a group, however, additional bidding serves only to guarantee a smaller overall return than before. It is the same in college athletics. No matter how many hundreds of millions of dollars institutions spend, only 20 teams will finish in the AP's top 20 in football each year, and only four teams will reach the final four in the NCAA basketball tournament.

The empirical literature does not rule out the possibility that a given institution's success in big-time college athletics might attract additional applicants or stimulate greater alumni giving. But even if both of those links were strong and positive at the individual level, they would essentially vanish from the perspective of institutions as a whole. Success, after all, is a purely relative phenomenon. Upward movements in the national rankings for some teams necessarily entail downward movements for other teams. If institutions in the first group attracted more applicants and larger donations as a result, the corresponding movements would be in the opposite direction for the institutions in the second group.

The NCAA and other athletic governing bodies have long since recognized the distinction between the incentives facing individual institutions and those facing institutions as a group. When, as in college athletics, reward depends on rank, institutions face powerful incentives to engage in costly "positional arms races."[24] The incentive to spend more may seem compelling from the perspective of each institution, even though each realizes that when all spend more, the competitive balance will be unaffected. The familiar stadium metaphor captures the essential idea: Each spectator stands to get a better view, but when all stand nobody sees any better than if all had remained seated.

Under these circumstances, individual institutions can often achieve better outcomes by empowering a larger governing body to restrict their own behavior. Such "positional arms control agreements" are found in virtually every domain in which the rewards of individuals depend strongly on rank.[25] Even when the stakes in athletic competition are relatively modest, as in the Ivy League, governing bodies typically restrict their members' ability to compete freely.

As in the case of military arms control agreements, however, positional arms control agreements in athletics are often hard to enforce. Sometimes the problem is that the governing body's jurisdiction is too narrow. A case in point was the Ivy League's decision to abandon a rule that prevented its members from holding football practice in the spring. The rationale for the rule was that if any one institution held practice in the spring, others would be forced to follow suit. Student-athletes would lose time from their studies, yet the competitive advantage each team sought to achieve would vanish in the end. Half of all teams would still lose on any given fall Saturday, and half would win. The difficulty was that Ivy League football schedules included not just opponents from within the league but also from outside it. At the time, Ivy League teams were losing consistently to rivals from the Colonial League, which allowed spring football practice. The ban was finally lifted in response to complaints from angry alumni.

A second problem is that positional arms control agreements are often mistaken by the antitrust authorities as unlawful cartel behavior. Many elite institutions, for example, were once party to an agreement whereby they pledged to target limited financial aid money for those students with the greatest financial needs. This was essentially a positional arms control agreement to curb competition among member institutions for students with elite credentials. Animated by its belief that unbridled competition always and everywhere leads to the best outcome, the Justice Department took a dim view of this agreement. And it brought an antitrust suit that led to its termination.

Once we appreciate the logic of the financial incentives that confront participants in winner-take-all markets, however, we may feel less inclined to embrace the mantra that all outcomes of open competition must be good. The problem, as noted, is that when reward depends on rank, behavior that looks attractive to each individual often looks profoundly unattractive from the perspective of the group. Collusive agreements to restrain these behaviors can create gains for everyone. Of course, cooperative agreements to limit competition can also cause harm, as in the notorious price-fixing cases of antitrust lore.

The challenge, of course, is to make informed distinctions. Antitrust authorities might consider a retreat from their uncritical belief that unlimited competition necessarily leads to the greatest good for all. Manifestly it does not. Collective agreements should be scrutinized not on quasi-religious grounds, but according to the practical test of whether they limit harmful effects of competition without compromising its many benign effects. The collective agreement among universities to concentrate financial aid on families with the greatest financial need was a positional arms control agreement that clearly met this test.

Because the reward structure in college athletics is so strongly rank dependent, the design and implementation of positional arms control agreements are by far the most important policy decisions that athletics governing bodies such as the NCAA must confront. And these decisions would take essentially the same form irrespective of the strength of the individual links between athletic success, on the one hand, and indirect benefits, such as larger applicant pools and greater alumni giving, on the other. A review of

the empirical literature suggests that these indirect benefits constitute at most only a small fraction of the total revenue stream generated by big-time college athletic programs. If those indirect benefits were found either not to exist at all, or else to be larger than existing studies suggest, participating institutions would still find themselves embroiled in a positional arms race with very high stakes.

CONCLUDING REMARKS

To observe that the reward structure in big-time college athletics gives rise to costly positional arms races is in no way to deny that athletic programs generate numerous real benefits to the institutions that sponsor them. As a report recently commissioned by the athletics subcommittee of the board of trustees at Rice University noted, for example,

> *Athletic competitions serve as focal points to which diverse constituencies of the University, who might otherwise never share a common experience, can relate. . . . Athletics also helps achieve the diversity goals of the school—athletes often bring a completely different set of social, ethnic, economic, and experiential backgrounds to the University. Finally, NCAA athletics provide a phenomenal training ground for participants, with valuable instruction in teamwork, leadership, discipline, and goal setting.*[26]

For policy purposes at the collective level, however, the important point is that each and every one of these benefits would occur with equal measure if every institution were to reduce its expenditures on big-time college athletics by half. Any institution that made such a cutback unilaterally would substantially increase its risk of fielding consistently losing teams. But if all institutions cut back in tandem, competitive balance would be maintained.

Policies that curtail positional arms races promise large benefits for participating institutions at little or no cost to the spectators who consume big-time college athletics. For these consumers, it is much less the absolute performance of teams that matters than the fact of there being spirited contests. (If absolute performance were of primary concern to spectators, they would have long since deserted college athletic contests in favor of their professional counterparts.) So if governing bodies such as the NCAA were able (or were permitted by the antitrust authorities) to create incentives for each program to limit its expenditures, resources can be diverted to meet other pressing ends without sacrificing any of the real benefits that college athletic programs generate.

The most forceful conclusion that can be drawn about the indirect effects of athletic success is that they are small at best when viewed from the perspective of any individual institution. Alumni donations and applications for admission sometimes rise in the wake of conspicuously successful seasons at a small number of institutions, but such increases are likely to be both small and transitory. More to the point, the empirical literature provides not a shred of evidence to suggest that an across-the-board cutback in spending on athletics would reduce either donations by alumni or applications by prospective students.

References

Henning, Lynn. "Martin Charting New Course at U-M," *The Detroit News,* February 4, 2004: www.detnews.com/2001/um/0102/05/d01-183919.htm.

Lowitt, Bruce. "Flutie's 'Hail Mary' Shocks Hurricanes," *St. Petersburg Times,* October 20, 1999: http://www.sptimes.com/News/102099/Sports/Flutie_s__Hail_Mary__.shtml.

Litan, Robert E., Jonathan M. Orszag, and Peter R. Orszag. "The Empirical Effects of College Athletics: An Interim Report," Commissioned by the NCAA, August 2003.

McCormick, R., and M. Tinsley. "Athletics versus Academics? Evidence from SAT Scores," *Journal of Political Economy,* volume 95, 1987: 1103–1116.

Mixon, Franklin G. "Athletics versus Academics? Rejoining the Evidence from SAT Scores," *Education Economics,* December 1995, volume 3: 277–304.

Mixon, Franklin G., and Hsing, Yu. "College Student Migration and Human Capital Theory: A Research Note," *Education Economics,* 1994, volume 2: 65–74.

Mixon, Franklin G., and Rand W. Ressler. "An Empirical Note on the Impact of College Athletics on Tuition Revenues," *Applied Economics Letters,* October 1995, volume 2, number 10: 383–87.

Murphy, Robert G., and Gregory A. Trandel. "The Relation between a University's Football Record and the Size of Its Applicant Pool," *Economics of Education Review,* 1994, volume 13: 265–70.

Rhoads, Thomas A. and Shelby Gerking. "Educational Contributions, Academic Quality, and Athletic Success," *Contemporary Economic Policy,* April, 2000, volume 18, issue 2: p. 248 ff.

Sigelman, L., and R. Carter. "Win One for the Giver? Alumni Giving and Big-Time College Sports," *Social Science Quarterly,* 1979, volume 60, issue 2: 284–294.

Sigelman, L., and S. Bookheimer. "Is It Whether You Win or Lose? Monetary Contributions to Big-Time College Athletic Programs," *Social Science Quarterly,* 1983, volume 64, issue 2: 347–359.

Smith, Adam. *An Inquiry Into the Nature and Causes of the Wealth of Nations* (1776), http://www.online-literature.com/adam_smith/wealth_nations/.

Svenson, O. "Are We All Less Risky and More Skillful Than Our Fellow Drivers?" *Acta Psychologica,* 47, 1981: 143–48.

Sylwester, Mary Jo and Thomas Witoski. "Athletic Spending Grows as Academic Funds Dry Up," *USA Today,* February 18, 2004. http://www.usatoday.com/sports/college/2004-02-18-athletic-spending-cover_x.htm.

Tiger, Lionel. *Optimism,* New York: Simon & Shuster, 1979.

Toma, J. Douglas and Michael Cross. "Intercollegiate Athletics and Student College Choice: Understanding the Impact of Championship Seasons on the Quantity and Quality of Undergraduate Applicants." ASHE Annual Meeting Paper. 1996. http://www.edrs.com.

Tucker, Irvin, and Louis Amato. "Does Big-Time Success in Football or Basketball Affect SAT Scores," *Economics of Education Review,* 1993, volume 12: 177–181.

Turner, S., L. Meserve, and W. Bowen. "Winning and Giving: A Study of the Responsiveness of Giving At Selective Private Colleges and Universities," *Social Science Quarterly,* December 2001, volume 82, issue 4: 812–826.

Tversky, Amos and Daniel Kahneman. "Judgment Under Uncertainty: Heuristics and Biases," *Science,* 185, 1974: 1124–1131.

Weinstein, N. D. "Unrealistic Optimism about Future Life Events," *Journal of Personality and Social Psychology,* 39, 1980: 806–820.

Weinstein, N. D. "Unrealistic Optimism about Susceptibility to Health Problems," *Journal of Behavioral Medicine,* 5, 1982: 441–60.

Weinstein, N. D. and E. Lachrendo. "Egocentrism and Unrealistic Optimism About the Future," *Personality and Social Psychology Bulletin,* 8, 1982: 195–200.

Wylie, R. C. *The Self-Concept,* Vol. 2, Lincoln, NE: University of Nebraska Press, 1979.

Young, Steve. Statement On the issue of Fundamental Fairness and the Bowl Championship Series (BCS) Before the House Judiciary Committee September 4, 2003. http://www.house.gov/judiciary/young090403.htm.

Notes

1. Henning, 2004.

2. Sylwester and Witosky, 2004. These figures, which omit capital expenditures, are likely to substantially understate the overall rate of athletic spending growth.

3. Young, 2003.

4. Sylwester and Witosky, op. cit.

. . . .

6. Smith, 1776, Book I, Chapter 10, part I.

. . . .

14. Gilovich, 1991, p. 77.

15. The anthropologist Lionel Tiger, for example, takes this approach in his 1979 book. See also Gilovich, 1991, chapter 5.

. . . .

17. Tversky and Kahneman, 1974.

18. USAToday, op. cit.

. . . .

20. In papers with different co-authors (Mixon and Ressler, 1994; and Mixon and Hsing, 1995), Mixon argues that athletic success stimulates additional applications primarily from out-of-state residents who are shopping, in effect, for pleasurable consumption experiences.

21. Toma and Cross define a national football championship as a first-place finish in either the AP poll or the CNN/USA Today poll.

22. 1996, p. 21.

23. Cite.

24. See Frank, 1992.

25. Again, see Frank, 1992.

. . . .

THE IMPACT OF COLLEGE SPORTS SUCCESS ON THE QUANTITY AND QUALITY OF STUDENT APPLICATIONS

Devin G. Pope and Jaren C. Pope

1. INTRODUCTION

Since the beginning of intercollegiate sports, the role of athletics within higher education has been a topic of heated debate.[1] Whether to invest funds into building a new football stadium or to improve a school's library can cause major disagreements. Lately the debate has become especially contentious as a result of widely publicized scandals involving student athletes and coaches and because of the increasing amount of resources schools must invest to remain competitive in today's intercollegiate athletic environment. Congress has recently begun to question the National Collegiate Athletic Association's (NCAA) role in higher education and its tax-exempt status. Representative Bill Thomas asked the president of the NCAA, Dr. Myles Brand, in 2006: *"How does playing major college football or men's basketball in a highly commercialized, profit-seeking, entertainment environment further the educational purpose of your member institutions?"*[2]

Some analysts would answer Representative Thomas's question by suggesting that sports does not further the academic objectives of higher education. They would argue that intercollegiate athletics is akin to an "arms race" because of the rank-dependent nature of sports, and that the money spent on athletic programs should be used to directly influence the academic mission of the school instead. However, others suggest that because schools receive a variety of indirect benefits generated by athletic programs, such as student body unity, increased student body diversity, increased alumni donations, and increased applications, athletics may act more as a complement to a school's academic mission than a substitute for it. Until recently, evidence for the indirect benefits of the exposure provided by successful athletic programs was based more on anecdote than empirical research.[3] Early work by Coughlin and Erekson (1984) looked at athletics and contributions but also raised interesting questions about the role of athletics in higher education. Another seminal paper (McCormick and Tinsley 1987) hypothesized that schools with athletic success may receive more applications, thereby allowing the schools to be more selective in the quality of students they admit. They used data on average SAT scores and in-conference football winning percentages for 44 schools in "major" athletic conferences for the years 1981–1984 and found some evidence that football success can increase average incoming student quality.[4] Subsequent research has further tested the increased applications (quantity effect) and increased

selectivity (quality effect) hypotheses of McCormick and Tinsley but has produced mixed results.[5] The inconsistent results in the literature are likely the product of (1) different indicators of athletic success, (2) a limited number of observations across time and across schools, which has typically necessitated a cross-sectional analysis, and (3) different econometric specifications.

This study extends the literature on the indirect benefits of sports success by addressing some of the data limitations and methodological difficulties of previous work. To do this we constructed a comprehensive data set of school applications, SAT scores, control variables, and athletic success indicators. Our data set is a panel of all (approximately 330) NCAA Division I schools from 1983 to 2002. Our analysis uses plausible indicators for both football and basketball success, which are estimated jointly in a fixed effects framework. This allows a more comprehensive examination of the impact of sports success on the quantity and quality of incoming students. Using this identification strategy and data, we find evidence that both football and basketball success can have sizeable impacts on the number of applications received by a school (in the range of 2–15%, depending on the sport, level of success, and type of school), and modest impacts on average student quality, as measured by SAT scores.

Because of concerns with the reliability of the self-reported SAT scores in our primary data set, we also acquired a unique administrative data set that reports the SAT scores of high school students preparing for college to further understand the average "quality" of the student that sports success attracts. These individual-level data are aggregated to the school level and allow us to analyze the impact of sports success on the number of SAT-takers (by SAT score) who sent their SAT scores to Division I schools. Again, the panel nature of the data allows us to estimate a fixed effects model to control for unobserved school-level variables. The results of this analysis show that sports success has an impact on where students send their SAT scores. This analysis confirms and expands the results from the application data set. Furthermore, this data makes it clear that students with both low and high SAT scores are influenced by athletic events.[6]

Besides increasing the quality of enrolled students, schools have other ways to exploit an increased number of applications due to sports success: through increased enrollments or increased tuition. Some schools that offer automatic admission to students who reach certain quality thresholds may be forced to enroll more students when the demand for education at their school goes up. Using the same athletic success indicators and fixed effects framework, we find that schools with basketball success tend to exploit an increase in applications by being more selective in the students they enroll. Schools with football success, on the other hand, tend to increase enrollments.

Throughout our analysis, we illustrate how the average effects that we find differ between public and private schools. We find that this differentiation is often of significance. Specifically, we show that private schools see increases in application rates after sports successes that are two to four times higher than seen by public schools. Furthermore, we show that the increases in enrollment that take place after football success are mainly driven by public schools. We also find some evidence that private schools exploit an increase in applications due to basketball success by increasing tuition rates.

We think that our results significantly extend the existing literature and provide important insights about the impact of sports success on college choice. As Siegfried and Getz (2006) recently pointed out, students often choose a college or university based on limited information about reputation. Athletics is one instrument that institutions of higher education have at their disposal that can be used to directly affect reputation and the prominence of their schools.[7] Our results suggest that sports success can affect the number of incoming applications and, through a school's selectivity, the quality of the incoming class. Whether or not the expenditures required to receive these indirect benefits promote efficiency in education is certainly not determined in the present analysis. Nonetheless, with the large and detailed data sets we acquired, combined with the fixed effect specification that included both college basketball and football success variables, while controlling for unobserved school-specific effects, it is our view that the range of estimates showing the sensitivity of applications to college sports performance can aid university administrators and faculty in better understanding how athletic programs relate to recruitment for their respective institutions.

Section 2 of this article provides a brief literature review of previous work that has investigated the relationship between a school's sports success and the quantity and quality of students that apply to that school. Section 3 describes the data used in the analysis. Section 4 presents the empirical strategy for identifying school-level effects due to athletic success. Section 5 describes the results from the empirical analysis. Section 6 concludes the study.

2. LITERATURE REVIEW

Athletics is a prominent part of higher education. Yet the empirical work on the impact of sports success on the quantity and quality of incoming students is surprisingly limited. Since the seminal work by McCormick and Tinsley (1987), there have been a small number of studies that have attempted to provide empirical evidence on this topic. In this section we review these studies to motivate the present analysis.

Table 13 provides a summary of the previous literature.[8] The table is divided into two panels. Panel A describes the studies that have directly or indirectly looked at the relationship between sports success and the quantity of incoming applications. These studies have found some evidence that

basketball and football success can increase applications or out-of-state enrollments. Panel B describes the studies that have looked at the relationship between sports success and the quality of incoming applications. These studies all reanalyze the work of McCormick and Tinsley (1987) using different data and control variables. The results of these studies are mixed. Some of these analyses find evidence for football and basketball success affecting incoming average SAT scores; whereas, others do not.

Differences in how the studies measured sports success make it difficult to compare the primary results of these studies. For example, Mixon and Hsing (1994) and McCormick and Tinsley (1987) use the broad measures of being in either various NCAA and National Association of Intercollegiate Athletics (NAIA) athletic divisions or "big-time" athletic conferences to proxy prominent and exciting athletic events at a university. Basketball success was modeled by Bremmer and Kesselring (1993) as being the number of NCAA basketball tournament appearances prior to the year the analysis was conducted. Mixon (1995) and Mixon and Ressler (1995), on the other hand, use the number of rounds a basketball team played in the NCAA basketball tournament. Football success was measured by Murphy and Trandel (1994) and McCormick and Tinsley as within-conference winning percentage. Bremmer and Kesselring used the number of football bowl games in the preceding 10 years. Finally, Tucker and Amato (1993) used the Associated Press's end-of-year rankings of football teams. While capturing some measures of historical athletic success, many of these variables may fail to capture the shorter-term episodic success that is an important feature of college sports.

Perhaps more important to the reliability of the results of these studies than the differences in how sports success was measured are the data limitations they faced and the resulting identification strategies employed. All of the analyses except for that of Murphy and Trandel (1994) use a single year of school information for a limited set of schools.[9] For example, Mixon and Ressler (1995) collected data from Peterson's Guide for one year and 156 schools that participate in Division I-A collegiate basketball. The lack of temporal variation in these data necessitates a cross-sectional identification strategy. A major concern with cross-sectional analyses of this type is the possibility that there is unobserved school-specific information, correlated with sports success, that may bias estimates. In fact, much of the debate surrounding differences in estimates in these cross-sectional analyses hinges on arguments about the "proper" school quality controls to include in the regressions. Another concern is the college guide data typically used. It is widely known that the self-reported data (especially data on SAT scores) from sources such as *U.S. News & World Report* and Peterson's can have inaccuracies or problems with institutions not reporting data.[10]

. . . .

Table 13 Summary of Previous Literature

Study	Years	Schools	Source of Data
Panel A: Sports Success and the "Quantity" Question			
Mixon and Hsing (1994)	One year (1990)	220 schools. 70% participated in Division I of the NCAA, 8% in Division II, 12% in Division III, and 10% in the NAIA.	Peterson's Guide to America's Colleges and Universities
Mixon and Ressler (1995)	One year (1993)	156 schools that participate in Division I-A Collegiate Basketball	Peterson's Guide to America's Colleges and Universities
Murphy and Trandel (1994)	10 years (1978–1987)	42 schools that participate in six major college football conferences	Peterson's Guide to America's Colleges and Universities
Panel B: Sports Success and the "Quality" Question			
McCormick and Tinsley (1987)	One year (1971)	Analysis 1: Approximately 150 schools	American Universities and Colleges (1971)
	One trend (1981–1984)	Analysis 2: 44 schools that particpate in seven major athletic conferences	Peterson's Guide to America's Colleges and Universities
Bremmer and Kesselring (1993)	Analysis 1: one year (1989); Analysis 2 uses one trend (1981–1989)	Reanalysis of McCormick and Tinsley. Analysis 1 uses 132 schools, and Analysis 2 uses 53 schools.	Barron's Profiles of American Colleges
Tucker and Amato (1993)	Analysis 1: 1 year (1989); Analysis 2 uses one trend (1980–1989)	Reanalysis of McCormick and Tinsley. Analysis 1 uses 63 schools for one year (1989), and Analysis 2 uses the same 63 schools for one trend (1980–1989)	Peterson's Guide to America's Colleges and Universities
Mixon (1995)	One year (1993)	Reanalysis of McCormick and Tinsley's Analysis 1 using 217 schools	Peterson's Guide to America's Colleges and Universities

Study	Identification Strategy	Primary Results
Panel A: Sports Success and the "Quantity" Question		
Mixon and Hsing (1994)	Cross-sectional Tobit model. LHS: % enrollment of out-of-state students. RHS: school quality control variables and a dummy variable equal to1 if the school is in one of 63 "big-time" athletic schools.	Some evidence that out-of-state students appear to favor higher division sports
Mixon and Ressler (1995)	Cross-section OLS model. LHS: % enrollment of out-of-state students. RHS: school quality control variables and a variable equal to the total number of rounds a school participated in NCAA basketball tournament from 1978 to 1992.	100% increase in the number of basketball tournament rounds results in 6% increase in out-of-state enrollment
Murphy and Trandel (1994)	Fixed-effects OLS with school-level fixed effects. LHS: number of applications of potential incoming freshmen. RHS: control variables and a variable denoting within-conference winning percentage of the football team, lagged one year.	Increasing within-conference football winning percentage by 25% results in a 1.3% increase in applications
Panel B: Sports Success and the "Quality" Question		
McCormick and Tinsley (1987)	Cross-sectional OLS model. LHS: average SAT scores of entering freshmen. RHS: school quality control variables and a dummy variable equal to1 if the school is in one of 63 "big-time" athletic schools. Cross-sectional OLS model. LHS: change in average SAT scores of entering freshmen between 1981 and 1984. RHS: control variables and the trend of in-conference football winning percentage.	Schools with "Big-time" athletics have a 3% increase in SAT scores Upward trend of in-conference football winning percentage marginally increases average incoming SAT scores
Bremmer and Kesselring (1993)	Cross-sectional OLS model. LHS: change in average SAT scores of entering freshmen between 1981 and 1989. RHS: school quality control variables and the number of basketball tournament appearances and football bowl games in the preceding 10 years were used as athletic success indicators.	No evidence was found that basketball or football success impacted average SAT scores
Tucker and Amato (1993)	Cross-sectional OLS model. LHS: change in average SAT scores between 1980 and 1989 freshmen. RHS: school quality control variables and the sum of end-of-year AP top 20 rankings over the previous 10 years for success in basketball and football were used as athletic indicators.	Football success (accumulating 31 points over the 10 years) resulted in a 3% increase in SAT scores by 1989. No evidence was found for basketball success.
Mixon (1995)	Cross-sectional OLS model. LHS: change in average SAT scores of entering freshmen between 1980 and 1989. RHS: school quality control variables and the number of rounds the basketball team played in the NCAA tournament in the 15 years prior to 1993.	Playing more rounds in the NCAA basketball tournament over the previous 15 years led to higher average incoming SAT scores

LHS = left-hand side; RHS = right-hand side.
Source: Southern Economic Journal. Used with permission.

3.   PRIMARY DATA SOURCES

. . . Athletic success likely has two primary components that affect college choice decisions: historic athletic strength and episodic athletic strength. The data sets we use allow us to control for historic athletic strength and analyze episodic athletic strength.

We use three primary data sets to conduct our empirical analysis. Each of these data sets is compiled so that the unit of observation is an institution of higher education that participates in Division I basketball or Division I-A football. The first data set is a compilation of sports rankings, which are used to measure athletic success. The second data set provides school characteristics, including the number of applications, average SAT scores, and the enrollment size for each year's incoming class of students. The third data set provides the number of SAT scores sent to each institution of higher education. The main features of these three data sets are discussed in more detail below.

Football and Basketball Success Indicators

Our indicator of football success is the Associated Press's college football poll. . . .

It is widely agreed that the greatest media exposure and indicator of success for a men's college basketball team (particularly on a national level) comes from the NCAA college basketball tournament. "March Madness," as it is often called, takes place at the end of the college basketball season during March and the beginning of April. It is a single elimination tournament that determines who wins the college basketball championship. Before 1985, 48–53 teams were invited to the tournament each year. Since 1985, 64 teams have been invited to play each year.[13] We collected information on all college basketball teams that were invited to the tournament between 1980 and 2003. From these data we created dummy variables that indicate the furthest round in which a team played. In our analysis, we use the rounds of 64, 16, 4, and champion. A team's progress in the NCAA tournament provides a good proxy of a basketball team's success in any given year during the time frame of the data.

. . . .

College Data

As discussed in Section 2, a weakness of earlier studies on the impacts of athletic success was the limited number of observations across time and across schools. In an attempt to rectify this shortcoming, we purchased access to a licensed data set from the Thomson Corporation that contains detailed college-level data. Thomson Corporation is the company that publishes the well-known "Peterson's Guide to Four Year Colleges." . . .We restrict the data set to the 332 schools that participated in NCAA Division I basketball or Division I-A football between 1983 and 2002.

. . . .

SAT Test-Takers Database

The third data set that we use is derived from the College Board's Test-Takers Database (referred to as SAT database in the remainder of the paper).[15] . . . .

After completing the test and questionnaire, students may indicate up to four colleges where their test scores will be sent for free. Students may also send their scores to additional schools at a cost of $6.50 per school. The data set identifies up to 20 schools to which a student has requested his scores be sent.[18] . . . .

The SAT data set will allow us to further explore how college applicants with different SAT exam scores are affected by football and basketball success. Unlike the self-reported data from sources such as Peterson's Guide, all the data in the SAT database are reported, and inaccuracies are almost nonexistent. These data also allow us to better analyze the impact of sports success on the SAT score sending of students with high, middle, and low SAT scores. By aggregating these high-quality individual-level data to the school level, the impact of sports success on the quality of incoming SAT scores that a school receives can be analyzed. These results will complement the analysis conducted with the applications database.[20]

4.   EMPIRICAL STRATEGY

Many school characteristics cannot be observed by the econometrician, yet these unobservables are likely correlated with both indicators of sports success and the number of applications received by a school. The unobservable component is likely to include information about scholastic and athletic tradition, geographic advantages, and other information on the true quality of the school. Without adequately controlling for these unobservables, they would likely confound the ability to detect the impact of athletic success on the quantity and quality of incoming students. The nature of the data we have compiled allows us to plausibly control for the unobservables associated with each school.

Even after including school fixed effects and linear trends for each school, it is always worrisome that schools that perform well in sports in a given year are schools that have recently improved academically as well. If this is the case, the effects of sports success on application rates and student quality may be spurious. To try and deal with this issue, we include one-year lead sports dummy variables in our regression to estimate the effect that having sports success next year has on this year's applications. If the results suggest that future sports success does not predict current admission figures, this would lend credibility to our empirical strategy.

. . . .

Timing of the Impact of Athletic Success

. . . .

The NCAA Division I-A football season finishes at the beginning of January. The NCAA basketball tournament finishes at the end of March or beginning of April. Therefore, if these sports influence the number of applicants a school receives, we would expect an effect on the current year variables. This means that a successful football team that finishes in January or a successful basketball team that finishes in March will affect application decisions for students enrolling that fall. However, given the timing of when applications were likely prepared and submitted, and the football and basketball seasons, one would possibly expect an equally large impact of football and basketball to be on the first lag of an athletic success variable (especially for basketball, which ends three months after football). The second and third lags will give an indication of the persistence of the athletic success which occurred two to four years earlier.

5.   RESULTS

Results Using Peterson's Data

. . . For basketball, the results suggest that being one of the 64 teams in the NCAA tournament yields approximately a 1% increase in applications the following year, making it to the "Sweet 16" yields a 3% increase, the "Final Four" a 4–5% increase, and winning the tournament a 7–8% increase. The impact of the athletic lags is as we expected. Although there is an effect of winning on the current year's applications, the largest effect comes in the first lag. By the third lag, the effect has usually diminished substantially. . . . For football, the results suggest that ending the season ranked in the top 20 in football yields approximately a 2.5% increase in applications the following year, ending in the top 10 yields a 3% increase, and winning the football championship a 7–8% increase. The largest effect is on the current football sports variable, along with a small effect on the first lag. . . . The results from these regressions suggest that for basketball private schools receive two to four times as many additional applications than public schools as they advance through the NCAA tournament, while the results for football are less conclusive. Furthermore, the application impact for private schools appears to be more persistent. For example, when a private school advances to the Sweet 16, it enjoys an 8–14% increase in applications for the next four years; whereas, a public school sees only a 4% increase for the next three years.

Besides being more selective, schools might react to increased applications by increasing their enrollment or tuition levels. . . . The results indicate that teams that have basketball success do not enroll more students the following year. However, schools that perform well on the football field in a given year do increase enrollment that year. Teams that finish in the top 20, top 10, and champion in football on average enroll 3.4%, 4.4%, and 10.1% more students, respectively. These results are all significant . . . this is largely driven by public schools. This increased enrollment could come from the fact that many public schools give guaranteed admission for certain students. For example, a school that guarantees admission for in-state students with a certain class rank or test score may be required to enroll many more students if demand suddenly spikes. Another possible reason for the increased enrollment is that more of the students that a university admitted decide to actually attend that year (higher matriculation rate), which would increase enrollment.

. . . . The results suggest that private schools increase tuition following trips to the Final Four (results are also suggestive for tuition increases by private schools after winning the basketball championship) but not for football success. There is no consistent evidence that public schools adjust tuition because of sports success. However, this is likely because many public schools have political constraints on increasing tuition.

. . . . [S]chools that do well in basketball are able to recruit an incoming class with 1–4% more students scoring above 500 on the math and verbal portions of the SAT. Similarly, these schools could also expect 1–4% more of their incoming students to score above 600 on the math and verbal portions of the SAT. . . . [H]owever, to examine the effect of sports success on SAT score categories in the Peterson's data set, approximately 1600 observations of the 5335 are dropped due to missing SAT data. Therefore it is important to further examine the "quality" effect using the SAT data set.

Results Using SAT Database

. . . . The results indicate that sports success increases SAT-sending rates for all three SAT subgroups. However, the lower SAT scoring students (less than 900) respond to sports success about twice as much as the higher SAT scoring students. For example, schools that win the NCAA basketball tournament see an 18% increase a year later in sent SAT scores less than 900, a 12% increase in scores between 900 and 1100, and an 8% increase in scores over 1100. Also, private schools tend to see a larger increase in sent SAT scores after sports success than for public schools (although this does not appear to be true for the basketball championship and high SAT scores). For example, it can be seen that when a private school reaches the Sweet 16 in the NCAA basketball tournament, they have two to three times as many SAT scores sent to them as the public schools in the first and second periods after the basketball success. Furthermore, the effect tends to persist longer for the private schools than the public schools, as can be seen on lags 2 and 3. . . . A similar difference between public and private schools can be seen for football. The championship round cannot be compared, as there were no private schools that won the football championship during this time period.

Overall, these results suggest that schools that have athletic success are not receiving extra SAT scores solely from low performing students. The results also greatly strengthen the SAT results derived from the Peterson's data. It appears that athletic success does indeed present an opportunity to schools to be either more selective in their admission standards or enroll more students while keeping a fixed level of student quality.

. . . .

6. CONCLUSION AND FUTURE RESEARCH

"How does playing major college football or men's basketball in a highly commercialized, profit-seeking, entertainment environment further the educational purpose of your member institutions?" Fully answering Representative Thomas's question that he posed to the president of the NCAA is beyond the scope of this study. However, the analysis presented above does provide a set of estimates about the impact of sports success on the quantity and quality of student applications at schools participating in the premier divisions of NCAA basketball and football. These estimates reflect several indirect benefits from these high-profile college sports.

Using two unique and comprehensive data sets in conjunction with an econometric design that controls for the unobservable features of schools, we find that football and basketball success increases the quantity of applications to a school after that school achieves sports success, with estimates ranging from 2% to 8% for the top 20 football schools and the top 16 basketball schools each year.[24] We also provide evidence that the extra applications are composed of students with both low and high SAT scores. Additional evidence suggests that schools use these extra applications to increase both student quality and enrollment size. There is some evidence that private schools adjust tuition levels in response to receiving extra applications from basketball success.

A related paper (Pope and Pope 2007) shows that sports success has a heterogeneous impact on various subgroups of the incoming student population. For example, we found that males, blacks, and students that played sports in high school are more likely to be influenced by sports success than their peers. This finding, combined with the results of this paper, provides a much broader picture of the impact of sports success on the composition of the incoming student body. These results significantly extend the existing literature and provide important insights about the impact of sports success on college choice. Using identification strategies that exploit the temporal variation in our data sets and that control for unobserved school heterogeneity, it is increasingly clear that sports success does have an impact on the incoming freshman classes. It is also clear that this impact is often short lived, and that it differs by student type. This may reflect differences in the ability of various student subgroups to acquire quality information that would affect school choice, or it may simply reflect preferences for high-quality athletics.

Whether or not the expenditures required to receive these short-run indirect benefits promote efficiency in higher education was not determined in the present analysis. Indeed, the raw summary data . . . would suggest that athletically successful schools actually saw slightly slower long-run growth in applications and enrollments. Future work directed at understanding the arms-race nature of athletics within higher education and its relation to economic efficiency would certainly be valuable. Nonetheless, the results presented in this paper should be important to college administrators. Athletics is one instrument that institutions of higher education have at their disposal that can be used to directly affect reputation and the prominence of their schools. It is hoped that these results provide information that can aid administrators in making decisions about athletic programs and help them to further understand the role of athletics within higher education.

. . . .

References

Avery, C., and C. Hoxby. 2004. Do and should financial aid decisions affect students' college choices? In *College choices: The new economics of choosing, attending, and completing college,* edited by Caroline Hoxby. Chicago: University of Chicago Press, pp. 239–299.

Bremmer, D., and R. Kesselring. 1993. The advertising effect of university athletic success—A reappraisal of the evidence. *Quarterly Review of Economics and Finance* 33:40–21.

Card, D., and A. Krueger. 2004. Would the elimination of affirmative action affect highly qualified minority applicants? Evidence from California and Texas. NBER Working Paper No. 10366.

Chapman, D. 1981. A model of student college choice. *Journal of Higher Education* 52:490–503.

Coughlin, C., and O. Erekson. 1984. An examination of contributions to support intercollegiate athletics. *Southern Economic Journal* 51:180–95.

Curs, B., and L. D. Singell. 2002. An analysis of the application and enrollment process for in-state and out-of-state students at a large public university. *Economics of Education Review* 21:111–24.

Fuller, W., C. Manski, and D. Wise. 1982. New evidence on the economic determinants of post secondary schooling choices. *Journal of Human Resources* 17:477–95.

Goidel, R., and J. Hamilton. 2006. Strengthening higher education through gridiron success? Public perceptions of the impact of national football championships on academic quality. *Social Science Quarterly* 87:851–62.

McCormick, R., and M. Tinsley. 1987. Athletics versus academics? Evidence from SAT scores. *Journal of Political Economy* 95:1103–16.

McEvoy, C. 2006. The impact of elite individual athletic performance on university applicants for admission in NCAA Division I-A football. *The Sport Journal* 9(1).

Mixon, F. 1995. Athletics versus academics? Rejoining the evidence from SAT scores. *Education Economics* 3:277–83.

Mixon, F., and Y. Hsing. 1994. The determinants of out-of-state enrollments in higher education: A Tobit analysis. *Economics of Education Review* 13:329–35.

Mixon, F., and R. Ressler. 1995. An empirical note on the impact of college athletics on tuition revenues. *Applied Economics Letters* 2:383–7.

Mixon, F., and L. Trevino. 2005. From kickoff to commencement: The positive role of intercollegiate athletics in higher education. *Economics of Education Review* 24:97–102.

Mixon, F., L. Trevino, and T. Minto. 2004. Touchdowns and test scores: Exploring the relationship between athletics and academics. *Applied Economics Letters* 11:421–4.

Murphy, R., and G. Trandel. 1994. The relation between a university's football record and the size of its applicant pool. *Economics of Education Review* 13:265–70.

Pope, D., and J. Pope. 2007. Consideration set formation in the college choice process. Unpublished paper, The Wharton School and Virginia Tech.

Savoca, E. 1990. Another look at the demand for higher education: Measuring the price sensitivity of the decision to apply to college. *Economics of Education Review* 9:123–34.

Siegfried, J., and M. Getz. 2006. Where do the children of professors attend college? *Economics of Education Review* 25:201–10.

Tucker, I. 2004. A reexamination of the effect of big-time football and basketball success on graduation rates and alumni giving rates. *Economics of Education Review* 23:655–61.

Tucker, I. 2005. Big-time pigskin success. *Journal of Sports Economics* 6:222–9.

Tucker, I., and L. Amato. 1993. Does big-time success in football or basketball affect SAT scores? *Economics of Education Review* 12:177–81.

Tucker, I., and L. Amato. 2006. A reinvestigation of the relationship between big-time basketball success and average SAT scores. *Journal of Sports Economics* 7:428–40.

Zimbalist, A. 1999. *Unpaid professionals: Commercialism and conflict in big-time college sports.* Princeton, NJ: Princeton University Press.

Notes

1. For example, a history of the NCAA provided on the NCAA's official web site states, "The 1905 college football season produced 18 deaths and 149 serious injuries, leading those in higher education to question the game's place on their campuses" (http://www.ncaa.org/wps/portal). The 1905 season led to the establishment of the Intercollegiate Athletic Association of the United States (IAAUS), which eventually became the NCAA in 1910.

2. Bill Thomas is a Republican congressman from California and previous chairman of the tax-writing House Ways and Means Committee. The full letter was printed in an article entitled "Congress' Letter to the NCAA" on October 5, 2006, in *USA Today*.

3. A leading example of the anecdotal evidence has been dubbed "the Flutie effect," named after the Boston College quarterback Doug Flutie, whose exciting football play and subsequent winning of the Heisman Trophy in 1984 allegedly increased applications at Boston College by 30% the following year. Furthermore, Zimbalist (1999) notes that Northwestern University's applications jumped by 30% after they played in the 1995 Rose Bowl, and George Washington University's applications rose by 23% after its basketball team advanced to the Sweet 16 in the 1993 NCAA basketball tournament.

4. The ACC, SEC, SWC, Big Ten, Big Eight, and PAC Ten conferences were typically considered the "major" conferences in college basketball and football at that time. Today the ACC, SEC, Big Ten, Big Twelve, Big East, PAC Ten, and independent Notre Dame are considered the major conferences/teams.

5. More detail about this literature is provided in the next section.

6. In Pope and Pope (2007), we use these data to also show that sports success has a differentiated impact on various demographic subgroups of students and to illustrate the limited awareness that high school students may have with regards to the utility of attending different colleges.

7. Reputation can be thought of as either academic reputation or as social/recreational reputation.

8. Other papers in this literature (as pointed out by a referee) include Mixon, Trevino, and Minto (2004), Tucker (2004, 2005), Mixon and Trevino (2005), Goidel and Hamilton (2006), McEvoy (2006), and Tucker and Amato (2006). These papers adopt similar identification strategies for estimating the quantity and quality effects as those described in Table 13.

9. Temporal variation typically enters the regression via a variable that reflects the aggregate sports success over the 10–15 years prior to the year of the school data.

10. See, for example, Steve Stecklow's April 5, 1995, article in the *Wall Street Journal* entitled "Cheat Sheets: Colleges Inflate SATs and Graduation Rates in Popular Guidebooks."

. . . .

13. Forty-eight teams were invited in 1980, 1981, and 1982. In 1983, 52 teams were invited. In 1984, 53 teams were invited. Currently 65 teams are invited, but one of two teams is required to win an additional game before entering the round of 64.

. . . .

15. We thank David Card, Alan Krueger, the Andrew Mellon Foundation, and the College Board for help in gaining access to this data set.

. . . .

18. Less than 1% of students sent their scores to more than 14 schools.

. . . .

20. Sending an SAT score to a school is not the same as applying to that school. However, it may be a good proxy. Card and Krueger (using the same SAT test-takers data set) tested the validity of using sent SAT scores as a proxy for applications. They compared the number of SAT scores that students of different ethnicities sent with admissions records from California and Texas and administrative data on the number of applications received by ethnicity. They conclude that "trends in the number of applicants to a particular campus are closely mirrored by trends in the number of students who send their SAT scores to that campus, and that use of the probability of sending SAT scores to a particular institution as a measure of the probability of applying to that institution would lead to relatively little attenuation bias" (2004, p. 18).

. . . .

24. To put this quantity effect into perspective, the application elasticity of changes in the price of attending college found in the literature typically range from –.25 on the low end to –1.0 on the high end (see, e.g., Savoca 1990; Curs and Singell 2002). These elasticities suggest that tuition/financial aid would have to be adjusted somewhere in the range of 2–24% to obtain a similar increase in applications.

FUNDRAISING

SCOREBOARDS VS. MORTARBOARDS: MAJOR DONOR BEHAVIOR AND INTERCOLLEGIATE ATHLETICS

Jeffrey L. Stinson and Dennis R. Howard

INTRODUCTION

A recent NCAA report indicated that charitable contributions to athletic departments at Division IA schools have more than doubled over the past decade . . . Despite the substantial growth, a number of fundamental questions regarding charitable contributions to athletic programs remain relatively unexplored:

1. Who gives to educational institutions in support of academic and/or athletic programs? Is it primarily non-alumni who contribute to intercollegiate athletics programs? Is it primarily alumni who contribute to academic programs?

2. Does the improved performance of intercollegiate athletic teams, specifically high profile sports including football and/or men's and women's basketball, affect both types of giving to the educational institution?

3. Does increased giving to athletics by alumni and non-alumni have a negative impact on charitable giving to educational programs at the same institution?

This study is based on an in-depth analysis of donor behavior at a major public university whose athletic teams compete at the Division IA level. The institution under study offers a unique window of opportunity for examining the extent to which improved team performance may impact both athletic and academic fund raising. Over the past decade, the university's athletic teams, in particular football and men's and women's basketball, have achieved unparalleled success, moving from perennial middle of the pack status to regularly contending for conference and, occasionally, national championships.

A review of the literature suggests that formal hypothesis development regarding the basic questions addressed in this study is premature. Many of the assertions concerning donor behavior found in the literature lack credible empirical support, and others offer contradictory findings. The current study seeks to offer an empirical foundation for future hypothesis development and testing.

Research Question 1: Do Alumni Donors Give Primarily to Academics and Non-Alumni Donors Give Primarily to Athletics?

At Big-time U's, a small percentage, usually in single digits, of alumni contribute to the school's intercol-legiate athletics program (a similarly low percentage donates to its educational programs). However, often the main contributors to athletic departments are boosters—rabid sports fans who, unlike alumni, never attended the institution and whose interest in it focuses almost exclusively on its college sports teams (Sperber 2000, p. 258).

In two books discussing the impact of "big-time intercollegiate athletics" on colleges and universities, Sperber (1990, 2000) commented extensively on donor behavior toward both academics and athletics. Sperber (1990) asserted that fewer than 2% of alumni contribute to their alma mater's athletics program; the majority instead focused their giving on their school's academic programs. Non-alumni, on the other hand, donated almost exclusively to the intercollegiate athletic program.

This distinction in giving behavior assumes alumni are less susceptible to fluctuations in giving with changes in athletic success, as "alumni giving is independent of college sports success or failure" (Sperber 2000, p. 256). Instead, alumni giving is driven by their academic relationship to the institution. Graduates are assumed to be proud of their degrees, and wish to repay the institution through their donations. Sperber argued that schools located at or near the top of *U.S. News & World Report's* annual ranking of alumni giving at American colleges and Universities (as a percentage of alumni making a gift in the previous year) rankings tend to be known for their educational reputation as opposed to their athletic reputation. In contrast, schools with top college sports teams (Wisconsin, Michigan, and UCLA are cited), all have far lower rankings on the alumni-giving list.

The Identity Salience Model of Nonprofit Relationship Marketing Success offers one plausible explanation for this giving discrepancy (Arnett, German, & Hunt, 2003). Identity salience, a measure of the importance of an identity to self, is proposed to mediate the relationship between relationship-inducing factors and donating behavior. In the case of alumni donors, to the extent that such relationship-inducing factors as participation and organizational prestige are centered around the academic mission of the institution, as Sperber argues is the case with the *U.S. News and World Report* top schools, one would expect a more salient donor identity with academics and more charitable giving directed at academic programs.

A recent study offered empirical support for the notion that alumni giving is more heavily influenced by academic-related factors than athletic success. Rhoads and Gerking's (2000) 10-year study of 87 NCAA Division IA institutions found that academic tradition and status had a far greater impact on alumni giving than the performance of athletic teams. Carnegie level I institutions, which represent the highest level of research institution in the Carnegie

Foundation's classification system, were found to receive 41% more support per student than other institutions. Additionally, a 100-point increase in incoming student average SAT scores correlated with 51% more alumni support per student.

Brown (1991) in a study of Ball State University alumni found that the academic reputation of the institution was a primary determinant of donor behavior. A substantial majority (61%) of the alumni donors equated the university's reputation with the quality of its faculty and educational programs. Intercollegiate athletics were insignificant in determining the donor behavior of this group.

Although some evidence supports Sperber's view that alumni donations are driven by academics rather than athletics, available literature (Rhoads & Gerking 2000, Brown 1991) does not substantiate his assertion that non-alumni (sometimes referred to as boosters) give exclusively to athletics. No empirical evidence was found to support this claim. In addition, research on institutional giving to date has not recognized that alumni and non-alumni can direct a portion of their institutional gifts to both academics and athletics. It is conceivable that the pattern of institutional giving may be more complex than the simple either/or differentiation suggested in previous studies. Therefore, this research will examine the donor behavior of both alumni and non-alumni, and the extent to which each of these donor groups split their annual donations across athletics and academics.

Research Question 2: Does Winning Have a Significant Impact on Alumni Giving?

Of the three research questions examined in this study, the relationship between winning and alumni giving has received the most attention. Despite this, there is still no clear answer to how athletic success impacts alumni academic giving. The many studies conducted on this topic often contradict each other and taken together produce equivocal results as to whether successful intercollegiate athletic teams influence alumni to donate more to their alma maters.

The aforementioned Rhoads and Gerking (2000) study also examined the impact of year-to-year changes in athletic success on total giving by alumni. Significant increases in alumni donations were associated with increased athletic success. Contributions were measured as *dollars per student currently enrolled* to control for institution size. A football bowl game win was found to raise alumni contributions per student by 7.3%, while alumni contributions fell 13.6% when a basketball team was placed on probation.

Grimes and Chressanthis (1994) also offered support for the positive impact of athletic success. The authors studied the giving patterns of Mississippi State University alumni from 1962-1991, and found that total contributions were positively related to the overall winning percentage of major (basketball, football, and baseball) intercollegiate athletic teams. The researchers found that each one percent increase in overall winning percentage of the three teams

was correlated with a substantial, significant increase in total giving to the institution.

In contrast, several studies have concluded that no significant relationship exists between athletic success and giving to the institution. As part of a comprehensive study of higher education, Shulman and Bowen (2001) examined giving data from eight private, academically selective colleges and universities that compete athletically at the NCAA Division IA level. Athletic success was found to be an insignificant factor in alumni giving. However, it is quite possible that the findings were a function of the elite academic nature of the schools included in Shulman and Bowen's study. All eight schools were among the most prestigious higher education institutions in the U.S., including several Ivy League schools, Stanford, and Northwestern. Each of these schools has higher levels of academic than athletics prestige. Some of the schools offer only academic scholarships. Consistent with the Arnett et al.'s (2003) Identity Salience Model, we expect donor behavior to follow the institutional focus on academics at these institutions and donors to direct their dollars to maintain the academic prestige of the university.

Two earlier studies also support the general lack of relationship between athletic success and charitable behavior among alumni. In a study of the annual campaigns of 135 schools, Sigelman and Carter (1979) found no relationship between athletic success and increased alumni giving. Gaski and Etzel (1984) examined 99 NCAA Division I institutions for donor behavior by alumni status (alumni vs. non-alumni) and fund type (annual fund vs. other), concluding that there was no evidence of the impact of athletic success on overall giving. While the influence of winning on alumni donor behavior is not clear, Gaski and Etzel (1984) remains the only study to date that has examined athletic team performance on the donor behavior of non-alumni.

The current study provides an empirical basis for examining whether winning has a differential influence on alumni *and* non-alumni and how such differences manifest themselves in the giving behavior of the two groups. Are non-alums, with few or no academic ties to the university, more sensitive to the fortunes of the institution's athletic teams? Does winning encourage greater overall financial support to just the institution's athletic program or does athletic success also spur more giving to academic programs? The intent of this study is to examine these questions and provide a deeper understanding of the relationship between intercollegiate athletic success and donor behavior.

Research Question 3: Does Athletics Giving Undermine Giving to Academics?

Sperber (2000) asserted that athletic departments "actively undermine efforts to raise money from alumni for educational programs" (p. 259). Labeling this the "college-sports-equals-alumni-giving myth," he noted an increasing focus by athletic departments on wealthy alumni to support larger programs and facilities. He contended that after securing a major gift for a new athletic facility from a particular alumnus it would be unlikely for that same individual to donate a major gift to an academic unit of the institution.

Additionally, Sperber (2000) suggested that the highly publicized athletic programs of most Division IA institutions could result in alumni cutting their gifts in times of negative publicity. He offered the case of Southern Methodist University where alumni giving to academics dropped following the football team receiving the death penalty—the severest of NCAA sanctions that completely shuts down a program for a period of time—in the 1980s. Furthermore, during the pre-scandal winning years, alumni giving to academics did not increase.

The opposite side of the spectrum is offered by Shulman and Bowen (2001), who write, "There is certainly no indication in the data we have collected that private giving to athletics today is so substantial (in either the number of donors or the size of the average gift) that it is likely to detract in any substantial way from fundraising for broader educational purposes" (Shulman & Bowen, 2001, p. 215).

As the quote indicates, Shulman and Bowen (2001) found no significant impact of giving to athletic programs on giving to academic programs at the eight Division IA schools included in their sample. The authors classified alumni gifts as either athletic or academic. There was no significant reduction in giving to academics associated with giving to athletics; thus, the authors concluded that no relationship between the two types of giving exists.

However, their findings might be a function of the very narrow range of schools in the sample. All eight schools included in their analysis are heavily endowed, academically elite, private institutions, leading the authors to note "the practices and leading issues in the Division IA schools are qualitatively different from those of the other institutions [in this study]" (p. xxiv). If the assumption that alumni donors give predominantly to academic programs is true, the schools in this sample may be less susceptible to any decline in academic giving as athletic contributions rise. It remains untested whether such a situation would hold at a public institution with much lower levels of alumni support. Yet these factors seem to contribute to the authors conclusion that "[i]t would be comforting to assume that the apparent lack of competition for gifts between athletics and other institutional purposes would continue into the future. Unfortunately, we do not think such confidence is warranted" (Shulman & Bowen, 2001, pg. 38).

Finally, one earlier study by McCormick and Tinsley (1990) found that giving to athletics had a positive impact on academic giving, estimating that a 10% increase in giving to athletics was associated with a 5% increase in academic giving. The authors examined alumni giving data at Clemson University, in South Carolina, for the time period 1979–1983.

As with the impact of athletic success on donor behavior, the limited empirical evidence considering the impact of donations to athletics on academic giving is less than clear. The current study seeks to directly examine the relationship between the two types of giving for both alumni and non-alumni.

AN EXAMINATION OF UNIVERSITY OF OREGON DONORS

The sample for this study includes all donors making gifts of $1000 or more between 1994 and 2002 to the Annual Giving Program at the University of Oregon. The university conducted a capital campaign ending in 1998. However, large, non-recurrent capital gifts (both athletic and academic) donated as part of the campaign were not classified as annual gifts and, therefore, not included as part of the database used in this study.

A minimum $1000 gift to the Annual Giving Program entitles the donor to membership in the President's Club and represents the first category of major donation at the University of Oregon. The number of major donors has grown from 779 in 1994 to 2,309 in 2002. In addition, major donors were found not only to give more but to also give more consistently than those making smaller annual contributions. Major donors had a significantly greater propensity to make recurrent annual gifts than minor donors, making this subset of donors a more relevant sample for examining the research questions under consideration in this study. Furthermore, while major donors constitute only 4.3% of the total number making gifts to the University, these donors contribute 72% of the total charitable revenues.

The entire giving history of each donor making an annual gift of $1000 or more during the selected time frame was extracted from the University's Benefactor database, compiled and managed by the University of Oregon Foundation, which is the academic fundraising body at the university. Each gift was subsequently coded as made by an alumnus or non-alumnus, and donations were divided into three giving areas.

- *Athletic gifts* represent gifts directed towards the athletic department, including all gifts made to the athletic fundraising entity, the Duck Athletic Fund.

- *Academic gifts* represent all gifts directed towards an academic program or unit, as well as all undirected gifts that may be used at the discretion of the university president.

- *Other gifts* are those donations directed at a non-academic, non-athletic unit of the University. Examples include the university theatre, the art museum and the Oregon Bach Festival.

Fiscal year 1994 was selected as the starting point for analysis as it represented the first year for which reliable giving data on all donors to the University of Oregon Foundation was available.

The University of Oregon is a mid-size public research institution that sponsors 15 National Collegiate Athletic Association (NCAA) Division I varsity athletic programs. Oregon offers a unique and interesting opportunity to examine the relationship between athletic success, athletic fundraising, and academic fundraising. The combination of unprecedented athletic success and major athletic fundraising efforts during the sampling period provides a rare window in which to examine the research questions of interest. No major changes in the university's academic program (i.e., change in Carnegie classification) occurred during the time period considered in this study, creating an unintended natural experimental condition in which to examine the potential influence of athletic-related success on academic fundraising.

The 1994 season began an unprecedented run of success for the Oregon football program. The team played in the Rose Bowl for the first time in 40 years in 1995. Over the next seven seasons, the Oregon football team compiled a 69 and 27 record, winning two conference championships and playing in five bowl games. In 2001, the Oregon football team compiled an 11 and 1 record and ended the season ranked #2 in the nation. In 2002, the athletic department completed a $90-million expansion of Autzen Stadium. In the ten years prior to 1994, the Oregon football team had only four winning seasons, compiling a record of 58 wins and 57 losses. In 1995, the men's basketball team advanced to the NCAA Championship tournament for the first time in 34 years. From 1995–96 through 2001–02, the Oregon basketball team played in four post-season tournaments, advancing to the National Invitational Tournament Final Four in 1999 and to the NCAA Elite Eight in 2002. A campaign to fund construction of a new basketball arena was announced in early 2003.

The fortunate circumstance of having detailed donor records available at the onset of the athletic teams' run of success provided a unique opportunity for directly examining the relationship between team performance and donor behavior related to both academic and athletic giving. As noted by Grimes and Chressanthis (1994) and Brooker and Klastorin (1981), while the focus on a single institution may result in the loss of reliability in generalizing the results, universities that share many common characteristics are more likely to experience similar patterns in the receipt of charitable donations. Stake (1983) argued that when there is a need to generalize only to similar cases as opposed to a population of cases, a single-institution study is an acceptable form of inquiry. The University of Oregon shares many characteristics with other public research institutions supporting NCAA Division I athletic programs, and while future research should include additional institutions, only the data from one school were considered in this study. Therefore, while the specific results of this study may not be generalizable to other institutions, similar findings at similar institutions would not be surprising.

Research Question 1

. . . [T]he data indicate that both alumni and non-alumni give to both academics and athletics, though, clearly, there are significant differences in the giving behavior of the two groups. In all but two years (1994, 1996), alumni made significantly higher gifts to academics than non-alumni, and in every year since 1994, alumni allocated a significantly larger portion of their total gift to academics than non-alumni. On the other hand, non-alumni allocated a significantly higher percentage of their total gift to athletics every sample year. However, in terms of actual average gift amount, non-alums only made a significantly higher gift to athletics in the final year of the sample (2002). Thus, the assumption that alumni give primarily to academic programs while non-alumni give primarily to intercollegiate athletic programs partially holds. Alumni do give predominantly more to academics, but they also donate large amounts, both in terms of average gift amount and percent of total gift, to intercollegiate athletics.

Further analysis shows that in the most recent year, 38.7% of alumni allocated their entire gift to the athletics program and 69.5% of alumni allocated at least a portion of their gift to athletics, suggesting higher alumni participation in athletic fundraising at Oregon than the 2% asserted by Sperber (2000). Over 36% of non-alumni in 2002 allocated at least a portion of their gift to a non-athletic program. Together, these results clearly demonstrate that both alumni and non-alumni give to both academics and athletic programs, and that a simple alumni/non-alumni dichotomy is not an adequate explanation of donor behavior.

The data were then analyzed by allocation groups . . . : a group allocating their entire gift to academics, a group allocating their entire gift to athletics, and a group making a split gift (both athletic and academic). No statistical differences were found between alumni and non-alumni allocating their entire gift to athletics or academics. It appears that only in the case of split gifts is the alumni/non-alumni distinction significant in donor behavior.

Research Question 2

In this era of increasing athletic success at the University of Oregon, more alumni give more to athletics, suggesting that alumni giving may indeed be influenced by athletic success. In 1994, 58.5% of alumni donors in the sample allocated at least a portion of their gift to the intercollegiate athletics program. This percentage has risen steadily to the 69.5% of alumni donors in the sample making a gift to athletics in 2002. In terms of real donors, 297 alumni donors donated to athletics in 1994; 962 alumni made a gift to athletics in 2002. This was in a time period where growth in total alumni donors making annual gifts of $1000 or more increased by 877 donors, suggesting that virtually every new alumni donor at this level allocated at least a portion of their gift to athletics, in addition to some previous donors who began allocating some of their gift to athletics. Finally, the average donation to athletics by this group grew from $1010.11 in 1994 to $1773.55 in 2002. In almost every way, alumni giving to athletics has increased with an associated increase in success by the high profile intercollegiate athletic teams at the University of Oregon.

While more subtle, athletic success may also be influencing academic giving by alumni. . . . The percentage of alumni donors making an academic gift has fallen from 73.2% to 61.3% since 1994. The number of alumni donors making gifts of $1,000 or more to academics has increased during the time period from 372 to 863, an increase of 491. However, this lags far behind the increase of 666 alumni donors making a major gift to the athletic department during the same time period. Still, in terms of average academic gift amount, alumni have been relatively stable, with average gifts ranging from $1427.27 to $1710.00. These data suggest a possible neutral to negative influence of athletic success on academic giving by alumni. Either way, it is clear athletic success has not had a strong positive impact on alumni giving to academic programs.

Research Question 3

Thus, we turn to an examination of the relationship between giving to athletic programs and giving to academic programs. The data . . . provide strong support for the assumption that giving to athletics undermines giving to academics, particularly for non-alumni. Over the time period considered, the average academic gift by non-alumni has fallen significantly, while the average gift to athletics has significantly increased. Since 1994, the average academic gift by a non-alum has fallen $671.35, while the average non-alum gift to athletics has increased $962.88. While the effects of winning athletic seasons on alumni donations are not quite as dramatic, the trends suggest that amounts donated to athletics are negatively associated with alumni decisions related to academic giving. There has been no significant change in alumni giving to academics in terms of total dollars donated. However, alumni have significantly increased their giving to athletics, and now donate a significantly larger percentage of their gift to the athletic department. In 1994, 40.4% of the average alum gift was targeted to intercollegiate athletics. By 2002, alums donated 56.7% of their gift to athletics.

It is clear that proportional giving by alums increasingly favors athletics . . . . Fiscal year 2002 saw an *increase* in total dollars donated by alumni of over $840,000. Over 81% of this incremental revenue was directed toward the intercollegiate athletic department. This resembles the allocation of incremental revenue by non-alumni, who allocated 83.9% of their additional giving to athletics. For every $100 of new revenue raised from major donors by the University of Oregon, over 80% is being directed to the athletic department.

Even with the large increases in numbers of total donors since 1994, academic giving struggles to remain stable while donations to athletics experience huge growth. In three out of the past five years (1998, 2000, 2001), the total dollars donated to academics by non-alumni has fallen despite annual increases in the number of non-alumni donors. Total dollars donated to academics by alumni fell in only one year (2000), again despite an increase in the total number of donors. This suggests new donors are not making academic gifts, and current donors are shifting dollars from academic giving to donations directed to the athletic program. Additionally, as discussed above, proportional giving by alumni is predominantly directed to the athletic program. If these trends continue, total academic giving will fall for both alumni and non-alumni despite continued increases in the total numbers of both types of donors.

Further analysis examined the number of donors allocating their entire gift to either intercollegiate athletics or academics . . . . Since 1994, the percentage of alumni donors allocating their entire gift to athletics has increased from 26.8% to 38.7%. During that same time period, the percentage of alumni allocating their entire gift to academics has fallen from 41.5% to 30.5%. Together, these findings are most likely the result of one or both of the following effects: some alumni are reducing or eliminating gifts to academics while increasing gifts to athletics, and/or some previous academic donors have stopped contributing and new alumni donors are making more gifts to athletics than academics. The pattern is similar for non-alumni, where the percentage allocating their entire gift to athletics has risen from 42.1% to 63.5%, and the corresponding percentage of non-alumni donors allocating their entire gift to academics has fallen from 26.6% to 12.8%. Increased giving to athletics is negatively associated with the academic giving of both alumni and non-alumni at the University of Oregon.

Again, the data were further analyzed by reducing donors to a group donating their entire gift to athletics, a group donating their entire gift to academics and a group splitting their gift. As discussed above, for both alumni and non-alumni the percentage of donors allocating their entire gift to athletics has increased while the percentage allocating their entire gift to academics has decreased. The percentage of alumni split-gift donors has remained relatively stable. However, the percentage of non-alumni split-gift donors has fallen to less than 25%, suggesting that non-alumni donors making a first gift to athletics are not subsequently making gifts to academics.

Furthermore, alumni split-gift donors are favoring athletics in the allocation of their split gift . . . . The percentage of gift allocated by alumni split-gift donors to athletics has risen from 38.1% to 52.9% of the total gift, while the percentage allocated to academics has fallen from 55.4% to 31.7%. In terms of actual dollars, alumni split-gift donors made an average gift to athletics of $1183.33 in 1994. That amount rose to an average gift of $2237.66 in 2002. Academic gifts, on the other hand, fell from $1721.89 in 1994 to $1340.98 in 2002. Again, the data show an increase in giving to athletics associated with reduced academic giving—even by alumni.

The overwhelming conclusion that can be drawn from this data is, at least at the University of Oregon, the increasing success of athletics-related fundraising has been and is associated with reduced giving to the academic mission of the institution. Perhaps most troubling is the possible negative influence on alumni giving. While lagging behind the significant changes in non-alumni donor behavior, all of the trends suggest that alumni giving behavior is moving in a similar direction—toward athletics.

With respect to the three research questions, the following conclusions are offered:

- Both alumni and non-alumni make gifts to both athletic and academic programs. Nearly 70% of alumni donors examined made a gift to the intercollegiate athletic department, casting doubt on the assertion that only a small percentage of alumni make athletics related gifts.

- At least contextually, there is evidence that a winning program may significantly influence the giving behavior of alumni. Alumni appear to give significantly more to the athletics program as program success increases. Alumni academic giving may not be influenced as strongly, though there are some indications that athletic success may encourage a reallocation of donors' institutional contributions with a discernable shift toward athletics.

- Both alumni and non-alumni show an increasing preference toward directing their gifts to the intercollegiate athletics department - at the expense of the donations to academic programs. Sperber's (2000) assertion that giving to athletics undermines academic giving is strongly supported.

IMPLICATIONS

The current study yields several important implications for future research. Issues surrounding donor motivations and institutional cultivation strategies will be critical to both a conceptual and practical understanding of institutional fundraising.

Most studies investigating the motives of donors to athletic programs have found at least some component of tangible benefit to the donor as a main determinant of the donor's behavior. Most recently, Mahony, Gladden, and Funk (2003) and Gladden, Mahony, and Apostolopoulou (2003) identify priority seating for football and basketball as the most important motive for an athletic department contribution, overwhelming any social motives. Earlier research on the Athletics Contributions Questionnaire Revised Edition II (Staurowsky, Parkhouse, & Sachs, 1996) and the Motivation of Athletics Donors (Verner, Hecht, & Fansler, 1998) both revealed a social motive for giving, defined by Staurowsky, Parkhouse, and Sachs as "the social interaction that occurs for people who follow teams and attend games" (pg. 270). However, both studies included one or more factors that could be considered tangible in nature. The availability of tangible benefit to the potential donor may in fact be pulling donors to make gifts to athletics instead of academics, where tangible benefit often requires more significant giving. A focus on tangible benefits offers one possible explanation for our findings. In exchange for a $1000 gift to the University of Oregon athletic department, a donor receives access to preferential seating at athletic events, preferred parking, and invitations to athletics-related social events. On the other hand, a $1000 gift to an academic unit, while entitling the donor to recognition as a member of the President's Club is accompanied by little if any tangible benefit. Therefore, the exchange, from the donor's perspective, may be seen as more valuable for a gift to athletics than to academics. Interestingly, athletic donors in the Gladden et al. (2003) study listed both a desire to help student-athletes in the form of scholarships and educational opportunity, and supporting the university as a whole in the top five reasons for making a donation. Future research should examine both whether donors are aware of any separation in athletic versus academic giving, and if donor behavior would change if such distinctions were more salient. It is quite plausible that donors view a donation to the athletic department as the best of both worlds: the donor is helping students and the university while at the same time receiving significant personal benefit. Such a view would help explain the shifts to athletic donations observed at the University of Oregon.

Furthermore, it is possible that our results begin to offer clarification to the model of individual donor behavior proposed by Brady et al. (2002). The authors propose a joint effects model of donor behavior to higher education institutions, whereby donors use both a services model focused on service value and satisfaction, and a philanthropic effects model centered on organizational identification, perceived need, and philanthropic predisposition in forming intent to give. However, no clarification of when their services model or philanthropic effects model would predominate over the other in explaining donor behavior was offered. It seems plausible, if not likely, that donations made in exchange for tangible donor benefit would be more subject to the services model than to the philanthropic effects model. Such reasoning would be consistent with our results of increased athletic giving associated with increased athletic winning, and with earlier studies indicating a positive relationship between winning and giving (Rhoads & Gerking, 2000; Grimes & Chressanthis, 1994). Academic giving, on the other hand, appears to be more dominated by the philanthropic effects model, suggesting these donations may be less susceptible to the fluctuations in athletic success. Again, this argument would be consistent with the alumni academic giving at the University of Oregon.

In an environment of heavy competition for donors and their gifts (Greenfield, 2002), the ability of athletic departments to offer a valuable tangible benefit in exchange for a gift may attract donors who would otherwise make an academic gift. This suggests that the organizational structure of the institution's development department may be an important factor. Where athletic and academic development officers have differing reporting structures, competition may more easily ensue, allowing athletics to capitalize on the more valuable tangible benefits typically available to athletics donors than to academic donors. Where both athletics and academic fundraisers report through the same lines, more cooperation would be expected, perhaps minimizing the negative impact to academic giving, either by offering similar tangible benefit for academic gifts, or by controlling the extent to which tangible benefits are offered for athletics gifts.

Consistent with the above argument is a need to better understand the role of athletics fundraising in recruiting donors to the institution. Two commonly prevailing views of the benefit of athletic fundraising are that it brings new donors to the institution, and that it captures funds that would not have been donated to the institution through other mechanisms (i.e., academic giving). The evidence at the University of Oregon suggests that while athletics-based fundraising has been successful at recruiting new institutional donors, such recruitment is coming at a price to academic giving. Our data suggest the institution is not successfully transitioning new donors from athletics only into split donors (academics and athletics). Future research needs to more clearly examine if, when and how this transition takes place, both from a donor decision-making view, and from an institutional cultivation view. The literature on social identification and identity salience may be relevant, with a key question being: Is it possible to move from a state of identification with a specific team or department, to a broader relationship with the institution as a whole? To the extent that organizational identification and identity salience drive donor behavior (Arnett et al, 2003; Mael & Ashforth, 1992), the nature and direction of identification may be crucial determinants in cultivating athletic donors to also support the academic mission of the institution.

CONCLUSION

While the data considered in this study came from only one institution, and therefore lack generalizability, we would expect to identify similar trends at other, similar institutions across the U.S. The results of this single-institution study indicate the need for future research that includes a broader cross-section of NCAA IA institutions to clarify the impact of intercollegiate athletics and athletics-related giving on academic giving to the sponsoring institution.

Future work needs to focus on the differing decision processes and motives for giving by alumni and non-alumni, as well as differences between athletic, academic, and split-gift donors. The data considered in this study are entirely historical, and while valuable in identifying trends in giving behavior, they provide little insight into donor decision processes and motivations. Additionally, this work should be expanded and included in research on the impact of successful intercollegiate athletic teams on donor behavior. The role of athletic success in influencing giving behavior needs to be further clarified, considering the susceptibility of different groups to changing gift patterns based on athletic team success. Finally, this research only included donors making annual gifts of $1,000 more. Future research should investigate whether lower level donors exhibit similar or different giving behaviors.

References

Arnett, D. B., German, S. D., & Hunt, S. D. (2003). The identity salience model of relationship marketing success: The case of nonprofit marketing. *Journal of Marketing, 67*, 89–105.

Brady, M. K., Noble, C. H., Utter, D. J., & Smith, G. E. (2002). How to give and receive: An exploratory study of charitable hybrids. *Psychology & Marketing, 19*, 919–944.

Brooker, G., & Klastorin, T. D. (1981). To the victors belong the spoils? College athletics and alumni giving. *Social Science Quarterly, 62*, 744–50.

Brown, I. D. (1991). Targeting university alumni segments that donate for non-athletic reasons. *Journal of Professional Service Marketing, 7*, 89–97.

Fulks, D. L. (2000). *Revenues and expenses of Division I and II intercollegiate athletics programs: Financial trends and relationships—1999,* Overland Park, KS: The National Collegiate Athletic Association.

Gaski, I. E., Etzel, M. J. (1984). Collegiate athletic success and alumni generosity: Dispelling the myth. *Social Behavior and Personality, 12*, 29–38.

Gladden, J. M., Mahony, D. F., & Apostolopoulou, A. (2003). *Toward a better understanding of college athletic donors: What are the primary motives?* Unpublished manuscript.

Greenfield, I. M. (2002). *The nonprofit handbook: Fundraising,* 3rd Edition, New York: Wiley.

Grimes, P. W., & Chressanthis, G.A. (1994). Alumni contributions to academics: The role of intercollegiate sports and NCAA sanctions. *American Journal of Economics and Sociology, 53*, 27–41.

Mael, F., & Ashforth, B. E. (1992). Alumni and their alma mater: A partial test of the reformulated model of organizational identification. *Journal of Organizational Behavior, 13*, 103–123.

Mahony, D. F., Gladden, J. M., & Funk, D. C. (2003). Examining athletic donors at NCAA Division I institutions. *International Sports Journal, 7*(1), 9–27.

McCormick, R. E., & Tinsley, M. (1990). Athletics and academics: A model of university contributions. In B.L. Goff & R.D. Tollison (Eds.), *Sportometics* (pp. 193–206). College Station, TX: Texas A&M University Press.

Rhoads, T. A., & Gerking, S. (2000). Educational contributions, academic quality and athletic success. *Contemporary Economic Policy, 18*, 248–59.

Shulman, J. L., & Bowen, W. G. (2001). *The game of life.* Princeton, NJ: Princeton University Press.

Shulman, J. L., & Bowen, W. G. (2001). The misfortunes of collegiate athletics. *Case Currents,* (27), 34–41.

Sigelman, L., & Carter, R. (1979). Win one for the giver? Alumni giving and big-time college sports. *Social Science Quarterly, 60*, 284–94.

Sperber, M. (1990). *College sports inc.* New York: Henry Holt.

Sperber, M. (2000). *Beer and circus: The impact of big-time college sports on undergraduate education.* New York: Henry Holt.

Stake, R.E. (1983). The case study method in social inquiry. In G.F. Madaus, M. Scriven, & D.L. Stuffelbeam (Eds.), *Evaluation Models* (pp. 279–286). Boston: Kluwer-Nijhoff Publishing.

Staurowsky, E. J., Parkhouse, B., & Sachs, M. (1996). Developing an instrument to measure athletic donor behavior and motivation. *Journal of Sport Management, 10*, 262–277.

Verner, M. E., Hecht, J. B., & Fransler, A. G. (1998). Validating an instrument to assess the motivation of athletic donors. *Journal of Sport Management, 12*, 123–137.

EMPHASIS ON INTERCOLLEGIATE ATHLETICS

THE IMPACT OF RECLASSIFICATION FROM DIVISION II TO I-AA AND FROM DIVISION I-AA TO I-A ON NCAA MEMBER INSTITUTIONS FROM 1993 TO 2003

INTRODUCTION

Purpose of Study

Recent years have seen a number of National Collegiate Athletic Association (NCAA) Division II institutions seeking reclassification to Division I-AA and Division I-AA institutions moving to Division I-A. Yet, other schools that seem like natural candidates to reclassify have resisted.[1] The purpose of this study is to investigate the impact of the reclassification process on both the financial and non-financial well-being of the reclassifying institutions from 1993 to 2003. We discuss the differences between divisions, the reclassification process, and the perceived incentives for reclassification, and also address previous research validating and contradicting the perceived incentives for Division I membership in terms of financial wealth, enhanced stature, increased enrollment, higher academic standards for applicants, etc. Our analysis suggests that while revenues tend to increase after reclassification, they are subsumed by cost increases such that net profits decline for reclassifying institutions. Though we provide evidence of some increase in enrollment diversity, it is far from overwhelming. We conclude that the primary benefit of reclassifying is an unquantifiable perceived increase in prestige.

NCAA Division Differences

"A basic purpose of this Association is to maintain intercollegiate athletics as an integral part of the educational program and the athlete as an integral part of the student body and, by so doing, retain a clear line of demarcation between intercollegiate athletics and professional sports." (Bylaw 1.3.1)

The purpose of the NCAA is consistent across the 1,000 member institutions, but the application of this purpose varies philosophically, operationally and legislatively by the three membership divisions—Division I, II and III. An overgeneralization would describe Division I as the wealthiest division providing athletics scholarships and as the most heavily legislated. Division II also provides athletics scholarships

with fewer financial resources and less legislation. Division III is the least legislated and does not offer athletics scholarships.[2] The three divisions of the NCAA federated in 1996 to increase individual division autonomy. The separation included reconstruction of the governance structure and the legislative process. Each division has become more independent and unique as the following descriptions will demonstrate. (See **Figure 1** for NCAA Membership Requirements.)

Division II Membership

The Division II philosophy states that intercollegiate athletics should be based on educational principles and practices consistent with the mission of the university to serve the welfare of the student-athlete. The philosophy statement lists 10 principles with overriding commitments to the following:

- academic success and personal development of the student-athlete
- equitable athletics opportunities for all students
- competition against other Division II institutions
- proper balance between athletics and campus life
- the awarding of athletics financial aid
- institutional control of intercollegiate athletics
- embracing the Division II philosophy (Bylaw 20.10)

The Division II philosophy is paired with two operational membership requirements concerning 1) sport sponsorship and 2) financial aid allocation. Division II institutions must offer a total of 10 teams, which must consist of (a) four varsity sports consisting of two team sports of all-male or mixed teams of males and females; and (b) six varsity sports consisting of two team sports of all-female or mixed teams of males and females. Division II institutions can also choose to balance their sport sponsorship by offering five primarily male teams and five primarily female teams (Bylaw 20.10.3). To meet sport sponsorship requirements, the sport must provide the appropriate number of participant opportunities and meet the scheduled contests limits. In terms of athletically related financial aid, Division II institutions must award 50 percent of the maximum allowable equivalencies (or scholarships) in four separate sports, two of which must be for women's sports. The total expenditures for the athletically related financial aid must be worth a minimum of $250,000, including $125,000 in women's sports (Bylaw 20.10.1.2). Relative to Division I, Division II is less regulated, likely a result of

	Sports Sponsorship: Number of Sports			Football scheduling requirement	Football attendance requirement
	All-male or mixed-team sports	All-female sports	Minimum number of team sports		
Division I	7	7	2-All male/mixed 2-All female		
	OR				
	6	8			
Football Bowl Subdivision (FBS)	8 Including football	8	2-All male/mixed 2-All female	At least 60% of all games must be played against FBS members and at least five home games against members of FBS	Average 15,000 in actual or paid attendance for home football games over a rolling two-year period
	OR				
	7 Including football	9			
	OR				
	6 Including football	10			
Football Championship Subdivision (FCS)	7 Including football	7			
	OR				
	6 Including football	8	2-All male/mixed 2-All female	At least 50% of all games must be played against FBS or FCS members	NONE

*For institutions that depend on exceptional amounts of Federal assistance to meet students' financial needs, the institution must provide a minimum of one-half of the required grants or aggregate expenditures cited in (a), (b) or (c) above. This provision shall be applicable to an institution in a given year if the average per-student allotment of Pell Grant dollars for undergraduates reported to the U.S. Department of Education the previous September is more than one standard deviation above the mean for all reporting Division I member institutions that year. If an institution does not qualify under this provision after having been able to do so the previous year, the institution may continue to utilize this alternative for one year and shall not be required to meet the provisions of (a), (b) or (c) until the following year. This provision shall be applicable only to institutions that were members of Division I on September 1, 1990.

Figure 1   General Requirements for Division Membership

fewer concerns with competitive equity and more institutional control to govern athletically related activities.

Division I Membership

The Division I philosophy calls for a balance of competitive equity and student-athlete well-being. The philosophy statement lists eight principles committed to the following:

- academic quality
- athletics excellence
- service to the public
- extensive athletics opportunities
- spectator/revenue producing sport objectives
- competition against other Division I opponents
- self-sufficient operations
- respect for all divisions while sustaining Division I principles for current membership and for institutions aspiring to be Division I members

Men's basketball scheduling requirement		Women's basketball scheduling requirement		Scheduling requirement—sports other than football and basketball	Financial aid requirement*
Provisional member:	All but two games against Division I teams and except for the first two years of provisional membership, at least 1/3 of all contests must be played in home arena	Provisional member:	All but two games against Division I teams	Sports used to meet sports sponsorship criteria: Each contest against Division I team to meet minimum number of contests	a) 50% of maximum allowable grants in each sport** or b) Minimum aggregate expenditure of $1,148,451 (with at least $574,225 in women's sports) in 2009-10 (excluding football and men's and women's basketball). Grant value may not be less than 38 full grants (with at least 19 for women)*** or c) Equivalent of 25 full grants in men's sports and 25 full grants in women's sports (exclusive of grants in football and men's and women's basketball)****
Active member:	All but four games against Division I teams and at least 1/3 of all contests must be played in home arena	Active member:	All but four games against Division I teams	50% of remaining contests against Division I opponents	
					In addition to Division I requirement, a) Provide an average of at least 90% of permissible maximum number of football grants-in-aid over rolling two-year period and b) Annually offer a minimum of 200 athletics grants-in-aid or spend $4 million on athletics grants-in-aid annually
					No additional requirements

** If an institution uses indoor track and field, outdoor track and field and cross country to meet the financial aid criterion, it must award the equivalent of at least 80% of the full grants for men and 80% of the full grants for women in these sports. If the institution counts two of those three sports to meet the financial aid criterion, it must award the equivalent of at least 70% of the full grants for men and 70% of the full grants for women. If the institution counts indoor and outdoor track and field as one sport, it must award the equivalent of at least 50% of the full grants for men and 50% of the full grants for women.

*** If the institution does not sponsor men's or women's basketball, the minimum aggregate expenditure must be $758,213 in 2009-10 for men or for women, but no fewer than the equivalent of 29 full grants for men or for women.

**** If the institution does not sponsor men's or women's basketball, it must provide a minimum of 35 full grants in men's sports and 35 full grants in women's sports.

Figure 1 (*Continued*)

Source: 2009–2010 *NCAA Division I Manual*, Figure 20-1, p. 317. © National Collegiate Athletic Association. 2008–2010. All rights reserved.

The delicate balance between revenue production through the entertainment market and protection of the educational intent of intercollegiate athletics has led to increased legislation in personnel, amateurism, recruiting, eligibility, financial aid, awards and benefits, playing and practice seasons, and postseason competition. (See Division I Manual for further explanation).

Division I is further classified in terms of football sponsorship by Division I-A, Division I-AA and Division I-AAA. Division I-A offers the highest level of sponsorship in terms of number of participants and financial resources. Division I-AA offers fewer football scholarships than Division I-A and does not have the stadium attendance restriction. Division I-AAA institutions do not offer football, but can offer all other Division I athletics opportunities. The Division I membership requirements include sport sponsorship of 14 teams, competition scheduling against Division I institutions and financial aid requirements. Division I-A has additional football sponsorship requirements.

Division I-AA

Division I-AA institutions can choose to balance their 14-sport sponsorship by offering at least seven primarily male teams and seven primarily female teams (Bylaw

20.9.7). Division I-AA institutions must award 50 percent of the maximum allowable equivalencies (or scholarships) in 14 separate sports. The aggregated expenditures for the athletically related financial aid is a minimum of $877,000, ($438,000 for women's sports), excluding men's football and basketball, or in terms of full grants, 25 grants for men's sports, other than football and men's basketball, and 25 grants for women's sports (Bylaw 20.10.1.2).

Division I-A

A Division I-A institution must offer a total of 16 teams, which must consist of at least six varsity sports, containing two team sports of all-male or mixed teams of males and females and eight varsity sports, containing two team sports of all-female or mixed teams of males and females (20.9.6).

To meet sport sponsorship requirements, the sport must provide the appropriate number of participant opportunities and meet the scheduled contests limits. Athletics financial aid for sports other than football is the same as Division I-AA. Division I-A football, however, must allocate 90 percent of the 200 athletics grants over a two-year period, and these grants must total $4 million. Division I-A football requirements also include an average actual attendance of 15,000 for all home football games, and the institution must perform an annual certification audit to validate the attendance record.

Reclassification Process

The reclassification process is a five-year educational program with the purpose of assisting institutions with the transition to the philosophy of the new division and its rules compliance and operations. Institutions applying for Division I membership are reviewed by the Division I Management Council to ensure the "readiness" of becoming a Division I institution. The reclassification process is based on three principles: 1) to involve the institution's president, athletics director, faculty athletics representative, senior woman administrator and compliance personnel; 2) to establish a timeline for the transition; and 3) to provide guidance in terms of the Division I philosophy, Division I membership regulations, development of institutional compliance policies and promotion of campus-wide involvement.

Reclassification Requirements

The reclassification process contains seven educational activities that must be completed to meet active membership status in addition to meeting Division I legislative compliance. First, the institutional officials must attend annual orientation sessions for education on the Division I philosophy, membership requirements and issues concerning Division I athletics. Second, the institution must submit an annual strategic plan of implementing the Division I philosophy and operating principles. Third, annual attendance to the NCAA Convention by all of the institution's officials is required. Fourth, the institution must receive instruction in and

demonstrate knowledge of NCAA Division I rules. Fifth, the institution must devise a compliance education system and self-assessment plan to ensure Division I compliance in the future. Sixth, at the end of the reclassification process, the institution must complete an NCAA certification visit, during which the Division I certification team will visit the campus to evaluate the capacity of the reclassifying institution to operate at the Division I level. Seventh, the institution must verify it has met Division I membership requirements and formulated the key elements to operate athletics programs at the Division I level. . . .

Perceived Divisional Benefits

The literature suggests several reasons institutions may consider reclassifying. Given the cost of the reclassification process and the continuing increased level of expenses, the initial benefit to consider is increased revenue. Increases in revenues may come from increased ticket sales, conference distributions, postseason earnings and alumni/booster contributions. (It should be noted that research concerning the correlation of athletics success and alumni/booster contributions is inconclusive.) Although increased spending that accompanies reclassification is inevitable, it is hoped that the increases in revenues outpace the increases in expenditures.

Another potential benefit is increased exposure after reclassification, which may result in an increase in applications, an increased academic pool, greater diversity and immeasurable intrinsic benefits.

Finally, reclassification may yield an increase in reputation and prestige, as the perceived quality of an institution's academic program is often tied to the success of its athletics program. Related benefits, of course, are immeasurable and intrinsic. It should also be noted here that a recent study by Orszag and Orszag (2005) found that there is a significant increase in revenue after reclassification, but this is subsumed by an increase in spending. The Orszag study does not address nonfinancial ramifications of reclassifying, which is a primary contribution of this study.[3]

DATA COLLECTION

Eleven institutions were identified that reclassified from Division I-AA to Division I-A during the period from 1993 to 2003. Eighteen institutions were identified as having moved from Division II to I-AA. Of the latter, insufficient data were found for 10 of the schools, leaving eight for observation (see Appendix II).

The financial data collected for each institution included total revenues (after removal of direct institutional support) and total expenses. The resulting net operating profit or loss was then calculated. Direct institutional support represents transfers of funds from the institution's general fund, or other units, to athletics. It should also be noted that the operating expenses do not include debt service or capital expenditures.

The nonfinancial data collected included ethnicity and gender of the institution's student body, ethnicity and gender of the student-athletes, graduation rate of the student body, graduation rate of the student-athletes, and the number of varsity sports sponsored by the institution.

The data were collected from NCAA archives of the biennial Revenues and Expenses of Intercollegiate Athletics Programs report, the annual Graduation Rate Report, and the annual Equity in Athletics Disclosure Act (EADA) data.

RESULTS

Financial Observations

Based on the data collected and utilized for the 19 reclassifying schools, the following distinct trends were noted.

Division I-AA to Division I-A

In every instance, total revenues increased steadily during the years after reclassification. Moreover, in only one instance for each of three schools did total revenues decline from one year to the next, and each of those declines was minimal. Thus, the common belief that a change in division will enhance revenues is confirmed. We add, however, that statistically, there was no change in average adjusted revenues from the years before the reclassification to the years after. For comparison, we also examined how revenues changed for schools from the same division that did not reclassify. Average revenues for these schools increased by a greater amount over the same period. This finding is noteworthy, though it may be partially explained by the fact that the operating budgets of reclassifying schools were generally much larger than those of the control group and the fact that schools that reclassify likely build their monetary base in the years before the reclassification and therefore do not experience such a large change in revenues in the year after the reclassification.

Concomitantly, total operating expenses show similar but more dramatic steady increases after reclassification. Again, there appears only one year for each of three schools in which total expenses declined. Only one of these was substantial. On average, over all schools in our sample, expenses increased by a statistically significant $2.572 million from the years before the reclassification to the years after, which is well over the amount by which revenues increased. However, similar institutions that did not reclassify experienced a significant and quantitatively similar increase in expenses over the same period. The impact on net income or loss, of course, is determined by the extent to which revenues increase relative to operating expenses. It should be noted that all 11 of the reclassifying institutions were experiencing net operating losses before reclassifying. Although results are mixed, the majority of the schools (seven) experienced substantially greater net losses after reclassifying. Two of the schools show a reduction in their operating

loss, one remained stable, and another showed losses that fluctuated greatly from year to year. Statistically, after the reclassification, there was a significant decrease in average net profits, on the order of $1.732 million. In general, the financial picture of reclassifying schools does not improve. Rather, the scope of both total revenues and total expenses, and in most cases net losses, simply gets larger. [*Ed. Note: See Table 14.*]

Division II to Division I-AA

Although the financial level at which Divisions II and I-AA operate is significantly lower than that of Division I-A, the percentage change in revenues, expenses and net losses is much more dramatic for these reclassifying schools than for those above.

The percentage increases in revenues for the eight schools after reclassification are generally vast. One school experienced a 1,200 percent increase; another 600 percent; a third tripled its revenues; and another saw an increase of 214 percent. Only one of the eight saw its revenues remain stable. On average, revenues for schools reclassifying from Division II to Division I-AA increased by a statistically significant $1.741 million after the reclassification. Economically, the average revenue for reclassifying programs after the reclassification is also significantly greater than the average revenue for a random sample of Division II schools that did not reclassify.

Unfortunately, operating expenses grew at an even greater rate, as all eight schools saw total expenses almost double (or more) those before reclassifying. Many schools experienced even greater increases, as evidenced by the resulting net losses. As was the case for schools reclassifying from Division I-AA to Division I-A, average expenses increased by approximately $2.445 million after the reclassification, which is not only statistically significant, but economically significantly more than the $1.417 million average increase in expenses that nonreclassifying Division

Table 14   Financial Results of Schools Reclassifying from Division I-AA to I-A

	Prior Loss	Subsequent Loss
School A	$6,200,000	$5,800,000
School B	100,000	1,400,000
School C	3,700,000	5,500,000
School D	4,100,000	0
School E	600,000	1,700,000
School F	100,000	1,600,000
School G	0	5,700,000
School H	2,300,000	4,600,000
School I	2,800,000	3,400,000
School J	0	400,000
School K	4,000,000	3,000,000

Source: National Collegiate Athletic Association. © National Collegiate Athletic Association. 2008–2010. All rights reserved.

Table 15   Financial Results of Schools Reclassifying from Division II to I-AA

	Prior Loss	Subsequent Loss
School A	$3,600,000	$6,900,000
School B	2,100,000	4,900,000
School C	2,800,000	6,300,000
School D	3,700,000	5,500,000
School E	2,700,000	6,200,000
School F	2,500,000	3,700,000
School G	1,400,000	4,400,000
School H	1,600,000	3,600,000

Source: National Collegiate Athletic Association. © National Collegiate Athletic Association. 2008–2010. All rights reserved.

II institutions experienced over the same period. Net profits also decreased after the reclassification by nearly twice as much as they did for nonreclassifying schools. [*Ed. Note: See Table 15.*]

Nonfinancial Observations

Ethnic Diversity

Given the absence of financial benefits of reclassifying, institutions must rely on either intrinsic benefits or measurable nonfinancial benefits to justify their move. One often cited benefit is the potential to gain better diversity among the student population.

Data available for purposes of measuring ethnic diversity in an institution's student population include enrollment numbers in the following groups:

Black, non-Hispanic men
Black, non-Hispanic women
Asian or Pacific Islander men
Asian or Pacific Islander women
Hispanic men
Hispanic women
White, non-Hispanic men
White, non-Hispanic women
Total men
Total women
Total enrollment

Division I-AA to Division I-A

Before Versus After Reclassification. Total enrollments for both the reclassifying schools and the control group have been steadily increasing during the entire 10-year period reviewed. This also holds true when the total enrollment before reclassification is measured against the enrollment after reclassification. Both groups show substantial total enrollment increases and substantial increases for both groups in white men and white women. A significant difference between the two groups is found, however, in the increases in the number of Black, non-Hispanic men and women. The reclassifying schools show a significantly greater increase in these areas than the control group. This holds true only in terms of total student count, however. When viewed as a percentage of total enrollment, the increases (before and

after) are not significantly different for the two groups. The only significant "before and after" difference is found in the Asian or Pacific Island ethnic population. The decrease in this segment is significantly greater for the reclassifying schools than for the control group.

Only After Reclassification. More substantial differences between the two groups of schools are found in enrollment data during only the period after reclassification.

- Reclassifying schools experienced a greater increase in the number of Black, non-Hispanic men than the control group during the period after reclassification.
- Reclassifying schools experienced a greater increase in the number of Black, non-Hispanic women.
- The control group experienced a marginally greater increase in the number of Asian or Pacific Islander women.
- The control group experienced a greater increase in the number of Hispanic women.
- Reclassifying schools experienced a greater increase in the number of White, non-Hispanic men.
- Reclassifying schools experienced a greater increase in the number of White, non-Hispanic women.
- Reclassifying schools experienced a greater increase in Black, non-Hispanic men as a percentage of total enrollment.
- Reclassifying schools experienced a greater increase in Black, non-Hispanic women as a percentage of total enrollment.
- The control group experienced a greater increase in Asian or Pacific Islander men as a percentage of total enrollment.
- The control group experienced a greater increase in Asian or Pacific Islander women as a percentage of total enrollment.
- The control group experienced a greater increase in Hispanic men as a percentage of total enrollment.
- The control group experienced a greater increase in Hispanic women as a percentage of total enrollment.
- Reclassifying schools experienced a marginally greater increase in white men as a percentage of total enrollment.
- Reclassifying schools experienced a greater increase in total men as a percentage of total enrollment.

Tested Statistical Significance. Schools moving from Division I-AA to Division I-A generally saw a statistically significant increase in the average number of both male and female students (respective averages increased from 8225 males to 10,717 and 9270 females to 12,608).

Division II to Division I-AA

Tested Statistical Significance. Schools moving from Division II to Division I-AA also saw a statistically significant increase in the average number of men and women. Specifically, the respective averages for men and women increased from 417 males to 543 and from 465 females to 611 after the reclassification. Nonreclassifying schools witnessed a similar increase in the average number of men and women. Interestingly, in schools that did not reclassify, the percentage of white men as a portion of total men increased significantly, though this was not the case for schools that reclassified. In terms of percentages, none of the ethnic groups experienced a statistically significant change after the reclassification. While the control group experienced increases in the raw number of Hispanic men and women and white men and women, the control group only experienced a significant increase in the percentage of white men. Indirectly, this may suggest that reclassification may help sustain a certain element of diversity.

Somewhat noteworthy, looking only at the years after the reclassification for schools that reclassified as compared to schools that did not reclassify, the average percentage of black men (women) as a portion of the total number of men (women) is statistically significantly lower for reclassifying institutions. Nonetheless, the relative proportion of white women is greater after the reclassification.

Graduation Rates. It is also worth mentioning that, on average, for those schools reclassifying to Division I-AA, graduation rates for both the student body and student-athletes are significantly greater in the years after the reclassification for reclassifying schools than they are for the schools that did not reclassify. This could point to reclassifying institutions being able to attract better students (athletes and non-athletes) as a result of increased visibility or prestige. The fact that graduation rates among athletes are higher is also consistent with the idea that Division I schools have fewer transfer students, perhaps because they offer more scholarship money, resources and facilities, and have more stringent transfer rules.

Because of the NCAA use of a six-year consortium for graduation rate purposes, combined with the timing of the reclassifications to Division I-A, sufficient data are not yet available for investigating the impact of reclassification on these schools.

Sports Sponsorship

In response to questions concerning the impact of an institution's reclassification on the number of varsity sports sponsored by that institution, related data were collected for both the reclassifying and control groups for this study. Results are discussed below.

Division I-AA to I-A. For the 1993 fiscal year, the average number of varsity sports sponsored by Division I-A institutions was 10 men's teams and nine women's teams—a total of 19. For fiscal 2003, the average had fallen to eight men's teams and nine women's. For the reclassifying schools in this study, however, the average for the group moved from eight men's teams and eight women's teams (total of 16) in 1993 to eight men's teams and 10 women's teams (total of 18) in 2003. No school in the group saw a decline in total sports sponsored, although two remain the same. Rather, all 11 increased the number of women's teams sponsored, and four reduced the number of men's teams. The NCAA now requires that all Division I schools offer a total of 14 varsity sports—either seven men's and seven women's, or six men's and eight women's.

Division II to I-AA. For the 1993 fiscal year, the average number of varsity sports sponsored by all Division I-AA institutions was 10 men's sports and eight women's. For fiscal 2003, the averages were seven men's sports and eight women's. For the reclassifying group, the averages in 1993 were eight men's and seven women's, and in 2003 the averages were nine men's sports and 10 women's. Two schools show a drop in total sports sponsored, while all show an increase in women's offerings. Five show a reduction in men's offerings.

CONCLUSION

This study evaluates financial and nonfinancial benefits to reclassification. We find that for both Division II schools that reclassify to Division I, and for Division I-AA schools that reclassify to Division I-A, increased revenues from reclassification are more than offset by increased expenses, such that, on average, net losses after reclassification increase. This financial drain is greater for Division II schools. We also uncover some changes in the diversity of the student body.

More specifically, graduation rates increased significantly for institutions that reclassified to Division I-AA. Especially noteworthy in this context is that the increase was reflected among student-athletes and the student body. We attribute this to more stringent transfer requirements and to an ability to attract better students from a wider geographical base as a result of increased visibility. We also find that reclassified institutions sponsor more sports than the average institution in their new divisions, which may simply reflect that Title IX requires an increase in female athletes to match the increase in scholarships granted to football players. Regardless, these changes are not consistently significantly different from similar schools that did not reclassify during the same period.

Overall, our study suggests that there are neither obvious financial nor considerable nonfinancial *measurable* benefits from reclassification and that the primary motivation to reclassify is intangible (e.g., perceived increased prestige). Additionally, the findings in this study underscore the issue faced by school administrators who are considering reclassification. One significant and consistent finding is that

Table 16   Men's Basketball Record and Home Attendance in the First Year in Division I, 1998–2008

Year School Joined Division I	School	Conference	Record	Average Home Attendance
2008	Bryant	Northeast	8–21	934
	North Dakota	Great West	16–12	1809
	Seattle	Independent	21–8	966
	South Dakota	Great West	20–9	1463
	SIU Edwardsville	Ohio Valley	10–20	1052
2007	Cal. State Bakersfield	Independent	8–21	2145
	Florida Gulf Coast	Atlantic Sun	10–21	2014
	NC Central	Independent	4–26	1279
	Presbyterian	Big South	5–25	1562
	USC Upstate	Atlantic Sun	7–23	908
	Winston-Salem	MEAC	12–18	1138
2006	Central Arkansas	Southland	10–20	1171
	NJIT	Independent	5–24	482
2005	Kennesaw State	Atlantic Sun	12–17	894
	North Florida	Atlantic Sun	6–22	1046
2001	Binghamton	America East	14–14	972
	Morris Brown	None	6–23	700
	UC Riverside	Big West	8–17	1849
1999	Alabama A&M	SWAC	17–11	1428
	Albany	America East	6–22	1148
	Belmont	Atlantic Sun	13–15	648
	Elon	Big South	9–20	708
	High Point	Big South	8–20	1170
	Oakland	Mid-Continent	12–16	1664
	Stony Brook	America East	17–11	1193
1998	Ark.–Pine Bluff	SWAC	2–25	1405
	Denver	Sun Belt	10–18	1184
	IUPUI	Mid-Continent	11–18	1186
	Portland St.	Big Sky	9–18	790
	Quinnipiac	Northeast	6–21	1003

reclassification is a financial drain to the athletics department. The fact that schools choose to reclassify despite this suggests that nonmonetary perquisites, perceived increases in status, and a "keeping up with the Joneses" effect may serve as motivation for reclassification. Of course, it is possible that there exist financial benefits to the schools that are not reflected in our data that pertains solely to athletics departments. This may be an avenue for future research.

. . . .

APPENDIX II

Reclassification from Division I-AA to I-A (Date)

University of Alabama at Birmingham (9/1/96)
Boise State University (9/1/96)
University at Buffalo, the State University of New York (9/1/99)

University of Connecticut (9/1/02)
University of Idaho (9/1/98)
Marshall University (9/1/97)
Middle Tennessee State University (9/1/99)
North Texas State University (9/1/95)
Portland State University (9/1/02)
University of South Florida (9/1/01)
Troy University (9/1/02)

Reclassification from Division II to I-AA (Date)

University at Albany (9/1/99)
Fairfield University (9/1/96)
Jacksonville University (9/1/98)
La Salle University (9/1/97)
Monmouth University (9/1/94)
Sacred Heart University (9/1/99)
Southeast Missouri State University (9/1/91)
Stony Brook University (9/1/99)

Notes

1. As anecdotal evidence, George Mason University discussed but dismissed the idea of reclassification with the Board of Visitors several years ago, but has since faced increasing pressure to reclassify. The school's administration is currently preparing a presentation on the expected costs and benefits of reclassification, perhaps due in part to recent successes in men's basketball.

2. Division III membership is markedly different from those of Divisions I and II and will not be explored in this paper.

3. See Orszag, J. M. and Orszag, P. R., 2005, "Empirical Effects of Division II Intercollegiate Athletics", Competition Policy Associates, Inc.

OPERATIONAL ISSUES

CIRCUMSTANTIAL FACTORS AND INSTITUTIONS' OUTSOURCING DECISIONS ON MARKETING OPERATIONS

Willie J. Burden and Ming Li

INTRODUCTION

Historically, outsourcing was a strategic initiative used by the general business community as a solution to a particular problem (Gay & Essinger, 2000). However, during the past decade, the outsourcing of marketing operations has become a common practice in American college athletics. According to Li and Burden (2002), more than one half of all NCAA Division I-A athletic programs have outsourced some or all of their marketing operations and rights to a growing number of nationally prominent outsourcing agencies. Among the operations commonly outsourced are the production of radio game broadcasts, production of radio call-in shows, coaches' television shows, sales of media and venue advertising, sales of "official sponsorship" rights to corporations, and production and management of Internet websites, etc. (Li & Burden, 2002).

Outsourcing simply means acquiring services from an external organization instead of using internal resources (Butler, 2000). By using outsourced resources, organizations can gain a competitive advantage by using contingent staff to accomplish strategic goals without incurring the fixed overhead. By focusing on the leading edge and highly specialized skill sets, outsourcing providers can often offer services better, or at a lower price than the client organization. Typical reasons for outsourcing go beyond simple contingent staffing. Outsourcing providers are able to maintain economies of scale with regard to specialization (Butler, 2000).

The outsourcing movement has been energized by the increasing commercialization of intercollegiate athletics, largely a result of the enormous competition among the largest programs in the NCAA and their mandate to be successful, self-supporting, and economically profitable. Intercollegiate athletics has grown into a $3 billion-a-year annual industry (Padilla & Baumer, 1994; Sneath, Hoch, Kennett, & Erdmann, 2000) with more and more money being spent for new stadiums, celebrity coaches, and better training facilities, etc. Some schools have independent athletic departments that support themselves, but the majority is funded by the university. Approximately 100 athletic departments in Division I are "sucking money from the schools" (Rozin & Zegel, 2003). Those that cannot pay the bills are often forced into painful downsizing of their sports programs (Rozin & Zegel, 2003).

Since outsourcing in intercollegiate athletics is fairly new, the amount of information available regarding the advantages that athletic programs gain from outsourcing is limited. However, the information available concerning outsourcing and the broader business community is more abundant. With such characteristics as advantages and disadvantages, business strategies, business goals, quantity and types of functions outsourced, the availability of experienced service providers, and even the proportion of companies that have outsourced, outsourcing has affected intercollegiate athletics in similar as well as dissimilar ways as the general business community.

Many of the reasons that an intercollegiate athletics program might choose to outsource are the same as the general business community. In addition to the advantages previously stated, by outsourcing, organizations can alleviate time pressure, draw from a varied base of professional expertise including technology expertise, gain additional resources, remove internal political barriers, maintain cost effectiveness, and increase staff without all of the associated costs (Elmuti & Kathawala, 1998; Williams, 1998). Specifically, by outsourcing, an organization can free up valuable resources for other uses and can redirect its people and other resources to its core business activities that better serve the organization's mission, purposes, and goals. By outsourcing, the organization can reduce operating costs through the elimination of the need for it to try to do everything itself, which often incurs high research, development, marketing, and deployment expenses (Davy, 1998).

The advantages in outsourcing can be operational, strategic, or both. Operational advantages usually provide for short-term trouble avoidance, while strategic advantages offer long-term contributions in maximizing opportunities. Outsourcing can cost more than doing something in-house, but offer benefits that justify it, like saving money or saving time (Chin, 2003). On the other hand, colleges and universities, when managed traditionally, are usually much more constrained. Because businesses are motivated to build their enterprises, they can be extremely creative. Unlike campus service departments, they are not allocated a budget or fund and asked to administer it. They work all the time for the market they serve in order to provide more and enhanced products and services that may earn them more money. That's a very different kind of thinking than is typical of colleges and universities (Bartem & Manning, 2001).

The general business community has found it beneficial to outsource an ever-widening number of functions, including business processes, human resources services, personnel benefits, administrative services, and business services (Rombel, 2002). Historically, the focus of intercollegiate athletics programs has been on some aspect of marketing operations and rights that has included printed media, production of radio game broadcasts and call-in shows, coaches' TV shows, licensing, and sale of media advertising. Also, the sport organization can utilize outside experts to handle difficult-to-manage functions. Most importantly, by outsourcing, the sport organization is able to access resources that are not available to it otherwise. This is vital considering today's highly competitive athletic climate where many institutions, already understaffed, are experiencing hiring freezes or reduction in work force combined with the pressure to generate additional revenues to support expanding sports programs (e.g., NCAA Division I qualifications, gender equity requirements, and facility enhancements, etc.). The University of Virginia, for example, was able to take advantage of increased professional staffing while getting its needs met in the areas of corporate sponsorships, sales of radio and television rights, advertising sales such as signage and roadway billboards, and more promotions for Olympic sports. Additionally, by using an outsourcing agency, they were able to avoid the State of Virginia's tough procurement regulations. Via additional business contacts, outsourcing has enabled the university to generate significantly more revenue than it would have on its own.

The general business community can select from numerous well-established service providers within each particular industry. However, since outsourcing is still relatively new in intercollegiate athletics, there are only a handful of reputable, major companies to select from. . . .

There is a downside to outsourcing. One major international study concerning the biggest outsourcing deals of the 1990s concluded that more that 35 percent of the deals failed. The causes for the failures included degradation of services, biased business dealings in favor of the vendor, lack of input from management, loss of control, and problems related to selecting the right service provider to meet the organization's needs (Gay & Essinger, 2000). Therefore, outsourcing might not be the right option for everyone. In

addition, outsourcing does not always bring the anticipated benefits, and in some instances can be a risky proposition (Chin, 2003). Willcocks and Lacity (1998) stated that among its disadvantages are the potential loss of control over critical functions such as timeliness and quality of service, difficulty in monitoring vendor performance, difficulty in explaining the business needs to vendors, the potential for loss of company secrets as well as intellectual property, and the high cost of outsourcing contracts. Schools also risk developing a dependency on outside agencies, lowering employee morale, loss of development skills for employees, and having to face the prospect of managing relationships that go wrong (Kakabadse & Kakabadse, 2000; Hayes, 2001). By outsourcing, not only do schools lose some of the personal touch in servicing their employees but their clients as well (Rombel, 2002).

With respect to colleges, while outsourcing has become one of the measures taken by colleges to support their need to gain a competitive advantage, it has not always been the most ideal alternative for attaining marketing goals. The Air Force Academy is a good illustration of what could go wrong if a college makes a poor decision about outsourcing. By outsourcing, The Air Force Academy lost control over their radio network and team travel package, and from a competitive standpoint was disadvantaged by their partnership with the service provider. Their relationship with the business community soured and the outsourcing agency contracted sponsors that were a poor match for the Academy. Because the service provider benefited more from the arrangement than the athletic department it became necessary to dissolve their contract.

As mentioned previously, among the largest NCAA Division I programs, some schools have chosen the outsourcing option while others have not; outsourcing has advantaged some schools and not others; and, some schools have been successful while keeping everything in house and managing the job themselves. Under what circumstances should a school choose one option over the other? Burden and Li (2002) stated that circumstantial factors play a significant role in differentiating those athletics programs that have outsourced their marketing operations from those that have chosen to keep their operations in house.

OTHER CIRCUMSTANTIAL FACTORS AFFECTING OUTSOURCING DECISIONS

In addition to the perceived advantages outsourcing could bring to the institution, other situational issues play a significant role in the decision-making process. For example, the athletics director at Georgia Tech might outsource; however, if that same person subsequently takes the job at Washington, a school in a very different environment, he or she might easily decide against it. When the athletic administrators at a particular institution are contemplating whether or not they should outsource their marketing operations, they need to examine their institution's mission, assess the attractiveness of their athletic product, establish who controls the property rights, determine the nature and status of the relationship it has with its local business community, and determine whether or not in-house resources are sufficient to get the job done.

First, the institution's mission, philosophy, and goals, etc., should be consistent with an outsourcing strategy. Further, the mission defines the purpose and goals of the organization, what its products, services, markets, and customers will be. It describes what core competencies will be necessary to achieve the goals, how the organization will distribute the products and services, and how it will interact with customers (Greaver, 1999). A couple of questions administrators need to consider are "what is the organization in business to do?" and "what resources does the organization need in order to do what it is in business to do?" (Gay & Essinger, 2000, p. 30). If outsourcing plays a critical role in the organization's overall strategy or service offerings, then outsourcing makes good sense for the organization and administrators can more effectively align its outsourcing objectives with the organization's overall strategies (Issacs, 1999). Otherwise, in-house operations would be more appropriate.

Next, if the institution is to derive some benefits from outsourcing, it must be positioned to do so. Butler (2000) maintains that the decision to outsource or not really depends on various circumstances. In arriving at the correct solution, sport organizations contemplating the outsourcing option should examine their unique characteristics. For example, their athletic product needs to be attractive enough to attract a topnotch service provider as well as the interests of potential, new corporate partners. Outsourcing agencies are less likely to pursue a relationship with those programs that have few followers, are not widely recognized or do not command the interests of advertisers. To determine the attractiveness of their product, they need to evaluate such information as (1) the level of national or regional recognition and exposure of their athletic programs (e.g., number of games or events that have been televised by the national and regional media), (2) the level of success of all of their athletic programs, (3) the degree of alumni and fan support or following, (4) membership in one of the NCAA elite conferences, (5) national ranking of football and men's basketball programs, (6) availability and/or use of state of the art facilities, and (7) accessibility of high profile coaches and blue chip athletes, etc. One rule of thumb in determining the attractiveness of an institution's athletic program is to see whether or not the responses from outsourcing agencies to the institution's request for proposal (RFP) for outsourcing collaboration are favorable. If the athletic administrators do believe their product is attractive enough, they should move on to the next step. Otherwise, they should not go for the outsourcing option (Li & Burden, 2004).

Who controls the property rights? This is a fundamental question that needs to be answered after the attractiveness of the product has been determined. In most cases, the athletic department has complete control over the rights of their athletic properties (e.g., sales of media advertising and venue signage, coaches' TV shows, TV and radio game broadcasts, licensing and merchandising, "official" sponsorships and venue naming rights, luxury seating, and production and management of Internet web sites, etc.). Nevertheless, there are some colleges and universities whose administrations want to exercise close control over all property rights, including those in athletics. As such, the athletic department cannot make any unilateral decisions in terms of outsourcing. If the athletic department has the ultimate authority to determine the use of athletic properties then it can certainly exercise its right to do so. In this scenario, the relationship between the athletic department and the business community is the next issue that needs to be examined.

The depth of an institution's relationship with the business community is another important consideration (Li & Burden, 2004). If it is strong, the collaboration with an outsourcing agency will not diminish the relationship but increase leverage and synergy. If the relationship is weak, the institution risks losing support from local businesses by introducing an unfamiliar intermediary.

If the athletic administrator is still uncertain, then he or she should determine whether or not in-house resources are sufficient to get the job done. Finally, if it is determined that in-house resources are not sufficient, and, after all of the issues have been thoroughly reviewed, then outsourcing logically becomes a viable alternative for achieving the organization's goals. **Figure 2** is a flowchart illustrating the decision-making process for outsourcing recommended for intercollegiate athletic administrators in NCAA Division I institutions.

. . . .

SUMMARY

The fiercely competitive nature of intercollegiate athletics, escalating cost of doing business, and mandate that campus athletics programs be self sufficient has made outsourcing marketing functions fashionable in recent years. Outsourcing has been described as an important tool for attaining and maintaining a competitive edge in intercollegiate marketing programs. Additionally, outsourcing is growing in appeal to individual institutions because of a variety of reasons important to them. The advantages in outsourcing can be operational, strategic, or both, ranging from alleviating time pressure on understaffed departments to generating large sums of revenues that were not available to the institution before. The disadvantages include the potential loss of control over critical functions such as timeliness and quality of services to managing dysfunctional partnerships.

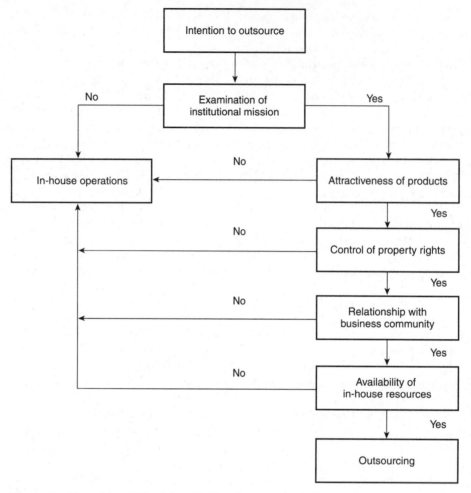

Figure 2   Flowchart of Decision-Making Process for Outsourcing

Source: Sport Marketing Quarterly. Used with permission from Fitness Information Technology.

This study discussed the process of making outsourcing decisions in intercollegiate athletics and proposes that the decision to outsource is circumstantial. Cases involving three NCAA Division I-A institutions were reviewed and used to support the central theme. Essentially, athletics administrators must complete a strategic analysis of their business environments to determine if outsourcing is a good fit for their institutions. However, according to Butler (2000) it must be emphasized that an organization's philosophy, goals, and strategic directions strongly influence the decision whether to outsource and what work to contract out. Consideration of these factors helps the institution determine whether it is advantageous to outsource or keep everything in-house.

Additionally, it is evident that outsourcing in intercollegiate athletics is an evolving process. Some schools are positioned to gain a competitive advantage by outsourcing. Others have the necessary resources in-house to get the job done. However, some schools still need to better position themselves if they are to gain benefits from outsourcing.

Also, what about those schools that do not have a top 10 athletics program, how do they retain their competitiveness? In order to address these issues future study is needed.

References

Bartem, R., & Manning, S. (2001). Outsourcing in higher education. *Change, 33*(1), 42.

Butler, J. (2000). *Winning the outsourcing game.* Boca Raton, FL: Auerbach.

Chin, T. (2003). The doctor is outsourcing. *American Medical News, 46*(30), 17.

Davy, J. (1998). Outsourcing human resources headaches. *Managing Office Technology, 43*(7), 6.

Elmuti, D., & Kathawala, Y. (1998). Outsourcing to gain a competitive advantage. *Industrial Management, 40*(3), 20–25.

Gay, C., & Essinger, J. (2000). *Inside outsourcing.* Naperville, IL: Nicholas Brealey.

Greaver, M. (1999). *Strategic outsourcing.* New York: American Management Association.

Hayes, F. (2001). A *light on ASPs computer world, 35*(34), 62.

ISP Website. ISP sports celebrates 10th birthday (n.d.). Retrieved May 25, 2004, from http://www.ispsports.com/news.cfm?id=8.

Issacs, N. (1999). Two companies, two outsourcing decisions. *InfoWorld, 2/*(24), 82.

. . . .

Kakabadse, N., & Kakabadse, A. (2000). Critical review—Outsourcing: A paradigm shift. *Journal of Management Development, 19*(8), 670–728.

Li, M., & Burden, W. (2002). Outsourcing sport marketing operations by NCAA Division I athletic programs: An exploratory study. *Sport Marketing Quarterly,11*(4), 226–232.

Li, M., & Burden, W. (2004). Institutional control, perceived product attractiveness, and other related variables in affecting athletic administrators' outsourcing decisions. *International Journal of Sport Management, 5*(4), 1–11.

Padilla, A., & Baumer, D. (1994). Big-time college sports: Management and economic issues. *Journal of Sport & Social Issues, 18*(2), 123.

Rader, A. (2002, June). *Working with an outside agency.* Paper presented at the 11th Annual Conference of the National Association of Collegiate Marketing Administrators, Dallas, Texas.

Rombel, A. (2002). Handing it over. *Global Finance,* 16(6), 42.

Rozin, S., & Zegel S. (2003, October 20). A whole new ball game? The push to reform and scale back collegiate athletics is gaining yardage. *Business Week, 3854,* 100.

Sneath, J. Z., Hoch, R.M., Kennett, P.A., & Erdmann, J.W. (2000). College athletics and corporate sponsorship: The role of intermediaries in successful fundraising efforts. *The Cyberjournal of Sport Marketing, 4*(3), 42.

Willcocks, L., & Lacity, M. (1998). Strategic sourcing of information systems: Perspectives and practices. New York: Wiley & Sons.

Williams, O. (1998). *Outsourcing: A CIO's perspective.* Boca Raton, LA: St. Lucie Press.

TAX ISSUES

TAX PREFERENCES FOR COLLEGIATE SPORTS, MAY 2009

The Congress of the United States, Congressional Budget Office

PREFACE

Colleges and universities generally qualify for preferential treatment under the federal income tax because their educational mission has important benefits for the public. But concerns have arisen that some activities undertaken by colleges and universities are only loosely connected to educating students and might be viewed as unrelated to the schools' tax-favored purpose. Long viewed as an integral component of higher education, sports in many universities have become highly commercialized. The large sums generated through advertising and media rights by schools with highly competitive sports programs raise the questions of whether those sports programs have become side businesses for schools and, if they have, whether the same tax preferences should apply to them as to schools in general.

This Congressional Budget Office (CBO) paper, which was prepared at the request of the Ranking Member of the Senate Finance Committee, compares athletic departments' share of revenue from commercial sources with that of the rest of the schools' activities to assess the degree of their commercialization. It also discusses the benefits of intercollegiate sports programs and some of the issues that might arise if the Congress decided to alter the treatment of those programs in the tax code. In accordance with CBO's

mandate to provide objective, impartial analysis, the paper makes no recommendations. . . .

CURRENT TAX TREATMENT OF THE ACTIVITIES OF COLLEGES AND UNIVERSITIES

As nonprofit institutions, colleges and universities are granted a variety of federal tax preferences that are designed to support their educational purpose, which has social as well as private benefits. Those preferences are not unlimited. The law has consistently attempted to balance the advantages of preferential federal tax treatment for nonprofit organizations against the possibility that those preferences could be used to engage in commercial activities that compete with taxable businesses.

Institutions of higher education, both public and private, benefit from several types of preferential tax treatment. Nonprofit private schools, like other nonprofits defined in section 501(c)(3) of the Internal Revenue Code, are exempt from the federal income tax, are eligible to receive charitable contributions that the donor may deduct, and may use tax-exempt debt to finance capital expenditures. Public colleges and universities receive broadly similar tax preferences; as state or local government entities, they are exempt from federal income taxation, are eligible for deductible contributions, and may have access to tax-exempt debt.

Like other nonprofit organizations, colleges and universities receive those preferences because they serve a public purpose. For institutions of higher learning, that public purpose is clearly education, which has traditionally included education through participation in athletics. Education is associated with a wide range of favorable outcomes. Investment in human capital through education confers a considerable private benefit on the individual, in the form of higher income and better health.[1] Education also creates public benefits for the community as a whole, including a more skilled workforce, increased economic growth, and greater social mobility.[2] An individual's decision regarding how much education to invest in will depend on his or her private benefit alone; in the absence of government intervention, that decision will yield fewer public benefits than is socially desirable. The favorable tax treatment of educational institutions, including those providing postsecondary education, is one way in which policymakers may be able to offset some of the potential underinvestment in human capital and subsidize the social benefits of education.

Because providing such benefits is the primary justification for nonprofit institutions' federal tax preferences, the government has a clear interest in ensuring that those preferences are used to facilitate activities that yield those benefits and not other activities. Thus, the federal income tax exemption for nonprofits is limited to income earned from the pursuit of the purpose that renders them eligible for the exemption, referred to as related income. Income earned from activities that are not substantially related to the performance of the exempt purpose is not tax-exempt and is subject to the corporate income tax on unrelated business income, commonly referred to as the unrelated business income tax (UBIT). That tax was enacted in 1950, at least partially in response to New York University's acquisition of Mueller's, the noodle and pasta company. The purchase of that previously taxable business contributed to the perception that nonprofit-owned businesses, facing lower costs because of their tax-exempt status and other federal subsidies, would be able to underprice taxable businesses, leading to unfair competition and the erosion of the corporate tax base.[3]

Policymakers at that time were also concerned that allowing charitable institutions to pursue commercial activities on a tax-exempt basis would encourage them to allocate an excessive amount of resources to those activities rather than to their charitable purpose. To that end, the law they enacted subjected income from commercial enterprises to the UBIT even if that income was used to finance the primary mission of an exempt organization. For colleges and universities, for example, the income they earn from tuition, research grants, passive investment income (which includes royalties, interest, and capital gains), contributions, and athletics is considered related to the exempt purpose and is therefore tax-exempt, but income earned from operating a restaurant that serves the general public is not, even if the profits are used to provide educational services for students.

Because public universities operate under the auspices of state governments, laws regarding state commercial enterprises may also be relevant to the commercialization of their activities. In general, the Internal Revenue Service (IRS) has never considered state commercial enterprises of any type taxable, even if they are separately incorporated, because their operation is invariably classified as an essential state function and the income accrues to the state government. The Internal Revenue Code, however, specifically makes state colleges and universities subject to the UBIT. That situation creates an anomaly: Any other state entity running a trade or business would not be subject to the UBIT and taxation, but a state college running the same unrelated business would be subject to the tax under current law.

Like the exemption from federal income taxation, the deductibility of charitable contributions to a nonprofit entity is subject to some limits when the contribution resembles a commercial transaction. In general, contributions given to a nonprofit in exchange for a good or service are nondeductible for the donor. Some donations to athletic departments are made to obtain the right to buy game tickets or preferential seating, and in 1986 the IRS ruled that such contributions were in return for a "substantial benefit" and were therefore nondeductible. In 1988, however, the Congress enacted legislation that explicitly permitted donors to deduct 80 percent of those contributions under section 170 of the Internal Revenue Code.

COMPARING COMMERCIALIZATION IN ATHLETIC DEPARTMENTS AND OTHER UNIVERSITY ACTIVITIES

This paper does not consider the possible commercial nature of a college or university as a whole.[4] Rather, the analysis takes the primarily noncommercial nature of the entire institution as a given and focuses on the activities of athletic programs. Specifically, this analysis addresses the concern that athletic programs have become primarily commercial—that is, they regularly provide a good or service in exchange for a fee in a market that also includes businesses subject to taxation—rather than educational. To assess the commercial nature of sports programs, the Congressional Budget Office (CBO) first examined the sources of athletic departments' revenue for a subset of colleges and universities and then compared them with the sources of revenue for the schools as a whole. The data indicate that athletic departments at some schools are significantly more commercial than the schools' other activities.

Commercial Activity in Athletic Programs

The analysis focused on athletic departments at schools in Division I of the National Collegiate Athletic Association (NCAA)—a voluntary organization through which colleges and universities govern their sports programs. Division I comprises the schools that have the largest sports programs—they must meet NCAA minimum standards for the number of sports played and for the amount of financial aid awarded to athletes—and are therefore most likely to engage in commercial activities. The division is further divided into three subdivisions—Divisions IA, IAA, and IAAA—that are relevant only for football.[5] To participate in Division IA, schools must meet certain minimum standards for football programs, including home game attendance and scheduled games against other members of the subdivision.

Information on athletic departments' budgets is available for 164 of the 327 schools that were members of Division I in academic year 2004–2005. The data were collected by the *Indianapolis Star* newspaper in 2006. The *Star* requested, under the Freedom of Information Act (FOIA), the budget reports that the NCAA requires from the athletic departments in all schools in Division I. The 112 private schools in the division

were exempt from the requests, as were public schools in Pennsylvania and Delaware, by state law.[6]

The *Star* data show that the largest source of athletic departments' revenue is ticket sales, followed by contributions, distributions by athletic conferences of revenue from championship games (including the sale of television rights for those games), and student fees. Large differences exist within the group, however. Division IA schools receive a considerably higher share of revenue from ticket sales (25.4 percent), contributions (20.8 percent), and conference distributions (15.6 percent) than the two other subgroups. That result is not surprising, considering the much higher profile of the football teams in Division IA (see **Table 17**).

Table 17   Sources of Revenue for NCAA Division I Athletic Programs, Academic Fiscal Year 2004–2005

	Average Revenue (Millions of Dollars)				Share of Revenue (Percent)			
Source	All	IA	IAA	IAAA	All	IA	IAA	IAAA
Commercial[a]								
Ticket sales	5.1	8.9	0.5	0.3	21.9	25.4	5.4	4.1
Conference distributions	3.2	5.5	0.5	0.3	13.7	15.6	4.8	3.8
Advertisements	1.3	2.1	0.3	0.2	5.4	5.8	3.1	3.1
Media rights	0.6	1.1	0	0	2.5	3.0	0.1	0.3
Guarantees	0.6	0.9	0.3	0.1	2.4	2.5	2.8	1.4
Items sold on game day	0.6	1.0	0.1	0	2.4	2.7	0.7	0.6
Investments	0.5	0.8	0.1	0.1	2.0	2.2	1.0	0.6
Sports camp	0.3	0.5	0.2	0.2	1.4	1.3	1.6	1.9
Third-party support	0.1	0.2	0	0	0.5	0.5	0.2	0.3
Other	0.5	0.8	0.2	0.2	2.3	2.4	2.0	2.0
Subtotal	12.7	21.6	2.1	1.4	54.4	61.5	21.7	18.1
Noncommercial								
Student fees	3.1	2.9	3.2	3.6	13.2	8.1	32.6	45.8
Institutional support	2.4	2.5	3.0	1.5	10.4	7.0	31.1	19.2
Facilities and administrative support	0.5	0.6	0.5	0.4	2.2	1.6	5.7	5.2
Government support	0.3	0.4	0.2	0.2	1.2	1.0	1.8	1.9
Subtotal	6.3	6.2	6.9	5.7	27.0	17.7	71.2	72.1
Contributions[b]	4.3	7.3	0.7	0.8	18.6	20.8	7.1	9.8
Average Total Revenue	**23.3**	**35.2**	**9.7**	**7.9**	**100.0**	**100.0**	**100.0**	**100.0**
Share of Revenue from Commercial Activities								
Contributions counted as noncommercial	n.a.	n.a.	n.a.	n.a.	54.4	61.5	21.7	18.1
Contributions counted as commercial	n.a.	n.a.	n.a.	n.a.	73.0	82.3	28.8	27.9
Memorandum:								
Numbers of Schools	164	90	41	33				
Total Revenue, All Schools	3,824	3,166	397	261				

Source: Congressional Budget Office based on data included in the budget reports that all Division I schools submit to the National Collegiate Athletic Association for their athletic programs. The data presented here, which include 164 of the 327 schools in Division I in academic fiscal year 2004–2005, were made available in response to a request by the *Indianapolis Star* newspaper under the Freedom of Information Act. Courtesy of the Congressional Budget Office.

Notes: The academic fiscal year typically runs from July 1 to June 30.

NCAA = National Collegiate Athletic Association; n.a. = not applicable.

a. Defined as revenue received in exchange for goods or services in a market that also includes taxed businesses.

b. Contributions can be commercial or noncommercial.

For its analysis of commercialization, CBO divided athletic departments' revenue into two main categories: commercial and noncommercial, described in more detail in **Box 1**. Revenue received in exchange for goods or services was classified as "commercial" revenue. Commercial sources include income from ticket sales, conference distributions (most of which derive from the sale of the rights to broadcast championship games), sales of team merchandise, and sales from advertisements. Support from the government and the school, the use of the school's facilities, and student fees were classified as "noncommercial."

Contributions to the athletic programs are more difficult to classify than the other sources. Although some contributions are given purely in support of the program, others guarantee the donor a tangible benefit in the form of a good or service. The data specifically count as contributions any amount paid in excess of the face value of a ticket; those excess values are typically paid in return for preferential seating at games. Payments may also be required before a fan can even become eligible to purchase premium tickets to games; such payments are legally considered partially deductible (80 percent) charitable contributions, despite the clear parallel to fee-for-service commercial transactions. The value of some donations of in-kind merchandise, such as apparel and soft drinks, are counted as contributions in the *Star* data, and those gifts represent an exchange in which the donor is paid with advertising and exposure when teams use their products. Contributions to the programs of the schools in Divisions IAA and IAAA, which have a lower profile, are unlikely to be related to premium ticketing or advertising, but over 90 percent of the total contributions to athletic departments go to Division IA schools, at which those factors are likely to be important. Most contributions thus seem to be related to the exchange of goods or services and therefore are primarily commercial. However, because the data do not specify which contributions are associated with a benefit to the donor and which are not, the tables in this report present the commercial share of revenue both with and without contributions.

When contributions are counted as commercial revenue, 73 percent of the revenue of athletic departments for Division I schools comes from commercial sources; when contributions are considered noncommercial, the share is about 54 percent. Within Division I, however, there are dramatic differences. Depending on whether contributions are considered commercial, athletic departments at Division IA schools receive about 60 percent to 80 percent of revenue from commercial sources, compared with 20 percent to 30 percent for schools in Divisions IAA and IAAA.

Commercial Activity in Other University Programs

The share of revenue from commercial activity in the rest of the university serves as a useful benchmark in determining whether athletic departments generate a disproportionately high share of revenue from commercial activity.

The Department of Education maintains the Integrated Postsecondary Education Data System (IPEDS), which contains data on revenue from most postsecondary institutions. CBO used those data to estimate the commercial share of total revenue for the entire school. IPEDS includes a category for revenue earned from auxiliary enterprises, defined as "revenues generated by or collected from the auxiliary enterprise operations of the institution that exist to furnish a service to students, faculty, or staff, and that charge a fee that is directly related to, although not necessarily equal to, the cost of the service."[7] Examples of auxiliary enterprises include residence halls, food services, and athletic departments; all revenue from those sources is classified as commercial.

Many university systems also have hospitals, which serve populations and missions that are somewhat different— though overlapping—from those served by the rest of the university. Although most hospital revenue is received in exchange for services, universities' hospital services are not typically viewed as a commercial enterprise. Whether hospitals should be considered a fundamental part of the universities' educational mission is unclear. . . .

With associated university hospitals excluded, the universities as a whole derive almost 11 percent of their revenue from commercial activities when contributions to the university are considered a noncommercial source of revenue. That share rises to about 14 percent when contributions are classified as commercial.[8]

A final consideration is the treatment of athletic programs' revenue within the overall university. For schools in Division IA, that revenue comes primarily from commercial sources, so including it boosts the share of revenue from commercial sources for the university as a whole. Because the IPEDS data do not have a separate category for the revenue of athletic programs, CBO used the *Indianapolis Star* data to estimate each category of revenue net of the effect of athletic programs.[9]

When athletic departments are removed from the calculation of commercial revenue for the university, the commercial share falls. Excluding hospitals, the share of university revenue from commercial sources is about 8 percent when contributions are considered noncommercial. That treatment of contributions may be more appropriate for the rest of the university than for the athletic department, although individuals or organizations making the largest donations to universities also tend to receive something, such as naming rights, in return. When contributions are considered commercial, the share of university revenue from those sources is about 11 percent.[10] Clearly, athletic departments derive a considerably higher share of their revenue from commercial activities than do other parts of universities. Depending on how it is calculated, the share of revenue from commercial sources is seven to eight times higher for Division IA athletic programs than for all other functions at those universities. For Divisions IAA and IAAA, the share

BOX 1

SOURCES OF REVENUE OF ATHLETIC DEPARTMENTS

The data the Congressional Budget Office (CBO) used to determine the sources of revenue of athletic departments in Division I of the National Collegiate Athletic Association (NCAA) are from the request made by the *Indianapolis Star* newspaper under the Freedom of Information Act in 2006. That request was for the budget reports that athletic departments are required to submit to the NCAA. The data include 164 of the 327 schools in Division I in academic year 2004–2005. CBO classified the sources as commercial or noncommercial, as described below; contributions, which can be commercial or noncommercial, were put in a separate category.

COMMERCIAL SOURCES OF REVENUE

Broadly defined, commercial activities provide a good or service in exchange for a fee in a market that also includes taxed businesses. For this paper, CBO classified the following activities as commercial:

Ticket sales. Ticket sales to the public, faculty, and students and money received for shipping and handling of tickets. Excludes ticket sales for conference and national tournaments.

Conference distributions. Revenue received from participation in bowl games, tournaments, and all NCAA distributions (for example, amounts received for direct participation or through a sharing arrangement with an athletic conference, including shares of conferences' television agreements).

Advertisements. Revenue from corporate sponsorships, sales of advertisements, trademarks, and royalties. Includes the value of in-kind products and services provided as part of a sponsorship (for example, equipment, apparel, soft drinks, water, and isotonic products).

Media rights. Institutional revenue received directly for radio and television broadcasts; Internet and e-commerce rights received through contracts negotiated by the institution.

Guarantees. Revenue received from home teams for participating in away games.

Items sold on game day. Revenue from the sale of programs, novelties, and food or other concessions and from parking fees.

Investments. Distributions from an endowment and other investment income in support of the athletic department.

Sports camp. Amounts received by the athletic department for sports camps and clinics.

Third-party support. All amounts provided by a third party and contractually guaranteed by the institution but not included on the institution's W-2 (for example, a stipend for the use of a car; membership in a country club; allowances for entertainment, clothing, and housing; speaking fees; compensation from camps; and income from radio, television, shoes, and apparel).

Other. Accounts for less than 5 percent of total revenue.

NONCOMMERCIAL SOURCES OF REVENUE

All sources of revenue not meeting the definition of "commercial" were classified as noncommercial:

Student fees. Fees assessed for support of (or the portion of overall fees allocated to) intercollegiate athletics.

Institutional support. Includes the value of institutional resources for the current operations of intercollegiate athletics; all unrestricted funds allocated to the athletic department by the university. That support may include state funds, tuition, tuition waivers, and transfers.

Facilities and administrative support. Includes the value of facilities and services provided by the institution and not charged to the athletic department (for example, an allocation for institutional administrative costs, facilities and maintenance, grounds and field maintenance, security, risk management, utilities, and debt service).

Government support. Includes state, municipal, federal, and other government appropriations made in support of the operations of intercollegiate athletics (including funding specifically earmarked for the athletic department by government agencies for which the institution has no discretion to reallocate).

CONTRIBUTIONS

Contributions were defined as amounts received directly from individuals, corporations, associations, foundations, clubs, or other organizations that are designated, restricted, or unrestricted by the donor for the operation of the athletic program. Examples of contributions are amounts paid in excess of a ticket's value (for example, to obtain premium seating), cash, marketable securities, and in-kind contributions. In-kind contributions may include automobiles provided by dealers (measured as the market value of the use of a car), apparel, and soft drinks for use by staff and teams.

Source: Courtesy of the Congressional Budget Office.

of commercial revenue for athletic programs is only two to three times as large as for the universities' other activities (assuming that the extent of commercial activity in those schools, apart from the athletic department, is comparable with that in Division IA schools).

Looking at the net income of athletic programs highlights the differences in the commercial nature of programs between the three Division I subgroups. Nearly 99 percent of total net income accrues to Division IA programs, according to the data reported by universities to the NCAA.[11] Average income for programs in Divisions IAA and IAAA is less than a tenth of that in the more commercial Division IA. Those differences in reported income are discussed later in the context of possible policy changes.

Even in that group of elite Division IA programs, however, more than a quarter of the athletic programs report a deficit each year. That result is more likely to reflect the conceptual difficulties in measuring income rather than a statement about the true underlying profitability of those programs. The correct allocation of revenue and expenses to athletic departments, and thus their net profit, is complicated. There are no rules or even standard practices delineating how schools divide revenue from parking, concessions, or licensing, for example, between the athletic department and the university.[12] On the cost side, schools generally list the full standard tuition as the cost of an athletic scholarship, even though that measure overstates the true cost of awarding the scholarship.[13] Because accounting practices vary, the reported profit or loss reported . . . may be a poor guide to the true financial status of athletic departments.

Competition with For-Profit Entities

Public and private colleges face relatively little competition from taxable competitors; for-profit postsecondary schools accounted for just 5 percent of total enrollment in degree-granting institutions in 2004.[15] When athletic departments function primarily as a part of the educational experience for students, they participate in that nonprofit market. However, highly competitive college sports teams with large-capacity stadiums and prime-time television events with advertising are more reasonably considered participants in the market for entertainment. They compete for entertainment spending with many other recreational options, but their most direct competitors are professional sports leagues.

Even though competitive university sports programs enter the same market with tax advantages unavailable to the taxable professional leagues, those leagues have never advocated removing tax preferences for the college programs. One reason may be that college sports tend to reduce costs for professional sports.[16] The two sports with the most active and commercial college programs—football and basketball—are each controlled by a single professional association that spends very little on training players. In many cases, all but the final polishing is done by the colleges while the players maintain amateur, nonpaid status.[17] If players

were not trained by colleges, the professional leagues would probably have to pay those players a salary and complete the training themselves. Particularly in football, the same lack of other leagues in the market—due at least in part to the partial antitrust exemptions granted to the National Football League (NFL)—has also facilitated explicit arrangements between the NCAA and the NFL that avoid direct competition so that they can jointly maximize revenue. For example, college and professional football teams play on different days of the week during the college season. Once the college football season is completed, professional teams play some games on Saturday, the day usually reserved for colleges.

THE BENEFITS OF COLLEGIATE ATHLETICS

Although this analysis focuses on the commercialization of university athletics, the favorable tax treatment of athletic departments within a university might also be evaluated in terms of the social benefit those programs provide to federal taxpayers, who finance the subsidies the universities receive. Research indicates that student athletes tend to underperform academically relative to their credentials, although there is no clear evidence about whether their participation in competitive athletics creates other types of human capital with social benefits.[18] If student athletes reap less academic benefit from higher education than other, similarly qualified students, the admission preferences they currently have represent a misallocation of education resources.

Collegiate athletics, like other extracurricular activities, may also enhance the quality of student life in various nonacademic ways that could also have social benefits. Supporters of university athletic programs cite the leadership skills, teamwork, and dedication that student athletes may learn through their participation.[19] Participating in and watching sporting events can also contribute to an institution's sense of community.

Athletics are unique among extracurricular activities, however, because of the expensive infrastructure support associated with providing such benefits to participants. Although some other activities also require facilities that are expensive to construct and maintain, salaries for coaches are higher than those for almost any other university employee, including college presidents, and no other extracurricular activities are provided with academic tutoring programs like those that focus on maintaining athletic eligibility.[20]

Athletic programs might also provide ancillary benefits (in addition to any direct profit from the programs themselves) to the schools, allowing them to further their mission of higher education. Athletic programs could benefit schools indirectly by improving their name recognition or reputation.[21] Successful athletic programs could also encourage increased giving by alumni to a school or improve the quality of the entering class by increasing the number of students who apply for admission. Although various empirical studies on both of those points have come to conflicting conclusions, overall the evidence indicates that the effect of successful programs on either of those measures at a specific school is likely to be positive but small (see the appendix).

Applying those conclusions to all university athletic programs in the nation—the appropriate level at which to evaluate a federal subsidy—is difficult. Most studies look at the relationship between success, defined by win-loss records or championship wins, and alumni giving or the number of applications at a specific school. Because athletic success is in general a zero-sum endeavor (championship games always have a winner), the relationships that hold for a single or small group of athletic programs may not hold for all athletic programs in the nation. There is no evidence suggesting that athletic programs increase the overall amount of charitable contributions (as opposed to shifting them between different schools or other nonprofit organizations) or the average quality of students attending all colleges.[22] Furthermore, the effect of athletic programs on either of those measures seems likely to be dwarfed by that of the many other federal subsidies for charitable giving and higher education. In fact, the current subsidy to athletic departments may simply encourage an "arms race" between schools, in which universities spend increasing resources on measures of athletic success that, at most, benefit their own institutions at the expense of others. Encouraging such competition within the higher education sector seems unlikely to benefit the federal taxpayers that ultimately pay for the subsidy.

POLICY OPTIONS

If the Congress decided that some or all of the activities undertaken by college athletic programs are primarily commercial, the rationale for providing preferential tax treatment to those activities would be eliminated or greatly reduced. Changes to the tax preferences could be achieved in one or more of the following ways:

- Limiting the deduction of charitable contributions,
- Limiting the use of tax-exempt bonds, or
- Limiting the exemption from income taxation, either for all or for certain types of income.

Several issues might arise if the Congress decided to eliminate or reduce those tax preferences. Most important, the position of athletic departments within larger nonprofit institutions affords many opportunities for shifting contributions, other revenue, or expenditures from one part of the university to another. The budgetary relationship between universities and their constituent parts would significantly reduce the effectiveness of most attempts to limit the general tax preferences for athletics while leaving those for the entire university intact. More targeted changes, such as limiting the types of income statutorily exempt from the unrelated business income tax, are more likely to have an impact but would still require assessing the commercialization of all of the university's activities rather than just those of the athletic department.

Limiting the Deduction of Charitable Contributions

Under the Internal Revenue Code, donors to college sports programs may deduct their contributions from their federal adjusted gross income. Many of those contributions, however, are made in order to become eligible to purchase game tickets or to ensure access to premium seating. In effect, the transaction is an exchange of money for valuable rights, and the benefits of the contribution accrue to the donor. Under current law, the donor may nonetheless deduct 80 percent of the value of such contributions.

If the Congress decided that contributions to athletic departments are primarily commercial, it could specify that contributions to universities' sports programs or to foundations that support them—either contributions given in exchange for certain benefits or all contributions—may not be deducted on the donor's federal tax return. Money can easily be moved between departments within the university, however, and a university administration can allocate a greater share of its own budget to its sports program. If that fact is well understood by donors and administrators, donations to sports programs might be unaffected by such a policy change; lower explicit donations to the athletic programs could simply be offset by indirect donations through the university.

Although such a response might completely offset the effects of a change in the deductibility of contributions, it would probably not do so. Total donations would be likely to decline to some extent, and a school's response would determine how the effects of that decline were shared between the athletic program and other parts of the budget.

Limiting the Use of Tax-Exempt Bonds

Although contributions can be given to or earmarked for sports programs directly, athletic departments generally do not have borrowing authority that is separate from that of the college or university as a whole. The borrowing is undertaken on behalf of the school and is earmarked for the sports program in the tax-exempt bond offering.

It would thus be more difficult for schools to move borrowing that is earmarked for another part of the university to the athletic department if the Congress prohibited the use of tax-exempt bonds to finance the capital facilities of sports programs. Even so, it might be possible for the university to borrow indirectly for the sports program. If the university could not use the proceeds from bonds directly for the sports program, it could still borrow for capital spending in other areas that would have been financed with operating revenue and use that operating revenue to finance the sports facilities. The major problem would be the large amount of revenue needed—the university might not have adequate capital facilities being financed with operating revenue to make the substitution. Thus, eliminating the direct use of tax-exempt bonds for sports facilities would be unlikely to eliminate their use but would probably have a bigger effect on the total amount of bonds a university issues than the elimination of charitable contributions would have on total charitable contributions.

Limiting the Exemption from Income Taxation

Attempts to end the exemption from income taxation for athletic departments would probably encourage universities to undertake significant efforts to avoid taxes. A sports program's position within a much larger institution makes successful taxation of its true net income a difficult undertaking. Changing the treatment of income from specific sources, such as royalty income or income from corporate sponsorships, might be effective, especially if the changes applied to the entire university rather than just the athletic program.

Subject the Income of Athletic Programs to the UBIT

The Congress could, by statute, reclassify collegiate athletic programs as unrelated commercial entities operated by a nonprofit organization, thereby subjecting them to the unrelated business income tax.[23] Because an athletic program in a nonprofit private or public postsecondary institution is part of a much larger economic entity that would remain classified as a nonprofit, the institution would have a substantial incentive to shift costs from the untaxed portion of the university to the taxable portion and to shift income in the other direction. Increased net income would have no tax consequences for the untaxed sector, and increased costs would reduce or eliminate taxable net income for the athletic program.[24]

Universities have other means of eliminating taxable income if cost shifting failed to do so completely. Unlike a for-profit enterprise, which has shareholders who expect managers to distribute a surplus as dividends or retain the surplus and distribute it in the future as capital gains, the nonprofit or public enterprise has no shareholders. If athletic programs still showed a profit even after income or cost shifting, that profit could be reduced or eliminated in two ways. First, the program could increase costs by paying higher wages to coaches or administrators or by spending more for other items, such as athletic facilities.[25] Second, the program could reduce revenues—for example, by lowering the price of game tickets. Directors of athletic programs might prefer to use one of those alternatives rather than pay taxes; all of the alternatives would reduce the income subject to tax.

Restructure the Relationship between Athletic Departments and the University

The schools' ability to shift income from one part of their budget to another is likely to prevent the net income of collegiate athletic programs from being taxed. To prevent such shifting, the Congress could require that the financial relationship between athletic programs judged to be commercial and their universities be severed completely. Like any commercial entity, the athletic programs could still lower their tax liability by reducing revenue or increasing costs, but they would be limited in doing so by their need to raise capital.

Such a major restructuring of the relationship between athletic departments and universities would present a variety of practical and political issues. Perhaps most important, it would be extremely difficult to implement effectively at the public universities that host most of the major sports teams. The Congress has made many changes to the exemption for nonprofit institutions, including imposing the unrelated business income tax. But the IRS has considered every commercial activity undertaken by a state or local government to be an essential public service and therefore not subject to taxation. Taxing a public entity would raise legal issues with regard to intergovernmental tax immunity. At the moment, the tax law treats nonprofit and public enterprises very differently. Therefore, a state institution of higher education operating a sports program classified as a commercial enterprise would be subject to the UBIT under that approach, but a state operating the identical sports program as a state entity not affiliated with its public university would not.

Reclassify Certain Types of Income

Instead of attempting to classify all net income from athletic programs as commercial and subject to the UBIT, the Congress could consider reclassifying certain types of income typically earned by those programs as unrelated income. For example, an athletic program earns royalty income when it receives a payment in exchange for allowing a for-profit enterprise to use its name. Current law excludes all royalty income from the UBIT because such income is considered passive. In general, passive income, which also includes income from investments, is not considered commercial because it is not derived from direct competition with commercial enterprises.

Some types of royalty income may reasonably be considered more commercial than others. The royalty income derived from the ownership of mineral and oil rights is usually a clear example of passive income; universities own the land to which such rights are attached but have little or no involvement in the ongoing commercial activity that occurs. In contrast, when colleges and universities license team names, mottoes, and other trademarks to for-profit businesses that supply apparel, accessories, and credit cards to the general public, they approve each product and use of their symbols and, in some cases, exchange information, such as donor lists, with the licensees to aid in their marketing. In 2005, the collegiate sector earned $203 million in that type of licensing revenue.[26] The manufacture or sale of such items would clearly be commercial—and subject to the UBIT—if undertaken directly by the schools. Schools' active involvement in generating licensing income could be the basis for considering such income as commercial and therefore subject to the UBIT. Even the income from mineral rights has been determined taxable if the university is substantially involved in the daily operation of such properties.

Bringing royalty income that accrues only to athletic departments under the UBIT would be problematic, however, for several reasons. First, schools could simply limit their licensing of the names and trademarks of their athletic teams and increase their licensing of the school's name and trademarks to minimize the amount of taxable activity, although doing so would be likely to decrease sales. More important, if royalty income from licensing team names to for-profit businesses was truly considered commercial and subject to the UBIT, the same arguments would apply in full force to licensing all other university names and trademarks. A consistent policy would subject all such income to the UBIT because of its commercial nature. Such a change in policy could affect many other nonprofits in addition to colleges and universities, although the amount of all commercial activity in athletic departments relative to that undertaken by universities and other nonprofits does provide a rationale for different treatment.

Income from corporate sponsorship is also explicitly excluded from the UBIT. Generally, sponsorship income arises from corporate payments made in exchange for associating the corporate name with the nonprofit or public institution. In the context of college athletics, most major college championship games, stadiums, and arenas have a corporate sponsor whose name is included in the name of the event or facility. The IRS considered subjecting such income to the UBIT in 1991. In the Taxpayer Relief Act of 1997, however, the Congress responded by excluding "qualified sponsorship payments" from the UBIT, defining such payments as those in return for no other benefit than the acknowledgment of the sponsor. The law makes a distinction between payments in return for advertising (which includes descriptions of the sponsor's products, locations, or other features) and payments in return for adding the sponsor's name to an event or facility (which is not considered a substantial benefit). The NCAA estimated that corporate sponsorship payments to all athletic programs totaled $275 million in academic year 2004–2005.[27]

The fact that sponsors of athletic facilities and bowl games are willing to pay large sums in qualified sponsorship payments suggests that they derive some benefit from the prominent location and display of their corporate trademarks during athletic contests and national broadcasts. If the Congress decided that those benefits were essentially similar to those conferred by advertising as defined in the law, it could reclassify such payments as taxable income from an unrelated business. Such a determination would be supported not only by the commercial nature of those specific transactions but also by the commercial nature of athletic departments themselves, in contrast to other nonprofits that earn some revenue from similar sources while remaining financed primarily by noncommercial activities.

However, not all payments for naming rights at athletic facilities really are in return for a substantial benefit; the benefit to the sponsor varies considerably among schools and is of course largest for the few schools whose athletic arenas attract extremely large crowds and host widely televised events. The range of success among programs—and thus the benefit in being a sponsor—implies that a blanket determination of "substantial benefit" from all sponsorships could be unreasonable. The situation is clearer in the case of sponsors of championship games. Title sponsors of widely televised events such as bowl games clearly receive a substantial benefit from their sponsorship. If the Congress determined that such transactions are commercial, it could specifically classify sponsorship payments for those particular athletic contests as taxable income.

Even reclassifying certain types of income might fail to be effective if the policy was intended to apply only to athletic departments. Unless the treatment of such income was consistent across the entire university, strong incentives would remain to shift income taxable to the athletic department to the nontaxed portion of the university. However, reclassifying certain types of income as unrelated, and therefore taxable, would have the advantage of focusing directly on the types of revenue that are associated with the relatively few highly commercial athletic departments rather than on the majority of athletic departments that engage in little commercial activity.

Notes

1. Claudia Goldin and Lawrence F. Katz (*Long Run Changes in the U.S. Wage Structure: Narrowing, Widening, Polarizing*, Working Paper No. 13568 [Cambridge, Mass.: National Bureau of Economic Research, November 2007]) document a rise in the return to education in general over the past several decades and, in particular, a rise in the return to postsecondary education. David M. Cutler and Adriana Lleras-Muney ("Education and Health: Evaluating Theories and Evidence," in Robert F. Schoeni and others, eds., *Making Americans Healthier: Social and Economic Policy as Health Policy* [New York: Russell Sage Foundation, 2008]) discuss the evidence for a positive relationship between education and health outcomes, with particular attention to the mechanisms through which education may be the cause of better health.

2. Eric Hanushek and Ludgar Woessmann (*Do Better Schools Lead to More Growth? Cognitive Skills, Economic Outcomes, and Causation*, Working Paper No. 14633 [Cambridge, Mass.: National Bureau of Economic Research, January 2009]) find empirical evidence of a causal relationship between educational attainment and economic growth rates across countries. For a discussion of the relationship between postsecondary education and social mobility, see Robert Haveman and Timothy Smeeding, "The Role of Higher Education in Social Mobility," *Future of Children*, vol. 16, no. 2 (2006), pp. 125–150.

3. Because the corporate income tax limits the deduction that corporate donors can take for their charitable donations, a commercial entity whose income accrues directly to a nonprofit parent would, in the

absence of the UBIT, pay lower taxes than a business that simply donated all of its profits to a nonprofit organization.

4. A previous Congressional Budget Office report, *Taxing the Untaxed Business Sector*, Background Paper (July 2005), discussed how those institutions are similar to for-profit businesses in important ways.

5. The NCAA has recently replaced the names IA, IAA, and IAAA with Football Bowl Subdivision, Football Championship Subdivision, and Division I Non-football, respectively. This paper uses the older terminology for brevity.

6. Very little information is available regarding the budgets of athletic departments at nonprofit private schools. Those schools and their athletic departments receive the same preferential tax treatment as public schools. The current lack of publicly available information about their programs makes a similar evaluation of their commercialization impossible and could be one justification for mandating additional disclosure of budget information from institutions registered as nonprofits.

7. Susan G. Broyles, *IPEDS Glossary* (Department of Education, National Center for Education Statistics, rev. August 1995), http://nces.ed.gov/pubs95/95822.pdf, p. 28.

8. When hospitals are included in the calculation, the commercial share of revenue is 9.5 percent with contributions considered noncommercial and 12.6 percent with contributions considered commercial.

9. In adjusting the universities' revenue to exclude revenue from athletic departments, CBO assumed that the schools that did not respond to the FOIA request were similar to those that did. CBO made the adjustment using averages from the *Indianapolis Star* data. For example, the calculation for all university revenue excluding athletics was made by subtracting the average revenue of athletic departments in the *Star* data, multiplied by the number of schools (101), from the total university revenue given in IPEDS. CBO used a similar process to calculate university revenue excluding athletics for contributions and auxiliary enterprises, using the *Star* data averages for contributions to athletic departments and commercial revenue from athletic departments, respectively.

10. Including hospitals, universities derive about 7 percent of revenue from commercial sources when contributions are considered noncommercial and 10 percent of revenue from commercial sources when contributions are considered commercial.

11. The majority of income is, of course, reinvested directly into the athletic programs—for example, into compensation for coaches and administrators. Because the athletes retain amateur status, there are strict limits on their compensation, and they are barred from receiving benefits that are proportional to the income that they earn for the university. Robert W. Brown and R. Todd Jewell ("Measuring Marginal Revenue Product in College Athletics: Updated Estimates," in John Fizel and Rodney Fort, eds., *Economics of College Sports* [Westport, Conn.: Praeger, 2004], pp. 153–162) estimate that universities earn $400,000 from each high-performing football player and over $1 million from each high-performing basketball player.

12. Robert Sandy and Peter Sloane, "Why Do U.S. Colleges Have Sports Programs?" in Fizel and Fort, eds., *Economics of College Sports*, pp. 87–110.

13. If class sizes are fixed, the cost of granting a scholarship to an athlete is the tuition that would have been paid by another student who cannot now be admitted, and the majority of students do not pay the listed tuition because they receive financial aid in the form of tuition discounting or grants. See Burton A. Weisbrod, Jeffrey P. Bal-

lou, and Evelyn D. Asch, *Mission and Money: Understanding the University* (Cambridge, U.K.: Cambridge University Press, 2008), Chapter 5. If class sizes are not fixed, the cost of granting a scholarship to an athlete could be even less than the net tuition that would be paid by another student, because the athlete's admission does not prevent any other applicant from being admitted.

. . . .

15. U.S. Department of Education, *Digest of Education Statistics*, http://nces.ed.gov/programs/digest/d07/tables/dt07_185.asp.

16. College baseball is an exception in that it competes for players with the minor leagues; even so, the collegiate and professional baseball seasons do not overlap the majority of the time.

17. The lack of compensation for college athletes (despite the substantial revenue that they earn for the university) is one factor encouraging basketball players to forgo college and instead improve their skills in professional leagues in other countries before returning to play for a professional team in the United States. If more athletes decided to play for foreign professional leagues rather than for colleges, the result could be both a decline in the commercialization of college basketball and a decline in its value to the domestic professional league.

18. See, for example, William G. Bowen and Sarah A. Levin, *Reclaiming the Game: College Sports and Educational Values* (Princeton, N.J.: Princeton University Press, 2003), Chapter 6. The authors concluded that after accounting for the influence of race, field of study, individual scores on the Scholastic Aptitude Test (SAT), and the average SAT score at the institution, athletes who are recruited achieve lower class rank relative to their academic credentials than do walk-on athletes or the general student body. The effect is most pronounced among football players and rowers. Others have noted that graduation rates for football and basketball team members in Division I are considerably lower than those for nonathletes or for athletes in other sports. See Weisbrod, Ballou, and Asch, *Mission and Money*, p. 231.

19. Letter from Myles Brand, President of the National Collegiate Athletic Association, to the Honorable William Thomas (November 13, 2006), www.ncaa.org/wps/ncaa?ContentID=44636, p. 4.

20. For a comparison of coaches' and university presidents' salaries, see Weisbrod, Ballou, and Asch, *Mission and Money*, pp. 221 and 251–277. For a discussion of spending on tutoring programs for athletes, which the NCAA requires of all Division I schools, see Zimbalist, *Unpaid Professionals*, pp. 43–44.

21. Goff, "Effects of University Athletics on the University," p. 91.

22. Total charitable donations to all sectors have remained roughly 2 percent of disposable income over time, suggesting that increased donations to higher education are offset by decreased giving to other nonprofits (Weisbrod, Ballou, and Asch, *Mission and Money*, p. 36).

23. For an in-depth discussion of the legal argument for applying the UBIT to college athletics under current law, see John D. Colombo, "The NCAA, Tax Exemption, and College Athletics" (*University of Illinois Law Review*, forthcoming; also available at http://papers.ssrn.com/abstract=1336727).

24. Joseph J. Cordes and Burton A. Weisbrod ("Differential Taxation of Nonprofits and the Commercialization of Nonprofit Revenues," in Burton A. Weisbrod, ed., *To Profit or Not To Profit* [Cambridge, U.K.: Cambridge University Press, 1998]) conclude that nonprofits

subject to the UBIT may shift expenses that are up to one-third of their gross profit to the taxable portion of the entity.

25. The large number of programs that currently post a loss . . . may suggest that those behaviors already occur; administrators and coaches may be able to extract higher salaries from those nonprofit programs because such programs have no incentive to show a profit.

26. Weisbrod, Ballou, and Asch, *Mission and Money*, p. 245.

27. Letter from Myles Brand to the Honorable William Thomas (November 13, 2006).

APPENDIX: RESEARCH ON CERTAIN BENEFITS OF INTERCOLLEGIATE SPORTS

Although the extent of commercialization in college sports provides one basis for evaluating athletic programs' access to federal subsidies intended for nonprofit organizations, other factors may also play a role. For example, many supporters of university athletics argue that a successful athletic department creates benefits for colleges and universities that are then passed on to the students. Numerous studies have attempted to prove or disprove that notion.

Athletic success is generally thought to benefit schools in one of two ways: by increasing donations to the school or by increasing the pool of applicants for admission. Research on the relationship between athletics and donations has used a variety of measures of athletic success and has come to conflicting conclusions. One study, for example, found that winning percentages in the major sports did not have a significant effect on donations.[1] A larger study reached a similar conclusion regarding winning records, but the authors documented a positive relationship between giving and appearances in championship games.[2] Using a panel data set of 320 institutions, a third study concluded that postseason success in football and basketball leads to increased gifts restricted for the use of the athletic department for some schools but no increase in unrestricted giving to the university.[3] Another study, using detailed data from a single large university, found little relationship between teams' general success and donations but found a significant increase in donations for some alumni when a sport in which they had participated was successful.[4] Overall, those studies seem to indicate that postseason success may increase restricted donations to the athletic department by particular alumni but that the effect on total giving to the university is likely to be small.

The results of research on the relationship between athletic success and the quality of entering classes are equally inconsistent. One study documented a positive relationship between advancing in the National Collegiate Athletic Association (NCAA) basketball tournament and Scholastic Aptitude Test (SAT) scores for the entering class.[5] In contrast, another study found that championships increased the number of applications but had no effect on the SAT scores

or grades of entering students.[6] A comprehensive study of the effects of athletic success on the quality of incoming students concluded that the percentage of games won was positively correlated with the quality of the students but that the effect was generally small and statistically insignificant; the authors also reached similar conclusions about the relationship between winning and alumni donations.[7]Another paper examined a separate mechanism through which athletic success could provide benefits to public schools—increased state funding. The author found that schools with a Division IA football program receive significantly more in state funding than those without one but that an increase in the success of the program does not raise the amount of appropriations it receives.[8]

Although the studies reach conflicting conclusions, even in the studies that find that successful athletic programs have a positive impact on the school overall, the measured impacts are generally quite small. In addition, studies that demonstrate a positive impact for a single school or a subset of schools do not address whether success in intercollegiate athletics increases donations or student quality at all schools—or simply shifts them between schools.

Notes

1. Paul W. Grimes and George A. Chressanthis, "Alumni Contributions to Academics: The Role of Intercollegiate Sports and NCAA Sanctions," *American Journal of Economics and Sociology*, vol. 53, no. 1 (1994), pp. 27–40.

2. Robert Baade and Jeffery Sundberg, "Fourth Down and Gold to Go? Assessing the Link Between Athletics and Alumni Giving," *Social Science Quarterly*, vol. 77, no. 4 (1996), pp. 789–803.

3. Brad R. Humphreys and Michael Mondello, "Intercollegiate Athletic Success and Donations at NCAA Division I Institutions," *Journal of Sport Management*, vol. 21, no. 2 (April 2007).

4. Jonathan Meer and Harvey S. Rosen, *The Impact of Athletic Performance on Alumni Giving: An Analysis of Micro Data*, Working Paper No. 13937 (Cambridge, Mass.: National Bureau of Economic Research, April 2008).

5. Franklin G. Mixon Jr., "Athletics versus Academics? Rejoining the Evidence from SAT Scores," *Education Economics*, vol. 3, no. 3 (December 1995), pp. 277–283.

6. J. Douglas Toma and Michael Cross, "Intercollegiate Athletics and Student College Choice: Understanding the Impact of Championship Seasons on the Quantity and Quality of Undergraduate Applicants" (paper presented at the 21st Annual Meeting of the Association for the Study of Higher Education, Memphis, Tenn., October 30–November 2, 1996).

7. Robert E. Litan, Jonathan M. Orszag, and Peter R. Orszag, *The Empirical Effects of Collegiate Athletics: An Interim Report* (prepared by Sebago Associates for the National Collegiate Athletic Association, August 2003), www.ncaa.org/databases/baselineStudy/baseline.pdf.

8. Brad R. Humphreys, "The Relationship Between Big-Time College Football and State Appropriations for Higher Education," *International Journal of Sport Finance*, vol. 1, no. 2 (May 2006).

Discussion Questions

1. What are the main causes of the annual deficits that most athletic departments face each year?

2. Are the NCAA deficit numbers actually accurate? Why or why not? How could one get an accurate figure?

3. What specific adjustments must be made in order for one to arrive at an accurate assessment of the amount a university makes or loses each year on its athletic programs? Explain each of these adjustments.

4. What are some of the positive effects that large football programs and men's basketball programs have on the publicity of an institution? Is there evidence of this? If so, what is it?

5. Does athletic success have an effect on student interest in an institution?

6. What led to the attempt by institutions to control expenditures rather than to distribute revenues? Was it successful? How so, or how not?

7. How does treating an athletic department as an auxiliary activity affect an institution?

8. How is the financial situation at Michigan likely to be different than at other Big Ten institutions? How about at Division I-A institutions not affiliated with the BCS?

9. What impact does a lack of athletic success have on institutional fundraising? If a member institution goes from being a losing athletic program to an intercollegiate power will that cause a positive shift in fundraising?

10. Are athletic department leaders such as directors and head coaches overpaid? How about relative to professors and other academics? What is the basis for your opinions?

11. What are the key factors an academic institution should use in determining if reclassification is appropriate for them?

12. How does the opportunity for individual member institution to achieve financial success under the NCAA governance system differ from the opportunities NFL teams have in their governance system?

Gender Equity

INTRODUCTION

One of the major issues that intercollegiate athletic directors must factor into their operations is the elements that enable an institution to attain gender equity. The key issue for managers in this area is compliance. Gender equity is often accomplished by means of Title IX, the federal law that requires equal opportunity in school-related athletics. Title IX, enacted in 1972, establishes that: "No person in the United States shall, on the basis of sex, be excluded from participation in, be denied the benefits of, or be subjected to discrimination under any education program or activity receiving Federal financial assistance." The articles and documents contained in this chapter explain what gender equity means, highlight the difficulties managers encounter in achieving it, and discuss the issues the athletics administrator must confront in order to comply. The articles also provide insight on how one sector of insiders can view the effectiveness of these policies.

Title IX is "Exhibit A" for the unique issues that collegiate administrators must grapple with that draw them away from the traditional professional sports and business goals of focusing on the bottom line or even exclusively on winning. Federal law mandates that gender equity be an essential element of the operational equation. This priority can have short- and long-term monetary impacts, particularly during transitional phases as an institution expands through NCAA divisions.

The chapter opens with an excerpt that provides a broad overview of the law related to Title IX in Rosner's "The Growth of NCAA Women's Rowing: A Financial, Ethical and Legal Analysis." Rosner also provides the specifics of the applicability of Title IX in relation to rowing. Rowing is referred to by some as the equivalent of football in terms of the numbers of athletes that participate and the difficulty that it causes in efforts to ensure equality.

The next three documents provide the U.S. government's interpretation of the law. Insight is gained by looking at various letters interpreting the rules as issued by the United States Department of Education's Office for Civil Rights (OCR), the federal administrative agency responsible for the oversight of Title IX. Arguably, these documents are the first step in attempting to understand the complexities of Title IX. The federal courts evaluating the merits of Title IX litigation have shown them great deference. The first is "Clarification of Intercollegiate Athletics Policy Guidance: The Three-Part Test." It is this three-part test that determines whether an academic institution is in compliance with Title IX. The OCR later issued additional clarification related to financial aid in a document referred to as the "Letter Clarifying Apportionment of Financial Aid in Intercollegiate Athletics." The next OCR-produced document is a letter that was designed to provide "Further Clarification of Intercollegiate Athletics Policy Guidance Regarding Title IX Compliance." This provides the most recent "final word" and guidance to the athletics administrator for Title IX. This letter was issued following contemplation of a report titled "Open to All: Title IX at Thirty," which was issued by a special commission created by the Secretary of Education to study Title IX 30 years after its passage. The Secretary's Commission on Opportunities in Athletics was charged to investigate and report back with "recommendations on how to improve the application of the current standards for measuring equal opportunity to participate in athletics under Title IX." The report was issued in early 2003. The letter included in this chapter from U.S. Assistant Secretary of Education for Civil Rights Gerald A. Reynolds essentially calls for no radical changes. However, it is clear that the guidelines and requirements—although now much more clearly defined—continue to evolve.

The final excerpt, from Rhode and Walker's article "Gender Equity in College Athletics: Women Coaches as a Case Study," provides a clear look at the impact of Title IX after 35 years via the results of an extensive survey of 450 coaches of women's intercollegiate sports.

OPERATIONAL ISSUES

THE GROWTH OF NCAA WOMEN'S ROWING: A FINANCIAL, ETHICAL, AND LEGAL ANALYSIS

Scott R. Rosner

. . . .

III.   LEGAL ASPECTS

A.   History of Title IX

Title IX of the Education Amendments of 1972 is a federal law prohibiting sex discrimination in education programs and activities receiving or benefiting from federal funding.[70] While not specifically mentioned in the law itself, athletics are covered by Title IX.[71] Consequently, this law has been the primary method by which women have achieved equal opportunity in high school and college athletics, and it has played a vital role in opening competition to female athletes.[72] Though signed into law on June 23, 1972,[73] the Department of Health, Education and Welfare's final Title IX regulations[74] did not go into effect until July 21, 1975, and were not enforced until the three-year compliance period expired in 1978.[75] In order to clarify the requirements of Title IX and to provide schools with guidance on their obligations under the law, the Office for Civil Rights (OCR) issued its final Policy Interpretation on December 11, 1979.[76] This outlines a detailed set of standards to be adhered to in three separate areas: student interests and abilities, athletic benefits and opportunities, and athletic financial assistance.[77]

Though the Policy Interpretation is not a rule of law, it has been given substantial deference by courts determining the rights of female athletes.[78] After the period of enforcement that followed the issuance of the Policy Interpretation, female athletes suffered a setback when athletic programs were removed from coverage under Title IX by *Grove City v. Bell.*[79] As a result of this judicial setback, OCR immediately cancelled all forty of its ongoing Title IX athletics investigations and ignored any new complaints regarding athletics.[80] Congress acted rather quickly to correct the narrowing of Title IX that *Grove City* had accomplished and enacted the Civil Rights Restoration Act in 1988,[81] overriding a veto by President Reagan.[82] The Act served the purpose of reversing the Supreme Court's decision in *Grove City* by stipulating that Title IX applies to all programs of an educational institution that receive any federal financial assistance.[83] The revitalization of Title IX was fortified by the Supreme Court's decision in *Franklin v. Gwinnett County Public Schools,*[84] which allowed private plaintiffs to receive monetary damages and attorney fees for an intentional violation of Title IX.[85]

In addition to these agency regulations and legislative and judicial statements, Title IX has been shaped by three other policy documents issued by OCR:[86] the Title IX Investigator's Manual;[87] the Clarification of Intercollegiate Athletics Policy Guidance: The Three-Part Test;[88] and a letter offering guidance regarding the issuance of athletics scholarships.[89] . . . [*Ed. Note: See these two latter documents beginning on p. 622.*]

B.   Analysis and Application of Title IX to Women's Rowing

1. Student Interests and Abilities

As previously mentioned, compliance with Title IX is measured in three separate areas: student interests and abilities, athletic benefits and opportunities, and athletic financial assistance.[90] Under Title IX, the athletic interests and abilities of male and female students must be equally and effectively accommodated.[91] OCR will assess whether an institution is in compliance with this aspect of Title IX through the application of the following three-part test:

(1) Whether intercollegiate level participation opportunities for male and female students are provided in numbers substantially proportionate to their respective enrollments; or

(2) Where the members of one sex have been and are underrepresented among intercollegiate athletes, whether the institution can show a history and continuing practice of program expansion which is demonstrably responsive to the developing interest and abilities of the members of that sex; or

(3) Where the members of one sex are underrepresented among intercollegiate athletes, and the institution cannot show a continuing practice of program expansion such as that cited above, whether it can be demonstrated that the interests and abilities of the members of that sex have been fully and effectively accommodated by the present program.[92]

An institution may choose any one of the three benchmarks established by this test in order to satisfy the accommodation requirement.[93] OCR also considers the quality of competition available to members of both sexes,[94] but it is this three-part test that has been the most litigated aspect of Title IX in determining whether the interests and abilities of an institution's students are effectively accommodated.[95]

Under part one of the three-part test, OCR looks at whether an institution's participation opportunities for its male and female students are substantially proportionate to their full-time undergraduate enrollments.[96] Although OCR will find that an institution with a closely mirrored image between these two figures is effectively accommodating the interests and abilities of its students, very few institutions have been able to take advantage of this "safe harbor."[97] In 1997, only fifty-one institutions in NCAA Division I were within even five percentage points of achieving substantial proportionality.[98] For many institutions, this is due to the presence of football. The number of participation opportunities in football is unmatched by any other sport.[99] An institution would typically have to sponsor at least three women's teams in order to match the number of athletes on a football team.[100] Thus, it becomes extremely difficult for an institution sponsoring a Division I-A football team to comply with the first benchmark.[101]

The growth of women's rowing in the NCAA is primarily attributable to its positive impact on institutions attempting to comply with the interests and abilities aspect of Title IX via the substantial proportionality test.[102] The large roster size of a women's rowing team has made it an extremely attractive alternative for athletic administrators looking to increase the number of participation opportunities afforded to an institution's female students.[103] The average roster size of a women's rowing team is the largest of any NCAA women's sport—nearly twice that of outdoor track and field, which has the second largest roster of any women's sport.[104] It is not uncommon for a crew to have 100 rowers.[105] Therefore, rowing is "women's football" in terms of roster size. It is a "quick fix" for institutions looking to offer substantially proportionate athletic opportunities to its female students.

While the first benchmark has been the focus of both litigants and courts, the dearth of institutions satisfying this test requires that attention be given to part two of the three-part test of Title IX compliance—whether an institution has a history and continuing practice of program expansion for the underrepresented sex. OCR reviews an institution's previous and ongoing remedial efforts to determine its compliance with this benchmark.[106] Of primary importance is ascertaining whether an institution has expanded its program over time in a manner that is demonstrably responsive to the developing interests of the underrepresented sex.[107] To do so, OCR will review if the school has added or elevated women's teams to intercollegiate status, added participation opportunities for female athletes, and its responses to female students' requests to add or elevate sports.[108] In determining

whether an institution has a continuing practice of program expansion that is demonstrably responsive to the developing interests of the underrepresented sex, OCR looks to whether the institution has effectively communicated to students a procedure for requesting the addition or upgrading of a sport.[109] In addition, the current implementation of an institution's plan to expand an underrepresented program is viewed favorably by OCR.[110] In *Boucher v. Syracuse University*,[111] the court held that the institution's addition of women's lacrosse, soccer, and softball between 1996 and 1999 was evidence that it had a history and continuing practice of program expansion for its female athletes.[112] Syracuse University is the first . . . institution to successfully rely on this benchmark in proving its compliance with Title IX.[113]

Women's rowing is beneficial to those institutions choosing to comply with the second benchmark. The tremendous growth of the sport at the intercollegiate level allows those schools that have recently begun to sponsor it to claim a history of program expansion.[114] The addition or elevation of a women's rowing team, and the numerous participation opportunities added for female athletes via the sport, will be evaluated positively by OCR.[115] At those institutions that have added or elevated the sport upon the request of its students, the affirmative response will receive similar approval from OCR.[116] The large number of NCAA institutions that are able to make these claims because of women's rowing is reflected in the sport becoming the first to move from Emerging to Championship status.[117] In addition, there are several institutions that have announced plans to add or elevate a women's rowing team in the near future.[118] These institutions may claim a continuing practice of program expansion through their implementation of a plan to add the sport.

In part three of the three-part test, an institution may claim that it is fully and effectively accommodating the interests and abilities of its female students even though it has neither achieved substantial proportionality nor demonstrated a history and continuing practice of program expansion.[119] In reviewing this claim, OCR evaluates whether there is unmet interest in a particular sport, sufficient ability to sustain a team in the sport, and a reasonable expectation of competition for a team.[120] First, OCR looks at several indicators to determine whether there is unmet interest in a particular sport at an institution.[121] These indicators include whether the institution has been requested to add or elevate a particular sport by its current or admitted students; participation in a particular club or intramural sport at the institution; participation in certain interscholastic sports by admitted students; and sports participation rates in the high schools, amateur athletic groups, and community sports leagues in the areas from which an institution draws most of its students.[122] Second, OCR looks at the potential ability of either an existing club team or interested students to evaluate if there exists a sufficient ability to sustain an intercollegiate team in the sport.[123] Third, OCR reviews if there is a reasonable expectation of intercollegiate competition available for a team in both the institution's conference and surrounding geographic area.[124] If there is unmet interest in a particular sport, sufficient ability to sustain a team in the sport, and a reasonable expectation of competition for a team, then the institution has not fully and effectively accommodated the interests and abilities of its female students.[125]

Women's rowing may or may not help an institution satisfy the third benchmark of Title IX compliance. There are many strong club teams at the college level.[126] If one of them requests elevation to the intercollegiate level, and the institution is located in an area with a high participation rate at both the high school and intercollegiate levels, then the institution could not refuse to elevate the women's rowing team and still claim that it is fully and effectively accommodating the interests and abilities of its female students.[127] This is due to the fact that all three compliance requirements would have been met by the women's rowing team.[128] However, there are several potential problems with this analysis that may allow an institution faced with a request to add a women's rowing team to refuse to do so with no Title IX impunity. There is likely to be a paucity of feeder rowing programs in many institutions' normal recruiting area, as there are so few club and high school programs throughout the country.[129] Depending on the geographic location of the institution and its conference affiliation, there may not be a reasonable expectation of intercollegiate competition in the institution's vicinity.[130] Thus, there would be no unmet interest or reasonable expectation of competition. Under these circumstances, the institution could claim that it is fully and effectively accommodating the interests and abilities of its female students without adding a rowing team.

2. Athletic Benefits and Opportunities

The second area of concern for Title IX compliance is the parity of athletic benefits and opportunities between male and female students.[131] Though only one court has issued a decision addressing these requirements at the intercollegiate level thus far, they are an important aspect of Title IX compliance that are likely to be the future focus of the courts.[132] In addition to looking at student interests and abilities, the law specifies that OCR examine other factors in determining whether there is equal opportunity in athletics.[133] The Policy Interpretation requires the following factors to be considered in determining whether an institution is providing equality in athletic benefits and opportunities: provision and maintenance of equipment and supplies; scheduling of games and practice times; travel and per diem expenses; opportunity to receive coaching and academic tutoring; assignment and compensation of coaches and tutors; provision of locker rooms and practice and competitive facilities; provision of medical and training services and facilities; provision of housing and dining services and facilities; publicity;

provision of support services; and recruitment of student athletes.[134] Each of these factors is evaluated by comparing an institution's entire male and female athletic program with respect to the availability, quality and kinds of benefits, opportunities, and treatment afforded.[135] While identical benefits, opportunities and treatments are not required, the effects of any differences must be negligible.[136]

The impact of women's rowing on any one particular aspect of this area of Title IX compliance is relatively small. However, any inequity in the women's rowing program is magnified because of the large number of participation opportunities provided by the sport.[137] Because a significant percentage of the female athletes at an institution may be rowers, the impact of women's rowing on this area may be considerable.[138] Of primary concern is the effect of women's rowing on the provision and maintenance of equipment and supplies, scheduling of games, and the construction of practice and competitive facilities.[139]

Perhaps the most compelling of these components are equipment and supplies.[140] The quality of equipment offered to both male and female athletes must be similar.[141] However, the cost of the equipment used in women's rowing is quite high.[142] As a result, many institutions opt to purchase used equipment to lower their expenses, especially when beginning a program.[143] If a women's rowing program is using inferior equipment for a sustained period of time, the institution may encounter difficulty establishing compliance with this component. The amount of equipment provided to male and female athletes also must be similar.[144] It seems logical to expect that there should be enough equipment to ensure that all members of a team will be able to practice at the same time. Providing enough boats for the entire team to be on the water at the same time becomes an expensive proposition for a rowing team. Due to this expense, many institutions have opted not to purchase a sufficient number of rowing shells; the rowers must "take turns" on the water.[145] Institutions engaging in this practice may find it similarly difficult to prove compliance with this component.

One of the ways in which the maintenance of equipment and supplies is measured is by how equipment is repaired.[146] Men's and women's teams should have their equipment repaired in the same manner.[147] If there is a professional equipment manager, repairs should be done for a similar number of men's and women's teams.[148] The specialized nature of rowing requires a trained individual to repair and maintain the equipment.[149] While some institutions employ either a part-time or full-time rigger, in many cases these repair duties are the responsibility of the coach. This may be a compliance problem for an institution, because its equipment repair policy may result in inequality between the men's and women's teams. Replacement of equipment typically must be done on the same schedule for men's and women's teams unless there is a difference justified by the nature of the sport.[150] While rowing may be of a sufficiently unique nature to justify a different replacement schedule, this difference must not cause an inequity between male and female athletes if the institution wishes to remain in compliance with Title IX.[151] The expense of purchasing new rowing equipment is likely to make it tempting for athletic administrators to delay this transaction. Nevertheless, administrators must not shy away from replacing old rowing equipment because of the expense involved if it results in inequitable treatment of female athletes.

Compliance with Title IX also implicates the procedures adopted by an institution for scheduling games and practice time for the women's rowing team.[152] The time of day during which competitive events and practices are scheduled should be equally convenient for the men's and women's teams.[153] Since most regattas are scheduled on weekends, the women's rowing team facilitates an institution's compliance with this component.

Women's rowing impacts upon the provision of practice and competitive facilities as well.[154] Practice and competitive facilities must be of equivalent quality and availability.[155] The assignment of a women's team to a poorer quality facility is a common compliance problem.[156] This is manifested in the sport of women's rowing by the type of boathouse facility used by many crews. Construction or renovation of a boathouse is a very expensive proposition.[157] Instead of engaging in such a project when adding or elevating a women's rowing team, many institutions choose to look at alternatives to incurring these large capital expenses. The institution may enter into a rental agreement with an existing boathouse or utilize an older boathouse that was previously used by the institution's men's or women's club rowing team. If these options prove unattractive, the institution may store equipment in a semi-trailer in close proximity to the practice water[158] or simply transport equipment to and from the institution to the practice water on boat trailers every day.[159] Engaging in these practices may make it extremely difficult for an institution to comply with this component; the poor quality of many of these facilities likely creates an inequity between male and female athletes. The availability of practice facilities involves the scheduling and location of these facilities. The location of the practice facility is of concern if the facility for a team of one sex is off campus and in an inconvenient location.[160] Most boathouses fit this description, as they tend to be located some distance from campus.[161] While the nature of the sport may justify some inconvenience in the availability of the practice facility, the institution should attempt to minimize this burden as much as possible so as to reduce any inequities between male and female athletes.

3. Athletic Financial Assistance

The final area of concern for Title IX compliance is athletic financial assistance.[162] Though only 46 institutions are in compliance,[163] this area has also received little judicial attention.[164] None of the three courts that have reviewed cases involving athletic financial assistance has found a violation of Title IX.[165] OCR presumes compliance in this area if the total amount of athletic scholarship dollars awarded to male and female athletes is within one percent of their respective participation rates in intercollegiate athletics at the institution.[166] Women's rowing may play an important role in an institution's compliance with this standard due to the large number of athletic scholarships that can be awarded. The NCAA allows for the equivalent of twenty full athletic scholarships to be awarded in women's rowing.[167] This is the largest of any women's sport.[168] When all sports are taken into consideration, only football offers more scholarships.[169] Thus, the presence of a women's rowing team is the single greatest ally to an institution hoping to comply with the athletic financial assistance standard established by OCR.

Notes

. . . .

70. 20 U.S.C. 1681 provides in relevant part that "no person in the United States shall, on the basis of sex, be excluded from participation in, be denied the benefits of, or be subjected to discrimination under any education program or activity receiving Federal financial assistance. . . ."

71. See 34 C.F.R. 106.41 (1975).

72. Masteralexis, supra note 16, at 184.

73. History of Title IX Legislation, Regulation and Policy Interpretation, at bailiwick.lib.uiowa.edu/ge/history.html (last visited May 24, 1999).

74. 34 C.F.R. 106.41 (1975).

75. Id.

76. The Office for Civil Rights within the U.S. Department of Education is responsible for the enforcement of Title IX. Letter from Dr. Mary Francis O'Shea, National Coordinator for Title IX Athletics, Office for Civil Rights, to Nancy Foster, General Counsel, Bowling Green State University (July 23, 1998), available at bailiwick.lib.uiowa .edu/ge/.

77. 44 Fed. Reg. 71413 (1979). See also Requirements Under Title IX, supra note 12. These requirements will be discussed further in Part III.B infra.

78. See Robert D'Augustine, A Loosely Laced Buskin?: The Department of Education's Policy Interpretation For Applying Title IX To Intercollegiate Athletics, 6 Seton Hall J. Sport L. 469, 473-80 (1996).

79. 465 U.S. 555 (1984). The Supreme Court limited the application of Title IX to programs or activities that received direct federal financial assistance. See id. As most athletic departments do not receive such direct funding, they were removed from coverage under Title IX.

80. History of Title IX Legislation, Regulation and Policy Interpretation, supra note 73.

81. Pub. L. No. 100-259, 102 Stat. 28 (1988) (codified at 20 U.S.C. 1687).

82. History of Title IX Legislation, Regulation and Policy Interpretation, supra note 73.

83. Id.

84. 503 U.S. 60 (1992).

85. Id.

86. Valerie Bonnette, Title IX Basics, available at www.ncaa.org/library/ general/achieving_gender_equity/ (n.d.).

87. Valerie Bonnette and Lamar Daniel, Office for Civil Rights, Title IX Investigator's Manual (1990).

88. Office for Civil Rights, Clarification of Intercollegiate Athletics Policy Guidance: The Three-Part Test, January 16, 1996, available at www.ncaa.org/library/general/achieving_gender_equity/ [hereinafter 1996 Clarification Letter].

89. 1998 Guidance Letter, supra note 76.

90. 44 Fed. Reg. 71413 (1979), See also Requirements Under Title IX, supra note 12.

91. Requirements Under Title IX, supra note 12.

92. 44 Fed. Reg. 71418 (1979).

93. 1996 Clarification Letter, supra note 88, at II-25.

94. Id.

95. See e.g., Cohen v. Brown Univ., 991 F.2d 888 (1st Cir. 1993); Boucher v. Syracuse Univ., 164 F.3d 113 (2d Cir. 1999); Pederson v. La. State Univ., 201 F.3d 388 (5th Cir. 2000).

96. 1996 Clarification Letter, supra note 88, at II-26. In doing so, OCR considers only the actual number of participants in intercollegiate athletics, including the walk-ons who make a squad and practice but do not compete. Id. OCR excludes intramural sports and any un- filled roster slots from this calculation. Id. An individual who quits after two weeks of practice is not counted as a participant. Bonnette, supra note 86. Women's rowing has a high attrition rate because of the demanding nature of the sport. See Brett Johnson, A Look at the University of Louisville's First Year (Part II), USRowing, June 2000, at 21-23 [hereinafter Johnson (Part II)]. A large number of individu- als who attend practices in the preseason quit the sport before the competitive schedule begins; these individuals are not counted as participants. See id. Thus, the number of participation opportunities provided by women's rowing is somewhat limited because of its dif- ficulty.

97. See Gender Equity Creative Solutions; A Case Study of What Edu- cation Institutions Can Do In Order To Comply With The Regula- tions of Title IX, at www.womenssportsfoundation.org (last visited May 12, 2000). Less than 9% of Division I institutions are able to do so. Id. An example is often helpful in understanding this aspect of the law. An institution with 10,000 full-time undergraduate stu- dents - 5200 women and 4800 men - must offer 52% of its partici- pation opportunities in intercollegiate athletics to women to be in strict compliance with part one. See 1996 Clarification Letter, supra note 88. OCR makes the determination of whether an institution is in compliance with part-one on a case-by-case basis, as there is no strict statistical cut-off for a finding of substantial proportionality. See id.

98. Chronicle of Higher Education, Participation: Proportion of Fe- male Students on Athletic Teams, at http://www.chronicle.com/ search97cgi/s97_cgi (last visited Jan. 19, 2001).

99. See NCAA, 1998–99 Participation Study—Men's Sports (2000), available at http://www.ncaa.org/participation_rates/1998-99_m_ partrates.pdf (last visited May 16, 2000). The average roster size for football is 113.4 in Division I-A and 92.7 in Division I-AA. Id.

100. Brewington, supra note 1.

101. See Chronicle of Higher Education, Participation: Proportion of Female Students on Athletic Teams, supra note 98. Only 18 insti- tutions in Division I-A and 20 institutions in Division I-AA were

within five percentage points of achieving substantial proportional- ity. Id.

102. Carton, supra note 59.

103. Brewington, supra note 1.

104. 1998-99 Participation Study, supra note 10.

105. Wallace, supra note 9.

106. 1996 Clarification Letter, supra note 88, at II-27. An institution cannot meet the requirements of part two simply by cutting men's teams or participation opportunities. Id. Nor can a school cut women's teams or participation opportunities without replacing them with additional teams or opportunities. Id. "Part two considers an institution's good-faith remedial efforts through actual program expansion." Id.

107. See supra note 92 and accompanying text.

108. 1996 Clarification Letter, supra note 88, at II-28. While no defini- tive time frame is mentioned by OCR, it is clear that the addition or elevation must be relatively recent. See id.

109. 1996 Clarification Letter, supra note 88, at II-28.

110. Id. Mere promises to expand the program do not suffice. Id.

111. 164 F.3d 113 (2d Cir. 1999).

112. Id. at 119.

113. Carol Barr, Still Afloat, Athletic Business, Oct. 1999, at 26-28.

114. This takes the form of an addition of a women's team at those in- stitutions where there was no club team prior to the formation of an intercollegiate women's rowing team; at institutions that upgrade a club team to the intercollegiate level, the decision is considered an elevation. See 1996 Clarification Letter, supra note 88, at II-28.

115. See 1996 Clarification Letter, supra note 88, at II-28.

116. Id. Any institution doing so may also be able to claim that it has a continuing practice of program expansion if it had a policy or proce- dure in place for requesting the addition or upgrading of sports that was effectively communicated to students. Id.

117. See supra note 42 and accompanying text.

118. Jeff Metcalfe, ASU Wet Behind Ears But Aims to be Water Power, The Arizona Republic, Sept. 8, 1999, at C1. Arizona State Univer- sity will add a rowing team in 2001–02. Id.

119. 1996 Clarification Letter, supra note 88, at II-29. This includes stu- dents who have been accepted but are not yet enrolled at the institu- tion. Id.

120. 1996 Clarification Letter, supra note 88, at II-29. An institution that has recently eliminated a viable intercollegiate women's team is highly unlikely to satisfy part three. Id.

121. Id.

122. Id.

123. Id.

124. 1996 Clarification Letter, supra note 88, II-30-31.

125. Id. at II-30.

126. American Rower's Almanac, supra note 3, at 489-94.

127. See Bonnette, supra note 86.

128. See id. "Compliance with this third method is unlikely if there is a sport not currently offered to the underrepresented sex for which there is sufficient competition in the institution's normal competi- tive regions and; a club team; and/or significant participation at high schools in the institution's normal recruitment area; and/or substan- tial intramural participation." Id.

129. See supra note 3 and accompanying text.

130. See supra notes 53-54 and accompanying text.

131. 44 Fed. Reg. 71413 (1979).

132. See Cook v. Colgate Univ., 802 F. Supp. 737 (N.D.N.Y. 1992), vacated as moot, 992 F.2d 17 (2d Cir. 1993) (College women's hockey team established a prima facie Title IX violation by coming forth with evidence that the university had provided significantly superior funding and equipment to the men's team).

133. 44 Fed. Reg. 71413 (1979).

134. Id.

135. Id.

136. Id.

137. See supra notes 103-05 and accompanying text. This is especially important given that the analysis of compliance with Title IX often focuses on whether the equivalent quality and quantities of benefits and services are provided to equivalent percentages of female and male athletes. See Bonnette, supra note 86. Many athletic administrators focus on comparing similar sports with each other for the purpose of this area of analysis, as they find that it is the easiest method by which to ensure compliance. See id. at II-2. Football creates a problem for these administrators because it is usually afforded better benefits than any other sport, yet does not have a similar women's sport to provide a basis for comparison. See id. at II-3. Thus, the administrators must provide "football-like" benefits to several sports in order to be in compliance with this area. See id.

Although the sports are dissimilar in nature, football and women's rowing are similar in the number of participation opportunities that they provide; this allows for an easier comparison between men's and women's athletics and, therefore, facilitates compliance with this area of Title IX. See generally id. at II-9-24. Even this comparison is not flawless; it is likely that football will still receive greater benefits in areas such as compensation of coaches, medical and training services, publicity, recruitment, and support services. However, the institution has available numerous justifications for the differences in the provisions of these services. See generally, Bonnette, supra note 86, at II-9-24.

138. See supra notes 103-05 and accompanying text.

139. See 44 Fed. Reg. 71414 (1979). See also Fed. Reg. 71416 (1979).

140. See 44 Fed. Reg. 71414 (1979). "Compliance will be assessed by examining, among other factors, the equivalence for men and women of: (1) the quality of equipment and supplies; (2) the amount of equipment and supplies; (3) the suitability of equipment and supplies; (4) the maintenance and replacement of the equipment and supplies; and (5) the availability of equipment and supplies." Id.

141. See id.

142. The specific equipment costs are discussed at length. . .

143. See infra. . .

144. See 44 Fed. Reg. 71414 (1979).

145. See Hale, supra note 52.

146. See 44 Fed. Reg. 71414 (1979).

147. Bonnette, supra note 86, at II-10.

148. Id.

149. Sue Rochman, Journey Towards Equity, Athletic Management, June/July 1998, at 23. This individual is referred to as a rigger. Id.

150. Bonnette, supra note 86, at II-10.

151. See id.

152. See 44 Fed. Reg. 71416 (1979). "Compliance will be assessed by examining, among other factors, the equivalence for men and women of: (1) the number of competitive events per sport; (2) the number and length of practice opportunities; (3) the time of day competitive events are scheduled; (4) the time of day practice opportunities are scheduled; and (5) the opportunities to engage in available pre-season and post-season competition." Id.

153. See Valerie Bonnette, Title IX Basics, available at www.neaa.org/library/general/achieving_gender_equity/ (n.d.) at II-11.

154. See 44 Fed. Reg. 71417 (1979). "Compliance will be assessed by examining, among other factors, the equivalence for men and women of: (1) quality and availability of the facilities provided for practice and competitive events; (2) exclusivity of use of facilities provided for practice and competitive events; (3) availability of locker rooms; (4) quality of locker rooms; (5) maintenance of practice and competitive facilities; and (6) preparation of facilities for practice and competitive events." Id.

155. Id. There is some flexibility in evaluating this standard depending on the nature of the facility used. See Bonnette, supra note 86, at II-16.

156. Id.

157. The specific construction costs are discussed at length. . .

158. United States Rowing Ass'n, Women's Rowing 2 (1995).

159. Telephone interview with Rob Catloth, Head Women's Rowing Coach, University of Kansas (June 2, 1999).

160. Bonnette, supra note 86, at II-17. The scheduling of the boathouse will not be of concern unless there are rental terms that stipulate that the facility only be used by the institution at times that are inconvenient for the athletes. Id.

161. Johnson (Part II), supra note 96. Louisville's team travels 43 miles to practice. Id. The rowing team at Robert Morris College practices at a boathouse eighteen miles from campus. Rochman, supra note 149, at 26.

162. 44 Fed. Reg. 71414 (1979) requires that the amounts spent on scholarships be offered on a "substantially proportional basis to the number of male and female participants in the institution's athletic programs." Id.

163. *Chronicle of Higher Education,* Participation: Proportion of Female Students on Athletic Teams, at http://www.chronicle.com/search97cgi/s97_cgi (last visited Jan. 19, 2001).

164. See Judith Jurin Semo and John F. Bartos, A Guide to Recent Developments in Title IX Litigation - February 15, 2000, Achieving Gender Equity at III-2, at http://www.ncaa.org/library/general/achieving_gender_equity/ (n.d.) (discussing Gonyo v. Drake Univ., 837 F. Supp. 989 (S.D. Iowa 1993); Beasley v. Ala. State Univ., 3 F. Supp.2d 1325 (M.D. Ala. 1998); Boucher v. Syracuse Univ., 164 F.3d 113 (2d Cir. 1999)).

165. Id.

166. 1998 Guidance Letter, supra note 76. Therefore, if females constitute 55 percent of the athletes at an institution, then they must receive between 54 and 56 percent of the athletic scholarship dollars awarded by institution. Id. OCR allows variations of larger than one percent under several circumstances, including during the phase-in period for scholarships that are awarded by a new team. Id.

167. NCAA Manual, supra note 11, 15.5.3.1.2. The NCAA classifies sports into two categories for the purpose of athletic scholarships. Head count sports are those sports in which only full athletic scholarships may be awarded if they are awarded at all. Id. at 15.5.2, 15.5.4, 15.5.5. In Division I, football, men's basketball, and wom-

en's basketball, gymnastics, tennis, and volleyball are head count sports. Equivalency sports are sports in which partial athletic scholarships may be awarded. All other NCAA sports are equivalency sports. Id. at 15.5.3.

168. Id.

169. NCAA Manual, supra note 11, 15.5.5.1, 15.5.5.2. A football team in Division I-A may award 85 scholarships, while a team in Division I-AA may offer the equivalent of 63 scholarships to 85 individuals. Id.

LEGAL FRAMEWORK

CLARIFICATION OF INTERCOLLEGIATE ATHLETICS POLICY GUIDANCE: THE THREE-PART TEST (JANUARY 16, 1996)

United States Department of Education, Office for Civil Rights

The Office for Civil Rights (OCR) enforces Title IX of the Education Amendments of 1972, 20 U.S.C. § 1681 et seq. (Title IX), which prohibits discrimination on the basis of sex in education programs and activities by recipients of federal funds. The regulation implementing Title IX, at 34 C.F.R. Part 106, effective July 21, 1975, contains specific provisions governing athletic programs, at 34 C.F.R. § 106.41, and the awarding of athletic scholarships, at 34 C.F.R. § 106.37(c). Further clarification of the Title IX regulatory requirements is provided by the Intercollegiate Athletics Policy Interpretation, issued December 11, 1979 (44 Fed. Reg. 71413 et seq. (1979)).*

The Title IX regulation provides that if an institution sponsors an athletic program it must provide equal athletic opportunities for members of both sexes. Among other factors, the regulation requires that an institution must effectively accommodate the athletic interests and abilities of students of both sexes to the extent necessary to provide equal athletic opportunity.

The 1979 Policy Interpretation provides that as part of this determination OCR will apply the following three-part test to assess whether an institution is providing nondiscriminatory participation opportunities for individuals of both sexes:

1. Whether intercollegiate level participation opportunities for male and female students are provided in numbers substantially proportionate to their respective enrollments; or

2. Where the members of one sex have been and are underrepresented among intercollegiate athletes, whether the institution can show a history and continuing practice of program expansion which is demonstrably responsive to the developing interests and abilities of the members of that sex; or

3. Where the members of one sex are underrepresented among intercollegiate athletes, and the institution cannot show a history and continuing practice of program expansion, as described above, whether it can be demonstrated that the interests and abilities of the members of that sex have been fully and effectively accommodated by the present program.

Thus, the three-part test furnishes an institution with three individual avenues to choose from when determining how it will provide individuals of each sex with nondiscriminatory opportunities to participate in intercollegiate athletics. If an institution has met any part of the three-part test, OCR will determine that the institution is meeting this requirement.

It is important to note that under the Policy Interpretation the requirement to provide nondiscriminatory participation opportunities is only one of many factors that OCR examines to determine if an institution is in compliance with the athletics provision of Title IX. OCR also considers the quality of competition offered to members of both sexes in order to determine whether an institution effectively accommodates the interests and abilities of its students.

In addition, when an "overall determination of compliance" is made by OCR, 44 Fed. Reg. 71417, 71418, OCR examines the institution's program as a whole. Thus, OCR considers the effective accommodation of interests and abilities in conjunction with equivalence in the availability, quality, and kinds of other athletic benefits and opportunities provided male and female athletes to determine whether an institution provides equal athletic opportunity as required by Title IX. These other benefits include coaching, equipment, practice and competitive facilities, recruitment, scheduling of games, and publicity, among others. An institution's failure to provide nondiscriminatory participation opportunities usually amounts to a denial of equal athletic opportunity because these opportunities provide access to all other athletic benefits, treatment, and services.

---

*The Policy Interpretation is designed for intercollegiate athletics. However, its general principles, and those of this Clarification, often will apply to elementary and secondary interscholastic athletic programs, which are also covered by the regulation. *See* 44 Fed. Reg. 71413.

This Clarification provides specific factors that guide an analysis of each part of the three-part test. In addition, it provides examples to demonstrate, in concrete terms, how these factors will be considered. These examples are intended to be illustrative, and the conclusions drawn in each example are based solely on the facts included in the example.

THREE-PART TEST—PART ONE: ARE PARTICIPATION OPPORTUNITIES SUBSTANTIALLY PROPORTIONATE TO ENROLLMENT?

Under part one of the three-part test (part one), where an institution provides intercollegiate level athletic participation opportunities for male and female students in numbers substantially proportionate to their respective full-time undergraduate enrollments, OCR will find that the institution is providing nondiscriminatory participation opportunities for individuals of both sexes.

OCR's analysis begins with a determination of the number of participation opportunities afforded to male and female athletes in the intercollegiate athletic program. The Policy Interpretation defines participants as those athletes:

a. Who are receiving the institutionally-sponsored support normally provided to athletes competing at the institution involved, e.g., coaching, equipment, medical and training room services, on a regular basis during a sport's season; and

b. Who are participating in organized practice sessions and other team meetings and activities on a regular basis during a sport's season; and

c. Who are listed on the eligibility or squad lists maintained for each sport, or

d. Who, because of injury, cannot meet a, b, or c above but continue to receive financial aid on the basis of athletic ability.

OCR uses this definition of a participant to determine the number of participation opportunities provided by an institution for purposes of the three-part test.

Under this definition, OCR considers a sport's season to commence on the date of a team's first intercollegiate competitive event and to conclude on the date of the team's final intercollegiate competitive event. As a general rule, all athletes who are listed on a team's squad or eligibility list and are on the team as of the team's first competitive event are counted as participants by OCR. In determining the number of participation opportunities for the purposes of the interests and abilities analysis, an athlete who participates in more than one sport will be counted as a participant in each sport in which he or she participates.

In determining participation opportunities, OCR includes, among others, those athletes who do not receive scholarships (e.g., walk-ons), those athletes who compete on teams sponsored by the institution even though the team may be required to raise some or all of its operating funds, and those athletes who practice but may not compete. OCR's investigations reveal that these athletes receive numerous benefits and services, such as training and practice time, coaching, tutoring services, locker room facilities, and equipment, as well as important non-tangible benefits derived from being a member of an intercollegiate athletic team. Because these are significant benefits, and because receipt of these benefits does not depend on their cost to the institution [or] whether the athlete competes, it is necessary to count all athletes who receive such benefits when determining the number of athletic opportunities provided to men and women.

OCR's analysis next determines whether athletic opportunities are substantially proportionate. The Title IX regulation allows institutions to operate separate athletic programs for men and women. Accordingly, the regulation allows an institution to control the respective number of participation opportunities offered men and women. Thus, it could be argued that to satisfy part one there should be no difference between the participation rate in an institution's intercollegiate athletic program and its full-time undergraduate student enrollment.

However, because in some circumstances it may be unreasonable to expect an institution to achieve exact proportionality—for instance, because of natural fluctuations in enrollment and participation rates or because it would be unreasonable to expect an institution to add athletic opportunities in light of the small number of students that would have to be accommodated to achieve exact proportionality—the Policy Interpretation examines whether participation opportunities are "substantially" proportionate to enrollment rates. Because this determination depends on the institution's specific circumstances and the size of its athletic program, OCR makes this determination on a case-by-case basis, rather than through use of a statistical test.

As an example of a determination under part one: If an institution's enrollment is 52 percent male and 48 percent female and 52 percent of the participants in the athletic program are male and 48 percent female, then the institution would clearly satisfy part one. However OCR recognizes that natural fluctuations in an institution's enrollment and/ or participation rates may affect the percentages in a subsequent year. For instance, if the institution's admissions the following year resulted in an enrollment rate of 51 percent males and 49 percent females, while the participation rates of males and females in the athletic program remained constant the institution would continue to satisfy part one because it would be unreasonable to expect the institution to fine tune its program in response to this change in enrollment.

As another example, over the past five years an institution has had a consistent enrollment rate for women of 50 percent. During this time period, it has been expanding its program for women in order to reach proportionality. In the year that the institution reaches its goal—i.e., 50 percent of the participants in its athletic program are female—its enrollment rate for women increases to 52 percent. Under these circumstances, the institution would satisfy part one.

OCR would also consider opportunities to be substantially proportionate when the number of opportunities that would be required to achieve proportionality would not be sufficient to sustain a viable team, i.e., a team for which there is a sufficient number of interested and able students and enough available competition to sustain an intercollegiate team. As a frame of reference in assessing this situation, OCR may consider the average size of teams offered for the underrepresented sex, a number which would vary by institution.

For instance, Institution A is a university with a total of 600 athletes. While women make up 52 percent of the university's enrollment, they only represent 47 percent of its athletes. If the university provided women with 52 percent of athletic opportunities, approximately 62 additional women would be able to participate. Because this is a significant number of unaccommodated women, it is likely that a viable sport could be added. If so, Institution A has not met part one.

As another example, at Institution B women also make up 52 percent of the university's enrollment and represent 47 percent of Institution B's athletes. Institution B's athletic program consists of only 60 participants. If the University provided women with 52 percent of athletic opportunities, approximately 6 additional women would be able to participate. Since 6 participants are unlikely to support a viable team, Institution B would meet part one.

THREE-PART TEST—PART TWO: IS THERE A HISTORY AND CONTINUING PRACTICE OF PROGRAM EXPANSION FOR THE UNDERREPRESENTED SEX?

Under part two of the three-part test (part two), an institution can show that it has a history and continuing practice of program expansion which is demonstrably responsive to the developing interests and abilities of the underrepresented sex. In effect, part two looks at an institution's past and continuing remedial efforts to provide nondiscriminatory participation opportunities through program expansion.*

OCR will review the entire history of the athletic program, focusing on the participation opportunities provided

for the underrepresented sex. First, OCR will assess whether past actions of the institution have expanded participation opportunities for the underrepresented sex in a manner that was demonstrably responsive to their developing interests and abilities. Developing interests include interests that already exist at the institution.[†] There are no fixed intervals of time within which an institution must have added participation opportunities. Neither is a particular number of sports dispositive. Rather, the focus is on whether the program expansion was responsive to developing interests and abilities of the underrepresented sex. In addition, the institution must demonstrate a continuing (i.e., present) practice of program expansion as warranted by developing interests and abilities.

OCR will consider the following factors, among others, as evidence that may indicate a history of program expansion that is demonstrably responsive to the developing interests and abilities of the underrepresented sex.

- An institution's record of adding intercollegiate teams, or upgrading teams to intercollegiate status, for the underrepresented sex;

- An institution's record of increasing the numbers of participants in intercollegiate athletics who are members of the underrepresented sex; and

- An institution's affirmative responses to requests by students or others for addition or elevation of sports.

OCR will consider the following factors, among others, as evidence that may indicate a continuing practice of program expansion that is demonstrably responsive to the developing interests and abilities of the underrepresented sex:

- An institution's current implementation of a nondiscriminatory policy or procedure for requesting the addition of sports (including the elevation of club or intramural teams) and the effective communication of the policy or procedure to students; and

- An institution's current implementation of a plan of program expansion that is responsive to developing interests and abilities.

OCR would also find persuasive an institution's efforts to monitor developing interests and abilities of the underrepresented sex, for example, by conducting periodic nondiscriminatory assessments of developing interests and abilities and taking timely actions in response to the results.

In the event that an institution eliminated any team for the underrepresented sex, OCR would evaluate the

---

*Part two focuses on whether an institution has expanded the number of intercollegiate participation opportunities provided to the underrepresented sex. Improvements in the quality of competition, and of other athletic benefits provided to women athletes, while not considered under the three-part test, can be considered by OCR in making an overall determination of compliance with the athletics provision of Title IX.

[†]However, under this part of the test an institution is not required, as it is under part three, to accommodate all interests and abilities of the underrepresented sex. Moreover, under part two an institution has flexibility in choosing which teams it adds for the underrepresented sex, as long as it can show overall history and continuing practice of program expansion for members of that sex.

circumstances surrounding this action in assessing whether the institution could satisfy part two of the test. However, OCR will not find a history and continuing practice of program expansion where an institution increases the proportional participation opportunities for the underrepresented sex by reducing opportunities for the overrepresented sex alone or by reducing participation opportunities for the overrepresented sex to a proportionately greater degree than for the underrepresented sex. This is because part two considers an institution's good faith remedial efforts through actual program expansion. It is only necessary to examine part two if one sex is overrepresented in the athletic program. Cuts in the program for the underrepresented sex, even when coupled with cuts in the program for the overrepresented sex, cannot be considered remedial because they burden members of the sex already disadvantaged by the present program. However, an institution that has eliminated some participation opportunities for the underrepresented sex can still meet part two if, overall, it can show a history and continuing practice of program expansion for that sex.

In addition, OCR will not find that an institution satisfies part two where it established teams for the underrepresented sex only at the initiation of its program for the underrepresented sex or where it merely promises to expand its program for the underrepresented sex at some time in the future.

The following examples are intended to illustrate the principles discussed above. At the inception of its women's program in the mid-1970s, Institution C established seven teams for women. In 1984 it added a women's varsity team at the request of students and coaches. In 1990 it upgraded a women's club sport to varsity team status based on a request by the club members and an NCAA survey that showed a significant increase in girls high school participation in that sport. Institution C is currently implementing a plan to add a varsity women's team in the spring of 1996 that has been identified by a regional study as an emerging women's sport in the region. The addition of these teams resulted in an increased percentage of women participating in varsity athletics at the institution. Based on these facts, OCR would find Institution C in compliance with part two because it has a history of program expansion and is continuing to expand its program for women in response to their developing interests and abilities.

By 1980, Institution D established seven teams for women. Institution D added a women's varsity team in 1983 based on the requests of students and coaches. In 1991 it added a women's varsity team after an NCAA survey showed a significant increase in girls' high school participation in that sport. In 1993 Institution D eliminated a viable women's team and a viable men's team in an effort to reduce its athletic budget. It has taken no action relating to the underrepresented sex since 1993. Based on these facts, OCR would not find Institution D in compliance with part two. Institution D cannot show a continuing practice of program expansion that is responsive to the developing interests and abilities of the underrepresented sex where its only action since 1991 with regard to the underrepresented sex was to eliminate a team for which there was interest, ability, and available competition.

In the mid-1970s, Institution E established five teams for women. In 1979 it added a women's varsity team. In 1984 it upgraded a women's club sport with twenty-five participants to varsity team status. At that time it eliminated a women's varsity team that had eight members. In 1987 and 1989 Institution E added women's varsity teams that were identified by a significant number of its enrolled and incoming female students when surveyed regarding their athletic interests and abilities. During this time it also increased the size of an existing women's team to provide opportunities for women who expressed interest in playing that sport. Within the past year, it added a women's varsity team based on a nationwide survey of the most popular girls high school teams. Based on the addition of these teams, the percentage of women participating in varsity athletics at the institution has increased. Based on these facts, OCR would find Institution E in compliance with part two because it has a history of program expansion and the elimination of the team in 1984 took place within the context of continuing program expansion for the underrepresented sex that is responsive to their developing interests.

Institution F started its women's program in the early 1970s with four teams. It did not add to its women's program until 1987 when, based on requests of students and coaches, it upgraded a women's club sport to varsity team status and expanded the size of several existing women's teams to accommodate significant expressed interest by students. In 1990 it surveyed its enrolled and incoming female students; based on that survey and a survey of the most popular sports played by women in the region, Institution F agreed to add three new women's teams by 1997. It added a women's team by 1991 and 1994. Institution F is implementing a plan to add a women's team by the spring of 1997. Based on these facts, OCR would find Institution F in compliance with part two. Institution F's program history since 1987 shows that it is committed to program expansion for the underrepresented sex and it is continuing to expand its women's program in light of women's developing interests and abilities.

THREE-PART TEST—PART THREE: IS THE INSTITUTION FULLY AND EFFECTIVELY ACCOMMODATING THE INTERESTS AND ABILITIES OF THE UNDERREPRESENTED SEX?

Under part three of the three-part test (part three) OCR determines whether an institution is fully and effectively accommodating the interests and abilities of its students who are members of the underrepresented sex—including students who are admitted to the institution though not yet enrolled. Title IX provides that a recipient must provide equal athletic opportunity to its students. Accordingly, the Policy Interpretation does not require an institution to accommodate the interests and abilities of potential students.*

While disproportionately high athletic participation rates by an institution's students of the overrepresented sex (as compared to their enrollment rates) may indicate that an institution is not providing equal athletic opportunities to its students of the underrepresented sex, an institution can satisfy part three where there is evidence that the imbalance does not reflect discrimination, i.e., where it can be demonstrated that, notwithstanding disproportionately low participation rates by the institution's students of the underrepresented sex, the interests and abilities of these students are, in fact, being fully and effectively accommodated.

In making this determination, OCR will consider whether there is (a) unmet interest in a particular sport; (b) sufficient ability to sustain a team in the sport; and (c) a reasonable expectation of competition for the team. If all three conditions are present OCR will find that an institution has not fully and effectively accommodated the interests and abilities of the underrepresented sex.

If an institution has recently eliminated a viable team from the intercollegiate program, OCR will find that there is sufficient interest, ability, and available competition to sustain an intercollegiate team in that sport unless an institution can provide strong evidence that interest, ability, or available competition no longer exists.

a)   Is there sufficient unmet interest to support an intercollegiate team?

[First,] OCR will determine whether there is sufficient unmet interest among the institution's students who are members of the underrepresented sex to sustain an intercollegiate team. OCR will look for interest by the underrepresented sex as expressed through the following indicators, among others:

- Requests by students and admitted students that a particular sport be added;

- Requests that an existing club sport be elevated to intercollegiate team status;

- Participation in particular club or intramural sports;

- Interviews with students, admitted students, coaches, administrators, and others regarding interest in particular sports;

- Results of questionnaires of students and admitted students regarding interests in particular sports; and

- Participation in particular interscholastic sports by admitted students.

In addition, OCR will look at participation rates in sports in high schools, amateur athletic associations, and community sports leagues that operate in areas from which the institution draws its students in order to ascertain likely interest and ability of its students and admitted students in particular sport(s).* For example, where OCR's investigation finds that a substantial number of high schools from the relevant region offer a particular sport which the institution does not offer for the underrepresented sex, OCR will ask the institution to provide a basis for any assertion that its students and admitted students are not interested in playing that sport. OCR may also interview students, admitted students, coaches, and others regarding interest in that sport.

An institution may evaluate its athletic program to assess the athletic interest of its students of the underrepresented sex using nondiscriminatory methods of its choosing. Accordingly, institutions have flexibility in choosing a nondiscriminatory method of determining athletic interests and abilities provided they meet certain requirements. These assessments may use straightforward and inexpensive techniques, such as a student questionnaire or an open forum, to identify students' interests and abilities. Thus, while OCR expects that an institution's assessment should reach a wide audience of students and should be open-ended regarding the sports students can express interest in, OCR does not require elaborate scientific validation of assessment.

An institution's evaluation of interest should be done periodically so that the institution can identify in a timely and responsive manner any developing interests and abilities of the underrepresented sex. The evaluation should also take into account sports played in the high schools and communities from which the institution draws its students both as an indication of possible interest on campus and to permit the institution to plan to meet the interests of admitted students of the underrepresented sex.

b)   Is there sufficient ability to sustain an intercollegiate team?

Second, OCR will determine whether there is sufficient ability among interested students of the underrepresented sex to sustain an intercollegiate team. OCR will examine indications of ability such as:

- The athletic experience and accomplishments—in interscholastic, club, or intramural competition—of

---

*However, OCR does examine an institution's recruitment practices under another part of the Policy Interpretation. See 44 Fed. Reg. 71417. Accordingly, where an institution recruits potential student athletes for its men's teams, it must ensure that women's teams are provided with substantially equal opportunities to recruit potential student athletes.

---

*While these indications of interest may be helpful to OCR in ascertaining likely interest on campus, particularly in the absence of more direct indications, the institution is expected to meet the actual interests and abilities of its students.

students and admitted students interested in playing the sport;

- Opinions of coaches, administrators, and athletes at the institution regarding whether interested students and admitted students have the potential to sustain a varsity team; and

- If the team has previously competed at the club or intramural level, whether the competitive experience of the team indicates that it has the potential to sustain an intercollegiate team.

Neither a poor competitive record nor the inability of interested students or admitted students to play at the same level of competition engaged in by the institution's other athletes is conclusive evidence of lack of ability. It is sufficient that interested students and admitted students have the potential to sustain an intercollegiate team.

c) Is there a reasonable expectation of competition for the team?

Finally, OCR determines whether there is a reasonable expectation of intercollegiate competition for a particular sport in the institution's normal competitive region. In evaluating available competition, OCR will look at available competitive opportunities in the geographic area in which the institution's athletes primarily compete, including:

- Competitive opportunities offered by other schools against which the institution competes; and

- Competitive opportunities offered by other schools in the institution's geographic area, including those offered by schools against which the institution does not now compete.

Under the Policy Interpretation, the institution may also be required to actively encourage the development of intercollegiate competition for a sport for members of the underrepresented sex when overall athletic opportunities within its competitive region have been historically limited for members of that sex.

CONCLUSION

This discussion clarifies that institutions have three distinct ways to provide individuals of each sex with nondiscriminatory participation opportunities. The three-part test gives institutions flexibility and control over their athletics programs. For instance, the test allows institutions to respond to different levels of the interest by its male and female students. Moreover, nothing in the three-part test requires an institution to eliminate participation opportunities for men.

At the same time, this flexibility must be used by institutions consistent with Title IX's requirement that they not discriminate on the basis of sex. OCR recognizes that institutions face challenges in providing nondiscriminatory participation opportunities for their students and will continue to assist institutions in finding ways to meet these challenges.

LETTER CLARIFYING APPORTIONMENT OF FINANCIAL AID IN INTERCOLLEGIATE ATHLETICS PROGRAMS (JULY 23, 1998)

United States Department of Education, Office for Civil Rights

Ms. Nancy S. Footer
General Counsel
Bowling Green State University
308 McFall Center
Bowling Green, Ohio 43403-0010

Dear Ms. Footer:

This is in response to your letter requesting guidance in meeting the requirements of Title IX specifically as it relates to the equitable apportionment of athletic financial aid. Please accept my apology for the delay in responding.

As you know, the Office for Civil Rights (OCR) enforces Title IX of the Education Amendments of 1972, 20 U.S.C. § 1682, which prohibits discrimination on the basis of sex in education programs and activities. The regulation implementing Title IX and the Department's Intercollegiate Athletics Policy Interpretation published in 1979—both of which followed publication for notice and the receipt, review, and consideration of extensive comments—specifically address intercollegiate athletics. You have asked us to provide clarification regarding how educational institutions can provide intercollegiate athletes with nondiscriminatory opportunities to receive athletic financial aid. Under the Policy Interpretation, the equitable apportioning of a college's intercollegiate athletics scholarship fund for the separate budgets of its men's and women's programs—which Title IX permits to be segregated—requires that the total amounts of scholarship aid made available to the two budgets are "substantially proportionate" to the participation rates of male and female athletes. 44 Fed. Reg. 71413, 71415 (1979).

In responding, I wish (1) to clarify the coverage of Title IX and its regulations as they apply to both academic and athletic programs, and (2) to provide specific guidance about the existing standards that have guided the enforcement of Title IX in the area of athletic financial aid, particularly the Policy Interpretation's "substantially proportionate" provision as it relates to a college's funding of the athletic scholarships budgets for its men's and women's teams. At the outset, I want to clarify that, wholly apart from any obligation with respect to scholarships, an institution with an intercollegiate athletics program has an independent Title IX obligation to provide its students with nondiscriminatory athletic participation opportunities. The scope of that separate obligation is not addressed in this letter, but was addressed in a Clarification issued on January 16, 1996.

TITLE IX COVERAGE: ATHLETICS VERSUS ACADEMIC PROGRAMS

Title IX is an anti-discrimination statute that prohibits discrimination on the basis of sex in any education program or activity receiving federal financial assistance, including athletic programs. Thus, in both academics and athletics, Title IX guarantees that all students, regardless of gender, have equitable opportunities to participate in the education program. This guarantee does not impose quotas based on gender, either in classrooms or in athletic programs. Indeed, the imposition of any such strict numerical requirement concerning students would be inconsistent with Title IX itself, which is designed to protect the rights of all students and to provide equitable opportunities for all students.

Additionally, Title IX recognizes the uniqueness of intercollegiate athletics by permitting a college or university to have separate athletic programs, and teams, for men and women. This allows colleges and universities to allocate athletic opportunities and benefits on the basis of sex. Because of this unique circumstance, arguments that OCR's athletics compliance standards create quotas are misplaced. In contrast to other antidiscriminatory statutes, Title IX compliance cannot be determined simply on the basis of whether an institution makes sex-specific decisions, because invariably they do. Accordingly, the statute instead requires institutions to provide equitable opportunities to both male and female athletes in all aspects of its two separate athletic programs. As the court in the Brown University case stated, "[i]n this unique context Title IX operates to ensure that the gender-segregated allocation of athletic opportunities does not disadvantage either gender. Rather than create a quota or preference, this unavoidable gender-conscious comparison merely provides for the allocation of athletic resources and participation opportunities between the sexes in a non-discriminatory manner." *Cohen v. Brown University*, 101 F.3d 155, 177 (1st Cir. 1996), cert. denied, 117 S. Ct. 1469

(1997). The remainder of this letter addresses the application of Title IX only to athletic scholarships.

Athletics: Scholarship Requirements

With regard to athletic financial assistance, the regulations promulgated under Title IX provide that, when a college or university awards athletic scholarships, these scholarship awards must be granted to "members of each sex in proportion to the number of students of each sex participating in . . . intercollegiate athletics." Since 1979, OCR has interpreted this regulation in conformity with its published "Policy Interpretation: Title IX and Intercollegiate Athletics." The Policy Interpretation does not require colleges to grant the same number of scholarships to men and women, nor does it require that individual scholarships be of equal value. What it does require is that, at a particular college or university, "the total amount of scholarship aid made available to men and women must be substantially proportionate to their [overall] participation rates" at that institution. It is important to note that the Policy Interpretation only applies to teams that regularly compete in varsity competition.

Under the Policy Interpretation, OCR conducts a "financial comparison to determine whether proportionately equal amounts of financial assistance (scholarship aid) are available to men's and women's athletic programs." The Policy Interpretation goes on to state that "[i]nstitutions may be found in compliance if this comparison results in substantially equal amounts or if a disparity can be explained by adjustments to take into account legitimate nondiscriminatory factors."

A "disparity" in awarding athletic, financial assistance refers to the difference between the aggregate amount of money athletes of one sex received in one year, and the amount they would have received if their share of the entire annual budget for athletic scholarships had been awarded in proportion to their participation rates. Thus, for example, if men account for 60% of a school's intercollegiate athletes, the Policy Interpretation presumes that—absent legitimate nondiscriminating factors that may cause a disparity—the men's athletic program will receive approximately 60% of the entire annual scholarship budget, and the women's athletic program will receive approximately 40% of those funds. This presumption reflects the fact that colleges typically allocate scholarship funds among their athletic teams, and that such teams are expressly segregated by sex. Colleges' allocation of the scholarship budget among teams, therefore, is invariably sex-based, in the sense that an allocation to a particular team necessarily benefits one sex to the exclusion of the other. Where, as here, disparate treatment is inevitable and a college's allocation of scholarship funds is "at the discretion of the institution," the statute's nondiscrimination requirements obliges colleges to ensure that men's and women's *separate* activities receive equitable treatment.

Nevertheless, in keeping with the Policy Interpretation allowance for disparities from "substantially proportionate" awards to the men's and women's programs based on legitimate nondiscriminatory factors, OCR judges each matter on a case-by-case basis with due regard for the unique factual situation presented by each case. For example, OCR recognizes that disparities may be explained by actions taken to promote athletic program development, and by differences between in-state and out-of-state tuition at public colleges, 44 Fed. Reg, at 71415. Disparities might also be explained, for example, by legitimate efforts undertaken to comply with Title IX requirements, such as participation requirements. See, e.g., *Gonyo v. Drake Univ.* 879 F. Supp. 1000, 1005–06 (S.D. Iowa 1995). Similarly, disparities may be explained by unexpected fluctuations in the participation rates of males and females. For example, a disparity may be explained if an athlete who had accepted an athletic scholarship decided at the last minute to enroll at another school. It is important to note it is not enough for a college or university merely to assert a nondiscriminatory justification. Instead, it will be required to demonstrate that its asserted rationale is in fact reasonable and does not reflect underlying discrimination. For instance, if a college consistently awards a greater number of out-of-state scholarships to men, it may be required to demonstrate that this does not reflect discriminatory recruitment practices. Similarly, if a university asserts the phase-in of scholarships for a new team as a justification for a disparity, the university may be required to demonstrate that the time frame for phasing-in of scholarships is reasonable in light of college sports practices to aggressively recruit athletes to build start-up teams quickly.

In order to ensure equity for athletes of both sexes, the test for determining whether the two scholarship budgets are "substantially proportionate" to the respective participation rates of athletes of each sex necessarily has a high threshold. The Policy Interpretation does not, however, require colleges to achieve exact proportionality down to the last dollar. The "substantially proportionate" test permits a small variance from exact proportionality. OCR recognizes that, in practice, some leeway is necessary to avoid requiring colleges to unreasonably fine-tune their scholarship budgets.

When evaluating each scholarship program on a case-by-case basis, OCR's first step will be to adjust any disparity to take into account all the legitimate nondiscriminatory reasons provided by the college, such as the extra costs for out-of-state tuition discussed earlier. If any unexplained disparity in the scholarship budget for athletes of either gender is 1% or less for the entire budget for athletic scholarships, there will be a strong presumption that such a disparity is reasonable and based on legitimate and nondiscriminatory factors. Conversely, there will be a strong presumption that an unexplained disparity of more than 1% is in violation of the "substantially proportionate" requirements.

Thus, for example, if men are 60% of the athletes, OCR would expect that the men's athletic scholarship budget would be within 59–61% of the total budget for athletic

scholarships for all athletes, after accounting for legitimate nondiscriminatory reasons for any larger disparity. Of course, OCR will continue to judge each case in terms of its particular facts. For example, at those colleges where 1% of the entire athletic scholarship budget is less than the value of one full scholarship, OCR will presume that a disparity of up to the value of one full scholarship is equitable and nondiscriminatory. On the other hand, even if an institution consistently has less than a 1% disparity, the presumption of compliance with Title IX might still be rebutted if, for example, there is direct evidence of discriminatory intent.

OCR recognizes that there has been some confusion in the past with respect to the Title IX compliance standards for scholarships. OCR's 1990 Title IX Investigator's Manual correctly stated that one would expect proportionality in the awarding of scholarships, absent a legitimate, nondiscriminatory justification. But that Manual also indicated that compliance with the "substantially proportionate" test could depend, in part, upon certain statistical tests. In some cases, application of such a statistical test would result in a determination of compliance despite the existence of a disparity as large as 3–5%.

We would like to clarify that use of such statistical tests is not appropriate in these circumstances. Those tests, which are used in some other discrimination contexts to determine whether the disparities in the allocation of benefits to different groups are the result of chance, are inapposite in the athletic scholarship context because a college has direct control over its allocation of financial aid to men's and women's teams, and because such decisions necessarily are sex-based in the sense that an allocation to a particular team will affect only one sex. See *Brown,* 101 F.3d at 176–78 (explaining why college athletics "presents a distinctly different situation from admissions and employment," and why athletics requires a different analysis than that used in such other contexts "in order to determine the existence vel non of discrimination"). In the typical case where aid is expressly allocated among sex-segregated teams, chance simply is not a possible explanation for disproportionate aid to one sex. Where a college does not make a substantially proportionate allocation to sex-segregated teams, the burden should be on the college to provide legitimate, nondiscriminatory reasons for the disproportionate allocation. Therefore, the use of statistical tests will not be helpful in determining whether a disparity in the allocations for the two separate athletic scholarship budgets is nondiscriminatory.

While a statistical test is not relevant in determining discrimination, the confusion caused by the manual's inclusion of a statistical test resulted in misunderstandings. Therefore, OCR is providing this clarification regarding the substantial proportionality provision found in the 1979 Policy Interpretation to confirm the substance of a longstanding standard. In order to ensure full understanding, OCR will apply the presumptions and case-by-case analysis described in this letter for the 1998–99 academic year. OCR strongly encourages recipients to award athletic financial assistance to women athletes in the 1997–98 academic year consistent with this policy clarification, both as a matter of fairness and in order to ensure that they are moving towards the policy clarification stated in this letter.

I trust that this letter responds to the questions the University has regarding the "substantially proportionate"

provision of the Policy interpretation in the context of the funding for an institution's two separate athletic scholarship budgets for male and female athletes. . . .

Sincerely yours,
Dr. Mary Frances O'Shea
National Coordinator for Title IX Athletics

FURTHER CLARIFICATION OF INTERCOLLEGIATE ATHLETICS POLICY GUIDANCE REGARDING TITLE IX COMPLIANCE

United States Department of Education, Office for Civil Rights

July 11, 2003

Dear Colleague:

It is my pleasure to provide you with this Further Clarification of Intercollegiate Athletics Policy Guidance Regarding Title IX Compliance.

Since its enactment in 1972, Title IX has produced significant advancement in athletic opportunities for women and girls across the nation. Recognizing that more remains to be done, the Bush Administration is firmly committed to building on this legacy and continuing the progress that Title IX has brought toward true equality of opportunity for male and female student-athletes in America.

In response to numerous requests for additional guidance on the Department of Education's (Department) enforcement standards since its last written guidance on Title IX in 1996, the Department's Office for Civil Rights (OCR) began looking into whether additional guidance on Title IX requirements regarding intercollegiate athletics was needed. On June 27, 2002, Secretary of Education Rod Paige created the Secretary's Commission on Opportunities in Athletics to investigate this matter further, and to report back with recommendations on how to improve the application of the current standards for measuring equal opportunity to participate in athletics under Title IX. On February 26, 2003, the Commission presented Secretary Paige with its final report, "Open to All: Title IX at Thirty," and in addition, individual members expressed their views.

After eight months of discussion and an extensive and inclusive fact-finding process, the Commission found very broad support throughout the country for the goals and spirit of Title IX. With that in mind, OCR today issues this Further Clarification in order to strengthen Title IX's promise of non-discrimination in the athletic programs of our nation's schools.

Title IX establishes that: "No person in the United States shall, on the basis of sex, be excluded from participation in, be denied the benefits of, or be subjected to discrimination under any education program or activity receiving Federal financial assistance."

. . . .

In its 1979 Policy Interpretation, the Department established a three-prong test for compliance with Title IX, which it later amplified and clarified in its 1996 Clarification. . . .

First, with respect to the three-prong test, which has worked well, OCR encourages schools to take advantage of its flexibility, and to consider which of the three prongs best suits their individual situations. All three prongs have been used successfully by schools to comply with Title IX, and the test offers three separate ways of assessing whether schools are providing equal opportunities to their male and female students to participate in athletics. If a school does not satisfy the "substantial proportionality" prong, it would still satisfy the three-prong test if it maintains a history and continuing practice of program expansion for the underrepresented sex, or if "the interests and abilities of the members of [the underrepresented] sex have been fully and effectively accommodated by the present program." Each of the three prongs is thus a valid, alternative way for schools to comply with Title IX.

The transmittal letter accompanying the 1996 Clarification issued by the Department described only one of these three separate prongs—substantial proportionality—as a "safe harbor" for Title IX compliance. This led many schools to believe, erroneously, that they must take measures to ensure strict proportionality between the sexes. In fact, each of the three prongs of the test is an equally sufficient means of complying with Title IX, and no one prong is favored. The Department will continue to make clear, as it did in its 1996 Clarification, that "[i]nstitutions have flexibility in providing nondiscriminatory participation opportunities to their students, and OCR does not require quotas."

In order to ensure that schools have a clear understanding of their options for compliance with Title IX, OCR will undertake an education campaign to help educational institutions appreciate the flexibility of the law, to explain that each prong of the test is a viable and separate means of compliance, to give practical examples of the ways in which schools can comply, and to provide schools with technical assistance as they try to comply with Title IX.

In the 1996 Clarification, the Department provided schools with a broad range of specific factors, as well as illustrative examples, to help schools understand the flexibility of the three-prong test. OCR reincorporates those factors, as well as those illustrative examples, into this Further Clarification, and OCR will continue to assist schools on a case-by-case basis and address any questions they have about Title IX compliance. Indeed, OCR encourages schools to request individualized assistance from OCR as they consider ways to meet the requirements of Title IX. As OCR works with schools on Title IX compliance, OCR will share information on successful approaches with the broader scholastic community.

Second, OCR hereby clarifies that nothing in Title IX requires the cutting or reduction of teams in order to demonstrate compliance with Title IX, and that the elimination of teams is a disfavored practice. Because the elimination of teams diminishes opportunities for students who are interested in participating in athletics instead of enhancing opportunities for students who have suffered from discrimination, it is contrary to the spirit of Title IX for the government to require or encourage an institution to eliminate athletic teams. Therefore, in negotiating compliance agreements, OCR's policy will be to seek remedies that do not involve the elimination of teams.

Third, OCR hereby advises schools that it will aggressively enforce Title IX standards, including implementing sanctions for institutions that do not comply. At the same time, OCR will also work with schools to assist them in avoiding such sanctions by achieving Title IX compliance.

Fourth, private sponsorship of athletic teams will continue to be allowed. Of course, private sponsorship does not in any way change or diminish a school's obligations under Title IX.

Finally, OCR recognizes that schools will benefit from clear and consistent implementation of Title IX. Accordingly, OCR will ensure that its enforcement practices do not vary from region to region.

OCR recognizes that the question of how to comply with Title IX and to provide equal athletic opportunities for all students is a challenge for many academic institutions. But OCR believes that the three-prong test has provided, and will continue to provide, schools with the flexibility to provide greater athletic opportunities for students of both sexes.

OCR is strongly reaffirming today its commitment to equal opportunity for girls and boys, women and men. To that end, OCR is committed to continuing to work in partnership with educational institutions to ensure that the promise of Title IX becomes a reality for all students.

Thank you for your continuing interest in this subject.

Sincerely,
Gerald Reynolds
Assistant Secretary for Civil Rights

IMPACT ON COACHES

GENDER EQUITY IN COLLEGE ATHLETICS: WOMEN COACHES AS A CASE STUDY

Deborah L. Rhode and Christopher J. Walker

INTRODUCTION

As Title IX celebrates its thirty-fifth anniversary, few would doubt its importance in changing the landscape of women's athletics. Since its enactment, female participation in high school sports increased from 294,000 athletes in 1971 to 2.9 million in 2006.[1] During roughly the same period, female participation in intercollegiate sports soared from 16,000 in 1970 to over 180,000 in 2005.[2] The effects of increased opportunity are also reflected in America's Olympic and world championship medals in both individual and team sports, including basketball, gymnastics, ice hockey, soccer, softball, volleyball, water polo, skiing, golf, speed skating, swimming, tennis, track and field, and wrestling.[3] Not all of this progress is, of course, directly attributable to Title IX.

Broader cultural changes in the status of women are at work and are themselves responsible for the statute's enactment and implementation. But few doubt the legislation's powerful role in transforming the landscape of women's athletics.

Despite this impressive legacy, however, considerable frustration persists in how the statute has, or has not, been implemented. Some complain that the pace of change has been too slow and that substantial gender disparities persist in participation rates and expenditures. Others are unhappy that progress for women's sports appears to have come at the expense of men's sports. Too little attention has, however, focused on one of the most ironic byproducts of Title IX: as opportunities for female students have increased, opportunities for female professionals have declined. Only 42% of women's teams have a female head coach, compared to over 90% in 1972. The number of men's teams with a female head coach remains at fewer than 2%, a figure unchanged since the 1970s. That leaves less than a fifth (17.7%) of all college teams with a woman in charge.[4] Furthermore, women coaches of women's teams win fewer championships than their male counterparts. At last count, six intercollegiate women's sports, including volleyball and swimming, have never had a team win the national championship with a female head coach; soccer has had only one.[5] Women have also lost departmental control of women's collegiate sports programs. Almost all are now merged with men's, and less than a fifth of top administrative jobs go to women.[6]

This Article focuses on the barriers that still confront women in college athletics, particularly those who seek professional positions in coaching and administration. . . . . Part II.A discusses the declining representation and lower success rate of women coaches. . . . Part III presents the findings of the empirical research conducted for this Article. We surveyed 462 coaches of women's collegiate teams to better understand their needs, priorities, and opinions on coaching and the role of Title IX. Part IV situates these findings in light of other research on barriers for women in male-dominated settings, including coaching, and concludes with potential policy prescriptions.

[*Ed. Note: Authors' historical overview of gender equity and Title IX is omitted.*]

. . . .

II. WOMEN COACHES IN COLLEGE ATHLETICS

A. The Representation and Success of Women Coaches

As noted earlier, the increase in resources for women athletes has brought a dramatic increase in men's interest in coaching them, and a corresponding decrease in coaching opportunities for women. Female head coaches lead only 42% of women's teams, as opposed to over 90% in 1972 when Title IX was first enacted.[58] Most of the decline occurred in the 1970s, but the trend persists: 2006 registered the lowest ever proportion of female coaches for women's teams.[59] This decline does not appear attributable to an absence of women's interest in coaching positions because the percentage of female assistant coaches has remained constant since the 1990s.[60] As one commentator puts it, women are entering the ranks, but the "professional finish line . . . continues to elude them."[61] The situation is bleaker still for women seeking head coach positions of men's teams: the number in that role has remained at 2% since the 1970s.[62] The result is that only 17.7% of all teams have a female head coach.[63]

Women are underrepresented not only in head coaching positions, but in those that produce the most competitive successes in women's sports. **Table 1** details the success rate of women coaches.[64]

The first two columns compare 1995–1996 figures with 2003–2004 figures for the percentage of women head coaches for women's teams. The third column demonstrates the percentage of women coaches who successfully coached their teams into the NCAA tournament during the 2003–2004 season, while the final column portrays the percentage of women coaches of national championship teams

Table 1   Sport-by-Sport Breakdown of Women Coaches of Women's Collegiate Teams

Sport	Head Coaches Women (%)		In Tourney (%)	Winners (%)
	1995–96	2003–04	2003–04	Through 2005
Basketball	63.7%	67.6%	72%	79%
Bowling	n/a	55	38	0
Cross Country	20.4	21.2	18	12
Fencing	25	5.9	9	4
Field Hockey	89.1	96.5	94	100
Golf	57	51	79	48
Gymnastics	38.8	44.8	67	63
Ice Hockey	n/a	42.9	50	100
Lacrosse	87.5	88.5	88	88
Rifle	5.3	21.1	22	47
Rowing	n/a	45.3	50	50
Skiing	26.7	20	18	0
Soccer	36.7	34.7	32	4
Softball	68.5	69	59	64
Swimming	21.1	16.8	14	0
Tennis	38.4	33.6	36	12
Track, Indoor	19.3	24.7	20	33
Track, Outdoor	17.7	23.9	19	21
Volleyball	61.7	0.5	39	0
Water Polo	n/a	35	0	0
Total	**42.3%**	**39.9%**	**41.2%**	**36.3%**

Source: "Gender Equity in College Athletics: Women Coaches as a Case Study" by Deborah L. Rhode and Christopher J. Walker. Copyright 2008 by *Stanford Journal of Civil Rights and Civil Liberties.* Reproduced with permission of *Stanford Journal of Civil Rights and Civil Liberties* in the format Textbook via Copyright Clearance Center.

during the past twenty-five years. These sport-by-sport statistics, although useful to a point, fail to capture some complexities in women's sports, because some sports have been dominated mostly by female head coaches, while in others they are almost nonexistent. Moreover, the gender difference in success rates should not be taken to imply gender differences in coaching capabilities. Rather, it may reflect women's underrepresentation in positions with the greatest access to resources and talented athletes. Still, the lack of women coaches, together with their lack of relative success, raises several grounds for concern.

The first involves the violation of meritocratic principles and the injustice for women who aspire to such professional positions. What little empirical evidence is available finds that women coaches are more qualified than their male counterparts in terms of training, experience, and achievement.[65] As subsequent discussion suggests, women's underrepresentation may be more attributable to unconscious biases, exclusionary recruiting networks, and inflexible working structures than to objective qualifications. Their poorer success rates may also partly reflect lack of mentoring and institutional support. A further concern is the impact that this underrepresentation has on female athletes. Many young women benefit from the distinctive experiences, coaching style, and role models supplied by female coaches. Dena Evans, former head coach of Stanford's cross-country team, notes that many women, particularly those in Division I, "will spend more time with the coaches in their sport than they will with any professor."[66] The lack of female role models in coaching and athletic leadership sends a disturbing message to female athletes about their own likely professional opportunities. Finally, the underrepresentation of women in key athletic positions may work against alternative conceptions of sporting excellence that focus less on revenues and more on participation and the benefits that it can foster.

[*Ed. Note: Authors' discussion of legal remedies for gender discrimination against women coaches is omitted.*]

. . . .

III. FINDINGS FROM A NATIONAL SURVEY OF WOMEN COLLEGIATE COACHES

As noted earlier, little empirical research is available on the state of women coaches in collegiate athletics.[92] This Article fills some of the gaps by providing a data set from perhaps the most important source: the coaches themselves. Although the results are far from conclusive, they do highlight some of the challenges still facing women seeking professional careers in college athletics and, together with other research reviewed in Part IV, suggest some avenues for change.

A. Survey Methodology

An electronic survey . . . was mailed to coaches of women's collegiate teams in March and April 2006.[93] We targeted coaches of women's teams via email correspondence, website postings, and listserv distributions.[94] Although the surveys were anonymous, participants had an option of including their email address in order to receive the results of the survey. Participants were also provided our contact information if they had further questions or comments.[95]

Hundreds of surveys were sent via email to coaches of women's collegiate teams with the request that they forward the survey link on to their colleagues. Of the 701 surveys submitted, 239 surveys had to be discarded due to incomplete responses. Of those 462 remaining participants who completed the survey, a quarter were male (24.3%), and three-quarters were female (75.7%).[96]

. . . For present purposes, the most relevant characteristics are as follows: about three-quarters of the respondents were head coaches and 60% were in Division I schools. Over half the female coaches and a quarter of the male coaches

were single. About 11% of the women and 4% of the men reported having domestic partners. Slightly over a quarter of the women and over half of the men had children. This profile is consistent with national data on coaches, which indicates that female coaches are significantly less likely than male coaches, or women in general, to be married or to have children.[97] As survey findings suggest, this gender difference may be partly attributable to the difficulties of reconciling coaching demands with family responsibilities, which still fall disproportionately on women. About 90% of the coaches who responded were white, a proportion again representative of coaches in the nation as a whole.[98]

Almost half of the participants were thirty-five or younger, and about the same percentage had graduate degrees and at least ten years of coaching experience. No significant gender differences in age, ethnicity, or qualifications emerged, except that women had significantly better athletic performance records in college. This last finding is consistent with the research noted earlier, finding that women coaches have higher qualifications than their male counterparts. And as subsequent discussion suggests, such gender differences may also suggest that women need higher credentials in order to advance within the coaching profession.

Participants came from sixteen different sports and relatively high performing programs. About four-fifths of the men, compared with two-thirds of the women, reported coaching at least "above average" teams. This finding is also consistent with other research summarized in Part II indicating that female coaches are less likely to be in positions yielding greatest competitive success.

B. The Role of Title IX in Promoting Women's Athletics and Women Coaches

The survey began by asking coaches to evaluate the impact of Title IX on various aspects of gender equity in collegiate athletics. Virtually all (96%) reported that Title IX has had a "strong" or "very strong" effect on the "number of female athletes and athletic teams on college campuses." Another four-fifths (81%) of coaches found a similar "strong" or "very strong" effect on the "general interest in, and significance of, women's athletic teams on college campuses." Four-fifths also reported a strong or very strong positive effect on the fair allocation of resources between men's and women's teams; one in five coaches (21%) believed that Title IX has had no effect or a negative effect on resource allocation.

Assessments of Title IX's impact on coaching and leadership opportunities are somewhat more qualified. About three-fourths felt that Title IX had a positive effect on "the resources college coaches of women's teams have to be successful." Two-thirds thought that the statute had positively affected leadership opportunities, and three-fifths believed that it had had similar impact on "the number and likelihood of women coaching at the collegiate level." However, as **Table 2** indicates, assessments of the value of Title IX for women coaches were more mixed.

Gender differences in these results were minimal except with respect to the effect of Title IX on women coaches. Two-thirds (66%) of male respondents believed that Title IX had a positive effect on women coaches, while only about half (54%) of female respondents agreed. Only 6% of men indicated that Title IX had a negative effect on women coaches, and another 27% reported no effect. By contrast, 18% of women coaches believed it had a negative effect, and 28% felt it had no effect. Head coaches also offered less positive assessments than assistant coaches: almost half reported no effect (30%) or a negative effect (16%) on women coaches, while only a third of assistant coaches saw no effect (18%) or a negative effect (15%).

Coaches had an opportunity to explain their views in response to an open-ended question: "If you do not think that Title IX has had a favorable (or sufficiently favorable) effect, why not and what reforms would be appropriate?" Of the 462 coaches surveyed, 169 responded. Many prefaced their concerns by acknowledging significant positive effects of Title IX. As one coach noted, "I would not have a job without it." But considerable frustration surfaced with the way that the statute had, or had not, been enforced. One cluster of grievances involved the failure of Title IX to secure true equality for women. Other concerns involved the adverse affect on men.

According to many respondents, a central limitation of Title IX involved the absence of oversight of schools' data reporting and the lack of penalties for noncompliance:

There is not enough backbone to it.

There is no strong policing. Reporting is just a shell game from the Athletic Director's perspective. There is never a check and balance on that reporting. There needs to be some kind of audit . . .

There are no repercussions for schools that don't comply . . .

Check out the debacles on the high school and city recreation level . . . It's a nightmare.

A related frustration involved continued inequalities in salaries, program support, and leadership opportunities. As some coaches put it, athletics was still under the control of an "old boys network" and "they take care of each other." The few women who were in high positions could not necessarily serve as effective Title IX advocates because their focus had to be on "making money, raising money, winning games." Many respondents also noted a double-edged byproduct of the increased status, compensation, and "professionalism" of women's sports: their increased attractiveness to male coaches. As more men came in, more women lost out. An equally unhappy consequence was the pressure to boost female participation rates beyond what resources

Table 2   Role of Title IX in Promoting Women Collegiate Athletics (In Order of Strongest Effect)

Question: In your opinion, what effect has Title IX had on the following?

	Very Strong Negative Effect	Some Negative Effect	No Effect	Strong Positive Effect	Very Strong Positive Effect	Response Average
Women in Sports: the number of female athletes and athletics teams on college campuses	0% (1)	2% (7)	2% (11)	47% (216)	**49% (226)**	4.43
Interest in Women's Teams: general interest in, and significance of, women's athletics teams on college campuses	0% (1)	3% (12)	16% (73)	**55% (252)**	26% (121)	4.05
Allocation of Resources: the fair allocation of resources between men's and women's teams based on interest and ability	2% (8)	5% (25)	14% (62)	**59% (270)**	20% (94)	3.91
Coaching Resources: the resources college coaches of women's teams have to be successful	1% (3)	3% (14)	22% (103)	**57% (260)**	17% (78)	3.86
Leadership: the representation of women in leadership positions in college athletics (head coaches, athletic directors, and so forth)	2% (10)	9% (40)	22% (103)	**51% (236)**	15% (70)	3.69
Female Coaches: the number of women coaching at the collegiate level	3% (15)	12% (56)	28% (126)	**43% (198)**	14% (63)	3.52

Source: "Gender Equity in College Athletics: Women Coaches as a Case Study" by Deborah L. Rhode and Christopher J. Walker. Copyright 2008 by *Stanford Journal of Civil Rights and Civil Liberties*. Reproduced with permission of *Stanford Journal of Civil Rights and Civil Liberties* in the format Textbook via Copyright Clearance Center.

permitted. As one coach put it, "we are required to carry more [athletes] without the necessary funds/staff to take care of more." An example was a golf team that had to carry twelve members but only had travel support for five. Adding women just to improve an institution's "equity numbers" adversely affected "team chemistry" and compromised talented athletes' access to playing and coaching time.

By contrast, other respondents regretted that Title IX had "limited opportunities for men while increasing opportunities for women." The main concern was the reduction in non-revenue male sports:

> *Men's programs suffer because schools cannot find a female sport to balance [them] out. [What is unfortunate about Title IX is that] there are a lot more young men than women interested in playing sports and a lot more men than women talented enough to play sports at the college level. . . . Every year I have to turn talented men away because I have roster limits, [while] I scour the nation trying to find good female golfers. . . . The reluctance to make meaningful reform to the quota system is destroying men's teams. . . . As a woman, I am ashamed that my success has to come at the expense of male athletes that have trained hard throughout their life only to find that their collegiate opportunities keep getting smaller.*

A related concern was the impact of Title IX on male applicants for coaching positions:

> *Some schools fill positions with women who are not necessarily qualified but fill a quota because they are female and to me that's an injustice to those of us that are good.*
>
> *I have served on a search committee to find prospective Head Coaches and some of the first comments out of the administration are that they do not want the typical "white male" filling the role.*
>
> *I have seen and experienced much difficulty for qualified men candidates to get a job because of a desire to increase/maintain the number of female coaches within a department.*

Other respondents, however, noted precisely the opposite form of favoritism: male athletic directors who hired male "friends or friends of friends" or coaches with "less experience [who would] . . . teach the girls to play like a guy." Several survey participants challenged the "misconception" that Title IX was to blame for the demise of male sports. From their vantage, the statute was a convenient "scapegoat," an "excuse to drop programs instead of raising revenues" or curbing expenses of college football.

One striking aspect of these responses is the absence of reform strategies. Apart from general calls for more enforcement and less curtailment of male programs, survey participants had little to say about how to avoid the problems

they identified. None suggested how to address the decline in female coaches. To gain insight into that problem, the remainder of the survey focused on the keys to coaching success and ways to assist women in gaining equal opportunity in athletic leadership positions.

C. The Keys to Coaching Success

Coaches were asked to identify what they need to succeed at the collegiate level, and nine in ten coaches reported that the following were "very important" or "most important" to success: (1) institutional support (from college, athletics director) (92%); (2) financial resources for program operations (91%); and (3) resources for recruiting (90%). Another four-fifths (82%) found staffing resources to be "very important" or "most important," while only half found the same for mentorship/professional development resources. Only one in three (32%) found childcare and flexibility for coaches' family concerns to be "very important" or "most important," although three in four (76%) coaches found this need to be at least "important." **Table 3** breaks down these findings in more detail. Fifty-one coaches also identified other important resources, primarily facilities, but also scholarships.

Again, some noteworthy gender differences emerged in the responses. Unsurprisingly, male and female coaches differed in the priority they attached to childcare and family concerns: close to half of both men and women (45%) considered these issues important, but less than a fifth (19%) of male coaches indicated that this was "very important" or "most important"—in comparison to over a third (36%) of women coaches. Women coaches also gave higher priority to mentoring and professional development; about three-fifths (58%) considered it "very important" or "most important," while only a third of men put it in that category. Women were also somewhat more likely to find staffing resources to be "very important" or "most important" (83%) than their male counterparts (77%).[99]

Coaches had an opportunity to expand on their views in response to an open-ended question: "Please comment on any of these above-listed resources or others that are not listed. What makes them so important to program success? Who is in the best position to provide the most important resources?" Of the 462 coaches surveyed, 232 responded. Money was the dominant and nearly universal concern. As one respondent put it, "Financial resources are the gateway to success in other areas." They made possible adequate salaries, facilities, scholarships, staff, equipment, travel, recruiting, marketing, and other operational support. The following responses are typical:

> *Financial resources are by FAR, the most important item in any college sport. Without equal across the board funding, a program cannot be expected to be highly competitive or of championship caliber.*
>
> *It is difficult to win if the resources are not there . . . plain and simple.*

Table 3   Resources Needed to Build Successful Programs (Listed in Order of Importance)

Question: Please indicate the importance of each of the following resources for a coach's success in collegiate athletics:

	Not Important	Not Very Important	Important	Very Important	Most Important	Response Average
Institutional Support (from College, Athletics Director)	0% (0)	1% (3)	8% (37)	40% (184)	**52% (239)**	4.42
Financial Resources for Program Operations	0% (0)	0% (2)	9% (40)	**50% (232)**	41% (189)	4.31
Resources for Recruiting	0% (0)	1% (5)	9% (42)	**50% (232)**	40% (184)	4.29
Staffing Resources (assistant coaches, administrative support)	0% (2)	2% (8)	16% (74)	**55% (255)**	27% (124)	4.06
Salary and Benefits for Coaches	1% (3)	2% (9)	29% (135)	**57% (265)**	11% (51)	3.76
Mentorship/Professional Development Resources	0% (1)	5% (25)	41% (192)	**46% (212)**	7% (33)	3.54
Childcare Needs/Flexibility for Coaches' Family Concerns	5% (25)	18% (85)	**44% (205)**	25% (117)	7% (31)	3.1

Source: "Gender Equity in College Athletics: Women Coaches as a Case Study" by Deborah L. Rhode and Christopher J. Walker. Copyright 2008 by *Stanford Journal of Civil Rights and Civil Liberties.* Reproduced with permission of *Stanford Journal of Civil Rights and Civil Liberties* in the format Textbook via Copyright Clearance Center.

Low funding means low performance.

Pardon . . . the way this sounds but money talks. If you do not have it they will not come.

There is, in short, no substitute for financial support in building effective athletic programs. The more time coaches have to spend raising funds, the less time they have for what they are being "paid to do and that is COACH THE GAME." The minority of respondents who mentioned child care also felt strongly about its importance. In order to keep women with children "in the ranks," some support was critical, especially during the peak season. Most survey participants viewed the athletic director as the key player in making sure resources were adequate, followed by the college president. The "Senior Woman Administrator" was almost never mentioned, even though the NCAA began to require members to create this position in 2001 partly to address such concerns.[100]

D.   The State of Coaches' Athletic Programs

In addition to identifying what coaches need for successful programs, we sought to understand how often coaches had the necessary support. To that end, the survey asked "How far away is your program from the ideal situation?" with respect to eight important factors. **Table 4** details coaches' responses.

What is perhaps most surprising about these responses is that they reflect no significant gender differences.[101] This is all the more striking because as Part III indicated, fewer women reported coaching high quality teams. It is also noteworthy that relatively little dissatisfaction surfaced about work family/conflicts; it may be that those who experience difficulty leave their positions.

Survey participants also had the chance to expand on their views in response to three open-ended questions:

- If there is one thing you could change about your program (or personal situation affecting your program), what would that be? (382 responses)

- What do you feel is the most important ingredient for the successes you have had with your program? (396 responses)

- Please comment on any of the keys (or barriers) to success that you have experienced. We are particularly interested in identifying "best practices" and "common pitfalls" here, so any additional information would be greatly appreciated. (307 responses)

Predictably, what coaches wished to change most about their program involved money. Most financial concerns fell into two clusters: more competitive salaries for themselves and their assistants, and additional resources for scholarships, recruiting, facilities, and staff positions. In addition to financial concerns, many coaches mentioned insufficient recognition, respect, and general appreciation for their team, their sport, and their hard work. The barriers to success took similar form. Inadequate budgets for scholarships, salaries, recruiting, and facilities were the dominant concern. The keys to progress followed obviously from that diagnosis: more support from their department and institution. A striking omission from the list was attention to factors that disproportionately affect women. Only two respondents put childcare benefits or more flexible schedules among their key concerns. And only a few mentioned inequalities in relation to men's teams, such as access to facilities or budgets. One objected to the pressure to expand team membership beyond what was productive for competition prior to a Title IX compliance review. However, as subsequent discussion notes, many of these issues surfaced when respondents were asked to focus on women's status, and their responses suggest that gender bias may help account for the insufficiency of support and respect that were key concerns.

In identifying the most important ingredient for success in their programs, coaches overwhelmingly cited personal qualities—their own and their players'. Hard work,

Table 4 State of Athletic Program (In Order of Accordance)

Question: Please indicate your level of accordance with the following statements:

	Strongly Disagree	Somewhat Disagree	Somewhat Agree	Strongly Agree	Response Average
My job provides enough flexibility to allow me to take care of my familial and other personal responsibilities.	3% (15)	14% (65)	**44% (202)**	39% (179)	3.18
My athletes have the resources they need to succeed.	5% (24)	16% (75)	**53% (244)**	26% (119)	2.99
I have had access to mentors and other professional development opportunities that have helped me succeed.	6% (28)	21% (96)	**47% (218)**	26% (119)	2.93
The school administration supports my program and understands my program's needs.	7% (33)	23% (108)	**48% (222)**	21% (97)	2.83
My institution allocates budgets and support fairly between men's and women's teams, given their respective interests and abilities.	12% (52)	26% (119)	**37% (166)**	25% (114)	2.76
I have the resources needed to recruit effectively.	15% (71)	26% (118)	**39% (179)**	20% (93)	2.64
My program receives the financial (and administrative) resources necessary to succeed.	16% (74)	28% (130)	**40% (183)**	16% (74)	2.56
I receive salary and benefits that meet my needs and fairly compensate me for my efforts/performance.	21% (96)	32% (150)	**33% (151)**	14% (65)	2.4

Source: "Gender Equity in College Athletics: Women Coaches as a Case Study" by Deborah L. Rhode and Christopher J. Walker. Copyright 2008 by *Stanford Journal of Civil Rights and Civil Liberties*. Reproduced with permission of *Stanford Journal of Civil Rights and Civil Liberties* in the format Textbook via Copyright Clearance Center.

dedication, perseverance, and commitment were key characteristics. Building a positive team dynamic and recruiting talented athletes were also crucial. A few respondents singled out an NCAA women coaches academy as particularly helpful in career development.[102] Several also mentioned developing the ability to "do more with less." Ironically, however, success along those lines could be double edged. As one coach explained, "If you win a lot with less," the department will not give you more.

E. Gender Inequalities in Coaching and Administration

Survey participants had several opportunities to directly address gender disparities in athletic leadership, and over three-fourths of the sample (353) responded. One question asked about student athletes' gender preferences in coaching. Another open-ended question asked: "Why do you think that women are underrepresented at leadership levels in collegiate athletics (e.g., head coaches, athletic directors, etc.)?" A related question asked "What more needs to be done to get more female coaches in college athletics?" Taken together, these responses offer an unusually rich account of women's professional status in college sports.

First, as **Table 5** indicates, over 90% of coaches agreed that male athletes prefer male coaches, and almost two-thirds disagreed that they accept female coaches. By contrast, about two-thirds thought that female athletes prefer female coaches, but almost all believed that female athletes accept male coaches. Men and women coaches agreed to roughly the same degree on all of these responses.

Obviously, student preferences account for some of the gender inequality in coaching, but they cannot of themselves explain the decline in female coaches of female teams over the last two decades. In responding to the question about what accounts for women's underrepresentation in athletic leadership, virtually no respondents blamed athletes. A significant minority thought that time was the major explanation:

Women have not been around long enough.

It takes a very long time to see big strides made in any area where you're looking to turn around decades and even centuries of a prevailing mind set.

Women's sports are just gaining real national recognition. Men and male sports have received this recognition for over a hundred years.

Table 5   Perceptions of Athletes' Gender Preferences in Coaching

Question: Please indicate your level of accordance with the following statements:

	Strongly Disagree	Somewhat Disagree	Somewhat Agree	Strongly Agree	Response Average
Male athletes prefer male coaches.	2% (9)	6% (27)	28% (126)	**65% (296)**	3.55
Female athletes accept male coaches.	1% (3)	2% (10)	45% (207)	**52% (237)**	3.48
Female athletes prefer female coaches.	3% (14)	31% (143)	**55% (253)**	10% (47)	2.73
Male athletes accept female coaches.	20% (93)	**43% (198)**	31% (142)	5% (23)	2.21

Source: "Gender Equity in College Athletics: Women Coaches as a Case Study" by Deborah L. Rhode and Christopher J. Walker. Copyright 2008 by *Stanford Journal of Civil Rights and Civil Liberties*. Reproduced with permission of *Stanford Journal of Civil Rights and Civil Liberties* in the format Textbook via Copyright Clearance Center.

Most of those responding assumed that time was the answer as well as the explanation for women's unequal status. The large increase in women's participation "will eventually filter into the leadership levels but it takes time." "Simply put, [women] started way behind but they are now catching up." Other survey participants, however, noted a countervailing trend. "As a result of Title IX, salaries for women's teams have increased, therefore men are now becoming interested in those positions." Although athletic directors and team members were happy to have men as coaches in women's sports, "a woman will never be hired to coach a men's team." It was simply "not going to happen. [The women's] playing field is narrow." The result is that women face more competition for coaching positions, and they are locked out of the high revenue sports that are gateways to leadership in most athletic departments. Because the teams that have the largest support groups (alumni, parents, etc.) appear to be mostly male sports—they are still the "money makers for the schools—they get more respect and appear to have more influence on who runs the show—men."

A relatively small minority of respondents felt that women were simply not as interested as men in the opportunities that were available, or were not as "aggressive," "competitive," or "self-confident" in pursuing them. Some believed that "women will not apply for a job unless they feel highly qualified." A few thought that women often lacked adequate judgment or experience for leadership positions, and several pointed to examples of female coaches who were "underqualified" or had been "promoted too soon" and couldn't succeed. But the vast majority of respondents felt that the root of the problem was not women's lack of interest or ability, but family responsibilities and gender bias that made current leadership opportunities seem undesirable, unrealistic, or otherwise unattainable.

Many coaches stressed the inherent difficulty of balancing the time and travel demands of coaching with family obligations:

The lack of flexibility and time requirements.

Coaching is not family friendly.

Women want to do it all but find they cannot.

Job [is] not flexible for working moms.

Family responsibilities make it hard for females to have 24/7 job schedules (which any coaching or administrative job is).

Other respondents thought that the problem was not just the structure of the job but also the lack of support for working mothers:

Without flexibility within the workplace or administrative support it's just not an appealing career.

Very few women have the support they need on the home front to stay in these demanding positions.

Male spouses are often not supportive of the time demands that coaching requires of their spouses.

Without help at home it gets tricky. Most women don't get that support.

Unlike fathers, who are expected "to work long hours and are normally not the primary care giver to children," mothers are expected to put family first. One respondent summarized widespread views: "After all is said and done, many female coaches choose family over career when there are issues at home." At many institutions, inadequate salaries contribute to that choice: the pay isn't enough to compensate for the long hours and childcare costs.

Yet the most frequent explanation that survey participants offered for women's underrepresentation was neither time nor families, but gender bias. Over fifty respondents used some variant of the phrase "old boys club" to describe a cluster of problems, and many others captured the same concerns in less colloquial terms. As coaches often noted, men dominate athletic leadership, and "men hire men." They prefer "people they know or people who are similar to them." Informal networks add to men's advantages. "Guys look out for each other and help their friends into better positions." By contrast, women "haven't established the good old girls network enough." There aren't enough women in leadership positions to help all those who need it. Several respondents also pointed out that most university presidents and major athletic donors are men who generally preferred men as athletic directors. Female candidates were frequently channeled into Senior Woman Administrator positions. Survey participants who commented on those positions generally viewed their presence as "tokenism" or "just for show" and lacking in real influence.

Respondents offered different explanations for these dynamics. Some attributed the problem to men's discomfort with women "in power positions": "Male coaches don't want to be told what to do by a woman." Others thought that men were "afraid of no longer having a 'boys club' work environment." That discomfort created comparable problems for women. They ended up in what was "not a friendly or enjoyable atmosphere to work in," which often led to career changes. Male resistance also constrained the efforts of the small number of women who managed to occupy positions of power. As one respondent noted, "It is difficult to break into the higher levels and . . . [those] who do may not want to jeopardize their position by rocking the boat."

Other respondents saw the main problem as adverse stereotypes about competence and commitment. Some felt women were not "respected" or had to be "twice as hardworking" and "twice as successful" as male counterparts to earn that respect. Men were assumed to have greater expertise; women had to "do more to get the same recognition," and their performance was more often "under a microscope." In athletics, like other leadership contexts, women suffered from the double bind of being too assertive or not assertive enough: "They get characterized as too tough or too soft, and get passed over." An equally common assumption was that women would not be as "capable working the 'old boy' network of alumni donors." Others stressed how difficult it was "to rise above the stereotypes and stigma if you are a mother . . . . They will look at you as not competent to do the job." Women who might become mothers also suffered from that stigma because those doing the hiring "don't want to go through the search process multiple times in a few years" to replace coaches who leave for family reasons.

Bias against lesbians was more pronounced, and could also affect "strong confident competitive women" who were suspected to be lesbians:

The glass ceiling of homophobia is very real.

I am not afraid to talk about the pink elephant in the room. There are very few places to work that support this. Female coaches and administrators are forced to stay in the closet just to keep their jobs. There is no freedom for [people] to be who they really are.

Many respondents linked these patterns with broader cultural forces. As they noted, "women are underrepresented at all leadership levels from politics to college athletics." It did not, however, follow that athletic departments were powerless to address the issue. A number faulted the profession in general or their own institutions in particular for failing to mentor women. As one put it, "there is plenty of focus on development of female players but not much in terms of developing female coaches." Female athletes and young assistant coaches "are not seeing enough encouragement to continue."

Responses to the question about what more could be done to attract women coaches suggested a variety of ways to address these problems. As **Table 6** indicates, men and women generally agreed on the need for more mentoring/professional development (66.5% women, 56.5% men, and 64.3% total). However, on other issues, significant gender differences emerged. Only a third (31.5%) of male coaches thought that more institutional support was necessary, and only a quarter identified a need for more female-friendly environments (23.9%) or more flexible coaching commitments (26.1%). By contrast, a majority of female coaches cited institutional support (59.8%) and more female-friendly environments (57.4%) as necessary, and about 40% thought more flexible coaching commitments would help.

Eighty-nine coaches mentioned other factors. The most common suggestion was to provide higher or more equitable salaries. Many respondents stressed the need to make hiring women a priority, to expand searches, and to encourage more women to go into coaching. Others felt that the problem was that there were not enough women who were interested or committed. Those who were should "stop whining about not having enough opportunities and work their hardest with the opportunities that [they] have." To deal with work/family conflicts, several respondents proposed more childcare services. One offered a cheaper solution: "Find coaches who don't want children because when you get right down to it the mother is more likely to want to be home once she has children."

Table 6   Resources Women Coaches Need To Succeed

Resource	Total by Gender (%)		
	Male	Female	Total
Mentorship/ Professional Development of Prospective Female Coaches	56.5%	66.5%	64.3%
Institutional Support of Prospective Female Coaches	31.5	59.8	53.8
More Female-Friendly Environments in Athletics Department	23.9	57.4	50.5
More Flexible Coaching Commitments	26.1	40.8	37.6
Other	26.1	19.3	20.9

Source: "Gender Equity in College Athletics: Women Coaches as a Case Study" by Deborah L. Rhode and Christopher J. Walker. Copyright 2008 by *Stanford Journal of Civil Rights and Civil Liberties.* Reproduced with permission of *Stanford Journal of Civil Rights and Civil Liberties* in the format Textbook via Copyright Clearance Center.

Some respondents felt that "nothing could be done" or that time would take care of the problem. Others thought broader shifts in cultural attitudes would be necessary to even the playing field:

More respect for women in positions of authority.

A continued change in societal views of a woman's role in the family structure.

Radical decrease in cultural misogyny.

Addressing homophobia issues.

A number of respondents, however, objected to the question. As one put it, "Why is that you have to have more women coaches? If a man can do that same job more effectively then he should get it. I am totally against any bias." Others similarly stressed that "the best person should get the job" and noted that a "female coach isn't always right for the job, just because she is a woman."

On the whole, however, there remains significant dissatisfaction about the enforcement of Title IX and its effect on both female and male athletes. There is comparable frustration with the barriers confronting women in coaching and athletic administration. Taken together with other research, these survey findings highlight the obstacles to equity that persist, and suggest some plausible directions for reform.

IV.   GENDER EQUITY AND ATHLETIC OPPORTUNITY

A.   Barriers to Women in Coaching and Athletic Administration

Many themes of this survey take on additional significance when viewed in the context of other data on women's opportunities for leadership in general and athletic positions in particular. As noted earlier, recent empirical research on coaching and athletic administration is sparse. Much of what is available involves small interview samples or broad demographic findings.[103] However, a rich literature exists on women in upper-level management and professional settings, which bears on women seeking positions in male-dominated athletic departments. Our survey, together with this body of research, reported cases, and press accounts, suggests barriers along three dimensions: adverse stereotypes; in-group favoritism in hiring, mentoring, and support networks; and work/family conflicts. Our more general findings about problems in equal opportunity enforcement structures also bear relevance for women professionals in fields other than athletics.

The first barrier involves the mismatch between stereotypes associated with women and those associated with leadership. Men continue to be rated higher than women on most of the qualities associated with leadership.[104] People more readily credit men with leadership ability and more readily accept men as leaders.[105] What is assertive in a man seems abrasive in a woman, and female leaders risk seeming too feminine or not feminine enough.[106] An overview of more than a hundred studies confirms that women are rated lower as leaders when they adopt authoritative, seemingly masculine styles, particularly when the evaluators are men, or when the role is one typically occupied by men.[107] In effect, women face tradeoffs that men do not.

These stereotypes are very much in play in athletic settings. Some coaches in our survey, like those in other studies, attributed women's underrepresentation in head coaching and upper level administration to women's lack of assertiveness, competitiveness, and drive to obtain such positions.[108] Both coaches and student athletes also report that women have more difficulty than men in commanding respect.[109] One reason that athletes prefer male coaches is that they appear more authoritative and less emotional than their female counterparts.[110] Yet women's attempts to act authoritatively can be off-putting, especially to men, and may evoke homophobic biases.[111] The adverse stereotypes associated with lesbians are a widely reported problem in athletics, and undoubtedly help account for women's attrition and underrepresentation in key positions.[112]

A related bias involves in-group favoritism. Extensive research documents the preferences that individuals feel for members of their own groups. Loyalty, cooperation, favorable evaluations, and the allocation of rewards and opportunities all increase in likelihood for in-group members.[113] A key example is the presumption of competence that dominant groups accord to their members but not to outsiders. Even in experimental situations where male and female performance is objectively equal, women are held to higher standards, and their competence is rated lower.[114] In-group favoritism is also apparent in the informal networks of mentoring, contacts, and support that are critical for advancement. People generally feel most comfortable with those who are like them in important respects, including gender. Women in traditionally male-dominated settings often remain out of the loop of advice and professional development opportunities, and women of color are particularly likely to experience isolation and exclusion.[115]

Virtually all surveys of female coaches report problems stemming from these forms of favoritism, a problem colloquially labeled as "the old boys' network." Many women feel they need to work twice as hard and be twice as successful to get the same recognition as their male counterparts.[116] This perception is consistent with frequently held beliefs that women are underrepresented in head coaching positions because they lack the qualifications and are too often hired for reasons of affirmative action rather than merit.[117] Whether there is a basis for these beliefs is open to question. As noted earlier, surveys find that female head coaches are more qualified than their male counterparts in terms of professional experience and training.[118] Although women also have poorer success records, it is unclear whether the cause is different levels of competence or different quality teams and institutional support. Given the subjectivity of hiring decisions, the influence of adverse stereotypes is difficult to expose.[119]

In any event, women have reason to see favoritism running in the opposite direction. Their perception that men favor men in hiring is consistent with surveys finding that women's chances of obtaining a coaching position are lower under male than female directors.[120] Women also have more difficulty advancing to positions of athletic director.[121] So too, women often experience difficulty gaining support and mentoring in male-dominated athletic settings, which can translate into burnout and early attrition.[122] Such problems may be compounded by backlash, stemming from the sense widely reported in our own and other surveys that Title IX has given women an unfair share of athletic resources.[123] When such attitudes undermine compliance with gender equity requirements, women's frustration and attrition increase. Unsurprisingly, survey evidence suggests that coaches who perceive a lack of compliance are less likely to be satisfied with their position and to plan to stay in coaching.[124]

A final set of obstacles involves work/family conflicts. Part of the problem involves the persistent gender inequalities in family roles. Despite an increase in men's assumption of domestic responsibilities, women continue to shoulder a disproportionate burden in dual career couples.[125] In one particularly illuminating study of high-achieving women, four out of ten felt that their husbands created more work than they contributed.[126] Unequal domestic burdens pose particular problems for women in workplaces with highly demanding and inflexible schedules. Inability to accommodate family responsibilities is a major reason why professional women step off the leadership track.[127]

It is also a primary explanation for women's underrepresentation in head coaching positions. Respondents in our survey, like those in other studies, noted the unrelenting and inconvenient schedules of athletic competition as a major obstacle for women with significant childrearing responsibilities. "Jobs that never end," expectations of "24/7" availability, and "family unfriendly" environments were typical observations.[128] Stories of the "faster than the speeding bullet" maternity leave are legendary: a coach who visited a recruit while in labor and another who was courtside six hours after giving birth.[129] According to Census data, average workloads for female coaches are 2400 hours a year and 2600 for male coaches, which are both well above the national average for full-time workers.[130] At the same time, average hourly pay scales are well below the national average, which makes it difficult for many families to afford child care to cover extended schedules.[131]

Not all of these problems are easily addressed, and some will require broader changes in cultural norms and institutional priorities. But as discussion below suggests, at least some are within reach of plausible reform strategies.

B.   Problems in Title IX Enforcement

Title IX has failed to adequately address the barriers to women in collegiate coaching. Many participants in our survey cited problems in enforcement that ran in opposite directions. One involved failures in oversight structures: the lack of sanctions for noncompliance with Title IX, and the lack of independent checks on compliance data. The converse problem involved the negative byproducts of enforcement, primarily the effect on male sports and talented male athletes who were deprived of competitive opportunities. But, some women's teams suffered as well. The pressure to expand participation beyond the resources available often compromised morale and performance. Although the result might be to improve the school's perceived compliance with Title IX, it also subverts the purpose of the statute to equalize opportunities for a successful athletic experience.

At the root of this problem are financial constraints. Those same constraints were the source of most coaches' unhappiness with the state of their current programs. The vast majority of participants in our survey viewed additional resources as essential for success. Most who expressed a view on how to solve the problem felt that the appropriate response was to "equalize up"—to add resources for women's sports without taking away opportunities from men.

This is also the preferred response by many women's rights advocates and the Secretary's Commission on Opportunity in Athletics. The Commission's report concluded, "Enforcement of Title IX needs to be strengthened toward the goal of ending discrimination against girls and women in athletics, and updated so that athletic opportunities for boys and men are preserved."[132] As other commentators have noted, cutting male programs to finance female teams creates backlash against women and weakens support for Title IX enforcement.[133] Yet how this result can be avoided under current budgetary constraints is a question on which few participants in our survey commented. The few who commented suggested curtailing football expenditures, an approach commonly proposed by commentators.[134] The political feasibility of this response, along with other reform strategies, deserves closer scrutiny.

C.   Strategies for Reform

The policy recommendations that emerge from our survey and related research fall along a continuum. Some would require shifts in attitudes and increases in resources by institutions and government enforcement agencies. Progress along those lines will to some extent depend on broader changes in cultural values. However, some strategies involve relatively modest budgetary commitments and programmatic restructuring. In the long run, institutions as well as individual athletes will benefit from initiatives that even the playing field for women, and broaden the talent pool of coaches and athletic administrators.

Calls for heightened enforcement, sanctions, and oversight of compliance data face significant difficulties in the current political climate. Given the substantial other claims on government resources, the lack of widespread public concern, and the likelihood of resistance by higher education constituencies, major changes in enforcement practices seem unlikely.[135] However, continued pressure by athletic and women's rights organizations, together with recently strengthened legal protections from retaliation for coaches who raise compliance issues, may make incremental progress possible.

Finding ways to increase financial resources for women's programs without curtailing men's programs poses comparable difficulties. The vast majority of higher education institutions confront escalating costs and flat or declining revenues.[136] Few of these institutions can realistically expect to find substantial additional support for female sports through increased alumni contributions or profit-generating athletic activities.[137] The only alternatives will be to use general funds or to reduce expenditures on male programs. Many college leaders are likely to view men's athletics as "just as good a source . . . [of increased budgets for women] as dollars that are spent on other important educational activities like need-based financial aid, reductions in class sizes, or expanded library and computing resources . . . . This is especially true if men have enjoyed more athletic opportunities in the past because of discrimination against female athletes."[138]

One possible source of funds could come from curbing the arms race in football expenditures, which some experts believe already ill serves colleges' collective interest.[139] The difficulty, of course, is that individual schools are reluctant to make cuts that might affect performance and jeopardize their reputation and relations with alumni, students, state government funders, and the broader community. An obvious response would be organizational or legislative initiatives that would encourage capping certain expenditures for all institutions.[140] However, in the absence of such initiatives, and in the 40% of NCAA schools that do not field football teams, it may be difficult to secure the resource increases that participants in our survey advocated.[141] However, institutions can at least focus on initiatives that will enhance opportunities for women coaches without requiring major budget expansions.

One set of strategies should involve improved recruitment, hiring, promotion, and professional development processes. Greater exposure to coaching and administrative career paths should be available through special outreach programs, internships, and volunteer opportunities with younger athletes.[142] Employment-related decision-making should be formalized to reduce reliance on the "old boys network." Standardizing job requirements and developing coaching certification systems could enhance both the fact and appearance of fairness.[143] Soccer, the only major sport with a clear certification process, is also the only one in which women's representation in coaching has not declined.[144] Institutions can also establish formal mentoring programs and provide financial support for attendance at career development programs for women in coaching and athletic administration.[145]

A second cluster of strategies should focus on making athletic careers more responsive to family commitments.

We do not lack for appropriate models across a wide range of professional, academic, and athletic contexts. Relevant initiatives include:

- Adequate family leaves;
- Part-time, job-sharing, and flexible-hour arrangements;
- Additional childcare subsidies, referral networks, placement opportunities, back-up assistance, and stipends for special arrangements during travel; and
- Work schedules and meeting times that are as responsive as possible to coaches' family obligations.

It bears noting that almost half the participants in our survey considered child care and flexibility in meeting family concerns to be "important," and another third felt that they were "very" or "most important" in building a successful program. Experience in many workplace contexts suggests that family-friendly initiatives can be highly cost-effective in boosting recruitment, retention, and job satisfaction.[146]

A final group of strategies should aim to build more inclusive athletic environments and to hold leadership accountable for the results. A wide array of research finds that a key factor in ensuring equal opportunities is a commitment to that objective, which is reflected in workplace priorities, policies, and reward structures.[147] Athletic department leaders need to acknowledge the importance of diversity and equity, to assess progress in achieving them, and to address obstacles that stand in the way. Institutions tend to get what they measure, and too few athletic departments are measuring gender equity for women coaches and athletic administrators. Decision makers need to know whether men and women are being recruited, hired, and promoted in equal numbers; whether they feel equally well supported in career development; whether they experience gender, race, or sexual orientation bias; and whether work/family initiatives are adequate.

V. CONCLUSION

This is not a modest agenda, but it is essential if we are serious about achieving gender equity in college athletics. Women are unlikely to develop their full potential as athletes unless they see career paths that can make use of their talents. Equalizing leadership opportunities in competitive athletics may also be one step toward achieving the broader objectives of full participation, physical health, and psychological benefits that early leaders of female physical education envisioned. Diversifying the leadership of intercollegiate sports could provide opportunities to rethink its priorities. Title IX at midlife has achieved enormous progress, but its promise remains unmet. The challenge now is to ensure that athletes who have been the statute's beneficiaries find a way to pass on their skills and commitments to the generations that follow.

Notes

1. *See* NAT'L COAL. FOR WOMEN & GIRLS IN EDUC., TITLE IX ATHLETICS POLICIES: ISSUES AND DATA FOR EDUCATION DECISION MAKERS 6 (2007).

2. LINDA JEAN CARPENTER & R. VIVIAN ACOSTA, WOMEN IN INTERCOLLEGIATE SPORT 10 (2006), available at http://webpages.charter.net/womeninsport/.

3. Cohen v. Brown Univ., 101 F.3d 155, 188 (1st Cir. 1996), *cert. denied*, 520 U.S. 1186 (1997); *see Int'l Olympic Comm., Olympic Medal Winners,* http://www.olympic.org/uk/athletes/results/search r uk.asp (last visited Nov. 5, 2007).

4. CARPENTER & ACOSTA, *supra* note 2, at 20.

5. See Dena Evans, *Coaching Gap Widens: A Generation After Title IX, Too Many Female Coaches Still Benched,* http://www.womenssportsfoundation.org/cgi-bin/iowa/issues/coach/article.html?record=1119 (last visited Oct. 25, 2007). Coach Evans has been a tremendous help to this project - in framing the initial research question, beta-testing the survey instrument, and distributing the survey to fellow coaches of women's teams.

6. CARPENTER & ACOSTA, *supra* note 2, at 2, 25. Before the merger, women held almost all administrative positions in women's sports. *See* Deborah Brake, *Revisiting Title IX's Feminist Legacy: Moving Beyond the Three-Part Test,* 12 AM. U.J. GENDER SOC. POL'Y & L. 453, 460-61 (2004); see also Welch Suggs, *Women's Athletic Departments Verge on Extinction,* CHRON. HIGHER EDUC., Nov. 19, 2004, at A33 (noting absence of women's programs).

. . . .

38. Wolverton, *supra* note 37, at A26. Some evidence suggests that if football, basketball, and ice hockey are excluded, salaries for male and female head coaches would be nearly equal. ROBERT DRAGO ET AL., FINAL REPORT FOR CAGE: THE COACHING AND GENDER EQUITY REPORT 11 (2005), available at http://lser.la.psu.edu/workfam/CAGEfinalreport.doc.

. . . .

58. CARPENTER & ACOSTA, *supra* note 2, at 15.

59. *Id.*

60. *Id.* at 26.

61. Evans, *supra* note 5.

62. CARPENTER & ACOSTA, *supra* note 2, at 24.

63. Id. at 20-23.

64. Table 1 is based on Coach Evans's data, on file with authors.

65. KANE, *supra* note 15, at 121-22; see also Cynthia A. Hasbrook et al., *Sex Bias and the Validity of Believed Differences Between Male and Female Interscholastic Athletic Coaches,* 61 RES. Q. EXERCISE & SPORT 259 (1990).

66. Evans, *supra* note 5.

. . . .

92. Indeed, even surveys by women's coaches associations are rare. A comprehensive literature review found only one. See CAROLYN LEHR, WOMEN'S BASKETBALL COACHES ASS'N, BASKETBALL COACHES SURVEY REPORT (2000), available at http://www.ncaa.org/genderequity/resourcematerials/Employment/WBCACoachCompStudy.pdf (documenting disparity between men and women coaches of college basketball teams based on panel survey data from 1994, 1997, and 1999).

93. An electronic version of the survey was created and carried out utilizing an online survey instrument from www.surveymonkey.com. The complete results are on file with the authors.

94. Because the URL link to the online survey was distributed via email, website postings, and listserv mailings and because respondents were encouraged to forward the survey link to other coaches of women's teams, an accurate response rate is not quantifiable here.

95. We took several steps to reduce the subjective nature of the survey instrument. First, we utilized an online application that would not allow participants to return to prior questions to change answers. See THOMAS MANGIONE, MAIL SURVEYS: IMPROVING THE QUALITY (1995). Furthermore, the survey was anonymous, so that there would be no pressure to submit a less-than-accurate answer. See generally FLOYD FOWLER, IMPROVING SURVEY QUESTIONS: DESIGN AND EVALUATION (3d ed. 2002); LAWRENCE M. FRIEDMAN & STEVEN MACAULAY, LAW AND BEHAVIORAL SCIENCES (2d ed. 1997); SURVEY RESEARCH METHODS: A READER (Eleanor Singer & Stanley Presser eds., 1989).

96. Five other survey respondents completed the survey but chose not to disclose their gender.

97. In the CAGE Final Report, based on a 2000 census of those who identified themselves as full-time coaches or scouts in higher education, 65.8% of men were married and 40% had children; none had gay living arrangements. Of women, 29.8% were married, 17.8% had children and 3.2% had lesbian living arrangements. DRAGO ET AL., *supra* note 38, at 44.

98. In the CAGE census data, 90.8% of the full-time female coaches and 84.4% of the full-time male coaches were white. *Id.* at 43.

99. By contrast, no noteworthy differences emerged with respect to how head coaches and assistant coaches valued these resources—though head coaches were more likely to list other needed resources. The differences between Division I and non-Division I were similarly insignificant—again Division I coaches were more likely to list other needed resources than their non-Division I counterparts.

100. *See* NAT'L COLLEGIATE ATHLETICS ASS'N, 2006–07 NCAA DIVISION I MANUAL § 4.02.4 (provision adopted Nov. 1, 2001).

101. Similarly, no significant differences emerged between head and assistant coaches or between Division I and non-Division I coaches.

102. See NCAA Women Coaches Academy Website, http://www.coachesacademy.org/ncaa.php (last visited Nov. 9, 2007).

103. The most comprehensive study involved focus groups with about 40 coaches and 40 student athletes as well as an analysis of U.S. Census data to estimate characteristics of male and female college coaches, such as work hours, marital status, sexual orientation, and dependent children. *See* DRAGO ET AL., *supra* note 38. A study of the relationship between Title IX compliance and coaching turnover rates relied on 273 questionnaires. Michael Sagas & Paul Batista, *The Importance of Title IX Compliance on the Job Satisfaction and Occupational Turnover Intent of Intercollegiate Coaches,* 15 APPLIED RES. IN COACHING & ATHLETICS ANN. 15 (2001). Other surveys rely on still smaller data sets. See Sue Inglis et al., *Multiple Realities of Women's Work Experiences in Coaching and Athletic Management,* 9 WOMEN IN SPORT & PHYSICAL ACTIVITY J. 1 (2000) (relying on interviews with eleven women).

104. CATALYST, WOMEN "TAKE CARE," MEN "TAKE CHARGE:" STEREOTYPING OF BUSINESS LEADERS EXPOSED (2005); Linda L. Carli & Alice H. Eagly, *Overcoming Resistance to Women Leaders: The Importance of Leadership Styles, in* WOMEN AND LEADERSHIP: THE STATE OF PLAY AND STRATEGIES FOR CHANGE 127, 128 (Barbara Kellerman & Deborah L. Rhode eds., 2007); Peter Glick et al., *Ambivalent Sexism, in* ADVANCES IN EXPERIMENTAL SOCIAL PSYCHOLOGY 115, 115 (Mark P. Zanna ed., 1999).

105. Carli & Eagly, *supra* note 104; Laurie A. Rudman & Stephen E. Kilianski, *Implicit and Explicit Attitudes Toward Female Authority,* 26 PERSONALITY & SOC. PSYCHOL. BULL. 1315 (2000).

106. LINDA BABCOCK & SARA LASCHEVER, WOMEN DON'T ASK: NEGOTIATION AND THE GENDER DIVIDE 87-88 (2003); Alice H. Eagly & Steven Karau, *Role Congruity Theory of Prejudice Toward Female Leaders,* 109 PSYCHOL. REV. 574 (2002).

107. JEANETTE N. CLEVELAND ET AL., WOMEN AND MEN IN ORGANIZATIONS: SEX AND GENDER ISSUES AT WORK 106, 107 (2000); D. Anthony Butterfield & James P. Grinnell, *Reviewing Gender Leadership, and Managerial Behavior: Do the Decades of Research Tell Us Anything?, in* HANDBOOK OF GENDER AND WORK 223, 235 (Gary N. Powell ed., 1998); Alice H. Eagly et al., *Gender and the Evaluation of Leaders,* 111 PSYCHOL. BULL. 17 (1992).

108. Kane, *supra* note 15, at 125.

109. DRAGO ET AL., *supra* note 38, at 29-31.

110. *Id.*

111. For homophobic biases, see *id.* at 5; Kane, *supra* note 15, at 125-35.

112. DRAGO ET AL., *supra* note 38, at 5, 60; Kane, *supra* note 15, at 135-37; Robin Wilson, *Where Have All the Women Coaches Gone?,* CHRON. HIGHER EDUC., May 4, 2007, at 40, 42.

113. *See generally* Marilyn B. Brewer & Rupert J. Brown, *Intergroup Relations, in* THE HANDBOOK OF SOCIAL PSYCHOLOGY, 554, 554-94 (Daniel T. Gilbert et al. eds., 1998); Susan T. Fiske, *Stereotyping, Prejudice and Discrimination, in* THE HANDBOOK OF SOCIAL PSYCHOLOGY, *supra,* at 357, 357-414; Laura M. Graves, *Gender Bias in Interviewers' Evaluations of Applicants, in* HANDBOOK OF GENDER AND WORK, *supra* note 107, at 145, 154-55; Barbara Reskin, *Rethinking Employment Discrimination and its Remedies, in* THE NEW ECONOMIC SOCIOLOGY: DEVELOPMENTS IN AN EMERGING FIELD 218, 218-44 (Mauro Guillen et al. eds., 2000).

114. Martha Foschi, *Double Standards in the Evaluation of Men and Women,* 59 SOC. PSYCHOL. Q. 237 (l996); Jacqueline Landau, *The Relationship of Race and Gender to Managers' Rating of Promotion Potential,* 16 J. ORG. BEHAV. 391 (1995). In experimental settings, resumes are rated more favorably when they carry male rather than female names. *See* BABCOCK & LASCHEVER, *supra* note 106, at 94; Rhea Steinpreis et al., *The Impact of Gender on the Review of the Curriculum Vitae of Job Applicants and Tenure Candidates: A National Empirical Study,* 41 SEX ROLES 509 (1999).

115. Deborah L. Rhode & Barbara Kellerman, *Women and Leadership: The State of Play, in* Women and Leadership, *supra* note 104, at 10-11; *see also* AM. BAR ASS'N COMM'N ON WOMEN IN THE PROFESSION, VISIBLE INVISIBILITY: WOMEN OF COLOR IN LAW FIRMS 17 (2006) (finding that 62% of women of color and 60% of white women felt excluded from informal networks); Christopher J. Walker, *Female Entrepreneurship and Business Consortiums: Prospective Solutions for Argentina's Economic Challenges,* 16 J. INT'L & PUB. AFF. 94, 96-97 (2005) (finding similar trends for women entrepreneurs and business leaders). For surveys of upper-level American managers, which find that almost half of women of color and close to a third of all women cite a lack of influential mentors as a major barrier to advancement, see CATALYST, WOMEN IN CORPORATE LEADERSHIP: PROGRESS AND PROSPECTS 37, 42 (1996); CATALYST, WOMEN OF COLOR IN CORPORATE MANAGEMENT 21 (2000). *See generally* IDA O. ABBOTT, NAT'L ASS'N FOR LAW PLACEMENT, THE LAWYERS' GUIDE TO MENTORING (2000); Belle Rose Ragins, *Gender and Mentoring Relationships: A Review and Research Agenda for the Next Decade, in* HANDBOOK OF GENDER AND WORK, *supra* note 107, at 347, 350-62; Timothy O'Brien, *Up the Down Staircase,* N.Y. TIMES, Mar. 19, 2006, at A4.

116. Inglis et al., *supra* note 103, at 8; Wilson, *supra* note 112, at 42.

117. Kane, *supra* note 15, at 121, 124.

118. *Id.* at 121-22 (citing surveys).

119. JAY COAKLEY, SPORT IN SOCIETY 220 (7th ed. 2001).

120. DRAGO ET AL., *supra* note 38, at 13; Kane, *supra* note 15, at 123.

121. Warren A. Whisenant et al., *Success and Gender: Determining the Rate of Advancement for Intercollegiate Athletic Directors,* 47 SEX ROLES 485 (2002). Women also have had difficulty obtaining interscholastic athletic director positions at the high school level. Warren A. Whisenant, *How Women Have Fared as Interscholastic Athletic Administrators Since the Passage of Title IX,* 49 SEX ROLES 179 (2003).

122. Kane, *supra* note 15, at 124; *see also* DRAGO ET AL., *supra* note 38, at 8, 14 (noting lack of support and mentoring for collegiate women athletes).

123. Kane, *supra* note 15, at 131.

124. Sagas & Batista, *supra* note 103, at 33, 37.

125. *See* BUREAU OF LABOR STATISTICS, AMERICAN TIME USE SURVEY (2004); Donald G. McNeil, *Real Men Don't Clean Bathrooms,* N.Y. TIMES, Sept. 19, 2004, at E3.

126. SYLVIA A. HEWLETT, CTR. FOR WORK-LIFE POL'Y, HIGH ACHIEVING WOMEN 2 (2001); SYLVIA A. HEWLETT, CREATING A LIFE: PROFESSIONAL WOMEN AND THE QUEST FOR CHILDREN 143 (2002).

127. Sylvia A. Hewlett & Carolyn Buck Luce, *Off Ramps and On Ramps: Keeping Talented Women on the Road to Success,* HARV. BUS. REV., Mar. 2005, at 43-45; Claudia Wallis, *The Case for Staying Home,* TIME, Mar. 22, 2004, at 52.

128. DRAGO ET AL., *supra* note 38, at 4-5, 18, 49.

129. Wilson, *supra* note 112, at 43.

130. *Id.* at 41.

131. The average hourly earnings of full-time, full-year male coaches was $16.22 compared with a national average of $19.99 for male employees. The average hourly earnings for female coaches was $12.88, compared with $14.94 for female employees. *Id.* at 40.

132. COMM'N ON OPPORTUNITY IN ATHLETICS, *supra* note 34, at 22.

133. Brake, *supra* note 6, at 467.

134. Rhode, *supra* note 13, at 15-16; John C. Weistart, *Can Gender Equity Find a Place in Commercialized College Sports?,* 3 DUKE J. GENDER L. & POL'Y 191, 225, 249-51 (1996); *see also* Sudha Setty, *Leveling the Playing Field: Reforming the Office for Civil Rights to Achieve Better Title IX Enforcement,* 32 COLUM. J.L. & SOC. PROBS. 331, 350-52 (1999) (discussing treatment of football).

135. Rhode, *supra* note 13, at 17 (summarizing comments about resource constraints by David Black, Deputy Assistant Secretary for Enforcement, Office for Civil Rights).

136. See DEBORAH L. RHODE, IN PURSUIT OF KNOWLEDGE 153-54 n.14 (2006).

137. John J. Cheslock & Deborah J. Anderson, *Lessons from Research on Title IX and Intercollegiate Athletics, in* SPORTING EQUALITY, *supra* note 48, at 138.

138. *Id.*

139. Rhode, *supra* note 13; Brake, *supra* note 6; Weistart, *supra* note 134, at 249-51.

140. Changes in antitrust law to permit such collective action may be a necessary first step. *See* Ralph D. Mawdsley & Charles J. Russo,

Antitrust Law and Limiting Coaches' Salaries, 131 EDUC. L. REP. 895 (1999).

141. Cheslock & Anderson, *supra* note 137, at 138.

142. DRAGO ET AL., *supra* note 38, at 25.

143. *Id.* at 50-51.

144. *Id.* at 28.

145. For discussion of mentoring programs, *see* Rhode & Kellerman, *supra* note 115, at 29-30. For discussion of coaching and administrative programs, such as the NCAA Women Coaches Academy, *see* DRAGO ET AL., *supra* note 38, at 52. Several respondents in our survey commented on the value of such programs.

146. Deborah L. Rhode & Joan Williams, *Legal Perspectives on Employment Discrimination, in* SEX DISCRIMINATION IN THE WORKPLACE 235 (Faye J. Crosby et al. eds., 2007).

147. CATALYST, ADVANCING WOMEN IN BUSINESS 6, 12-13 (1998); KAREN KLENKE, WOMEN AND LEADERSHIP 173 (1996); Rhode & Kellerman, *supra* note 115, at 27; Cecilia L. Ridgeway & Shelley J. Correll, *Limiting Inequality Through Interaction,* 29 CONTEMP. SOC. 118 (2000).

. . . .

Discussion Questions

1. What is the purpose of Title IX?
2. How does a college president know whether his or her institution is in compliance with Title IX?
3. How do the operational strategies of the athletic director differ from that of the general manager of a Major League Baseball franchise?
4. Could and should any form of gender equity guidelines apply to professional sports franchises?
5. Describe the various budgetary impacts of Title IX.
6. What has been the impact of Title IX on the gender breakdown of coaching staffs across all sports?
7. What steps could be taken in relation to football to move schools closer to gender equity?
8. Should football be exempted from the Title IX equation?
9. Based on the results of Rhode and Walker's survey and other historical actions discussed in this book, what steps should be taken to promote gender equity in collegiate coaching?

Amateurism and Reform

INTRODUCTION

At the heart of the push for reforming collegiate sports is changing views of amateurism. As the readings that follow highlight, for most of the time that organized collegiate sports have existed, Americans have believed that there should be a class of athletes that participate in sports for the glory of the games alone. Even as the Olympic Games have moved away from this view, collegiate sports, under the governance of the NCAA, continue to hold fast, as the readings in this chapter highlight.

The excerpt from Kenneth L. Shropshire's "Legislation for the Glory of Sport: Amateurism and Compensation" provides a historic overview of amateurism and the mythology and misconceptions associated with its lofty status. The article briefly traces the history that provides the foundation for the lingering beliefs of the righteousness of what are arguably outdated concepts of amateurism. Once the reality of amateurism is grasped, the important question becomes whether any reforms recognizing this reality will improve college sports.

The next excerpt, from Peter Goplerud III, provides an examination of the possibilities of "pay for play"; that is, paying student-athletes based on their athletic abilities. Christopher A. Callanan's "Advice for the Next Jeremy Bloom: An Elite Athlete's Guide to NCAA Amateurism Regulations" discusses the issue of athlete compensation by examining the case of a unique two-sport athlete.

The chapter concludes with three selections focused on reform in collegiate sports. The first is an excerpt from James L. Shulman and William G. Bowen's *The Game of Life*. The piece focuses on the findings of their extensive study of the role of athletics in America's colleges and universities and, particularly, insight on the participating athletes. The next selection is part of a report from The Knight Foundation Commission on Intercollegiate Athletics entitled "A Call to Action: Reconnecting College Sports and Higher Education." This document, published in June 2001, is probably the best-known effort focused on the reform of collegiate sports. Many individuals believe that the Knight Commission's ongoing efforts led to college presidents taking greater control of their athletic programs. The final excerpt is the Executive Summary from a 2009 Knight Commission report. The focus of this excerpt is on cost containment by university presidents in the Football Bowl Subdivision.

LEGISLATION FOR THE GLORY OF SPORT: AMATEURISM AND COMPENSATION

Kenneth L. Shropshire

. . . .

B. ORIGIN OF THE RULES AGAINST COMPENSATION

1. Ancient Greeks

A common misconception held by many people today is that the foundation of collegiate amateurism had its genesis in the Olympic model of the ancient Greeks. . . . The "myth" of ancient amateurism held that there was some society, presumably the Greeks, that took part in sport solely for the associated glory while receiving no compensation for either participating or winning.[10] In his book, *The Olympic Myth of Greek Amateur Athletics,*[11] classicist David C. Young reported finding "no mention of amateurism in Greek sources, no reference to amateur athletes, and no evidence that the concept of 'amateurism' was even known in antiquity. The truth is that 'amateur' is one thing for which the ancient Greeks never even had a word."[12] Young further traces the various levels of compensation that were awarded in these ancient times including a monstrous prize in one event that was the equivalent of ten years worth of wages.[13]

The absence of compensation was not an essential element of Greek athletics.[14] Specifically, the ancient Greeks "had no known restrictions on granting awards to athletes."[15] Many athletes were generously rewarded. Professor Young asserts that the only real disagreement among classical scholars is not whether payments were made to the athletes but only when such payments began.

The myth concerning ancient Greek athletics was apparently developed and perpetuated by the very same individuals that would ultimately benefit from the implementation of such a system.[16] The scholars most often cited for espousing these views of Greek amateurism were those who sought to promote an athletic system they supported as being derived from ancient precedent.[17] In his work, Professor Young systematically proves these theories false by countering with direct evidence and an analysis of the motivation for presenting inaccurate information. Similar faults by other scholars led to the inevitable development of fallacious cross-citations with each relying upon the other for authority.[18] One scholar is believed to have actually created a detailed account of an ancient Greek athlete which Professor Young concluded was a "sham" and "outright historical fiction."[19] The reasoning behind such deliberate falsehoods was apparently designed to serve as "a moral lesson to modern man."[20]

In simplest terms, these scholars were part of a justification process for an elite British athletic system destined

THE IDEAL

to find its way into American collegiate athletics. "They represent examples of a far-flung and amazingly successful deception, a kind of historical hoax, in which scholar[s] joined hands with sportsm[e]n and administrator[s] so as to mislead the public and influence modern sporting life."[21] With amateurism widely proclaimed by the scholars of the day, the natural tendency was for non-scholars to join in and heed the cry as well.

The leading voice in the United States espousing the strict segregation of pay and amateurism was Avery Brundage, former President of both the United States Olympic Committee (USOC) and the International Olympic Committee (IOC).[22] Brundage believed that the ancient Olympic Games, which for centuries blossomed as amateur competition, eventually degenerated as excesses and abuses developed attributable to professionalism.[23] "What was originally fun, recreation, a diversion, and a pastime became a business. . . . The Games . . . lost their purity and high idealism, and were finally abolished. . . . Sport must be for sport's sake."[24] Brundage was firmly against amateurs receiving any remuneration, justifying his belief upon the Greek amateur athletic fallacy. Brundage took extraordinary action during his tenure as president of the USOC and the IOC to ensure such a prohibition. . . .

Professor Young and other like-minded scholars contend that the development of the present day system of collegiate amateurism is not modeled after the ancient Greeks. Rather, today's amateurism is a direct descendant of the Avery Brundages of the world and is actually much more reflective of the practices developed in Victorian England than those originated in ancient Greece.

2. England

In 1866, the Amateur Athletic Club of England published a definition of the term "amateur."[26] Although the term had been in use for many years, this was, perhaps, the first official definition of the word. The definition which was provided by that particular sports organization required an amateur to be one who had never engaged in open competition for money or prizes, never taught athletics as a profession, and one who was not a "mechanic, artisan or laborer."[27]

The Amateur Athletic Club of England was established to give English gentlemen the opportunity to compete against each other without having to involve and compete against professionals.[28] However, the term "professional" in Victorian England did not merely connote one who engaged in athletics for profit, but was primarily indicative of one's social class.[29] It was the dominant view in the latter half of the nineteenth century that not only were those who competed for money basically inferior in nature, but that they were "also a person of questionable character."[30] The social distinction of amateurism, attributable to the prevailing aristocratic attitude

Student-athletes shall be amateurs in an intercollegiate sport, and their participation should be motivated primarily by education and by the physical, mental and social benefits to be derived. Student participation in intercollegiate athletics is an avocation, and student-athletes should be protected from exploitation by professional and commercial enterprises.

Figure 1   NCAA Constitution, Article 2.9—The Principle of Amateurism

Source: 2009–2010 *NCAA Division I Manual*, p. 4. © National Collegiate Athletic Association. 2008–2010. All rights reserved.

Only an amateur student-athlete is eligible for intercollegiate athletics participation in a particular sport.

Figure 2   NCAA Bylaw 12.01.1—Eligibility for Intercollegiate Athletics

Source: 2009–2010 *NCAA Division I Manual*, p. 61. © National Collegiate Athletic Association. 2008–2010. All rights reserved.

at the time, provided the incentive for victory. "When an amateur lost a contest to a working man he lost more than the race. . . He lost his identity. . . His life's premise disappeared; namely that he was innately superior to the working man in all ways."[31] Thus, concepts of British amateurism developed along class lines, and were reinforced by the "mechanics clauses" that existed in amateur definitions. These clauses typically prevented mechanics, artisans, and laborers from participation in amateur sport. The reasoning behind the "mechanics clause" was the belief that the use of muscles as part of one's employment offered an unfair competitive advantage.[32] Eventually, under the guise of bringing order to athletic competition, private athletic clubs were formed that effectively restricted competition "on the basis of ability and social position" and not on the basis of money.[33] Over the years this distinction has been used to identify those athletes who are ineligible for amateur competition, because their ability to support themselves based solely on their athletic prowess has given them a special competitive advantage.[34] It is from these antiquated rules that the modern eligibility rules of the NCAA evolved. Any remaining negative connotations regarding professionalism owe their continued existence to these distinctions.

3.   United States

The amateur/professional dilemma confronting today's American universities is based on the presumption that if a college competes at a purely amateur level it will lose prestige and revenue, as it loses contests. However, open acknowledgement of the adoption of professional athleticism would result in a loss of respectability for the university as a bastion of academia. The present solution to this dilemma has been for collegiate athletic departments to "claim amateurism to the world, while in fact accepting a professional mode of operation."[35]

Two sports, baseball and rowing, were the first to entertain the questions of professionalism versus amateurism in the United States. Initially, the norm for organized sports in this country was professionalism. Baseball was played at semiprofessional levels as early as 1860, and the first professional team, the Cincinnati Red Stockings, was formed in

1868.[36] The first amateur organization, the New York Athletic Club, was established in the United States in 1868.[37]

In 1909, the NCAA (which had successfully evolved from the Intercollegiate Athletic Association, established in 1905) recommended the creation of particular amateur/professional distinctions.[38] With the subsequent adoption of these proposals, England's Victorian amateur and professional delineations were incorporated into American intercollegiate athletics. [*Ed. Note: See **Figures 1** and **2**.*]

Prior to the adoption of the NCAA proposals, "professionalism" abounded. For example, in the 1850s Harvard University students rowed in a meet offering a $100 first prize purse, and a decade later they raced for as much as $500.[39] Amateurism, at least as historically conceived, was largely absent from college sports in the beginning of the twentieth century. Competition for cash and prizes, collection of gate revenue, provisions for recruiting, training, and tutoring of athletes, as well as the payment of athletes and hiring of professional coaches had invaded the arena of intercollegiate athletics.[40] . . . The sheer number of competing American educational institutions was, in itself, a major reason that athletics in the United States developed far beyond the amateurism still displayed [by their] learned British counterparts. In England, an upper level education meant one of two places, either Oxford or Cambridge. With each institution policing the other, the odds of breaching the established standards of amateurism were not high. In the United States, while the Ivy League schools competed strongly amongst themselves, there was also the rapid emergence of many fine public colleges and universities.[42] Freedom of opportunity, a pervasive factor in the genesis of American collegiate athletics, made it increasingly more difficult for the Harvards and Yales to maintain themselves as both the athletic and the intellectual elite within the United States.[43]

According to some scholars, the English system of amateurism, "loosely" derived from the Greeks, simply did not have a chance of success in the United States. As noted above, one factor contributing to its demise was increased competition among a larger number of institutions. Another was the difference in egalitarian beliefs between the two nations:

> Member institutions' athletics programs are designed to be an integral part of the educational program. The student-athlete is considered an integral part of the student body, thus maintaining a clear line of demarcation between college athletics and professional sports.

Figure 3 NCAA Bylaw 12.01.2—Clear Line of Demarcation

Source: 2009–2010 NCAA Division I Manual, *p. 61.* © National Collegiate Athletic Association. 2008–2010. All rights reserved.

The English amateur system, based upon participation by the social and economic elite . . . would never gain a foothold in American college athletics. There was too much competition, too strong a belief in merit over heredity, too abundant an ideology of freedom of opportunity for the amateur ideal to succeed. . . . It may be that amateur athletics at a high level of expertise can only exist in a society dominated by upper-class elitists.[44]

In spite of the ideological conflicts, the early post-formative years of the NCAA were spent attempting to enforce the various amateur standards. The first eligibility code sought only to insure that those who participated in collegiate athletics were actually full-time registered students who were not being paid for their participation.[45] This initial set of amateur guidelines was largely ignored by the NCAA member institutions. After establishing this initial code, the NCAA sought on numerous occasions to further define its views on amateurism. An intermediate step was the formal adoption of the Amateur Code into the NCAA constitution.[46] The impetus behind the adoption was "to enunciate more clearly the NCAA's purpose; to incorporate the amateur definition and principles of amateur spirit; and to widen the scope of government."[47] As the monetary resources of the NCAA grew, so too did its enforcement power. The prime targets of those enhanced enforcement powers were the principles of amateurism as incorporated into the NCAA constitution. [*Ed. Note: See **Figure 3**.*]

The motivation to cheat existed even in the formative years of collegiate sports. Winning athletic programs had the potential to return high revenues to the institution. In its early years as a national football power, Yale University made $105,000 from its successful 1903 football program.[48] Thus, the financial incentive to succeed existed even then, and has continued to serve as a strong incentive for many schools to break the rules in order to obtain the best talent.

[*Ed. Note: The author's discussion of the Sanity Code is omitted. See discussion of the Sanity Code in Chapter 13.*]

. . . .

The NCAA was an organization formed to promote safety in collegiate sports. It later adopted the prevailing views of amateurism and is currently the largest sports organization to prohibit member athletes from receiving compensation. [*Ed. Note: See **Figures 4** and **5**.*] The lack of compensation for the student participant permeates virtually all decisions in collegiate athletics today. Although the NCAA does not deliberately promote or associate itself with the tales of Greek amateurism, nothing has been done to correct popular misconceptions.

Notes

. . . .

10. David C. Young, The Olympic Myth of Greek Amateur Athletics 7 Ares Publishers (1985).

11. Id.

12. Id.

An individual loses amateur status and thus shall not be eligible for intercollegiate competition in a particular sport if the individual:

(a) Uses his or her athletics skill (directly or indirectly) for pay in any form in that sport;

(b) Accepts a promise of pay even if such pay is to be received following completion of intercollegiate athletics participation;

(c) Signs a contract or commitment of any kind to play professional athletics, regardless of its legal enforceability or any consideration received;

(d) Receives, directly or indirectly, a salary, reimbursement of expenses or any other form of financial assistance from a professional sports organization based upon athletics skill or participation, except as permitted by NCAA rules and regulations;

(e) Competes on any professional athletics team (per Bylaw 12.02.4), even if no pay or remuneration for expenses was received; (*Revised: 4/25/02 effective 8/1/02*)

(f) After initial full-time collegiate enrollment, enters into a professional draft (see Bylaw 12.2.4); or (*Revised: 4/25/02 effective 8/1/02, 4/24/03 effective 8/1/03 for student-athletes entering a collegiate institution on or after 8/1/03*)

(g) Enters into an agreement with an agent. (*Adopted: 4/25/02 effective 8/1/02*)

Figure 4 NCAA Bylaw 12.1.2—Amateur Status

Source: 2009–2010 NCAA Division I Manual, *pp. 62–63.* © National Collegiate Athletic Association. 2008–2010. All rights reserved.

A student-athlete may receive athletically related financial aid administered by the institution without violating the principle of amateurism, provided the amount does not exceed the cost of education authorized by the Association; however, such aid as defined by the Association shall not exceed the cost of attendance as published by each institution. Any other financial assistance, except that received from one upon whom the student-athlete is naturally or legally dependent, shall be prohibited unless specifically authorized by the Association.

Figure 5   NCAA Constitution, Article 2.13—The Principle Governing Financial Aid

Source: 2009–2010 *NCAA Division I Manual*, p. 5. © National Collegiate Athletic Association. 2008–2010. All rights reserved.

13. Id. He notes later that in a single running event the winner received enough money to buy six or seven slaves, 100 sheep or three houses. Id. at 127.

14. Id. at 7.

15. Eugene Glader, Amateurism and Athletics 54 Human Kinetics (1978).

16. Young, supra note 10, at 8.

17. Professor Young cites an article written by classical scholar, Paul Shorey, in The Forum as an example of one of the first misstatements of the actual history:

And here lies the chief, if somewhat obvious, lesson that our modern athletes have to learn from Olympia . . . . They must strive . . . only for the complete development of their manhood, and their sole prizes must be the conscious delight in the exercise . . . and some simple symbol of honor. They must not prostitute the vigor of their youth for gold, directly or indirectly. . . . [T]he commercial spirit . . . is fatal, as the Greeks learned . . . . Where money is the stake, men will inevitably tend to rate the end above the means, or rather to misconceive the true end . . . the professional will usurp the place of the amateur . . . . [emphasis in original]. Id. at 9.

Shorey's article was written prior to the first modern Olympiad held in Athens in 1896 and it was directed at the potential Olympians. Id. at 9. Young maintains further that this was not, in fact, the first revival of the Olympics. Id. He writes that as early as 1870 a modern Olympiad took place in Athens in which cash prizes were awarded. Id. at 31.

18. Id. at 12.

19. Young at 12, 13. See Harold Harris, Greek Athletes and Athletics Greenwood (1964).

20. Young, supra note 10, at 13. The lesson is apparently somewhat self-serving and designed to present in a favorable light the values of the gentlemen amateur athletes of Victorian England. Id.

21. Id. at 14.

22. Id. at 85. Brundage was in strong opposition to Jim Thorpe recovering his forfeited Olympic medals. The irony behind his losing the medals is evident in Thorpe's own statements referring to the semi-professional baseball games in which he participated. "I did not play for the money . . . but because I liked to play ball." Id. While other athletes participated in the same games under a variety of aliases, Thorpe did not even realize he was jeopardizing his amateur and Olympic eligibility. See Pachter, Champions of American Sport 195 (1981).

23. Avery Brundage, USOC Report of the Games of the XIV Olympiad (1948).

24. Id.

. . . .

26. Glader, Amateurism and Athletics 100 (1978).

27. Id. at 100. See also H. Hewitt Griffin, Athletics 13–14 (1891); H.F. Wilkinson, Modern Athletics 16 (1868).

28. Young, supra note 10, at 19.

29. Id.

30. Glader, supra note 26, at 15. The title "amateur" became a badge for upper class gentlemen seeking to evidence their good social standing. Young, supra note 10, at 18.

31. Young, supra note 10, at 18 n. 17.

32. Glader, supra note 26 at 17. See also Ronald A. Smith, Sports & Freedom: The Rise of Big Time College Athletics 166, Oxford University Press (1998) (stating that the eligibility rules of the British Amateur Rowing Assoc. in 1870 contained a similar clause).

33. Glader, supra note 26, at 17. The laborer was classified as a professional due to his unfair physical advantage. Id.

34. Id.

35. Smith, supra note 32, at 166. Although the reference is made to a "professional mode of operation," university scholarship athletes are not allowed to receive compensation above what amounts to tuition, room, board, and educational fees. Id.

36. H. Savage, American College Athletics (1929), at 36.

37. Young, supra note 10, at 22.

38. Savage, supra note 36, at 42. Specifically:

1. An amateur in athletics is one who enters and takes part in athletic contests purely in obedience to the play impulses or for the satisfaction of purely play motives and for the exercise, training, and social pleasure derived. The natural or primary attitude of mind in play determines amateurism.

2. A professional in athletics is one who enters or takes part in any athletic contest for any other motive than the satisfaction of pure play impulses, or for the exercise, training or social pleasures derived, or one who desires and secures from his skill or who accepts of spectators, partisans or other interests, any material or economic advantage or reward. Id.

39. Smith, supra note 32, at 169 (citing Alexander Agassiz, Rowing Fifty Years Ago, Harv. Graduates Mag., Vol. XV, at 458 (March 1907)); see also Charles W. Eliot, In Praise of Rowing, Harv. Graduates Mag., Vol. XV, at 532 (March 1907); B. W. Crowninshield, Boating, F.O. Vaille; H.A. Clark, The Harvard Book 263 (1875).

40. Smith, supra note 32, at 171.

. . . .

42. Id. at 173.

43. Id. Refusal to compete against other athletically developing schools would have caused Harvard and Yale to lose their athletic "esteem and prestige." Id.

44. Id. at 174.

45. NCAA Constitution, art. VII, Eligibility Rules (1906). The first NCAA Eligibility Code is set forth below:

    The following rules . . . are suggested as a minimum:

    1. No student shall represent a college or university in any intercollegiate game or contest, who is not taking a full schedule of work as prescribed in the catalogue of the institution.

    2. No student shall represent a college or university . . . who has at any time received, either directly or indirectly, money, or any other consideration, to play on any team, or . . . who has competed for a money prize or portion of gate money in any contest, or who has competed for any prize against a professional.

    3. No student shall represent a college or university . . . who is paid or received, directly or indirectly, any money, or financial concession, or emolument as past or present compensation for, or as prior consideration or inducement to play in, or enter any athletic contest, whether the said remuneration be received from, or paid by, or at the instance of any organization, committee or faculty of such college or university, or any individual whatever.

    4. No student shall represent a college or university . . . who has participated in intercollegiate games or contests during four previous years.

    5. No student who has been registered as a member of any other college or university shall participate in any intercollegiate game or contest until he shall have been a student of the institution which he represents for at least one college year.

    6. Candidates for positions on athletic teams shall be required to fill out cards, which shall be placed on file, giving a full statement of their previous athletic records. Id.

46. Paul Lawrence, Unsportsmanlike Conduct: The National Collegiate Athletic Association and the Business of College Football 24, Praeger (1987).

47. Id. (citing 1922 NCAA Proceedings at 10.)

48. Benjamin G. Rader, American Sports from the Age of Folk Games to the Age of Spectators 268–269, Prentice-Hall (1983).

REFORM

SYMPOSIUM: SPORTS LAW AS A REFLECTION OF SOCIETY'S LAWS AND VALUES: PAY FOR PLAY FOR COLLEGE ATHLETES: NOW, MORE THAN EVER

Peter Goplerud III

I. INTRODUCTION

Imagine a large group of employees in a company working long hours, some of them far from home, going to school full-time, and helping bring in millions of dollars to their employer. Does this sound like a sweat shop . . . ? Actually, this describes the typical athlete in a revenue producing sport at a National Collegiate Athletic Association (NCAA) member institution.

Approximately one year ago this author wrote an article advocating a change in the Constitution and Bylaws of the NCAA to provide for the payment of stipends to some athletes at some of its member institutions.[1] Specifically, the article proposed the payment of $150 per month to scholarship athletes in the revenue-producing sports of football and men's basketball and to a comparable number of scholarship athletes in women's sports. The stipend rule would have applied only to Division I member schools. An underlying premise of the article was that the concept of amateurism, a cornerstone of the NCAA, is essentially a sham due to the commercial nature of the end product. The athletes are used, abused, and then thrown out, while the schools make millions on television money, gate receipts, and sales of licensed products, many directly tied to particular players. The article suggested several legal, political, and financial hurdles that must be considered prior to implementing a policy of providing stipends for players. Included were legal concerns associated with employees, which the athletes would become under the proposal; among these would be workers' compensation, labor, taxation, antitrust, and gender equity issues. The article also noted the internal politics of the NCAA would be an obstacle, but also opined that the new restructuring might facilitate movement towards the concept of paying players. It also attempted to calculate the costs of providing stipends to approximately 200 athletes at each Division I school. Finally, sources of revenue to pay for the proposal were suggested, notably corporate sponsors and the possibility of a Division I football playoff.

In the intervening time numerous other voices have been heard on the subject and the NCAA itself has considered several alternatives and even adopted what its membership believes to be a compromise between the status quo and the instant proposal.[2] However, no substantial or significant progress has been made to this point. The purpose of this article is to renew the call for a change in the rules. At this point, however, a slightly different proposal will be presented. Since this author now believes the current structure and the former proposal both present serious antitrust issues, the proposal will focus on a market-based approach to awarding stipends. It will still be limited to those athletes in revenue-producing sports and proportionate numbers of women athletes.

While there was much talk on the subject of athletes' rights and the creation of a special task force during the remainder of 1996, the NCAA did very little at the recently completed final convention prior to restructuring. Only a modest change and an arguably ill-conceived concession to costs of attendance was approved with regard to restrictions on work during the school year by athletes on scholarship.[3]

It thus becomes relevant . . . to revisit the issue. . . . The basic premise will remain the same as before: the athletes at Division I schools, particularly those in revenue-producing sports, are exploited on a regular basis and must be compensated beyond the scholarship and beyond the cost of attendance.

II.   INTERCOLLEGIATE ATHLETICS AND COMMERCIALISM

[*Ed. Note: The author's discussion of NCAA regulations and commercialism is omitted.*]

. . . .

C.   The Proposal

It is time to give more serious consideration than ever before to stipends for collegiate athletes. As noted above, the proposal developed a year ago has flaws, mostly legal, which require modification. A market component must be inserted in the stipend, but the proposal must also provide for a certain amount of restraint and competitive balance in keeping with the NCAA's long-standing concerns for both factors within collegiate athletics. Therefore, the NCAA should develop legislation providing for stipends for athletes in major revenue-producing sports at the Division I level. The stipends should be available to men in football and basketball, and women in basketball, volleyball, and other sports in sufficient numbers to satisfy gender equity requirements. The exact amount of the stipend to an individual athlete would be within the discretion of the individual school. However, the schools should have a limit on the total amount of money allocated to student-athletes. This "salary cap" would be set at an average of $300 per month per scholarship athlete, with half of the money going into a trust fund to be paid to those athletes receiving degrees within five years of matriculation. Those schools with football programs would calculate their football amounts separately with the total amount varying depending upon whether a school is Division I-A or I-AA. These athletes would also be able to work, as under the new rule, with the stipend not counting against the cost of attendance. Schools may, of course, spend less than the cap or may choose not to pay the stipend to any athletes. In addition, scholarship athletes in the non-revenue sports would be allowed to be employed during the school year, even in campus settings, and would have no cap on their earnings. The only stipulation would be that the jobs must be available to non-athlete students as well as athletes.

III.   LEGAL ISSUES WHICH ARISE FROM THE PROPOSAL

A.   Antitrust Questions

An issue which could arise should the association choose to enact legislation allowing for the payment of players would be a question of price-fixing. The proposal made a year ago is flawed in this respect. It is quite believable that an athlete in a revenue-producing sport would become disgruntled with only receiving $150 per month while competing, and find a resourceful attorney willing to bring an action under the antitrust laws. For reasons discussed below, it is likely that such an action would be successful. Thus, the more prudent legislative action would be the salary cap approach which allows for individual decision-making based upon market determinations developed by the member institutions.

The NCAA has found itself as a defendant in antitrust actions on numerous occasions, with mixed results. Section 1 of the Sherman Antitrust Act provides that: "every contract, combination in the form of trust or otherwise, or conspiracy, in restraint of trade or commerce among the several States, or with foreign nations, is hereby declared to be illegal."[31] The Supreme Court has long held that only unreasonable restraints of trade are proscribed by the act.[32] Some restraints on economic activity are viewed by the Court as so inherently anti-competitive that they are deemed per se illegal. Examples of this type of conduct would be group boycotts, market divisions, tying arrangements, and price-fixing.[33]

It is arguable that most of the regulatory activity in which the NCAA engages is per se illegal. Actions such as the establishment of limits on the type and amount of financial aid appear to be price-fixing. Certainly a fixed stipend such as proposed previously appears to be price-fixing. However, in the context of intercollegiate athletics the Supreme Court has recognized that certain types of restrictive activity by the NCAA may, under appropriate circumstances, be allowed under the act.[34] The very nature of competitive sports is such that in order to promote competition, some actions which would normally be viewed as restraints will be allowed to exist. The Court has said that "what the NCAA and its member institutions market . . . is competition itself—contests between competing institutions" and thus, it is "an industry in which horizontal restraints on competition are essential if the product is to be available at all."[35] Any number of rules relating to the size of playing fields, squad size, length of seasons, number of scholarships, academic standards, and the like must be agreed upon in order to market a product, collegiate sports, which might not otherwise be available. The Court, therefore, in reviewing a challenge to the NCAA's actions in entering into a television contract for football, did not apply the per se rule, instead choosing to use a "rule of reason" analysis. The rule of reason analysis has been utilized in all recent antitrust cases involving the NCAA as well.[36]

The rule of reason analysis requires the court to determine if the harm from the restraint on competition outweighs the restraint's pro-competitive impact.[37] The plaintiff bears the initial burden of showing the restraint causes significant anti-competitive effects in a relevant market.[38] If this burden is met, the defendant must then produce evidence of the restraint's pro-competitive effects.[39] If this is done, the plaintiff must finally show that any legitimate objectives of the restraint can be met through less restrictive means.[40]

To date, the courts have also been consistent in upholding, against antitrust challenge, every regulatory action of the NCAA which has directly impacted athletes.[41] The Supreme Court has, on the one occasion noted above, ruled against the NCAA in an antitrust action involving its proprietary action in entering into contracts for the televising of football games.[42] There is, perhaps, reason to believe that even some of the NCAA's regulatory activities may now be suspect under the Sherman Act.

[*Ed. Note: The author's analysis of* Law v. NCAA *is omitted.*]

. . . .

The NCAA's limitations on scholarships, in so far as they prohibit stipends, are part of its regulatory program. The association would no doubt contend that these are non-commercial and, therefore, out of the purview of the Sherman Act. One jurist has labeled a similar assertion in regard to the NCAA's rules on eligibility and the professional football draft "incredulous."[57] It is quite clear that the rules act as a restraint on a relevant market, the labor market for collegiate athletes. They are obviously an attempt to perpetuate the amateur nature of collegiate athletics. But, this overlooks the key to the NCAA and collegiate athletics:

> *Intercollegiate athletics programs shall be maintained as a vital component of the educational program, and student-athletes shall be an integral part of the student body. The admission, academic standing and academic progress of student-athletes shall be consistent with the policies and standards adopted by the institution for the student body in general.[58]*

Amateurism has certainly been a significant part of the NCAA's programs, but there have been and continue to be exceptions to this requirement. As recently as the 1960s, the NCAA allowed schools to provide athletes on scholarship with "laundry money."[59] And, the NCAA has long allowed athletes who are clearly professionals, to continue to compete in collegiate athletics in other sports. The only restriction is that they may not receive financial aid from

the school.[60] Collegiate athletics could survive if stipends were paid to the athletes. The strong allegiances to individual schools and traditions would survive if the athletes in certain sports received a stipend in addition to their tuition and room and board. The athletes would still be required to be full-time students. The stipend would not change the competition on the field, only the nature of the competition for players.

The present system is clearly a restraint. Many athletes do not have the funds to buy clothing, cannot fly home without going to the special assistance fund (except in an emergency), and often struggle to meet ordinary financial requirements of life.[61] The restrictions are not necessary to maintain collegiate athletics; as noted there is already precedent for chipping away at the amateur nature of the venture. And, a stipend, coupled with a "salary cap," is a less restrictive means of promoting collegiate athletics and maintaining competitive balance. It would not be possible under this proposal for a school to offer unlimited amounts of money and, in effect, act like a professional sports team during free agent signing periods.

B.   Workers' Compensation Issues

If the proposal is adopted, even in some modified form, by the NCAA, it is likely that in most jurisdictions the athletes receiving stipends would then be covered by the workers' compensation laws of those states. Coverage brings with it legal and financial considerations for the athletic departments impacted.[62]

Workers' compensation laws are state statutes enacted to compensate workers or their estates for job-related injuries or death, regardless of fault. The underlying premise of this legislation is that accidents in the workplace are inevitable, particularly in the industrial setting, and the burden of injuries caused by such accidents should be borne by the industries that benefit from the labor rather than the employees who are injured.[63] This philosophy is implemented by providing an employee with a guaranteed remedy of benefits and medical care in the event of an injury occurring in the course of employment. Employers are generally required to self-insure, contract with a private insurance carrier, or pay into the state workers' compensation fund.[64] Under these statutes, each state has developed its own jurisprudence, and the determination of coverage under particular circumstances would necessitate analysis of the particular statute relevant to a particular circumstance.

[*Ed. Note: The author's analysis of various state provisions is omitted.*]

. . . .

Under most state statutes, if the NCAA adopts a stipend provision the athletes on scholarship would probably fall within existing definitions of "employee." The stipend appears to be a wage paid for services rendered. Intent would, of course, be an issue in that a court would look to whether the stipend was any more tied to services rendered than the rest of the scholarship package. The analysis in *Rensing* focused on the amateur nature of collegiate athletics and the NCAA's prohibition on payment of players.[95] Such reasoning would no longer be available to a court. . . . As noted, collegiate athletics is big business. If additional money is paid to players, it is likely that the school will attempt to exercise more control over them. Control, of course, is a factor used in determining whether an employment relationship exists. Arguably, a college scholarship which includes a stipend begins to look more like a professional sports contract that happens to include tuition, fees, room, board, and books as well as a cash component. Under most definitions a recipient of this type of "scholarship" would be an employee.[96]

The best comparison would be to graduate assistants or teaching assistants on college campuses. The comparison is a valid one in that a graduate assistant in an English department or engineering college will often receive a tuition scholarship plus a stipend. The stipend and the scholarship are awarded in exchange for the student's serving as a teacher for a set number of classes or laboratory sessions. In the athletic setting, the scholarship and the proposed stipend would be awarded in exchange for the student's participation in the school's athletic program. This would include all practice sessions, team meetings, games, and off-season conditioning programs. Failure to participate would, of course, be cause for loss of the scholarship, as would failure to maintain a certain level of competence.[97] At the University of Oklahoma, and perhaps many other universities, graduate assistants are treated as any other person on the payroll.[98] In other words, the university includes them within its workers' compensation coverage.[99] It is difficult to understand how collegiate athletes would be treated any differently.

C.   Other Legal Issues Arising from the Proposal

1. Gender Equity.

Gender equity measures must be taken into account when adopting the proposal. Title IX requires not only equal opportunities for participation, but equal treatment and benefits for athletes with intercollegiate programs.[100] Violations of the law will produce actions for injunctive relief and even for monetary damages. It is quite clear that schools providing stipends under the proposal would have to provide the stipends for a proportionate number of women athletes. Any disparities will wave red flags and likely subject the school to sanctions under the law.

2. Labor Law Issues.

Another question which arises in the context of consideration of stipends for collegiate athletes is whether the athletes would then be employees for purposes of the National Labor Relations Act.[101] The act essentially gives employees of businesses engaging in interstate commerce the right to

organize and engage in concerted activity for the purpose of collective bargaining or other mutual aid.[102] The act further defines "employee" to mean any employee unless otherwise excluded by the act.[103] The courts have construed the act to give the National Labor Relations Board great latitude in determining who is an employee under the act.[104] In analyzing the question with regard to collegiate athletes receiving stipends along with their scholarships, one would have to look at the conditions of that scholarship.

Scholarships for collegiate athletes typically require enrollment as a full-time student, compliance with NCAA rules, compliance with athletic department rules, and requirements established by the coaches of the particular sport. The athlete does receive some benefits similar to those of a traditional employee. If the local definition of "employee" required additional benefits to be paid to an athlete, the stipend proposed would be added support for the determination that the athlete is an employee for federal labor law purposes. Certainly the "tools of the trade" are supplied by the athletic department and the university provides the place and time of work. No athlete could be viewed as an independent contractor. The only issue is whether this stipend is for services rendered or simply a part of the scholarship. Consistent with the position taken above, the stipend must be viewed as being paid for services rendered, just as would be the case for a traditional employee. The athlete in a Division I revenue-producing sport is at her institution to participate in sports, and, oh, by the way, get an education. Again, the comparison to a graduate assistant in an academic department is instructive. The stipend paid to the graduate assistant appears to trigger tax consequences and workers' compensation consequences similar to a traditional employee. It should also trigger labor law consequences, should the athletes desire to take advantage of them.[105]

It is not hard to imagine the reaction throughout the world of collegiate sports should a court determine that college athletes have the right to form unions. What would be the bargaining unit? Would the linebackers be a separate unit or would they have to organize with the rest of the defensive squad? Again, one would expect significant efforts to influence Congress with regard to specific exclusions for intercollegiate athletics.

3. Taxation Issues.

Currently, athletic scholarships are not taxable to the athlete. Based upon experience with graduate assistants, it is clear that if the stipend is added, at least that portion of the scholarship would constitute taxable income to the athlete.[106] This would also add the burden of withholding for income tax as well as for social security and Medicare. It might further provide fuel for those who advocate the general removal of the tax-exempt status of collegiate athletics. Providing the stipend could have an impact on evaluations of unrelated business income for NCAA member institutions.

IV. PRACTICAL FINANCIAL CONCERNS AND WHY IT WON'T HAPPEN OVERNIGHT

Assume for the moment that the legal issues raised above do not deter the membership's consideration of the proposal. There are nonetheless several serious political and practical concerns. The history and culture of the NCAA have for decades revolved around the concept of amateurism and the notion of the "student-athlete." Athletics are an integral part of the educational experience. Further professionalizing the programs, the argument goes, destroys this concept. The purists argue that any denigration of the amateurism concept is a giant step towards the destruction of intercollegiate athletics. The former president of the association, Joseph Crowley, said, "the day our members decide it's time to pay players will be the day my institution stops playing."[107] Even some people who favor increased attention to athletes' welfare believe that paying athletes is not a good idea.[108]

There are, however, some very respected coaches who believe it is time to support the concept of paying stipends to athletes. Tom Osborne of the University of Nebraska has argued for many years that players should be able to receive money for living expenses.[109] . . . However, even many who conceptually support the proposal acknowledge the enormous practical and financial difficulties presented. . . .

There are sources of revenue or ideas for revenue redistribution which could support the proposal. As noted, the NCAA budget is $239 million for 1996–97.[111] That figure will go up in the coming years. [*Ed. Note: The NCAA budget for 2009–2010 was $710 million.*] The bowl games following the 1996 college season paid out over $100 million to participating schools and their conferences.[112] Estimates are that licensed products generate over $2 billion annually in sales, providing generous royalties for colleges and universities. Corporate sponsorship agreements with individual schools provide additional funds. The NCAA Basketball Championship generates in excess of $50 million annually for the member schools; and, if the NCAA ever approves a national football championship playoff system, an additional $100 million or more will be available for distribution to the schools. Finally, there are television contracts and gate receipts that add to the revenues of most of the Division I schools.

The other side of the equation begins with the reality that many of the Division I schools lose money on their athletic programs.[113] Even those making money argue they have very little flexibility in their budgets, particularly those with gender equity pressures.[114] The proposal as structured above would cost approximately $29 million annually, with the impact as high as $400,000 for Division I-A football schools.[115]

While there is no doubt that absorbing these costs would be difficult for most schools, there are sources of revenue which could support the proposal. It will require athletic administrators to be creative and to look for ways to cut costs in existing programs without cutting quality and equality. It is arguable that many, if not most, Division I athletic programs have unnecessary extravagance and duplication. It may also be time to suggest to the professional sports leagues that direct subsidies are due their "minor leagues," the college athletic programs. Corporate sponsors such as McDonald's or Nike should be considered as potential benefactors of this program. For the present, however, these outside sources are not available in any meaningful way. Therefore, existing funding would have to be utilized to implement the proposal for stipends for athletes.

The cost of the stipend is not the only cost presented. If the athlete is viewed as an employee in a given state for workers' compensation purposes, the schools may have to purchase insurance coverage. There may also be additional insurance or fringe benefit costs associated with a determination of employee status. If the program begins to look more professional than amateur, there may be tax consequences to the schools with very significant price tags. If athletes had success with either the potential claims under the Sherman Act or those under Title IX, costs would escalate. Then there is the possibility of added leverage through unionization and collective bargaining. This too would have additional costs.

It is difficult to be sympathetic to concerns for the loss of amateurism in collegiate sports as a result of consideration for stipends. When a school makes an estimated $4 million in revenues directly traceable to the participation of one basketball player, concerns over the loss of amateurism are difficult to swallow.[116] Intercollegiate athletics revolves around big money. Winning brings more money to programs and, thus, coaches are under pressure to produce. Those who do produce at the Division I level can expect six and seven figure annual incomes. Athletes spend twelve months a year playing, practicing, and training for their particular sport. For approximately eight months per year they are also students. The athletes are primarily responsible for the generation of the revenues used to pay the aforementioned coaches and programs. In return, they receive, relatively speaking, incredibly poor compensation. The days of sports at the collegiate level, at least in Division I programs, being "just a game" are long gone.[117] Sports have a way of putting educational institutions on the map. How many people would know of the College of Charleston without basketball?

Finally, it is suggested that amateurism in and of itself is not the reason most fans watch collegiate sports.[118] Loyalties to educational institutions and to tradition are very important. Ticket prices for collegiate events are more affordable than for professional events, and a modest stipend for athletes will not alter that situation. Rivalries and the national championships sanctioned by the NCAA are a natural attraction. A retreat from pure amateurism will not detract from this attraction.

More attention must be paid to athletes' welfare. The relaxation of the work restrictions is well-intentioned, but is misdirected. It is counter to the association's own concerns over the amount of time the athletes have in a day for sports, school, and life. It throws one more factor into the mix, which is a mistake. There are, of course, natural concerns over athletes having jobs under this rule which pay good wages for little or no work. Policing will be a nightmare.

It is time for collegiate athletes to receive monthly stipends as part of their scholarship package. Even Walter Byers, former longtime Executive Director of the NCAA, now calls for fair treatment of athletes, including relaxation of restrictions on compensation and outside income.[119] We are no longer in an age of innocence where there is no commercialism in college athletics. It is big business and those most responsible for the product put on the field, the players, should be compensated.

Notes

1. C. Peter Goplerud, Stipends for Collegiate Athletes: A Philosophical Spin on a Controversial Proposal, 5 Kan. J.L. & Pub. Pol'y 125, 127 (1996).

2. See Steve Wulf, Tote That Ball, Lift That Revenue; Why Not Pay College Athletes, Who Put in Long Hours to Fill Stadiums—and Coffers?, Time, Oct. 21, 1996, at 94 (recognizing that the colleges and coaches make money at the athletes' expense); see also Ray Yasser, Essay: A Comprehensive Blueprint for the Reform of Intercollegiate Athletics, 3 Marq. Sports L.J. 123 (1993) (examining the NCAA and proposing reform).

3. See Jack L. Copeland, Delegates OK Key Athlete-Welfare Legislation, NCAA News, Jan. 20, 1997, at 1.

. . . .

31. Sherman Act, 15 U.S.C. 1 (1990).

32. See Standard Oil Co. v. United States, 221 U.S. 1, 56 (1911).

33. See White Motor Co. v. United States, 372 U.S. 253, 259-260 (1963).

34. See NCAA v. Board of Regents of the Univ. of Okla., 468 U.S. 85, 119 (1984).

35. NCAA v. Board of Regents of the Univ. of Okla., 468 U.S. 85, 101 (1984).

36. See Banks v. NCAA, 977 F.2d 1081, 1086 (7th Cir. 1992); McCormack v. NCAA, 845 F.2d 1338, 1344 (5th Cir. 1988); Law v. NCAA, 902 F. Supp. 1394, 1403 (D. Kan. 1995); Gaines v. NCAA, 746 F. Supp. 738, 746 (M.D. Tenn. 1990).

37. See Hairston v. Pacific 10 Conference, 101 F.3d 1315, 1319 (9th Cir. 1996).

38. See id.

39. See id.

40. See id.

41. See, e.g., Banks, 977 F.2d at 1094; McCormack, 845 F.2d at 1345; Justice v. NCAA, 577 F. Supp. 356, 383 (D. Ariz. 1983).

42. See Board of Regents of the Univ. of Okla., 468 U.S. at 88.

. . . .

57. Banks v. NCAA, 977 F.2d 1081, 1098 (7th Cir. 1992). (Flaum, J., concurring in part and dissenting in part).

58. 1996–1997 NCAA Manual (1996), at 2.5.

59. Steve Wulf, Tote That Ball, Lift That Revenue; Why Not Pay College Athletes Who Put in Long Hours to Fill Stadiums and Coffers? Time, Oct. 21, 1996, at 94.

60. See NCAA Manual, supra note 58, at 12.1.2.

61. See, e.g., Brian Carnell, Another View: Free the Athletes and Scrap the NCAA, Detroit News, Jan. 23, 1997, at A15 (arguing that the players do most of the work and assume all of the risk, yet are prevented from sharing in the results of their labor); Ron Maly, Hawkeyes' Verba: Players Feeling Cheated, Des Moines Reg., Jul. 28, 1996, at Big Peach 4 (describing the financial struggles of scholarship athletes); Michael Costello, Some Cheating: Sharing the Booty with Athletes, Lewiston Morning Trib., Mar. 16, 1996, at A12 (stating that students "grind their bones into dust for next to nothing").

62. See generally Goplerud, supra note 1, at 127-128 (discussing workers' compensation as it would relate to student athletes on a stipend). Much of the following discussion appeared initially in the Kansas article and is used here with permission of the journal.

63. See generally Richard A. Epstein, The Historical Origins and Economic Structure of Workers' Compensation Law, 16 Ga. L. Rev. 775 (1982) (commenting upon the central features of the history and of the debate that workers' compensation law has generated); Ray Yasser, Are Scholarship Athletes At Big-Time Programs Really University Employees?—You Bet They Are!, 9 Black L.J. 66 (1984) (exploring how courts treat the relationship between athletes and educational institutions when the student-athlete is injured and tries to recover against the school under local workers' compensation laws); Sean Alan Roberts, Comment, College Athletes, Universities, and Workers' Compensation: Placing the Relationship in the Proper Context by Recognizing Scholarship Athletes as Employees, 35 S. Tex. L. Rev. 1315 (1996) (focusing on the applicability of the Texas workers' compensation statute to scholarship athletes).

64. See Arthur Larson, Workers' Compensation Law: Cases, Materials, and Text 795 (1992).

. . . .

95. Rensing v. Indiana State Univ. Bd. of Trustees, 444 N.E.2d 1170 (Ind. 1983) at 1172–73.

96. See generally Alan Roberts, Comment, College Athletes, Universities, and Workers' Compensation: Placing the Relationship in the Proper Context by Recognizing Scholarship Athletes as Employees, 35 S. Tex. L. Rev. 1315 (1996), at 1341 (noting Texas' liberal definition of employee on a quid pro quo basis); Ray Yasser, Essay: A Comprehensive Blueprint for the Reform of Intercollegiate Athletics, 3 Marq. Sports L.J. 123 (1993), at 137 (calling an athletic scholarship an oxymoron and comparing it more to a one-year renewable contract).

97. Today, scholarships are one-year awards. During the typical recruitment process the athlete is promised a four- or five-year scholarship. This is actually delivered on a year- to-year basis and there are some schools or coaches that do not renew scholarships to certain players. This can be done under current rules so long as there is notice and some opportunity to discuss the non-renewal of the scholarship.

98. See Telephone Interview with Sandy Pruett, Administrative Assistant to the Director of Personnel, University of Oklahoma (Feb. 28, 1996).

99. See id.

100. See Cohen v. Brown Univ., 101 F.3d 155, 166-67 (1st Cir. 1996).

101. 29 U.S.C. § 151 (1994).

102. See id. § 157. It is assumed no one will argue that the NCAA is not engaged in interstate commerce.

103. See id. § 152.

104. See generally NLRB v. O'Hare-Midway Limousine Serv., Inc., 924 F.2d 692 (7th Cir. 1991) (holding that whether an individual is an employee is a factual matter focusing on the employer's ability to control the purported employee and analyzing characteristics of an employer-employee relationship, including how payment for services is determined; whether the employer provides benefits; who provides tools or other materials to perform the work; who designated where the work is done, and whether the relationship is temporary or permanent).

105. Periodically, there are calls for college athletes to strike over some issue. Indeed, Bob Knight, the legendary Indiana University basketball coach has recently suggested such a move to respond to mistreatment of athletes by the NCAA. See Fish, supra note 56, at E6. Application of the labor laws to athletes receiving a stipend would likely allow the athletes to organize and, under appropriate circumstances, strike.

106. See 26 U.S.C. § 117 (1994).

107. Curry Kirkpatrick, The Hoops Are Made of Gold, Newsweek, Apr. 3, 1995, at 62.

108. See John Eisenberg, NCAA On The Right Track With New Part-Time Job Rule, Baltimore Sun, Jan. 20, 1997, at C1.

109. See Paying College Athletes a Bad Idea: Scholarship Rules Could Be Fairer, Omaha World Herald, Jan. 18, 1995, at 18.

. . . .

111. See Fish, supra note 56, at E6.

112. See id.

113. See Maly, supra note 61, at Big Peach 4; Ed Graney, Scheduling Changes Hit Aztecs in Pocketbook, San Diego Union-Trib., Oct. 8, 1996, at D1; John Williams, Mounting Defeat Threatens UH Sports Programs, Hous. Chron., June 27, 1996, at A1.

114. David Nakamura, Equity Leaves Its Mark on Male Athletes; Some Schools Make Cuts to Add Women's Sports, Wash. Post, Jul. 7, 1997, at A1.

115. See Bob Hurt, Paying College Athletes Has Major Obstacles, Ariz. Republic, May 5, 1995, at E2.

116. See W. D. Murray, NCAA's Top Product Faces Big Challenge—Top Players Leave for More Compensation, Seattle Times, Mar. 30, 1997, at D2.

117. At least one judge has clearly noticed the change:

The NCAA would have us believe that intercollegiate athletic contests are about spirit, competition, camaraderie, sportsmanship, hard work ... and nothing else .... Players play for the fun of it, colleges get a kick out of entertaining the student body and alumni, but the relationship between players and colleges is positively noncommercial .... The NCAA continues to purvey, even in this case, an outmoded image of intercollegiate sports that no longer jibes with reality. The times have changed. College football is a terrific American institution that generates abundant nonpecuniary benefits for players and fans, but it is also a vast commercial venture that yields substantial profits for colleges, ... both on and off the field. Banks v. NCAA, 977 F.2d 1081, 1098-99 (7th Cir. 1992) (Flaum, J., concurring in part and dissenting in part).

118. See generally Mitten, supra note 56 (arguing that limitations on scholarships currently a part of the NCAA rules are violative of antitrust laws). Professor Mitten notes

It is unlikely that the tremendous popularity of intercollegiate sports is a result of the amateur status of college athletes. Other factors seem to be more significant in accounting for the strong national public interest in college sports. For example, alumni pride and loyalty, tradition, long-standing rivalries, national rankings, conference and national championship tournament competition, and exciting play probably contribute to the public obsession with college sports more than the "amateur" status of college athletes.

Id. at 78.

119. See Walter Byers, Unsportsmanlike Conduct: Exploiting College Athletes (University of Michigan Press 1995).

ADVICE FOR THE NEXT JEREMY BLOOM: AN ELITE ATHLETE'S GUIDE TO NCAA AMATEURISM REGULATIONS

Christopher A. Callanan

INTRODUCTION

Jeremy Bloom presented a unique challenge to the National Collegiate Athletic Association (NCAA) regulations on amateurism because, as a world-class freestyle moguls skier and Division I football player, he was a marketable athlete.[1] By declaring Bloom ineligible to compete as an NCAA football player in the event he accepted the customary financial benefits of professional skiing, the NCAA created myriad issues for similarly situated athletes. Although Bloom was among the first athletes to raise the issue, he will be by no means the last. Emerging nontraditional sports, particularly action sports, attract younger athletes. These sports are aggressively marketed to young audiences through the endorsement of young athletes. Thus, more and more athletes at younger ages receive opportunities to participate in activities that, without careful consideration, can jeopardize present and future athletic eligibility at the scholastic and collegiate level.

As a result of Jeremy Bloom's case (*Bloom v. National Collegiate Athletic Association*), individual sport, Olympic, and action sport athletes as well as other talents who also compete (or hope to compete) in scholastic and NCAA sports must exercise particular caution. Given the detail of NCAA Bylaws, it is impossible to cover every scenario or exception here. Instead, the following is intended to introduce athletes and their families to common issues that arise and to suggest strategies for informed decision-making in light of the *Bloom* decision.

KNOW THE RULES: THEY APPLY SOONER THAN YOU THINK

Any athlete who is or hopes to be eligible to participate in collegiate athletics is bound by the NCAA Bylaws.[2] Conduct before and during NCAA participation can jeopardize eligibility.[3] In addition, each state regulates scholastic eligibility. Most states follow the NCAA Bylaws as they relate to amateurism, so this discussion focuses on NCAA regulation. However, every pre-high school and high school athlete must consider both state regulations and the NCAA Bylaws.

AGENTS AND LAWYERS: WHAT ADVICE IS PERMITTED?

Bylaws 12.1.1(g)[4] and 12.3[5] declare an athlete ineligible if he or she enters into an agreement with an agent to market his or her reputation or ability in that sport. An agreement that does not limit itself to a particular sport makes an athlete ineligible in all sports.[6] An athlete may secure advice from a lawyer concerning a proposed professional sport, contract, so long as the lawyer does not also represent the athlete in negotiations for that contract.[7]

"SALARIED" PROFESSIONAL ATHLETES: PROHIBITIONS AND EXCEPTIONS

Bylaw 12.1.1[8] characterizes the activities that destroy amateur status required for NCAA eligibility. Using skill in a sport for pay (12.1.1.(a)), accepting a promise of pay (12.1.1.(b)), signing a professional contract (12.1.1.(c)), and agreeing with an agent (12.1.1.(g)), are among the activities that destroy athletic eligibility. A specific exception to this rule permits many athletes to play minor league baseball while retaining eligibility to play college football.[9] Several well-known athletes have used this exception to their advantage, such as Chris Weinke, Cedric Benson, Drew Henson, and Ricky Williams. Bylaw 12.1.2 permits a professional athlete in one sport to retain eligibility in another sport.[10] However, the athlete cannot receive financial aid in the eligible sport if he or she is still involved with professional athletics, receives any pay from any professional sports organization, or has any active contractual relationship.[11]

NAVIGATING THE MURKY WATERS OF ENDORSEMENT AND PROMOTIONAL INCOME: JEREMY BLOOM'S CHALLENGE TO THE NCAA

Jeremy Bloom argues that the 12.1.2 exception for "professional athletes in another sport" should permit him to accept the customary income for professional skiing—product endorsements and marketing activities—without jeopardizing his eligibility to play NCAA Division I football.[12] Bloom compared the salary paid to a minor league baseball player to the endorsement and marketing income customarily earned by a professional skier.[13] Both are customary forms of payment in the respective professional sports. In rejecting his claim, the NCAA cited two regulations dealing with commercial activity to distinguish permissible salary income from prohibited marketing income.

Bylaw 12.5.2.1(a) prohibits a college athlete, subsequent to enrollment from accepting pay for or permitting the use of his or her name or picture "to advertise, recommend or promote directly the sale or use of a commercial product."[14] Bylaw 12.5.2.1(b) prohibits receiving pay for endorsing a commercial product or service through the athlete's use of the product or service.[15] These bylaws prohibit any college athlete from endorsing a product or service by using the product or service or lending the athletes' name, image, or likeness to promote the product or service.[16]

Bylaw 12.4.1.1, the "Athletics Reputation" rule[17] prohibits a student-athlete from receiving compensation from anyone (not just an advertiser or marketer) in exchange for the value that the student-athlete provides to the employer for the athlete's "publicity, reputation, fame or personal following" obtained because of athletic ability.[18] This rule prohibits commercial activity by a student-athlete even if it does no[t] involve promotion, endorsement, or product use, but exists in part as a result of the athlete's goodwill as an NCAA athlete.

Through these bylaws, the NCAA distinguishes salary income in a sport like baseball or football from endorsement, promotional, or reputation income.[19] In deciding the *Bloom* case, the Colorado Court of Appeals noted that the NCAA Bylaws consistently prohibit student-athletes from engaging in any form of paid endorsement or media activity.[20] The court enforced the bylaws as written because, despite their disproportionate impact on athletes of different sports, the Bylaws are unambiguous and consistent in prohibiting any form of commercial activity by any athlete.[21]

The *Bloom* decision suggests that the NCAA and courts asked to interpret NCAA Bylaws will continue to strictly interpret amateurism regulations to forbid marketing, endorsement, or media-related income (or activity) by student-athletes regardless of the circumstance. The continued prevalence of endorsement and media activity in popular culture is unlikely to generate change in the NCAA system. It will only increase the number of athletes who knowingly or inadvertently face the consequences of strictly interpreted bylaws.

One practical difficulty in likening endorsement income to salary income is that it is impossible to determine the degree to which an athlete's marketability derives from his or her simultaneous status as an NCAA athlete. In his case, Bloom could not show that none of his marketability resulted from his Colorado football career. As a result, he was unable to convince the court that his proposed activity complied with otherwise unambiguous bylaws prohibiting any kind of commercial activity by student-athletes.

Even if the NCAA could measure the source of an athlete's marketability or if it decided to undertake the effort to distinguish permissible kinds of income to be fairer to skiers and other similar athletes, it has no financial incentive to do so. Allowing student-athletes to accept paid endorsement or media income provides marketers an alternative (and likely cheaper) way to associate with the goodwill of college sports. Given the present system's great financial reward to the NCAA and its institutions, neither is likely to voluntarily change the present system. These realities create great risk for athletes who participate in sports (or other similar activities) where endorsement and media income are customary.

BEWARE THE BREADTH OF COMMERCIAL ACTIVITY

Aaron Adair's story demonstrates the breadth of commercial activity as interpreted by the NCAA.[22] Adair was a Texas high school baseball star and highly touted professional prospect when he was diagnosed with brain cancer.[23] After a successful treatment, rehabilitation and arduous comeback, Adair worked his way back to competitive baseball.[24] He ultimately accepted a scholarship to play Division I baseball at the University of Oklahoma.[25] While he was in college, Adair lost his father to leukemia.[26] Adair authored a book, *You Don't Know Where I've Been*, chronicling his own struggle to overcome cancer and to deal with the loss of his father.[27] While promoting the book throughout Texas and Oklahoma, the University, through its NCAA compliance officer, informed Adair that he was engaging in prohibited commercial activity—the promotion and sale of his book.[28] Adair's book ended his NCAA eligibility and baseball career.

Athletes involved in the performing arts must also be vigilant. Many of the arguments raised by Jeremy Bloom were originally made by Northwestern University football player Darnell Autry. Autry successfully overcame the NCAA's objection to his participation in a feature film, *The Thirteenth Angel*.[29] Autry, a theatre major, obtained an injunction permitting him to act by showing that the opportunity was relevant to his studies and anticipated career, did not result from or relate to his athletic reputation, and would not result in payment beyond expense reimbursement.[30] Addressing similar issues, bylaw 12.5.1.3 permits an athlete to continue modeling activities unrelated to athletic activity that the athlete participated in prior to enrollment under specific conditions.[31] Similar issues have arisen with athletes who publish local restaurant reviews and participate in music videos. Although each circumstance is different, the degree to which each opportunity relates to athletic ability or to one's student-athlete status is always an important factor in determining permissibility. As athletes continue to participate in various activities that generate commercial and media attention, challenges to traditional definitions of amateurism will continue.

. . . .

Notes

1. Bloom v. NCAA, 93 P.3d 621 (Colo. Ct. App. 2004). For instructive discussion of the Bloom litigation and controversy, see Christian Dennie, Amateurism Stifles a Student-Athlete's Dream, 12 SPORTS LAW. J. 221 (2005); Alain Lapter, Bloom v. NCAA: A Procedural Due Process Analysis and the Need for Reform, 12 SPORTS LAW. J. 255 (2005); Gordon E. Gouveia, Making a Mountain Out of a Mogul: Jeremy Bloom v. NCAA and Unjustified Denial of Compensation Under NCAA Amateurism Rules, 6 VAND. J. ENT. L. & PRAC. 22 (2003).

2. NCAA BYLAWS, reprinted in NAT'L COLLEGIATE ATHLETIC ASS'N, 2005-2006 NCAA DIVISION I MANUAL (2005), available at http:// www.ncaa.org/library/membership/division_i_manual/2005-06/2005-06_d1_ manual.pdf [hereinafter NCAA MANUAL].

3. "Amateurism" states that: "A student-athlete shall not be eligible for participation in an intercollegiate sport if the individual takes or has taken pay, or has accepted the promise of pay in any form, for participation in that sport or if the individual has violated any of the other regulations related to amateurism set forth in Bylaw 12." Id. § 14.01.3.1 (emphasis added). Bylaw 12.01.3 states that "NCAA amateur status may be lost as a result of activities prior to enrollment in college." Id. § 12.01.3.

4. Id. § 12.1.1(g).

5. Id. § 12.3.

6. Id. § 12.3.1.

7. Id. § 12.3.2.

8. Id. § 12.1.1.

9. Id. § 12.1.2.

10. Id.

11. Id.

12. Bloom v. NCAA, 93 P.3d 621, 625 (Colo. Ct. App. 2004).

13. Id. at 625.

14. NCAA BYLAWS § 12.5.2.1(a), reprinted in NCAA MANUAL, supra note 2.

15. Id. § 12.5.2.1(b).

16. Id.

17. Id. § 12.4.1.1.

18. Id.

19. Bloom v. NCAA, 93 P.3d 621, 625-26 (Colo. Ct. App. 2004).

20. Id. at 626.

21. Id.

22. See Aaron Adair Website, http://www.aaronadair.com (last visited Apr. 23, 2006) (providing an account of Mr. Adair's story); see also Dennie, supra note 1.

23. Aaron Adair Website, supra note 22.

24. Id.

25. Id.

26. Id.

27. Id.; see also AARON ADAIR, YOU DON'T KNOW WHERE I'VE BEEN (2003); Description and Reviews of You Don't Know Where I've Been, http://www.amazon.com/gp/product/1553955145/qid=1145890634/sr=1-1/ref=sr_1_1/103-2448975-0787006?s=books&v=glance&n=283155 (last visited May 10, 2006).

28. Dennie, supra note 1, at 236-37.

29. Description of The Thirteenth Angel, http:// www.imdb.com/title/tt0119055/ (last visited May 10, 2006).

30. Dennie, supra note 1, at 233.

31. NCAA BYLAWS § 12.5.1.3, reprinted in NCAA MANUAL, supra note 2.

THE GAME OF LIFE

James L. Shulman and William G. Bowen

KEY EMPIRICAL FINDINGS

. . . We have used the extensive institutional records of the 30 academically selective institutions in the study to learn about the pre-collegiate preparation of athletes and other students in the 1951, 1976, and 1989 entering cohorts and their subsequent performance in college. We have also followed the approach suggested more than a century ago by the Walter Camp Commission on College Football and analyzed the experiences and views of both former athletes and other students who attended these schools. In seeking to move the debate over intercollegiate athletics beyond highly charged assertions and strongly held opinions, we use this chapter to summarize the principal empirical findings that we believe deserve the attention of all those who share an interest in understanding what has been happening over the course of the past half century.

. . . .

Scale: Numbers of Athletes and Athletic Recruitment

1. *Athletes competing on intercollegiate teams constitute a sizable share of the undergraduate student population at many selective colleges and universities, and especially at coed liberal arts colleges and Ivy League universities.* In 1989, intercollegiate athletes accounted for nearly one-third of the men and approximately one-fifth of the women who entered the coed liberal arts colleges participating in this study; male and female athletes accounted for much smaller percentages of the entering classes in the Division I-A scholarship schools, which of course have far larger enrollments; the Ivies are intermediate in the relative number of athletes enrolled, with approximately one-quarter of the men and 15 percent of the women playing on intercollegiate teams. Some of the much larger Division I-A schools, public and private, enrolled a smaller absolute number of athletes than either the more athletically oriented coed liberal arts colleges or the Ivies—primarily because a number of the Division I-A schools sponsor fewer teams.

2. *The relative number of male athletes in a class has not changed dramatically over the past 40 years, but athletes in recent classes have been far more intensely recruited than used to be the case.* This statement holds for the coed liberal arts colleges as well as the universities. In 1989, roughly 90 percent of the men who played the High Profile sports of football, basketball, and hockey said that they had been recruited (the range was from 97 percent in the Division I-A public universities to 83 percent in the Division III coed liberal arts colleges), and roughly two-thirds of the men who competed in other sports such as tennis, soccer, and swimming said that they too had been recruited. In the '76 cohort, these percentages were much lower; there were many more "walk-ons" in 1976 than in 1989, and there were surely fewer still in the most recent entering classes.

3. *Only tiny numbers of women athletes in the '76 entering cohort reported having been recruited, but that situation had changed markedly by the time of the '89 entering cohort; recruitment of women athletes at these schools has moved rapidly in the direction of the men's model.* Roughly half of the women in the '89 cohort who played intercollegiate sports in the Ivies and the Division I-A universities reported that having been recruited by the athletic department played a significant role in their having chosen the schools they attended. The comparable percentages in the coed colleges and the women's colleges were much lower in '89, but women athletes at those schools are now also being actively recruited.

Admissions Advantages, Academic Qualifications, and Other "Selection" Effects

1. *Athletes who are recruited, and who end up on the carefully winnowed lists of desired candidates submitted by coaches to the admissions office, now enjoy a very substantial statistical "advantage" in the admissions process—a much greater advantage than that enjoyed by other targeted groups such as*

underrepresented minority students, alumni children, and other legacies; this statement is true for both male and female athletes. At a representative non-scholarship school for which we have complete data on all applicants, recruited male athletes applying for admission to the '99 entering cohort had a 48 percent greater chance of being admitted than did male students at large, after taking differences in SAT scores into account; the corresponding admissions advantage enjoyed by recruited women athletes in '99 was 53 percent. The admissions advantages enjoyed by minority students and legacies were in the range of 18 to 24 percent.

2. *The admissions advantage enjoyed by men and women athletes at this school, which there is reason to believe is reasonably typical of schools of its type, was much greater in '99 than in '89, and it was greater in '89 than in '76.* The trend—the directional signal—is unmistakably clear.

3. *One obvious consequence of assigning such a high priority to admitting recruited athletes is that they enter these colleges and universities with considerably lower SAT scores than their classmates.* This pattern holds for both men and women athletes and is highly consistent by type of school. The SAT "deficit" is most pronounced for men and women who play sports at the Division I-A schools, least pronounced for women at the liberal arts colleges (especially the women's colleges), and middling at the Ivies. Among the men at every type of school, the SAT deficits are largest for those who play the High Profile sports of football, basketball, and hockey.

4. *Admitted athletes differ from their classmates in other ways too, and there is evidence of an "athlete culture."* In addition to having weaker academic qualifications, athletes who went on to play on intercollegiate teams were clearly different in other ways at the time they entered college. They were decidedly more competitive than students at large. The male athletes were also more interested than students at large in pursuing business careers and in achieving financial success (this was not true, however, of the women athletes); athletes placed considerably less emphasis on the goals of making original contributions to science or the arts. The differences between athletes and their classmates along many of these dimensions have widened with the passage of time. In addition, athletes who compete in the Lower Profile sports (such as track, swimming, lacrosse, and tennis) had begun, by the time of the '89 cohort, to share more of the attributes of the athlete culture that earlier were found mostly among the High Profile athletes. Similarly, whereas women athletes in the '76 cohort were largely indistinguishable from their classmates in most

respects, by the time of the '89 cohort women who played sports had more and more in common with the male athletes (for example, entering college with both lower standardized test scores and more politically conservative views than other women students).

5. *Contrary to much popular mythology, recruitment of athletes has no marked effect on either the socioeconomic composition of these schools or on their racial diversity.* Male athletes (especially those who play High Profile sports at the Division I-A schools) are more likely than students at large to come from modest socioeconomic backgrounds and to be African Americans. Nonetheless, elimination of the athletic contribution to racial diversity in the '89 cohort would have caused the percentage of African American men enrolled at these schools to decline by just 1 percentage point—an estimate obtained by recalculating the percentage of African American students who would have been enrolled had the racial mix of athletes been the same as the racial mix of students at large. There would even be an opposite effect among the women, since the share of African American women playing college sports is much lower—often half the corresponding percentage—of African American women students at large. Moreover, until very recently, women athletes were more likely than other women students to come from privileged backgrounds. Those men who play Lower Profile sports continue to come from more advantaged backgrounds than either the other athletes or the rest of their male classmates.

Graduation Rates, Underperformance in the Classroom, and Choice of Major

1. *Despite their lower SATs, athletes who attended the selective schools included in this study, along with their classmates who participated in other time-intensive extracurricular activities, graduated at very high rates.* The national problem of low graduation rates—which has attracted the attention of both the NCAA and the public—does not afflict most athletes or other students who attend these schools.

2. *When we examine grades (rank-in-class), an entirely different picture emerges: the academic standing of athletes, relative to that of their classmates, has deteriorated markedly in recent years.* Whereas male athletes in the '51 cohort were slightly more likely than other students to be in the top third of their class, only 16 percent of those in the '89 cohort finished in the top third, and 58 percent finished in the bottom third. Women athletes in the '76 cohort did as well academically as other women, but women athletes in the '89 cohort were more likely than other women to be in the bottom third of the class. This pattern is especially pronounced in those sets of schools where women

athletes were highly recruited; the women's colleges are alone in showing no gap at all in academic performance between women athletes and other women students in the '89 cohort.

3. *Only part of this decline in the academic performance of athletes can be attributed to their lower levels of aptitude or preparation at the time they began college; they consistently underperform academically even after we control for differences in standardized test scores and other variables.* Academic underperformance among athletes is a pervasive phenomenon. In the '89 cohort, it is found among both male and female athletes and among those who played all types of sports (not just among the men who played football, basketball, and hockey); it is more pronounced within the Ivy League and the coed liberal arts colleges than it is within the Division I-A schools.

4. *Academic underperformance in college has roots in high school academic performance, in the priority assigned by athletes to academics, and in the "culture of sport."* The degree of underperformance varies not only with precollege academic indicators, but also with how many other athletes who played on the same teams underperformed (possible peer effects) and whether athletes cited a coach as a principal mentor. The "culture of sport" interpretation of this pattern is supported by evidence showing that students who were active in other time-intensive extracurricular activities overperformed academically, relative to their SAT scores and other predictors.

5. *Male athletes have become highly concentrated in certain fields of study, especially the social sciences, and female athletes have started to show different patterns of majors as well.* At one Ivy League university, 54 percent of all High Profile athletes majored in economics or political science as compared with 18 percent of male students at large. When considered in the light of differences in career and financial goals, many of the choices of field of study by male athletes seem to be driven by a desire for something akin to a business major. More generally, this evidence on academic concentrations is consistent with other data on rooming patterns in suggesting a greatly increased tendency for athletes to band together. In the 1950s, male athletes were much more broadly distributed across fields of study and, in general, were more like their classmates in all respects.

Advanced Degrees, Careers, and Earnings

1. *Women athletes in the '76 cohort (but not in the '89 cohort) were more likely than their peers to earn advanced degrees of every kind; this was not true of the men, however.* Male athletes were more likely than other male students to earn no advanced degree and also more likely to earn MBAs; they were less likely to earn Ph.D.s. Differences between athletes and other students in advanced degree attainment must be seen in context: all students who attended these selective schools, athletes and others, were far more likely to earn advanced degrees than were most graduates of four-year colleges.

2. *Consistent with patterns of advanced degree attainment, male athletes are more likely than other men in their classes to have chosen jobs in business and finance and less likely to have become scientists, engineers, academics, or doctors or lawyers.* These differences were smaller in the '51 cohort than in the '76 cohort (to the extent they existed at all in the 1950s), and they are magnified when we look at the early vocational choices made by the members of the '89 cohort. High Profile athletes have always been somewhat more interested in careers in marketing than either other athletes or students at large, and this vocational preference appears to have intensified in the most recent cohort. Athletes in the '89 cohort were appreciably less likely than their classmates to work in computer science and other technologically driven fields.

3. *Male athletes consistently earned more money than their classmates.* The average earnings of former athletes exceed the average earnings of students at large in the '51, '76, and '89 cohorts. This pattern is also found in every type of school, ranging from the coed liberal arts colleges to the Division I-A public universities. These consistent differences are on the order of 10 percent.

4. *The earnings advantage of male athletes is attributable to both pre-college differences and post-college choices.* Athletes are more likely than students at large to work in the for-profit and self-employment sectors; moreover, within the for-profit sector, the earnings advantage of athletes is highly concentrated in financial services occupations. There is no significant difference in the average earnings of athletes and of students at large in law and medicine, among those who are CEOs of for-profit enterprises, or in any of the fields within the not-for-profit and governmental sectors. Thus the earnings advantage of male athletes is not an across-the-board phenomenon, and its location in financial services suggests that it is mainly a function of some combination of (a) the vocational interests of male athletes; (b) the special advantages of athlete-alumni networks in fields such as financial services; and (c) the special contribution to marketplace success in these fields of personal traits often associated with being an athlete (such as a high level of competitiveness, discipline, focus on achieving well-defined goals, and ability to take direction and work in teams).

5. *In general, the earnings of male athletes are not associated with how many years they played sports in college.* This lack of any association leads us to believe that the earnings advantages enjoyed by athletes are related more to who they were, what they had already learned, and what they wanted when they entered college than to the amount of further "training" ("treatment") that they received by playing college sports. One clear exception to this pattern is that the small number of High Profile athletes who played for four years earned appreciably more than their teammates—a finding that we suspect indicates the presence of a kind of "credentialing" or "celebrity" effect. Those male athletes who earned letters for four years in the High Profile sports are likely to be the visible stars, who are most likely to have been known by alumni and who may then have had especially good opportunities to enter high-paying occupations in fields where connections are often especially useful.

6. *Intensity of the level of play does not translate into superior later life outcomes for male athletes, as measured by earnings.* On the contrary, the earnings advantage enjoyed by athletes is smallest among those who played at the Division I-A public universities and, if anything, larger for the men who played at the Division III level in coed liberal arts colleges than for those who participated in more elaborate programs in the Ivies or in the Division I-A private universities. Also, there is no relation between the won–lost record of the team on which a student played and how much that student earned later in life.

7. *Women athletes in the '76 cohort were more likely than their female peers to be working full-time, to be either doctors or academics (unlike the male athletes, who were disproportionately found in business fields), and, like the men who played sports, to enjoy a sizable earnings advantage over their women classmates; moreover, within the for-profit sector, the relative earnings advantage of the '76 women athletes is even larger than the earnings advantage of their male counterparts.* These patterns reflect both the high overall academic achievements of these '76 women athletes (who were only rarely recruited as athletes and met the same admissions requirements as all other women students) and the atypically high levels of drive and ambition often associated with playing college sports. In many respects, these '76 women athletes resemble the men who played sports in the 1950s.

8. *In contrast, women athletes in the '89 cohort are no more likely than other women to have earned, or to be earning, advanced degrees, and they do not enjoy any earnings advantages over their peers.* These women are of course at very early stages in their post-college lives, and much may change over time. But the '89 women athletes differ from their predecessors in having been more actively recruited as athletes, in having entered with weaker academic profiles, and in having subsequently underperformed academically. The experiences to date of the '76 women athletes may be poor predictors of what latter-day women athletes will go on to do.

9. *There is no evidence that earnings for women athletes are enhanced by larger "doses" of athletic framing in college.* There is no consistent association of any kind between years of play and earnings; nor is there any association between the earnings advantages enjoyed by women athletes and the intensity of the level of play. In fact, the Division I-A private universities are the only group of schools at which women athletes enjoyed *rio* earnings advantage; conversely, the highest earnings advantage accorded college athletes in the '76 cohort is found in the women's colleges.

Leadership

1. *Athletes were more likely than other students to rate themselves highly as leaders before college began and were also more likely to say, after college, that leadership had played an important role in their lives; yet, surprisingly, neither this greater inclination to provide leadership, nor this stronger expression of its importance, is associated with evidence of having actually provided more leadership.* Athletes and their classmates seem about on a par in this regard. Athletes were no more likely than other students to become CEOs, to earn top salaries in professional fields like law and medicine (where earnings may serve as a proxy for leadership), or to be leaders in most civic activities.

2. *Athletes are leaders in exceptionally large numbers in two specific arenas—alumni/ae activities and youth groups (men only)—and having been a college athlete appears to have measurable effects on the priorities that these leaders emphasize.* This is clearest in the case of alumni/ae leadership. Former athletes who now serve as trustees and in other leadership capacities are more likely to favor increasing the emphasis their school places on intercollegiate athletics than are other alumni leaders, alumni at large, or even other alumni who played sports in college.

3. *In the aggregate, alumni/ae from all three eras and from all types of institutions want their schools to place less, not more, emphasis on intercollegiate athletics than the schools do at present.* When asked about their schools' institutional priorities, the alumni/ae consistently wanted more emphasis placed on

undergraduate teaching, residential life, and extracurricular activities—but not on intercollegiate athletics. Former athletes, on the other hand, favor placing more emphasis on intercollegiate athletics.

Giving Back to the College or University

1. *In common with high academic achievers and students who were heavily involved in extracurricular activities, former athletes have generally had above-average general giving rates.* All three of these groups have "bonded" more closely with their schools than have most students, in part because they may feel that they had unusually successful and enjoyable experiences as undergraduates. Such feelings of attachment may be the primary reason why these groups have been so supportive of the broad educational purposes of their institutions.

2. *The High Profile athletes at the Division I-A schools are a revealing exception to this pattern: they are much less likely than others to be contributors.* The main reason, we suspect, is that these High Profile athletes are more likely to be focused on their athletic pursuits and may see themselves as a group apart from the larger academic community (and may even disidentify with it). General giving rates among High Profile athletes have declined over time, relative to the giving rates of others, at both the Division I-A private universities and the coed liberal arts colleges (although not in the Ivies)—a finding that may reflect what appears to be a growing separation of athletes on many campuses from the rest of the campus community. Striking evidence in support of this interpretation is provided by the lack of any decline in general giving rates on the part of either the academic high achievers or the students active in extracurricular activities.

3. *The data flatly contradict one of the strongest myths about college athletics—namely, that winning teams, and especially winning football teams, have a large, positive impact on giving rates.* Winning football teams do not inspire increased giving on the part of alumni/ae at Division I-A private universities or Ivy League schools. Surprisingly, it is only at the coed liberal arts colleges, where teams generally receive less recognition, that winning is associated with increased alumni/ae giving, a finding that can be attributed mainly to the exceptionally large number of former athletes found among the alumni/ae of these schools.

The Financial Equation: Costs and Revenues Associated with Intercollegiate Sports

1. *Expenditures on intercollegiate athletics, excluding capital costs, vary tremendously depending on the level of play at which the institution competes.* Total expenditures, excluding capital costs, reach the $50 million level at a university such as the University of Michigan, which offers a wide range of highly competitive big-time programs; $20 to $25 million at a more "standard" Division I-A university; $10 million at an Ivy League university; and $1.5 million at a coed liberal arts college.

2. *Level of play has a surprisingly large effect on expenditures on sports such as tennis, swimming, and field hockey, as well as on football and basketball.* Direct annual expenditures on one of these Lower Profile sports may range from $350,000 at a Division I-A university, to $125,000 in the Ivy League, to $40,000 at a coed liberal arts college. Thus the budgetary consequences of choosing one level of competition over another are considerable.

3. *Revenues from athletics, including gate receipts and television and bowl revenues, can offset most, and sometimes all, of the costs of big-time programs if (and only if) teams are consistently successful; even in these settings, most schools lose money, and it is unlikely that any school comes close to covering its full costs if proper allowances are made for the capital-intensive nature of athletics.* We estimate that the overall net costs of an intercollegiate sports program, exclusive of capital costs, may range from zero for the most competitively successful big-time programs, to $7 to $8 million at both the "standard" Division I-A private universities and the Ivies, to $1.5 million at a coed liberal arts college. Net spending ranges from $2500 per intercollegiate athlete per year at a coed liberal arts college, to $9000 per year at an Ivy League school, to $18,000 per year at a "standard" Division I-A private university.

4. *Athletic budgets, seen on a "net" basis, should be regarded as expenditures by the institution that must be justified in terms of the contribution they do or do not make to the core educational mission of the school.* In only the rarest case can athletic expenditures be justified as an "investment" that will somehow benefit the institution's bottom line. Moreover, the increasing volatility of athletic revenues (at those schools where revenues from sponsorships and licensing are consequential) means that the financial risk factor associated with big-time programs cannot be ignored.

A CALL TO ACTION: RECONNECTING COLLEGE SPORTS AND HIGHER EDUCATION

Report of the Knight Foundation Commission on Intercollegiate Athletics

FOREWORD

In 1989, as a decade of highly visible scandals in college sports drew to a close, the trustees of the John S. and James L. Knight Foundation were concerned that athletics abuses threatened the very integrity of higher education. In October of that year, they created a Commission on Intercollegiate Athletics and directed it to propose a reform agenda for college sports.

In announcing this action, James L. Knight, then chairman of the Foundation, emphasized that it did not reflect any hostility toward college athletics. . . . "Our interest is not to abolish that role but to preserve it by putting it back in perspective. . . ."

To understand their concern and the subsequent work of the Commission, it is necessary to look back on the extent to which corruption had engulfed big-time college sports in the 1980s.

In a cover story shortly before the Commission was created, *Time* magazine described the problem as ". . . an obsession with winning and moneymaking that is pervading the noblest ideals of both sports and education in America." Its victims, *Time* went on to say, were not just athletes who found the promise of an education a sham but "the colleges and universities that participate in an educational travesty—a farce that devalues every degree and denigrates the mission of higher education."

Here are some broad outlines of the problems the Commission saw then:

- In the 1980s, 109 colleges and universities were censured, sanctioned, or put on probation by the National Collegiate Athletic Association (NCAA). That number included more than half the universities playing at the NCAA's top competitive level—57 institutions out of 106.

- Nearly a third of present and former professional football players responding to a survey near the end of the decade said they had accepted illicit payments while in college, and more than half said they saw nothing wrong with the practice.

- Another survey showed that among the 106 institutions then in the NCAA's Division I-A, 48 had graduation rates under 30 percent for their men's basketball players and 19 had the same low rate for football players.

At times it seemed that hardly a day passed without another story about recruiting violations . . . , under-the-table payoffs . . . [or] players who didn't go to classes or who took courses that would never lead to a meaningful degree. Even crime sprees at some athletic powerhouses were added to the list.

It was small wonder that eight out of 10 Americans questioned in a Louis Harris poll in 1989 agreed that intercollegiate sports had spun out of control. They agreed that athletics programs were being corrupted by big money, and felt that the many cases of serious rules violations had undermined the traditional role of universities as places where young people learn ethics and integrity.

A 1989 series in the *New York Times* raised another warning flag:

> *"High school athletics have become the latest entree on the American sports menu, served up to help satisfy the voracious appetite of the fan. As a result, scholastic athletes are on the verge of becoming as important to the billion-dollar sports industry as their college brothers and sisters—and just as vulnerable to big-time exploitation."*

Somehow, the Knight Foundation concluded, sanity had to be restored to this bleak scene and the values of higher education put above all else in the world of intercollegiate athletics.

. . . .

The Commission laid out an analysis of the problems facing college sports and proposed a "new model for intercollegiate athletics." This analysis was straightforward: Following decades of presidential neglect and institutional indifference, big-time college sports were "out of control." The reform agenda Commission members proposed was equally straightforward, the "one-plus-three" model—presidential control directed toward academic integrity, financial integrity, and independent certification.

No claim was made that their recommendations would solve all the problems tarnishing college sports, or even that all problems would ever be solved to everyone's satisfaction. "Reform is not a destination but a never-ending process," said the Commission's last report.

. . . .

The report that follows presents the Commission's findings from a series of meetings in 2000 and 2001 with NCAA representatives, university presidents, a trustee board chair, faculty, conference commissioners, athletics directors, coaches, athletes, authors, professional sports executives, television officials, a sports apparel representative, a gambling lobbyist, leaders of national higher education associations, and a U.S. senator.

After assessing those hearings, the Commission concludes with some satisfaction that the NCAA has moved a long way toward achieving the goals laid out in the Commission's earlier reports. . . . Many reform efforts have been undertaken over the last decade with sincerity and energy. We reiterate our strong conviction that college sports, when properly conducted, are worth saving. Sports at all levels have been a source of immense satisfaction, self-discipline, and achievement for tens of thousands of young men and women.

. . . .

TEN YEARS LATER

It is tempting to turn away from bad news. To the cynic, corruption has been endemic in big-time sports as long as they have existed. To the rationalizer, reform is already under way and things are not nearly as bad as the critics make them out to be. More time is all that is needed. But to the realist, the bad news is hard to miss. The truth is manifested regularly in a cascade of scandalous acts that, against a backdrop of institutional complicity and capitulation, threaten the health of American higher education. The good name of the nation's academic enterprise is even more threatened today than it was when the Knight Commission published its first report a decade ago. Despite progress in some areas, new problems have arisen, and the condition of big-time college sports has deteriorated.

Consider as an example some simple statistics: As noted in the foreword, 57 out of 106 Division I-A institutions (54 percent) had to be censured, sanctioned, or put on probation for major violations of NCAA rules in the 1980s. In the 1990s, 58 out of 114 Division I-A colleges and universities (52 percent) were similarly penalized. In other words, more than half the institutions competing at the top levels continue to break the rules. Wrongdoing as a way of life seems to represent the status quo.

The fact that such behavior has worked its way into the fiber of intercollegiate sports without provoking powerful and sustained countermeasures from the many institutions so besmirched speaks for itself. It appears that more energy goes into looking the other way than to finding a way to integrate big-time sports into the fabric of higher education.

At the heart of these problems is a profound change in the American culture of sports itself. At one time, that culture was defined by colleges, high schools, summer leagues, and countless community recreational programs. Amateurism was a cherished ideal. In such a context, it made sense to regard athletics as an educational undertaking. Young people were taught values ranging from fitness, cooperation, teamwork, and perseverance to sportsmanship as moral endeavor.

All of that seems somehow archaic and quaint today. Under the influence of television and the mass media, the ethos of athletics is now professional. The apex of sporting endeavor is defined by professional sports. This fundamental shift now permeates many campuses. Big-time college basketball and football have a professional look and feel—in their arenas and stadiums, their luxury boxes and financing, their uniforms and coaching staffs, and their marketing and administrative structures. In fact, big-time programs have become minor leagues in their own right, increasingly taken into account as part of the professional athletics system.

In this new circumstance, what is the relationship between sport and the university as a place of learning?

At the time the Knight Commission was formed in 1989, the answers to that question were already sounding alarm bells. For example, the late A. Bartlett Giamatti, a former president of Yale who went on to become commissioner of major league baseball, said that "failures of nerve, principle and purpose" were threatening to "engulf higher education in ways unfair and dangerous." He argued that what had been "allowed to become a circus—college sports—threatens to become the means whereby the public believes the whole enterprise is a sideshow."

Now, in this new millennium, informed critics are equally scathing in their evaluations. James Duderstadt, president emeritus of the University of Michigan, put it this way before the Knight Commission in late 2000: Major college sports "do far more damage to the university, to its students and faculty, its leadership, its reputation and credibility than most realize—or at least are willing to admit." The ugly disciplinary incidents, outrageous academic fraud, dismal graduation rates, and uncontrolled expenditures surrounding college sports reflect what Duderstadt and others have rightly characterized as "an entertainment industry" that is not only the antithesis of academic values but is "corrosive and corruptive to the academic enterprise."

. . . .

The most glaring elements of the problems outlined in this report—academic transgressions, a financial arms race, and commercialization—are all evidence of the widening chasm between higher education's ideals and big-time college sports.

Academics

When the accretions of centuries of tradition and the bells and whistles of the modern university have been stripped away, what remains is the university's essential mission as an institution for teaching, learning, and the generation of new knowledge. This is the mission that big-time college sports often mock and, in some cases, deliberately undermine.

Big-time athletics departments seem to operate with little interest in scholastic matters beyond the narrow issue of individual eligibility. They act as though the athletes' academic performance is of little moment. The historic and vital link between playing field and classroom is all but severed in many institutions. Graduation rates for athletes in football and basketball at the top level remain dismally low—and in some notable cases are falling. While the Commission recognizes that graduation rates for athletes subject to the NCAA's more stringent eligibility standards effective in the mid-1990s are not yet available, we cannot ignore these facts: The graduation rate for football players in Division I-A fell 3 percent last year and 8 percent in the last five years. The rate for men's basketball players at Division I-A institutions remained stable over the last year, but fell 5 percent over the last five years.

Graduation rates for both were already abysmal. The most recent NCAA graduation rate report reveals that 48 percent of Division I-A football players and 34 percent of men's basketball players at Division I-A institutions earned degrees. The graduation rate for white football players was 55 percent, the lowest since the Student Right to Know Act mandated that such records be made public. Only 42 percent of black football players in Division I-A graduate, according to the most recent figures.

Derrick Z. Jackson, a columnist for the *Boston Globe,* analyzed the graduation rates of African-American players on the 64 teams in the 2001 NCAA men's basketball tournament. He reports these shameful figures from the latest NCAA graduation rate report: Twenty-six of the 64 teams graduated fewer than 35 percent of their African-American players. Seven teams had African-American graduation rates of zero. Furthermore, he writes, "Of the 64 teams, a school was nearly twice as likely to have suffered a decline in its African-American player graduation rate since the mid-1990s than enjoy an increase. The rate in the 2000 NCAA graduation rate report was lower for 35 schools than the rate in the 1996 report. It was higher for only 19 schools."

An academic official at a Division I-A institution told Jackson in regard to the 10 percent graduation rate of its men's basketball team, "We have not in the past had the same high expectations of athletes in academics and not held them to as high a standard in the classroom."

In the face of these facts, many defend the overall graduation rates of Division I-A football and basketball players because in some instances they compare favorably to those of the student body as a whole. The Commission is unimpressed with this comparison of apples and oranges. The fact is that the rest of the student body does not have the advantage of full scholarships and the often extensive academic support services extended to athletes. Data from the U.S. Department of Education indicate that approximately 75 percent of high school graduates who enroll full-time in college immediately after graduation (and continue full-time in the same institution) will receive a bachelor's degree within five and a half years. This group of young full-time students is the appropriate comparison for Division I-A athletes.

Athletes are often admitted to institutions where they do not have a reasonable chance to graduate. They are athlete-students, brought into the collegiate mix more as performers than aspiring undergraduates. Their ambiguous academic credentials lead to chronic classroom failures or chronic cover-ups of their academic deficiencies. As soon as they arrive on campus, they are immersed in the demands of their sports. Flagrant violation of the NCAA's rule restricting the time athletes must spend on their sport to 20 hours a week is openly acknowledged. The loophole most used is that of so-called "voluntary" workouts that don't count toward the time limit. In light of these circumstances, academic failure, far from being a surprise, is almost inevitable.

Sadly though, it comes as a rude surprise to many athletes yearning for a professional sports career to learn that the odds against success are astronomically high. Approximately 1 percent of NCAA men's basketball players and 2 percent of NCAA football players are drafted by NBA or NFL teams—and just being drafted is no assurance of a successful professional career. "Student-athletes" whose sole and now failed objective was to make the pros suddenly find themselves in a world that demands skills their universities did not require them to learn.

The academic support and tutoring athletes receive is too often designed solely to keep them eligible, rather than guide them toward a degree. The instances of tutors or other counselors bending and breaking rules on athletes' behalf is a well-publicized scandal. NCAA case books clearly reveal multiple infractions stemming from "tutoring" involving completing athletes' assignments, writing their papers, and pressuring professors for higher grades. Beyond the breaking of the rules is the breaking of the universities' implicit covenant with all students, athletes included, to educate them. Despite new NCAA satisfactory progress requirements effective in the mid-1990s, press and NCAA reports repeatedly document instances of athletes being diverted into courses that provide no basis for meaningful degrees. A faculty member at a Division I-A institution who has recently spoken out against the transgressions she has witnessed on her campus said, "There are students on our football team this year [2000] who will graduate when both faculty and students know they cannot read or write."

The Arms Race

NCAA President Cedric Dempsey, along with many others, has been outspoken about what he calls an ever-growing "arms race" of spending and building to reach impractical financial goals. There is evidence to support these concerns. The NCAA's latest study of revenues and expenses at Divisions I and II institutions shows that just about 15 percent operate their athletics programs in the black. And deficits are growing every year.

"Clearly, the rising revenues on most campuses have been overwhelmed by even higher costs," Dempsey told the NCAA convention this year. "At the more than 970 NCAA member schools, we are bringing in just over $3 billion a year, but we're spending $4.1 billion in that same period."

A frantic, money-oriented modus operandi that defies responsibility dominates the structure of big-time football and basketball. The vast majority of these schools don't profit from their athletics programs: At over half the schools competing at the NCAA's Division I-A level in 1999, expenses exceeded revenues by an average of $3.3 million, an increase of 18 percent over the previous two years. On the other hand, for the 48 Division I-A institutions where revenues exceeded expenses, the average "profit" more than doubled, increasing 124 percent from $1.7 million to $3.8 million from 1997 to 1999. In considering all these data, moreover, it must be understood that they do not take into consideration the full costs of athletics programs, in that the reported expenses do not include capital expenditures, debt service, and many indirect program costs. Nevertheless, competitive balance is crumbling as the gap between the haves and the have-nots widens. While a relative few programs flourish, many others have chosen to discontinue sports other than football or basketball to make ends meet. Even some of the "haves" react to intense financial pressure to control costs by dropping so-called minor sports.

Too much in major college sports is geared to accommodating excess. Too many athletic directors and conference commissioners serve principally as money managers, ever alert to maximizing revenues. And too many have looked to their stadiums and arenas to generate more money. In the last seven years, capital expenditures at Division I-A institutions (e.g., construction or remodeling of athletics facilities, capital equipment, etc.) increased 250 percent. From east to west, north to south, the test becomes who can build the biggest stadiums, the most luxurious skyboxes. Every one of the 12 schools in one major conference has built a new football stadium or refurbished its old one in recent years. All seem to have assumed they could not afford to do otherwise. The building boom in college sports facilities now under way across the nation will cost well over $4 billion, with the resulting debt stretching far into the future.

The arms race isn't entered into by NCAA fiat. Institutions, not the NCAA, decide what's best for themselves, and for many that means joining the arms race. Presidents and trustees accept their athletics department's argument that they have to keep up with the competition. When one school has a $50 million athletic budget and another gets along on $9 million, how can there be any pretense of competitive parity? And what about on-campus parity? A five-part series, "The Price of Winning," published by the Philadelphia Inquirer in fall 2000 revealed average annual costs as high as nearly $90,000 per athlete at one Division I-A institution. At some Division I-A schools, annual costs per football player are well over $100,000. How can such expenses be justified when the average salary of fully tenured professors at U.S. public research universities barely exceeds $84,000? And what does higher education sacrifice when a school names its football stadium after a pizza chain or its new stadium club after any other commercial product or corporation? To what purpose, indeed, are luxury skyboxes built? Not to satisfy any legitimate institutional need; certainly not to accommodate more students, in whose name and for

whose benefit collegiate sports were originally introduced. The central goal is to garner greater fiscal windfalls from wealthy boosters and alumni willing to spend thousands of dollars to acquire not only luxury boxes but choice seating throughout the stadium, while students are often relegated to the end zone if they can get tickets at all. Interestingly, repeated studies indicate that most contributions to colleges and universities come from those to whom athletic records have little import. Big athletic boosters, conversely, are far less likely to support other aspects of the universities' life and mission, again according to these studies.

There is a tangible downside to this arms race for most schools, that is, for the majority whose big-time programs are less successful and cannot pay for themselves. They must siphon funds from general revenue to try to keep up with the Joneses. Pursuit of success in this context jeopardizes not only the universities' moral heritage but also their financial security.

A glaring symptom of the arms race run amok is the salaries of so-called "star" coaches. At last count, some 30 college football and men's basketball coaches are paid a million dollars or more a year. A few are nearing twice that, or are already there. The irony is not lost on the critics. A college provost points out that his school spent more money hiring the head football coach than it did hiring five department heads—combined. A trustee laments that his university signed the basketball coach to a salary three times greater than its president's. Many players join the complaining chorus when they compare their scholarships to their coaches' salaries, and when their coaches break contracts and jump from team to team—just as their professional counterparts do. Some dissatisfied players have begun to organize in an attempt to increase their clout and have aligned with the United Steelworkers of America for help in doing so.

But coaches have quite a different perspective. They consider the pressures put on their teams' performance when football and basketball revenues are expected to produce the lion's share of the athletic department's budget. They weigh the dismissal rate of those in their ranks who do not win—or do not win soon enough, or big enough—in a win-at-any-cost environment. And they conclude that their salaries are justified.

The logical question for academia emerges: Is there any other department at a university where so much money is spent and justified primarily by reference to the nonacademic performance of its students, staff, or instructors? That is the crux of the matter. Coaches' salaries, like numerous athletics department expenditures, are considered as though they have nothing to do with the traditions and principles of the universities in which they are housed. This lack of academic connection is the fundamental corruption of the original rationale for both sports and coaches on campus: that they are integral components of a well-rounded student life and a useful complement to the universities' other central pursuits. What we have now is a separate culture of performers and trainers, there to provide bread and circuses but otherwise unconnected to the institution that supports them.

Commercialization

Over the last decade, the commercialization of college sports has burgeoned. Vastly larger television deals and shoe contracts have been signed, and more and more space in stadiums and arenas has been sold to advertisers. In too many respects, big-time college sports today more closely resemble the commercialized model appropriate to professional sports than they do the academic model. The NCAA's Dempsey warned the NCAA membership recently that "the level of cynicism over the commercialization of our most visible athletics programs has reached epidemic proportions."

Beginning in 2002, CBS will pay the NCAA $6.2 billion over an 11-year period for broadcast rights primarily for its Division I men's basketball tournament. Television accounts for nearly 80 percent of the NCAA's revenue. When all sources of revenues are accounted for, the Division I men's basketball tournament alone generates well over 90 percent of the NCAA's operating budget. . . . .

With the money comes manipulation. Schools and conferences prostrate themselves to win and get on television. There is a rush now to approve cable and television requests for football and basketball games on weekday evenings, on Sundays, in the morning, and late at night. So much for classroom commitments. On the field, the essential rhythms of the games are sacrificed as play is routinely interrupted for television commercials, including those pushing the alcoholic beverages that contribute to the binge drinking that mars campus life.

Arguments that higher education should be above this commercial fray largely go unheeded, but concern is growing over the economic realities. The television money, when parceled around, never seems to be enough, and the benefits are never evenly distributed. The rich—that is, the schools more in demand by network schedule-makers—get richer, the poor go deeper into debt. Disparities have widened to the point where many underfunded programs trying to compete at the top level are perpetual losers, both on and off the field.

The winners are primarily those institutions that belong to the founding conferences in the Bowl Championship Series (BCS), namely, the Atlantic Coast Conference (ACC), the Big East, the Big Ten, the Big 12, the Pacific-10, and the Southeastern Conference (SEC). The BCS is a consortium originally designed and instituted in the early 1990s by conference commissioners to control Division I-A postseason football. The NCAA has no role in the BCS, and even presidents of BCS member institutions are marginalized: for negotiation of BCS television contracts, for example, only conference commissioners and representatives of the television network are at the table, with bowl representatives brought in for the revenue distribution discussions that

follow. A small group of conference commissioners controls distribution of all Division I-A postseason football revenues. Conference commissioners are rewarded for successfully generating postseason revenues and so have little incentive to consider other priorities. In allowing commercial interests to prevail over academic concerns and traditions, presidents have abdicated their responsibilities.

Meanwhile, equipment manufacturers inundate prominent coaches and universities with goods and money in exchange for exposure—advertisements of all kinds on campuses, stadiums, and field houses, and logos on uniforms, shoes, and every other conceivable piece of equipment.

There is a clear and sharp message in such deals: This is business; show us the money. Over the last decade, the amounts of money involved have grown tremendously. The University of Michigan's latest contract with Nike, for example, doubled its cash payments from the shoe and apparel company to $1.2 million a year. With royalties, uniforms, and equipment added to that, the seven-year deal is expected to be worth $25 million to $28 million.

The sellout has made at least one longtime manufacturer's representative openly disdainful. He told the presidents on the Commission that they and their counterparts had "sold their souls" to him in the 1970s when he came bearing gifts, and it was their lack of courage to make changes in the interim that put them so deeply into the morass.

The influence of sneaker companies is now pervasive in high school sports as well, both in schools and in summer basketball leagues. These companies have become part of the college recruiting process in many instances, and contribute to the special treatment of athletes from a young age. This special treatment raises players' expectations, shields them from the consequences of their own actions, and teaches them that the rules applied to everyone else don't necessarily apply to them. It exploits athletes as they are eased through high school and college, finishing their years in school with no semblance of the education needed to negotiate life when their playing days are over.

High school sports today can reflect the worst of their collegiate counterparts. In addition to commercial influences, recruitment and transfer of high school players is far too common, leading to disjointed academic experiences and absurdly dominant teams in some communities. Academic compromises are made for high school athletes as well, leaving them with a diploma but ill prepared for college-level work. And throughout high school sports, as throughout colleges and universities, the young athletes' ultimate goal has increasingly become a successful career at the professional level, with all the single-minded focus that requires.

College sports as an enterprise with vested commercial interests contradicts the NCAA's stated purpose: to maintain intercollegiate athletics "as an integral part of the educational program, and the athlete as an integral part of the student body, [and to] retain a clear line of demarcation between intercollegiate athletics and professional sports." The more that line is crossed, the more likely government intervention in the form of IRS challenges to the institutions' tax-exempt status becomes. . . .

The NCAA Manual also says that postseason play is meant to be controlled to "prevent unjustified intrusions on the time student-athletes devote to their academic programs, and to protect [them] from exploitation by professional and commercial enterprises." Yet the number of postseason bowl games has grown from 18 to 25 over the past 10 years, and the men's Division I basketball tournament is three weeks long. Seasons now extend from August until January for football, and from October to April—nearly six months—for basketball.

Sports as big business is suitable for the marketplace and has proved to be a profitable way to tap into the national psyche. Sports as big business for colleges and universities, however, is in direct conflict with nearly every value that should matter for higher education. In the year 2001, the big business of big-time sports all but swamps those values, making a mockery of those professing to uphold them.

A CALL TO ACTION

. . . .

The Commission has pursued this work over the years because it believes the nation's best purposes are served when colleges and universities are strong centers of creative, constant renewal, true to their basic academic purposes. In the opening years of the new century, however, those basic purposes are threatened by the imbalance between athletic imperatives and the academy's values. To say it again, the cultural sea change is now complete. Big-time college football and basketball have been thoroughly professionalized and commercialized.

Nevertheless, the Commission believes that the academic enterprise can still redeem itself and its athletic adjunct. It is still possible that all college sports can be reintegrated into the moral and institutional culture of the university. Indeed, in sports other than football and basketball, for the most part that culture still prevails. Athletes can be (and are) honestly recruited. They can be (and are) true "student-athletes," provided with the educational opportunities for which the university exists. The joys of sport can still be honorably celebrated.

But the pressures that have corrupted too many major athletic programs are moving with inexorable force. If current trends continue, more and more campus programs will increasingly mirror the world of professional, market-driven athletics. What that could look like across the board is now present in high-profile form: weakened academic and amateurism standards, millionaire coaches and rampant commercialism, all combined increasingly with deplorable sportsmanship and misconduct.

Even if the larger picture is not yet fully that bleak, the trend is going in entirely the wrong direction. As it accelerates, so too does the danger that the NCAA might divide—with the major programs forming a new association to do business in very much the same way as the professional sports entertainment industry.

Perhaps 40 to 60 universities (mostly those with large public subsidies) could and might indefinitely operate such frankly commercial athletic programs. Critics might say good riddance. But the academic and moral consequences implicit in such an enterprise are unacceptable to anyone who cares about higher education in this nation.

Such a division must not be allowed to happen. It is time to make a larger truth evident to those who want bigger programs, more games, more exposure, and more dollars. It is this: Most Americans believe the nation's colleges and universities are about teaching, learning, and research, not about winning and losing. Most pay only passing attention to athletic success or failure. And many big donors pay no attention at all to sports, recognizing in Bart Giamatti's words that it is a "sideshow."

Part of this larger truth requires understanding something that sports-crazed fans are inclined to ignore or denigrate: Loss of academic integrity in the arenas and stadiums of the nation's colleges and universities is far more destructive to their reputations than a dozen losing seasons could ever be.

Time has demonstrated that the NCAA, even under presidential control, cannot independently do what needs to be done. Its dual mission of keeping sports clean while generating millions of dollars in broadcasting revenue for member institutions creates a near-irreconcilable conflict. Beyond that, as President Cedric Dempsey has said, the NCAA has "regulated itself into paralysis."

The Need to Act Together

The plain truth is that one clear and convincing message needs to be sent to every member of the academic community: What is needed today is not more rules from above, but instead a concerted grassroots effort by the broader academic community—in concert with trustees, administrators, and faculty—to restore the balance of athletics and academics on campus.

But a grassroots effort cannot be expected to flourish campus by campus. As long as there is an athletics arms race, unilateral disarmament on the part of one institution would most assuredly be punished swiftly by loss of position and increased vulnerability. Change will come, sanity will be restored, only when the higher education community comes together to meet collectively the challenges its members face.

Presidents and trustees must work in harness—not wage the battles so commonplace today over control of the athletic enterprise. Presidents cannot act on an issue as emotional and highly visible as athletics without the unwavering public support of their boards. As John Walda, president of the Indiana University board of trustees, told the Commission in early 2001:

> *"Trustees must insist that their presidents not only be dedicated to recapturing control of college sports, but that they stand up to the media, the entertainment industry, coaches, and athletics directors when the institution's values are threatened. And when a president takes bold action . . . trustees must support and defend their president and his or her decision."*

National higher education associations such as the American Council on Education (ACE) and the Association of Governing Boards of Universities and Colleges (AGB), in particular, can and should do more to help resolve the persistent problems addressed in this report. Intercollegiate athletics should loom larger in their programming priorities. New and creative programs and services should be offered directly to institutions and their governing boards through joint collaboration among these associations.

Conferences and the NCAA must work together as well. Tensions between conference commissioners and the NCAA must be resolved so that the best interests of intercollegiate athletics and higher education prevail. Power struggles for control of big-time football, revenue distribution, and other matters reflect a culture dominated by competitive rather than academic concerns, and one that often ignores the welfare of the athletes representing their institutions.

Faculty, too, have a critical role to play. Above all, they must defend the academic values of their institutions. Too few faculty speak out on their campus or fight aggressively against meaningless courses or degrees specifically designed to keep athletes eligible, suggesting they have surrendered their role as defenders of academic integrity in the classroom. Further, the academy has capitulated on its responsibility and allowed commercial interests—television, shoe companies, corporate sponsors of all sorts—to dictate the terms under which college sports operate. No academic institution would allow television to arrange its class schedule; neither should television control college athletic schedules. There are scattered signs of faculty awakening, but on many campuses, faculty indifference prevails even when informed critics make their case.

Athletics directors and coaches bear a huge responsibility. Directors of athletics steer the enterprise for their institutions and, in that regard, are in the best position to monitor its direction and raise flags and questions when it heads off course. Coaches are closest to the athletes and have the most influence on the quality of their collegiate experiences. Clearly, pressures on athletics directors and coaches to generate revenues and win at all costs must be mitigated. In turn, athletics directors must see to it that athletics programs are conducted as legitimate and respected components of their institutions. And coaches, quite simply,

need to be held more accountable for what goes on around them. They set the tone. "When the cheating starts," the legendary Bear Bryant used to say, "look to the head coach. He's the chairman of the board."

Alumni pressure to escalate athletics programs and produce winning teams distorts and ultimately compromises the values of the institutions they claim to cherish. Alumni must offer strong and visible support to the president and trustees of their alma mater as they work to balance athletics and academics on their campuses. Alumni, better than anyone, should realize that the reputation of their institution depends not on its won–lost record but on its reputation for integrity in all that it undertakes.

A Coalition of Presidents

The Commission understands that collective action is key to overcoming the dynamic of the athletics arms race. No single college or university can afford to act unilaterally, nor can one conference act alone. But a determined and focused group of presidents acting together can transform the world of intercollegiate athletics. Just as Archimedes was convinced he could move the world with the right fulcrum for his lever, presidents from a group of powerful conferences could, in collaboration with the NCAA, create the critical mass needed to bring about the fundamental changes this Commission deems essential.

In its earlier reports, the Commission defined a "one-plus-three" model, with the "one"—presidential control—directed toward the "three"—academic integrity, financial integrity, and certification. The Commission here proposes a new "one-plus-three" model for these new times—with the "one," a Coalition of Presidents, directed toward an agenda of academic reform, de-escalation of the athletics arms race, and de-emphasis of the commercialization of intercollegiate athletics. The Coalition of Presidents' goal must be nothing less than the restoration of athletics as a healthy and integral part of the academic enterprise.

The creation of the Coalition is the first order of business, but its creation will be no panacea in and of itself. Given the enormous scope of this reform effort, the Commission recognizes that change will have to be accomplished in a series of steps over time. As in its earlier reports, the Commission feels no obligation to rewrite the NCAA Manual or propose solutions to every problem on campus. Starting from the broad principle that athletic departments and athletes should be held to the same standards, rules, policies, and practices that apply elsewhere in their institutions, the Commission makes the following recommendations for the Coalition's agenda:

Academics

Our key point is that students who participate in athletics deserve the same rights and responsibilities as all other students. Within that broad framework, the Coalition should focus on the following recommendations:

- Athletes should be mainstreamed through the same academic processes as other students. These specifically include criteria for admission, academic support services, choice of major, and requirements governing satisfactory progress toward a degree.

- Graduation rates must improve. By 2007, teams that do not graduate at least 50 percent of their players should not be eligible for conference championships or for postseason play.

- Scholarships should be tied to specific athletes until they (or their entering class) graduate.

- The length of playing, practice, and postseasons must be reduced both to afford athletes a realistic opportunity to complete their degrees and to enhance the quality of their collegiate experiences.

- The NBA and the NFL should be encouraged to develop minor leagues so that athletes not interested in undergraduate study are provided an alternative route to professional careers.

These recommendations are not new. What is novel is the Commission's insistence that a new and independent structure is needed to pursue these proposals aggressively.

The Arms Race
The central point with regard to expenditures is the need to insist that athletic departments' budgets be subject to the same institutional oversight and direct control as other university departments. The Coalition should work to:

- Reduce expenditures in big-time sports such as football and basketball. This includes a reduction in the total number of scholarships that may be awarded in Division I-A football.

- Ensure that the legitimate and long-overdue need to support women's athletic programs and comply with Title IX is not used as an excuse for soaring costs while expenses in big-time sports are unchecked.

- Consider coaches' compensation in the context of the academic institutions that employ them. Coaches' jobs should be primarily to educate young people. Their compensation should be brought into line with prevailing norms across the institution.

- Require that agreements for coaches' outside income be negotiated with institutions, not individual coaches. Outside income should be apportioned in the context of an overriding reality: Advertisers are buying the institution's reputation no less than the coaches'.

- Revise the plan for distribution of revenue from the NCAA contract with CBS for broadcasting rights to the

Division I men's basketball championship. No such revenue should be distributed based on commercial values such as winning and losing. Instead, the revenue distribution plan should reflect values centered on improving academic performance, enhancing athletes' collegiate experiences, and achieving gender equity.

Again, the recommendations put forth here have been heard before. The Coalition offers a chance to make progress on them at long last.

Commercialization
The fundamental issue is easy to state: Colleges and universities must take control of athletics programs back from television and other corporate interests. In this regard, the Coalition should:

- Insist that institutions alone should determine when games are played, how they are broadcast, and which companies are permitted to use their athletics contests as advertising vehicles.

- Encourage institutions to reconsider all sports-related commercial contracts against the backdrop of traditional academic values.

- Work to minimize commercial intrusions in arenas and stadiums so as to maintain institutional control of campus identity.

- Prohibit athletes from being exploited as advertising vehicles. Uniforms and other apparel should not bear corporate trademarks or the logos of manufacturers or game sponsors. Other athletic equipment should bear only the manufacturer's normal label or trademark.

- Support federal legislation to ban legal gambling on college sports in the state of Nevada and encourage college presidents to address illegal gambling on their campuses.

The Commission is not naïve. It understands that its recommendations governing expenditures and commercialization may well be difficult to accept, even among academics and members of the public deeply disturbed by reports of academic misconduct in athletics programs. The reality is that many severe critics of intercollegiate athletics accept at face value the arguments about the financial exigencies of college sports. In the face of these arguments, they conclude that little can be done to rein in the arms race or to curb the rampant excesses of the market.

Nothing could be further from the truth. The athletics arms race continues only on the strength of the widespread belief that nothing can be done about it. Expenditures roar out of control only because administrators have become more concerned with financing what is in place than rethinking what they are doing. And the market is able to invade the academy both because it is eager to do so and because overloaded administrators rarely take the time to think about the consequences. The Coalition of Presidents can rethink the operational dynamics of intercollegiate athletics, prescribe what needs to be done, and help define the consequences of continuing business as usual.

Membership and Financing

The Commission recommends that the president of the American Council on Education (ACE), working with the NCAA and the Association of Governing Boards of Universities and Colleges (AGB), bring together presidential and trustee leadership drawn from ACE, the NCAA, AGB, and Division I-A conferences to establish the Coalition of Presidents. We emphasize the importance of the commitment and active involvement of presidents; Coalition members must be drawn from their group. This is an extraordinary undertaking that cannot be delegated to conference commissioners or the executive staffs of the organizations represented. As we said in our initial report 10 years ago, "The Commission's bedrock conviction is that university presidents are the key to successful reform."

The presidents who must step forward should represent the conferences conducting the most visible and successful athletics programs—in terms of national championships and revenues produced. These are the conferences representing the lion's share of big-time programs. They include: the Atlantic Coast Conference (ACC), the Big East, the Big Ten, the Big 12, the Pacific-10, and the Southeastern Conference (SEC). But membership must not be restricted to presidents from those conferences alone. Institutional compromises in favor of athletics are not limited to the biggest sports schools. Coalition membership, therefore, should be strengthened by presidents from conferences that are not founding members of the BCS but that also compete at the Division I-A level.

The Coalition of Presidents should work collaboratively with the NCAA Division I Board of Directors, meeting jointly from time to time to identify priorities for review and discussion, focus on reform solutions, and develop a comprehensive timeline for appropriate action by the Division I board and by the officers of other higher education associations.

To protect the Coalition's objectivity and the credibility of its recommendations, it is absolutely critical in the Commission's view that it be financially independent of the athletics enterprises it is designed to influence, namely, the NCAA and the conference offices. The Commission believes the Coalition should be financed independently with assessments and dues from its member institutions, support from the higher education associations, and perhaps grants from the philanthropic community.

To complement and support the critical work that must be done, we recommend that the Knight Foundation consider helping fund the Coalition of Presidents with matching grants based on performance to the American Council on Education, and establishing, perhaps with other foundations and the Association of Governing Boards, a separate and independent body—an Institute for Intercollegiate Athletics. The Commission envisions the Institute not as an action agency but as a watchdog to maintain pressure for change. It should keep the problems of college sports visible, provide moral leadership in defense of educational integrity, monitor progress toward reform goals, and issue periodic report cards.

A Final Word

This Commission concludes its work with an admission and an exhortation. The admission first: Most of us who serve on the Knight Commission have held leadership positions while the excesses we deplore here have distorted American higher education. We offer our indictment of the existing situation painfully aware that it calls us, no less than others, to account.

The exhortation involves a strong reaffirmation of the role and purpose of higher education in enhancing the well-being of our nation. That role is best filled and these purposes best achieved when integrity, character, and honor are the hallmarks of academic activities across the board—on the playing field as much as in the classroom and laboratory.

There are no downsides to thoroughgoing reform. When and if accomplished, athletic contests would still be attended by their fans and covered by the media even if the players were students first and athletes second. None of the measures proposed here will diminish competitiveness. The games will continue and be just as exciting—perhaps more so if played without television timeouts interrupting and changing the very nature of the game. Although there might be some grumbling in the short term, the enthusiasm of students and alumni will not be abated over the long haul, largely because most will not notice the difference.

But if there is no downside to deep and sustained reform, continued inattention to the problems described here is fraught with potential dangers. Failure to engage in self-corrective action may leave higher education vulnerable to external interventions, especially legislative. In some areas that would be welcome, as in steps to control the influence of gambling. In others, it would be unwelcome, as in a possible attack on college sports' tax-exempt status.

Worse, some predict that failure to reform from within will lead to the collapse of the current intercollegiate athletics system. Early warning signs of just that are abundant and should not be ignored. If it proves impossible to create a system of intercollegiate athletics that can live honorably within the American college and university, then responsible citizens must join with academic and public leaders to insist that the nation's colleges and universities get out of the business of big-time sports.

The Knight Foundation Commission on Intercollegiate Athletics trusts that day will never arrive. The search now is for the will to act. Surely the colleges and universities of the land have within their community the concerned and courageous leaders it will take to return intercollegiate athletics to the mainstream of American higher education. If not, it is not the integrity of intercollegiate sports that will be held up to question, but the integrity of higher education itself.

[*Ed. Note: The commission's discussion in Appendix A of additional issues that were raised for its consideration for which no specific recommendations were made is omitted. These issues included freshman ineligibility, recruiting restrictions, need-based financial aid, early departures to the NBA, certification and accreditation, and antitrust exemptions.*]

. . . .

APPENDIX B: ACTION ON KNIGHT COMMISSION RECOMMENDATIONS OF MARCH 1991

Presidential Control

Trustees should explicitly endorse and reaffirm presidential authority in all matters of athletics governance, including control of financial and personnel matters. Trustees should annually review the athletics program and work with the president to define the faculty's role in athletics.

Implementation of this recommendation requires action on individual campuses. Following the release of the Commission's first report, more than 100 institutions and organizations reported adoption of these principles. Additionally, the Association of Governing Boards of Universities and Colleges (AGB) has worked to educate trustees about their appropriate role in intercollegiate athletics through articles and white papers in its periodicals and publications, and via speakers and meetings focused on this topic.

Presidents should act on their obligation to control conferences.

Based on testimony before the Commission during 2000–2001, presidents do not in practice control at least a handful of Division I-A conferences. At the national level, the 1992 NCAA convention amended the NCAA Constitution to require presidential approval of conference-sponsored legislative initiatives.

Presidents should control the NCAA.

In 1997 the NCAA restructured, giving presidents full authority for the governance of intercollegiate athletics at the national level. The Association's top body, the Executive Committee, is comprised entirely of CEOs, and the NCAA's three divisions are led by presidential groups.

Presidents should commit their institutions to equity in all aspects of intercollegiate athletics.

Opportunities for women to compete for NCAA member institutions in NCAA championship sports increased 57 percent between 1991 and 2000. Despite this tremendous progress, during the 1998–1999 academic year (the most recent year for which data are available), 41 percent of these varsity athletes were women even though women comprise 52 percent of the undergraduates at NCAA member institutions.

Women at the Division I level in 1999–2000 — where they represent 53 percent of the student body—received 43 percent of athletic scholarship dollars and 32 percent of overall athletics budgets. Overall, 48 percent of all participants in NCAA-sponsored championships in 2000–2001 were women and 52 percent were men.

Presidents should control their institutions' involvement with commercial television.

Presidents have been actively involved with contract negotiations with CBS, which broadcasts the Division I men's basketball tournament, and with ESPN. Their involvement, however, has not led to institutional control over the commercial aspects of televised sports. Further, testimony before the Commission during 2000–2001 indicated that presidents are not actively involved in negotiations for televising the Bowl Championship Series (BCS) postseason football bowl games.

Academic Integrity

The NCAA should strengthen initial eligibility requirements:

The number of required units of high school academic work for initial eligibility should be raised from 11 to 15.

The 1992 NCAA convention raised the Divisions I and II core curriculum requirements from 11 to 13 units, effective in 1995.

High school students should be ineligible for reimbursed campus visits (or signing a letter of intent) until they show reasonable promise of being able to meet degree requirements.

Between 1991 and 1997 the NCAA adopted seven proposals related to proof of a prospect's academic credentials required before an official (expense paid) visit. Criteria included minimum required test scores and core academic courses completed. In 1997, however, in response to concerns expressed by the U.S. Department of Justice, the NCAA eliminated specific academic criteria and instead requires only that the prospect submit a test score and academic transcript prior to an official visit.

Junior college transfers who did not meet NCAA initial eligibility requirements upon graduation from high school should sit out a year of competition after transfer.

This recommendation has not been adopted by the NCAA. In 1996, however, the NCAA adopted higher minimum percentage of degree requirements for all junior college transfers in Division I football and men's basketball. These athletes must have completed 35 percent—versus 25 percent—of their degree requirements to be immediately eligible in their third year of collegiate enrollment (see below).

The NCAA should study the feasibility of requiring that the range of academic abilities of incoming athletes approximates the range of abilities of the entire freshmen class.

In its first five-year cycle, the NCAA certification program gathered data related to this recommendation by requiring that institutions compare the academic profiles of all incoming athletes with the rest of the incoming class as a whole. The next certification cycle improves upon this assessment by requiring that comparisons be made on a sport-by-sport basis, as well as by gender and racial subgroups. Significant differences in academic profiles must be noted and explained.

The letter of intent should serve the student as well as the athletics department.

Since 1991, no changes have been made in the national letter of intent program. However, athletes are permitted to appeal the terms and conditions of the letter of intent. Approximately 20,000 such documents are signed each year by prospects planning to attend NCAA Division I and II institutions. During the 1999–2000 academic year—a typical year—170 letters of intent were appealed: 86 percent of the appeals were approved, 12 percent of the athletes were granted a partial release, and 2 percent of the appeals were denied. These data indicate flexibility in the administration of the national letter of intent program.

Athletics scholarships should be offered for a five-year period.

No action to date.

Athletics eligibility should depend upon progress toward a degree.

The 1992 NCAA convention adopted new Division I requirements stipulating minimum percentages of credits earned toward a specific degree, as well as a minimum grade point average toward that degree, for athletes' third and fourth years of eligibility, effective in 1996. Further, the permissible number of credits earned during the summer to maintain eligibility was capped, and the new satisfactory progress toward degree requirements was made applicable to midyear transfer students after a semester rather than a year on campus.

Graduation rates of athletes should be a criterion for NCAA certification.

NCAA certification incorporates graduation rates as a criterion. In the program's first five-year cycle, however, graduation rates of all athletes were compared with the student body as a whole. The next certification cycle improves upon this assessment by requiring that comparisons be made on a sport-by-sport basis, as well as by gender and racial subgroups. Significant differences in graduation rates must be noted and explained.

Financial Integrity

All funds raised and spent in connection with intercollegiate athletics programs will be channeled through the institution's general treasury. The athletics department budget will be developed and monitored in accordance with general budgeting procedures on campus.

Implementation of this recommendation requires action on individual campuses. Data concerning its adoption are unavailable. The NCAA certification program, however, addresses these issues specifically in the first operating principle under the Financial Integrity section of the program's self-study document, which each Division I institution must address in detail.

Athletics costs must be reduced.

Some efforts to reduce costs have been made, such as reducing the number of allowable scholarships in certain sports and limiting assistant coaches' salaries in men's basketball. In the latter instance, however, the salary caps were successfully challenged as a violation of antitrust law; the NCAA settlement with the coaches cost over $50 million. At the institutional level, athletics costs rose steadily during the 1990s, such that the NCAA's latest financial study reports that roughly just 15 percent of Divisions I and II institutions operate in the black. From 1997 to 1999, deficits at Division I-A institutions where expenses exceeded revenues increased 18 percent.

Athletics grants-in-aid should cover the full cost of attendance for the very needy.

No action to date, although the NCAA's Special Assistance Fund available to needy athletes has increased from $3 million in 1991 to $10 million in 1998, and is scheduled to increase to $10.4 million in 2002. Additionally, in 2002 the NCAA will institute a new $17 million Student Opportunity Fund, which can be broadly used for anything that benefits athletes but not, specifically, on salaries or facilities. Each fund is scheduled to increase annually throughout the duration of the NCAA's 11-year CBS contract.

The independence of athletics foundations and booster clubs must be curbed.

Implementation of this recommendation requires action on individual campuses. Data concerning changes in the numbers of independent athletics foundations and booster clubs are unavailable.

The NCAA formula for sharing television revenues from the Division I men's basketball tournament must be reviewed by university presidents.

The NCAA Executive Committee and the Division I Board of Directors, both composed entirely of presidents, have been actively involved in review of the formula for distribution of revenues from the new $6.2 billion CBS contract. The formula was approved in early 2001 by the NCAA Executive Committee.

All athletics-related coaches' income should be reviewed and approved by the university.

The 1992 NCAA convention adopted legislation requiring annual, prior written approval from the president for all athletically related income from sources outside the institution. That legislation, however, was eliminated in 2000 as part of an NCAA deregulation effort.

Coaches should be offered long-term contracts.

Implementation of this recommendation requires action on individual campuses. While it appears that more long-term contracts are being offered to big-time football and men's basketball coaches, the pressure to win has not diminished.

Institutional support should be available for intercollegiate athletics.

Progress in this regard has been minimal. The NCAA Division I Philosophy Statement, for example, still contains language recommending that its members strive "to finance [their] athletics programs insofar as possible from revenues generated by the program itself." Moreover, several states have laws prohibiting the use of state funds on intercollegiate athletics programs. In Division I-A, institutional support, direct government funding, and student activity fees have increased as a percentage of total revenues from 14 percent in 1993 to 16 percent in 1997.

Certification

The NCAA should adopt a certification program for all institutions granting athletics aid that would independently authenticate the integrity of each institution's athletics program.

Division I institutions must undergo NCAA certification of their athletics departments. When the program was first adopted, institutions were meant to be certified once every five years; since then, the cycle has been extended to once every 10 years. Division II institutions, which also award athletics aid, have not adopted the certification program.

Universities should undertake comprehensive, annual policy audits of their athletics programs.

The Division I certification program requires an annual compilation of athletics policy audits and other data.

The certification program should include the major themes advanced by the Knight Commission, i.e., the "one-plus-three" model.

The NCAA certification program substantially incorporates the fundamental principles of the "one-plus-three" model. The four major components of athletics certification are: governance and commitment to rules compliance; academic integrity; fiscal integrity; and equity, welfare, and sportsmanship.

QUANTITATIVE AND QUALITATIVE RESEARCH WITH FOOTBALL BOWL SUBDIVISION UNIVERSITY PRESIDENTS ON THE COSTS AND FINANCING OF INTERCOLLEGIATE ATHLETICS: REPORT OF FINDINGS AND IMPLICATIONS, OCTOBER 2009

Knight Commission on Intercollegiate Athletics

. . . .

III.   EXECUTIVE SUMMARY

The following provides a summary of key findings from the quantitative and qualitative research.

A.   The Dilemma of Reform

It is clear from the quantitative and qualitative research that presidents recognize the need for reform; few, however, are sanguine about the possibilities for positive change. What was striking in many of our findings was the lack of any clear idea of the best way to effect change or the most appropriate entity to move reform efforts forward.

While the quantitative research revealed strong presidential support for studies of policy changes regarding a number of concerns, such as the number of coaches and athletic contests, the qualitative research revealed a sense of powerlessness to effect the kind of change that is needed at the conference and national levels to contain the athletics arms race and address critical issues regarding sustainability, such as rapidly escalating coaches' salaries. The quantitative research also shows that a high percentage of presidents who believe that sustainability is problematic for their own institution or for their conference or the FBS as a whole believe that sweeping change is necessary across the FBS.

In sum, presidents would like serious change but don't see themselves as the force for the changes needed, nor have they identified an alternative force they believe could be effective.

While serious problems are recognized, beyond limited actions they can take on their own campuses, presidents are at a loss to describe solutions that will address the broader FBS problems. The following are chief among their concerns:

- Presidents believe they have limited power to effect change on their own campuses regarding athletics financing and the larger problems it has created, much less for the FBS as a whole. Indeed, nearly three-quarters interviewed in the quantitative research believe that athletics presents unique challenges as compared to schools, divisions, or other parts of the university when trying to control costs.

- While antitrust exemption and other political solutions have some appeal, these are seen as political impossibilities by many FBS presidents.

- Outside sources of income for intercollegiate athletics, such as extremely lucrative television contracts, have diminished presidents' authority over athletics and their ability to influence reform.

- While there is some satisfaction with the steps taken by their conferences, there is also serious doubt that the conferences will make decisions or take actions that are against the self-interest of the most successful conference institutions.

A majority of presidents interviewed in the quantitative research favor studying the following policy initiatives to explore how these might help control costs and make FBS athletics more sustainable:

- Reduce the number of coaches and sports-specific personnel for revenue-producing sports (supported by roughly two-thirds of presidents).

- Reduce the number of contests for non-revenue producing sports (supported by roughly two-thirds of presidents).

- Reduce the level of financial commitment required for FBS membership (supported by over three-quarters of presidents).

- Change BCS and NCAA revenue distribution policies (supported by nearly two-thirds of presidents).

B.   Sustainability

Based on findings from the quantitative and qualitative research, it is clear that the question for a majority of presidents of equity and non-equity institutions alike is not whether or not the current model is sustainable but, given the forces at work, *how long it can be sustained.*

In terms of their own institutions, two-thirds of FBS presidents expressed confidence that, considering current trends in athletics revenues and expenses, athletics operations are sustainable in their current form. However, this confidence was not extended to other institutions in their conferences or to the FBS as a whole. And even in the context of their own programs, nearly half of all respondents (48%) expressed concern that the current outlook will affect the number of varsity sports their institution can retain in the future.

In the qualitative research respondents voiced broad concerns regarding the sustainability of all athletics programs in the face of what a number of presidents described in the qualitative interviews as an "arms race" that is driving up costs for athletics programs and creating tensions that cannot be clearly measured in other areas. These concerns were shared by a majority of those presidents interviewed regardless of their athletics programs' financial outlook.

Issues identified by presidents as key factors in the accelerating costs of competing at the FBS level include the following:

- Increases in coaches' salaries and privileges as well as the increasing costs of the expanding number of sports-specific personnel.

- Commercialization, including TV contracts and other corporate interests which have injected substantial revenue into intercollegiate athletics.

- Costs of building more and better appointed facilities.

Presidents also identified a number of challenges associated with the increasing costs of FBS participation, chief among them,

- Difficulties in balancing the athletic budget and keeping costs under control. This pressure is increasingly felt by non-equity presidents, two-thirds of whom reported a concern about the proportion of institutional resources used to fund athletics on their campus.

- Insidious and growing cultural divide between academics and athletics in which athletics is in an increasingly privileged position. This has created mounting tensions and concerns about conflicts with institutional mission and values.

- Growing imbalance between the "haves and have-nots" both within equity conferences and between equity and non-equity institutions. Presidents of less competitive institutions feel that their programs are being unfairly exploited.

- Concern that competitive and financial pressures created by the "arms race" are having an increasingly negative impact on student athletes.

- Challenges for some programs to continue to be competitive or even to maintain their Division I status.

C.   Implications of Increases in Coaches' Salaries and Sports-Specific Personnel

When asked about salaries across FBS institutions nationally, an overwhelming majority of FBS presidents (85%) indicated that they felt compensation was excessive in the context of higher education for football and basketball coaches.

The qualitative research suggests that presidents see the issue of coaches' salaries as a key contributor to the "arms race" in intercollegiate athletics. *Coaches' salaries are seen as the greatest impediment to sustainability.* In addition to placing strains on the institutional finances, increases in coaches' salaries and, to a lesser extent, increases in the numbers of other sports-specific personnel required for the athletic enterprise in the FBS were seen to create a public-relations challenge with regard to other internal and external university constituencies.

Presidents are pessimistic about their ability to control these costs. A majority (56%) feels that as the use of private monies to compensate coaches has increased, their control over these salaries has decreased. A majority of presidents do not support attempts to change federal legislation to allow some level of control on coaching staff salaries. This seems to be tied to presidents' skepticism about the political possibility of intercollegiate athletics being granted an exemption from anti-trust legislation.

D. Budget Pressures Produced by Increasing Costs of Operating Successful Athletic Programs

Quantitative and qualitative results suggest that the increasing costs of operating successful athletic programs, especially in the current economic climate, present serious challenges to FBS presidents. For presidents of non-equity institutions, which operate with far less athletics revenue, these challenges are especially daunting.

Most presidents reported making athletics budget cuts in the most recently completed fiscal year, and a significant number anticipate continuing declines in revenues through next year. A majority of presidents (62%) believe the recession has affected athletics budgets at the same level as other units of their university. Key factors associated with the recession's impact on FBS campuses include the following:

- The recession affected both public and private funding sources.

- Most universities athletics budgets reductions equated roughly proportionally to cuts being made in other units of the institution.

- Presidents have largely delegated responsibility for determining details of budget cuts to their Athletics Director.

- Despite widespread concern over financial stresses created by the "arms race" and exacerbated by the recession, the most common sentiment expressed by presidents regarding current levels of spending was their desire to increase revenue rather than opt out of the system or push for systemic change.

E. Cross-Institutional Benefits of Successful Athletics Programs

Despite the concerns expressed by presidents regarding the pressures placed on their institution through its participation in the FBS, competing at this level is seen to carry considerable financial as well as less tangible benefits. Although a number of presidents are aware of scholarly research questioning the relationship between big-time athletics and non-athletic benefits, personal experience plays a much more powerful role in defining presidents' attitudes toward athletics than do the results of these studies.

A significant majority of FBS presidents believe that athletics success provides substantial benefits to their institutions. These include tangible benefits such as increasing applications, quality of the student body, and donations to the university.

Presidents also see indirect benefits stemming from athletics success, including enhancing school spirit and raising the profile of the institution with regard to the general public, public officials, and other university presidents. Some of these latter benefits are seen to provide leverage for more concrete benefits such as helping to generate higher levels of giving and helping to attract more and better qualified students.

Presidents do not view fundraising for athletics and academics as a zero-sum game, in which financial gains for athletics programs are made at the expense of the academic side of the house. Despite research suggesting that athletics are taking a larger share of donations, some 80 percent of presidents expressed the belief that athletic fundraising *does not* take from the same pool of money that would otherwise go to general university fundraising.

F. Transparency

With regard to the financial information currently available, a majority of presidents (95%) agree that they are confident in the accuracy of the financial information they receive from their athletics departments, with a vast majority of these (82%) being *very* confident. Presidents expressed lower levels of confidence regarding the financial information reported by their peer institution (61% were "somewhat" confident this information was accurate).

Their confidence in data currently available notwithstanding, *nearly 8 in 10 presidents agree that greater transparency of athletics operating and capital costs is needed.*

Many presidents, particularly those at public universities already required to comply with state standards regarding financial data, are convinced that their programs currently practice transparency, although some acknowledged that not all information is readily available. Furthermore, there is a lack of consensus regarding what constitutes transparency and a recognition that it is possible to game the system regarding the nature and appearance of financial data. That said, generally, presidents agree that standards should be set regarding reporting of individual institutional data so that measures are consistent.

Nearly 9 out of 10 FBS presidents have reviewed the NCAA financial dashboard indicators for their institutions. The NCAA is viewed as a key player in providing even greater transparency, particularly in a way that provides a reliable basis for cross-institutional and conference comparisons that would be available to the media and general public.

Discussion Questions

1. Which constituency is the most likely to be able to effectuate a change in intercollegiate athletics? Which is the least likely to effectuate change?

2. What is the likelihood that the reform measures suggested by the Knight Commission will be adopted by the NCAA?

3. Why do people cling to antiquated (and mythological) notions of amateurism when discussing intercollegiate athletics?

4. What, if any, reforms would you make to intercollegiate athletics? How could you make these reforms economically feasible?

5. What would be the impact if athletes in revenue-generating sports were paid a stipend?

6. What problems would arise if only athletes in men's basketball and football were paid?

7. Are there any potential racial repercussions to not fully contemplating pay for student-athletes?

8. Should the revenues of profitable sports be used to support those that are not profitable?

9. What justifications exist for the continuation of the existing amateurism model in collegiate sports?

10. Discuss the "athletic arms race" that universities are facing, including the aggravating factors and any suggestions that you feel would properly address the situation.

11. What factors have led to the commercialization of college sports? What are the implications of this commercialization?

12. What would be the impact of NCAA regulations targeting coaching and sport personnel?

Part IV

Sociological Considerations

Race

INTRODUCTION

Sports business leaders, who face greater public exposure and scrutiny than executives in other industries, have long been confronted with pressure to ensure that their industry is diverse. The diversity emphasis has been focused primarily on race and gender. In recent years, a global diversity element has come into play as well. In general, sports has attained a leadership position for its on-field diversity, but has long lagged in diversity in the front office and ownership.

Well before Jackie Robinson integrated Major League Baseball in 1947, municipalities, led by New York City, often raised racial discrimination issues. The National Association for the Advancement of Colored People made a number of pronouncements as well. Questions of policy were raised, including why publicly financed facilities should be used by enterprises that discriminate.

Even as far back as the search to find a "Great White Hope" to battle the first black heavyweight champion, Jack Johnson, race has been an ever-present part of the business of sports. Early in the last century, the race of the boxers in a bout was used to sell tickets and inspire interest. The race-baiting formula has been used over and over again, including, notably, the Larry Holmes–Gerry Cooney heavyweight championship bout decades later. Race sells in the marketing of a sporting contest.

In the United States, the elimination of racial discrimination in sports largely occurred for practical reasons, not from any dramatic evolution of society's hearts and minds. In post–World War II baseball, part of the motivation to recruit ballplayers from the Negro Leagues was simply to fill the need for more talent. Eventually it became the desire to expand the talent pool, as owners came to realize that much of the best talent was black. Ironically, this led to the demise of the Negro Leagues. That realization of the value of black talent ultimately occurred in other leagues as well.

Table 1 shows the racial composition of players among leagues and in intercollegiate athletics in recent years.

The issue of racial diversity has evolved from players to management and ownership. In recent years, the NFL has shown dramatic success in the hiring of African American head coaches. This success has largely been attributed to the so-called "Rooney Rule." This league-imposed rule requires that whenever a position for a head coach occurs at least one minority candidate must be interviewed for the job. Since the implementation of the rule in 2002, the number of African American head coaches has grown from a low of two to a high of seven. In 2009, the rule was expanded to apply to general manager positions as well.

When the ownership barrier in major league sports was knocked down by Bob Johnson in the NBA and Arte Moreno in Major League Baseball, it was done with little ceremony. Once those barriers were broken it became clear that, for the most part, the only color barrier to ownership in the new millennium was green—economics. That barrier is obviously not one that exclusively impacts sports.

Diversity has become a global issue as well. Soccer has formed a number of organizations, including Football Against Racism in Europe (FARE), to battle racism, which permeates many of its venues, particularly on game days. Similar to American sports, coaches and managers of color have been underrepresented in soccer as well.

Non-race-related diversity issues have evolved over time as well. The 1973 Billie Jean King–Bobby Riggs "Battle of the Sexes" tennis match held in the then-novel Houston Astrodome is symbolic of some of the barriers that have been overcome in these other areas. That spectacle revealed to many that the potential of women's sports could extend beyond the moral obligation to promote gender equality to the realization of profit. This certainly led to a number of women's sports leagues. Many of these are discussed in Chapter 4, "Emerging and Niche Leagues." Other important

Table 1 Racial Composition of Players in Major Sports Leagues

	NBA	NFL	MLB	NHL	MLS
2008–2009					
White	18%	31%	—	—	—
African American	77%	67%	—	—	—
Latino	3%	1%	—	—	—
Asian	1%	2%	—	—	—
Other	1%	< 1%	—	—	—
International	18%	2%	—	—	—
2007–2008					
White	20%	31%	60.4%	—	62%
African American	76%	66%	10.2%	—	20%
Latino	3%	1%	27.0%	—	16%
Asian	< 1%	2%	2.4%	—	1%
Other	1%	< 1%	0.0%	—	1%
International	18%	2%	28.7%	—	32%
2006–2007					
White	21%	31%	59.8%	—	59%
African American	75%	67%	8.2%	—	22%
Latino	3%	0.5%	29.1%	—	14%
Asian	< 1%	1.5%	2.8%	—	1%
Other	1%	0%	0.0%	—	3%
International	19%	1%	31.0%	—	31%
2005–2006					
White	22%	31.5%	59.5%	—	61%
African American	73%	65.5%	8.4%	—	17%
Latino	3%	< 1%	29.4%	—	15%
Asian	< 1%	2%	2.4%	—	3%
Other	1%	< 1%	0.3%	—	3%
International	19%	1%	31.0%	—	21%
2004–2005					
White	23%	—	60%	—	58%
African American	73%	—	9%	—	18%
Latino	2%	—	29%	—	20%
Asian	< 1%	—	3%	—	1%
Other	1%	—	0%	—	3%
International	19%	—	30%	—	28%
2003–2004					
White	22%	29%	63%	—	64%*
African American	76%	69%	9%	—	17%*
Latino	1%	1%	26%	—	14%*
Asian	< 1%	1%	2%	—	1%*
Other	0%	0%	0%	—	4%*
International	17%	—	27%	—	—
2002–2003					
White	—	—	—	—	—
African American	—	—	—	—	—
Latino	—	—	—	—	—
Asian	—	—	—	—	—
Other	—	—	—	—	—
International	—	—	—	—	—

Table 1   *(Continued)*

	NBA	NFL	MLB	NHL	MLS
2001–2002					
White	20%	33%	60%	98%	60%
African American	78%	65%	10%	1%	16%
Latino	< 2%	< 1%	28%	0%	22%
Asian	< 1%	1%	2%	< 1%	1%
Other	0%	< 1%	0%	< 1%	1%
2000–2001					
White	21%	—	59%	98%	59%
African American	78%	—	13%	2%	19%
Latino	1%	—	26%	< 1%	20%
Other	0%	—	1%	< 1%	2%
1999–2000					
White	22%	32%	60%	98%	63%
African American	78%	67%	13%	2%	15%
Latino	< 1%	< 1%	26%	0%	21%
Other	0%	< 1%	< 1%	< 1%	1%
1998–1999					
White	21%	32%	60%	98%	65%
African American	78%	66%	13%	1%	16%
Latino	1%	< 1%	26%	0%	18%
Other	0%	1%	< 1%	1%	1%
1997–1998					
White	23%	33%	59%	98%	62%
African American	77%	65%	15%	1%	16%
Latino	< 1%	< 1%	25%	0%	21%
Other	0%	1%	1%	1%	1%
1996–1997					
White	20%	31%	58%	—	—
African American	79%	66%	17%	—	—
Latino	< 1%	< 1%	24%	—	—
Other	< 1%	2%	1%	—	—
1995–1996					
White	20%	31%	62%	—	—
African American	80%	67%	17%	—	—
Latino	0%	0%	20%	—	—
Other	< 1%	< 2%	1%	—	—
1994–1995					
White	18%	31%	62%	—	—
African American	82%	68%	19%	—	—
Latino	0%	0%	19%	—	—
Other	0%	1%	0%	—	—
1993–1994					
White	21%	35%	64%	—	—
African American	79%	65%	18%	—	—
Latino	0%	0%	18%	—	—
1992–1993					
White	23%	30%	67%	—	—
African American	77%	68%	16%	—	—
Latino	0%	< 1%	16%	—	—
Other	0%	1%	< 1%	—	—

(continued)

Table 1   *(Continued)*

	NBA	NFL	MLB	NHL	MLS
1991–1992					
White	25%	36%	68%	—	—
African American	75%	62%	17%	—	—
Latino	0%	2%	14%	—	—
1990–1991					
White	28%	39%	68%	—	—
African American	72%	61%	18%	—	—
Latino	0%	0%	14%	—	—
1989–1990					
White	25%	40%	70%	—	—
African American	75%	60%	17%	—	—
Latino	0%	0%	13%	—	—

WNBA

2008	
White	24%
African American	76%
Latina	0%
Asian	0%
Other	0%
International	15%
2006	
White	36%
African American	63%
Latina	0%
Asian	0%
Other	1%
International	17%
2005	
White	34%
African American	63%
Latina	1%
Asian	0%
Other	1%
International	19%
2004	
White	33%
African American	66%
Latina	1%
Asian	0%
Other	0%
International	16%
2002	
White	35%
African American	61%
Latina	< 3%
Asian	< 1%
Other	< 1%

Table 1   *(Continued)*

WNBA	
2000	
White	34%
African American	63%
Latina	3%
Other	0%
1999	
White	33%
African American	65%
Latina	2%
Other	0%
1998	
White	32%
African American	64%
Latina	3%
Other	1%

College Student-Athletes (Male): Division I**			
	Basketball	**Football**	**Baseball**
2006–2007			
White	32.5%	46.0%	84.5%
African American	60.4%	45.9%	6.0%
Latino	1.8%	2.2%	5.4%
American Indian/Alaskan Native	0.4%	0.4%	0.4%
Asian	0.4%	1.6%	1.2%
Non-Resident Aliens	N/A	N/A	N/A
Other	4.7%	2.9%	2.5%
2005–2006			
White	29.9%	47.1%	84.6%
African American	58.9%	45.4%	5.7%
Latino	1.8%	2.1%	5.0%
American Indian/Alaskan Native	0.3%	0.9%	0.4%
Asian	0.5%	1.6%	1.1%
Non-Resident Aliens	6.2%	2.4%	1.0%
Other	2.3%	0.4%	2.5%
2004-2005			
White	31.9%	47.7%	83.7%
African American	57.8%	45.4%	6.5%
Latino	1.5%	2.3%	5.4%
American Indian/Alaskan Native	0.6%	0.3%	0.3%
Asian	0.4%	1.6%	1.2%
Non-Resident Aliens	5.4%	0.4%	1.0%
Other	2.5%	2.3%	1.9%
2003–2004			
White	31.6%	48.3%	83.8%
African American	58.2%	44.3%	6.1%
Latino	1.5%	2.4%	4.9%
American Indian/Alaskan Native	0.3%	0.4%	0.3%
Asian	0.2%	1.6%	1.2%
Non-Resident Aliens	5.7%	0.6%	1.3%
Other	2.5%	2.4%	2.1%

(continued)

Table 1 *(Continued)*

	Basketball	Football	Baseball
2002–2003			
White	32.3%	49.3%	84.1%
African American	57.9%	43.8%	6.1%
Latino	1.3%	2.2%	5.1%
American Indian/Alaskan Native	0.4%	0.4%	0.3%
Asian	0.2%	1.6%	1.2%
Non-Resident Aliens	5.3%	0.5%	1.2%
Other	2.6%	2.3%	2.0%
2001–2002			
White	32.3%	50.1%	83.4%
African American	57.7%	42.6%	6.9%
Latino	1.5%	2.1%	5.2%
American Indian/Alaskan Native	0.3%	0.4%	0.4%
Asian	0.2%	1.4%	1.1%
Non-Resident Aliens	4.8%	0.5%	1.1%
Other	3.2%	2.8%	1.9%
2000–2001			
White	32.5%	49.4%	81.3%
African American	57.1%	42.1%	6.7%
Latino	1.4%	2.1%	5.6%
American Indian/Alaskan Native	0.4%	0.4%	0.4%
Asian	0.2%	1.3%	0.9%
Non-Resident Aliens	5.1%	1.7%	2.1%
Other	3.3%	2.9%	3.0%
1998–1999			
White	34.0%	46.9%	88.1%
African American	55.9%	46.4%	2.8%
Latino	1.4%	1.9%	4.7%
American Indian/Alaskan Native	0.3%	0.4%	0.5%
Asian	0.3%	2.0%	0.8%
Non-Resident Aliens	5.5%	1.0%	1.4%
Other	2.6%	1.9%	1.7%
1996–1997			
White	33.8%	46.9%	89.5%
African American	57.3%	47.6%	3.0%
Latino	1.5%	1.9%	4.3%
American Indian/Alaskan Native	0.2%	0.3%	0.5%
Asian	0.3%	1.2%	0.6%
Non-Resident Aliens	4.4%	0.6%	0.9%
Other	2.5%	1.5%	1.2%
1991–1992			
White	34.5%	53.2%	90.0%
African American	61.8%	42.7%	4.3%
Latino	0.8%	1.4%	3.9%
American Indian/Alaskan Native	0.2%	0.3%	0.3%
Asian	0.2%	1.0%	0.7%
Non-Resident Aliens	***	***	***
Other	2.5%	1.4%	0.8%

*Received from EEO MLS self-report, April 2005.

**Data provided by the NCAA. Historically Black institutions excluded. Only student-athletes receiving financial aid are included in this report.

***Not recorded at this date.

Source: Institute for Diversity and Ethics in Sport, Racial and Gender Report Card.

issues related to women and diversity are discussed in Chapter 16, "Gender Equity."

The first selection in this chapter, Edward Rimer's "Discrimination in Major League Baseball: Hiring Standards for Major League Managers, 1975–1994," illustrates some of the history of disparate standards used in managerial hiring decisions. At the time of its publication, it delivered a clear message to managers to beware of applying disparate standards in hiring. A more recent study by Janice Madden examines the issue in the NFL, focusing on the baseball manager equivalent, the head coach. The Madden study, and updates, may be viewed at http://www.findjustice.com/UserFiles/File/Report_-_Superior_Performance_Inferior_Opportunities.pdf. That research is described further in the article by Jeremi Duru which appears in this chapter. Since the publication of that earlier research, Madden has conducted a follow-up study to determine the impact of the Rooney Rule. Her conclusion is that the statistical bias that was found earlier against the hiring of African American head coaches no longer exists. This success must, in part, be attributed to the Rooney Rule. See **Figure 1** for a snapshot of those original findings.

The readings in this chapter provide the sports business leader with a broad swipe at these issues as well as some of the approaches used to address them. Duru's article, "The Fritz Pollard Alliance, The Rooney Rule, and the Quest to 'Level the Playing Field' in the National Football League," provides insight into the Rooney Rule. The excerpt from Shropshire, "Diversity, Racism, and Professional Sports Franchise Ownership: Change Must Come from Within," focuses on ownership. The discussion in this selection highlights the limitations of the law in bringing about change. The piece was written before Bob Johnson (and now Michael Jordan) and Arte Moreno obtained their respective ownership interests. However, no other African Americans or Latinos have yet acquired a controlling ownership interest in a major North American team sport. The excerpt from Kahn, "The Sports Business as a Labor Market Laboratory," focuses on salary discrimination and contract termination issues. The selection provides an overview of the research available on the issue of differences in pay to players based on race. Race and sports is a global issue, too. The article by Ryan, "The European Union and Fan Racism in European Soccer Stadiums: The Time Has Come for Action" examines the race issue in European soccer. The lessons from all of these excerpts are applicable to broader diversity issues as well.

MANAGERS AND COACHES

DISCRIMINATION IN MAJOR LEAGUE BASEBALL: HIRING STANDARDS FOR MAJOR LEAGUE MANAGERS, 1975–1994

Edward Rimer

In 1975, the Cleveland Indians hired Frank Robinson to be their manager, the first Black to hold such a position in Major League Baseball. This occurred 28 years after Jackie Robinson had successfully integrated professional baseball. As befalls most managers, Frank Robinson was fired and, subsequently, was rehired by two other teams [*Ed. Note: now three*]. Although other Blacks have become managers and there have been several Hispanic managers, there remains a belief that minorities are not given an equal opportunity to assume administrative and managerial positions in the major leagues. [*Ed. Note: See Figure 1 for racial comparisons of coaches in the NFL.*]

The purpose of this article is twofold. First, I analyze the backgrounds of those individuals who were managers during the past 20 years (1975–1994) to ascertain what were the implicit standards, if any, that the owners used in making their hiring decisions. Second, having identified such standards, I compare the backgrounds of Black, White, and Hispanic managers to determine whether the standards were applied equally to all managers.

This study differs from previous work in that it seeks to determine what were the standards used to hire managers and whether such standards were applied equally to Blacks, Hispanics, and Whites. The focus is on the hiring actions of the teams, and on whether the qualifications were applied uniformly to all who became managers, rather than on the behaviors of individuals seeking managerial positions.

Historically, employers have used two methods to screen out and discriminate against applicants for certain positions. Applicants [first] may be asked to possess some non-job-related attributes. Courts have continually ruled that employers must demonstrate that the requirements for a job must be essential for its successful completion.

Second, these job-related requirements must be applied equally to all applicants. Personnel management law is replete with edicts that standards must be applied equally in diverse areas such as hiring, firing, compensation, and benefits. In fact, current human resource management theory posits that other functions, such as performance appraisal, also suffer when dissimilar standards are used to evaluate employees. Employers have been able to defend their personnel actions when they have been able to demonstrate that the qualifications are job related and applied equally to all applicants.

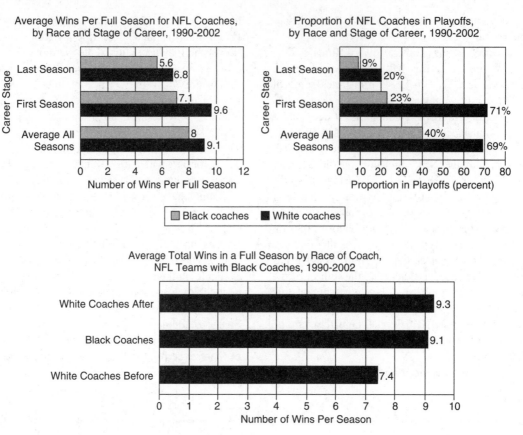

Figure 1   Black vs. White Coaching Success in NFL

Source: Journal of Sport and Social Issues. Used with permission.

. . . This study attempts to determine whether the job-related requirements were applied equally to all who became managers between 1975 and 1994. In this manner, we would have some indication as to how the courts might rule should an individual seek legal remedies against a team alleging discriminatory hiring/promotion practices.

This is accomplished by comparing the prior job-related work experiences of Whites, Blacks, and Hispanics who were managers during the past 20 years, 1975–1994. The purpose of this study is to ascertain whether White, Black, and Hispanic professional baseball players had to possess different attributes to be hired as major league managers. Further, I discuss the extent to which these different hiring standards may preclude or facilitate future success as a manager.

Managerial Skills, Knowledge, and Abilities

Managers need to possess a knowledge of baseball so that they can make strategic decisions as the game progresses. This normally involves setting the starting lineup, determining the starting pitching rotation, and determining when to pinch hit, remove the pitcher, and numerous other options (steal, hit-and-run, etc.) that may occur during a game. Whereas the average fan may have some rudimentary understanding of these aspects of the game, the manager is expected to make these decisions while being cognizant of his team's abilities as well as what the opposition will do to counter his actions. This knowledge of the game can be gained by anybody playing the game. It is not limited to those who play for specific teams or at certain positions.

Managers also serve as teachers, assisting their players in some of the finer points of the game. Aspects of hitting, fielding, and pitching are all within the purview of the manager. It is common to hear players give credit to their managers and to see photographs in the newspapers (particularly during spring training) of a manager holding a bat and demonstrating a swing or gripping a bat while a circle of players is gathered around him. Managers must also possess leadership abilities. Although their specific styles may differ, managers must be able to instill in their players the confidence and loyalty to perform at their peak performance levels. The ability to teach and be an effective leader is not limited to certain types of players. The literature on both teaching and leadership indicates that there is more than one effective style, and a cursory review of baseball history indicates that infielders, outfielders, pitchers, and catchers have been effective managers.

Whereas knowledge of the job, knowledge of the jobs of those they supervise (the players), and the ability to lead are quite similar to the case of generic management, baseball is unique in that the prior job-related experiences of managers (as players and/or coaches) are readily available and easily quantifiable. The ability to quantify performance has been an essential part of the studies on salary discrimination. Here, however, prior records are evaluated in terms of qualifications for the job as manager. Three distinct prior job-related experiences are analyzed. Specifically, I compare the records of the managers as players, focusing on longevity and several career performance statistics to measure their knowledge of Major League Baseball and potential ability to be major league managers.

Longevity provides the individual with a greater opportunity to learn about the game, leadership techniques, and the like. Managerial experience at the minor league level is used to assess previous opportunities to exercise leadership, and major league coaching background is used as a measure of their teaching and instructional expertise.

The Managerial Pool, 1975–1994

Between 1975 and 1994, 140 different individuals held the position of manager of a Major League Baseball team. Of these 140, 39 had managed prior to 1975; Frank Robinson was the only new manager to begin the 1975 season. In 1975, there were 24 teams. Two teams were added to the American League in 1977, and two teams were added to the National League in 1993. During this 20-year time period, major league teams changed managers 210 times, creating an average of more than 10 opportunities per year for major league teams to hire new managers. Of the 24 managers who started the 1975 season, none was managing the same team at the conclusion of the 1994 season. Of the original 24 managers in 1975, 20 were subsequently rehired by other teams after being terminated. There was a constant turnover of managers, thus providing ample opportunity for the hiring of Black and Hispanic managers.

Of the 140 managers, there were 7 Black managers (Don Baylor, Dusty Baker, Larry Doby, Cito Gaston, Hal McRae, Frank Robinson, and Maury Wills) and 5 foreign-born Hispanic managers (Felipe Alou, Preston Gomez, Marty Martinez, Tony Perez, and Cookie Rojas). [*See Table 2*.] In addition, 12 individuals managed fewer than 42 games or 25% of a full season. Marty Martinez, who managed 1 game with Seattle in 1986, is the only Black or Hispanic who managed fewer than 42 games. Many of these individuals who managed a limited number of games were hired on an interim basis. This is taken into account when I compare their managerial experiences.

Table 2   Racial Differences in Managerial Selection

Major League Baseball Managers: 1975–1994		
	Number	Percentage
White	128	91.4
Black	7	5.0
Hispanic	5	3.6
Total	140	100.0

Major League Baseball Managers and Major League Playing Experience: 1975–1994		
	Number	Years
White	89	9.0
Black	7	16.6
Hispanic	5	12.8
All managers	101	9.8

Managers with Major League Playing Experience			
	Total	Major League Experience	Percentage
White	128	103	80.4
Black	7	7	100.0
Hispanic	5	5	100.0
Total	140	115	82.1

Source: Journal of Sport and Social Issues. Used with permission.

RESULTS

Managers as Major League Players

The most notable prerequisite to being a major league manager is to have played in the major leagues. By performing at the major league level, players demonstrate their abilities under the most repetitive conditions and gain firsthand knowledge of how the game is played and the performance required to succeed at the highest level.

Of the 140 managers, 25 never played at the major league level. Of the remaining 115, 6 were pitchers. Consistent with earlier findings, most played second base or shortstop (47), followed by catcher (25). . . . All 25 who did not have major league experience as players were White. All 6 managers who were pitchers in the major leagues were White.

A comparison of the experience of White, Black, and Hispanic managers as major league players reveals that the Black and Hispanic managers have had more extensive and productive careers than have their White counterparts. This is true even after eliminating from the comparison all of the White managers who never played at the major league level. . . .

Even after excluding White managers who never played at the major league level and therefore raising the mean experience for Whites, Black managers have approximately twice as much major league experience as do White managers (i.e., 84% longer, 136% more games, and 159% more at bats). The major league careers of Hispanic managers are 42% longer, having played in 72% more games and with 82% more plate appearances.

Because there is a limited number of Black and Hispanic managers compared to White managers, and because the analysis includes the entire population, no test for statistical significance was performed. I did calculate the standard deviation of each mean to reveal the extent to which there is variation within the White, Black, and Hispanic managers. The greatest variance is among the Hispanic managers, whereas the least is among the Black managers.

As with career longevity, Black and Hispanic managers outperformed the White managers in all offensive categories [as major league players]. Blacks, on average, scored more than twice as many runs and had 176% more hits, 406% more home runs, 249% more runs batted in, and a batting average 7% higher than did White managers. Hispanics also outperformed White managers, but not to the same extent as did the Black managers: 88% more runs, 91% more hits, 163% more home runs, 120% more runs batted in, and a batting average 5% higher than those of White managers. Interestingly, there is less variance among White managers regarding the performance criteria, with Hispanics showing the greatest variance.

Minor League Managerial Experience

In addition to being a player, managing at the minor league level is often considered a prerequisite for obtaining a major league managerial job. It is as a manager that the individual gains experience in game strategy, leadership, and interactions with team administration. Of the 140 managers, almost 70% had managed at the minor league level. . . .

Felipe Alou, Frank Robinson, and Preston Gomez are the only minority major league managers with prior experience as minor league managers. . . .

Whereas the length of experience and performance appears similar, the percentage of Blacks and Hispanics with minor league managerial experience is less than the percentage of Whites with minor league managerial experience. The variance between those who have managed at the minor league level is also similar.

. . . .

DISCUSSION

Standard employment practices compel employers to demonstrate that requirements for a position are job related and that such job requirements are applied equally to all candidates for the position. Baseball managers need to have a knowledge of the game, the ability to teach, and the ability to lead. I identified three prior job-related experiences

that are likely to provide the individual with these necessary skills, knowledge, and abilities: major league playing experience, minor league managerial experience, and major league coaching experience.

All but one of the men who managed between 1975 and 1994 had some experience as either a major league player, a minor league manager, or a coach of a major league team. The lone exception, Atlanta Braves owner Ted Turner, managed for one game in 1977. It thus appears that these three conditions are used by teams as part of the hiring process and are considered to be job-related prerequisites for employment as a manager. It is also evident from the analysis that these three qualifications are not considered to be an absolute requirement. Only 55 of the 140 managers (39%) had experience in all three areas studied. Some combination of playing experience, minor league managerial experience, and major league coaching experience is deemed appropriate to be hired as a manager.

The requirement that a manager have major league playing experience was not applied equally to all who were managers between 1975 and 1994. All Black and Hispanic managers had to have played at the major league level and had to have had longer and more productive careers as players than was the case with White managers. This is true even after eliminating from consideration the 25 White managers who never played major league baseball. Only 80% of the White managers had major league playing experience, whereas 100% of the minority managers had performed at the major league level. The data reveal that heightened expectations regarding length of time in the major leagues were applied consistently to all Black managers.

Previous studies would lead one to conclude that this difference in the performance standards is attributable to position segregation. Seven of the minority managers were primarily outfielders (58% of all minority managers as compared to only 9% of White managers were outfielders), and outfielders have consistently had to be more productive in terms of offensive performance. The data reveal, however, that minority outfielders who became managers had longer and more productive careers than did White outfielders who became managers.

. . . .

Between 1975 and 1994, only 18 outfielders became managers. This is consistent with previous research regarding position centrality. However, the total playing, coaching, and minor league managerial experience of minority and White outfielders is different. The minority outfielder/managers spent an average of 23 years as player, coach, and minor league manager; whereas the average was 17 years for the White outfielders with major league playing experience who became managers. There were several White managers who were outfielders but had not played at the major league level.

Minority outfielders who became managers were coaches for an average of 4 years, whereas the White outfielder/

managers were coaches for an average of 2 years. Only 28% of the minority outfielder/managers had minor league managerial experience, whereas 55% of the White outfielder/managers managed at the minor league level. The average number of years of managing in the minor leagues was almost equal: 1.8 for the minority outfielders and 2.7 for the White outfielders. The limited number of Black or Hispanic managers who played positions other than outfielder precludes any meaningful comparison to the White managers.

The data show that no marginal Black players, either those who did not make it to the major leagues or those who had limited major league careers, were ever selected to be major league managers during the past 20 years. Although it is not known with any certainty who may have applied for these positions, there are several Blacks with limited playing careers who became coaches but never became managers (e.g., Tommie Aaron, Gene Baker, Curt Motton, and, most recently, Tom Reynolds).

A cursory look at the White managers who did not play at the major league level indicates that a lengthy playing career cannot be considered an essential prerequisite for superior performance as a manager. Two of the more successful managers in the past and present, Earl Weaver and Jim Leyland, are among the 25 who never played Major League Baseball. This leads one to consider the impact on the effectiveness of minority managers who, it appears, are required to possess certain characteristics that are not necessarily correlated with success as a manager. Further analysis of the relationship between a manager's playing career and managerial record is necessary.

The situation is somewhat reversed when we examine managerial experience in the minor leagues. Although it is the weakest of the three elements (only 69% of all managers had minor league managerial experience), the majority of Black and Hispanic managers did not have an opportunity to manage in the minor leagues. The length and performance of those who did are similar for Blacks, Whites, and Hispanics.

Star players may be hesitant to spend time in the minor leagues, even if it is as the manager of the team. Data on player performance at the major league level indicate that most of the minority managers could be considered star players. Offers to coach at the major league level may appeal to both the player and team, as the player is more visible to the fans. It should be noted that there are numerous star White players who became managers without first obtaining managerial experience in the minor leagues. Yogi Berra, Alvin Dark, Toby Harrah, and Pete Rose are some of the more prominent to follow this career path. Further study is needed to determine the extent to which being a minor league manager provides invaluable experience that is not obtained by either playing or coaching.

. . . .

The large variance in the means for player longevity, performance categories, and years and games managed in the minor leagues indicates the absence of precise prerequisite criteria. A total of 65 managers (46%) had experience in two of the three categories. In addition, 20 were players and minor league managers, 30 were players and had prior coaching experience, and 15 had managed minor league teams and coached. Previous studies of managerial performance have taken into account the abilities of the players managed and the teams' won–lost records (Horowitz, 1994; Jacobs & Singell, 1993; Kahn, 1993; Porter & Scully, 1982), and neglected to include the backgrounds of the individual managers. Porter and Scully's evaluation of managers with 5 or more years of experience between 1961 and 1980 determined that Earl Weaver, Sparky Anderson, and Walter Alston were the most efficient. Horowitz's methodology also concluded that Weaver and Alston were among the best major league managers. Given that these three had limited, if any, major league experience as players (Alston, 1 at bat; Anderson, 1 year with 477 at bats; Weaver, no major league playing experience), we should be cautious before assuming that playing can substitute for minor league [managing] or coaching experience. To the extent that Blacks and Hispanics have longer playing careers and limited coaching and previous managerial experience, they may be at a disadvantage in terms of the training and background necessary to succeed as a manager. Further study is needed to determine what combination of the three job-related activities is most closely related to superior performance as a manager. Additionally, further study is needed to determine whether and to what extent the position played at the major league or minor league level affects the number of years considered appropriate experience and, therefore, the need to be a minor league manager or major league coach before becoming a major league manager.

This study examined the background of all major league managers from 1975 through 1994. Specifically, it compared the playing records, minor league managerial experience, and coaching experience of all those who managed during the past 20 years. All but one (Ted Turner, a team owner) had some combination of the specified job-related experiences. We can thus conclude that these criteria are considered by owners when they hire managers. The amount of experience required as a player, minor league manager, or coach was different for Black, White, and Hispanic managers. Blacks and Hispanics had longer and more productive careers as players than did their White counterparts. Further, there were differences between the minority and White outfielders who became managers. A comparison of the playing careers of the minority and White outfielders who became managers revealed that the minority outfielder/managers outperformed the Whites in all offensive categories and had nearly an identical batting average. Minority managers tended to be outfielders, a position in which they are overrepresented but a position that has produced a limited number of managers. Black and Hispanic managers had less minor league managerial experience than did White managers and had similar experience as major league coaches. It would appear that major league baseball teams, although using appropriate job-related criteria in the hiring of managers, did not apply these criteria in an equitable manner.

References

Horowitz, I. (1994). Pythagoras, Tommy Lasorda, and me: On evaluating baseball managers. *Social Science Quarterly, 75,* 187–194.

Jacobs, D., & Singell, L. (1993). Leadership and organizational performance: Isolating links between managers and collective success. *Social Science Research, 22,* 165–189.

Kahn, L. (1993). Managerial quality, team success, and individual player performance in major league baseball. *Industrial and Labor Relations Review, 46,* 531–547.

Porter, P., & Scully, G. (1982). Measuring managerial efficiency: The case of baseball. *Southern Economic Journal, 49,* 642–650.

THE FRITZ POLLARD ALLIANCE, THE ROONEY RULE, AND THE QUEST TO "LEVEL THE PLAYING FIELD" IN THE NATIONAL FOOTBALL LEAGUE

N. Jeremi Duru

INTRODUCTION

The National Football League (the "NFL" or the "League"), like the National Basketball Association ("NBA") and Major League Baseball ("MLB"), has a long history of racial exclusion.[1] And like these other long-standing American professional sport leagues, desegregation among players preceded desegregation among coaches.[2] As slowly increasing numbers of minorities assumed NBA head coaching positions and MLB managing positions toward the end of the twentieth century, however, minority NFL coaches were less likely to receive head coaching opportunities than their basketball and baseball counterparts.[3] Indeed, as of 2002, only two minorities held head coaching positions in the thirty-two team NFL, and only five, including those two, had held head coaching positions during the League's modern era.[4] Four years later, however, the NFL had more than tripled its number of minority head coaches and shone as a model for other athletic institutions seeking to provide head coaching candidates equal employment opportunities.[5]

This article seeks to explore the history of racial exclusion in the NFL, the particular barriers minority coaches seeking NFL head coaching positions have faced, and the effort to level the playing field for such coaches. . . . Part II explores the travails of the NFL's first three post-reintegration coaches of color as well as statistical evidence revealing that, as of 2002, NFL coaches of color generally suffered inferior opportunities despite exhibiting outstanding performance. Part III examines the campaign launched by attorneys Cyrus Mehri and Johnnie L. Cochran, Jr. to alter NFL teams' hiring practices, the creation of the Rooney Rule (the "Rule"), and the birth of the Fritz Pollard Alliance of minority coaches, scouts, and front office personnel in the NFL. Finally, Part IV traces the Rooney Rule's success in creating equal opportunity for coaches of color in the NFL.

[*Ed. Note: The author's discussion of the history of racial exclusion in the NFL is omitted.*]

. . . .

In 2002, civil rights attorneys Johnnie L. Cochran, Jr.[50] and Cyrus Mehri[51] commissioned University of Pennsylvania economist Dr. Janice Madden to analyze the performance of NFL head coaches during the fifteen years between 1986 and 2001 and to compare the success of the five black head coaches who coached during that period against the success of the eighty-six white head coaches who coached during the same period.[52] Dr. Madden concluded that, by any standard, the black head coaches outperformed the white head coaches: "No matter how we look at success, black coaches are performing better. These data are consistent with blacks having to be better coaches than the whites in order to get a job as head coach in the NFL."[53]

Indeed, *in every category Dr. Madden studied,* black coaches outperformed white coaches.[54] In terms of total wins per season—the primary category upon which a head coach's performance is assessed—[55] black coaches averaged over nine wins, while white coaches averaged eight wins.[56] While the 1.1 win differential might, at first blush, seem a minor matter, considering that NFL teams play only sixteen games during each regular season, one additional win is extremely significant.[57] Further, no win is more significant than the ninth, as, during the fifteen years studied, sixty percent (60%) of teams winning nine games advanced to the playoffs while only ten percent (10%) of teams winning eight games advanced to the playoffs.[58]

The disparity in success is even more pronounced when considering coaches' success in their first seasons with a team.[59] In their first seasons, black coaches averaged 2.7 more wins than did white coaches in their first seasons and, accordingly, were far more likely to advance their teams to the playoffs than were white coaches.[60]

In addition, in their last seasons before being fired, black coaches outperformed their white counterparts.[61] Black coaches won an average of 1.3 more games in their terminal years than white coaches, and while twenty percent (20%) of the black coaches who were fired led their teams to the playoffs in the year of their firing, only eight percent (8%) of white coaches did the same.[62]

III. THE CAMPAIGN TO CHANGE THE NFL

Based on Dr. Madden's results, Cochran and Mehri authored a report titled, *Black Coaches in the National Football League: Superior Performances, Inferior Opportunities*. They concluded, based on Dr. Madden's results, that black head coaches faced more exacting standards than white head coaches and were often dismissed under circumstances that would not have resulted in white head coaches' dismissals.[63] As stark as Madden's results were, Mehri and Cochran, of course, did not conclude black head coaches were somehow inherently better than white head coaches. Rather, they concluded that because barriers to entry facing black coaches seeking head coaching positions were more formidable than those facing white coaches, the black coaches able to surmount those barriers were exceedingly well equipped to succeed as head coaches. And, of course, as a consequence of those exceedingly high barriers, they argued, many black assistant coaches never received serious consideration for head coaching jobs.[64] Cochran and Mehri's report ultimately concluded that despite statistically "superior performance," black coaches have received "inferior opportunities": "In case after case, NFL owners have shown more interest in—and patience with—white coaches who don't win than black coaches who do."[65]

Armed with this conclusion and statistically significant analyses to support it, Cochran and Mehri possessed critical information in confronting employment discrimination: persuasive evidence that the discrimination actually exists. Over forty years after Congress issued broad-based anti-discriminatory legislative edicts, Americans are reluctant to acknowledge discrimination existing in their organizations.[66] Racial bias and discrimination in America is now more subtle than overt, and, according to some scholars, often sub-conscious.[67] Consequently, the suggestion of racial discrimination's existence may, and often does, strike institutions' executives as inaccurate and offensive, prompting fierce denials and dampening the possibility of sincere and meaningful settlement negotiations.[68]

Statistically significant evidence of systemic discrimination buttressed by anecdotal evidence of that discrimination's impact—as opposed to anecdotal evidence alone—is often crucial in prompting institutions to honestly confront the existence of discrimination. Cochran and Mehri had just that, which was sufficient to convince the NFL, which had to its credit previously expressed concern as to the lack of diversity among its head coaches,[69] that some level of cooperation, as opposed to confrontation, was in order. And, indeed, shortly after the report's publication, the NFL displayed leadership by creating a committee dedicated to increasing equal employment opportunity for NFL coaching candidates.[70] Consisting of the owners of several of the League's teams and chaired by Pittsburgh Steelers owner Dan Rooney, the Workplace Diversity Committee set out to consider the remedial recommendations Cochran and Mehri proffered.[71]

A. Crafting the Rooney Rule

The most notable of Cochran and Mehri's recommendations was the mandatory interview rule. Arguing that racial bias, whether conscious or unconscious, was steering teams away from head coaching candidates of color, Cochran and Mehri contended NFL teams should be made to do what few had theretofore done—grant candidates of color meaningful head coach job interviews.[72] Given the opportunities, they believed, coaching candidates of color would exhibit preparedness for head coaching jobs; the coaches of color simply needed the opportunities to compete for positions.[73] Cochran and Mehri, therefore, suggested that each NFL team searching for a head coach be required to interview at least one minority candidate before making its hire.[74] Crucial to the suggestion was that the interview be *meaningful*—that it be an in-person interview and that the interviewers be among the team's primary decision-makers.[75]

After some deliberation, the Workplace Diversity Committee recommended the Rule to the broader group of NFL team owners, and the owners agreed by acclamation to implement the suggested rule.[76] All parties agreed the rule should require nothing beyond a meaningful interview, and that if after the interview the interviewing team chose to hire a non-minority coach, the choice was its to make.[77] In December of 2002, the NFL announced its mandatory interview rule, which would come to be known as the Rooney Rule in honor of the Workplace Diversity Committee's chairman, Dan Rooney,[78] and which would prove to fundamentally change the NFL.[79]

From the start, the Rooney Rule met with significant skepticism.[80] Indeed, criticism rained down from all quarters. NFL insiders questioned the League's decision to take its lead in pursuing diversity from two lawyers previously unaffiliated with the League and its internal mechanisms. If anyone should guide the League on these issues, they argued, he or she should be from the football community—from a group of NFL alums or from the League's, or one of its team's, front offices. Others, recognizing the Rule contained no accompanying penalty mechanism, wondered whether teams would bother to heed the rule, and if they didn't, whether the League would do anything about their failures to do so.[81] Still others argued that even assuming teams followed the Rule, because the interviewing team had no obligation to hire a minority coach, the interview would prove merely ornamental.[82] Burdened with these criticisms, the Rooney Rule's early life was shaky.

B. The Birth of an Alliance

Those questioning the propriety of the NFL's reliance on outsiders with no connection to the NFL community to guide its equal employment opportunity efforts would soon be silenced.

Shortly after Cochran and Mehri issued their report, Floyd Keith, the Executive Director of the Black Coaches

Association ("BCA"), an advocacy organization of black collegiate coaches,[83] suggested the lawyers consult with John Wooten, a former NFL All-Pro offensive lineman well-known throughout the League for his tenacity and intellectual acuity both on and off the field.[84] While Wooten was a remarkable player, he made his most lasting impact in NFL front offices, where he worked in various high-level capacities with the Dallas Cowboys, the Philadelphia Eagles, and the Baltimore Ravens over the course of almost thirty years.[85] More impressive than Wooten's success as a player or front office executive, however, was his unwavering and expressed commitment to racial equality in the NFL. For years, Wooten decried the almost entirely homogenous composition of the NFL's head coaching ranks. Having played with and against scores of fellow black players whom he knew would, if given the opportunity, excel as NFL head coaches, Wooten was incensed at their exclusion.

Cochran and Mehri's report offered quantitative support for what Wooten knew: with a fair chance to take the reins of an NFL team, black head coaches would perform as well, if not better than, white head coaches. Wooten also knew that many black coaches in the League who had consistently been passed over for head coaching positions were anxious to meaningfully compete for those positions and would support the lawyers' efforts. Wooten committed to assisting Cochran and Mehri's work in any way he could and suggested they travel to Indianapolis, Indiana, in February of 2003 to meet with the NFL's black coaches during the NFL Scouting Combine. The Combine, which serves as a nearly week-long tryout for collegiate players seeking NFL jobs,[86] is the one occasion on which all of the League's teams and their staffs can be counted on to be in one place and, therefore, presented the perfect opportunity for Cochran and Mehri to meet and share ideas with the individuals they were hoping to help. The lawyers recognized that in order to initiate true reform in the NFL, the primary stakeholders would have to engage in the battle, and they hoped a meeting at the Combine would galvanize their interest in organizing as a unit.

Although Cochran was unable to attend, Mehri represented them both at the Combine. What Mehri imagined would be a gathering of a few dozen black coaches turned out to be a meeting of over one hundred black coaches, scouts, and front office personnel, all deeply concerned about equity in the NFL. The group, though, was not a monolith. Some in the room expressed reluctance to push the NFL and its teams too vociferously for fear of backlash. Others, exceedingly frustrated with lack of opportunity, felt no push could be hard enough. Still others staked out middle ground positions. Overwhelmingly, however, those in the room supported increased organization among them. They wanted to maintain a connection in order that there be a forum in which to engage issues that they, as black coaches, scouts, and front office personnel in the NFL, shared. And

they did so, forming an organization and naming it in honor of the individual who preceded and inspired them all. They became the Fritz Pollard Alliance ("FPA"), an affinity group dedicated to equal opportunity of employment in the coaching, scouting, and front office ranks of the NFL.[87]

There was little doubt Wooten would serve as the fledging organization's chairman, guiding its vision and maintaining a strong relationship with the NFL, where he previously worked and maintained many close contacts and personnel friendships. And when Wooten considered who might effectively manage the organization's affairs and serve as its public face, a few individuals came to mind, but none more compelling than Kellen Winslow, Sr.

Winslow, one of the NFL's all time great players, was a tight end with the League's San Diego Chargers from 1979–1987, during which time he set numerous League records and revolutionized the position.[88] Whereas tight ends before Winslow were primarily utilized as blockers and rarely called upon to catch anything other than short passes, Winslow combined superior blocking skill with speed and pass-catching ability to rival even the best wide receivers.[89] Along with his physical abilities, Winslow mixed intelligence, dogged persistence, and compelling leadership ability to become a Hall of Fame player;[90] the type of player capable of willing his team to win.[91] Because of these characteristics and his tremendous success as a player, Winslow naturally presumed he would, upon retirement, have opportunities to work in the NFL or in major conference collegiate football.[92] Retirement, however, brought with it a crushing realization when the opportunities he envisioned did not materialize. As Winslow described in his foreword to *In Black and White: Race and Sports in America*, Kenneth Shropshire's incisive investigation of the intersection of race and sport:

> As long as I was on the field of play I was treated and viewed differently than most African-American men in this country. Because of my physical abilities, society accepted and even catered to me. Race was not an issue. Then reality came calling. After a nine-year career in the National Football League, I stepped into the real world and realized . . . I was just another nigger . . . the images and stereotypes that applied to African-American men in this country attached to me.[93]

Winslow's revelation led him to channel his talents toward exposing inequity in the sports industry, and when he agreed to serve as the FPA's Executive Director, he carried that passion with him. . . .

As a consequent of the FPA's support, the Rule, which was just a few months earlier decried as the brainchild of outside agitators, suddenly enjoyed endorsement from a body representing coaches, scouts, and front office personnel of color throughout the League. The Rooney Rule had gained instant credibility.

IV. THE ROONEY RULE: APPLIED

Credibility, however, offered no guarantee of efficacy, and if the Rule were to be effective, it would need teeth. Detroit Lions' General Manager Matt Millen's approach to hiring a new head coach in 2003 would ensure that it had them. In January of that year, the Lions fired their head coach Marty Mornhinweg, after the team suffered through a lackluster season during which they lost thirteen games and won only three.[95] Three weeks earlier, the San Francisco 49ers had fired their longtime head coach, Steve Mariucci.[96] Millen wanted Mariucci to lead the Lions and he expressed little interest in maintaining an open mind to other potential candidates. In his single-minded pursuit of Mariucci, Millen hired Mariucci without interviewing any candidates of color.[97] While such a hiring process would have been unobjectionable just a few months earlier, under the Rooney Rule it was facially non-compliant.

The NFL's then-Commissioner, Paul Tagliabue, had his test case, and his response would determine the Rule's fate. If Tagliabue responded with inaction or an empty condemnation, the Rule would be rendered useless as a change agent. It would exist as little more than a symbolic gesture, creating the impression of a League dedicated to equal employment opportunity for coaches of color in the NFL, but having no actual impact. If, on the other hand, Tagliabue substantially punished the Lions, he would, in doing so, signal the NFL's commitment to the Rooney Rule and to the equity Cochran, Mehri, and the FPA sought to achieve.

Tagliabue's decision shocked even those hoping for a stout punishment. Explaining that Millen "did not take sufficient steps to satisfy the commitment that [the Lions] made" regarding the Rooney Rule, Tagliabue fined Millen $200,000, and explicated that Millen, not the team for which he worked, would have to pay the fine.[98] With the fine, Tagliabue made clear that as the Lions' principal decision-maker, Millen was responsible for following the League's mandatory interview guidelines, and he would have to pay account.

Notably, Tagliabue did not stop at issuing the fine. He went further still, moving away from the facts of the Lions' inadherence and issuing broad-based notice as to the League's unwavering commitment to the Rule. The next principle decision-maker to flout the Rule would, Tagliabue promised, suffer a $500,000 fine.[99]

While the FPA celebrated Tagliabue's response to the Lions' head coach hiring process as revealing that the "'Rooney Rule' ha[d] finally arrived,"[100] Tagliabue's actions sparked outrage among Rooney Rule opponents and others who felt it was excessive.[101] After all, it did not appear Millen was seeking to exclude from consideration minority candidates to the benefit of a group of Caucasian candidates. He was, rather, committed to hiring a particular person—Steve Mariucci—and was uninterested in considering any other candidate, regardless of race.[102] If the Rule applied in this circumstance, they argued, future decision-makers interested in a particular candidate would offer an interview to a minority candidate simply to fulfill the Rule and for no other reason.[103] And, indeed, this criticism exposed an obvious potential weakness in the Rule. While the Rule requires a team to grant a minority candidate a meaningful interview, in that the Rule is incapable of directing state of mind, it cannot require that a team grant a candidate meaningful *consideration*. Thus, the Rule is powerless to prevent the inconsequential interview—the interview with all the trappings of meaningfulness but whose outcome is predetermined.

The Rule's critics cited this reality as evidence the Rule would be ultimately ineffectual.[104] However, many commentators believe that, more often than one might initially intuit, a face-to-face, in-person, interview with an organization's primary decision-makers begets meaningful consideration—that sitting down together and discussing at length a common interest potentially melts away conscious or subconscious preconceptions and stereotypes that might otherwise color decision-makers' judgments.[105] As such, they argued that despite being a process-oriented rule with no hiring mandate, the Rooney Rule carried the power to markedly increase diversity among NFL head coaches.[106]

The proponents' belief was borne out. Indeed, over the course of the several years following its implementation, the Rule has markedly increased diversity among NFL head coaches.[107] As of the Rule's implementation in 2002, two minorities held NFL head coaching positions.[108] Four years later, during the 2006 season, minority head coaches led seven of the NFL's thirty-two teams.[109] *[Ed. Note: There were six minority head coaches at the start of the 2010 season.]* While this progress may not be entirely attributable to the Rule, the Rule has undoubtedly made a major impact, and at least a portion of that impact has occurred under circumstances Rooney Rule critics insisted would reveal the Rule as ineffectual—circumstances suggesting a "meaningful" interview would not spark truly meaningful consideration.

Consider the Cincinnati Bengals' 2003 search for a head coach. Prior to that year, the Bengals had never in franchise history hired a person of color for its head coach position.[110] In fact, during that period, the Bengals had never interviewed a person of color for its offensive coordinator or defensive coordinator positions, the two positions directly under the head coach in the football coaching hierarchy.[111] Under the Rooney Rule, therefore, the Bengals were obligated to do something they had never done nor indicated desire in doing—they were obligated to interview a minority candidate for their head coaching vacancy. With the opportunity to convince the Bengals of his merit, an opportunity history suggests would not have arisen absent the Rooney Rule, Marvin Lewis, a renowned defensive strategist and the then Washington Redskins defensive coordinator, interviewed for the position and became the Bengals' head coach.[112] And, in the year after his hire, Lewis transformed the Bengals, who were for years the NFL's worst team, into a playoff contender,[113] a feat for which he narrowly missed receiving the NFL's American Football Conference Coach of the Year Award.[114]

Although Lewis has not yet guided his team to the NFL's Super Bowl game—in which the American Football Conference Champion plays the League's National Football Conference Champion for the NFL title—another Rooney Rule beneficiary has. In 2004, the Chicago Bears hired Lovie Smith, formerly the St. Louis Rams' defensive coordinator, as the Bears' new head coach.[115] Smith inherited a weak team, which had, in the previous year, won only 7 games and lost 9.[116] In two seasons, however, Smith transformed the Bears' defense into arguably the best defensive unit in the NFL, and in January of 2007, Smith led his team to a victory in the National Football Conference Championship game and to a consequent Super Bowl berth.[117] The 2007 Super Bowl would prove an historic one, as Smith would join Tony Dungy, coach of the Indianapolis Colts team the Bears' would play on Super Bowl Sunday, as the first African American head coaches in Super Bowl history.[118]

By his own admission, without the opportunity the Rooney Rule produced, Smith may not have ascended to the NFL head coaching ranks.[119] Given an equal opportunity, however, he did so ascend and proceeded to establish himself among the NFL head coaching elite.

CONCLUSION

Five years after the Rooney Rule's emergence, the Rule is an established feature of the National Football League's teams' hiring processes. Indeed, recognizing the Rule's value, NFL teams have displayed commitment to interviewing candidates of color for their highest level front office positions despite no penalty adhering if they fail to do so.[120] And, just as diversity has increased among the League's head coaches, it has increased in the League's teams' front offices.[121]

In short, the Rooney Rule has succeeded. No team has flouted the Rule since Millen did so in 2003, the Rule has produced increased diversity throughout the League, and the Rule's beneficiaries have met with substantial success. As such, the Rule is enjoying greater buy-in than ever before—both among those affiliated with the NFL and NFL outsiders committed to ensuring equal employment opportunity in other contexts. Most notably, in October of 2007, the NCAA's Division I Athletic Directors' Association, concerned that minorities are disproportionately scarce among the nation's Division I head football coaching positions, have turned to a form of the Rooney Rule in hopes of increasing equal employment opportunity among minority head coaching candidates.[122] The organization's members have committed to including candidates of color among the

interviewees for their universities' head football coaching vacancies.[123] Whether the athletic directors' commitment will translate into greater diversity among Division I head coaches is untold, but if the NFL's experience with the Rooney Rule is any indicator, prospects are bright.

As Cyrus Mehri and Johnnie L. Cochran, Jr. pressed the NFL to adopt the Rooney Rule, they insisted they had "provided the basis for meaningful change" and that it was the "obligation of the National Football League to see that change happen[ed]."[124] They were correct, and the League has, indeed, changed. Once an embarrassment among its peer leagues regarding equal employment opportunity for minority coaches, the NFL now stands as a model for other organizations seeking the change it has enjoyed.

Notes

1. *See* KENNETH L. SHROPSHIRE, IN BLACK AND WHITE: RACE AND SPORTS IN AMERICA 29-31 (1996) (discussing history of discrimination in all three sports). The NHL, America's fourth premier sports league, has had a discriminatory history as well, but in that athletes of color have historically played little hockey, discrimination in hockey has been rooted in national origin, dividing "French-Canadian and European players from their American and Anglo-Canadian counterparts." Kenneth L. Shropshire, *Minority Issues in Contemporary Sports*, 15 STAN L. & POL'Y REV. 189, 191 n.9 (2004) (citing Lawrence M. Kahn, *Discrimination in Professional Sports: A Survey of the Literature*, 44 INDUS. & LAB. REL. REV. 395 (1991)).

2. *See* JOHNNIE L. COCHRAN, JR. & CYRUS MEHRI, BLACK COACHES IN THE NATIONAL FOOTBALL LEAGUE: SUPERIOR PERFORMANCE, INFERIOR OPPORTUNITIES 1 (2002), http://www.findjustice.com/files/Report_-_Superior_Performance_Inferior_Opportunities.pdf. (noting as of 2002, only 1.5% of the 400 coaches in NFL history were African American).

3. *See* Brian W. Collins, *Tackling Unconscious Bias in Hiring Practices: The Plight of the Rooney Rule*, 82 N.Y.U. L. REV. 870, 877-884 (2007) (discussing coaching opportunities for African Americans in the NBA and NFL); Shropshire, *supra* note 1, at 203-05 (noting baseball was "impetus" for diversity initiatives creating opportunities for African Americans in managerial and coaching positions).

4. Tony Dungy and Herman Edwards were the NFL's only head coaches of color in 2002. Chris Myers, *Sunday Morning QB: Black Coaches Try to Get in the Game*, N.Y. DAILY NEWS, Oct. 6, 2006, at 70. Art Shell, Dennis Green, and Ray Rhodes join them as the only people of color to have held NFL head coaching positions in the League's modern era. *Id.*

5. Steve Wieberg, *Division I-A Tackles Minority Hiring: Unlike NFL's Rooney Rule, ADs' Directive Will Only Encourage, Not Require, Action*, USA TODAY, Oct. 3, 2007, at 1C. Electronic copy available at: http://ssrn.com/abstract=1109176.

. . . .

50. Johnnie L. Cochran, Jr.—Biography, *available at* http://www.cochranfirm.com/pdf/CochranBrochure.pdf, at 2.

51. Cyrus Mehri—Biography, *available at* http://www.findjustice.com/about/attorneys/mehri/.

52. COCHRAN, JR. & MEHRI, *supra* note 2, at i-ii.

53. *Id.* Exhibit B at 3.

54. *See id.* Exhibit B at 1 ("Find[ing] that, by any measure used, black coaches were more successful than white coaches").

55. *See id.* at ii (noting wins and losses are "the currency of football and all team sports").

56. *Id.* at 2.

57. *See id.* (recognizing a one-win difference often determines whether a team is successful in reaching the playoffs).

58. *Id.*

59. *Id.* at 3.

60. *Id.*

61. *Id.* at 4.

62. *Id.*

63. *See id.* at i-ii.

64. *See id.* at 8-10.

65. *Id.* at ii.

66. *See* KENNETH SHROPSHIRE, IN BLACK AND WHITE: RACE AND SPORTS IN AMERICA 10 (1996) (discussing various methods individuals use to underplay their discriminatory hiring practices).

67. Charles R. Lawrence III, *The Id, the Ego, and Equal Protection: Reckoning with Unconscious Racism*, 39 STAN. L. REV. 317, 323 (1987); R.A. Lenhardt, *Understanding the Mark: Race, Stigma, and Equality in Context*, 79 N.Y.U L. REV. 803, 829 (2004).

68. *See* William L. Kandel, *Practicing Law Institute: Litigation and Administrative Practice Course Handbook Series*, 682 PRACTICAL L. INST. 469, 483 (2006) (explaining that attacking the character of executives in negotiations as racist often hampers the ability to reach meaningful solutions).

69. *See* Collins, *supra* note 3, at 884 (noting ex-NFL commissioner Paul Tagliabue's efforts to increase minority hiring before the Rooney Rule's inception).

70. *Id.* at 886.

71. *Id.*

72. *See* COCHRAN & MEHRI, *supra* note 2, at 15.

73. *See id.* at 14.

74. *See id.* at 15.

75. *See* Collins *supra* note 71 at 901-04 (discussing problem of "sham" interviews with the Rooney Rule and difficulty of measuring franchises' good faith efforts in interviewing minority candidates during hiring process).

76. *See id.* at 886 (noting that the NFL Committee on Workplace Diversity's suggestions were adopted by all thirty-two NFL owners).

77. *Id.*

78. Greg Garber, *Thanks to the Rooney Rule, Doors Opened*, ESPN .COM, Feb. 9, 2007, http://sports.espn.go.com/nfl/playoffs06/news/story?id=2750645

79. *See id.* (discussing the effect of the Rooney Rule on the NFL).

80. *E.g.* Jay Nordinger, *Color in Coaching*, NATIONAL REVIEW, Sept. 1, 2003, *available at* http://www.nationalreview.com/flashback/nordlinger200504200048.asp.

81. *See* Collins *supra* note 71, at 871 (noting that the Rooney Rule appeared "vague and inefficient" at first).

82. *Id.* at 902.

83. In 2007, the Black Coaches Association changed its name to the Black Coaches and Administrators, and now encompasses black collegiate sports administrators as well. Erika P. Thompson, *Black Coaches Association Announces Name Change*, BLACK COACHES & ADMINISTRATORS, Jul. 6, 2007, http://bcasports.cstv.com/genrel/072007aaa.html. (last visited January 15, 2008).

84. *See Fritz Pollard Alliance John Wooten Biography*, http://www.fpal .org/wooten.php (last visited November 27, 2007) (noting Wooten's various work as a football player and front office executive).

85. *Id.*

86. NFL Scouting Combine, http://www.nflcombine.net/ (last visited November 27, 2007).

87. Collins, *supra* note 71, at 887.

88. *See* Jay Paris, *Browns' Winslow is the Mouth that Roars*, NORTH COUNTY TIMES, Nov. 2, 2006 (claiming that Kellen Winslow revolutionized the tight end position).

89. *See NFL 1980 League Leaders*, http://www.pro-football-reference .com/years/leaders1980.htm (last visited Nov. 27, 2007) (showing Winslow second in the league in receiving yards).

90. The Pro Football Hall of Fame inducted Winslow in 1995. Pro Football Hall of Fame Kellen Winslow Biography, http://www .profootballhof.com/hof/member.jsp?player_id=233 (last visited Nov. 27, 2007).

91. Winslow's capability in this regard is perhaps best illustrated by his performance in a 1982 Chargers playoff victory over the Miami Dolphins, a performance ranking among the greatest individual performances in NFL history. *See* PAGE 2 STAFF, *The List: Best NFL Playoff Performances*, ESPN, http://espn.go.com/page2/s/list/NFLplayoffperform.html (last visited Nov. 30, 2007) (ranking Winslow's performance the second greatest playoff performance of all time). During that game, Winslow refused to allow his team to lose. Despite being treated throughout the game for severe cramps, dehydration, a pinched nerve in his shoulder, and a gash in his lower lip requiring stitches, Winslow caught 13 passes for 166 yards, scored a touchdown, and blocked a Miami Dolphin field goal that would have given the Dolphins the victory. Dan Ralph, *The Reluctant Superstar*, NFL CANADA, Oct. 16, 2007, http://www .nflcanada.com/News/FeatureWriters/Ralph_Dan/2007/archive.html.

92. SHROPSHIRE, *supra* note 1, at xii.

93. *Id.* at xi.

. . . .

95. ESPN 2002 NFL Standings, http://sports.espn.go.com/nfl/standings?season=2002&breakdown=3&split=0 (last visited November 28, 2007).

96. CBC SPORTS, *Lions Hire Mariucci as Head Coach*, CANADIAN BROADCASTING CENTRE, Feb. 5, 2003, http://www.cbc.ca/sports/story/2003/02/03/mariucci030203.html.

97. Collins, *supra* note 71, at 900-01. Ironically, Mariucci, the coach Millen pursued with such myopia, performed quite poorly as the Lions head coach. During his two-plus seasons with the team, Mariucci amassed a record of fifteen wins and twenty-eight losses and was ultimately terminated in the middle of the 2005 season. Skip Wood, *After Digesting Turkey Day Debacle, Lions Fire Mariucci*, USA TODAY, Nov. 28, 2005.

98. Bram A. Maravent, *Is the Rooney Rule Affirmative Action?: Analyzing the NFL's Mandate to its Clubs Regarding Coaching and Front Office Hires*, 13 SPORTS LAW J. 233, 243 (2006).

99. ASSOCIATED PRESS, *Millen Fined for not Interviewing Minority Candidates*, ESPN, July 5, 2003, http://espn.go.com/nfl/news/2003/0725/1585560.html.

100. SPORTSLINE.COM WIRE REPORTS, *Millen Fined $200K for not Interviewing Minority Candidates*, CBS SPORTS, July 5, 2003, http://cbs.sportsline.com/nfl/story/6498949.

101. Curt Sylvester, *Detroit Lions Owner Lashes Out at NFL in Response to Diversity Fine*, DETROIT FREE PRESS, July 29, 2003.

102. Indeed, it merits noting that Millen did invite candidates of color to interview for the Lions' head coaching position, but recognizing that Millen had already decided to hire Mariucci and that the interviews to which they were being invited would be pro forma, and thus not meaningful, none of the invitees accepted. Collins, *supra* note 71, at 901.

103. *See id.* at 902 (discussing the possibility of "sham" interviews for minority coaching candidates).

104. Nordlinger, *supra* note 82.

105. *See* SHROPSHIRE, *supra* note 1, at 37-38 (discussing positive effect of Carol Moseley Braun's election to the United States Senate on the sensitivity to issues affecting minorities).

106. *See* COCHRAN, JR. & MEHRI, *supra* note 2, at 17 (noting that their proposal for changes in NFL's hiring process had the capability to promote "meaningful change").

107. *See* Collins, *supra* note 71, at 907-11 (discussing statistical effect of Rooney Rule).

108. Maravent, *supra* note 101, at 245.

109. Collins, *supra* note 71, at 907.

110. Geoff Hobson, *The Torch Has Been Passed*, CINCINNATI BENGALS, http://www.bengals.com/team/coach.asp?coach_id=7 (last visited Nov. 28, 2007).

111. Mark Curnutte, *Coughlin, Lewis Come to Town*, CINCINNATI ENQUIRER, Jan. 10, 2003, 1C.

112. Damon Hack, *Bengals Draw Praise for Hiring of Lewis*, N.Y. TIMES, Jan. 17, 2003.

113. *See* Jim Corbett, *Lewis Confident in Untested Palmer*, USA TODAY, May 29, 2004.

114. Cincinnati Bengals Marvin Lewis Biography, http://www.bengals.com/team/coach.asp?coach_id=7 (last visited November, 28. 2007).

115. ASSOCIATED PRESS, *Bears Hire Smith to be Head Coach*, USA TODAY, Jan. 14, 2004.

116. ESPN 2003 NFL Standings, http://sports.espn.go.com/nfl/standings?season=2003&breakdown=3&split=0.

117. John Mullin, *Super Bowl Bound*, CHICAGO TRIBUNE, Jan. 21, 2007, *available at* http://www.chicagotribune.com/sports/football/bears/cs-070121bearsgamer,0,188867.story?coll=chihomepagepromo440-fea.

118. Jarrett Bell, *Coaches Chasing Super Bowl—And History*, USA TODAY, Jan. 17, 2007.

119. Clifton Brown, *NFL Roundup: Bears Hope Takeaways Lead Them to Title*, N.Y. TIMES, Jan. 30, 2007.

120. Although the NFL has strongly encouraged its member teams to interview candidates of color for front office positions, it has stopped short of requiring such interviews. Mark Maske, *Expansion of 'Rooney Rule' Meets Resistance*, WASH. POST, Apr. 13, 2006, at D1. Indeed, the League's commitment to the Rooney Rule and its underlying principles is so complete that the League committed to interviewing candidates of color when seeking a replacement for former League Commissioner Tagliabue. *See* Scott Brown, *Rooney Rule Helping Minority Coaching Candidates*, PITTSBURGH TRIBUNE-REVIEW, Jan. 11, 2007, http://www.pittsburghlive.com/x/pittsburghtrib/sports/steelers/s_488048.html (noting that minority candidate, Fred Nance, was among the five finalists considered to replace Tagliabue) (last visited January 15, 2008).

121. *See* Maske, *supra* note 120, at D1 (noting "the Rooney Rule, or the spirit of it, has led to more opportunities for minorities in NFL front offices").

122. Steve Wieberg, *Major-College ADs Tackle Minority Hiring*, USA TODAY, Oct. 2, 2007.

123. *Id.*

124. COCHRAN, JR. & MEHRI, *supra* note 2, at 17.

OWNERS

DIVERSITY, RACISM, AND PROFESSIONAL SPORTS FRANCHISE OWNERSHIP: CHANGE MUST COME FROM WITHIN

Kenneth L. Shropshire

One possible path for decreasing actual or perceived racism against African Americans in any business setting is to increase African American ownership. The broad assumption underlying the advocacy of this remedy is that increased diversity in the ownership of an industry will decrease occurrences of discrimination.

. . . .

II. IDEAL STATE: VALUE OF DIVERSITY IN OWNERSHIP

A. General Benefit

What would be the primary benefits of greater African American ownership in professional sports? Two of the major benefits would be (1) the social value of diversity and (2) the financial value of diversity. The social value of diversity consists of both the actual value that diversity can bring to an enterprise through the presentation of different points of view and the perceived value that diversity may have in improving the image of an almost all white ownership. The financial value of diversity includes allowing minorities access to a piece of the lucrative sports ownership pie and front office employment, expanding the individual franchise revenues by attracting more fan support and attendance from minorities, and bringing about equity in player salaries without regard to race.

[*Ed. Note: The author's discussion of the actual and perceived values of diversity is omitted.*]

. . . .

C. Ownership Glass Ceilings and Differential Racism

Glass ceilings are present in much of American society. Part of the reason for the existence of such ceilings is the discomfort that many white Americans feel with African Americans in positions of power. African Americans may not be treated dramatically differently by whites in the business setting until they seek a position of power—until they seek to break through the glass ceiling. This has been referred to as a form of "differential racism."

. . . .

Just as this glass ceiling, or differential racism, may be the reason for an absence of African Americans in top-level positions on the field in sports, in politics, in corporate America, and in the entertainment industry, glass ceilings that keep African Americans from acquiring ownership interests in sports franchises probably exist as well.

III. LEGAL RECOURSE: CAN THE LAW COMPEL DIVERSITY?

. . . . One may question whether existing law provides any possible causes of action or remedies by which to increase diversity and African American ownership of professional sports franchises. The conclusion is that present law can only play a limited role in bringing about increased African American ownership in professional sports.

[*Ed. Note: The author's discussion of affirmative action and other applicable laws is omitted.*]

. . . .

It cannot be disputed that trust and confidence among fellow owners of a sports league is desirable for the efficiency and success of the league. A bad choice can doom the partnership. There are thirty [*now 32*] or fewer franchises in each of the professional leagues. Consequently, individuals who enter into a partnership or who expand their partnerships are very selective of whom they permit to join, and the courts are aware of this selectivity. The necessary trust and confidence will not exist if the partnership is compelled by force of law to admit an individual whom the partnership does not want. There will just be too much bad blood and distrust. Once a legal action is brought, the possibility that the petitioner and the partners could work together harmoniously is minimal. Moreover, such legal action could jeopardize the partnership. This is why reinstatement is a

disfavored remedy for high-level employees, both in the employment and partnership contexts, and why a judicial mandate of minority sports franchise ownership is even more unlikely.

Thus, antidiscrimination law provides only limited protections to minorities seeking to own professional sports franchises. Title VII does not apply directly, because there will normally not be an existing employer–employee relationship at stake, and Section 1981 only prevents owners from flagrantly discriminating on the basis of race in choosing their co-owners.

. . . .

As it currently stands, the law is clear that the owners in a given league may sell or grant franchises to whomever they choose, and, provided nothing in their decision-making process violates any . . . laws . . . , no legal action can force the existing owners to sell to a particular group. The plaintiffs in . . . two cases based their actions on antitrust laws, arguing against the anti-competitive nature of a league not accepting them as franchise owners. Neither bidder was African American, and neither was successful.

In both the existing franchise purchase and expansion areas, the choice as to which potential owners to bring on board is that of the respective league owners. Just as in any other business, courts are reluctant to compel business owners to take on new partners. So long as the reason for rejection is not illegal, courts are not likely to intervene.

[*Ed. Note: The author's discussion of the impact of litigation and litigation threats is omitted.*]

. . . .

IV. WILL IT HAPPEN? NEED FOR VOLUNTARY EFFORTS

As the previous section indicates, courts are not likely to interpret existing law as a mandate to compel existing professional club owners to admit minority ownership into their league memberships without flagrant racism. . . . What is likely to be much more effective—at least in the short term—is increased commitment from existing owners and players to recognize the important benefits that diverse ownership in sports can bring about.

V. CONCLUSION

There are many difficulties in breaking African Americans into the ownership ranks of professional sports. The greatest obstacles are not financial but structural. The owners themselves must somehow be compelled to desire change; however, they likely suffer from the same levels of conscious and unconscious racism as the rest of society. Indeed, the issues discussed in this article are applicable to businesses beyond sports.

The key barrier to change is the legally protected club-biness of the owners. They have the nearly exclusive right to select their co-owners. There is no requirement, unless self-imposed, that the owners accept the best financial offer. As a group, the owners of any league certainly could mandate that any multiowner group seeking a franchise must include African American investors. . . .

It will be difficult to use legal pressure to compel greater African American ownership. No current legislation on either the state or federal level regulates sports franchise ownership. Given the constitutional problems that would arise if such legislation were implemented and the recent public backlash against affirmative action in general, it does not appear that the lack of diversity in franchise ownership will be addressed by statute. In addition, although Section 1981 offers protection from flagrant discrimination, it is ineffective to put any real pressure on the owners to diversify their group.

The burden is thus on league leaders and the athletes to bring about such change.

SALARIES

THE SPORTS BUSINESS AS A LABOR MARKET LABORATORY

Lawrence M. Kahn

Among the forms of discrimination in sports, salary discrimination is the most studied issue. The typical research design—similar to much work in this area in labor economics—is a regression in which log salary is the dependent variable, and the independent variables include performance indicators, team characteristics, and market characteristics, with a dummy variable for white race. If the coefficient on the white indicator is positive and significant, then this potentially offers evidence of discrimination. Alternatively, some researchers have used separate regressions for white and nonwhite players, testing the possibility that performance is rewarded differently by race.

A major difficulty for all labor market research on discrimination is the problem of unobserved or mismeasured variables, such as the quality of schooling among workers in general. However, such problems must surely be less severe in sports than elsewhere. For example, the *Baseball Encyclopedia* and other baseball data sources allow one to control for very detailed performance indicators like batting average, stolen bases, home runs, career length, team success, and many more. "Occupation" in baseball is one's position, a far more detailed indicator than, say, "machine operative." The accuracy of the compensation data in sports, in many cases supplied by the relevant players' union that keeps copies of the actual player contracts, is very high.

The sport where regression analyses have produced the most evidence of salary discrimination is professional basketball. In the mid-1980s, several studies found statistically significant black salary shortfalls of 11–25 percent after controlling for a variety of performance and market-related statistics (for example, Kahn and Sherer, 1988; Koch and Vander Hill, 1988; Wallace, 1988; Brown, Spiro, and Keenan, 1991).* However, by the mid-1990s, there were no longer any overall significant racial salary differentials in the NBA, holding performance constant (Hamilton, 1997; Dey, 1997; Bodvarsson and Brastow, 1998). One caveat to this finding is seen in Hamilton's (1997) results from quantile regressions, which estimate the extent of discrimination at different points of the salary distribution, conditional on productivity. He did not find evidence of discrimination at the 10th, 25th, and 50th salary percentiles, but there was a significant white salary premium of about 20 percent, other things equal, at the 75th percentile of the salary distribution and above.[†]

Customer preferences may have something to do with the racial pay gap observed in basketball in the 1980s. For example, Kahn and Sherer (1988) found that, all else equal, during the 1980–86 period each white player generated 5,700 to 13,000 additional fans per year. The dollar value of this extra attendance more than made up for the white salary premium, a finding consistent with the existence of monopsony. Other researchers found a close match between the racial makeup of NBA teams in the 1980s and of the areas where they were located, again suggesting the importance of customer preferences (Brown, Spiro, and Keenan, 1991; Burdekin and Idson, 1991; Hoang and Rascher,

---

*While there may still be omitted variables that could have explained the *ceteris paribus* white salary advantage, reverse regression tests, which can under some restricted circumstances take account of such problems (Goldberger, 1984), showed even larger apparent discrimination coefficients against black players (Kahn and Sherer, 1988). In fact, these larger effects suggest that black players had better unmeasured productivity characteristics than whites, at least under the statistical assumptions outlined by Goldberger (1984).

[†]Logically, if there is no *ceteris paribus* pay gap on average, and white stars receive a premium, then blacks at the bottom should earn more than whites. Hamilton (1997) finds point estimates in this direction, but they are not statistically significant.

1999). However, by the 1990s, customer preferences for white players were less evident. Dey (1997), for example, found that all else equal, white players added a statistically insignificant 60 fans apiece per season during the 1987–93 period. This evidence is consistent with the decline in the NBA's overall unexplained white salary premium from the 1980s to the 1990s, although Hamilton's (1997) results suggest that it is possible that white stars add fans even if the average white player does not.

If NBA fans do have preferences for white players, having white benchwarmers may be a cheap way for teams to satisfy such demands. While early research found that white benchwarmers had longer careers than black benchwarmers (Johnson and Marple, 1973), more recent work does not find that benchwarmers are disproportionately white (Scott, Long, and Somppi, 1985).

In contrast to these findings in basketball, similar regression analyses of salaries in baseball and football have not found much evidence of racial salary discrimination against minorities. For example, in baseball, these kinds of analyses never seem to find a significantly positive salary premium for white players. Among nonpitchers, some studies actually have found significantly negative effects of being white in the late 1970s and 1980s (Christiano, 1986, 1988; Irani, 1996); however, my own reanalysis of the same data used in one of these studies found that these differentials disappeared when a longer list of productivity variables was added (Kahn, 1993). In football in 1989, Kahn (1992) found only very small salary premia (discrimination coefficients) in favor of whites of only 1–4 percent, and these differences were usually not statistically significant. However, nonwhite NFL players earned more in areas with a larger relative nonwhite population than nonwhites elsewhere, and whites earned more in more white metropolitan areas than whites elsewhere. These findings suggest the influence of customers, but they did not add up to large overall racial salary differences in the NFL.[††]

Although little evidence exists of a discriminatory salary premium in baseball or football, there is evidence of other forms of discrimination in sports, some of it among customers, and also in hiring, retention, and assignment of players. For example, a larger number of white players seem to lead to added baseball fans, over the time period from the mid-1950s through the 1980s (Hanssen, 1998; Irani, 1996). Moreover, baseball cards for white players sold at

a significantly higher price than those of comparable black players in 1989 (Nardinelli and Simon, 1990).

On hiring, there is indirect evidence that black players went later in the NFL draft than whites of equal playing ability during the 1986–91 period (Conlin and Emerson, 1998). However, in basketball, a study found only small, insignificant racial differences in draft order among NBA players on rosters in 1985, conditional on college performance—and these differences favored black players (Kahn and Sherer, 1988). All studies of drafts suffer somewhat from the fact that there is no systematic information available on those not drafted and not on rosters.

On player retention, Jiobu (1988) found that from 1971 to 1985, black players in Major League Baseball had a significantly higher exit rate than whites, other things equal, and Hoang and Rascher (1999) obtained a similar result for the NBA for 1980–91. A reasonable interpretation of these differences in exit rates is that they reflect team decisions not to offer players a new contract. . . .

References

Bodvarsson, Orn and Raymond T. Brastow. 1998. "Do Employers Pay for Consistent Performance?: Evidence from the NBA." *Economic Inquiry.* 36:1, pp. 145–60.

Brown, Eleanor, Richard Spiro, and Diane Keenan. 1991. "Wage and Nonwage Discrimination in Professional Basketball: Do Fans Affect It?" *American Journal of Economics and Sociology.* 50:3, pp. 333–45.

Burdekin, Richard C. K. and Todd L. Idson. 1991. "Customer Preferences, Attendance and the Racial Structure of Professional Basketball Teams." *Applied Economics.* 23:1, Part B, pp. 179–86.

Christiano, Kevin J. 1986. "Salary Discrimination in Major League Baseball: The Effect of Race." *Sociology of Sport Journal.* 3:2, pp. 144–53.

Christiano, Kevin J. 1988. "Salaries and Race in Professional Baseball: Discrimination 10 Years Later." *Sociology of Sport Journal.* 5:2, pp. 136–49.

Conlin, Mike and Patrick M. Emerson. 1998. "Racial Discrimination and Organizational Form: A Study of the National Football League." Working Paper, Cornell University.

Dey, Matthew S. 1997. "Racial Differences in National Basketball Association Players' Salaries: Another Look." *The American Economist.* 41:2, pp. 84–90.

Goldberger, Arthur S. 1984. "Reverse Regression and Salary Discrimination." *Journal of Human Resources.* 19:3, pp. 293–318.

Hamilton, Barton Hughes. 1997. "Racial Discrimination and Professional Basketball Salaries in the 1990s." *Applied Economics.* 29:3, pp. 287–96.

Hanssen, Andrew. 1998. "The Cost of Discrimination: A Study of Major League Baseball." *Southern Economic Journal.* 64:3, pp. 603–27.

Hoang, Ha and Dan Rascher. 1999. "The NBA, Exit Discrimination, and Career Earnings." *Industrial Relations.* 38:1, pp. 69–91.

Irani, Daraius. 1996. "Estimating Customer Discrimination in Baseball Using Panel Data," in *Baseball Economics: Current Research.* John Fizel, Elizabeth Gustafson, and Lawrence Hadley, eds. Westport, CT: Praeger, pp. 47–61.

Jiobu, Robert M. 1988. "Racial Inequality in a Public Arena: The Case of Professional Baseball." *Social Forces.* 67:2, pp. 524–34.

Johnson, Norris R. and David P. Marple. 1973. "Racial Discrimination in Professional Basketball: An Empirical Test." *Sociological Focus.* 6:4, pp. 6–18.

Jones, J. C. H. and William D. Walsh. 1988. "Salary Determination in the National Hockey League: The Effects of Skills, Franchise Characteris-

---

[††]A lively literature has developed on the issue of discrimination against French Canadians in the National Hockey League. Some authors have found apparent salary discrimination against this group in Canadian cities outside Quebec province, a pattern consistent with the notion of customer discrimination (Jones and Walsh, 1988; Longley, 1995). Yet others have disputed this interpretation and the findings as well (Krashinsky and Krashinsky, 1997). There is also a debate over whether French Canadians face entry barriers into the NHL (Walsh, 1992; Lavoie, Grenier, and Coulombe, 1992).

tics, and Discrimination." *Industrial & Labor Relations Review.* 41:4, pp. 592–604.

Kahn, Lawrence M. 1992. "The Effects of Race on Professional Football Players' Compensation." *Industrial & Labor Relations Review.* 45:2, pp. 295–310.

Kahn, Lawrence M. 1993. "Free Agency, Long-term Contracts and Compensation in Major League Baseball; Estimates from Panel Data." *The Review of Economics and Statistics.* 75:1, pp. 157–64.

Kahn, Lawrence M. and Peter D. Sherer. 1988. "Racial Differences in Professional Basketball Players' Compensation." *Journal of Labor Economics.* 6:1, pp. 40–61.

Koch, James V. and C. Warren Vander Hill. 1988. "Is There Discrimination in the 'Black Man's Game'?" *Social Science Quarterly.* 69:1, pp. 83–94.

Krashinsky, Michael and Harry A. Krashinsky. 1997. "Do English Canadian Hockey Teams Discriminate Against French Canadian Players?" *Canadian Public Policy-Analyse de Politiques.* 23:2, pp. 212–6.

Lavoie, Marc, Gilles Grenier, and Serge Coulombe. 1992. "Performance Differentials in the National Hockey League: Discrimination Versus

Style-of-Play Thesis." *Canadian Public Policy-Analyse de Politiques.* 18:4, pp. 461–69.

Longley, Neil. 1995. "Salary Discrimination in the National Hockey League: The Effects of Team Location." *Canadian Public Policy-Analyse de Politiques.* 21:4, pp. 413–22.

Nardinelli, Clark and Curtis Simon. 1990. "Customer Racial Discrimination in the Market for Memorabilia: The Case of Baseball." *Quarterly Journal of Economics.* 105:3, pp. 575–95.

Scott, Jr., Frank A., James E. Long, and Ken Somppi. 1985. "Salary vs. Marginal Revenue Product Under Monopoly and Competition: The Case of Professional Basketball." *Atlantic Economic Journal.* September 13:3, pp. 50–59.

Wallace, Michael. 1988. "Labor Market Structure and Salary Determination Among Professional Basketball Players." *Work and Occupations.* 15:3, pp. 294–312.

Walsh, William D. 1992. "The Entry Problem of Francophones in the National Hockey League: A Systemic Interpretation." *Canadian Public Policy-Analyse de Politiques.* 18:4, pp. 443–60.

EUROPEAN FOOTBALL

THE EUROPEAN UNION AND FAN RACISM IN EUROPEAN SOCCER STADIUMS: THE TIME HAS COME FOR ACTION

Michael Ryan

I. INTRODUCTION

Unlike in America, where there has been a substantial decrease in the incidence of spectator racism at sporting events over the last thirty years, racially motivated incidents still occur frequently at European soccer matches.[1] The prevalence of racist abuse varies from match to match, but at times it can get quite brutal. In one famous episode, Spanish fans pelted Cameroonian player Samuel Eto'o with bottles as he prepared to take a corner kick, and made ape sounds at him every time he touched the ball.[2] After enduring this abuse for most of the game, Eto'o finally snapped and threatened to walk off the field in protest, despite the fact that there was still nearly fifteen minutes to play. Eventually, he was talked out of doing so by players from both teams,[3] but in interviews after the game, Ronaldinho, Eto'o's teammate and arguably the finest player in the world, revealed that had Eto'o left the field, he would have followed him.[4]

Unfortunately, the abuse of Eto'o was hardly an isolated event. In another incident, Spanish spectators threw bananas at Cameroonian goalkeeper Carlos Kameni.[5] At the same time, other fans used bullhorns to taunt Kameni for going to the press to complain about previous racist abuse he had endured.[6] What made this abuse particularly galling, however,

was that it did not come from opposing fans, but instead from supporters of Kameni's own team.[7]

The problems of spectator racism are hardly just a Spanish problem. The racist chants of Italian fans in Milan caused Ivorian defender Marc Zoro to break down in tears during the middle of a game.[8] Croatian fans have been known to form human swastikas in the stands.[9] Dutch fans have hung banners suggesting that African players should go "to a banana tree" instead of playing.[10] In short, fans from virtually every country in Europe have engaged in some type of racist or anti-Semitic abuse.[11] Despite the efforts of European soccer authorities, the problem has shown no signs of abating.[12]

Because of soccer's inability to eliminate spectator racism, the European Union (EU) has expressed an increased interest in enacting measures to combat such abuse. Traditionally, the EU has stayed out of sports-related issues and deferred to the judgment of the organizations that run European sports.[13] Since 1995, however, the EU has shown an increased willingness to challenge the rules and practices of sports organizations when they affect important Community principles,[14] such as the protection of human rights.[15] Therefore, it should be of little surprise that the EU is considering whether to take action to combat spectator racism in soccer.

As a practical matter, however, the EU's power is limited. Under the current treaty system, the EU has no direct authority over sport. Therefore, before it can act, the EU must identify a provision in one of its treaties that authorizes it to take the desired action. Article 13 EC of the Treaty of Amsterdam, however, authorizes the EU to take measures designed to eliminate racial discrimination;[16] therefore, Article 13 EC could be interpreted to permit the EU to enact measures to combat spectator racism. This Article argues that it is both necessary and proper to use Article 13 EC as a basis for EU action, and assesses the likely components of an EU anti-spectator racism instrument.

Part II of this Article provides a brief overview of the governing structure of European soccer, as well as the anti-racism measures adopted at each level. Part III examines the history of the EU's involvement in sports as a whole, and details that body's increased willingness to address problems in soccer, including spectator racism. Part IV details the components of Article 13 EC, which prohibits discrimination on the basis of race, as well the free movement and equal rights provisions that could potentially serve as the basis for any EU action on this topic. This part also assesses the likelihood that each provision will actually be used to produce spectator anti-racism legislation. Part V proposes that the EU enact legislation enabling the Member States to impose stiffer penalties for teams whose fans behave in a racist manner. This Article concludes with an assessment of the criticisms most likely to be leveled at the proposed EU instrument and argues that those criticisms are unwarranted.

. . . .

[*Ed. Note: Author's overview of the governing structure of European soccer and the ineffective efforts made to eliminate spectator racism at each level—UEFA, national association, league and club—is omitted.*]

III. THE EU'S INCREASING WILLINGNESS TO GOVERN SPORT AND SPECTATOR RACISM

Founded in the wake of World War II, Europe's oldest multinational political organization,[54] the Council of Europe, was founded primarily to prevent future acts of war on the continent.[55] In the past fifty years, however, the goals of Europe's multinational organizations have broadened considerably. As the events of the last decade indicate, the EU in particular has expressed an increased willingness to assert jurisdiction over sport even though no treaty provision expressly authorizes it to do so.

In 1995, the EU took its first major action with respect to sport in Bosman. In Bosman, an out-of-contract[56] Belgian soccer player challenged a rule that required his new team to pay a transfer fee to his old team on the grounds that the requirement for payment impeded his right of free movement.[57] In analyzing Bosman's claim, the European Court of Justice (ECJ) explained that the EU typically defers to the decisions of sports governing bodies in many areas where EU law might otherwise apply. The court further stated, however, that when sporting rules affect economic activity (such as those that deal with the ability of professionals to obtain future employment), then sport will be subject to scrutiny under Community law.[58] After applying

EU legal principles, the ECJ concluded that the rule that requires a new team to pay an original team for the rights to an out-of-contract player is "likely to restrict the freedom of movement of players who wish to pursue their activity in another Member State by preventing or deterring them from leaving" their current clubs.[59] Therefore, the rule was invalidated.[60]

Two years later, in 1997, the EU took another step toward asserting jurisdiction over sport, as it included its first official reference to sport in the Final Act to the Treaty of Amsterdam. The document falls well short of giving the EU general jurisdiction over sport, yet it notes that sport plays a significant role in European society, and called on the institutions of the EU to "listen to sports associations when important questions affecting sport are at issue."[61]

At that time, much as today, a major issue facing soccer was spectator racism. Therefore, especially given the proclamation from the Treaty of Amsterdam, it is unsurprising that the EU chose the same year to get involved with efforts to eliminate spectator racism in football. Specifically, the EU granted 20,000 to a grass-roots anti-racism group, which produced an anti-racism movie in which more than fifty professional players discussed the effect of spectator racism on the game.[62] The EU's funding for this matter was critical to its success. The extra funds allowed the group to feature a number of prominent players, which made the film more effective with young children.[63]

Two years later, the European Council, in a formal response to the inclusion of sport in the Treaty of Amsterdam, invited the Commission to prepare a report "with a view [toward] safeguarding current sports structures and maintaining the social function of sport within the Community."[64] The subsequent Commission report, entitled the Helsinki Report, made several important observations. First, while acknowledging that none of the EU's treaties specifically reference sport, the Commission stressed that many aspects of EU law still applied to sporting organizations.[65] The Commission also explained, however, that despite the EU's ability to reach some areas of sport under the existing treaty system, the Community did not have the authority to implement any large-scale sports intervention because of the lack of a treaty provision giving it direct jurisdiction over athletics.[66] Despite this limitation, the Commission went on to explain that the EU still had an important role to play in the administration of European sport, particularly when such intervention could be conducted in a manner consistent with the Community's core values.[67] In this vein, the Commission observed that existing EU programs could make use of sport in its efforts to combat racism since such action would promote "social democracy."[68]

After receiving the Helsinki Report, the European Council promulgated the Nice Declaration in 2000. The vast majority of the declaration merely reiterated the Commission's conclusions: that sports organizations and the individual Member States have primary control over sports, but that the Community should make an effort to preserve the critical social role of sport in Europe.[69] With respect to racism and xenophobia, however, the Council appeared reluctant to endorse the Community action endorsed by the Commission. Instead of agreeing that the EU should take action, the Council explained that sports federations (such as UEFA or the national associations) should take the lead in formulating measures to combat racism and xenophobia.[70] Despite this apparent step back, however, the Council left the door open for future EU action to address racism in soccer, as it explained that the EU should continue to examine its policies in order to ensure protection for the benefits of sport.[71]

In keeping with the Helsinki Report's focus on the social effects of sport, two years later the European Monitoring Center on Racism and Xenophobia (EUMC) released a report examining the extent to which fans used the Internet to make racist remarks about players. In the report, the EUMC found that approximately eleven percent of the team-related web sites they examined had at least some racist content, including several that had strong racist themes.[72] The EUMC concluded that this percentage was significant because it believed that the expression of online racism was likely to mirror the abuse expressed in stadiums.[73] In addition to its findings, the study also made a key observation. It noted that the countries with individual laws prohibiting online racism had been the most effective at eliminating racism on fan sites.[74] Therefore, the EUMC suggested that a resolution be passed at the European level that would require all countries to recognize the crime of spreading racist ideas through the internet.[75] Although not directly related to spectator racism, this suggestion was significant, given that it marked the first time an EU institution had suggested that the EU take specific action with respect to racist soccer fans.[76]

Soon after the EUMC's report, the Member States moved toward providing a firm basis for an EU spectator anti-racism action by including a provision in the 2004 Constitutional Treaty that would have given the EU competence over areas related to sport. Specifically, the Constitutional Treaty would have allowed the EU to "contribute to the promotion of European sporting issues" by "protecting the physical and moral integrity" of citizens through the use of European laws to establish incentives for Member State compliance.[77] Despite being signed by the heads of government in 2004, the Treaty is not effective because it has not been ratified by all of the Member States.[78] If ratified, however, this section will allow the EU to protect the educational and social values in sport by taking action to counter abuses in sport, especially those that cannot be adequately dealt with at a national level.[79]

Finally, in 2006, the EU took its first formal action with respect to spectator racism when the European Parliament issued a declaration strongly condemning fan racism in soccer.[80] Using the increasing number of racist incidents as an impetus for its action, the declaration noted that

Article 13 of the EC Treaty provides that one of the main objectives of the EU is to prevent discrimination based on racial or ethnic origin, and that according to ECJ jurisprudence, football players, like all other workers have a right to a racism-free work environment.[81] Therefore, Parliament used the declaration to call on UEFA to punish national associations and club teams whose fans continually engage in racist abuse.[82] In addition, the declaration expressed Parliament's support for a program that would allow referees to stop matches marred by racial abuse.[83] Unfortunately, the declaration had no authority to change existing law.[84] Nevertheless, Parliament's action is significant because it marks the first time that a major EU institution has specifically addressed the issue of spectator racism with a formal legal instrument.

Also in 2006, the ECJ continued its extension of free market law into the world of sports through its decision in Meca-Medina. In Meca-Medina, two suspended swimmers challenged their suspensions for the use of performance-enhancing drugs on the basis that the suspensions violated the free movement provisions embodied in Articles 39 and 49 EC.[85] Reaffirming its holding in Bosman, the ECJ explained that professional sports are generally required to comply with the provisions of EU law when sport involves economic activity.[86] The ECJ went on to refine this holding slightly. It noted that although most sports rules probably have some tangible economic effect, certain rules, such as the anti-doping rule in this case, were based predominantly on legitimate, non-economic grounds (such as ensuring the fairness of the game) and were therefore consistent with EU law.[87] This narrow exception articulated by the court is critical because it raises the possibility that if a player were to challenge the weak punishment rules currently in place for spectator racism as being an obstacle to the free movement of services, the proponents of the rule would have to justify the leniency of its punishments on legitimate, non-economic grounds. This is something that UEFA and the national associations may find very difficult to do given the robust economic health of soccer as a whole.

Yet again in 2006, the UK Presidency of the EU released its Independent European Sports Review, a report that was designed to look at the implementation of the Nice Declaration.[88] The report makes several critical observations. First, it recognizes that in certain areas, the discretion of sports organizers should be given extreme deference.[89] In particular, the report identifies the rules regulating the functioning of competitions, the integrity of sport and competitive balance as those that should generally be left to administrator discretion.[90] Despite this deference, however, the report suggests that there may be a role for the EU to play in the governance of sport, particularly since racism and violence have flared up in stadiums around Europe.[91] Therefore, the report suggests that the EU enact measures to harmonize the Member States' approach to hooliganism (and other issues related to fan violence).[92] Furthermore, the report explains that both

UEFA and the national associations should enact stricter rules designed to deter racist behavior, and that those parties should cooperate with the EU to ensure safety and security in football stadiums around Europe.[93]

Building off the momentum from this report, in 2007 the Commission made its first proposal to deal with sport-specific issues in its 2007 White Paper on Sport.[94] The White Paper deals with a wide range of sports issues. With respect to spectator racism, the Commission explains that the EU should look at the possibility of enacting new legal instruments to prevent misbehavior at sporting events, including spectator racism.[95] The Commission did not, however, propose a legal basis for such action.[96] In the White Paper, the Commission also suggests that existing educational programs regarding fan violence should be examined and that the EU should provide support for successful programs.[97] Much like Parliament's Directive, the White Paper creates no binding legal duties. It is nevertheless significant because the Commission uses white papers to make proposals for Community action.[98] Therefore, the White Paper suggests that the Community may be prepared to take formal action to eliminate spectator racism in soccer.

IV. POSSIBLE AVENUES FOR EU ACTION ON RACISM IN SOCCER

After the issuance of the White Paper on Sport, the EU appears poised to take action to curtail spectator racism at soccer matches. The EU, however, does not have general lawmaking authority; rather, it only has competence in areas where it has been granted jurisdiction by treaty.[99] Unfortunately, no EU treaty expressly provides the EU with jurisdiction over sport. However, if the EU could locate a generally-applicable section in one of its treaties that could be interpreted as applying to sport, it would be able to take action to eliminate spectator racism. Four major legal provisions could potentially give the EU jurisdiction over this matter: Article 39 EC (ensuring the free movement of workers), Article 13 EC (general anti-discrimination), the European Convention on Human Rights and the Charter of Fundamental Rights.[100] Each of these four potential bases will be analyzed.

A. Free Movement of Workers

The free movement of workers is "one of the fundamental freedoms guaranteed by Community law."[101] The pertinent part of the treaty that ensures the freedom of movement for workers mandates "the abolition of any discrimination based on nationality between workers of the Member States as regards employment, remuneration and other conditions of work and employment."[102] Free movement rights allow workers to accept offers of employment actually made, to move freely within the Community for the purpose of accepting work, and to stay in another Member State in

accordance with provisions governing the employment of nationals.[103] This right is not without exception. Free movement can be limited due to public policy, public security or health grounds, and does not apply to employment in the public service.[104]

It might seem like a stretch to link an anti-racism plan to a treaty provision aimed at ensuring free movement for workers, yet such action may be rationalized by explaining that the failure of teams and national associations to eliminate overt acts of spectator racism may make minority players less likely to accept employment in a different country, thereby acting as an obstacle to the exercise of their free movement rights.[105] In fact, this proposition appears to be supported by accounts from former players, some of whom have explained that spectator racism played a prominent role in their decision to turn down offers from foreign teams.[106] Therefore, there appears to be at least some modicum of objective evidence that the EU could use to describe fan racism as an obstacle to free movement.

The protection offered by Article 39 of the EC Treaty is appealing as a basis for EU action for a number of reasons. First, as the plain text of Article 39 indicates, protection is provided for "workers;" the ECJ has interpreted this term broadly, in that both part-time and full-time workers are considered protected.[107] Therefore, professional soccer players will surely be considered "workers" under the terms of the article. Second, the article has been interpreted as prohibiting both direct and indirect discrimination, although indirect discrimination can be justified if there is an objective reason for doing so.[108] Given the practical ramifications of a team or league openly supporting racism, it seems unlikely that a player will ever be able to prove that crowd racism is an act of direct discrimination. By prohibiting indirect discrimination as well, however, it is conceivable that a league or team's inaction could be interpreted as providing implicit support for such behavior and therefore, constitute a violation of the article. Lastly, Article 39 EC may be particularly appealing as a platform for anti-racism action because the treaty explicitly provides that it can serve as the basis for Community action. Specifically, Article 40 EC explains that the Council can issue directives or make regulations in order to ensure the free movement of workers in the Community.[109] Historically, the Council has used this power to promulgate secondary legislation, such as Directive 68/360.[110] Therefore, at least initially, Article 39 EC may be an excellent provision upon which to base an EU spectator racism action.

Despite this optimism, there would be three major problems if the EU were to rely on Article 39 EC to give itself a legal basis to act. First, the right of free movement for workers does not apply to persons who are not nationals of an EU Member State.[111] Whether someone is considered a national of a particular state is determined based on the law of that country.[112] Although many European countries have given the term "national" a broad reading by allowing descendants of nationals to be considered nationals themselves,[113] these provisions would not appear to aid many of the targets of racial abuse: players of African descent.[114] Therefore, if African players want to gain the protection of EU law, they would be required to acquire dual citizenship in an EU country through the naturalization process. Attaining dual citizenship is easier said than done. Many countries require immigrants to reside in their "new" country for five to ten years before they can obtain citizenship rights.[115] The length of the residency requirement, particularly given the short length of most professional athletes' careers, may prove to be a significant obstacle to providing many minority players any type of protection.

Moreover, the plain language of the article only prohibits discrimination on the basis of nationality.[116] It makes no mention of discrimination based on race.[117] Although the difference between nationality and race is often minimal (at least in the eyes of the public), as a legal matter, it would be difficult for a black French player, for example, to argue that the abuse he receives is based on his nationality rather than his race. While it may be within the spirit of this provision to prevent discrimination based on racism, the fact remains that the plain text does not allow such an expansive interpretation.

Despite the fact that there is evidence to suggest that spectator racism affects some players' willingness to play in a new country, the ECJ decision in Germany v. Parliament and Council (Tobacco Directive) seriously limits the EU's ability to use free movement provisions for such broad purposes.[118] In Tobacco Directive, the EU enacted a directive prohibiting various types of advertising for tobacco products.[119] The Directive was based on a treaty provision responsible for protecting the internal market.[120] However, in the case, the ECJ annulled the Directive, which had been enacted pursuant to Article 95 EC.[121] The ECJ found that the directive's primary purpose was to improve public health rather than to protect the internal market.[122] In other words, under the ECJ's case law, an instrument enacted pursuant to Article 95 EC (and perhaps any other market-based provision of the treaty by way of analogy) must actually improve the conditions for the establishment of the internal market, rather than serving as a basis for tangentially-related policy concerns.[123]

Arguably, any EU action with respect to spectator racism could be distinguished from the EU action taken in the Tobacco Directive case in two ways. First, unlike in the directive in that case, which was based on Article 95 EC, this proposed action could be based on Article 39 EC. This difference could be significant because Article 39 explicitly prohibits discrimination, and therefore has at least some reference to social concerns, while Article 95 EC appears focused solely on economic matters.[124] In other words, due to this difference, the ECJ could conceivably require a higher quantum of proof of economic effect before allowing a provision under Article 95 EC than it would in review of

an instrument promulgated under Article 39 EC. This in turn might make it easier for the EU to pass an anti-racism action under Article 39 EC. As a practical matter, however, the Tobacco Directive case has been heralded by commentators as signaling the EU's intent to finally take "jurisdictional boundaries seriously."[125] If this is the case, the EU may have a very difficult time basing this social policy on an economic treaty provision.

Alternatively, unlike in Tobacco Directive, where the directive prohibited certain types of advertising and therefore did not actually facilitate trade in tobacco products, any anti-racism action will facilitate rather than prevent the free movement of services by eliminating discriminatory treatment. Despite this distinction, however, the case appears to limit the reach of the EU's free movement provisions to cases in which there is an "appreciable" impact on competition.[126] While there is some anecdotal evidence to suggest that fan racism has had an impact on some individual players' decision to play or not play in a particular country, it is likely that the EU would have to provide more evidence from players who made similar decisions in order to show the requisite level of impact on the free market. In other words, the EU would simply need to provide more information on the effects of fan racism before the ECJ would be likely to uphold the action. As it stands right now, however, such legislation would almost certainly be struck down. Therefore, given these problems, the EU may be better off relying on an alternative basis for taking action with respect to spectator racism.

B. Anti-Discrimination Provisions

Like the free movement provision detailed above, treaty provisions prohibiting discrimination could also serve as the basis for an EU spectator anti-racism instrument. In pertinent part, Article 13 EC provides that the Council can take "appropriate action" to eliminate racial discrimination.[127] The plain text of the article does not specify whether there are any limits to the types of discrimination that the EU may address, other than to say such action must be "within the limits of the powers" given to the Community.[128] A procedural limitation to such action, however, is that measures taken pursuant to Article 13 EC must be agreed upon unanimously.[129] Despite this limitation, Article 13 EC has already served as the basis for one important European Council anti-discrimination measure: Directive 2000/43/EC (Race Directive). Therefore, Article 13 EC may be a particularly promising provision upon which to base an anti-discrimination measure related to spectator racism.

The Race Directive, which was the first piece of binding Community legislation designed to eliminate racial discrimination,[130] was enacted to ensure that EU Member States respect the principle of equal treatment.[131] This principle requires Member States to eliminate discrimination based on racial or ethnic origin,[132] including discrimination related to employment.[133] Specifically, the directive prohibits three types of discrimination: direct discrimination, indirect discrimination, and harassment.[134] Direct discrimination occurs when a person is treated less favorably than another because of racial or ethnic origin.[135] In contrast, indirect discrimination occurs when an apparently neutral provision puts a person of a particular racial or ethnic origin at a disadvantage that cannot be "objectively justified by a legitimate aim."[136] Lastly, harassment is considered discriminatory when it is racially motivated and is intended to or has the effect of "violating the dignity of a person" or creates "an intimidating, hostile, degrading, humiliating or offensive environment."[137] Member States, however, have the option of applying their own definition of harassment if they see fit.[138] Pursuant to this directive, Member States were required to take measures to eliminate racial discrimination by July 2003.[139]

Given the breadth of the Race Directive, the basis for such action, Article 13 EC, appears to be an excellent candidate for the EU to utilize to take action to eliminate spectator racism. In fact, if the Race Directive were broadly interpreted, spectator racist acts would almost certainly already constitute unlawful discrimination under the Race Directive. Therefore, because the Race Directive has been applied by the ECJ in its jurisprudence, it seems reasonable to conclude that if the EU were to adopt a similar anti-discrimination provision, it would have the competence to do so under Article 13 EC.

C. European Convention on Human Rights

Alternatively, the European Convention on Human Rights (ECHR) could theoretically serve as the basis for EU action. The ECHR was originally signed in 1950 under the authority of the Council of Europe.[140] Designed to provide international protection for human rights, the Convention has since been ratified by 47 European countries, including all of the Member States of the EU.[141] In pertinent part, Article 14 of the ECHR states that the rights and freedoms set forth in the Convention cannot be abridged based on any type of discrimination, including racial discrimination.[142]

Despite the presence of this promising language, the ECHR's ability to serve as a basis for a Community anti-racism instrument is limited for three reasons. First, the Convention does not recognize a right to employment.[143] Therefore, acts of discrimination that affect a person's ability to work do not appear to be covered by the ECHR. Second, although all of the countries comprising the EU have signed the ECHR, the EU itself has not signed or ratified the document.[144] Furthermore, the ECJ has held that the EU does not have competence to accede to the Convention.[145] This is significant because if the EU is not able to accede to the ECHR, it does not have the ability to rely on its provisions as a basis for enacting laws pertaining to human rights.[146] Finally, even if the EU were able to accede to the ECHR, the ECHR by itself may not be capable of serving as a platform for positive action in the absence of a European Court of Human Rights (CHR) decision requiring it to do

so.[147] Given the fact that the CHR only hears complaints related to the ECHR,[148] and that the ECHR does not cover the right to work,[149] the chances of the CHR handing down a decision protecting the right to work seem highly unlikely. Therefore, if the ECHR can only serve as the basis for positive action following a case in the CHR, the ECHR's utility with respect to this problem is nearly non-existent.

Although the ECHR cannot serve as the basis for Community action, it may still have persuasive value. While the EU cannot accede to the ECHR, the Treaty of Amsterdam calls for Member States to respect fundamental rights as laid out in the ECHR.[150] Therefore, while an anti-racism provision could not be based on the ECHR, the ECHR is nevertheless indicative of the Community's willingness to take the action necessary to protect human rights, and could potentially be used to persuade the opponents of any anti-racism action that such action would be consistent with the ideas behind the EU.

D. Charter of Fundamental Rights

Building off the momentum from the 50th anniversary of the enactment of the ECHR, the EU revisited its treatment of fundamental rights when a number of individual countries signed the Charter of Fundamental Rights (ECFR) in December 2000.[151] The ECFR differs from the ECHR in two significant ways. First, unlike the ECHR, which was adopted by the Council of Europe, the ECFR was promulgated by the EU, which has fewer members than the Council of Europe.[152] Second, the ECFR constitutes a significant expansion in human rights protection over the ECHR, in that the ECFR provides greater protection for the civil, economic, political and social rights of EU residents.[153]

The ECFR explicitly prohibits all racial discrimination.[154] And because the ECFR was incorporated into the draft constitution, which has since been signed by all of the heads of the Member States,[155] it could theoretically provide the basis of an EU spectator anti-racism provision. Until the provisions incorporated in the Constitutional Treaty are deemed legally effective via ratification by each of the Member States, however, the ECFR, like the ECHR, can only be used in a persuasive, rather than substantive manner.[156]

V. THESIS: WHAT EU ACTION SHOULD LOOK LIKE?

Absent a limiting provision in the treaty article providing the basis for the action, the EU can produce a wide range of secondary legislation to effectuate its goals. There are two major types of secondary legislation: regulations and directives. Regulations are generally applicable, and are binding in their entirety on all Member States.[157] In contrast, directives set goals for the Member States to which they are addressed, but leave the exact method for achieving those goals to the discretion of the Member States themselves.[158] Therefore, while regulations are immediately grafted into each individual country's law, directives allow each individual nation to select the best way to achieve a goal for itself. Because soccer's organizing bodies have failed to eliminate the problem of fan racism despite "trying" to do so for a number of years, the ideal way to handle this issue would be for the EU to pass a regulation mandating stiff penalties for spectator racism. The requirement of unanimous agreement[159] for measures based on Article 13 EC, however, renders this possibility extremely remote, since many countries like to retain as much control as possible over the exact measures used to implement Community goals.[160] Therefore, any EU action taken pursuant to this article will likely take the form of a directive.

The Race Directive is a major EU anti-racism provision based on Article 13 EC. In fact, the Race Directive, if broadly read, could be interpreted as already prohibiting spectator racism. As a practical matter, however, the Race Directive has had no effect on the expression of such attitudes at soccer stadiums across Europe since its enactment in 2000. This suggests that the Race Directive has been unable to address this problem, and that some type of additional measure - one that is focused specifically on spectator racism - is required to effectively police spectator racism.

Because the validity of its provisions have never been challenged in the ECJ,[161] it would seem reasonable to assume that an EU directive on spectator racism, although different, could look very much like the Race Directive and be legally acceptable. In fact, it might even be possible to amend the Race Directive to reach the problems of spectator racism. As a practical matter, however, the EU should probably promulgate a separate directive as opposed to amending the Race Directive. This is the case because dealing with spectator racism seems to require more intrusive intervention than was necessary to deal with racism generally under the Race Directive. For example, reports have suggested that the Race Directive has been very effective despite the fact that "harassment" can be defined in accordance with the law of an individual Member State;[162] however, to reach spectator behavior and to make the clubs liable for such behavior, the definition of harassment would have to be broadened considerably to ensure spectator behavior and club liability for such behavior come within the purview of the directive's prohibition. In other words, amending the Race Directive to reflect the broader definition of harassment that would be required to stymie spectator racism is simply unnecessary for the Race Directive to be effective. Therefore, because the principle of proportionality requires that the EU take action only when it is absolutely necessary, a separate directive, which broadens the definition of harassment only with respect to fan racism, may be more desirable than an amendment that affects provisions related to racism generally.[163]

The Race Directive has been effective despite the fact that it does not establish the maximum penalties for violation of the directive, instead choosing to leave all questions regarding penalties to the discretion of the Member States. Again, the Race Directive appears to have been successful despite its use of a hands-off approach with respect to penalties; for soccer, however, one of the major problems with the current enforcement scheme is that the penalties available to the national associations are simply not severe enough to encourage clubs to root out racist behavior amongst their fans. Therefore, while setting higher maximum penalties appears necessary in soccer, similar amendments to the Race Directive, at least thus far, appear unnecessary. In other words, the amendments that would be required to allow the Race Directive to effectively police spectator behavior would broaden the directive's reach well beyond what is necessary for the provision to reach its general goals, and again may make the Race Directive a poor candidate for amendment.

Although amending the Race Directive would probably be a poor idea, many of the provisions of a new directive would likely mirror some aspects of the Race Directive. For example, the proposed directive would also likely begin with a purpose statement. In short, the proposed directive's purpose statement would explain that its purpose is to lay a framework for combating racism in soccer as expressed by spectators before, during and after matches, with a view toward effectuating the principle of equal treatment. Then, the Council could explain that the principle of equal treatment requires the elimination of all acts of racism or discrimination in soccer stadiums.

In addition, the proposed directive, like the Race Directive, should carefully define the scope of its authority. In the proposed directive, the EU should broadly construe the substantive reach of the directive by applying it to all spectators, teams and national associations playing or organizing professional soccer within the EU, which is the widest scope possible. Unfortunately, limiting the scope in this way will prevent the EU from reaching much of the most virulent racism taking place in Eastern Europe, as many of the countries with the most offensive fans are not yet Member States and are therefore not subject to EU law.[164] Since many of those countries have expressed interest in joining the EU,[165] however, the fact that the EU has taken such action may encourage those countries to voluntarily comply.[166]

Furthermore, given the complicated nature of this problem, the Member States should be given up to three years to adopt the provisions necessary to comply with the proposed directive, just as they were when the Race Directive's prohibition on discrimination was enacted. Obviously, if an individual country wanted to comply more quickly, it would have the option to do so; but as many commentators have noted, spectator racism is a problem caused by a number of factors.[167] Therefore, the Member States, in conjunction with UEFA, the national associations and the clubs, will likely need a period of time during which they can try any number of tactics to eliminate this problem without having to fear incurring EU sanctions. Therefore, it may be wise to provide a short grace period, in which the Member States can determine which anti-racism measures work best, and allow them to implement those measures before compliance with the directive is required.

Although any Council action would likely be similar to the Race Directive in a number of ways, the proposed directive should also differ from the Race Directive in order to target its effects to the problem of spectator racism. For example, the new directive should adopt a broader definition of the term "harassment" and make the revised definition a floor under which no Member State can go below. In the Race Directive, "harassment" is defined as conduct that violates the dignity of a person or creates a hostile, degrading or offensive environment.[168] This definition appears broad enough to encompass acts of spectator racism. The last sentence of the definition provides, however, that Member States may use their own definition in lieu of the EU standard. This raises the possibility that a state could adopt a more narrow definition, and therefore eviscerate the protection intended by the directive.[169] In order to prevent Member States from adopting a lower standard, the new directive should adopt most of the Race Directive's definition of harassment. It should remove the exception that allows the term to be defined in accordance with the law of the Member States.

Additionally, the Council should add a provision that explains that the failure of a club to eliminate spectator racism is considered harassment by the club, and therefore constitutes unlawful discrimination and subjects the club to punishment. This clarification is necessary because it ensures that clubs will be held responsible for the failure of their fans to act in an appropriate manner. As a matter of policy, attributing the racist acts of a team's fans to the team itself is reasonable because UEFA has traditionally held teams accountable for their fans' racist behavior. Furthermore, holding a team accountable is an appropriate measure because it will encourage the clubs, who make a great deal of money selling tickets to fans, to behave more responsibly when determining who to sell to.

Lastly, the proposed directive should permit the Member States to impose stiff criminal penalties on teams that fail to comply with the directive.[170] As explained above, the current system, in which the national associations and UEFA have been left with the authority to impose penalties, has led to punishments that are laughable at best. Therefore, the proposed directive should suggest that Member States use their general powers of governance to themselves punish teams and national associations that do not eliminate spectator racism.

Under the current system, the penalties that teams currently incur for racist fan behavior have been imposed by the national associations or UEFA,[171] so the possibility of governmental sanctions would certainly be a significant change. There is no mechanism, however, to make an EU directive require an organization such as UEFA to adopt higher maximum penalties because directives are addressed to the Member States.[172] Given that the Member States are generally required to transpose its obligations into national law, however, it is only reasonable to allow the same national governments to impose penalties on teams and fans that behave inappropriately.

While it might seem counter-intuitive to establish higher maximums rather than a higher minimum penalty, doing so will finally allow more significant fines to be imposed.[173] Interestingly, there is no section in the Race Directive that enumerates the maximum penalties available for violation. There is, however, a precedent for such action in the anti-racism area. The EU recently enacted a separate measure that enumerates the maximum allowable penalty for people who intentionally incite others to commit racial violence.[174] This suggests that the EU could properly take similar action with respect to the penalties for spectator racism. Therefore, like the EU's recent action to prevent the incitement of racial incidents, I would introduce a penalty system which would provide a range of maximum penalties for teams whose fans behave in a racist manner.

Furthermore, with respect to the exact contents of a discipline system, the EU should propose a progressive system. In other words, the maximum penalty that can be imposed for a violation of the directive should increase with each successive violation, with additional increases possible depending on the severity of the incident. For a first offense, Member States should be able to individually ban offending fans for up to five years, fine the offending club up to the equivalent of five games' gate receipts, and require stadium closure for up to three games; for each successive offense, another decade can be added to the fan's ban, and another game's gate receipts or ground closure can be assessed to the team. Looking at each component individually, a ban is an effective tool because it allows the removal of an offending fan from soccer stadiums for an extended period of time, whereby he or she will no longer be capable of inciting spectator racism inside the stadium.[175] Also, by increasing the amount that clubs can be fined, many teams will now have the financial motivation that may be required for them to root out racist fans. This is especially appropriate because one of each team's primary sources of income comes from ticket sales. In assessing these fines, however, it is important to recognize that different teams have different size fan bases and therefore, different abilities to pay; in other words, rather than fining teams in absolute monetary figures, the amount of a team's fine should be based on the average per game gate receipts of the offending team. Similarly, by allowing the closure of an offending team's stadium, the directive will provide yet another powerful incentive for teams to comply. This seems appropriate in an era where some teams make more than $5 million every time that their stadium opens for a game.[176] Thus, teams will have an incredible financial incentive, in addition to paying fines, to comply with the anti-discrimination requirement.

VI. POTENTIAL OBJECTIONS TO THIS PLAN

Although an EU anti-spectator racism directive would appear to have a sound legal foundation, critics of the directive could theoretically object for at least three major reasons. In short, critics could argue that the directive violates the principles of subsidiarity and proportionality, both of which are formal limits on EU action. Furthermore, UEFA and the national associations could argue that while the EU may technically have the legal authority to take this action, as a policy matter it should not because EU authorities have traditionally deferred to sports organizations on a number of matters. However, all three of these objections are unlikely to be persuasive.

A. Principle of Subsidiarity

In recognition of the fact that the EU is a body of limited legislative competence, Article 5 of the EC provides that the EU should take action only when doing so is consistent with the principle of subsidiarity.[177] The principle of subsidiarity requires that the Community take action only when the objectives of the proposed action cannot sufficiently be achieved by the Member States, and when the scale of the effects of the proposed action can be better achieved by Community action.[178] Therefore, one potential objection to the proposed directive is that such action would violate the principle of subsidiarity because effective measures could be taken at the national level.

Practical experience, however, explains that the Member States (as well as UEFA and the national associations) have not dealt with this problem adequately. Extensive accounts of the racial abuse inflicted upon minority players appear as far back as the 1970s.[179] Therefore, assuming that UEFA and the national associations have been paying attention to what happens at the games they organize, soccer's current governing structure has had knowledge of this problem for over thirty years, yet the problem persists. This suggests that the current scheme, in which national authorities are left with complete discretion to punish such behavior, is incapable of providing the protection of basic human dignity that the EU and its corresponding treaties require. In contrast, in areas where the EU has acted to reduce racial discrimination outside of sport, its efforts appear to have been quite effective.[180] Therefore, it appears reasonable to conclude that the EU may provide an effective means to combat spectator racism that the Member States are simply incapable of equaling.

Furthermore, the evidence in areas where the EU has acted suggests that its action in the area of racial discrimination have been quite effective. For example, the above-mentioned Racial Equality Directive required Member States to enact domestic legislation by the end of 2006.[181] In looking at the effects of Member State compliance, the study found that after the enactment of harmonizing measures, nearly every country experienced a significant increase in the number of racist crimes, which could suggest that countries are more willing to take action to combat such behavior.[182] Furthermore, the report suggested that those countries which had taken stronger measures to implement the EU's requirements, such as the provision for a special racial adjudication body, were far more likely to have effective sanctions against racism.[183] Therefore, this report suggests that action at the EU level may provide a useful way to combat racism that cannot be achieved by the Member States alone.

B. Principle of Proportionality

Protocol 30 of the Treaty of Amsterdam provides that Community measures should leave as much scope for national decision as possible, so long as it can leave discretion to the Member States while ensuring that the requirements of the Treaty are met.[184] In other words, when there is a choice between several appropriate measures recourse must be had to the least onerous, and the disadvantages caused must not be disproportionate to the aims pursued.[185] Therefore, a challenger to this proposed directive could argue that it does not meet the requirements for the principle of proportionality on three grounds: that the measure is not suitable to achieve a legitimate goal, that the measure is not necessary to achieve that goal, and that the measure has an excessive effect on other interests.[186]

With respect to the first complaint, eliminating crowd racism is a legitimate goal for the EU to undertake, as in recent years, it has made the protection of human rights one of its most fundamental goals.[187] In fact, it is difficult to imagine a goal that is more legitimate for the EU to undertake than to eliminate racism, given its history of human rights protection.[188]

Furthermore, as mentioned in the previous section, the proposed directive is absolutely necessary to prevent additional racist acts. In the absence of EU legislation, neither UEFA nor the national associations have taken effective steps toward eliminating fan racist behavior. Given the success of the EU's other efforts to stop racism, however, it appears likely that the EU may be capable of taking such action in an effective manner.

The proposed directive is consistent with the principle of proportionality because it does not have an excessive effect on the private interests of UEFA or the national associations. By adopting a directive as opposed to a regulation, the Member States will retain the ability to establish comprehensive anti-racism programs that best serve their own, individual needs. And although the Member States, at least in the eyes of the EU, will be responsible for implementing measures to eliminate fan racism, as a practical matter, since most countries have allowed their national associations to govern almost all other aspects of soccer, one would expect the national associations to work with the Member States to formulate their anti-racism plan. In other words, because the directive does not require the government to authorize a certain type of penalty in all situations, national associations and UEFA could still potentially have a say in the penalties that the Member States will choose to assess for racist behavior. Furthermore, nothing in the directive prohibits UEFA or the national associations from imposing fines of their own; therefore, their own discretion in this matter will not be limited at all. Finally, by giving Member States three years to determine which anti-racism measures will be most effective, both UEFA and the national associations will have a great deal of time in which to persuade the Member States to use its preferred methods to achieve the EU's goal. Therefore, although soccer's governing bodies will no longer have complete control over the game, they will still have a sufficient opportunity to protect their interests.

C. Other Objections from UEFA/ National Associations

In the fallout from Bosman, European soccer authorities loudly voiced their displeasure with the EU's willingness to interfere with soccer-related affairs. In fact, for more than one year after the Bosman decision, UEFA refused to amend its rules to comport with the ECJ's decision.[189] UEFA's reaction to the ECJ decision reflected a constant theme underlying its attitude toward the EU: that UEFA should have control over European football, and that the EU should leave it alone to do so.[190] Therefore, it would not be unreasonable to believe that UEFA would lobby against any EU action designed to limit its discretion in soccer-related matters.

In the decade since the Bosman decision, however, UEFA's stance toward the EU has softened considerably, particularly with regard to matters related to spectator racism. For example, in 2003, UEFA opened an office in Brussels in order to facilitate its ability to work with the EU on all matters related to soccer, including racism.[191] Furthermore, in 2005, when the European Parliament was considering whether to pass its resolution regarding racism in soccer, UEFA made a public statement indicating it intended to support the tougher penalties suggested in the declaration.[192] In 2007, Jonathan Hill, who serves as UEFA's delegate to the EU, publicly suggested that UEFA should work with the EU to eliminate spectator racism.[193] In other words, while UEFA often resists EU intervention in sport, it might actually be willing to accept EU intervention to help deal with this problem. Therefore, this directive could meet minimal resistance, or perhaps even garner support, from UEFA.

VII. CONCLUSION

Spectator racism, despite the continuing efforts of European soccer's governing bodies, remains a serious problem. Over the past few years, however, the EU has taken steps toward enacting legislation to combat this problem. With the publication of the 2007 White Paper on Sport, it actually seems poised to do so. Although this is not an area in which the EU has traditionally acted, its current jurisprudence on discrimination suggests that it has the power to adopt a measure that would require Member States to adopt measures designed to eliminate crowd racism. Furthermore, given that the EU has committed itself to protecting basic human rights, it would be necessary and appropriate for the EU to take action, particularly when Member States have not been able to adequately address this problem. Therefore, the EU should take steps to address spectator racism before it further tarnishes the sport and again make soccer enjoyable for all.

Notes

1. ESPN Sportscenter: Beautiful Game Turned Ugly (ESPN television broadcast June 4, 2006), available at http://www.youtube.com/watch?v=W-iRLmaZf4A [hereinafter Beautiful Game Turned Ugly]. But see Phoebe Weaver Williams, Performing in a Racially Hostile Environment, 6 Marq. Sports L.J. 287, 287 n.2 (1996) (detailing the prevalence of fan racism in America).

2. Sid Lowe, Eto'o on Verge of Walking Off After Racist Abuse at Zaragoza, Telegraph, Feb. 27, 2006, http://www.telegraph.co.uk/sport/main.jhtml?xml=/sport/2006/02/27/sfnrac27.xml.

3. Id.

4. Id.

5. Beautiful Game Turned Ugly, supra note 1.

6. Id.

7. See id. The abuse can hardly be blamed on the quality of Kameni's play; he was named the African Goalkeeper of the Year in 2006/07. See Jon Carter, African Nations Cup 2008, ESPN Soccernet, Jan. 14, 2008, http://soccernet.espn.go.com/columns/story?id=488562&root=global&&cc=5901.

8. Zoro Suffers More Racist Abuse, BBC Sport, Nov. 27, 2005, http://news.bbc.co.uk/sport2/hi/football/africa/4476412.stm.

9. Mark Irwin, Nasty Croats Form Swastika, The Sun, Oct. 10, 2006, http://www.thesun.co.uk/sol/homepage/sport/football/article66475.ece.

10. Racist Banner Mars Match, Football Against Racism in Europe (FARE), Feb. 17, 2005, http://www.farenet.org/default.asp?intPageID=7&intArticleID=463.

11. European Union Distressed by Pre-World Cup Racism, (National Public Radio broadcast, June 4, 2006), available at http://www.npr.org/templates/story/story.php?storyId=5450741.

12. See id.

13. See Stratis Camatsos, European Sports, The Transfer System and Competition Law: Will They Ever Find a Competitive Balance, 12 Sports Law. J. 155, 155 (2005) (explaining that in the past few years, "there has been increased judicial and legal analysis of [soccer] and its rules").

14. Ken Foster, European Law and Football: Who's in Charge?, 1 Soccer & Soc'y 39, 39–40 (2000).

15. Activities of the European Union: Human Rights, http://europa.eu/pol/rights/indexen.htm (last visited Oct. 11, 2008).

16. Treaty of Amsterdam Amending the Treaty on European Union, the Treaties Establishing the European Communities and Certain Related Acts, Oct. 2, 1997, 1997 O.J. (C 340) 1 [hereinafter Treaty of Amsterdam].

. . . .

54. See Sophie Lobey, The History, Role and Activities of the Council of Europe: Facts, Figures and Information Sources, http://www .nyulawglobal.org/globalex/Council of Europe.htm#A2 (last visited Oct. 13, 2008).

55. The History of the European Union: 1945–1959, http://europa.eu/ abc/history/1945-1959/index en.htm (last visited Oct. 13, 2008).

56. An out-of-contract player is one who no longer has a valid, enforceable contract with his or her team. In most American professional sports, these players would be free to sign with any team they wish; under the rule challenged in Bosman, however, a new team was required to pay a player's old team as compensation if the new team wanted to sign the player, despite the fact that the new team technically had no enforceable contractual rights to that player. See Football Industry Group, Fact-Sheet One: The Bosman Case, EU Law, and the Transfer System, http://www.liv.ac.uk/footballindustry/ bosman.html (last visited Oct. 13, 2008).

57. Case C-415/93, Union royale belge des societes de football association ASBL v. Bosman, 1995 E.C.R. I-04921.

58. Id.

59. Id.

60. Id.

61. Treaty of Amsterdam, supra note 16.

62. Jon Garland & Michael Rowe, Racism and Anti-Racism in Football 61 (2001).

63. Id.

64. Report from the Commission to the European Council: The Helsinki Report on Sport, at 3, COM (1999) 644 final (Dec. 10, 1999).

65. Id. at 6.

66. Id.

67. Id. at 5-6.

68. Id. at 5. Generally speaking, social democracy "is a political outlook that promotes welfare of all citizens and prevents wide disparities among citizens." Furthermore, "social democracy usually results in considerable control by government to address social inequalities." See Arthur R. Pinto, Globalization and the Study of Comparative Corporate Governance, 23 Wis. Int'l L.J. 477, 494 (2005).

69. European Council, The Nice Declaration, available in European Sport Review, supra note 17, at 141.

70. Id. at 142.

71. Id. at 144.

72. Carlo Balestri, Racism, Football and the Internet 6-7, available at http://fra.europa.eu/fra/material/pub/football/Football.pdf (last visited Oct. 10, 2008).

73. Id. at 9.

74. Id. at 7-8.

75. Id. at 10.

76. See id. at 4 (stating that the report is the first time even research has been done in the area).

77. Treaty Establishing a Constitution for Europe, art. 3-282, Oct. 29, 2004, 2004 O.J. (C 310) 1.

78. Jean-Claude Piris, The Constitution of Europe: A Legal Analysis 7-9 (noting that both France and the Netherlands have not ratified the Treaty, leaving it ineffective).

79. European Year of Education Through Sport: Mid-term Review as Sport Gets Its Place in the Constitution (June 22, 2004), http:// europa.eu/rapid/pressReleasesAction.do?reference=IP/04/774&form at=HTML&aged=0&languag e=EN&guiLanguage=en (last visited Oct. 11, 2008).

80. Declaration of the European Parliament on Tackling Racism in Football, Parliament Declaration P6 TA(2006)0080 (2006).

81. Id.

82. Id.

83. Id.

84. See Damian Chalmers et al., European Union Law 137 (2006) (explaining that declarations are generally considered "soft law," as they have "no legally binding force but which nevertheless may have practical effects").

85. Case C-519/04 P, Meca-Medina v. Comm'n, 2006 E.C.R. I-06991.

86. Id.

87. See id. (explaining that "purely sporting rules have never been excluded generally by the Court of Justice from the scope of the provisions of the Treaty." Id. at *14. And, that "the provisions of Community law concerning freedom of movement for persons and freedom to provide services do not preclude rules or practices justified on non-economic grounds which relate to the particular nature and context of certain sporting events"). Later in the opinion, the ECJ reiterated that "the mere fact that a rule is purely sporting in nature does not have the effect of removing from the scope of the Treaty the person engaging in the activity governed by that rule or the body which has laid it down." Id.

88. European Sport Review, supra note 17, at 21.

89. Id. at 31.

90. Id. at 32-33, 53.

91. Id. at 147.

92. Id. at 129, 132.

93. European Sport Review, supra note 17, at 136.

94. Commission White Paper on Sport, at 2, COM (2007) 391 final (July 11, 2007).

95. Id. at 8.

96. Id.

97. Id. at 8-9.

98. Europa Glossary White Paper, http://europa.eu/scadplus/glossary/ white paper en.htm (last visited Oct. 11, 2008).

99. Treaty Establishing the European Community art. 5, Nov. 10, 1997, 1997 O.J. (C 340) 3 [hereinafter EC Treaty].

100. EC Treaty arts. 39, 13; Convention for the Protection of Human Rights and Fundamental Freedoms, opened for signature, Nov. 4, 1950, Europ. T.S. No. 005 [hereinafter ECHR]; Charter of Fundamental Rights of the European Union, Dec. 18, 2000, 2000 O.J. (C 364) 1. If Article 95 EC were to be given an extremely broad interpretation, perhaps it too could serve as the basis for EU action in this area. In pertinent part, Article 95 EC permits "[t]he Council . . . [to] adopt the measures for the approximation of the provisions laid down by law, regulation or administrative action in Member States which have as their object the establishment and functioning of the internal market." EC Treaty art. 95(1). Therefore, at least initially, it appears that if spectator racism can be proven to have an effect on the internal market, Article 95 EC could potentially serve as the basis for EU action. However, the other provisions of the article, as well as its judicial interpretation likely preclude such an expansive reading of the treaty. For example, the next section of Article 95 EC, explicitly states that the previous section does "not apply . . .

to [provisions related to] the free movement of persons nor to those relating to the rights and interests of employed persons." EC Treaty art. 95(2). However, the provisions relating to the free movement of workers are probably one of the most likely ways to produce EU action in this area. See EC Treaty art. 39. Furthermore, the ECJ has explained that measures based on Article 95(1) must genuinely have the object of eliminating "appreciable" distortions in competition. See Case C-376/98, Germany v. Parliament and Council, 2000 E.C.R. I-8419 [hereinafter Tobacco Directive]. In other words, the EU cannot allow other policies to "piggy-back" on to Article 95 by claiming the instrument is designed to address a miniscule distortion in competition. Chalmers et al., supra note 84, at 473. Given this interpretation of Article 95 EC, under which the ECJ was unwilling to allow the EU to take measures to deter the advertising of tobacco products (which is exactly the type of social policy, like an anti-racism policy, which would seem likely to garner widespread support), the likelihood of Article 95 EC providing a sound legal basis for EU anti-racism action seems improbable at best. See id. (noting that the ECJ was "unwilling to allow [Article 95] to be used . . . as a basis for a full-blown anti-tobacco policy"). Therefore, this Article does not include Article 95 EC within the foregoing discussion.

101. European Commission, Free Movement of Workers and the Principle of Equal Treatment, http://ec.europa.eu/employment social/free movement/index/en.htm (last visited Oct. 11, 2008).

102. EC Treaty art. 39(2).

103. EC Treaty art. 39(3).

104. EC Treaty art. 39(3)-(4).

105. Unfortunately, a recent search of the ECJ web site did not locate any cases in which "indirect discrimination" was interpreted to include actions by third parties as opposed to employers. One recent case, however, explained that Article 39 "prohibits not only overt discrimination by reason of nationality but also all covert forms of discrimination which, by the application of other distinguishing criteria, lead in fact to the same result." See Case C-237/94, O'Flynn v. Ajudication Officer, 1996 E.C.R. I-2617. The failure of teams and national associations to effectively eliminate fan racism, therefore, certainly seems like it could be interpreted to be the type of "covert" discrimination that constitutes discriminatory treatment in violation of Article 39.

106. See Richie Moran, Racism in Football: A Victim's Perspective, in The Future of Football: Challenges for the Twenty-First Century 190, 190 (Jon Garland et al. eds., 2000) (detailing the decision of British player Richie Moran's decision to quit soccer because of racism); see also University of Leicester Center for the Sociology of Sport, Fact Sheet 6: Racism and Football (June 2002), http://www.le.ac.uk/so/css/resources/factsheets/fs6.html (last visited Oct. 12, 2008) (detailing the decision of British player Dalian Atkinson's decision to leave his prominent Spanish team after being subjected to racist abuse).

107. EC Treaty art. 39; Case 53/81, D.M. Levin v. Staatssecretaris van Justitie, 1982 E.C.R. 01035.

108. Freidl Weiss & Frank Wooldridge, Free Movement of Persons within the European Community 43 (Kluwer Law International 2002).

109. EC Treaty art. 40.

110. Weiss & Wooldridge, supra note 108, at 41. In 2004, Directive 68/360, which had abolished "restrictions on movement and residence within the Community for workers or Member States and their families," was repealed when its contents were merged into Directive 2004/38/EC in substantially the same form. See General Provisions for Movement and Residence of Workers and Their

Families (Feb. 28, 2004), http://europa.eu/scadplus/leg/en/lvb/l23011a.htm (last visited Oct. 12, 2008).

111. Weiss & Wooldridge, supra note 108, at 41.

112. See Case C-369/90, Micheletti v. Delegacion del Gobierno en Cantabria, 1992 E.C.R. I-4239 (noting that "it is for each Member State, having due regard to Community law, to lay down the conditions for the acquisition and loss of nationality").

113. See Ralph H. Folsom, Principles of European Union Law 131 (2005).

114. A number of black European players have been subjected to racist abuse by spectators. See Beautiful Game Turned Ugly, supra note 1 (detailing French player Thierry Henry's battle with fan racism). African players, such as Samuel Eto'o and Marc Zoro, whose stories were detailed earlier in this Article, would not be protected by a change in EU law based on this provision. See Lowe, supra note 2; see Zoro Suffers More Racist Abuse, supra note 8.

115. Michael A. Becker, Managing Diversity in the European Union: Inclusive European Citizenship and Third Country Nationals, 7 Yale Hum. Rts. & Dev. L.J. 132, 152 n.109 (2004).

116. See EC Treaty art. 39(2).

117. See id.

118. See Tobacco Directive, supra note 100.

119. Id.; Council Directive 98/43/EC, arts. 1, 3, 1998 O.J. (L 213 9).

120. See Tobacco Directive, supra note 100.

121. Id.

122. Id.

123. See Chalmers et al., supra note 84, at 473.

124. See EC Treaty art. 95.

125. Mattias Kumm & Victor Ferreres Comella, The Primacy Clause of the Constitutional Treaty and the Future of Constitutional Conflict in the European Union, 3 Int'l J. Const. L. 473, 484 (2005).

126. See Tobacco Directive, supra note 100. The ECJ explained that such a requirement was necessary to prevent the "unlimited" extension of Community powers into areas in which the EU was not intended to have competence. See id.

127. EC Treaty art. 13(1).

128. Id.

129. Chalmers et al., supra note 84, at 875.

130. Mark Bell, Beyond European Labor Law?, Reflections on the EU Racial Equality Directive, 8 Eur. L.J. 384, 384 (2002).

131. Council Directive 2000/43, art. 1, 2000 O.J. (L 180) 22, 24 (EC).

132. Id. art. 2(1).

133. Council Directive 2000/78/, pmbl., 2000 O.J. (L 303) 16, 16 (EC). This directive, which prohibits employment discrimination, does not list race as a prohibited ground for discrimination; however, this omission is explained by the fact that the Council considers racial employment discrimination to already be prohibited by the Race Directive. Id.

134. Council Directive 2000/43/, art. 2, 2000 O.J. (L 180) 22, 24 (EC).

135. Id. art. 2(2)(a).

136. Id. art. 2(2)(b).

137. Id. art. 2(3).

138. Id. For example, the UK has arguably adopted a definition for harassment that is more narrow than what is set forth in the Race

Directive. See Lizzie Barnes, Constitutional and Conceptual Complexities in UK Implementation of the EU Harassment Provisions, 36 Indus. L.J. 446, 452 (2007).

139. Council Directive 2000/43/, art. 16, 2000 O.J. (L 180) 22, 26 (EC).

140. European Convention on Human Rights (ECHR), http://europa.eu/scadplus/glossary/eu human rights convention/en.htm (last visited Oct. 12, 2008).

141. Council of Europe, Convention for the Protection of Human Rights and Fundamental Freedoms, http://conventions.coe.int/Treaty/Commun/ChercheSig.asp?NT=005&CM=&DF=&CL =ENG (listing the 47 countries that have ratified the ECHR) (last visited Oct. 12, 2008).

142. ECHR art. 14, supra note 100.

143. See generally id.

144. See Kumm & Comella, supra note 125, at 486.

145. See Opinion 2/94, Opinion Pursuant to Article 228(6) of the EC Treaty, 1996 E.C.R. I-1759.

146. See id.

147. See Damira Kamchibekova, State Responsibility for Extraterritorial Human Rights Violations, 13 Buff. Hum. Rts. L. Rev. 87, 97 (2007).

148. See Jason N.E. Varuhas, One Person Can Make a Difference: An Individual Petition System for International Environmental Law, 3 N.Z. J. Pub. & Int'l L. 329, 331 (2005) (explaining that the CHR only hears complains based on the ECHR).

149. See ECHR, supra note 100 (detailing the rights protected, but including no provision creating an affirmative right to work).

150. Id.

151. Justice & Home AFF., Eur. Comm'n, The Charter of Fundamental Rights of the EU: All Personal, Civil, Political, Economic and Social Rights in One Simple Text, http://www.ec.europa.eu/justicehome/fsj/rights/charter/fsjrightscharteren.htm [hereinafter Charter of Fundamental Rights of the EU] (last visited Sept. 16, 2008).

152. Id.

153. Id.

154. Charter of Fundamental Rights of the European Union art. 21(1), 2000 O.J. (C 364) 1.

155. Ingolf Pernice, Integrating the Charter of Fundamental Rights into the Constitution of the European Union: Practical and Theoretical Propositions, 10 Colum. J. Eur. L. 5, 5 (2003).

156. Charter of Fundamental Rights of the EU, supra note 151.

157. EC Treaty art. 249.

158. Id.

159. See supra text accompanying note 129.

160. See Neil S. Siegel, Commandeering and Its Alternatives: A Federalism Perspective, 59 Vand. L. Rev. 1629, 1658 (2006) (noting that "member states tend to prefer directives to regulations").

161. In fact, this provision has only been referenced in four judgments published in the Official Journal since its enactment in 2000. See http://curia.europa.eu/jurisp/cgi-bin/form.pl?lang=en to search for ECJ case law (last visited Oct. 13, 2008).

162. See infra notes 180-83 and accompanying text.

163. See infra Part VI.B.

164. See Beautiful Game Turned Ugly, supra note 1. Much of the worst spectator racism occurs in Eastern Europe, where few countries have had the opportunity to join the EU.

165. At various points, a number of Eastern European countries with serious spectator racism problems have expressed a desire to join the EU. See, e.g., Croatia's EU Hopes: MEP's to Vote in Strasbourg on State of Play, European Parliament, Apr. 17, 2007, http://www.europarl.europa.eu/news/public/story page/030-5248-106-04-16-903-20070412STO05232-2007-16-04-2007/default en.htm (detailing Croatia's hopes of joining the EU); EU Opens Entry Talks with Turkey, CNN.com, Oct. 4, 2005, http://www.cnn.com/2005/WORLD/europe/10/03/eu.turkeytalks/index.html (detailing Turkey's efforts to join the EU); Ukraine Wants to Join EU While Preserving Ties with Russia: Kuchma, EUbusiness.com, May 17, 2003, http://www.eubusiness. com/Ukraine/110410 (detailing the statement of the Ukrainian President); Yugoslavia Aims to Join EU, CNN.com, Nov. 15, 2000, http://archives.cnn.com/2000/WORLD/europe/11/15/yugoslavia.eu/index.html (reporting the remarks of Yugoslavian President Kostuncia).

166. See Ryan Moshell, And Then There Was One: The Outlook for a Self-Regulatory United States Amidst a Global Trend Toward Comprehensive Data Protection, 37 Tex. Tech. L. Rev. 357, 364 n.57 (explaining that in the field of data protection, many of the aspiring EU members in Eastern Europe adopted laws based on EU legislation, despite the fact that they were not bound to do so).

167. See European Union Distressed by Pre-World Cup Racism, supra note 11 (blaming mass immigration and inexperience dealing with blacks as some of the causes of spectator racism).

168. Council Directive 2000/43, art. 2, 3, 2000 O.J. (L 180) 22,24.

169. Chalmers et al., supra note 84, at 901-02.

170. Again, the Member States would not necessarily have to impose stiffer penalties, but they would be allowed to do so under the directive.

171. See supra text accompanying notes 21-25.

172. Chalmers et al., supra note 84, at 133.

173. See, e.g., Racism Punished, The Times (London), Nov. 9, 2005, at 83 (explaining that the maximum fine that the Spanish soccer federation could impose on a team with racist fans was just €6000).

174. See Press Release, Council of the European Union, Framework Decision on Racism and Xenophobia (Apr. 19, 2007), http://www.consilium.europa.eu/ueDocs/cmsData/docs/pressData/en/misc/93739.pdf (requiring the Member States to ensure that racist conduct is "punishable by criminal penalties of a maximum of at least between 1 and 3 years of imprisonment.").

175. See Football Ban Orders Take Effect, BBC News, Aug. 29, 2006, http://news.bbc.co.uk/1/hi/scotland/5293288.stm (recounting the quotes of Scottish Justice Minister Cathy Jamieson following the enactment of a new rule allowing the police to ban fans for up to ten years for behaving inappropriately).

176. Stadium Move Boosts Arsenal Figures, SKYNews, Sept. 24, 2007, http://news.sky.com/skynews/article/0,,30400-1285410,00.html (noting that Arsenal takes in "an average of 3.1m per game").

177. EC Treaty art. 5.

178. Id.

179. See Garland & Rowe, supra note 62, at 38-44.

180. Eur. Union Agency for Fundamental Rights, Report on Racism and Xenophobia in the Member States of the EU 123-24 (2007), http://fra.europa.eu/fra/material/pub/racism/ report racism 0807en.pdf [hereinafter EUAFR]. In looking at the effects of the Race Directive, this study found that after the Member States enacted harmonizing measures, nearly every country experienced a significant increase in the number of racist crimes, which could suggest that coun-

tries are more willing to take action to combat such behavior. Id. Furthermore, the report suggested that the countries which had taken stronger measures to implement the EU's requirements, such as the provision for a special racial adjudication body, were far more likely to have effective sanctions against racism. Id.

181. Id. at 19.

182. Id. at 123-24.

183. Id. at 38.

184. Treaty of Amsterdam protocol 30, supra note 16.

185. Case C-331/88, R v. Minister of Agriculture, Fisheries and Food ex parte Fedesa, 1990 E.C.R. I-4023.

186. Chalmers et al., supra note 84, at 449.

187. See Elizabeth F. Defeis, Human Rights and the European Union: Who Decides? Possible Conflicts Between the European Court of Justice and the European Court of Human Rights, 19 Dick. J. Int'l L. 301, 302 (2001).

188. See generally supra note 16 and accompanying text.

189. See Lindsey Valaine Briggs, UEFA v. The European Community: Attempts of the Governing Body of European Soccer to Circumvent EU Freedom of Movement and Antidiscrimination Labor Law, 6 Chi. J. Int'l L. 439, 447-48 (2005).

190. See Gianni Infantino, Meca-Medina: A Step Backwards for the European Sports Model and the Specificity of Sport? (2006), http://www.uefa.com/multimediafiles/download/uefa/keytopics/480401download.pdf (explaining that UEFA's position on the holding in this case was not that sport should be "above the law," as had been contended in the past).

191. See UEFA Opens on EU Doorstep, BBC Sport, Nov. 26, 2003, http://www.sportbusiness.com/news/153234/uefa-opens-on-eu-doorstep.

192. UEFA Backs New EU Anti-Racism Law, BBC Sport, Nov. 30, 2005, http://news.bbc.co.uk/sport1/hi/football/africa/4485282.stm.

193. Jonathan Hill, UEFA, Research Lecture at Loughborough University 3 (Mar. 21, 2007) (transcript available at www-staff.lboro.ac.uk/euojd/Jonathan%20Hill%20at%20Loughborough%20University%20March%202007.doc).

Discussion Questions

1. Will the election of Barack Obama have any impact on race-related issues in sports? Explain your answer.
2. What are the benefits of the Rooney Rule and Tagliabue's precedent?
3. What are the implications if racism in European soccer is not effectively addressed?
4. What use can sports business leaders make of the statistics presented in the article by Rimer?
5. Is there business value to increased minority sports franchise ownership?
6. Not too long ago, a key diversity issue was the absence of African American NFL quarterbacks. Why has this issue, and many related player diversity issues, largely disappeared?
7. Why doesn't the law compel greater diversity at the ownership level?
8. What impact does the addition of two owners of color—Arte Moreno and Robert Johnson—have on the overall sports diversity picture?
9. Why are there fewer minorities in niche and individual sports than in team sports?
10. If you were to begin a league from scratch today, how might you avoid many of the diversity issues confronting leaders in existing sports enterprises?
11. What is the primary barrier to preventing top level anti-racism regulations in European soccer? Explain the complexity of this barrier.

Ethics

INTRODUCTION

No modern day business plan or existing enterprise is complete or current without the incorporation of ethical guidelines. Arguably, the most public ethical issues in sports have involved the use and regulation of performance-enhancing drugs. Historically, this issue was primarily the province of the Olympic Games and collegiate athletics. In recent years, the media focus has predominantly been on the use of these drugs in Major League Baseball.

It is now the case that the teaching of ethics at America's colleges and universities has moved from being the exclusive domain of philosophy departments to being a required part of undergraduate and graduate business programs. The names Enron, WorldCom, and Arthur Andersen have played no small role in this development.

The Enron–WorldCom–Arthur Andersen–Olympic–college stew makes this an important area of study for sports business leaders. Most of the issues are generic in that they involve questions of honesty, deception, and corruption. However, some ethical issues only impact sports. The pervasive use of performance-enhancing drugs and point-shaving and game-fixing scandals are unique to sports, but at their core are the moral standards of the individuals involved. It is these unique issues that the readings in this chapter focus upon.

The role of sports in this ethical realm is made even more complex because of the lessons many of us expect these games to teach our children. Right or wrong, virtually every aspect of sport is held on an ethical pedestal.

The first selection, "The Ethical Issues Confronting Managers in the Sport Industry" by Hums, Barr, and Gullion, provides a broad overview of the ethical issues confronting sports business leaders. The article is useful in giving readers a list of topics to pause and reflect upon in their ethical overview of sports-related business decisions.

The second selection, Smith's "The Olympics and the Search for Global Values," provides a micro view of ethics in a specific sector of the sports business. The piece is, noticeably, highly opinionated and critical of former IOC President Juan Antonio Samaranch, who led the organization from 1980–2001. It should be noted that he was succeeded by Jacques Rogge, whose leadership has also been criticized, albeit less for its integrity and more for its alleged ineffectiveness. The article relates two bits of business well. First, it appropriately positions the sports ethics issue in the global setting. As leagues globalize, an understanding of these issues becomes increasingly important. Second, and probably most important, the article points to the need for the improvement of ethics issues to begin at the top of an organization. It is now broadly understood, outside of the sports context, that ethical standards in business entities are most successful when clearly mandated from the top down.

The final selection in this chapter focuses specifically on ethics issues related to gambling, match-fixing, biased refereeing, and doping. In "Doping in Sports: Legal and Ethical Issues: Corruption: Its Impact on Fair Play," McLaren reviews these issues as they impact major sporting enterprises.

THE ETHICAL ISSUES CONFRONTING MANAGERS IN THE SPORT INDUSTRY

Mary A. Hums, Carol A. Barr, and Laurie Gullion

PROFESSIONAL SPORT

. . . . Professional sport has very different ethical issues than amateur or school sport, since the purposes of professional sport are entertainment and profits. Sport managers working in professional sport face ethical issues in relation to a number of different constituencies, specifically: 1) local communities which support teams, 2) the players, and 3) the front office personnel.

Local Communities

What obligations do professional sport organizations have to their fans and the communities in which the organizations reside? One ethical decision sport managers face is determining ticket prices for fans. Every year teams raise ticket prices. Factors influencing ticket prices come from both outside and inside sport, and range from economic recessions and world wars to team success, strikes, and moving into new facilities. It is in this last category where many questions arise. When new stadiums and arenas are built, they have a positive impact on attendance. Given the predictable increase in ticket prices however, a not so obvious change occurs in the fan base. Fans who were able to have season tickets in the past, but who cannot afford to renew them when the new arena is constructed, are effectively shut out of the new arena, and replaced by fans with higher disposable incomes. In effect, the consumption of spectator sport in person is beginning to become an activity for the elite, while others are denied access. . . . The underlying question here is who really are the team's "most valuable customers"—the casual attendees who come to the game only when their disposable income allows a ticket purchase, the traditional season ticketholders, the new higher income season ticketholders, or the corporate luxury box holders? The answer to that question speaks to the stance teams take in the industry. Is it only about increasing corporate revenues or is there still some consideration for the average fan on whom the success of these teams was originally built?

What commitments do professional franchises have to the communities in which they do business? The recent rash of "free agent franchises" has brought this question to the forefront. Cities such as Baltimore, Cleveland, and Los Angeles, which lost NFL teams, as well as Canadian cities like Quebec City and Winnipeg, which have lost NHL franchises, have been left with empty stadiums and arenas while teams and their owners move on to more lucrative locations. . . . Why are owners lured to new locations? In a nutshell, owners look to determine if they can acquire: 1) better lease arrangements including greater cuts of parking and concessions, 2)

public financing of the project which relieves them of any debt incurred in stadium or arena construction, and 3) an increased number of luxury boxes. And how do owners convince cities that a sport franchise is a "good" use of public dollars? Usually three arguments are made—1) the city will benefit from direct spending on events, 2) the city will benefit from money spent by fans as that money recycles through the economy via the multiplier effect, and 3) the city needs the franchise to have a "major league" image. Research by a number of authors . . . has indicated that these arguments may not always hold up. The bottom line question remains—who really profits from franchise relocation? The answer is the owners. So the question becomes for sport managers—is this an ethical stance to take? Is it ethical to "hold cities hostage" with the threat to leave for a better offer, oftentimes leaving the cities with massive amounts of long-term debt and an empty facility to maintain?

Players

Volumes have been written relating to the recent labor unrest and work stoppages in Major League Baseball and the National Hockey League. Whether one sides with management or labor in these discussions, there are still the same questions of fundamental fairness involved in any labor dispute. What made these disputes different to the general public was the fact [that] the "laborers" in these cases happened to be highly paid professional athletes instead of coal miners or factory workers. What constitutes fair working conditions for these athletes? Just how much control is management allowed to have over them? And where does the phrase "in the best interest of the game" enter into the discussion? Although the salaries are high, sport managers must still keep in mind the basic principles of fairness when dealing with these athlete-employees.

[*Ed. Note: The authors' discussion of the HIV issue is deleted.*]

. . . .

Front Office Personnel

Finally, there are ethical issues related to front office staffs of professional franchises. The most important has to do with diversification of front office staffs. Traditionally, professional sport management has been the exclusive realm of white males. Sport is often regarded as one of society's most traditionally male institutions. Given the changing face of the international workforce, sport managers now must make ethical decisions in hiring in order to make the management of sport more inclusive for women, minorities, and people with disabilities.

. . . .

In addition to diversifying the workforce in terms of women and minorities, special attention needs to be turned to increasing opportunities for people with disabilities.

While athletes with disabilities continue to make slow progress with recognition and acceptance on the playing field, relatively little data is available on the numbers of people with disabilities in sport management positions. The following suggestions have been offered . . . for increasing opportunities for people with disabilities in sport management positions:

1. Value diversity within the organization.

2. Redefine who is a "Qualified Individual" by:

   a) Being knowledgeable of existing labor laws related to discriminatory work practices.

   b) Increasing knowledge and awareness of multiculturalism in general.

   c) Being knowledgeable and supportive of issues of importance to all groups in the workplace.

   d) Writing statements about valuing diversity into the organization's code of ethics.

   e) Expanding personal and professional networks.

   f) Acting as a "mentor" or "womentor" to people with disabilities in one's sport organization.

3. Create organizational visions inclusive of people with disabilities.

4. Create organizational mission statements inclusive of people with disabilities.

5. Actively recruit and retain people with disabilities as employees.

INTERCOLLEGIATE ATHLETICS

The world of intercollegiate athletics is certainly not without its share of ethical issues. Examples of ethical issues within intercollegiate athletics include, but are not limited to, 1) whether student-athletes are being exploited by not being paid for their athletic endeavors, 2) the courting of amateur student-athletes by professional player agents, 3) gender equity, 4) diversity issues, and 5) improprieties by intercollegiate coaches and administrators.

Paying Student-Athletes

The National Collegiate Athletic Association's (NCAA) 1995–96 budget projected revenues of $234.2 million. [*The 2009–10 budget was $710 million.*] Of this total, $180.9 million or 77% came from television rights fees, with $178.3 million directly attributed to the NCAA's broadcast contract with CBS covering the men's basketball tournament. [*Ed. Note: In 2009–2010, $639 million came from television rights fees from the CBS contract.*] Thus, 64 college basketball teams and their roughly 12–15 student-athletes per team generate nearly 77% [*Ed. Note: now 90%*] of the NCAA's total revenue. This figure does not include revenue the NCAA collects from ticket sales, merchandise

sales, or sponsorship deals connected with the men's basketball tournament. In addition, base salaries of Division I men's basketball coaches . . . exceed the six-digit mark. Including additional shoe and apparel contracts, TV and radio contracts, and endorsement deals, this base salary is likely to more than double or even triple. Some of these contracts, such as shoe and apparel deals, involve the student-athlete to a greater extent than the coach, and yet the coach receives the paycheck while the athlete is required to wear the shoes and apparel.

Bylaws 15.02.5 and 15.2.4.1 of the NCAA rules prohibit a college student-athlete on an athletic scholarship from receiving anything more than the monetary equivalent of tuition, room, board, books, and fees plus Pell Grant money up to the student-athlete's full cost of attendance. . . . In 1989, University of New Haven sociology professor Allen Sack surveyed approximately 3,500 current and former professional athletes. Of the 1,182 athletes who responded, nearly one-third admitted receiving illegal payments while they were in college.

. . . . The more controversial and difficult issue may not be determining whether student-athletes should be paid, but rather determining *which* student-athletes should get paid and how much. Should differences be put in place for male versus female student-athletes, football players versus field hockey players, starters or star players versus second or third string athletes? The actual implementation of a system may be the more difficult of the ethical concerns surrounding the paying of student-athletes.

Player Agents

A growing problem within intercollegiate athletics is the courting of highly talented student-athletes by professional player agents. Player agents, depending upon the athlete's sport, receive between 3% and 15% of a professional athlete's salary. This income potential is extremely enticing to the professional player agent. Many player agents, therefore, disregard the NCAA rules restricting a collegiate student-athlete from signing or accepting anything from a player agent and instead use various methods to lure the student-athlete into signing with them. NCAA Bylaw 12.3.1 states that an individual shall be ineligible for participation in an intercollegiate sport if he or she ever has agreed (orally or in writing) to be represented by an agent for the purpose of marketing his or her athletics ability or reputation in a sport. Player agents have been known to offer cash, cars, airline tickets, and other amenities to the student-athlete in exchange for the student-athlete signing with them. Player agents have also used "runners" who act on behalf of the player agent trying to persuade the student-athlete to sign with that particular player agent. These "runners" exert pressure on the student-athlete by getting close to the student-athlete and his/her family or friends, and attempting to persuade the student-athlete to sign with the player agent.

This problem is compounded because of lack of regulation of player agents. The NCAA lacks any authority or enforcement power over the player agents. The NCAA can punish the school and student-athlete, but possesses no enforcement power over the player agent. Individual states have become more involved in this area by passing their own legislation and/or agent registration systems. The state of Florida has already handed down fines and jail sentences to agents who contacted Florida's student-athletes without first registering with the state. Individual colleges and universities are also getting more involved by instituting their own agent registration systems and trying to educate student-athletes as to illicit player agent behavior.

Gender Equity

Perhaps the most important phrase . . . in intercollegiate athletics is "gender equity," that is, offering equal opportunities for both men and women to participate in sport. A piece of legislation referred to as Title IX provides guidelines for gender equity. Title IX prohibits sex discrimination in any educational program or activity receiving federal financial assistance. A 1990–91 NCAA Gender Equity study found that although college campuses were comprised of approximately 50% male students and 50% female students, college athletic departments were comprised of 70% male athletes and 30% female athletes. In addition, the male student-athletes were receiving 70% of the athletic scholarship money, 75% of the operational budget, and 80% of the recruiting moneys available. [*Ed. Note: A 2005–2006 NCAA Gender Equity study found that college campuses were comprised of 45.6% male and 54.4% female students, but that male athletes comprised 55% of the athletes in Division I-A, 58% of the athletes in I-AA, 50% of the athletes in I-AAA, 59% of the athletes in Division II, and 58% of the athletes in Division III. In Division I overall, the male student-athlete received 55% of the athletic scholarship money, 66% of the operational budget, and 68% of the recruiting dollars.*] Institutions have been slow to comply with Title IX, though, given the potential financial impact of instituting a new women's sport program, increasing scholarship, operational, and recruiting funding for women, or instituting other changes dictated by Title IX legislation involving areas such as facilities, equipment, travel and per diem, or coaches' compensation. A 1994–95 NCAA participation study found the percentage of female athletes has increased to 36.9% of all athletic participants, but this number still lacks in comparison to the 63.1% of student-athletes who are male. [*Ed. Note: In 2005–2006, females comprised 45% of college athletes.*]

Gender equity also involves coaches and administrators. In 1972, the year Title IX was passed, more than 90% of women's teams were coached by women. In 1994, 49.4% of women's teams were coached by women and only about 2% of the head coaches of men's teams within the NCAA were women with almost all of these sport programs involving combined gender teams. [*Ed. Note: In 2005, 42% of women's teams were led by a woman head coach and less than 2% of men's teams were coached by a woman.*] In 1972, more than 90% of women's programs were directed by a female head administrator. In 1994, 20.98% of women's programs were directed by a woman, and the average number of women included in the athletic administrative structure at each school was less than one. [*Ed. Note: Less than 20% of top administrative positions were held by women in 2005.*]

Historically, although Title IX is the law, its enforcement policy was weak, therefore it was often simply ignored by college athletic directors. It became an ethical choice for athletic directors to attempt to comply with the law, and many athletic directors, for reasons including money or tradition or sexism, simply chose not to comply. Others, however, made the ethical choice to increase opportunities for female athletes, simply because it was the right thing to do.

Diversity

The NCAA's Minority Opportunity and Interests Committee studied the minority composition of intercollegiate student-athletes, coaches, and administrators and found in 1993–94 that Black student-athletes comprised 25.3% of Division I college scholarship student-athletes, but accounted for only 4.1% of athletic directors and 4.4% of head coaches when predominantly Black institutions were excluded. These percentages were an increase from a 1990–91 study which found 2.2% of athletic directors and 3.3% of head coaches were Black, but still fall short of the percentage of Black student-athletes which has remained unchanged since 1990–91. [*Ed. Note: In 2005–2006, the percentage of Black male student athletes in Division I was 24.6%, and the percentage of Black female student-athletes in Division I was 15.7%. Only 5.5% of Division I athletic directors and head coaches of 11.6% of men's teams and 10.6% of women's teams were Black, when excluding historically Black institutions.*]

Improprieties

On June 28, 1996, *The Chronicle of Higher Education* reported 23 institutions on NCAA probation. [*Ed. Note: Twelve institutions were on probation in the spring of 2008.*] Violations included improper academic certification of student-athletes, playing ineligible student-athletes, recruiting violations, providing extra benefits to student-athletes, lack of institutional control, and unethical conduct by head and assistant coaches. A "win at all costs" attitude still dominates intercollegiate athletics, pressuring coaches and even administrators to violate NCAA rules in an attempt to sign highly talented student-athletes or win big games. The financial payoff associated with athletic success still dominates in "big-time" football and basketball. Coaches and athletic administrators feel pressure from alumni, boosters, and even university administrators to win. The enforcement and investigative staff of the NCAA is small and cannot keep up with the many activities of the 991 *[Ed. Note: now 1,055]* member institutions. Coaches may feel the odds of not being caught are in their favor, and administrators may look the other way in order to keep the revenue streams flowing.

[Ed. Note: The authors' discussion of facility management ethical issues is omitted.]

. . . .

SPORT MANAGERS AND ETHICAL DECISION MAKING

. . . .

An adaptation of Zinn's[1] ethical decision-making model has also been suggested, which could be applied across the different industry segments:

1. Identify the correct problem to be solved.
2. Gather all the pertinent information.
3. Explore codes of conduct relevant to one's profession or to this particular dilemma.
4. Examine one's own personal values and beliefs.
5. Consult with peers or other individuals in the industry who may have experience in similar situations.
6. List decision options.
7. Look for a "win-win" situation if at all possible.
8. Ask the question, "How would my family feel if my decision and how I arrived at my decision were printed in the newspaper tomorrow?"
9. Sleep on it. Do not rush to a decision.
10. Make the best decision possible, knowing it may not be perfect.
11. Evaluate the decision over time.

The development of an ethical decision-making model for sport managers is obviously an area ripe for additional research and thought.

CONCLUSION

As illustrated above, the sport industry is a broadly defined industry encompassing a number of diverse segments. Managers in each of these segments, professional sport, intercollegiate sport, the health and fitness industry, recreational sport and facility management, are challenged daily by the changes occurring in the industry as it grows and matures. Along with growth comes an increasing number of complicated ethical questions, many of which are unique to given segments of the industry. Sport managers need to stay current with the ethical issues they may confront, so they will be proactive in their approaches rather than reactive.

Note

1. Zinn, Z. M. "Do the Right Thing: Ethical Decision Making in Professional and Business Practice," *Adult Learning* 5, 7–8, 27.

THE OLYMPICS AND THE SEARCH FOR GLOBAL VALUES

John Milton Smith

Disillusionment with the Olympics mirrors the mounting disenchantment with the values of globalization. Indeed, the recent history of the Games has been characterized by the growth of a culture which reifies the worst features of global competition, including: winning at any price, commercial exploitation by MNCs, corruption, intense national rivalry, [and] the competitive advantage of advanced nations.

There can be little argument that the global institutions have been a miserable failure in dealing with the social and ethical consequences of globalization. Their performance has been particularly dismal in addressing issues involving poverty, terrorism, environmental protection, natural disasters and humanitarian crises involving the weak and defenseless.

[Ed. Note: The author's background discussion on Olympic corruption is deleted.]

. . . .

THE IOC'S LEADERSHIP CHALLENGE

Ironically, the last vestige of amateurism associated with the Games is its management. Despite the scandals and controversies of recent years, the IOC [International Olympic Committee] displays few signs of the professional management techniques and processes which characterize the successful international business organizations of today. The IOC has not been proactive in addressing the key corporate governance issues such as accountability, social responsibility, risk management, transparency, and the implementation of codes of conduct. Furthermore, the Olympic leadership has failed to define and communicate a clear unifying purpose. The Olympic ideals remain at the level of platitude;

they do not constitute a unifying sense of purpose. There has been no rigorous public discussion of the multiple and sometimes conflicting objectives of the Games. Not only is there a lack of vision and coherent mission, there are also no major mechanisms in place to provide for public input into planning processes.

Despite heavy emphasis on the so-called Olympic ideals, the leaders of the movement have singularly failed to articulate its core values and relate them to contemporary mores and behavior. Again, by comparison with management best practiced in major MNCs, the IOC has lagged badly. This is further reflected in the lack of a comprehensive Code of Conduct and ethics training regime. Only recently, after an extremely damaging period of adverse publicity, has an Ethics Commission been established, and there is still no regular ethics auditing system. Instead, President Samaranch continues to talk paternalistically about "the Olympic Family" and of the need for more loyalty and better housekeeping. The "family" analogy is doubly unfortunate because, on the one hand, it implies a degree of unity which clearly does not exist and, on the other, a closed community with the potential to become a corrupt, self-serving community more akin to the Mafia than to a modern, professional organization.

Juan Antonio Samaranch, the long-standing President of the IOC, has been the architect of the Olympic Games as a scandal-ridden media spectacle and business enterprise. *[Ed. Note: Samaranch served as President from 1980–2001 and was replaced by Jacques Rogge in 2001.]* It is claimed that he has transformed the Games "from a global sporting get-together to a corporate spectacle sadly replete with corruption and kickbacks." Aloof, arrogant, and imperious, Samaranch operates not as an inspiring leader but as a banana-republic dictator, cultivating a shameless culture of extravagance and excess around him. Once a senior member of General Franco's fascist regime, he presides over the IOC as if it were a personal fiefdom. Until the Salt Lake City kickback scandal, Samaranch expected to be called "Excellency," demanded a royal standard of hospitality wherever he traveled, and turned a blind eye to the blatant corruption of his colleagues.

As President of the IOC, Samaranch has clearly failed to provide inspiring values leadership. Instead, the Olympic Games are enveloped in a culture of shame, disappointment, and uncertainty. While Samaranch has certainly succeeded in addressing the commercial challenges facing the Games as a global sporting event, he has been much less successful in articulating what they stand for or in realizing their potential influence as a moral force. Apart from vague rhetoric about Olympic ideals, he has never been convincing as the champion for Olympic values. Despite his long tenure, Samaranch has not created a transcending Olympic ethos based on human excellence, and he himself falls far short of what such a challenge demands of a leader.

Despite intense world-wide interest in the Games and attraction to the values they are perceived to represent, they have failed dismally in recent years to celebrate and reinforce the values which are embedded in their history. The opportunity is still there for a future leader to tap into this history and to liberate the massive moral authority and potential ethical influence which it contains. Above all, and certainly more than any other regular global event, the Olympic Games are a potential forum for rekindling the human spirit, lifting morale, and bringing people together in pursuit of common goals. They are also a reaffirmation of the importance of setting ambitious objectives, having a sense of purpose, making painful sacrifices, persevering when the going gets tough, giving loyalty to one's teammates, and being proud of doing one's best.

Unfortunately, the administration of the Games has become remote from the world of the athletes and a source of embarrassment to virtually every group of stakeholders. Based on their track record, most senior officials are perceived to be self-seeking power brokers rather than inspiring leaders. How could this sad situation be transformed, and what changes would be required to convert the Olympic ideology and rhetoric into practical reality?

The most important change would be in the area of leadership. Rekindling and revitalizing the Olympic spirit will involve much more than the sort of leadership which produces plans and profits. Character and credibility will be critical success factors, as will the communication skills needed to articulate the Olympic values and create an uplifting ethos. . . . This should not be a purely top-down exercise.

Instead, all stakeholders should be given the opportunity to provide input and discuss options openly and without intimidation. In reviewing the Mission and charting the future direction of the Olympic Games, participants from all over the world would come together in developing a set of global human values which could become the touchstone for future international relations and problem-solving. At every level—local, national, regional, global—the key to transforming society is to reform the critical organizations first. And that is why there is such an urgent need for an outstanding leader at the helm of the IOC.

In defining the task and revising the position description for the next President of the IOC, there is an exciting opportunity to conceptualize the Games as a major vehicle and catalyst for developing and propagating a set of widely shared global ethical standards.

The transformation of the Games will require nothing short of a leadership revolution. Apart from changes to the decision-making process and a radical restructuring, the new leadership must have the ability to create an inspiring global festival of human attainment.

. . . .

The reinvention of the Games will require not only transformational leadership but also a solid framework of strategic management as well. This will entail a more focused and well-defined mission, more democratic and representative structures, more transparent and accountable processes, and more emphasis upon the creation of brand equity. Because the strength and credibility of the Olympic brand hinges so heavily upon core values, high priority should be given to the development of a code of practice, to the role of the new Ethics Commission and to the use of audit mechanisms.

There is still an opportunity for a visionary IOC leader to seize the initiative in making the Games a platform for promoting positive global values. Such a leader will need to be a strategic thinker and an outstanding communicator. Just as the most recent leaders of the UN, IMF, and the World Bank have begun to reshape the agendas of their organizations to place greater emphasis upon human rights and the welfare of people, so the IOC needs a leader who is able to create a shared vision for the Games which is a beacon for inspiring people all over the world to strive for excellence and to work together in harmony. As Sir Roger Bannister, the first person to run a four-minute mile, has put it: "The Olympic Games should remain one of the great hopes of the world."

DOPING IN SPORTS: LEGAL AND ETHICAL ISSUES: CORRUPTION: ITS IMPACT ON FAIR PLAY

Richard H. McLaren

I. INTRODUCTION

A difference between sport and entertainment is the unpredictability of sporting outcomes versus the planned and executed event that provides entertainment. Corruption attempts to alter this equation and make sport more of an entertainment event with a greater certainty of outcome. This equation is altered when corruption is centered on match fixing or gambling; biased refereeing; and, to a similar but different degree, when sporting results are affected by the use of performance enhancing drugs. Corruption, in any of the foregoing forms, robs sport of its essential feature of uncertainty of the outcome and accelerates its spin into the forum of entertainment, and thus it no longer is sport. Corruption gnaws away at the fundamental foundations of sport and therefore of sporting integrity. It becomes essential to protect that integrity to ensure that sport is free from any corrupt influence that might cast doubt over the authenticity and unpredictability of the sporting result.

Integrity is, in a large measure, a perception, although there is a real intangible existence to it.[1] Once lost it is very difficult to ever retrieve. The perception of integrity must be present for the sports enthusiast to believe that the outcome of a sporting competition is genuine.[2] Match fixing, gambling, biased refereeing, and doping have all recently posed serious threats to the integrity of sports. In many parts of the world betting has become a mainstream leisure activity through the use of the internet. Cheating sports personalities can lead to corrupt betting practices, and has been associated with attempts to fix matches and alter the results of sporting competitions. Nowhere is this truer than in the recent outbreak of scandals in tennis relating to accusations, which are often founded, on betting by players. Biased refereeing, alleged in wrestling, boxing, and women's soccer at the Beijing Olympics, is unfair to the individual players in matches, and is the antithesis of the concept of a fair and impartial observer during play. Doping unfairly enhances the performance of those who engage in such practices, and causes cynicism among the viewing public of the natural abilities of athletes. Each of these forms of corruption will be discussed and analyzed with recent examples of scandals in the international sporting world traced out. The resulting discussion will demonstrate how corruption is gnawing away at the integrity of modern day professional and elite sports. The examples form the backdrop for a discussion of recent proactive measures taken by sports regulatory bodies. The paper will conclude with some further suggestions that may help to improve the integrity of sports.

II. MATCH-FIXING AND GAMBLING

Integrity in sport is crucial to its success and to the enjoyment of participants and spectators. Sports are a global activity providing entertainment and enjoyment to an international audience who watch with intense passion. There are isolated occasions where the players involved have been tempted to cheat to gain an advantage over fellow competitors. Even such isolated events have, in the past decade, shaken the integrity of some sports and caused severe and serious setbacks. Match fixing is engaged in to benefit some form of gambling on the outcome. No other aspect of sports corruption works so quickly to destroy the integrity of a sport, which often has taken decades to build. Betting on sport, including professional tennis, various events in the Olympic Games, soccer, and basketball, is now an established leisure activity in many parts of the world, and corrupt betting practices can lead to cheating by athletes, referees, and others to fix matches and alter the results of competitions.

A. Tennis

Recently in tennis, reports of match-fixing attempts point towards an undeniable problem that poses a serious threat to the integrity of the sport.[3] In recent years, the international professional tennis regulatory bodies have been aware of this growing concern. The tennis community, along with the international media, has drawn public attention to concerns about the integrity of the sport, especially concerning allegations of players betting on their own and others' matches, and of players "throwing matches" in order to facilitate these corrupt betting practices. There was explosive worldwide media attention when allegations were made against Russian tennis player Nikolay Davydenko, although they were subsequently found by the Association of Tennis Professionals[4] ("the ATP Tour") to be unfounded.

The international media devoted much attention to the investigation relating to betting irregularities concerning an August 2, 2007 match at the Prokom Open in Sopot, Poland, between Davydenko and Martin Vassallo Arguello, an Argentinian tennis player. In an unprecedented move, the British online betting company, Betfair, voided all bets placed on the second-round match between the then 4th in the world, Davydenko, and then 87th-ranked Arguello. Betfair reported it received about seven million dollars (US) in wagers on the match, which was ten times the usual amount for a similar level match, and most of the money was on Arguello to win, even after Davydenko had won the first set 6-2. Arguello won the second set 6-3, and was leading 2-1 in the third when Davydenko retired, stating he aggravated a left foot injury in the second set. Two days after the match, the ATP Tour launched a formal investigation into the suspicious gambling activity. However, after over a year of intense investigation into the case, on September 11, 2008 both Davydenko and Arguello were cleared of any involvement in match-fixing.[5]

Allegations of gambling and match fixing in tennis did not begin with Davydenko, but had surfaced in the past. At Wimbledon in 2006, Betfair reported irregular betting patterns surrounding a first-round match between British wild card player, Richard Bloomfield, and the higher ranked Carlos Berlocq of Argentina, who had lost in straight sets. Berlocq, who was ranked 170 places higher than Bloomfield, lost 6-1, 6-2, 6-2. Most of the bets placed were on Berlocq to lose. The International Tennis Federation (ITF), which oversees Grand Slam tournaments, investigated the matter but found no illicit wrongdoing.[6]

Earlier, in 2003, bookmakers reportedly suspended betting six hours before a match in Lyon, France, between Russian player, Yevgeny Kafelnikov, and Spanish player, Fernando Vicente, after a big wager was placed on Vicente. Vicente, who had been winless for several months, won in straight sets. There was no suggestion that either player was involved in wrongdoing, and no investigation was made by the ATP.[7]

Finally, several Russian tennis players were photographed with Alimzhan Tokhtakhounov, a suspected mobster from the former Soviet republic of Uzbekistan, who was accused of fixing the pairs and ice dancing events at the 2002 Salt Lake City Olympics.[8] Photographs of Tokhtakhounov with Yevgeny Kafelnikov, Marat Safin, and Andrei Medvedev were taken off Medvedev's website in 2002 after Tokhtakhounov's arrest. Tokhtakhounov spent nearly a year in an Italian prison, but escaped extradition to the United States in 2003 on the Olympic rigging charges.[9]

Moreover, since August of 2007, and the alleged Davydenko scandal, several players went public with stories of people offering them money to throw matches for gambling purposes. For example, Belgian tennis player Gilles Elseneer stated that he was approached in the locker room at Wimbledon in 2005, and was offered over $140,000.00 to throw his first round match against Italian player, Potito Starace.[10] Another Belgian player, Dick Norman, admitted that he has been pressed for tips that could be useful to bettors, such as inside information on injuries.[11] Russian tennis player Dmitry Tursunov alleged he was approached twice with bribe offers,[12] while French player Michael Llodra said he hung up on an anonymous call to his hotel room in the summer of 2007 which had encouraged him to "be relaxed" in his next match. The recently retired U.S. tennis player Paul Goldstein stated that he was approached and asked to influence the outcome of a match sometime during the past two years. Finally, British player Arvind Parmar told *The Times* of London that he was offered an unspecified amount of money to throw a lower-level Challenger's series match.[13]

i.   What Is Being Done?

Since 2003, the ATP Tour has had an arrangement with Betfair and the European Sports Security Association, which covers ten online gambling companies, to provide confidential account information when suspicious betting activity occurs. Additionally, ATP's Tennis Anti-Corruption Program bans all players and "support personnel" from betting on any amateur or professional tennis matches. Rule 7.05 C.i.a of the 2007 ATP Official Rulebook sets out the "corruption offense" of wagering. According to the ATP's rules, players and their personnel cannot bet on any matches, and also cannot "solicit, induce, entice, persuade, encourage or facilitate" anyone else to affect the outcome of matches.[14] The penalty for a wagering offense is determined by the Anti-Corruption Hearing Officer and is punishable under Rule 7.05 G.1.a of the Code. The penalty may include: a fine of up to 100,000 dollars plus an amount equal to the value of any winnings or other amounts received by the player or his player support personnel; ineligibility for participation in any competition or match at any ATP tournament, competition, or other event or activity authorized or organized by the ATP, for a period of up to three years; and permanent ineligibility.[15]

In an effort to describe the issues and reform the sport, the tennis regulatory bodies took the proactive measure of establishing a commission of inquiry. Their report was published in May of 2008, entitled "Environmental Review of Integrity in Professional Tennis."[16] The ATP, the Women's Tennis Association (WTA), the ITF, and the Grand Slam Committee (GSC), comprising the President of the ITF and the Chairman of the four official International Championships of Australia, France, Great Britain and the United States, which are also known, individually and collectively, as the Grand Slams, launched this independent analysis of professional tennis' integrity regulations and procedures, along with the nature of the current threat posed by gambling. The initiative was led by Jeffrey Rees and Ben Gunn, leading sports integrity experts. The Review examined seventy-three matches over the past five years involving suspected betting patterns. Patterns of suspected betting activity have been noted on twenty-seven accounts in two different countries, and there are emerging concerns about some players which would warrant further attention.[17]

The Review strongly suggested a uniform anti-corruption program, with a regulatory structure and an integrity unit.[18] Before the publication of the Review, the regulation of international professional tennis was overseen by numerous bodies, including the four Grand Slams, the ITF, the ATP, and Sony Ericsson WTA Tour. Each of the international tennis regulatory bodies had their own sets of regulations and codes of conduct. The Review suggested the harmonization of these various regulations and codes of conduct for professional tennis internationally. The principal objective of the Anti-Corruption Programme is to maintain and enhance the integrity of professional tennis worldwide by investigating and, where necessary, prosecuting breaches of the regulations.

Accordingly, on August 23, 2008, the Sony Ericsson WTA Tour, the ATP, the ITF, and the Grand Slam Committees announced the appointment of Jeff Rees as Director of the sport's newly formed Tennis Integrity Unit and the landmark adoption of a uniform Tennis Anti-Corruption Code across the sport.[19] As Director of the Tennis Integrity Unit, Rees is responsible for the development of the unit's intelligence and investigative strategies, as well as the hiring and oversight of core staff. The Unit has global responsibility for the detection and investigation of integrity issues across tennis. Rees reports to a committee of four senior executives representing each of the ATP, the ITF, Sony Ericsson WTA Tour, and GSC. This single, uniform Anti-Corruption Code forms one of the cores of the sport's Tennis Anti-Corruption Programme, and is designed to ensure that a single set of rules, procedures, penalties and investigative processes are applied across all of professional tennis to players, officials, tournament staff, agents, coaches and family members. Under the Code, the most serious corruption offences will be punishable by a lifetime ban from the sport, and those subject to the Code will have a duty to report any information regarding suspected corrupt activities.[20]

Likely influenced by the explosive media attention that Davydenko's alleged scandal created, the ATP began to stringently enforce its anticorruption rules, leading to a number of players being suspended or fined for betting on both their own matches and the matches of other players. On November 10, 2007, then ranked 124th in the world, Alessio di Mauro was the first player to be sanctioned for betting.[21] He was found to have made 120 bets with an online

bookmaker involving approximately 340 ATP matches from November 2, 2006, to June 12, 2007, and was caught as a result of an investigation beginning in April of 2007. Although the bets were made on both football games and ATP matches, Di Mauro claimed never to have placed bets on any of the tennis matches in which he competed.

Following a hearing held before the Anti-Corruption Hearing Officer of the ATP, Dr. Peter Bratschi, Di Mauro was declared to have violated the ATP's Tennis Anti-Corruption Program for betting. In his decision, dated November 9, 2007, Dr. Bratschi concluded that a rule violation had occurred "in a gross negligent way" and declared a sanction of nine months ineligibility and a fine of US $60,000.[22] However, on November 29, 2007, Di Mauro filed a Statement of Appeal, under Rule 7.05 H.3 of the ATP Code, to the Court of Arbitration for Sport (CAS). Having admitted the violation and his personal culpability for having misunderstood "the real content of the anti-corruption rules," Di Mauro requested only the re-consideration of the penalty.[23] In his view, the sanction was excessive when compared with his misconduct, arguing that it was his first offense and that there was no intention to break the rules or to injure the integrity of the game. Although he did not deny the fact that he opened the betting account and placed all of the modest bets under his own name, the stakes were "made for leisure only" and to "pass the time," and he never bet on his own matches.[24]

The CAS Panel stated that general prevention is best achieved by imposing a just individual sanction.[25] If the term of ineligibility and the amount of the fine were not reduced in this case, the punishment imposed upon Di Mauro would place the proportionality of the sanction in question and vitiate the preventive purposes which it intends to achieve. For this reason, the Panel partially granted the appeal, reducing the term of ineligibility from nine months to seven months and the fine from 60,000 dollars (US) to 25,000 dollars (US).[26]

Potito Starace and Daniele Bracciali were also sanctioned by the ATP in December of 2007. Starace wagered on matches from February to May of 2006, while Bracciali's bets were from May 2004 to January 2005. Starace made five bets totalling one hundred thirty dollars (US), and Bracciali made about fifty bets of seven dollars (US). The Italian tennis federation stated that both players bet on matches involving others, and also that they were unaware that the wagers violated ATP regulations. Starace, ranked 31st, was suspended by the ATP for six weeks and fined 30,000 dollars (US), while Bracciali, ranked 258th, was banned for three months and fined 20,000 dollars (US).[27]

Giorgio Galimberti was subsequently sanctioned in February of 2008, suspended for 100 days and fined 35,000 dollars (US). The ATP stated that he bet on tennis from June 2003 to January 2006, wagering 401 times on 1,796 tennis matches.[28] Federico Luzzi was also sanctioned in February of 2008. He was suspended 200 days and fined 50,000 dollars (US) by the ATP for betting. An ATP investigation, launched in August 2007, found that Luzzi had wagered 273 times on 836 tennis matches between May 2004 and April 2007. Of these 273 bets, one was a €3 bet, placed on him to win. The ATP found no evidence of any attempt by Luzzi to affect the outcome of any tennis match; this was a conclusion shared by the independent Anti-Corruption Hearing Officer, Dr. Bratschi.[29] Luzzi also appealed to CAS relating to this sanction, but the Panel deemed the appeal withdrawn.[30]

Frantisek Cermak and Michal Mertinak were both sanctioned by the ATP in July 2008. Neither of the players had bet on their own matches, and the investigation found no evidence of any intent to affect the outcome of the matches wagered upon. Cermak was suspended for ten weeks and fined 15,000 dollars (US); Mertinak was suspended for two weeks and fined 3,000 dollars (US) for betting on tennis matches in October 2006.[31]

Finally, in August 2008, Mathieu Montcourt was suspended from participation in the ATP Tour for a period of eight weeks, and fined 12,000 dollars (US) after the ATP determined that he bet on matches. Launched in November 2007, the ATP investigation found that he wagered on tennis matches during a period dating from June 2005 through September of the same year. Montcourt did not wager on his own matches, and the investigation found no evidence of any intent to affect the outcome of any matches wagered upon.[32] Montcourt appealed this decision to CAS.[33]

B. Olympic Games Events

Gambling and match fixing are certainly not confined to tennis or even athletes. Referees, coaches, and officials are also involved in this form of corruption in various sports. The Chinese badminton coach, Li Yongbo, came forward in the spring of 2008 admitting that he had fixed a badminton match at the 2004 Athens Olympic Games.[34] Li Yongbo told China Central Television's sports channel that the 2004 Olympics semi-final was fixed to improve China's chances of winning a gold medal. Two Chinese players, Zhou Mi and Zhang Ning, were drawn together in the semi-final tie. After watching Zhang win the first game, the coaching staff decided that she would have a better chance at winning the final against a non-Chinese opponent rather than Zhou. Yongbo subsequently told Zhou Mi to throw the game and let Zhang into the final. Zhang won the gold as planned over Mia Audina from the Netherlands.[35]

During the 2008 Beijing Olympic Games in boxing, the International Boxing Association (AIBA) Executive Director, Ho Kim, stated that the AIBA leadership had received information that Rudel Obreja, the Romanian deputy technical delegate of the Beijing Olympic boxing competition, tried to influence select referees. Obreja alleged that the organization brought in an extra employee to monitor the random computer selection of match judges and referees and, in many cases, changed the assignments to suit particular boxers. AIBA excluded the suspicious referees

from certain bouts. Obreja then held an "unauthorized press conference" on the sidelines of the boxing competition, and accused some judges and referees of match-fixing. The AIBA Executive Committee Bureau charged Obreja with corruption, misconduct toward judges and referees, and disparagement of AIBA's reputation and interests at the disciplinary commission.[36]

i. What Is Being Done?

International Olympic Committee (IOC) President, Jacques Rogge, has called for a united front of the international sports federations to combat the problem of match-fixing. He stated: "This is something we have to address. The purpose of the IOC is to have a common approach to that with all international sports federations and the national Olympic committees. This is what we did in the fight against doping."[37] At the 2008 Beijing Olympic Games, the IOC created a special unit to watch for suspicious betting patterns during the Olympic Games. For the first time agreements were signed with major betting companies to monitor any irregular gambling during Olympic events.[38] The IOC also created a special investigative unit that had the authority to impose sanctions for individuals who violated Article A.5 of the Code of Ethics. That provision of the Code of Ethics concerns the prohibition on betting at the Olympic Games, which states that "[a]ll forms of participation in, or support for betting related to the Olympic Games, and all forms of promotion of betting related to the Olympic Games, are prohibited."[39] The special IOC investigative unit had the power to confront those involved, and then turn their findings over to the executive board, which was enabled to make sanctions.

C. Professional Soccer

In soccer, Declan Hill, an investigative journalist and academic, exposed several potentially explosive stories of sports corruption in his study of match-fixing in professional soccer. His book, *The Fix: Soccer and Organized Crime*,[40] exposes fixed matches in the 2006 World Cup Games between Ghana–Italy, Ghana–Brazil, and Italy–Ukraine.[41] In his research for this book, Hill interviewed more than two hundred people, including professional gamblers, Mafia hitmen, undercover police, top-level international soccer players, referees, and officials, and also came into contact with the multibillion-dollar illegal Asian gambling industry. Through his investigation, Hill discovered that gambling fixers have successfully infiltrated professional soccer, including major international matches.

In professional soccer, corruption began with the illegal Asian gambling industry, which has infiltrated the sport and organized some of the largest and most extensive match-fixes. At the top of this gambling structure sits a prominent businessman or politician who provides protection from the government and the police. These individuals may not be involved in the day-to-day running of the gambling industry, but they do provide political protection and influence. Such powerful individuals help to protect organized crime groups and bookies to fix matches.[42] Alongside this prominent businessman or politician is the triad underworld, which provides the muscle to collect debts or provide protection from other groups. The national level bookies, as well as the more localized gambling level, include regional bookies in counting centers. The runners, who each have between fifteen and one hundred clients, supply the bookies with internet technology, collect money from losing bets, and pay off the winning bets. At the bottom of the structure are the punters, who are the millions of bettors, wagering on European and local football leagues, four-digit lotteries, horse-racing, and other events.[43]

For the larger European soccer matches, the television audience in Asia climbs to more than the entire population of Western Europe. With the rise of the internet, this large television population has the ability to bet on games anywhere in the world. Asian match-fixers have capitalized on this phenomenon by successfully operating in Europe.[44] An investment of a few thousand Euros could net a potential return of millions for a match-fixer. A match-fixer will scan the European leagues for matches that allow for corruption. The tournaments involved will include early Champions League, the Union of European Football Associations (UEFA) Cup, and Intertoto Cup matches. During the preliminary rounds of these tournaments, teams from smaller and poorer European countries play one another in hopes of advancing in the competition. Largely due to the fact that there are no other high-level soccer games during June and July, these games between relatively obscure teams attract more gambling than normal.[45]

In Europe, the Asian gambling structures facilitate match-fixing in numerous ways. Most gambling fixers do not actually directly meet with the players; instead, they use what are known as "runners." Runners are often former players known to officials and players, and thus are trusted. Accordingly, they do not create suspicion. Whereas an outsider would not be able to pass security, a former player with a well known reputation can easily gain access to any team event or hotel. They are the connectors between the illegal gambling world and the potentially corrupt soccer team.[46]

Once this runner has infiltrated a corrupt member of the team, the corrupt member of the team is contacted by the bookie. The bookie discloses to the corrupt player which game to lose, offering him money to distribute to himself and the other corrupt players involved. This player then approaches the other corrupt players on the team, offering them money if they help him lose the game. This central corrupt player receives the money, ensures the game is lost, and then distributes the money to his fellow corrupt players. This central player must be an influential player, and is often one of the top players of the team. Fixers want to work with these players, since they often have the influence and prestige on the team that prevents the other players from refusing their scheme. As such, they are able to build a corrupt network on the team.[47]

This central corrupt player must have at least three to five other players to help fix the match. In soccer, fixes normally include five to seven players. A successful fix, however, must at minimum include the goalkeeper, a defender, and a striker.[48] For goalkeepers, the key strategy to throw a game is simple: leave his area as much as possible. A corrupt goalkeeper may rush out of his net and allow the forward to step around him and score. Another tactic used by goalkeepers is to drop the ball or pat it loose in a crowded penalty area. Defenders must also be involved, as one mistake by a defender can easily lead to a goal. One tactic used by defenders includes placing the ball too far away for the goalkeeper to clear or gather it, but near enough to the opposing forward for him to run in and score a goal.[49] Forwards must also be involved in the fix in order for the fix to be successful. If forwards score too many goals, the fix becomes very obvious. As a result, fixers have various strategies for forwards to follow, including dribbling the ball straight at the opponent players thereby allowing them to take away the ball, and missing goal opportunities by either kicking directly at the goalkeeper or missing the goal altogether.[50]

Under Hill's analysis midfielders do not have as direct an influence on the fix as goalkeepers, defenders, and forwards. Their role is to control the fix. It is difficult for a strong team to lose credibly against a weak team. In recent years, the skill of controlling a game is becoming increasingly important, as match-fixers are asking the players not only to lose the game, but also to change the game depending on the time of the match. Match-fixers will have far higher odds than just a win or loss when they are able to predict total goals scored in the match or the timing when those goals will be scored. Strategies used by corrupt midfielders include keeping the ball for a long time to allow the other team to take it away, interrupting the system of playing by passing the ball back to the defense and keeping the ball in his area and not allowing the ball to get open.[51]

Match-fixers rely on various methods to gain access and credibility with players, such as manoeuvring their accommodation so as to share the same hotel corridor as the players and officials. Others do it less directly by deploying runners to ensure access between the fixer and the players. These two methods allow the match-fixer to gain access to as wide an assortment of players as possible.[52] The next stage is to approach the player by a telephone call to the targeted player at their hotel and proposing the match-fixing deal. The alternative is a personal approach when the match-fixer is able to develop a relationship with the player and over time persuade the player to participate in the nefarious scheme on an ongoing basis.[53]

The most explosive match-fixing scandal exposed in Hill's book is the 2006 World Cup Finals. According to Hill, the tournament was fixed at an anonymous Kentucky Fried

Chicken restaurant in northern Bangkok between four men, including one man who Hill identified as "Lee Chin," who is known to have been fixing games for more than fifteen years. According to Chin, during the 2004 Olympic Games in Athens, some of his associates were able to infiltrate the Ghana team, persuading them to agree to throw their last game against Japan. As a result, Chin had a close relationship with various corrupt Ghanaian players.[54] Chin alleged that the game between Ghana and Italy was fixed,[55] along with the game between Ghana and Brazil.[56] The book also exposes a fixed match between Ukraine and Italy. One of Chin's associates persuaded a few corrupt players on the Ukrainian team to throw the game against Italy.[57] Chin told Hill the essential results of these three matches before they were even played. The games all followed a particular pattern; all of the matches were between relatively poor underdogs and heavily favoured teams.

In another recent soccer scandal, a Spanish judge, Judge Baltasar Garzon, sent German prosecutors information suggesting that Russian mobsters fixed a UEFA Cup semi-final game last season between the Russian teams Zenit St. Petersburg and Bayern Munich.[58] A probe by Judge Garzon exposed a taped telephone conversation of suspected Russian gang member Gennady Petrov, mentioning that fifty million of an unspecified currency had been paid to Bayern. Previously, one of Petrov's aides, Leonid Khristoforov, boasted to Petrov that he knew the result of the match in St. Petersburg would be 4-0 in Zenit's favour. The final score was in fact 4-0, with Zenit winning. Petrov was one of twenty people arrested in Spain in June 2008 in raids ordered by Judge Garzon. The detainees are suspected members of the Tambov gang, which is considered one of the world's most powerful Russian Mafia groups, with Petrov alleged to be the head of the group. They were accused of laundering proceeds from crimes that included contract killings and arms and drug trafficking. In another conversation, another detained suspect, Vitaly Izguilov, talked of making money on the transfer of one of Zenit's players. The other person in the call mentioned the transfer of four players, but it was not clear if this concerned the Russian league champion.[59]

i. What Is Being Done?

In soccer, some of the major European gambling companies, including Betfair, have now signed agreements with UEFA and the International Federation of Association Football (FIFA) in order to share any information about possible match-fixes. FIFA states that its early warning system is an efficient net to catch any potential match-fixes.[60] The development of integrity units similar to those involved in other sports would be of great assistance in bringing these problems under more control. UEFA has recently approved a special investigative unit to stamp out match-fixing and illegal betting in soccer by examining reported situations of irregular betting in European competitions. At the end of last year, UEFA submitted a ninety-six page report to Interpol detailing match-fixing suspicions of twenty-six matches in the Champions League, UEFA Cup, and Intertoto Cup. Of these twenty-six matches, fifteen remain under investigation.[61]

D. Professional Basketball

During the summer of 2007, Tim Donaghy, a National Basketball Association (NBA) referee, was found to have used confidential information to bet on NBA games, and provided this confidential information to bookies and gamblers in violation of NBA rules, policies, and procedures. The League first learned that an NBA referee was connected with illegal gambling from the Federal Bureau of Investigation (FBI) and the United States Attorney's Office for the Eastern District of New York. On June 20, 2007, an FBI agent contacted Bernie Tolbert, the NBA's Senior Vice President of Security, to alert the League that the FBI had interviewed a current NBA referee in connection with a federal investigation of illegal gambling.[62] On June 21, 2007, Commissioner David Stern and other senior members of NBA management met with the FBI.[63] The FBI explained that Donaghy, who had been with the League for thirteen seasons, had placed bets on NBA games, including games he had officiated. The FBI also informed the League that Donaghy had disclosed confidential NBA information, including player injuries and the names of the referees assigned to specific games, to individuals for use in betting on NBA games.[64]

On August 15, 2007, Donaghy pleaded guilty before Judge Carol Bagley Amon in the United States District Court for the Eastern District of New York to two felonies: conspiracy to commit wire fraud by denying his employer the intangible right to his honest services and conspiracy to transmit wagering information.[65] Donaghy made picks on sixteen NBA games that he officiated during the 2006–2007 season, and bet on thirty to forty games that he officiated in each of the prior three seasons. On February 8, 2008, Donaghy's co-conspirators, James Battista and Thomas Martino, were also indicted in the U.S. District Court for the Eastern District of New York. Like Donaghy, Battista and Martino were charged with conspiracy to commit wire fraud by denying the NBA the intangible right to its employee's honest services and conspiracy to transmit wagering information.[66] Martino was also charged with two counts of perjury for lying to a grand jury regarding his involvement in the conspiracies. On April 16, 2008, Martino pleaded guilty to conspiracy to commit wire fraud, and, on April 24, 2008, Battista pleaded guilty to conspiracy to transmit wagering information.[67] On July 24, 2008, Battista was sentenced to a prison term of fifteen months, and Martino was sentenced to a prison term of twelve months and one day. On July 29, 2008, Donaghy was sentenced to a prison term of fifteen months. The defendants were also ordered to serve supervised release terms of three years each after their imprisonment and to pay $217,266.94 in restitution to the NBA as the victim of their crimes.[68]

i. What Is Being Done?

For many years, the NBA Constitution has prohibited team owners and employees, including players and coaches, and League employees, including referees, from betting, directly or indirectly, on NBA games.[69] The NBA also prohibits the intentional disclosure of confidential League or team information.[70] The NBA's Board of Governors adopted amendments to the NBA Constitution on April 18, 2008, and the League has made other changes to its rules. These changes strengthen and clarify the ban on gambling on NBA games and the prohibition on sharing confidential League information with individuals outside the NBA. The League is also in the process of hiring a full-time Compliance Officer who will be responsible for assuring enforcement by appropriate personnel of the League's compliance policies and procedures and overseeing the League's anti-gambling efforts.[71] Also, starting this season, a "hotline" is available for League and team employees, including referees, coaches, trainers, players and other NBA employees, to anonymously raise questions and report problems concerning gambling and game integrity issues.[72] Finally, ongoing gambling education efforts continue to be enhanced.[73]

As in tennis, the NBA initiated a report by Lawrence B. Pedowitz, called the "Report to the Board of Governors of the National Basketball Association," published on October 1, 2008.[74] As a result of Donaghy's conduct, Commissioner David Stern and the Audit Committee of the NBA's Board of Governors engaged Pedowitz and his colleagues at Wachtell, Lipton, Rosen & Katz to conduct a review of the League's officiating program. This review focused on three areas, including a risk review of issues related to the integrity of the game. They further sought to identify ways that the League could enhance a culture of compliance to the NBA's rules and regulations and underscore the importance of protecting the game's integrity and the NBA's reputation.[75]

III. BIASED REFEREEING

Biased refereeing occurs when the officials monitoring a match weigh more heavily towards one competitor than the other. It can take many forms, and may be subtle enough to go undetected by both the viewing audience and the players involved. Methods used include unnecessary penalties, missed calls, and inaccurate points awards, all of which are able to effect or even entirely shift the eventual outcome of the match. Biased refereeing was alleged to have occurred in wrestling, boxing, and women's soccer at the Beijing Summer Olympics, although not all of these instances have progressed beyond mere accusations. Outlined below are some recent cases that have been brought forward, demonstrating the nature of biased refereeing and its consequences.

A. Wrestling and Boxing at the Olympics

i. Ara Abrahamian

Ara Abrahamian was a member of the Swedish wrestling team for the 2008 Summer Olympic Games in Beijing. He had successfully advanced from the early rounds in his class, but then lost during the men's Greco Roman 84 kg semi-final match. During that match, Abrahamian had initially been assigned a point for the round, which would have required a third period to determine the winner of the bout overall. However, the officials issued a warning to the wrestler at the end of the second period, resulting in him losing the match. The Swedish team responded to the call by requesting for a video check to see if the warning was justified, as allowed by the International Federation of Associated Wrestling Styles (FILA) rules, but was denied this request. The Swedish team later attempted to file a formal protest to FILA and the competition committee alleging that the officials had made a departure from proper procedures, yet FILA refused the protest. The Swedish team eventually appealed to CAS, who accepted the appeal.[76]

This case demonstrates the role that effective refereeing plays in keeping matches fair. Officials may act or be perceived to have acted rather one-sidedly in judging the bout, and their actions seem to have favoured a win against one of the opponents as may have happened to the Swedish wrestler. Both the issuing of a late penalty and the denial of a video check can be characterised as raising suspicions surrounding the motivations of the officials, and could possibly demonstrate biased judging of the event.

The episode was escalated beyond the match in question. Although Abrahamian went on to fight in the bronze medal bout and win, his disappointment with the earlier outcome was not extinguished. The wrestler expressed his protest against the officials and FILA by walking out of the medal ceremony and placing his medal on the floor. As a repercussion for these actions, he was disqualified from the Olympics and stripped of his medal by the IOC. Abrahamian has since appealed to CAS that these sanctions be lifted.[77] Additionally, FILA banned both Abrahamian and his coach, Leo Myllari, from the sport for two years, and also banned the Swedish wrestling federation from hosting any international events for two years.[78] These later events can be labelled as ripple effects from the biased refereeing during the semi-final match, demonstrating how fundamental fair, independent judging with neutrality is in maintaining the integrity of sports. In high level competitions such as the Olympics, when emotions run high and reputations are at stake, referees control the outcome of much more than the matches they are judging.

ii. Other Cases

A second biased refereeing case, *Samurgashev v. FILA* which involves a Russian wrestler, was raised towards the end of the Beijing Olympics, and has since been sent to be determined by CAS in Lausanne.[79] The wrestler in this case is seeking the payment of damages from FILA further to the alleged misconduct of an umpire.

Several other complaints were made concerning the officiating of boxing at Beijing. This was nothing new, as Olympic boxing has come under suspicion several times in the past regarding outcomes.[80] Speculations often center on matches being fixed, with referees determining the outcome unfairly for one fighter. As an attempt to repair the flawed refereeing, a new scoring system was implemented at the Beijing Games.[81] However, the new scoring system was actually alleged to have caused more problems than it resolved; fighters who deserved a point did not receive any, and undeserving fighters would often score a point. Additionally, referees awarded points to fighters that seemed like poor or undeserved calls, and at times inconsistent with other calls. Another tactic that was employed to counter biased refereeing was a special unit created by the IOC to monitor any suspicious betting patterns that occurred during the Games.[82]

B. Salt Lake Judging Scandal

One of the most widely publicized cases of judging bias occurred during the 2002 Olympic Winter Games in the pairs figure skating competition. The Canadian pair was said to have skated a flawless performance, and were expected to win gold before the scores for their program were revealed. However, to the surprise of the crowd and many commentators on various networks, the Canadians did not receive the highest scores, and the gold was instead awarded to the Russian pair. Doubts concerning the reliability of the judging were immediately expressed in the aftermath of the event. It was reported that the French judge, upon being confronted by International Skating Union (ISU) members, admitted to having been pressured to score highly for the Russian pair. The ISU announced that it would further examine the details of the judging decision. The ISU and IOC quickly decided to upgrade the Canadian pair from a silver medal to gold. The Canadians shared the gold medal with the Russian pair. However, there were still many, including several judges from the panel, who thought that the Russians were in fact the rightful winners.[83]

This case differs from those discussed above during the Beijing Games in that the players affected by the biased judging were not the ones to commence any action. The catalyst that brought the matter to a resolution was the application of the Canadian Olympic Committee for preliminary relief from the CAS Ad Hoc Division to make an order that certain individuals be compelled to appear before CAS to provide evidence and that a decision be issued that would enable the United States Court to issue subpoenas to various referees and judges to appear and give evidence.[84] Once it was recognized that the CAS would act in such a fashion, the Salt Lake scandal was dealt with swiftly by both the ISU and the IOC, by awarding a co-gold medal to the Canadian

pair for their performance and suspending the judge in question for her misconduct. At the time of the incident, the case was covered extensively by the world press with many sympathetic to the Canadian pair. Several factors help to explain the extent of coverage: figure skating is one of the most popular events in the Winter Olympics, and typically not associated with judging scandals; the fact that the pair was Canadian attracted a lot of media attention from the large North American broadcasters; and the Soviet Union and Russian teams had dominated the pairs figure skating event for the previous ten Winter Olympics. The IOC and the ISU had no choice but to act to resolve the problem.

IV. DOPING

When athletes engage in the use of substances to enhance their performance, it places those that train and compete legitimately, and with sporting integrity, at a considerable disadvantage. Not only does doping tarnish fair play, but it also creates skepticism whenever an athlete is able to perform at a high ability and surpass past benchmarks; eyebrows are almost always raised with doubts centered on doping. The exceptional performances of Michael Phelps[85] and Usain Bolt[86] at the Beijing Summer Games, both excelling in their sports, immediately drew accusations that doping must have played a role. The public is unwilling to accept remarkable feats as being attributable to human ability, and mistrust of athletes is escalating.[87] . . . [R]elease of the Mitchell Report covering steroid use in professional baseball demonstrated the depth and breadth of doping in that professional sport. The Report makes the point that doping is a form of corruption,[88] much like gambling, in that it gnaws at the integrity of professional baseball. When big name players who have broken past records are mentioned in the Mitchell Report, the entire professional sporting organization is cast in a shadow of doubt.

A. Azerbaijan Women's Field Hockey Team

At the Beijing Summer Olympics, the Ad Hoc Division of CAS dealt with a matter of eligibility for the Olympics[89] that focused on an issue of doping. An application was filed to CAS by the Azerbaijan National Olympic Committee (ANOC), the Azerbaijan Field Hockey Federation (AFHF), and the players of the Azerbaijan Field Hockey Team against the International Hockey Federation (FIH).[90] ANOC and AFHF requested authorization for the women's team to be able to participate in Beijing by challenging a decision issued by the FIH judicial committee in relation to an alleged doping case committed by two Spanish players during the Women's World Hockey qualifying tournament.

The Azerbaijan Women's Field Hockey Team had participated in the Women's World Hockey Qualifier in Baku, Azerbaijan. The Spanish team defeated Azerbaijan and thereby qualified to participate in the Olympics. Subsequently, it was alleged that two Spanish players had committed doping infractions. The FIH Judicial Committee found that one Spanish player, Gloria Comerma, had committed a doping infraction without fault or negligence, while the other player was exonerated from any anti-doping rule violation—as such her name cannot be released. Although not a party to the doping case between the Spanish players and the International Federation, the Azerbaijan team called for a new hearing. They submitted that both Spanish players had committed anti-doping rule violations and were therefore asking that the entire Spanish team be disqualified from the event, and that the Azerbaijan team be proclaimed the winner and designated replacement at the Olympics.[91]

The CAS Panel found that the Azerbaijan team did not have any standing to bring an application affecting the Spanish players and dismissed the appeal. No eligible parties, such as the IOC or WADA, raised an appeal, so the ruling was upheld. The Azerbaijan team was therefore not eligible to participate in the Olympic Games. The case merely skims the surface of an apparently greater problem and issue than was before the Ad Hoc Division. The only reason that the Azerbaijanis were denied the appeal was that they had no standing to raise the application; CAS never ruled on the issue of doping in this matter.[92]

B. Austrian Ski Team

Ten members of the Austrian ski team were placed on trial in Italy in October 2008 for allegations of doping at the 2006 Winter Olympics in Turin.[93] The case involved blood doping by the athletes to enhance their performances, which was thought to be a well organized strategy that involved several people in various positions within the organization. The accused group included athletes, trainers, medics and officials, including the president of the Austrian Skiing Federation. The five accused athletes among the group were all banned for life by the IOC. At the time of writing, the cases were pending before the Italian courts and obviously no applications had yet been brought to CAS.

C. Testing at Beijing

A team consisting of ten independent observers was hired to monitor and report on the drug testing procedures undertaken during the Beijing Games. The results of the official report, which were presented to the World Anti-Doping Agency (WADA), revealed several issues. The most striking of these was the allegation that "around 300 test results were missing [from the WADA accredited Laboratory] in comparison to the doping control forms," and that the IOC was also missing some reports.[94] Additionally, the report raised the concern that the Laboratory failed to catch a quality control sample that contained a prohibited substance.[95] The matter was quickly cleared-up by WADA and the IOC with all of the missing tests, including the quality control sample, being traced and sent to the team of independent observers. No new negative test results were revealed within these

tests. WADA released an addendum to the report addressing these issues and their explanations.[96]

There were additional issues mentioned in the independent observers' report that were not justified in the addendum. The observers pointed out that the Beijing Laboratory was unable to test for insulin, which is a banned substance.[97] Additionally, nearly half of the National Olympic Committees (NOCs) present at the Games failed to provide important whereabouts information of their athletes to enable effective pre-Games and out of competition testing programs.[98] The report also pointed out several occasions where doping control was over rigorous, specifically through the monitoring of athletes by doping control officers (DCOs) and chaperones. Some notable instances included: a chaperone running behind an athlete to do a lap of honor around the hockey pitch with the entire team;[99] another chaperone who joined a victorious team's huddle after a basketball match;[100] and a DCO that was unfamiliar with the use of tampons by females concerned that it was a form of manipulation device during a urine sample.[101]

The Independent Observer process is an excellent prophylactic methodology. It ought to be adopted as a control mechanism in more sports situations involving many of the activities discussed in this article. The methodology goes a long way to ensuring neutrality and independence in the sporting organization and how it carries out its functions. There is no better method of protecting integrity in sport.

V. CONCLUSION

Sports regulatory bodies are attempting various initiatives to help remedy the problems associated with corruption. Players must be educated and aware of the threats to the integrity of the sport, along with education and awareness of the rules and regulations against betting, gambling, and performance enhancing drugs. A crucial aspect of addressing the threats to integrity in sports is an effective education and awareness program for all players, players' support staff, officials and other relevant persons.[102] Players and all those connected with the sport must understand the nature of the threats and the penalties if caught, as well as the need to act responsibly in enhancing the integrity of the sport. A strong message must be delivered that each player, official, and coach has a role to play in maintaining and enhancing the integrity of sport.

The examples highlighted throughout this paper illustrate the grim realities of the level of corruption that have infiltrated the modern day professional sporting and elite athlete world. The undesirable actions of a few are negatively affecting the outcomes for many. Professional sports provides a means to make a legitimate living for well more than just the athletes involved in the matches: coaches, assistants, trainers, officials, venue staff, and television commentators provide only a short list of the careers created through the large sporting network. When the integrity of sports is corrupted and tested, the livelihood of a great body of people is destabilized. The measures suggested here must be taken and strengthened in order to successfully fight off corruption and stop sport from becoming merely a form of entertainment, having lost the element of unpredictability of outcome.

Notes

1. For example, the integrity of professional basketball was tried as a result of the recent betting scandal. Please refer to the discussion on this topic within the match fixing section . . . for further analysis.

2. Sir Paul Condon, Report on Corruption in International Cricket (2001), http://www.yehhaicricket.com/news/eyecatchers/topl.html; Ben Gunn & Jeff Rees, Environmental Review of Integrity in Professional Tennis (2008).

3. Gunn & Rees, supra note 2.

4. Formed in 1972 to protect the interests of male professional tennis players.

5. Davydenko Cleared of Match-Fixing, BBC Sport, Sept. 12, 2008, http://news.bbc.co.uk/sport2/hi/tennis/7612536.stm.

6. Officials Look Into Irregular Betting on Match ESPN.com, June 28, 2006, http://sports.espn.go.com/sports/tennis/wimbledon06/news/story?id=2502709.

7. ATP Chief Skeptical of Player Involvement, ESPN.com, Oct. 14, 2003, http://sports.espn.go.com/tennis/news/2003/1014/1637964.html.

8. For a discussion regarding the outcome of the 2002 pairs figure skating event, see infra.

9. Tennis officials investigate irregular betting on match, ESPN.com, Aug. 3, 2007, http://sports.espn.go.com/sports/tennis/news/storyid=2959748.

10. ATP Says Sport Is Clean In Light of Recent Gambling Reports, ESPN.com, Sept. 27, 2007, http://sports.espn.go.com/sports/tennis/news/story?id=3039436.

11. Id.

12. John Barr, For Davydenko, It's Déjà vu Down Under, ESPN.com, Jan. 10, 2008, http://sports.espn.go.com/sports/tennis/aus08/news/storyid=3190154.

13. Paul Newman, Murray Attacks Match-Fixing as ATP Gets Tough, The Independent, Oct. 10, 2007, http://www.independent.co.uk/sport/tennis/murray-attacks-matchfrxing-as-atp-gets-tough-396432.html.

14. The 2007 ATP® Official Rulebook, Rule 7.05.

15. Id. Rule 7.05(G).

16. GUNN & REES, supra note 2.

17. Id.

18. Id. at 22-36.

19. Tennis Governing Bodies Appoint Jeff Rees As Director Of Tennis Integrity Unit & Adopt Uniform Anti-Corruption Code, Tennis Life Magazine, Aug. 22, 2008, http://www.tennislife.com/news/industryinsider/articles/08-05/wn-08-08-27-1.html.

20. Id.

21. Nine-Month Ban For Italy's di Mauro Is First Under New Rules, Associated Press, Nov. 10, 2007.

22. Nine-Month Ban for Italy's di Mauro Is First Under New Rules, ESPN.com, Nov. 10, 2007, http://sports.espn.go.com/sports/tennis/news/story?id=3 103462.

23. Id.

24. Id.

25. Alessio Di Mauro v. ATP Tour Inc., CAS 2007/A/1427.

26. Id.

27. Players Bet on Tennis, But Not Their Own Matches, ESPN.com, Dec. 27, 2007, http://sports.espn.go.com/sports/tennis/news/story?id=3165719.

28. William Weinbaum, ATP: Galimberti Bets Included Wagers on Own Matches, ESPN.com, Feb. 19, 2008, http://sports.espn.go.com/sports/tennis/news/storyid=3253331.

29. Luzzi Fined $50,000, Suspended 200 Days, ESPN.com, Feb. 29, 2008, http://sports.espn.go.com/sports/tennis/news/story?id=3271281.

30. Federico Luzzi v. ATP Inc. CAS 2008/A/1529.

31. ATP Suspends Doubles Titlists Cermak, Mertinak for Betting, ESPN.com, July 21, 2008, http://sports.espn.go.com/sports/tennis/news/story?id=3498511.

32. Montcourt Suspended 2 Months, Fined $12K for Betting on Matches, ESPN.com, Aug. 8, 2008, http://sports.espn.go.com/sports/tennis/news/story?id=3525837.

33. Mathieu Montcourt v. ATP, CAS 2008/A/1630. The case was pending before CAS at the time of writing this article.

34. China Admits Throwing Olympic Badminton Match, Gulf Daily News, June 11, 2008, 2008 WLNR 15430567.

35. China Coach Admits Match Fixing, Yahoo! Sports, Mar. 23, 2008, http://uk.eurosport.yahoo.com/23032008/58/china-coach-admits-match-fixing.html.

36. Romanian Boxing Official Rudel Obreja to Resort to CAS After Cheat Jibe, The Australian, Sept. 3, 2008, http://www.theaustralian.news.com.au/story/0,25197,24286751-5013449,00.html.

37. IOC Calls for Common Front Against Match-Fixing, Sport Business International, Dec. 13, 2007, http://www.sportbusiness.com/news/163107/ioc-calls-for-common-front-againstmatch-fixing.

38. Major Steps Taken to Fight Olympic Match-Fixing, CBC, June 6, 2008, http://www.cbc.ca/olympics/badminton/story/2008/06/06/f-olympics-news-matchfixing-prevent.html.

39. International Olympic Committee, Rules for the Application During the Olympic Games in Beijing of Article A.5 of the Code of Ethics Concerning the Prohibition on Betting Linked to the Olympic Games, (2008), available at http://multimedia.olympic.org/pdf/en-report1323.pdf.

40. Declan Hill, The Fix: Soccer and Organized Crime (2008).

41. The 1984 UEFA Cup semi final match is also claimed to have been fixed. See id. at 93.

42. Id. at 51-53.

43. Id. at 58.

44. Id. at 84-85.

45. Id. at 97.

46. Id. at 21.

47. Id. at 22-23.

48. Id. at 23.

49. Id. at 29-31.

50. Id. at 31-32.

51. Id. at 32-33.

52. Id. at 139-140.

53. Id. at 142-143.

54. Id. at 226-229.

55. Id. at 236-237.

56. Id. at 248-249.

57. Id. at 251.

58. Russian Mob Suspected of Fixing UEFA Cup Soccer Match, TheStar.com, Oct. 1, 2008, http://www.thestar.com/Sports/article/509616.

59. Id.

60. Hill, supra note 40, at 176. The efficiency of this, however, is limited. Hill points out those Asian fixers do not bet with Betfair, the English betting companies, or European sports lotteries. Instead, they bet on the Asian gambling market.

61. UEFA to Set Up Special Unit to Stamp Out Corruption, MSN Sport, Sept. 26, 2008, http://sport.sg.msn.com/article.aspx?cp-documentid=1697889.

62. Lawrence B. Pedowitz, Report to The Board of Governors of the National Basketball Association 1 (2008)

63. Id. at 2.

64. Id.

65. United States v. Donaghy, 570 F. Supp. 2d 411 (E.D.N.Y. 2008).

66. United States v. Battista & Martino, 570 F. Supp. 2d 411 (E.D.N.Y. 2008).

67. Transcript of Guilty Plea 23:17-24:14, United States v. Martino, No. 08 Cr. 86 (CBA) (E.D.N.Y. April 16, 2008). During his guilty plea, Battista made a similar statement. Transcript of Guilty Plea 18:20-19:6, United States v. Battista, No. 08 Cr. 86 (CBA) (E.D.N.Y. April 24, 2008).

68. See Donaghy, 570 F.Supp.2d 411.

69. National Basketball Association, NBA Const., Art. 35A(g). Article 35(f) covers players.

70. National Basketball Association, NBA Legal Compliance Policy and Code of Conduct, § II.C.

71. Pedowitz, supra note 62, at 109.

72. Id.

73. Id.

74. Id.

75. Id.

76. See Swedish NOC & Abrahamian v. FILA, CAS OG 08/007.

77. See National Olympic Committee of Sweden and Abrahamian v. IOC, CAS 1647/A/2008. At the time of writing, this case was still in process.

78. Wrestler Banned 2 Years For Olympic Medal Protest, International Herald Trib., Nov. 6, 2008, http://www.iht.com/articles/ap/2008/11/06/sports/OLY-WRE-Abrahamian-Banned.php.

79. At the time of writing, this case was still in process.

80. For example, at the 1988 Summer Olympics in Seoul, American boxer Roy Jones Jr. was robbed of a gold medal due to a highly disputed decision that resulted in the three match judges being suspended. See Gary Smith, One Tough Bird, Sports Illustrated, June 26, 1995, available at http://vault.sportsillustrated.cnn.com/vault/article/magazine/MAGI 006753/l/index.htm.

81. The system involved a panel of five judges sitting ringside with controls to touch to indicate that a boxer deserved to score a point. In order for a point to be received, three of the five judges were required to touch the control within one second or else no point was awarded.

82. Please see the above subsection dealing with solutions to match fixing . . . for a more in-depth discussion of the IOC gambling unit.

83. 2002 Olympic Winter Games Figure Skating Scandal, http://www.nationmaster.com/encyclopedia/2002-Olympic-Winter-Games-figure-skating-scandal.

84. Canadian Olympic Association v. International Skating Union, CAS OG 2002/004.

85. American swimmer who won eight gold medals and set seven new world records.

86. Jamaican sprinter who won gold medals in the 100, 200, and 4 x 100 meter races, and set two new world records.

87. Three cyclists from the Tour de France 2008 were found long after the race was over on reevaluation testing to have produced Adverse Analytical Findings for CERA, an advanced version of the blood-booster EPO. See Stephen Wilson, IOC Exec: Cycling's Olympic Future in Limbo, Yahoo! Sports, Oct. 6, 2008, http://sports.yahoo.com/olympics/news?slug-ap-cyclingsfuture&prov=ap&type=lgns. The IOC announced on 8 October 2008 it was to retest many samples from the Beijing Olympics for the same substance. See IOC to Further Analyse Beijing 2008 Samples, Olympic.org, Oct. 8, 2008, http://www.olympic.org/uk/news/olympic news/fullstory-uk.asp?id=2828.

88. George J. Mitchell, Report to the Commissioner of Baseball of an Independent Investigation into the Illegal Use of Steroids and Other Performance Enhancing Substances by Players in Major League Baseball, Sec. II.B, page 11, Dec. 13, 2007, available at http://mlb.mlb.com/mlb/news/mitchell/index.jsp.

89. See Azerbaijan Field Hockey Federation & Azerbaijan National Olympic Committee, and Players v. Federation Internationale de Hockey, CAS OG N' 08/001, 004 & 005. All three decisions are the subject of a judicial review application brought before the Swiss Federal Tribunal in October of 2008. The outcome of that proceeding was unknown at the time of writing this article.

90. See Azerbaijan Field Hockey Federation, CAS OG 08/001.

91. Id.

92. Id.

93. 10 Austrians Handed Notice In Turin-Doping Probe, Austria Today, Oct. 8, 2008, available at http://austriantimes.at/index.php?id—9010.

94. World Anti-Doping Agency, Report of the Independent Observers, XXX Olympic Games, Beijing 2008, Section 1.1, page 5, available at http://www.wada-ama.org/rtecontent/document/WADA_10_ReporLBeijing_2008_FINALFINAL.pdf (last visited December 10, 2008).

95. Id. at 25, §3.10, comment VII.

96. See World Anti-Doping Agency, Addendum to the 2008 Olympic Games Independent Observer Report, available at http://www.wada-ama.org/rtecontent/document/ADDENDUM-IOReport2008-27October2008.pdf (last visited December 10, 2008).

97. Report of the Independent Observers, supra note 94, at 25.

98. Id. at 4, §.1.

99. Id. at 17, §3.6.4.

100. Id.

101. Id. at 21, §3.8.1, comment V.

102. See Pedowitz, supra note 62, at 107-109.

Discussion Questions

1. What obligations do professional teams have to the communities in which they play? What about college teams?
2. What ethical dilemmas are raised by not paying college athletes? What dilemmas would be raised by paying them?
3. What are the ethical issues associated with Title IX? What are the ethical issues associated with diversity generally?
4. What are the elements of the suggested model to confront ethical issues as a sports business leader?
5. What are the unique ethical problems of the leaders in the Olympic movement?
6. How might the Olympic-related ethical guidelines presented in the readings apply to the NFL, the NCAA, and the WTA?
7. Why is it "good" to have a major league franchise move into your home city? Who actually benefits?
8. As a local middle-class citizen would it *really* be good for a team to move to your city? Why or why not?
9. Why is it more common to see fans side against "athletes" when it is quite common for the masses to side with "laborers" when dealing with work stoppages? Who do you tend to side with during a work stoppage in sports?
10. What are the risks associated with franchise relocation that are faced by owners?
11. Why is there not more internal self-regulation by NCAA member institutions?

Index

Note: Page numbers followed by *f* indicate figures; page numbers followed by *t* indicate tables.